The
Politics
of
Nonviolent
Action

A study prepared
under the auspices of
Harvard University's Center
for International Affairs

The
Politics
of
Nonviolent
Action

Gene Sharp

With the editorial assistance of
Marina Finkelstein

Extending Horizons Books
PORTER SARGENT PUBLISHER
11 Beacon St. • Boston, MA 02108 • USA

Library of Congress Catalog Number 72-95483
ISBN 0-87558-068-8

Preface

There is no pretense that this study is exhaustive. The historical material on nonviolent action which is used here only scratches the surface of past experience, for example. This volume is, however, the most comprehensive attempt thus far to examine the nature of nonviolent struggle as a social and political technique, including its view of power, its specific methods of action, its dynamics in conflict and the conditions for success or failure in its use. The historical material is used primarily in assisting the inductive construction of the analyses, theories and hypotheses. It is hoped that this book will stimulate many other studies and explorations of the nature of this technique and of its potentialities as a substitute for political violence.

This study was begun out of a view that alternatives to violence in meeting tyranny, aggression, injustice and oppression are needed. At the same time it appeared evident that both moral injunctions against violence and exhortations in favor of love and nonviolence have made little or no contribution to ending war and major political violence. It seemed to me that only the adoption of a substitute type of sanction and struggle as a functional alternative to violence in acute conflicts—where important issues are, or are believed to be, at stake—could possibly lead to a major reduction of political violence in a manner compatible with freedom, justice and human dignity.

But mere advocacy of nonviolent alternatives will not necessarily produce any change either—unless they are accurately perceived as being at least as effective as the violent alternatives. That, too, is not a matter for sermonizing or declarations. Therefore, a very careful examination of the nature, capacities and requirements of nonviolent struggle was necessary, which needed to be as objective as possible. This study is my primary contribution to that task. This work should not be regarded as final, but as a tool for increasing our understanding and knowledge; its propositions, classifications, analyses and hypotheses should be subjected to further examination, research and critical analysis.

Since this book is focused almost exclusively on the nature of the nonviolent technique of action, several closely related areas are not treated here. For example, relationships between this technique and ethical problems, and between the technique and belief systems exhorting to nonviolent behavior, are for the most part not discussed here. This study may be, however, the basis for a fresh look at those problems.[1] The political implications and potentialities of nonviolent action, including for social change and for national defense,[2] have also been left for separate exploration; it is hoped that this study will assist those investigations.[3]

This book is the culmination of studies which began in 1950 while I was a student at Ohio State University. A lengthy draft of a book manuscript with the present title was completed at St. Catherine's College, Oxford in 1963, partially based on work done earlier in Norway, first at the Institute of Philosophy and the History of Ideas of the University of Oslo, and, then, for two-and-a-half years, at the Institute for Social Research. After much further research, a full revision and expansion of major parts of the 1963 draft was completed in 1968 at the Center for International Affairs of Harvard University. This became also my doctoral thesis at the University of Oxford, for which I was awarded the degree of D. Phil. in November 1968. This book is a thorough revision and rewriting of that 1968 thesis, with expansion of certain chapters and a restructuring of the whole book and of individual chapters. That rewriting took nearly three years further due to teaching responsibilities.

This study has been possible because of the encouragement and assistance of others. My parents, Eva M. and Paul W. Sharp, merit first place in thanks for their understanding and kindnesses in many ways over the years.

Most of the research and drafting has been done at four institutions: the Institute for Social Research in Oslo, Norway; the Institute of Philosophy and the History of Ideas of the University of Oslo; St. Catherine's College of the University of Oxford; and the Center for International Affairs of Harvard University; each of these, the members of their staffs and faculties, and their libraries deserve special appreciation. Mr. Erik Rinde, former Director of the Institute for Social Research, merits individual mention.

Very particular gratitude is also due to five men whose encouragement, help, advice, and infinite patience at various stages enabled me to continue study of this field: Professor Kurt H. Wolff of Brandeis University; Professor Arne Naess of the University of Oslo; Mr. Alan Bullock, Master of St. Catherine's College and Vice-Chancellor of the University of Oxford; Professor John Plamenatz of All Souls College, Oxford; and Professor Thomas C. Schelling of the Center for International Affairs of Harvard University, and now Chairman of the Public Policy Program of the John F. Kennedy School of Government of Harvard University. Without their help I could not have carried on.

Thanks must also go to the various sources of financial assistance which provided funds and loans over the years to enable me to continue.

I should also like to thank for their various kindnesses Sir Isaiah Berlin, President, Wolfson College, Oxford; Mr. Wilfrid Knapp and Mr. B. E. F. Fender of St. Catherine's College, Oxford; the members of the Board of the Faculty of Social Studies of the University of Oxford; Mr. Christopher Seton-Watson of Oriel College, Oxford; Professor J. C. Rees of University College, Swansea (then visiting All Souls College, Oxford); Dr. Robert L. Jervis of the Center for International Affairs of Harvard University; and Dean Richard Fontera of Southeastern Massachusetts University. Most of the individual academic acknowledgements are made in footnotes, but George Lakey and John L. Sorenson—both of whom have researched in this field—should be mentioned here for their suggestions of specific methods or examples which have been incorporated in the text and are not specifically credited. Individual members of the staff of the Center for International Affairs who merit special mention for help in typing, proofreading, reproduction and suggestions are Moira Clarke, Margaret Rothwell, James Havlin, Katherine Brest and especially Jeanette Asdourian. Dennis Brady searched libraries to help provide references to pagination in both British and American editions wherever possible.

The index has been prepared by John Hearn, William Singleton, Walter Conser, Ronald McCarthy, Ken Feldman and myself. Ronald McCarthy also ably assisted in other ways in getting the final manuscript to press, including steps in the obtaining of permissions for quotations. Walter Conser and Jessie

Jones helped considerably in proofreading and other tasks. From Porter Sargent Publisher, I wish to thank for their kindnesses and assistance in various ways Debbie Rose, Pat Roberts, Tom Murray, Jan Boddie, Jennie Fonzo, and F. Porter Sargent himself. Robert Reitherman, formerly a student at Harvard University, has drawn the charts and helped in diverse ways, not the least of which was encouragement. This also came generously from April Carter, Theodor Ebert, Adam Roberts and Sandi Tatman who volunteered special advice and help. Various of my students, from the University of Massachusetts at Boston, Tufts University, Brandeis University, Harvard University and Southeastern Massachusetts University, have offered helpful comments and suggestions.

During four of my years as Research Associate and Research Fellow at the Center for International Affairs of Harvard University, while the 1968 draft was being completed, I received funds from grants for projects of Professor Thomas C. Schelling made to Harvard University from the Ford Foundation and from the Advanced Research Projects Agency of the U.S. Department of Defense, Contract No. F44620-67-C-0011. Some persons may find either the availability or the acceptance of such funds surprising; I have been arguing for years that governments and defense departments—as well as other groups—should finance and conduct research into alternatives to violence in politics and especially as a possible basis for a defense policy by prepared nonviolent resistance as a substitute for war. As acceptance of such Defense Department funds involved no restrictions whatever on the research, writing, or dissemination of the results, I willingly accepted them. I welcome further research by governments and defense departments of all countries into alternatives to violence and war. After the completion of that draft, the Center for International Affairs provided an office and typing and editorial assistance for the rewriting of this volume.

The final rewriting of this book has only been possible because of the perceptive intellect, skillful pen, and friendly candor of Dr. Marina S. Finkelstein, Editor of Publications at the Center from 1968 until her death in 1972.

It is my hope that this book will serve as a contribution to the beginning of new research, investigation and development of effective nonviolent alternatives to domestic violence and international war.

Gene Sharp
Harvard University
Center for International Affairs
Cambridge, Massachusetts
June 1972.

NOTES

1. See Gene Sharp, "Ethics and Responsibility in Politics: A critique of the present adequacy of Max Weber's classification of ethical systems," in **Inquiry** (Oslo), vol. VII, no. 3 (Autumn 1964), pp. 304-317; Gene Sharp, "Dilemmas of Morality in Politics," in **Reconciliation Quarterly** (London), First Quarter 1965, no. 128, pp. 528-535; Reinhold Niebuhr, **Moral Man and Immoral Society** (New York: Charles Scribner's Sons, 1960 [orig. 1932] and London: S.C.M. Press, 1963) pp. 167, 238, 250-251, and 254; Gene Sharp, "Gandhi's Defence Policy," in T. K. Mahadevan, Adam Roberts and Gene Sharp, eds., **Civilian Defence: An Introduction** (Bombay: Bharatiya Vidya Bhavan and New Delhi: Gandhi Peace Foundation, 1967), pp. 15-52; and Gene Sharp, "Non-violence: Moral Principle or Political Technique?" in **Indian Political Science Review** (Delhi), vol. IV, no. 1 (Oct. 1969-Mar. 1970), pp. 17-36. On belief systems which reject violence, see Gene Sharp, "Types of Principled Nonviolence" in A. Paul Hare and Herbert H. Blumberg, eds., **Nonviolent Direct Action: American Cases: Social-Psychological Analyses** (Washington, D.C. and Cleveland: Corpus Books, 1968), pp. 273-313.
2. For introductory studies of civilian defense, see Gene Sharp "The Political Equivalent of War"–Civilian Defense, 67 pp., **International Conciliation**, no. 555 (Nov. 1965, whole issue), New York: Carnegie Endowment for International Peace; Gene Sharp, **Exploring Nonviolent Alternatives** (Boston: Porter Sargent, 1970), pp. 47-72; and Adam Roberts, ed., **Civilian Resistance as a National Defense** (Harrisburg, Pa.: Stackpole Books, 1968; paperback: Harmondsworth, Middlesex, England and Baltimore, Md.: Penquin Books, 1969). Original British edition titled **The Strategy of Civilian Defense** (London: Faber & Faber, 1967).
3. For basic terminology in this whole field of nonviolent action and civilian defense, see Gene Sharp, **An Abecedary of Nonviolent Action and Civilian Defense** (Cambridge, Mass.: Schenkman, 1972). For research areas on nonviolent action and its application, see Sharp, **Exploring Nonviolent Alternatives**, pp. 73-113. For a classified guide to the existing literature, see *ibid.*, pp. 133-159.

CONTENTS

Chapter Two

NONVIOLENT ACTION: AN ACTIVE TECHNIQUE OF STRUGGLE

PART TWO: THE METHODS OF NONVIOLENT ACTION
POLITICAL JIU-JITSU AT WORK

Chapter Three

THE METHODS OF NONVIOLENT PROTEST AND PERSUASION

Chapter Four

THE METHODS OF SOCIAL NONCOOPERATION

Chapter Five

THE METHODS OF ECONOMIC NONCOOPERATION:
(1) ECONOMIC BOYCOTTS

CONTENTS xiii

Chapter Six

THE METHODS OF ECONOMIC NONCOOPERATION:
(2) THE STRIKE

Chapter Seven

THE METHODS OF POLITICAL NONCOOPERATION

Chapter Eight

THE METHODS OF NONVIOLENT INTERVENTION

CONTENTS xv

PART THREE: THE DYNAMICS OF NONVIOLENT ACTION

Chapter Nine

LAYING THE GROUNDWORK FOR NONVIOLENT ACTION

Chapter Ten

CHALLENGE BRINGS REPRESSION

Chapter Eleven

SOLIDARITY AND DISCIPLINE TO FIGHT REPRESSION

Chapter Twelve

POLITICAL JIU-JITSU

Chapter Thirteen

THREE WAYS SUCCESS MAY BE ACHIEVED

Chapter Fourteen

THE REDISTRIBUTION OF POWER

Introduction
by Professor Thomas C. Schelling,
Harvard University

The original idea was to subject the entire theory of nonviolent political action, together with a full history of its practice in all parts of the world since the time of Christ, to the same cool, detailed scrutiny that military strategy and tactics are supposed to invite. Now that we have Gene Sharp's book, what we lack is an equally comprehensive, careful study of the politics of violent action.

Violence gets plenty of attention. But purposive violence, violence for political effect, is rarely examined in print with anything like the care and comprehensiveness, the attention to detail and the wealth of historical examples, that Gene Sharp brings to nonviolent action.

It is too bad that we haven't that other book, the one on violent action. It would be good to compare the two in detail. This book's analysis of nonviolent action might be even more impressive if it had a competitor.

Nonviolence can hardly compete with violence in total effect—it rarely produces disasters of the magnitude that violence has made familiar—but what we would want to compare is not some gross potency but the achievement of political purpose and the costs of the achievement. And we would need detailed comparisons in a multitude of contexts, to learn the strengths and weaknesses of both kinds of action in differing circumstances.

The difference is not like the difference between prayer and dynamite. Political violence, like political nonviolence, usually has as its purpose making somebody do something or not do something or stop doing something. The aim is to influence behavior. Violent action tries to do it mainly by intimidating people—large numbers or a few, followers or leaders, common citizens or officials. (The people to be intimidated need not be the direct victims of the violence.) The violence does not directly make people behave or perform or participate; it can only make it hurt if they don't. Indeed, the most skillful use of violence may produce, precisely because it is skillful, comparatively little violence.

The violent actions and the nonviolent are different methods of trying to make it unrewarding for people to do certain things, and safe or rewarding to do other things. Both can be misused, mishandled, or misapplied. Both can be used for evil or misguided purposes. "Nonviolent action" furthermore, as developed in this book, is not merely all the kinds of political activity in which violence is absent or unintended; so "violent action" and "nonviolent action" do not exhaust the possibilities. A comparison of the two would not be just a way of picking a favorite, but rather a way of highlighting similarities and differences in different contexts and illuminating political processes themselves.

This book does shed some light on the theory of violent action. The more coercive nonviolent techniques, in particular, have something in common with the techniques based on violence. (They can even entail a latent threat of violence, although often it is the people "nonviolently" posing the threat who would be the victims if violence broke out.)

Discipline, command and control; intelligence about the adversary; careful choice of weapons, targets, terrain and time of day; and, especially, avoiding impetuous recourse to provoked or purposeless violence, are critical to success in violent as in nonviolent action. Most of what are usually called the "principles of war" are chapter headings rather than rules to follow—things like economy, concentration, purpose, initiative, and surprise—and, as topical headings, are about as appropriate to the study of nonviolent action as to the violent.

One of the main differences is that violent action often requires hot blood, while the nonviolent depends more on cool heads. That is why the violent is so much easier to engage in, but perhaps harder to engage in with a clear and sustained consciousness of purpose. The violent tends to make demands on morale that are incompatible with dispassionate calculation or continual assessment of goals. The victims of violence get to be seen as enemies or criminals. The scoring system is corrupted; and accomplishment comes to be measured negatively, by how much an enemy has been frustrated and hurt, not by how effectively someone has been influenced into accommodating, participating, or whatever it was that the violence was supposed to make him do.

There is probably a corresponding effect in nonviolence, a tendency to count one's own risk and suffering as accomplishment. But in terms of effectiveness, as political action, neither the hurting nor the being hurt should be mistaken as the ultimate goal or the accomplishment of political purpose.

What Gene Sharp's book does at every step is to relate the methods of nonviolent action, and the organizational requirements, the logistics and the leadership and the discipline, the recruitment of members and the choice of targets, to political purpose. Nonviolence as a source of sheer personal gratification gets little attention, just as inflicting pain for its own sake, as sheer retribution, should get little attention in that other book on the politics of violent action.

The book does not attempt to convert you to a new faith. It is not about a compassionate political philosophy that, if only enough of us believed it, would make the walls come tumbling down. It offers insight, by theory and example, into a complex field of strategy. There is a coherence to the theory and an integrity to the book as a whole; but no one has to accept all the principles developed or to assume the author's point of view in order to get a new appreciation of politics and its methods. The book offers insight into the past and it illuminates a multitude of contemporary events that, whether or not they affect us, we are witnesses to. And many of them do affect us. And some of them we are engaged in.

And if the book should fall into the wrong hands, and begin to inform and enlighten our adversaries, we can be doubly thankful for the work Gene Sharp has done. Whatever the contest, there is a good chance that one is better off confronting a skillful and effective recourse to nonviolent action than a savagely ineffectual resort to violence.

PART ONE:
Power and Struggle

INTRODUCTION
TO PART ONE

Some conflicts do not yield to compromise and can be resolved only through struggle. Conflicts which, in one way or another, involve the fundamental principles of a society, of independence, of self-respect, or of people's capacity to determine their own future are such conflicts. For their resolution, regular institutional procedures are rarely available; it is even doubtful that they could be completely adequate. Instead, in the belief that the choice in these types of conflicts is between abject passive surrender and violence, and also that victory requires violence, people turn to the threat and use of violence. The specific means used will vary: they may include conventional military action, guerrilla warfare, regicide, rioting, police action, private armed offense and defense, civil war, terrorism, conventional aerial bombings and nuclear attacks, as well as other forms. Whether threatened, used with restraint, or applied without controls, these means of violence are designed to injure, kill, demolish and terrorize with maximum efficiency. Century by century, then decade by decade, and now year by year, this efficiency has grown as people and governments have applied talents and resources to that end.

The fact is, however, that it is not true that violence is the only effective means of action in crucial conflict situations. Throughout history, under a variety of political systems, people in every part of the world have waged conflict and wielded undeniable power by using a very different technique of struggle—one which does not kill and destroy. That technique is nonviolent action. Although it has been known by a variety of names, its basis has always been the same: the belief that the exercise of power depends on the consent of the ruled who, by withdrawing that consent, can control and even destroy the power of their opponent. In other words, nonviolent action is a technique used to control, combat and destroy the opponent's power by nonviolent means of wielding power. Although much effort has gone into increasing the efficiency of violent conflict, no comparable efforts have yet gone into making nonviolent action more effective and hence more likely to be substituted for violence.

And yet nonviolent action has already had a long history, which has remained largely unknown because historians have been so overwhelmingly concerned with other matters. In fact, there was until recently so little awareness of the tradition and history of nonviolent struggle that nonviolent actionists have, by and large, improvised their responses independently of past practice. This situation is only now beginning to change.

That there is a rich lode of material awaiting the analyst and actionist is abundantly clear. Even at the present early stage of investigation, he who looks can find numerous examples, ranging from ancient Rome to the civil rights struggle in the United States and the resistance of the Czechs and Slovaks to the Russian invasion of 1968. By searching diligently through scattered sources, he can find mention of plebeian protests against Rome as far back as the fifth century B.C.; he can trace the resistance of the Netherlands to Spanish rule in mid-sixteenth century Europe. But the history of nonviolent struggle in these centuries still remains to be written. What we have now are only brief glimpses.

In more modern times, however, the picture becomes more crowded. Important examples of nonviolent action and struggle occur in extremely varied settings. For example, to an extent which has on the whole been ignored, the American colonists used nonviolent resistance in their struggle against Britain, refusing to pay taxes and debts, refusing to import, refusing to obey laws they considered unjust, using independent political institutions, and severing social and economic contact with both the British and pro-British colonists.

Later, especially in the late nineteenth and early twentieth centuries, working people in many countries used noncooperation in the form of strikes and economic boycotts to improve conditions and to gain greater power. The Russian Revolution of 1905 is full of nonviolent responses to the events of "Bloody Sunday": paralyzing strikes, refusal to obey censorship regulations, establishment of "parallel" organs of government—these were only some of the pressures which led the Tsar's government to the promise of a more liberal governmental system. When the collapse of the tsarist system came in 1917 it was because it had disintegrated in face of an overwhelmingly nonviolent revolution—months before the Bolsheviks seized control in October. Nor does nonviolent pressure always have to be "against"; it can also be "for" as was made clear in Berlin in 1920, when the bureaucracy and population, who remained loyal to the existing Ebert government, brought down the militarist Kapp *Putsch* by refusing to cooperate with it.

Gandhi, who was the outstanding strategist of nonviolent action, regarded nonviolent struggle as a means of matching forces, one which had the greatest capacity for bringing real freedom and justice. The classic national Gandhian struggle was the 1930-31 campaign, which began with the famous Salt March as a prelude to civil disobedience against the British monopoly. A year-long nonviolent campaign followed. It shook British power in India and ended with negotiations between equals.

Despite highly unfavorable circumstances, nonviolent resistance sometimes also produced political tremors in certain Nazi-occupied countries during World War II. Occasionally—as in Norway—where Quisling's effort to set up a Corporative State was thwarted by nonviolent resistance—it won some battles. Covert noncooperation and, very rarely, nonviolent defiance even helped save the lives of Jews. During the same period, on the other side of the world, popular nonviolent action was being used successfully to dissolve the power of two Central American dictators. Communist systems, too, have felt the power of nonviolent action in the East German Rising in 1953, in strikes in Soviet prison camps, and in the nonviolent phase of the 1956 Hungarian Revolution. In the United States nonviolent action has played a major role in the struggles of Afro-Americans from the Montgomery bus boycott on. And in 1968, one of the most remarkable demonstrations of unprepared nonviolent resistance for national defense purposes took place in Czechoslovakia after the Russian invasion. The struggle was not successful, but the Czechs and Slovaks were able to hold out far longer—from August to April—than they could have with military resistance; even in defeat, it is a case meriting careful study. The achievements and victories of past nonviolent struggles, although often inadequate, have nevertheless frequently been remarkable, especially when one considers the usually small number of actual participants, and the general improvised, unprepared character of the resistance.

Another characteristic of nonviolent action is its great variety, in degree of success and in purpose and method. Sometimes nonviolent action may be used to achieve reforms or limited objectives (as in the Montgomery bus boycott); sometimes to destroy a whole regime (as in Russia in February–March 1917); sometimes to defend a government under attack (as in Czechoslovakia). Often deliberate efforts may be made to keep the struggle nonviolent, while in other cases nonviolence is not premeditated. Although the range of methods available in this type of struggle is vast, effective utilization of a considerable number of methods in the same case has taken place only rarely, as in the Russian revolutions. Only in a few cases (as in the Continental Association, the nonviolent "battle plan" of the First Continental Congress, and in India's 1930–31 campaign) has there been planned strategic phasing of the development of the struggle. Only once in a while—as with Gandhi—has there been conscious use of both strategic and tactical planning. Only rarely, as in Germany in the 1920s, during World War II in the case of governments-in-exile, and in Czechoslovakia in 1968, has there been official government backing for nonviolent resistance to usurpers. Many other variations in nonviolent action exist and will continue.

However, implicitly or explicitly, all nonviolent struggle has a basic assumption in common and that is its view of the nature of power and how to deal with it.

1

The Nature
and Control
of Political Power

INTRODUCTION

Unlike utopians, advocates of nonviolent action do not seek to "control" power by rejecting it or abolishing it. Instead, they recognize that power is inherent in practically all social and political relationships and that its control is "the basic problem in political theory"[1] and in political reality. They also see that it is necessary to wield power in order to control the power of threatening political groups or regimes. That assumption they share with advocates of violence, although they part company with them on many other points.

Social power may be briefly defined as the capacity to control the behavior of others, directly or indirectly, through action by groups of people, which action impinges on other groups of people.[2] Political power is that kind of social power which is wielded for political objectives, especially by governmental institutions or by people in opposition to or in support of such institutions. Political power thus refers to the total authority, influence, pressure and coercion which may be applied to achieve or prevent the implementation of the wishes of the power-holder.[3] In this book, when used alone, the term power is to be understood as referring to political power.

WHAT IS THE BASIC NATURE
OF POLITICAL POWER?

All types of struggle, and all means to control governments or to defend them against attack, are based upon certain basic assumptions about the nature of power. These are not usually explicit. In fact, so little do people stop to think about these assumptions that people are rarely aware of them and would often find it hard to articulate them. This is true of advocates of both nonviolent and violent action. Nevertheless, all responses to the "how" of dealing with an opponent's power are rooted in assumptions about the nature of power. An erroneous or inadequate view of the nature of political power is unlikely to produce satisfactory and effective action for dealing with it.

Basically, there appear to be two views of the nature of power. One can see people as dependent upon the good will, the decisions and the support of their government or of any other hierarchial system to which they belong. Or, conversely, one can see that government or system dependent on the people's good will, decisions and support. One can see the power of a government as emitted from the few who stand at the pinnacle of command. Or one can see that power, in all governments, as continually rising from many parts of the society. One can also see power as self-perpetuating, durable, not easily or quickly controlled or destroyed. Or political power can be viewed as fragile, always dependent for its strength and existence upon a replenishment of its sources by the cooperation of a multitude of institutions and people—cooperation which may or may not continue.

Nonviolent action is based on the second of these views: that governments depend on people, that power is pluralistic, and that political power is fragile because it depends on many groups for reinforcement of its power sources. The first view—that people depend on governments, that political power is monolithic, that it can really come from a few men, and that it is durable and self-perpetuating—appears to underlie most political violence. (A notable exception is guerrilla war in its predominently political stages.) The argument of this chapter is that the theory of power underlying nonviolent action is sounder and more accurate than the theory underlying most violent action, especially military struggle. In contrast to the pluralistic-dependency theory of nonviolent action—to which the bulk of this chapter is devoted—we might call this other view the "monolith theory."

The "monolith theory" of power assumes that the power of a government is a relatively fixed *quantum* (i.e. "a discrete unit quantity of energy"), a "given," a strong, independent, durable (if not indestructable), self-reinforcing, and self-perpetuating force. Because of these assumed characteristics, it follows that in open conflict such power cannot in the last analysis be controlled or destroyed simply by people but only by the threat or use of overwhelming physical might. The opponent's power may increase somewhat in the course of the struggle, or it may be somewhat reduced. But it is almost an axiom that in severe crises a hostile government's power can be significantly reduced, obstructed, or demolished only by destructive power—something like blasting chips or chunks off a solid stone block with explosives until it has been brought down to size or obliterated. War is based on this view of the nature of political power: faced with the actual or potential destruction of men, weapons, cities, industries, transport, communications and the like, the enemy will be forced to accept a settlement or to surrender (unless *he* has the greater destructive capacity). Nuclear weapons are the extreme development of the approach to control and combat based on this monolith view of the nature of political power.

If it were true that political power possesses the durability of a solid stone pyramid, then it would also be true that such power could only be controlled by the voluntary self-restraint of rulers (discussed below), by changes in the "ownership" of the monolith (the State)—whether with regular procedures (such as elections) or with irregular ones (regicide or *coup d'état),* or by destructive violence (conventional war). The monolith view would not allow for the possibility of other types of effective pressure and control. But the monolith view of a government's power is quite inaccurate and ignores the nature of the power of any ruler or regime.

Nor can belief in the monolith theory by the rulers themselves make it come true. That theory can only alter reality when both the subjects and the opponents of a regime presenting this monolithic image of itself can be induced to believe the theory. Then, if the "owners" of the monolith refused to grant concessions, dissidents would either have to submit helplessly or resort only to the destructive attack called for by that theory of power. However, since the monolith theory is factually not true, and since *all* governments are dependent on the society they rule, even a regime which believes itself to be a monolith, and *appears* to be one, can be weakened and shattered by the undermining and severance of its sources of power, when people act upon the theory of power presented in this chapter.

If the monolith theory is not valid, but nevertheless forms the basic assumption of modern war and other types of control, the resulting underlying fallacy helps to explain why war and other controls have suffered from disadvantages and limitations. Relying on destructive violence to control political power is regarded by theorists of nonviolent action as being just as irrational as attempting to use a lid to control steam from a caldron, while allowing the fire under it to blaze uncontrolled.

Nonviolent action is based on the view that political power can most efficiently be controlled *at its sources*. This chapter is an exploration of why and how this may be done. It will lead us to basic questions concerning the roots of political power and the nature of government. It will finally lead us to the distinctive way of looking at the problem of how to control power on which nonviolent action rests. This conceptual framework is both old and new.[4] It is rooted in the insights of some of the most respected political thinkers concerned with the nature of society and politics.

SOCIAL ROOTS OF POLITICAL POWER

An error frequently made by students of politics is to view political decisions, events and problems in isolation from the society in which they exist.[5] If they are studied within their social context, however, it may be found that the roots of political power reach beyond and below the formal structure of the State into the society itself. If this is so, it will follow that the nature of the means of controlling power will differ radically from those most suitable if it were not true.

It is an obvious, simple, but often forgotten observation of great theoretical and practical significance that the power wielded by individuals and groups in highest positions of command and decision in any government —whom we shall for brevity call "rulers"[6]—is not intrinsic to them. Such power must come from outside them. True, some men have greater personal qualities or greater intelligence, or inspire greater confidence than others, but this in no way refutes the fact that the political power which they wield as rulers comes from the society which they govern. Thus if a ruler is to wield power, he must be able to direct the behavior of other people, draw on large resources, human and material, wield an apparatus of coercion, and direct a bureaucracy in the administration of his policies. All these components of political power are external to the person of the power-holder.

The situation is essentially that described by the sixteenth-century

French writer Étienne de La Boétie, in speaking of the power of a tyrant: "He who abuses you so has only two eyes, has but two hands, one body, and has naught but what has the least man of the great and infinite number of your cities, except for the advantage you give him to destroy you."[7] Auguste Comte also argued in the early nineteenth century that the then popular theory was not correct in attributing to rulers a permanent, unchanging degree of power. On the contrary, while granting the influence of the political system on the society as a whole, Comte insisted that the power of a ruler was variable and that it depended on the degree to which the society granted him that power.[8] Other, more recent writers have made the same point.[9]

A. Sources of power

If political power is not intrinsic to the power-holder, it follows that it must have outside sources. In fact, political power appears to emerge from the interaction of all or several of the following sources:

1. Authority   The extent and intensity of the ruler's authority among the subjects is a crucial factor affecting the ruler's power.

Authority may be defined as the ". . . right to command and direct, to be heard or obeyed by others,"[10] voluntarily accepted by the people and therefore existing without the imposition of sanctions. The possessor of authority may not actually be superior; it is enough that he be perceived and accepted as superior. While not identical with power, authority is nevertheless clearly a main source of power.

2. Human resources   A ruler's power is affected by the number of persons who obey him, cooperate with him, or provide him with special assistance, as well as by the proportion of such persons in the general population, and the extent and forms of their organizations.

3. Skills and knowledge   The ruler's power is also affected by the skills, knowledge and abilities of such persons, and the relation of their skills, knowledge and abilities to his needs.

4. Intangible factors   Psychological and ideological factors, such as habits and attitudes toward obedience and submission, and the presence or absence of a common faith, ideology, or sense of mission, all affect the power of the ruler in relation to the people.

5. Material resources   The degree to which the ruler controls property, natural resources, financial resources, the economic system, means of communication and transportation helps to determine the limits of his power.

6. Sanctions   The final source of a ruler's power is the type and extent of sanctions at his disposal, both for use against his own subjects and in conflicts with other rulers.

As John Austin wrote, sanctions are "an enforcement of obedience,"[11] used by rulers against their subjects to supplement voluntary acceptance of their authority and to increase the degree of obedience to their commands. They may be violent or not; they may be intended as punishment or as deterrence. Citizens may sometimes apply sanctions against their governments or against each other (these will be discussed below). Still other sanctions may be applied by governments against other governments and may take a variety of forms, such as the breaking of diplomatic relations, economic embargoes, military invasions and bombings. Violent domestic sanctions, such as imprisonment or execution, are commonly intended to punish disobedience, not to achieve the objective of the original command, except insofar as such sanctions may inhibit future disobedience by other persons. Other violent sanctions sometimes, and most nonviolent sanctions usually, are intended to achieve the original objective; this is often the case in conventional war, strikes, political noncooperation and boycotts. Sanctions are usually a key element in domestic and international politics.

It is always a matter of the *degree* to which some or all of these sources of power are present; only rarely, if ever, are all of them completely available to a ruler or completely absent. But their availability is subject to constant variation, which brings about an increase or decrease in the ruler's power. Baron de Montesquieu observed that "those who govern have a power which, in some measure, has need of fresh vigor every day . . ."[12] To the degree that the sources of power are available without limitation, the ruler's power is unlimited. However, the opposite is also true: to the degree that the availability of these sources is limited, the ruler's political power is also limited.[13]

B. These sources depend on obedience

A closer examination of the sources of the ruler's power will indicate that they depend *intimately* upon the obedience and cooperation of the subjects. Let us, for example, consider *authority* from this point of view. Authority is necessary for the existence and operation of any regime.[14] No matter how great their means of physical coercion, all rulers require an acceptance of their authority, their right to rule and to command.[15] The key to habitual obedience is to reach the mind.[16] Thomas Hill Green points out that "obedience will scarcely be habitual unless it is loyal, not forced."[17] Because authority must by definition be voluntarily accepted by the people, the authority of the ruler will depend upon the goodwill of the subjects and will vary as that goodwill varies.

If a ruler's need for acceptance of his authority is basic, loss of authority will have serious consequences for his position and power. Just as subjects may accept a ruler's authority because they believe it is merited on grounds of morality and of the well-being of their society or country, subjects may for the same reasons at times deny the ruler's claims to authority over them. The weakening or collapse of that authority inevitably tends to loosen the subjects' predisposition toward obedience. Obedience will no longer be habitual; the decision to obey or not to obey will be made consciously, and obedience may be refused.

If the subjects deny the ruler's right to rule and to command, they are withdrawing the general agreement, or group consent, which makes possible the existing government.[18] This loss of authority sets in motion the disintegration of the ruler's power.[19] That power is reduced to the degree that he is denied authority. Where the loss is extreme, the existence of that particular government is threatened.

A second point to be considered is *the contribution of the subjects to the established system.* Clearly, every ruler must depend upon the cooperation and assistance of his subjects in operating the economic and administrative system. Every ruler needs the skill, knowledge, advice, labor and administrative ability of a significant portion of his subjects. The more extensive and detailed the ruler's control is, the more such assistance he will require. These contributions to the ruler's power will range, for example, from the specialized knowledge of a technical expert, the research endeavors of a scientist, and the organizational abilities of a department head to the assistance of typists, factory workers, transportation workers, and farmers. Both the economic and the political systems operate because of the contributions of many people, individuals, organizations and subgroups.

The ruler's power depends on the continual availability of all this assistance, not only from individual members, officials, employees and the like,[20] but from the subsidiary organizations and institutions which compose the system as a whole. These may be departments, bureaus, branches, committees and the like. Just as individuals and independent groups may refuse to cooperate, so too these unit organizations may refuse to provide sufficient help to maintain effectively the ruler's position and to enable him to implement his policies.[21] "Thus no complex can carry out a superior order if its members (either unit organizations or individuals) will not enable it to do so . . ."[22]

If the multitude of "assistants" reject the ruler's authority, they may then carry out his wishes inefficiently, or may take unto themselves certain decisions, or may even flatly refuse to continue their usual assistance.[23] In efforts to ensure the desired degree of assistance and cooperation, sanctions may, of course, be applied. But because rulers need more than grudging, outward forms of compliance by this multitude of subjects, efforts to obtain this assistance by compulsion will inevitably be inadequate as long as the extent and intensity of the ruler's authority among these subjects is limited.[24]

Because, then, of dependence on other people to operate the system, the ruler is continually subject to influence and restriction by both his direct assistants and the general populace. This control will be greatest where his dependence is greatest.

It remains to discuss the relation between *sanctions* and submission. If, in the face of serious unrest, the regime does not make changes to meet popular demands, increased reliance will have to be placed on enforcement. Such sanctions are usually possible despite dissatisfaction with the regime because very often while one section of the populace rejects the ruler's authority another section remains loyal and willing to help the regime to maintain itself and carry out its policies. In such a case a ruler may use the loyal subjects as police or soldiers to inflict sanctions on the remainder of the people.[25] However, sanctions, even in such a case, will not be the determining force in maintaining the regime—for several reasons. The ruling group (foreign or domestic) will itself still be united by something other than sanctions.[26] Furthermore, any ruler's ability to apply sanctions at home or abroad arises from and depends upon a significant degree of help from the subjects themselves.

Sanctions *are* important in maintaining a ruler's political power—especially in crises. But *the ability to impose sanctions* itself derives from the obedience and cooperation of at least some subjects; also, *whether those sanctions are effective* depends on the subjects' particular pattern of submission. Let us discuss each of these.

Without various types of cooperation and assistance, no ruler could impose sanctions, either on the people he wishes to rule in his own country, or internationally on foreign enemies. This ability depends to a considerable degree on whether his subjects are willing to become police and soldiers for him, and if so, upon the degree of efficiency with which they carry out commands to impose sanctions.[27] Furthermore, the material weapons themselves are social products. Once one gets much beyond bows and arrows, the manufacturing process for weapons—guns, bombs, planes, tanks and so on—depends on social cooperation, often of many people and of diverse organizations and institutions. Even technology has not changed this. New developments in communications and weaponry may in the future reduce the extent of assistance needed at a given moment to inflict sanctions, and may change the types of sanctions. The relationship of dependency will not be reduced or abolished, however.

Finally, the effectiveness of even enthusiastic police and troops in carrying out their tasks is often highly influenced by the degree to which the general population gives them voluntary support or obstructs their efforts.[28] As W.A. Rudlin points out, it is not that the State rests on "force," but that the State possesses "force" as long as most of its subjects deem this desirable.[29] Therefore, the capacity to *impose* sanctions rests on cooperation. But the *effectiveness* or ineffectiveness of sanctions when available and used also depends on the response of the subjects against whom they are threatened or applied.

Thus, the compliance pattern of the subjects will largely determine the extent to which sanctions are "required" to bolster obedience and even their relative effectiveness when used. We are speaking here of the degree to which people obey without threats, and the degree to which they continue to disobey despite punishment. Speaking of the general pattern of obedience under "normal" conditions, Karl W. Deutsch has argued that the chances of detection and punishment, even when small, help to strengthen and reinforce the pattern of obedience. This general obedience is sufficiently widespread and strong to make enforcement practical and probable in the minority of cases of disobedience. Enforcement and obedience are, then, interdependent: the greater the voluntary obedience, the greater the chances of detection and punishment of deviations.[30] Compliance and enforcement thus reinforce each other: the stronger the compliance pattern, the more effective the enforcement (and conversely). Also the weaker the compliance pattern, the less effective the enforcement (and conversely), with a continual range of variations. This applies to all types of regimes, including totalitarian systems.[31]

The ruler's power, we may summarize from the above discussion, is therefore not a static "given" *quantum*. Instead, his power varies because the number, type and quality of the social forces he controls varies. "The internal stability of a regime can be measured by the ratio between the number and strength of the social forces that it controls or conciliates, in a word, represents, and the number and strength of the social forces that it fails to represent and has against it."[32]

Similarly, the variations in the ruler's power are in turn directly or indirectly associated with the willingness of the subjects to accept the ruler, to obey, to cooperate with him and to carry out his wishes.[33] So important is the cooperation of the subjects in determining the availability of the sources of power, and hence the extent and capability of any ruler's power, that Bertrand de Jouvenel has put the ruler's political power, the sources of his power and the obedience of the subjects on an almost mathematical basis of equality.[34]

WHY DO MEN OBEY?

The most important single quality of any government, without which it would not exist, must be the obedience and submission of its subjects. Obedience is at the heart of political power. The relationships between the ruler and the subjects, and the ancient question of why some men obey other men, therefore become relevant to our analysis.

Many people often assume that the issuance of a command and its execution form a single, more or less automatic operation and therefore that the wielding of political power is an entirely one-way relationship. If this were true, any suggestion that a ruler's power might be controlled by reducing and withdrawing obedience and cooperation would be absurd, for the command and its implementation would be inseparable. However, such an assumption is not true: the relationship between command and obedience is always one of mutual influence and some degree of inter-action—which is "mutually determined" action[35] involving a two-sided relationship between the ruler and the subjects.

Sanctions for disobedience are more severe in the relationship between ruler and subject than is usual in other relationships between persons who are superior in rank (superordinates) and those who are under the controls or orders of a superior (subordinates).[36] Nevertheless, certain basic similarities of interaction and dependence do exist between the ruler-subject relationship and all other superordinate-subordinate relationships. Professor Harold Lasswell, the German sociologist Georg Simmel and Chester I. Barnard, the American analyst of *The Functions of the Executive,* have all offered insights into the nature of this interaction and dependence. Professor Lasswell has described this mutual influence as "cue-giving" and "cue-taking."[37] He cites the orchestra as an example, observing that just as a conductor may impose penalties upon members who fail to follow his cues, so the orchestra if dissatisfied with the conductor can impose penalties and "by deliberate noncooperation or hostile agitation . . . may get him fired."[38] Lasswell adds that without the expected conformity by the subordinates (whether in the form of "passive acquiescence or active consent") the power relationship is not complete, despite the threat or infliction of sanctions.[39]

Simmel has offered other examples of interaction, which occur even where least expected.[40] He cites the relationship between the speaker and his audience, the teacher and his class, and the journalist and his readers as instances in which the subordinates actually influence the superordinate in a major way. "Thus, a highly complex interaction . . . is hidden here beneath the semblance of pure superiority of the one element and a purely passive being-led of the other."[41] Even in the case of certain types of personal relationships in which the exclusive function of one person is to serve the other, he says, and even in the case of the relation between the hypnotist and the hypnotized, an element of reciprocity and mutual dependence is involved. As he puts it, ". . . appearance shows an absolute influence, on the one side, and an absolute being-influenced, on the other; but it conceals an interaction, an exchange of influences . . ."[42] He concludes that ". . . even the most miserable slave . . . in some fashion at least, can still in this sense react to his master."[43]

Barnard has also pointed out that the same type of interaction takes place *between institutions* and between the various units *within a complex organization.*[44] Because the superordinate body is dependent on its subordinate members or suborganizations to carry out orders and tasks, he describes their operation as a "cooperative effort."[45]

The same type of interaction takes place in the State: commands and orders are not automatically obeyed. This is true in the relationship between ruler and subjects, between ruler and the regime's various departments and agencies, among the various departments, and, within each of them, between its head and its subordinate members.[46] The power relationship exists only when completed by the subordinates' obedience to the ruler's commands and compliance with his wishes. As we shall see, this does not always take place. Even where political power is backed by sanctions, some degree of interaction *always* exists between the rulers or superiors-in-rank and those to whom they give orders and commands.[47] The wielding of political power is *not*, therefore, a one-way process in which the ruler issues commands which are inevitably carried out. "Since political power is the control of other men," Franz

Neumann wrote, "political power . . . is always a two-sided relationship."[48] Furthermore, the interaction between ruler and subject takes place within a political and social setting in which a variety of factors may influence its course and outcome.

The variables in this interaction are generally three: the ruler (or leader), the subject (or follower), and the situation.[49] All are subject to constant mutual influence, changes in one altering the reactions of the other two, and in turn requiring a new response from the original factor. The degree to which the ruler succeeds in wielding power and achieving his objectives thus depends upon the degree of obedience and cooperation emerging from this interaction. Both domestically and internationally a regime's power "is in proportion to its ability to make itself obeyed and win from that obedience the means of action. It all turns on that obedience. Who knows the reasons for that obedience knows the inner nature of Power."[50]

Having established the fact that obedience is necessary if the command is to be carried out and also the fact that obedience is not inevitable, we come to the ancient question: why do the many obey the few?

How is it that a ruler is able to obtain and maintain political domination over the multitude of his subjects? Why do they in such large numbers submit to him and obey him,[51] even when it is clearly not in their interest to do so? How is it that a ruler may even use his subjects for ends which are contrary to the subjects' own interests?[52] All these questions are not new. But in asking them here as though they were new, we may rediscover old insights and explore afresh their implications. The answers will be important in determining what solutions are to be offered to the problem of how to control political power. As the sociologists Hans Gerth and C. Wright Mills have concluded, ". . . from a psychological point of view the crux of the problem of power rests in understanding the origin, constitution, and maintainance of voluntary obedience."[53]

Thomas Hobbes' answer in the seventeenth century to the question of obedience was simple. Subjects obey their rulers because of fear, he wrote, either fear of the ruler himself or of one another.[54] Were fear the only reason for obedience there would be only two possible means of control of the sovereign's power: either inducing in the ruler self-imposed limitations, or threatening or using superior fear-instilling power. Today these means are often seen to be inadequate. Their inadequacy may be rooted in an erroneous or incomplete understanding of the reasons for obedience. Hobbes' view, taken by itself, is not true. Other factors in addition to fear have played a significant role in the development of governments and the maintenance of obedience. It is necessary to look beyond Hobbes' conceptual framework to discover the reasons for obedience.

A. The reasons are various and multiple

Actually there is no single self-sufficient explanation for obedience to rulers. Nor can political obedience be explained solely in rational terms. The reasons are multiple, complex and interrelated; different combinations and proportions of reasons produce obedience in various situations. A number of specific answers and explanations have, however, been offered. We can learn much from them, provided we remember that no one answer can be totally adequate, and that each must be seen in the perspective of the others.

1. Habit   One reason why men obey is that obedience has long been the practice of humanity, and it has become a habit. In the opinion of some, the habit of obedience is in fact "the essential reason" for continued obedience.[55] David Hume said that habit consolidates what other principles of human nature have imperfectly founded. Once accustomed to obedience, he wrote, men "never think of departing from that path in which they and their ancestors have constantly trod, and to which they are confined by so many urgent and visible motives." [56]

No one claims, however, that habit is the sole cause of obedience. Convincing reasons felt over a long period are necessary to make obedience habitual. Such obedience, Austin suggested, is the consequence of a combination of various factors such as custom, prejudice, utility, and a perception of the expediency of political government.[57] Further, in times of political crisis, or when the demands of the ruler increase sharply, habit ceases to be a complete explanation of obedience.[58] Unless other adequate reasons for obedience also exist, it may then cease.

2. Fear of sanctions   The fear of sanctions has been widely acknowledged as a source of obedience.[59] While sanctions may take various forms, such as social and economic pressures, we are here largely concerned with the sanctions provided in the law and practice of the State. These generally involve the threat or use of some form of physical violence against the disobedient subject, and induce obedience by ". . . power merely coercive, a power really operating on people simply through their fears . . ."[60]

The intent behind such sanctions may be both to provide a punishment or reprisal for failure to meet an obligation (thus, sanctions applied against subjects are usually not primarily intended to achieve the objective of the original command) and also to encourage the continued compliance of *other* subjects by inspiring in them, through exemplary cases, a fear of the sanctions for disobedience.[61] Fear of violent internal sanctions against individuals and the existence of means for waging violent conflict against groups (both internally and externally) have often been regarded as important in the origin of the State and of political obedience.[62] The role of fear of sanctions is especially important when other reasons for obedience have become weakened. Yet political power cannot be reduced simply to physical might, and fear of sanctions in support of laws and commands is not the sole reason for obedience.

3. Moral obligation   A third reason for obedience is that subjects feel a moral obligation to obey. This is distinct from a legal obligation to do so, although certain types of moral obligation may be associated with a legal obligation. A sense among the subjects of a moral obligation to obey is a common quality of all forms of political organization.[63]

A sense of moral obligation to obey is partly a product of the normal process by which the individual absorbs the customs, ways and beliefs of his society as he grows up,[64] and partly the result of deliberate indoctrination.[65] The line between these processes is not always clear. They produce in the subject an inner "constraining power"[66] which leads him to obedience and submission.[67] This sense of moral obligation may not originate with the ruler but, instead, come from general views about the welfare of the whole society or from religious principles. On the other hand, because of the limited effectiveness of fear, rulers may try to influence "the most efficacious of all" restraints, that of "a man's own conscience."[68] The ruler's "secret of success" then becomes the subject's mind, and propaganda becomes "the indispensable adjunct of the police."[69]

The origins and effects of such feelings vary, but generally they may arise from four considerations:[70]

a) The common good of society. Belief that constraint by government is for the common good is always an element in political obedience.[71] Hume described this as the motive which first produced submission and obedience to governments and one which continued to do so.[72] Obedience makes protection from antisocial persons possible,[73] and promotes the good of all. As T.H. Green put it, both morality and political subjection originate in general rational recognition of "a common well-being," embodied in rules to restrain those who would violate it.[74] This view includes both belief in the benefits of government in general and of a particular government as compared to any possible alternative.[75]

Belief that political obedience is for the common good—held by both the general population and those able to impose sanctions for disobedience—thus "gives great security to any government."[76] Without this belief, says Green, no one would recognize any claim to the common obedience of the subjects.[77]

The degree to which the law or the particular regime is identified with the common good will help to determine the degree of loyal obedience.[78] However, a considerable discrepancy may be tolerated, for belief in the advantages of government makes people averse to resistance and displeased when others resist.[79] Although dissatisfied, people may therefore continue to obey for fear that resistance might entail still greater evil and that government itself might collapse.[80]

b) Suprahuman factors. A second source of moral obligation leading to political obedience lies in the identification of the lawgiver or ruler with suprahuman qualities, powers, or principles which make disobedience inconceivable. These qualities may originate in magic, supernatural beings, deities, or "true-believer" ideologies (both political and religious). But the effect on obedience is similar. The ruling system thus takes on the character of a religious or nonreligious "theocracy"—a development which significantly contributes to obedience,[81] for disobedience then becomes heresy, impiety, a betrayal of race, nation, or class, or a defiance of the gods,[82] of History, or of Truth. Various methods, such as rituals, may be used to keep alive deference and belief in the particular suprahuman qualities, powers, or principles identified with the lawgiver or ruler.

c) Legitimacy of the command. Commands are also obeyed because they are considered legitimate owing to their source[83] and their issuer.[84] If the command is given by someone in an accepted official position, if it is seen as being in accordance with tradition, established law and constitution, if the ruler has obtained his position through the established procedure, then the subject will usually feel a greater obligation to obey than he would if these conditions were not present.[85] More rarely, by contrast, in revolutionary situations legitimacy may derive not from tradition but from "the people," "the revolution," and activities during the struggle against the previous, now "illegitimate," ruler or system. There are also other sources of legitimacy[86] which contribute to obedience by increasing the ruler's authority.

d) Conformity of commands to accepted norms. The fourth source of feelings of moral obligation to obey rulers lies in the conformity of their commands to accept norms of conduct. People then obey because the behavior commanded by the ruler is what they believe to be right in any case, such as not stealing or not killing. The law is then obeyed because of the "rationality of its contents."[87] As Green puts it, the law corresponds to the "general sense of what is equitable and necessary."[88]

4. Self-interest Nonpolitical organizations and institutions—business, educational, scientific and the like—often obtain the desired cooperation of individuals by offering incentives, such as money, position and prestige. Similarly, incentives may also be important in political institutions, including the State, as they help to procure the obedience, cooperation and active assistance of subjects. Hume lists self-interest as a secondary, supporting, reason for obedience which operates in combination with other reasons.[89] People who dislike a ruler or system may nevertheless continue not only to obey passively, but even to serve actively in what they consider to be their own positive self-interest. There may also be a negative type of self-interest, involving the avoidance of molestation and inconvenience; this is related to sanctions and is discussed under that topic.

Positive self-interest is most important if the ruler is to obtain the various types of assistants and helpers he needs to run the government and to rule. Once the ruler is established, he is able to encourage the expectation of rewards.[90] Normally his ministers and military force, for example, "find an immediate and visible interest in supporting his authority."[91] Such self-interest may also be especially important for persons who occupy secondary governmental positions in administration, enforcement and the like, as well as nongovernmental intermediary positions in the society.

Self-interest may be appealed to in terms of: *prestige* (the hope for titles, decorations and various honors); *relative power position* (maintenance and improvement of one's status in the political and social pyramid);[92] or *direct or indirect financial gain* ("every man is supposed to have his price").[93] These rewards especially help the ruler to obtain the services of the minority, which he will use to rule and control the majority.[94]

While direct economic rewards have generally been limited to relatively small numbers of persons, economic self-interest may now in certain societies be an increasingly important motive for obedience among a larger percentage of the population. With the multiplication of government jobs and controls over the economy, more people may find it to their interest to remain loyal, to obey, and to cooperate. Also, indirect economic rewards may encourage general submission; higher standards of living and increasing material benefits in highly industrialized countries may contribute significantly to continuing political obedience and positive assistance for the system and regime.

5. Psychological identification with the ruler   Subjects may also obey and cooperate because they have a close emotional identification with the ruler or with the regime or system. This identification may be stronger and more usual in societies in which the common beliefs and sense of purpose have broken down; people often need something or someone to believe in and some source of purpose and direction in their lives. Deutsch refers to persons who look "upon the government in some manner as an extension of themselves or upon themselves as an extension of the government . . . the triumphs and successes of the government are felt as personal triumphs by its subjects; its defeats are experienced as personal dishonor or misfortune . . ."[95] This phenomenon is not limited to any particular political system.

6. Zones of indifference   Although subjects do not obey all laws with equal thoroughness or enthusiasm, it does not follow that all those laws which do not arouse enthusiastic obedience will be poorly obeyed in the absence of threats of sanctions. This is because, in Robert M. MacIver's words, "there is a margin of indifference and a margin of tolerance."[96] Barnard also observes that one reason that it is possible to achieve enduring cooperation is the existence of " 'a zone of indifference' within which each individual will accept orders without consciously questioning their authority . . ."[97] How wide this zone is will vary, depending on a number of social and political conditions and the inducements offered for obedience.

7. Absence of self-confidence among subjects   Many people do not have sufficient confidence in themselves, their judgment and their capacities to make them capable of disobedience and resistance. Having no strong will of their own, they accept that of their rulers, and sometimes prefer rulers who will direct their lives and relieve them of the task of making decisions. The subjects may be disillusioned, exhausted, apathetic, or possessed of inertia, or they may lack a belief system which makes it possible both to evaluate when one ought to obey and disobey, and also to give confidence in one's right and ability to make such a decision. Lack of self-confidence may also be influenced by a belief that the ruling group is more qualified to make decisions and to carry them out than are the subjects. This attitude may be based on perceived greater competence,[98] social customs and class distinctions,[99] or conscious indoctrination.[100]

One consequence of the lack of self-confidence is a tendency to avoid responsibility, to seek to delegate it upward and to attribute greater authority to superiors in the hierarchy than is in fact merited.[101] People lacking self-confidence may seek a ruler, a leader, a despot, a tyrant who will relieve them of responsibility for guiding their present and their future.[102] Wrote Rousseau: "Slaves lose everything in their chains, even the desire of escaping from them: they love their servitude, as the comrades of Ulysses loved their brutish condition."[103] Even where subjects wish to alter the established order, they may remain submissive because they lack confidence in their ability to act effectively in bringing about the desired changes. As long as people lack self-confidence they are unlikely to do anything other than obey, cooperate with, and submit to their rulers.

B. Obtaining the ruler's functionaries and agents

Every ruler uses the obedience and cooperation he receives from *part* of the society to rule the *whole*. He is assisted by a "veritable army of underlings,"[104] a complex graded organization of subordinates, functionaries and agents,[105] who help to subject the society as a whole to his domination.[106] This requires and produces a hierarchical system.[107] Because of the key role of this section of the population, brief special attention to their motives for obedience and cooperation is required. As with the general populace, these motives are various and multiple: habit, fear of sanctions, moral obligation, self-interest, identification with the ruler, indifference within very broad limits to particular policies, and insufficient self-confidence to refuse. While the preceding discussion of these motives also applies here, it seems that for this group a particular motive may be of either more or less importance than among the general population. Feelings of moral obligation to obey and to provide help may be especially important. Within the ruling group, which includes this organization of functionaries and agents, "some common sentiment," "something like voluntary consent" is needed.[108] As already noted, self-interest may play a disproportionately large role; Boétie observed that there may be "as many people to whom tyranny seems profitable, as those to whom liberty would be agreeable."[109] Today, many people have vested in the continuance of established regimes and therefore continue to serve them.

Fear of sanctions is probably less important among the functionaries and agents than among the general populace. (An exception might be soldiers who are drafted into the army against their wishes and face severe sanctions should they mutiny.) Generally, however, violent sanctions are not decisive in obtaining the special assistance of functionaries and agents; other motives predominate. This may be important in getting them to refuse to assist groups which have illegally seized the State apparatus by a *coup d'état,* for example.

C. Obedience is not inevitable[110]

Obedience to a ruler's command, though usual, is not inevitable. It always varies in degree with the individual concerned and with the social and political situation. Obedience is never universally practiced by the whole population. Many people sometimes disobey the law. Some people do so frequently. The degree of general compliance varies widely. The most powerful ruler receives no more than the habitual obedience of the bulk of the subjects.[111] Publicized cases of mass disobedience, defiance and noncooperation are simply more extensive dramatic evidences of this general truth. They are demonstrations that the wielding of political power is indeed a case of interaction.

People are generally law-abiding, except when "unmoored by catastophic events or by social convulsions."[112] At any given point in a given society there are limits within which a ruler must stay if his commands are to be obeyed. These limits are subject to change throughout the history of a society.[113] To the degree that the law and the ruler's general policies agree with the needs of a society and the general sense of what is desirable and tolerable, obedience will be widespread. But, Rudlin observed, "Obedience can be enforced only while the mass of men are in some sort of agreement with the law. There is no lack of examples of opposition and successful opposition, to government decision."[114]

It follows that under certain conditions subjects may be willing to put up with inconvenience, suffering and disruption of their lives rather than continue to submit passively or to obey a ruler whose policies they can no longer tolerate. Having long been accustomed to receiving widespread obedience, rulers do not always anticipate these eventualities.[115]

THE ROLE OF CONSENT

In light of the above discussion, it is reasonable to view the political obedience on which a ruler's power is ultimately dependent as a consequence of a combination of a fear of sanctions and free consent—the latter arising either from a more or less nonrational acceptance of the standards and ways of one's society, or from a more or less rational consideration of the merits of the regime and the reasons for obeying it. This is compatible with discussions by several theorists who describe obedience as arising from a mixture of "coercion" and "consent."[116] Clearly sanctions *alone* could not produce the necessary degree, extent and constancy of obedience. Yet if *other* reasons for obedience are present, an increase in sanctions may increase compliance.[117] Nevertheless, the fact remains that sanctions do not *always* produce an increase in obedience. This may be because in order to produce obedience, sanctions must also operate through the volition, or will, of the subject. This possibility merits further exploration. If true, it has important political implications.

Let us first admit that there is a meaningful sense in which obedience is *not* voluntary, in which the individual is a more or less helpless victim of vast social and political forces which impinge upon him—even determining his beliefs, his moral standards, his attitudes to social and political events, and consequently his obedience to the State. If these forces are insufficient to produce obedience, there is always the repressive power of the State, which he has learned to fear. This combination of pressures, controls and repression is, more often than not, seen as a conclusive reason for the view that obedience follows more or less automatically from the issuance of commands. As we have seen, however, the wielding of political power involves social interaction, and obedience is by no means as uniform or universal as this deterministic view of obedience would lead us to expect. The reason for this inconsistency may be simple: the view that political obedience is constant, that it is determined by these social and political forces (or, if all else fails, will at least be produced by sanctions) is fallacious.

A. Obedience is essentially voluntary

In reviewing the reasons for obedience we find that although they are highly influenced by various social forces, each reason must operate through the will or the opinion of the individual subject to be effective. If he is to obey, the subject must accept a combination of the current reasons for obeying as in fact being sufficient for obedience. Because sanctions do not automatically produce obedience, the subject's evaluation of the reasons for obedience will even include sanctions. The will or opinion of the individual is not constant and may change in response to new influences, events and forces. In varying degrees the individual's own will may then play an active role in the situation. There is thus an important sense in which the obedience of subjects is essentially the result of an act of volition.[118]

Even in the case of obedience by habit, the subject accepts the view that it is best to continue to obey without consciously trying to examine why he should do so. Feelings of moral obligation, a psychological identification with the ruler, and acceptance of a "zone of indifference" all involve a basically voluntary acceptance of the ruler's wishes. The role of self-interest in procuring obedience may vary, depending upon the relative importance given (more or less consciously) to it by the subject, in the context of a variety of other attitudes. In certain situations the subject may even conclude that it is in his self-interest to *disobey* a regime—especially if he foresees its collapse. The degree of his lack of self-confidence also varies and may be influenced by changes in the attitudes of other subjects.

Even in the case of sanctions, there is a role for an act of will, for choice. The sanction must be *feared* and its consequences be seen as more undesirable than the consequences of obedience. This is not to deny that there is always "a margin of obedience which is won only by the use of force or the threat of force."[119] Even Gandhi would admit that "consent is often forcibly procured by the despot."[120] To say there is a role for will or choice even in the case of sanctions is to say that one can choose to obey, thus avoiding the sanctions threatened for disobedience. Or one can choose to disobey and risk receiving the threatened sanctions.

Here a distinction must be made between obedience and coercion by direct physical violation. If, for example, a man who is ordered to go to prison refuses to do so and is physically dragged there (that is, if he is coerced by direct physical violation), he cannot be said to obey, argued Austin. But if he *walks* to prison under a command backed by *threat* of a sanction, then he in fact obeys and consents to the act, although he may not approve of the command.[121] *Obedience thus exists only when one has complied with or submitted to the command.*

Physical compulsion affecting only the body therefore does not obtain *obedience.* Only certain types of objectives can be achieved by direct physical compulsion of disobedient subjects—such as moving them physically, preventing them from moving physically, or seizing their money or property. Even to achieve such limited objectives in the face of a larger number of disobedient subjects would require a vast number of enforcement agents able to force or constrain each of them physically. Most other objectives of commands, and certainly active cooperation, cannot be produced by even continuous direct physical violation of persons—whether the command is to dig a ditch, obey traffic signals, work in a factory, offer technical advice, or arrest political opponents. The overwhelming percentage of a ruler's commands and objectives can only be achieved by inducing the subject to be *willing* for some reason to carry them out. Punishment of one who disobeys a command does not achieve the objective (for example, the ditch remains undug even if the men who refused to dig it have been shot).

The threat of physical compulsion or sanctions produces obedience and consent only when the threat affects the subject's mind and emotions —in other words, when the subject fears the sanctions and is unwilling to suffer them. This was Simmel's point too: he argued that despite penalties for disobedience, the choice to obey or to disobey is always possible.[122] *It is not the sanctions themselves which produce obedience but the fear of them.*[123] In Robert Michels' words: "Even when authority rests on mere physical coercion it is accepted by those ruled, although the acceptance may be due to a fear of force."[124] Of course, it is almost axiomatic that most people in most situations are quite unwilling to suffer the penalties for disobedience. Even when their dislike of the status quo is high, there will be hesitation. Gandhi, for example, on the basis of his efforts to produce large-scale disobedience and voluntary acceptance of imposed sanctions, observed that feelings must be very intense to make possible the acceptance of such sacrifice.[125] However, disobedience sometimes occurs despite sanctions, as will be described later in more detail.

If, then, choice and volition are present even where obedience is largely produced by sanctions—where one could least expect an act of will —the obedience of subjects in general can be regarded as voluntary and as arising from consent. This is especially so because generally people obey for reasons other than the threat of sanctions. Clearly, permanent obedience cannot be produced only by threat of sanctions.[126] It is reasonable to conclude with Austin that obedient subjects *will* the obedience they render, that they obey because of some motive, that they consent to obey. Their obedience is therefore essentially voluntary.[127] This is one of the significant characteristics of government.

The conclusions of the discussion thus far may be put succinctly. A ruler's power is dependent upon the availability of its several sources. This availability is determined by the degree of obedience and cooperation given by the subjects. Such obedience and cooperation are, however, not inevitable, and despite inducements, pressures, and even sanctions, obedience remains essentially voluntary. Therefore, *all government is based upon consent.*[128]

Support for this view comes from widely diverse political thinkers and actionists. For example, Austin wrote that the view "that every government continues through the people's consent" simply means that in every society "the people are determined by motives of some description or another, to obey their government habitually . . ."[129] William Godwin, an earlier and more libertarian thinker, argued that people can be held in subjection only insofar as ". . . they are willing to be subject. All government is founded in opinion."[130] Acceptance of this view came even from Adolf Hitler: "For, in the long run, government systems are not held together by the pressure of force, but rather by the belief in the quality and the truthfulness with which they represent and promote the interests of the people."[131]

To say that every government depends on consent of the people does not, of course, mean that the subjects of all rulers *prefer* the established order to any other which might be created. They *may* consent because they positively approve of it—but they may also consent because they are unwilling to pay the price for the refusal of consent.[132] Refusal requires self-confidence and the motivation to resist and may involve considerable inconvience[133] and social disruption,[134] to say nothing of suffering.

The degree of liberty or tyranny in any government is, it follows, in large degree a reflection of the relative determination of the subjects to be free and their willingness and ability to resist efforts to enslave them.

Three of the most important factors in determining to what degree a ruler's power will be controlled or uncontrolled therefore are: 1) the relative desire of the populace to control his power; 2) the relative strength of the subjects' independent organizations and institutions; and 3) the subjects' relative ability to withhold their consent and assistance.

Ultimately, therefore, freedom is not something which a ruler "gives" his subjects. Nor, in the long run, do the formal institutional structures and procedures of the government, as prescribed by the constitution, by themselves determine the degree of freedom or the limits of the ruler's power. A society may in fact be more free than those formal arrangements would indicate. Instead, the extent and intensity of the ruler's power will be set by the strength of the subjects and the condition of the whole society. Those limits may themselves, in turn, be expanded or contracted by the interplay between the actions of the ruler and those of the subjects.

The political conclusions to be drawn from these insights into the power of all rulers are simple but they are of fundamental significance in establishing control over dictators and finding a substitute for war. Errol E. Harris has formulated them succinctly. He argues that political power "can never be exercised without the acquiescence of the people—without the direct cooperation of the large numbers of people and the indirect cooperation of the entire community."[135] Therefore, tyranny has "flourished only where the people through ignorance, or disorganization, or by actual connivance and complicity, aid and abet the tyrant and keep him in power by allowing themselves to be the instruments of his coercion."[136]

> . . . a nation gets the government which it deserves, and those to whom this dictum is distasteful are either the small minority of dissidents, too few to influence the popular will of which they are the victims, or else those whose discontent is inconsistent with their practice, and who cooperate with the tyranny they deplore in spite of themselves and often without realizing it.[137]

Leo Tolstoy had such insights into the nature of all government in mind when he wrote about the English subjection of India:

> A commercial company enslaved a nation comprising two hundred millions. Tell this to a man free from superstition and he will fail to grasp what these words mean. What does it mean that thirty thousand men . . . have subdued two hundred million . . . ? Do not the figures make it clear that it is not the English who have enslaved the Indians, but the Indians who have enslaved themselves?[138]

It was not simply English military might which subjected India to English rule, argued Tolstoy; this subjection could not be understood except in the context of the condition of Indian society which led the Indians to cooperate with, submit to, and obey the new *Raj*.

Such obedience and cooperation are not offered automatically, for people do not give equal obedience and help to every person and group which lays claim to governing them. Nor does any particular ruler necessarily receive equal obedience and assistance throughout his reign.

B. Consent can be withdrawn

We have seen that obedience by the subject is the consequence of the mutual influence of various causes operating through his will. These causes of obedience are not, however, constant. The reasons for obedience are variable and may be strengthened or weakened. For example, the degree of a ruler's authority will vary. Other reasons for obedience may increase or decrease. Conditions and outlooks, the state of the subjects' knowledge, their attitudes and emotions—all may change. They may alter the subjects' willingness to submit or to resist. Even fear of sanctions is not constant. Such fear may grow because of increased severity or personal insecurity. Or it may decrease, because of reduced severity or increased willingness to accept sanctions because of overriding goals. The subjects' willingness to submit to a particular policy or to a whole regime may also be altered because of new beliefs (or new insights into old ones) and because of changes in perceptions of the established system. As a result of all these possible variations, the necessary consent of the subjects is unstable. It is always characterized by minor variations; it may at times be characterized by major changes.

Obedience therefore varies. For example, decline in the ruler's authority may undermine the subjects' willingness to obey and also weaken their voluntary cooperation.[139] When one or more reasons for obedience lose strength, the ruler may seek to counteract that loss by efforts to increase other reasons for obedience, such as by making sanctions harsher and more frequent or by increasing rewards for loyal service.[140] If such efforts are not successful, the continued decline in grounds for obedience may lead to the disintegration of the particular regime.

The change in the subjects' wills may lead to their withdrawing from the ruler their service, cooperation, submission and obedience. This withdrawal may occur among both the ordinary subjects and the ruler's agents and administrators. There is abundant historical evidence that changes in the opinions of the subjects and agents have led to reduced obedience and cooperation with the established ruler and, in turn, to the weakening of the regime.

The attitudes and beliefs of the ruler's agents are especially important here. Destroy the opinion of the supporting intermediary class that it is in their interest to support the ruler, urged Godwin, "and the fabric which is built upon it falls to the ground."[141] Likewise, he argued, any army, domestic or foreign, which is used to hold a people in subjection may be influenced by the opinions and sentiments of the people at large. The army may then decline to provide the ruler with assistance in suppressing the people, just as the general populace may withhold its assistance.[142]

Gandhi, who experimented widely with the political potentialities of disobedience, emphasized the importance of a change of will as as a prerequisite for a change in patterns of obedience and cooperation. There was, he argued, a need for: 1) a psychological change away from passive submission to self-respect and courage;[143] 2) recognition by the subject that his assistance makes the regime possible;[144] and 3) the building of a determination to withdraw cooperation and obedience.[145] Gandhi felt that these changes could be consciously influenced, and he therefore deliberately set out to bring them about. "My speeches," he said, "are intended to create 'disaffection' as such, that people might consider it a shame to assist or cooperate with a government that had forfeited all title to respect or support."[146]

Changes in the attitudes of workers in factories or of citizens in politics, for example, which result in withdrawal of obedience and cooperation can create extreme difficulties for the system. It can be disrupted or paralyzed. At times this can happen even when the ruler's own agents continue their loyal obedience. The sheer difficulties of maintaining the normal working of any political unit when its subjects are bent upon an attitude of defiance and acts of obstruction are sufficient to give any ruler cause for thought. Without the obedience, cooperation, assistance and submission of the subjects and agents, power-hungry men claiming to be rulers would be "rulers" without subjects, and therefore only "objects of derision."[147]

If a ruler's power is to be controlled by withdrawing help and obedience, noncooperation and disobedience must be widespread and must be maintained in the face of repression aimed at forcing a resumption of submission. However, once there has been a major reduction of or an end to the subjects' fear, and once there is a willingness to suffer sanctions as the price of change, large-scale disobedience and noncooperation become possible. Such action then becomes politically significant,[148] and the ruler's will is thwarted in proportion to the number of disobedient subjects and the degree of his dependence upon them. The answer to the problem of uncontrolled power may therefore lie in learning how to carry out and maintain such withdrawal despite repression.

TOWARD A THEORY OF NONVIOLENT CONTROL OF POLITICAL POWER

Many people may readily admit that noncooperation and disobedience may create minor and temporary problems for rulers, but deny that such action can do more. If such were the limits of the impact of noncooperation and disobedience, then reliance would have to be placed elsewhere for control of the power of governments. Indeed, a number of political theorists have pointed to very different means of control over ruler's powers, and their theories have gained wide acceptance.

A. Traditional controls

Because a discussion of these more traditional means of control can, by comparison and contrast, help to point up important characteristics of the nonviolent approach, they should be briefly surveyed here. Generally speaking, they fall into three categories: voluntary self-restraint by rulers themselves, institutional arrangements designed to limit the exercise of power, and the application of superior power of the same type, as in violent revolution or war.

1. Self-restraint   Self-restraint has long been one of the important restraining or limiting influences on rulers: the ruler voluntarily accepts some limits on the scope of his power and on the means he would use to wield that power. Beyond such limits he would be unwilling to go, because of a belief that to do so would violate moral and other standards accepted by the ruler and by society. This self-restraint has operated both alone and in combination with other controls, especially certain institutional arrangements which are discussed below.

Among contemporary writers, Martin J. Hillenbrand has placed special emphasis on the importance of self-control in rulers, regarding it as one of the two fundamental ways of controlling "the power of force" (the other being "the superior power of force").[149] He calls this "the internal control of self-restraint in the use of power based on some criterion or theory of conduct."[150] Hillenbrand concludes that for the present and in the future "the essential solution" to the problem of the control of power "must lie in the inducement of restraint in the·possessors of power so that they will use it only in accordance with certain criteria."[151]

2. Institutional arrangements   The second traditional means to control the abuse of power has been the attempt to establish "a principle or a set of institutions by which governments might be restrained."[152] This has involved setting up procedures for selecting the power-holder, determining government policy, and regulating government actions. The institutional and constitutional arrangements of liberal democracies have been the prime contributions toward this type of control. The legislature is elected by the subjects, and then either the executive is chosen by the legislature (as a prime minister and his cabinet) or the chief executive is elected directly by the subjects (as the American president). Governmental powers and procedures have been enumerated in the constitution, laws and traditions of such systems. In the American system differing tasks have been assigned to separate branches of the government, and the rights of the subjects have been enumerated. The judiciary has often been authorized to defend the rights of the subjects and to limit the actions of the government. These are only examples. Such systems are based on the assumption that in the last analysis the elected government is willing to abide by such restrictions on its power, and that powerful internal forces do not handicap seriously or disrupt the normal functioning of the system.

3. Applying superior means of violence   Where all other means of asserting influence and control over a political ruler have failed, the traditional solution has been to threaten or to use superior violence against his forces. As we noted, Hillenbrand speaks of "the threat of, or the actual use of, superior power of force" as one of "two fundamental ways by which the power of force may be controlled."[153] Violence for this purpose has taken a variety of forms, including rioting, assassination, violent revolution, guerrilla warfare, *coup d'état*, civil war and international war.

The need for some further means of control beyond these three has often been admitted. Jouvenel, for example, has spoken of the difficulty of finding "some practical method" for controlling power,[154] and Jacques Maritain has posed "the problem of the means through which the people can supervise or control the State."[155]

This is not an easy task, for an alternative technique of control over political power ought to contain the potential for dealing with extreme situations as well as minor ones. The remainder of this chapter, therefore, surveys briefly a small part of the evidence from existing theory and practice which indicates that withdrawal of cooperation, obedience and submission may threaten the ruler's position and power.

B. Theorists on withdrawal of support

Several political theorists have also argued that the withdrawal of obedience, cooperation and submission by subjects, if sustained, will produce a crisis for the ruler, threatening the very existence of the regime. These include Boétie, Machiavelli and Austin. The similarities of their views to the conclusion reached to this point in our analysis are striking.

Boétie—the least known of these theorists—argued that refusal of assistance to tyrants cuts off the sources of their power, and continued refusal causes tyrants to collapse without need for violence against them. ". . . if they are given nothing, if they are not obeyed, without fighting, without striking a blow, they remain naked and undone, and do nothing further, just as the root, having no soil or food, the branch withers and dies."[156] Boétie maintained that people could deliver themselves from a tyrant by casting off servility: ". . . just don't support him, and you will see him like a great colossus whose base has been stolen, of his own weight sink to the ground and shatter."[157] Boétie's views—reputedly written at the age of eighteen—exerted a great influence upon Thoreau and Tolstoy.[158] Through Tolstoy, those views also influenced Gandhi who saw in them a confirmation of the theory of power he had already grasped, and the political potential which he had already begun to explore.

A few years before Boétie, Machiavelli also pointed to the dangers which disobedience (by both his agents and his ordinary subjects) presented to a prince, especially in times of transition from a civil to an absolute order of government. The prince must then depend on the uncertain goodwill of his agents (magistrates), who may refuse to assist him, or of his subjects, who may not be "of a mind to obey him amid these confusions."[159] Machiavelli argued that the prince ". . . who has the public as a whole for his enemy can never make himself secure; and the greater his cruelty, the weaker does his regime become."[160]

Marat, writing in the *Ami du Peuple* on June 30, 1790, warned the "aristocracy of rich men" that, instead of taking revenge, the poor should simply leave the rich to themselves, for ". . . to take your place, we have only to stand with folded arms. Reduced, as you will then be, to working with your hands and tilling your own fields, you will become our equals . . ."[161]

Percy B. Shelley, poet and son-in-law of Godwin, was similarly convinced that by noncooperation numerically overwhelming subjects might control their rulers. His wife, Mary Wollstonecraft Shelley, has written: "The great truth that the many, if accordant and resolute, could control the few . . . made him long to teach his injured countrymen how to resist."[162]

Jouvenel, one of today's major political philosophers, has emphasized the dependence of earlier rulers on their subjects. How could a feudal king have waged "war if the barons had not mustered their contingents? What use to condemn a notable if his peers were certain to refuse to cooperate in the execution of the sentence?"[163] Not only the nobility but also the common people possessed power over the ruler through noncooperation: ". . . how could a feudal king have mustered an army if the barons . . . had not received obedience in their domains? And how could the industrialists have paid their taxes if their workers had stopped work?"[164]

It is almost axiomatic that in the face of such noncooperation and disobedience from anything less than the total population, the ruler will inflict severe sanctions through those agents remaining faithful to him. Repression of the subjects in such situations may force a resumption of submission. But repression will not necessarily ward off the danger to his position and power. As we have seen, disobedient subjects may still refuse to submit and may be willing to endure the repression and to continue their resistance in order to achieve some overriding objective. The subjects may then win, for, as Tocqueville argued, "A government which should have no other means of exacting obedience than open war must be very near its ruin . . ."[165]

Austin was similarly convinced:

> For if the bulk of the community were fully determined to destroy it [the government], and to brave and endure the evils through which they must pass to their object, the might of the government itself, with the might of the minority attached to it, would scarcely suffice to preserve it, or even to retard its subversion. And though it were aided by foreign governments, and therefore were more than a match for the disaffected and rebellious people, it hardly could reduce them to subjection, or constrain them to permanent obedience, in case they hated it mortally, and were prepared to resist it to the death.[166]

"It is easier to conquer than to rule," observed Rousseau.[167]

C. Clues to the political impact of noncooperation

There is considerable historical evidence that the theoretical insights of Boétie, Machiavelli, Austin, Jouvenel and others are valid and that, at least in certain circumstances, noncooperation can be effective in controlling governments and other bodies that wield political power. Let us explore a few examples which show in diverse situations the dependence of the titular ruler on his bureaucracy and then on the mass of the general populace.

1. Bureaucratic obstruction   Three cases are offered to show the dependence of power-holders on their bureaucracy. The first of these involves the withholding of cooperation in a political situation with a high degree of support for the ruler (the American presidency). The second is an intermediary case, with civil servants acting in an atmosphere of reservation and hostility (Russia in 1921–22). In the third there is a high degree of outright resistance (the German bureaucracy against the Kapp *Putsch*).

The United States.   Richard Neustadt has documented the actual limitations on the power of the American president, especially those imposed by his own aides, bureaucracy and Cabinet. After analyzing several important cases in the administrations of Presidents Truman and Eisenhower, Neustadt concludes: *"The same conditions that promote his leadership in form preclude a guarantee of leadership in fact."*[168] The president has a "power problem":

> This is the classic problem of the man on top of any political

POWER

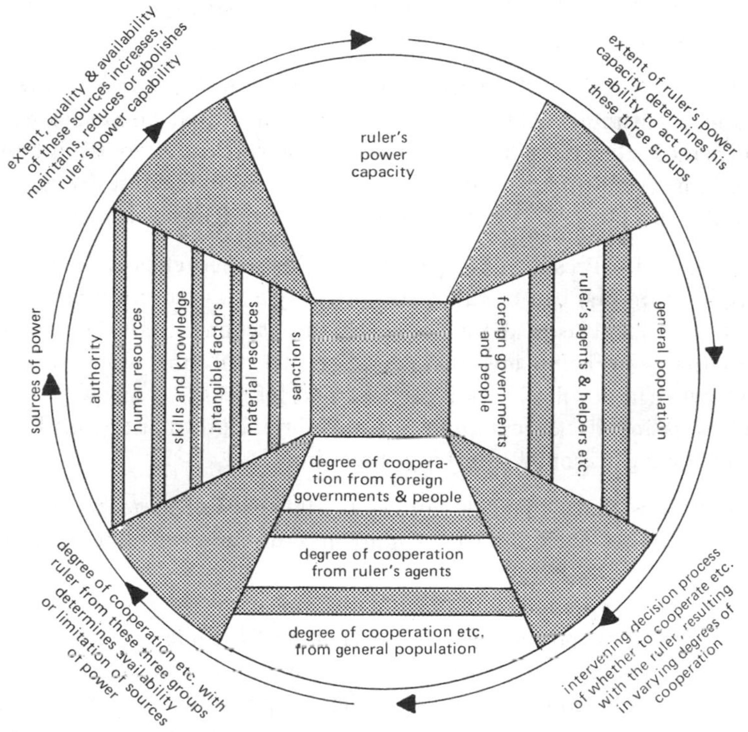

extent, quality & availability of these sources increases, maintains, reduces or abolishes ruler's power capability
ruler's power capacity
extent of ruler's power capacity determines his ability to act on these three groups
sources of power
authority
human resources
skills and knowledge
intangible factors
material resources
sanctions
foreign governments and people
ruler's agents & helpers etc.
general population
degree of coopera-tion from foreign governments & people
degree of cooperation from ruler's agents
degree of cooperation etc. from general population
degree of cooperation etc. with ruler from these three groups determines availability or limitation of sources of power
intervening decision process of whether to cooperate etc. with the ruler, resulting in varying degrees of cooperation

CHART ONE

THIS IS A CONTINUAL PROCESS WHICH INCREASES OR DECREASES THE RULER'S POWER CAPACITY. THIS PROCESS ENDS ONLY WHEN THAT POWER IS DISINTEGRATED.

system: how to be on top in fact as well as name. It is a problem common to Prime Ministers and Premiers, and to dictators, however styled, and to kings who rule as well as reign. It is a problem also for the heads of private "governments," for corporate presidents, trade union leaders, churchmen.[169]

True, the position of the president gives him important persuasive and bargaining advantages, but these do not guarantee that his wishes will be implemented; all sorts of limitations and counterpressures confront him.[170] These come even from his executive officials, including White House aides and Cabinet members. Neustadt quotes a former Roosevelt aide:

> Half of a President's suggestions, which theoretically carry the weight of orders, can be safely forgotten by a Cabinet member. And if the President asks about a suggestion a second time, he can be told that it is being investigated. If he asks a third time, a wise Cabinet officer will give him at least part of what he suggests. But only occasionally, except about the most important matters, do Presidents ever get around to asking three times.

Neustadt adds that "this rule applies to staff as well as to the Cabinet, and certainly has been applied by staff in Truman's time and Eisenhower's."[171]

The limiting pressures on the effective power of the president extend, of course, far beyond the executive branch and include the attitudes and actions of private citizens, a variety of publics, and a vast network of institutions, political organizations, officials, personalities, and even foreign governments. Real government power "is influence of an effective sort on the behavior of men actually involved in making public policy and carrying it out"; the president's "power is the product of his vantage points in government, together with his reputation in the Washington community and his prestige outside."[172] Even clear commands are not always carried out, and command is a form of persuasion not suitable for everyday use.[173] While in office President Truman once said: "I sit here all day trying to persuade people to do things they ought to have sense enough to do without my persuading them. . . . That's all the powers of the President amount to." This limitation, Neustadt writes, points to "the essence of the problem," for " 'powers' are no guarantee of power . . ."[174]

In the summer of 1952, before the heat of campaign, President Truman contemplated the problems of a general-become-president should Eisenhower win the election: "He'll sit here," (tapping his desk for emphasis), "and he'll say, 'Do this! Do that!' *And nothing will happen.* Poor Ike—it won't be a bit like the Army. He'll find it very frustrating."[175]

Even as late as 1958 President Eisenhower still experienced " 'shocked surprise' that orders did not carry themselves out" and that the assistance of others had to be deliberately cultivated in order to produce "effective power."[176] Of course, it is possible to cultivate the art of inducing others to provide necessary help. However, the necessity to do this helps to confirm the pluralistic-dependency theory of power, the need of a power-holder to receive his power from others.

The Soviet Union. In March 1922, at the Eleventh Congress of the Russian Communist Party, Lenin presented the Political Report of its Central Committee. In very clear terms Lenin stated that "the political lesson" of 1921 had been that control of the seats of power does not necessarily mean control of the bureaucracy. Asking what constituted Communist strength and what the Party lacked, Lenin observed that "We have quite enough political power . . . The main economic power is in our hands." Nevertheless, something was missing. This, it was "clear," was lack of culture among the stratum of Communists who perform the functions of administration." In Moscow there were 4,700 responsible Communists and also the Russian government's "huge bureaucratic machine, that huge pile." But, Lenin said, "we must ask: Who is directing whom?" Were the Communists directing? No, said Lenin. "To tell the truth, they are not directing, they are being directed." Remarkably, Lenin compared this domestic power problem to the international power problem of occupation of a defeated country by a foreign conqueror—something they had learned in their history lessons as children, said Lenin. The nation that conquers appears to be the conqueror and the nation that is vanquished appears to be the conquered nation. However, what really happens then depends, said Lenin, on the relative cultural level of the two nations. Despite the military realities, if the vanquished nation is more "cultural" than the conquering nation "the former imposes its . . . culture upon the conqueror."

Lenin then asked: "Has something like this happened in the capital of the R.S.F.S.R? Have the 4,700 Communists (nearly a whole army division, and all of them the very best) become influenced by an alien culture?" The "culture" of the "vanquished," though "at a miserably low and insignificant level," was, nevertheless, higher than that of the "responsible Communist adminstrators, for the latter lack administration ability."

Communists who are put at the head of departments—and sometimes artful saboteurs deliberately put them in these positions in order to use them as a shield—are often fooled. This is a very unpleasant admission . . . but . . . this is the pivot of the question. I think that this is the political lesson of the past year; and it is around this that the struggle will rage in 1922.

Will the responsible Communists of the R.S.F.S.R. and of the Russian Communist Party realize that they cannot administer; that they only imagine that they are directing, but actually, they are being directed? If they realize this they will learn, of course; for this business can be learnt. But one must study hard to learn it and this our people are not doing. They scatter orders right and left, but the result is quite different from what they want.[177]

Germany. The monarchist–military Kapp *Putsch* of 1920 against the new German Weimar Republic was defeated. According to the eminent German historian Erich Eyck, victory for the republic against this attempted *coup d'état* was won principally by "the general strike of the workers and the refusal of the higher civil servants to collaborate with their rebel masters."[178] Particular attention will be given here to the refusal of assistance by these civil servants and certain other key groups. A further description is offered in Chapter Two.

At the onset of the *Putsch*, the legal Ebert government had proclaimed that German citizens remained under obligation to be loyal to and obey it alone.[179] The resulting resistance of the civil servants took a variety of forms. The officers of the *Reichsbank* refused Kapp's request for ten million Marks because it lacked an authorized official signature—all the undersecretaries in the ministries had refused to sign. The bank's cashier rejected Kapp's own signature as worthless,[180] even though his troops occupied the capital and the legal government had fled.

Unable to obtain the cooperation of qualified men to form the promised cabinet of experts, the Kappists asked public patience with a government of inexperienced men.[181] Some cabinet posts were never filled.[182] Many officials already in government bureaus refused to assist the Kapp regime; those in the government grain bureau, for example, threatened to strike unless Kapp retired.[183]

Even lesser civil servants were not very helpful to those who had seized the pinnacle of power; as a result, hopelessly incompetent men were appointed to lesser but nonetheless important posts, such as directorship of the press bureau;[184] this weakened the Kapp regime. Even the noncooperation of clerks and typists was felt. When Kapp's daughter, who was to draft the new regime's manifesto to the nation, arrived at the Reich Chancellery on Saturday, March 13, she found no one to type for her—no one had turned up for work that day—and no typewriter; as a result, Kapp's manifesto was too late for the Sunday papers.[185] Many offices of the Defense Ministry were also vacant that day.[186] Toward the end even the Security Police turned against Kapp, demanding his resignation.[187]

Combined with a powerful general strike, the impact of such noncooperation was considerable. A specialist in the history of the *coup d'état* and a historian of the Kapp *Putsch*, Lieutenant Colonel D.J. Goodspeed, writes: "No government can function long without a certain necessary minimum of popular support and cooperation."[188]

2. Popular noncooperation   The need for popular cooperation and the danger to the regime when it is absent are suggested by two cases: the Indians under the British in 1930 and the Soviet peoples under the Germans, 1941–45. In both cases we shall cite the views of the occupation officials.

India. Jawaharlal Nehru's experience with noncooperation in the Indian struggle for independence led him to conclude: "Nothing is more irritating and, in the final analysis, harmful to a government than to have to deal with people who will not bend to its will, whatever the consequences."[189] Gandhi wrote: "If we are strong, the British become powerless."[190]

The British government seems to have agreed with Nehru and Gandhi. British officials saw large-scale noncooperation and civil disobedience as a threat and recognized the great potential of nonviolent struggle for the control of political power. Addressing both Houses of the Indian Legislative Assembly on July 9, 1930, during the noncooperation and civil disobedience movement of 1930-31 for independence (the *Swaraj satyagraha),* the British Viceroy, Lord Irwin (who was later to become Lord Halifax), rejected the view that this was "a perfectly legitimate form of political agitation."

In my judgment and that of my Government it is a deliberate attempt to coerce established authority by mass action, and for this reason, as also because of its natural and inevitable developments, it must be regarded as unconstitutional and dangerously subversive. Mass action, even if it is intended by its promoters to be nonviolent, is nothing but the application of force under another form, and, when it has as its avowed objective the making of Government impossible, a Government is bound either to resist or abdicate. The present Movement is exactly analogous to a general strike in an industrial country, which has for its purpose the coercion of Government by mass pressure as opposed to argument, and which a British Government recently found it necessary to mobilize all its resources to resist.

But in India the noncooperators had gone further; the All-India Working Committee of the Indian National Congress had "insidiously" attempted to undermine the allegiance of the government's police and troops. As a result, the Viceroy continued, the government had "no option" but to proclaim that body illegal. India needed to be protected from "principles so fundamentally destructive . . ."

Therefore it is that I have felt bound to combat these doctrines and to arm Government with such powers as seem requisite to deal with the situation. I fully realize that in normal times such special powers would be indefensible. But the times are not normal, and, if the only alternative is acquiescence in the result of efforts openly directed against the constituted Government of the King-Emperor, I cannot for one moment doubt on which side my duty lies . . . So long as the Civil Disobedience Movement persists, we must fight it with all our strength.[191]

It is remarkable to find the British Viceroy in essential agreement with Nehru, Gandhi and Tolstoy on the nature of British power in India and on the effective means of destroying the foreign *Raj*.

The Soviet Union. Conditions and events during the German occupation of major sections of the Soviet Union during World War II differed vastly from those prevailing in India during the British occupation. However, German experiences also led certain officials of Nazi agencies and officers of the army to the view that the cooperation and obedience of the population of these territories were needed in order to maintain the occupation regime.

In accordance with their racial ideology and policies (especially that of replacing the existing population with Germans), for a long time the Nazis did not even seek cooperation from the Eastern *Untermenschen* (subhumans). This case therefore represents an absence of cooperation by the population of the occupied areas rather than a deliberate refusal of cooperation when sought. The situation is not always clear, for many factors influenced the course of the occupation. The role of the absence of cooperation in the occupied territories is itself sometimes difficult to isolate, because of the war and guerrilla activities in these territories. Nevertheless, despite ideology, Nazi policies and war, some German officials and officers very significantly concluded that the subjects' cooperation was needed.

In his study of the occupation Alexander Dallin is able to cite many instances of Nazi officials and army officers who came to realize the need for such cooperation. For example, Kube, the *Reichskommissar* in Belorussia, slowly and reluctantly concluded that at least the passive support of the population was needed. In 1942 he became convinced, Dallin reports, "that German forces could not exercise effective control without enlisting the population." [192] Dallin also quotes a statement by German military commanders in the Soviet Union in December 1942: "The seriousness of the situation clearly makes imperative the positive cooperation of the population. Russia can be beaten only by Russians." [193] Captain Wilfried Strik-Strikfeldt expressed similar views in lectures before a General Staff training course: "Germany, Strik-Strikfeldt concluded, faced the choice of proceeding with or without the people: it could not succeed without them if only because such a course required a measure of force which it was incapable of marshalling." General Harteneck wrote in May 1943: "We can master the wide Russian expanse which we have conquered only with the Russians and Ukrainians who live in it, never against their will." [195]

Reviewing the history of the German occupation of the Soviet Union, Dallin writes:

> While the whip continued to be the rather universal attribute of German rule, there slowly matured an elementary realization that the active cooperation of the people was needed for maximum security and optimal performance. A pragmatic imperative, perceived primarily in the field, dictated a departure from the practice, if not the theory, of Nazi-style colonialism. [196]

This departure is all the more significant because it was diametrically opposed to the Nazi ideological position, which called the East Europeans subhumans, and to the earlier plans for exterminating the original population of major areas in order to provide empty territory for colonization, *Lebensraum* for the German *Volk*.

D. Toward a technique of control of political power

In May 1943 Hitler told Alfred Rosenberg that in the occupied East, German policy needed to be so tough as to numb the population's political consciousness. [197] However, in July he also declared that:

> . . . ruling the people in the conquered regions is, I might say, of course a psychological problem. One cannot rule by force alone. True, force is decisive, but it is equally important to have this psychological something which the animal trainer also needs to be master of his beast. They must be convinced that we are the victors. [198]

What follows from Hitler's admission that "force" alone is inadequate in ruling people in conquered territories if the people refuse to accept the militarily successful invaders as their political masters? Hitler's emphasis on the psychological nature of occupation rule very significantly coincides with the views of the political thinkers which have already been presented: that in order to rule it is necessary to reach the subjects' minds. These theoretical insights into power indeed have practical implications. Noncooperation and defiance by subjects, at least under certain conditions, can create serious problems for rulers, thwart their intentions and policies, and even destroy their government.

If this is true, then *why* have people not long since abolished oppression, tyranny and exploitation? There appear to be several reasons. First, such victims of a ruler's power usually feel helpless in the face of his capacity for repression, punishment and control. These feelings of helplessness arise from several causes.

The subjects usually do not realize that they are the source of the ruler's power and that by joint action they could dissolve that power. Failure to realize the role they play may have its roots either in innocent ignorance or in deliberate deception by the ruler. If the subjects look at their ruler's power at a given moment, they are likely to see it as a hard, solid force which at any point may fall upon them in their helplessness; this short-range view leads them to the monolith theory of power. If they were to look at their ruler's power both backward and forward in time, however, and note its origins and growth, its variations and fragility, they would begin to see their role in the genesis, continuance and development of that power. This realization would reveal that they possess the capacity to destroy that power.

It is also often in the ruler's power-interest to keep the people deceived about the fragile nature of political power and their capacity to dissolve it. Hence, rulers may sometimes seek to keep this knowledge from them. Tolstoy argued that the people, on whose cooperation the oppressive regime ultimately depended, continued to serve it by becoming soldiers and police, because "from long continued deception they no longer see the connection between their bondage and their own share in the deeds of violence." [199] In his day Hume similarly anticipated that rulers would themselves see the dangers of this view of power to their own position:

> Were you to preach, in most parts of the world, that political connections are founded together on voluntary consent or a mutual promise, the magistrate would soon imprison you, as seditious, for loosening the

ties of obedience, if your friends did not before shut you up as delirious, for advancing such absurdities.[200]

Hobbes saw something of the power of disobedience and, anticipating that it would destroy *all* government (not only a particular one), he turned away horrified, arguing firmly for the universal (or near universal) unquestioning submission of subjects to rulers.[201]

Unjust or oppressive rulers have every reason to keep knowledge of this theory from their subjects, and there are signs that they deliberately do so. (It is much less obvious that governments which genuinely reflect the will of their subjects have good reason for such restriction.) Even small-scale strikes and trade unions were widely illegal until union organization became too strong to suppress. The frequent reactions of governments when confronted with general strikes and mass popular action are worth noting. Do they not react with disproportionately intense determination not to give in, to defeat such actions—*even when these actions have majority support* and are aimed at relatively minor objectives? Do not such governments often refuse to negotiate until the general strike has been called off? Even when concessions are made, are these not often attributed to causes other than the popular noncooperation? It would seem that at least part of the explanation for such reactions is that the governments often object less to granting the demands than they do to the popular withdrawal of cooperation and obedience, and that they fear the spread of an awareness of the power of noncooperation in controlling political power. This would also explain, among other things, why rulers who pride themselves on their liberalism and who acknowledge the right of individual dissent, even in conscientious objection to military service, may react so strongly when a number of individuals act collectively in noncooperation and disobedience.

We are assuming that, under at least certain circumstances, ethical justification for disobedience of commands of rulers, and even for the abolition of whole regimes, exists. This is an assumption which not everyone will grant, but it is not a question which any longer requires much debate. Always to deny such a right of disobedience or revolution is to say that once Hitler's Nazi regime came to power, it was the duty of all Germans to obey it completely and carry out all its plans efficiently, that no matter what it did, there was no right of resistance or revolution. Few today will accept so extreme an interpretation of one's duty to obey. If they do not accept it, they implicitly grant that disobedience and defiance may be morally justified, at least under certain conditions.

The right to disobey and resist has been argued, however, on other grounds as well. Hume, for example, believed that constitutional government, with its separation and limitation of powers, depended on some form of resistance to keep it democratic, for "every part or member of the constitution must have a right of self-defence, and of maintaining its ancient bounds against the encroachments of every other authority." It is, he argued,

a gross absurdity to suppose in any government a right without a remedy, or allow that the supreme power is shared with the people, without allowing that it is lawful for them to defend their share against every invader. Those, therefore, who would seem to respect our free government, and yet deny the right of resistance, have renounced all pretensions to common sense, and do not merit a serious answer.[202]

The problem of finding remedies which are not in the long run worse than the evils they are intended to remove—a problem which concerned Hobbes—is still a difficult one. It is important to examine all proposed courses of action in that light, including the technique on which this book is focused. Examination of specific political potentialities of this technique lies outside the scope of this study, which is limited to exploration of the nature of nonviolent action; but an understanding of nonviolent action and its theory of power requires that this point be briefly answered. There is no reason to assume, as Hobbes did, that the withdrawal of obedience and cooperation to deal with a tyrant, for example, necessarily destroys all future capacity to maintain social order and democratic government. There are important reasons for believing that this is not true; these will become clearer as we consider in the concluding chapters the actual operation of the technique of action based upon this theory of power. There is even evidence that the alternative forms of behavior—violent counteraction or passive submission to oppression—may be more destructive of society than nonviolent action, especially under modern conditions.

Long before he became Chancellor, Hitler wrote that "one must not imagine that one could suddenly take out of a briefcase the drafts of a new State constitution" based on the leader-principle and impose them dictatorially on the State by command, "by a degree of power from above. One can try such a thing, but the result will certainly not be able to live, will in most cases be a stillborn child."[203] What would happen if people realized this on a wide scale, knew that they could prevent the imposition on them of unwanted policies and regimes, and were skillfully able to refuse to assist, in open struggle? It has been suggested that such knowledge could lead to the abolition of tyranny and oppression. Gandhi, for example, though referring specifically to economic issues, certainly had in mind wider implications when he wrote:

> The rich cannot accumulate wealth without the cooperation of the poor in society. If this knowledge were to penetrate to and spread amongst the poor, they would become strong and would learn how to free themselves by means of nonviolence from the crushing inequalities which have brought them to the verge of starvation.[204]

Harris has observed that people do not realize that ". . . political power is their own power. . . . Consequently, they become its accomplices at the same time as they become its victims. . . . If sufficient people understood this and really knew what they were about and how to go about it, they could ensure that government would never be tyrannical."[205] It is not without significance, perhaps, that the first issue of the first illegal resistance newspaper in Nazi-occupied Norway included this sentence near the conclusion of its first policy article: "We are convinced that a system which builds on hate, injustice and oppression never can last."[206]

The central political implications of our analysis point to control of political power by, in Green's words, "withdrawal by the sovereign people of power from its legislative or executive representatives."[207] It is control of the ruler's power by withdrawal of consent. It is control, not by the infliction of superior violence from on top or outside, not by persuasion, nor by hopes of a change of heart in the ruler, but rather by the subjects' declining to supply the power-holder with the sources of his power, by cutting off his power at the roots. This is resistance by noncooperation and disobedience. If it can be applied practically and can succeed despite repression, this would seem to be the most efficient and certain means for controlling power.

If this theory of power is to be implemented, the question is *how*. Lack of knowledge of how to act has also been one reason why people have not, long since, abolished tyranny and oppression.

First, the citizens' rejection of the tyrannical government must be actively expressed in refusal to cooperate. This refusal may take many forms; few of these will be easy, each will require effort, many will be dangerous, and all will need courage and intelligence. And there must be group or mass action. As Gaetano Mosca pointed out, the ruling minority is unified and can act in concert, whereas the ruled majority is "unorganized"[208]—or, we may add, often lacks independent organization. The result is that the subjects are usually incapable of corporate opposition and can be dealt with one by one. Effective action based on this theory of power requires *corporate* resistance and defiance—which may or may not be preceded by opportunity for advance specific preparations.

But generalized obstinacy and collective stubbornness are not effective enough. General opposition must be translated into a strategy of action, and people need to know how to wage the struggle which will almost inevitably follow their initial act of defiance. This includes how to persist despite repression. They will need to understand the technique based on this insight into power, including the methods of that technique, its dynamics of change, requirements for success and principles of strategy and tactics. The implementation must be skillful. We need, therefore, to examine in detail how the technique of nonviolent action—which is built on this insight into power—operates in struggle.

Therefore, we first turn to the exploration of the basic characteristics of the nonviolent technique and a survey of its history. This will lead us, in Part Two, into the multitude of specific nonviolent "weapons," or methods, included in its armory. The chapters of the concluding Part will examine in detail the dynamics and mechanisms of nonviolent struggle, and the factors which in a particular conflict determine its failure or its success.

NOTES

1. Martin J. Hillenbrand, **Power and Morals** (New York: Columbia University Press, 1949), p. 12.
2. Robert M. MacIver, **The Web of Government** (New York: Macmillan, 1947), p. 87.
3. *Ibid.*, p. 83.
4. A number of respected political and social theorists and prominent political activists have assumed this view of the nature of power, although there have been few systematic presentations of it. One reason for this lack appears to be that many of the theorists have presumed the view to be so obvious that detailed analysis was thought to be unnecessary.
   For a brief presentation of this view of power, see Errol E. Harris, "Political Power," *Ethics,* vol. XLVIII, no. 1 (Oct. 1957). pp. 1-10. Dr. Harris' article came to my attention sometime after the early drafts of this analysis were completed.

5. Auguste Comte pointed to the close relationship between the society and the political system and their mutual influence on each other, emphasizing the need to view political systems in the context of "the coexisting state of civilization." (Auguste Comte, The Positive Philosophy of Auguste Comte. Freely trans. and condensed by Harriet Martineau, with an Introduction by Frederic Harrison, 2 vols. [London: George Bell & Sons, 1896], vol. II, pp. 220-223.) He lamented that "the existing political philosophy supposes the absence of any such interconnection among the aspects of society . . ." *(Ibid., p. 225.)*

T. H. Green maintained that political theorists have often erred in focusing their attention solely on a coercive State and isolated individuals, ignoring other forms of community and the important role of society in influencing the nature of political power. (Thomas Hill Green, Lectures on the Principles of Political Obligation. [London: Longmans, Green & Co., 1948 (orig. 1882)], pp. 121 ff.) "The notion that force is the creator of government," argued MacIver, "is one of those part-truths that beget total errors." (MacIver, The Web of Government, p. 15.)

More recently Errol E. Harris has written: "Physical force itself is the instrument only, not the essence, of political power. Brawn, guns, and batons are but the tools employed. Power itself is not a physical phenomenon at all, it is always and only a social phenomenon . . ." (Harris, "Political Power," p. 3.)

6. The term "ruler" or "rulers" is used here as a kind of shorthand to describe the individuals or groups which occupy the highest positions of decision and command in a given government. At times this "ruler" may be, or come close to being, a single person – as is usually assumed to have been true in the case of Hitler and Stalin. In other cases the "ruler" may be a small elite or an oligarchy. Most of the time, however, a very large number of persons, with complex interrelationships, may collectively occupy the position of "ruler." In a case of pure direct democracy, the position of "ruler" as separated from the "ruled" would not exist. Intermediary forms and gradations also exist.

7. Etinne de La Boetie, *"Discours de la Servitude Volontaire,"* in Oeuvres Completes d'Etienne de la Boetie (Paris: J. Rouam & Cie.,1892), p. 12. See also Boetie, Anti-Dictator: The *Discours sur la servitude volontaire"* Of Etinne de La Boetie, trans. by Harry Kurz (New York: Columbia University Press, 1942), pp. 11-12. That translation differs slightly from the one in the text of this volume which was made by Madeline Chevalier Emerick.

8. Comte saw "every social power" as being "constituted by a corresponding assent . . . of various individual wills, resolved to concur in a common action, of which this power is the first organ, and then the regulator. Thus, authority is derived from concurrence, and not concurrence from authority . . . so that no great power can arise otherwise than from the strongly prevalent disposition of the society in which it exists . . ." The degree of disposition in the society toward a ruler, Comte believed, would determine the relative strength or weakness of the power-holder. (Comte, The Positive Philosophy of Auguste Comte, pp. 222-223.)

9. Two contemporary American writers argue similarly to Comte. Harold D. Lasswell writes: "Power is an interpersonal situation; those who hold power are empowered. They depend upon and continue only so long as there is a continuing stream of empowering responses . . . power is . . . a process that vanishes when the supporting responses cease.

"The power relationship is . . . giving-and-taking. It is a cue-giving and cue-taking in a continuing spiral of interaction." (Harold D. Lasswell, Power and Personality [New York: W. W. Norton & Co., 1948], p. 10.)

MacIver says it this way: "... social power is in the last resort derivative, not inherent in the groups or individuals who direct, control or coerce other groups or individuals. The power a man has is the power he *disposes;* it is not intrinsically his own. He cannot command unless another obeys. He cannot control unless the social organization invests him with the apparatus of control." (MacIver, **The Web of Government,** pp. 107-108.)

10. Jacques Maritain, **Man and the State** (Chicago Ill.: University of Chicago Press, 1954, and London: Hollis and Carter, 1954), U.S. ed., p. 126; British ed., pp. 114-115.

11. John Austin, **Lectures on Jurisprudence or the Philosophy of Positive Law** (Fifth ed., rev. and ed. by Robert Campbell; 2 vols; London: John Murray, 1911 [1861], vol. I, p. 89.

12. Charles Louis de Secondat, Baron de Montesquieu, **The Spirit of the Laws** (Trans. by Thomas Nugent; Introduction by Franz Neumann; New York: Haffner, 1949), vol. I, p. 313.

13. Arthur Livingstone emphasized the closeness of the relationship between possession of the sources of power and being a ruler: "A man rules or a group of men rules when the man or the group is able to control the social forces that, at the given moment in the given society, are essential to the possession and retention of power." Social forces are defined by Livingstone as "any human activity or perquisite that has a social significance – money, land, military prowess, religion, education, manual labor, science – anything." (Arthur Livingstone, Introduction to Gaetano Mosca, **The Ruling Class** (Trans. by Hannah D. Kahn; ed. and rev. with an Introduction by Arthur Livingstone; New York and London: McGraw-Hill, 1939), p. xix.

14. Rousseau speaks "of morality, of custom, above all of public opinion" as "the real constitution of the State" upon which "success in everything else depends." (Jean Jacques Rousseau, "The Social Contract," in **The Social Contract and Discourses** [New York: E. P. Dutton & Co., 1920, and London: J. M. Dent & Sons, Ltd., 1920], p. 48.)

15. While acknowledging the role of coercive force, David Hume points out that "nothing but their own consent, and their sense of the advantages resulting from peace and order" could be responsible for the subjection of multitudes to a ruler. (Frederick Watkins, ed., **Hume: Theory of Politics** [Edinburgh: Thomas Nelson & Sons, Ltd., 1951], p. 196.) It is, Hume says, "on opinion only that government is founded," including not only the most free and popular, but also the most despotic and military ones. *(Ibid.* p. 148.)
William Godwin argues that it is precisely *because* government is based upon opinion and consent that rulers use various pressures to influence the subjects to accept their authority. (William Godwin, **Enquiry Concerning Political Justice and its Influence on Morals and Happiness** [Sec. ed.; London: G. G. and J. Robinson, 1796], vol. I, p. 98.)

16. Bertrand de Jouvenel, **On Power: Its Nature and The History of its Growth** (Trans. by J. F. Huntington; Boston: Beacon Paperback, 1962), p. 355. British edition: **Power: The Natural History of its Growth** (Revised; London: The Batchworth Press, 1952), p. 302.

17. Green, **Lectures . . . ,** p. 103. Habitual obedience, he argued, arises from "the common will and reason of men," and only rarely needs backing by coercive force. *(Ibid.;* see also p. 98.) Coercive force, says Green, is not the most important thing about governments; it is not coercive power operating on the fears of the subjects "which determines their habitual obedience." *(Ibid.,* pp. 98 and 103.)

That would require far, far more police than there are; Jouvenel says as many police as subjects. (Jouvenel, On Power, p. 376. Br. ed.: Power, p. 317.) Even where people have been conquered by military might, the dominance cannot last if it depends solely upon such means (MacIver, The Web of Government, p. 16; Chester I. Barnard, The Functions of the Executive [Cambridge, Mass.: Harvard University Press, 1948], p. 149). Even the power of undemocratic regimes depends on acceptance of their authority. (Harris, "Political Power" p. 6.) Rousseau insisted: "The strongest is never strong enough to be always master, unless he transforms his strength into right, and obedience into duty." (Rousseau, "The Social Contract," p. 8.)

Niccolo Machiavelli speaks repeatedly in The Prince of the need to keep subjects satisfied and loyal, to maintain or win their good will, and of the importance of avoiding their hatred. (Machiavelli, The Prince [New York: E. P. Dutton & Co., Everyman's Library, 1948, and London: J. M. Dent & Sons, Everyman's Library, 1948], pp. 16, 74-77, 81-82, 129 and 146-147.) In his Discourses Machiavelli writes that the prince "who has the public as a whole for his enemy can never make himself secure; and the greater his cruelty, the weaker does his regime become. In such a case the best remedy he can adopt is to make the populace his friend." (Machiavelli, "The Discourses on the First Ten Books of Livy," The Discourses of Niccolo Machiavelli [London: Routledge and Kegan Paul, 1950]), vol. I, p. 254.

18. W. A. Rudlin, "Obedience, Political," Encyclopedia of the Social Sciences, (New York: Macmillan, 1935), vol. XI, p. 415.

19. Says Green: "If a despotic government comes into anything like habitual conflict with the unwritten law which represents the general will, its dissolution is beginning . . ." (Green, Lectures . . . , p. 313.)

Jouvenel points out that in the extremity of the total rejection of the ruler's claimed authority, he would simply not have the attributes of a ruler. The State "falls to pieces as soon as the authority of the sovereign loses its hold on a part of the subject mass, which bestows its allegiance elsewhere." (Bertrand de Jouvenel, Sovereignty: An Enquiry into the Political Good [Chicago, Ill.: University of Chicago Press, 1959, and London: The Batchworth Press, 1952], p. 4.)

Without authority, says MacIver, organizations can "carry no function whatever." (MacIver, The Web of Government, p. 84.) "Even the most ruthless tyrant gets nowhere unless he can clothe himself with authority." (Ibid., p. 83.) In a situation where a considerable portion of the subjects rejects the ruler's authority while another considerable portion continues to accept it, his political power will be seriously weakened, but not necessarily destroyed. Two States will then tend to form and will engage in some form of struggle which will lead to the destruction of one (as in a civil war), or to some kind of accommodation (ranging from reforms to separation into two independent States, e.g., in colonial conflicts).

20. Max Weber, "Politics as a Vocation," in From Max Weber: Essays in Sociology (Trans., ed. and with an Introduction by H. H. Gerth and C. Wright Mills; New York: Oxford University Press, Galaxy Book, 1958 [orig. 1946], and London: Kegan Paul, Trench, Trabner and Co., 1948), p. 81.

21. See Bernard, The Functions of the Executive, pp. 181-182.

22. Ibid., p. 182.

23. Herbert Goldhamer and Edward A. Shils point out that full control is rarely possible over a large subordinate staff, and hence the subordinates may assume a certain amount of independence and initiative in wielding power. This,

combined with the ruler's dependence on them, ". . . tends to set up a bilateral power relation between the chief power-holder and his subordinates, giving the latter power over the chief power-holder in addition to any independent power they may exercise over the mass. Subordinate power-holders, to the extent that they exercise independent power in the sphere claimed by the chief power-holder, will limit the power of the latter, and to that extent lose their character of subordinates." (Herbert Goldhamer and Edward A. Shils, "Power and Status," in The American Journal of Sociology, vol. XLV, no. 2 [September 1939], p. 177.) A ruler, over a period of time, must therefore come to terms with his subjects and adjust to some degree to their needs and aspirations. (See Jouvenel, On Power, p. 110; Br. ed.: Power, p. 101.)

24. Barnard insists: ". . . no absolute or external authority can compel the necessary effort beyond a minimum insufficient to maintain efficient or effective organization performance." (Barnard, The Functions of the Executive, p. 182.) He argues that this need for contributions is a common characteristic of all institutions including the State. Most attempted organizations fail because "they . . . cannot secure sufficient contributions of personal efforts to be effective or cannot induce them on terms that are efficient." Such failure occurs, in the last analysis, because "the individuals in sufficient numbers . . . withdraw or withhold the indispensable contributions."*(Ibid.,* pp. 164-165).

25. Jouvenel, Sovereignty, p. 4.

26. MacIver, The Web of Government, p. 16.

27. As Harris has pointed out: ". . . there is no such thing as political enforcement which is not a socially exercised activity in which a considerable proportion of the members of the group on which it is imposed participate." (Harris, "Political Power," p. 6.) Both the manufacture and the use of the instruments applied in inflicting violent political sanctions depend on "that very social organization which the political power is needed to maintain." *(Ibid.,* p. 4; see also pp. 3-5).

28. Karl W. Deutsch, "Cracks in the Monolith," in Carl J. Friedrich, ed., Totalitarianism (Cambridge, Mass.: Harvard University Press, 1954), p. 315.

29. Rudlin, "Obedience, Political," p. 416.

30. Deutsch, "Cracks in the Monolith," pp. 314-315.

31. Deutsch writes: "At one end of this spectrum, we could imagine a situation where everybody obeys habitually all commands or decisions of the totalitarian regime, and no enforcement is necessary; at the other end . . . we could imagine a situation where nobody obeys voluntarily any decision of the totalitarian system, and everybody has to be compelled to obey at pistol point, or under conditions of literally ever-present threat and ever-present supervision.
"In the first of these cases, enforcement would be extremely cheap and, in fact, unnecessary; in the second, it would be prohibitively expensive, and in fact no government could be carried on on such a basis. Even the behavior of an occupying army in wartime in enemy territory falls far short of this standard; even there, many of its orders are obeyed more or less habitually by an unwilling population in situations where immediate supervision is not practicable. If the occupying army had to put a soldier behind every man, woman, and child of the local population, it would be extremely difficult for the army to keep sufficient numbers of its men detached from such occupation duties to continue with further military operations. Somewhere in the middle between these extremes of universal compliance and ubiquitous enforcement is the range of effective government. There a majority of individuals in a majority of

situations obeys the decisions of the government more or less from habit without any need for immediate supervision." *(Ibid.,* pp. 313-314.)

32. Livingstone, "Introduction," to Mosca, **The Ruling Class,** p. xix.

33. As Jeremy Bentham put it: "The efficacy of power is, in part at least, in proportion to the promptitude of obedience . . ." (Jeremy Betham, **A Fragment on Government** [Ed. with an Introduction by F. C. Montague; London: Oxford University Press, Humphrey Milford, 1931 (orig. 1891)] ,p. 168.) The degree of political power is established by "neither more nor less . . . than a habit of, and disposition to obedience . . ." *(Ibid.,* p. 223.)

    The need for obedience is not limited to free societies argued Montesquieu: In despotic states, the nature of government requires the most passive obedience . . ." (Montesquieu,**The Spirit of the Laws,**vol. I, p. 2.)

    Weber said it concisely: "If the state is to exist, the dominated must obey the authority claimed by the powers that be." (Weber, "Politics as a Vocation," p. 78.)

34. Jouvenel, **On Power,** p. 18; Br. ed.: **Power,** pp. 27-28.

35. Kurt H. Wolff, editor and trans., **The Sociology of Georg Simmel** (Glencoe, Ill.: Free Press, 1950), p. 183.

36. **The Shorter Oxford English Dictionary on Historical Principles,** Third Edition, revised, 2 vols. (Oxford: The Clarendon Press, 1959), vol. II, pp. 2060 and 2084.

37. "Although cue-giving is highly concentrated in the conductor, commanding officer or foreman, the function is not wholly monopolized by any of them. The conductor, for instance, is continuously responsive to what comes to his attention from the orchestra; and neither the drill master nor the foreman is oblivious to the behavior of his men. And the members of the orchestra, the squad or the work-team are attentive to one another, adapting themselves to one another's performance." (Lasswell, **Power and Personality,** pp. 10-11.)

38. *Ibid.,* p. 12.

39. *Ibid.,* p. 16.

40. Wolff, ed., **The Sociology of Georg Simmel,** p. 183.

41. *Ibid.,* p. 186.

42. *Ibid.*

43. *Ibid.,* p. 250.

44. Barnard, **The Functions of the Executive,** pp. 181-182.

45. *Ibid.,* p. 182.

46. These same principles apply despite the fact that on relatively minor issues the supporting units of the State will usually support "law and order" regardless of the merits of the case, and despite the fact that the pressure on individual subjects to conform will be strong. *(Ibid.,* p. 183.)

47. E. V. Walter writes: "A power relation . . . is a dynamic interaction in which at least some control may be exercised by all parties. It is clear, of course, that each does not control the others to the same degree, nor do they control the same thing." (E. V. Walter, "Power and Violence," **American Political Science Review,** vol. LVIII, no. 2, [June 1964] , p. 352.)

48. Franz Neumann, **The Democratic and The Authoritarian State: Essays in Political and Legal Theory** (Ed. and with a Preface by Herbert Marcuse; Glencoe, Ill.: Free Press and Falcon's Wing Press, 1957), p. 3.

49. Paul Pigors offers a fourth variable: the presence of absence of a common cause uniting the ruler and subject. This factor is here included in the situation. See

Paul Pigors, **Leadership or Domination** (New York: Houghton Mifflin Co., 1935, and London: George G. Harrap, 1935), p. 195. See also Mary Follett, **Creative Experience** (New York and London: Longmans, Green & Co., 1924), p. 61.

50. Jouvenel, **On Power,** p. 17; Br. ed.: **Power,** p. 27. Jouvenel uses the term "Power" with a capital "P" as approximately the same as "the State."

51. "Discipline on such a scale as this," wrote Jacques Necker, "must astound any man who is capable of reflection. This obedience on the part of a very large number to a very small one is a thing singular to observe and mysterious to think on." (Necker, **Du Pouvior Executif dans les Grandes Etats** [1792], pp. 20-22; quoted in Jouvenel, **On Power,** p. 19; Br. ed.: **Power,** pp. 28-29.)
It was Hume's question too: "Nothing appears more surprising, to those who consider human affairs with a philosophical eye, than the easiness with which the many are governed i, ṭhẹ few, and the implicit submission with which men resign their own sentiments and passions to those of their rulers." (Watkins, ed., **Hume,** p. 148.)
Contemporary political thinkers are still asking the same question. Hans Gerth and C. Wright Mills have written: "Since power implies that an actor can carry out his will, power involves obedience. The general problem of politics accordingly is the explanation of varying distributions of power and obedience, and one basic problem of political psychology is why men in their obedience accept others as the powerful. Why do they obey?" (Hans Gerth and C. Wright Mills, **Character and Social Structure** [New York: Harcourt, Brace & Co., 1953, and London: Routledge and Kegan Paul, 1954], p. 193.)

52. In the sixteenth century Boetie marvelled at the phenomenon of obedience to oppressors: ". . . what happens in every country, by all men, and in all eras, that one man abuses a hundred thousand and deprives them of their liberty, who would believe it, if only he heard of it, and did not see it? And if it only happened in strange and distant lands and that it was spoken of, who would not suppose that it was somewhat false and made up, not really true?" (Boetie, *"Discours de la Servitude Volontaire,"* p. 8; see also, Boetie, **Anti-Dictator,** p. 9.)

53. Gerth and Mills, **Character and Social Structure,** p. 194.

54. Thomas Hobbes, Leviathan (Reprinted from the edition of 1651; New York: E. P. Dutton, 1950 and Oxford: Clarendon Press, 1958), U.S. ed., p. 167; Br. ed., p. 152.

55. Jouvenel, **On Power,** p. 22; Br. ed.: **Power,** p. 30. See also Deutsch, "Cracks in the Monolith," p. 314; MacIver, **The Web of Government,** p. 76; Green, **Lectures . . . ,** pp. 101 and 126; Austin, **Lectures . . . ,** pp. 292-294; and Necker, quoted in Jouvenel, **On Power,** p. 21-22; Br. ed.: **Power,** p. 30.

56. Watkins, ed., **Hume,** p. 155. See also p. 197.

57. Austin, **Lectures . . . ,** p. 294.

58. Jouvenel, **On Power,** pp. 23-24; Br. ed.: **Power,** p. 32.

59. See, e.g., Neumann, **The Democratic and the Authoritarian State,** p.8; MacIver, **The Web of Government,** pp. 76-77; Jouvenel, **Sovereignty,** p. 2; Deutsch, "Cracks in the Monolith," p. 314; Rudlin, "Obedience, Political," p. 417; Austin, **Lectures . . . ,** p. 298; Watkins, ed., **Hume,** pp. 201-206; Godwin, **Enquiry . . . ,** vol II, pp. 43-44; and Hobbes, **Leviathan,** U.S. ed., p. 167; Br. ed., p. 152.

60. Green, **Lectures . . . ,** p. 98.

61. Machiavelli, although emphasizing the need for the goodwill of the populace if a prince were to maintain his power, believed that under certain conditions

obedience could be produced by sufficient violence and threat of violence. (See, e.g., Machiavelli, **The Prince,** p. 67.) Leo Tolstoy, too, emphasized the role of fear of sanctions in obtaining obedience to the State, especially in cases where obedience was not in the interest of the subjects. (See, e.g., Leo Tolstoy, **The Kingdom of God Is Within You** [New York: Thomas Y. Crowell, 1899, and London: William Heinemann, 1894], U.S. ed., pp. 154-155, 263-264, 266; Br. ed., pp. 237, 413, 417.

62. See e.g., Watkins, ed., **Hume,** pp. 154-155; Mosca, **The Ruling Class,** pp. 53-54; and Bertrand Russell, **Power: A New Social Analysis** (New York: W. W. Norton & Co., 1938; and London: Geo. Allen and Unwin, 1938), U.S. ed., p. 184; Br. ed.: p. 190.

63. Montesquieu, for example, found it under both monarchies and republics, (See, Montesquieu, **The Spirit of the Laws,** vol. I, p. 34). Contemporary writers such as Jouvenel, have found it "varying in liveliness and effectiveness from one individual to another, among the members of any political society." (Jouvenel, **Sovereignty,** p. 87.)

64. See MacIver, **The Web of Government,** p. 77, and Green, **Lectures . . . ,** pp. 123-124.

65. Feelings of moral obligation as a cause of obedience may be variously interpreted; ranging from Green's view that this is largely a recognition of the objective social benefits of government, to the anarchist view that this is always a means of deception used to hold the people in subjection. (See Godwin, **Enquiry . . . ,** vol. I, p. 98, and Emma Goldman's pamphlet **The Individual, Society and the State** (Chicago: Free Society Forum, n.d.), p. 5.

66. Green, **Lectures . . . ,** pp. 123-124.

67. See Barnard, **The Functions of the Executive,** pp. 152-153.

68. Jouvenel, **On Power,** p. 376; Br. ed.: **Power,** p. 317.

69. *Ibid.,* p. 302.

70. See Hume's two-fold classification of (1) "opinion of interest," including consideration (a) in this text, and (2)"opinion of right," including (b), (c), and (d). Watkins, ed., **Hume,** pp. 148-150.

71. Green, **Lectures . . . ,** p. 125.

72. Watkins, ed., **Hume,** pp. 102 and 213.

73. *Ibid.,* p. 101.

74. Green, **Lectures . . . ,** pp. 124-125. Green acknowledged the existence of objections and certain qualifications to the theory concerning the general good and obedience, while insisting on its general validity. (See *ibid.,* pp. 126-128 and 131-135.) Similar observations are made by Jouvenel (**On Power,** pp. 25-26; Br. ed.: **Power,** pp. 32-33); Simmel (Wolff, ed., **The Sociology of Georg Simmel,** p. 284); and Robert M. MacIver (**The Modern State** [Oxford at the Clarendon Press, 1926; London and New York: Oxford University Press, 1964], p. 154).

75. Watkins, ed., **Hume,** pp. 148-149.

76. *Ibid.*

77. Green, **Lectures . . . ,** pp. 103 and 109.

78. *Ibid,.* p. 109.

79. Watkins, ed., **Hume,** p. 104.

80. See Austin, **Lectures . . . ,** p. 293 and Rudlin, "Obedience, Political," p. 417.

81. Jouvenel, **On Power,** p. 355 (see also pp. 41-42); Br. ed.: **Power,** p. 301 (see also p. 45).

82. One of the conditions described by Mosca in which resistance to rulers was seen as impossible was "When the leaders of the governing class are the exclusive interpreters of the will of God or the will of the people and exercise sovereignty in the name of those abstractions in societies that are deeply imbued with religious beliefs or with democratic fanaticism . . ." (Mosca, **The Ruling Class,** p. 134.)

83. MacIver, **The Web of Government,** p. 76.

84. Jouvenel, **On Power,** p. 24; Br. ed.: **Power,** p. 32.

85. Goldhamer and Shils, "Power and Status," p. 173; Jouvenel, **Sovereignty,** p. 5; Pigors, **Leadership or Domination,** p. 311; Godwin, **Enquiry . . . ,** vol. I, p. 250. Several sources of authority described by Hume clearly refer to ways in which the legitimacy of the ruler may be established. In addition to the supposed role of original contract, he discusses five other sources: (a) time ("long possession in any one form of government or succession of princes"), (b) present possession, (c) right of conquest, (d) right of succession, and (e) "positive laws" enacted by the legislature to fix a form of government or succession of princes. These sources, Hume stated, may appear in combinations and in varying degrees. (See Watkins, ed., **Hume,** pp. 106-113 and 197-198.)

86. Max Weber has distinguished three "pure types" of "ruling power, profane and religious, political and apolitical," on the basis of the type of legitimacy claimed by the ruling power. These are: (a) charismatic authority "a rule over men, whether predominantly external or internal, to which the governed submit because of their belief in the extraordinary quality of the specific *person*"), (b) traditionalist authority (domination resting upon "piety for what actually, allegedly, or presumably has always existed"), and (c) legal authority ("based upon an *impersonal* bond to the generally defined and functional 'duty of office,' " the official duty being fixed "by *rationally established* norms, by enactments, decrees, and regulations, in such a manner that the legitimacy of the authority becomes the legality of the general rule, which is purposely thought out, enacted, and announced with formal correctness"). (Gerth and Mills, eds., **From Max Weber,** pp. 294-301.)

87. MacIver, **The Web of Government,** p. 76.

88. Green, **Lectures . . . ,** p. 101.

89. Watkins, ed., **Hume,** p. 150.

90. *Ibid.*

91. *Ibid.,* p. 155.

92. MacIver, **The Web of Government,** p. 76.

93. Godwin, **Enquiry . . . ,** vol. II, p. 45; see also pp. 42-45.

94. Tolstoy, **The Kingdom of God is Within You,** U.S. ed., p. 302, Br. ed., p. 474.

95. Deutsch, "Cracks in the Monolith," p. 315.

96. MacIver, **The Web of Government,** p. 76.

97. Barnard, **The Functions of the Executive,** p. 167.

98. See Pigors, **Leadership or Domination,** p. 311, and Mosca, **The Ruling Class,** p. 53.

99. See Alexis de Tocqueville, **Democracy in America** (Trans. by George Lawrence, and ed. by J. P. Mayer; Garden City, N.Y.: Doubleday & Co., Anchor Books, 1969), p. 658.

100. Tolstoy, **The Kingdom of God is Within You,** U. S. ed., pp. 293-294; Br. ed., pp. 459-460. Arguing that English education increased Indian submission to the

colonial system, Gandhi wrote: "Culturally, the system of education has torn us from our moorings, our training has made us hug the very chains that bind us." (Quoted, Gene Sharp, **Gandhi Wields the Weapon of Moral Power** (Ahmedabad: Navajivan, 1960), p. 54.

101. See Barnard, **The Functions of the Executive,** p. 170.

102. See Sebastian de Grazia, The **Political Community: A Study of Anomie** (Chicago: University of Chicago Press, 1948), especially p. 177; Jouvenel, **On Power,** p. 11; Br. ed.: **Power,** p. 22; Wolff, ed., **The Sociology of Georg Simmel,** p. 193; Machiavelli, **The Discourses . . . ,** vol. I, p. 496; Tocqueville, **Democracy in America,** pp. 257 and 701-702; and especially Erich Fromm, **Escape From Freedom** (New York: Holt Rinehart and Winston, 1961; Br. ed.: **The Fear of Freedom,** London: Routledge and Kegan Paul, 1961 [orig. 1942]).

103. Rousseau, "The Social Contract," p. 7.

104. Jouvenel, **On Power,** p. 20; Br. ed. **Power,** p. 29. See also Pigors, **Leadership or Domination,** p. 197. MacIver, **The Modern State,** p. 47; Tolstoy, **The Kingdom of God is Within You,** U.S. ed., pp. 276 and 294; Br. ed., pp. 434 and 460; and Mohandas K. Gandhi, **Hind Swaraj or Indian Home Rule** (Ahmedabad: Navajivan, 1958 [orig. 1909]), pp. 56-57.

105. This has not always been a characteristic of all political systems. For centuries, says Jouvenel, Rome had no permanent officials or standing army within its walls and only a few lictors (Jouvenel, **On Power,** p. 20; Br. ed.: **Power** p. 29). Montague also mentions the absence of State means of enforcement. (See his Introduction to Bentham, **A Fragment on Government,** p. 73.)

106. Jouvenel, **Sovereignty,** pp. 32-33.

107. See MacIver, **The Modern State,** p. 47.

108. Bertrand Russell, **Authority and the Individual: The Reith Lectures for 1948-1949** (New York: Simon & Schuster, 1949 and London: George Allen and Unwin, 1949), U.S. ed., p. 14: Br. ed., p. 30. See also MacIver, **The Web of Government,** p. 16, and Watkins, ed., **Hume,** p. 148.

109. Boetie, quoted in Leo Tolstoy, **The Law of Violence and the Law of Love** (Trans. by Mary Koutouzow Tolstoy; New York: Rudolph Field, 1948), p. 44; a slightly different wording appears in Boetie, **Anti-Dictator** (trans. Harry Kurz), p. 43.

110. Austin argued that "no conceivable motive will *certainly* determine to compliance, or no conceivable motive will render obedience inevitable." (Austin, **Lectures . . . ,** vol. I, p. 90.)

111. Montague, "Introduction" to Bentham, **A Fragment on Government,** p. 74.

112. MacIver, **The Web of Government,** p. 76.

113. Jouvenel, **On Power,** p. 18; Br. ed.: **Power,** p. 27.

114. Rudlin, **"Obedience, Political,"** p. 417.

115. Russell, **Power,** p. 177; Br. ed., p. 183.

116. See, e.g., Tocqueville, **Democracy in America,** p. 139; Watkins, ed., **Hume,** pp. 155-156; Jouvenel, **Sovereignty,** p. 2; Russell, **Power,** pp. 117-118; Br. ed., p. 120.

117. See Austin, **Lectures . . . ,** vol. I, p. 90; Jouvenel, **Sovereignty,** p. 33; and Deutsch, "Cracks in the Monolith," p. 314.

118. Austin insisted that ". . . every *forbearance* is *intended;* and is either the effect of an aversion from the consequences of the act forborne, or is the effect of a preference of that act. Consequently, every forbearance, like every act, is the

consequence of a desire." (Austin, **Lectures** . . . , p. 453.)

119. Jouvenel, **Sovereignty,** p. 33.

120. Mohandas K. Gandhi, **Young India,** 30 June 1920; quoted in Nirmal Kumar Bose, **Selections from Gandhi** (Ahmedabad: Navajivan, 1948), p. 116.

121. Austin, **Lectures** . . . , pp. 295-297.

122. Within a relationship of subordination, the exclusion of all spontaneity whatever is actually rarer than is suggested by such widely used popular expressions as 'coercion,' 'having no choice,' 'absolute necessity,' etc. Even in the most oppressive and cruel cases of subordination, there is still a considerable measure of personal freedom. We merely do not become aware of it, because its manifestation would entail sacrifices which we usually never think of taking upon ourselves. Actually, the 'absolute' coercion which even the most cruel tyrant imposes upon us is always destinctly relative. Its condition is our desire to escape from the threatened punishment or from other consequences of our disobedience. More precise analysis shows that the super-subordination relation destroys the subordinate's freedom only in the case of direct physical violation. In every other case, this relationship only demands a price for the realization of freedom — a price, to be sure, which we are not willing to pay. It can narrow down more and more the sphere of external conditions under which freedom is clearly realized, but except for physical force [i.e. direct physical violation], never to the point of the complete disappearance of freedom." (Wolff, ed., **The Sociology of Georg Simmel,** p. 183.)

123. Austin: "Our desire of avoiding the evil which we might chance incur by disobedience makes us will the act which the command enjoins, makes us forbear from the act which the command forbids." (Austin, **Lectures** . . . , p. 453.)
    Hobbes is prominent among those who have recognized the role of fear of the ruler's punishment in securing consent. The case "where a Sovereign Power is acquired by Force" occurs, he said, "when a man singly, or together by plurality of voyces, for fear of death, or bonds, do authorise all the actions of that Man, or Assembly, that hath their lives and liberty in his Power." (Hobbes, **Leviathan,**U.S. ed., p. 167; Br. ed., p. 152.)

124. Robert Michels, "Authority," **Encyclopedia of the Social Sciences** (New York: MacMillan, 1935), vol. II, p. 319.

125. Gandhi, **Young India,** 18 August 1920; quoted in Gandhi, **Non—Violent Resistance** (U.S. ed.: New York: Schocken Books, 1957; Indian ed.: **Satyagraha,** Ahmedabad, India: Navajivan, 1951), p. 157.

126. See MacIver, **The Web of Government,** p. 16; William Laud, quoted in Gerth and Mills, **Character and Social Structure,** p. 194; and Green, **Lectures** . . . , p. 126.

127. Austin, **Lectures** . . . , vol. I, pp. 295-296.

128. "Since, then, a government continues through the obedience of the people," argued Austin, "and since the obedience of the people is voluntary or free, every government continues through the consent of the people or the bulk of the political society." *(Ibid.,* vol. I, p. 296.)

129. *Ibid.,* vol. I, pp. 295-297.

130. Godwin, **Enquiry** . . . , vol. I, p. 145.

131. Adolf Hitler, **Mein Kampf** (New York: Reynal and Hitchcock, 1941), p. 388.

132. Austin, **Lectures** . . . , vol. I, p. 297.

133. *Ibid.,* pp. 296-297.

134. The nature of this disruption may vary considerably with the precise means used.

135. Harris, "Political Power," p. 6.

136. *Ibid.*, p. 8.

137. *Ibid.*, pp. 8-9.

138. Leo Tolstoy, " A Letter to a Hindu," in The Works of Tolstoy, vol. 21, **Recollections and Essays,** (London: Oxford University Press, Humphrey Milford, 1937), p. 427; Indian ed.: Kalidas Nag, **Tolstoy and Gandhi** (Patna, India: Pustak Bhandar, 1950), pp. 92-93.

139. Jouvenel, **Sovereignty,** p. 33.

140. *Ibid.*

141. Godwin, **Enquiry . . . ,** vol. I, pp. 145-146.

142. *Ibid.*, vol. I, p. 254.

143. "The moment the slave resolves that he will no longer be a slave, his fetters fall. He frees himself and shows the ways to others. Freedom and slavery are mental states. Therefore, the first thing is to say to yourself: 'I shall no longer accept the role of a slave. I shall not obey orders as such but shall disobey them when they are in conflict with my conscience.' " (Gandhi, **Harijan,** 24 February 1946; quoted in M. K. Gandhi, **Nonviolence in Peace and War,** vol. II [Ahmedabad, India: Navajivan, 1949], p. 10.)

144. "It is not so much British guns that are responsible for our subjection as our voluntary cooperation." (Gandhi, **Young India,** 9 February 1921; quoted in Bose, **Selections from Gandhi,** p. 116.)

145. "I believe, and everybody must grant, that no Government can exist for a single moment without the cooperation of the people, willing or forced, and if people suddenly withdraw their cooperation in every detail, the Government will come to a standstill." (Gandhi, **Young India,** 18 August 1920; quoted in Gandhi, **Nonviolent Resistance,** p. 157; Indian ed.: **Satyagraha, p. 157.**

146. Quoted in Clarence Marsh Case, **Nonviolent Coercion: A Study in Methods of Social Pressure** (New York: Century Co., 1923), pp. 391-392.

147. Godwin, **Enquiry . . . ,** vol. I, pp. 253-254.

148. Gandhi, **Young India,** 16 June 1920; quoted in Gandhi, **Nonviolent Resistance,** pp. 114-115; Ind. ed.: **Satyagraha,** pp. 114-115.

149. Hillenbrand, **Power and Morals,** p. 5.

150. *Ibid.*, p. 10.

151. *Ibid.*, p. 22.

152. David Spitz, **Democracy and the Challenge of Power** (New York: Columbia University Press, 1958), p. viii.

153. Hillenbrand, **Power and Morals,** p. 5.

154. Jouvenel, **On Power,** p. 42; Br. ed.: **Power,** p. 45.

155. Maritain, **Man and the State,** U. S. ed., p. 64; Br. ed., pp. 58-59.

156. Boétie, *"Discours de la Servitude Volontaire,"* pp. 8-11; see also Boétie, **Anti-Dictator,** pp. 9-10.

157. Boétie, *"Discours de la Servitude Volontaire,"* pp. 12-14; see also, Boétie, **Anti-Dictator,** pp. 12-13.

158. The influence on Tolstoy, and through him on Gandhi is indisputable, as Tolstoy quotes from Boétie. The influence on Thoreau, however, I have not seen documented, although it is frequently stated to have been the case.

However, the close friendship between Emerson and Thoreau and the certainty of Emerson's familiarity with that essay makes it almost without doubt that Thoreau also knew it.

159. Machiavelli, **The Prince,** p. 77.

160. Machiavelli, **The Discourses . . . ,** p. 254.

161. Gaetano Salvemini, **The French Revolution 1788-1792** (trans. by I. M. Rawson; New York: Henry Holt and Co., 1954, and London: Jonathan Cape, 1963), p. 162.

162. Thomas Hutchinson, ed., **The Complete Poetical Works of Percy Bysshe Shelley** (Oxford: Clarendon Press, 1904). p. 364. See esp. Shelley's "The Mask of Anarchy" in *ibid.)*

163. Jouvenel, **On Power,** p. 180; Br. ed.: **Power,** p. 154.

164. Jouvenel, **On Power,** p. 161; Br. ed.: **Power,** p. 138-139.

165. Tocqueville, **Democracy in America,** p. 139.

166. Austin, **Lectures . . . ,** vol. I, p. 296.

167. Rousseau, "The Social Contract," p. 64.

168. Richard E. Neustadt, **Presidential Power: The Politics of Leadership** (New York and London: John Wiley and Sons, 1960), p. 7 (italics in the original).

169. *Ibid.,* pp. vii-viii.

170. *Ibid.,* pp. 36-37.

171. *Ibid.,* p. 41. The statement by A. Roosevelt Aide is from Johnathan Daniels, Frontier on the Potomac (New York: MacMillan, 1946), pp. 31-32.

172. *Ibid.,* p. 179.

173. *Ibid.,* pp. 26 and 32.

174. *Ibid.,* p. 9-10.

175. *Ibid.,* p. 9.

176. *Ibid.,* p. 163.

177. V. I. Lenin, "Political Report of the Central Committee of the Russian Communist Party (Bolsheviks)" delivered March 27, 1922, at the Eleventh Congress of the Russian Communist Party (Bolsheviks), **V. I. Lenin; Selected Works in Three Volumes** (New York: International Publishers, 1967), vol. III, pp. 692-693, and in Nikolai Lenin (sic), **The Essentials of Lenin in Two Volumes** (London: Lawrence and Wishart, 1947), vol. II, pp. 788-789.

178. Erich Eyck, **A History of the Weimar Republic,** vol. I. **From the Collapse of the Empire to Hindenburg's Election** (Cambridge, Mass.: Harvard University Press, 1962), p. 151.

179. S. William Halperin, **Germany Tried Democracy: A Political History of the Reich from 1918 to 1933** (Hamden, Conn. and London: Archon Books, 1946), p. 180.

180. Eyck, **A History of the Weimar Republic,** vol. I, pp. 151-152.

181. W. H. Crook, **The General Strike: A Study of Labor's Tragic Weapon in Theory and Practice** (Chapel Hill: University of North Carolina Press, 1931), p. 512.

182. D. J. Goodspeed, **The Conspirators: A Study in the Coup d'Etat** (New York: Viking Press, 1962; Toronto: Macmillan Co. of Canada, 1962), p. 131.

183. Crook, **The General Strike,** p. 515.

184. Halperin, **Germany Tried Democracy,** p. 179.

185. Goodspeed, **The Conspirators,** p. 130 and John W. Wheeler-Bennett, **The**

Nemesis of Power: The German Army in Politics, 1918-1945 (New York: St. Martin's Press, 1954 and London: Macmillan, 1953), p. 77.

186. Goodspeed, The Conspirators, p. 131.

187. Wheeler-Bennett, The Nemesis of Power, p. 79.

188. Goodspeed, The Conspirators, p. 211.

189. Jawaharlal Nehru, Toward Freedom (Rev. ed.; New York: The John Day Co., 1942), p. 249.

190. Quoted in D. G. Tendulkar, Mahatma: Life of Mohandas Karamachand Gandhi (New rev. ed.; Delhi: Publications Division, Ministry of Information and Broadcasting, Government of India, 1962), vol. VI, p. 88.

191. Government of India, India in 1930-31: A Statement Prepared for Presentation to Parliament in accordance with the requirements of the 26th section of the Government of India Act (5 & 6 Geo. V, Chapter 61) (Calcutta: Central Publication Branch, Government of India, 1932), pp. 80-81.

192. Alexander Dallin, German Rule In Russia, 1941-1945: A Study of Occupation Policies (New York: St. Martin's Press, 1957, and London: Macmillan, 1957), p. 218.

193. Ibid., p. 497.

194. Ibid., p. 516.

195. Quoted in ibid., p. 550.

196. Ibid., p. 663.

197. Ibid., p. 580.

198. Quoted in ibid., p. 498.

199. Tolstoy, The Law of Violence and the Law of Love, p. 47.

200. Watkins, ed., Hume, p. 198.

201. Hobbes' recognition of the power of disobedience apparently frightened him and encouraged his authoritarian view of government. In a discussion of "the poyson of seditious doctrines; whereof one is, That every private man is Judge of Good and Evill actions," Hobbes argues that this doctrine will lead men to decide to obey or disobey "the commands of the Commonwealth . . . as in their private judgements they shall think fit. Whereby the Common-wealth is distracted and Weakened." (Hobbes, Leviathan, U.S. ed., pp. 277-278; Br. ed., p. 249.)
Hobbes clearly placed obedience at the heart of political power and believed that disobedience therefore would lead to the ruler's collapse: "For the prosperity of a People ruled by an Artistocraticall, or Democraticall assembly, commeth not from Aristocracy, nor from Democracy, but from the Obedience, and Concord of the Subjects: nor do the people flourish in a Monarchy, because one man has the right to rule them but because they obey him. Take away in any kind of State, the Obedience, (and consequently the Concord of the People,) and they shall not only not flourish, but in a short time be dissolved. And they that go about by disobedience, to doe no more than reforme the Common-wealth, shall find they do thereby destroy it . . ."(Ibid., U.S. ed., pp. 291-292; Br. ed., p. 261.)

202. Watkins, ed., Hume, p. 115.

203. Hitler, Mein Kampf, pp. 872-873.

204. Gandhi, Harijan, 25 August 1940; quoted in Bose, Selections from Gandhi, p. 79.

205. Harris, "Political Power," p. 10.

206. **Vi Vill Oss et Land,** October 1940. Quoted in Hans Luihn, **De Illegale Avisene: Den Frie, Hemmilige Pressen i Norge Under Okkupasjonen** (Oslo and Bergen: *Universitetsforlaget,* 1960), p. 18.

207. Green, **Lectures . . . ,** p. 77.

208. Mosca, **The Ruling Class,** p. 53.

2

Nonviolent Action: an Active Technique of Struggle

INTRODUCTION

In political terms nonviolent action is based on a very simple postulate: people do not always do what they are told to do, and sometimes they do things which have been forbidden to them. Subjects may disobey laws they reject. Workers may halt work, which may paralyze the economy. The bureaucracy may refuse to carry out instructions. Soldiers and police may become lax in inflicting repression; they may even mutiny. When all these events happen simultaneously, the man who has been "ruler" becomes just another man. This dissolution of power can happen in a wide variety of social and political conflicts. The factory manager's power dissolves when the workers no longer cooperate. Political power disintegrates when the people withdraw their obedience and support. Yet the ruler's military equipment may remain intact, his soldiers uninjured, the cities unscathed, the factories and transport systems in full operational capacity, and the government buildings undamaged. But everything is changed. The human assistance which created and supported the regime's political power has been withdrawn. Therefore, its power has disintegrated.[1]

When people refuse their cooperation, withhold their help, and persist in their disobedience and defiance, they are denying their opponent the basic human assistance and cooperation which any government or hierarchical system requires. If they do this in sufficient numbers for long enough, that government or hierarchical system will no longer have power. This is the basic political assumption of nonviolent action.

CHARACTERISTICS OF NONVIOLENT ACTION

Nonviolent action is a generic term covering dozens of specific methods of protest, noncooperation and intervention, in all of which the actionists conduct the conflict by doing—or refusing to do—certain things without using physical violence. As a technique, therefore, nonviolent action is not passive. It is *not* inaction. It is *action* that is nonviolent.

The issue at stake will vary. Frequently it may be a political one—between political groups, for or against a government, or, on rare occasions, between governments (as in imposition of embargoes or resistance to occupation). It may also be economic or social or religious. The scale and level of the conflict will also vary. It may be limited to a neighborhood, a city, or a particular section of the society; it may at other times range over a large area of a country or convulse a whole nation. Less often, more than one country and government may be involved. Whatever the issue, however, and whatever the scale of the conflict, nonviolent action is a technique by which people who reject passivity and submission, and who see struggle as essential, can wage their conflict without violence. Nonviolent action is not an attempt to avoid or ignore conflict. It is *one* response to the problem of how to *act* effectively in politics, especially how to wield power effectively.

A. A special type of action.

It is widely assumed that all social and political behavior must be clearly either violent or nonviolent. This simple dualism leads only to serious distortions of reality, however, one of the main ones being that some people call "nonviolent" anything they regard as good, and "violent" anything they dislike. A second gross distortion occurs when people totally erroneously equate cringing passivity with nonviolent action because in neither case is there the use of physical violence.

Careful consideration of actual response to social and political conflict requires that all responses to conflict situations be initially divided into those of *action* and those of *inaction,* and not divided according to their violence or lack of violence. In such a division nonviolent action assumes its correct place as *one* type of *active* response. *Inaction,* which may include passivity, submission, cowardice and the like, will not detain us, for it has nothing to do with the nonviolent technique which is the subject of this book. By definition, nonviolent action cannot occur except by the replacement of passivity and submissiveness with activity, challenge and struggle.

Obviously, however, important distinctions must be made *within* the category of *action.* Here, too, a dichotomy into *violent* or *nonviolent* is too simple. Therefore, let us set up a rough typology of six major classes of the forms of action in conflicts, one of them nonviolent action, the technique with which we are concerned. This (rather crude) classification includes: 1) simple verbal persuasion and related behavior, such as conciliation; 2) peaceful institutional procedures backed by threat or use of sanctions: 3) physical violence against persons; 4) physical violence against persons plus material destruction; 5) material destruction only; and 6) the technique of nonviolent action. Obviously, each of these classes may itself be subclassified. People may shift back and forth between types of action, or back and forth between action and inaction. However, it is crucial to understand that the basic dichotomy of social and political behavior is between action and inaction, rather than between nonviolence and violence.

It is also important to see why and how nonviolent action as a technique differs from milder peaceful responses to conflicts, such as conciliation, verbal appeals to the opponent, compromise and negotiation. These responses may or may not be used with nonviolent action or with any of the other five kinds of action, but they should not be identified with the nonviolent technique as such. Conciliation and appeals are likely to consist of rational or emotional verbal efforts to bring about an opponent's agreement to something, while nonviolent action is not verbal—it consists of social, economic and political activity of special types. For example, asking an employer for a wage increase is an act of attempted simple verbal persuasion, but refusal to work until the wage increase is granted is a case of nonviolent action. Nor should nonviolent action be confused with compromise, which involves settling for part of one's objectives. Compromise is not a form of conflict or struggle, as is nonviolent action. As with violence, nonviolent action may or may not lead to a compromise settlement, depending on the issues,

SIX CLASSES OF ACTION
IN CONFLICTS

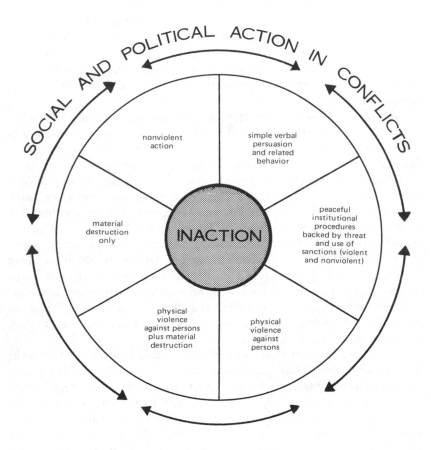

CHART TWO

power relationships, and the actionists' own decision. Similarly, negotiation is not a form of nonviolent action. Negotiation is an attempt at verbal persuasion, perhaps utilizing established institutional procedures, but always involving an implied or explicit threat of some type of sanction if an acceptable agreement is not reached. Negotiation could, therefore, precede a strike or a civil disobedience campaign, as it can a war. But such negotiation is an approach which must be distinguished from a strike, civil disobedience, or other form of nonviolent action.

Nonviolent action is so different from these milder peaceful responses to conflicts that several writers have pointed to the general similarities of nonviolent action to military war.[2] Nonviolent action is a means of combat, as is war. It involves the matching of forces and the waging of "battles," requires wise strategy and tactics, and demands of its "soldiers" courage, discipline, and sacrifice. This view of nonviolent action as a technique of active combat is diametrically opposed to the popular assumption that, at its strongest, nonviolent action relies on rational persuasion of the opponent, and that more commonly it consists simply of passive submission. Nonviolent action is just what it says: *action* which is nonviolent, not *inaction*. This technique consists, not simply of words, but of active protest, noncooperation and intervention. Overwhelmingly, it is group or mass action. Certain forms of nonviolent action may be regarded as efforts to persuade by action; others, given sufficient participants, may contain elements of coercion.

Another characteristic of nonviolent action which needs emphasis is that it is usually extraconstitutional; that is to say, it does not rely upon established institutional procedures of the State, whether parliamentary or nonparliamentary. However, it is possible to incorporate the technique into a constitutional system of government at various points, and it is also possible to use it in support of an established government under attack. Nonviolent action must not be confused with anarchism. That "no-State" philosophy has traditionally given inadequate thought to the practical problem of how to achieve such a society and to the need for realistic means of social struggle which differ in substance from those employed by the State.

B. Motives, methods and leverages

The motives for using nonviolent action instead of some type of violent action differ widely. In some cases violence may have been rejected because of considerations of expediency, in others for religious, ethical, or moral reasons. Or there may be a mixture of motivations of various types.

Nonviolent action is thus not synonymous with "pacifism." Nor is it identical with religious or philosophical systems emphasizing nonviolence as a matter of moral principle. Adherents to some of these belief systems may see nonviolent action as compatible with their convictions and even as a fulfillment of them in conflicts. Adherents to certain other creeds which also emphasize nonviolence may, however, find this technique too "worldly" or "coercive" for them. Conversely, nonviolent action has often been practiced, and in a vast majority of the cases led, by nonpacifists who saw it only as an effective means of action. The popular idea that only pacifists can effectively practice nonviolent action —a view sometimes pressed with considerable conceit by pacifists themselves—is simply not true.

Furthermore, in many cases motivations for using nonviolent action have been mixed, practical considerations being combined with a *relative* moral preference for nonviolence (although violence was not rejected in principle). This type of mixed motivation is likely to become more frequent if nonviolent action is increasingly seen to have important practical advantages over violence.

It is frequently assumed that nonviolent actionists seek primarily to convert their opponent to a positive acceptance of their point of view. Actually, there is no standard pattern of priority for either changes in attitudes and beliefs, or policy and structural changes. Sometimes the nonviolent group may seek to change the opponent's attitudes and beliefs as a preliminary to changing his policies or institutions. Or the nonviolent action may be an expression of the determination of the members of the group not to allow the opponent to change their own attitudes or beliefs. Or the actions may be aimed primarily at changing policies or institutions or at thwarting the opponent's attempts to alter them, whether or not his attitudes and beliefs have first been changed (these cases appear to be in the majority). In still other cases, the nonviolent group may seek to change attitudes and policies simultaneously.

Nonviolent action may involve: 1) *acts of omission*—that is, people practicing it may refuse to perform acts which they usually perform, are expected by custom to perform, or are required by law or regulation to perform; 2) *acts of commission*—that is, the people may perform acts which they do not usually perform, are not expected by custom to perform, or are forbidden by law or regulation to perform; or 3) *a combination* of acts of omission and acts of commission.[3]

There are in the technique three broad classes of methods. 1) Where the nonviolent group uses largely symbolic actions intended to help persuade the opponent or someone else, or to express the group's disapproval and dissent, the behavior may be called *nonviolent protest and persuasion*. In this class are such demonstrations as marches, parades and vigils. These particular methods may be used either in an attempt to change opinions or to express disagreement, or both. 2) Where the nonviolent group acts largely by withdrawal or the withholding of social, economic, or political cooperation, its behavior may be described as *noncooperation*. This class contains three subclasses which include *social* noncooperation, *economic* noncooperation (economic boycotts and strikes), and *political* noncooperation. 3) Where the nonviolent group acts largely by direct intervention its action may be referred to as *nonviolent intervention*. The nonviolent group in this class clearly takes the initiative by such means as sit-ins, nonviolent obstruction, nonviolent invasion and parallel government. The technique may be applied by individuals, by small or large groups, and by masses of people.

Just as there is diversity among the many specific methods which constitute this technique, so also wide variation exists in the intensities of pressures and the types of leverage exerted by this technique. When successful, nonviolent action produces change in one of three broad ways, which we call *mechanisms of change*. In *conversion* the opponent reacts to the actions of the nonviolent actionists by finally coming around to a new point of view in which he positively accepts their aims. In *accommodation* the opponent chooses to grant demands and to adjust to the new situation which has been produced without changing his viewpoint. Where *nonviolent coercion* operates, change is achieved against the opponent's will and without his agreement, the sources of his power having been so undercut by nonviolent means that he no longer has control. These three mechanisms are discussed in detail in Chapter Thirteen.

To a degree which has never been adequately appreciated, the nonviolent technique operates by producing power changes. Both the relative power and the absolute power of each of the contending groups are subject to constant and rapid alterations. This power variability can be more extreme and occur more rapidly than in situations where both sides are using violence. As may be expected, the actionists seek continually to increase their own strength and that of their supporters. They will usually seek and gain assistance and active participation also from among the wider group affected by the grievances. In addition, the nature of nonviolent struggle makes it possible for the actionists also to win considerable support even in the camp of the opponent and among third parties. This potential is much greater than with violence. The ability to gain these types of support gives the nonviolent group a capacity to influence—and at times to regulate—*their opponent's* power, by reducing or severing the power of the opponent at its sources. Usually the results of these complex changes in the relative power positions of the contenders will determine the struggle's final outcome.

Nonviolent discipline must be viewed in the context of the mechanisms of change of this technique and the ways in which these power shifts are produced. The maintenance of nonviolent discipline in face of repression is not an act of moralistic naïveté. Instead, it contributes to the operation of all three mechanisms and is a prerequisite for advantageous power changes. As a consequence, nonviolent discipline can only be compromised at the severe risk of contributing to defeat. Other factors are, of course, highly important too, and it should not be assumed that maintenance of nonviolence will alone inevitably produce victory.

C. Correcting misconceptions

It is widely assumed that nonviolent action must always take a very long time to produce victory, longer than violent struggle would take. This may be true at times, but not necessarily so, and at times the situation even seems reversed. Violent struggle may take many months or years to defeat the opponent, assuming that it eventually does so. In a variety of cases nonviolent struggle has won objectives in a very short time indeed. The 1766 repeal of the Stamp Act, which the American colonists resisted, came in a very few months. The 1920 Kapp *Putsch* in Germany was defeated in days. In 1942 Norwegian teachers within months defeated the Quisling regime's first effort at establishing a fascist Corporative State. In 1944 the dictators of El Salvador and Guatemala were ousted in a matter of days. Economic boycotts in American cities have often very quickly induced significantly increased hiring of Afro-Americans. The time taken to achieve victory depends on diverse factors —primarily on the strength of the nonviolent actionists.

By examining and correcting misconceptions about nonviolent action we are often able to bring out more sharply positive characteristics. 1) As has been pointed out above, this technique has nothing to do with passivity, submissiveness and cowardice; just as in violent action, these must first be rejected and overcome. 2) Nonviolent action is not to be equated with verbal or purely psychological persuasion, although it may use action to induce psychological pressures for attitude change; nonviolent action, instead of words, is a sanction and a technique of struggle involving the use of social, economic and political power, and the matching of forces in conflict. 3) Nonviolent action does not depend on the assumption that man is inherently "good"; the potentialities of man for both "good" and "evil" are recognized, including the extremes of cruelty and inhumanity. 4) People using nonviolent action do not have to be pacifists or saints; nonviolent action has been predominantly and successfully practiced by "ordinary" people. 5) Success with nonviolent action does not require (though it may be helped by) shared standards and principles, a high degree of community of interest, or a high degree of psychological closeness between the contending groups; this is because when efforts to produce voluntary change fail, coercive nonviolent measures may be employed. 6) Nonviolent action is at least as much of a Western phenomenon as an Eastern one; indeed, it is probably more Western, if one takes into account the widespread use of strikes and boycotts in the labor movement and the noncooperation struggles of subordinated nationalities. 7) In nonviolent action there is no assumption that the opponent will refrain from using violence against nonviolent actionists; the technique is designed to operate against violence when necessary. 8) There is nothing in nonviolent action to prevent it from being used for both "good" and "bad" causes, although the social consequences of its use for a "bad" cause may differ considerably from the consequences of violence used for the same cause. 9) Nonviolent action is not limited to domestic conflicts within a democratic system; it has been widely used against dictatorial regimes, foreign occupations, and even against totalitarian systems.

D. A neglected type of struggle

Nonviolent action has not always brought full, or even partial, victory. People using nonviolent action have been defeated. It is no magic ritual. This is also true of violent action, however, including military struggle. No type of struggle guarantees short-term victory every time it is used. Failure in specific cases of nonviolent action, however, may be caused by weaknesses in a group employing the technique or in the strategy and tactics used—as may be the case in military action. If the group using nonviolent action does not as yet possess sufficient internal strength, determination, ability to act, and related qualities to make nonviolent action effective, then repetition of phrases and words like "nonviolence" will not save it. There is no substitute for genuine strength and skill in nonviolent action; if the actionists do not possess them sufficiently to cope with the opponent, they are unlikely to win. Considering the widespread ignorance of the nature and requirements of nonviolent action and the absence of major efforts to learn how to apply it most effectively, it is surprising that it has won any victories at all. Comparative studies are urgently needed of cases of "failure" and "success," and of possible ways to improve effectiveness.

It is clear, however, that the failures of nonviolent action do not adequately explain its widespread nonrecognition as a viable technique of struggle. This nonrecognition has taken several forms. One is a lack of attention to the history of nonviolent action. This technique has been widely used. It has a long history. At the moment of its use, its power and effectiveness have frequently been widely acknowledged; but once the particular case is over these characteristics are often forgot. Even the memory of them recedes. It is difficult to find good factual accounts of past nonviolent struggles.

The roots of this nonrecognition are hard to pinpoint, to separate one from the other and to trace to specific neglect. Suggested explanations can only be tentative at this stage of investigation. On a popular level it is easy to romanticize the more dramatic and heroic acts of violence for good causes, and the memory of such bravery has its influence on how the present is viewed, and therefore the past. Although nonviolent action may be equally heroic and dramatic, rarely do its deeds and heroes become romanticized as examples for future generations. There are also other, perhaps more fundamental, possible reasons for this nonrecognition. Some of the neglect of nonviolent struggle by historians may be rooted in their personal preconceptions and their acceptance of their society's assumption that violence is the only really significant and effective form of combat. In addition, where historians have been closely allied to established oppressive systems and ruling elites and have allowed that alliance to influence their writing, their neglect of these forms of struggle may be traced to consideration of the best interests of the ruling minority. The detailed recounting of forms of struggle usable by people who lack military weapons might be thought of as actual instruction in an antielitist technique which the people could use against their rulers. Furthermore, by recording effective continuing noncooperation, for example, the historian might cast aspersions on the established ruler and administration by implying that they were either inefficient or unpopular.

Anthropologists have revealed great cultural diversity among human societies, which include quite opposite attitudes and behaviors toward violence and nonviolence. Were it not for this diversity it would be difficult to avoid the conclusion that human nature is more violent than nonviolent. Many people accept this conclusion. Such a view influences not only what is done, but also how we interpret what happens. The conclusion that human beings are basically violent is, however, a distortion of reality, for in its assumptions Western civilization is biased toward violence. Indeed, when people in our society are confronted with situations in which violence obviously suffers from grave disadvantages and where significant evidence shows that nonviolent alternatives exist, a large number of people will still say that they *believe* violence to be necessary—a resort to conviction rather than evidence. This built-in bias toward violence may also contribute to the nonrecognition of the viability of nonviolent action.

There is one more possible explanation of the nonrecognition of nonviolent action as a significant political technique, a much simpler one. Why has not any new way of viewing the world been accepted earlier? Why, although apples had fallen from trees for centuries, did it remain for Newton to formulate the law of gravity? How is it that slavery could be accepted for many centuries as a right and necessary social institution? So one might ask similar questions about diverse approaches to understanding reality and viewing society. The explanation of the neglect and nonrecognition of nonviolent action—its practice, nature and potential—may be very similar to answers to these different questions.

In addition, until very recently no overall conceptual system existed to reveal relationships between diverse and apparently dissimilar historical events which are now grouped as cases of nonviolent action. We can now see, not simply a multitude of separate and unrelated events and forms of action, but one common technique of action. The resistance of Roman plebeians, the defiance of American colonials, the boycotting by Irish peasants, the strikes by workers of St. Petersburg, the fasts of Algerian nationalists, the civil disobedience by Gandhians, the refusal of Afro-Americans to ride buses in Montgomery, Alabama, and the arguments of students in Prague with Russian tank crews—all are different aspects of essentially the same type of behavior: nonviolent action. For the many forms of military struggle an overall conceptual tool has long existed, and this itself may have contributed to the detailed attention which wars have received. Attention to war has included historical and strategic studies which could help in future wars. But, until very recently, nonviolent action has had no comparable self-conscious tradition. Such a tradition would probably have brought attention to many of these neglected struggles and might well have provided knowledge to be used in new cases of nonviolent action.

There has been, then, little or no awareness of the history of nonviolent action, not only among the general public but also among future leaders of nonviolent struggles. Contrary to earlier assumptions, before undertaking his own campaigns Gandhi had a general knowledge of sev' eral important nonviolent struggles, especially in Russia, China and India; but even so he lacked the detailed knowledge that could have been gained from such conflicts.[4]

Another form of nonrecognition of nonviolent action is the general practice of unfairly comparing it with violence by using different standards of assessment for the two techniques. Sometimes when violence has had no chance of succeeding (even despite preparations), nonviolent action has been used, despite highly unfavorable conditions—including the usual lack of preparations, as in Czechoslovakia in 1968. Then when it failed, nonviolent action has later been criticized or condemned *as a whole* because its accomplishments were limited, slow to appear, or even absent. When violence fails, or when its achievements are limited or take time, *specific* inadequacies or factors are frequently blamed—not the technique itself. This rarely happens when nonviolent action is used, however. Rarely are the violent and nonviolent techniques carefully and fairly compared in terms of time, casualties, successes and failures (using specific criteria), adequacy of preparations, type of strategy, and the like. In cases where nonviolent action has produced partial or full successes, the tendency is to forget, minimize, or dismiss these as irrelevant. Full successes are sometimes written off, without careful analysis, as having been unique and without significance for future politics. This was the case with the downfall of the tsarist regime in Russia in 1917 and the collapse of the dictators of El Salvador and Guatemala in 1944. Who remembers these as victories won by nonviolent struggle? Where past struggles *are* remembered, their victories are forgotten or denied or minimized (as with the American colonists' struggles and the United States civil rights campaigns); or they are explained as having been unrelated to the nonviolent struggle or only partially so (as with the Gandhian struggles in India). Partial successes are often regarded as total failures —for example, the Ruhr struggle against the French and Belgian occupation in the period after World War I. In other cases, the nonviolent struggles may not be deliberately belittled, but greater attention may be paid to the less successful or less important violent struggles which preceded the nonviolent action (as in nineteenth-century Hungary) or which occurred alongside it (as in Nazi-occupied Norway).

Articulate opposition to the technique has often been based on misunderstanding and lack of information. Supposed "friends of nonviolent means"—such as some pacifists—have often by their own distortions and lack of knowledge discouraged others from taking this technique seriously. Generally, however, past nonviolent action has been ignored in contemplating how to face the conflicts of the future.

ILLUSTRATIONS FROM THE PAST

Despite its widespread practice, nonviolent action has therefore remained an underdeveloped political technique. Very little deliberate effort has been given to increasing knowledge of its nature and how it works. Practically no research and planning have been carried out to promote its development and refinement. This is in sharp contrast to military war, guerrilla struggle, and the procedures of representative democracy. To date what we have in nonviolent action is essentially a raw, unrefined, intuitive technique—a type of struggle which still awaits efforts to increase its effectiveness and expand its political potential.

Nevertheless, in the past hundred years nonviolent action has risen to unprecedented political significance throughout the world. People using it have amassed major achievements. Higher wages and improved working conditions have been won. Old traditions and practices have been abolished. Government policies have been changed, laws repealed, new legislation enacted, and governmental reforms instituted. Invaders have been frustrated and armies defeated. An empire has been paralyzed, a seizure of power thwarted, and dictators overthrown. Sometimes, too, this technique has been used—as by Deep South segregationists—to block or delay changes and policies regarded by others as desirable and progressive.

A. Some early historical examples

Much of the long history of nonviolent action has been lost for lack of interest in recording and recounting these struggles. Even existing historical accounts and other surviving information have not been brought together. The result is that a comprehensive history of the practice and development of the technique does not yet exist. Therefore, in this section we can only outline the history of nonviolent action in broad terms and illustrate it with more detailed sketches of a few especially interesting or significant cases. These were not necessarily influential in later struggles, for much of the use of this technique has been independent of earlier practice.

Nonviolent action clearly began early: examples go back at least to ancient Rome. In 494 B.C., for example, the plebeians of Rome, rather than murder the consuls in an attempt to correct grievances, withdrew from the city to a hill, later called "the Sacred Mount." There they remained for some days, refusing to make their usual contribution to the life of the city. An agreement was then reached pledging significant improvements in their life and status.[5] Theodor Mommsen offers an account of a similar Roman action in 258 B.C. The army had returned from battle to find proposals for reform blocked in the Senate. Instead of using military action, the army marched to the fertile district of Crustumeria, occupied "the Sacred Mount," and threatened to establish a new plebeian city. The Senate gave way.[6]

Although occasionally there are in the literature other references to instances of nonviolent action in the ancient Mediterranean world, they are not detailed; a few will be cited later as examples of specific methods of this technique. No systematic attempt has been made to locate and assemble early cases of nonviolent action, not only from Rome, but from a variety of civilizations and countries. Nonviolent action certainly occurred between Roman times and the late eighteenth century, when the case material becomes rich—for example, the Netherlands' resistance to Spanish rule from 1565 to 1576 is one very prominent such struggle—but we lack a coherent account of instances of nonviolent action during these centuries. This still remains to be written. Careful search from this perspective even in existing historical studies might reveal a great deal.

B. The pre-Gandhian expansion of nonviolent struggle

We can, however, see that a very significant pre-Gandhian expansion of the technique took place from the late eighteenth to the early twentieth centuries. During this period the technique received impetus from four groups. The first consisted of nationalists (and others who were ruled from distant capitals) who found nonviolent action useful in resisting a foreign enemy or alien laws. The struggles of the American colonists before 1775 furnish highly important cases of such nonviolent resistance. In this period Daniel Dulany of Maryland, for example, advocated economic resistance in order to force Parliament to repeal offensive laws. In his proposals he urged the colonists to accept principles of action which are basic to this technique: "Instead of moping, and puling, and whining to excite Compassion; in such a Situation we ought with Spirit, and Vigour, and Alacrity, to bid Defiance to Tyranny, by exposing its Impotence, by making it as contemptible, as it would be detestable."[7]

Nationalist examples include the Hungarian resistance against Austria between 1850 and 1867 and the Chinese boycotts of Japanese goods in the early twentieth century. Both the American and the Hungarian struggles were extremely significant and effective, yet the degree to which the Americans won their demands and British power was immobilized by noncooperation is today not often fully recognized.[8] The nonviolent Hungarian resistance led by Deák is largely forgotten and is even lacking, it is said, a good historian; while the earlier, very unsuccessful, violent resistance under Kossuth is remembered and idealized.

The second source of impetus in the development of the nonviolent technique in this period came from trade unionists and other social radicals who sought a means of struggle—largely strikes, general strikes and boycotts—against what they regarded as an unjust social system, and for the improvement of the condition of working men. An examination of the histories of the labor movement and of trade union struggles, and an awareness of the current use of such methods, quickly reveal the vast extent to which strikes and economic boycotts have been and are still used. Indeed, it was action based on awareness that withdrawal of labor was a powerful instrument of struggle which not only made possible improved wages and working conditions, but frequently also contributed to an extension of the right to vote, to the political power of working people, and to reform legislation. The significance of this frequently escapes us today, when people are often more conscious of the inconveniences to themselves which strikes may involve. However real these may often be, it has been fortunate both for the labor movement and for society as a whole that predominantly strikes and boycotts have been used to right economic grievances, instead of physical attacks on factory managers and owners, arson, riots, bombings and assassinations. Today these may seem unlikely tools for such ends, but this is a reflection of the degree to which violent means of struggle have in this area been replaced with nonviolent ones in order to induce the desired concessions in negotiations. Today it is also largely forgotten that nonviolent struggle in the form of general strike, for example, had its exponents among advocates of major political and economic change.

A third source of impetus in the development of the nonviolent technique on the level of ideas and personal example came from individuals such as Leo Tolstoy[9] in Russia and Henry David Thoreau[10] in the United States, both of whom wanted to show how a better society might be peacefully created.

Thoreau, for example, sketched in the political potentialities of disobedience of "immoral" laws. "Let your life be a counter-friction to stop the machine," he wrote. Speaking of disobedience and willingness to go to prison as a means of struggle against slavery in the United States, he continued: "A minority is powerless while it conforms to the majority; it is not even a minority then; but it is irresistible when it clogs by its whole weight." He also envisaged that such disobedience would be practiced by the ruler's agents: "When the subject has refused allegiance, and the officer has resigned his office, then the revolution is accomplished."[11]

Tolstoy's argument in his "A Letter to a Hindu"—that it was the submissiveness and cooperation of the Indians which made British rule of India possible—is known to have made a great impression on Gandhi. In terms of political impact, however, the use of nonviolent action against foreign rulers and by the labor movement was far more important than such men as Thoreau and Tolstoy.

A fourth group which contributed more or less unconsciously to the pre-Gandhian development of nonviolent struggle were opponents of despotism which originated, not abroad, but in their own country. Their contribution may be seen most clearly in the defeated Russian Revolution of 1905. This case deserves detailed and careful research and analysis, and its lessons may be much more profound than the ones usually offered: that the "situation was not ripe," or that a full-scale violent revolution was needed.

C. Early twentieth-century cases

A sense of reality and political substance can perhaps best be infused into the generalizations about the nature of nonviolent action and this sketchy historical survey by illustrating it with brief accounts of a few of the cases which have occurred in the twentieth century, beginning with the Russian Revolution of 1905.

1. Russian Empire—1905-06[12]   The Russian Empire, which had been long ruled by tsars who believed in their divine duty to govern, had been shaken by internal unrest and by humiliating defeats in the Russo-Japanese War. The years immediately before 1905 had already seen expressions of dissatisfaction among the peasants, workers, students and the intelligentsia. There had been more demands for representative government. Strikes by industrial workers had occurred.

In January 1905 thousands joined a peaceful march to the Winter Palace in St. Petersburg to present a mild petition to the Tsar. The guards fired into the crowd; over a hundred persons were killed and over three hundred wounded. The day became known as "Bloody Sunday." A predominantly nonviolent revolution followed spontaneously. There was violence, especially among the peasants, but the year-long struggle was largely expressed in a multitude of forms of nonviolent action, especially strikes. The major strikes, which repeatedly paralyzed St. Petersburg and Moscow and the railway and communications systems, were only the most obvious forms of resistance. (Many of these are described in later chapters.) Whole provinces and nationalities broke away from tsarist control and set up independent governments.

By October the country was paralyzed. The Tsar finally issued the October Manifesto, granting an elected legislature, with admittedly incomplete but nevertheless significant powers—something he had vowed never to do. The revolution, however, continued. Newspapers and magazines ignored censorship regulations. Trade unions made rapid growth. Councils (called *soviets*) became popular organs of parallel government and were much more representative than the established regime. There had already been limited mutinies among soldiers and sailors; the loyalty of troops wavered, and upon their obedience or large-scale mutiny depended in part the continued life or complete collapse of the regime. About two-thirds of the government troops were unreliable at this point, reports one historian.

During a widespread strike movement the Bolsheviks and Mensheviks succeeded in getting the Moscow *Soviet* to endorse a plan to transform the city's general strike, in early December 1905, into an armed rising. In face of this rebel violence, with their own lives in danger, the soldiers in Moscow largely obeyed orders. The violent rising was crushed. The regime made this victory for the tsar the beginning of a counteroffensive against the revolution. The strikers had also faced other problems, but major historians cite the defeat of the Moscow rising as the beginning of the end of the 1905 revolution.

Certain forms of struggle persisted into 1906. The downfall of the tsarist autocracy was, however, postponed until the predominantly nonviolent revolution of February 1917—which as in 1905 took the political parties espousing revolution by surprise.

Gandhi's struggles began in South Africa in 1906 against white supremacist oppression of Indians and continued in India after his return home in 1915 until his assassination in 1948. This historical contribution will be discussed shortly. It is important to note, however, that non-Gandhian contributions to the development of the technique of nonviolent action and its political potentialities continued even after Gandhi's struggles had begun.

2. Berlin—1920[13]   The rightist Kapp *coup d'état* (or *Putsch)* against the young Weimar Republic of Germany was defeated by nonviolent action. This action was launched in support of the legitimate government after that government had fled Berlin. These events—which took place without advance preparation or training—merit attention, even though the *coup* itself was rather amateurish and the improvised resistance something less than a perfect model. The case also illustrates the point that nonviolent action may be used to defend and preserve a regime or political system as well as to oppose it.

From the start the new Weimar Republic faced immense difficulties associated with the loss of the war: economic dislocation, military unrest, and attempts at revolution. In these circumstances, a right-wing promonarchist *coup d'état* was planned by Dr. Wolfgang Kapp and Lieutenant-General Freiherr Walter von Lüttwitz with the backing of General Erich von Ludendorff and various other army officers. On March 10, 1920, General Lüttwitz presented President Friedrich Ebert with a virtual ultimatum. This was rejected by the government, and it became apparent that a *Putsch* would be attempted. Minister of Defense Gustav Noske warned Lüttwitz that if orders were disobeyed and troops were used in an attempt to overthrow the Republic, the government would call a general strike. A meeting of generals showed that they were unwilling to use military force to defeat a rightist *Putsch*. They would not defend the Republic.

The same day—March 12—the Kappists, despite their limited preparations, began their march on Berlin. Police officers sided with the conspirators. There was grave doubt that government soldiers would fire on the advancing troops from the Baltic Brigades. The Ebert government abandoned Berlin without a fight, going first to Dresden and then to Stuttgart. Berlin was occupied on Saturday, March 13. The Kappists declared a new government. However, the *Länder* (states) were directed by the Ebert government to refuse all cooperation with the Kapp regime and to maintain contact only with the legal government.

When *Freikorps* (independent para-military units) troops occupied the offices of two progovernment newspapers on Sunday afternoon all Berlin printers went on strike. Other workers in Berlin by scores of thousands also spontaneously went on strike. Later that Sunday a call for a general strike against the *coup* was issued under the names of the members of the Executive Committee of the Social Democratic Party (S.P.D.) and the S.P.D. members of the Ebert Cabinet: "There is but one means to prevent the return of Wilhelm II: the paralysis of all economic life. Not a hand must stir, not a worker give aid to the military dictatorship. General Strike all along the line."[14] The general strike was supported by workers of all political and religious groups. (The Communists, however, had at first refused to support it.) No "essential services" were exempted. As described in Chapter One, the bureaucracy itself noncooperated. The

Kappist regime lacked money, and ordinary civil servants struck or otherwise refused to head ministries under Kapp, who was unable to obtain cooperation from the bureaucracy. Workers tried to influence the Kappist troops.

On the fifteenth of March the Ebert government rejected proposals for a compromise. The limited power of the occupiers of the Berlin government offices became more obvious. Some *Reichswehr* (German army) commanders resumed loyalty to the government. Leaflets entitled "The Collapse of the Military Dictatorship" were showered on Berlin from an airplane. The strike continued to spread despite severe threats and actual deaths by shooting. On the morning of the seventeenth the Berlin Security Police demanded Kapp's resignation.

Later that day, Kapp did resign and fled to Sweden, leaving General Lüttwitz as Commander-in-Chief. Bloody clashes took place in many towns. That evening most of the conspirators left Berlin in civilian clothes and Lüttwitz resigned from his new post. The next day the Baltic Brigades—now under orders of the Ebert government—marched out of Berlin but did not hesitate to shoot and kill some civilians who had jeered at them. The *coup* was defeated and the Weimar Republic preserved. The Ebert government faced continuing unrest, however, as bloody conflicts between government troops and an armed "Red" army in the Rhineland took many lives.

An authority on the *coup d'état,* Lieutenant Colonel D.J. Goodspeed, has pointed to one of the central lessons to be learned from the Kapp *Putsch:* after having seized the machinery of government, the conspirators must "obtain the required minimum of consent for their own administration."

> The Kapp *putsch* is the episode where this question of popular support is seen at its clearest . . . to all intents and purposes the *coup* seemed to have succeeded. Yet it was broken, very largely because the people would not obey the new government.[15]

The distinguished German historian Erich Eyck has also concluded that "the strike . . . brought the *coup* of Kapp and company to an end after only four days. Since the regular tools of the state had been found wanting, only immediate intervention by the populace could have saved it so soon."[16]

3. The Ruhrkampf—1923[17]   The resistance to the Kapp *Putsch* was followed quickly by another very significant nonviolent struggle in support of legitimate government. This was the German resistance, in 1923, to the French and Belgian occupation of the Ruhr. During this remarkable struggle, trade unionists, industrialists, German civil servants, officials and many other people refused to obey or cooperate with the occupation regime. French repression was very severe.

Besides noncooperation, the situation was also complicated at certain stages by various types of sabotage. And there were economic problems for all of Germany. The country's economic situation was endangered by the severance of the industrial and coal-mining belt from the rest of Germany, as well as by the financing of the resistance by unsupported paper money.

The *Ruhrkampf* has been widely regarded as a failure. However, France found her ability to control the Ruhr and extract its resources and products frustrated, expenses in the attempt exceeding the economic gains. The French government fell, in part at least because of French domestic revulsion over the severe repression practiced by its occupation troops and officials. French troops evacuated the Ruhr after the German government agreed to call off the passive resistance campaign. The success-failure ratio seems to have been mixed for each side.

D. Gandhi's contribution

It was Gandhi who made the most significant personal contribution in the history of the nonviolent technique, with his political experiments in the use of noncooperation, disobedience and defiance to control rulers, alter government policies, and undermine political systems. With these experiments the character of the technique was broadened and its practice refined. Among the modifications Gandhi introduced were greater attention to strategy and tactics, a more judicious use of the armory of nonviolent methods, and a conscious association between mass political action and the norm of nonviolence. For participants, however, this association was not absolutist in character, and clearly most took part because this technique was seen to offer effective action. As a result of Gandhi's work the technique became more active and dynamic. With his political colleagues and fellow Indians, Gandhi in a variety of conflicts in South Africa and India demonstrated that nonviolent struggle could be politically effective on a large scale.

Gandhi used his nonviolent approach to deal with India's internal problems as well as to combat the British occupation of his country, and he encouraged others to do likewise. One of the well-known local uses of his *satyagraha* took place at Vykom in South India in 1924 and 1925; it was conducted by some of Gandhi's supporters to gain rights for the untouchables. In this case there was a considerable attempt to change the attitudes and feelings of the orthodox Hindus. Gandhi's frequent exhortations on the need to convert, not coerce, the opponent were well implemented in this case. Emphasis on conversion is not usual in nonviolent action, however, nor is this case typical of the Gandhian struggles. However, it is significant precisely because of the attempt to convert the opponent group despite the extreme "social distance" between the Brahmans and the untouchables.

1. Vykom—1924-25[18]   In Vykom, Travancore, one of the states ruled by an Indian maharajah instead of the British, untouchables had for centuries been forbidden to use a particular road leading directly to their quarter because it passed an orthodox Brahman temple. In 1924, after consultations with Gandhi, certain high-caste Hindu reformers initiated action. Together with untouchable friends, this group walked down the road and stopped in front of the temple. Orthodox Hindus attacked them severely, and some demonstrators were arrested, receiving prison sentences of up to a year. Volunteers then poured in from all parts of India. Instead of further arrests, the Maharajah's government ordered the police to keep the reformers from entering the road. A cordon was therefore placed across it. The reformers stood in an attitude of prayer before it, pleading with police to allow them to pass. Both groups organized day and night shifts. The reformers pledged themselves to nonviolence and refused to withdraw until the Brahmans recognized the right of the untouchables to use the highway. As the months passed, the numbers of the reformers and their spirits sometimes rose and sometimes fell. When the rainy season came and the road was flooded, they stood by their posts, shortening each shift to three hours between replacements. The water reached their shoulders. Police manning the cordon had to take to boats.

When the government finally removed the barrier, the reformers declined to walk forward until the orthodox Hindus changed their attitude. After sixteen months the Brahmans said: "We cannot any longer resist the prayers that have been made to us, and we are ready to receive the untouchables." The case had widespread reverberations throughout India, it is reported, assisting in the removal of similar restrictions elsewhere and strengthening significantly the cause of caste reform.

2. Gandhi's theory of power   Gandhi is better known, however, for his struggles against British domination. In these struggles he operated on the basis of a view of power and avowedly based his newly developed approach to conflict—*satyagraha*—upon a theory of power: "In politics, its use is based upon the immutable maxim that government of the people is possible only so long as they consent either consciously or unconsciously to be governed."[19] This constituted the basic principle of his grand strategy.

In Gandhi's view, if the maintenance of an unjust or nondemocratic regime depends on the cooperation, submission and obedience of the populace, then the means for changing or abolishing it lies in the noncooperation, defiance and disobedience of that populace. These, he was convinced, could be undertaken without the use of physical violence, and even without hostility toward the members of the opponent group. In *Hind Swaraj or Indian Home Rule,* an early pamphlet written in 1909, Gandhi expressed his theory of control of political power in a passage addressed to the British rulers:

> You have great military resources. Your naval power is matchless. If we wanted to fight with you on your own ground, we should be unable to do so, but if the above submissions be not acceptable to you, we cease to play the part of the ruled. You may, if you like, cut us to pieces. You may shatter us at the cannon's mouth. If you act contrary to our will, we shall not help you; and without our help, we know that you cannot move one step forward.[20]

A resolution drafted by Gandhi, approved by the All-India Working Committee of the Indian National Congress (the nationalist party), and passed by public meetings on the Congress-declared Independence Day, January 26, 1930, contained this statement on noncooperation and the withdrawal of voluntary submission to the British *Raj:*

> We hold it to be a crime against man and God to submit any longer to a rule that has caused this fourfold disaster to our country. We recognize, however, that the most effective way of gaining our freedom is not through violence. We will therefore prepare ourselves by withdrawing, so far as we can, all voluntary association from the British Government, and will prepare for civil disobedience, including nonpayment of taxes. We are convinced that if we can but withdraw our voluntary help and stop payment of taxes without doing violence, even under provocation, the end of this inhuman rule is assured.[21]

Later that same year, Gandhi, at the request of the Indian National Congress, launched a movement of noncooperation and disobedience for the attainment of *swaraj, i.e.,* "self-rule." This campaign was based upon the above theory, the seditious nature of which Gandhi had nearly ten years earlier openly avowed.

> . . . sedition has become the creed of the Congress. Every noncooperator is pledged to preach disaffection towards the Government established by law. Noncooperation, though a religious and strictly moral movement, deliberately aims at the overthrow of the Government, and is therefore legally seditious in terms of the Indian Penal Code.[22]

This withdrawal of support, Gandhi said, should be in proportion to "their ability to preserve order in the social structure" without the assistance of the ruler.[23] The way to control political power therefore became, in his view, "to noncooperate with the system by withdrawing all the voluntary assistance possible and refusing all its so-called benefits."[24] On this basis he had formulated *satyagraha.*

While he sought to convert the British, Gandhi had no illusions that there could be an easy solution without struggle and the exercise of power. Just before the beginning of the 1930-31 civil disobedience campaign he wrote to the Viceroy:

> It is not a matter of carrying conviction by argument. The matter resolves itself into one of matching forces. Conviction or no conviction, Great Britain would defend her Indian commerce and interests by all the forces at her command. India must consequently evolve force enough to free herself from that embrace of death.[25]

It was by no means inevitable that the Indian struggle would be nonviolent, and there are strong indications that in the absence of Gandhi's alternative grand strategy the terrorists would probably have carried the day. (This seems so despite the fact that nonviolent resistance played a significant role in the analyses and actions of Indian nationalists *before* Gandhi.)

Ranganath R. Diwakar, a participant in the independence struggle and author of several books on Gandhi's *satyagraha,* has written:

> In fact, if Gandhiji had not been there to guide and lead India, awakened and conscious as she was, she would certainly have adopted the usual methods of armed revolt against her alien oppressors. . . . it would have been inevitable. . . . A choice had to be made and at the psychological moment Gandhiji presented this unique weapon of satyagraha.[26]

Even after Gandhi's program of action had been accepted by the Indian National Congress and mass nonviolent campaigns had been launched, the terrorists continued to act, and there was wide support for advocates of violent revolution, especially for Subhas Chandra Bose, who was even elected president of the Congress in 1939. In 1928 Jawaharlal Nehru was still in favor of a violent war of independence. Contrary to many sentimental comments by both Indians and Westerners, this was the political context within which Gandhi's grand strategy was adopted and within which Gandhi formulated a series of nonviolent campaigns. One of these, the 1930–31 independence campaign, which began with the famous Salt March, remains a classic example of a nationwide nonviolent struggle.

3. India—1930–31[27]   For the 1930 campaign Gandhi formulated a program of political demands and a concrete plan for nonviolent rebellion, including civil disobedience. Pleas to the Viceroy produced no concessions.

Focusing initially on the Salt Act (which imposed a heavy tax and a government monopoly), Gandhi set out with disciples on a twenty-six day march to the sea to commit civil disobedience by making salt. This was the signal for mass nonviolent revolt throughout the country. As the movement progressed, there were mass meetings, huge parades, seditious speeches, a boycott of foreign cloth, and picketing of liquor shops and opium dens. Students left government schools. The national flag was hoisted. There were social boycotts of government employees, short strikes *(hartals),* and resignations by government employees and Members of the Legislative Assembly and Councils. Government departments were boycotted, as were foreign insurance firms and the postal and telegraph services. Many refused to pay taxes. Some renounced titles. There were nonviolent raids and seizures of government-held salt, and so on.

The government arrested Gandhi early in the campaign. About one hundred thousand Indians (including seventeen thousand women) were imprisoned or held in detention camps. There were beatings, injuries, censorship, shootings, confiscation, intimidation, fines, banning of meetings and organizations, and other measures. Some persons were shot dead. During the year the normal functioning of government was severely affected, and great suffering was experienced by the resisters. A truce was finally agreed on, under terms settled by direct negotiations between Gandhi and the Viceroy.

Although concessions were made to the nationalists, the actual terms favored the government more than the nationalists. In Gandhi's view it was more important, however, that the strength thus generated in the Indians meant that independence could not long be denied, and that by having to participate in direct negotiations with the nonviolent rebels, the government had recognized India as an equal with whose representatives she had to negotiate. This was as upsetting to Winston Churchill as it was reassuring to Gandhi.

Jawaharlal Nehru, who was later to become Prime Minister of independent India, was no believer in an ethic of nonviolence or Gandhi's philosophy or religious explanations. However, like many other prominent and unknown Indians, he became a supporter of Gandhi's nonviolent "grand strategy" for obtaining a British evacuation from India, and he spent years in prison in that struggle. Nehru wrote in his autobiography:

> We had accepted that method, the Congress had made that method its own, because of a belief in its effectiveness. Gandhiji had placed it before the country not only as the right method but as the most effective one for our purpose . . . .
>
> In spite of its negative name it was a dynamic method, the very opposite of a meek submission to a tyrant's will. It was not a coward's refuge from action, but a brave man's defiance of evil and national subjection.[28]

E. Struggles against Nazis

Independent of the continuing Gandhian campaigns, significant nonviolent struggles under exceedingly difficult circumstances also emerged in Nazi-occupied Europe. Almost without exception these operated in the context of world war and always against a ruthless enemy. Sometimes the nonviolent forms of resistance were closely related to parallel violent resistance; occasionally they took place more independently. Often the nonviolent elements in the resistance struggles were highly important, sometimes even overshadowing the violent elements in the resistance.

Nonviolent resistance in small or large instances took place in a number of countries but was especially important in the Netherlands,[29] Norway[30] and, probably to a lesser degree, in Denmark.[31] In no case does there appear to have been much if anything in the way of special knowledge of the technique, and certainly no advance preparations or training. The cases generally emerged as spontaneous or improvised efforts to "do something" in a difficult situation. Exceptions were certain strikes in the Netherlands which the London-based government-in-exile requested in order to help Allied landings on the continent.

1. Norway—1942[32]   The Norwegian teachers' resistance is but one of these resistance campaigns. During the Nazi occupation, the Norwegian fascist "Minister-President," Vidkun Quisling, set out to establish the Corporative State on Mussolini's model, selecting teachers as the first "corporation." For this he created a new teachers' organization with compulsory membership and appointed as its Leader the head of the *Hird,* the Norwegian S. A. (storm troopers). A compulsory fascist youth movement was also set up.

The underground called on the teachers to resist. Between eight thousand and ten thousand of the country's twelve thousand teachers wrote letters to Quisling's Church and Education Department. All signed their names and addresses to the wording prescribed by the underground for the letter. Each teacher said he (or she) could neither assist in promoting fascist education of the children nor accept membership in the new teachers' organization.

The government threatened them with dismissal and then closed all schools for a month. Teachers held classes in private homes. Despite censorship, news of the resistance spread. Tens of thousands of letters of protest from parents poured into the government office.

After the teachers defied the threats, about one thousand male teachers were arrested and sent to concentration camps. Children gathered and sang at railroad stations as teachers were shipped through in cattle cars. In the camps, the Gestapo imposed an atmosphere of terror intended to induce capitulation. On starvation rations, the teachers were put through "torture gymnastics" in deep snow. When only a few gave in, "treatment" continued.

The schools reopened, but the teachers still at liberty told their pupils they repudiated membership in the new organization and spoke of a duty to conscience. Rumors were spread that if these teachers did not give in, some or all of those arrested would be killed. After difficult inner wrestling, the teachers who had not been arrested almost without exception stood firm.

Then, on cattle car trains and overcrowded steamers, the arrested teachers were shipped to a camp near Kirkenes, in the Far North. Although Quisling's Church and Education Department stated that all was settled and that the activities of the new organization would cease, the teachers were kept at Kirkenes in miserable conditions, doing dangerous work.

However, their suffering strengthened morale on the home front and posed problems for the Quisling regime. As Quisling once raged at the teachers in a school near Oslo: "You teachers have destroyed everything for me!" Fearful of alienating Norwegians still further, Quisling finally ordered the teachers' release. Eight months after the arrests, the last teachers returned home to triumphal receptions.

Quisling's new organization for teachers never came into being, and the schools were never used for fascist propaganda. After Quisling encountered further difficulties in imposing the Corporative State, Hitler ordered him to abandon the plan entirely.

2. Berlin—1943 It is widely believed that once the "Final Solution," the annihilation of Europe's Jews, was under way, no nonviolent action to save German Jews occurred and that none could have been effective. This belief is challenged by an act of nonviolent defiance by the non-Jewish wives of arrested Berlin Jews. This limited act of resistance occurred in the midst of the war, in the capital of the Third Reich, toward the end of the inhuman effort to make Germany free of Jews—all highly unfavorable conditions for successful opposition. The defiance not only took place, but was completely successful, even in 1943. The following account is by Heinz Ullstein, one of the men who had been arrested; his wife was one of the women who acted:

The Gestapo were preparing for large-scale action. Columns of covered trucks were drawn up at the gates of factories and stood in front of private houses. All day long they rolled through the streets, escorted by armed SS men. . . . heavy vehicles under whose covers could be discerned the outlines of closely packed humanity . . . On this day, every Jew living in Germany was arrested and for the time being lodged in mass camps. It was the beginning of the end.

People lowered their eyes, some with indifference, others perhaps with a fleeting sense of horror and shame. The day wore on, there was a war to be won, provinces were conquered, "History was made," we were on intimate terms with the millennium. And the public eye missed the flickering of a tiny torch which might have kindled the fire of general resistance to despotism. From the vast collecting centers to which the Jews of Berlin had been taken, the Gestapo sorted out those with "Aryan kin" and concentrated them in a separate prison in the Rosenstrasse. No one knew what was to happen to them.

At this point the wives stepped in. Already by the early hours of the next day they had discovered the whereabouts of their husbands and as by common consent, as if they had been summoned, a crowd of them appeared at the gate of the improvised detention center. In vain the security police tried to turn away the demonstrators, some 6,000 of them, and to disperse them. Again and again they massed together, advanced, called for their husbands, who despite strict instructions to the contrary showed themselves at the windows, and demanded their release.

For a few hours the routine of a working day interrupted the demonstration, but in the afternoon the square was again crammed with people, and the demanding, accusing cries of the women rose above the noise of the traffic like passionate avowals of a love strengthened by the bitterness of life.

Gestapo headquarters was situated in the Burgstrasse, not far from the square where the demonstration was taking place. A few salvoes from a machine gun could have wiped the women off the square, but the SS did not fire, not this time. Scared by an incident which had no equal in the history of the Third Reich, headquarters consented to negotiate. They spoke soothingly, gave assurances, and finally released the prisoners.[33]

F. Latin American civilian insurrections

Latin America is more famous for its political violence than for nonviolent action. This may be an unbalanced view. There have apparently been a large number of instances in Latin America of general strikes and several cases of nonviolent civilian insurrections. For example, within a few weeks in 1944 two Central American dictators, in El Salvador and Guatemala, fell before massive civil resistance. These cases are especially important because of the rapidity with which the nonviolent action destroyed these entrenched military dictatorships. Attention here is focused on the Guatemalan case.

1. Guatemala—1944[34]   With the help of the secret police General Jorge Ubico had ruled Guatemala since 1931. Ubico was extolled in some U.S. magazines as a "road-and-school dictator"; the men who had faced his political police knew better. *Time* magazine called him an admirer of Hitler's 1934 blood purge, and quoted Ubico: "I am like Hitler, I execute first and give trial afterwards . . ."[35]

During World War II many U.S. troops were in Guatemala, which had joined the Allies. The Americans there promoted ideas of democracy for which, they said, the war was being fought. These appealed especially to Guatemalan students and young professional men. Other changes were undermining Ubico's position. Seizure of German-owned coffee *fincas* (plantations) in 1942 removed some of his supporters. Domestic issues were causing unrest, both among workers and within the business community. The dictator of nearby El Salvador, Martinez, had fallen a few weeks previously in the face of widespread nonviolent resistance. That proved to be a dangerous and contagious example. Action began in Guatemala, mildly—at first.

In late May 1944 forty-five lawyers asked the removal of the judge who tried most political opponents of the regime brought before a civil court. Ubico asked for specific charges against the judge. Surprisingly, one newspaper was allowed to publish them.

On the day prior to the annual parade of teachers and schoolchildren in tribute to the dictator, two hundred teachers petitioned Ubico for a wage increase. Those who drafted the petition were arrested and charged with conspiracy against the social institutions of the supreme government. The teachers replied with a boycott of the parade; they were fired.

On June 20 a manifesto announced the formation of the Social Democrat Party and called for opposition parties, social justice, lifting of the terror, and hemispheric solidarity. Students petitioned for university autonomy, rehiring of two discharged teachers and release of two imprisoned law students. Unless the demands were granted within twenty-four hours, they threatened a student strike.

Ubico declared a state of emergency. He called the opposition "nazi-fascist." Fearful, many student leaders sought asylum in the Mexican Embassy. However, young lawyers and professional men refused to submit to intimidation, and supported the students. On June 23 the schoolteachers went on strike.

Ubico had once said that if three hundred respected Guatemalans were to ask him to resign he would do so. On June 24 two men delivered the *Memorial de los 311* to Ubico's office. The three hundred and eleven prominent signers had risked their lives. The document explained the reasons for unrest, asked effective constitutional guarantees, and suspension of martial law. The same day, students marched past the U.S. Embassy and emphasized reliance on nonviolent means. Officials seemed surprised at the form of this demonstration. A peaceful meeting that evening demanded Ubico's resignation. Later that night, however; police beat and arrested hundreds at a neighborhood religious and social celebration. Some blamed "drunken bandits, previously coached by the police"; others pointed to clashes between persons shouting anti-Ubico slogans and the dictator's strong-arm men.

The next day the foreign minister summoned to the National Palace the two men who had delivered the *Memorial de los 311"*—Carbonell and Serrano. The ex-head of the secret police joined the meeting. Simultaneously, a demonstration took place before the National Palace; against it the government massed platoons of soldiers, cavalry, tanks, armored cars, machine guns, and police armed with guns and tear-gas bombs. Carbonell and Serrano were asked to "calm the people." Although all meetings had been banned, the men were permitted to meet with other "leaders" of the movement to seek a solution to the crisis.

That afternoon women dressed in deep mourning prayed for an end to the night's brutalities at the Church of San Francisco in the center of Guatemala City. Afterward they formed an impressive silent procession; the cavalry charged and fired into the crowd. An unknown number were wounded and one, María Chincilla Recinos, a teacher, was killed. She became the first martyr. "... the mask had been torn from the Napoleonic pose, revealing Ubico and his regime standing rudely on a basis of inhumanity and terror."[36]

Guatemala City responded with a silent paralysis. The opposition broke off talks with the government. Workers struck. Businessmen shut stores and offices. It was an economic shutdown. Everything closed. The streets were deserted.

After attempts at a new parley failed, at Ubico's request the diplomatic corps arranged a meeting that afternoon between the opposition and the government. The delegates told Ubico to his face that during his rule "Guatemala has known nothing but oppression." Ubico insisted: "As long as I am president, I will never permit a free press, nor free association, because the people of Guatemala are not ready for a democracy and need a strong hand."[37] The possibility of Ubico's resigning and the question of a succession were discussed. The delegates were to sample public opinion.

The opposition later reported to Ubico by letter the unanimous desire of the people that he resign. They again demanded the lifting of martial law, freedom of press and association, and an end to attacks on the people. Petitions and messages from important people poured into the palace; they also asked Ubico to resign. The silent economic shutdown of Guatemala City continued. The dictator's power was dissolving.

On July 1 Ubico withdrew in favor of a triumvirate of generals. Immediate and unaccustomed political ferment followed. Labor and political organizations mushroomed, and exiles returned. General Ponce, one of the triumvirate, tried to install himself in Ubico's place. In October he faced another general strike and a student strike and was ousted by a *coup d'état*. Difficult times were still ahead.

The victory over Ubico was not well utilized to establish democracy. But it had been a victory, both for the people and for their type of struggle. Mario Rosenthal writes:

> Energetic and cruel, Jorge Ubico could have put down an armed attack . . . He could have imposed his will on any group of disgruntled, military or civilian, and stood them up against a wall. But he was helpless against civil acts of repudiation, to which he responded with violence, until these slowly pushed him into the dead-end street where all dictatorships ultimately arrive: kill everybody who is not with you or get out.[38]
>
> The movement that brought Waterloo to Guatemala's Napoleon was, fittingly, a peaceful, civilian action; the discipline, serenity and resignation with which it was conducted made it a model of passive resistance.[39]

Rosenthal also paid tribute to the intelligence with which it was directed and to the solidarity shown by Guatemalans of all social classes, and ethnic and political backgrounds.

G. Risings against Communist regimes

Nonviolent forms of struggle have also emerged in several Communist-ruled countries. While always producing something less than total success and sometimes obvious defeat, these predominantly spontaneous corporate acts of defiance and resistance have sometimes shaken the regime to its core. The largely nonviolent East German Rising of June 1953 is a clear case in point.[40] During the Hungarian Revolution of 1956-57 the great variety of methods of nonviolent action applied, under severe conditions—methods such as the general strike, massive demonstrations, and the shifting of loyalty from the old government to the incipient parallel government of the workers' councils—had a powerful impact, and together they constituted an extremely important component in the total combat strength. The general strike was able to continue in Budapest for some time after the Russians had crushed the military resistance. Today it is often forgotten that nonviolent methods of struggle were very important in the Hungarian Revolution.[41]

1. Vorkuta—1953[42]   There was also a significant wave of strikes in the prison labor camps, especially among political prisoners, in the Soviet

Union itself in 1953.[43] In some of these there was a great deal of violence. In all there was repression, though apparently it was less severe where the prisoners were predominately nonviolent. Perhaps the most important of these strikes was at Vorkuta.

Strikes against poor conditions had long been considered among the 250,000 political prisoners in the coal-mining camps at Vorkuta. The decision was precipitated just after Stalin's death in 1953 by the announcement of the M.V.D. (Ministry of Internal Affairs) at Vorkuta that political prisoners ought not to expect an amnesty, as their liberation would jeopardize State security.

Many waverers then cast their lot with those advocating nonviolent resistance; by the end of May, strike committees had been secretly established in several camps. They were mainly composed of three groups of prisoners: Leninist students, anarchists, and the *Monashki* (a postrevolutionary pacifist Christian group resembling the early Quakers), as well as some prisoners representing no group.

The fall of Beria, the head of the secret police, while the prisoners were organizing encouraged more waverers. Strike committees were set up in coal-mining pits where they worked. It was agreed that the strike was to demand abolition of the camps and change of the prisoners' status to that of free colonists under contract. Before the strike began the central leadership was arrested and removed to Moscow. A new central strike committee was elected.

On July 21 many prisoners remained in their barracks, refusing to work. They insisted on presenting their demands to the general who was commandant of all the Vorkuta camps. They did so two days later, after thirty thousand had joined the strike. After the demands were presented the general made a long speech containing vague promises and specific threats.

A week passed without decisive action; no clear orders came from Moscow. Food would continue only while existing supplies lasted, it was announced. A strike leaflet appeared by the thousands of copies, urging self-reliance to gain freedom and the strike as the only possible means of action. Sympathetic soldiers helped to spread these and to maintain contacts between the camps. Twenty big pits were shut down.

Russian-speaking troops were then withdrawn and replaced by soldiers from Far Eastern sections of the Soviet Union, who did not speak Russian. With the strike at its peak in early August, the State Prosecutor arrived with several generals from Moscow and offered minor concessions: two letters home a month (instead of two a year), one visitor a year, and removal of identification numbers from clothes and iron bars from barracks windows.

In an open letter the strike leadership rejected these. The Prosecutor spoke at the camps, promising better food, higher pay, shorter shifts. Only a few wavered. The Strike Committee leaders went to an interview with the commanding general—but never returned. Some strikers were shot.

After the prisoners had held out for over three months the strike finally ended in the face of food and fuel shortages. However, considerable material improvements resulted. A spokesman of the International Commission on Concentration Camp Practices declared that the strike action in this and other camps was one of the most important factors in the improvement in the lot of the political prisoners.

H. American civil rights struggles

In the United States in the mid-1950s there emerged among Afro-Americans and civil rights workers a very significant, large, and reasonably effective movement of nonviolent action against segregation and discrimination against Afro-Americans. The nonviolent action took a variety of forms—bus boycotts, various economic boycotts, massive demonstrations, marches, sit-ins, freedom rides and others. This movement dates from the Montgomery bus boycott, which remains significant despite changes in resistance methods in recent years.

1. Montgomery, Alabama—1955-56[44]   On December 1, 1955, four Negroes in Montgomery were asked, as was usual, to give up their bus seats to newly boarded whites and stand. Three complied, but Mrs. Parks, a seamstress, refused.

A one-day boycott of the buses on December 5 in protest against her arrest was nearly 100 percent effective. It was decided to continue the boycott until major reforms were made. Evening mass meetings in churches overflowed. The response, in numbers and spirit, exceeded all hopes.

Negroes walked, took taxis, and shared rides, but stayed off the buses. A new spirit of dignity and self-respect permeated the Negro community. The whites were confronted by qualities they had not believed the Negroes possessed. The aim became improvement of the whole community. The appeal was to Christian love. The young Rev. Martin Luther King, Jr., and his co-workers found themselves thrust into leadership and international prominence.

Negotiations failed. The use of taxis at reduced fares was prohibited.

A car pool of three hundred vehicles was organized. Money began to pour in, and a fleet of over fifteen new station wagons was added. Many Negroes preferred to walk to express their determination.

Unfounded rumors were spread about the movement's leaders, along with false reports of a settlement. Negro drivers (including Dr. King) were arrested for minor, often imaginary, traffic violations. Police intimidation became common. Over thirty threats a day reached the leaders. King's home was bombed; Negroes nearly broke into violence. Another home was bombed. Then nearly one hundred Negro leaders were arrested, charged with violating an antiboycott law.

Fear, long known by Southern Afro-Americans, was cast off. Many went to the sheriff's office, hoping to be among those "wanted." The trial of the arrested leaders, which received world attention, became a testimony of fearlessness and a recounting of grievances. The movement gained new momentum. On June 4 the Federal District Court, acting on a suit filed by the Negroes, declared the city bus segregation laws to be unconstitutional, but the city appealed. The bus protest continued, now to bring a full end to bus segregation. Insurance policies on the station wagons were canceled; a London firm issued new policies. City officials declared the car pool illegal. The same day, November 13, the United States Supreme Court declared bus segregation laws unconstitutional.

In the evening two simultaneous mass meetings emphasized love, dignity, and refusal to ride on the buses until segregation was abolished. That night the Ku Klux Klan rode through the Negro district. Instead of dark, locked houses of terrified Negroes, the K.K.K. found the lights on, the doors open and people watching the Klan parade. A few even waved. Nonplussed, the Klan disappeared.

With the car pool prohibited, each area worked out its own share-the-ride plan, and many people walked. The buses remained empty. In the mass meetings detailed plans were presented for resuming—after over a year—the use of the buses on an integrated basis. There must be courtesy. This was a victory, not over the white man, but for justice and democracy.

The Supreme Court's antisegregation order reached Montgomery on December 20. On the first day of integration, there were no major incidents. Then the white extremists began a reign of terror. Shots were fired at buses; a teen-age girl was beaten; a pregnant Negro women was shot; the Klan paraded again and burned crosses. But the Negroes' fear had gone. The homes of more leaders and several Negro churches were bombed. This terrorism repelled many whites. The local newspaper, several white ministers, and the businessmen's association denounced the bombings.

The Negroes kept nonviolent discipline. More bombs exploded. Although arrested whites were quickly found "not guilty," the terrorism abruptly ceased. Desegregation then proceeded smoothly, a compliance virtually inconceivable a year before.

CONTINUING DEVELOPMENT

Throughout the world there has also been other significant nonviolent action, some of which occurred before these examples and some of it since. Other important cases are likely to have occurred before this book is in print. Major strikes and nonviolent demonstrations in Franco's Spain are scarcely mentioned here, for example, and there appear to be a large number of unstudied Latin American, as well as African, cases.

In the non-Gandhian development of nonviolent action in the mid-twentieth century particular struggles were often tinged with violence. Sometimes the nonviolent action took place side by side with violence. Sometimes it occurred before or after the violence—both in the case of Hungary in 1956-57. Nevertheless, the power of these various struggles has been predominantly rooted in mass solidarity and popular nonviolent defiance. The reasons for this essentially nonviolent quality have varied. Sometimes people recognized the practical limitations of violence—for example, in 1968 Czechs and Slovaks recalled the violent phase of the 1956 Hungarian Revolution as a pattern not to be imitated. Sometimes people have felt a revulsion against cruelty and killing for political ends, having seen so much of it. For example, some East Germans in June 1953 shouted: "We want a *decent* revolution." More frequently, probably, people have simply seen methods of nonviolent action as ways to act, ways which gave them a sense of their own power and perhaps also offered a reasonable chance of success in gaining their objectives. This seems to have been the case, for example, in Norway in 1942 and in El Salvador and Guatemala in 1944.

The development of nonviolent action of various types continues throughout the world, arising from different roots, taking numerous forms in response to a multitude of situations and problems. Struggles against war, for civil liberties, for social revolution, against home-grown and foreign-imposed dictatorships, and for a determining voice in their own lives by people who feel powerless are now leading to a continuing application of nonviolent action. This type of resistance is also likely to be used by persons and groups who find the direction or speed of change distasteful. In addition, as knowledge of this technique spreads, groups who attempt to suspend constitutional government gracefully or to destroy it blatantly may find themselves confronted with unexpectedly effective resistance.

The experiments made under Gandhi's political leadership, and also his thought and activities, still sometimes stimulate or strongly influence new nonviolent struggles. But even in such cases the Gandhian component has often been modified in new cultural and political settings. Frequently, as in anti-Nazi resistance movements and in Czechoslovakia in 1968, there is no clear link between the Gandhian experiments and new cases of nonviolent struggle. As those *satyagraha* campaigns recede into history they are less and less a direct factor in these new struggles. It is always possible, however, that this might be reversed if serious new interest should develop in Gandhi as a political strategist. It must be noted, however, that whatever may be the stimuli and motivations, in the twentieth century a remarkable expansion has taken place in the use of nonviolent struggle as a substitute for violence in a widening variety of political conflicts.

Needless to say, there have been setbacks in this development. At times there has appeared a clear trend toward the abandonment of nonviolent action in favor of violence. For example, the limited and sporadic use of nonviolent action both by nonwhites in South Africa[45] and by Afro-Americans in the United States was followed in each case by advocacy of violence. Nevertheless, when seen in historical perspective there has been a relative burst of development in this technique in the twentieth century. However unevenly, the process continues. One of the evidences for this was the unprepared use for some weeks of widespread and courageous nonviolent resistance by the Czechs and Slovaks following the invasion by the Soviet Union and her allies on August 21, 1968.

A. Czechoslovakia—1968[46]

The Soviet leaders expected that the massive invasion of Czechoslovakia by more than half a million Warsaw Treaty Organization troops would overwhelm the much smaller Czechoslovak army within days, leaving the country in confusion and defeat. The invasion would also make possible a *coup d'état* to replace the reform-minded Dubček regime with a conservative pro-Moscow one. With this in mind, the Soviet

K.G.B. (State Police) kidnapped the Communist Party's First Secretary, Alexander Dubcek; the Prime Minister, Oldrich Černik; the National Assembly President, Josef Smrkovsky; and the National Front Chairman, František Kriegel. The Soviet officials held under house arrest the President of the Republic, Ludvik Svoboda, who was a popular soldier-statesman in both Czechoslovakia and the Soviet Union. They hoped that he would give the mantle of legitimacy to the new conservative regime. The kidnapped leaders might have been killed once the *coup* had been successful, as happened in Hungary in 1957.

But the country was not demoralized as a result of military defeat, for it was a different type of resistance which was waged. Nor did a puppet regime quickly replace the kidnapped leaders. The Czechoslovak officials sent emergency orders to all the armed forces to remain in their barracks. The Soviet leaders had expected that the situation would be so effectively under control within three days that the invading troops could be then withdrawn. This did not happen, and as a result there were serious logistical and morale problems among the invading troops. Owing to resistance at several strategic points a collaborationist government was prevented, at least for about eight months—until April 1969 when the Husak regime came in.

Resistance began in early hours of the invasion. Employees of the government news agency (Č.T.K.) refused orders to issue a release stating that certain Czechoslovak party and governmental officials had requested the invasion. Also, President Svoboda courageously refused to sign the document presented to him by the conservative clique. Finally, it was possible through the clandestine radio network to convene several official bodies, and these opposed the invasion.

The Extraordinary Fourteenth Party Congress, the National Assembly, and what was left of the government ministers all issued statements similar to the emergency statement by the Party Presidium before the arrival of the K.G.B.—that the invasion had begun without the knowledge of party or governmental leaders; there had been no "request." Some of the bodies selected interim leaders who carried out certain emergency functions. The National Assembly went on to "demand the release from detention of our constitutional representatives . . . in order that they can carry out their constitutional functions entrusted to them by the Sovereign people of the country," and to "demand immediate withdrawal of the armies of the five states."[47]

The clandestine radio network during the first week both created many forms of resistance and shaped others: it convened the Extraordinary Fourteenth Party Congress, called one-hour general strikes, requested the rail workers to slow the transport of Russian tracking and jamming equipment, and discouraged collaboration within the Č.S.S.R. State Police. There is no record of any collaboration among the uniformed Public Police; indeed, many of them worked actively with the resistance. The radio argued the futility of acts of violence and the wisdom of nonviolent resistance. It instructed students in the streets to clear out of potentially explosive situations and cautioned against rumors. The radio was the main means through which a politically mature and effective resistance was shaped. Colin Chapman has observed that "each form of resistance, however ineffective it might have been alone, served to strengthen the other manifestations,"[48] and through the radio different levels of resistance and different parts of the country were kept in steady communication. With many government agencies put out of operation by Russian occupation of their offices, the radio also took on certain emergency functions (such as obtaining manpower to bring in potato and hops harvests) and provided vital information. This ranged from assuring mothers that their children in summer camps were safe to reporting meager news of the Moscow negotiations.

Militarily totally successful, the Russians now faced a strong political struggle. In face of unified civilian resistance, the absence of a collaborationist government, and the increasing demoralization of their troops, the Soviet leaders agreed on Friday, the 23rd, that President Svoboda would fly to Moscow for negotiations. Svoboda refused to negotiate until Dubček, Černik, and Smrkovsky joined the discussions. In four days a compromise was worked out. This left most of the leaders in their positions but called for the party to exercise more fully its "leading role," and left Russian troops in the country. The compromise seems also to have included the sacrifice of certain reform-minded leaders and reforms.

That first week the entire people had in a thousand ways courageously and cleverly fought an exhilarating battle for their freedom. The compromise, called the Moscow Protocol, created severely mixed feelings among the people. Observers abroad saw this as an unexpected success for the nation and its leaders; an occupied country is not supposed to have bargaining power. But most Czechs and Slovaks saw it as a defeat and for a week would not accept it. The leaders were apparently doubtful of the disciplined capacity of the populace for sustained resistance in the face of severe repression.

Despite the absence of prior planning or explicit training for civilian resistance, the Dubček regime managed to remain in power until April

1969, about eight months longer than would have been possible with military resistance. The Russians subsequently gained important objectives, including the establishment of a conservative regime. The final outcome of the struggle and occupation remains undetermined at this writing. Nevertheless, this highly significant case requires careful research and analysis of its methods, problems, successes and failures.

SEEKING INSIGHT

This brief sketch of the historical development of nonviolent action does not convey the extent and significance of the past use of this technique. Nevertheless, even this survey and the various illustrative cases cited throughout the remainder of this book are sufficient to call into question and even to refute some of the main misconceptions which have been widely accepted concerning this type of action.

Extensive use of nonviolent action has occurred despite the absence of attention to the development of the technique itself. Its practice has been partly spontaneous, partly intuitive, partly vaguely patterned after some known case. It has usually been practiced under highly unfavorable conditions and with a lack of experienced participants or even experienced leaders. Almost always there were no advance preparations or training, little or no planning or prior consideration of strategy and tactics and of the range of methods. The people using it have usually had little real understanding of the nature of the technique which they sought to wield and were largely ignorant of its history. There were no studies of strategy and tactics for them to consult, or handbooks on how to organize the "troops," conduct the struggle, and maintain discipline. Under such conditions it is not surprising that there have often been defeats or only partial victories, or that violence has sometimes erupted—which, as we shall see, helps to bring defeat. With such handicaps, it is amazing that the practice of the technique has been as widespread, successful and orderly as it has.

Some men and women are now trying to learn more of the nature of this technique and to explore its potentialities. Some people are now asking how nonviolent action can be refined and applied in place of violence to meet complex and difficult problems. These intellectual efforts are a potentially significant new factor in the history of this technique. It remains to be seen what consequences this factor may have for the future development of nonviolent action.

NOTES

1. For a fuller discussion of this theory of controlling the power of rulers, see Chapter One.

2. See, for example, Bart. de Ligt, **The Conquest of Violence: An Essay on War and Revolution** (New York: E. P. Dutton & Co., 1938, and London: George Routledge & Sons, 1937), pp. 26-27; Richard Gregg, **The Power of Nonviolence** (Second rev. ed.; New York: Schocken Books, Schocken Paperback, 1966, and London: James Clarke & Co., 1960), pp. 93-94 and 98-100; Krishnalal Shridharani, **War Without Violence: A Study of Gandhi's Method and Its Accomplishments** (New York: Harcourt Brace & Co., 1939, and London: Victor Gollancz, 1939), U.S. ed., pp. 276-294; Br. ed., pp. 237-246; and T. K. Mahadevan, Adam Roberts and Gene Sharp, eds., **Civilian Defence: An Introduction** (New Delhi: Gandhi Peace Foundation and Bombay: Bharatiya Vidya Bhavan, 1967) Appendices Four and Five (consisting of quotations on the point from R. R. Diwakar, N. K. Bose, K. Shridharani, and R. Gregg), pp. 249-254.

3. This is a revision of the definition first published in Gene Sharp, "The Meanings of Nonviolence: A Typology (revised)," **Journal of Conflict Resolution,** vol. III, no. 1 (March 1959), pp. 44-45. The definition is largely compatible with, although not based upon, that offered by Niels Lindberg, *"Indledning og Problemstilling,"* in Karl Ehrlich (pseud. of Karl Raloff), Niels Lindberg and Gammelgaard Jacobson, **Kamp Uden Vaaben: Ikke-Vold som Kampmiddel mod Krig og Undertrykkelse** (Copenhagen: Levin & Munksgaard, Ejnar Munksgaard, 1937), pp. 9-13.

4. See Gene Sharp, "The Origins of Gandhi's Nonviolent Militancy" (review-essay on **Gandhi's Truth** by Erik Erikson). **Harvard Political Review,** vol. II, no. 1 (May 1970), pp. 13-14 and 34-39.

5. F. R. Cowell, **The Revolutions of Ancient Rome** (New York: Frederick A. Praeger, 1962, and London: Thames and Hudson, 1962), pp. 42-43. Cowell's account is based on Livy.

6. Theodor Mommsen, **The History of Rome,** trans. William Purdie Dickson, rev. ed. (London: Richard Bentley & Son, 1894), vol. I, pp. 346-350. An excerpt appears in Mulford Q. Sibley, ed., **The Quiet Battle: Writings on the Theory and Practice of Non-violent Resistance** (Garden City, N.Y.: Doubleday, Anchor Books, 1963), pp. 108-110.

7. Daniel Dulany, **Considerations upon the Rights of the Colonists to the Privileges of British Subjects** (New York, 1766), p. 47, quoted in Edmund S. and Helen M. Morgan, **The Stamp Act Crisis: Prologue to Revolution** (Rev. ed.; New York: Collier Books, 1963), p. 118.

8. See esp. Morgan and Morgan, **The Stamp Act Crisis;** Arthur M. Schlesinger, **The Colonial Merchants and the American Revolution, 1763-1776** (New York: Frederick Ungar, 1966); and Lawrence Henry Gipson, **The British Empire Before the American Revolution,** vol. X, **The Triumphant Empire: Thunderclouds Gather in the West, 1763-1766,** vol. XI, **The Triumphant Empire: The**

Rumbling of the Coming Storm, 1766-1770, and vol. XII, The Triumphant Empire: Britain Sails into the Storm, 1770-1776 (New York: Alfred A. Knopf, 1961-1965).

9. See Leo Tolstoy, The Kingdom of God is Within You, and "A Letter to A Hindu."

10. See Henry David Thoreau, On the Duty of Civil Disobedience (pamphlet; Introduction by Gene Sharp; London: Peace News, 1963).

11. *Ibid.,* pp. 11 and 13.

12. On the 1905 Revolution, see Sidney Harcave, First Blood: The Russian Revolution of 1905 (New York: Macmillan, 1964, and London: Collier-Macmillan, 1964); Solomon M. Schwarz, The Russian Revolution of 1905: The Workers' Movement and the Formation of Bolshevism and Menshevism. Trans. by Gertrude Vakar, with a Preface by Leopold H. Haimson (Chicago and London: University of Chicago Press, 1967), esp. pp. 129-195. Also see Richard Charques, The Twilight of Imperial Russia (London: Phoenix House, 1958), pp. 111-139; Leonard Schapiro, The Communist Party of the Soviet Union (New York: Random House, 1960, and London: Eyre & Spottiswoode, 1960), pp. 63-70 and 75; Hugh Seton-Watson, The Decline of Imperial Russia, 1855-1914 (New York: Fredcrick A. Praeger and London: Methuen & Co., 1952), pp. 219-260; Bertram D. Wolfe, Three Who Made a Revolution (New York: Dial Press, 1948, and London: Thames and Hudson, 1956), pp. 278-336; and Michael Prawdin, The Unmentionable Nechaev: A Key to Bolshevism (London: Allen and Unwin, 1961), pp. 147-149.

13. See Wilfred Harris Crook, The General Strike, pp. 496-527; Goodspeed, The Conspirators, pp. 108-143 and 211-213; Halperin, Germany Tried Democracy, pp. 168-188; Eyck, A History of the Weimar Republic, vol. I, pp. 129-160; Karl Raloff (pseud.: Karl Ehrlich), *"Den Ikkevoldelige Modstand, der Kvalte Kapp-Kupet,* in Ehrlich, Lindberg and Jacobson, Kamp Uden Vaaben, pp. 194-213; and Wheeler-Bennett, The Nemesis of Power, pp. 63-82.

14. Crook, The General Strike, p. 513.

15. Goodspeed, The Conspirators, pp. 211-213.

16. Eyck, A History of the Weimar Republic, vol. I, p. 154.

17. On the *Ruhrkampf,* see Wolfgang Sternstein, "The *Ruhrkampf* of 1923: Economic Problems of Civilian Defence," in Adam Roberts, ed., Civilian Resistance as a National Defense: Nonviolent Action Against Aggression (Harrisburg, Pa.: Stackpole Books, 1968); British edition: The Strategy of Civilian Defence: Nonviolent Resistance to Aggression (London: Faber and Faber, 1967), pp. 106-135. (Note: the paperback edition is entitled Civilian Resistance as a National Defense [Baltimore, Md. and Harmondsworth, Middlesex, England: Penguin Books, 1969] but all page references cited in notes in this volume refer to the hardbook editions.) See also Karl Raloff (psud.: Karl Ehrlich), "Ruhrkampen," in Ehrlich, Lindberg and Jacobsen, Kamp Uden Vaaben, pp. 181-193; Wheeler-Bennett, The Nemesis of Power, pp. 102-109; Halperin, Germany Tried Democracy, pp. 246-260 and pp. 288-289; and Eyck, A History of The Weimar Republic, vol. I, pp. 232-306 *passim.*

18. This account was originally published in Gene Sharp, "Creative Conflict in Politics," The New Era, January 1962; pamphlet reprint ed., p. 4 (London: Housmans, 1962). See Joan V. Bondurant, Conquest of Violence: The Gandhian Philosophy of Conflict (Princeton, N.J.: Princeton University Press, 1958), pp. 46-52; Gandhi, Non-violent Resistance; Ind. ed.: Satyagraha, pp. 177-203; and Mahadev Dcsai, The Epic of Travancore (Ahmedabad: Navajivan, 1937).

19. M. K. Gandhi, **Indian Opinion**, Golden Number, 1914; quoted in Gandhi, **Non-violent Resistance**, p. 35; Ind. ed.: **Satyagraha**, p. 35.

20. M. K. Gandhi, **Hind Swaraj or Indian Home Rule**, p. 100.

21. Quoted in Sharp, **Gandhi Wields the Weapon of Moral Power**, p. 54.

22. Gandhi, **Young India**, 29 September 1921; quoted in Clarence Marsh Case, **Non-violent Coercion**, p. 392.

23. Gandhi, **Young India**, 4 August 1920; quoted in Gandhi, **Non-violent Resistance** p. 127; Ind. ed., **Satyagraha**, p. 127.

24. Gandhi, **Young India**, 27 March 1930; quoted in Sharp, **Gandhi Wields . . .** , p. 82.

25. All-India Congress Committee, **Congress Bulletin**, 7 March 1930, no. 5; quoted in Sharp, **Gandhi Wields . . .** , p. 64. For a brief discussion of some popular misconceptions about Gandhi and his activities, see Gene Sharp, "Gandhi's Political Significance Today," in G. Ramachandran and T. K. Mahadevan, eds., **Gandhi: His Relevance for Our Times** (Berkeley, Calif.: World Without War Council, 1971, and New Delhi: Gandhi Peace Foundation, and Bombay: Bharatiya Vidya Bhavan, 1967), pp. 137-157.

26. Ranganath R. Diwaker, **Satyagraha: Its Technique and History** (Bombay: Hind Kitabs, 1946), p. 55.

27. This account was also originally published in "Creative Conflict in Politics." See Sharp, **Gandhi Wields The Weapon of Moral Power**, pp. 37-226, and S. Gopal **The Viceroyalty of Lord Irwin, 1926-1931** (London: Oxford University Press, 1957), pp. 54-122.

28. Jawaharlal Nehru, **Toward Freedom**, p. 80.

29. See for example, Warmbrunn, **The Dutch Under German Occupation 1940-1945**. Further references are cited.

30. See, for example, Magne Skodvin, "Norwegian Nonviolent Resistance During the German Occupation," in Roberts, ed., **Civilian Resistance as a National Defense**, pp. 136-153; Br. ed.: **The Strategy of Civilian Defence**, pp. 136-153. Further references are cited.

31. See for example, Jeremy Bennett, "The Resistance Against the German Occupation of Denmark 1940-5," in Roberts, ed., **Civilian Resistance as a National Defense** pp. 154-172; Br. ed.: **The Strategy of Civilian Defence**, pp. 154-172. Further references are cited.

32. This sketch also was originally published in "Creative Conflict in Politics." See Sharp, **Tyranny Could Not Quell Them** (pamphlet) (London: Peace News, 1958 and later editions). Norwegian sources include: Magnus Jensen, "Kampen om Skolen," in Sverre Steen, general editor, **Norges Krig** (Oslo: Gyldendal Norsk Forlag, 1947-50), vol. III, pp. 73-105, and Sverre S. Amundsen, gen. ed., **Kirkenes Ferda, 1942** (Oslo: J. W. Cappelens Forlag, 1946).

33. From Heinz Ullstein's memoirs **Spielplatz meines Lebens** (Munich: Kindler Verlag, 1961), pp. 338-340. This passage (translated by Hilda Morris) is reprinted from Theodor Ebert, "Effects of Repression by the Invader," **Peace News**, 19 March 1965.

34. This account is based upon Mario Rosenthal, **Guatemala: The Story of an Emergent Latin-American Democracy** (New York: Twayne Publishers, 1962) pp. 191-214, and Ronald M. Schneider, **Communism in Guatemala 1944-1954** (New York: Frederick A. Praeger, 1958), pp. 5-14.

35. Rosenthal, **Guatemala**, p. 201.

36. *Ibid.*, p. 210.

37. *Ibid.,* p. 211.

38. *Ibid.,* p. 200.

39. *Ibid.,* pp. 201-202.

40. See, for example, Theodor Ebert, "Nonviolent Resistance Against Communist Regimes?" in Roberts, ed., **Civilian Resistance as a National Defense**, pp. 175-194; Br. ed.: **The Strategy of Civilian Defence**, pp. 175-194. Further references are cited.

41. See, for example, **Report of the Special Committee on the Problem of Hungary** (New York: United Nations, General Assembly Official Records, Eleventh Session, Supplement No. 18-A/3592, 1957).

42. This sketch also was originally published in "Creative Conflict in Politics." See Brigitte Gerland, "How the Great Vorkuta Strike was Prepared," and "The Great Labor Camp Strike at Vorkuta," in the weekly *The Militant* (New York), 28 February and 7 March 1955, and Joseph Scholmer, "Vorkuta: Strike in a Concentration Camp," in Sibley, ed., **The Quiet Battle**, pp. 187-204, reprinted from Scholmer, *Vorkuta* (New York: Henry Holt & Co., 1955).

43. **Monthly Information Bulletin of the International Commission Against Concentration Camp Practices** (Brussels), no. 4 (August-November 1955); See especially Paul Barton's article "The Strike Mechanism in Soviet Concentration Camps."

44. This sketch was originally published in Sharp, "Creative Conflict in Politics." See, for example, Martin Luther King, Jr., **Stride Toward Freedom: The Montgomery Story** (New York: Ballantine Books, 1958, and London: Victor Gollancz, 1959).

45. For a discussion of strategic problems of resistance in South Africa, and the potentialities of nonviolent action there, see Sharp, "Can Non-Violence Work in South Africa?", "Problems of Violent and Non-Violent Struggle," "Strategic Problems of the South African Resistance," and "How Do You Get Rid of Oppression?", in the weekly *Peace News* (London) 21 June, 28 June, 5 July, and 25 October 1963.

46. This account is based on a draft prepared by Carl Horne. The following sources may be consulted for further details of this case: Robert Littell, ed., **The Czech Black Book** (New York: Frederick A. Praeger, 1969); Robin Alison Remington, ed., **Winter in Prague** (Cambridge, Mass.:M.I.T. Press,1969); Joseph Wechsberg, **The Voices** (Garden City, N.Y.: Doubleday, 1969); and Philip Windsor and Adam Roberts, **Czechoslovakia 1968** (New York: Columbia University Press, 1969 and London: Chatto & Windus, 1969).

47. Remington, ed., **Winter in Prague,** p. 382.

48. Colin Chapman, **August 21st** (Philadelphia: Lippincott, 1968), p. 44.

PART TWO:
The Methods of Nonviolent Action: Political Jiu-Jitsu at Work

INTRODUCTION
TO PART TWO

Nonviolent action "works" in very special ways which must be grasped if the technique itself is to be understood, evaluated intelligently, and applied most effectively. These ways diverge significantly from popular assumptions about conflict and struggle—in particular the assumption that violence can be effectively met only with violence.

Nonviolent action is designed to operate against opponents who are able and willing to use violent sanctions.[1] There is no assumption in this technique that such opponents will, when faced with nonviolent action, suddenly renounce their violence, or even that they will consistently restrict their use of violent repression.

However, the use of nonviolent means against violent repression creates a special, asymmetrical, conflict situation, in which the two groups rely on contrasting techniques of struggle, or "weapons systems"—one on violent action, the other on nonviolent action. To have the best chance of success, the nonviolent actionists must stick with their chosen technique. An extensive, determined and skillful application of nonviolent action will cause the opponent very special problems, which will disturb or frustrate the effective utilization of his own forces. The actionists will then be able to apply something like *jiu-jitsu* to their opponent, throwing him off balance politically, causing his repression to rebound against his position, and weakening his power. Furthermore, by remaining nonviolent while continuing the struggle, the actionists will help to improve their own power position in several ways.

It is sometimes assumed that the nonviolent technique inevitably leads to high public exposure and high vulnerability to punishment. Therefore, it is concluded, only a minority of persons is likely to use it. It is true that where nonviolent actionists are few in number and lack the support of majority opinion, the actionists may well be in an exposed and vulnerable position. (The use of violence in such a case would make them even more exposed and vulnerable.) However, the situation is very different where nonviolent actionists are acting in support of general public opinion and themselves constitute a large part of the population. In that situation there is less exposure, and the chances of any one person's being singled out for punishment may be disproportionately reduced. But the opponent is unlikely to submit meekly.

There should, in fact, be no dismay or surprise at repression: it is often the result of the opponent's recognition that the nonviolent action is a serious threat to his policy or regime. Nonviolent actionists must be willing to risk punishment as a part of the price of victory. The severity and chances of repression will vary. This risk is not unique to nonviolent action, however. There are also risks when both sides use violence —some similar to and some different from those faced by nonviolent actionists. One difference is that in violent action risks are incurred in the course of attempting to injure or kill the opponents, while in nonviolent action, this is not the case. Some people erroneously understand that to mean that the nonviolent group is helpless. This is not true. This difference in the treatment of the opponent should not lead to feelings of impotence or frustration, especially if the nonviolent actionist understands that remaining nonviolent makes it more possible for him to gain increased control over the opponent, reduce the violence against the nonviolent group, and increase the chances of winning.

The fact is, of course, that repression does not necessarily produce submission. For sanctions to be effective, they must operate on people's minds, produce fear, and create willingness to obey. However, lack of fear, or some overriding loyalty or objective, may cause the actionists to persist despite repression. (This is also true in military struggle.) When the nonviolent actionists so persist, the opponent's problems may be aggravated in a number of ways. Most of his usual means of repression have been designed to deal with violent disobedience and violent rebellion. Because the dynamics and mechanisms of violent and nonviolent struggle differ, however, very different effects will result from repression against nonviolent actionists. For example, men imprisoned in a nonviolent struggle—whether Gandhi, King, Dubček, or students sitting-in at lunch counters—are widely regarded as still in the "front lines," and not as removed from the battle. Instead of trying to avoid provoking repression, nonviolent actionists may seek to exhaust the opponent's means of repression—such as by filling the jails—and thus to demonstrate his incapacity to rule even with such means. Repression against nonviolent action *may* be effective, of course. But depending on conditions, it also *may not*. If it is not, the opponent may be in difficulties. There will also be other sources of his troubles, however.

The opponent facing nonviolent action may be in a very awkward position if his own policies are hard to justify, if the nonviolent action involves the optimal combination of quality of behavior and number of actionists, and if, in face of repression, the nonviolent group is able to maintain a disciplined and determined persistence in its intended course. If the defiance is widespread or especially daring, the opponent cannot really ignore it without appearing to be helpless in face of defiance and thereby risking its spread. Yet repression may not only *not* strengthen his position, but may in certain circumstances set in motion forces which may actually weaken it further. These problems may make him wish that the rebels had chosen violent rather than nonviolent means, for violence does not pose the same kind of enforcement problems.

The opponent's difficulties in coping with nonviolent action do not depend on his being surprised by the nonviolence or on unfamiliarity with the technique. The opponent's knowledge of the operation of nonviolent struggle, for example, does not on its own give him the capacity to defeat the actionists: as in military conflicts, both sides may seek to utilize for their own ends knowledge of the technique of struggle they are using. With more knowledge, the opponent may become more sophisticated, and perhaps less cruel. But the nonviolent group also may learn how to struggle more skillfully and effectively.

The opponent's difficulties in dealing with nonviolent action are primarily associated with the special dynamics and mechanisms of the technique, and their tendency to maximize the influence and power of the nonviolent group while undermining those of the opponent. For example, partly because extremely brutal repression against a nonviolent group is more difficult to justify, the opponent's repression may be more limited than it would be against a violent rebellion. Furthermore, overreacting in repression may, instead of weakening the resisters, react against sources of the opponent's own power, and thus weaken *his* power position. The opponent may therefore prefer that the rebels use violent, rather than nonviolent, action and may deliberately seek to provoke the resisters to violence, perhaps by severe repression intended to break the nonviolent discipline or by spies and *agents provocateurs.*

If the nonviolent actionists nevertheless maintain their discipline and continue the struggle, and if they involve significant sections of the populace, the results of their behavior may extend far beyond individual example and martyrdom. They may effectively block the opponent's will and make it impossible for him to carry out his plans, even with the aid of repression. The arrest of leaders may simply reveal that the nonviolent movement can carry on without a recognizable leadership. The opponent may make new acts illegal, only to find that he has opened new opportunities for defiance. He may find that while he has been attempting to repress defiance at certain points, the nonviolent actionists have found sufficient strength to broaden their attack on other fronts to the extent of challenging his very ability to rule. Instead of mass repression forcing cooperation and obedience, he may find that the repression is constantly met by refusal to submit or flee; repression may repeatedly be demonstrated to be incapable of inducing submission. Furthermore, in extreme cases his very agencies of repression may be immobilized by the massive defiance; there may be too many resisters to control, or his own troops may mutiny. All these possible effects are examples of a process which may be called "political *jiu-jitsu.* "

The nonviolent actionists deliberately refuse to challenge the opponent on his own level of violence. Violence against violence is reinforcing. The nonviolent group not only does not need to use violence, but they must not do so lest they strengthen their opponent and weaken themselves. They must adhere to their own nonviolent "weapons system," since nonviolent action tends to turn the opponent's violence and repression against his own power position, weakening it and at the same time strengthening the nonviolent group. Because violent action and nonviolent action possess quite different mechanisms, and induce differing forces of change in the society, the opponent's repression—given a maintenance of nonviolent discipline and of persistence in the nonviolent group—can never really come to grips with the kind of power wielded by the nonviolent actionists. Gandhi has compared the situation with that of a man violently striking water with a sword: it was the man's arm which was dislocated.[2]

This is part of the reason why it is important for the actionists to maintain nonviolent discipline even in face of brutal repression. By maintaining the contrast between the violent and nonviolent techniques, the nonviolent actionists can demonstrate that repression is incapable of cowing the populace, and they can undermine the opponent's existing support. This can lead to weakening of his ability or will to continue with the repression and to defend his objectives and position.

To sum up: Repression of a nonviolent group which nevertheless persists in struggle and also maintains nonviolent discipline may have the following effects. As cruelties to nonviolent people increase, the opponent's regime may appear still more despicable, and sympathy and support for the nonviolent side may increase. The general population may become more alienated from the opponent and more likely to join the resistance. Persons divorced from the immediate conflict may show increased support for the victims of the repression. Although the effect of national and international public opinion varies, it may at times lead to significant political and economic pressures. The opponent's own citizens, agents, and troops, disturbed by brutalities against nonviolent people, may begin to doubt the justice of his policies. Their initial uneasiness may grow into internal dissent and at times even into such action as strikes and mutinies. Thus, if repression increases the numbers of nonviolent actionists and enlarges defiance, and if it leads to sufficient internal opposition among the opponent's usual supporters to reduce his capacity to deal with the defiance, it will clearly have rebounded against him. This is political *jiu-jitsu* at work.

Whether or not this is achieved hinges on the capacity of the nonviolent actionists to continue their struggle by the use of *their own* "weapons system." These "weapons," or specific methods of opposition, are also capable of altering the selected social, economic, or political relationships, whether or not changes in the balance of forces are also produced by political *jiu-jitsu*. There are a multitude of such methods, which collectively constitute the technique of nonviolent action; it is to a classification of these to which the focus of this study now shifts.

Such a classification is useful in a number of ways. For one thing, it assists us in understanding better the nature of the nonviolent technique, while also revealing very clearly the important distinctions and classes which exist within it. Some methods are basically symbolic actions, some involve a withdrawal of particular types of cooperation, others are largely direct interventions in a conflict situation. Classification also reveals the very large number and variety of methods of action the technique encompasses;[3] the present listing is certainly not exhaustive. The terminological refinement and definition of specific methods will also make possible future comparative analyses of the operation of different methods, or of the same method in different situations. In addition, a detailed classification provides something of a checklist of the main methods of nonviolent action thus far practiced.[4] Such a listing may assist actionists in the selection of methods most appropriate for use in a particular situation. It may also give groups faced with nonviolent opposition an idea of the methods which may be used against them, possibly reducing nervousness and brutalities. In addition, the list may give researchers and persons evaluating the political potentialities of the nonviolent technique a greater grasp of its armory of methods of struggle.

The broad classification of the particular methods of action under the general categories of *protest and persuasion, noncooperation* and *intervention* ought not to be regarded as rigid, but simply as generally valid. In particular circumstances one method may more correctly fall into a different category than the one under which it is classified in this study. In some situations one method may in the course of action develop into another, so there is no clear dividing line between them. Or two distinct methods may in a particular case be so closely combined as to be inseparable, even for analytical purposes.

Neither should the listing of specific methods be regarded as complete for all time. Doubtless some have been missed altogether, and a number of unlisted variations exist on those methods which are included. Perhaps more important, new forms of nonviolent action may be deliberately developed or improvised in the course of struggle. The "reverse strike," for example, in which people do without pay additional work they are not expected to do, is probably only about twenty years old. The examples of the specific methods offered in these chapters should be regarded as only illustrative. They are not intended to be representative, either geographically or historically, and they include both "successful" and "unsuccessful" cases. They do, however, indicate something of the widely differing historical, political and cultural conditions under which the technique of nonviolent action has already been used. Further research could doubtless provide additional examples from many cases not even mentioned in this study.

Which methods will be used in a particular case, and how many of them, will vary widely depending on such factors as 1) the traditions of the people involved; 2) the extent and depth of the knowledge of, and experience with, methods of nonviolent action possessed by the general population, the direct participants in the struggle and their leaders; 3) the general social and political situation; 4) the degree of repression which the general population, the actionists and the leaders are prepared to suffer; 5) the nature of the opponent's objectives; 6) the resources at the opponent's disposal (including his administrative system, agents of repression, and so on; 7) the degree of ruthlessness the opponent is prepared to use; 8) the degree of the opponent's dependence on members of the nonviolent opposition; 9) the numbers of participating actionists and the degree of support they receive from the population; 10) the quality of the actionists and leaders; 11) the nature of the grievance; and 12) the physical details of the specific situation in which action is contemplated.

Let us now turn to an examination of our first category of the methods of this technique: nonviolent protest and persuasion.

NOTES

1. Cases in which *both* sides use nonviolent means are discussed in Chapter Eleven.
2. M. K. Gandhi, **Non-violent Resistance,** p. 57; Ind. ed.: **Satyagraha,** p. 57.
3. The terms "method" and "form" are used interchangeably here, although generally "method" is used and recommended. There are precedents for the use of these terms in the way we apply them here. Joan Bondurant **(Conquest of Violence,** p. 36) uses the phrase "forms of nonviolent action" to describe the phenomena discussed in these chapters. Carl von Clausewitz **(On War,** [New York: Barnes and Noble, 1956, and London: Routledge & Kegan Paul, 1956], vol. I, pp. 125 and 166, and vol. II, p. 409) refers to those types of action in war which are in their relationship to the over-all struggle roughly comparable to these "forms" in nonviolent struggles as "methods." Despite the vast differences between military and nonviolent struggles there is sufficient

similarity in the role of the respective "methods" or "forms" in the over-all conflict to justify, and for clarity even require, the use of the same or similar terminology.

4. This catalog of methods of nonviolent action has no precedent in the literature. There are, however, separate listings of various types of strikes and of economic boycotts in the literature, and these are cited in the appropriate chapters. But for nonviolent action as a general technique, earlier listings were extremely limited. See, for example, Shridharani, **War Without Violence,** pp. 28-62 (fifteen methods, at least two of which "negotiations and arbitration" and "self-purification" are not classified within the technique here), and Lindberg, Jacobsen and Ehrlich, **Kamp Uden Vaaben,** p. 10 (seven methods, including sabotage which is excluded here, some of which are here discussed in whole chapters).

3

The Methods
of Nonviolent Protest
and Persuasion

INTRODUCTION

Nonviolent protest and persuasion[1] is a class which includes a large number of methods which are mainly symbolic acts of peaceful opposition or of attempted persuasion, extending beyond verbal expressions but stopping short of noncooperation or nonviolent intervention. Among these methods are parades, vigils, picketing, posters, teach-ins, mourning and protest meetings.

Their use may simply show that the actionists are *against* something; for example, picketing may express opposition to a law which restricts dissemination of birth control information. The methods of this class may also be applied *for* something; for example, group lobbying may support a clean-air bill pending in the legislature or overseas aid. Nonviolent protest and persuasion also may express deep personal feelings or moral condemnation on a social or political issue; for example, a vigil on Hiroshima Day may express penance for the American atomic bombing of that Japanese city. The "something" which the nonviolent protestors may be concerned with may be a particular deed, a law, a policy, a general condition, or a whole regime or system.

The act may be intended primarily to influence the *opponent*—by arousing attention and publicity for the issue and thereby, it is hoped, support, which may convince him to accept the change; or by warning him of the depth or extent of feeling on the issue which is likely to lead to more severe action if a change is not made. Or the act may be intended primarily to communicate with the *public,* onlookers or third parties, directly or through publicity, in order to arouse attention and support for the desired change. Or the act may be intended primarily to influence the *grievance group*—the persons directly affected by the issue—to induce them to do something themselves, such as participate in a strike or an economic boycott. A method of nonviolent protest and persuasion such as a pilgrimage may also be associated with some other type of activity, such as collections of money for famine victims. Certain mild methods of this class are intended to persuade in order to produce a stronger action by someone else: leafleting may be aimed at inducing participation in an economic boycott, and fraternization within the context of resistance may be intended to help induce later mutiny by occupation soldiers, for example.

In summary, within the context of this class of methods, emphasis may be placed on being for or against something; the grievances may be diverse; the group to whom the act is primarily directed may vary; the types of influence will differ; the intended result may range widely; the act may be an independent one or closely combined with some other method (or methods) of nonviolent action.

Behavior in such demonstrations clearly extends beyond personal verbal expressions of opinion, either by reason of the corporate nature of the act or the form of action or, in a few cases, the circumstances which give an individual act a corporate significance. Yet the methods of nonviolent protest and persuasion usually remain (unless combined with other methods) expressions in action of a point of view, or an attempt in action to influence others to accept a point of view or to take a certain action. This is distinguished from the social, economic, or political pressures imposed by noncooperation or nonviolent intervention. There are political circumstances in which some of the forms of nonviolent protest, such as marches, for example, are illegal. Under such circumstances their practice would merge the method with civil disobedience and possibly other forms of political noncooperation.

The impact of these methods of nonviolent protest and persuasion, which depend on influencing the attitudes of someone, will vary considerably. It is possible that where a particular method is common, its impact on any one occasion may be less than may be the case where the method has hitherto been rare or unknown. The political conditions in which it occurs are also likely to influence its impact, with dictatorial conditions making an act of nonviolent protest less possible, more dangerous and rarer; hence if it does occur, the act may be more dramatic and gain greater attention than it would where the act is common or carries no penalty. Demonstrations of protest and persuasion may precede or accompany acts of noncooperation or nonviolent intervention, or may be practiced in their absence.

What, then, are the specific methods of nonviolent action which may be classified as nonviolent protest and persuasion? Fifty-four methods are included in this listing; they are grouped here in ten subclasses.

FORMAL STATEMENTS

Normally, written or oral statements, whether by an individual, group or institution, are simply verbal expressions of opinion, dissent or intention, and not acts of nonviolent protest and persuasion as defined above. However, certain circumstances may give such statements a greater than usual impact and such an act may then fall within this class. Whether this happens or not will depend on the political situation in which the statement is issued, the status of the person or body issuing the statement, the nature of the statement itself, the degree of conformity and nonconformity in the political society, and the risk taken in issuing such a statement. As with many if not all acts of nonviolent action, such statements may be primarily for, or against, some issue, regime, system, policy or condition. They take various forms, and on the basis of these we distinguish six specific methods. These statements are primarily addressed to the opponent or to the person or body which is being supported or opposed, but secondarily they may influence some wider public.

1. Public speeches

Some public speeches may become significant acts of nonviolent protest. They may be spontaneous in some unexpected situation, they may be formal addresses, or they may be sermons delivered during religious services. In 1934, for example, when the Nazis were simply a minority in a coalition cabinet headed by Hitler as Chancellor, the non-Nazi Vice-Chancellor was Franz von Papen. In a dramatic, rather untypical act, Papen in a speech to students at the University of Marburg on June 17, 1934, expressed his alarm at the course of events since Hitler's accession to the chancellorship and called for an end to Nazi terror and a restoration of some freedoms, especially freedom of the press.[2] Coming from the Vice-Chancellor himself, this was an unexpected act of opposition which, despite censorship, received widespread support within Germany and major publicity abroad.

In Berlin on November 11, 1941, a sixty-five-year-old Roman Catholic priest, Provost Lichtenberg, declared in a sermon in St. Hedwig's Cathedral that he wished to share the fate of the Jews and be deported to the East in order to be with them to pray for them.[3] His wish was granted. Another incident on November 18, 1943, was recorded in his diary by Joseph Goebbels, Nazi Propaganda Minister: "During the burial of victims of the last bomb attack on the Bulgarian capital, the Bishop of Sofia delivered a speech in which he attacked the Bulgarian Government rather severely."[4]

2. Letters of opposition or support

Letters as a method of this class may take several forms. These include primarily private letters to a certain person or body, conveying a particular political viewpoint or declaration of intention. These letters may be from individuals or from groups; or similar or identical letters may be sent by many people. At times private letters may deliberately or otherwise become public knowledge. Or the letter may be published as an "open letter"—written to a particular person but intended equally or primarily to influence the general public which reads it.

Letters usually gain sufficient significance to be classed as a method of nonviolent protest because of the status of the signer or signatories, because of the number of persons signing the letter or sending identical or similar letters, or because the political situation has heightened the significance of such an act. In the Netherlands in December 1941, for example, over four thousand physicians signed and sent a letter to *Reichskommissar* Arthur Seyss-Inquart asking that plans to set up a compulsory National Socialist organization of physicians be abandoned.[5] And in occupied Norway *Reichskommissar* Josef Terboven received, in May 1941, a letter signed by representatives of forty-three organizations and associations, citing a series of specific actions by the Quisling regime in support of their general charge that "the acting ministers have in a series of cases issued decrees and made decisions that are in open conflict with international law, Norwegian law, and the general Norwegian understanding of justice . . ."[16] Also in Norway in 1942 (as described in detail in the previous chapter), in addition to individually written form letters to the Church and Education Department from Norwegian teachers rejecting membership in the new fascist teachers' organization, tens of thousands of signed letters of protest were sent to the department by the parents of the pupils.[7]

Among other examples, Bulgarian protest against Nazi antisemitic measures during World War II might be cited. For example, when the anti-Jewish "Law in Defense of the Nation" was introduced, opposition "was expressed in floods of letters and telegrams addressed to parliament, cabinet ministers, statesmen, and social and political leaders." In addition to such letters from individuals, the Union of Bulgarian Writers sent a letter to the government and parliament asking that the bill not be made law, for it would "enslave part of the Bulgarian people and would blemish Bulgaria's modern history." Similar objections came from the Executive Council of the Union of Bulgarian Writers and the Executive Council of Bulgarian Doctors.[8]

To come to more recent history, on August 22, 1968, delegates of the Extraordinary Fourteenth Congress of the Communist Party of Czechoslovakia sent a letter of support to Alexander Dubček, First Secretary of the Party, who was then in Moscow.[9] On the same day, the Ambassador to Prague of the German Democratic Republic (East Germany) refused to receive a letter from the Czechoslovak National Assembly addressed to the parliament and government of the German Democratic Republic, protesting the presence of their troops in Czechoslovakia.[10] Two days later, on August 24, the Presidium of the Central Council of the Czechoslovak Trade Unions wrote to Aleksandr Shelepin, the Chairman of the All-Union Central Council of Soviet Trade Unions, asking that Soviet trade unionists demand an immediate withdrawal of Soviet and Warsaw Pact troops.[11] Similar letters were sent to officials and citizens of the Soviet Union, among them an open letter to the President of the Academy of Sciences of the Soviet Union from the Chairman of the Czechoslovak Academy of Sciences.[12]

3. Declarations by organizations and institutions

One of the forms such declarations have taken has been that of pastoral letters and similar official church statements. During World War II, in Vichy France, for example, in August and September 1942, protest declarations against the deportation of Jews were read by priests from their pulpits in Toulouse and in the Lyons diocese.[13] On February 16, 1941 a pastoral letter was read in the majority of Norwegian pulpits (and widely circulated in printed form), protesting fascist violations of principles of government under law and interference by Quisling's government with the priests' duty of silence regarding confessions of parishioners. The letter exhorted the regime "to end all which conflicts with God's holy arrangements regarding justice, truth, freedom of conscience and goodness and to build entirely on God's law of living."[14] In February 1943 the Dutch Reformed Church and the Roman Catholic Church in the Netherlands, in a similar declaration and pastoral letter, urged their listening congregations toward civil disobedience and the refusal of collaboration as religious duties.[15] Goebbels was later to call this "an exceptionally insolent pastoral letter."[16] Anti-Nazi pastoral letters were also read on a number of occasions in churches in Germany itself.[17]

Public declarations of support for the Dubček regime and of opposition to the Soviet-led invasion of Czechoslovakia were widespread and important in the early days of the occupation. They were among the factors which made it impossible for a collaborationist regime to be created at the time. The first day after Warsaw Pact troops crossed the borders, the Presidium of the National Assembly addressed a declaration to the governments and parliaments of the five invaders, denouncing the act and demanding "immediate withdrawal."[18] A whole series of bodies issued formal statements in support of the Dubček regime and in opposition to the invasion.[19]

4. Signed public statements

A declaration directed primarily to the general public, or to both the public and the opponent, and released with the signatures of supporters is a method of nonviolent protest and persuasion. The signatures may be those of persons from particular organizations, occupations or professions, or of people from various parts of the society.

Thus, in St. Petersburg, following the events of "Bloody Sunday" (January 9, 1905), sixteen members of the Academy of Sciences publicly declared their belief that events had created a need for a change in government. They were joined by 326 leading university professors and lecturers in circulating the "Statement of the 342," which affirmed that Russia would enjoy the benefits of education only after "freely elected representatives of the people are given the power to make laws and keep a check on the administration." This was endorsed by 1,200 of the country's most noted scholars, and has been called "an outstanding, and perhaps

the most effective, action in stirring the educated to a sense of the urgent
need for change . . ."[20]

About fourteen hours after the invasion of Czechoslovakia, a statement supporting the legal constitutional and political authorities and denouncing the invasion as an "illegal act" was issued with signatures of
fourteen members of the Czechoslovak Government. Certain other officials
had already been seized by the Russians.[21]

5. Declarations of indictment and intention

Certain written statements of grievance or future intentions to produce a new situation, or a combination of both, are seen to be of such
a quality or to meet such a response that the document itself becomes
influential in influencing people's loyalties and behavior. The American
Declaration of Independence is one such document; it was adopted by the
Second Continental Congress on July 4, 1776. Another is the South African "Freedom Charter" adopted at the Congress of the People at Kliptown, Johannesburg, South Africa, on June 25-26, 1955. Dr. Albert
Luthuli, leader of the South African National Congress, has written that
"nothing in the history of the Liberatory movement in South Africa quite
caught the popular imagination as this did, not even the Defiance Campaign." [22] During this period the anti-*Apartheid* movement was committed to nonviolent means. After a moving list of the social and political objectives of these opponents of *Apartheid,* the document concluded:
"These freedoms we will fight for, side by side, throughout our lives, until we have won our liberty."[23]

6. Group or mass petitions

Group or mass petitions are written requests or suplications seeking
the redress of a specific grievance, signed by a large number of individuals
or by a smaller number of individuals acting on behalf of organizations,
institutions or constituencies. (Petitions from individuals normally do not
fall within "nonviolent protest and persuasion," since they are usually simply personal efforts to persuade. Exceptions may occur, however.) Of the
multitudes of examples, we offer here a few of the less known in order to
illustrate some of the diversity in the use of this method. Examples of
petitions go back at least as far as the Roman Empire. In one instance, in
the years A.D. 183-185, during the reign of Emperor Commodus, son of
Marcus Aurelius, the peasant tenants of one of the imperial estates of Africa
sought relief from the amount of compulsory work required of them by

petitioning the Emperor directly; they sent their petition to Rome by a plenipotentiary who was a Roman citizen. They expressed confidence in the Emperor and hatred for their oppressors (the farmer-general and the procurators) and appealed to the Emperor for relief. The tenants asked protection of the *Lex Hadriana* and insisted on their rights. This petition was successful, though others were not. [24]

Another example from ancient history is the petition to the Roman Emperor Septimius from the village of Aga Bey in Lydia (Asia Minor). In their position the peasant tenants of an imperial estate sought two objectives, one of which was relief from municipal duties which had been imposed on them even though they did not reside in cities, as well as other forms of relief. The peasants threatened the Emperor with a work stoppage by means of a mass "flight" from the estate. (That method is described in Chapter Four.) Relief from the municipal duties was granted. [25]

M. Rostovtzeff describes another petition of the same period, this one in A.D. 201. The petition was from the *navicularii* of Arelate, who probably transported men and supplies by sea from Gaul to the East during the second Parthian expedition. The petition from the *navicularii* complained bitterly of "the vexations and exactions to which they were subjected in performing their service to the state," Rostoztzeff reports. It is likely, he adds, that repeated complaints, coupled with threats of a strike, induced Septimius to revise, complete, and even extend some of the privileges granted to this important group. [26]

A millennium and a half later the American colonists repeatedly petitioned the British officials for relief from their grievances, sometimes in the form of addresses from colonial assemblies, sometimes as petitions from merchants. In November 1766, for example, 240 merchants of the city of New York petitioned the House of Commons for major changes in the trade and navigation system. [27] As part of a struggle among the poor back-country people in North Carolina against the group which was in power in that province, two hundred sixty inhabitants of Anson County signed a petition to the colony's Assembly, listing the grievances from which they sought relief and saying that "we . . . have too long yielded ourselves slaves to remorseless oppression." [28]

African slaves in the Province of Massachusetts Bay also petitioned, addressing the Governor (General Gage), the Council, and the House of Representatives on May 25, 1774. They asserted that in common with all other men they had a right to their freedom. Therefore they asked for legislation to grant that freedom, "our Natural right," and particularly that their children should be set at liberty when they reached the age of twenty-one years. [29]

In more modern times petitions have been used both by nationalists objecting to foreign rule, as in Finland and Egypt, and in grievances against Communist governments. For example, in 1898, five hundred thousand Finns (out of a total population of three million) signed a petition protesting a new Russian law drafting Finnish youths into Russian army units and subjecting them to five years of military duty.[30] Despite British prohibition, two million signatures were gathered for a petition in Egypt aimed at achieving a popular mandate for a national delegation which sought the right to participate in the Versailles peace conference after World War I.[31]

In the German Democratic Republic (East Germany) on July 7, 1953, 1,500 workers at the Zeiss factory at Jena signed a petition demanding the release of Eckhardt Norkus (who had been sentenced to three years in prison after an arbitrary arrest following the June rising) and the release within three days of every striker against whom a criminal charge could not be proved.[32]

A "Memorandum" signed by several dozen of the elite of Hungary's Communist writers and artists in early November 1956 requested the Central Committee of the Communist Party to stop officials from applying "anti-democratic methods which cripple our cultural life," and expressed the view that ". . . the only basis for eliminating difficulties and wrong opinions . . . is a free and sincere and healthy and democratic atmosphere imbued with the spirit of popular rule."[33] As with the other methods in this chapter, illustrations could go on indefinitely.

COMMUNICATIONS WITH A WIDER AUDIENCE

Several of the methods of this class are designed primarily to communicate ideas, viewpoints and information to a wider audience. The objective may be to influence the opponent group, gain sympathy and support from third parties, or gain converts, members, or assistance for the nonviolent group. Persuasion is the aim at least as often as protest. Both visual and oral forms are included in these six methods.

7. Slogans, caricatures and symbols

Among the very common forms of nonviolent protest are slogans, caricatures and symbols. They may be written, painted, drawn, printed, mimed, gestured, or spoken. From the summer of 1941 to May 1942 a resistance group of Jewish youths in Berlin, the Baum Group, carried out such activities without a single arrest, Professor Ber Mark reports.

Going out with buckets of paint and brushes at night was a very risky business. Still, the young fighters went eagerly to post the leaflets and paint the slogans on the walls. The group considered such acts as a test of one's revolutionary ardor, and as the best way to strengthen the revolutionary daring and the spirit of self-sacrifice of the members.[34]

Painted symbols on walls, rocks or fences are often used to express protest. During the Nazi occupation, for example, H VII for the exiled Norwegian King Haakon VII, were so displayed. The nuclear disarmament symbol and the Nazi swastika may also be seen in various countries.[35] In Munich in early 1943 young student members of the *Weisse Rose* (White Rose) resistance group wrote "DOWN WITH HITLER" on walls.[36] In occupied Poland, a group of young boys called "The Little Wolves" in 1942 used indelible paint to decorate German trucks and automobiles, German residences, and even the backs of Germans themselves with inscriptions, such as "POLAND FIGHTS ON," which appeared in Warsaw every morning. Caricatures and posters were also displayed. According to one Polish commentator: "The mischievous and diabolically efficient little pack did much to sustain the psychological atmosphere of contempt for the Germans and fostered the spirit of resistance."[37] After the Russian invasion of Czechoslovakia, in August 1968, one of the slogans that was written on walls widely in Prague was "LENIN, WAKE UP! BREZHNEV HAS GONE MAD."[38]

8. Banners, posters and displayed communication

Written, painted or printed communications such as banners, posters and displayed signs are similar enough to be classed together, but the range of variations is fairly large. During President Wilson's address to Congress on December 4, 1916, five members of a woman suffragist organization, Congressional Union, unrolled a yellow sateen banner from the Visitors' Gallery saying, "MR. PRESIDENT, WHAT WILL YOU DO FOR WOMAN SUFFRAGE?"[39] In India during the struggle in 1930-31, sidewalks and even paved streets served as blackboards for notices of the Indian National Congress.[40] During the *Ruhrkampf*, German resistance fighters tore down French occupation proclamations and posters, replacing them with their own.[41] In Rotterdam in 1942 signs plastered on walls urged the people to show respect for Jews on the street who were wearing the required yellow star.[42] During the Moncton Commission's visits to Northern Rhodesia and Nyasaland in 1960 to review for the

British government the future of the Federation of Rhodesia and Nyasa-land (which was hated by black Africans as an instrument of European control), posters urging a boycott of the commission frequently appeared in towns and cities.[43]

On the night of August 23-24, 1968, the Warsaw Pact occupation troops went throughout Prague tearing down resistance posters and patriotic appeals to the citizens to resist, and putting up their own proclamations. The paper *Svoboda* reported that this was: "To no avail! New ones were up by morning. Prague is like one huge poster. 'Occupiers go home!' "[44] One tall smokestack in the Prague-Vrsovice railroad depot was decorated with the sign "FRIENDSHIP, NOT OCCUPATION."[45] On the morning of August 25, the Prague city buses began their routes bearing the signs: "U.N.: S.O.S." Shop windows in the center of the city had been turned into huge display areas for the posting of notices. A car drove by carrying the sign: "THEY OCCUPIED CHARLES UNIVERSITY."[46]

9. Leaflets, pamphlets and books

The publication and distribution of leaflets, pamphlets or books which have as their main purpose the expression of a point of view in opposition to, or in support of, particular or general policies, or to the regime as a whole may in political conditions of repression and struggle become a method of nonviolent action. The distribution of leaflets is perhaps the most common method of communication used by dissenting groups, but under conditions of censorship, books may also be involved. (Literature which calls for active resistance, as distinct from making a general case, is classified below as a separate method, under political noncooperation, because of the content and consequences of such calls.)

For example, the centennial celebration of the Declaration of Independence in Philadelphia was invaded by a group of woman suffragists who distributed leaflets to the assembly and chairman containing a Declaration of Women's Rights.[47] In the section of Nazi-occupied Poland known as the *General Gouvernement,* the underground in 1942(?) counteracted a new Nazi propaganda campaign to acquaint Poles with all types of German achievements by preparing exact duplicates with the original contents radically altered into a biting satire which cited a series of Nazi cruelties and executions.[48] Protest letters which had been sent by Norwegian organizations to *Reichskommissar* Joseph Terboven in early 1941 were printed in Norway from texts broadcast back to Norway from England, and circulated throughout the country in thousands of copies. [49] They were reported to have had a strong and stimulating influence.

In 1941 and 1942 the Baum Group of Jewish resisters in Berlin had as one of their five fields of activity the publication and distribution of various leaflets, brochures and pamphlets which they sent to private homes and offices, distributed to workers, and posted at night on walls.[50] In Munich the student *Weisse Rose* group published several anti-Nazi leaflets and distributed them in Munich and several other South German cities. The leaflets usually were placed in letter boxes, and finally, in 1943, were openly distributed in the University of Munich.[51] In April and May 1959, the Direct Action Committee Against Nuclear War carried a mass leaflet distribution in the Norfolk area of England.[52] Leaflets demanding that the Warsaw Pact armies leave Czechoslovakia, asserting loyalty to the legal governments, and urging resistance were widespread in the early days of the occupation.[53] An "Appeal to the Warsaw Pact Soldiers!" urged them to "leave our territory as friends and do not interfere with our internal development."[54] The Russians also waged a leaflet campaign, distributing them by helicopter and motor vehicles; the resisters' Czechoslovak Radio reported that the fraudulent leaflets over the names of Czechoslovak representatives had been distributed by the occupation forces.[55]

Books, too, may be important in arousing and expressing opinions in times of conflict and in contributing to wider actions and changes. Such influences may occur whether the book is officially allowed or has been prohibited under censorship. In the latter case, books have circulated in manuscript, typescript, or in printed editions published illegally within the country or smuggled in from without. One such book was N.G. Chernyshevsky's *What Is To Be Done?,* a novel which expressed important ideas of revolutionary populism. It was written in prison in 1862 and 1863. It was approved by the censor without reading it, as he thought other officials had already examined it. Published in serial form in the journal *Sovremennik,* it "moulded a whole generation of Populist students and revolutionaries. It became a blueprint of life for the young intelligentsia." It pointed to activities which revolutionaries should undertake, and the need for firm opposition to despotism.[56] A multitude of books have wielded considerable influence in social, economic, religious or political conflicts.

10. Newspapers and journals

Journals and newspapers, both legal and illegal, constantly recur throughout the history of social and political conflicts as media for advancing the views and causes which their publishers espouse. The very existence of such publications is at times illegal, and in such cases this method merges with civil disobedience and the general class of political noncooperation.

The publication and distribution of illegal newspapers and journals played a very important role in the Russian revolutionary movement in the nineteenth and early twentieth centuries.[57] Illegal newspapers and news sheets were also widely published and circulated in Norway during the Nazi occupation,[58] as was the case in other countries such as Denmark,[59] the Netherlands,[60] and Poland.[61] Where politically possible, articles and advertisements in regular papers and journals may also be used to communicate views.

11. Records, radio and television

Under certain conditions records, radio and television themselves become instruments of nonviolent protest and persuasion. Phonograph records may convey ideas through music, speeches or declarations. Much of the American rock music of the 1960s conveyed dissent and dissatisfaction, as did Bob Dylan's song *Blowin' in the Wind*.

In that song Dylan poignantly asked:

— how often can any man turn away as if he hadn't noticed;

— how many times must the cries of suffering be heard before a man pays attention;

— how much time must pass with people in their present conditions before they experience freedom? [62]

Recorded songs with explicit political lines and objectives have been distributed by various political groups for some decades. In 1968 newly released phonograph records were available in Prague on the morning of August 24, carrying the statement of the Extraordinary Fourteenth Party Congress which had been issued on August 22; that declaration, addressed to the citizens of the country, condemned the invasion, rejected Soviet justifications, and demanded release of all detained officials and withdrawal of the foreign troops: "Socialist Czechoslovakia will never accept either a military occupation administration or a domestic collaborationist regime dependent on the forces of the occupiers."[63]

Although radio broadcasts to the populations and resisters in occupied countries were widespread during World War II, Czechoslovakia in 1968 provided the most advanced use to date of radio and television broadcasts originating *within* the occupied country. The clandestine radio network, some of which was able to continue operating for a full two weeks, not only conveyed information about what was happening, but broadcast declarations of opposition to the invasion. The radio also called for specific acts of resistance, warned against violence and urged peaceful discipline in the struggle, opposed collaboration, cautioned against rumors, and took over certain emergency administrative functions. Television broadcasts (which were made from private apartments and other locations away from the regular studios where they would have been subject to Soviet controls) continued into the first days of September.[64]

12. Skywriting and earthwriting[65]

These are words or symbols communicated to people over large distances by writing them in the unusual media of the sky or earth. Skywriting by airplane was used on October 15, 1969, to place a large nuclear disarmament symbol in the sky over the rally against the war in Vietnam, which was then taking place on the Common in Boston, Massachusetts.[66] Earthwriting was used by a California rancher, Edwin Frazer, who lived near San Diego, when his milder protests against sonic booms from planes based at the nearby Miramar Naval Air Station had been ignored. In huge letters in his back pasture he ploughed the word QUIET. (It didn't work either.)[67] Variations could be achieved by planting contrasting crops, trees and the like in the desired pattern, or by arranging such materials as rocks or shrubs in the form of a word or symbol on hillsides or mountains.

GROUP REPRESENTATIONS

Groups may make representations for or against some policy, etc., in a variety of ways. Four of the five methods listed in this category involve the physical presence of those making the representations; in one method this is not the case.

13. Deputations

Protest and disapproval may be expressed by a group of self-selected individuals or of representatives of one or various organizations who go to meet with an official (or his representative) who is particularly responsible for the grievance. On occasion, deputations may seek consideration or adoption of a new policy or measure.

In a district near China's imperial capital in about 1890, taxpayers responded to repeated malpractice by the tax collector (who arbitrarily regulated the exchange rate between copper cash and silver in his favor) by sending a deputation to the capital with documents prepared by a local committee. The first delegation was a failure and the members received fifty blows of the bamboo and a fine. The second deputation was successful; the tax collector was fired and banned from future government employment.[68]

After Tsar Nicholas II had autocratically enacted a law which incorporated the Finnish army into the Imperial Russian army and had declared in a manifesto, on February 15, 1899, his "right" to enact laws for Finland regardless of the views or decision of the Finnish Diet, a deputation of five hundred men carried a protest petition with 523,000 signatures (nearly half the adults of the country) to the Tsar. He refused to receive them.[69]

On November 1, 1958, a London organization called the Geneva Committee of Parents sent a delegation of women to Geneva to see the representatives at the forthcoming test ban conference to press for a permanent end to nuclear testing.[70] Following a demonstration in which between three and four hundred African students marched to the Kremlin on December 18, 1963, a deputation of Ghanaian students went to the Ministry of Education to protest against racial discrimination in Moscow. It was received by the Minister of Education and the Minister of Health.[71]

On August 24, 1968, the Presidium of the Prague City Committee of the Communist Party sent a delegation to the Soviet Embassy to demand the release of Comrade Bohumil Simon, a member of the newly elected Presidium of the Central Committee and the leading secretary of the Prague City Committee. After initial denial of all knowledge of Simon, the Soviet attaché later made assurances that he was all right and that everything was being done to achieve his release.[72]

14. Mock awards[73]

Satirical "awards" may be presented to opponents in order to publicize grievances and perhaps also to appeal to the recipient of the "honor" to correct the grievance. For example, in Massachusetts in November 1969, while hearings on industrial pollution were in progress, the Boston Area Ecology Action campaign presented to the Boston Edison Company a "Polluter of the Month" award. Numerous complaints had previously been made against this electric company on charges of excessive pollution of the atmosphere from its generating plants.[74]

15. Group lobbying

Lobbying in the sense of personal visits to a parliamentary representative by his constituent in an effort to influence his voting in the parliament or assembly is normally simply a verbal expression of opinion. When done as a group action, however, lobbying becomes a form of corporate nonviolent action, because in addition to persuasion of the legislator, the gathering of a fairly large group of people in order to lobby itself becomes a demonstration. This may take the form of *small group lobbying* when a series of individuals or groups in moderate numbers on one occasion, or over a period of time, or on several occasions visit their representatives in an effort to influence them. For example, in the spring of 1966, under the sponsorship of the Friends Committee on National Legislation, persons and groups visited their congressmen and senators in Washington each Wednesday for several weeks to discuss U.S. policy in Vietnam.[75] Or lobbying may be organized to focus on getting very large numbers on a particular day. This is *mass lobbying.* For example, the Anti-*Apartheid* Movement held a "mass lobby" of members of the House of Commons in London on March 8, 1965. Its supporters urged Members of Parliament to press for a firm official stand against South Africa by such means as an arms embargo, collective economic sanctions, and other measures.[76]

16. Picketing

Picketing is an effort to persuade others to do or not to do a particular act, or a method of protest by means of one's physical presence at a place significantly related to the matter in question. The picketing may be conducted by standing, sitting, or walking back and forth. Placards may or may not be carried, and leaflets may or may not be distributed. The pickets may or may not try to talk with others as a means of promoting their end.

Especially in the West, picketing has been widely associated with strikes, largely in an effort to ensure that strikebreakers did not accept the jobs of the strikers or that strikers did not return to their jobs before an agreed settlement. As Lloyd G. Reynolds, a writer on labor economics, put it:

> The device which unions have developed to keep workers out of a struck plant is the picket line. Strikers patrol back and forth in front of the plant entrance, advertising the existence of a strike by placards and word of mouth. Workers entering the plant are greeted with

pleas not to go to work. As a worker leaves the plant at the end of the shift, a picket may walk alongside him for a few steps and urge him not to come to work the next day. Under experienced direction picketing is an effective method of peaceful persuasion, though it can also degenerate into physical conflict. . . . picketing necessarily involves moral pressure if it is to be fully effective. It is not merely a method of reasoning with the would-be strike-breaker, but is intended also to shame him and perhaps alarm him.[77]

In such circumstances the picketing may also be a means of informing the public of the existence of the strike and the issues at stake, and of seeking to enlist their sympathy and support.

Picketing may also be associated with the boycott and political non-cooperation. This was especially the case in India during the nonviolent struggles for freedom. In 1930 the law courts were picketed by the nationalists, the litigants being urged to go instead to the *Panchayats* (village-five or town-five tribunals revived by the India National Congress); government schools and colleges were picketed, and the students were urged to attend "national institutions" which were independent of the British government; shops selling boycotted goods were picketed to discourage purchases of the boycotted items; government buildings were picketed, Indians holding government jobs being urged to give them up in the cause of India's freedom; opium and liquor shops were picketed, usually by women urging the prospective customer not to buy.[78]

Picketing may also be a means of protesting against particular policies, acts, or general policies of the government, or those of the body whose office, headquarters, or the like is being picketed. For the first time in the country's history the White House was picketed on January 10, 1917, and for several days thereafter by woman suffragists who sought to point to President Wilson's lack of commitment to votes for women. In March of that year nearly one thousand women picketed the White House.[79] When President Eisenhower arrived at the San Francisco Civic Auditorium in October 1958, he was greeted by a picket line of two hundred persons from the Northern California Committee for the Abolition of Nuclear Weapons.[80] In some northern U.S. cities, writes Arthur Waskow, white parents have picketed school boards trying to end *de facto* segregation in the school system.[81]

Even picketing may, of course, be illegal (as may most of the methods). Its exercise has been restricted even in parliamentary democracies —it was, for example, in Britain for nearly twenty years prior to 1946. The Trade Disputes and Trade Union Act of 1927, enacted after the British General Strike of 1926, contained a section which, writes Julian Symons, "limited the right to picket, in terms so vague that almost any form of picketing might be liable to prosecution."[82] (It was repealed in 1946.)

In countries with considerable civil liberties, picketing is often used as a means of public protest against the policies of both the government and foreign governments. Embassies, consulates, courts, legislatures, government departments, agencies, and so on may all be the focal point for protests involving picketing. Picketing varies considerably in a number of respects, such as how long the action is continued, the degree to which it is intended to be persuasive or obstructive, and the numbers involved—ranging from a token group to mass picketing. In a particular situation, picketing may be combined with other methods, such as strikes, boycotts and fasts.

17. Mock elections

The final method of making group representations described here is the mock election. An opposition group may, as a means of protest, hold extralegal elections or direct popular balloting on a topical issue. Special "polling" places at which to "vote" may be established, or the "votes" may be collected in some other way, such as by house-to-house calls. This method may be used by large minorities or by majorities when restrictions on the operation of the regular constitutional electoral system prevent the opposition from participating, either fully or in any form at all. Or minorities with full access to the regular electoral system may also, or instead, use the mock election when they feel that they need additional means of reaching the public about the issue which concerns them.

This approach was used in Mississippi in 1963 and 1964. Civil rights groups set up "freedom registration" for any Mississippian who wanted to register, regardless of the legal restrictions which were widely used to disfranchise Negroes. (Only seven percent or 23,000 of all voting-age Negroes were legally registered to vote in regular elections at the time.) About 83,000 people did "freedom register" and cast their "freedom ballot" for governor and lieutenant governor, choosing among official Democratic and Republican candidates and a civil rights slate. "More than a dramatic gimmick to attract national attention," wrote James Farmer, former head of the Congress of Racial Equality, "the mock election proved a superb educational device for instructing Mississippi Negroes in the ways and means of voting."[83] Arthur Waskow has pointed out that if they had been cast for the minority candidate in a regular gubernatorial election, that many votes could have changed the result, and that therefore the mock election "proved how considerable their own [the Negroes'] strength might be if they were ever able to enter the regular political system."[84]

Denied a place on the regular ballot, the predominantly Negro Freedom Democratic Party staged its own "election" in the autumn of 1964, inviting all Missississians to vote and listing all the regular candidates plus the Freedom Democratic Party candidates—who won among the nearly eighty thousand "voters." Three "newly elected" F.D.P. congresswomen then unsuccessfully challenged the seating of regularly elected congressmen in the U.S. House of Representatives, charging the denial of voting rights in Mississippi, where forty-three percent of the citizens of voting age were barred from participation.[85]

SYMBOLIC PUBLIC ACTS

There are many ways in which the viewpoint of nonviolent actionists or their grievances may be expressed in symbolic behavior. These forms of action have been popular over the years, and the specific methods listed here do not exhaust the possibilities.

18. Displays of flags and symbolic colors

The display of the flag of a national, religious, social or political group, or the colors of such a group, or the flag or colors with some other type of symbolism is a common type of nonviolent protest. Such displays are often motivated by or arouse deep emotions.

On the visit of Emperor Franz Josef to the capital of Hungary on June 6, 1865, inhabitants of Pesth at first displayed only a very few flags of the Empire, as they opposed Austrian domination and sought home rule for Hungary. At the urging of the pro-Austrian governor, Palffy, the whole city was beflagged, which pleased the Emperor when he left the Agricultural Exhibition he had visited—until he realized that the flags were the green, white and red official flag of independent Hungary.[86]

Black flags have been used as symbols of protest and disapproval on numerous occasions: in India in 1928 by nationalists who were refusing to cooperate with the visiting British parliamentary Simon Commission,[87] in Ceylon in 1957 by the minority Tamils,[88] and in Pakistan in condemnation of the incorporation of Kashmir with India.[89]

In India the nationalists observed Independence Day on January 26, 1930, with the hoisting of the national flag at numerous demonstrations and celebrations.[90] In December 1956 students at Jena University in

East Germany in solidarity with Hungarian revolutionaries displayed the national colors of Hungary in the hall selected for their winter dance.[91]

Flags also played an important role in the 1963 Buddhist campaign against the Diem regime in South Vietnam, with government objections to the display of the Buddhist flag being important in the genesis of the conflict. On September 9 of that year students at the Chu Van An boys' high school, in the largely Chinese Cholon section of Saigon, tore down the government flag and hoisted the Buddhist flag, after which more than one thousand students were arrested.[92] In the first days of the August 1968 Czech resistance, flags and national colors were displayed in symbolic resistance. The morning of August 21, only hours after the invasion, crowds carried Czechoslovak flags in the streets of Prague, flags decorated the statue of St. Wenceslas, and the students carried a bloodstained flag into Wenceslas Square. Four days later flags throughout the city of Prague were flying at half-mast.[93]

Flags indicating political views are sometimes displayed in unusual ways. The morning of January 19, 1969, a Viet Cong flag was discovered flying from the top of the 240-foot central spire of Notre Dame Cathedral in Paris. The flag was fifteen feet by six feet; a helicopter from the Paris Fire Department was required to remove it.[94]

19. Wearing of symbols

Political dissent may be expressed by wearing on one's person some item of clothing, a color, a badge, a flower, or the like. For example, in France during the winter of 1792 the "red cap of liberty" became fashionable among the *sans-culottes*.[95] In World War II red, white and blue caps—imitations of the R.A.F. roundel—were worn by students in Denmark as symbols of opposition to the Nazi occupation,[96] while red caps were worn in Norway for the same purpose.[97] Occasionally, non-Jews in Germany and France wore the yellow star out of sympathy after it had been made compulsory for Jews.[98] In the Netherlands sympathy was shown by the wearing of yellow flowers in the lapel.[99] Symbols worn in Norway ranged from a flower on King Haakon's seventieth birthday to paper clips in the lapel ("keep together"), with considerable variations.[100] In the early days after the Russian invasion, Prague citizens wore the patriotic colors as tricolor bands on their lapels and elsewhere on their clothing.[101]

A related form of protest used in South Vietnam involves not wearing of some object, but the altering of one's appearance as a form of symbolic protest. During the 1963 Buddhist struggle against the Diem regime, the Foreign Minister, Vu Van Mau, resigned his post and "shaved his head in protest against the violent policy of that regime," Thich Nhat Hanh reports. "After that many professors and students did the same. The movement among students and professors was deeply influenced by that act." [102]

The way one who wears an article of clothing, or whether or when one wears it, may also symbolically convey a certain viewpoint. For example, at the inaugural session of the States General on May 5, 1789, when the French king replaced his hat, followed as usual by the clergy and the nobles, instead of remaining bareheaded (according to ancient custom) deputies of the Third Estate also "defiantly placed their hats on their heads." [103]

20. Prayer and worship

Prayer and worship may be so conducted that the participants by their religious act express moral condemnation and even political protest. This may be made clear by the content of the prayer or worship service, the immediate situation (as when an order to disperse has been given or demonstrators are arrested), the place in which the prayer is made, or the day on which it is made.

On learning of the planned British closure of the port of Boston in Massachusetts Bay Province on June 1, 1774 (an act taken in retaliation for resistance in that city), the Virginia House of Burgesses on May 24 resolved that June 1 be set aside as a "day of fasting, humiliation and prayer." Arthur Schlesinger writes: "Governor Dunmore, suspecting rightly that the fast was intended to prepare the minds of the people to receive other and more inflammatory resolutions, dissolved the House two days later." [104]

In occupied Poland in 1942 the Germans destroyed all monuments which commemorated Polish heroes or patriotic events. "By common consent all Poles made conspicuous detours around the spots where these monuments had been located. Prayers would even be offered up at these spots, to the outrage of the German officials." [105]

In South Africa during the 1952 Defiance Campaign prayer constituted an important part of the movement, as Leo Kuper reports:

Thus, in July at Uitenhage, during the trial of ten resisters, hundreds knelt and prayed, led by an old African woman in a red shawl. At East London, some 250 singing and praying Africans gathered outside the Magistrates Court while eighty-five of their fellow campaigners were charged with not being in possession of night passes . . . about 1,000 Africans gathered outside the courtroom in Port Elizabeth, and sang hymns and prayed for the accused. In August, again at Port Elizabeth, some 5,000 Africans prayed for the success of the campaign, after welcoming 250 volunteers released from prison.[106]

Albert Luthuli reports that in 1959 African women demonstrating at Ixopo, when ordered by the police to disperse, "fell down on their knees and began to pray! The police hung around helplessly."[107]

In Trafalgar Square in London, on November 12, 1961—Remembrance Sunday for the war dead—a public service of worship with an anti-war, pro-nuclear-disarmament orientation was held with about one thousand participants, under the joint auspices of Christian Action and the Christian Group of the Campaign for Nuclear Disarmament.[108]

Six civil rights workers knelt and prayed on the steps of the city hall in Albany, Georgia, in August 1962.[109] Public prayers were made on several occasions during the 1963 campaign in Birmingham, Alabama; on Sunday evening, May 5,

> A little before sunset the crowd of about two thousand Negroes came out [of the new Pilgrim Baptist Church] and faced the police. They knelt in silence as one of the ministers prayed solemnly: "Let them turn their water on. Let them use their dogs. We are not leaving. Forgive them, O Lord."
>
> Perhaps for a moment this touched something in Bull Connor, for he let the Negroes cross the police line and spend fifteen minutes in a small park near the city jail, where they prayed and sang hymns within hearing of the hundreds of demonstrators inside. Afterward, they returned to the church, where it was announced that the children would definitely march on Monday.[110]

During the 1963 Buddhist struggle against the Diem regime, Father Cao Van Luan, a Roman Catholic and rector of the Hué University, led students to the Buddhist Tu Dam pagoda to pray, in symbolic protest against the government.[111] In June 1966, Buddhists in Hué and Quan-tri, South Vietnam, erected altars in the middle of streets and conducted religious observances there, even though government troops wished to have full use of the streets to facilitate control of the city.[112] Thich Nhat Hanh describes the carrying of family altars into the streets to oppose tanks as an act "no less tragic than the self-immolation of the Venerable Thich Quang Duc." It was, he said, the use of "traditional values to oppose inhumanity and violence."[113] This also has elements of psychological intervention. That year prayer ceremonies were conducted throughout Vietnam in opposition to the war. These are described as having a "tremendous effect."[114]

On June 30, 1966, in the U.S. Senate Visitors' Gallery, after the Senate had adjourned twelve members of the Society of Friends held a silent Quaker Meeting for prayer and worship in protest against the recess of that body while the bombing of North Vietnam was being intensified. Their two-and-a-half-hour Meeting and wait-in were combined with trespass for refusing to leave when ordered, for which they were arrested.[115]

During the Great October Strike of the 1905 Russian Revolution, young schoolchildren on one occasion made their political protest in a related but rather different way:

> Tsarskoe Selo, a small city almost completely dominated by the imperial residence, had its day also: local secondary school boys went out on strike and were joined by the pupils of the girls' secondary school; and the primary school children registered their feelings by refusing to say their morning prayers and, when the prayers were read to them, responding with the favored Russian form of disrespect, whistling.[116]

21. Delivering symbolic objects

The delivery of an object which symbolizes a grievance or an objective to the official or office associated with the issue has been used in various ways to advance the views of the protesters. For example, in Chicago a few years ago when "The Woodlawn Organization" (T.W.O.)—a neighborhood organization in a black slum area—sought action from Mayor Daley to deal with bad conditions in their district, they piled rats on the steps of City Hall, Saul Alinsky reports.[117] In protest against Soviet nuclear weapons tests, Committee of 100 supporters in London in October 1961 brought hundreds of bottles of milk, each labeled "DANGER—RADIOACTIVE" in red letters, and left them in front of the Soviet Embassy.[118]

President Kennedy in 1963 had not yet fulfilled his 1960 campaign promise to eliminate discrimination in federally assisted housing (made in his "stroke of the pen" statement, in which he promised to issue and sign such an executive order). James Farmer writes that there was reliable information that an executive order on the subject, drafted by his staff, had lain unsigned in the President's office since 1961. The Congress of Racial

Equality then joined the wider campaign on the issue. Farmer writes: "We figured JFK's pen had run dry, and we sent thousands of bottles of ink to the White House."[119]

22. Protest disrobings

One of the rarer old—but newly reactivated—forms of nonviolent protest is the public removal of clothes as a means of expressing one's religious dissapproval or political protest. During the Quaker "invasion" of the intolerant Massachusetts Bay Colony in the seventeenth century, Lydia Wardel entered Newbury Church naked as a protest.[120] Members of the Sons of Freedom sect of the Doukhobors in British Columbia, Canada, have been credited with "uncounted nude parades" and in some cases individual women have disrobed in front of their own burning homes, to which they set fire as a protest against alleged government interference or prosecution of their husbands for resistance activities, including demolitions.[121] When Prime Minister John Diefenbaker was attending a political rally at Trail, British Columbia, on May 28, 1962, Doukhobor women whose husbands were awaiting trial for terrorist acts interrupted the meeting, tearfully protesting "unfair treatment" of their group, and took off their clothing as part of their protest.[122]

One of several cases of protest disrobing in the United States in recent years by young people in the antiwar and social protest movements took place at Grinnell College, in Grinnell, Iowa, on February 5, 1969. The students staged a "nude-in" during a speech by a representative of *Playboy* magazine, in protest against the magazine's "sensationalism of sex."[123]

23. Destruction of own property

An unusual method of nonviolent protest is the voluntary destruction of *one's own* property in order to demonstrate the intensity of one's feelings of opposition. Where there is danger from the act of destruction, all persons are removed to safety in advance so that there is no physical harm to anyone.

Early American colonial patriots publicly destroyed letters when they disliked their political contents. When New York merchants in July 1770 decided to break with the general policy of nonimportation of British goods, they sent letters of their decision to Philadelphia and Boston. "When a copy of the letter reached Princeton, James Madison and his fellow-students garbed in black gowns, solemnly witnessed the burning of the letter by a hangman while the college bell tolled funereal peals."[124] "At Boston, a meeting of the trade at Faneuil Hall voted unanimously that the New York letter, 'in just indignation, abhorrence and detestation, be forthwith torn into pieces and thrown to the winds as unworthy of the least notice,' which was accordingly done."[125]

In support of the movement for economic sanctions against England, the merchants in Charleston, South Carolina, promoted an association for the nonconsumption of India teas, whether or not duty had been paid on them, beginning on November 1, 1774. At the instigation of the merchants, schoolboys collected tea from private houses and it was publicly burned on November 5, Gunpowder Plot Day—the anniversary of an attempt to blow up the Houses of Parliament in London.[126] In Providence, Rhode Island, on March 2, 1775, the day after the total halt to the use of tea became effective, a bonfire was made of three hundred pounds of tea which had been collected from the inhabitants.[127]

In the Province of Massachusetts Bay in February 1775, Colonel Leslie, a British officer, sailed from Boston to Marblehead to seize artillery which colonists had taken to Salem for safekeeping.

He landed his detachment successfully on a Sunday morning; but, when the alarm reached the nearest meeting-house, the congregation turned out and took up a position upon some water which barred his route. They refused to lower the draw-bridge on the plea that there was no public right of way across it; and when Leslie attempted to lay hands on a couple of barges, the owners proceeded to scuttle them. The soldiers drew their bayonets, and inflicted some wounds . . .[128]

A segment of the Doukhobor religious group in Canada has a long record of burning their own homes in protest against government regulation or government repression for (sometimes more violent) acts of resistance.[129]

In 1918 and 1919 woman suffragist members of the Women's Party publicly burned copies of President Wilson's speeches in Washington, D.C., on the gounds that he advocated freedom and democracy while not, in their opinion, doing everything possible to give women the vote at home.[130]

Other examples of symbolic acts include the burning of imported cloth during the nonviolent Indian struggles (as a symbol of renunciation of dependence on foreign countries and of determination to build a free, self-reliant India)[131] and the destruction of the statue of Stalin in Budapest during the Hungarian Revolution.[132]

In some cases this method may include destruction of documents provided by and technically owned by the government or some organization, which persons are required or expected to keep their possession or carry for long periods of time—for most practical purposes such items thereby become the property of such persons. Examples are passes, party membership cards, passports, identity cards, and conscription registration and classification cards. For purposes of this classification the item in question is seen as *de facto* the property of the person who has it in his possession, although *de jure* it belongs to the government, party or other body.

For example, in 1960 following the launching by the Pan Africanist Congress of the campaign against the pass laws in South Africa, the rival African National Congress called for the burning of passes. "We did not desire to leave our shackles at home," wrote Albert Luthuli. "We desired to be rid of them. I burned my Reference Book, others burned theirs and the bonfires began to grow in number."[133]

On October 15, 1965, during an antiwar rally outside the Army Induction Center in New York City, a youth burned his draft card while Federal agents looked on.[134] *The New York Times* reported that during anti-Vietnam war rallies throughout the country on August 16, 1967, five young men burned draft cards as a protest in Philadelphia, sixty-seven did so at the Arlington Street Church in Boston, and in Los Angeles at least eight burned their cards. In the latter city several veterans were reported to have burned their certificates of discharge. Many other draft cards were turned in undamaged throughout the country to offices of Selective Service or U.S. Attorneys.[135]

24. Symbolic lights

Torches, lanterns and candles are often carried in protest parades and marches and have sometimes also been used in other types of protest activities. For example, in South Africa on June 26, 1953, the anniversary of the launching of the 1952 Defiance Campaign, the African National Congress leader Chief Albert Luthuli appealed to Africans and their allies to light bonfires or candles or lanterns outside their homes "as a symbol of the spark of freedom which we are determined to keep alive in our hearts, and as a sign to freedom-lovers that we are keeping the vigil on that night."[136]

Three days after burning himself in opposition to the Soviet invasion, Jan Palach died on January 19, 1969. Young people then marched in a candlelight ceremony in Wenceslas Square, Prague, where the self-immolation had taken place. They quietly carried black flags and the

Czechoslovak red, white and blue flag to the fountain in the square where the burning had happened, in front of the National Museum which still bore scars of Soviet bullets. Alvin Schuster reported in *The New York Times:*

> Hundreds of somber people, many of whom had placed candles and wreaths on the fountain, surrounded it in silence. Others gathered around the statue of Wenceslas, fifty yards away, the site of an informal memorial to those killed in the August invasion. It, too, was aglow with candles.[137]

25. Displays of portraits

The public display of pictures of resistance heroes or persons who otherwise symbolize the objectives of the movement is sometimes used as a means of communicating to others one's political loyalties. During the Indian 1930-31 struggle, photographs of the national leaders—Gandhi, Nehru and others—were widely sold and displayed in homes and shops.[138] Similarly, in Czechoslovakia in August 1968, buildings in Prague displayed portraits of President Svoboda and of Dubček, First Secretary of the Czechoslovak Communist Party.[139]

26. Paint as protest

During the East German Rising, on June 17, 1953, the night shift at the Stralsund shipyard covered the name of a new lugger, *Walter Ulbricht,* with thick black paint, and the ceremony scheduled for the next day to launch that new boat for the herring fleet had to be canceled.[140] In 1962 in Eisenbach, East Germany, someone altered a huge picture of Walter Ulbricht by painting a rope around his neck.[141]

27. New signs and names

Erecting signs where there have been none or replacing old street names with new ones of symbolic significance are among the forms which this method may take. (Complete removal of all street, highway, town, and railroad station signs, or their replacement with erroneous ones, is not simply symbolic but an act of noncooperation, and hence is classified under political noncooperation.) In occupied Poland in 1942, for example, "The Little Wolves" group of youthful resisters stole many of the "FOR GERMANS ONLY" signs which were displayed at the best cafés, cinemas, and hotels in Warsaw, and also prepared many copies. One morning the signs appeared on hundreds of the city's lamp posts and trees—where the Germans had frequently hung Polish patriots.[142] On orders of a branch of the underground government, the Poles renamed most of the country's streets. "Overnight, on the walls, on street corners and lamp posts, inscriptions and placards appeared bearing new names, the heroes or statesmen of this war whom the Poles admired: Niedzialkowski Avenue, Rataj Drive, Roosevelt Street, Churchill Boulevard." Patriots all used the new names, and the name someone used was a clue to his political opinion (unless he were an agent working with the Germans).[143]

28. Symbolic sounds

Oral or mechanical sounds may be used to convey ideas in a conflict situation. The tolling or simple ringing of bells has often been used in this way, as in the example cited above in which James Madison and other Princeton students witnessed the burning of a letter they did not like, "while the college bell tolled funereal peals."

A very different case occurred at the end of May 1917, when major mutinies of the French army had already taken place, even those units which were nominally obeying orders were often highly discontented. "Throughout the Zone of the Armies the units which could be persuaded to march forward to the trenches were baaing in imitation of lambs led to the slaughter, and their officers were helpless to prevent it."[144] Between 9:00 and 9:15 A.M. on August 26, 1968, bells and sirens were sounded throughout the whole of Czechoslovakia, reported *Lidova Demokracie,* as

a protest of the citizens of a sovereign state against a forcible occupation, against barbarism and the brute force of the occupiers. The wail of the sirens mingled with the majestic tolling of church bells. The Bishop of Ceske Budejovice, Dr. Josef Hlouch, called upon all the clergy of his diocese to support the negotiations of our statesmen in Moscow by the tolling of these bells. In the streets of Prague, even the cars of foreign visitors sounded their horns.

This Russian reaction was also reported:

The demonstration apparently frightened the occupation troops. At the main railroad station, Soviet officers with drawn pistols threw themselves on an engineer and tried to force him to stop the locomotive whistle. During the demonstration, a young woman was shot at Klarov. She was taken to a hospital, but she died.[145]

29. Symbolic reclamations

Certain types of acts may be carried out to demonstrate a creative alternative to the disputed existing use or ownership of the territory in question. Among the forms this may take are the planting of seeds, plants or trees, the cultivation of neglected or seized land, and the construction of a building whose intended use runs counter to existing and future policies for the arca. For example, in October 1962 demonstrators of the Committee of 100 in Britain, protesting nuclear weapons, planted seeds at the edge of the R.A.F. V-bomber base at Honington, England, as a symbol of their desire to reclaim the land for constructive civilian use.[146]

30. Rude gestures

There are many variations of rude gestures and behavior which convey insults. They may rarely be used in situations of political, and even international, conflict. One example comes from the Sino-Soviet conflict. According to Edmund Stevens, in January 1967

. . . each morning an entire platoon of Chinese soldiers would march out on the ice and lowering their trousers train their buttocks towards the Soviet side, the ultimate in Chinese insults. This exercise continued until one morning just as the Chinese assumed their positions the Russians set up large portraits of Mao facing in their direction. The Chinese hastily covered themselves and retired in confusion. There were no repetitions.[147]

PRESSURES ON INDIVIDUALS

Several methods may be used in attempts to put pressures on individual members of the opponent group, whether officials or ordinary soldiers, for example. These acts may be directed against specific persons or groups of persons, or may be intended to apply pressure on individuals who are part of a large body, such as an occupation army. The ones included here are not exhaustive. Certain other methods in this chapter, such as picketing, may also be used for that purpose, as may social boycotts and fasts, which are described in later chapters.

31. "Haunting" officials

As a means of reminding officials of the "immorality" of their behavior in repressing a nonviolent resistance movement and of the determination and fearlessness of the population, volunteers may sometimes follow and "haunt" officials everywhere they go, thus constantly reminding them of the population's determination. For example, as Joan Bondurant has reported, during the 1928 Bardoli campaign in India: "Volunteers followed officials everywhere, camping on roads outside official bungalows. When arrested, they were replaced by others until authorities tired of the process."[148]

32. Taunting officials

Instead of the predominantly silent and dignified behavior used in the above method, people may mock and insult officials, either at a certain place or by following them for a period. In the summer of 1942, for example, in Honan, China, under Kuomintang rule, tax collectors and soldiers seized grain from unwilling peasants who were facing a severe famine, having refused to accept either money or farm tools instead. As a result,

in many villages, more soldiers had to be called in before the tax-collectors dared remove all the grain. As they dragged it away, the peasants would follow like a pack of monkey scarecrows, bitterly mocking, and sometimes threatening, without a trace of "virtue and obedience."[149]

33. Fraternization

An alternative to a social boycott of the soldiers and police of the opponent is to fraternize with them, in the process subjecting them to intense influence and direct or indirect propaganda or both.[150] The objectives may be 1) to become personal friends with the soldiers and convince them that no personal hostility or desire to injure them is involved in the resistance; 2) to convince them that the objectives of the regime which they serve are unjust and immoral and that those of the nonviolent actionists are just and right; 3) to persuade the soldiers (or other agents of repression) to reduce the efficiency with which they carry out orders against the resisters and the population, or, eventually, to mutiny and refuse to carry them out; or 4) to provide information for the population and the resistance movement on the opponent regime's plans. Such fraternization is accompanied by noncooperation with the regime and disobedience of its regulations.

For example, during the 1956 Hungarian Revolution, even in a situation where both violent and nonviolent methods of resistance were being used, Hungarians made deliberate efforts at fraternization and at influencing Soviet soldiers, both by personal conversation and leaflets in Russian. These efforts seem to have had a degree of success. One journalist reported that as a result of Hungarians talking with Russian soldiers, "something like a bond of sympathy was arising."[151]

There were many direct attempts to influence Russian soldiers in the early stages of the invasion and occupation of Czechoslovakia in August 1968. A Czech journalist reported, in *Rude Pravo,* participating in conversations with a Soviet captain, a Soviet lieutenant colonel, two Russian ambulance attendants, a Czech captain, a Czech citizen, and Czech ambulance attendants. It was "a lively discussion":

> We presented our arguments [about the invasion], and when we parted we all said: "We shall not say *au revoir*, we shall not wish you luck, and we shall not even shake your hands." This was perhaps the ultimate argument. I actually saw tears in the eyes of the Soviet captain. There was even a small spasm in the lieutenant colonel's face. The soldiers who had earlier just listened stood about hanging their heads. As we were leaving, the captain followed us a few steps and said: "We shall all reflect about what we discussed here. I am afraid that you are right about a number of things. It is a terrible tragedy. And you can print this if you want to." "If that is really so," I said, "perhaps we shall shake hands after all some day."[152]

Within four days it proved necessary to rotate invasion troops and bring in replacements.[153]

34. Vigils

A vigil is an appeal normally addressed not to one or a few persons, but to many people. Like picketing, a vigil consists of people remaining at a particular place as a means of expressing a point of view. It differs from picketing, however, in that it is frequently maintained over a longer period of time, sometimes around the clock, and is associated with a more solemn attitude, often of a pleading or religious character. It often involves late hours and loss of sleep.

In 1917, for example, women in the Netherlands maintained a vigil for weeks outside the building where a new constitution for the country was being drafted, seeking a clause granting woman suffrage. The clause was not inserted, but woman suffrage was determined to be an issue on which a simple majority vote of the legislature could rule.[154] Other examples include the constant vigil for fourteen months at barricades preventing volunteers (including untouchables) from using a road passing a Hindu temple in 1924-25 at Vykom in South India, as described in Chapter Two;[155] the South African "black-sash" women, who in 1955 and 1956 stood, mute and still, outside government offices in protest against efforts to change the South African constitution in the direction of greater regimentation;[156] the nine-week day-and-night vigil outside the Aldermaston Atomic Weapons Research Establishment in England conducted from July to September 1958 by the Direct Action Committee Against Nuclear War;[157] the year-long silent "Appeal and Vigil" maintained from July 1, 1959, outside the germ warfare plant at Fort Detrick in Frederick, Maryland, by pacifists and others who protested against germ warfare research and preparations conducted there;[158] and the attempt by Western exponents of unilateral nuclear disarmament to hold an antinuclear weapons vigil with banners in Red Square, Moscow, on July 13, 1962.[159]

DRAMA AND MUSIC

Nonviolent protest and persuasion may be expressed also in acting and music. Variations are possible on the methods described here.

35. Humorous skits and pranks

Political humor may become a method of nonviolent action when expressed in some social form such as a humorous prank or a skit, or, conceivably, a play of political satire. In such cases the humor or satire ceases to be simply verbal political dissent (as often expressed in dictatorial countries in political jokes passed from one person to another) and becomes an act of public political protest.

It has been impossible to find documentation for the following, but the story is told that in Austria, prior to the peace treaty and while Soviet troops still occupied sections of Vienna and the countryside, students tied a suitcase to the arm of a statue of Stalin.

In late 1956 students at Jena University in East Germany included humorous skits which parodied the amateur theatricals used to further Communist propaganda in the cabaret program at their winter dance; these skits were received with high applause. One concerned a hunter and his dog. The dog was muzzled, the hunter said, as a protection against malignant wasps and the extremely short lead on the dog was a "bond of friendship." The hunter shot the dog for running away, but he said he had shot the wasps which had been attacking the dog; the hunter replied to criticisms of his earlier beating of the dog by calling them accusations of "over-critical harsh tongues." Someone then described the hunter as "a protector true" of dogs, whose work would be venerated by future generations.[160]

36. Performances of plays and music

Under certain political conditions, the performance of certain plays, operas, and other music may be a form of nonviolent political protest. For example, in early January 1923, in the opening stages of the *Ruhrkampf* against the French and Belgian occupation, "the performance of *Wilhelm Tell* at the municipal theater in Essen developed into a demonstration of the national will to resist, and finally occupation troops invaded the theater and dispersed the audience."[161]

Another example took place in January 1943 in Trondheim in Nazi-occupied Norway. It was three months after executions in the city by the Nazis, and as part of the citizens' protest, the city's theaters offering light plays were still empty despite official efforts to fill them. But when the musician Ingeborg Gresvik gave two concerts the same day at the church called *Fruekirka* (where Nazi permission was not required), the lines of people wanting to attend blocked two of the city's main streets; over 2,500 people were seated in the church itself to hear the heavy and somber piano music. The *Ballade* by the Norwegian composer Grieg was an example of the music played. As a Norwegian author put it, "the program must be regarded as a Norwegian cultural demonstration."[162]

37. Singing

Under appropriate conditions, singing may constitute a method of nonviolent protest—for example, singing while an unwanted speech is being made, singing national or religious songs and hymns, rival vocal programs to compete with boycotted ones organized by the opponent, singing while engaged in a march, civil disobedience, or some other act of opposition, and singing songs of social and political satire and protest.

In the midst of the Finnish disobedience movement against the Tsar's autocratically imposed, and from the Finns' view unconstitutional, new conscription law of July 1901 (which conscripted Finns into the *Russian* army), *Kagal* (the secret society directing the disobedience movement) called for noncooperation. Everyone was to refuse to cooperate: youths should refuse to report for induction, doctors should refuse to examine recruits, communes should refuse to elect members to draft boards, and the preachers should refuse to announce the military conscriptions from their pulpits. When most of the ministers disobeyed *Kagal*'s call and instead obeyed their archbishop's order to make the conscription announcements, "the parishioners drowned out the voice from the pulpit by singing hymns."[163]

In Denmark during the Nazi occupation, while the Danes boycotted concerts of German military music, they set up rival programs of community singing of traditional Danish songs.[164]

A Red Army officer who was among Jewish prisoners from the Soviet at the Sobibor extermination camp in eastern Poland reports two instances in which the inmates asserted defiance by singing. The officer, Alexander Pechersky, reports that on September 24, 1943, the morning after their arrival at the camp, *Oberscharführer* Franz ordered the Russian Jews to sing Russian songs:

> "We don't know which songs we're allowed to sing," I said.
>
> The kapo (a prisoner with the status of a policeman) translated my words.
>
> "Sing what you know," Franz replied.
>
> "Sasha, what shall we sing?" Tsibulsky turned to me. He was a Jew from Donbas, tall and with a round face.
>
> *"Yesli Zaftra Voina."* (If War Comes Tomorrow.)
>
> "What's the matter with you? They'll kill us."
>
> "I say sing. We don't know any other songs." Tsibulsky began:
>
> > "If war comes tomorrow
> > Tomorrow we march
> > If the evil forces strike—"
>
> All the others chimed in:
>
> > "United as one
> > All the Soviet people
> > For their free native land will arise."
>
> The guards came running out of the barracks when our column passed. In this camp of death and despair the Soviet song rang out like a clap of spring thunder. We felt refreshed and exhilarated, as though we had received happy tidings, a promise of victory, and liberation.[165]

After a large number of South African resistance leaders were arrested in early December 1956, a large crowd gathered outside the Drill Hall in Johannesburg on the first day of the Preparatory Examination: "Just before the proceedings began, [wrote Albert Luthuli,] the huge crowd began *Nkosi Sikelel' i Afrika,* the African National Anthem. It sounded like an angelic choir: to us the sound seemed to come from above."[166] In May 1963 more than three thousand Negro children converged on the downtown area of Birmingham, Alabama. "Groups of them trooped in and out of stores, singing 'Ain't gonna let nobody turn me 'round' and 'I'm on my way to freedom land.'"[167]

In Prague at eight in the morning on August 21, 1968, after the night invasion, in one corner of the Old Town Square a group of citizens sang the national anthem while others argued with a Soviet captain, urging him to go home. Thirty-five minutes later a column of Czechoslovak vehicles passed through Wenceslas Square headed for the Old Town Square; the vehicles carried people who were singing the Slovak national anthem: "There is lightning over the Tatras, and terrible thunder . . ."[168]

Satirical political songs, as well as folk poetry and wise sayings, were used as means of education and protest in the Buddhist struggles in South Vietnam, especially in 1963. Thich Nhat Hanh writes:

> Political satirical songs are easy to learn by heart and can be circulated very quickly. They were widely used during the struggle against Ngo Dinh Diem [who was ousted as head of the government in 1963]. There were hundreds of them. The most famous was *Nghe ve, nghe ve, nghe ve Nhu Diem,* a song dealing with corruption of that regime.[169]

Singing songs of satire and protest is not, however, a modern innovation, much less a Vietnamese one. They go back at least as far as the early fourteenth century, when they occurred in France, and probably much further. Alejandro Planchart, an authority on medieval music, refers to this as "one of the most troubled times in the history of France," a time of widespread corruption among clergy and nobility, the Hundred Years' War, the papal exile in Avignon, and the schism in the church.

> In contrast to the luxury of the courts famine swept the countryside and pillage was rampant. Thus besides the love songs of the court poets we have the thundering of the political pieces with their scathing attacks upon all-pervading corruption.[170]

Political protest music survives in a number of manuscripts, the most famous of which is *Le Roman de Fauvel;* the words are from a satirical poem written by Gervaise de Bus between 1310 and 1314. *Fauvel* is a symbolic animal, an ass, whose name is composed of the initials of *flaterie, avarice, vilanie, variété, envie,* and *lascheté.* The original poem was later modified with additions from other texts, and various musical accompaniments and arrangements were created for it. Some of these were in the form of motets, in which two different texts were sung simultaneously with a different instrumental melody. In one of these, while the first singer is condemning corruption in clerical life, the second is singing a comment on secular affairs, while the instrumental melody *Ruina* underlies both. The text of the second singer includes this passage:

> Presiding today in the thrones of the world are deceit and pillage. The soldiers of Hercules have stopped. The discipline of the church perishes. Arms push hymns out of the smallest corner. Rapaciousness and craftiness reign at home, growing rich on the blood of the small. The cornerstone lacks foundation. To what purpose? More often to proclaim: ruin is near! [171]

PROCESSIONS

Some of the best-known methods of nonviolent protest and persuasion are forms of processions, i.e., people walking or marching. Five ways this is commonly done are included here.

38. Marches

The march as a form of nonviolent protest and persuasion is practiced when a group of people walk in an organized manner to a particular place which is regarded as intrinsically significant to the issue involved. The duration of the march may vary from an hour or two to several weeks, or even longer. Posters and banners may or may not be carried, and leaflets may or may not be distributed to bystanders. In May 1765, fifty thousand English weavers convened at Spitalfields and marched by three different routes to Westminster, London, to petition for relief against competition from French silk.[172] Marches occurred several times during the 1905 Russian Revolution. During the Great October Strike of 1905, striking railroadmen in Tashkent marched on the governor-general's home and were turned back by troops without bloodshed.[173] Following the "October Manifesto" (in which the Tsar granted civil liberties, gave voting rights to groups hitherto excluded from them, and established the principle of *Duma* consent to laws and *Duma* supervision of officials), in many cities throughout the Russian Empire people marched to the residence of the governor or to the municipal *Duma* to celebrate and to make further demands, especially for the release of political prisoners.[174] Other examples include the several marches of three thousand persons which proceeded simultaneously to foreign consulate buildings in Seoul in 1919 to demonstrate to the world that the Koreans were opposed to Japanese rule.[175] Gandhi's 1930 Salt March to the beach at Dandi to commit civil disobedience by making salt,[176] and the six thousand mile march (December 1, 1960 to October 8, 1961) from San Francisco to Moscow by pacifists urging unilateral disarmament.[177]

An "Agreement for the Deportation of the First Batch of twenty thousand Jews to the East German Territories" was signed by a Bulgarian and a German official on February 22, 1943. But revolutionary groups in Sofia appealed to the Bulgarian people, urging them to stand before Jewish homes and crowd into the Jewish quarters, refusing to allow the Jews to be deported. On May 24, 1943, writes Matei Yulzari, the Jews of Sofia organized a protest in which many non-Jewish Bulgarians also participated:

> It started from the Jewish synagogue in one of the suburbs, where the gathering was addressed by Rabbi Daniel Zion and several young men. The crowd started an impressive march, which was intended to join the demonstration of the university students and make its way to the royal palace to protest against the outrages to which the Jews were subjected. Clashes with the police were followed by numerous arrests.
>
> This mass demonstration alarmed the authorities and they did not carry out the second stage of their deportation plan—deportation to Poland, where the Jews of Europe found their death. Fearing internal unrest, the Fascist government and the king were forced to give up their plan to send the Jews of Bulgaria to their doom in the death camps.[178]

In Oriente province of Cuba in late 1956, during the Batista regime, the bodies of twenty-nine Cuban youths are reported to have been delivered, badly mutilated, as government reprisals for the November uprising. Later there were other murders and countermurders in Santiago. On January 2, 1957, soldiers in Santiago seized William Soler, a fourteen-year-old boy; his badly tortured body was dumped in an empty lot the next night. Robert Taber writes:

> At ten o'clock in the morning [of January 4], some forty women dressed in black left the Church of Dolores . . . and moved in slow procession, praying in unison and fingering their rosaries, down Calle Aguilera . . . At their head marched the mother of William Soler, and with her the mothers of other youths slain by police and soldiers . . . Over their heads they carried a large white banner with the black inscription: *Cesen los asesinatos de nuestros hijos.* (Stop the murder of our sons.)
>
> As they moved on past the park and through the shopping dis-

trict, other women joined them. There were two hundred by the time they had passed the first block, then eight hundred, then a thousand. At every step more women left the shops to join the procession, pressing slowly forward through the narrow, cobbled street. A few policemen stood by, helpless, at the intersections. Men watched from the doorways and many wept with shame as the women passed by, the only sound of their murmured litany and the funereal tapping of their heels.

At one intersection, a jeep load of soldiers suddenly appeared, training a machine gun on the procession, blocking the way. The women waited, silently. The demonstration continued to grow until it overflowed into nearby streets, blocking all traffic.

When the soldiers tried to break up the manifestation, pushing their way into the dense crowd, the women simply opened aisles for them to pass through, and then closed ranks again. The mothers refused to be provoked into any overt act of physical resistance, but stood in quiet dignity until the soldiers gave up their futile efforts and, shamefaced, turned away. Then the women began, still silently, to disperse. Part of the procession continued on to the city hall and to the offices of several newspapers to leave petitions, demanding an end of the terror and the restoration of civil law. Then these women, too, went quietly home.

The mothers' protest march in Santiago had significance because it was the first public act to signal the beginning of organized civic resistance on a broad and effective scale in Cuba, under the aegis of the *fidelista* movement.[179]

39. Parades

A parade as a demonstration of protest or persuasion involves a group of people walking in an organized manner as a means of calling attention to their grievance or point of view. The parade is distinguished from the march in that, although it has a point of termination, that point is not of intrinsic significance to the demonstration. Banners, leaflets, posters, and the like may or not be used in conjunction with the parade. This type of demonstration may or may not be accompanied by bands providing music and by other types of activities.

The first parade for woman suffrage in Washington, D.C., was held in 1913 by the National American Woman Suffrage Association, with between eight thousand and ten thousand participants, including many senators and representatives with their wives. As it dispersed, the parades were assaulted by opponents, which resulted in a major press and political uproar.[180] Parades were often used during the Indian nonviolent struggles; for example, the parades of Muslims in Bombay on June 3, 1930, to demonstrate their support for the civil resistance movement.[181] An example from the West is the four-hour protest parade in London on November 4, 1956, against the invasion of Egypt.[182]

Six thousand supporters of the People's United Party paraded through the streets of Belize on August 24, 1958, in support of their demand for immediate self-government for British Honduras.[183] In South Africa, in June 1957, several thousand professors, lecturers and students at Capetown University paraded through the streets of Capetown in protest against the Universities' Apartheid Bill, which made multiracial university education illegal in the country.[184]

There are many possible variations on the parade. For example, during the boycott of tea (as part of the nonimportation campaign against the Townshend duties) the merchants of Marblehead, in the Province of Massachusetts Bay, on October 19, 1769 ceremoniously carted through the streets a chest of tea purchased from a Boston importer and then returned it to its starting point in Boston.[185] During the 1960 Japanese campaign against the revision of the United States-Japanese Security Pact, the student group *Zengakuren* developed other variations of the parade: "Zig-zag demonstration (snake-like parade), French style of demonstration (hand-in-hand parade), centripetal demonstration (parades starting from many points and finally centralizing at the Center . . ."[186]

40. Religious processions

A religious procession as a method of nonviolent action has the general characteristics of a march or a parade, plus certain religious qualities, which may take such forms as carrying religious pictures or symbols, singing religious songs, and significant participation by clergy and monks. The degree of religious as compared to other motivations may vary. In mid-nineteenth century China, following a serious flood in Kiangsu, a member of the gentry in Kao-yu district aroused the city's people to demand relief from the government, in defiance of the governor's memorial to the contrary. "The people gathered, refused to open their shops for trade, carried statues of the gods about the streets, and disturbed the yamen [government officials]."[187]

The several columns of petitioning Russians, led by Father Gapon, headed toward the Tsar's Winter Palace, on January 9, 1905, clearly took the form of a religious procession. According to carefully laid plans, several columns of workers with their families started from various points in St. Petersburg, to converge on Palace Square at 2 P.M. All these columns were "to advance as if in a Procession of the Cross, a dignified progression of devotees following their clergy, carrying icons and singing hymns . . ." One of these, led by Gapon himself, began marching about noon, after worship and prayers:

In orderly train, they followed their leader along the Peterhof Chaussée, holding aloft icons, religious standards, the Russian national flag, and portraits of the Tsar and the Tsarina. As they marched they sang such favorite hymns as "Our Father" and "Save, O Lord, Thy People." It was a decorous procession, and police along the route cleared the way for them, as was customary for religious processions, while the crowds who gathered to watch them made the customary signs of respect to religious and national symbols.[188]

According to official figures, well over a hundred of these demonstrators died from bullet wounds from the Tsar's troops and well over three hundred were wounded.[189] This action alienated the peasants from the Tsar and aligned most of the intelligentsia and even conservatives against the regime.

41. Pilgrimages

The pilgrimage as a form of moral condemnation has deep moral and religious qualities. It involves one or more persons walking 1) as a means of bringing a message to people, 2) as penance for some deed or policy which has been committed or pursued by the people or government, and 3) as a means of self-dedication to a program for altering the status quo. Often the pilgrimage will involve walking to a particular point of significance to the underlying beliefs or to the policy in question.

Such a pilgrimage usually lasts at least several days, and perhaps for months. Banners and posters are not usually used, although leaflets might be. At times some type of transportation may be combined with the walking. An example of a pilgrimage in the sense in which it is defined here is Gandhi's walking tour of the Noakhali district of Bengal in early 1947, undertaken in an effort to persuade Hindus and Muslims to halt their murderous rioting and to live together peacefully.[190]

42. Motorcades

A modern Western variation of the parade or march is the motorcade, which takes the form of the march or parade except that the participants drive cars at a very slow speed. The cars usually bear posters or banners. The motorcade may also be combined with a parade or march of people on foot. An example of this method is the motorcade organized by various pacifist groups which toured through Boston in November and December 1959, stopping at selected points to distribute leaflets and to urge people to support peace and disarmament.[191]

HONORING THE DEAD

Several methods of nonviolent protest and persuasion involve paying respect to the memory of deceased persons. The person so honored may be a hero from previous decades or centuries, or those remembered may have recently died in the course of participating in the struggle. One of these methods, a "mock funeral," is used to suggest that some cherished principle or social condition has been destroyed or is in danger, or to suggest that certain policies imperil human lives.

43. Political mourning

The same symbols which are used in mourning the death of an individual are often used for expressing political opposition and regret at particular events and policies. Public mourning was important during the American colonists' struggle against the Stamp Act in 1765. When the tax stamps for Pennsylvania, New Jersey and Maryland arrived by ship at Philadelphia on October 5, for example, all the ships in the harbor flew their flags at half-mast, and the city's bells tolled throughout the day.[192] When the Act was to go into effect, on November 1, the day was generally observed in the colonies as a day of mourning, again with the tolling of bells. In Boston, for example, the "Loyal Nine," or "Sons of Liberty," ensured that the day's protest was conducted in perfect order.[193]

During the Hungarian Protestants' resistance to Austrian attempts to destroy the autonomy of Hungary's Protestant churches, many arrests of pastors and bishops took place in February and March 1860, and church meetings were repeatedly broken up. Students went to the towns where these churchmen were to be tried and, dressed in black, conducted silent demonstrations.[194]

Sometimes the mourning may begin for the dead and gradually turn to political protest, as in this example from an eyewitness in Warsaw in November 1939:

At the corner of Marshall and Jerusalem Boulevards, in the heart of Warsaw and close to the Central Railroad Station, the paving stones had been uprooted and a huge mass grave dug for unknown soldiers. It was covered with flowers and surrounded by burning candles. A crowd of mourners knelt beside it, praying. I learned later that this unceasing vigil had been kept up since the burials had taken place three months ago.

During the next few weeks I continued to see the mourners by the side of the grave from dawn to the curfew hours. Gradually the ceremonies that took place ceased to be only a devotion to the dead;

they became tokens of political resistance as well. In December, the Nazi Gauleiter for Warsaw, Moser, realized the significance the grave had assumed and ordered the bodies disinterred and burried in a cemetery. But even after this measure, mourners would still come to kneel in prayer at this corner and candles would be lighted as if the spot had been hallowed by a presence the shovels of the Nazi soldiers could not expel.[195]

In Argentina, beginning in 1943, opponents of Perón's dictatorship demonstrated by wearing various black symbols of mourning: neckties, armbands, ribbons on lapels and coats, veils, headcloths, or small black handkerchiefs pinned on women's dresses. The numbers doing this rapidly multiplied, and this is credited with giving antiregime forces considerable encouragement.[196]

After the killings of Africans at Sharpeville, South Africa, when demonstrators defied the pass laws, Albert Luthuli called for an observance of March 28, 1960, as "a national day of mourning."

On this day I asked people to stay at home, and treat it as a day of prayer. The response was good, and in some centres it was magnificent. Moreover, it was multi-racial and went far beyond our usual allies.[197]

Luthuli for some days wore a black tie and black crepe as emblems of mourning.[198]

At the beginning of the 1963 Buddhist struggle against the Diem regime, following the killing of eight demonstrating Buddhists in Hué, the ancient Annamese capital, the predominantly Buddhist population wore white for mourning, in a situation in which the mourning seemed intended both for the dead and as opposition to the government which was discriminating against the Buddhists.[199]

44. Mock funerals

Political protest has also been expressed in the form of a "funeral" for some principle which the demonstrators cherish and which they accuse the opponent of violating. Or it may take the form of a mock funeral procession in which the participants seek to symbolize the seriousness of their protest both by restrained and serious demeanor and by including some of the paraphernalia of a real funeral procession, such as the use of black and the carrying of caskets.

Such a protest was held in Newport, Rhode Island, amid great tensions, at the time when the Stamp Act was officially to go into effect on

November 1, 1765. The event is described by Edmund S. and Helen M. Morgan, who quote from a contemporary newspaper:

On November first, in order to forestall any possible riot, the Sons of Liberty attempted to divert popular feeling into an orderly demonstration, by staging "a grand funeral of Freedom." A procession of mourners marched through the streets to the burying ground following a coffin marked "Old Freedom." Upon arrival at the place of interment, according to the description in the *Mercury*,

"A Son of LIBERTY emerging from the horrid Gloom of Despair, addressed himself thus: 'Oh LIBERTY! the Darling of my Soul! —GLORIOUS LIBERTY! admir'd, ador'd, by all true Britons!—LIBERTY dead! it cannot be!'—A groan was then heard, as if coming from the Coffin; and upon closer attention, it proved to be a Trance, for old FREEDOM was not dead—The Goddess Britannia had order'd a guardian Angel to snatch Old FREEDOM from the Jaws of frozen Death, to the Orb of the rising Sun, to remain invulnerable from the attacks of lawless Tyranny and Oppression."

After this agreeable diversion the afternoon was spent in rejoicing, with bells ringing and the courthouse ornamented with flags.[200]

Similar mock funerals were also held on the same occasion in Portsmouth, New Hampshire, Baltimore, Maryland, and Wilmington, North Carolina.[201]

In November 1961 on the day following the detonation of a Soviet superbomb, antitest demonstrators in Oslo, Norway, walked in a mock funeral procession with burning torches and black flags to the Soviet Embassy.[202] In March 1965 after a religious service in a small church at Lowndesboro, Alabama (near which Mrs. Viola Liuzzo was murdered), civil rights demonstrators took ten caskets in a funeral procession of automobiles to the state capital of Montgomery. The caskets symbolized the ten persons killed to date because of participation in the civil rights struggle in Alabama. The caskets were carried from the cars to a point near the capitol building, where prayers were said, and a black-clad woman brought flowers.[203]

45. Demonstrative funerals[204]

Under conditions of political unrest, memorial services and funerals —especially funeral processions for persons killed by political opponents or those who died of other causes in the course of the struggle—may express protest and moral condemnation. This may take place whether the person or persons killed were prominent opposition leaders or unknown demonstrators, whether the killers were a private individual or secret group on the one hand, or the police or troops of the regime on the other. Rarely, the occasion is the death of a person who has committed suicide as a protest. (This is not here regarded as a method of nonviolent action.) This method will usually take the form of a dignified walking procession.

There are a number of examples of this. During American colonial resistance to the Townshend Acts, on February 22, 1770, some boisterous school children in Boston were scolded by an "infamous Informer" named Richardson for placing a crude effigy in front of the door of an importer who was violating the boycott policy. Richardson failed to destroy the effigy, and a pelting exchange of rubbish between the children and Richardson, his wife and another man ended with Richardson's shooting several times into the crowd; he wounded one boy and killed Christopher Snider, eleven years old. Christopher Snider's funeral, reports Schlesinger, was made the occasion for a great demonstration, and he became the "little hero and first martyr to the noble cause."[205]

In the autumn of 1905 Prince Trubetskoi suddenly died; he had been a moderate liberal who led the delegation which, on behalf of the Third *Zemstvo* Congress, in June had urged the Tsar to establish the promised national assembly, the *Duma*. The Prince's death was used, by the revolutionaries and other opponents of the government, in the struggle against the regime. In St. Petersburg, Social Democrats organized six hundred students and workers to accompany the body, along with other deputations, when it was taken to the railroad station to be sent to Moscow for burial. In Moscow the funeral "was transformed into a great political demonstration," with many opponents of the regime speaking to crowds and organizing special memorial services to present much more extreme opinions than those held by the deceased Prince.[206] Later in the revolution, reports Harcave, whenever antigovernment demonstrators "were killed in the encounters, elaborate funerals would be arranged to honor them as martyrs." The Moscow funeral of Nicholas Bauman, a Bolshevik, on October 20, 1905, was one of the most dramatic, when "over one hundred thousand workers, students, *intelligents,* and even soldiers in uniform followed the cortège for nearly eight hours through the Moscow streets in what was clearly an anti-government demonstration."[207]

In late September 1917, Thomas Ashe, an imprisoned Irish nationalist, died after being forcibly fed for a week during a hunger strike of a number of prisoners. Edgar Holt describes the funeral:

> The funeral of Thomas Ashe on September 30, 1917, was the clearest sign of the resurgence of the Easter Week spirit that had yet been given. . . .
>
> In all, some 20,000 to 30,000 people followed the hearse together with several bands; for the most part the crowds watched in silence. . . .
>
> The Dublin police took no action as the forbidden uniforms [of the Citizen Army and the Irish Volunteers, of which Ashe had been a member] were flaunted before them. . . .
>
> The British authorities took no action over the funeral and burial of Thomas Ashe. But they were shocked by his death and at once made a number of changes in the treatment of Sinn Fein [nationalist party] prisoners.[208]

During the *Ruhrkampf* in 1923 the funeral procession for thirteen workers at a Krupp factory who were shot by occupation soldiers the Saturday before Easter became a demonstration of national mourning.[209]

News of the murder in the fall of 1940 of Rudi Arndt, who was a Jewish resistance leader in the Buchenwald concentration camp, by the S.D. *(Sicherheits-Dienst,* Security Service) did not reach Berlin underground circles until early in 1941. Herbert Baum then called a memorial meeting in his own home to honor Rudi Arndt, and later organized a memorial ceremony at the Jewish cemetery on the Weissensee. Professor Ber Mark describes these as both "tremendously effective" in that they raised the prestige of Baum's resistance group and "heightened the yearning for resistance." Some other Jewish leaders had thought that "such large gatherings were too risky"; normally attendance for an underground cell was limited to seven.[210]

In 1960 *Zengakuren* demonstrators against the United States-Japanese Security Pact held incense-burning demonstrations for the martyrs of their struggle.[211] Following the murder in May 1963 of Dr. Gregory Lambrakis, independent member of the Greek Parliament and strong opponent of nuclear weapons, a dignified and orderly procession at his funeral was formed by an estimated quarter of a million people to demonstrate respect for Lambrakis and solidarity with his political ideals.[212] (This murder was the basis for the novel and film *Z.)*

Following police firings into demonstrating crowds in East Berlin, on June 17, 1963, the body of the young man who was the first fatality was carried on a stretcher through the Petersstrasse with a wreath across his body, while onlookers threw flowers as the cortège passed.[213]

The funeral parlor of the Strasnice crematorium in Prague was the scene on August 26, 1968, of the funeral of a twenty-seven-year-old young man, a simple bystander who had been shot by a Soviet soldier. A group of weeping young people entered the parlor, carrying a Czechoslovak flag and a banner which read: "WE ARE COMING TO BURY THE VICTIM OF YOUR 'LIBERATION.'" Some of them spoke, swearing they would never forget those days and the victims. Then, reports a Prague newspaper, "the mother's heart-rending voice mingles with the strains of the national anthem: 'Do not leave me, my son . . .'"[214]

At least a half million people attended the funeral of Jan Palach in Prague on January 25, 1969, to honor the young student who had burned himself as an expression of his devotion to Czechoslovak freedom. At noon the day before the funeral, all of Prague stopped work for five minutes. Thousands of people, many weeping and many with flowers, filed past the coffin which lay in state in Charles University at the foot of a statue of Jan Hus. Hus, a Protestant reformer, had been burned at the stake for heresy in 1415.

Soviet troops were kept out of sight for the funeral, and Czechoslovak troops which had been called out to keep order were not needed. The government had not wanted the funeral to develop into civil disobedience to give the Russians the excuse to bring back tanks to Prague. The service began in Charles University; the procession then moved slowly through the streets of the Old Town to "Jan Palach Square," where the national anthem was played. Crowds stood in the cold drizzle for hours. National flags with black sashes were hung from windows. The students' own commentary on the funeral was broadcast from Radio Prague and other stations. Throughout the country, memorial services were held in factories, universities and public halls. A correspondent wrote: "This was the Czechoslovakia [which] the Russian leaders both fear and wish to crush—a quiet, disciplined people whose slightest gesture nevertheless cries out for freedom and self-respect."[215]

46. Homage at burial places

A visit to a person's burial place by a large number of people together or by a series of individuals and small groups may express political protest and moral condemnation when the dead has been in some way associated with the cause of the current struggle or when the dead has been killed by the opponent. For example, in St. Petersburg on October 4, 1861, a procession of students opposed to the tsarist regime carried a wreath to the tomb of Granovsky, the historian and friend of Alexander Herzen, the founder of Russian Populism.[216] On November 17, 1861, student revolutionaries from the University of Petersburg called "the Terrorist Section of the People's Will" sought to mark the fifth anniversary of the death of Dobrolubov, the comrade of Chernyshevsky (the great Russian Populist leader) by placing a wreath on his grave, but were prevented by the police and Cossacks.[217] During the Nazi occupation of Czechoslovakia on the "anniversaries of Thomas Garrigue Masaryk's birth and death, people used to go . . . in thousands to his grave at Lany near Prague to put flowers on his grave," writes Josef Korbel. "They also would go to the monument of Jan Hus in the center of the old city of Prague and do the same."[218] In France the bodies of hostages executed by the Nazis were dispersed among inaccessible cemeteries, apparently to avoid large-scale visiting of their graves.[219]

On December 4, 1956, one month after the second attack on Budapest by Soviet troops, Hungarian women, many black-veiled, walked to the tomb of Hungary's Unknown Soldier in Heroes' Square, in Budapest, where they heaped flowers on the tomb to pay tribute to the recent dead. The women sang the old national anthem and recited Sándor Petöfi's poem "Up, Hungarians!"[220] which contains these lines:

> Up, Hungarians! It's your country calling.
> Now's the moment, now or never!
> Shall we be slaves? Shall we be free?
> That's the question—what's your answer?
> In God's great name we swear, we swear,
> No more shall we be slaves—no more![221]

(Petöfi, poet-hero of the 1848 rebellion, died in battle with the Russians in 1849.)

PUBLIC ASSEMBLIES

When people have been concerned to express their viewpoint to a larger public or to an opponent, one of the most common ways they have chosen is to gather together in some type of assemblage or meeting.

47. Assemblies of protest or support

Opposition to the policies or acts of an opponent, or support for certain policies, may be expressed by public assembly of a group of people at appropriate points, which are usually in some way related to the issue. These may be, for example, government offices, courts, or prisons. Or people may gather at some other place, such as around the statue of a hero or villain. Depending on the particular laws and regulations and on the general degree of political conformity, such an assemblage may be either legal or illegal (if the latter, this method becomes combined with civil disobedience).

Students of the University of St. Petersburg, both protesting and seeking details of the rumored but unannounced new regulations which would virtually eliminate all freedom within the university, on September 24, 1861, assembled in the courtyard seeking to speak with the Curator. When the Curator told them he was no longer in office, the students marched in long orderly files across the bridge over the River Neva toward his home—in what Venturi says was the first demonstration in St. Petersburg.[222]

Following a protest by the Pesth county council against the dissolution of the Hungarian Parliament by Emperor Franz Josef, the council was ordered dissolved; then, having ignored the order and continued to meet, it was evicted from its council chambers by Austrian soldiers in August 1861. A supporting crowd of Hungarians gathered, first outside the chambers and then, after a march through the streets, at the home of the chairman of the council, who declared: "We have been dispersed by tyrannic force—but force shall never overawe us."[223]

In one case during the *Ruhrkampf* a crowd of thousands gathered outside a court to express solidarity with arrested resisters.[224] In Norway solidarity with arrested noncooperating teachers was expressed by children who gathered at railway stations the prison train carrying the teachers would pass on its way to the ship which would take them to a prison camp in northern Norway.[225] In Berlin in 1943—as described in Chapter Two—about six thousand non-Jewish wives of arrested Jews assembled outside the gate of the improvised detention center near the Gestapo headquarters demanding release of their husbands.[226] And in the entry for March 6, 1943, Goebbels wrote in his diary: "Unfortunately there have been a number of regrettable scenes at a Jewish home for the aged, where a large number of people gathered and in part even took sides with the Jews."[227]

In 1956 a massive demonstration against applying the South African pass system to women was held in Pretoria, the administrative capital, with women of all races from every part of the country taking part. They sang: "Strijdom, you have struck a rock!"[228]

In Algiers on August 31, 1962, a crowd of twenty thousand gathered in a square to protest the quarrel raging between the leaders of the newly independent country and approved a resolution calling for a general strike for an indefinite period in case of civil war.[229]

48. Protest meetings

Another method of protest and persuasion is to conduct protest meetings. These may vary considerably in size and nature, ranging from open-air street meetings to small local meetings, from the well-organized fairly formal protest meetings to the mass open-air protest meetings of thousands. As most of the people attending such meetings are already agreed on the need to protest, the speeches are usually of secondary importance and the protest itself consists of people assembling together as a means of expressing their views. Protest meetings are associated with a wide variety of causes and opposition groups. The meeting may be an end in itself or associated with other methods of action.

Mass meetings played a significant role in the American colonists' struggles in the 1760s and 1770s, often merging with the established town meeting system in which each enfranchised man had a voice and a vote. In protest against the customs' seizure of John Hancock's sloop *Liberty,* charged with illegal importation of Madeira wine, the Sons of Liberty in Boston, for example, called a meeting at the Liberty Tree on June 13, 1768. This was adjourned to Faneuil Hall, where a legal town meeting could be held, and thence to South Church because of the large numbers attending. The meeting adopted a petition to Governor Bernard seeking the rights of Englishmen under the British constitution, which, they claimed, had established that "no man shall be governed by laws, nor taxed, but by himself or representative legally and fairly chosen, and to which he does give his own consent. In open violation of these fundamental rights of Britons, laws and taxes are forced on us, to which we not only have not given our consent, but *against* which we have firmly remonstrated."[230]

Mass meetings, such as those in Philadelphia, Boston, and New York in October, November and December,[231] were also very important in the struggle in 1773. On December 16, for example, two thousand persons met in New York despite bad weather and resolved to establish a Committee of Correspondence to communicate with the other provinces.[232] A meeting of eight thousand people in Philadelphia in late December directed the captain of a tea ship arriving during the boycott of tea not to enter the vessel at the customhouse but to leave for England at once.[233]

After the tsarist regime had, during the 1905 Revolution, conceded the reestablishment of immunity rights on the premises of universities and other higher schools, student leaders, in cooperation with socialists and liberals, in early September 1905 turned their buildings into political meeting places. As many as ten thousand persons—students, workers, intelligentsia—met in a single evening in the lecture halls, laboratories and auditoriums of the universities in St. Petersburg and Moscow; smaller meetings were held elsewhere.[234] On October 14, 1905, in St. Petersburg, as a general strike got under way, the halls and courtyards of the University and the Academy of Arts were filled with mass meetings attended by about fifty thousand persons, and the city's high schools were also overflowing with striking workers and their supporters.[235]

In May 1917 improvised meetings were often held by mutinying French troops, rebelling against the vast and hopeless slaughter of the soldiers. When the troops of the 370th Infantry Regiment were notified in the morning that shortly after midnight they were to be sent to the front lines, some of the soldiers made inflammatory speeches urging the men to refuse to board the trucks which would take them to the trenches. By 11 P.M. the troops were drunk on wine they had looted and were milling in the streets of Soissons (sixty-five miles northwest of Paris). Two trucks, belonging to other regiments, then appeared filled with soldiers waving red flags and shouting *"À bas la guerre!"* The trucks stopped and became platforms for antiwar speakers.

In wine-thickened voices the speakers ranted about the butchery of war, about the peace offers spurned by a French government in the grip of the profiteers, about the politicians who callously sent troops to their death merely to prevent the inevitable encroachment of a truly socialist system. Instead of the 370th Regiment moving forward to attack the Chemin des Dames, it might be better employed in cleaning out the nest of vipers who were the government in Paris!

For a moment the men around the trucks were silent, and then there began an ominous roar. "We march on Paris!" "Get the deputies out of Parliament!" *"À bas la guerre!"* In another moment the drunken mob of five hundred men was surging down the cobblestone streets toward the railroad station.[236]

In the early 1940s, when fewer than four hundred Negroes in New Orleans, Louisiana, were registered to vote, mass outdoor meetings were called to hear victims of police brutality describe their experiences, and to protest the repeated instances of such brutalities. These meetings, called by a Negro labor leader, were on occasion attended by police representatives, and assurances of investigations and action were often forthcoming.[237] The open-air meetings against *Apartheid* and in support of the resistance held throughout South Africa in 1952 before and during the Defiance Campaign are also examples: mass open-air meetings in Sophiatown, Capetown, Port Elizabeth, East London, Pretoria and Durban held on April 6, 1952, while the whites were celebrating the three hundred years of their presence in the country,[238] as well as the meeting held in Durban on November 9, 1952, in support of the Defiance Campaign.[239]

In China in 1957, during the "Hundred Flowers Blossoming" period, eight thousand students in Peking held a rally on May 4 to celebrate the thirty-eighth anniversary of the student May Fourth Movement—claimed by the Communists to have been Socialist-inspired. Students used the meeting, however, to charge the Communists with "suppression of freedom and democracy in all the country's educational institutions" and called for nationwide agitation against the regime.[240]

Protest meetings were widely used in England in 1961–62 by the Committee of 100, on both a small and a large scale. The North-West Committee of 100, for example, in November 1962 held a "public assembly" at the Victoria Monument in Manchester in support of its policies.[241] In London, on October 29, 1961, the Committee held a mass forum in Trafalgar Square on the need for and nature of civil disobedience attended by about five thousand people.[242] On Sunday, February 25, 1962, at the time of the prosecution of six of its leaders for organizing civil disobedience, the Committee of 100 held a public assembly, again in Trafalgar Square, where it presented its case against the government, including statements by some witnesses which had been disallowed in the court.[243]

49. Camouflaged meetings of protest

Under certain political conditions gatherings of protest may be held under the (sometimes undisguised) pretense that the gathering is for some other more legal and approved purpose. (Sometimes everyone may be aware of the pretense.) This may happen when the regime is a relatively moderate type of tyranny, neither liberal enough to allow open meetings of protest nor tyrannical enough to act ruthlessly against persons attending a gathering which is ostensibly legal and approved, although the real purpose of the gathering may be well understood. Camouflaged meetings of protest may take various forms. For example, the meeting may occur under the auspices of an organization which has some totally different and quite innocent purpose, such as sport, amusement, art or religion. Or the gathering may take the form of a social affair. For example, on several occasions in France in 1847 and 1848, when meetings of open protest were not permitted, camouflaged meetings of protest were held under the pretense that they were banquets. The *Gauche Dynastique* and their moderate republican allies sought to mobilize public opinion to force government action against famine conditions by launching, in Paris and the provinces, a successful "campaign of banquets," beginning on July 9, 1847. The last of the banquets, which had been planned by others in 1848, was forbidden by the government, a ban which helped to precipitate the 1848 Revolution.[244]

Political banquets were also widespread during the 1905 Revolution in Imperial Russia. They began in October 1904 on the call of the Council of the Union of Liberation (liberals) at a time when many types of meetings were illegal. As part of a wider political campaign, the Liberationists set November 20—the fortieth anniversary of the Judicial Statutes, which had established a modern system of courts—as the date for the banquets. A surviving paraphrase of the original text of the plan called on Liberationists to "organize banquets on that day in Petersburg, Moscow, and as many other cities as possible, at which must be adopted constitutional and democratic resolutions much more decisive in tone than could be expected from a congress of *zemstvo* and municipal leaders."[245] That is, at the banquets their members would propose resolutions calling for a popularly elected national assembly to create a democratic constitution. Similar banquets attended by the intelligentsia were also held on that date in other cities, including Kiev, Saratov, Odessa, Kaluga, Rostov-on-Don, Baku, Kostroma, Tiflis, Nizhny Novgorod and Tashkent.

[Later,] ingenious liberals found additional occasions, for banquets —the anniversary of the founding of the Medico-Surgical Academy in St. Petersburg, perhaps, or the sesquicentennial of the opening of the University of Moscow. Almost any anniversary provided the excuse for a banquet; and a banquet, the opportunity for long and impassioned antiregime speeches and strongly worded resolutions . . . .

The opposition had never been so outspoken, nor had the attack on the regime and its policies ever been so open.[246]

Such banquets continued in December and into 1905 following "Bloody Sunday."[247]

50. Teach-ins

A teach-in and a protest meeting have certain features in common. In each case the topic for discussion is one on which there is considerable controversy. A teach-in, however, differs from a public protest meeting in that various political viewpoints are represented both among the speakers and those attending, and the speakers may be high-level specialists on the subject or otherwise regarded as especially able to provide, not only a capable presentation of their own attitude to the issue, but important factual and background information relevant to the issue. Teach-ins may thus have a larger number of speakers and extend for longer periods of time than ordinary meetings. Their aim, also, is not simply protest—although the holding of a teach-in on a topic of important public controversy recognizes the existence of differing views on the issue and provides a platform for all of these. An important aim of a teach-in is to provide the opportunity for people to hear various viewpoints and obtain relevant information in order to be able to make up their own minds. Confrontation of opposing viewpoints, questioning of the speakers, and discussion from the floor constitute important aspects of a teach-in. Teach-ins were widely held throughout the United States[248] and England in 1965, when the teach-in was a fresh and unusual method: in Washington, D.C., on May 15[249]; at the University of California at Berkeley, on May 21[250] at the University of Minnesota on June 4[251]; and at Oxford University in mid-June 1965.[252]

WITHDRAWAL AND RENUNCIATION

The final subclass of methods of nonviolent protest and persuasion includes those forms in which the people briefly, or in a very limited way, withdraw from certain usual behavior or renounce some honor they hold. These forms already possess limited characteristics of noncooperation, especially of methods of social noncooperation. However, the element of noncooperation is predominantly symbolic, and these methods are intended to express protest and to persuade.

51. Walk-outs

A group of persons, a delegation, or even an individual may express his political objections by walking out of a conference, assembly, meeting, or discussion before it has been adjourned. In 1920, for example, there was considerable opposition among Russian trade unionists, including members of the Communist Party, to the extension of government control over trade unions and their activities. This opposition was expressed by a walkout when the enlarged plenum of *Tsektran* (the Joint Central Transport Committee) met in December; the "communist representatives of the water transport workers together with a large number of railwaymen left the conference room as a protest."[253] On at least two occasions the normally subservient Field Marshal Wilhelm Keitel, then Chief of the German High Command, walked out on Hitler. In April 1940, for instance, he walked out of the conference chamber when Hitler rebuked him in front of others after Keitel had opposed the transfer of the administration of occupied Norway from the German commander-in-chief there to *Gauleiter* Josef Terboven, who then became *Reichskommissar.* [254] And following Hitler's angry repudiation of his memorandum opposing a war with the Soviet Union, and his offer of resignation in late August 1940, Keitel again "walked out of the room without a word."[255]

52. Silence

Corporate silence has also been used as a method of expressing moral condemnation. The silence may be a main method for expressing the attitude, or it may be an auxiliary method combined with another, for example, a march or stay-at-home demonstration. There are several German examples among those cited here.

During the Kapp *Putsch* in Berlin in 1920, Berliners would have nothing to do with the few apologists for the usurpers. When one pro-Kapp enthusiast climbed on the Potsdamer Bridge and spoke against the legitimate regime, calling the President "King Ebert," icy silence was all he evoked from the crowd.[256] On September 27, 1938, Berliners who believed that war over Czechoslovakia was imminent received the parade of armored troops down the Wilhelmstrasse for review by Hitler with clear hostility; they either scattered and refused to watch or stood "in utter silence."[257]

On June 16, 1953, a column of at least two thousand protesting East Berlin workers passed the new Soviet Embassy on the Unter den Linden in silence.[258] After the crushing of the rising, workers at the Zeiss factory at Jena met the speeches and pleas of Socialist Unity Party representatives with "a wall of sullen, obstinate silence."[259]

Aware of unrest and revolt in Poland, Hungarians on October 22, 1956, held a silent demonstration outside the Polish Embassy.[260] Later, during the Hungarian Revolution of 1956 "silent hour" demonstrations were observed between 1 and 2 P.M. in many parts of Budapest; after notification by poster, leaflet or word of mouth, many people hurried home to be off the streets during that hour, or went into doorways at the apppointed time.[261] In England, the last mile of the eight thousand-strong first Aldermaston March in 1958 was observed in silence, as the marchers approached the nuclear weapons research establishment.[262]

In 1962, in response to a leaflet call for the women of Madrid to show solidarity with tens of thousands of striking workers in the Asturias mines, the Basque provinces, and other parts of Spain, women went to Madrid's historic central square, the Puerta del Sol, to show "silent support." Singly or in pairs they walked around the plaza on that day, May 15, 1962. The secret police quietly arrested seventy of them—many very prominent women and wives of important public figures. The next day they were fined from one thousand to twenty-five thousand pesetas.[263]

When a militant Cuban at the Twenty-third Congress of the Communist Party in Moscow advocated taking all risks to defeat the Americans in Vietnam, his speech was greeted with silence rather than applause.[264]

During the 1964 free speech controversy at the University of California at Berkeley, one night (about October 1) a crowd of students opposed to the free speech movement heckled and molested student demonstrators and threw eggs and lighted cigarette butts at them. The demonstrators responded with simple silence, and after forty-five minutes of provocations the hecklers left.[265]

Silence was a main characteristic of the mourning for Jan Palach, the student who in January 1969 burned himself to protest the Russian occupation. The student action committee said: "In the circumstances, a complete silence will be the best way of showing our real feelings."[266] The funeral itself was described as "marked by perfect silence and order." "Bells from scores of churches tolled over the quiet city."[267]

53. Renouncing honors

One method of communicating one's views to others has been the renunciation of special honors which had been conferred by, or new ones which were offered by, the government against which the campaigns were conducted. This may involve the voluntary renunciation of titles of honor, medals and honorary offices, and resignation from prestigious societies closely identified with the opponent's cause. Such renunciation may be regarded as a means of self-sacrifice for the cause and weakening the authority of the government.

During the Indian nonviolent struggles, for example, Sikh soldiers in large numbers returned their war medals, and thousands of other Indians relinquished their titles.[268] The famous poet Rabindranath Tagore surrendered his title of British knighthood.[269] During the Korean national demonstration against Japanese rule in 1919-22 some Koreans who had been given titles of nobility by the Japanese also resigned them.[270] Bertrand Russell returned the Carl von Ossietzky peace medal awarded in 1963 by the East German Peace Council because the East German officials refused to release Heinz Brandt who had been long imprisoned by both the Nazis and the Communists. (Brandt was later named "Prisoner of the Year" by Amnesty International.)[271]

54. Turning one's back

Silent disapproval may be emphasized by turning one's back (whether standing or sitting) to the person or persons who are or represent the opponent. For example, in his proclamation of a day of fasting and prayer in 1771 Governor Hutchinson of Massachusetts Bay had included a call for thanks for the "Continuance of our Privileges," the radicals took this as an open insult because of the implication of support for British policies. The proclamation was to be read in the churches, but, Philip Davidson writes, "Dr. Pemberton alone of the Boston pastors read the proclamation—and he did so simply because the Governor was a member of his congregation—and he did so with evident embarrassment, for many of the members turned their backs or left the building."[272]

After the dramatic days of the June 16-17 East German Rising, on June 18, 1953, East Berlin strikers returned to their factories but refused to work. "They squatted in front of their lathes and benches and turned their backs on Party officials."[273]

These latter methods have shown symbolic withdrawal of cooperation with the opponent. The overwhelming majority of the methods of nonviolent action, however, are more substantial forms of action in which people refuse to begin new cooperation of some type with an opponent, or in which they withdraw some type of cooperation which they have previously been providing. It is to these methods to which our attention now turns.

NOTES

1. This is a modification of previous titles I have given to this class. The title of "nonviolent protest and persuasion" has been adopted at the risk of clumsiness in order to be more accurate. Adam Roberts has pointed out that my previous title "nonviolent protest" was misleading since many of these methods are often used to persuade instead of protest. In fact, the same method may in different situations be used for both purposes.

2. William L. Shirer, **The Rise and Fall of the Third Reich** (New York: Simon and Schuster, 1960, and London: Secker and Warburg, 1962), p. 218.

3. Gerard Reitlinger, **The Final Solution: The Attempt to Exterminate the Jews of Europe, 1939-1945** (New York: A. S. Barnes & Co., 1961), p. 90.

4. Louis P. Lochner, ed., **The Goebbels Diaries, 1942-1943** (Garden City, New York: Doubleday & Co., 1948), p. 517.

5. Warmbrunn, **The Dutch Under the German Occupation, 1940-1945**, p. 154.

6. Magne Skodvin, "Norwegian Nonviolent Resistance During the German Occupation," in Roberts, ed., **Civilian Resistance as a National Defense**, p. 142; Br. ed.: **The Strategy of Civilian Defence**, p. 142, and Thomas Chr. Wyller, **Nyordning og Motstand: Organisasjonenes Politiske Rolle Under Okkupasjonen** (Oslo: Universitetsforlaget, 1958), pp. 29-33. Other comparable letters by Norwegian organizations are also described by Wyller.

7. Gene Sharp, **Tyranny Could Not Quell Them** (pamphlet; London: Peace News, 1959 and later editions). It is potentially significant that the receipt by a German language paper in Poland in October 1942 of a single unsigned postcard from a Jew expressing outspoken hostility because of the sufferings of the Jews caused considerable disturbance and the "Propaganda Division feared that it was the beginning of a flood of postcards . . ." Raul Hilberg, **The Destruction of the European Jews** (London: W. H. Allen, 1961), p. 332.

8. Matei Yulzari, "The Bulgarian Jews in the Resistance Movement," in Yuri Suhl, ed., **They Fought Back: The Story of the Jewish Resistance in Nazi Europe** (New York: Crown Publishers, 1967), p. 276.

9. Littell, ed., **The Czech Black Book**, p. 81.

10. *Ibid.*, p. 91.

11. *Ibid.*, pp. 149-150.

12. *Ibid.*, pp. 163-164.

13. Hilberg, **The Destruction of the European Jews**, p. 409.

14. Bjarne Høye and Trygve M. Ager, **The Fight of the Norwegian Church Against Nazism** (New York: Macmillan, 1943), pp. 24-25.

15. Werner Warmbrunn, **The Dutch Under German Occupation, 1940-1945**, pp. 160-161.

16. Lochner, ed., **The Goebbels Diaries**, p. 278.

17. See *ibid.*, pp. 20 and 374; also p. 388 for another French case.

18. Littell, ed., **The Czech Black Book**, p. 41.
19. Among the bodies which issued statements in support of the Dubcek regime and in opposition to the invasion were the Association of Anti-Fascist Fighters, the Presidium of the Union of Czechoslovak Journalists, the Central Trade Union Council, the National Assembly, the Extraordinary Fourteenth Party Congress, the Presidium of the Prague City Committee of the National Front, the All-Unit Committee of the Communist Party in the main administration of the State Security, the editors of **Rude Pravo** (the official Party paper) and other papers, the Central Labor Union Council, and the Central Committee of the Trade Union Organizations, the Presidium of the Central Trade Union Council, the University Committee of the Communist Party, the Presidium of the Central Committee of the Communist Party, and the Czechoslovak Writers Union. *Ibid.,* 32-34, 42-44, 48-49, 80-81, 90-91, 150-51, 158-60, 170-71, 191-92, and 203-04.
20. Harcave, **First Blood**, p. 101. For other public declarations see pp. 104-105.
21. Littell, ed., **The Czech Black Book**, p. 47.
22. Albert Luthuli, **Let My People Go: An Autobiography** (New York: McGraw Hill Co., 1962, and London: Collins, 1962), p. 159.
23. *Ibid.,* pp. 239-243.
24. M. Rostovtzeff, **The Social and Economic History of the Roman Empire.** Second ed. revised by P. M. Fraser. (Oxford: Clarendon Press, 1957), vol. I, p. 398.
25. *Ibid.,* p. 409.
26. *Ibid.,* p. 408.
27. Gipson, **The British Empire Before the American Revolution**, vol. XI, **The Triumphant Empire, The Rumbling of the Coming Storm, 1766-1770,** pp. 54-55.
28. *Ibid.,* p. 521.
29. Joanne Grant, ed., **Black Protest: History, Documents, and Analyses 1619 to the Present** (Greenwich, Conn.: Fawcett, 1968), pp. 29-30.
30. Hugh Seton-Watson, **The Decline of Imperial Russia, 1855-1914,** p. 165.
31. A. Fenner Brockway, **Non-co-operation in Other Lands** (Madras: Tagore & Co., 1921), pp. 29-30.
32. Stefan Brant, **The East German Rising** (New York: Frederick A. Praeger, 1957, and London: Thames & Hudson, 1955), pp. 161-162.
33. For the "Document" in full and the story of its significance, see Tamas Aczell and Tibor Meray, **The Revolt of the Mind: A Case History of Intellectual Resistance Behind the Iron Curtain** (New York: Frederick A. Praeger, 1969, and London: Thames & Hudson, 1960), pp. 345-368.
34. Ber Mark, "The Herbert Baum Group: German Resistance in Germany in the Years 1937-1942," in Suhl, **They Fought Back,** p. 62.
35. Personal observations.
36. Jacques Delarue, **The Gestapo: A History of Horror** (New York: William Morrow, 1964), p. 317.
37. Jan Karski, **Story of a Secret State** (Boston: Houghton Mifflin Co., 1944), p. 301.
38. Littell, ed., **The Czech Black Book**, p. 184.
39. Inez Haynes Irwin, **The Story of the Woman's Party** (New York: Harcourt,

Brace and Co., 1921), p. 181. I am grateful to George Lakey for this reference.

40. Sharp, **Gandhi Wields the Weapon of Moral Power,** p. 114.
41. Sternstein, "The *Ruhrkampf* of 1923," in Roberts, ed., **Civilian Resistance as a National Defense,** p. 118; Br. ed., **The Strategy of Civilian Defence,** p. 118.
42. Hilberg, **The Destruction of the European Jews,** p. 374.
43. Report of the Advisory Commission on the Review of the Constitution of Rhodesia and Nyasaland, Cmnd. 1148 (London: H. M. Stationery Office, 1960), p. 8.
44. Littell, ed., **The Czech Black Book,** p. 144.
45. *Ibid.,* p. 116.
46. *Ibid.,* pp. 184 and 188.
47. George Lakey, "Cultural Aspects of the American Movement for Woman Suffrage, Militant Phase," unpublished mss., Philadelphia, 1968, p. 8.
48. Karski, **Story of a Secret State,** pp. 302-303. For another leaflet, see *ibid.,* pp. 127-128.
49. Wyller, **Nyordning og Motstand,** pp. 27, 29, 36 and 45.
50. Ber Mark, "The Herbert Baum Group," in Suhl, **They Fought Back,** p. 61.
51. A personal account by the sister of the executed Hans and Sophie Schol, together with the text of leaflets, is contained in Inge Schol, **Six Against Tyranny,** trans. by Cyrus Brooks (London: John Murray, 1955). The leaflets sometimes advocated "passive resistance" as the means of struggle, in one case listing specific recommended activities. An American edition of **Six Against Tyranny** was published in German by Houghton Mifflin of Boston in 1955.
52. *Peace News* (London), 1 May 1959.
53. Littell, ed., **The Czech Black Book,** pp. 50-51.
54. *Ibid.,* p. 51.
55. *Ibid.,* pp. 138, 146-147, 172-173, and 185.
56. Franco Venturi, **Roots of Revolution: A History of the Populist and Socialist Movements in Nineteenth Century Russia** (New York: Alfred A. Knopf, 1960 and London: Weidenfeld and Nicolson, 1960), pp. 178-179 and 748-749, n. 134.
57. See *ibid.;* Hugh Seton-Watson, **The Decline of Imperial Russia, 1855-1914;** and Leonard Schapiro, **The Communist Party of the Soviet Union.**
58. Skodvin, "Norwegian Nonviolent Resistance During the German Occupation," pp. 143-144, and Hans Luihn, **De Illegale Avisene.**
59. Hans Kirchoff, Henrik S. Nissen and Henning Poulsen, **Besaettelsestidens Historie** (Copenhagen: Forlaget Fremad, Danmarks Radios Grundbøger, 1964), pp. 113 ff., and their reference to Leo Buschardt, Albert Frabritius and Helge Tønnesen, *Besaettelsestidens illegale blade og bøger,* 1954 and supplement 1960.
60. Warmbrunn, **The Dutch . . . ,** pp. 221-258.
61. Karski, **Story of a Secret State,** pp. 236 and 264-274.
62. New York: M. Whitmark and Sons, 1965. This discussion is stimulated by an unpublished paper, "Music and Nonviolent Action: A Means of Nonviolent Protest," by Kenneth King, a student of mine in 1969 at the University of Massachusetts at Boston.
63. Littell, ed., **The Czech Black Book,** pp. 80-81.
64. See Littell, ed., **The Czech Black Book,** and Royal D. Hutchinson, **The Radio**

and the Resistance: A Case Study from Czechoslovakia (Hellerup, Denmark: Institute for Peace and Conflict Research, 1970).

65. This category and description are based on papers by Michael Schulter, then a student of mine at Tufts University, prepared in 1969 and 1970.

66. Personal observation.

67. *Life,* 3 July 1964. A large photograph is published with the story.

68. Hsiao Kung-ch,un, **Rural China: Imperial Control in the Nineteenth Century** (Seattle: University of Washington Press, 1960), p. 123.

69. Eino Jutikkala, with Kauko Pirinen, **A History of Finland.** Trans. by Paul Sjoblom. (New York: Frederick A. Praeger, 1962, and London: Thames and Hudson, 1962), pp. 230-232.

70. *Peace News,* 24 October 1958 and 7 November 1958.

71. Ruth Daniloff in *Peace News,* 3 January 1964.

72. Littell, ed., **The Czech Black Book,** pp. 134-135.

73. This section is based on a suggestion and draft by Michael Schulter.

74. *Boston Herald Traveler,* 26 November 1969, p. 3.

75. *War/Peace Report,* April 1966, p. 18.

76. *Peace News,* 26 February 1965.

77. Lloyd G. Reynolds, **Labor Economics and Labor Relations** (Englewood Cliffs, N.J.: Prentice-Hall, 1959), pp. 288 and 290. See also on picketing in connection with strikes: John Stueben, **Strike Strategy** (New York: Gaer Associates, Inc., 1950), pp. 289-294; John A. Fitch, "Strikes and Lockouts," **Encyclopedia of the Social Sciences** (New York: Macmillan, 1935), vol. XIV, p. 422; Florence Peterson, **American Labor Unions: What They Are and How They Work** (New York: Harper and Bros., 1945), p. 264; and James Myers and Harry W. Laidler, **What Do You Know About Labor?** (New York: John Day Co., 1956), pp. 74-75.

78. Sharp, **Gandhi Wields . . . ,** pp. 37-226. On the role of picketing in satyagraha, see Diwakar, **Satyagraha,** p. 48; Shridharani, **War Without Violence,** U.S. ed. pp. 18-19, Br. ed., pp. 39-40; and Gandhi, **Non-violent Resistance,** pp. 333-341; Indian ed.: Gandhi, **Satyagraha,** pp. 333-341.

79. Lakey, "Cultural Aspects of the American Movement for Woman Suffrage, Militant Phase," p. 12.

80. *Peace News,* 31 October 1958.

81. Arthur I. Waskow, **From Race Riot to Sit-In: 1919 and the 1960's** (Garden City, N.Y.: Doubleday, 1966), p. 280.

82. Julian Symons, **The General Strike, A Historical Portrait** (London: The Cresset Press, 1957), p. 226.

83. James Farmer, **Freedom — When?** (New York: Random House, 1965), p. 185.

84. Waskow, **From Race Riot to Sit-In,** p. 264.

85. Farmer, **Freedom — When?,** p. 187.

86. Arthur Griffith, **The Resurrection of Hungary: A Parallel for Ireland** (Dublin: Wheland & Son, 1918, Third ed., pp. 39-40.

87. Sharp, **Gandhi Wields . . . ,** p. 38.

88. *The Times* (London), 7 January 1957.

89. *Ibid.,* 28 January 1957.

90. Sharp, **Gandhi Wields . . . ,** pp. 54-55.

91. Rainer Hildebrandt, **2 x 2 = 8: The Story of a Group of Young Men in the**

Soviet Zone of Germany (Bonn & Berlin: Federal Ministry for All-German Affairs, 1961), p. 45.

92. Adam Roberts, "The Buddhist Revolt: The Anti-Diem Campaign in South Vietnam in 1963" (London: The Author, duplicated, 1964), p. 32. Sources for the event cited are the *New York Times* and *The Guardian* (Manchester and London), 10 September 1963.

93. Littell, ed., **The Czech Black Book,** pp. 35, 37, 39 and 50.

94. *New York Times,* 20 January 1969, p. 1.

95. George Lefebre, **The French Revolution from its Origins to 1793** (New York: Columbia University Press, 1962 and London: Routledge & Kegan Paul, 1962), p. 230.

96. Bennett, "The Resistance Against the German Occupation of Denmark 1940-1945," p. 159.

97. Skodvin, "Norwegian Nonviolent Resistance During the German Occupation," p. 141.

98. Reitlinger, **The Final Solution,** pp. 90 and 313-314.

99. Hilberg, **The Destruction of the European Jews,** p. 374.

100. Sharp, **Tyranny Could Not Quell Them.**

101. Littell, ed., **The Czech Black Book,** pp. 111 and 188.

102. Thich Nhat Hanh, **Love in Action: The Nonviolent Struggle for Peace in Vietnam** (pamphlet, mimeo; Paris [?] : Overseas Vietnamese Buddhists Association, 1967 or later), p. 13.

103. Gaetano Salvemini, **The French Revolution, 1788-1792,** p. 122.

104. Schlesinger, **The Colonial Merchants . . . ,** p. 363.

105. Karski, **The Story of a Secret State,** pp. 301-302.

106. Kuper, **Passive Resistance in South Africa** (New Haven: Yale University Press, 1957, and London: Jonathan Cape, 1956), p. 131.

107. Luthuli, **Let My People Go,** p. 196.

108. *Peace News,* 17 November 1961.

109. *Ibid.,* 31 August 1962.

110. Miller, **Nonviolence,** p. 334.

111. Adam Roberts, "Buddhism and Politics in South Vietnam," in *The World Today* (London), vol. 21, no. 6 (June 1965), p. 246.

112. *New York Times,* 10, 11, 14 and 23 June 1966.

113. Hanh, **Love in Action,** p. 13.

114. *Ibid.,* pp. 10-11.

115. *Washington Post,* 1 July 1966.

116. Harcave, **First Blood,** pp. 184-185.

117. Saul Alinsky, a conversation with Marion K. Sanders, "The Professional Radical, 1970," *Harpers Magazine,* January 1970, p. 38.

118. *Peace News,* 3 November 1961.

119. James Farmer, **Freedom — When?,** p. 40.

120. Harvey Seifert, **Conquest by Suffering: The Process and Prospects of Nonviolent Resistance** (Philadelphia: Westminster Press, 1965), p. 142.

121. *New York Times,* 11 March 1962, 8 May 1962, 24 June 1962. Disrobing as a method of political protest was also used on at least one occasion by African women in Northern Rhodesia (now Zambia) prior to independence, but I have not been able to trace the precise reference for this.

122. *The Times* (London), 29 May 1962.

123. *New York Times,* 19 February 1969 and *Esquire,* January 1970.

124. Schlesinger, The Colonial Merchants . . . , p. 227.

125. *Ibid.*

126. *Ibid.,* p. 525.

127. *Ibid.,* p. 486.

128. Sir George Otto Trevelyan, The American Revolution (New York, London and Bombay: Longmans, Green & Co., 1908), vol. I, p. 282.

129. *New York Times,* 11 March and 9, 11, 18 and 24 June 1962.

130. Lakey, "Cultural Aspects of the American Movement for Woman Suffrage," p. 14, and Doris Stevens, Jailed for Freedom (New York: Boni and Liverwright, 1920), p. 277.

131. Sharp, Gandhi Wields . . . , p. 41 and *passim.*

132. George Mikes, The Hungarian Revolution (London: Andre Deutsch, 1957), p. 82.

133. Luthuli, Let My People Go, p. 223.

134. *New York Times,* 16 October 1965, p. 1.

135. *Ibid.,* 17 Oct. 1967.

136. Leo Kuper, Passive Resistance in South Africa, p. 145.

137. *New York Times,* 20 January 1969, pp. 1 and 11.

138. Sharp, Gandhi Wields . . . , p. 180.

139. Littell, ed., The Czech Black Book, p. 111.

140. Brant, The East German Rising, p. 129.

141. Miller, Nonviolence, p. 353.

142. Karski, The Story of a Secret State, p. 301.

143. *Ibid.,* p. 259.

144. Richard M. Watt, Dare Call It Treason (New York: Simon and Schuster, 1963), p. 194.

145. Littell, ed., The Czech Black Book, pp. 196 and 192.

146. *Peace News,* 26 October 1962.

147. *Sunday Times* (London), 19 March 1967.

148. Bondurant, Conquest of Violence, p. 57 and Mahadev Desai, The Story of Bardoli (Ahmedabad, India: Navajivan Publishing House, 1929), pp. 188-189.

149. Graham Peck, Two Kinds of Time (Boston: Houghton Mifflin, 1950), pp. 394-395.

150. On the possible use of fraternization in resistance, see Ligt, The Conquest of Violence, p. 217.

151. *The Times,* 14 December 1956; *Observer* (London), 16 December 1956; M. Fejto in *France Observateur* (Paris), 15 November 1956; and Report of the Special Committee on the Problem of Hungary, pp. 25 and 82-83. See also Miller, Nonviolence, pp. 357-358.

152. Littell, ed., The Czech Black Book, pp. 63-64. This book contains other references to attempts to influence Russian troops. Not all reports suggest that the soldiers were easily influenced.

153. *Ibid.,* pp. 134 and 212.

154. *Suffragist,* 1917 (organ of the Women's Party, Washington, D.C.). I am grateful to George Lakey for this reference.

155. Bondurant, **Conquest of Violence,** pp. 48-49, and Diwaker, **Satyagraha,** pp. 115-117.
156. *Time,* vol. 66, 26 September 1955, p. 31, and vol. 67, 27 February 1956, pp. 35-36, and *Manchester Guardian,* 20 February 1956.
157. *Peace News,* 4 July-22 August 1958.
158. *Peace News,* 9 October 1959, and 1 January and 29 July 1960, and Jeanne Bagby, "Witness Against Germ Warfare," *Christian Century,* vol. 76, 23 September 1959.
159. *Peace News,* 13, 20 and 27 July 1962.
160. Hildebrandt, **2 x 2 = 8,** pp. 39-45.
161. Sternstein, "The *Ruhrkampf* of 1923," p. 113.
162. Hans Jørgen Hurum, **Musikken Under Okkupasjonen,** 1940-1945 (Oslo: H. Aschehoug, 1946), p. 176.
163. Jutikkala, **A History of Finland,** pp. 232-235.
164. Bennett, "The Resistance Against the German Occupation of Denmark 1940-5," p. 159.
165. Alexander Pechersky, "Revolt in Sobibor," in Suhl, ed., **They Fought Back,** pp. 13-14 (italics added). See also *Ibid.,* pp. 27-28, for instance.
166. Luthuli, **Let My People Go,** p. 167.
167. Miller, **Nonviolence,** p. 336.
168. Littell, ed., **The Czech Black Book,** pp. 34 and 38.
169. Hanh, **Love in Action,** p. 11.
170. Alejandro Planchart, **The Ars Nova,** commentary to the phonograph recording of the same title (New York: *Experiences Anonymes,* 1966), p. 1. I am grateful to Michael Schulter for this example and reference.
171. Translation of the motet, "Super Cathedram/Presidentes/Ruina" which appears in **Le Roman de Fauvel,** quoted in *ibid.,* p. 2, from Leo Schrade, **Polyphonic Music of the Fourteenth Century** (Monaco: 1956-68), vol. I.
172. Gipson, **The British Empire Before the American Revolution,** vol. X, **The Triumphant Empire: Thunderclouds Gather in the West,** 1763-1766, p. 279.
173. Harcave, **First Blood,** p. 184.
174. *Ibid.,* pp. 195-196 and 200.
175. Carlton W. Kendall, **The Truth About Korea** (San Francisco: Korea National Association, 1919), p. 29.
176. Sharp, **Gandhi Wields . . . ,** pp. 70-86.
177. *Peace News,* 20 October 1961, pp. 5-12.
178. Matei Yulzari, "The Bulgarian Jews in the Resistance Movement," in Suhl, **They Fought Back,** pp. 277-278.
179. Robert Taber, **M-26: Biography of a Revolution** (New York: Lyle Stuart, 1961), pp. 86-87. I am grateful to William Hamilton for this example.
180. Carrie Champman Catt and Nettie Rogers Shuller, **Woman Suffrage and Politics: The Inner Study of the Suffrage Movement** (New York: Charles Scribner's Sons, 1923), pp. 242-243. I am grateful to George Lakey for this example.
181. *New York Times,* 4 June 1930.
182. *Peace News,* 9 November 1956.
183. *The Times,* 25 August 1958.
184. *Manchester Guardian,* 8 June 1957.

185. Schlesinger, The Colonial Merchants . . . , p. 197.

186. Michiya Shimbori, "Zengakuren: A Japanese Case Study of a Student Political Movement," Sociology of Education, vol. 37, no. 3 (Spring 1964), p. 247.

187. Chang Chung-li, The Chinese Gentry: Studies in Their Role in Nineteenth-Century Chinese Society (Seattle: University of Washington Press, 1955), p. 55.

188. Harcave, First Blood, p. 89.

189. Ibid., p. 93.

190. Pyarelal (Nayar), Mahatma Gandhi: The Last Phase (Ahmedabad, India: Navajivan, 1956), vol. I, pp. 353-529.

191. Christian Science Monitor, 11 November 1959.

192. Lawrence Henry Gipson, The Coming of the Revolution, 1763-1775 (New York and Evanston: Harper & Row, 1962), p. 102.

193. Ibid., p. 103, and Morgan and Morgan, The Stamp Act Crisis, p. 173.

194. Miller, Nonviolence, p. 235.

195. Karski, The Story of a Secret State, p. 52.

196. R. H. Post (then second secretary of the U.S. Embassy in Buenos Aries), "Mourning Becomes Patriotic," in Win (New York), vol. 3, no. 13, July 1967, p. 23.

197. Luthuli, Let My People Go, p. 222.

198. Ibid., p. 224.

199. Newsweek, 27 May 1963, cited in Roberts, "The Buddhist Revolt." p. 8.

200. Morgan and Morgan, The Stamp Act Crisis, pp. 247-248.

201. Ibid., pp. 257-258, and Gipson, The British Empire Before the American Revolution, vol. X, p. 317.

202. Peace News, 17 November 1961.

203. Dagbladet (Oslo), 31 March 1965 (a U.P.I. dispatch).

204. The term "demonstrative funeral" is used by J. H. L. Keep, The Rise of Social Democracy in Russia (Oxford: Clarendon Press, 1963), p. 237.

205. Schlesinger, The Colonial Merchants . . . , p. 180.

206. Harcave, First Blood, pp. 117-179.

207. Ibid., p. 200.

208. Edgar Holt, Protest in Arms (London: Putnam & Co. Ltd., 1960), pp. 145-147. I am grateful to William Hamilton for this example.

209. Sternstein, "The Ruhrkampf of 1923," p. 120.

210. Mark, "The Herbert Baum Group," in Suhl, ed., They Fought Back, pp. 60-61.

211. Shimbori, "Zengakuren," p. 247.

212. Peace News, 31 May and 7 June 1963.

213. Brant, The East German Rising, p. 108. Other examples are described by Venturi, Roots of Revolution, pp. 568-569, and Peace News, 30 July 1965.

214. Littell, ed., The Czech Black Book, p. 194.

215. Sunday Times (London), 26 January 1969, p. 1; see also, Observer (London), 26 January 1969, and The Times (London), 24, 25, and 27 January 1969.

216. Venturi, Roots of Revolution, pp. 229-230.

217. Avrahm Yarmolinsky, Road to Revolution: A Century of Russian Radicalism (New York: Macmillan Co., 1959, and London: Cassell, 1957), p. 330. See also Venturi, Roots of Revolution, passim.

218. Personal letter from Josef Korbel (during World War II with the Czechoslovak Government-in-exile in London), 22 December 1966.

219. Edward Crankshaw, **Gsetapo: Instrument of Tyranny** (London: Putman & Co., 1956), p. 213.

220. *New York Times*, 5 December 1956 (cited by Bondurant, **Conquest of Violence**, pp. 226-227), and *The Times* (London), 5 December 1956.

221. **Report of the Special Committee on the Problem of Hungary**, p. 80.

222. Venturi, **Roots of Revolution**, p. 227.

223. Griffith, **The Resurrection of Hungary**, pp. 30-31.

224. Sternstein, "The *Ruhrkampf* of 1923," p. 114.

225. Sharp, **Tyranny Could Not Quell Them.**

226. See the description by Heinz Ullstein above in Chapter Two.

227. Lochner, ed., **The Goebbels Diaries**, p. 276.

228. Luthuli, **Let My People Go**, p. 192.

229. *Guardian* (London and Manchester) 1 September 1962.

230. Gipson, **The British Empire Before the American Revolution**, vol. XI, p. 153.

231. Schlesinger, **The Colonial Merchants . . .** , pp. 279-293.

232. *Ibid.*, pp. 292-293.

233. *Ibid.*, p. 290.

234. Harcave, **First Blood**, p. 176.

235. *Ibid.*, p. 183.

236. Watt, **Dare Call It Treason**, 189-190.

237. Daniel Thompson, **The Negro Leadership Class** (Englewood Cliffs, New Jersey: Prentice Hall, 1963), p. 99.

238. Luthuli, **Let My People Go**, pp. 115-116.

239. Kuper, **Passive Resistance in South Africa**, pp. 10-17.

240. Robert Loh (as told to Humphrey Evans), **Escape from Red China** (New York: Coward-McCann, 1962), p. 299. I am grateful to Margaret Jackson Rothwell for this example.

241. *Peace News,* 16 November 1962,

242. *Ibid.*, 3 November 1961.

243. *Ibid.*, 2 March 1962.

244. John Plamenatz, **The Revolutionary Movement in France, 1815-1871** (London: Longmans, Green & Co., 1952), pp. 61 and 67.

245. Schwartz, **The Russian Revolution of 1905**, p. 33.

246. Harcave, **First Blood**, p. 59.

247. See *ibid.*, pp. 57, 59, 62 and 117, and Schwartz, **The Russian Revolution of 1905,** pp. 33-35.

248. See Louis Menashe and Ronald Radosh, eds., **Teach-ins: U.S.A.: Reports, Opinions, Documents** (New York: Frederick A Praeger, 1967).

249. *Peace News,* 21 and 28 May 1965.

250. *Ibid.*, 21 May 1965.

251. *Ibid.*, 4 June 1965.

252. *Ibid.*, 25 June 1965.

253. Leonard Schapiro, **The Origin of the Communist Autocracy: Political Opposition in the Soviet State, First Phase 1917-1922** (Cambridge, Mass.: Harvard

University Press, 1955, and London: G. Bell & Sons, The London School of Economics and Political Science, 1956), p. 275.

254. Walter Gorlitz, ed., The Memoirs of Field-Marshal Keitel (trans. by David Irving; New York: Stein and Day, 1966), pp. 105-106.

255. *Ibid.*, p. 123.

256. Eyck, **A History of the Weimar Republic,** vol. I, p. 151.

257. William L. Shirer, **Berlin Diary: The Journal of a Foreign Correspondent, 1934-1941** (New York: Alfred A. Knopf, 1941), pp. 142-143. See also other references in John W. Wheeler-Bennett, **The Nemesis of Power: The German Army in Politics 1918-1945** (New York: St. Martin's Press, 1953, and London: Macmillan, 1953), p. 421, n. 2.

258. Brant, **The East German Rising,** p. 63.

259. *Ibid.*, p. 162.

260. Miller, **Nonviolence,** p. 356.

261. *New York Times,* 7 December 1956.

262. *Peace News,* 11 April 1958.

263. *The Times,* 16 and 17 May 1962.

264. Abraham Katz (formerly with the U.S. Embassy, Moscow), talk at the Center for International Affairs, Harvard University, 20 October 1966.

265. "The Berkeley Free Speech Controversy," prepared by "A Fact-Finding Committee of Graduate Political Scientists," the authors, mimeo., 1964, supplemented by information from Dr. Robert Jervis, one of the authors of that report.

266. *The Times* (London) 25 January 1961, p. 1.

267. *Observer* (London), 26 January 1969, p. 1.

268. Case, **Non-violent Coercion,** p. 386.

269. For Tagore's statement on this, see *ibid.*, pp. 384-385.

270. *Ibid.*, p. 293.

271. *Peace News,* 17 January 1964.

272. Philip Davidson, **Propaganda and the American Revolution** (Chapel Hill: University of North Carolina Press, 1941). I am grateful to William Hamilton for this example.

273. Brant, **The East German Rising,** p. 109.

4

The Methods
of Social Noncooperation

Chapter Four
The Methods of Social Noncooperation

INTRODUCTION

Overwhelmingly, the methods of nonviolent action involve noncooperation with the opponent. That is, the actionists deliberately withdraw the
usual forms and degree of their cooperation with the person, activity,
institution, or regime with which they have become engaged in conflict.
People may, for example, totally ignore members of the opposition
group, looking through them as though they did not exist. They may
refuse to buy certain products, or they may stop work. They may disobey
laws they regard as immoral, sit down in the streets, or refuse to pay
taxes. The actionists conduct their struggle by reducing or ceasing their
usual cooperation, or by withholding new forms of assistance, or both;
this produces a slowing or halting of normal operations. In other words,
noncooperation involves the deliberate discontinuance, withholding, or
defiance of certain existing relationships—social, economic or political.

The action may be spontaneous or planned in advance, and it may be legal or illegal.

The methods of noncooperation are divided below into three main classes: 1) methods of *social noncooperation* (which include social boycotts); 2) methods of *economic noncooperation* (which are subdivided into economic boycotts and strikes); and 3) methods of *political noncooperation* (which might also be called the methods of the political boycott).

This chapter deals with the first of these classes, the methods of social noncooperation. These involve a refusal to carry on normal social relations, either particular or general, with persons or groups regarded as having perpetrated some wrong or injustice, or to comply with certain behavior patterns or social practices. In addition to the methods of social noncooperation listed here, others are likely to emerge from reflection, research and invention. The fifteen specific methods included here in this, at present the smallest, class of nonviolent action methods, are grouped in three subclasses: ostracism of persons, noncooperation with social events, customs and institutions, and withdrawal from the social system as a means of expressing opposition.

OSTRACISM OF PERSONS

55. Social boycott

The most common method in this class, the social boycott, is characterized by a refusal to continue usual social relations with a person or group of persons. Such refusal is also called ostracism. This term derives from the ancient Athenian practice in which citizens voted to send into exile (for ten years, and in a later period only five years) those persons who had become too powerful or popular. The citizens voted by writing the person's name on tiles or on potsherds, called *ostrakon;* to banish by this practice was called *ostrakizein.*

In modern England the social boycott is called being "sent to Coventry" and has been used especially by trade unionists against workers who have refused to take part in strikes and other such activities. The social boycott has also been frequently associated with religious groups. The extent to which this ostracism is carried, and the spirit in which it is practiced, vary considerably. For example, at times it has been accompanied by hatred and vindictiveness; occasionally the boycotters may avow love of the rejected persons who, they hope, will alter their behavior to one acceptable to the boycotting group. The effectiveness of the social boycott seems to depend in large part on how vital or important the social relations in question are to the persons or groups being ostracized. In the context of a political struggle, the social boycott is usually a temporary practice, rarely lasting more than some months or occasionally years. However, in certain social or religious systems, a particular group such as the untouchables in India may be subjected to social boycott for centuries. This should remind us that social boycott—like other methods of nonviolent action—may be used for ignoble causes. For example, in early 1904 a brief social boycott took place against Jews in Limerick, Ireland; it was denounced by the Irish nationalist, Michael Davitt.[1]

Among the various uses to which social boycotts have been put, three stand out as especially significant within the context of resistance movements. This method has been used: 1) to induce large sections of a population to join in resistance activities; 2) to induce particular persons and groups to refrain from, or cease, some special collaboration with or service to the opponent group; and 3) to apply pressure on—and also often to communicate intense rejection or hatred to—the opponent's representatives or especially his police or troops. Let us now explore some examples of each of the uses.

Among the cases where social boycotts have been applied to induce resistance from reluctant sections of one's own population, the American colonies, Finland and India provide good examples. American colonials used social boycotts widely in their struggles with the Mother Country, both to encourage participation in noncooperation campaigns and to punish those who were judged too pro-British. These boycotts took many forms and were frequently combined with economic boycotts. The term social boycott did not come into use until over a century after these events; instead, the term frequently used at this time was "discountenancing," which indicated showing disfavor, putting to shame, showing disapprobation, and withdrawing one's good will and moral support.

During the Stamp Act campaign, for example, "The maids of Providence and Bristol [Rhode Island] displayed the extent of their resolution by bravely agreeing to admit the addresses of no man who favored the Stamp Act."[2] Later, social boycotts—discountenancing—were used to unify colonial nonviolent resistance against the Townshend Acts.

The town meeting in Providence on December 2, 1769, determined to enforce its strong nonimportation, nonconsumption and austerity plan with a discountenancing—"in the most effectual but decent and lawful Manner"—of anyone who refused to sign or obey the new regulations for the campaign.[3] And the previous March Philadelphians had pledged not only to buy no goods imported in violation of the agreement, but also to discountenance "by all lawful and prudent measures" anyone who violated it.[4] Publication of names of violators during this period was also a common form of expressing disapproval and of communicating the names of persons to be socially boycotted. In Boston in July 1769, for example, it was resolved to print the names of violators of the economic boycott agreement.[5]

Social boycotts were again used during 1774-75 to gain compliance with the program of economic and political noncooperation known as the Continental Association, adopted in October 1774 by the First Continental Congress. For example, the Maryland convention in December 1774, in seeking means to enforce the nonimportation, nonconsumption and nonexportation policy of the Continental Association, resolved that lawyers should not prosecute suits for persons who violated this policy and should not seek to recover debts for stores where such violators served as managers.[6] Similar action in support of the Continental Association campaign was also reported from Pennsylvania, New York, Massachusetts Bay, New Hampshire and Maryland.[7] In Massachusetts Bay, persons who had in violation of the colonists' policy of political noncooperation accepted Crown appointments as members of the Council were branded as "infamous Betrayers ·of their Country" whose names should be published "as Rebels against the States," in order that they might be "handed down to Posterity with the Infamy they deserve . . . ."[8]

Following Tsar Nicholas II's autocratic abolition of the Finnish constitution by the February Manifesto of 1901, the Finns split into two groups: the "Compliants," who approved of submission to the change, and the "Constitutionalists," who favored uncompromising rejection of the new system and refusal to obey laws or decrees issued under it. During the disobedience campaign which followed, the underground leadership group, known as *Kagal,* called for social boycott of the "Compliants":

> According to the "Citizen's Catechism" published by the *Kagal,* those who advocated compliance should be treated in daily life like carriers of the plague or violent criminals. Contacts between relatives and friends were broken off if they happened to take opposite sides in the conflict; they did their shopping in different stores and deposited their savings in different banks; and, in one town, a new secondary school was founded because families belonging to opposite political camps did not want their children to attend the same institution.[9]

The social boycott was also used by Indian nationalists against Indians who refused to join the noncooperation movement during the nonviolent struggles for independence. In this case the avowed aim was not to penalize the dissenter but to remind him constantly of his antisocial attitude and behavior, which put him beyond the pale of social intercourse. No physical harm was done to him or his relatives; in fact, the *satyagrahis* usually saw to it that all his primary needs, such as food, shelter, clothing, and water, were filled. The boycotted person had a standing invitation to see his error, correct it, and "rejoin" the community. (Gandhi strongly reproved the occasionally overzealous enforcers of the social boycott during the 1930–31 campaign, especially when the boycotted persons were denied food.)

After Gandhi's imprisonment early in that struggle, V.J. Patel, a prominent Indian nationalist, urged the social boycott of all government employees for the duration of Gandhi's imprisonment. On June 27, 1930, the All-India Working Committee of the Congress called upon the people ". . . to organize and enforce a strict social boycott of all Government officials and others known to have participated directly in the atrocities committed upon the people to stifle the national movement." [10] In Gandhi's view the social boycott could be permissible or not, depending upon the spirit and manner in which it was carried out. Boycotted persons, for example, should be supplied with food, water and medical care, and the boycotters should not feel hatred or vindictiveness against those boycotted; instead, the attitude should be sorrow, concern and hope that they would rejoin the community by stopping their help to the British government. When Gandhi returned from the Round Table Conference in 1931, the All-India Working Committee modified its earlier instructions by reminding the people that: "Social boycott with the intention of inflicting injury on Government officers, police or anti-nationalists should not be undertaken and is wholly inconsistent with the spirit of nonviolence." [11]

Now we turn to the second use of social boycotts in resistance movements. Individual members of one's own group who have served the opponent in particular ways seen to be traitorous (as political police or puppet officials) or who have clearly defied instructions for a specific noncooperation campaign (as strikebreakers) have often been subjected to social boycott. For example, early twentieth-century American trade unionists often refused to work with nonunionists and practiced social boycott against strikebreakers ("scabs") by avoiding their boardinghouses and restaurants. The local unions circulated lists of strikebreakers to others of the same trade in different cities, thus preventing their admittance to membership. [12]

There are also Irish, Polish, and Czech examples. In the struggle against British rule of Ireland, the social boycott was directed against members of the Royal Irish Constabulary and their families in 1919. Unlike the British police, the R.I.C. carried guns, and many of the members were quartered in barracks throughout Ireland. Charles L. Mowat reports: "A policy of ostracism, including the refusal to sell food to members, demoralized the force far more than a few murders or the threat of more; the men were mostly Irish and resigned in large numbers, and no new recruits came forward." This was described by Mowat as "the most successful weapon in 1919 . . ." [13] The social boycott was similarly used in Poland during the Nazi occupation. There, the underground government's Directorate of Civilian Resistance, which was charged with keeping Poland clear of traitors and collaborators during the German occupation, used the sentence of "infamy" as an alternative to a death sentence:

A Pole was sentenced to "infamy" who did not follow the prescribed "stiff attitude toward the occupant" and was unable to justify his conduct when asked to do so by us. It meant social ostracism, and was also the basis for criminal proceedings to be held after the war. [14]

As an example, one might cite the sentence of "infamy" which was imposed on a Polish actress who kept a theater open in violation of the underground's specific orders. Her name was published in all the underground papers. [15]

In late August 1968, after the Russian invasion, social boycott and the public "naming" of Czech collaborators or potential collaborators were important means in helping to prevent the early establishment of a pro-Russian puppet government. The Czech Union of Journalists urged in a printed leaflet, probably on August 24: "Help each other and stand together. Ostracize the traitors, ostracize their families. Do not help them." [16] Posters in Prague streets named persons believed to be collaborators; as a result, one of these persons, Karel Mestek, sent a letter to the National Assembly dissociating himself from the occupiers. [17]

Officials, police and troops of a foreign regime are often subjected to social boycott—the third use we are exploring. This is sometimes applied to members of visiting delegations or commissions. For example, in Northern Rhodesia and Nyasaland noncooperation with the 1960 visiting Monckton Commission from London was frequently extended beyond political noncooperation to refusal to have any social relationship with its members. [18] Then there is the case of the policemen who were stationed in the town of Kilmallock, Ireland, during a rent strike in June 1881. The British had not provided them with means of travel and the villagers would have nothing to do with them, with the following results:

> These men had much difficulty in providing themselves even with food, being "boycotted." The licensed publicans refused them the use of any public conveyance, which rendered the men almost powerless to act on an emergency outside the town. [19]

During the 1923 *Ruhrkampf,* members of the French and Belgian occupation forces in the Ruhr were boycotted socially by Germans; when the soldiers entered a tavern for a drink, the German guests would promptly leave. [20] Similar treatment was also accorded German troops in Denmark during the Nazi occupation. Throughout the four years of occupation, some soldiers were never spoken to by civilians in Denmark; the Danes would walk away without replying when spoken to by Germans, and shoppers would either remain silent or leave when Germans entered a store. [21] In Norway the social boycott was sometimes carried to such an extreme that Norwegians would look right through German soldiers as though they did not even exist and would never speak. Refusal to sit beside German soldiers on streetcars was widespread, and it was finally made an offense to stand when there was an empty seat. [22] In addition, social boycott was also at times used against Norwegians who either collaborated with the opponent or refused to join resistance activities. [23]

In 1959 Breton peasants in France used various types of social boycott. Under syndicalist leadership, the artichoke growers attempted to raise prices of that vegetable by reducing the supply of artichoke buds to growers elsewhere. The Artichoke Committee proposed forms of the social boycott as means of enforcing this ban, Suzanne Berger reports. In a circular to district leaders, the Artichoke Committee recommended that a peasant who violated the ban should first be visited by a few of his neighbors. If he persisted in selling the buds for growing artichoke plants, the entire neighborhood was to visit him. That failing, he should be removed as a member of all agricultural organizations, ostracized, refused all neighborly help, and publicly shamed. (Provision was also made for final resort to certain minor acts of damage to property, such as deflating tires or putting sugar in gasoline, if the social boycott provisions failed.) [24]

After a short period during which the Czechs and Slovaks engaged in extensive arguments with Russian soldiers in Prague in late August 1968, a period of deliberate ostracism of Soviet soldiers followed. This was urged on Czechs and Slovaks by the resistance radio and leaflets. By August 23 (troops invaded the night of August 20) it was already reported that "nobody talks to the Soviet soldiers any more. The people are passing by and pay no attention to them. But you can see everywhere written in large letters in the Russian alphabet: 'Go HOME!' 'DON'T SHOOT AT US!'" [25]

56. Selective social boycott

Instead of a social boycott being total or near-total, it may be restricted to one or more particular types of relationship. These particular relationships may have been chosen as a result of a tactical decision, or they may simply happen to be the main points of contact between the particular resisters and the opponent. Thus, shopkeepers or traders may be willing to speak to occupation troops but refuse to sell them anything. This type of social noncooperation differs from a "traders' boycott," which is an economic boycott, because here it is not a refusal to sell the *item* in question, but to sell it to the *particular person*. Hence the act is not economic but social noncooperation. During the *Ruhrkampf,* for example, shopkeepers refused to serve French and Belgian soldiers. [26] And in 1956 during the British and French occupation of Port Said at the time of the Suez invasion, Egyptian street peddlers observed a complete boycott of British and French forces, and Egyptian merchants in the European quarter of the city closed down their shops. [27]

A selective social boycott may, of course, take quite different forms having nothing to do with trading. Following the shooting of peaceful demonstrators in St. Petersburg on "Bloody Sunday," January 9, 1905, for example, the Merchants Club barred its doors to Guards officers because of their participation in the firings. [28] In January 1917 a sharp exchange took place at the Winter Palace between the President of the *Duma,* M.V. Rodzyanko, and the Minister of the Interior, A.D. Protopopov (who was regarded as Enemy Number One of the "progressive forces"). Later, while waiting for the Tsar, Protopopov approached Rodzyanko, obviously intending to shake hands. An eyewitness reported the following scene:

In one of these groups I saw the heavy figure of Rodzyanko. Protopopov approached him, and wishing him a happy New Year, proffered his hand. The impolite Rodzyanko, without even turning, pronounced in a resounding voice: "Go away! Do not touch me."

. . . . The incident at once became known all over the palace, and by that evening was the talk of all Petrograd.

George Katkov describes this refusal to shake hands as "a calculated discourtesy with political significance." [29]

On March 7, 1917, five days after the abdication of Tsar Nicholas II, a special commission from the *Duma* arrived at Mogilev, where Nicholas then was, with the news that the Provisional Government had decided to put him under arrest. The delegation and the ex-Tsar, accompanied by ten soldiers, then traveled by train from Mogilev to the palace at Tsarskoe Selo. There Nicholas invited the *Duma* Commissars to dinner. The invitation was refused. [30]

57. Lysistratic nonaction

The prescription for stopping war contained in Aristophanes' play *Lysistrata*—that wives should refuse sexual relations with their bellicose husbands—is so special a form of selective social boycott that it merits individual classification. This method has been applied on at least two known occasions. Stan Steiner reports that at the beginning of the seventeenth century the women of the Iroquois Indian nation conducted the "first feminist rebellion in the U.S.":

The year was 1600, or thereabouts, when these tribal feminists decided that they had had enough of unregulated warfare by their men. Lysistratas among the Indian women proclaimed a boycott on lovemaking and childbearing. Until the men conceded to them the power to decide upon war and peace, there would be no more warriors. Since the Iroquois men believed that women alone knew the secret of birth, the feminist rebellion was instantly successful. [31]

In late December 1963 the African women in the Mpopoma township in Bulawayo, Southern Rhodesia, sought the wider agreement of wives to deny their husbands all marital rights until an outbreak of bombings and explosions had ceased. [32]

58. Excommunication [33]

One of the forms of social and religious sanctions which churches may apply is excommunication, that is, excluding an individual or group from membership and the associated privileges and participation. This form of social noncooperation is initiated by the leadership of the church, rather than individual members. While such action may at times be prompted by purely personal factors (i.e., excommunication of an individual for conduct considered morally objectionable), in other instances these forms of social noncooperation have been used in political and social struggles.

Excommunication and interdict (discussed below) were both politically crucial sanctions in Europe during the medieval period, when the Church had a great share in temporal power and final political as well as religious allegiance belonged to the Pope. Thus excommunication of a secular ruler might lead to a popular withdrawal of authority and revolution.

During the late eleventh century there was a struggle between Pope Gregory VII and Emperor Henry IV of the Holy Roman Empire (an area now centering upon present-day Germany and Austria). After Henry had associated with excommunicates (a form of social disobedience), he drove an invested archbishop from Milan; in 1076, at a council at Worms, he referred to the Pope as a false monk. At this point:

> Gregory answered by excommunicating and deposing Henry himself —and the news made all men tremble. Henry's rebellious subjects in Saxony made it so clear that they would throw off the yoke of an excommunicate prince, that Henry was driven to circumvent them by submitting. Making a hasty winter journey into Lombardy, and finding Gregory at Canossa, one of the Alpine strongholds of the countess Matilda of Tuscany, he waited three days in the snow of the courtyard as a penitent, imploring release from excommunication. He had appealed from the statesman in Gregory to the priest, and on the fourth day, against the interests of the statesman, Gregory absolved him.[34]

Nevertheless, certain of the Saxon rebels elected a rival emperor in 1077. After a civil war in which neither side accepted the intervention of the Pope, Gregory again excommunicated Henry in 1080, and Henry reacted by designating a rival pope and establishing him in Rome. The struggle was never finally decided.[35]

Excommunication was also used in the United States as a weapon of antislavery forces during the struggle over abolition in the mid-nineteenth century. Often slaveholders were either excommunicated or prevented from joining churches on account of their practice.[36]

59. Interdict

The interdict is the suspension of religious services and other religious activities in a given district or country for a specific period, by the decision of the leadership of the church.

An interdict, although it may be partially punitive in nature, usually has as its primary goal the coercion of a government or population to rectify specific grievances, which may be either strictly religious or (more often) partially political. The pressure is imposed by depriving the district of religious services, sacraments, or canonical burial, or a combination of these. A canon of Pope Innocent II described the interdict as *cessatio a divinorum celebratione.*[37] Edward B. Krehbiel, an authority on the interdict, has written that

> . . . the purpose of the interdict is to secure compliance with demands made by the church on some offender against the welfare of society, church, or priesthood, or against the laws of faith and morals. It is compulsion by a form of passive resistance. It is not an aggressive act and not a punishment; it is a defensive act by which the church withdraws from public service until society "plays fair."[38]

Thus Innocent III placed under interdict London and the land under the barons who opposed King John after he repudiated the Magna Charta; the Lombard cities were disciplined for reforming their league with the intention of resisting Frederick II; and as early as 1031 the Council of Limoges threatened interdiction for the robber barons who fought in violation of the Peace of God.[39]

NONCOOPERATION WITH SOCIAL EVENTS, CUSTOMS AND INSTITUTIONS

60. Suspension of social and sports activities

Social noncooperation may take the form of cancellation of, or refusal to arrange, social and sports activities. This type of social noncooperation may be intended either as a protest by renunciation (hence related to the methods of nonviolent protest and persuasion), or as an attempt to counter efforts (usually by the government) to initiate new controls over the society (hence related to political noncooperation). This method is classed here because it is social in form, although it may be political in intent or result.

During the 1940–45 occupation Norwegians continually refused in one way or another to cooperate in sports activities, both with the Germans and with the Norwegian fascist party, the *Nasjonal Samling.*[40] As early as the summer of 1940 German officers sought to have German-Norwegian football matches. Only a few were played before they were halted, in accordance with a policy adopted in 1939 by both national Norwegian sports organizations prohibiting matches with foreign teams, in support of strict Norwegian neutrality. The prohibition provided a good basis for declining German overtures.

Germans then tried to join Norwegian sports clubs, and officers especially sought out tennis clubs. Everywhere the Norwegians succeeded in declining such an influx of unwanted members. Where German pressure was most persistent, it was settled that the Germans might requisition or rent the tennis courts one or two days a week, but club members stayed away on those days, thwarting Nazi attempts to build friendships with their "Germanic brothers in the North."

Various Norwegian fascist and German attempts were made in September 1940 to establish controls over sports organizations. On October 1 the new Minister of Labor Services and Sports, Axel Stang, ordered the prohibition against international sports contests lifted. Sports organizations' officials, however, insisted on continued freedom and self-determination of sports organizations, without party agitation or interference. On November 4 the annual meetings of sports organizations were banned by the Department for Labor Services and Sports. The steering committee of Norway's Sports Association sent a circular letter to their branches concerning the fascist efforts to establish party control over the sports organizations, and announced that the committee felt unable to continue its activities. No instructions or recommendations for action were given to members. On November 22, Stang announced State control of Norway's Sports Association, with prohibition of dissolution of the constituent organizations; there would be no more elected officials and "Leaders" would be named for each sports organization. A protest letter was drafted by sports officials and sent to Stang; this was later distributed in circulars and illegal papers throughout the country. These officials withdrew, stating that all responsibility now lay with the State Minister.

The members of sports clubs throughout the country now took the initiative—action occurred almost immediately. Plans for wrestling matches between Norway and Denmark had already begun. When the *Nasjonal Samling* (N.S.) official arrived in Tønsberg, where the matches were to be held, he was told that the sixty-four scheduled Norwegian wrestlers had all stayed away. "And thereby the sports front was really created," wrote Olaf Helset, who had been the Chairman of Norway's Sports Association before N.S. control. "Now it was clear that the active sports youths would have nothing to do with the 'New Order.' Now it was necessary to hold the front." [41] With few exceptions, all the activities of the fascist-controlled sports organizations were boycotted, including participation in and attendance at official sports events and contests. The sports strike was not simply conducted on the basis of orders from above, but arose from the rank-and-file members in the sports clubs throughout the country. Illegal and unofficial sports contests in track, skiing, football and tennis were held, however, with high attendance, while official matches attracted almost no spectators.

Helset, later a Major General in the Norwegian Army, described the sports strike as: ". . . the unconditional *no* to every demand for participation in sports contests in which Germans were present, and to the edict to be part of the sports movement for the 'New Order' . . ." Furthermore, he added, "its moral significance for the whole resistance movement lay both in that it was the first organized rally against the German administrative attack and in that it continued under all pressures as long as the war lasted." [42] Thomas Wyller, a Norwegian political scientist analyzing the occupation resistance, points out that the action of the sportsmen "became an example which showed the way when other organizations later were confronted with the choice between existing in a new form or laying down their activities." The sports strike conveyed throughout the whole country the eye-opening message that the Norwegian people were still involved in struggle. [43]

One of the most prominent historians of this period, Magne Skodvin, writes:

> The sports strike extended over the whole country and gathered the greater part of the youth. When the sports people disappeared from the sports grounds—and from the newspaper columns, when they stopped appearing officially completely, then one had either to be very stupid, or very much like a hermit, not to notice it. The Germans and N.S. suffered a serious defeat when the sportsmen refused to play, and no tolerably awake Norwegian could be blind to the pattern which was thereby given. [44]

The sports strike was not officially broken until June 3, 1945, when parades of thousands of sportsmen and crowds of people all over Norway celebrated the end of the struggle and the initiation of new uninhibited sports activities. (Parts of this example are also associated with political noncooperation.)

This method took a somewhat different form in Portugal where in the spring of 1962 students in Coimbra suspended their social and sports activities as a protest against the government; this was intended as a protest by renunciation rather than as an attempt to counter governmental efforts to initiate new controls.[45]

61. Boycott of social affairs

A spirit of resistance may also be expressed by a corporate refusal to attend certain social affairs, such as receptions, banquets, parties, concerts and the like. During the Nazi occupation, for example, the Danes refused to attend concerts of German military music.[46] In late 1940 and early 1941 a wave of "cinema strikes" occurred in Norway in which patrons boycotted the cinemas. These began in Stavanger, where the local cinema board was dismissed for refusing to allow members of Quisling's elite organization (the *Hird*) to enter free. Cinema-going was then suspended elsewhere, culminating in the Oslo cinema strike in February.[47] (This example is also related to the economic boycott.) In Poland during the same period the underground forbade Poles to patronize cinemas and theaters which had been started by the Germans. In 1942 the underground determined that Polish theaters as well as German-operated theaters should be boycotted, and that no Pole should operate such a theater. Jan Karski reports that the predominant reason was that "no Pole could be allowed to forget, even for two hours, what was happening in his country, or to amuse himself. It was forbidden to interrupt the fight and insurrection in permanence against the invader."[48]

62. Student strike

Students and pupils of all types of schools, from elementary schools to universities, may as a means of protest or resistance temporarily refuse to attend classes. Or they may refuse to cooperate in a related way—by boycotting only some, not all, lectures, for example;[49] or students may attend classes but refuse to pay attention, as was done at the University of Madrid in 1965 as part of the campaign for an independent student union.[50] Possible variations are legion. It is more usual, however, for all classes to be boycotted. (Student strikes are also called school boycotts or class boycotts.)

The student strike has long been widely used in China, Latin America, and to a lesser degree Africa;[51] in 1970 following the United States' invasion of Cambodia it became a prominent part of university life in the United States. The student strike is not a modern invention, as the Chinese examples show. Student strikes in China have sometimes taken the form of refusal to take the examinations, sometimes in protest against the lack of impartiality by the examiners. In an edict of 1673, for example, the K'ang-hsi emperor noted that "young scholars in the provinces often went on strike in the local examinations, as a result of their quarrel with local functionaries." The Yung-cheng emperor also noted the same type of action in 1734. This type of student strike was also reported from districts of Kwangtung in 1851, this time in protest against action of the magistrates on taxes and money matters.[52]

Other examples include the strike in May 1935 of students at the Belleville Township High School, near St. Louis, in the United States, in protest against the firing for political reasons of teachers with seniority;[53] the 1960 walkout of half the students at the Jesuit secondary school at Chikuni, Northern Rhodesia, in protest against the expulsion of fourteen boys who, in connection with political agitation, had refused to obey orders;[54] and the sit-down strike by pupils at the Fort Jameson Secondary and Grades Schools, Northern Rhodesia (now Zambia), in March 1960, for the purpose of asking that "political" visits to the schools, such as by the visiting Monckton Commission, be stopped.[55]

In 1899 there was a student strike in all universities of the Russian Empire, in protest against the flogging of some students by the police in St. Petersburg.[56] During the 1905 Revolution the student strike which had begun in February was called off in the autumn in order to open the lecture halls to the public for revolutionary talks and discussions in the evenings.[57] During the Egyptian noncooperation movement of 1919, strikes of schoolboys and students became so frequent that the government had to issue a special order to counter them.[58] The noncooperation movement which toppled Guatemalan strongman Jorge Ubico in June 1944 began with a strike of students at the National University.[59] In the Netherlands in the winter of 1940–41 students at Delft and Leiden went on strike in protest against the dismissal of Jewish professors.[60] Early in 1955 students at the East German University of Greifswald went on strike against a government decree transforming the medical faculty into a military school of medicine directed by the "People's Police."[61]

Student strikes may also be directed against certain grievances directly associated with the schools. This was the case in Glasgow in the autumn of 1963 when parents refused to send their children to school because of school arrangements requiring children to cross a dangerous unfenced canal. Instead, the parents organized their own classes.[62] Similar student strikes have been held in the United States to protest *de facto* racial segregation and bad conditions in schools; this happened in New York City on January 3, 1964, when nearly a half million pupils stayed at home[63] and on February 3, 1964, when forty-four percent of the city's total school population was absent. In the latter case substitute private "freedom schools" were held for the children.[64] In neither case were the teachers on strike. In Chicago on October 22, 1963, 224,000, or ninety percent, of the Negro children stayed away as a protest, and on February 25, 1964, also in Chicago, 172,000 Negro pupils were absent.[65] New York City whites have also applied short-term school boycotts in protest against steps to desegregate neighborhood schools.[66]

Following the United States invasion of Cambodia in May 1970, American colleges and universities, and even some high schools, experienced a wave of student strikes without precedent in United States history. According to the *Newsletter* of the National Strike Information Center at Brandeis University, as of May 10 there were 142 high schools on strike or scheduled to strike, and on May 9, 431 colleges and universities were reported on strike.[67]

63. Social disobedience[68]

This is the disobedience of social customs or the rules, regulations, or practices of a nongovernmental social institution (a religious body, club, economic organization, or the like).[69] Such social disobedience may take many forms—for example, breaking factory regulations (short of striking) or disobeying ecclesiastical orders or violating standard forms of speech, dress and behavior. In other cases, persons who disapprove of a social boycott against certain people may fraternize with them, thereby practicing social disobedience. Persons in India who reject untouchability have often deliberately fraternized with untouchables, defying both the religious taboo and social customs. Although social disobedience may not challenge the government at all, or do so only indirectly, there may nevertheless be a counteraction from those offended by the disobedience. Such retaliation may or may not involve action by police. Violation by U.S. civil rights workers of social taboos against social equality between Negroes and "whites" has sometimes aroused extreme violent responses from archsegregationists. The murder in Mississippi, during the 1964 campaign for Negro voter registration, of James Chaney, Andrew Goodman and Michael Schwerner, one Mississippi Negro and two New York "whites," is one example.[70]

64. Withdrawal from social institutions

During conflicts members of various types of social organizations and institutions may, as a means of expressing their views, either resign membership or withhold participation in the body without actually canceling membership. The examples here refer to religious groups, but this method may be applied to other institutions.

In the 1830s, after the failure of attempts to persuade the churches in the United States to take a stronger stand against slavery, many Garrisonian abolitionists took the radical step of withdrawing membership from their traditional denominations: thus in 1840 an abolitionist editor named Rogers withdrew from the Congregational Church of Plymouth, New Hampshire, after having urged it to no avail to denounce all slaveholding congregations and ministers, and fellowship with them. General Agent Wright of the Nonresistance Society (a group actually dedicated to moral nonviolent resistance) excommunicated his church in the same year before it had a chance to excommunicate him; and Congregational deacon Amos Wood, also a member of the Nonresistance Society in Concord, New Hampshire, had withdrawn from his church and was attending "a little meeting of anti-slavery worshippers." [71] (Where members withdraw because a political party or the State has taken control over their organization, this is classed as boycott of government-supported organizations, a method of political noncooperation.)

WITHDRAWAL FROM THE SOCIAL SYSTEM

65. Stay-at-home

The stay-at-home is often applied in close association with forms of the strike or the *hartal,* although it may be practiced entirely after working hours. In this form of noncooperation the population as a whole remains at home for a set period, usually for a political motive. Normally, the stay-at-home will last a short period, such as one or two days. It is usually organized, although it may be spontaneous. In addition to reducing the chances of "incidents," it may serve to demonstrate to the opponent the degree of unity and self-discipline among the population.

This method has been used in South Africa on several occasions. A one-day stay-at-home was held in that country on June 26, 1950, for example, to protest against the Group Areas Bill and the Suppression of

Communism Bill, and also to mourn the dead of the liberation struggle. It was especially effective in Johannesburg, Port Elizabeth and Durban.[72] Another was held following the shootings in Sharpeville, in March 1960.[73] After the Hungarian Revolution of 1956 was crushed and it was announced that former Premier Imre Nagy and others had been executed, people in Budapest conducted a stay-at-home in the evenings, leaving the streets and places of entertainment deserted.[74]

66. Total personal noncooperation

Very rarely, there have been cases in which a prisoner has literally refused to do almost everything except breathe because he believed his arrest to be unjust for moral or political reasons. The best known case is that of Corbett Bishop, an American religious conscientious objector during World War II. Bishop had initially cooperated with the alternative service program provided for conscientious objectors—Civilian Public Service—but over a period of time he concluded that his beliefs required him to discontinue cooperation in *any* form. Refusing to continue C.P.S. work, Bishop was arrested on September 9, 1944; he announced that his spirit was free and that if the arresting officers wanted his body, they would have to take it without any help from him. In the federal prison at Milan, Michigan, he refused to eat, stand up or dress himself. He was force-fed by tube. After eighty-six days he was brought to trial for walking out of C.P.S. camp, but the judge released him without bond until a decision could be made. Bishop refused to return to court and was rearrested in Philadelphia on February 20, 1945. Bishop then went limp and remained limp during his later hearings. He told the U.S. Commissioner: "I am not going to cooperate in any way, shape or form. I was carried in here. If you hold me, you'll have to carry me out. War is wrong, I don't want any part of it." His limp body was carried into the court in Philadelphia on February 26. Shortly afterward, he was returned to Grand Rapids, where he was fined and sentenced to four years in prison. Bishop continued his complete personal noncooperation and finally, after 144 days, he was paroled without signing any papers or making any promises, under the Special Parole Plan of Executive Order 8641. He was, however, expected to work on a cooperative farm in Georgia, and when he refused to do so he was again arrested, on September 1 in Berea, Ohio, this time as a parole violator. Bishop again went limp, resumed his full noncooperation, and was returned to the Milan prison to finish his uncompleted sentence. After continued refusal by Bishop to do *anything,* and considerable newspaper publicity, the Department of Justice on March 12, 1946, released him on parole, with no conditions and without his signing anything; he returned to his home in Hamilton, Alabama, thus ending 193 days of continuous and total personal noncooperation. [75]

67. "Flight" of workers

This precursor of the strike involved both a cessation of work by the peasants or workers and their leaving their homes and fleeing elsewhere, without demands or conditions being stated for their return. In the Egyptian cases described below the withdrawal seems usually to have been intended to be temporary, though not necessarily short, while in the Russian cases the "flight" seems to have been intended to be permanent, as was usually the case with African slaves in America.

When peasant conditions were intolerable in ancient Egypt the peasants resorted to "flights to the temples to seek the protection of gods or to the swamps and the desert . . ." [76] These cases have important features in common with the next method in this class, "sanctuary." This was a "characteristic feature of Egyptian life" and continued at least into the second century A.D. [77] M. Rostovtzeff writes:

> When the demands [of the State] became intolerable and made life a heavy burden for any group of natives, they resorted to passive resistance, to strikes. A strike was a resolve to submit the case to the judgement of the god, and was effected by leaving their usual place of residence and taking refuge in a temple. Here the strikers remained in idle resignation until the wrong was redressed or compulsion was used to make them resume work. In Greek terminology these strikes were called "secessions" . . . [78]

Under the severe conditions prevailing in the Roman Empire during the first and second centuries, ". . . we hear repeatedly of villages refusing to pay taxes or to perform compulsory work and resorting to the ancient Egyptian practice of striking, that is to say, leaving the villages and taking refuge in the swamps of the Delta." [79] During the reign of Emperor Commodus (176-192 A.D.), "The numbers of those who fled from the villages of Egypt to the swamps of the Delta to escape the burden of levies, compulsory work, and taxes became so large that the fugitives . . . , under the leadership of a priest, could challenge the imperial government." [80]

"Flight" as a type of strike in the Roman Empire was not limited to Egypt, however, for one petition to Emperor Commodus from tenants-peasants on an imperial estate elsewhere in North Africa warned that if their grievances were not righted, "we will flee to some place where we may live as free men." [81]

In the 1860s and 1870s Russian workers of peasant origin sometimes rebelled against extremely severe working conditions by collectively leaving their jobs and returning to peasant life. In 1860 and 1861, for example, mine workers and those engaged in constructing roads and new railway lines refused to continue to work under existing conditions:

> The most serious cases involved not so much abstention from work as "flight"—desertion, intended to be irrevocable, by those who had some hope or possibility of obtaining a piece of land and so resuming their normal lives as peasants. Movements of this kind occurred, for instance, among the men digging the New Canal at Ladoga and other similar undertakings. In one case, in 1861, at least fifty workers were flogged for leaving their work. [82]

Venturi reports that "a few concessions" quickly ended most of these protests. This particular method continued to be used for some years. It clearly was not regarded as a means by which individuals changed jobs, but rather as a means for collective resistance. Venturi adds that between 1870 and 1879 in the Russian Empire there were forty-nine cases in which desertion of work was carried out in an "organized way." [83] "'Flight' was still the means of defence to which the workers sometimes resorted to escape from conditions when they became too oppressive." [84] Where the withdrawal is permanent, this method is closely related to the method of protest emigration described below, although a change in political jurisdiction may not be involved.

Temporary or permanent flight was also used by African slaves in the United States. Slaves who were hired out by their owners to other masters sometimes ran away from the new masters, either returning to their owner or remaining in hiding until they decided to return to work. [85] U.B. Phillips also reports this type of resistance by African slaves:

> Occasionally, . . . a squad would strike in a body as a protest against severities. An episode of this sort was recounted in a letter of a Georgia overseer to his absent employer: "Sir: I write you . . . to let you know that six of your hands has left the plantation. . . They

displeased me with their work, and I give some of them a few lashes . . . On Wednesday morning they were missing. I think they are lying out until they can see you or your uncle Jack . . . ."

The slaves could not negotiate directly at such a time, but while they lay in the woods they might make overtures to the overseer through slaves on a neighboring plantation as to terms upon which they would return to work, or they might await their master's post-haste arrival and appeal to him for a redress of grievances. Humble as their demeanor might be, their power of renewing the pressure by repeating their act could not be ignored.[86]

Frederick Olmsted, a traveler through the slave states in the 1850s, reported cases of flights to "the swamp" by slaves in response to excessive work demands or cruel treatment.

> The slave, if he is indisposed to work, and especially if he is not treated well, or does not like the master who has hired him, will sham sickness—even make himself sick or lame—that he need not work. But a more serious loss frequently arises, when the slave, thinking he is worked too hard, or being angered by punishment or unkind treatment, "getting the sulks," takes to "the swamp," and comes back when he has a mind to. Often this will not be till the year is up for which he is engaged, when he will return to his owner, who, glad to find his property safe, and that it has not died in the swamp, or gone to Canada, forgets to punish him, and immediately sends him for another year to a new master.[87]

The importance of "flight" in the slave struggle is also emphasized by Herbert Apteker, who points to its role in producing bargaining:

> The method most commonly pursued was for the Negroes to flee to outlying swamps or forests, and to send back word that only if their demands—perhaps for better food or clothes, or fewer beatings, shorter hours, or even a new overseer—were met (or, at least, discussed) would they willingly return. It is interesting to observe that during the Civil War the slaves added a new demand, the payment of money wages, and at times won, thus "lifting themselves by their own boot-straps" from chattels to wage workers.[88]

The latter is potentially of extreme significance as it points to the possibility of self-liberation by nonviolent struggle by the slaves themselves.

African slaves in the United States also undertook "flight" as a means of full escape from slavery by leaving slave territory. One of the early places to which they went was Spanish Florida. In the 1730s many slaves escaped into the Spanish territory of Florida, where they had been promised—and received—freedom under Spanish law. A royal decree had been issued in 1733 to the effect that all fugitive slaves reaching Florida would be permitted to live there as freemen.[89]

Later, many slaves, often with the help of abolitionist groups, escaped to Northern states and frequently went on to Canada. The escape network, called the Underground Railroad, enabled many to reach freedom. Their legal status in Northern states, however, varied from state to state and changed with legislation and court decisions; these particular "flights" therefore have characteristics of both "flight" and protest emigrations in varying proportions.

68. Sanctuary[90]

Sanctuary is an unusual method whereby an individual or, more often, a group of people important to the opponent withdraws to a place where they cannot be touched without violation of religious, moral, social or legal prohibitions. Such violation would, in turn, put the opponent in a new and difficult situation. Temples, churches and other holy places have frequently been such places of refuge. When ancient Egyptian peasants took "flight" to temples, as described in the preceding method, they were using a combination of flight and sanctuary; when they went to hide in the swamps they were using only the method of "flight." There are examples within both the Christian and the Islamic traditions.

In medieval Christian Europe even professed murderers and felons, as well as the innocent, could obtain safety within the sanctuary of shrines and sacred places. The present status of sanctuary in Roman Catholic ecclesiastical law is defined in canon 1179 of the still authoritative *Codex juris canonici* promulgated by Pope Benedict XV in 1917, which is based on earlier codes and laws.[91]

During 1968 the idea of sanctuary was revived in the United States within the context of resistance to military conscription. First in churches and later in universities, a kind of symbolic sanctuary was offered to young men wanted for arrest on grounds of disobedience to military conscription orders. The Rev. William Sloane Coffin delivered a sermon which discussed the subject at a "Service of Acceptance" at the Arlington Street Unitarian-Universalist Church in Boston, when three hundred young men turned their draft cards over to clergymen. Coffin said:

Now if in the Middle Ages churches could offer sanctuary to the most common of criminals, could they not today do the same for the most conscientious among us? . . . . should a church declare itself a "sanctuary for conscience" this should be considered less a means to shield a man, more a means to expose a church, an effort to make a church really a church.

For if the state should decide that the arm of the law was long enough to reach inside a church there would be little church members could do to prevent an arrest. But the members could point out what they had already dramatically demonstrated, that the sanctity of conscience was being violated.[92]

On May 20, 1968, that Boston church offered sanctuary to Robert Talmanson and William Chase, both wanted for acts of disobedience to military duty. On May 23 they were arrested. Talmanson, going limp, was carried from the pulpit where he was reading from the writings of Lao-tse. A Roman Catholic priest, Father Anthony Mullaney, told arresting officers as they entered that they were about "to violate a moral sanctuary." He and another priest were among those beaten outside the church and arrested.

Similar cases of sanctuary took place in Providence, Rhode Island, and churches in New York City, Detroit and San Francisco declared themselves open to those seeking sanctuary.[93] After sanctuaries were provided in chapels at the Harvard Divinity School and Boston University, a nonreligious sanctuary was conducted in the Student Center of the Massachusetts Institute of Technology. Other university sanctuaries were held as far apart as the City College of New York and the University of Hawaii. Noting that in the United States there was no legal recognition of the custom of sanctuary, which had once existed both in Europe and in old Hawaii, the University of Hawaii Resistance group stated: "Yet as a symbol of resistance to injustice, sanctuary remains effective today in stirring the conscience of man."[94]

Probably the most politically significant cases of the use of sanctuary occurred in the Persian Revolution in 1905-06,[95] in combination with certain other methods including the closing of bazaars. These Persian examples are sufficiently important to merit fairly detailed descriptions. Such sanctuary was powerful because the Shah's authority was believed to derive from religious sources; hence, when Islamic leaders of Persia went into sanctuary they were in fact withdrawing the religious basis of his right to rule.

There had been various grounds for dissatisfaction with the Shah, Muzaffaru'd-Din: he was disliked for his extravagance, his love of foreign travel, the tariffs imposed by his imported Belgian officials and their arrogance, the exploitation of the country by foreign *concessionnaries,* and the tyranny of his main Minister, Grand Vizier Abdu'l Hamíd, who was known by his title, *'Aynu'd-Dawla.* This powerful nobleman was also believed to be cooperating with the Belgians and Russians against Persian interests.

When the Shah in April 1905 undertook a pilgrimage to Mashhad, he traveled through Russian territory to reach it and was accompanied by a Russian official; there was disapproval in the Persian capital of Tehran. Many merchants therefore retired to Sháh 'Abdu'l-'Azím, a holy shrine near Tehran, and the bazaars were closed for five days.

Later, various new grievances developed. One of those was the government violence at Mashhad under the oppressive rule of *Áṣaf'd-Dawla.* This official had ordered his soldiers to fire on a crowd of people who in protest against his exactions had taken refuge within the holy precincts of the Shrine of Imám Rizá. *Mullás* (Islamic teachers) and businessmen also had been beaten (bastinadoed).

As a result, in December 1905 a large number of merchants took sanctuary in the Royal Mosque, called Masjid-i-Shah. They were shortly joined by many of the chief *mullás.* The *Imám-Jum'a,* or prayer leader of the congregation, himself a wealthy relative of the Shah, was asked by the Grand Vizier to disperse them. After violent eviction by the followers of the *Imám-Jum'a,* the expelled *mullás* and a few others left the city and took refuge in the holy shrine of Sháh 'Abdu'l-Azím. There was a difference in kind between a mosque and a holy shrine, a shrine being far more sacred. They were joined at the shrine by many others, *mullás* and students, including Shaykh Fazlu'lláh, who was to become famous as one of the three founders of the Constitutional Movement. The aim of this action, however, was simply the dismissal of the disliked *'Aynu'd-Dawla,* the Grand Vizier; for this there was wide support.

The taking of sanctuary was known in Persian as *bast,* and those taking sanctuary were called *bastis.* Three prominent persons including the Crown Prince, Mohamed Ali Mirza, contributed large sums of money for food and other supplies for the *bastis.* The Crown Prince is reported also to have urged the *mullás* of Tabriz to support the *bast.* Despite efforts of *'Aynu'd-Dawla* to prevent new volunteers and supplies from reaching the sanctuary, both got through. More *mullás* and theological students, as well as merchants and traders, joined in the *bast.* The Shah's threats and promises failed to induce them to return to the capital of Tehran, and even a personal trip by the Amír Bahadur Jang, an army commander, accompanied by three hundred horsemen, failed to persuade the *bastis* to return from sanctuary.

The historian Edward G. Browne writes of the events of January 1906:

> At length the scandal became so grave and the inconvenience so intolerable that the Sháh sent them a *dast-khatt*, or autograph letter, promising to dismiss *'Aynu'd-Dawla;* to convene the 'Adálat-khána, or "House of Justice," which they now demanded, and which was to consist of representatives elected by the clergy, merchants and landed proprietors, and presided over by the Shah himself; to abolish favouritism and to make all Persian subjects equal in the eyes of the law. [96]

After photographic copies of this letter had been distributed throughout the country, the *bastis* returned to Tehran with great pomp, the leaders riding in the royal carriages, and were received by the Shah, who verbally renewed his promises. However, soon there were attempts to interpret away certain of these concessions; the "House of Justice" had never been intended to be a Legislative Assembly, it was said, but only a judicial court. As the weeks went on, there were new grounds for dissatisfaction, including currency problems. Toward the end of April 1906 the *mullás* of Tehran presented a petition to the Shah, asking that the promised reforms be implemented and that he use his executive power in accord with the laws. The petition was published in the official *Gazette,* but it had no results. Things steadily got worse. Spies were everywhere. Cossacks and soldiers filled the streets. A curfew was imposed three hours after sunset. There were more protests against the Grand Vizier, *'Aynu'd-Dawla,* and Islamic leaders preached sermons against autocracy and tyranny. A free National Library was set up to educate the people in patriotic ideas, and a secret society was formed.

The Shah suffered a paralytic stroke, and *'Aynu'd-Dawla* decided on repression. Annoyed by the denunciations of himself from the pulpit, the Grand Vizier expelled Ágá Sayyid Jamal, who then retired to the theological center of Qum, built around the shrine of an important female saint. Then *'Aynu'd-Dawla* also decided to expel Shaykh Muhammad, a very effective preacher *(Wá'iz),* who was very popular among the artisans and humble folk of the bazaars. A crowd of people gathered around the preacher and the soldiers and attempted to prevent his removal. After

Shaykh Muhammad had been imprisoned in a guardhouse, a student who was a descendant of Mohammed rushed at the door trying to free him. The soldiers disobeyed orders and refused to fire, but an officer personally killed the young man. The date was June 21, 1906. The body of the dead Sayyid Husayn was then carried through the streets and bazaars; there were rioting and clashes between people and soldiers who had tried to stop the procession. Fifteen people were killed by shootings into the crowd. The soldiers succeeded in clearing the streets and occupied the whole town. But a large number of *mullás, rawza-khwáns* (who recite to the common people narratives about the sufferings of Mohammed's spiritual descendants), students, merchants, tradesmen, artisans and humble people then took sanctuary in the Masjid-i-Jami, the Mosque of Assembly, in the city's center. There they buried the body of the dead student. They were besieged by soldiers for three or four days, after which the Shah granted their request for permission to leave the city and to retire to Qum, ninety miles to the south.

They left for Qum about July 21. Thousands of people joined the clerical leaders in this procession from the capital to Qum; one Persian author said the road between the two places "was like the street of a town." Among Persians this is known as "the Great Exodus" *(Hijrat-i-Kubrá)*. One historian of Persia writes: "This action amounted to a withdrawal of religious sanction for the regime and thus challenged its legitimacy." [97] The Shah's permission for the *bastis* to leave the Masjid-i-Jami to go to Qum had been given on the condition that the *mujtahids* ("supreme religious judges" of the dominant Shia sect of Islam) depart from the mosque alone. On their way to Qum, these *mujtahids* issued a notice threatening to leave Persia completely unless the Shah fulfilled his promises. General Percy Sykes reports: "As their absence would stop all legal transactions, this threat was really a serious one, for it would be equivalent to placing the land under an interdict." [98]

Meanwhile the bazaars and shops had been closed in protest, and *'Aynu'd-Dawla* had ordered them to open, under threat of looting. On July 19 a few bankers and merchants were assured by the British *Chargé d'Affaires* that if they took refuge in the British Legation in the capital, they would be allowed to remain symbolically under British protection. A few of them proceeded at once to the Legation garden and encamped there. By July 23 their numbers had increased to 858; three days later there were five thousand, all in the Legation grounds. These merchants demanded, as the price for their return to their homes and normal activities, the dismissal of Grand Vizier *'Aynu'd-Dawla,* the promulgation of a Code of Laws, and the recall from Qum of the ecclesiastical leaders.

The Shah, greatly vexed and perplexed, decided on July 30 so far to yield to the popular demands as to dismiss *'Aynu'd-Dawla,* appoint in his place the popular and liberal Mirza Nasru'lláh Khán, *Mushiru'd-Dawla,* and invite the *mullás* to return from Qum to the capital . . .[99]

The people no longer trusted the Shah, however, and demanded a regular constitution, a representative National Assembly, and satisfactory guarantees of the Shah's good faith. By August 1 there were thirteen thousand persons in sanctuary at the British Legation, and the number still grew, reaching at least fourteen thousand (some said sixteen thousand). During the *bast* at the Legation, according to a British eyewitness, there were tents everywhere. People policed themselves "in a most remarkable manner" and gave little trouble; meals were cooked in enormous caldrons; and at night old, old stories were told.[100] For a long time the *bastis* refused direct negotiations with the Government. Finally, through the good offices of the British representative, an acceptable document was drafted. On August 5, his birthday, the Shah, Muzaffaru'd-Din, granted all the demands of the *bastis,* who then left the Legation. The hated Grand Vizier was ordered to proceed to his estate. The document the Shah issued that day has been called "The *Magna Charta* of Persia."[101]

This same eyewitness to the events reports that the 1905 Russian Revolution had had "a most astounding effect here. Events in Russia have been watched with great attention, and a new spirit would seem to have come over the people. They are tired of their rulers, and, taking examples of Russia, have come to think that it is possible to have another and better form of government."[102] The writer also added, evaluating the whole moment, that after the riots, which followed the killing of the student, Sayyid:

> Finding that they were unable to oppose armed resistance to the Government, the people decided to take *bast* in the British Legation, and this proved a very successful method of obtaining their ends. . . . the exiled *mullás* have asked to return, and will be brought back in triumph, and the Courts of Justice are to be established.[103]

In short, writes General Sykes, "without bloodshed or civil war, the Persians had gained on paper everything demanded by their leaders."[104]

Shortly after the Shah yielded, the religious leaders from Qum returned to the capital escorted by *'Aṣudu'l-Mulk* (who later became Regent) and Ḥájji Niẓamu'd-Dawla. It was a day of great rejoicing over the "National Victory" *(Fath-i-Milli)*. On August 19 the new House of Parliament was opened by the ailing Shah, in the presence of high ecclesiastical authorities who were the Shah's guests for three days. A few days earlier, a proclamation had been issued announcing the establishment as well of a National Consultative Assembly.

About September 8, 1906, fresh friction arose when the *mullás* refused to accept the ordinances drafted by the Prime Minister, and the Shah refused to allow the changes they demanded. Again *bastis* took sanctuary in the British Legation, and the bazaars were closed. The Shah gave way to the demands concerning electoral districts, membership in the *Majlis* (parliament), and qualifications for election. On September 17, the Shah accepted the proposed ordinance concerning the constitution of the *Majlis,* setting up a parliament of 156 members elected every two years (directly in the capital and by colleges of electors in the provinces), and providing that the deputies were to be inviolable. "Thus," writes Richard Cottam, "by utilizing the time-honored, almost sacrosanct, institution of *bast* the merchants and clergy were able to force their demands for a constitution upon the government." [105] Many problems still remained, but parliamentary constitutional government was thereby established.

69. Collective disappearance

At times the population of a small area, such as a village, may choose to cut off any social contact with the opponent by disappearing and abandoning their homes and village. As one example, the peasants of Kanara in South India used this method in 1799 and 1800 in opposing British attempts to establish rule over them. The British officer in charge, Sir Thomas Munro, wrote that ". . . whenever I approached a village, the inhabitants went to another, so that I was sometimes several weeks in a district without seeing one of them . . ." [106]

E.C. Barber, a nineteenth century English writer, reported an incident of collective disappearance which took place in central China in 1883:

"In very early times," it was said, the magistrate of a *hsien* in central China was directed by the governor "to institute a census of the population." Being dissatisfied with the returns sent in by his subordinates the magistrate undertook to count the inhabitants himself.

The population "alarmed at the pertinacity of the [official] and apprehensive that he was coming to levy some oppressive tax, fled from the city and hid themselves in the fields." The official was thus frustrated in his efforts, and hanged himself to escape the expected punishment. He left the following note:

"Men .... none
Women .... none
Children under 14 years of age, of both sexes .... none

Total .... none" [107]

George Taylor, in describing North China during the Japanese occupation in 1939, also cited similar instances:

So well organized are the villages now that when the Japanese approach, the people evacuate the village completely, bury their food, remove all animals and utensils, and retire into the hills. The Japanese must, therefore, bring with them everything they need. [108]

70. Protest emigration *(hijrat)*

Protest emigration, called *hijrat* in India, is a deliberate emigration from the jurisdiction of the State responsible for certain injustices or oppression in the eyes of the resisters with the objective of expressing their disapproval and protest by this complete severance of all forms of social cooperation. Hence, only certain special cases of emigration are included here. It is sometimes intended to be permanent and at other times is intended to be temporary, especially where the opponent needs cooperation of some type from the emigrants. Joan Bondurant calls this method "voluntary exile." [109] Arabic in origin, the term *hijrat* (also spelled *hizrat)* derives from *hejira,* the flight of Mohammed from Mecca to Medina, which he chose instead of submission to the tyranny in Mecca. [110]

Hijrat (also called in India *deshatyaga*—giving up the country) [111] was extensively used in India during the various campaigns against specific injustices and for independence during British rule. There it was a spontaneous, though peculiar, offshoot of the various "no-tax" campaigns. In terms of Gandhi's teachings, the bravest course was for the *satyagrahis* cheerfully to suffer the worst repression which might be meted out to them, in the belief that this would have the greatest effect in achieving their goals and in melting the hearts of the opponent. However, if the resisters and population felt oppressed and unable to have self-respect while living under such circumstances and if they lacked the strength to bear such repression—strength which came either from a deep inner conviction in *ahimsa* (nonviolence) or from the capacity (though not the willingness) to defend themselves violently—then Gandhi felt there was nothing immoral, dishonorable, or cowardly about self-imposed exile. *Hijrat* was a physical withdrawal from the territory controlled by the State, at the sacrifice of all interests which the emigrants had there. It provided a nonviolent way out of an unbearable situation.[112] This method has been interpreted as a final effort of noncooperation. Clearly, where large portions of the population are involved, this method becomes a form of political noncooperation and not simply an instance of nonviolent protest.

Hijrat was used by the peasants of Gujarat who migrated to Baroda (where the British had no jurisdiction) during the repression following their refusal to pay taxes during the 1930-31 campaign.[113] Similarly, it was used during the 1928 Bardoli tax-refusal campaign, when peasants from Bardoli district also emigrated temporarily to Baroda.[114]

Other examples of protest emigrations range from that of the plebians in 494 B.C. to secure reforms from the patricians of the Roman Republic,[115] described in Chapter Two, to those of various persecuted religious and political groups from Europe to America,[116] and the mass emigrations from Hungary during the 1956 Revolution.[117] It is also reported by Clarence Marsh Case that similar methods were considered in China for combatting foreign control of pockets along the Chinese coast in the days when the Western powers had gained territorial enclaves in China; it was proposed to organize the population of these areas to participate in a "wholesale exodus from foreign concessions" as a drastic means of protest.[118]

Japanese peasants, especially around the middle of the nineteenth century, during the Tokugawa Period, resorted to this type of method to deal with oppressive feudal barons and corrupt officials. The peasants migrated out of the jurisdiction of their opponents and into a neighboring fief or province. These actions were called "desertions," or *chō-san*.[119] Hugh Borton writes:

> Originally, individuals would secretly desert into a neighbouring village or fief to avoid some specific grievance or hardship, but gradually the habit developed into an organized group of one or more villages leaving en masse. If the villagers crossed into the neighbouring fief or province, they would petition the lord of that fief that they

either be allowed to remain within his domain, or that he intervene on their behalf. [120]

Chōsan was most prevalent in the early part of the Tokugawa Period (1603–1867) [121]; the largest such case of the Period occurred in 1853, when some peasants in the north of the Nambu fief at Morioka, angry at the general corruption among the fief officials and their monopoly of all transactions, deserted to Sendai, a neighboring fief, asking to be allowed to live there and finally presenting their complaints to the Sendai officials. [122] It is reported that *chōsan* were illegal and that the feudal barons would send officials out to bring back the peasants who had fled into another fief, but it is not clear whether the permission of the neighboring baron was required for such recapture. The whole feudal structure depended on the ability of the peasant to produce, and hence officials were reluctant to punish the returned peasants whose rice-producing capacity was much needed. [123] One estimate is that *chōsan* constituted 9.2 percent of the peasant uprisings of the Tokugawa Period. [124]

In addition to the large-scale general migration from the German Democratic Republic (East Germany) prior to the building of the Berlin Wall, protest emigration from East Germany also occurred because of specific measures. For example, East German farmers in 1952 expressed their opposition to the introduction of Soviet-like cooperative farms by emigration to the West; between January and April 22, 852 farmers left. [125]

Protest emigrations in large numbers may, as the above Chinese plan suggests, take on the character of political noncooperation. For example, when Frederick William of Prussia threatened them with compulsory military service in 1723, Mennonites living in East Prussia emigrated to Pennsylvania in such large numbers that the project was abandoned. New regulations of 1787 and 1801 which were intended to check the growth of the Mennonites led to a new emigration, this time to Russia, so the government again made concessions. [126] Action thus intended to enable the believers to maintain their religious principles by a total withdrawal from all relations with the interfering government, nevertheless produced political concessions.

The more usual forms of noncooperation in modern societies, however, are not social but economic, and sometimes political. It is to the two main types of economic noncooperation to which we now turn our attention.

NOTES

1. F. Sheehy-Skiffington, **Michael Davitt: Revolutionary, Agitator and Labor Leader** (London and Leipsic: T. Fisher Unwin, 1908), p. 232.
2. Schlesinger, **The Colonial Merchants and the American Revolution,** p. 77.
3. *Ibid.,* p. 111-112.
4. *Ibid.,* p. 129-130.
5. *Ibid.,* p. 162.
6. *Ibid.,* pp. 504-505.
7. See *ibid.,* pp. 292, 301, 316, 319, 324 and 352, and Gipson, **The British Empire Before the American Revolution,** vol. XII, **The Triumphant Empire, Britain Sails into the Storm, 1770-1776,** pp. 162, 170 and 196.
8. Gipson, **The British Empire . . .** vol. XII, p. 162.
9. Jutikkala, **A History of Finland,** pp. 233-234.
10. B. Pattabhi Sitamarayya, **The History of the Indian National Congress, 1885-1935** (Madras: Working Committee of the Congress, 1935), vol. I, p. 684.
11. *Ibid.,* p. 869.
12. Reynolds, **Labor Economics and Labor Relations,** p. 33.
13. Charles Loch Mowat, **Britain Between the Wars, 1918-1940** (London: Methuen & Co. Ltd., 1955), p. 64. I am grateful to William Hamilton for this reference.
14. Karski, **The Story of a Secret State,** p. 235.
15. *Ibid.,* pp. 260-261.
16. Littell, ed., **The Czech Black Book,** p. 151.
17. *Ibid.,* p. 145.
18. **Report of the Advisory Commission on the Review of the Constitution of Rhodesia and Nyasaland,** Cmnd. 1148 (London: H.M. Stationery Office, 1960), pp. 8 and 17.
19. Clifford Lloyd, **Ireland Under the Land League: A Narrative of Personal Experiences** (Edinburgh and London: William Blackwood & Sons, 1892), p. 78.
20. Sternstein, "The *Ruhrkampf* of 1923," p. 116.
21. Conversation with Hagbard Jonassen, Virum, Denmark, March 1957 and Bennett, "The Resistance Against the German Occupation of Denmark 1940-5," p. 159.
22. Conversation with Haakon and Lotta Holmboe, Asker, Norway, 1957, and various later conversations with others.
23. Wyller, **Nyordning og Motstand,** p. 63.
24. Suzanne Berger, **Peasants Against Politics: Rural Organization in Brittany, 1911-1967** (Cambridge, Mass.: Harvard University Press, 1972), p. 204.
25. Littell, ed., **The Czech Black Book,** p. 111. See also pp. 75 and 114.
26. Sternstein, "The *Ruhrkampf* of 1923," p. 116.

27. *New York Times,* 6 December 1956.
28. Harcave, **First Blood,** p. 101.
29. George Katkov, **Russia 1917: The February Revolution** (New York: Harper & Row, 1967), pp. 211, 211 n. 1, and 218.
30. *Ibid.,* p. 351.
31. Stan Steiner, **The New Indians** (New York: Harper & Row, 1968), p. 220. My attention was called to this by Margaret DeMarco, "The Use of Non-violent Direct Action Tactics and Strategy by American Indians," unpublished research paper, Upland School of Social Change, Upland, Pa., July 1968).
32. *Guardian* (Manchester and London), 31 December 1963, and *Peace News,* 10 January 1964.
33. This section and the next on interdict are based on a draft by Michael Schulter.
34. Margaret Deanesly, **A History of the Medieval Church, 590-1500** (London: Methuen and Co. Ltd., 1965), pp. 102-103.
35. *Ibid.,* p. 103.
36. Carleton Mabee, **Black Freedom: The Nonviolent Abolitionists from 1830 Through the Civil War** (New York: Macmillan Co., 1970), pp. 217-221.
37. Edward B. Krehbiel, **The Interdict, Its History and Its Operation** (Washington: American Historical Association, 1909), pp. 13 and 9.
38. *Ibid.,* pp. 11-12.
39. *Ibid.,* pp. 26-27.
40. This description is largely based upon Major General Olaf Helset, "Idretts-fronten," in Steen, gen. ed., **Norges Krig,** vol. III, pp. 7-34.
41. *Ibid.,* p. 25.
42. *Ibid.,* p. 8.
43. Wyller, **Nyordning og Motstand,** p. 11.
44. Magne Skodvin, "Det Store Fremstot," in Steen, gen. ed., **Norges Krig,** vol. II, pp. 640-641.
45. *Peace News,* 18 May 1962.
46. Bennett, "The Resistance Against the German Occupation of Denmark 1940-5," p. 159.
47. Magne Skodvin, "Det Store Fremstot," p. 624.
48. Karski, **The Story of a Secret State,** p. 260.
49. Michael Prawdin, **The Unmentionable Nechaev,** p. 21.
50. *Peace News,* 5 March 1965.
51. Case, **Non-violent Coercion,** p. 333, and L. L. Bernard, **Social Control in its Sociological Aspects** (New York: Macmillan, 1939), pp. 387-388.
52. Hsiao, **Rural China,** pp. 246-247.
53. Bernard, **Social Control in its Sociological Aspects,** p. 388.
54. *The Observer* (London), 20 March 1960.
55. *Ibid.,* 13 March 1960.
56. Seton-Watson, **The Decline of Imperial Russia,** p. 145, and Keep, **The Rise of Social Democracy in Russia,** p. 70.
57. Keep, **The Rise of Social Democracy in Russia,** pp. 217-218.
58. Brockway, **Non-co-operation in Other Lands,** p. 35.
59. *New York Times,* 24 and 27 June 1944.
60. Warmbrunn, **The Dutch Under German Occupation,** p. 105.

61. Brant, **The East German Rising**, p. 181.

62. *Peace News,* 29 November 1963.

63. *Ibid.,* 14 February 1964.

64. *Ibid.,* 21 February 1964.

65. *Ibid.,* 6 March 1964.

66. Waskow, **From Race Riot to Sit-In,** p. 280.

67. National Strike Information Center (Brandeis University, Waltham, Mass.), *Newsletter,* no. 8, 12 May 1970, p. 9 and dittoed 6 pp. memo "Colleges on Strike — State by State Breakdown," 9 May 1970.

68. This description is based upon a draft prepared by Michael Schulter.

69. This is a more narrow usage than suggested by Seifert, **Conquest by Suffering,** pp. 17-18.

70. *Newsweek,* 17 August 1964, p. 28.

71. Mabee, **Black Freedom,** pp. 221-243. I am grateful to Michael Schulter for these examples.

72. Luthuli, **Let My People Go,** pp. 108-110. See also pp. 170 and 182.

73. *The Times,* 29 and 30 March 1960.

74. Lajos Lederer, *The Observer,* 22 June 1958.

75. Mulford Q. Sibley and Philip E. Jacob, **Conscription of Conscience: The American State and the Conscientious Objector, 1940-1947** (Ithaca, N.Y.: Cornell University Press, 1952), pp. 401-409.

76. Rostovtzeff, **The Social and Economic History of the Roman Empire,** vol. I, p. 179. I am grateful to Margaret Jackson Rothwell for these references.

77. *Ibid.,* vol. II, p. 677, n. 52.

78. *Ibid.,* vol. I, p. 274.

79. *Ibid.,* p. 348.

80. *Ibid.,* p. 374.

81. *Ibid.,* 398.

82. Venturi, **Roots of Revolution,** p. 507.

83. *Ibid.,* p. 509.

84. *Ibid.,* p. 510.

85. Raymond A. and Alice H. Bauer, "Day to Day Resistance to Slavery," **Journal of Negro History,** vol. XXVII, no. 4 (Oct. 1942), pp. 400-401.

86. Ulrich Bonnell Phillips, **American Negro Slavery: A Survey of the Supply, Employment and Control of Negro Labor as Determined by the Plantation Regime** (New York: Peter Smith, 1952 [orig. 1918], pp. 303-304.

87. Frederick Law Olmsted, **A Journey in the Seaboard Slave States, with Remarks on Their Economy** (New York: Dix and Edwards, 1856, and London: Sampson Low, Son & Co., 1856), p. 100. I am grateful to Ron McCarthy for this illustration.

88. Herbert Apteker, **American Negro Slave Revolts** (New York: International Publishers, 1964), p. 142. I am grateful to Marilyn Saunders for this citation.

89. Apteker, **American Negro Slave Revolts,** p. 174.

90. This section is based on a suggestion by James Prior, who has also provided the cited references, and clarified certain matters related to Persian terms and religious customs.

91. George Huntston Williams, "The Ministry and the Draft in Historical Perspective," in Donald Cutler, ed., **The Religious Situation** – **1969** (Boston: Beacon Press, 1969), pp. 464-512.

92. Quoted in J. Dennis Willigan, S. J., "Sanctuary: A Communitarian Form of Counter-Culture," *Union Seminary Quarterly Review,* vol. XXV, no. 4 (Summer, 1970), p. 532. See esp. his discussion on pp. 531-539. For further discussion and case material, see Cutler, ed., **The Religious Situation** – **1969**, pp. 513-537.

93. *Ibid.,* p. 534.

94. *Ibid.,* p. 539.

95. This account is based upon the following sources: Edward G. Browne, **The Persian Revolution of 1905-1909** (Cambridge, England: University Press, 1910), pp. 111-124; Brigadier-General Sir Percy Sykes, **A History of Persia** (London: Macmillan & Co. Ltd., 1963), vol. II, pp. 394-405; and Richard W. Cottam, **Nationalism in Iran** (Pittsburgh: University of Pittsburgh Press, 1964), pp. 139-141.

96. Browne, **The Persian Revolution of 1905-1909,** p. 114.

97. Cottam, **Nationalism in Iran,** p. 141.

98. Sykes, **A History of Persia,** p. 402.

99. Browne, **The Persian Revolution of 1905-1909,** p. 119.

100. *Ibid.,* p. 120.

101. Sykes, **A History of Persia,** p. 403. The full text of that document is published on pp. 403-404.

102. Browne, **The Persian Revolution of 1905-1909,** p. 120.

103. *Ibid.,* p. 121.

104. Sykes, **A History of Persia,** p. 404.

105. Cottam, **Nationalism in Iran,** p. 141.

106. Quoted by Diwaker, **Satyagraha,** p. 147.

107. E. C. Baber, "China in Some of Its Physical and Social Aspects," **Proceedings of the Royal Geographical Society,** N. S., V, (1883), pp. 442-43. Quoted in Hsiao, **Rural China,** p. 582, n. 143. Hsiao comments that although "this story may not literally be true, . . .the situation which it illustrates is authentic."

108. George R. Taylor, **The Struggle for North China,** p. 171. New York: Institute of Pacific Relations, 1940.

109. Bondurant, **Conquest of Violence,** p. 41.

110. On the origin of the term *hijrat* see Shridharani, **War Without Violence,** U.S. ed., p. 28; Br. ed., p. 47.

111. Bondurant, **Conquest of Violence,** p. 119.

112. For Gandhi's views on *hijrat,* see for example Gandhi, **Non-violent Resistance** pp. 212 and 289; Ind. ed.: **Satyagraha,** pp. 212 and 289.

113. Sharp, **Gandhi Wields . . . ,** pp. 188, 190 and 197-198.

114. Shridharani, **War Without Violence,** U. S. ed., pp. 97-98; Br. ed., p. 101.

115. Cowell, **The Revolutions of Ancient Rome,** pp. 41-43.

116. Allan Nevins and Henry Steele Commander, **America: The Story of a Free People** (Boston: Little, Brown and Co., 1943), pp. 12-13 and 29.

117. George Mikes, **The Hungarian Revolution,** pp. 172-173.

118. Case, **Non-violent Coercion**, pp. 345-346. For another example, see Pieter Geyl, **The Revolt of the Netherlands, 1555-1609** (New York: Barnes and Noble, 1958, and London: Ernest Benn, 1962), p. 201.

119. Hugh Borton, **Peasant Uprisings in Japan of the Tokugawa Period** (Second ed.; New York: Paragon Book Reprint Corp, 1968 [First published in **The Transactions of the Asiastic Society of Japan** (Second Ser.), vol. XVI, 1938.]) Preface [p. iii]. I am grateful to Carl Horne for calling my attention to this reference.

120. *Ibid.,* pp. 30-31.

121. *Ibid.,* Preface, [p. iii].

122. *Ibid.,* p. 31.

123. *Ibid.,* Preface [pp. iii-iv].

124. *Ibid.,* p. 31, n. 53. For other details, see also pp. 65-66 and 144 ff.

125. Brant, **The East German Rising,** p. 37.

126. Margaret E. Hirst, **The Quakers in Peace and War** (New York: George H. Doranco, 1923, and London: Swarthmore Press, 1923), p. 32.

5

The Methods
of Economic
Noncooperation:
(1) Economic Boycotts

INTRODUCTION

Economic forms of noncooperation are much more numerous than the forms of social noncooperation, identified above. Economic noncooperation consists of a suspension of or refusal to continue specific economic relationships. The first subclass within the broad class of economic noncooperation is that of economic boycotts—the refusal to continue or to undertake certain economic relationships, especially the buying, selling, or handling of goods and services. The second subclass consists of various forms of the strike, which involves the restriction or suspension of labor. The next chapter is devoted to the strike, while our focus here is on economic boycotts.

Economic boycotts may be spontaneous, or they may be deliberately initiated by a particular group. In either case, they usually become organized efforts to withdraw, and to induce others to withdraw, economic cooperation in ways which restrict the buying or selling market of an individual or group.[1] Although the word boycott did not come into use until 1880, when it originated with the name of a Captain Boycott against whom the peasants of Mayo County, Ireland, were protesting,[2] examples of this method of noncooperation go back much earlier. The boycott has been practiced on local, regional, national and international levels both by persons directly involved in the grievance and by sympathetic third parties. Motivations and objectives have varied from economic and political to social and cultural.

Economic boycotts have been practiced mainly in labor struggles and national liberation movements, although their use in other situations is not unknown. The economic boycott in industrial disputes had its origin in the American trade union movement,[3] where it emerged in 1880 "almost without warning . . . to become for the next ten or fifteen years the most effective weapon of unionism. There was no object so mean and no person so exalted as to escape its power."[4]

Economic boycotts for nationalist objectives against foreign powers appear to have been most frequently used in China; those cases seem to have drawn upon earlier Chinese experience in economic noncooperation, as Professor John K. Fairbank suggests. He writes that "in Chinese life the boycott had been a widely used form of passive resistance, or nonviolent coercion, by which organized groups such as merchant guilds could exert their influence upon officialdom. In the twentieth century they began to be used as expressions of anti-foreignism." As examples he cites the boycott of American products sponsored in 1905 by the merchant guilds of Canton in protest against the exclusion of Chinese from the United States, the boycotts of Japanese goods in 1908 and 1915 in protest against that country's policies, and the prolonged boycott and strike against the British which began in Hong Kong in 1925.[5]

One way of viewing economic boycotts is to divide them into primary and secondary boycotts. The primary boycott is the direct suspension of dealings with the opponent or a refusal to buy, use, or handle his goods or services (sometimes accompanied by efforts to persuade others to do likewise). The secondary boycott is the economic boycott of third parties in an effort to induce them to join in the primary boycott against the opponent. It occurs "where those who fail to support the original movement are themselves boycotted."[6] Leo Wolman defines a secondary boycott as "a combination to withdraw patronage from a person in order to force that person in turn to withdraw his patronage from that individual or firm with whom the union is primarily at odds."[7]

A secondary boycott took place in the United States in 1921 when the International Association of Machinists boycotted not only the Duplex Printing Co., with which it was involved in a conflict, but also all those firms which continued to use the products made by that company.[8] Another American example of a secondary boycott occurred in period preceding the War of Independence, when merchants and other persons were themselves boycotted economically if they did not observe the boycott of English commodities which was part of the resistance to the Stamp Act and the Townshend Acts. Such action sometimes also affected economic relations between the colonies. In 1766, for example, a group in Charleston, South Carolina, agreed that no provisions should be shipped "to that infamous Colony Georgia in particular nor any other that make use of Stamp Paper."[9] When the Boston town meeting heard in May 1770 that traders in Newport, Rhode Island, were importing goods from both England and the East Indies, it voted to sever all commercial relations with that town.[10]

The remainder of this chapter will not distinguish between primary and secondary economic boycotts because different criteria are used to distinguish the specific methods of economic boycotts. Frequently one method of economic boycott may be applied either as a primary or as a secondary boycott.

Since the term economic boycott covers a considerable variety of specific acts, it is desirable to subdivide the classification; this can most usefully be done in terms of the nature of the group responsible (at least primarily so) for conducting the boycott. This classification should not be regarded as rigid, however, for one type often blends into another, and frequently several methods, or action by several groups, may be combined. Economic boycotts may also be combined with a great variety of other methods of nonviolent action.

ACTION BY CONSUMERS

71. Consumers' boycott

The consumers' boycott involves a refusal by consumers to purchase certain goods or services. There may be many reasons for such a boycott: 1) the price may be regarded as too high; 2) the item may not be available to all persons and groups on equal terms; 3) the boycotted item may furnish a convenient symbolic point for expressing a wider grievance or a general discontent with the status quo; 4) the particular boycotted item may be regarded as having certain "immoral" qualities; 5) there may be objection to the conditions, especially of labor, under which the item has been produced; 6) there may be objection to the use to which the profits from such sales will be put; and 7) there may be other less noble motives, including prejudices and political differences. The motives for economic boycotts may, therefore, vary considerably in their origin, which may be economic, political, social, or cultural, or a combination of these.

Examples of consumers' boycotts, taken almost at random, include the New York housewives' boycott of meat in protest against high prices in 1936;[11] the 1907 boycott initiated by U.S. trade unionists against the products of Buck's Stove and Range Co.;[12] the six-year boycott initiated in 1893 by the Knights of Labor against the products of the Liggett & Myers Tobacco Co.;[13] the Socialists' boycott in the late nineteenth century of German inns which refused to let rooms for meetings of the Social Democratic Party;[14] the Berlin workers' boycott, in 1894, of beer produced by members of the Brewers' Employers' Association (this was so effective, Leo Wolman reports, that the secretary of the Association stated that the emergence of the boycott added a new and extraordinarily effective weapon to the methods of social and industrial warfare).[15]

Other examples are the 1934 boycott of "immoral" films, organized in the United States by Protestants and the Roman Catholic Legion of Decency;[16] the fifteen-day bus boycott in Barcelona, Spain, in January 1957, to express dissatisfaction with the regime;[17] the famous bus boycott in Montgomery, Alabama, by the city's Afro-Americans, which lasted 381 days (from 1955 to 1957);[18] the boycott in 1959 by Africans in Buganda of all Asian shopkeepers and a few non-African goods;[19] and the June–July 1959 boycott by British businessmen of a grill in Singapore whose name had been changed from "Elizabethan Grill" to "Epicurean" and from which the portrait of the Queen had been removed.[20]

Numerous examples can be drawn from Nazi-occupied Europe, also. Patriotic citizens of Prague, for example, refused to buy German-controlled newspapers during the week of September 14–21, 1941. The call for this boycott (planned for several weeks by a patriotic organization in the city) was broadcast by the Czechoslovak government from London. "It proved to be a tremendous success," reports Josef Korbel, who was then working with the Czech government-in-exile.[21] From time to time during the German occupation the streetcars in Prague were boycotted to such an extent that they traveled completely empty.[22] As a means of testing the discipline of the Poles during the Nazi occupation, during certain periods the underground forbade them to read on Fridays the German newspapers printed in Polish. This order was highly effective all over Poland. (It was often enforced, however, by hostile or even violent action. Sometimes abusive signs were placed on the purchaser's back or home; or after he left the newsstand a brick might be thrown at him.)[23]

Various types of consumers' boycotts have also been used in South Africa by black Africans. Objecting to a slight increase in bus fares, Africans of the township of Alexandra outside Johannesburg on January 7, 1957, launched a total boycott of the bus line, choosing instead to cycle, accept rides with sympathetic motorists, or, most usually, walk (often eighteen miles a day). Despite severe police harassment and some fourteen thousand arrests, the boycott spread elsewhere, including to Pretoria, and eventually involved sixty thousand Africans. The boycott ended after twelve weeks when the Chamber of Commerce negotiated with the Joint Boycott Committee for a working compromise pending an investigation. Full victory for the boycotters came later with the passage in Parliament of an Act which doubled the employers' levy to subsidize African transport, so that fares were kept at the previous rate.[24] Encouraged, the African National Congress (which had not been involved in launching the bus boycott) called for a wide economic boycott of Nationalist-controlled firms and their products.[25] Also, Africans carried out a three-month boycott of their staple food, potatoes, which were largely grown in the Eastern Transvaal and elsewhere by the labor of African prisoners, many of them jailed for violations of the pass laws. The market was glutted with potatoes. Efforts to break the boycott were unsuccessful, and it continued until called off by Albert Luthuli.[26]

Other examples which indicate the widespread use of this method are numerous. Peasant serfs in tsarist Russia in 1859 sought to express in economic ways their hatred for serfdom by "starting a temperance movement so as to deprive the State of its revenues from the vodka monopoly."[27] The German population in the Ruhr refused during the 1923 struggle to ride on the few trains that the occupation authorities managed to get rolling despite the workers' resistance.[28] In 1938, as part of a jobs-for-Negroes movement led by the Rev. Adam Clayton Powell, A. Philip Randolph, and the Rev. William Lloyd Imes, Negroes in Harlem, New York City, conducted a "blackout boycott" every Tuesday night by turning off electricity and lighting candles to induce Consolidated Edison Co. to hire Negroes in jobs above the unskilled level.[29] In Nashville, Tennessee, shortly before Easter 1960, Negroes supporting a student sit-in to integrate lunch counters decided not to buy new Easter clothes as a means of influencing Nashville merchants. On May 10 the lunch counters of the six downtown stores were integrated.[30] During the summer of 1960 about 250,000 people in the Philadelphia area carried out a "selective patronage program" against the Tasty Baking Co. of Philadelphia, in order to obtain equal job opportunities for Negroes.[31] Faced with further boycotts, the Pepsi-Cola Company and Gulf Oil in Philadelphia then quickly capitulated and hired Negroes for positions from which they had previously been excluded.[32]

Consumers' boycotts may sometimes involve the publication of "unfair," "black," "closed," "we don't patronize," and "fair" lists or the use of a union label as a means of guiding purchasing power.[33] "Selective buying campaigns" encouraging patronage of named firms with nondiscriminatory hiring practices—as distinct from listing firms *not* to be patronized—have sometimes been used as means of sidestepping laws against boycotts in some American states.[34]

72. Nonconsumption of boycotted goods

Rejection of boycotted products may be extended to the point of not using them even though they are already in one's possession, when their use would therefore not involve any further purchase. Nonconsumption of boycotted goods cannot exist without a consumer's boycott, but the latter can exist without the former. The nonconsumption method facilitates social pressure against purchase of the goods, for no one can excuse himself by saying he already had the items. Although it is rare and is largely auxiliary to a consumers' boycott, this method has been regarded as a distinctive type of action—for example during the American colonial noncooperation struggles. Nonconsumption was then listed with the nonimportation of British products and the various other "non's" in the program. For example, one of the clauses of the Continental Association, the plan of resistance adopted by the First Continental Congress at Philadelphia in September 1774, declared:

> As a non-consumption agreement, strictly adhered to, will be an effectual security for the observation of the non-importation, we, as above, solemnly agree and associate, that, from this day, we will not purchase or use any tea, imported on account of the East-India company, or any on which a duty hath been or shall be paid; and from and after the first day of March next, we will not purchase or use any East-India tea whatever; nor will we, nor shall any person for

or under us, purchase or use any of those goods, wares, or merchandise, we have agreed not to import, which we shall know, or have cause to suspect, were imported after the first day of December, . . . [except for goods imported · between December 1 and February 1 and sold at the direction of the local committee, with profits going to the relief of the poor suffering from the closure of the port of Boston].[35]

73. Policy of austerity

The voluntary giving up of luxuries as part of a nonviolent action struggle contains elements of both symbolic nonviolent protest and of economic boycott. Such austerity may have one or more consequences. It may demonstrate to the opponent and to vacillating potential resisters the depth of the actionists' feelings. Austerities may also have certain psychological influences on the people practicing them, such as increasing the intensity of their commitment to the struggle. Very frequently too— and this is the reason for classifying this method among economic boycotts—giving up the use and purchase of luxuries may have a detrimental economic effect on the opponent.

One of the most important instances of the use of this method was by American colonists. Austerities were then very closely associated with various types of economic boycotts, especially the nonimportation of British goods. One prominent form which the policy of austerity took during the struggle against the Stamp Act in 1765-66 was the extreme simplification of the mourning practices, which at the time were very elaborate and involved expensive imported English goods. Costly mourning clothes for the widow or widower were abandoned, for example, as was the practice of handing out fancy gloves and scarves to other mourners. An agreement to practice this type of austerity, along with others, was signed by fifty Boston merchants in 1764 in anticipation of the enactment of the Stamp Act. Once this austerity was in operation, expensive mourning was soon abandoned in New Hampshire, Rhode Island, New Jersey, New York and Philadelphia. Such renunciation was estimated at the time to have saved more than ten thousand pounds sterling a year.[36] Imported laces and ruffles were also discarded, and expensive lamb was given up in order to make mutton more plentiful. Native substitutes for tea were encouraged, and local manufactures, including American linen, were encouraged.[37]

The use of American products and the adoption of austerities were recommended in another nonviolent campaign several years later: the Continental Association, adopted by the First Continental Congress. The

Continental Association document included a long paragraph on a policy of austerity:

> We will, in our several stations, encourage frugality, economy, and industry, and promote agriculture, arts, and the manufacturers of this country, especially that of wool; and will discountenance and discourage every species of extravagance and dissipation, especially all horse-racing, and all kinds of gaming, cock-fighting, exhibitions of shews, plays, and other expensive diversions and entertainments; and on the death of any relation or friend, none of us, or any of our families, will go into any further mourning-dress, than a black crape or ribbon on the arm or hat, for gentlemen, and a black ribbon and necklace for ladies, and we will discontinue the giving of scarves at funerals.[38]

Such recommendations were widely applied throughout the colonies, taking such forms as abandoning public college commencements, closing at least one puppet show, discouraging public dancing and feasting, refusing to use foreign liquors and imported beers, canceling public balls and fairs, discouraging gambling and horse racing, and encouraging considerable efforts to promote American manufactures.[39]

74. Rent withholding

The withholding of rent is a form of economic boycott practiced by persons renting land or property who feel they have a just grievance against the landlord. Individually or collectively they may withhold payment of further rent until a satisfactory agreement has been reached. This is sometimes also called "rent refusal" or "rent strike." The withholding may be for only a short period, after which the back rent is paid up in full—in which case the withholding becomes a token demonstration. If the rent refusers intend to press the issue, however, they must be willing to face eviction and prosecution. In some states of the United States rent withholding has in recent years been legalized under some conditions to enforce housing codes and so on.

Withholding rent has been widely practiced: in colonial New York, Russia, Ireland, Wales, and modern New York City. In June 1766 between four and five hundred farmers from Dutchess County, Province of New York, and others from Albany and Westchester counties, resolved to refuse to pay rent. They went further and decided also to rescue the men already imprisoned for nonpayment of rent and threatened to march on New York City.[40] When the Tsar decreed the emancipation of the serfs in 1861, many of them were highly disappointed at the decree's failure to acknowledge that the land belonged to them, as they believed, even though they had themselves been owned by the nobility. Many of them expected that a new, more liberal decree including this point would be forthcoming, and therefore refused to comply with certain new regulations imposed on them. This refusal included nonpayment of money due to their former masters in exchange for the land which the ex-serfs still used, as well as refusal to render further services to them or to sign agreements with them.[41]

Refusal by Irish peasants to pay "unjust rents" was one of the main methods of resistance adopted by the National Land League, founded in Dublin in October 1879, under the leadership of Charles S. Parnell, M.P., for the purpose of achieving "a reduction of rack-rents" and "to facilitate the obtaining of the ownership of the soil by the occupiers of the soil."[42] A leaflet of the Land League addressed "To THE PEO-PLE OF IRELAND" read, in part:

> The Government of England has declared war against the Irish people. The organization that protected them against the ravages of land-lordism has been declared "unlawfully criminal." A reign of terror has commenced. Meet the action of the English Government with a determined passive resistance. The No Rent Banner has been raised, and it remains with the people now to prove themselves dastards or men,
>
> PAY NO RENT.
AVOID THE LAND COURT.[43]

Speaking widely throughout Ireland, Parnell stressed the self-reliance of the Irish and the need for persistence if victory was to be won:

> Depend upon it that the measure of the Land Bill of next session will be the measure of your activity and energy this winter—it will be the measure of your determination not to pay unjust rents. . . . If you refuse to pay unjust rents, if you refuse to take farms from which others have been evicted, the land question must be settled, and settled in a way that will be satisfying to you. It depends therefore, upon yourselves, and not upon any Commission or any Government.[44]

In early 1965 the owners of 234 house trailers renting sites from St. Donats Holiday Estates, in Nash, Monmouthshire, Wales, refused to pay their rents in protest against a rent increase, as well as deteriorating conditions and facilities.[45]

The final example of rent refusal offered here began in 1963 in Harlem, New York City, as a protest against extreme slum conditions and the failure of landlords to make repairs; the rent strike was led by Mr. Jesse Gray. On November 1 the tenants of sixteen buildings were taking part, but by mid-January 1964, five thousand families in three hundred buildings were reported to be refusing to pay their rent. Furthermore, the strike was reported to have spread to the Lower East Side, Brooklyn and the Bronx. Early that month a New York City civil court judge ordered the tenants to continue withholding rent from landlords and to pay them to the court, which would in turn release the money to landlords only for the purpose of making repairs. Mayor Robert Wagner proposed legislation which would in effect make rent strikes legal in cases of substandard conditions if the money was paid into a special fund to be used for repairs and services—for which the landlord would be charged.[46]

75. Refusal to rent

In contrast to refusal to pay rent for an existing tenancy, refusal to rent involves the refusal of the prospective tenant to rent a residence or land as part of a collective action of noncooperation. In the late 1870s, for example, in pressing for an improvement in their status, Russian peasants "collectively refused to rent even the most indispensable fields when offered at ruinous prices."[47] The Irish no-rent campaign, described in the previous method, included a refusal to rent land from which others had been evicted.

76. National consumers' boycott

The national consumers' boycott involves a refusal by a major part of the consumers of a single country to buy products or use services from another country with which they are in conflict. Such a boycott may be practiced by the people of an independent country, a colony, or an otherwise subjected country seeking to regain its independence.

Motivation for such a boycott may be 1) to weaken or refuse to strengthen the opponent economically; 2) to strengthen the home economy by increased use of home-produced products; 3) to seek self-purification for past preference for foreign goods which may have contributed to the loss of economic independence and hence of political independence; 4) to symbolize revolt against political suppression or injustices; 5) to supplement a broader noncooperation movement against the foreign power, aimed at a restoration of political independence; 6) to force the opponent to right specific wrongs and to desist from such wrongs in the future; or 7) a combination of these. The general motivation is thus national—to weaken the opponent country and to strengthen one's own country in order to achieve some national goal. The national boycott may be against specific goods or services, against all the goods and services of the offending country, or against foreign products in general. Several of the methods of the economic boycott described in this chapter may be used simultaneously.

As already noted, China is often regarded as the classic home of the national consumers' boycott. The Chinese boycotts against Japan in 1908, 1915 and 1919 are examples.[48] However, the Americans were doing very well at this type of boycott in the late eighteenth century. They quite effectively used the national economic boycott (along with nonimportation, nonexportation and nonconsumption of boycotted products) on a wide scale in several campaigns—achieving thereby the repeal of the Stamp Act and the Townshend Acts taxes (except on tea). A still more comprehensive plan for national economic boycott was contained in the Continental Association, adopted by the First Continental Congress in October 1774. This included refusal by the American colonials to import from Britain, export to Britain, or use British and certain other imported products. The Continental Congress declared that this program constituted "the most speedy, effectual and peaceable measures" for righting the colonists' grievances.[49] (The various measures were to be put into effect in stages, with the nonexportation provisions not becoming operative until September 10, 1775—by which time there had been a major shift toward violent rebellion, so that the plan was not fully implemented.)

The spirit behind national consumers' boycotts may vary considerably. This is clear from the cases mentioned and also is reflected in Gandhi's thinking about such boycotts during the Indian struggles. The Indian noncooperation movement of 1920 included a call for merchants and traders to sever foreign trade relations by boycotting foreign goods and actively encouraging home industries.[50] In the 1930-31 campaign Gandhi backed an immediate and complete boycott of all foreign cloth. However, Gandhi then still regarded an extensive economic boycott of the opponent as coercive and hence not permissible under his code of nonviolence. With Gandhi in prison in 1930, however, the nationalist movement turned to a wider boycott of British goods and services than Gandhi would have sanctioned at the time. This included a boycott of almost all British goods, State-owned post offices, and British-owned or -operated telegraph systems, shipping lines, streetcars, and banking and insurance institutions.[51] In January 1932, after Gandhi had returned from the second Round Table Conference, the All-India Working Committee of the Indian National Congress once more sanctioned the extension and renewal of the extensive boycott of goods and services. Its resolution stated:

> Even in nonviolent war, boycott of goods manufactured by the oppressors is perfectly lawful, inasmuch as it is never the duty of the victim to promote or retain commercial relations with the oppressor. Therefore, boycott of British goods and concerns should be resumed and vigorously prosecuted.[52]

Gandhi gradually became more sympathetic to an extensive economic boycott of the opponent and eventually favored an economic boycott of an aggressor nation.

77. International consumers' boycott

A consumers' boycott operating in several countries against the products of a particular country because of a given grievance may be called an international consumers' boycott. In contrast to the above method, not only are consumers in several countries involved, but the issue itself is normally a broader humanitarian one of international concern. It is distinguished from government embargoes, which are discussed later in this chapter. Examples of the international consumers' boycott include the boycott of Spanish goods in 1909 in protest against the execution of Francisco Ferrer,[53] the boycott of Hungarian goods in 1920 in protest against the Hungarian government's repression of labor,[54] and the boycotts of South African goods from 1960 on.[55]

ACTION BY WORKERS AND PRODUCERS

78. Workmen's boycott

This involves a refusal by workers to work with supplies or tools "which have been manufactured under conditions objectionable to organized labor and whose continued manufacture is interpreted by such labor as constituting a menace to its welfare."[56] This type of boycott has been used against foreign products, prison-made goods and materials, goods made by new machinery regarded as a threat to jobs, goods produced by nonunion men, and inferior goods produced under bad working conditions.[57] In 1830, for example, the journeymen stone cutters of New York imposed a boycott on convict-cut stone and also made efforts to get others to refuse to work stone from the state's prisons.[58] In 1885 members of the Knights of Labor on the Union Pacific Railroad, its branches, and Jay Gould's Southwestern system refused to handle or repair the rolling stock of the Wabash Railroad Co. because of that company's hostility to the Knights of Labor.[59] About 1900 the U.S. Journeymen Stone Cutters Association required its members not to finish or set machine-cut stone, which was seen as contributing to the loss of jobs for the stone cutters.[60] From 1896 to about 1910 the United Brotherhood of Carpenters and Joiners refused to install building trim manufactured in nonunion mills which employed women and children.[61]

79. Producers' boycott

The producers' boycott, or "selling strike," [62] involves a refusal by producers to sell or otherwise deliver their products. It may even involve a refusal to produce the product, so that delivery becomes impossible. This form of noncooperation may be practiced by any type of producer, from farmers to manufacturers. The reasons may vary. In one case the motive may be a desire to boost prices by reducing available goods on the market. In another it may be a means of supporting boycotted fellow producers. At other times the producers' boycott may be part of a wider noncooperation movement directed against a hostile or occupying regime.

The examples offered here range from the days of the Roman Empire to Nazi-occupied Netherlands and Japanese-occupied China. Toward the end of the second century A.D., at Ephesus in Asia Minor, the shop managers of bakeries (most of whom were also owners) held meetings which were apparently concerned with common grievances, and collectively stopped making bread. These activities were the subject of an edict of the Roman Proconsul of Asia: he forbade them to hold meetings, demanded that they obey the regulations, and ordered them "to supply the city unfailingly with the labour essential for bread-making." [63]

Norwegian peasants in the eleventh century refused to deliver to the king either men or provisions for his military expeditions against Denmark, Sweden and England. As a consequence, the wars were brought to a complete halt.[64] In the American colonies a few American newspapers suspended publication after November 1, 1765, when the Stamp Act went into effect, in order to avoid the legal requirement to use such tax stamps on each newspaper.[65]

In 1886 in the United States the Brewers' Association attempted to counter union-initiated consumer boycotts of particular breweries by ruling that no member of the association could sell "beer, porter or ale" to any retail customers of another brewery in the association which was involved in a boycott; the aim was thus to force retailers to buy the boycotted beer by cutting off other supplies.[66] In 1932 there was widespread refusal by farmers in the United States to sell milk and livestock until prices had improved.[67]

This type of economic boycott occurred also in Nazi-occupied Europe. In the Netherlands in late April 1943, in solidarity with striking anti-Nazi urban workers Dutch farmers refused to deliver milk to dairy factories.[68] And in Poland during at least the early years of the German occupation, despite many pressures, "the peasants developed many ways of outwitting them [the Nazis], managing by shrewd devices to save food for themselves and either to turn over to the Germans the most inferior produce or to destroy what they could not salvage."[69] In occupied North China it had proved impossible for the "Border Government"—which was a kind of resistance organization-*cum*-parallel government—to prevent the sale of the 1937 cotton crop to the Japanese. Therefore, it instructed peasants to reduce cotton production by about seventy percent and to use the land so released to produce food, which the peasants did—and hence there was less cotton for the Japanese.[70]

ACTION BY MIDDLEMEN

80. Suppliers' and handlers' boycott

A suppliers' and handlers' boycott involves a refusal by workers or middlemen (wholesalers, jobbers and distributors) to handle or supply certain goods. The reasons for this refusal may include: 1) objection to the use to which the goods are to be put, such as by struck firms or in wars or by antipathetic regimes; 2) objection to the intrinsic nature of the goods; and 3) objection to the conditions under which the goods have been produced (slavery, *Apartheid* or oppression, or milder conditions deemed unfair to organized labor, such as sweatshops or employment of strikebreakers).

There are many examples of this form of boycott in support of strikes. In 1912 in Italy, for instance, a boycott was called in support of a marble quarry strike. By refusing to load sand destined for the boycotted quarry the workmen in neighboring towns made it impossible to cut marble, even had the firm successfully obtained strikebreakers.[71] Also, trade unions have often made efforts to convince producers and suppliers to refuse supplies to firms against which they were conducting a consumers' boycott.[72]

K.G.J.C. Knowles regards such a refusal to handle goods as a form of the sympathetic strike,[73] and there are situations in which the suppliers' and handlers' boycott and the sympathetic strike merge, primarily if the former is carried out on a large scale. In the summer of 1894, for example, the American Railway Union headed by Eugene V. Debs ordered its members to refuse to work on any train to which a Pullman car was attached, thus indicating their support for the striking employees of the Pullman Palace Car Co. This soon developed into a major sympathetic strike, as nearly all trains to Chicago included Pullman cars.[74]

A handlers' boycott was imposed on coal in Britain in 1925. The owners of the coal mines had given a one-month notice of the termination of the National Wages Agreement of 1924—the end of which would have cut earned wages between ten and twenty-five percent. Unionists responded with a ban on the movement of coal after July 31, when the notice went into effect, imposed by the General Council of the Trades Union Congress.[75]

In 1942 on the island of Lewis, also in Britain, dockworkers belonging to the same union as the island's spinners refused to handle not only imported weaving yarn sold at prices which threatened the economic welfare of the spinners, but also the finished cloth made from this cheap yarn.[76] British dockworkers in 1920 refused to load arms destined for use against Russian revolutionaries; in 1937-38 dockers at Liverpool, Glasgow and Southampton refused to load arms to be used by Japan against China; and in 1946 New Zealand and Australian trade unionists refused to load arms for use against the Indonesians.[77] In 1943 Portuguese cinema owners refused to show German films; ultimately Goebbels concluded that Germany would have to buy its own motion picture theatres in Portugal.[78] This method has also been given atypical expression on two occasions, when American brokerage firms refused to sell bonds from Southern states involved in brutal actions against civil rights workers. After June 1964—the time of the civil rights murders in Philadelphia, Mississippi—Baxter & Co. of New York and Cleveland refused to handle bonds from Mississippi and Alabama; and in the spring of 1965—after Governor Wallace had announced that the state did not have enough money to protect civil rights marchers from Selma to Montgomery—Childs Security Corporation informed the governor that it would not deal in the state's bonds since his statement had made clear that it was a poor financial risk.[79]

A very different case of handler's boycott by paper mill workers, combined with a selective strike by linotypists, was applied by Communist-controlled trade unions in Czechoslovakia in the period before the

Communist *coup.* "Several times, as the result of an article critical of the Soviet Union or the policy of the Communist Party, workers in paper mills refused to deliver paper to democratic newspapers in Prague and Bratislava or to load or unload it, and linotypists refused to set up the paper."[80] In February 1948—still in the pre-*coup* period—similar action was taken again. "In Bratislava, the capital of Slovakia, printers refused to run the Democratic Party presses. In Bohemia, workers in several paper mills refused to produce paper for National Socialist and Catholic newspapers; railwaymen refused to load and unload it."[81]

During the 1951-53 conflict which followed Iran's nationalization of the Anglo-Iranian Oil Co., the international oil cartel gave notice that shipping firms which allowed their tankers to transport oil from Iran's newly-nationalized oil company would receive no more shipping business from companies affiliated with the cartel. As a consequence, no more than forty tankers dared to transport Iranian oil overseas during the whole period of Mossadegh's government (April 1951-August 1953).[82]

ACTION BY OWNERS AND MANAGEMENT

81. Traders' boycott

The traders' boycott involves a refusal by retailers to buy or sell certain goods. Just as producers and suppliers may refuse to sell their products to particular firms in furtherance of their economic interests, so retailers may elect to make their purchases from particular producers and wholesalers for similar reasons.[83] Political motives or national grievances may also furnish reasons for such actions.

The traders' boycott may in addition involve a refusal to sell certain products even though they may already be in his possession. Such refusal may be carried out, for example, in support of widespread consumers' boycotts of foreign goods during wider national struggles. In 1930, in addition to canceling foreign orders, Indian cloth merchants sometimes refused to sell foreign cloth already on their shelves because of the extensive consumers' boycott of such cloth during the campaign for independence.[84] During the Chinese boycott of Japanese goods in 1919, Chinese merchants also refused to buy or sell Japanese goods, even when they had them in stock.[85]

The American colonists' Continental Association of 1774 pledged that from December 1 of that year traders would ". . . wholly discontinue the slave trade, and will neither be concerned in it ourselves, nor will we hire our vessels, nor sell our commodities or manufactures to those who are concerned in it."[86]

82. Refusal to let or sell property

Owners of houses or other buildings or property may refuse to offer them for rent or sale to certain persons or groups for a variety of reasons. This method, which has been widely applied in the United States against Negroes and other groups, was also widely used in nineteenth century China against Christian missionaries—for Westerners were regarded as "barbarians" and "foreign devils." A missionary reported that in August 1868 efforts to rent some thirty different houses in Yang-chou, Kiangsu province, had failed before one was found which the owner would rent to the missionary; the house was later attacked by a mob.[87]

83. Lockout

In a lockout the employer—not the workers—initiates the work stoppage when he temporarily closes down the operation of a particular firm or other economic unit as a means of forcing employees into line.[88] The shutting down of operations of this type is clearly within nonviolent action. However, the use of public or private armed police or troops in behalf of the management would introduce violence into the lockout, just as violence by workers or employers would bring violence into strike situations. In strikes, of course, it is the workers who bring the operations to a halt by withdrawal of their labor, as described in detail in the next chapter. In a particular industrial conflict it is sometimes difficult to determine whether the stoppage began as a strike or a lockout.

A lockout may be applied by a single firm. It has also been applied simultaneously by a large number of employers in an area or industry, using a kind of sympathetic lockout in an effort to deal with workers. For example, in England in the 1860s employers' associations instituted a general lockout of *all* men in a particular industry in order to bring under control dissident employees in one or two firms. This was particularly widespread in 1865 when Staffordshire ironworkers and shipbuilding operatives on the Clyde in Scotland were locked out.[89]

The lockout is usually applied in industry but not always. In England when farm laborers attempted to form unions in 1833-34 the employers' response was frequently a lockout, such as one near the village of Chipping Norton in Oxfordshire. Similarly, in 1874, when the agricultural unions sought payment of thirteen to fourteen shillings for a fifty-four-hour week, there was an immediate widespread lockout in the Eastern and Midland counties, with over ten thousand union members put out of work.[90] These examples make clear that a lockout occurs when the employer suspends his activities as employer, not simply when certain doors are physically locked against the employees.

Lockouts were used in the United States against the Knights of Labor, especially in 1886. In New York State in that year fifteen thousand laundry workers were put out of work by lockouts in Troy, and twenty thousand knitters at Cohoes and Amsterdam, while in Chicago twenty thousand packinghouse workers were locked out.[91] In Russia, as the tide of the 1905 Revolution ebbed, industrialists formed organizations to resist trade union advance by means of common action which included lockouts.[92]

84. Refusal of industrial assistance

Economic or political opposition may under special circumstances be expressed by the refusal to provide desired economic and technical assistance and advice. For example, in 1936, in an effort to counter the demand by steel industrialists for a significant price rise, Göring sought to establish a new government steel plant, the Hermann-Göring-Works. The majority of steel producers in Germany, however, tried to defeat Göring's new project by proposing that "none of the private steel firms should lend any assistance" to the new government steel plant. (Krupp and Röchling, however, fully cooperated with the Göring-Works).[93]

85. Merchants' "general strike"

Whereas a general strike involves a withdrawal of labor by workers, a paralysis of the economy of a city or region may also be caused by the simultaneous closing of stores and businesses by the merchants. Such action would not only affect small shops and stores run by a single person or family, but would also close larger businesses without the initiative of the employees. For example, in 1742 a general strike of merchants *(pa-shih)* took place in several districts of northern Kiangsu, China, in disapproval of the way the local official had conducted relief work following a flood.[94] When a merchants' "general strike" is combined with a general strike of workers, the result is an "economic shutdown," which is described in the following chapter on strikes.

ACTION BY HOLDERS OF FINANCIAL RESOURCES

86. Withdrawal of bank deposits

Money deposited in private or government banks or government savings systems may be withdrawn either as an expression of protest against the government or as a means of noncooperation intended to help overthrow an unsteady government. For example, the withdrawal of bank deposits was called for at least twice during the 1905 Revolution in Russia—first by the All-Russian Peasant Union at its founding conference in midsummer 1905, in case the government should seek to repress the Union,[95] and second, by the St. Petersburg Soviet on December 2, 1905. This was designed to weaken foreign confidence in the Russian economy and government and thus prevent the government from obtaining a foreign loan to be used to combat the revolution. To the embarrassment of the government, there were extensive withdrawals of funds from banks in the following weeks, apparently as a result of the call.[96]

In a very different context, in December 1966 a moderately successful appeal was made to depositors of the First National City Bank and the Chase Manhattan Bank, urging them to withdraw their deposits from those banks and to place them elsewhere, because of the banks' financial involvement in the South African economy.[97]

87. Refusal to pay fees, dues and assessments

Individuals, groups, or governments may on occasion deliberately refuse to pay fees, dues, or assessments to a private organization, public institution, government, or international body. Norwegian teachers in 1942 refused to make voluntary payments to a new fascist-controlled teachers' organization.[98] Japanese students in 1947 used the refusal to pay university fees as a means of demonstration.[99] Probably the best-known example is the refusal of Soviet bloc countries, France, Belgium and Portugal to pay their share of the costs of the United Nations forces in the Congo, on the ground that *ad hoc* expenses of that special operation could not legally be regarded as "expenses of the organization" under the terms of the Charter, payment of which was obligatory for members.[100]

88. Refusal to pay debts or interest

Nonpayment of debts (or, rarely, refusal to pay only the interest due) has also been used as a method of economic boycott. This primarily occurs when the debts are owed to an opponent or to persons or firms in a country whose government is the opponent. Sometimes an attempt has been made to apply this method to government debts; people have been urged not to pay taxes for government debts, or foreign creditors have been warned that if they loan money to a tottering regime, the debt will not be honored when the government falls. This was attempted in the Financial Manifesto of the St. Petersburg Soviet in December 1905[101] and in the Vyborg Manifesto, signed by about two-thirds of the members of the *Duma* after the Tsar and dissolved it on July 21, 1906:

> Therefore, now that the Government has dissolved the Duma, you [the people] are justified in giving neither money nor soldiers. If the Government contracts loans to procure funds, these loans are invalid without the consent of the people's representatives. The Russian people will never recognise them and will not feel itself called upon to repay them. [102]

Nonpayment of debts has been most demonstrably effective, however, where it was applied to private debts to private persons or firms in the course of a political struggle with a government, that is, in the American colonists' struggles against British rule from London. This method was used especially in 1765 and 1766, in the struggle against the Stamp Act. Most of the trade between Britain and British North America was on credit, with the latter a heavy borrower. Clearly, stopping trade would have had severe economic repercussions in England; but stopping payment of debts resulted in a more severe and a more rapid economic squeeze. Payment of debts was halted well before the Act went into effect, for by August 1765 a Bristol merchant already reported: "We have no Remittances, and are at our Witts End for Want of Money to fulfill our Engagement with our Tradesmen." [103]

One of the reasons that English merchants were later unable to use the courts to collect debts, as usual, was that frequently the courts themselves closed rather than use the tax stamps on legal documents or operate without them in defiance of the law. Sometimes the decision to close the courts had been taken to prevent their being used to collect debts to English merchants. George Washington clearly suggested this tactic on September 20, 1765, several weeks before the Stamp Act went into effect:

> Our Courts of Judicature must inevitably be shut up; for it is impossible . . . under our present Circymstances that the Act of Parliament can be complied with . . . and if a stop be put to our judicial proceedings I fancy the Merchants of G. Britain trading to the Colonies will not be among the last to wish for a Repeal of it. [104]

Horace Walpole later described the situation which resulted:

> But the weapon with which the Colonies armed themselves to most advantage, was the refusal of paying the debts they owed to our merchants at home, for goods and wares exported to the American provinces. These debts involved the merchants of London, Liverpool, Man-

chester, and other great trading towns, in a common cause with the Americans, who forswore all traffic with us, unless the obnoxious Stamp Act was repealed. [105]

Gipson reports that the debts amounted to some four million pounds sterling and that these "were now wielded as a club with telling force." [106] In the summer of 1774, prior to the First Continental Congress, there was discussion in the newspapers of New York and Philadelphia as whether once again to use this method in the then current conflict. [107] Some local bodies had already begun to refuse to pay debts or to allow use of the courts for collecting them. For example, on May 25 of that year, following the British closure of the port of Boston, a meeting of inhabitants of Annapolis resolved that, in addition to a nonimportation and nonexportation agreement, no suit in law be brought "for the recovery of any debt due from any inhabitant of this province to any inhabitant of Great-Britain, until the said act be repealed." [108] One of the resolves passed by Westmoreland County, Virginia, under the leadership of men like Richard Henry Lee, the county's representative in the House of Burgesses, was that for the duration of the planned nonexportation agreement, the lawyers of the county should not "bring any writ for the Recovery of Debt, or push to a Conclusion any such Suit already brought." [109]

An instance of refusal to pay interest on loans, while continuing to repay the principle of the loan, took place in Germany shortly before the Nazi rise to power, when the "Nazified leaders" of middle-class organizations organized not only campaigns against the foreclosure of farms, but also collective refusal by the farmers to pay interest on their bank loans. [110]

89. Severance of funds and credit

Economic pressures can also be exerted by cutting off the opponent's sources of money, such as salaries, appropriations, loans and investments. This may be done by individuals, firms, or governments. In certain American colonies, the assemblies withheld appropriations for the salaries of governors and judges as a means of keeping them from acting too much out of line with the assemblies' political wishes. [111]

Segregationist whites in the southern United States have cut off bank credit as well as other types of credit to individual Negroes who have been active in abolishing segregation. [112] Also, when school officials in Prince Edward County, Virginia, were ordered in May 1955 to integrate the school system, in which fifty-three percent of the pupils were Negro, the officials immediately and unanimously cut off all funds for the operation of public schools in that county. Without public schools, there could be no integration in public schools.[113] When the Virginia legislature met in August 1956 to consider thirteen antiintegration bills, House Bill No. 1 proposed by Governor Thomas Stanley was to cut off state school funds from any school district which integrated. State money amounted to forty-two percent of operating costs. The bill passed both houses, though only narrowly in the Senate.[114] Later, Prince Edward County officials resumed appropriation of funds to operate the schools, but not on the usual annual basis. Instead, appropriations were made on a monthly basis, "with a publicly declared intention of discontinuing that appropriation if schools in the county are mixed racially at this time," reported Federal Judge Sterling Hutcheson in a decision on January 23, 1957.[115] Opposition to the abandonment of public education developed, however, and that form of resistance was discontinued.

Federal funds and contracts have been withheld or withdrawn from various types of activities—such as welfare and education—which did not conform to established federal standards or practices, especially where there was racial discrimination. James Farmer has described "the withdrawal of financial support from any discriminatory activity" as the "most powerful weapon" available to the federal government. "If the threat of economic withdrawal were made palpable, an army of Southern bigots would alter their ways."[116] There have also been various calls for the withdrawal of foreign investments from South Africa as a means of abolishing *Apartheid*.[117]

90. Revenue refusal

This method involves a refusal by the resisters to provide the government with revenue voluntarily. Since such revenue is owed to a government, or an agency of it, and is required by statute or regulation, this method may also be classed as political noncooperation. Where this action is more than symbolic its most important characteristic usually is the withholding of financial resources from the government; where the political disobedience element is dominant, however, this method would fall primarily within political noncooperation. But it is both economic and political in form.

This method involves the refusal to pay various types of taxes—including income taxes, property taxes (rates), sales or purchase taxes—or the refusal to purchase certain required licenses (dog, car, radio, television, and the like) either as a protest against a particular injustice directly related to the license in question or as a symbol of a wider protest against the government. Revenue refusal might also involve the boycott of goods on whose sale there is a sales or purchase tax. Where land or property rent is paid to the government, these may also be refused. A related way of denying funds to the government (though not technically revenue) is to refuse to purchase government loans and bonds, national savings accounts, and so on, and the withdrawal of such existing loans and deposits.

In advanced stages of a struggle, the resister may sell taxed items but refuse to collect or pay the tax. Whereas the refusal to purchase loans or to use national savings accounts as a means of providing revenue to the government is usually legal, the refusal to pay taxes or rents to the government is illegal—this is a direct refusal of supplies to the government. The refusal of revenue is usually regarded as a very strong expression of disapproval of the government. Where it is undertaken in large numbers it may become a severe threat to the existence of the government, either because of the threat to the State's treasury or because of the extent and depth of the population's refusal to submit to the regime, as indicated by the extremity of their resistance. Collective refusal of taxes is probably an ancient method, as reports from Egypt are frequent as early as the second century, for example.[118]

Norwegian peasants rebelled against greatly increased taxes demanded by the Danish King Christian II to support his war against Sweden from 1515. The peasants refused to pay taxes and killed tax collectors; in turn, they were severely repressed.[119] Widespread peasant tax refusal, especially along the Norwegian coast around the 1630s, led to both repression and tax reform.[120] Another major tax rebellion occurred in Norway in 1764 and 1765 in protest against high taxes, presumed corruption of the tax collectors, and such practices as government seizure for tax payments of the farmers' and fishermen's indispensable tools. In Romsdal "the peasants absolutely refused to pay and drove the tax-collectors away. In 1764 there was unrest along the whole coast, and everywhere less and less of the tax went in," although the 1762 and 1763 taxes had been fully paid. There was a massive demonstration in Bergen and intimidation of officials. Even in the period after repression less than half the assessed taxes were collected in most places.[121]

Refusal to pay certain taxes by boycotting the taxed goods, especially during the Stamp Act struggle, was one of the methods of resistance used prior to the American War of Independence, as has been mentioned repeatedly in examples of other methods. During the French Revolution of 1789 refusal to pay taxes and feudal dues was very widespread.[122] When the Third Estate, joined by some clergy, constituted itself as the National Assembly on June 17, 1789, it attempted to protect itself from counterattack by the King by authorizing refusal to pay taxes; only future taxes approved by the National Assembly were legal, and existing taxes were payable only while it continued in session.[123] By the end of 1789 "everyone refused to pay former taxes and fees."[124]

Both Hsiao Kung-ch,üan and Chang Chung-li report in their studies of their studies of nineteenth-century Chinese society that several cases of organized tax refusal occurred in China around 1860.[125] In Hungary in 1861 there was massive resistance to the collection of taxes under Austrian laws, the tax collectors being politely told that they were "illegal persons."[126] During the first two and a half years of the 1902 and 1914 tax refusal campaign in England that was directed against tax aid for parochial schools, 70,000 summonses were issued, and there were 254 imprisonments.[127]

During the 1905 Russian Revolution payment of taxes was often refused by the populace seeking the overthrow of the tsarist regime. In Georgia, for example, neither taxes nor dues were paid.[128] On two occasions the revolutionaries offically launched refusal of taxes as a major part of a resistance program to topple the regime. The first was urged by the St. Petersburg Soviet on November 23 and December 2, 1905 (the Financial Manifesto), and was stimulated by Parvus' study of the regime's economic problems.[129] The second was the famous Vyborg Manifesto signed by about two-thirds of the members of the dissolved *Duma* on July 23, 1906. Since consent of the people's representatives gave government its right to tax and to conscript soldiers ". . . now that the Government has dissolved the *Duma,* you are justified in giving neither money nor soldiers . . . . Be firm in your refusal . . ."[130]

Tax refusal was also an important form of resistance during the Indian independence struggles, in both local and national campaigns.[131] In Germany, prior to the Nazi rise to power, the pro-Nazi leaders of certain middle-class organizations used tax strikes (among other means) to oppose "unfair" competition, foreclosure of farms, and the like.[132] Nonpayment of taxes was part of the nonviolent resistance program adopted in April 1953 by the Nyasaland African Congress to defeat the imposition of the Central African Federation despite united black African opposition.[133] In 1956 ten Welshmen were prosecuted for having refused to pay for their radio licenses because the British Broadcasting Corporation maintained the Welsh Service on a wavelength which was subject to serious evening interference from an East German station.[134] Africans were being arrested in Northern Rhodesia in September 1962 for refusing to pay the poll tax and for not having identity certificates, which they had burned in 1961 as a sign of defiance against the government.[135]

A case of tax refusal in 1966 has been reported from Eastern Angola, where it took place at a time when guerrilla warfare was the major means of African resistance to the Portuguese. This account, from the American peace worker James Bristol, is based on his conversations with an Angolan nationalist leader in Lusaka, Zambia:

> Recently, he told me, they had been able to organize a tax refusal movement in a group of villages. Apparently, the system has called for the chiefs to collect taxes from the people and then turn the money over to the Portugese. Twelve chiefs refused to demand the taxes from the people; they stated that there was unemployment on a large scale, and that as long as this unemployment continued and they could see no tangible benefits from the taxes they paid, they would refuse to give orders to their people to pay taxes. The 12 chiefs were arrested, and taken away by plane to another part of Angola. As they were in the plane, the Portugese pointed out to them how powerful they, the Portugese, were; they had weapons, they had these big planes; the Angolans had nothing. The chiefs replied that the Portugese still could not force the people to do what they had decided not to do. They were put in jail; they were questioned; they were threatened, but still they refused to give the order for the people to pay the taxes. Finally, the Portugese said that they would release them and take them back to their villages, on condition that the chiefs engage in no further subversive action. The chiefs replied that they *would continue to oppose* the payment of unjust taxes and other injustices imposed by the Portugese. But after a time the Portugese released them anyhow, and returned them to their villages. [The Angolan leader] . . . said that the Portugese know how to handle the guerrillas, but not how to deal with this sort of united resistance by the villagers themselves.[136]

Refusal of revenue can also take the form of refusing to pay fines and court costs. For example, in Americus, Georgia, in the fall of 1963, the local Sumter County civil rights movement announced: "Don't forget that our fines and court costs every morning are helping to pay for new police cars and extra policemen who are just here to intimidate Negroes." In consequence, for weeks the income from payment of fines, court costs, and bail bonds averaged only five hundred dollars weekly instead of the normal two to three thousand dollars.[137]

91. Refusal of a government's money

This method is the refusal, as a political act, to accept a government's printed money, either completely or in all but minor transactions. In other situations the motives could be partly economic (in case of high inflation). Alternatives to the printed money might be gold, silver, barter, and the like. This method appears to have been deliberately used with the intent of undermining a regime only rarely. The Financial Manifesto of the St. Petersburg Soviet, referred to in the discussion of the preceding method, not only asked that gold be demanded when deposits were withdrawn from banks, but also urged people to demand gold in payment for wages and in all major financial transactions.[138]

ACTION BY GOVERNMENTS

92. Domestic embargo

A domestic embargo may be briefly defined as an economic boycott initiated by the government to operate within its own country. This method of noncooperation was applied, for example, in Nazi Germany between 1933 and 1935 as part of the Nazi cartel program. In July 1933 two cartel laws were issued, one of which authorized the State to form compulsory cartels and to regulate investments, while the other authorized the Minister of Economics to supervise cartel prices and to deal with firms which were not cartel members. One way this supervision operated was to limit the firms allowed to trade in coal, both as wholesalers and retailers. No firm not a cartel member could expect delivery of coal. Dealers not on the approved list because they were deemed unsuitable or unnecessary were driven out of business, both by a boycott (apparently a consumers' boycott) and by the delivery embargoes imposed by the cartel court in accordance with the above laws, or, after a decree from the Minister of Economics, simply by the court's chairman. As a result of these and other government measures, approximately 2,000 of 54,000 coal dealers were put out of business in two years. Similar action occurred in the radio industry; in one year during this time the number of radio retailers was reduced from 60,000 to 37,000, and of radio wholesalers, from 1,500 to 750.[139]

93. Blacklisting of traders[140]

During wartime or during a policy of embargo, one government may seek to block indirect transfer of embargoed good through firms or individuals in a neutral country by prohibiting trade with them as well as with the enemy country itself. A blacklist of such traders is normally published, and transactions with them prohibited. At times, however, the blacklist remains unpublished, becoming a "graylist" which may cause a listed firm to "lose time waiting for a deal to go through before it realizes that it has been listed and seeks other arrangements," as Professor Thomas C. Schelling has written. These were standard United States practices during World War II.

94. International sellers' embargo

An international sellers' embargo is a refusal by government decision to sell certain or all products to another country. The action may be taken by one or several governments; it is normally national and the effect international. The motives may vary from objections to the existence of the regime itself (arising from its political orientation or from the means it used to come to power or to maintain itself) to objections to a particular policy or action of the country. In some cases, however, the international seller's embargo may be an attempt to halt or prevent a war or, under the guise of that objective, to assist one side by preventing sales of arms to the weaker side.

When the British King on October 17, 1807, proclaimed the right of impressment of neutral merchant vessels, measures stronger than the recent ban on importation of various articles of British manufacture were deemed to be necessary in the United States. In accordance with "Jefferson's doctrine, that foreign nations could be coerced by peaceable means into respect for neutral rights . . . ," the President obtained from Congress the permanent Embargo Act, which was intended to coerce Europe by stopping supplies to West Indian colonies and by halting the export of cotton and corn to Europe. This was to be done by placing an embargo on all shipping owned by United States citizens to prevent them from transporting such supplies for sale. Jefferson was successful in getting the country to adopt "the experiment in peaceable coercion." (Various Republicans had argued that a standing army would be dangerous to popular liberties.) "In the scheme of President Jefferson's statesmanship, non-intercourse was the substitute for war—the weapon of defense and coercion which saved the cost and danger of supporting an army or navy and spared America the brutalities of the Old World." The embargo encountered widespread economic problems, and evasion and violation by Americans; the army and navy had to be used to enforce it at home. Jefferson and his policy became highly unpopular, and after the election of

Madison as President the embargo laws were repealed [141] but replaced with a similar nonintercourse policy.

The embargo on arms during the Chaco War of 1933–36 between Bolivia and Paraguay is another example of this method. [142] Attempts to apply economic sanctions against Italy during its attack on Ethiopia in 1935–36 constitute a further example. [143] In 1950 the United States government imposed an embargo on Communist China, prohibiting ships registered in the United States from calling at Chinese ports and banning United States exports to Communist China. [144] This remained in force without major relaxation for about twenty years.

95. International buyers' embargo

The international buyer's embargo involves the prohibition of general or particular purchases from a specific country. Again, the motives vary: the intent may be to produce a change in a particular policy, to force a broader modification in the regime, or to contribute to the downfall of the regime. Examples of an international buyer's embargo include the Non-Importation Act of April 18, 1806 (before the Embargo Act), which prohibited the import of various articles of British manufacture and made their possession illegal. As the historian Henry Adams put it:

> The measure was in its nature coercive. The debates in Congress showed that no other object than that of coercion was in the mind of the American government; the history of the Republican Party and the consistent language of Jefferson, Madison, and the Virginian school proclaimed that the policy was their substitute for war. England was to be punished, by an annual fine of several million dollars, for interference with American trade to the continent of Europe. [145]

Stronger measures were required, however, before this Act could really take effect, and the Embargo Act was pushed through Congress. It was repealed on March 1, 1809, by the Non-Intercourse Act, which also contained provisions to exclude all British and French vessels from United States waters and forbade the import of British and French goods. [146]

96. International trade embargo

An international trade embargo is a combination of the international seller's embargo and the international buyer's embargo. It involves a total prohibition of trade with the opponent country, or a near-total ban, exempting perhaps medicines and the like. For example, after the news of the armed engagements at Lexington and Concord, the British government passed the Prohibitory Bill, which barred all trade and commerce with the rebellious colonies, under the threat of the seizure of all ships and cargoes. [147] (Where this ban was effective because of voluntary acceptance or possible economic sanctions against British violators, it falls within this technique; however, the use of naval power to enforce the ban combines the economic sanction with military action.)

International economic sanctions have been seen by various American political leaders as alternatives to military action. Sometimes their recommendations have clearly referred to a complete cessation of all trade: at other times the extent and types of the embargoes recommended have been left more flexible. Halt to international trade of all types by government initiative was seen by Thomas Jefferson as an alternative to war sometime before the particular measures cited under the two methods above. As early as March 1793, in a letter to James Madison, Jefferson contemplated what action should be taken if the naval powers blockaded France, at the time of the French Revolution, stopping imports of supplies and provisions. Jefferson wrote:

> Should this be formally notified I should suppose Congress would be called, because it is a justifiable cause of war, & as the Executive cannot decide the question of war on the affirmative side, neither ought it to do so on the negative side, by preventing the competent body from deliberating on the question. But I should hope that war would not be their choice. I think it will furnish us a happy opportunity of setting another precious example to the world, by showing that nations may be brought to do justice by appeals to their interests as well as by appeals to arms. I should hope that Congress instead of a denunciation of war, would instantly exclude from our ports all the manufactures, produce, vessels & subjects of the nations committing this aggression, during the continuance of the aggression & till full satisfaction made for it. This would work well in many ways, safely in all, & introduces between nations another umpire than arms. It would relieve us too from the risks & horrors of cutting throats. [149]

Referring to the means of enforcing the antiwar provisions of the League of Nations Covenant, President Woodrow Wilson said in the autumn of 1919:

> If any member of the League breaks or ignores these promises with regard to arbitration and discussion, what happens? War? No, not war but something . . . more tremendous than war . . . .
>
> Apply this economic, peaceful, silent, deadly remedy and there will be no need for force . . . .

The boycott is what is substituted for war. [149]

In 1932 John Foster Dulles, who later became Secretary of State, wrote:

The great advantage of economic sanctions is that on the one hand they can be very potent, while on the other hand, they do not involve that resort to force which is repugnant to our objective of peace.

If any machinery can be set up to ensure that nations comply with their covenant to renounce war, such machinery must be sought primarily in the economic sphere. [150]

On February 3, 1962, the United States government applied an international trade embargo against Cuba. Under the Department of State declaration of October 1960, American exports to Cuba had already been prohibited. The Presidential proclamation of February 3, 1962, however, extended its scope by placing an embargo on *all* trade with Cuba. [151]

International embargoes of all three types have not produced many notable successes. Peter Wallensteen points to the small proportion of successes they had between 1933 and 1967. [152] How much of this lack of success is a result of intrinsic limitations of these methods and how much is a consequence of insufficient care in their application and an unwillingness to apply them seriously remain to be investigated. [153]

Wallenstein cites two successful cases during this period. British economic sanctions against the Soviet Union in 1933 ended with a negotiated agreement between the governments, removal of the sanctions, and release of arrested British subjects. [154] The other case involved the Dominican Republic in 1960-62, with economic action being imposed by the United States and the Organization of American States in condemnation of Dominican participation in an attempt to assassinate President Betancourt of Venezuela. The real objective, however, was condemnation of the Trujillo dictatorship in the Dominican Republic itself. In May 1961 Trujillo was assassinated, but apparently this was unconnected with the economic sanctions, which were continued for six more months, until all members of the Trujillo family had left the country to ensure a real change in the regime. [155]

A very large number of the methods of economic noncooperation involve the withdrawal of labor, and we now turn to the various methods of the strike.

NOTES

1. This definition is adapted from those offered by Harry Laidler, "Boycott," **Encyclopedia of the Social Sciences** (New York: Macmillan, 1935, vol. II, pp. 662-66; Laidler, **Boycotts and the Labor Struggle, Economic and Legal Aspects** (New York: John Lane Co., 1913), pp.27 and 55; Leo Wolman, **The Boycott in American Trade Unions**, Johns Hopkins University Studies in Historical and Political Science, Series XXXIV, No. 1 (Baltimore: Johns Hopkins Press, 1916), pp. 11-12; and Clarence Marsh Case, **Non-violent Coercion: A Study in Methods of Social Pressure** (New York: Century Co., 1923), pp. 320-24.

2. See Case, **Non-violent Coercion**, p. 305.

3. *Ibid.*, pp. 314-15; Wolman, The Boycott in American Trade Unions, p. 41.

4. Wolman, **The Boycott in American Trade Unions**, p. 24; see also Laidler, "Boycott," pp. 663-664; and Philip Taft, **The A.F. of L. in the Time of Gompers** (New York, Harper and Bros., 1957) pp. 264-266.

5. John King Fairbank, **The United States and China** (Cambridge, Mass.: Harvard University Press, 1958) pp. 167-168. I am grateful to Carl Horne for this reference.

6. Case, **Non-violent Coercion**, p. 316.

7. Wolman, **The Boycott . . . ,** p. 14; see also Reynolds, **Labor Economics and Labor Relations**, p. 134.

8. Laidler, "Boycott," p. 665.

9. Schlesinger, **The Colonial Merchants and the American Revolution**, p. 82.

10. Gipson, **The Coming of the Revolution, 1763-1775**, p. 204.

11. L. L. Bernard, **Social Control in Its Sociological Aspects** (New York, Macmillan Co., 1939), p. 386.

12. Case, **Non-violent Coercion**, pp. 332-340; Taft, **The A. F. of L. in the Time of Gompers**, pp. 268-271; and Wolman, **The Boycott . . . ,** pp. 80-82.

13. Wolman, **The Boycott . . . ,** p. 28.

14. *Ibid.*, p. 41.

15. *Ibid.*

16. Bernard, **Social Control . . . ,** pp. 393-395.

17. *The Times* (London), 31 January 1957.

18. Martin Luther King, Jr., **Stride Towards Freedom.** The boycott is reported to have cost the bus company between $3,000 and $3,500 a day, in addition to major financial losses to the white-owned businesses in the center of Montgomery. (William Peters, **The Southern Temper**, [Garden City, N.Y.; Doubleday & Co., 1959], p. 232.)

19. *Observer*, (London) 23 August 1959.

20. *The Times*, 6 July 1959.

21. Josef Korbel, **The Communist Subversion of Czechoslovakia 1938-1948: The**

Failure of Coexistence (Princeton, N.J.: Princeton University Press, 1959), p. 57. Also a personal letter dated 22 December 1966.

22. Josef Korbel, personal letter dated 22 December 1966.

23. Karski, **The Story of a Secret State**, p. 259.

24. Miller, **Nonviolence**, pp. 273-275, and Luthuli, **Let My People Go**, pp. 174-178.

25. Miller, **Nonviolence**, p. 275.

26. *Ibid.*, and Luthuli, **Let My People Go**, pp. 217-219.

27. Venturi, **Roots of Revolution**, p. 191.

28. Sternstein, "The *Ruhrkampf* of 1923", p. 116.

29. Arna Botemps, **100 Years of Negro Freedom**, (New York: Dodd, Mead & Co., 1962) p. 254.

30. Louis E. Lomax, **The Negro Revolt** (New York: New American Library, Signet Book, 1963), p. 143.

31. *Peace News,* 26 August 1960.

32. Hannah Lees, "The Not-Buying Power of Philadelphia's Negroes," **The Reporter**, vol. 24, no. 10 (11 May 1961), pp. 33-35.

33. Wolman, **The Boycott . . .**, pp. 33, 34 and 42; and Laidler, **Boycotts and the Labor Struggle**, pp. 60-63.

34. Waskow, **From Race Riot to Sit-in**, p. 239.

35. Text quoted from Schlesinger, **The Colonial Merchants . . .**, p. 609.

36. Morgan and Morgan, **The Stamp Act Crisis**, p. 50. See also Schlesinger, **The Colonial Merchants . . .**, p. 77.

37. Schlesinger, **The Colonial Merchants . . .**, pp. 73-74, 76-77.

38. *Ibid.*, p. 610.

39 *Ibid.*, pp. 483, 486, 492, 500-503, 508-509, 518-519, and 528.

40. Gipson, **The British Empire Before the American Revolution**, vol. XI, **The Triumphant Empire: The Rumbling of the Coming Storm,1766-1770**, p. 49.

41. Venturi, **Roots of Revolution**, p. 101.

42. G. Locker-Lampson, **A Consideration of the State of Ireland in the Nineteenth Century** (New York: E. P. Dutton & Co., 1907, and London: Archibald Constable & Co., Ltd., 1907), p. 372.

43. H. O. Arnold Forster, **The Truth About the Land League, Leaders and its Teaching** (pamphlet - London: National Press Agency, Ltd., published for the Property Defence Association, 1883), p. 57.

44. From a speech at Ennis on September 19, 1880. Quoted in Patrick Sarsfield O'Hegarty, **A History of Ireland Under the Union, 1880-1922** (with an Epilogue carrying the story down to the acceptance in 1927 by the De Valera of the Anglo-Irish Treaty of 1921) (London: Methuen Press, 1952) p. 491.

45. *Peace News,* 5 February 1965.

46. Nat Hentoff, **The New Equality** (New Edition; (New York: Viking Press, 1965) pp. 201-202. See also **New York Times**, 7 January 1964.

47. Venturi, **Roots of Revolution**, p. 576.

48. Case, **Non-violent Coercion**, pp. 330-342.

49. Schlesinger, **The Colonial Merchants . . .**, p. 608. These boycott campaigns are highly significant, in terms not only of early American history, but of the history of nonviolent action generally and the potentialities of economic boycotts. For details of these campaigns, see the following studies, all of which

contain references to original sources: Schlesinger, **The Colonial Merchants . . . ,** esp. pp. 78, 97, 104-121, 157, 179, 185, 194, 215-219, 300-301, 312-315, 324, 339-340, 344, 351-353, 356-357, 360-363, 366, 369, 398-399, 402, 414-419, 427 and 608-609. Gipson, **The Coming of the American Revolution,** esp. 104, 106-107, 114-115, 187-188, 196-198, 203-205, 208-209, and 230. Gipson, **The British Empire ....** Vol. XI esp. pp. 84, 143, 145, 181-190, 242, 254, and 256n. *Ibid.,* vol. XII, **The Triumphant Empire, Britain Sails Into the Storm, 1770-1776,** esp., pp. 152-153, 207, 217, 251, and 254.

50. Case, **Non-violent Coercion,** p. 383.

51. Sharp, **Gandhi Wields the Weapon of Moral Power,** pp. 125-127.

52. Pattabhi Sitamarayya, **The History of the Indian National Congress, 1885-1935,** vol. I, p. 870.

53. Laidler, "Boycott," p. 666.

54. *Ibid.*

55. See William A. Hance, "Efforts to Alter the Future Economic Action" for a good discussion of international economic boycott and other economic sanctions in relation to South Africa, in Amelia C. Leiss, editor, **Apartheid and United Nations Collective Measures,** (New York: Carnegie Endowment for International Peace, 1965) pp. 95-130.

56. Wolman, **The Boycott . . . ,** p. 43.

57. *Ibid.,* pp. 44-49.

58 *Ibid.,* p. 23.

59. *Ibid.,* p. 59.

60. *Ibid.,* p. 45.

61. *Ibid.,* pp. 49-52.

62. Bernard, **Social Control . . . ,** p. 385.

63. W. H. Buckler, "Labour Disputes in the Province of Asia Minor", in W. H . Buckler and W. M. Culder, eds., **Anatolian Studies Presented to Sir William Mitchell Ramsay** (Manchester, England: The University Press, 1923), p. 31. See also, Rostovtzeff, **The Social and Economic History of the Roman Empire,** vol. II, p. 621, no. 45.

63. Andreas Holmsen, *Norges Historie Fra de Eldste Tider til 1660,*(Third Edition; Oslo and Bergen: *Universitetsforlaget,* 1964), p. 179. Professor Holmsen has written to me about this case: "What is maintained on p. 179 in my book about the farmers' opposition against Harald Hardråde's frequent raids against Denmark around 1050, is only a reasonable conclusion based on the fact that gradually the raids had to be abandoned. There are no sources specifically saying that this was caused by the farmers' opposition."

64. Morgan and Morgan, **The Stamp Act Crisis,** p. 241.

66. Wolman, **The Boycott . . . ,** p. 39.

67. Bernard, **Social Control . . . ,** p. 385.

68. L. de Jong, "Anti-Nazi Resistance in the Netherlands," in **European Resistance Movements 1939-1945. First International Conference on the History of the Resistance Movements held at Liege-Brusseles-Breendonk, 14-17 September 1958** (Oxford: Pergamon Press, 1960), p. 141.

69. Karski, **The Story of a Secret State,** p. 255.

70. Taylor, **The Struggle for North China,** pp. 114-115. I am grateful to Abraham Halperin for this reference and certain others on China.

71. Wolman, **The Boycott . . . ,** p. 42.

72. Laidler, **Boycotts and the Labor Struggle**, pp. 64-65.
73. K.G.J.C. Knowles, **Strikes – A Study in Industrial Conflict with Special Reference to British Experience Between 1911 and 1945** (New York: Philosophical Library, 1952; Oxford: Basil Blackwell, 1954), p. 17.
74. Case, **Non-violent Coercion**, p. 315, and Wolman, **The Boycott in American Trade Unions**, p. 32, and Almont Lindsey, **The Pullman Strike: The Story of a Unique Experiment and of a Great Labor Upheaval** (Chicago and London: University of Chicago Press, Phoenix Books, 1964 [orig. 1942]).
75. Symons, **The General Strike**, pp. 13-15.
76. Knowles, **Strikes**, p. 17.
77. *Ibid.*
78. Lochner, ed., **The Goebbels Diaries**, pp. 508-509.
79. James Farmer, **Freedom – When?**, p. 117.
80. Korbel, **The Communist Subversion of Czechoslovakia**, p. 144.
81. *Ibid.*, p. 227.
82. Bahman Nirumand, **Iran: The New Imperialism in Action** (New York and London: Modern Reader Paperback, 1969), p. 70. I am grateful to James Prior for this reference.
83. Laidler, **Boycotts and the Labor Struggle**, p. 49.
84. Sharp, **Gandhi Wields . . .** , p. 166.
85. Case, **Non-violent Coercion**, pp. 337-339.
86. Schlesinger, **The Colonial Merchants . . .** , pp. 608-609.
87. Hsiao, **Rural China**, pp. 488 and 496.
88. Fitch, "Strikes and Lockouts."
89. Sidney and Beatrice Webb, **The History of Trade Unionism. Revised Edition to 1920** (New York: Longmans, Green & Co., 1920), pp. 255-256.
90. *Ibid.*, pp. 332-334.
91. Joseph G. Rayback, **A History of American Labor**, (New York: Macmillan, 1964), p. 174.
92. Seton-Watson, **The Decline of Imperial Russia**, p. 228.
93. Arthur Schweitzer, **Big Business in the Third Reich** (Bloomington; Indiana University Press, 1964; London: Eyre & Spottiswoode, 1964), p. 539.
94. Hsiao, **Rural China**, p. 247.
95. Seton-Watson, **The Decline of Imperial Russia**, p. 230.
96. Richard Charques, **The Twilight of Imperial Russia** (London: Phoenix House, 1958), p. 135, and Harcave, **First Blood**, p. 232.
97. "An Appeal" (leaflet), issued in New York City by the Committee of Conscience Against Apartheid and a list of sponsors.
98. Sharp, **Tyranny Could Not Quell Them.**
99. Shimbori, *"Zengakuren,"* p. 247. Shimbori does not supply any details.
100. King Gordon, **U. N. in the Congo: A Quest for Peace** (New York: Carnegie Endowment for International Peace, 1962), p. 150, and Catherine Hoskyns, **The Congo Since Independence: January 1960-December 1961** (London: Oxford University Press, 1965), pp. 295 and 467.
101. Harcave, **First Blood**, p. 232.
102. This is quoted from the text of the Manifesto, from R. W. Postgate, **Revolution**

from **1789 to 1906** (New York, Harper Torchbooks, Harper & Brothers, 1962), p. 391.

103. Gipson, **The Coming of the Revolution**, p. 106.

104. Quoted by Gipson, **The British Empire Before the American Revolution**, vol. X, **The Triumphant Empire: Thunder-Clouds Gather in the West, 1763-1766**, p. 360.

105. Quoted by *Ibid.*, pp. 106-107.

106. *Ibid.*, p. 107.

107. Schlesinger, **The Colonial Merchants . . .** , pp. 404-405.

108. Quoted by Gipson, **The British Empire . . .** , vol. XII, p. 194.

109. *Ibid.*, p. 202.

110. Arthur Schweitzer, **Big Business in the Third Reich** (Bloomington, Ind.: Indiana University Press, 1964 and London: Eyre and Spottiswood, 1964) p. 88.

111. Gipson, **The Coming of the American Revolution**, p. 175.

112. Waskow, **From Race Riot to Sit-in**, p. 279.

113. Benjamin Muse, **Virginia's Massive Resistance** (Bloomington: Indiana University Press, 1961), p. 13.

114. *Ibid.*, pp. 29-30.

115. Quoted by *Ibid.*, pp. 59-60.

116. Farmer, **Freedom – When?**, p. 178.

117. Luthuli, **Let My People Go**, p. 210.

118. Rostovtzeff, **The Social and Economic History of the Roman Empire**, vol. I, p. 348.

119. Holmsen, *Norges Historie Fra de Eldste Tider til 1660*, pp. 386-387. See pp. 413-414 for a fairly localized case of tax refusal by Norwegian peasants in Gauldal, Trøndelag, from 1573.

120. *Ibid.*, p. 451.

121. Magnus Jensen, *Norges Historie Under Eneveldet 1660-1814* (Third Ed.; Oslo and Bergen: *Universitetsforlaget, 1963*) , pp. 83-84.

122. Lefebvre, **The French Revolution from its Origins to 1793**, pp. 120, 127, 157-158 and 184, and Salvemini, **The French Revolution, 1788-1792**, pp. 120, 131, 165, 170 and 209.

123. Salvemini, **The French Revolution, 1788-1792**, p. 124.

124. Lefebvre, **The French Revolution from its Origins to 1793**, p. 134.

125. Hsiao, **Rural China**, p. 305, and Chang, **The Chinese Gentry**, p. 46.

126. Griffith, **The Resurrection of Hungary**, p. 32.

127. Case, **Non-violent Coercion**, pp. 230-231.

128. Keep, **The Rise of Social Democracy in Russia**, p. 160.

129. *Ibid.*, pp. 240-241 and Charques, **The Twilight of Imperial Russia**, p. 135.

130. The full text appears in R. W. Postgate, **Revolution from 1789 to 1906**, p. 391.

131. See Desai, **The Story of Bardoli**, and S. Gopal, **The Viceroyalty of Lord Irwin 1926-1931**, pp. 19-34. Pattabhi Sitaramayya, **The History of the Indian National Congress, 1885-1935**, vol. I, p. 605, and, Sharp, **Gandhi Wields . . .** pp. 106-211 *passim*.

132. Schweitzer, **Big Business in the Third Reich**, p. 88.

133. **Report of the Nyasaland Commission of Inquiry** Cmnd. 814 (London: H. M. Stationery Office, 1959), p. 11.

134. **Bulletin of the Non-violence Commission of the Peace Pledge Union** (London), no. I, March 1956.

135. *Guardian,* 5 September, 1962.

136. Letter from James Bristol dated 8 October 1966, from Lusaka, Zambia, to Stewart Meacham.

137. Nat Hentoff, **The New Equality,** p. 55.

138. Harcave, **First Blood,** p. 232.

139. Schweitzer, **Big Business in the Third Reich,** pp. 269-287.

140. This section is based upon discussion by Thomas G. Schelling, **International Economics** (Boston: Allyn and Bacon, 1958), pp. 488-489.

141. Henry Adams, **History of the United States During the Second Administration of Thomas Jefferson** (New York: Charles Scribners' Sons, 1890), vol. II, pp. 166-177, and Adams, **The Formative Years** (Cond. and ed. by Herbert Agar; London: Collins, 1948), vol. I, pp. 458-466, and vol. II, 487-542. The quotations are respectively from **The Formative Years,** vol. I, p. 461; **History . . . ,** vol. II, p. 176; **The Formative Years,** vol. II, p. 495.

142. The Royal Institute of International Affairs, **International Sanctions** (London: Oxford University Press, 1938), pp. 27-30, and F. P. Walters, **A History of the League of Nations** (London: Oxford University Press, 1960), pp. 131, 393-395, 525-536, and 787.

143. Walters, **A History of the League of Nations,** pp. 623-691; Royal Institute of International Affairs, **Sanctions** (Second Edition; London: R.I.I.A., 1935), and R.I.I.A., **International Sanctions;** and G. W. Baer, **The Coming of the Italian-Ethiopian War** (Cambridge, Mass.: Harvard University Press, 1967), see esp. Chapt. 12.

144. See **American Foreign Policy, 1950-1955: Basic Documents** (Washington: Department of State, 1957), vol. II, p. 2595, and **American Foreign Policy: Current Documents, 1956** (Washington: Department of State, 1959), pp. 1085-1095.

145. Adams, **History of the United States During the Second Administration of Thomas Jefferson,** vol. II, pp. 165-166.

146. Adams, **The Formative Years,** vol. II, pp. 540-542.

147. Gipson, **The British Empire . . . ,** vol. XII, pp. 346-349.

148. H. A. Washington, ed., **The Writings of Thomas Jefferson** (Washington, D. C.: Taylor and Maury, 1853), vol. III, p. 519. I am grateful to Michael Schulter and Ron McCarthy for this information.

149. Hamilton Foley, **Woodrow Wilson's Case for the League of Nations** (Princeton: Princeton University Press, 1933, and London: Humphrey Milford, Oxford University Press, 1933), pp. 67, 71 and 72.

150. John Foster Dulles, "Practicable Sanctions," in Evans Clark, ed., **Boycotts and Peace** (New York and London: Harper & Bros., 1932), p. 21.

151. See **American Foreign Policy: Current Documents, 1960** (Washington, D.C.: Department of State, 1964), pp. 240-241, and Department of State **Bulletin,** vol. XLVI, pp. 283-284.

152. Peter Wallensteen, "Characteristics of Economic Sanctions," **Journal of Peace Research** (Oslo), 1968, no. 3, pp. 250-51.

153. The reader is referred to other literature specifically dealing with international economic sanctions, including the following: Baer, **The Coming of the Italian-Ethiopian War**, especially Chapter 12; Clark, ed., **Boycotts and Peace** (this report contains a bibliography); Johan Galtung, "On the Effects of International Economic Sanctions, with Examples from the Case of Rhodesia," **World Politics**, vol. XIX, no. 3 (April 1967), pp. 378-416; Frederik Hoffmann, "The Functions of Economic Sanctions, A Comparative Analysis," in **Journal of Peace Research, 1967, no. 2,** pp. 140-60; Amy Leiss, ed., **Apartheid and the United Nations: Collective Measures** (New York: Carnegie Endowment for International Peace, 1965); Ronald Segal, ed., **Sanctions Against South Africa** (Baltimore: Penguin Books, 1964); Rita Falk Taubenfeld and Howard J. Taubenfeld, "The 'Economic Weapon': The League and the United Nations," **Proceedings of the American Society of International Law,** 1964, pp. 184-205 (this article is largely based on the cases of Italy, Cuba, Dominican Republic, China, and South Africa); Wallensteen, "Characteristics of Economic Sanctions," pp. 248-67; Walters, **A History of the League of Nations.**

154. Wallensteen, "Characteristics of Economic Sanctions," p. 251.

155. *Ibid.*

PART TWO: METHODS

6

The Methods
of Economic
Noncooperation:
(2) The Strike

INTRODUCTION

The second general subclass of methods of economic noncooperation is the strike. The strike[1] involves a refusal to continue economic cooperation through work. It is a collective, deliberate and normally temporary suspension of labor designed to exert pressure on others within the same economic, political and, sometimes, social or cultural unit. That is to say, though the issues are normally economic, they are not necessarily so, even though the means of action are economic. The aim of a strike is to produce by this leverage some change in the relationships of the conflicting groups. Usually this takes the form of granting of certain demands made by the strikers as a precondition for their resumption of work. It is the collective nature of the strike which gives this type of noncooperation its characteristics and power. Strikes are largely associated with modern industrial organizations; they also occur, however, in agricultural conflicts and within various institutions. Strikes are possible wherever people work for someone else.

Strikes are almost always specific, in the sense of being *for* or *against* something which is important to the strikers. In theory any number of workers might act together to produce a strike, but in practice the number of strikers must be sufficiently large to disrupt seriously or to make impossible continued operations of at least that economic unit. As with violence and other more powerful forms of nonviolent action, the mere *threat* of a serious strike may be sufficient to induce concessions from the opponent group; some examples of such threats are included in this chapter. Strikes may be spontaneous or planned, "official" (authorized by the unions) or "wildcat" (not authorized by the unions).

The motives for strikes vary considerably. Economic motives, which include wages, working conditions, union recognition, and hours, have been predominant. Even these types of strikes may be directed against a government agency, though an employer is usually the target. Political and social aims may accompany economic objectives or may be independent of them. Those wider issues may take many forms.

Now to the classification of the forms of the strike. The broad categories which must be used in classifying the many methods of nonviolent action are too rigid to suit the reality, as we noted at the beginning of Part Two. Consequently, in every general class and subclass—such as the strike—there are some methods which also have one or more characteristics of another class (or do so under certain conditions) or which differ in at least one respect from the general characteristics of its class. This is especially true in the case of the strike. Normally, the strike is a temporary withdrawal of labor, but there are methods in which the withdrawal is, or at least is intended to be, permanent. Also, some methods are combinations of economic boycotts and strikes. Other methods operate by withdrawing labor but do so only symbolically, so that they might also be included within the class of nonviolent protest and persuasion. One solution might be to develop a much more complicated classification system than that offered in this book; that indeed needs to be done, for there are many methods which should have at least dual classifications. Also, the effects and leverages of particular methods differ with the situation in which they are applied and the manner in which they are conducted. For our purposes here, however, several methods which fall on a borderline between classes or which have mixed characteristics are grouped within the strike, coming closer to belonging here than in any other class or subclass of the methods. This is instructive and humbling, for the reality of social dynamics is always more complex and flexible than the intellectual tools which we use in efforts to understand it. Three of the groupings of methods of the strike which follow consist of such borderline forms or are offspring of mixed parentage. These are often some of the fresher, more imaginative ones; because they are less usual or because they combine more than one type of leverage or population group, they may also make a disproportionate impact.

SYMBOLIC STRIKES

97. Protest strike

In a protest strike,[2] also called token strike[3] and demonstration strike,[4] work is stopped for a preannounced short period—a minute, an hour, a day, or even a week—in order to make clear the feelings of the workers on a particular issue: economic, political, or other.[5] No set demands are made. The aim is to demonstrate that the workers feel deeply about a certain matter and that they possess strength to strike more effectively if necessary, thus warning the officials that they had best take the workers' feelings into consideration. An additional aim may be to catch the imagination of workers and the public. This method may also be used in the early stages of a protracted struggle to accustom the workers to the idea of striking on the issue involved; in instances in which the unions are not prepared for a longer strike; where longer strikes would incur more severe retaliation than the workers are, at that particular point, prepared to suffer; or where serious damage to the economy is not desired. The token strike may be varied by combining it with periods of silence, "stay-at-home" days, or other methods. There may be protest general strikes, protest industry strikes, protest sympathy strikes and the like.

On January 15, 1923, four days after the Franco-Belgian invasion of the Ruhr, the population of the Ruhr area and the occupied Rhineland held a thirty-minute protest strike to express their will to resist.[6] A one-day strike to protest the ill-treatment of the Jews was called in Amsterdam on February 25-26, 1941.[7] Other examples include a one-hour strike on April 10, 1959, by about five hundred building workers in a factory making rockets in Stevenage, Hertfordshire, England, in support of the unilateral renunciation of nuclear weapons;[8] the ten- to fifteen-minute work stoppage by nine million people in Belgium (half the population), as a demonstration against nuclear weapons, which occurred at 11 A.M. on May 8, 1962;[9] the one-day strike (except on ships at sea, troop carriers, and relief ships) by various U.S. maritime unions in protest against delays in bringing servicemen home after World War II.[10]

Protest strikes were frequent during the Russian 1905 Revolution. In February, for example, streetcar workers in Astrakhan held a one-day strike,[11] and in October the printers in St. Petersburg held a three-day strike to show sympathy for the striking printers of Moscow.[12] A conservative bureaucrat described the November strike movement in the capital: "One day the barbers would strike; another day it would be the restaurant and hotel employees. No sooner would these strikes end than the newsboys would strike; then it would be the salesmen in stores."[13]

A twenty-four-hour protest general strike was held in Ireland on April 23, 1918, and was solidly observed throughout the country, except in Belfast. "Factories stood idle, shops and bars were closed, transport was stopped," writes Edgar Holt. "It was now clear that Southern Ireland had no intention of standing patiently by in the remote hope that conscription, when the Government chose to impose it, would be accompanied by Home Rule."[14]

Several short protest strikes were conducted in Czechoslovakia the week after the Russian invasion in August 1968. On August 21 at 12 noon, only hours after the invasion, in response to a call for a two-minute protest strike issued by representatives of the creative artists' unions and broadcast on television and radio, all movement on the streets of Prague came to a halt.[15] A broadcast plea from the North Bohemian region brought about a one-hour general strike starting at noon the following day.[16] The Declaration of the Extraordinary Fourteenth Party Congress of the Communist Party of Czechoslovakia on August 22 contained a call for a one-hour protest strike at noon on Friday, August 23. Appeals were posted that morning that everyone leave the streets of Prague during that hour. "Prague is to become a dead city." The Communist Party newspaper *Rude Pravo* reported that strike as seen in the center of Prague:

> From the National Museum, a line of young people marches down Wenceslas Square. They are holding hands and shouting: "Evacuate the streets!" Behind them there is only the empty, wide space of the Square. The sirens begin to wail; car horns join them. The soldiers in tanks look around. They don't know what is going on. They are scanning buildings on either side, watching the windows. Some of the tanks are closing their hatches. The machine guns and cannon are turning around, looking for targets. But there is no one to shoot at; nobody is provoking them. The people have begun a general strike, as proclaimed by our Communist Party.
>
> All of a sudden Wenceslas Square is empty; only dust, papers,

posters rise up in the wind. All that is left are tanks and soldiers. Nobody around them, none of our people.[17]

98. Quickie walkout (lightning strike)

Short, spontaneous protest strikes undertaken without deliberation to "let off steam" or to protest over relatively minor issues have come to be known as quickie walkouts in the United States[18] and lightning strikes in England;[19] they rarely last more than a few hours or involve more than a few workers in a plant. This is one of the form which wildcat strikes may take. They were fairly common in the United States during World War II in situations where major strikes were banned. Jack Barbash cites an example of such a walkout by department store workers because of inconveniences in a new pay system and the company's misrepresentation of the union's attitude toward the employment of a handicapped worker.[20] In the summer of 1963 a lightning strike occurred on the Paris *Métro*. (The government in turn sought legislation to require at least five days' strike notice.)[21]

AGRICULTURAL STRIKES

99. Peasant strike

Under feudal and semifeudal conditions peasants have collectively refused to continue to work on the properties of their landlords. The examples here are Russian. In 1861 peasants in the department of Kazan were influenced by Anton Petrov, a peasant political prophet, to begin a series of actions in which they would rely on themselves alone to improve their living conditions. These included peasant strikes. "The peasant communities met together in assemblies and began by deciding on collective abstention from all work on the landlords' properties."[22] During the 1905 Revolution, the second congress of the Peasants' Union resolved upon the "refusal of conscript military service and peasant strikes on the large landed estates"[23] as methods for advancing their demands for a change in the system of land ownership and for an early constituent assembly. In the autumn of 1905, strikes by agricultural laborers were reported from the provinces of Kiev, Volhynia, Podolia, Kharkov, Poltava, Chernigov, Saratov, Samara, Orlov, Kursk, Tambov, Moscow, Nizhny Novgorod, and Penza, and also from the Don Cossack region. At the time there was still relatively little looting and burning of estates.[24]

Peasant strikes are among the means of protest and resistance frequently used in Latin America, Solon Barraclough has written.[25] For example, in July and August 1952 Indian *campesinos* (farm workers) in Bolivia refused to work and applied other methods of nonviolent action: organizers from the Ministry of Rural Affairs and various political parties had been active among the peasants.[26] Peasant unions in Northeast Brazil in 1962 conducted a strike of over 200,000 peasants. Landlords made many concessions, and various national and regional proposals for agrarian reforms were stimulated. It has also been claimed that this strike was one factor in the military *coup* two years later; the new military regime is reported to have backed the organizations of the large farmers and to have suppressed peasant union activity. Peasant leaders were jailed, exiled, or murdered.[27]

In Peru during 1960-63, peasant strikes were conducted in the valley of La Convención. Led by Hugo Blanco, permanent laborers on the large plantations of the valley simply withdrew the labor they had provided to landlords for almost no wages. Some of the peasants were able to work instead on the plots assigned for their own use, and thereby even increased their incomes while on strike. Leaders were jailed and military force was used to crush the movement. However, a special decree was issued breaking up the large holdings in that area and selling them to peasants, and a first attempt at agrarian reform legislation for all Peru passed the legislature.[28]

100. Farm workers' strike

Farm workers hired for wages may, like any other group, withdraw their labor by striking with the aim of achieving certain objectives. The years 1929 to 1935 witnessed in California "a series of spectacular strikes" stimulated by the wage cuts of the Depression and expectations aroused by policies of the new Roosevelt administration. Carey McWilliams writes: "Beyond question, the strikes of these years are without precedent in the history of labor in the United States. Never before had farm laborers organized on any such scale and never before had they conducted strikes of such magnitude and such far-reaching social significance."[29] Migrant farm laborers expressed their unrest in spontaneous strikes, as well as organized ones.

These strikes were frequently failures and usually resulted in severe repression by both local government and unofficial groups. In January and February, 1930, for example, in the Imperial Valley two spontaneous strike movements occurred among Mexican and Filipino field workers and American workers in the packing sheds: the issues were wage reductions and demands for wage increases and improved conditions. Trade union organizers became active during the strikes and were arrested on suspicion and watched. After the strikes failed, the union called for a conference of agricultural workers for April 20, but six days before that there were raids on residences and public meeting places. Over a hundred workers were arrested and kept on forty thousand dollars bond; eight of them were convicted under the Criminal Syndicalism Act. The union was crippled. [30]

In November 1932 Communist Party organizers of the Cannery and Agricultural Workers' Industrial Union led fruit workers at Vacaville in a strike, which was met with "formidable intimidation, beatings and prosecution." Six strike leaders were kidnapped, were flogged with tug straps, had their heads clipped with sheep clippers, and had red enamel poured over them. Communists arriving in the area found 180 deputized armed vigilantes and also strikebreakers carrying gas pipes and pruning shears. After this strike was broken, other strikes occurred during 1933. Three thousand pea pickers striking in April also met wholesale arrests, floggings and general intimidation, but nevertheless they forced payment for a "hamper" (about thirty pounds) of peas up from ten cents to seventeen and twenty cents. One man was dead, however, and many injured. [31]

Repression against other farm workers' strikes included severe beatings, broken bones, shootings (resulting in injuries and death), arrests, acquittal of identified murderers of strikers, excessive bail for strikers, misuse of various laws and regulations to harass and prosecute strikers, tear gas, raiding parties, jailing of strikers in a stockade, forcible eviction from a strike camp, and burning of strikers' shacks. Agricultural workers involved in strikes during this period included pickers of various tree fruits as well as pickers of grapes, cotton and vegetables. During 1933 about fifty thousand strikers were involved; of the thirty-seven recorded strikes (there were many more), gains for strikers resulted in twenty-nine cases; in the union-led strikes the wage rates were increased from fifteen cents an hour to an average of twenty-five cents. [32]

The most famous agricultural strike in the United States in recent years has been that of the grape workers of Delano, California, under the leadership of Cesar Chavez. The strike began in September 1965, and it was not until the summer of 1970 that growers of table grapes in large numbers signed union contracts. Leading the National Farm Workers' Association, and later the United Farm Workers' Organizing Committee,

A.F.L.-C.I.O., Chavez repeatedly insisted on adherence to nonviolent discipline. The strike was supplemented by a nationwide consumers' boycott—first of all California grapes, then, after the first union contracts, of nonunion grapes. In March 1966 the strikers conducted a 250 mile pilgrimage from Delano to the state capital at Sacramento to protest the spraying of pickets with insecticides and fertilizer and to publicize the boycott. Evening rallies were held along the way. At each rally the union plan was read:

> We are suffering. . . We shall unite. . . We shall strike. . . . We shall overcome . . . Our pilgrimage is the match that will light our cause for all farm workers to see what is happening here, so that they may do as we have done.[33]

STRIKES BY SPECIAL GROUPS

101. Refusal of impressed labor

Demands that certain people perform impressed labor for others have on occasion been met with a refusal to do such work. Refusal has usually been aimed at the abolition of impressed labor, rather than merely at improved conditions. In 1921, for example, in the district of Kotgiri (or Kotgarh) in India, an organized, disciplined campaign of nonviolent refusal was conducted against the very old system of *begar,* or forced labor. This system had allowed Europeans to demand at will that poor cultivators perform hard labor at extremely low wages, despite the consequent detrimental effect on the agriculture of the hill tribes. The cultivators' demands were met; a strict limitation was placed on the types of service that Europeans could demand, and reasonable rates of pay were fixed for any work performed.[34]

During the American War of Independence, the British sought to revive the former French system of *corvée* (compulsory unpaid labor) in the province of Quebec. For two years, from 1776 to 1778, Quebec farmers and villagers, such as those in Chambly, often simply refused to work on the roads or to carry out any other military transport duties. Then the British withdrew the law and abolished *corvée,* providing payment for those already "hired."[35] In 1781 in Yang-ku, Shantung, China, a scholar *(sheng-yüan)* incited villagers to refuse to do river-dredging work. (The villagers, however, also took out their anger on government property—they attacked the prison and destroyed the tax collector's office.)[36]

102. Prisoners' strike

Prisoners have also at times refused to do work required of them by prison officials; the refusal may have various motives: an objection to being incarcerated at all, an effort to improve specific conditions in the prison, or other motives. During World War II a number of strikes by conscientious objectors took place in U.S. prisons. One of these, by nineteen prisoners, began at the Federal Correctional Institution at Danbury, Connecticut, on August 11, 1943, in protest against the official policy of racial segregation at meals. After 133 days of restriction to their cells, with only limited exercise, a monotonous diet, and restrictions on visits, the prisoners noted the gradual introduction of a cafeteria system, which the strikers expected would permanently eliminate the policy of segregation.[37] During the summer of 1953 coal-mining prisoners at the huge camp at Vorkuta, U.S.S.R., conducted a strike for improved conditions,[38] as described briefly in Chapter Two. Because the area industry (coal) was involved and this was a one-industry complex, this case had additional characteristics of both the industry strike and the general strike.

103. Craft strike

"A craft strike is a suspension by the workers of a single craft in one or in many shops of a local, regional, national, or international area. The variations in geographic scope may be indicated as shop craft strike, local craft strike, regional craft strike, etc."[39] The craft strike almost always takes place where the union is a craft union rather than an industrial union which includes all the workers in a plant or industry.[40] Examples of the craft strike include the following: In 1741 the New York City master bakers struck against municipal regulation of the price of bread (the first American strike);[41] Boston journeymen carpenters struck in 1825 for a ten-hour day;[42] in January 1890 over three thousand New York cloak makers struck against sweatshop conditions;[43] and fifteen thousand shirtwaist and dress makers in New York struck from November 1909 to February 1910 for improved wages and conditions.[44]

104. Professional strike

Groups of salaried persons or self-employed persons in a particular profession may go on strike for economic, political, or other reasons. Where the motive is political, the professional strike usually takes place within the context of a wider struggle involving other sections of the population and other methods of nonviolent action, which may precede, accompany, or follow the professional strike.

An early example of a professional strike took place in Oxyrhynchus, Egypt, in A.D. 260. M. Rostovtzeff writes:

> . . . the tremendous depreciation of the currency led to a formal strike of the managers of the banks of exchange. . . They closed their doors and refused to accept and to exchange the imperial currency. . . The administration resorted to compulsion and threats. The *strategus* issued an order to the bankers and to other money-changers "to open their banks and to accept and exchange all coin except the absolutely spurious and counterfeit." The trouble was not new, for the *strategus* refers to "penalties already ordained from them in the past by his Highness the Prefect." [45]

About 200 A.D. shipmasters who took cargoes of grain from Asia Minor to Rome apparently threatened a professional strike if certain demands were not met. The Minister of Food *(praefectus annonae)* wrote to a provincial subordinate that the seafaring shipmasters of the five unions of Arles were "virtually giving notice that their service will shortly be suspended if the grievance continues." [46]

The suspension of practice by lawyers as part of a political struggle has occurred on several occasions. For example, when the courts in the American colonies were required under the Stamp Act to use tax stamps —which the colonists refused to do—lawyers frequently responded by suspending practice and seeking closure of the courts. [47] Lawyers in St. Petersburg, Russia, reacted to "Bloody Sunday" in January 1905 by refusing to appear in court and by issuing a formal protest against the "pitiless hand of the government." [48] The following October various government employees went on strike in the city: printers for the navy, actors, port and customs staff, and the State Bank's local staff. [49]

Other groups which have used the professional strike are teachers, doctors and civil servants. The teachers in Mayfield Borough, Pennsylvania, struck in January and April 1934, after working six and a half months without receiving salaries. [50] In December 1956 the general strike and economic shutdown directed against the attempt of Haitian strongman General Paul E. Magliore to stay in power despite constitutional restrictions included strikes by civil servants and bank and school employees, as well as the refusal of lawyers to accept court cases. [51]

ORDINARY INDUSTRIAL STRIKES

105. Establishment strike

An establishment strike "involves all the crafts in one or more plants under one management irrespective of their spatial distribution." [52] Examples of the establishment strike include: the strike, in February and March 1936, of Goodyear rubber workers in Akron, Ohio, for union recognition;[53] and the strike of five hundred Scandinavian Airlines System workers in Norway in March and April 1954, on the issue of wage increases.[54]

106. Industry strike

An industry strike is a suspension of all the establishments of an industry (e.g., mining, printing, etc.) of a local or other area." [55] Local and regional industry strikes have occurred frequently. Examples include: the strike in 1902 of the United Mine Workers against the operators of the "anthracite monopoly" in eastern Pennsylvania;[56] the strike in 1912 of textile workers employed by several companies in Lawrence, Massachusetts, led by the Industrial Workers of the World;[57] the dockworkers' strike in June–July 1959, led by several unions, in Colombo, Ceylon;[58] and the July–August 1953 strike of the Cannery Workers Union (A.F.L. Teamsters), which closed sixty-eight canneries affiliated with the Canners Association in Northern California.[59] Other examples include: politically motivated strikes in the coal mines during the *Ruhrkampf*;[60] the Dutch shipyard workers' strike on February 17 and 18, 1941, which "forced local German authorities to abandon the plan of deporting workers to Germany against their will;"[61] the strike of Dutch railway workers which, beginning in September 1944 and continuing into 1945, was called for by the Dutch government-in-exile to aid the Allied armies;[62] and the Spanish strike movement in the Asturian mines in April–May 1962.[63]

107. Sympathetic strike

In a sympathetic strike workers withdraw their labor, not to help themselves, but to support the demands of fellow workers by bringing additional pressure to bear upon the employer. The two groups of workers may or may not have a common employer; the sympathetic strikers may simply believe that their participation may force other employers, the public, or the government to bring sufficient pressure to bear on the employer directly involved so that he will grant the desired concessions.[64] The sympathetic strike is reported to have originated about 1875, although the present name for it was not adopted until 1886.[65] Sympathetic strikes were illegal in Britain between 1927 and 1946.[66]

Fred Hall elaborates on motivations for the sympathetic strike:

> A sympathetic strike receives its name not so much because its motive is sympathy only . . . but because its motive is not selfish only . . . The ordinary striker protests against an injury which affects, or definitely threatens to affect, some fellow workmen, but which, he believes, will affect himself at some more or less definite time in the future. . . . Sympathetic strikers object, not to their employer's attitudes to *them,* but to his attitude toward *certain other parties*—an attitude which is hostile to labor.[67]

Examples of the sympathetic strike include: the railroad system strike in 1886, which originated on the Texas and Pacific Railroad and soon extended sympathetically to cover the entire Missouri Pacific Railroad as well;[68] and the 1924 Norwegian paper mill workers' strike in sympathy with locked-out transport workers.[69] In Imperial Russia in July 1903, sympathetic strikes were declared in Odessa, Kiev, Nikolaev and Ekaterinoslav, in support of strikes for increased wages and shorter hours in Baku, Tiflis and Batum.[70] In an unusual case, Guatemalan railroad workers in late June 1944 went on sympathy strike in support of the student strike at the National University. The ostensible purpose of this student strike was to oust the university rector, but the basic aim was to oust President Jorge Ubico, who had suspended five constitutional articles concerned with political freedoms,[71] with the consequences described in Chapter Two.

RESTRICTED STRIKES

108. Detailed strike

In the detailed strike, as originally understood, the workers one by one stop work or take up other jobs, until the employer is compelled to inquire about their grievance and is informed of their demands. This type of detailed strike was practiced by English craft unions in the middle of the nineteenth century—for example, in the case of the Flint glass makers in the years following 1854. Their magazine described the effect of this form of strike: "As man after man leaves . . . then it is that the proud and haughty spirit of the oppressor is brought down and he feels the power he cannot see." [72]

According to E.T. Hiller, the term detailed strike has come to include any piecemeal stoppage by persons engaged in a dispute. Where a strike is to cover a number of factories in a single industry (or, conceivably, in a number of industries), it may be organized in such a way that the workers in one factory or industry after another stop work on succeeding days or weeks, progressively increasing the strike. Allowance is made, however, for the possibility of a settlement before the full working force is withdrawn. Another variation of this method would be the withdrawal, each day, of a certain number of workers from a plant, the number being gradually extended accumulatively to include all the workers.

This method enables the unions to concentrate their forces on particular points, plants, or firms, while other workers either remain at work or are made jobless by a strike in which they are technically not participating—and hence, in some countries, they are eligible for unemployment benefits.

Examples of the detailed strike include: the strike of United Auto Workers at the General Motors plant in Flint, Michigan, in the summer of 1938, in which only the skilled tool-and-die workers struck; under the existing regulations the other then-unemployed "nonstriking" production workers could draw unemployment insurance;[73] the detailed strike by American cigar makers union in 1886;[74] and finally a New York clothing strike (1914?) in which the pants-makers struck one day, the vest-makers the next, and finally the coat-makers, as a means of demonstrating the workers' power and obtaining optimum impact.[75]

109. Bumper strike

A type of strike closely related to the detailed strike is the bumper strike, in which the union strikes only one firm in an industry at a time; by dealing with the firms individually, the union exposes each struck firm to the competition of rivals during the strike.[76] The bumper strike was used in the British radio industry in 1946.[77]

110. Slowdown strike

In the slowdown strike (also known as the go–slow and in Britain and elsewhere by the Welsh word *ca'canny*[78] instead of leaving their jobs or stopping work entirely, the workers deliberately slow down the pace of their work until the efficiency is drastically reduced.[79] In an industrial plant this slowdown has its effects on profits; in governmental offices it would, if continued, reduce the regime's capacity to rule.

Slowdowns in work by African slaves in the United States are reported in statements by ex-slaves and others. Raymond and Alice Bauer summarize these:

> The amount of slowing up of labor by the slaves must, in the aggregate, have caused a tremendous financial loss to plantation owners. The only way we have of estimating it quantitatively is through comparison of the work done on different plantations and under different systems of labor. The statement is frequently made that production on a plantation varied more than 100 percent from time to time. Comparison in the output of slaves in different parts of the South also showed variations of over 100 percent.[80]

Russian serfs in 1859 showed their opposition to their serfdom by doing less work,[81] and two years later in the early weeks of 1861, following an explicit promise of emancipation, the peasants conducted go-slows on the *corvées*.

> The peasants carried out these duties, from which they thought they would soon be exempted, more and more slowly and more and more reluctantly. A sort of spontaneous strike, aimed at loosening the bonds of serfdom, and making submission to the local administrative authorities less specific, accompanied, and often partly replaced an open but sporadic refusal to yield to the landlord's will.[82]

Franz Neumann describes the *ca'canny* or the slowdown as "one of the decisive methods of syndicalist warfare" and claims that its first large-scale use—he presumably means in industrial conflicts—was by Italian railway workers in 1895.[83] It had, however, previously been used by Glasgow dockers after an unsuccessful strike in 1889.[84]

During the Nazi occupation, "Dutch factory workers went slow, particularly when they were forced to work in Germany . . ."[85] In 1942 Sir Stafford Cripps broadcast an appeal to workers in Nazi-occupied Europe to "go slow" in their work. Goebbels thought silence the best means of fighting the appeal, since he wrote, "the slogan of 'go slow' is always much more effective than that of 'work fast.'"[86] German workers themselves appear to have used slowdown strikes very effectively in 1938 and 1939. Go-slows by the coal miners during that period led to a significant drop in production, which in turn prodded the government to launch efforts to raise production and to grant significant wage increases.[87] The wage freeze of September 1939, other worsening labor conditions, and the "clear . . . intention of the regime at the outbreak of the war . . . to abolish all social gains made in decades of social struggle" led to similar more widespread action by German workers. Neumann writes:

> . . . it is at this point that passive resistance[88] seems to have begun on a large scale. The regime had to give way and to capitulate on almost every front. On 16 November 1939, it reintroduced the additional payments for holiday, Sunday, night, and overtime work. On 17 November 1939, it reintroduced paid holidays and even compensation to the workers for previous losses. On 12 December 1939, the regime had finally to enact new labor-time legislation, and strengthen the protection of women, juveniles, and workers as a whole.[89]

In Nazi-occupied Czechoslovakia, "there was of course also in general the go-slow campaign when workers would either absent themselves from work or reduce the tempo of their work."[90]

111. Working-to-rule strike

The working-to-rule strike is "the literal carrying out of orders in a way calculated to retard production and reduce the employer's profit margin."[91] The workers remain at their jobs but meticulously observe all the rules and regulations of the union, employer, and the contract concerning how the work should be done, safety regulations, and so on, with the result that only a fraction of the normal output is produced. It is thus a variation of the slow-down strike under the technical excuse of doing the job extremely well. Neumann (who lumps the work-to-rule together with the broader slowdown strike) states that this kind of strike was applied successfully by the Austrian railway workers in 1905, 1906 and 1907 in the form of "scrupulous compliance" with all traffic and security regulations[92] It was also used in a series of local railway disputes in Britain preceding the General Strike in 1926, and during the 1949 British railway wage dispute.[93]

112. Reporting "sick" (sick-in)

Where strikes are prohibited by law, decree, or contract, or are not feasible for other reasons, workers may achieve anything from a slowdown of production to the equivalent of a full strike by falsely claiming to be sick. This is an especially useful method when sick leave has been granted in the contract or law but strikes have been prohibited.

A great deal of feigned illness was reported among African slaves in the southern United States, sufficient to have had considerable economic impact. Sometimes the illness ratio was nearly one sick to seven well. Slaves were frequently sick on Saturday but rarely on Sunday, which was not a normal workday; more sickness often occurred when the most work was required. Although there was a great deal of genuine illness among the slave population, it is also clear that much of it was feigned in order to get out of work, to avoid being sold to an undesirable master, or to get revenge on a master (by feigning a disability while on the auction block and hence fetch a lower price). Women pretending pregnancy received lighter work and increased food. The Bauers write:

> Of the extent to which illness was feigned there can . . . be little doubt. Some of the feigning was quite obvious, and one might wonder why such flagrant abuses were tolerated. The important thing to remember is that a slave was an important economic investment. Most slave owners sooner or later found out that it was more profitable to give the slave the benefit of the doubt. A sick slave driven to work might very well die. [94]

Another example is reported from China in late 1952. In this instance the workers, although lacking an independent union, by the very strength of their numbers maintained a capacity to act.

> Gradually the workers learned to offer passive resistance, which, although never on a planned or organized basis, nevertheless became a serious problem for the regime. Basically the passive resistance was expressed in a kind of slowdown. Outwardly, the workers seemed animated with the zeal demanded by the authorities but both the quantity and the quality of production fell noticeably.
>
> The most noticeable aspect of the resistance was absenteeism. Taking advantage of the stipulation in the Labor Insurance Regulations that only a small reduction in pay would result from medically approved sick leave, the workers now formed long queues outside the clinics. Most of the "patients" had undiagnosable symptoms which the doctors dealt with by authorizing a few days' leave. [95]

Caught between the pressure of officials and legal responsibility if a genuinely ill patient had an accident after having been refused sick leave, the doctors tended to grant leave. In many factories absenteeism ran as high as twenty percent. After the Health Committee of the Trade Unions organized "Comfort Missions" to visit every sick worker to determine whether he was really ill, absenteeism in one group of flour mills dropped from sixteen to five percent; but in a few weeks it returned to the original rate, after families learned to keep a lookout for the visit of the "Comfort Mission." "Thus by the time we arrived," said one such visitor, "the patient is always having a severe attack of pain." [96]

113. Strike by resignation

Another means of bypassing contractual or legal prohibitions against strikes (it may be used also on other occasions), is the strike by resignation. In this method a significant proportion of the personnel involved formally submit individual resignations. These may be timed so that the dates on which the resignations are submitted or go into effect are phased, so that the total number of resigned personnel steadily increases. Alternately, the whole group may resign simultaneously. At the end of August 1967 in Haverhill, Massachusetts, 85 nurses out of a nursing staff of 175 at Hale Hospital submitted resignations after the failure of negotiations over wages and working conditions. Fifty-eight of the resignations went into effect immediately, while the remainder were postponed for a few weeks. This was believed to be the first case of mass resignation by nurses during wage negotiations in the state. Haverhill City Manager J.P. Ginty called the nurses' action "tantamount to a strike." [97]

114. Limited strike

In the limited strike, which has also been called a "running-sore strike," the workers continue to perform most of their normal duties in an efficient way, but refuse to perform certain marginal work (either within or beyond their required working hours) or refuse to work on certain days. Such a strike may involve, for example, a refusal to work overtime or to work longer than is deemed reasonable. Transport workers have on occasion refused to operate the last scheduled bus, either for a predetermined period or until a settlement was reached. [98]

In 1870 miners in Fifeshire, Scotland, refused to work longer than eight hours a day. [99] Workers in St. Petersburg in October and November 1905 introduced the eight-hour day by "the simple expedient of ceasing work eight hours after they had reported for duty." [100] Strikes limited by refusal to work certain whole days are illustrated by the "Sundays only" strikes by British railway workers in 1945 and 1949, [101] and the alternative days" strike of Argentine railway workers in November 1947. [102] In 1942 Dutch mine workers in the strongly Catholic province of Limburg refused to work on Sundays, not primarily for religious reasons but because of opposition to the Nazi occupation. [103]

When German officials in Denmark in World War II met increased public opposition and sabotage with executions, prohibitions of all meetings and groups of more than five in the streets, and a curfew of 8 P.M. to 5 A.M., workers at Burmeister and Wain in Copenhagen, Denmark's largest shipyard, retaliated with a type of limited strike. On June 26, 1944, they left their places of work and sent a message to *Dagmarhus,* the Nazi headquarters, saying that since the Germans could not guarentee enough food, the workers had to tend their garden plots—and therefore had to leave work early. They were not striking, they said; but the potatoes and vegetables from their gardens were more important to them than the German war industry. These became known as the "go-home-early-strikes." [104]

115. Selective strike

In a selective strike workers refuse only to do certain *types* of work, often because of some political objection. The objection is to the tasks themselves, not hours, conditions, or the like. The intent is thus both to prevent the work itself from being carried out- and to induce the employer in the future not to request the workers to do that type of work.

The first example here, from the American colonies, occurred in the interim between the appointment of delegates to the First Continental Congress (elections began in June 1774) and its adjournment on October 26. In the commercial provinces, Arthur M. Schlesinger writes, "the most striking development was the combination of workingmen of two of the chief cities to withhold their labor from the British authorities at Boston. Early in September 1774, Governor Gage sought to hire Boston workingmen for fortifying Boston Neck, but was met with refusals wherever he turned." New York workers were persuaded not to go to Boston to work on the fortifications. General Gage's brief success in getting a few days' work done on barracks by Boston carpenters and masons was shortlived; the workmen left the jobs, and a meeting of committees of thirteen towns adopted a labor boycott program. Under this program they resolved that should anyone from Massachusetts or any other province supply the troops at Boston with labor or materials which would enable them "to annoy or in any way distress" the citizens, such persons would be deemed "most inveterate enemies" and should be "prevented and defeated." The leading towns at the meeting appointed Committees of Observation and Prevention for enforcement, and the resolves were sent to all towns in the province. As a result, "the labor boycott was made effective," and the barracks were not completed until November—and then only because workers had been brought from Nova Scotia, and a few from New Hampshire. [105]

In other examples, German rail workers refused to take coal trains to France during the *Ruhrkampf,* and the personnel of the coal-shipping companies joined them in that refusal. When occupation officials imposed a Franco-Belgian administration to run the railroads in the Ruhr, in March 1923, only 400 of the 170,000 preinvasion rail employess were willing to work for it. [106] In August 1943 Danish dockworkers at Odense refused to repair German ships. [107] At Gothenburg, Sweden, in the summer of 1963, dockers refused to unload 180 tons of South African canned fruit after dockers at Copenhagen and Aarhus, Denmark, had similarly refused. [108]

MULTI-INDUSTRY STRIKES

116. Generalized strike

When several industries are struck simultaneously as part of a general grievance but the strikers constitute less than a majority of the workers in the important industries of the area, the strike may be termed a generalized strike. [109] For example, because of common involvement in government wage regulations and procedures, several industries may be struck simultaneously, as happened in the metal, textile, shoe, mining and building industries in Norway in 1926 and again in 1927, in protest against wage reductions; the Norwegian strikes in 1931 again involved several industries, including newspapers, breweries and the tobacco industry. [110]

117. General strike

The general strike is widespread stoppage of labor by workers in an attempt to bring the economic life of a given area to a more or less complete standstill in order to achieve certain desired objectives. [111] The method may be used on a local, regional, national, or international level. Wilfred Harris Crook defined the general strike as "the strike of a major ity of the workers in the more important industries of any one locality or region." [112] When confined to a city it may be called a localized general strike, such as occurred in Seattle, Washington, and Winnipeg, Canada, in 1919 and Vienna in 1927. [113] While a general strike is usually intended to be total, certain vital services may be allowed to operate, especially those necessary for health, such as provision of milk, water, and food; sewage disposal; and hospital services. Crook distinguishes three broad types of the general strike—political, economic, and revolutionary:

> There is the *political* general strike, with the aim of exacting some definite political concession from the existing government, as the demand for universal suffrage in the Belgian General Strikes, or, more rarely, for the purpose of upholding the existing government against a would-be usurper, as the German strike against the *Kapp-Putsch* in 1920. The *economic* type is perhaps the most common form, at least at the beginning of the strike, and is exemplified by the Swedish strike of 1909. The *revolutionary* general strike, aiming at the definite overthrow of the existing government or industrial system, may be revolutionary in its purpose from the very start, or it may develop its revolutionary purpose as it proceeds. It is more likely to be found in countries where labor has not been long or extensively organized, or where the influential leaders of labor are largely syndicalist or anarchist in viewpoint, as Russia in 1905, Spain or Italy.[114]

The general strike has been widely advocated in radical socialist, syndicalist and anarchist thought; it has been practiced by English, Russian and Scandinavian socialists, and French, Italian, Spanish and South American anarchists and syndicalists.[115]

There are a large number of examples of general strikes, with considerable geographical and political variations. The Belgian general strikes of 1893, 1902 and 1913 supported demands for political reforms, including universal manhood suffrage.[116] Early general strikes in Imperial Russia were held at Rostov-on-Don in 1902 and Odessa in 1903,[117] and general strikes were widely used during the 1905 Russian Revolution. Perhaps the largest and most important of these was the Great October Strike of 1905, involving most of the cities of Imperial Russia that had any degree of industrial life.[118] The situation in Moscow is illustrative:

> Within a week, Moscow was virtually isolated, and most of her important public activities were at a standstill. All train connections were severed. All telegraphic connections along the lines emanating from the city were silent. Only the central General Telegraph Office remained in operation in the city to provide communication with the outside and the railroadmen were planning to close it.[119]

The general strike was also used against the Kapp *Putsch* in Weimar Germany in 1920, as we saw in Chapter Two.

By the late afternoon of March 14, 1920, the greatest strike the world had ever seen was a reality. The economic life of the country came to a standstill. . . Kapp attempted to break the strike . . . [and] made picketing a capital offense. But his efforts proved totally ineffectual. [120]

The general strike in Norway in 1921 was against wage reductions, [121] and the Chinese general strike of 1925 was over economic and nationalist grievances. [122] The British General Strike of May 3-12, 1926, was the outgrowth of unsatisfied claims of the coal miners, and developed into a major test of power between workers and the government, complicated by the capitulation by the trade union leaders. [123]

In Amsterdam a general strike was held on Febrary 25 and 26, 1941, to protest maltreatment of the city's Jews. [124] The 1943 Dutch general strike, or wave of strikes, from April 29 to as late as May 8 in some places, involved a majority of industrial workers, who opposed the planned internment of Dutch army veterans in Germany. [125] In Copenhagen, too, the general strike was applied during the Nazi occupation, from June 30 to about July 4, 1944, with the aim of forcing the Germans to withdraw the state of martial law and to remove the hated Danish fascist *Schalburgkorps* from the country. Negotiations led to German concessions, though not to the granting of the full demands. [126]

General strikes played a very important role in many cities and towns during the East German Rising of June 1953. [127] A general strike in Haiti in February 1957 ousted the temporary president, Pierre Louis. [128]

COMBINATION OF STRIKES AND ECONOMIC CLOSURES

118. The hartal

The *hartal* is an Indian method of nonviolent action in which the economic life of an area is temporarily suspended on a voluntary basis in order to demonstrate extreme dissatisfaction with some event, policy, or condition. It is used not to wield economic influence, but to communicate sorrow, determination, revulsion, or moral or religious feelings about the matter in question. Although the form of this method is largely economic, the effect is one of symbolic protest. The *hartal* is usually limited to a duration of twenty-four hours; it may rarely be extended to forty-eight hours or even longer in an extremely serious case. The *hartal* is usually city-wide or village-wide, although it may occur over a more extended area, including the whole nation. Generally speaking, there is greater emphasis in the *hartal* than in the general strike on its voluntary nature, even to the point of the laborers abstaining from work only after obtaining permission from their employers. Also, shop owners and businessmen fully participate by closing their establishments and factories.

This is one of the forms of nonviolent action known to ancient India, where it was used against the prince or king to make him aware of the unpopularity of a certain edict or other government measure. [129] The *hartal* is also used at a time of national mourning. Gandhi employed this ancient method in resistance movements he led. He often used the *hartal* at the beginning of a struggle with the intent of purifying participants in the struggle, of testing their feelings on the issue, and arousing the imagination of the people and the opponent. It was used, for example, at the beginning of the nationwide *satyagraha* campaign in India against the Rowlatt Bills in 1919, [130] and at the beginning of and during the 1930–31 *satyagraha* campaign for independence, especially to protest the arrest of important leaders. [131]

119. Economic shutdown

An economic shutdown occurs, producing economic paralysis, when the workers strike while management, businessmen, commercial institutions, and small shopkeepers simultaneously halt their economic activities ; this method thus includes characteristics of both strikes and economic boycotts. Tendencies in this direction may occur in general strikes for widely supported political objectives. Economic shutdowns vary in the extent to which the different types of economic activities are shut down and the extent to which businessmen, management, and so on, participate, just as participation in the general strike ranges widely.

In late 1905 a national economic shutdown was a factor in the restoration of Finnish autonomy within Imperial Russia; Finnish employers expressed their solidarity by paying their employees wages for the duration of the strike. [132] J. Hampden Jackson writes:

> Trains stopped, telegraphs went dead, factories stood empty. This lead was followed spontaneously by the whole nation: shops, offices, schools, restaurants were shut. The police went on strike and . . . university students formed a corps to maintain order . . . . There was no bloodshed; it was merely passive resistance with a whole nation behind it. [133]

After six days constitutional government with free elections was granted, although several years later the Tsar's regime once more attempted Russification.[134]

In Esbjerg, Denmark, an economic shutdown broke out on July 11, 1943, "where not only the workers, but also the functionaries went home, and the traders closed the stores."[135] In Port-au-Prince, Haiti, in December 1956, General Paul Magliore, strongman since 1946, was confronted with an economic shutdown to protest his modified martial law; this involved a general strike of workers and closure of businesses by owners or managers. Almost all concerns shut down, including gasoline and oil works, docks, most of the public market, downtown shops, schools and banks; civil servants were on strike and lawyers refused to take court cases; there were even strikes in some hospitals. "The resistance was completely passive. Haitians simply stayed away from their jobs." After Magliore's resignation from the presidency on December 12, the shutdown continued with the demand that he also resign from the army, which he did after additional support for the resignation demand came from the army itself and the Papal Nuncio. On December 14 it was reported that Magliore had left for exile in Jamaica.[136]

During the Buddhist struggle against the Diem regime in 1963, the majority of shops in Hué closed down on at least two occasions in support of the opposition movement, although it is not clear to what degree this was or was not accompanied by the shutdown of other sections of the city's economic life.[137]

Certain examples of strikes show that they have been used for political objectives, and in some cases (as when civil servants have gone on strike) the events themselves have become mixed with aspects of political noncooperation. Where certain methods of the strike have been illegal or have continued despite government edicts to the contrary (say, in a case of an economic shutdown intended to destroy a government), there has also been a mixture of economic and political forms of noncooperation. Let us now turn to methods of political noncooperation and examine them in detail.

NOTES

1. This general definition of the strike is based upon the following studies: Fitch, "Strikes and Lockouts," pp. 419-426; Jack Barbash, **Labor Unions in Action: A Study of the Mainsprings of Unionism,** (New York, Harper and Bros., 1948) pp. 124-141; Florence Peterson, **Survey of the Labor Economics,** rev. ed. (New York, Harper and Bros., 1951), pp. 565-572; E. T. Hiller, **The Strike: A Study in Collective Action** (Chicago: University of Chicago Press, 1928), esp. pp. 12-24 and 278; Steuben, **Strike Strategy;** and Reynolds, **Labor Economics and Labor Relations,** pp. 284-286.

2. The term is used by Warmbrunn, **The Dutch Under German Occupation,** p. 108.

3. Knowles, **Strikes,** p. 11.

4. Barbash, **Labor Unions in Action,** p. 129.

5. This inclusion of political issues as possible motivations in the protest strike diverges from Barbash, **Labor Unions in Action,** p. 131. Here the form of the strike rather than its motivation is regarded more significant in developing a classification.

6. Sternstein, "The *Ruhrkampf* of 1923", p. 111.

7. Warmbrunn, **The Dutch . . . ,** p. 110.

8. *Peace News,* April 10 and 17 April 1959.

9. *Ibid.,* 18 May 1962.

10. Barbash, **Labor Unions in Action,** p. 130.

11. Harcave, **First Blood,** p. 134.

12. *Ibid.,* p. 178.

13. Vladimir Gurko, quoted in Harcave, **First Blood,** p. 198.

14. Edgar Holt, **Protest in Arms,** p. 157. I am grateful to William Hamilton for this reference.

15. Littell, ed., **The Czech Black Book,** pp. 41 and 45-46.

16. *Ibid.,* pp. 76 and 85.

17. *Ibid.,* p. 115. On the announcements, see also pp. 81 and 112.

18. Barbash, **Labor Unions in Action,** pp. 126-127.

19. Knowles, **Strikes,** p. 11.

20. Barbash, **Labor Unions in Action,** pp. 126-127.

21. *Peace News,* 19 July 1963.

22. Venturi, **Roots of Revolution,** pp. 214-215.

23. Charques, **The Twilight of Imperial Russia,** p. 138.

24. Harcave, **First Blood,** pp. 170-171.

25. Solon L. Barraclough, "Agricultural Policy and Land Reform" (mimeo), (Conference on Key Problems of Economic Policy in Latin America, University of Chicago, November 6-9, 1966), p. 45. I am grateful to Jeffrey B. Peters for this and the following references.

26. Dwight B. Heath, Charles J. Erasmus and Hans C. Buechler, **Land Reform and Social Revolution in Bolivia** (New York: Frederick A. Praeger, 1969), pp. 42-44.

27. Barraclough, "Agricultural Policy and Land Reform," pp. 45-46; and Barraclough, "Farmers' Organizations in Planning and Implementing Rural Programs" (unpublished paper, n.d., prepared for a reader on rural development being edited by Professor Raanan Weitz) pp. 11-12.

28. Barraclough, "Farmers' Organizations in Planning and Implementing Rural Programs," pp. 11-12.

29. Carey McWilliams, **Factories in the Field: The Story of Migratory Farm Labor in California** (Boston: Little, Brown & Co., 1939), p. 211.

30. *Ibid.*, pp. 213-14.

31. *Ibid.*, pp. 215-16.

32. *Ibid.*, pp. 210-229.

33. John Gregory Dunne, **Delano: The Story of the California Grape Strike** (New York: Farrar, Straus & Giroux, 1967), p. 133. Also on the grape strike, see Peter Matthiessen, **Sal Si Puedes: Cesar Chavez and the New American Revolution** (New York: Random House, 1969).

34. Diwakar, *Satyagraha*, pp. 124-126.

35. Dan Daniels, "Nonviolent Actions in Canada," in **Our Generation Against Nuclear War** (Montreal), vol. 3, no. 1 (June 1964), p. 70.

36. Hsiao, **Rural China**, pp. 247-248.

37. Mulford C. Sibley and Asa Wardlaw, "Conscientious Objectors in Prison," in Staughton Lynd, ed., **Nonviolence in America: A Documentary History**, (Indianapolis, etc.: Bobbs-Merrill Co., 1966), pp. 301-302. See also James Peck, **Freedom Ride** (New York: Simon and Schuster, 1962), pp. 39-41.

38. Brigitte Gerland, "How the Great Vorkuta Strike Was Prepared" and "The Great Labor Camp Strike at Vorkuta," *The Militant* (New York), 28 February and 7 March 1955.

39. Steuben, **Strike Strategy**, p. 278.

40. On craft unions and industrial unions, see Peterson, **American Labor Unions,** pp. 71-75.

41. Selig Perlman, **A History of Trade Unionism in the United States** (New York: Macmillan Co., 1923), p. 3.

42. *Ibid.*, p. 8.

43. Benjamin Stalberg, **Tailor's Progress: The Story of A Famous Union and the Men Who Made It** (New York: Doubleday, Doran and Co., 1944), p. 38.

44. *Ibid.*, pp. 59-64.

45. Rostovtzeff, **The Social and Economic History of the Roman Empire,** vol. I, p. 472.

46. Buckler, "Labour Disputes in the Province of Asia Minor," p. 29.

47. Morgan and Morgan, **The Stamp Act Crisis,** pp. 223-224.

48. Harcave, **First Blood,** p. 101.

49. *Ibid.*, p. 183.

50. David Ziskind, **One Thousand Strikes of Government Employees** (New York: Columbia University Press, 1940), pp. 75-76.

51. *New York Times,* 12, 13 and 14 December 1956.

52. Hiller, **The Strike,** p. 278.

53. McAlister Coleman, **Men and Coal** (New York: Farrar and Rienhart, 1943), pp. 164-166.

54. Harriet Holter, "Disputes and Tensions in Industry" (reprint from **Scandinavian Democracy** [Copenhagen], 1958, pp. 3 4.

55. Hiller, **The Strike**, p. 278.

56. Herbert Harris, **American Labor** (New Haven: Yale University Press, 1938), pp. 120-129.

57. Foster Rhea Dulles, **Labor in America: A History** (New York: Thomas Y. Crowell, Co., 1949), pp. 215-219.

58. *The Observer* (London), 5 July 1959.

59. *Militant,* 10 and 17 August 1953.

60. Sternstein, "The *Ruhrkampf* of 1932," pp. 118-119.

61. Warmbrunn, **The Dutch . . .** , p. 108.

62. Jong, "Anti-Nazi Resistance in the' Netherlands," in **European Resistance Movements 1939-1945,** pp. 141-142. The failure of Field-Marshal Montgomery's military plan and German counter measures to the strike led to over 15,000 deaths from starvation, de Jong reports. Warmbrunn **(The Dutch . . . ,** pp. 141-146) offers a more detailed account and evaluation.

63. *The Times,* 3, 7, 8, 10, 14, 16, 17, 21, 22, 23, 24, 26, 28 and 29 May 1962.

64. Peterson, **American Labor Unions,** p. 270, and **Survey of Labor Economics,** pp. 568-569.

65. Fred S. Hall, **Sympathetic Strikes and Sympathetic Lockouts** (New York: Published Ph.D. dissertation in Political Science, Columbia University, 1898), pp. 11-12.

66. Symons, **The General Strike,** p. 226.

67. Hall, **Sympathetic Strikes and Sympathetic Lockouts,** pp. 14-15.

68. *Ibid.,* pp. 82-84.

69. Walter Galenson, **Labor in Norway** (Cambridge, Mass.: Harvard University Press, 1949), p. 165.

70. Seton-Watson, **The Decline of Imperial Russia,** p. 130.

71. *New York Times,* 23, 24 and 27 June 1944.

72. *Flint Glass Makers' Magazine,* July 1850, quoted by Hiller, **The Strike,** p. 136.

73. Irving Howe and B. J. Widick, **The U.A.W. and Walter Reuther** (New York: Random House, 1949), pp. 78-79.

74. Hiller, **The Strike,** p. 137.

75. *Ibid.*

76. Knowles, **Strikes,** pp. 12-13.

77. *Ibid.*

78. Knowles, **Strikes,** pp. 18-19.

79. Peterson, **American Labor Unions,** p. 268.

80. Raymond A. Bauer and Alice H. Bauer, "Day to Day Resistance to Slavery," **The Journal of Negro History,** vol. XXVII, no. 4 (Oct. 1942), p. 397.

81. Venturi, **Roots of Revolution,** p. 191.

82. *Ibid.,* pp. 207-208.

83. Franz Neumann, **Behemoth: The Structure and Practice of National Socialism 1933-1944** (New York: Octagon Books, 1963), p. 344.

84. Knowles, **Strikes,** p. 19.

85. Jong, "Anti-Nazi Resistance in the Netherlands," in **European Resistance Movements 1939-1945** p. 144. On slow-downs by Dutch miners, see Warmbrunn, **The Dutch . . . ,** p. 138.

86. Lochner, ed., **The Goebbels Diaries,** p. 107. Diary entry by Goebbels for 1 March 1942.

87. Neumann, **Behemoth,** pp. 344-345.

88. Neumann uses this term as identical with the *ca'canny* and the slow-down.

89. *Ibid.,* p. 347. Neumann (p. 348) offers reasons for believing that the concessions followed from the workers' action, while he acknowledges a possible primary role for reduced demands resulting from the "phoney" war of 1939.

90. Personal letter from Josef Korbel, 22 December 1966.

91. Knowles, **Strikes,** p. 18.

92. Neumann, **Behemoth,** p. 344.

93. Knowles, **Strikes,** p. 18.

94. Bauer and Bauer, "Day to Day Resistance to Slavery," p. 408.

95. Loh, **Escape from Red China,** pp. 109-111. I am grateful to Margaret Jackson Rothwell for this reference.

96. *Ibid.*

97. *Boston Globe,* 27 and 29 August 1967.

98. Knowles, **Strikes,** pp. 11-12.

99. *Ibid.,* p. 12.

100. Keep, **The Rise of Social Democracy in Russia,** p. 237, and Harcave, **First Blood,** p. 224.

101. Knowles, **Strikes,** p. 12.

102. *Ibid.*

103. Warmbrunn, **The Dutch . . . ,** p. 138.

104. Kirchhoff, et al., *Besættelsestidens Historie,* p. 204.

105. Schlesinger, **The Colonial Merchants and the American Revolution,** pp. 386-388.

106. Sternstein, "The *Ruhrkampf* of 1923," p. 115.

107. Reitlinger, **The Final Solution,** p. 346.

108. *Peace News,* 19 July 1963.

109. Hiller, **The Strike,** pp. 139, 243-244 and 278.

110. Galenson, **Labor in Norway,** pp. 166-168.

111. For more detailed discussion of the general strike, see esp. Wilfred H. Crook, "General Strike," **Encyclopedia of the Social Sciences,** vol. VI, pp. 607-612; Crook, **The General Strike;** and Crook, **Communism and the General Strike** (Hamden, Connecticut: The Shoe String Press, 1960).

112. Crook, **The General Strike,** p. vii.

113. *Ibid.*

114. *Ibid.,* pp. vii-viii.

115. Ligt, **The Conquest of Violence,** pp. 110-111 and Peterson, **American Labor Unions,** p. 257, for example.

116. Crook, **The General Strike,** pp. 54-103.

117. Seton-Watson, **The Decline of Imperial Russia,** pp. 128 and 130.

118. See Harcave, **First Blood,** pp. 180-186.

119. *Ibid.,* p. 181.

120. Halperin, **Germany Tried Democracy,** pp. 179-180.

121. Galenson, **Labor in Norway,** p. 162.

122. Crook, "General Strike," p. 610.

123. Symons, **The General Strike,** and Crook, **The General Strike,** pp. 367-445.

124. Jong, "Anti-Nazi Resistance in the Netherlands," p. 140, and Warmbrunn, **The Dutch . . . ,** pp. 106-111.

125. Warmbrunn, **The Dutch . . . ,** pp. 113-118. Jong, "Anti-Nazi Resistance in the Netherlands," p. 141 and personal letter confirming the participation of a majority of industrial workers from Dr. L. de Jong, 7 July 1966.

126. Kirchhoff, **et al.,** *Besættelsestidens Historie,* pp. 206-209.

127. Brant, **The East German Rising,** pp. 69-136 *passim.*

128. *Time,* 18 February 1957, p. 23.

129. Bondurant, **Conquest of Violence,** pp. 118-119.

130. *Ibid.,* p. 79.

131. *Ibid.,* p. 94 and Sharp, **Gandhi Wields . . . ,** pp. 91, 104, 109, 121 and 132.

132. Eino Jutikkala, **A History of Finland,** pp. 240-242.

133. J. Hampden Jackson, **Finland** (New York: Macmillan, 1940), pp. 74-75.

134. Miller, **Nonviolence,** p. 248.

135. Kirchhoff, **et al.,** *Besaettelsestidens Historie,* pp. 168-169.

136. *New York Times,* 7-14 December 1956.

137. Adam Roberts, "Buddhism and Politics in South Vietnam," in **The World Today** (London), vol. 21, no. 6 (June 1965), p. 246.

7

The Methods
of Political
Noncooperation

INTRODUCTION

Political noncooperation is the third subclass of methods of noncooperation; these methods involve refusals to continue the usual forms of political participation under existing conditions. Sometimes they are known as political boycotts. Individuals and small groups may practice methods of this class. Normally, however, political noncooperation involves larger numbers of people in corporate, concerted, usually temporary suspension of normal political obedience, cooperation and behavior. Political noncooperation may also be undertaken by government personnel and even by governments themselves. The purpose of suspension of political cooperation may simply be protest, or it may be personal dissociation from something seen as morally or politically objectionable, without much consideration as to consequences. More frequently, however, an act of political noncooperation is designed to exert pressure on the government, on an illegitimate group attempting to seize control of the government apparatus, or sometimes on another government. The aim of the political noncooperation may be to achieve a particular limited objective or a change in broader government policies. Or it may be to change the nature or composition of that government, or even to produce its disintegration. Where political noncooperation is practiced against usurpers, its aim may be to defend and to restore the legitimate government.

The political significance of these methods increases in proportion to the numbers participating and to the need for their cooperation for the operation of the political system. In actual struggles this class of methods is frequently combined with other forms of nonviolent action.

Political noncooperation may take an almost infinite variety of expressions, depending upon the particular situation. Basically they all stem from a desire not to assist the opponent by performance of certain types of political behavior. The thirty-eight methods included here are grouped into six subclasses: rejection of authority, citizens' noncooperation with government, citizens' alternatives to obedience, action by government personnel, domestic governmental action, and international governmental action. Many other possible forms have not been included here. For example, among the forms not specifically listed in this chapter which have to do with only one particular area of behavior—responses to arrest, fines, court orders, and the like—are refusal to accept bail, refusal to pay securities, suspension of publication of newspapers when faced with restrictions, refusal to make parole rounds, defiance of restraining and prohibition orders, and refusal to buy confiscated property. There is room for much more research.

REJECTION OF AUTHORITY

120. Withholding or withdrawal of allegiance

This form of political noncooperation involves a refusal to recognize a particular regime as legally or morally deserving of allegiance. A clear illustration is to be found in Hungarian resistance to Austrian rule in the nineteenth century. For instance, Emperor Franz Josef was not accepted as King of Hungary as long as he was unwilling to abide by the Hungarian constitution and had not been crowned King of Hungary.[1] Therefore, the members of the Hungarian parliament refused to recognize the legality of its dissolution by Franz Josef. When the Pesth County Council protested the dissolution of the parliament, it was itself dissolved, though it refused to recognize this dissolution and continued to meet.[2] When the County

Councils, which had refused to carry out ordinances issued by the Austrians,[3] were generally dissolved, their members refused to transfer their services to the Austrians.[4]

The conscious withdrawal by the people of authority from their rulers was also seen during the struggle of the Netherlands against Spanish rule in the sixteenth century. In 1565, for example, "lampoons were circulated, branding Philip as a perjurer who violated the privileges, and to whom, following the old law of the 'Joyous Entry,' no further allegiance was due."[5] In the summer of 1581 the States General meeting in The Hague passed a resolution

> whereby Philip, on account of his tyrannical rule and his trampling underfoot of the privileges of the country, was deposed from domination over his Netherland provinces. Following this resolution all authorities, officials, military commanders, and the like, were required to take a new oath, in the absence of Anjou, to the United Provinces . . . . The "Placard of Dismissal" . . . was a brilliant, though late, expression of the sturdy medieval tradition of freedom . . . [6]

The American colonists' rejection of the British government's authority over them was also a crucial point in the establishment of American independence. Thomas Jefferson wrote in 1774: "The true ground on which we declare their [Parliament's] acts void is, that the British parliament has no right to exercise authority over us."[7] This denial of authority to the British government, and its bestowal elsewhere, seem to have been highly important supportive factors in John Adams' later declaration 'that "the revolution was complete in the minds of the people, and the Union of the colonies, before the war commenced in the skirmishes of Concord and Lexington on the 19th April, 1775."[8]

Sometimes the withdrawal of allegiance may be expressed by a symbolic act, as on November 13, 1905, when the Russian cruiser *Ochakov* "raised the red flag in a dramatic gesture of 'non-recognition' of the government . . ."[9] The same month "in Vilna the two thousand delegates to the Lithuanian nationalist congress declared that they did not recognize the legitimacy of the Russian government under which they were living."[10]

During the *Ruhrkampf* Germans withheld allegiance from the French and Belgian occupation regime, denying the legality and therefore the validity of occupation decrees and orders. On January 19, 1923, the German government declared that "all state, provincial and local authorities were forbidden to obey any orders issued by the occupation authorities, and were told to confine themselves strictly to directions given by the appropriate German authorities." As one expression of this refusal of allegiance, German policemen refused to salute foreign officers.[11]

American Indians have frequently and in a variety of ways rejected the authority of the United States and Canadian governments over them. A number of these cases have been collected by Margaret DeMarco,[12] who writes that in 1921 Canadian Iroquois of the Six Nations Confederacy refused to become Canadian citizens and, asserting their sovereignty, brought a petition against the Dominion Government to the League of Nations.[13] Again, in the 1940s and 1950s American as well as Canadian members of the Confederacy sought both hearings before and membership in the United Nations. A band of Chippewas seeking a hearing in a treaty rights case appealed to the U.N. in 1946,[14] and another band of the same tribe requested a U.N. seat in 1960.[15]

In the early days after the August 1968 Russian invasion of Czechoslovakia, citizens and officials of that country refused to acknowledge that the Russians had any authority over political activities in that country. For example, on August 24 the lord mayor of Prague simply refused to see the occupation forces sent to negotiate with him.[16] Two days later, Communists working for State security asserted that they accepted the authority only of their own, not the Russian, officials:

> The All-Unit Committee of the Communist Party in the main administration of State Security in Sadova Street [Prague] declares again that it stands fully behind the legitimate Czechoslovak constitutional and Party organs and that it is guided in its work solely by the orders of Minister of Interior Josef Pavel.[17]

121. Refusal of public support

There are political circumstances in which failure to express openly support for the existing regime and its policies becomes an act of political noncooperation. Under political conditions of organized unanimity and coerced enthusiasm, silence may often be dangerously noticeable. Even where the regime is not fully totalitarian, some individuals may be expected or ordered to express their public support for the regime; their refusal to do so may be regarded as an act of opposition. During the 1963 Buddhist struggle against the Diem regime in South Vietnam, for example, government-staged demonstrations of support for the regime failed, and at least once a general did not appear at an announced press conference at which he was to declare his support for government raids on Buddhist pagodas.[18] It was clear that his "support" was not very enthusiastic.

Following the defeat of the 1956 Hungarian revolution, the country's writers publicly demonstrated their lack of support for the imposed regime by maintaining a "writers' silence" and submitting nothing for publication. In the circumstances, the publication of articles, stories, or books with their names listed as authors would have implied that the writers were passively accepting, or positively endorsing, the new regime. Conversely, their silence made it clear that they were refusing to give it their support. In late January 1957 François Fejto wrote: "One seeks in vain the signature of any reputed writer in all the official newspapers and periodicals. The voluminous Christmas issue of *Nepszabadsag* was published without a single article or poem by any known living writer." [19]

During the spring of 1968, when Russian broadcasts aimed at Czechoslovakia had been stepped up, it was reported that Czechoslovak employees working for the Soviet Union in Moscow as broadcasters refused to broadcast polemics critical of the liberalization taking place at home. Soviet spokesmen later denied the report. News accounts also indicated that Czechoslovak Radio had sent a legal adviser to Moscow to assist those employees concerning their legal status with the Soviet radio. [20]

122. Literature and speeches advocating resistance

In many situations, the making of speeches and the publication and distribution of literature which call on people to undertake some form of nonviolent noncooperation or nonviolent intervention themselves become acts of defiance and resistance. This is especially so in those countries where any call for resistance, especially for illegal acts of resistance, is itself illegal or seditious.

In England, for example, six members of the Direct Action Committee Against Nuclear War were imprisoned in December 1959 for distributing leaflets calling upon people illegally to enter a rocket base site at Harrington. [21] In Madrid fourteen men from Murcia province were charged with incitement to military rebellion and sentenced to imprisonment for terms of from six months to six years for distributing leaflets calling for a nationwide general strike on June 18, 1959. [22]

CITIZENS' NONCOOPERATION WITH GOVERNMENT

123. Boycott of legislative bodies

In undemocratic systems, legislative bodies may be used to bolster the regime's prestige and influence and to offer the appearance of democracy.

A resistance movement may then decide on a permanent or temporary boycott of participation in such bodies. Nonparticipation would be designed to: 1) remove the facade of democracy; 2) increase the degree of noncooperation with the opponent regime; 3) obtain the active participation in the resistance movement of those politicians who would otherwise spend time attending legislative sessions which produce no changes; and 4) offer by withdrawal a symbolic or newsworthy protest in cases where defeat of the dissident minority in the legislature seems certain. Frequently, of course, withdrawal from the legislature simply means that the opponent group can proceed without legislative opposition.

A national minority may similarly boycott participation in a multinational or imperial parliament of an "oppressor" State. This form of boycott may be undertaken by the nationalists on grounds of principle—a refusal to recognize or accept the political integration of their country with the "oppressor." Or, the boycott may be based on strategy, as an action intended to protest or achieve a particular point, or as part of a program of noncooperation intended to make the foreign rule unworkable. In 1861, for example, the elected Hungarian representatives refused to attend the Imperial Parliament in Vienna and insisted on sitting as the parliament of Hungary alone. [23] In Serbia, the Radicals precipitated a crisis in early 1882 by leaving the parliament after their demand for an investigation of a railroad scandal had been rejected[24] Prior to the *Duma's* voting of war credits to the Russian Tsar's regime in mid-1914, the Social Democratic deputies walked out of the chamber. [25]

During the 1930–31 campaign in India there was strong effort to get members of the provincial Legislative Councils and the national Legislative Council to refuse to attend further sessions and to resign their seats. [26] On March 18, 1967, when the new parliament was opened by President S. Radhakrishnan in New Delhi, over one hundred opposition members boycotted the session in protest against the way Prime Minister Indira Gandhi's government had prevented a non–Congress party ministry from being formed in the state of Rajasthan. This was the first legislative boycott since the Indian constitution had been established seventeen years previously. [27]

Anthony de Crespigny reports two additional European cases of boycott of particular sessions of legislatures. In December 1961, in Greece, over one hundred newly elected opposition deputies boycotted the opening of parliament by King Paul as a means of calling attention to their challenge to the validity of the elections. In May 1962 various legislators withdrew from a plenary session of the West German *Bundestag,* preventing a quorum and thus blocking approval of the Cabinet's decision to cut tariffs on foreign cars. [28]

124. Boycott of elections

Where there is reason to believe that an election will not be conducted fairly or where there is refusal to recognize the authority of the regime conducting the election, an opposition movement may refuse to put up candidates and may urge people to refuse to vote. The aim of such a boycott is usually to protest the use of the election to deceive people as to the degree of democracy present; or it may be an attempt to prevent the "real" issue or issues, as seen by the resistance group, from being overshadowed by "lesser" issues. Sometimes election boycotts have also been attempted by minority groups seeking to deprive the elected government of legitimacy and thereby making it more vulnerable to later attack by various means, including guerrilla warfare.

When the Jacobins sought in 1793 to calm political discontent by submitting to a plebiscite a constitution which declared that after the emergency Frenchmen could once again choose their form of government, three out of four citizens abstained from voting. [29] Later the electors acted similarly: "The result of the illegalities of *fructidor* made the election of 1798 almost farcical. Practically all the moderates abstained from voting. What was the use of voting if the Directors refused to accept the results of the elections?" [30]

Following the Russian Tsar's manifesto of 1905, which contained very limited steps toward greater local autonomy for Finland, the Finnish Social Democrats returned to their earlier minimum demand for a Constituent Assembly and boycotted the elections to the new Diet. [31] Socialist Revolutionaries meeting in Russia in January 1906 told their followers to boycott the elections to the *Duma,* though most of them voted anyway. [32]

Another example is that of the Puerto Rican Nationalists, who for many years boycotted elections because they refuse to recognize the United States government's right to control the island and to operate the election machinery. [33]

Crespigny reports three cases from the years 1961 and 1962. [34] In November 1961 the opposition in Portugal withdrew from the coming parliamentary elections and urged citizens not to vote, in order to avoid the false appearance of a fair election. [35] In Uganda, in April 1962, the rulers of Ankole, Bunyoro, Toro and Busoga threatened election boycotts in an effort to gain full federal status for their territories. [36] That same month all major opposition parties boycotted the federal elections of the Central African Federation (also called the Federation of Rhodesia and Nyasaland), as part of their eventually successful campaign for the federation's breakup.[37] Also in April 1962 the opposition party in El Salvador refused to take part in the presidential election, declaring that the election of 1961 had been fraudulent: the government's candidates had won all seats.[38]

Militant Vietnamese Buddhist leaders in mid-August 1966 called on their followers not to vote in the election of a constitutional assembly on September 11, charging that the Ky government was trying to exploit the election in order "to form a dictatorial regime to serve foreign interests."[39]

A variation on this approach was the "Voters' Veto" campaign in Britain during the 1959 General Election, in which there was no opposition to candidates being nominated or to the holding of the election, but there was a refusal to support any candidates, of whatever party, who did not clearly state their willingness to vote in Parliament for unconditional unilaternal nuclear disarmament. In practice this meant a boycott of all candidates in most constituencies.[40]

125. Boycott of government employment and positions

This type of political noncooperation occurs when people refuse to assist the government by serving it in some job or post. They may either resign from current positions or refuse to accept new ones—either all posts (as in a dictatorial or foreign regime) or only particular ones associated with an objectionable policy. In either case, the objections to government service are normally more serious than the usual run of strike demands. The posts boycotted may range widely, from government ministries to quite menial jobs.

This method produces in varying degrees a withdrawal of labor, skills and other support by individuals; at times such resignations or withholding of aid may cumulatively involve a large number of people, or they may be the result of a corporate resistance strategy. But this is not a form of strike, which is normally a short-term (or relatively so) withdrawal of labor to achieve certain demands, rather than a voluntary quitting of the opponent's employ. The boycott of government employment and positions is *not* a conditional and temporary suspension of activities while in government employ, but a resignation from, or refusal to accept, government employment. The noncooperation is long-term: it may be permanent; it may last for the duration of the regime or policy; on occasion it may last only for some months during a particular campaign of resistance.

This method may be applied by individuals with or without regard to political consequences, simply to dissociate themselves from something they regard as immoral. When used as a method of corporate resistance, however, the aim of this type of political boycott is to reduce the number of officials and employees willing to carry out the policy or assist a regime regarded as oppressive. Effectiveness will therefore depend largely on the numbers involved and their particular talents, skills, positions, or influence.

Examples of this method range fairly widely. When the Austrians in 1861 seized goods to pay the taxes refused by the Hungarians, they found that Hungarian auctioneers refused to work for the Austrian government in selling the confiscated goods.[41] In the Soviet Union on December 9, 1920, dissident Communist representatives of water transport workers opposed centralized government control by resigning from *Tsektran* (the Joint Central Transport Committee).[42]

From Nazi Germany there are a series of individual resignations, as well as threats to resign and unsuccessful attempts to resign, both by prominent officials and by subordinate aides who found themselves opposed to one or another of Hitler's policies or actions, or who simply could not continue to carry out particularly distasteful duties.[43] There was also a plan to use this method on a large scale in an African colonial situation. On August 31, 1962, as part of a "master plan" to dismantle the Central African Federation (of Northern and Southern Rhodesia and Nyasaland, under white rule), Kenneth Kaunda, then President of the United National Independence Party (later to become President of Zambia), announced that he intended to call upon Northern Rhodesia's 11,000 civil servants employed by the Federal government to resign.[44] It did not, however, prove necessary to carry out this master plan.

Resignations for political reasons have also occurred among staffs of government-sponsored universities, especially in protest against government interference in the university. In 1911, for example, about a hundred members of the faculty of Moscow University resigned in protest against political suppression by the Minister of Education and the forced resignations of the rector and vice-rector.[45] During the Buddhist struggle in Vietnam against the Diem regime in 1963, forty-seven faculty members of Hué University resigned in protest against the dismissal of Father Cao Van Luan, the Catholic rector of the University who had supported the Buddhist struggle.[46]

Sometimes the members of a government agency or institution may resign *en masse* because of opposition to acts and policies of the regime. For example, when Louis XV of France forbade the thirteen *parlements* (roughly, courts of justice) to regard themselves as representatives of the nation and to supervise the work of other branches of the government, the members of the *parlement* of Paris resigned in a body in 1770. When they and members of other *parlements* persisted in their noncooperation, these institutions were suppressed.[47] During the Nazi occupation, between February and April 1942, Norwegian bishops, deans and pastors resigned as employees of the State church in protest against violations of Norwegian constitutional priciples and government interference with the church. However, they continued to hold their spiritual positions and to carry out their pastoral duties—in effect disestablishing the church and making it for the time an independent body.[48]

High ranking officials and ministers may resign their posts and new candidates may refuse to accept appointment to such posts because of opposition to government policies. Modern examples have a forerunner in the Netherlands' struggle against Spanish rule in the 1560's: on two occasions the Prince of Orange, the Count of Egmont, and the Count of Hoorn withdrew from the Council of State in order to press King Philip II of Spain to correct various grievances.[49] On August 9, 1943, Danish Premier Scavenius threatened to resign if the Germans required Danish courts to try the men arrested after a wave of anti-German strikes and riots; on August 28 he and his government did resign, in the political context of increased repression and resistance.[50] African Members of the Legislative Council in preindependence Kenya refused to accept ministerial posts, especially in March 1960, because of their opposition to the British-imposed Lennox-Boyd constitution.[51] In the summer of 1963 the Vietnamese Foreign Minister and the Ambassador to the United States both resigned in support of the Buddhist struggle against the Diem regime.[52]

There are relatively few examples of attempts to destroy a regime by corporate withholding or withdrawal of assistance by current or potential employees and officials. During the Indian nonviolent campaigns, however, there were frequent efforts to induce government employees to resign their positions, whether they were village headmen or top departmental officers in New Delhi. These efforts were particularly strong during the 1930–31 campaign.[53]

A case in which there was a stillborn attempt to overthrow a regime by widespread resignations suggests a possible alternative to both the *coup d'état* and regicide, and therefore merits mention in discussion of this particular method even though it was not actually carried out. In 1938 the Chief of the German General Staff, Colonel-General Ludwig Beck, opposed the impending Nazi attack on Czechoslovakia, fearing an unwanted general European war. Beck not only decided to resign himself; he also sought to obtain the resignation and support of Commander-in-Chief Walter von Brauchitsch. With his full support (seen as crucial) Beck planned to provoke a mass resignation of Germany's senior commanding generals and the conservative members of the coalition government—that is, Minister of Economics Schacht, Foreign Minister Neurath, Finance Minister Krosigk, and Minister of Justice Gürtner. Beck resigned, but Brauchitsch refused either to resign or to play the role Beck had intended for him, that he appeal for support for the plan to the full conference of the High Command of the Army, and that he then lead the officers to a direct personal confrontation with Hitler.[54]

126. Boycott of government departments, agencies and other bodies

In refusing to recognize the authority of the government or to support one of its particular policies, the resisters may refuse to cooperate with all government departments or only with the governmental bodies responsible for the particular objectionable policy. Such noncooperation may sometimes be conducted even at the financial expense of the noncooperators. This type of boycott may involve either withholding new forms of cooperation or severing existing forms of cooperation. Many types of departments, agencies and bureaus may be boycotted. This method may also involve a refusal to accept government loans, grants-in-aid, and the like.[55]

It is frequently applied in colonial conflicts, as our examples from Egypt, India and Central Africa show. Lord Milner's mission to Egypt in 1919 to prepare a constitution for the then-British protectorate met with such complete boycott that after three months it had to return to Britain without having consulted a single representative Egyptian.[56] Similarly, in 1928 the Indian nationalists carried out a complete boycott of the Simon Commission which had been instructed to make recommendations concerning the future status of India, but had no Indian members. There were refusals to give evidence. "Go back, Simon," was a popular slogan.[57] During noncooperation campaigns the Indian nationalists promoted a boycott of the British law courts by lawyers, solicitors and litigants and encouraged the alternative of settling civil disputes by private arbitration, including by the *panchayat* (the village-five advisory council.)[58]

The Central African Federation (or the Federation of Rhodesia and Nyasaland) has already been referred to in this chapter. From the time that this Eupropean-dominated Federation was first proposed at the beginning of the 1950's, African nationalists from the constituent territories undertook a policy of noncooperation. Although this did not prevent its establishment, their refusal to accept and cooperate with the new federal government ultimately led to its dissolution. This African noncooperation provides three examples of the use of this particular method. Africans from Northern Rhodesia and Nyasaland refused to participate in the April-May meetings in London which were to draft the Federal Scheme. They similarly refused to attend the meeting in London in January 1953 which prepared the final Scheme for the Federation. When the Monckton Commission visited the Federation in 1960 to gather information needed to make recommendations concerning the review of the federal constitution, African political organizations in Northern Rhodesia and Nyasaland maintained an effective boycott of the Commission and refused to give evidence before it. [59]

This method has also been used in other types of situations, including cases of political revolution, resistance to foreign occupation, guerrilla struggle, and resistance to government control over business. During the Russian 1905 Revolution, the Mensheviks organized in Georgia, and especially in Kutais province, a successful boycott of the Russian administration, courts and schools. It was the summer of 1906 before Russian authority and control were reestablished. [60] During the *Ruhrkampf*, despite an acute food shortage Germans refused to use the soup kitchens and shops set up by the occupation authorities. [61] In Quang Nang province, Vietnam, in September-November 1964, Buddhists repeatedly refused to cooperate with the National Liberation Front administration and were finally left alone. [62]

Another example of this form of boycott comes from Nazi Germany in 1935 and derives from an attempt by the Nazi Party's Labor Front to establish party control over both large and small business organizations. To this end, a decree issued on June 13 by Dr. Robert Ley, head of the Labor Front, formed the National Chamber of Labor and eighteen regional chambers, an act which was intended to give the party's Labor Front a counterpart to the Chambers of Industry. Ley ordered employers to become individual members, and the Minister of War was invited to delegate officers to attend the meetings of the regional chambers. These new chambers were intended to be used to control private business. The business groups, however, boycotted the Chambers of Labor, and the Minister of War authorized only civilian officials to attend. The boycott was effective, and this attempt at establishing effective control over private business failed. [63]

When the U.S. House of Representatives Committee on Internal Security in July 1970 requested 177 colleges and universities to supply it with the names of radical speakers, their sponsors, fees and sources of the funds, they were met with sharp noncooperation from Tufts University, in Medford, Massachusetts, and milder lack of help from Harvard University. Tufts Vice-President John W. Scheetz declared:

> We feel the request immediately suggests grave and ominous implications involving constitutionally guaranteed rights of free speech and other freedoms which the university has traditionally enjoyed and protected. . . . To avoid possible infringement on these freedoms of such deep concern to us all, Tufts University chooses not to respond to the committee's request.

The Harvard reply, from Charles P. Whitlock, simply stated that the university had no information on the speakers invited to the campus by student organizations. The *Boston Globe* editorially called these acts of noncooperation "new blows for political as well as academic freedom." [64]

This type of political boycott has sometimes also been practiced within various nongovernmental international organizations. For example, a brief boycott of a session in Geneva of the International Labor Organization took place on June 22, 1966, when African delegates, followed by delegates from many other countries, walked out during a discussion of a committee report on the ways member governments abide by I.L.O. obligations. These Africans and other delegates were protesting Portugal's denial of independence to African colonies; charges of forced labor were especially prominent. [65] The same day it was announced that the delegation to the I.L.O. from the American Federation of Labor and Congress of Industrial Organizations would end its boycott of the I.L.O. and would attend that agency's executive board meeting on June 23. Mr Faupl of the A.F.L.-C.I.O. had boycotted the three-week conference in protest against the election at the I.O.L.'s annual session of a representative from Poland, the first to be elected from a Communist delegation. [66]

127. Withdrawal from government educational institutions

The permanent or indefinite withdrawal of children and youths from schools owned or controlled by the government during a major campaign of resistance to that government is also a method of political noncooperation. This was done, for example, during the Indian independence struggle.[67] Such withdrawal may have the fourfold effect of: 1) contributing to the establishment and growth of "national" schools and colleges independent of the established authority; 2) checking the influence of the authorities and those in educational circles still loyal to the old order, who might use their positions to seek to instill loyalty to the established regime in their pupils and students; 3) providing the resistance movement with youthful recruits who would otherwise have been occupied with studies; and 4) contributing to the general disruption of the *status quo* and increasing the totality of noncooperation with the government. The National Conference of the African National Congress in 1954 called for a boycott of educational institutions as long as the South African government's Bantu Education policy remained in force—which meant indefinitely.[68]

128. Boycott of government-supported organizations

This type of political noncooperation expresses itself in a refusal to join, or decision to resign from, organizations which are regarded as instruments of the government or political movement which is being opposed. One example is the refusal of the Norwegian teachers in 1942 to join the Quisling government's new teachers' organization, which was to be used as the cornerstone of the Corporative State and as a wedge for indoctrinating the children.[69] As the Quisling government, still pursuing the plan for the Corporative State, sought to take control of various existing Norwegian organizations, the great bulk of members resigned: estimates for the summer of 1941 range from seventy to ninety percent of the total membership of individual organizations.[70] Following the crushing of the June 1953 Rising, East German workers practiced a related type of resistance; as a body they refused to pay membership dues to government-controlled trade unions.[71]

129. Refusal of assistance to enforcement agents

It is fairly common for the general population, in areas where there is either sympathy with criminal elements or fear of them, to refuse to provide information to the police or to disclose the whereabouts of wanted persons. Similarly, the general population living under foreign occupation or a domestic dictatorship may refuse to supply the police with information on political and patriotic resisters. This constitutes an act of political noncooperation.

Americancolonistsrepeatedly refused to inform against persons wanted for committing various acts of destruction against British property or resistance to political control. This was illustrated on two prominent occasions. When, in late 1771, a group of disguised men captured a boat and its contents which had been seized in the lower Delaware by a revenue vessel, even the offer of a reward of two hundred pounds sterling by Pennsylvania's Lieutenant Governor Richard Penn for information leading to their arrest failed to bring forward any informers. In Rhode Island waters, when the revenue vessel *Gaspée* ran aground on June 8, 1772, a group of undisguised and prominent citizens of Providence boarded it (after having openly organized the action), injured the commander, overpowered the crew, and burned the vessel; despite a royal proclamation offering a large reward and setting up a royal commission to investigate the incident, the guilty parties "were so well shielded both by their fellow citizens and by the government of the colony that no evidence could be obtained against them." [72]

This method may also involve the refusal of other types of assistance. For example, during the 1928 Bardoli revenue-refusal campaign in India, Joan V. Bondurant reports:

> Peasants met revenue collectors with closed doors, or receiving them, read extracts aloud from Patel's speeches and tried by argument to persuade them that they could not collect the revenue. When police reenforcements broke down doors and carried away equipment, peasants began to dismantle carts and other equipment, hiding the parts in different places. [73]

In the summer of 1881 Irish tenants took various actions in order not to assist the seizure of property for back rent, which was being refused. An eyewitness reports one such case:

> After the men's dinners, the sheriff again started, protected by a considerable force, for the farm of one Murnane, where a seizure was also to be made for rent due. When we arrived at the farm, which seemed to be one of some value, it was found that there was not a single head of cattle upon it . . . in fact, everything movable had been taken away.

The sheriff and his men had to leave empty-handed, but when they returned unexpectedly a few days later, they were able to seize the cattle which had been removed for the previous visit. [74]

Irish gypsies, camping with their horses and caravans on the outskirts of Dublin in January and February 1964, resisted eviction from certain sites by refusing to harness their horses to the caravans, so that each had to be pulled away from the sites by hand.[75]

Sometimes the refusal to assist enforcement agents has been applied by the persons being arrested themselves, in "going limp" when arrested. Martin Oppenheimer and George Lakey offer the following definition of this type of action:

> "Going limp" is just what the phrase implies. It is a relaxation of all the body in a kind of physical non-cooperation with the situation, so that the non-cooperator has to be dragged or carried to wherever authorities want him moved. It can be modified by putting hands in pockets, or in situations of violence by folding up (as in football) and covering up the head and other sensitive areas with your arms.[76]

130. Removal of own signs and placemarks[77]

The removal, alteration, or replacement of house numbers, street signs, placemarks, railway station signs, highway direction and distance signs, and the like may temporarily misdirect, impede, or delay the movement of foreign troops and police. Such efforts, which seem to have only a stalling potential, are most likely to be effective where the troops or police are quite unfamiliar with the territory, where the country or layout of streets is especially bewildering or complicated, and where the population is unwilling to provide accurate directions. One of the potential uses of this method is to delay the political police until wanted persons have had time to escape, or until resistance headquarters or equipment can be relocated. The time thus gained may be minimal in some cases, although a psychological impact on both occupation forces and the resisting population may remain a significant factor.

The clearest example of the use of such methods was in Prague the first week of the Russian occupation in August 1968. (Troops entered late on August 20.) Czechoslovak Radio reported on Friday, August 23, at 5:25 P.M., that arrests were expected during the night. An appeal was made to paint over or remove street signs and number plates on homes and to make name plates on apartments illegible. Highway direction signs throughout the country were to be repainted. Such action had already started, however. On Thursday night many street signs were already painted over, as were direction signs on the main highways. After noon on Friday Prague had been flooded with leaflets urging the removal or painting over of street signs and signs on important offices and plants. The newspaper *Prace* reported: "There was a lightning reaction to this appeal. Prague streets have lost their names!" [78] The paper *Lidova Demokracie* reported that hundreds of thousands of people had participated in such action:

> Prague names and numbers have died out. For the uninvited guests, Prague has become a dead city. Anyone who was not born here, who has not lived here, will find a city of anonymity among a million inhabitants. . . . let us follow the slogan: The mailman will find you, but evil-doers won't! Bravo Prague and other cities that followed and follow its example! [79]

The Communist Party paper *Rude Pravo* reported that many young boys had participated in the removal of signs or painting over them, "to see to it that the only people who find their way around the city are those who are supposed to." [80]

The Czech film *Closely Watched Trains,* made long before the Russian invasion, illustrated well the disruptive effects during the Nazi occupation of altering the names of railroad stations, when this is combined with disruptive assistance from railroad workers determined to see that a particular train does not reach its destination until hours or days later than scheduled.

131. Refusal to accept appointed officials

The political unit over which an official has been appointed to serve may on occasion refuse to accept the appointee. In the example to follow the appointee was persuaded to depart promptly, but in cases where this does not happen, this method would involve refusal to recognize the appointee in his official role and noncooperation with him if he attempts to carry out his duties. This example, which occurred in Ping-fang, Hupeh, China, in the 1840's, was reported by a Western missionary. Opposition to the appointment of a certain mandarin to the post of governor (magistrate) of the town was based upon his previous administration in another district, which had been corrupt, arbitrary and tyrannical. When a deputation to the Viceroy (governor-general) of the province failed to win cancellation of the appointment,

> The principle people assembled, and held a grand council. . . . It was decided that the new governor should not be permitted to install himself, and that he should be civilly ejected from the town. . . .
> Scarcely had he entered the tribunal, [when] . . . it was an-

nounced to him that the chief citizens of the town requested an audience. . . . The deputation prostrated themselves . . . before their new Prefect [magistrate]; then, one of them stepping forward, announced to him, with exquisite politeness and infinite grace, that they came in the name of the town, to request that he would set off directly to return whence he came, for they would have none of him.

The Prefect . . . endeavored first to soothe, and then to intimidate, the rebellious citizens, but all in vain. . . . The spokesman very calmly told him that they had not come there to discuss the matter; that the thing was settled, and they had made up their minds that he should not sleep in the town . . . the town would pay his traveling expenses, beside providing a brilliant escort to conduct him safely to the capital of the province.

Encouraged by a noisy crowd outside, the appointee yielded and left, escorted by the chief men of the town. They went directly to the Viceroy. After reading a petition signed by all the most important people of Pingfang, the Viceroy told the delegation that their arguments were reasonable and should be attended to.[81]

132. Refusal to dissolve existing institutions

When governments seek to abolish independent institutions in order to control the population better, to abolish a particular opposition movement, or to restructure the society on the basis of some ideological preconception, political, educational, labor, cultural and many other types of organizations may refuse voluntarily to accept such dissolution. They may then continue to operate either openly or secretly and keep up as many of their normal activities as they can, resisting collectively the governmental measures intended to destroy them. The widespread preservation of domestic institutions is a key objective in resisting foreign occupations seeking to remold the society. Refusal to disband such institutions may be combined with the boycott of government-supported institutions described above. Both methods may thus be used when nonviolent action is employed to defend a legitimate government and the society's institutions against illegitimate attack.

German Chancellor Prince Otto von Bismarck wrongly linked two assassination attempts against Emperor Wilhelm II to the Social Democrats and with this excuse induced the new parliament in 1878 to pass the Socialist Law. This enabled the government within eight months to dissolve many workingmen's unions and associations, suppress a multitude of publications, dissolve *bona fide* cooperative societies, prohibit political meetings of Social Democrats, imprison and expel Socialists, destroy the entire Social Democratic Party organization, and launch many forms of police harassment of people connected with the Social Democratic Party. After three years, however, the Socialists, refusing to accept the dissolution of their party, began meeting again secretly; they circulated literature smuggled from Switzerland and organized and nominated candidates for elections. At each election after 1881 there was a significant increase in the votes recorded, reports J. Ellis Barker, a historian of this period, "notwithstanding, or rather because of, all the measures taken against it by the Government." By 1890, when Bismarck was dismissed by the Emperor and the Socialist Law withdrawn, the Social Democratic vote had risen from 437,158 in 1878 to the new high of 1,427, 298. Barker writes: "The effect of the Socialist Law, with all its prosecution, was the reverse of what Bismarck had expected for it had made that party great." [83]

CITIZENS' ALTERNATIVES TO OBEDIENCE

133. Reluctant and slow compliance

Where opponents of regimes or policies do not feel able to resist unconditionally, they may at certain points postpone compliance as long as possible, finally complying with a marked lack of enthusiasm and thoroughness. Thus, while not entirely blocked, the ability of the regime to carry out its will may be slowed and somewhat limited. In East Germany, for example, when so-called voluntary plans for the collectivization of agriculture were announced by Walter Ulbricht in July 1952, opposition by farmers was expressed not only by thousands of emigrations to the West, but also by a widespread disinclination to join the new cooperatives. "Party speakers organized 'foundation meetings' in every village. Generally these functions were ignored or sparsely attended; often the speakers were shouted down; sometimes they were forced to withdraw in haste." In at least one case even the local mayor and Party secretary ignored invitations to attend. Although at the end of four months two thousand cooperative farms had been established, and six months later five thousand, the government plan had obviously been stalled. [84]

This type of behavior has often been applied to tax collection, although the motives in such cases are frequently less clearly political than economic. In both seventeenth and nineteenth century China, members of the gentry often deliberately postponed payment of their land tax or grain tribute to the government in hopes that they might eventually evade payment.[85] During the nineteenth century payment of the rice tribute was often made very reluctantly and in unhelpful ways. Not only were payments often late, but wet and impure rice was often substituted for dry, clean rice, less than the quantity required was often delivered, and sometimes even that was simply dumped outside the granaries. Occasionally a mild inquiry from the official or clerk at the granary would provoke a refusal to deliver the rice at all or formal charges against the clerk and complaints to a superior official.[86]

In a very different situation during World War II, on the evening of the violent revolt and escape by Jewish prisoners from the Sobibor extermination camp in Poland on October 14, 1943, German officials sent an urgent message by railway-telegraph: "SEND MILITARY REINFORCEMENTS AT ONCE TO PURSUE REBELS." A young woman telegrapher who received it at the nearby Chelm station withheld the telegram from the German contact for over four hours, even though she was risking her life.[87]

134. Nonobedience in absence of direct supervision

Another type of political noncooperation involves the population's ignoring and noncompliance with laws, edicts and regulations in all situations where there is no immediate, direct supervision or enforcement. When soldiers are around to see that a particular order is carried out, for example, the population obeys; but when the soldiers leave, the people resume their noncompliance. This is a method that has often been used in China against unpopular regimes and foreign invaders. But this type of behavior is very difficult to document.[88]

135. Popular nonobedience

There are a large number of instances in which the general population, or part of it, has consciously disregarded and violated laws or regulations, but in ways which do not amount to civil disobedience. One or more characteristics of either of the types of civil disobedience may be absent—for example, the disobeyed law may not be seen as illegitimate. Primarily, however, this method involves ignoring or disregarding the law or regulations more than blatant defiance, the resisters choosing not to flaunt their noncompliance. The acts may be open and unhidden but not advertised, the resisters preferring to remain, as far as possible, personally unknown and unpunished and to continue to be part of a larger opposition group. This method frequently takes the form of unobtrusively ignoring the law or regulation in question, often by large numbers of people, as though it did not exist.

Efforts in 1686 by King Christian V of Norway-Denmark to build Christiansand into a major city, as planned by Christian IV, were partially frustrated by the refusal of the inhabitants of Risør, Arendal, Mandal and Flekkefjord to comply with a clear order, backed by threats of severe punishments, to move to Christiansand within six months. "Not once did this help. The inhabitants continued living quietly, and the coastal towns thrived and bloomed." [89] During the French Revolution, in the late autumn of 1789, a decree reestablished freedom of the grain trade, but "no one obeyed it." [90] And on June 20, 1792, in defiance of a prohibition of a demonstration, people marched in front of the Assembly to celebrate the anniversary of the Tennis Court Oath and then invaded the Tuileries and sought out the King, whom they cursed and threatened. [91]

When the French government abolished the national workshops in June 1848, and then sought to avoid trouble and revolution by sending some of the workmen back into the country, "They refused to leave. On the 22nd of June, they marched through Paris in troops, singing in cadence, in a monotonous chant, 'We won't be sent away, we won't be sent away . . .'" Within days there was bloodshed. [92] During the 1905 Revolution in Imperial Russia, de facto freedom of the press was temporarily established late in the year by direct action in the form of popular nonobedience. All the censorship regulations were simply ignored and newspapers published what they liked. Without the required permission, new newspapers with strong political views sprang up. [93] Trade unions similarly ignored the law and operated openly. [94]

Acts of popular nonobedience also occurred during World War II. In the Netherlands, for example, German orders that the population turn in metal coins were generally disregarded, and private and illegal listening to broadcasts from Britain was regarded as an act of opposition to the German occupation. [95] In several sections of Copenhagen during the June 1944 strike and resulting German emergency measures, the populace simply ignored the curfew. [96] Among Jews deported from Belgium in November 1942 were some who had removed the required yellow star from their clothes[97] and in June 1942 there were various types of noncompliance with the decree requiring the wearing of the yellow star in occupied France:

Some of the Jews decided not to wear the star. Others wore it in the wrong way. Still others wore several stars instead of one. Some Jews provided their star with additional inscriptions. And, finally, a number of non-Jews took to wearing the star or something that looked like it. Angrily, the Germans arrested some of the Jewish offenders and their French supporters to intern them in one of the camps.[98]

One reason for the inefficiency of regulations aimed at preventing the rural people of China from migrating to urban areas between 1950 and 1958 reportedly was that frequently the regulations were "ignored altogether by those wishing to leave."[99]

136. Disguised disobedience

Disobedience of laws, regulations, or orders may be carried out in ways which give the disobedience the thinly disguised appearance of compliance. During the noncooperation campaign which achieved the nullification of the Stamp Act, the undisguised refusal of merchants, shippers and the like to use the required stamps on shipping documents generally brought the trading ports to a standstill when the law went into effect on November 1, 1765. But in Philadelphia a form of disguised disobedience was used which kept ships moving for some weeks—and without the hated stamps:

In Philadelphia, by an ingenious device not apparently thought of elsewhere, trade had been kept moving throughout November. In all colonial ports merchants had cleared out every ship they could load before November first, but in Philadelphia they cleared ships which were only partially loaded. Although clearances were not supposed to be granted until the entire cargo was declared, all the ships in Philadelphia which had any part of their cargoes aboard obtained clearance papers in the last days of October. When the cargoes had been completed, the owners went to the custom-house and had undated additions entered on their papers . . . . Since it normally took three to four weeks for a ship to complete her cargo, there was relatively little pressure in Philadelphia until the end of November.[100]

One way banned newspapers may practice disguised disobedience is by quickly reappearing with new names. This happened during the *Ruhrkampf,* when banned newspapers even sometimes adopted the names of other newspapers which had not been banned.[101] This also happened in Russia in 1905,[102] and in late spring of 1929 British suppression of *Forward,* a newspaper in Calcutta, was followed by the appearance of *New Forward;* upon its being banned, *Liberty* was issued.[103]

With jazz having been banned by the Nazis during World War II and defiant jazz musicians being hunted by the Gestapo, German jazz enthusiasts changed the names of American jazz numbers to innocent-sounding German titles, Richard W. Fogg reports. "Organ Grinder Swing" became *"Hofkonzert im Hinterhaus"* (Court Concert in the

Back Yard), "Tiger Rag" became *"Schwartzer Panther"* (Black Panther). "Black Bottom" became *"Schwartze Erde"* (Black Earth), and "Lady, Be Good" became *"Frau, Sei Gut."* One of these German jazz enthusiasts, Jutta Hipp, recalled: "We played American tunes, but we had to give the Nazis a list, so we translated the titles into German. . . . We translated them in the most stupid way, because we thought the whole idea of requiring a list and banning American music was stupid. Nobody found out, either. The Nazis listened and applauded it, and we laughed inside." One such number was even played by the official *Wehrmacht* (German army) band! [104]

Young men in Nazi Germany who did not wish to be conscripted into the army, but who also wanted to avoid outright resistance, claimed exemption on medical grounds as a "standard technique." They would obtain a certificate of ill-health from a *"Guten-Tag* doctor"—a doctor who greeted a new patient with *"Guten Tag"* rather than *"Heil Hitler."* One such young man, Horst Lippmann, who was also a jazz enthusiast, successfully used this technique for a year; he had to try to look sick when the inspector called at the house and (since unfit young men were not issued passes) had to stay off the streets. When he was later arrested for jazz activities, Lippmann's father got doctors to testify to the Gestapo that young Lippmann's health was too delicate for him to withstand a jail sentence. Young Horst was released. [105]

The remaining examples are Chinese. Indirect evidence is sometimes the only documentation available for such behavior. One such bit of evidence is found in the Chinese emperor's edicts issued in 1814. These stated that it had been the practice of provincial and local officials (especially those who registered the inhabitants) to present "a good appearance for the moment" but be negligent in carrying out their official duties. The emperor spoke of "officials [who] obey ostensibly and actually disregard Our wishes, i.e., . . . respond to a standing requirement with empty gestures." [106]

Another example of disguised disobedience is drawn from the late 1930s, after the Japanese had established the Hopei-Chahar Political Council in North China, a council which they hoped would be a willing political instrument in Japanese plans for economic development. The Chinese government, however, regarded the council as a buffer between it and the Japanese. Faced with Japanese economic demands, therefore, instead of simply rejecting them the Chinese adopted the device of stretching out the negotiations and stalling for time:

> When pressed with demands General Sung Cheh-yuan, Chairman of the Political Council, in order to evade the issue, retired to his native village "to sweep the graves of his ancestors." Such tactics inevitably exasperated the Japanese who spoke of "Chinese insincerity." They

soon came to realize that as a political instrument the Political Council would not serve the ends for which it was set up. [107]

In 1942 in Chungking the government closed ice cream and coffee parlors and prohibited the sale of coffee and soda pop; once more the response was a type of disguised disobedience:

> The very fancy "Sing Sing Café" reopened as the "Sing Sing Kitchen" and would serve ice cream only after plates and butter plates, water glasses, knives, forks and spoons had been set on the table to give it the look of a dessert after a full meal. Soda pop was served in soup plates and had to be eaten with soup spoons. [108]

Chinese soldiers, too, had learned comparable responses to orders, as Graham Peck observed in Chungking in December 1940:

> After a while a line of shabby soldiers in gray cotton uniforms and straw sandals came slogging up the hill, technically in double-time, but really mocking the quick step. For all their jogging up and down, they moved forward less rapidly than the burdened housewives. Like soldiers all over China, they were chanting numbers to keep in pace: "One, two, three . . . (step, step, step) . . . FOUR!" When their officer screamed at them to hurry it up, they began chanting faster and faster, out of time, while their feet pounded the road as slowly as ever. They all wore that smile. [109]

137. Refusal of an assemblage or meeting to disperse

A formal meeting or an informal gathering of some type may express opposition by refusing official or unofficial demands that it disperse. This method may at times be closely related to popular nonobedience or to civil disobedience of "illegitimate" laws, but this is not always the case.

On several occasions during the American colonists' struggles, town meetings, public assemblies and conventions formally defied specific orders to disperse, given by the governor or some other official. In one such case Lieutenant Governor Hutchinson, long disturbed at the activities of the city's merchants and the Boston town meeting, in January 1770 sent the sheriff to Faneuil Hall, where the merchants were meeting, with a message denouncing the gathering as unjustifiable "by any authority or colour of law," and condemning their house-to-house marchings as dangerous and conducive to terror. As representative of the Crown Hutchinson ordered them to disperse and "to forbear all such unlawful assemblies for the future . . ." The merchants paused in their meeting only long enough to vote unanimously that in their opinion the meeting was lawful; then they resumed their transactions. [110]

On June 23, 1789, in an atmosphere of popular rebellion against the powers of the French king and the nobility, Louis XVI gave a speech to the representatives of the three estates outlining their roles, and then he ordered the deputies to adjourn and to meet the next day in separate chambers. "When the King withdrew, the nobles and most of the clergy followed him, while the commons remained silently in their seats." Their spokesman told the King's representative that they had decided not to adjourn without a debate and that ". . . no one can give orders to the assembled nation." [111]

In a very different situation, on May 15, 1848, the Assembly in Paris was invaded by a crowd which sought to force the Assembly to "pronounce forthwith in favour of Poland." For hours there were no troops to evict the crowd, and while the Assembly refused to comply with the demand, it neither adjourned nor sought to evict the rebels. "During all this disorder in its midst, the Assembly sat passive and motionless on its benches, neither resisting nor giving way, silent and firm," reports Alexis de Tocqueville, an eyewitness. A vote for the motion would have dishonored the Assembly and shown it to be powerless; one against it would have risked cut throats among the members. "This passive resistance irritated and incensed the people; it was like a cold, even surface upon which its fury glided without knowing what to catch hold of . . ." The crowd finally shouted: "We can't make them vote!" After some chaos and the expectation that troops were coming, a member of the crowd declared the Assembly to be adjourned—without, however, the crowd's having achieved its objective. [112]

During the Hungarian Protestants' struggle against restrictive Austrian religious laws and efforts to subordinate them to imperial control, the Calvinists of the Trans-Tisza Church District played a prominent role. Defying a government order, their council met as scheduled in Debrecen on January 11, 1860, with five hundred church officials and thousands of laymen attending. William Robert Miller quotes a description of the occasion by Imre Révész, a church historian:

> Immediately after the opening prayer, the Austrian Imperial Government representative . . . stood up and called upon the meeting to disperse. The chairman [Deputy Bishop Peter Balogh] then asked those present whether they wished to disperse or not, whereupon the huge crowd roared in reply: "We shall hold the meeting; we will not disperse." Then as the meeting proceeded, fear began to show on the face of the Imperial representative, as he saw thousands of angry eyes turned in scorn upon him. Finally, he could bear the situation no longer, and got up and left; and no one did him harm. [113]

The gathering refusing to disperse, however, need not be an official assembly; it may simply be a public meeting or an improvised protest gathering. On February 17, 1959, for example, a crowd of from 150 to 200 Africans in the Kota Kota district of Nyasaland went to the police station to protest ten arrests for illegal acts which had taken place the previous day and to demand that they be arrested also; rejecting the District Commissioner's explanation for the arrests and his offer to receive a delegation, they refused orders to disperse. "The police then used tear smoke and made a baton charge." [114]

A variation on this refusal to disperse was applied by the Czechoslovak delegation which negotiated in Moscow following the 1968 invasion. At Moscow Airport they discovered that one of their members, Frantisek Kriegel, was missing. Kriegel was a liberal member of the Presidium of the Czechoslovak Communist Party and a Jew to whom the Soviet officials particularly objected. The remaining delegates refused to depart without Kriegel, and it was not until Soviet officials produced him that the delegation flew back to Prague. [115]

138. Sitdown

The sitdown is an act of noncooperation in which the participants actually sit down on the street, road, ground, or floor and refuse to leave voluntarily, for either a limited or an indefinite period of time. The sitdown may be a spontaneous act, or a reaction decided on in advance, as a response to orders for a march or other demonstration to disperse. Or it may be combined with civil disobedience to some regulatory law as a serious type of symbolic resistance. The sitdown may also be used to halt ordinary traffic or tanks, or to prevent workers or officials from carrying out their work. In these cases it becomes a method of nonviolent intervention (either nonviolent interjection or nonviolent obstruction, which are described in the next chapter). In recent years the sitdown appears to have been more widely used than previously.

Toward the end of April 1960, during the Algerian War, over five hundred demonstrators protested the internment of six thousand North Africans in France, without trial or hearing, by marching to the Centre de Tri de Vincennes (one of the French reception centers for Arabs) and sitting down in front of it. New waves of demonstrators came when the first persons were arrested and driven away in vehicles. [116] Demonstrators protesting the same policy held a sitdown near the Champs Elysées in Paris in late May, after the police had stopped their march toward the Ministry of the Interior. [117]

In the autumn of 1961 three hundred Norwegians opposing nuclear tests held a sitdown outside the Soviet Embassy in Oslo after the Soviet announcement of its intention to explode a fifty-megaton nuclear bomb.[118] In May 1962 about one thousand Lisbon University students staged a sit-down in protest against a decision by the Portuguese Minister of Education to ban their student-day celebrations.[119]

On June 19, 1964, about five hundred young Russian art fans attended the opening (delayed until 5 P.M.) at the Manege Gallery in Moscow of works by the controversial painter, Ilya Glazunov. When the Soviet Ministry of Culture announced that the scheduled public debate on the exhibited works had been postponed, the young people refused to leave, saying they would have their own discussion. When officials turned out the lights, the people sat down on the floor, first clapping in unison and then airing opinions of every kind. The militia finally induced them to leave three hours after the opening.[120] Students at Madrid University, campaigning for an independent student union, on February 24, 1965, first conducted a silent march and then sat down at the police barrier which blocked their way.[121]

A variation on the usual patterns occurred on at least two occasions during the Indian struggle in 1930–31 when the police who halted a march or parade of nonviolent actionists also staged a sitdown in the street or road to block their passage. On May 15, 1930, during the Dharasana salt raids, a group of *satyagrahis* headed for the salt depot under the leadership of the poet Sarojini Naidu was halted by a police superintendent who said to her: "We are going to stay here and offer Satyagraha . . . ourselves as long as you do." But after twenty-eight hours of a dual sitting confrontation, police patience wore out and they returned to more violent methods.[122] Some weeks later armed police in Bombay stopped a procession of about thirty thousand men, women and children who then sat down in the streets, whereupon the police also sat down, and they confronted each other for hours. When sympathizers brought food, water and blankets during the night's rain, the *satyagrahis* passed these on to the obstructing police as a token of good will. Finally the police gave in and the procession ended in a triumphant midnight march.[123]

139. Noncooperation with conscription and deportation

Opposition to various types of government conscription and deportation may be expressed by a refusal either to register as ordered, or to report for duty or participate in deportation. (The motives of the opponent in initiating deportation may vary: the opponent may want to depopulate the area, remove political dissidents, produce forced labor, or exterminate an unwanted group.) Such noncooperation may also be a form of civil disobedience or popular nonobedience. It is classified separately here because it is not the disobedience itself which is important but the refusal to cooperate with a program of conscription or deportation. This kind of noncooperation may include several specific types of acts, not simply disobedience.

Noncooperation with military conscription has been practiced on a number of occasions. For example, in Hungary from 1820 to 1825 there was a mass refusal to comply with a levy of troops imposed on the country by Austria,[124] and this happened again beginning in 1861.[125] In their struggle for autonomy from Imperial Russia, the Finns similarly refused military conscription. When the Russian conscription system was imposed on Finland by imperial decree in 1901, "The pastors refused to proclaim the law in the villages, the judges and lawyers to apply it, the conscripts to execute it."[126] To make the conscription less obnoxious, the Tsar decreed that with each conscription only one percent of the recruits (to be chosen by drawing lots) were to be taken into the army. Eino Jutikkala writes:

> Nevertheless, [during the conscription of 1902] three-fifths of the youths of conscription age—the proportion among the university students was as high as five-sixths—refused to report for the draft. . . .
>
> In the following two conscriptions, the resistance was less successful but still strong enough to cause the Russians to abandon their campaign in this field. . . . the Finns were released from personal military service, and Finland was obliged to pay a small annual tax to the imperial treasury as compensation.[127]

Finnish soldiers were consequently not available for the Russo-Japanese War or for service to the Tsar during the 1905 Revolution.

In New Zealand there was widespread refusal to be conscripted for military training in 1913, with many being sentenced to detention camps, and in 1930 some fifty thousand young men from fourteen to eighteen refused to take military instruction.[128]

This method of noncooperation has also been practiced against conscription and deportation for forced labor and against deportation for extermination. There were some cases (apparently only a minority) of Jews under Nazi rule refusing to register or report as ordered. Although there probably were 85,000 Jews in Belgium in May 1939, only about 42,000 registered with the police when ordered to do so in October 1940; Gerard Reitlinger attributes the bulk of this difference to a refusal to register.[129] In Athens in December 1943 only 1,200 Jews registered with the

Judenrat (Jewish Council) when ordered to do so, although eight thousand Jews were believed to be in the city.[130] For a period in August 1944 Jews in the Lodz ghetto in Poland noncooperated with German evacuation orders, refusing, for example, to collect their rations (i.e., report) at the local railroad station or the Central Prison.[131] When all surviving Jews in Bratislava, Czechoslovakia, were ordered on November 16, 1944, to report to the Bratislava *Rathaus* (town hall) for transfer to Sered camp, only fifty obeyed, while at least six thousand remained hidden in bunkers.[132] This method was also used by non-Jews against the Nazis. In the Netherlands only a few thousand of the ex-soldiers reported, as ordered, for deportation and internment in Germany, and about seventy percent of the students refused to report for work in Germany. It appears that the Germans did not make any special effort to arrest these students.[133]

140. Hiding, escape and false identities

Hiding, escape and false identities are not usually a part of nonviolent action. Normally they are not protest or resistance as such, and they commonly reflect fear which, as will be discussed in Chapter Nine, disrupts the effective operation of the technique. However, there are certain circumstances under which they may constitute a method of nonviolent action. These are largely political circumstances in which the regime seeks the arrest, internment and perhaps extermination of particular groups of people for ideological reasons or as part of a massive wave of repression. It could also apply to groups wanted as hostages or for reprisals, forced labor, or military duty. And of course escape by slaves is resistance to the institution of slavery. In certain circumstances members of the resistance movement might also seek to disappear.

In the United States before the Civil War escapes and assistance to escaped slaves from the South were reasonably effective methods of opposition to the institution of slavery. As many as 100,000 slaves are estimated to have successfully escaped in the generation before the Civil War, and despite the federal Fugitive Slave Law requiring the return of escapees, more slaves escaped in the 1850s than ever before, Carleton Mabee reports.[134]

As an act of political noncooperation this method was very widely practiced in the Netherlands during World War II. According to Dr. L. de Jong this method was practiced not only by members of the resistance groups who needed false identities, but also by large sections of the population who were wanted by Germans for one reason or another. Approximately 25,000 Dutch Jews went into hiding; those who "submerged" later included much larger groups in the population who were to be deported to Germany, such as members of the Dutch armed forces, students who had refused to declare loyalty to the new regime, and workers needed to boost German production. By the summer of 1944 there were more than 300,000 "underdivers" who had to be provided with shelter, false identity papers, food and usually ration cards. [135]

Some Dutchmen also used escape to counter Nazi measures, especially those Dutch students who—in contrast with those cited in the previous section—registered for work in Germany. Conditions for them in the camps in Germany were extremely bad. Some died. An escape route from Germany back to their own country was arranged, and before the end of the war most—one writer even says "by far the greater number"—had escaped and returned to the Netherlands. [136]

This method was one common means by which Jews in other parts of Europe also sought to counter Nazi measures. [137] When German forces invaded Belgium in May 1940, about one-third of the Jews in that country fled to France, and of the 52,000 remaining toward the end of 1940, German agencies managed to deport only 25,000. An important reason for German difficulties was, as a Foreign Office representative, Bargen, reported in September 1942, the large-scale evasions, including Jews hiding with Belgian families, the use of Belgian identification cards, and flights to occupied and unoccupied France. [138] Of the 8,000 Jews in Athens in December 1943, about 6,800 remained hidden when ordered to register on December 18; only a few hundred of these were later discovered. [139] For some months in 1941-42 the main activity of the Baum Group of young Jewish resisters in Berlin was the raising of money to obtain Aryan documents and foreign passports, largely forged, which enabled Jews to escape, or even to live on the outskirts of Berlin. [140] It is estimated that in Warsaw, 25,000 Jews posed as Aryans, using forged papers. Yuri Suhl describes how Simcha Poliakiewicz, who escaped from the Treblinka extermination camp, was provided with false papers by friendly Poles; these showed him to be Stanislaw Frubel, a Pole of German descent. [141] Several hundred Jews are estimated to have lived through those years in Slovakia either in hiding or by using false documents. [142]

In Canada during World War I, French Canadians resisted military conscription by sending their youths into hiding and refusing to disclose their whereabouts. Over forty percent of the registered draftees were never found and still others were never registered. [143]

141. Civil disobedience of "illegitimate" laws

Civil disobedience is a deliberate, open and peaceful violation of particular laws, decrees, regulations, ordinances, military or police instructions, and the like which are believed to be illegitimate for some reason. One of the most drastic forms of political noncooperation, civil disobedience is an expression of the doctrine that there are times when men have a moral responsibility to disobey "man-made" laws in obedience to "higher" laws. At least since Socrates,[144] members of religious and political groups have often experienced a conflict of loyalties in which they had to choose between obeying the laws of the established government, thus violating their own beliefs, and disobeying such laws, thus remaining true to their deeper convictions.

Sometimes civil disobedience is seen to be called for because of a belief that a certain law is illegitimate, the body or person which instituted the law having had no authority to do so. For example, in February 1766, Edmund Pendleton, one of Virginia's most notable lawyers (he was also a magistrate and a member of the House of Burgesses), wrote to James Madison, Sr., telling him his views on the current debate over whether the courts should noncooperate with the Stamp Act by open disobedience to it, or noncooperate without such disobedience. The courts could suspend activities, and hence not use the required tax stamps on certain documents, or they could operate normally but, in defiance of the law, refuse to use the tax stamps. Pendleton's view was that "he had taken an oath to determine cases according to the law, and since he believed that Parliament had had no authority to pass the Stamp Act, he could not regard that Act as a law and felt that it would be a violation of his oath if he refused to proceed because of it."[145]

In more modern times the theory of civil disobedience was refined and popularized through the action of Henry David Thoreau and a famous essay by him.[146] It was Gandhi, however, who made the greatest single contribution to developing civil disobedience as a means of social and political action on a mass scale. Gandhi wrote: "Disobedience to be civil has to be open and non-violent."[147] Civil disobedience is regarded as a synthesis of civility and disobedience, that is, it is disobedience carried out in nonviolent, civil behavior. It is generally used only after other attempts to remove the undesirable situation have failed and there appears to be no alternative, or in situations where the individual or group is placed in a position of deciding where their higher loyalty lies.

Modern justification for civil disobedience of this type is frequently based on a conviction that obedience would make one an accomplice to an immoral or unjust act or one which is seen to be, in the last analysis, itself illegal. A vivid expression of this view was offered by Pawel Herst in Poland in 1954, at the meeting of the Council of Art and Culture which ousted its Secretary-General, Jerzy Putrament, after he had imposed rigid controls on behalf of the Comminist Party. Herst declared: "If Putrament should tell me to jump out of the window, and I jumped, then we would both be guilty, he for giving the order, and I for obeying it." The phrase became widely repeated in Poland. [148]

Civil disobedience of "illegitimate" laws as a method of political noncooperation may be practiced by individuals, groups or masses of people, and by organized bodies, even governmental ones. The disobedience may be undertaken reluctantly by persons who have no real desire to disturb the status quo but desire only to remain true to their deepest beliefs *(purificatory civil disobedience)*. Or civil disobedience may be aimed at changing only a particular aspect of the regime's policies or a particular law or regulation regarded as immoral or unjust *(reformatory civil disobedience)*. Or it may be used during a major social or political upheaval as a means of undermining, paralyzing and disintegrating a regime which is seen as unjust or oppressive, with the aim of replacing it with a new system *(revolutionary civil disobedience)*. Or civil disobedience may be practiced against a new illegitimate regime (of domestic or foreign origin) and in defense of the legitimate regime or order *(defensive civil disobedience)*. These classifications may merge into each other.

Gandhi regarded civil disobedience as a potent way of helping to destroy unjust laws; he also felt that it could be applied far more widely than that objective. "Complete civil disobedience is rebellion without the element of violence in it," he said. [149] In his view civil disobedience could be 1) used to redress a local wrong, 2) applied as a means of self-sacrifice to arouse people's awareness and consciences about some particular wrong, or 3) focused on a particular issue as a contribution to a wider political struggle. [150] Gandhi regarded civil disobedience as dangerous to the autocratic State, but harmless in a democracy which is willing to submit to the will of public opinion. Furthermore, he regarded it as an "inherent right of a citizen" and stated that any attempt to put it down was an "attempt to imprison conscience." [151]

There are a multitude of examples of civil disobedience. The practice of publishing accounts of debates in the British Parliament, for example, was established by acts of civil disobedience. Orders by the House of Lords in 1660 and the House of Commons in 1661 had banned publication of reports of parliamentary debates; the Commons had reaffirmed the ban in 1723 and enforced it in 1760.

Nevertheless [writes Gipson], John Almon in 1768 had begun to give detailed accounts of proceedings in Parliament, and other daily and weekly papers had followed his lead. As a result, eight newspapers were prosecuted by the House of Commons during the early part of 1771. The issue became acute when printers John Wheble of the *Middlesex Journal* and Roger Thompson of the *Gazetteer* openly defied a House order for their arrests . . .

These two cases were dismissed when the men were brought before sympathetic magistrates, one of whom was John Wilkes. However, the Commons then committed two of these magistrates, who also happened to be members of the House, to imprisonment in the Tower of London:

The issue aroused the populace to such a degree that popular demonstrations were made not only against Lord North but even against the king. But the upshot of the matter was that the offending printers went unpunished and newspapers continued to print parliamentary debates.

Thus, although the old resolutions prohibiting parliamentary reporting were never officially rescinded, Parliament in 1771 permitted a constitutional amendment to come into being by not fully pressing the charges against the printers in the face of popular sentiment. [152]

The refusal of American colonial merchants to use the tax stamps would not have been civil disobedience had they merely refused to cooperate by suspending the various activities for which stamps were required; but when they continued business without using stamped papers and documents, their defiance became civil disobedience. [153]

Governmental bodies, too, may commit civil disobedience. Salem, in the Province of Massachusetts Bay, for example, held an official town meeting on August 20, 1774, in defiance of Governor Gage's orders. [154] As the Massachusetts Bay House of Representatives met to plan for the First Continental Congress, Governor Gage sent the Secretary of the province to the meeting to announce its dissolution. The members of the House, however, refused to unlock the doors, and continued their business until it was completed, with the Governor's messenger reduced to reading the proclamation of dissolution on the wrong side of the door. [155]

In North Carolina, Governor Martin's proclamation forbidding "illegal Meetings" of the towns and counties—and especially a planned meeting of the whole province—"had the same effect as the executive interdicts, in other provinces, of the right of the people to organize and act. The provincial convention of August 25 assembled at Newbern with a representation from thirty-two of the thirty-eight counties and two of the six towns, while the governor and his council sat futilely by." [156]

In Imperial Russia in 1875, the poor peasants in the villages in the Chigirin district near Kiev practiced a form of civil disobedience in the aftermath of the abolition of serfdom. Opposing the attempts of the richer peasants to legalize their possession of the larger holdings (which had been obtained by unfair means at the emancipation), the poorer peasants sought an equable redistribution of the land. Declining to seize the land by violence but firmly believing they were acting "in accordance with the Tsar's will, they refused to put their mark on the official deeds and some would not make the customary payments" despite severe repression, flogging and imprisonment. In the end they lost even their existing allotments. [157]

During the winter of 1914-15 in Sioux City, Iowa, eighty-three members of the Industrial Workers of the World were imprisoned for violating city restrictions on the holding of street meetings; many had come from other parts of the country specifically to break down the ban. [158] During the famous Toledo, Ohio, automobile strike in the 1930s, the strikers ignored an injunction and "quietly and voluntarily submitted to arrest and filled all police wagons and the jails to overflowing." [159]

In the 1930-31 campaign in India, civil disobedience was expressed in a number of ways, which included the making and public sale of salt in violation of the law, the sale and reading in public of prohibited and seditious literature, defiance of bans on parades and meetings, disobedience of ordinances and police orders, and the violation of a number of other selected laws. [160] During the 1952 Defiance Campaign in South Africa, in which over seven thousand persons went to prison for civil disobedience, the main points attacked were the pass law and apartheid regulations, mainly on the railroads. [161] In March 1960 the South African Pan-Africanist Congress called on Africans to leave their passes at home, to surrender themselves at the nearest police station (remaining completely nonviolent), and to repeat the process when released from prison. [162]

In 1965 American Indians, many of whom depended on fishing for their livelihood, conducted civil disobedience against restrictive regulations of the Conservation Department of the state of Washington by committing "fish-ins" in defense of their rights to fish in ancestral fishing areas. These rights had originally been unlimited and had even been acknowledged—by the Treaty of Medicine Creek of 1854 with the United States and later treaties. Planned by youthful college-educated Indians from various tribes, the direct action was also intended to counter the stereotyped image which American society had of the American Indians and which was held by the Indians themselves. One of the leaders, Mel Thom, said: "We decided to take direct action. We decided to show this country, and ourselves, that the Indians had guts." [163] On a cold day in March 1965 Indians set out with boats and forbidden nets, but without fishing licenses, to fish on the Quillayute River. Hundreds of Indians watched from the banks. The game wardens and state police were armed with warrants and guns. "The tribe was small," reports Stan Steiner. "It had never done anything this bold; for fishing off the reservation, without licenses, was an act of civil disobedience to the game laws. . . And the wardens were white with wrath." [164] Other fish-ins continued into 1966.

And before it ended the hundreds of Indians had swelled to thousands. There were Fish-Ins in half a dozen rivers. There were dozens of arrests, war dances on the steps of the capitol rotunda, an Indian protest meeting of several thousand at the state capitol. There were Treaty Treks on the streets of the cities and Canoe Treks, of sixty miles, through Puget Sound. There was a gathering of more than one thousand Indians from fifty-six tribes throughout the country who came to join their brothers. [165]

Several prominent non-Indians joined them, including film star Marlon Brando, comedian Dick Gregory, and the Rev. John J. Yaryan, Canon of Grace Cathedral of San Francisco.

Occasionally there was scattered minor violence—women and children throwing rocks, for example, and young men of the Yakimas carrying rifles to guard tribal fishermen—but the fish-in campaign was predominantly nonviolent. Mel Thom called it the "first tribal direct action in modern history." [166]

Nearly two-and-a-half years after the first fish-in, the United States Department of Justice appeared before the Supreme Court of Washington State "in behalf of a tribe which had been enjoined from exercising its treaty fishing rights." [167] The case was lost in 1968 in the United States Supreme Court. Stan Steiner quotes Patrick Hamilton, an Indian sociology student at the University of Washington, to show the mood of the Indian youth after the campaign had subsided:

The past decade has shown us the power of civil disobedience. Wake up! . . . . see what your people have done to us and then decide if breakage of a few fishing laws is justifiable. [168]

ACTION BY GOVERNMENT PERSONNEL

142. Selective refusal of assistance by government aides

Government employees, administrators, officials, agents and officers, individually or collectively, may refuse to carry out particular instructions or orders, and inform their superior officers of their refusal. The refusal is clear and open, at least to the superior officers, which is what distinguishes this method from the more hidden types of evasion and obstruction described below. The selective refusal of assistance may or may not be announced to the public.

The examples offered here are all associated in some way with Nazi Germany.[169] In March 1942, for example, Goebbels complained that whenever he requested the imposition of harsh measures of "justice," Schlegelberger, the undersecretary for such matters in the Ministry of Justice, "always refuses my requests on the grounds that there is no legal basis for action."[170] Later he wrote again of the need for "brutal punishment," but once more complained of the refusal of the Ministry to go along: "Our Ministry of Justice is unable to understand a line of reasoning that is so obvious. It still moves in formal grooves." A change in the law was made to eliminate the legal justification for such refusal of assistance.[171]

In late 1938 the Nazi Party in *Gau* (party district) Franken decided to take advantage of the anticipated expropriation of Jewish property; calling in Jews from the district, it sought to force them to sign documents transferring their property, almost without compensation, to the city of Fürth, the *Gau* or some other body. Some court officers, however, doubted the legality of this procedure and refused to enter the transactions in the real estate book *(Grundbuch)*—thus voiding the transfers.[172]

Hitler was sometimes confronted with the direct rejection of orders by his army officers, even after he had become Commander-in-Chief. In 1941, for example, he visited the headquarters of the Army Group Center at Borisov on the Russian front and was immediately confronted with a sharp difference of opinion concerning strategy and the utilization of available forces—Hitler wished to concentrate on Leningrad and the Ukraine, while his officers intended to concentrate the campaign on Moscow. When the *Führer* ordered the transfer of two Tank Armies, commanded by Hoth and Guderian, he "came up against a blank wall of refusal," backed by claims that the units needed two or three weeks for regrouping and repairs. The two commanders were supported by their colleagues, including the War Office and the Army Group Center, who "put up a united front to their Führer. He was convinced that they did not *want* to do it and had just claimed that they were not *able* to . . ." [173] Hitler seems to have been correct on this point. The German Army High Command *(O.K.H.-Oberkommando des Herres)* was appalled at the military risk and dangers involved in the invasion of Denmark and Norway proposed by Hitler, and "braving their *Führer*'s wrath, they flatly refused to participate in the preliminary preparations. The Scandinavian operation was subsequently planned entirely by O.K.W. [High Command of the Armed Forces—*Oberkommando der Wehrmacht]* . . ." [174]

The German officials in direct charge of the deportation of Danish Jews, having no forces of their own and unable to count on Danish help, obtained formations of the Order Police from Germany (there were no German police in Denmark), and then sought help from the German occupation army. But General Hermann von Hannecken refused to transfer his men for that task or to issue a decree ordering Jews to report at *Wehrmacht* (German army) offices for "work." This forced the police to undertake a door-to-door search. After Hannecken unsuccessfully sought postponement by intervention in Berlin, he agreed to cooperate only to the extent of providing a mere fifty soldiers to cordon off the harbor area during the loading of Jews on ships, arguing that this was for the maintenance of law and order, and not participation by the army in the "arrests" of Jews. [175]

143. Blocking of lines of command and information

The effective power of a ruler may be limited by his subordinates if they quietly block the relay downwards or execution of orders, or the passage of information from the lower echelons upwards. Members of different levels of the hierarchy may seriously interfere with the regime's capacity to deal with various problems and crises simply by not forwarding to appropriate superiors or departments the information needed to help the regime. Withheld information may concern a variety of matters, such as economic conditions, public opinion, and the state of supplies; it may also include a refusal to report secret resistance organizations, plans and activities.

In Nazi Germany, this blocking of information took an extreme form: presumably loyal officials kept quiet and even shielded men whom they knew to be plotting Hitler's overthrow and assassination, as Wheeler-Bennett describes:

. . . within O.K.W. . . . departmental chiefs—for example, Canaris and Thomas—were frankly disloyal to the regime to the extent of plotting its downfall, and in O.K.H. . . . both the Commander-in-Chief and Chief of the General Staff were cognizant of, if not participant in, subversive conversations and activities, which grew in volume and intent as the war progressed, and never reported them to Security authority.[176]

Even Fritz Fromm, Commander-in-Chief of the Home Army, refrained from reporting the conspiratorial activities of his subordinates Olbrich and Stauffenberg, although Fromm was unwilling to further the conspiracy by direct participation.[177] Field Marshall Keitel reported that officers in the War Office and in military intelligence had known of the July 20, 1944, attempt to assassinate Hitler but had not reported it.[178]

One way to block the chain of command is simply to fail to relay orders to one's subordinates, so that they never reach the men who are to carry them out. For example, the 1939 German generals' plot to prevent the planned offensive against the Western Allies and the invasions of Luxembourg, Belgium and the Netherlands, as a step toward peace, depended to a considerable degree on an act of noncooperation by them. Wheeler-Bennett writes: "On the understanding that they would receive a direct order from the Commander-in-Chief [General Walter von Brauchitsch, himself one of the plotters] they agreed to hamstring the offensive by the simple means of not transmitting to their subordinates the essential order to attack."[179]

As late as 1940 employees of the foreign organization of the Nazi Party had to be reminded to submit documents proving their Aryan ancestry. "Most employees in the office had simply ignored an earlier directive for submission of records, without even giving an excuse or explanation for failure to comply."[180]

The notorious Commissar Decree issued by Hitler in May 1941, which ordered the execution of captured Communist political officials and leaders in the occupied Soviet Union, including military prisoners, was reduced in effectiveness by the refusal of some officers to relay the instructions to their subordinates. Field Marshal Fedor von Bock, Commander-in-Chief of the Army Group Center, refused to issue it, as did others including Field Marshal Wilhelm von Leeb and Colonel-General Erich Hoepner.[181] Walter Görlitz reports that the Commissar Decree was complied with only partially, and then during the first months of the war in the East, but "it was then gradually and quietly dropped, so that by 1942 it was no longer valid.[182]

This method of noncooperation may also take the form of ignoring orders which have actually been received, rather than either obeying or blatantly refusing to obey them. This is neither simple forgetfulness nor accidental inefficiency: such orders are ignored because of lack of sympathy or outright opposition on the part of the person who is refusing to cooperate. One reason for the lax control of funds of various enterprises in Communist China from 1950-63 is reported to have been the tendency of plant managers to ignore most financial regulations; another was a lack of sympathy from even high party officials for tight financial controls.[183]

Reichskommissar Erich Koch of the Ukraine was directed by the East Ministry on September 7, 1942, to seize all Jewish and other abandoned property and to use former Ukrainian officers and civil servants for the job. Koch, however, ignored the order and on March 16, 1943, informed Alfred Rosenberg that the decree was a "political and organizational impossibility."[184] Rosenberg headed the *Ostministerium*, the civilian administration of the occupied East.

144. Stalling and obstruction

Administrative officers and other governmental employees may express political noncooperation by stalling and obstruction carried out under the guise of compliance with a particular order or policy. This method falls within the approach which Sir Basil Liddell Hart defined as "Apparent acquiescence that conceals, and is combined with, a strategy of noncompliance . . ." It may be also described as "Fabian tactics" and "polite procrastination." Liddell Hart argued that this approach can be "maintained more continuously and extensively than others, so as to yield the minimum to the occupying power and create a cumulative sense of frustration." It may be made all the more baffling if practiced "with a cheerful smile and an air of well-meaning mistake, due to incomprehension or clumsiness . . ."[185] The degree of outward appearance of support and compliance may vary.

Again, all the examples offered here except one are from within the Nazi regime itself (especially its bureaucracy) or within puppet or pro-Nazi governments. The final Czech example is very different.

Goebbels repeatedly complained about the lack of leadership and initiative for promoting Nazi measures shown by government ministries and departments,[186] particularly the Ministry of Justice, where, as we have already noted, he encountered problems. Goebbels wrote on March 19, 1942:

We propose a multitude of reforms, improvements, and drafts of laws, but they don't have the right effect because a sort of quiet sabotage is going on in the central offices. The bourgeois elements dominate there, and as the sky is high and the Fuehrer far away, it is very difficult indeed to prevail against this tough and solid bureaucracy. [187]

Hitler is reported by Goebbels to have been convinced of the need for drastic measures, not only in the administration of justice but "against certain types of swivel-chair generals and against the whole bureaucracy." [188] Nearly a year later, in March 1943, Goebbels reported that Hitler agreed with most of his proposals for waging "total war" against the Allies, but added: "He [the *Führer*] merely complains of resistance that is always offered to our measures by the bureaucracy. In some cases this resistance is simply intolerable . . ." [189] The specific cases here dealt with treatment of captured Allied fliers, efforts to develop nuclear weapons, and anti-Jewish measures.

Stalling and obstruction thwarted Hitler's two attempts to apply lynch law to the Allied so-called terror fliers. Görlitz describes this as a specific example of a general phenomenon—the blocking of Hitler's more extreme intentions by various uses of prevarication, stalling and postponement:

. . . often it will be found that the sole purpose of the central figures was to create a paper war around certain questions and prosecute this paper war for as long as was necessary for the whole matter to be dropped and filed, because Hitler had either forgotten all about it or had become interested in new problems. [190]

Hitler's attempt in the summer of 1944 to establish a systematic program of terror against captured Allied "terror fliers" was effectively stalled by the combined efforts of Field Marshal Keitel (Chief of the High Command), Colonel-General Jodl (Chief of Operations Staff O.K.W.), and *Reichsmarschall* Göring (Commander-in-Chief of the Air Force). This was done by pretending to clarify the concept of "terror flier" in international law and by prolonging the debate in memoranda, lengthy discussions and correspondence. In March 1945 Hitler again sought to establish such a policy, and again was thwarted (despite Martin Bormann's assistance) by the obstructive tactics of Jodl's aide, Air Staff Officer Major Herbert Büchs, Field Marshall Keitel, *Reichsmarschall* Göring and General Karl Koller, the Chief of the Air Force Operations Staff. In neither case was the order demanded by Hitler ever issued. [191]

One very important reason that Nazi Germany did not develop atomic weapons was that the nuclear scientists who worked on the task deliberately stalled and obstructed the effort. The German atomic researchers not only refused to push for the development of an atomic bomb but diverted attention from the idea. Their efforts, as described by Robert Jungk, were considered and deliberate. They refrained from passing on preparatory theoretical studies to their superiors, labeled suggestions from others as unrealistic though not impossible in principle, kept memoranda on research locked away, and kept the military departments in the dark about the imminent feasibility of making atomic bombs—all while pretending to cooperate. "It was considered that an open strike of research workers would be dangerous, as it would leave the field open for unscrupulous and ambitious persons. So long as a policy of delay and postponement proved practicable, it was resolved the risk should be taken." [192]

Various of the more extreme Nazi anti-Jewish measures, especially those concerning extermination, met a significant degree of stalling and obstruction. These obviously were not sufficiently widespread and effective to halt the whole effort, and the examples offered here are certainly not cited with any intent of whitewashing any individual or any group. It is, nevertheless, highly significant that these acts of noncooperation occurred and that they did save the lives of many Jews. Such stalling and obstruction occurred within the German bureaucracy, in the Foreign Office, among German occupation officials in the East, and among officials of Nazi-allied Bulgaria, Vichy France, and Mussolini's Italy.

Following the decisive Grosse Wannsee Conference of January 1942, at which Reinhardt Heydrich announced the necessity of "treatment" of those Jews who survived forced labor to prevent them from going free and beginning "a new Jewish development" (that is, he announced the extermination program, the "Final Solution"), "a wave of obstruction began to grow" within the various chancellories and ministries with the very limited aim of obtaining a series of exceptions to the policy which prevented its extension to partners of mixed marriages and their children. [193]

Within the Foreign Office, matters related to Jewish deportations were dealt with by the Department Deutschland, headed by Martin Luther. Nazi deportation policies had specifically excluded Jews of certain nationalities, but Foreign Minister Ribbentrop requested Luther to prepare a report on the possibility of extending the deportations to Jews of *all* nationalities. Baron Ernst von Weizsäcker (head of the Foreign Office under Ribbentrop) then sent Luther's report to Emil Albrecht, of the office's legal department, "in hope that it might be buried there for some time—a favorite device when dealing with Department Deutschland." [194]

Although by no means wholly innocent concerning the "Final Solution," *Reichskommissar* Heinrich Lohse in *Ostland* (an administrative district of occupied Eastern territories) contributed to the delay and prevented the completion of the Riga massacres. In October 1941 Lohse had been reported to Rosenberg's *Ostministerium* for impeding the massacres in Libau. On November 15 he requested a ruling on whether Jews under his jurisdiction were to be killed regardless of the economic situation; an affirmative reply was not received until over a month later. On November 7 Lohse telegraphed *Stadtkommissar* Hingst in Vilna calling attention to the protests of General Braemer; the latter on December 1 urged the civil commissars to stop the execution of irreplaceable Jews, and two days later Lohse distributed Braemer's manifesto. [195]

Various types of administrative and diplomatic stalling and obstruction were also used elsewhere—in Bulgaria (an Axis partner), [196] Vichy France, and Mussolini's Italy—to thwart Nazi extermination efforts. Italian occupation forces in France, for example, proved very obstructive in the face of German orders for the expulsion of Jews. Italian military officers reinterpreted German orders of December 1942 that they expel *all* Jews from French frontier and coastal areas to mean only *French* Jews. The Italian Fourth Army stopped the Prefect of Lyons from arresting from two thousand to three thousand Polish Jews in the Grenoble district and prevented their dispatch to Auschwitz. When German Foreign Minister Joachim von Ribbentrop objected about this to Mussolini himself, Mussolini replied that he sympathized with Ribbentrop's request; but he nevertheless refused to interfere with his generals, who continued to free the arrested Jews. The Italian military officers, Mussolini said, had a "different intellectual formation." When the Italian police did expel Jews from the coastal area, they placed them safely in hotels well within their zone. [197] There was similar Italian obstruction in the Italian Zone of Greece [198] and the Italian Military Zone II in Croatia. [199]

While sharing responsibility for the fate of many Jews who lived in France, the Vichy government nevertheless undoubtedly saved a great number by administrative and diplomatic stalling and obstruction; Pétain and Laval, as well as subordinate officials and police, contributed to these tactics. "The *Commissariat aux Questions Juives* was never sure of the support of the Vichy Government, and its police obtained less and less cooperation from the regular *gendarmerie.*" [200] Xavier Vallat, appointed by Vichy as its first Commissary for Jewish Affairs, early opposed any deportations of French (as distinct from foreign) Jews and the imposition of the Jewish badge—the wearing of which could not be enforced in Vichy territory even after full German occupation. [201] French police in Bordeaux arrested only stateless Jews for deportation (and then only 150 of them) so that Lieutenant-Colonel Karl Adolph Eichmann—who was in charge of the whole deportation system for exterminations—wondered whether he might have to give up France completely as a source of deportations. [202] Laval stalled on German demands for a decree to revoke post-1933 naturalized citizenship of Jews (such a revocation would have made them eligible for deportation). Finally, Laval informed the Germans that Pétain—whose approval was necessary—was disgusted with a decree to take French citizenship obtained by naturalization from women and children and told them that Laval himself had lost his copy of the draft decree. This meant that a three months' waiting period for Jewish objections would be necessary before a new draft could be submitted to the *Conseil de Ministres.* Italian approval would also be needed. During that period the French police could not help in roundups of Jews, he said. Gerald Reitlinger, in his study *The Final Solution,* says that the Gestapo suddenly appeared "singularly powerless" and were supported neither by the High Command nor the Foreign Office. Hitler must have lost interest in the extermination of French Jews, he writes. "This man, who cared nothing for the opinion of the world and who was unamenable to reason, could be undermined completely by slow obstruction." [203] No large-scale roundups were possible without the cooperation of the French police, and even after Italian protection of French Jews collapsed on September 8, 1943, only three transports left the departure station Dracy for Auschwitz. [204]

In the first days of the Russian occupation of Czechoslovakia, the hidden radio transmitters were extremely important in continuing support for the legitimate government and Communist Party, and in arousing nonviolent resistance against the occupation and any possible puppet regime. In order to counter this radio attack, the Russians sought to bring in by railroad jamming equipment (some reports said tracking equipment) to destroy the resistance broadcasts. An account of how its trip was "assisted" was published in Prague in *Politika* on August 27, 1968. It was written by a Czechoslovak rail worker who took part in the action:

I tell you frankly, that train should have been stopped at Cierna [near the border]. But there was nothing peculiar about it—except that it was so short, eight cars only. At first we wanted to throw it off the track, but that could have had terrible consequences. Near Olomouc, it got ahead of a long freight train. Then it accidentally broke up into three sections, and it took four hours to fix. Exactly according to all regulations. Then I collapsed. Another maintenance worker needed another four hours to fix it. Then it moved on to Trebova and, with repair work going on all the time, as far as Chocen. From there, we wanted to steer them on to Poland, but by that time they had maps.

Suddenly they were in a great hurry because they had eaten up everything they had in their two parlor cars. Before Moravany, we threw the trolley wires down, and the train got all tangled up in them. That took two maintenance squads, and they were unable to put it together. The Russians were quite nervous. They wanted the machine to run on batteries, and they could not understand why it should not be possible when all the various pieces of equipment seemed to be functioning all right. In Pardubice, they wanted steam, but we told them that that was an electrified line. In Prelouc, a piece of the track was dismantled, then a trolley thrown off, and they decided that they would go on by way of Hradec. In Steblova, again a thrown-off trolley; it's a single-track stretch so there was nothing to be done. Not too quickly, anyway. Six Soviet helicopters picked up our dispatchers as hostages. We put fifteen freight trains in front of them, and there is no yard in Prague that could take all of that. Our own trains suffered because of it; everything was delayed. I myself got to Kolin with a completely empty passenger train. Now they are somewhere around Lysa on the Elbe. But such a [Good Soldier] Schweik-type operation cannot last indefinitely. [205]

Czechoslovak radio reported on August 25 that the train was halted at Lysa nad Labem and that the jamming equipment was being reloaded into Russian helicopters. [206]

145. General administrative noncooperation

The great majority of a government's administrative personnel may refuse to cooperate with a usurping regime. This may be either an occupation government or a group which has seized control of the State apparatus by *coup d'etat* or other illegal means.

After the Bolsheviks seized power in October 1917 from the post-revolutionary Provisional Government headed by Kerensky, for instance, the new regime was immediately boycotted by the civil servants, who disobeyed the orders of the new occupants of the seats of power. In the Ministry of Public Welfare all but forty of the functionaries went on strike. [207] As has already been pointed out, this kind of noncooperation was instrumental in defeating the Kapp *Putsch* in 1920 against the Weimar Republic. [208]

146. Judicial noncooperation [209]

This method of intragovernmental noncooperation occurs when members of the judicial system—judges, jurors, and the like—refuse to carry out the will of the regime or of some other portion of the judicial system. An example of the latter would be the refusal of a jury to convict a political prisoner despite the wish of the presiding judge that he be convicted. In certain cases determination by a court that a given law or policy is unconstitutional would also be an act of political noncooperation with the regime. Or, a judge could refuse to convict or punish, despite the evidence and pleas of the prosecutor.

Resignation of an entire judicial institution may occur in reaction to interference with the court's independence by a usurper. In December 1940, for example, the Norwegian Supreme Court resigned in protest against the declaration by *Reichskommissar* Terboven that the Court had no right to declare his German occupation "laws" unconstitutional.[210]

Judicial noncooperation may also operate within the judicial system. A noteworthy case of nullification by judicial noncooperation was the abolition of capital punishment for petty theft in England during the early nineteenth century. The law specified a certain minimum value of goods at which the death penalty became applicable. Often the juries would find the value of the stolen goods to be just a penny or a shilling lower than the crucial figure—regardless of the actual value—in order to avoid a hanging. Arthur Koestler writes:

> The deterrent of the gallows affected the jury more than the criminal; the juries went on strike as it were. They made it a rule, when a theft of goods worth forty shillings was a capital offense to assess the value of the goods at thirty-nine shillings; and when, in 1827, the capital offense was raised to five pounds, the juries raised their assessments to four pounds and nineteen shillings.[211]

Some juries refused outright to convict persons for other crimes against property, such as forging banknotes. Merchants and bankers themselves demanded the abolition of capital punishment in order that there be some kind of effective punishment against such crimes. Finally, the legislation on capital punishment was altered, in 1837 and 1861, to abolish hanging for property crimes.

Occasionally, judicial noncooperation may involve open disobedience by a jury of a judge's instructions where they find them unreasonable. In 1670 William Penn and William Mead were arrested for "unlawfully and tumultously" assembling in a Quaker Meeting, which Penn addressed outdoors after the entrance to the house where the Meeting was to have been held had been barred by soldiers. The trial itself was a remarkable one, and when it came time for a verdict from the members of the jury, they found Mead "not guilty" and Penn simply "guilty of speaking or preaching to an assembly." The latter was not a crime; nor was this a legal verdict. The foreman refused to say whether the assembly to which Penn spoke was itself legal or illegal. After threats of indefinite confinement by the Recorder, one of the two justices in the case, the jury again returned the same verdict. The Recorder then announced:

> Gentlemen, you shall not be dismisst till we have a Verdict, that this Court will accept; and you shall be lock'd up, without Meat, Fire,

Drink, or Tobacco; you shall not think thus to abuse the Court; we shall have a verdict, by God, or you shall starve for it.[212]

After two nights of such detention the jury found Penn "not guilty." Both the defendants and the jury were then fined for contempt of court. A year later a higher court ruled that the jury was correct and that it had been illegally detained.

147. Deliberate inefficiency and selective noncooperation by enforcement agents

Police, soldiers and other enforcement officials may at times deliberately carry out their orders with less than full efficiency, either out of political motivation, sympathy for the resisters, or distaste for the repressive measures. Or, police and others may selectively refuse certain orders on a scale too limited to be described accurately as mutiny. To the degree to which this method of political noncooperation is practiced, the ruler's ability to implement his will is reduced and the effect of repression lessened. Let us first survey some examples of deliberate inefficiency. These come from tsarist Russia, British-occupied India, and German-occupied Norway.

A.T. Vassilyev, the former head of the *Ochrana*, the tsarist secret police, has reported that the law prohibiting Jews from settling in certain provinces of Imperial Russia "was constantly evaded, and that countless Jews, with the consent of the authorities, lived in towns that should have been closed to them. The Police looked upon the fact with benevolence and shut both eyes." [213]

And in India during the 1930 nonviolent raids on the salt depot at Dharasana, Indian police ordered to beat the nonviolent volunteers with *lathis* (heavy bamboo rods, often steel-shod) were not always efficient, as an eyewitness, Webb Miller, reports: "Much of the time the stolid native Surat police seemed reluctant to strike. It was noticeable that when the officers were occupied on other parts of the line the police slackened, only to resume threatening and beating when the officers appeared again." [214]

In 1941, in Hanover, former Gestapo chief Rudolf Diels refused the *Gauleiter*'s orders to arrest Jews, and Graf Faber-Castell refused to shoot five hundred Jews in Poland. Neither was harshly punished.[215] Lieutenant-General Hans Rauter of the S.S. complained in September 1942 that there was almost no cooperation from the Dutch police in the roundup of Jews in the Netherlands.[216]

In occupied Norway both Norwegian police and German soldiers were sometimes deliberately inefficient and either facilitated escapes or did less than was expected of them in making arrests. In one case a Norwegian policeman sent to arrest a Jew who happened to be out left a message that he would return at twelve noon—which gave the hunted man time to gather his belongings and get away. During this early roundup, large numbers of Jews were warned in advance of the arrests.[217] Similar events later took place prior to the arrests of the remaining Jews, including women and children, on November 26, 1942. Norwegian policemen informed resistance people of the impending arrests, and some personally went the night before to warn the Jews.[218] When many students at the University of Oslo were arrested on November 30, 1943, German soldiers sent to private homes often encouraged escapes by taking the word of someone answering the door that the wanted student was not at home and going away, rather than entering and searching the house, as was expected.[219]

In addition to such types of action, a certain amount of open refusal of cooperation and flouting of orders occurred among Norwegian police, although it would not be accurate to say that this was a model of full refusal of cooperation with fascism. These various acts of noncooperation have been reported by Lars L'Abée-Lund, who later became chief of criminal police in Oslo and an appeals court judge.

The very day on which the Germans entered Oslo, April 6, 1940, Vidkun Quisling, leader of the Norwegian fascist party, *Nasjonal Samling,* declared himself to be State Minister, and ordered Kristian Welhaven, the chief of police in Oslo, to meet him in conference. Chief Welhaven did not appear at Quisling's office, however. When Quisling phoned Welhaven the next day enquiring as to why he had not appeared, the police chief replied that he had indeed been at his own office and was at present, if Quisling wished to confer with him. For the moment Quisling had to back off, but in September *Reichskommissar* Terboven permitted Welhaven's dismissal and arrest. He was kept in Grini concentration camp in Norway until 1943, then in Gestapo headquarters in Berlin, and finally in Bavaria until he was released in early 1945 as a result of negotiations led by the Swede Count Folke Bernadotte. Not all Norwegian police officers followed Welhaven's example, however, and within a short time almost all higher police officials were members of the *Nasjonal Samling;* sixty percent of all officers, including assistant chiefs, voluntarily joined Quisling's *N.S.*[220] About forty percent of the other policemen also joined the party. Nevertheless, reports L'Abée-Lund, "the regime could not rely on the police apparatus."[221]

In July 1940 the police were ordered to salute fascist-style with outstretched right hand. "Bitterness among the police was great. In Oslo, the force at headquarters that was ready for duty refused to go out, and in Kristiansand the police chief, one of the few who was not a member of *Nasjonal Samling,* resigned. He was followed by his assistants."[222]

The Kristiansand chief was arrested and, after still refusing to comply, was imprisoned and deported to Germany.

In the autumn of 1941 three assistant chiefs of the Oslo criminal police refused to obey an order to confirm a confiscation of food that the *Hird,* Norwegian storm troops, had seized during the night. These officers were themselves jailed but later released, after which they set up in the district of Østlandet the core of a secret resistance organization of police. From the autumn of 1942 instructions were sent out from resistance leaders for police to boycott *N.S.* propaganda meetings and to refuse to apply for promotions when vacant police positions were listed for applicants.

When the fascists launched their program of labor mobilization of Norwegian citizens—the "National Work Effort"—in 1943, the underground gave instructions in June that every policeman should refrain from actions which would help this conscript labor program. Two months later Gunnar Eilifsen, assistant police chief in Oslo, refused to obey an order to bring in two young girls for the work effort. He was court-martialed and executed on August 16, 1943. The same day all the Oslo police—between six and seven hundred—were called to a meeting with Police Chief Jonas Lie, an *N.S.* member. Lie told them of Eilifsen's execution and demanded that they sign a statement promising to obey orders. *N.S.* members promptly signed, but some others simply marched past the table where they were expected to sign. After both friendly conversations and warnings that if they refused they would be shot the next day, fourteen policemen still refused. They were driven away in German cars but apparently not executed. [223]

In the autumn of 1943 the police set up an illegal police leadership organization, in line with *Milorg* (the military resistance group) and *Sivorg* (the civilian, nonviolent, resistance group). The police organization cooperated with *Milorg,* setting up an information service about coming police raids and arrests against home front personnel and organizations; they also operated to discover and "neutralize" agents who were working for the Nazis. [224]

148. Mutiny

In advanced stages of a noncooperation movement, the opponent's troops, police, or both may mutiny and flatly refuse to carry out orders to repress the resistance movement. In other situations mutiny has itself constituted a major—sometimes the dominant—method of resistance and revolutionary struggle where the army itself is in revolt. Whereas in essentially violent revolutions a mutiny may be followed by the troops joining in the violent struggle on the side of the revolutionaries, in an essentially nonviolent struggle, a mutiny may express itself entirely through the refusal to carry out usual functions of forcing the regime's will on the populace or waging war against a foreign enemy. This refusal may contribute to a paralysis of the regime's ability to rule, by increasing the totality of defiance and noncooperation, paralyzing the regime's organs of enforcement, and destroying its conventional military capacity.

During the Russian 1905 Revolution mutinies were not uncommon. The former head of the *Ochrana* reports an early mutiny in St. Petersburg on February 24, 1905:

> When the attempt was made to relieve the Police by employing detachments of Cossacks, a very serious state of matters was revealed: the Cossacks, who had once been the terror of a riotous crowd, now actually fraternized with the mob and gave not the least sign of taking serious measures against it. [225]

During this revolution (especially from November 1905 to mid-1906) troops returning across the Trans-Siberian Railway from the war with Japan often violated discipline:

> The soldiers disobeyed officers and fraternized with civilian radicals in centers where authority was being broken down—particularly Harbin, Chita, Krasnoyarsk, and Irkutsk. Their contempt for discipline ranged from simple gestures of insubordination to quite serious excesses—such as their retaliation at Chita for a general's insult to some railworkers: they detached his coach and left him there. [226]

The mutiny at Irkutsk in Siberia particularly appears to have displayed the characteristics of this nonviolent method; with virtually everyone opposed to the central government, the Social Democrats obtained official permission to address crowds of soldiers, who then refused to perform their military duties, J.H.L. Keep reports. [227]

During the February 1917 Revolution, mutinies of Russian troops played a very important role. For example, the Volynsky Regiment mutinied on February 27, after having fired, under orders, on nonviolent demonstrators in Znamensky Square, Petrograd, on the previous day and after the shooting of their officer the next morning by an unknown assassin: "The men of the Volynsky Regiment were firing their rifles into the air and proclaiming their support for the people's rising. But they soon lost their cohesion and mingled with the demonstrators to form part of the same motley crowd." [228] The mutiny spread to other units, and as patrols dispersed to their barracks for supper, "On the way they merged with the crowds." [229] The troops generally did not remain in their units and did not oppose the regime by military means:

> The soldiers who came out into the streets preferred the anonymity

of the milling crowd to an identifiable position in their units. They sold their rifles to the highest bidder, adorned their greatcoats with pieces of red ribbon, and joined one or other of the demonstrations, smashing police stations, opening up prisons, setting fire to court buildings, or indulging in other forms of "bloodless" revolutionary activity.[230]

The Army Headquarters no longer knew on which troops they could rely. On February 27 the Minister of War sent telegrams to the Tsar reporting the spreading mutiny, arson and total loss of control by Khabalov (the Commander of the Petrograd Military District), and asking for really reliable troops immediately in considerable numbers.[231] Occasionally, however, rebellious troops violently turned on loyal units, as in the ambush in Luga during this period.[232]

In May and June 1917 large-scale mutinies also took place in the French Army as a sign of general rebellion against the war and the immense casualties which were being suffered in the military stalemate. By official admission mutinies—or "collective indiscipline"—took place in almost exactly half the French fighting forces. "The revolts began as they would continue—spontaneous mutinies without a realizable objective, devoid of organized leadership, and without individual heroes or villains," writes Richard Watt.

The mutinies, which began on a small scale, provoked punishments. But as the numbers of mutineers increased vastly, the disobedient troops sensed that they were too numerous to be punished. The first full-fledged mutiny was that of the Second Battalion of the Eighteenth Infantry Regiment. This battalion had been ordered back into battle on April 29, less than two weeks after about four hundred of its six hundred men had been killed or injured. Even the approximately two hundred remaining alive and physically uninjured were badly shell-shocked. Finally, this battalion was induced to return to the front; later five men of the battalion were condemned to death with little regard as to whether they were in fact leaders of the rebellion. Mutiny, however, spread. "Almost overnight the entire basis of discipline had evaporated. The officers suddenly found that they were not in control of their men but were only scurrying about on the perimeter of what had become a huge, disorderly mob." Watt describes these mutinies as

. . . a kind of "professional strike," a strike stimulated by the fact that they suddenly and completely lost faith in their generals and their generals' strategies and were no longer willing to entrust their lives to a high command which they felt was indifferent and careless of their suffering.

The terrible casualties and the offensive without victory launched by the Commander-in-Chief, General Robert Nivelle, were important in bringing about the mutinies. The French government, appalled by both the mutinies and the failure of the offensive, on May 15, 1917, dismissed General Nivelle and appointed in his place General Henri Pétain.[223]

On April 23, 1930, during the 1930-31 campaign in India, a Garhwali regiment refused to fire on peaceful demonstrators in Peshawar, an act for which its members were prosecuted.[234]

DOMESTIC GOVERNMENT ACTION

149. Quasi-legal evasions and delays

Units of government may not directly defy the laws, court decisions, or the like which require them to carry out some policy or take some measure which they reject, but instead use the reality or appearance of some other law or regulation, or some quite different criteria than those which may be in dispute, in order to evade indefinitely, or at least delay as long as possible, compliance with the requirements of the law, order, or court decision being resisted. These measures are similar to stalling and obstruction, described above, except that these are not the acts of individuals, administrative units, and the like, but are actions by subordinate or constituent units of government as such.

These types of actions have been widely used in the United States South from the end of the post-Civil War Reconstruction period to the present writing. There is, however, nothing intrinsic to the method which limits it to the uses to which it has been put by its Southern segregationist practitioners. Although the Fifteenth Amendment to the United States Constitution denied to the states the authority to refuse Negroes the right to vote, various states pursued alternative means to achieve the same objective. For example, when Oklahoma in 1910 amended its constitution to set up a literacy test as a qualification for voting, the enacted law made a significant exception among the citizens required to take the literacy examination. No one "who was on January 1, 1866, or at any time prior thereto, entitled to vote under any form of government . . . and no *lineal descendant of such person* [was to be] denied the right to register and vote because of his inability to so read and write . . ." (italics added). "In other words," write A.P. Blaustein and C.C. Ferguson, Jr., in their study *Desegregation and the Law,* "the only persons who would be required to pass a difficult literacy test in order to vote were those whose grandfathers had been slaves."[235] This "Grandfather Clause" as a means of disfranchisement was declared unconstitutional by the U.S. Supreme Court. Then Oklahoma passed, in 1916, a statute to the effect that all persons hitherto denied the right to vote must register within a twelve day period. Again, this was intended to apply only to Negroes; various "practical difficulties" would keep many from voting. This was also declared unconstitutional. The U.S. Supreme Court wrote that the Fifteenth Amendment "nullifies sophisticated as well as simple-minded modes of discrimination." [236]

Various other means of a legal or quasi-legal character have been used by Southern states to bar Negroes from voting. The 1961 "Report to the U.S. Commission on Civil Rights" from the North Carolina State Advisory Committee cites sworn written complaints from Negroes in five counties that literacy tests were applied in a discriminatory manner in order to prevent their registration as voters. It has frequently been charged that Southern states enacted such literacy laws precisely to be used to that end. The "Report" states: "It was alleged that the reading and writing tests were applied to the complainants in a manner different from the way in which such tests were applied to white applicants, so as to discriminate against the complainants and deny them the privilege of registering and voting solely because of their race." In 1961 the North Carolina Supreme Court ruled that one of the complainants must be given another opportunity to register and that the examination which she had been given was beyond the intent of the law. [237]

Various states have used several legal and quasi-legal means of avoiding compliance with the United States Supreme Court ruling in 1954 which outlawed racial segregation in public schools. For example, Florida's Pupil Assignment Law allowed the Board of Education to set regulations to establish "uniform tests" for "classifying the pupils according to intellectual ability and scholastic proficiency," so that there would be in each school "an environment of equality among pupils" of similar qualifications. The tests were to take into consideration "sociological, psychological, and like intangible social scientific factors" in order to avoid any "socio-economic class consciousness" among pupils in any given school. Assignments of pupils to a particular school would consider "the psychological, moral, ethical and cultural background" of the pupil as compared with those already assigned to that school. [238]

During this period North Carolina set up a pupil assignment plan, authorizing the school boards to assign each pupil to a particular elementary or high school, subject to a very complicated and time-consuming system of appeal for pupils dissatisfied with their assignment. Blaustein and Ferguson write that this plan was "designed to take advantage of the fact that no proceedings can be begun in the federal courts until a plaintiff has exhausted all the possible remedies which might be available through the action of state courts." [239] When a suit brought under this law, on behalf of all Negro children in one district, finally reached the

North Carolina Supreme Court in May 1956, it was dismissed on the grounds that the given Act required proceedings on an individual basis, and hence such a group suit was outlawed. A separate suit would have to be commenced afresh in behalf of each of the children. [240]

150. Noncooperation by constituent governmental units

Where there is widespread opposition to and noncooperation with the central government, and where local, provincial or state governmental bodies are responsive to public opinion, they may themselves undertake official noncooperation with the central government. Crane Brinton believes that this was an important factor in the American Revolution, during which "town meetings and colonial legislatures were part of the legal government, but were often controlled by men active in the illegal government." [241] Probably the most extreme act of nonviolent government noncooperation during the American colonists' struggle occurred in Rhode Island, where in September 1765 the Assembly instructed the officials of the province to ignore the Stamp Act, resolving

> That all the officers in this colony, appointed by the authority thereof, be, and they are hereby, directed to proceed in the execution of their respective offices in the same manner as usual; and that this Assembly will indemnify and save harmless all the said officers, on account of their conduct, agreeably to this resolution. [242]

Not only did the Stamp Distributor for Rhode Island resign, but the Governor himself refused to take the required oath to help enforce the Stamp Act. [243] The colony's courts accordingly remained open and operated as usual without the use of the stamps (required by the law) on their documents. [244]

The New York General Assembly stalled and procrastinated when requested in 1766 to make provisions for quartering the King's troops, as required by the British Quartering Act; in an address replying to the Secretary of State for the Southern Department in London it pleaded that the expense of such provisions was excessive for the colony and its people, ". . . and therefore we humbly intreat your Excellency to set our Conduct . . . in its true Light, by representing that our Non Compliance on this Occasion proceeds entirely from a just Sense of what our Duty requires." [245]

Following the military occupation of Boston, which began on September 30, 1768,

> Boston, through its constituted authorities, met the invasion with pas-

sive, but most effective and irritating resistance [writes George Tre-velyan]. The Colonels called upon the Council to house and feed their men. They were reminded that under the statute the city was not bound to provide quarters or supplies until the barracks in the Castle were full; and the Council and the Colonels alike knew that the regiments had been sent, not to defend the Castle, (which stood on an island in the Bay,) but to occupy and annoy the city.

When the Commander-in-Chief in America, General Gage, went to Boston and saw his soldiers sleeping in tents on the Common, with winter fast approaching, he found it necessary to hire private houses at exorbitant rates, and the British Treasury had to pay.[246] Until the shift to military struggle in 1775, colonial town meetings and provincial legislatures themselves repeatedly took the initiative in launching and conducting various economic boycotts, which were used as primary weapons in the colonial struggles with the government in London.[247]

One of the early and crucial constitutional problems of the United States government after its establishment was the question of who would determine when a law or action had exceeded or violate the purposes and powers set out by the new Constitution. Although the Supreme Court soon assumed this role, this was not the only possibility. Thomas Jefferson and James Madison developed the doctrine of nullification, which said that the legislature of a given state could decide that an Act passed by Congress violated the Constitution, and hence was null and void within that state. This was the basis for the famous Virginia Resolutions of 1798 and the Kentucky Resolutions of 1798 and 1799.

Aroused by antidemocratic tendencies in the new United States government, of which he saw the Alien and Sedition Acts as only the beginning, Thomas Jefferson concluded that it was necessary to erect a strong barrier against the encroachments of the Federal Government. He privately participated in drafting these resolutions, introduced in both Kentucky and Virginia. (James Madison introduced them in the Virginia Assembly.) One of the 1798 Kentucky Resolutions declared:

> *Resolved,* that the several States composing the United States of America, are not united on the principle of unlimited submission to their general government; but that . . . they constituted a general government for special purposes . . . ; and that whensoever the general government assumes undelegated powers, its acts are unauthoritative, void, and of no force . . .

It further asserted that the constituent states, not the federal government itself, must be able to judge when the Constitution had been exceeded.[248]

One of the Virginia Resolutions of that year also asserted that when the Federal Government had exceeded its constitutionally authorized powers, "the states, who are parties thereto, have the right and are in duty bound to interpose for arresting the progress of the evil, and for maintaining within their respective limits the authorities, rights, and liberties appertaining to them." [249] The 1799 Kentucky Resolutions asserted that extension of the activities of the Federal Government beyond the bounds set by the Constitution would lead to "an annihilation of the state governments . . .", and that the doctrine that the Federal Government alone should judge the extent of its constitutionally delegated powers, not the constituent states, would lead to a process of increasing federal powers which would "stop not short of *despotism* . . ." [250]

This theory was the basis for the nullification doctrine adopted by Vice-President John C. Calhoun in 1828, when he denounced the tariff law of that year. Calhoun claimed the right of a state to declare inoperative within its boundaries any law that it judged to be unconstitutional. [251] He saw this as an alternative to secession and as a defense of the Constitution. This general doctrine was later extended by certain states to actual secession from the Union. By itself secession was not an act of war; it only became so when military clashes occurred between Union troops and secessionist soldiers. (Had slavery—an institution impossible to defend by nonviolent means—not existed in the South and had the South wished to secede on other grounds, it is theoretically possible that it might have done so and applied a widespread program of nonviolent noncooperation which would have been, given a very different type of society in the South, very difficult indeed for Federal forces to crush.)

When the Russian government sought to bring Finland under tighter control in 1910, it tried to avoid clear rejection by the Finnish parliament of the bill to achieve that aim which was then being considered in the Russian capital, St. Peterburg. The Finns were asked to deliver a *report* on the proposed new law which would formalize Finland's subordination to the Russian government—not to *vote* on the bill (that is, accept or reject it). The Finnish parliament, however, refused to draw up such a report on the grounds that it, not the Russians, held full legislative power over such matters. [252]

As described in Chapter Two, the various *Länder* (states) in Germany under the Weimar Republic, at the call of the legal Ebert government, refused to cooperate with the usurping group of putschists headed by Dr. Kapp and General Lüttwitz.

During the 1930-31 struggle for Indian independence the Municipal Board of Ahmedabad informed British officials that they were unable to cooperate with the coming census because the Indian National Congress had decided upon a boycott of it. Insisting that there was widespread and determined opposition to the census, they said they would lack full public cooperation should they take part in it. Furthermore, if the Board was supposed to represent the public, it ought not to take action in conflict with public opinion. [253]

INTERNATIONAL GOVERNMENTAL ACTION

A more thorough classification of the types of noncooperation between governments than that offered here should be undertaken, for a large number of variations appear even at first glance. The illustrative nature of the seven methods described here should be kept in mind. These methods range from relatively mild ones of largely symbolic significance to more extreme measures which may disrupt the normal international activities and functions of the country. The League of Nations Covenant imposed on its members the obligation of a *total* international embargo —diplomatic, political, social and economic, the severance of all intercourse—of any State resorting to war in violation of the Covenant, Crespigny reminds us. [254]

151. Changes in diplomatic and other representation

In order to express disapproval of the policies of another country, a government will at times recall its own diplomat or other officials without breaking diplomatic relations, or ask that a foreign diplomat be replaced. Sometimes one government will place at the head of its diplomatic corps in another country an official holding a rank so low as to be an insult to the host country. At other times a country will voluntarily close, or be requested by the host country to close, certain of its offices, such as consulates—again, without breaking diplomatic relations.

Or officials other than members of the diplomatic staff may be withdrawn. As the differences between the Soviet Union and Yugoslavia sharpened in 1948, after the Central Committee of the Yugoslav Communist Party rejected Stalin's demand that Yugoslavia and Bulgaria immediately establish a federation, the Soviet Union replied on March 18 by recalling its military advisers from Belgrade. [255]

The host country may ask for the withdrawal of an ambassador, as Sir Douglas Busk notes, "for political and not personal reasons, i.e., because of displeasure with the policy of his government." [256] Diplomatic matters in the host country are then handled by a subordinate official. On occasion a government's request for withdrawal of a certain ambassador has been rejected by his home government. As a result, writes Charles W. Thayer, "the host government simply ceases to do business with the ambassador and there is nothing much the sending government can do but retaliate by breaking relations." [257] Thus during the 1848 revolution, after the British Ambassador to Spain, Henry Bulwer, somewhat exceeding his instructions, had strongly intervened to halt repression of Spanish liberal politicians, the British government rejected Spain's demand for Bulwer's recall. After various diplomatic exchanges the two governments broke diplomatic relations. [258]

During World War I the German military attaché in Washington, Franz von Papen, was declared *persona non grata* for allegedly engaging in plots to blow up American ammunition plants and was consequently withdrawn by the German government. There are many other examples of requested withdrawal for alleged improper behavior by diplomats. [259]

The closing of consulates is also common. After the sinking by a German submarine of the U.S. merchant ship *Robin Moor* on May 21, 1941, for example, the U.S. government ordered all German and Italian assets in the United States frozen and also ordered the closing of all German and Italian consulates. Germany and Italy retaliated by closing U.S. consulates in their countries. [260]

During the period of United States dissatisfaction with Sweden's policy of opposing U.S. involvement in the war in Vietnam, the U.S. Ambassador, William Heath, was recalled in March 1968 for consultations with President Johnson. [261] Heath did not return, nor was he replaced with a new ambassador. In November 1969 the U.S. Consulate in Göteborg was closed, the official reason being to cut U.S. foreign spending. It was the oldest American consulate, having been established by George Washington in 1797 after Sweden became the first government to recognize the new U.S. government. [262] Then the Nixon administration, which came to office in January 1969, declined to appoint a new ambassador to Sweden for a time. The new Swedish Premier, Olof Palme, thought the U.S. policy rather "impractical": "If Washington really wants to explain where we are wrong, there should be someone here to do the explaining." [263] Finally Dr. Jerome Holland was appointed and took up his post as the new U.S. Ambassador to Sweden in the spring of 1970.

152. Delay and cancellation of diplomatic events

Governments may stall or completely halt certain negotiations, meetings, conferences and the like as a result of displeasure with the actions or policies of another government involved in such events. For example, Gordon A. Craig argues that in the past it has been the practice of the Soviet Union to prolong negotiations for months and even years, sometimes also shifting the level of negotiation (say, from the ambassadorial to the ministerial level, and then to heads of state), with the result that the issues at stake and original points of difference become blurred, with assistance from publicity efforts. Craig cites as examples "the repeated and protracted negotiations in the 1920s over the question of the Russian debts," which resulted in avoidance of payment without penalty, and later various negotiations concerning Berlin and Germany, especially during the time of Premier Khrushchev. [264]

As Stalin began to apply pressure in early 1948 against Yugoslovia, the Soviet Union canceled the planned April meeting at which Soviet-Yugoslav commercial agreements were to be renewed. [265]

The announcement in early May 1960 that a United States U-2 plane photographing the Soviet Union from a great height had been shot down by a Soviet rocket was followed by denunciations of "spy flights" by Premier Khrushchev and demands that those responsible be punished. He said that the summit conference then taking place in Paris between the Soviet Union, the United States, France and Great Britain could not go on unless the U.S. government gave a full apology. So "after a brief meeting on the morning of 16 May the summit conference of 1960 was at an end," Wilfrid Knapp writes. [266]

The North Vietnamese and the National Liberation Front's delegations canceled the sixty-sixth plenary session of the Vietnam peace talks in Paris on May 6, 1970, in protest against five days of renewed United States' bombing of North Vietnam, Nguyen Thanh Le, the North Vietnamese spokesman, described the extraordinary move as "a political decision." The date for the next scheduled session, May 14, was not immediately accepted by the United States and South Vietnamese delegations; the latter indicated that it might make this same type of threat itself. [267]

153. Withholding of diplomatic recognition

The general practice of governments to recognize other governments which are effectively in control of the countries they rule is sometimes replaced by deliberate refusal of diplomatic recognition. This is often because of objection to the way in which that government came to power or to its basic political character. President Woodrow Wilson, for example, refused United States' recognition of the Mexican regime of Victoriano Huerta, harsh spokesman of propertied groups, who had ousted the revolutionary regime of Francisco Madero and had been responsible for his murder in prison. Wilson declared: "My ideal is an orderly and righteous government in Mexico; but my passion is for the submerged eighty-five per cent of the people of that Republic who are now struggling toward liberty." [268]

After Japan seized China's Manchuria and proclaimed the puppet state of Manchukuo in February 1932, the United States pursued the Stimson (or Hoover-Stimson) Doctrine: nonrecognition of international changes produced by means contrary to the provisions of the Kellogg-Briand Pact, which outlawed wars of aggression. Consequently, although rejecting both proposed economic sanctions and military means, the United States refused diplomatic recognition to Manchukuo. The U.S., however, continued trade relations and kept consular officials there, although they remained accredited to the Chinese National government. [269] In March 1932 the Assembly of the League of Nations unanimously adopted a resolution against Japan which followed almost verbatim the Hoover-Stimson Doctrine of Nonrecognition, Thomas Bailey reports. [270] For many years the United States refused to recognize the Communist government of the Soviet Union, on the basis of various grievances and charges, until recognition was agreed to in 1933. [271]

United States' long refusal to grant diplomatic recognition to the Peoples' Republic of China is one of the best-known examples of the use of this method. Diplomatic nonrecognition was in this case intended to contribute to the collapse of the Communist regime, as the State Department statement of August 11, 1958, indicated: "The United States holds the view that communism's rule in China is not permanent and that it one day will pass. By withholding diplomatic recognition from Peiping it seeks to hasten that passing." [272] Secretary of State John Foster Dulles further explained the policy on December 4, 1958: "Such recognition and the seating of the Chinese Communists in the United Nations would so increase their prestige and influence in the Far East, and so dishearten our allies there, that the Communist subversive efforts would almost surely succeed." [273]

Refusal of diplomatic recognition to Israel has been a basic part of Arab policy since the establishment of Israel. In addition, they have used more severe means, such as refusing other direct dealings with the Israeli government, trying to block its membership in international organizations, and imposing economic embargoes. [274]

Following the crushing of the 1956 Hungarian Revolution, various Western governments imposed a diplomatic boycott on the Kadar regime which was not broken until January 1, 1958. Even thereafter, however, the United States maintained only a *chargé d'affaires* in Budapest. Ferenc Váli writes: "The Soviets have considered the refusal by the United States to grant full recognition to the post revolutionary Hungarian government as the greatest stumbling block in the way of eliminating the bitterness caused by its armed intervention." [275]

The threat by one country of permanent nonrecognition of a government has also been used to help defeat a *coup d'etat* in another country. For example, Major-General Sir Neill Malcolm, Head of the British Military Mission in Berlin, told General Lüttwitz on March 16, 1920, that Britain would never recognize the new Kapp regime which Lüttwitz was helping to impose, "and thereby completed its discomfiture," reports Wheeler-Bennett. [276]

One variation of this nonrecognition is to recognize the government in question, but to do so conditionally. Harold Nicolson in his book *Diplomacy* cites the case of the British government's recognizing the Portuguese Republic on the condition that the new regime be confirmed by a general election. [277]

154. Severance of diplomatic relations

Severance of diplomatic relations "normally involves the departure of the entire Missions from both capitals, though sometimes only the Ambassador or High Commissioner and some others are forced to leave," writes Busk. Consular officials may or may not be allowed to remain. If the entire diplomatic staff is withdrawn, another country is asked to represent the country's remaining interests in that land. [278] Nicholson points out that the breaking of diplomatic relations "is by no means always a prelude to war and is often resorted to as a means of expressing profound moral indignation. Thus the British Minister was withdrawn from Belgrade after the [June 1903] assassination of King Alexander and Queen Draga, even as a similar diplomatic rupture occurred when Colonel Plastiras murdered M. Gounaris and his ministers in November 1922." [279] After the German announcement on January 31, 1917, of a submarine campaign to sink *all* ships, including neutrals, in the war zone, in an effort to break the British blockade, President Wilson appeared before the United States Congress to announce the termination of diplomatic relations with Germany. [280]

In a very different case, on April 25, 1943, the Soviet Union broke diplomatic relations with the Polish government-in-exile in London. This followed the discovery by the Germans of the Katyn graves, where ten thousand Polish army officers who had been missing for two years were buried. The Polish government-in-exile was convinced of Russian guilt for the executions, and after the Polish Minister of Defense called for an investigation by "a proper international body, such as the International Red Cross" the Soviet Union broke diplomatic relations.[281]

155. Withdrawal from international organizations

Governments may withdraw from either membership in or the activities of various types of international organizations and conferences. The motive may be to express dissatisfaction with their policies or to give the withdrawing country the freedom to take action which might receive disapproval from those bodies. For example, on October 14, 1933, Hitler announced that because of a denial of equal rights to Germany, that country was withdrawing from the Disarmament Conference and also the League of Nations. He argued that the hoped-for reconciliation with former foes had not been achieved, nor had the restoration of equal rights to the German people; hence Germany could no longer tolerate humiliation. The same day Hitler announced that he would submit withdrawal from the League to a plebiscite on November 12, the day after the anniversary of the Armistice of 1918.[282]

In 1950 the Soviet Union's delegates withdrew from United Nations activities—but not from membership—in protest against the continued seating of Nationalist China's delegates instead of those of the Communist government which controlled mainland China. Knapp reports that after Jacob Malik, the Soviet representative to the U.N. walked out of the Security Council on this issue on January 10, 1950, "Malik announced that he would not participate in the work of the Security Council until the Kuomintang [Nationalist Chinese] delegate had been replaced. The Soviet delegates thereupon withdrew from all United Nations bodies of which China was a member."[283] The absence of the Soviet delegate to the Security Council enabled it to take rapid action against North Korea when the Korean War broke out.

During the Indonesian "confrontation" against Malaysia, Indonesia notified the President of the United Nations General Assembly and the Office of the Secretary-General on December 31, 1964, that it was withdrawing from membership in the U.N. because Malaysia had been elected to the Security Council. Despite various appeals and private talks, in late January 1965 Indonesia confirmed her withdrawal from the U.N. and also some of its specialized agencies. (There is no provision for withdrawal in the U.N. Charter.)[284]

156. Refusal of membership in international bodies

Governments may be refused membership by international institutions because of political rivalries, disapproval of the government in question, and other reasons. The most outstanding example of this was the refusal for more than twenty years by the United Nations to seat delegations from the Communist government of mainland China as the representatives of China, in place of the delegates from the Nationalist government, which controlled only the island of Formosa (Taiwan). By the end of 1949 the Communist government (the People's Republic of China) had gained control of all of mainland China, and the Nationalist government (the Republic of China) had moved to Formosa. Consequently, the delegate of the Soviet Union on the Security Council sought unsuccessfully to exclude the Nationalist delegation. [285] After 1961 the question of Chinese representation was regarded by the U.N. General Assembly as "an important question," thereby requiring a two-thirds majority approval, rather than a simple majority. [286] Under heavy pressure from the United States, United Nations bodies declined to seat representatives of the Chinese Communist government until 1971 when they replaced the Nationalist delegates.

157. Expulsion from international organizations

One sanction sometimes used by international bodies against States violating its policies or constitution is expulsion from membership. The League of Nations Covenant provided that any member which violated "any covenant of the League" might be declared to be no longer a member. [287] This was applied only once—against the Soviet Union following its attack on Finland in 1939. On December 14, 1939, the Assembly of the League, with the Soviet delegate absent, unanimously condemned the invasion and declared that "in virtue of Article 16 paragraph 4 of the Covenant [the Assembly] finds that, by its act, the U.S.S.R. had placed itself outside the League of Nations. It follows that the U.S.S.R. is no longer a member of the League." [288]

The United Nations Charter, Article 6, provides "A Member of the United Nations which has persistently violated the Principles contained in the present Charter may be expelled from the Organization by the General Assembly upon the recommendation of the Security Council." [289] The Soviet Union proposed inclusion of such a provision in the Charter during the Dumbarton Oaks Conference and strongly supported the proposal at the San Francisco founding conference. [290] This article has never yet been applied, although suggestions have been made to expel South Africa and Portugal.[291]

Expulsion of Yugoslavia from the *Cominform* (an international Communist organization) was one of the sanctions applied in 1948 when Tito refused to submit to Stalin.[292]

Political noncooperation has been the last of the three subclasses of methods of nonviolent noncooperation. Our attention now turns to the final class of methods of nonviolent action, those of "nonviolent intervention."

NOTES

1. Griffith, **The Resurrection of Hungary,** esp. pp. 22, 43 and 48.
2. *Ibid.,* p. 30.
3. *Ibid.,* p. xxiv.
4. *Ibid.,* p. 31.
5. Geyl, **The Revolt of the Netherlands, 1555-1609,** p. 84.
6. *Ibid.,* pp. 183-184.
7. Gipson, **The British Empire Before the American Revolution,** vol. XII, **The Triumphant Empire: Britain Sails into the Storm 1770-1776,** p. 243.
8. Gipson, **The Coming of the Revolution,** p. 231.
9. Charques, **The Twilight of Imperial Russia,** p. 135.
10. Harcave, **First Blood,** p. 225.
11. Sternstein, "The *Ruhrkampf* of 1923," pp. 114-115. See also Halperin, **Germany Tried Democracy,** p. 249.
12. Margaret DeMarco, "The Use of Non-violent Direct Action Tactics and Strategy by American Indians."
13. "Iroquois of Canada Refuse to Become Canadian Citizens," *New York Times,* 12 March 1921, p. 6.
14. "Chippewa Indians Seek Help of UN to Restore Sovereign Rights," *Philadelphia Evening Bulletin,* 18 November 1946.
15. "Indian Tribe Asks United Nations Seat," *Philadelphia Evening Bulletin,* 8 July 1960.
16. Littell, ed., **The Czech Black Book,** p. 143.

17. *Ibid.*, p. 191.

18. Adam Roberts, "Buddhism and Politics in South Vietnam," p. 247.

19. *France Observateur* (Paris), 24 January 1957; quoted from Miller, **Nonviolence,** p. 362.

20. *New York Times,* 5 June 1968. I am grateful to Carl Horne for this reference.

21. *Peace News,* 27 November and 18 December 1959.

22. *The Times,* 24 March 1960.

23. Griffith, **The Resurrection of Hungary,** pp. 24-28 and 36.

24. Seton-Watson, **The Decline of Imperial Russia,** p. 170.

25. Katkov, **Russia 1917,** p. 4, n.l.

26. Sharp, **Gandhi Wields the Weapon of Moral Power,** pp. 51-219 *passim,* and Pattabhi Sitaramayya, **The History of the Indian National Congress,** vol. I, p. 605.

27. *Sunday Times,* (London), 19 March 1967.

28. Anthony de Crespigny, "The Nature and Methods of Non-Violent Coercion," **Political Studies** (London), vol. XII, no. 2 (June 1964), pp. 264-65. The respective sources are *The Times* (London), 5 Dec. 1961 and 21 May 1962.

29. E. L. Woodward, **French Revolutions** (London: Oxford University Press [Humphrey Milford], 1939), p. 55.

30. *Ibid.*, p. 74.

31. Seton-Watson, **The Decline of Imperial Russia,** p. 242.

32. *Ibid.*, p. 249. See also Charques, **The Twilight of Imperial Russia,** pp. 145 and 174.

33. Personal conversations with Ruth Reynolds, New York 1954-55.

34. Crespigny, "The Nature and Methods of Nonviolent Coercion," p. 264. The following are sources for the particular cases. ˙

35. *New Statesman* (London), 10 Nov. 1961; *The Times* (London), 14 Nov. 1961.

36. *The Times,* 2 and 3 April 1962.

37. *The Observer* (London), 22 April 1962.

38. *The Times,* 30 April 1962.

39. *Washington Post,* 17 August, 1966.

40. *Peace News,* 11 July 1958 and 23 January, 6 and 27 February 1959.

41. Griffith, **The Resurrection of Hungary,** p. 32.

42. Schapiro, **The Origin of the Communist Autocracy,** p. 280.

43. See Lochner, ed., **The Goebbels Diaries,** p. 396; Reitlinger, **The Final Solution,** pp. 53, 97, 187 and 192; Schweitzer, **Big Business in the Third Reich,** pp. 142 and 183; Walter Gorlitz, ed., **The Memoirs of Field-Marshal Keitel** (New York: Stein & Day, 1966) pp. 100-102, 123, 163-164 and 247; Crankshaw, **Gestapo,** p. 166; Alan Bullock, **Hitler: A Study in Tyranny,** revised edition. (U.S. ed.: New York: Harper and Row, 1962, British ed.: London: Odhams, 1964), p. 300, and Wheeler-Bennett, **The Nemesis of Power,** p. 319.

44. *Guardian,* 1 September 1962.

45. Charques, **The Twilight of Imperial Russia,** p. 207.

46. Roberts, "Buddhism and Politics in South Vietnam," p. 246.

47. Salvemini, **The French Revolution, 1788-1792,** p. 86.

48. Høye and Ager, **The Fight of the Norwegian Church Against Nazism,** pp. 88-104.

49. Geyl, The Revolt of the Netherlands, pp. 75 and 78-79.

50. Reitlinger, The Final Solution, pp. 346-347.

51. *The Times*, 19 and 23 March 1960.

52. Roberts,"Buddhism and Politics in South Vietnam," p. 247.

53. Sharp, Gandhi Wields . . . , pp. 53-219 *passim.*, and Bondurant, Conquest of Violence, pp. 57-58 and 94.

54. Wheeler-Bennett, The Nemesis of Power, pp. 398-405.

55. Bernard, Social Control in its Sociological Aspects, p. 398.

56. A. Fenner Brockway,Non-co-operation in Other Lands, pp. 34-39.

57. Sharp, Gandhi Wields . . . , pp. 37-40 and Pattabhi Sitaramayya, The History of the Indian National Congress, vol. I, pp. 534-546.

58. Shridharani, War Without Violence, pp. 30, 18, 41, and 161, and Case, Non-violent Coercion, p. 383.

59. Report of the Advisory Commission on the Review of the Constitution of Rhodesia and Nyasaland, pp. 8, 14 and 16.

60. Seton-Watson, The Decline of Imperial Russia, p. 240.

61. Sternstein, "The *Ruhrkampf* of 1923," p. 117.

62. Roberts, "The Buddhists, the War and the Vietcong," pp. 219-220, in *The World Today*, vol 22, no. 5 (May 1966).

63. Schweitzer, Big Business in the Third Reich, pp. 147-148.

64. *Boston Globe,* 6 and 8 August 1970.

65. *New York Times*, 23 June 1966.

66. *Ibid.*

67. Case, Non-violent Coercion, p. 383, and Shridharani, War Without Violence, p. 49.

68.Luthuli, Let My People Go, p. 147.

69. Sharp, Tyranny Could Not Quell Them, and Amundsen, ed., *et al.,* Kirkenes Ferda 1942.

70. Wyller, Nyordning og Motstand, pp. 62-63.

71. Brant, The East German Rising, p. 161.

72. Gipson, The British Empire Before the American Revolution, vol. XII, p. 21, and Gipson, The Coming of the Revolution, pp. 208-209. See also Schlesinger, The Colonial Merchants and the American Revolution, pp. 252-253.

73. Bondurant, Conquest of Violence, p. 57.

74. Lloyd, Ireland Under the Land League, pp. 123-126.

75. *Peace News*, 5 June 1964.

76. Martin Oppenheimer and George Lakey, A Manual for Direct Action (Chicago: Quadrangle Books, 1965), p. 107n.

77. This section is based on a draft prepared by Michael Schulter.

78. Littell, ed., The Czech Black Book, p. 118.

79. *Ibid.,* pp. 118-19.

80. *Ibid.,* p. 185.

81. Quoted in Hsiao, Rural China, pp. 449-450.

82. This section is based on a draft prepared by Michael Schulter.

83. J. Ellis Barker, Modern Germany: Its Rise, Growth, Downfall and Future (New York: E. P. Dutton & Co.,1919), pp. 293-299.

84. Brant, **The East German Rising,** pp. 34-37.

85. Chang, **The Chinese Gentry,** p. 45.

86. Hsiao, **Rural China,** pp. 134-135.

87. Alexander Pechersky, "Revolt in Sobibor," in Suhl, ed., **They Fought Back,** p. 46.

88. It has not been possible to locate precise documentation or specific cases for this method, although several China authorities have assured me that it has been frequently applied in China. For example, Professor Wolfram Eberhard has written to me in a personal letter, dated 27 April 1966:
  "I am acquainted with the kind of 'non-obedience' which you are referring to. In class-room and other discussion I call this 'apathy' and I regard this attitude as a part of the conditions in a traditional society as I have briefly outlined it in the introduction to the second edition of my **Conquerors and Rulers.** The trouble is only, that one cannot expect that Chinese writers (being of the class of scholar/officials) write about this, because they either do not know conditions in villages or would not like to describe these conditions as a description would reflect upon their (non-) efficiency as administrators. The only references which you might be able to find, would be in non-Chinese sources, especially reports by travellers and officials (British) who worked or travelled in China during the 19th Century."
  There is evidence that the government during the Ming dynasty and later learned that taxes would not be paid unless a collector or some official was physically present to "prompt" payment. See Hsiao, **Rural China,** pp. 97-99.

89. Magnus Jensen, **Norges Historie: Norge Under Eneveldet 1660-1814,** p. 39.

90. Lefebvre, **The French Revolution from its Origins to 1793,** p. 134.

91. *Ibid.,* p. 234.

92. J. P. Mayer, ed. and trans., **The Recollections of Alexis de Tocqueville,** (New York: Meridian Books, 1959), pp. 151-152.

93. Schapiro, **The Communist Party of the Soviet Union,** p. 68 and Keep, **The Rise of Social Democracy in Russia,** p. 227, and Harcave, **First Blood,** p. 214.

94. Harcave, **First Blood,** p. 174.

95. Warmbrunn, **The Dutch Under German Occupation,** p. 112 and p. 105.

96. Kirchhoff *et al.,* **Besaettelsestidens Historie,** p. 204.

97. Hilberg, **The Destruction of the European Jews,** p. 388.

98. *Ibid.,* p. 405.

99. Dwight H. Perkins, **Market Control and Planning in Communist China** (Cambridge, Mass.: Harvard University Press, 1966), p. 141.

100. Morgan and Morgan, **The Stamp Act Crisis,** pp. 206-207.

101. Sternstein, "The *Ruhrkampf* of 1923," p. 118.

102. Harcave, **First Blood,** p. 215.

103. Sharp, **Gandhi Wields . . . ,** p. 43.

104. Richard W. Fogg, "Jazz Under the Nazis," in *Music 66, Down Beat's* annual, 1966, p. 99.

105. *Ibid.,* p. 98.

106. Hsiao, **Rural China,** p. 52.

107. Taylor, **The Struggle for North China,** p. 120.

108. Peck, **Two Kinds of Time,** p. 414.

109. *Ibid.,* p. 93.

110. Schlesinger, **The Colonial Merchants . . . ,** p. 177. For other examples see also

pp. 286 and 463-464, and Gipson, **The British Empire . . .** , vol. XII, pp. 79-80.

111. Salvemini, **The French Revolution,** p. 125.

112. Mayer, ed., **The Recollections of Alexis de Tocqueville,** pp. 126-132.

113. Miller, Nonviolence, pp. 234-235. The passage is from Imre Révész, History of the Hungarian Reformed Church (Washington, D. C.: Hungarian Reformed Federation of America, 1956), p. 128.

114. **Report of the Nyasaland Commission of Inquiry,** p. 61.

115. Littell, ed., **The Czech Black Book,** p. 223, n. 1.

116. *Peace News,* 6 May 1960.

117. *Ibid.,* 3 June 1960.

118. *Ibid.,* 17 November 1961.

119. *Ibid.,* 18 May 1962.

120. Ruth Daniloff, in *ibid.,* 3 July 1964.

121. *Peace News,* 5 March 1965.

122. Sharp, **Gandhi Wields . . . ,** pp. 136-137.

123. *Ibid.,* p. 167.

124. Griffith, **The Resurrection of Hungary,** p. xix.

125. *Ibid.,* p. 33.

126. Seton-Watson, **The Decline of Imperial Russia,** p. 165.

127. Jutikkala, **A History of Finland,** p. 237. See also Miller, **Nonviolence,** p. 246.

128. Ligt, **The Conquest of Violence,** p. 144.

129. Reitlinger, **The Final Solution,** p. 342.

130. *Ibid.,* p. 377.

131. *Ibid.,* pp. 302-303.

132. *Ibid.,* p. 394.

133. Warmbrunn, **The Dutch . . . ,** pp. 118 and 152.

134. Mabee, **Black Freedom,** p. 314.

135. Jong, "Anti-Nazi Resistance in the Netherlands," in **European Resistance Movements, 1939-1945,** p. 146.

136. Warmbrunn, **The Dutch . . . ,** pp. 152-53, and 301 n. 153.

137. Philip Friedman, "Jewish Resistance to Nazism: Its Various Forms and Aspects," in **European Resistance Movements 1939-1945,** p. 204.

138. Hilberg, **The Destruction . . . ,** pp. 387-388.

139. Reitlinger, **The Final Solution,** pp. 377-378.

140. Ber Mark, "The Herbert Baum Group," in Suhl, ed., **They Fought Back,** pp. 62-63.

141. Suhl, "The Evidence," pp. 144-46, in Suhl, ed., They Fought Back.

142. Emil F. Knieza, "The Resistance of the Slovak Jews," in Suhl, ed., **They Fought Back,** pp. 177-179.

143. Daniels, "Non-violent Actions in Canada," p. 68.

144. Isidore Abramowitz, ed., **The Great Prisoners: The First Anthology of Literature Written in Prison** (New York: E. P. Dutton and Co., 1946), pp. 2-27.

145. Morgan and Morgan, **The Stamp Act Crisis,** p. 222.

146. Thoreau, "On the Duty of Civil Disobedience," in **Walden and Other Writings of Henry David Thoreau,** pp. 635-663; or Thoreau "On the Duty of Civil Disobedience " (pamphlet).

147. M. K. Gandhi, **Young India** (Triplicane, Madras, India: S. Ganesan, 1922, vol. I, p. 22.

148. Flora Lewis, **The Polish Volcano: A Case History of Hope** (New York: Doubleday & Co., 1958 and London: Secker and Warburg, 1959), pp. 85-86.

149. Gandhi, **Young India,** vol. I, p. 938.

150. M. K. Gandhi, **The Constructive Programme** (pamphlet; Ahmedabad, India: Navajivan, 1941), p. 26

151. Gandhi, **Young India,** vol. I, p. 943.

152. Gipson, **The British Empire Before the American Revolution,** vol. XI, **The Triumphant Empire, The Rumbling of the Coming Storm, 1766-1770,** pp. 219-220.

153. Schlesinger, **The Colonial Merchants . . . ,** p. 70.

154. Gipson, **The British Empire . . . ,** vol. XII, p. 158.

155. *Ibid.,* p. 396, and Schlesinger, **The Colonial Merchants . . . ,** pp. 151-152.

156. Schlesinger, **The Colonial Merchants . . . ,** p. 372.

157. Yarmolinski, **Road to Revolution,** pp. 199-200.

158. Hiller, **The Strike,** pp. 237-238.

159. Myers and Laidler, **What Do You Know About Labor?,** p. 76.

160. Sharp, **Gandhi Wields . . . ,** pp. 51-219, *passim.*

161. Kuper, **Passive Resistance in South Africa,** esp. pp. 17-18, 20-22, 122 and 125-138.

162. *The Times,* 21 March 1960.

163. Steiner, **The New Indians,** p. 55.

164. *Ibid.,* p. 50.

165. *Ibid.*

166. *Ibid.,* p. 53.

167. *Ibid.,* p. 61.

168. *Ibid.,* p. 63.

169. Many other examples are, however, possible. For example, for Finnish examples, see Miller, **Nonviolence,** p. 248 and Jutikkala, **A History of Finland,** p. 238; as civil servants, etc., during the Kapp *Putsch,* see Goodspeed, **The Conspirators,** pp. 129-135; on withholding of *Duma* speeches from the police in 1917, see Katkov, **Russia 1917,** p. 291; and on a large number of acts of noncooperation of officials in the American colonies, see Morgan and Morgan, **The Stamp Act Crisis,** pp. 61, 67, 194, 206, 222 and 228, and Schlesinger, **The Colonial Merchants . . . ,** pp. 253, 305-306, 512 and 522.

170. Lochner, ed., **The Goebbels Diaries,** p. 133.

171. *Ibid.,* p. 229.

172. Hilberg, **The Destruction . . . ,** p. 86.

173. Görlitz, ed., **The Memoirs of Field-Marshal Keitel,** pp. 150-151. See also pp. 166-167 and 247, for other cases.

174. Wheeler-Bennett, **The Nemesis of Power,** p. 494.

175. Hilberg, **The Destruction . . . ,** pp. 360-362.

176. Wheeler-Bennett, **The Nemesis of Power,** p. 457.

177 *Ibid.,* pp. 585 and 625.

178. Görlitz, ed., **The Memoirs of Field-Marshal Keitel,** p. 193.

179. Wheeler-Bennett, **The Nemesis of Power,** p. 470.

180. Hilberg, **The Destruction . . .** , p. 49.

181. Wheeler-Bennett, **The Nemesis of Power,** p. 514, and Alexander Dallin, **German Rule in Russia 1941 and 1945,** p. 32.

182. Görlitz, "The Indictment," in Görlitz, ed., **The Memoirs of Field-Marshal Keitzel,** p. 252. Alexander Dallin even maintains that the order "did not become operative because of the tacit opposition of the generals." (Dallin, **German Rule in Russia 1941-1945,** p. 32.) Görlitz reports that the Commando Order, drafted by Hitler personally (which decreed that all members of Allied commando or sabotage units were to be killed, whether armed or unarmed, even if voluntarily surrendered) was only partially complied with Görlitz, *op. cit.* p. 257.

183. Perkins, **Market Control and Planning in Communist China,** p. 122.

184. Hilberg, **The Destruction . . .** , p. 240.

185. B. H. Liddell Hart, "Lessons from Resistance Movements – Guerilla and Nonviolent," in Roberts, ed., **Civilian Resistance as a National Defense,** p. 207; Br. ed.: **The Strategy of Civilian Defence,** p. 207.

186. Lochner, ed., **The Goebbels Diaries,** pp. 134, 312 and 373.

187. *Ibid.,* p. 128.

188. *Ibid.,* p. 192 (Entry for 27 April 1942).

189. *Ibid.,* p. 314.

190. Görlitz, "The Indictment," p. 261.

191. *Ibid.,* pp. 261-264.

192. Robert Jungk, **Brighter than a Thousand Suns: The Story of the Men who Made the Bomb** (New York: Grove Press Black Cat Edition, n.d.), pp. 88-97.

193. Reitlinger, **The Final Solution,** pp. 97 and 173-79.

194. *Ibid.,* p. 95.

195. *Ibid.,* pp. 218-219.

196. *Ibid.,* p. 380 and Hilberg, **The Destruction . . .** , pp. 478 and 481-484.

197. Reitlinger, **The Final Solution,** pp. 321-324.

198. *Ibid.,* pp. 375-376 n.

199. *Ibid.,* pp. 366-368.

200. *Ibid.,* p. 306.

201. *Ibid.,* pp. 307 and 313.

202. *Ibid.,* p. 320.

203. *Ibid.,* p. 321. See also p. 320, and Hilberg, **The Destruction . . .** , p. 417.

204. Reitlinger, **The Final Solution,** pp. 325-326.

205. Littell, ed., **The Czech Black Book,** pp. 215-16.

206. *Ibid.,* p. 170.

207. Isaac Deutscher, **Stalin: A Political Biography** (New York and London: Oxford University Press, 1961), p. 178.

208. Goodspeed, **The Conspirators,** pp. 130-132.

209. This section is based on a draft by Michael Schulter.

210. Magne Skodvin, "Norwegian Non-violent Resistance During the German Occupation," in Roberts, ed., **Civilian Resistance as a National Defense,** p. 142; Br. ed.: **The Strategy of Civilian Defence,** p. 142.

211. Arthur Koestler, **Reflections on Hanging** (New York: Macmillan, 1967), p. 51. See also pp. 27 and 52.

212. "Afterword," in **Contempt** (no author) (Chicago: Swallow Press, 1970), p. 250. On other details of this case, see pp. 245-254. On Irish juries refusing to bring in convictions, see Locker-Lampson, **A Consideration of the State of Ireland in the Nineteenth Century,** p. 373.

213. A. T. Vassilyev, **The Ochrana: The Russian Secret Police,** ed. by Rene Fülöp-Miller (Philadelphia and London: J. B. Lippincott Co., 1930), p. 100.

214. Sharp, **Gandhi Wields . . . ,** p. 141.

215. Reitlinger, **The Final Solution,** pp. 192-93 n.

216. *Ibid.,* p. 335. Concerning German police in the *Ruhrkampf,* see Halperin, **Germany Tried Democracy,** p. 250; on police etc., during the Kapp *Putsch,* see Goodspeed, **The Conspirators,** pp. 129-135.

217. Interview with Lars Porsholt, Oslo, February 1965.

218. Interview with Inge Ingebretsen (pseud.), Oslo, February 1965.

219. Interview with Professor Arne Næss, Oslo, 1965.

220. Police Inspector Lars L'Abee-Lund, *"Politiet over og Under Jorden,"* in Steen, gen. ed., **Norges Krig,** vol. III, pp. 276-77.

221. *Ibid.,* p. 278.

222. *Ibid.*

223. *Ibid.,* pp. 279-80.

224. *Ibid.,* pp. 281-82.

225. Vassilyev, **The Ochrana,** p. 213.

226. Harcave, **First Blood,** p. 223. On other mutinies, usually more violent, see also pp. 156-158, 190, and 220ff.

227. Keep, **The Rise of Social Democracy in Russia,** p. 263. See also pp. 246-247 and 258, and Charques, **The Twilight of Imperial Russia,** pp. 119 and 135.

228. Katkov, **Russia 1917,** p. 273.

229. *Ibid.,* p. 274.

230. *Ibid.,* p. 276.

231. *Ibid.,* pp. 306-307.

232. *Ibid.,* pp. 314-315. See also pp. 327-328.

233. Watt, **Dare Call It Treason,** pp. 175-211.

234. Sharp, **Gandhi Wields . . . ,** p. 196, and Muhammed Yunus, **Frontier Speaks** (Bombay: Hind Kitabs, 1947), p. 118.

235. Albert P. Blaustein and Clarence Clyde Ferguson, Jr., **Desegregation and the Law: The Meaning and Effect of the School Segregation Cases** (New Brunswick, N. J.: Rutgers University Press, 1957), p. 256.

236. *Ibid.*

237. **The Fifty States Report,** submitted to the Commission on Civil Rights by the State Advisory Committees, 1961 (Washington: U.S. Government Printing Office, 1961), p. 451. See also pp. 460-467.

238. Blaustein and Ferguson, **Desegregation and the Law,** pp. 253-254.

239. *Ibid.,* p. 250.

240. *Ibid.,* p. 251.

241. Crane Brinton, **The Anatomy of Revolution** (New York: Vintage Books, 1962), p. 142.

242. Morgan and Morgan, **The Stamp Act Crisis,** p. 133.

243. *Ibid.,* p. 194.

244. *Ibid.,* pp. 226-227.
245. Gipson, **The British Empire** . . ., vol. xi p. 53. See also pp. 48-63.
246. Trevelyan, **The American Revolution,** p. 88.
247. See Schlesinger, **The Colonial Merchants** . . . , esp. pp. 111-154, 181-182, 256ff, 323, 365-366, and 432-472.
248. Henry Steele Commager, ed., **Documents of American History** (New York and London: Appleton-Century-Crofts, 1948), p. 178.
249. *Ibid.,* p. 182.
250. *Ibid.,* p. 184.
251. *Ibid.,* pp. 250-251.
252. Jutikkala, **A History of Finland,** p. 246.
253. Sharp, **Gandhi Wields** . . . , pp. 195-196.
254. Crespigny, "The Nature and Methods of Non-violent Coercion," p. 261, n. 3.
255. André Fontaine, **History of the Cold War: From the October Revolution to the Korean War 1917-1950** (New York: Pantheon Books, 1968), p. 347.
256. Sir Douglas Busk, **The Craft of Diplomacy: How to Run a Diplomatic Service** (New York: Frederick A. Praeger, 1967), p. 15.
257. Charles W. Thayer, **Diplomat** (New York: Harper & Bros., 1959), p. 217.
258. *Ibid.,* p. 217.
259. *Ibid.,* pp. 217-219.
260. Thomas A. Bailey, **A Diplomatic History of the American People** (sixth ed.; New York: Appleton-Century-Crofts, 1958), pp. 724-725.
261. *Time,* vol. 91, 22 March 1968, p. 33.
262. *New York Times,* 29 Nov. 1969.
263. C. L. Sultzberger, "Foreign Affairs: The Missing Envoy," *New York Times,* 28 Nov. 1969.
264. Gordon A. Craig, "Totalitarian Diplomacy," in Lawrence W. Martin, ed., **Diplomacy in Modern European History** (New York: Macmillan Co. and London: Collier-Macmillan Ltd., 1966), pp. 90-91.
265. Fontaine, **History of the Cold War,** p. 347.
266. Wilfrid F. Knapp, **A History of War and Peace 1939-1965** (London, New York and Toronto: Oxford University Press, 1967), p. 480.
267. *New York Times,* 7 May 1970, pp. 1 and 11.
268. Quoted by Bailey, **A Diplomatic History of the American People,** p. 555.
269. Taylor, **The Struggle for North China,** p. 195.
270. Bailey, **A Diplomatic History of the American People,** pp. 694-699.
271. *Ibid.,* pp. 633-34 and 671-72.
272. Quoted in Robert Blum, **The United States and China in World Affairs** (ed. by A. Doak Barnett; New York: McGraw-Hill [for the Council on Foreign Relations], 1966), p. 121.
273. *Ibid.,* p. 122.
274. Charles D. Cremeans, **The Arabs and the World: Nasser's Arab Nationalist Policy** (New York and London: Fredrick A. Praeger [for the Council on Foreign Relations], 1963), pp. 195-197.
275. Ferenc A. Váli, **Rift and Revolt in Hungary: Nationalism versus Communism** (Cambridge, Mass.: Harvard University Press, 1961, and London: Oxford University Press, 1961), p. 484.

276. Wheeler-Bennett, **The Nemesis of Power**, p. 79. For references to continued efforts by the Kappists to obtain diplomatic recognition, see p. 79, n. 2.

277. Harold Nicholson, **Diplomacy** (sec. ed.; London, New York and Toronto: Oxford University Press, 1960 [orig. 1950]), p. 191.

278. Busk, **The Craft of Diplomacy**, pp. 15-16.

279. Nicholson, **Diplomacy**, p. 192.

280. Bailey, **A Diplomatic History of the American People**, pp. 590-91.

281. Knapp, **A History of War and Peace**, p. 44, n. 16, and Fontaine, **History of the Cold War**, pp. 184-85.

282. Bullock, **Hitler**, pp. 322-324.

283. Knapp, **A History of War and Peace**, pp. 198 and 200-201.

284. Leland M. Goodrich, Edvard Hambro and Anne Patricia Simons, **Charter of the United Nations: Commentary and Documents** (Third and rev. ed.; New York and London: Columbia University Press, 1969), p. 76.

285. *Ibid.*, pp. 77-80, 109-10, 200-201, 251, and 523.

286. U. S. Department of State *Bulletin,* vol. 59 (9 December 1968), p. 613, and Goodrich, Hambro and Simons, **Charter of the United Nations**, pp. 171-175, 174 n. 252.

287. Goodrich, Hambro and Simons, **Charter of the United Nations**, p. 99.

288. Knapp, **A History of War and Peace**, p. 4.

289. Goodrich, Hambro and Simons, **Charter of the United Nations**, p. 98.

290. *Ibid.*

291. *Ibid.*, p. 100 and n. 91.

292. Knapp, **A History of War and Peace**, p. 128.

8

The Methods
of Nonviolent
Intervention

INTRODUCTION

One final class of the methods of nonviolent action remains, that of nonviolent intervention. The forty-one methods in this class differ from those in the classes of protest and persuasion and of noncooperation in that in some way they *intervene* in the situation. Such methods of intervention operate both negatively and positively: they may disrupt, and even destroy, established behavior patterns, policies, relationships, or institutions which are seen as objectionable; or they may establish new behavior patterns, policies, relationships, or institutions which are preferred. Some of these methods contribute primarily to the first of these results, some to the second.

Compared with the methods of the classes of protest and persuasion and of noncooperation, the methods of nonviolent intervention pose a more direct and immediate challenge. *If successful,* the victory is likely to come quicker by the use of methods of this class than with the use of methods of the previous classes, because the disruptive effects of the intervention are harder to tolerate or withstand for a considerable period of time. For example, intervention by a sit-in at a lunch counter disrupts more immediately and completely than would, say, picketing or a consumers' boycott, though the objective of each of these actions be to end racial discrimination. However, though the challenge of methods of intervention is clearer and more direct, the result is not necessarily more rapid success; precisely because of the character of intervention, speedier and more severe repression may be a first result—which, of course, does not necessarily mean defeat.

In most cases, use of the methods of this class may induce change through the mechanisms of accommodation or of nonviolent coercion, i.e., without the opponent's being convinced that he *ought* to change his policy on the matter in question. However, certain of these methods (especially those classed as psychological intervention) and also the repression which frequently occurs against others (especially those of physical intervention) may contribute to the opponent's conversion, or at least to his becoming less certain of the rightness of his previous views. These mechanisms of conversion, accommodation and nonviolent coercion are discussed in detail in the final Part of this book.

To a greater degree than in the classes discussed earlier, methods of nonviolent intervention are associated with initiative by the nonviolent actionists. The methods of intervention may be used both defensively—to thwart an opponent's attack by maintaining independent initiative, behavior patterns, institutions, or the like—and offensively—to carry the struggle for the actionists' objectives into the opponent's own camp, even without any immediate provocation. These methods, therefore, are not simply defensive responses to the opponent's initiative.

The range of methods within this class is wide. In this chapter they have been classified according to the dominant manner of expression of the intervention itself: psychological, physical, social, economic, or political. This is quite often different from the influences the method may have. For example, an act of social intervention may have strong psychological influence. An act of psychological intervention may have a political impact. An act of physical intervention may have social repercussions, and so on. All the methods of nonviolent action are likely to have some type of psychological influence; as considered here, psychological intervention includes methods in which the psychological element is the dominant form of expression.

Obviously these five subclasses are somewhat arbitrary. Alternative classifications of particular methods are possible, especially in a given conflict situation. Furthermore, not every use of these methods will actually produce intervention. A given act may be too limited, weak, or restricted in time, numbers, or focus to constitute significant intervention, and may instead become primarily an act of nonviolent protest and persuasion. Of the five subclasses of intervention we turn first to psychological intervention.

PSYCHOLOGICAL INTERVENTION

The four methods of psychological intervention described here differ significantly from each other in attitudes toward the person or group to which they are directed, in the intended process of change, and in the actual types of behavior. They have in common only the characteristic that the intervention is predominantly or exclusively on a psychological level.

158. Self-exposure to the elements

Exposure of one's own body to discomfort or suffering from the elements, such as the heat of the sun, is one form which psychological intervention has taken. This method is one of the several forms in which self-retribution may be expressed. Self-retribution involves putting psychological, moral, or emotional pressure on others to induce them to change their attitudes or to take certain action, by voluntarily taking discomfort, humiliation, penalties, or suffering upon oneself. Other ways in which self-retribution is expressed within nonviolent action include protest disrobing, destruction of one's own property (as used by some Doukhobors) both already discussed, and the fast, which follows.

An example of self-exposure to the elements comes from the mid-nineteenth century China and concerns the action of a judge, Lu Chia-shu, who dealt with a "legal fight" between brothers. Ch'ien Yung recorded:

> There were two brothers who fought against one another without stopping (i.e. reconciliation). Mr. Lu told them: "If brothers are not harmonious, this represents a great change in the human relations. I am the father and mother of the people here. So this must be my fault, that I did not teach you well." Then he knelt down in the blazing sun. The fighting (parties) were touched and cried. From then on, they were good to one another. [1]

Professor Wolfram Eberhard, who provided this example, comments:

> The judge Lu, in this case, could have severely beaten both claimants for their violation of the Confucian rules of brotherly love. This would have been the normal action of the judges at the time. No judge would have looked into the case in order to find out who is right and who is wrong. Lu's actions (to take the guilt upon himself) shamed the brothers, corrected their behavior, and did not involve the expected violence. [2]

A related but much milder type of action was used, probably in the 1880s, by temporary farm laborers in the province of Kherson of Imperial Russia, in order to protest the poor diets provided by the landowners. Trotsky records seeing this as a child on his father's farm:

The laborers would leave the fields and collect in the courtyard. They would lie face downward in the shade of the barns, brandishing their bare, cracked, straw-pricked feet in the air, and wait to see what would happen. Then my father would give them some clabber, or watermelons, or half a sack of dried fish and they would go back to work again, often singing.[3]

In the summer of 1972 some English and American prisoners protested by staying for long periods, and with danger to themselves, on the slanting roofs of prison buildings, or even on top of the prison water-tower (as at the Federal Correctional Institution at Danbury, Connecticut).

159. The fast

The fast is often used as a method of psychological intervention. Abstention from certain or all foods may be undertaken for a number of reasons, including health, religion, penance, self-purification, and desire to achieve social and political objectives. The latter reason is most relevant here, although fasts undertaken for reasons of religion, penance and self-purification may under certain circumstances also constitute intervention. In addition, fasts may serve simply as a form of moral protest. Three types of the fast will be distinguished in this context: the *fast of moral pressure,* the *hunger strike,* and the *satyagrahic fast* as applied on some occasions by Gandhi.

The *fast of moral pressure* has characteristics which fall between the other two types. It is also much more likely not to fulfill completely the requirements of nonviolent intervention, and to become instead a form of nonviolent protest and persuasion (although for simplicity this form of the fast is not listed under both classes). Fasts of moral pressure are usually conscious attempts to exert moral influence on others to achieve an objective, though they lack the openly coercive intent of the hunger strike, and the full "conversion" intent of the satyagrahic fast. Many people have argued that the fast is incomprehensible in the West; however, there are a multitude of Western examples, and in cases where fasts have been initiated where they have been unfamiliar, the response has often been unexpectedly favorable. For example, in 1960 and 1961 exponents of nuclear disarmament and pacifists in England had argued that fasts should not be used in the disarmament campaign since they would be incomprehensible to Englishmen. However, when this method was introduced in 1962 in support of the unilateral nuclear disamament movement and simultaneously to raise money for famine relief, the number of fasts grew rapidly during that year and 1963, and they were received with considerable public understanding and sympathy.[4]

Examples of fasts of moral pressure are varied. St. Patrick once fasted against King Trián of Ulster to compel him to have compassion on his slaves. On another occasion he fasted three days and three nights against the Pelagian heresy in a city to compel the inhabitants to become orthodox.[5]

Fasting was on several occasions also practiced by American colonists. For example, on May 24, 1774, the Virginia House of Burgesses resolved to observe June 1 (the day the Boston Port Act was to go into effect) as a day of "Fasting, Humiliation, and Prayer." The objective was to implore divine interposition to avert the "destruction to our Civil rights, and the Evils of Civil War . . . and that the Minds of his Majesty and his Parliament, may be inspired from above with Wisdom, Moderation, and Justice, to remove from the loyal People of America all cause of danger, from a continued pursuit of Measures, pregnant with their ruin." Two days later, after the Governor had summoned the members of the House to meet with him immediately in the Council chamber, he declared that the resolve was conceived "in such Terms as reflect highly upon his Majesty and the Parliament of Great Britain," and thereupon he dissolved the House,[6] thus preventing its continuing to meet and preventing it from taking other "hostile" actions.

There is an interesting story behind this case which introduced fasting into the American colonists' struggles. Earlier, in response to the action of some Bostonians in dumping tea belonging to the East India Company into Boston harbor, the British government had decided to close the port of Boston on June 1, 1774, and published the Boston Port Act to that end. This news reached Virginia while the House of Burgesses was in session. Thomas Jefferson later wrote that the lead in the House was no longer being left to the older members. A small group of younger members which included Patrick Henry, Richard Henry Lee, Jefferson himself, and four or five others, met to consider what to do. They were determined to take a bold, unequivocal stand in support of Massachusetts. As Jefferson described it, they gathered to

> consult on the proper measures in the council chamber, for the benefit of [i.e. to have the use of] the library in that room. We were under conviction of the necessity of arousing our people from the lethargy into which they had fallen as to passing events; and thought that the appointment of a day of general fasting and prayer would be most likely

to call up & alarm their attention. No example of such a solemnity had existed since the days of our distresses in the war [against the French] of [17]55, since which a new generation had grown up. With the help therefore of Rushmore, whom we rummaged over for the revolutionary precedents & forms of the Puritans of that day, preserved by him, we cooked up a resolution, somewhat modernizing their phrases, for appointing the 1st day of June, on which the Port bill was to commense, for a day of fasting, humiliation & prayer, to implore heaven to avert from us the evils of civil war, to inspire us with firmness in support of our rights, and to turn the hearts of the King & parliament to moderation & justice. [7]

Edmund Randolph credits Jefferson and Charles Lee with originating the "fast to electrify the people from the pulpit." [8] The young men who drafted the resolution "were famed more for skill with the violin and grace in dancing than for piety and prayer." [9] In order, therefore, to avoid ridicule and defeat if they offered so grave a resolution, the next morning they persuaded Robert Carter Nicholas, the pious, elderly chairman of the committee of religion, to move the resolution. Mr. Nicholas did so the same day, and it was passed without opposition. [10] One opponent denounced the fast as "a Schem calculated to *inflame* and excite an *enthusiastic* zeal in the Minds of the People under a Cloak of Religion . . ." [11] After dissolution, the members of the House met elsewhere and agreed to call for a meeting of an American Congress of Deputies for all the colonies; and then they returned to their own districts to arouse the clergymen and people to patriotic feelings. When the first of June came, B.O. Flower writes:

the great fast day led to the crystallizing of the revolutionary sentiment of the colony, just as the leaders had predicted it would. Never before, and rarely since, have the clergy been so brave and outspoken. "The cause of liberty is the cause of God!" exclaimed one minister; and this was the sentiment echoed from ocean to mountain. [12]

Later Jefferson himself wrote: "The people met generally, with anxiety & alarm in their countenances, and the effect of the day thro' the whole colony was like a shock of electricity, arousing every man & placing him erect & solidly on his centre." [13]

In the summer of 1774, "a day of fasting and prayer, on account of the dark aspect of our publick affairs" was proclaimed in Rhode Island. [14] The next spring, on February 16, 1775, the Massachusetts Bay Provincial Congress (the unconstitutional legislature of members of the previous House of Representatives), meeting in Cambridge, set aside a day for fasting and prayer, with a request included for prayers for King George III, pointedly indicating the conflict was not with the King but with the King's government. Boston observed the day with "marked solemnity." However, while a religious service was in progress that day, the King's Own corps played their drums and fifes within ten yards of the church. [15]

There are many more examples of the fast of moral pressure. For example, in April 1962 a number of Frenchmen fasted for peace in Algeria, [16] and a French pacifist, Louis Lecoin, fasted in June of that year to obtain legal recognition of French conscientious objectors. [17]

Danilo Dolci has used both the individual and mass fast in his efforts to relieve poverty in Sicily. When a child died of malnutrition in December 1952, Dolci resolved to fast to draw attention to the misery and unemployment in Trappeto, and to refuse food until a certain amount of money had been received for the relief of the starving. On January 30, 1956, he led about one thousand unemployed fishermen in a twenty-four hour mass fast on the beach to call attention to their plight; the demonstration was broken up by the police. [18] On January 16, 1966, Dolci completed a seven-day fast against the Mafia; and he called for casting off the fear which imposed the *omertà* (the law of silence) and prevented the gathering of evidence on Mafia crimes. Dolci fasted in a traditional Sicilian one-room family habitation in Castellammare del Golfo in Western Sicily—the district whose parliamentary representative was Signor Mattarella, the former Minister for Foreign Trade who had been accused of connections with the Mafia. The fast was reported to have brought about a "revolution" in people's willingness to criticize authority and an increased willingness to defy the Mafia. [19]

Buddhists also used fasting in nonviolent struggles in South Vietnam during the 1960s. Sometimes individuals have fasted alone, sometimes a group, and sometimes thousands of people have taken part in the fast. On occasion only elders of the Buddhist church took part. Trich Nhat Hanh reports that the Venerable Thich Tri Quang fasted for one hundred days at the Duy Tan Clinic in 1966. Hanh continues: "The purpose of fasting is for prayer, for purifying one's heart and consolidating one's will, or for arousing the awareness and compassion latent within the people." [20]

The *hunger strike*, the second type of fast considered here, may be defined as a refusal to eat with the aim of forcing the opponent to grant certain demands but without any serious effort to convert him or to achieve a "change of heart." On this point it differs sharply from the satyagrahic fast, as applied by Gandhi, which is discussed next. The hunger strike may be undertaken for a set period of time, for an indefinite period, or unto death if the demand is not granted. Prisoners who feel they have no other powerful method of protest at their disposal often use the fast. The examples are many and varied.

According to the legal code of ancient Ireland it was the duty of an injured person, when all else had failed, to inflict punishment directly on the wrongdoer. In some cases before a settlement involving reimbursement by seizure of property (such as cattle or other effects),

> . . . the plaintiff *fasted* on the defendant; . . . and this process, called *troscad*, "fasting," was always necessary before distress [removal of goods in compensation] when the defendant was of chieftain grade and the plaintiff of an inferior grade. . . The plaintiff, having served due notice, went to the house of the defendant, and, sitting before the door, remained without food. It may be inferred that the debtor generally yielded before the fast was ended, i.e., either paid the debt or gave a pledge that he would settle the case. If the creditor continued to fast after an offer of payment, he forfeited all the debt due to him . . . .
>
> From some passages it would appear that the debtor was bound to remain fasting as long as the creditor or complainant fasted . . . it was considered disgraceful for a defendant not to submit to it: "He that does not give a pledge to fasting is an evader of all: he who disregards all things shall not be paid by God or man." (British Laws, I, 113).[21]

That is, he would be subjected to a complete social boycott.

This is closely related to the Indian practice of *dhurna* or sitting *dhurna,* described by Shridharani as follows:

> Every so often in the Middle Ages a moneylender, failing to receive his money back in due time, would sit in front of the house of the debtor, refusing to budge from his place or to take any food until the client paid in full. Since the interesting situation always gathered a crowd of idle curious, the debtor would make a supreme effort to pay rather than suffer a long drawn-out siege with its attendant embarrassment. The *Bhat* (bard of the royal court) used a similar method when he wanted his king to "be a man" and fight. When his ruler, out of cowardice or other considerations, refused to meet an invading or offending king in combat, the *Bhat* would sit in the palace gate [way] and start a hunger strike. In most cases, this compelled the king to fight.[22]

There were also a considerable number of Russian hunger strikes, as illustrated by the following examples. Political prisoners in the Peter-Paul Fortress in St. Petersburg went on a long hunger strike during the summer of 1875; following a number of deaths of hunger strikers, the Head of the Third Section (the branch of the police which had a vast network of informers and agents) was assassinated in revenge. [23] In another case, while imprisoned in the dungeon of the Peter-Paul Fortress the notorious revolutionary Sergei Nechaev at about the end of 1877, after four years in solitary confinement, went on a hunger strike to obtain books not in the prison library. [24] In July 1878, reports Peter Kropotkin, six prisoners at Kharkov prison "resolved to starve themselves to death" in an act of opposition against extreme jail conditions. After they had resisted efforts to feed them by injection, officials promised walking exercise for prisoners and the removal of the sick from irons. These promises were not kept, and "only later on, when several had died, and two went mad . . . the prisoners obtained the privilege of sawing some wood in the yard, in company with two Tartars, who understood not a word of Russian." [25] Kropotkin also reports that the right of prisoners in the Peter-Paul Fortress to have visits from relatives every fortnight in 1879 and 1880 was won "by the famous famine strike, during which a number of prisoners in the Trubetskoi bastion refused to take any food for five or six days . . ." and resisted all efforts to feed them by injections. [26]

While confined in Kherson in 1898 the youthful Trotsky persuaded his fellow political prisoners to go on a hunger strike to protest a police proposal that juvenile prisoners be released if their parents promised to give them a thrashing and keep them from political activities; according to Trotsky, this was "an insult to the honor of the juvenile revolutionary." [27] Early in 1922, when two thousand arrested Mensheviks were threatened with administrative mass exile to distant provinces, some of them went on hunger strike, and approximately twelve were eventually allowed to leave the country. [28]

However, the results were very different when similar action was attempted in the autumn of 1936. According to an eyewitness, Boris Podolak, whose testimony was given in 1951, a large, well-organized group of Trotskyist prisoners at Vorkuta, with participation of other political groups, participated in a hunger strike of four hundred prisoners. They remained lying on their bunks and also refused to work. They addressed their declaration to the internal police of the N.K.V.D., denounced the current political system as fascist, and stated demands. Although many of the other prisoners were sympathetic, the number of hunger strikers did not grow, but rather became smaller. After one-and-a-half or two months, most of them could no longer resist forced feeding. Only about forty held out until they died. In the autumn of 1937, the report continues, a special commission arrived from Moscow, and the former strike leaders together with many other prisoners were arrested. After being kept in a barracks, they were moved twenty miles away to an abandoned brickworks "which became a kind of death-isolator." By the end of February 1938 about seven hundred prisoners were being kept there. The first mass executions began the night of May 8-9 and continued. [29]

Hunger strikes have also occurred in the modern Irish nationalist movement. For example, in late September 1917 two Irish nationalists imprisoned for one year at hard labor at Mountjoy Gaol went on hunger strike. They were Thomas Ashe, an Irish Volunteer, and Austin Stack, a Kerry Volunteer, both charged with "attempting to cause disaffection among the civil population." In prison they organized a hunger strike in support of the demand that they be either treated as political prisoners or released. The jail officials, however, force-fed the hunger strikers: after a week of this Ashe collapsed, and within five hours of being hospitalized, died. [30] (A brief account of his funeral is offered in Chapter Three under the method demonstrative funeral.)

The British also applied other measures to deal with hunger strikers including the so-called cat-and-mouse act. This had been used to deal with women suffragists who frequently went on hunger strikes in England. [31] Weakening prisoners on hunger strikes were released, but when they regained their strength they were rearrested. Edgar Holt reports that "it was an effective measure . . . . and there were no more deaths from hunger strikes until 1920."

On Easter Monday, April 5, 1920, some one hundred Sinn Fein prisoners in Mountjoy Gaol began a mass hunger strike, this time demanding either that they be treated as prisoners of war or released. The official British attitude to this challenge was expressed in the House of Commons by Bonar Law, the leader of the House and Lord Privy Seal: "It would be perfectly futile if men are to be released because they choose to refuse food." In Ireland, however, support grew, for members of the Irish Labour Party called for a general strike for April 13 for support of the Mountjoy prisoners, and the Roman Catholic hierarchy publicly declared it to be "their solemn duty to call the attention of everyone to the appalling tragedy that seems imminent in Mountjoy Prison." After ten days, the government released the prisoners unconditionally. [32] One who did not fare so well that same year was the Lord Mayor of Cork, Terence McSweeney, who died after a fast of seventy-four days. [33]

In October 1944 several American conscientious objectors, imprisoned in the federal prison at Lewisburg, who objected to punishment imposed on them for their participation in a work strike against the parole system, organized a "rotation" hunger strike. In this, five men would refuse to eat for a definite but unannounced period, after which five others would take their place as hunger strikers.[34]

In May 1958 nearly thirteen thousand prostitutes in India threatened a mass hunger strike when brothels were closed under an Act prohibiting the letting of houses for prostitution.[35] In a similar case to "sitting *dhurna*" discussed earlier, in August 1959 a factory stoker in New Delhi undertook a fast unto death outside his employer's villa to protest low pay and poor working conditions.[36]

The final type of fast discussed here is the *satyagrahic fast,* predominantly practiced by Gandhi who distinguished his fasts for social objectives from the hunger strike, which he regarded as coercive. Although accused of failing to recognize coercive elements in his own fasts, Gandhi insisted that their objective was to convert. According to him, the *satyagrahi* may fast to "sting" the conscience of the wrongdoer (who may be an individual, a group of people, or even millions) through voluntary suffering only if he has exhausted all other nonviolent means. The satyagrahic fast may be for a set period of time, or unto death if the demand is not granted.

Gandhi sought to establish strict limits on this use of the fast; for example, it should not be applied against just anyone, regardless of the issue. Normally, one would not fast against one's opponent, especially if the opponent were a stranger or not one's friend. Gandhi thought that the wrongdoer and the fasting *satyagrahi* must have been close and have shared mutual affection for this self-imposed form of suffering to be justified and to have the intended conversion effect. Under special circumstances, however, the fast could be applied to others, primarily if the opponent's repression and restrictions closed other avenues of approach. *Satyagrahis* who as prisoners were subjected to inhuman treatment might, for example, fast for the removal of such treatment—though they might not, in Gandhi's view, fast for their release. In either case, the "mistake" of the individual or group against whom the fast is undertaken must have been gross and have moved the *satyagrahi* to the very depth of his being.

Gandhi believed that considerable spiritual preparation and service were necessary before one was justified in undertaking a satyagrahic fast, and that a fast unto death was to be used only when every other form of *satyagraha* had failed. Examples of Gandhi's use of the satyagrahic fast include his fast during the Ahmedabad labor strike in February–March 1918, undertaken to arouse striking workers who had weakened in their resolve to keep their pledges to him to continue the strike until their demands had been granted.[37] His final fast at Delhi in January 1948, for Hindu-Muslim unity in the midst of the riots, is a clearer example of the characteristics he avowed for this instrument.[38] In this Gandhi sought to restore by his fast an awareness of the worth of the lives of all Indians and to arouse feelings of brotherhood between Hindu and Muslim.

160. Reverse trial

Another form of psychological intervention is the reverse trial. Sometimes the combination of circumstances and the behavior during the trial of those prosecuted for political, religious, or other reasons significantly reverses the roles of prosecution and defender in the trial. The defendants become the prosecutors, and the trial is turned into a demonstration against the government and is used by the prosecuted to publicize their beliefs, program and indictment of the established order. This is what we call a reverse trial.

This reversal of roles has taken place in a wide variety of political cases. In Russia, in each of the "great trials of 1877" of revolutionaries the accused were able to conduct themselves in such a way as to arouse public sympathy and support. The first of these, the trial of the demonstrators of the Square of Our Lady of Kazan in St. Petersburg, brought great sympathy for those on trial. In the second trial, of "the fifty" in March in Moscow, observers compared the accused with early Christian martyrs. And in the 1877-78 St Petersburg "trial of the hundred and ninety-three" members of the movement "to go to the people" with the revolutionary message, the events of the trial made an important public impact despite strict censorship. Part of this impact resulted from the speech of Ippolit Nikitch Myshkin, one of the accused, on the ideas and program of socialism. Myshkin, in another speech, also denounced the tribunal itself as "a useless comedy" and "more shameful than a brothel . . ." The revolutionary S.M. Kravchinsky later wrote: "After his words the tribunal was annihilated." [39]

In a very different style, when he was on trial, Gandhi behaved in such a way that even when he pleaded guilty to the charge he gave the impression that he had only been guilty of doing the right thing; this occurred, for example, in 1922, during his trial for writing three seditious articles in his journal, *Young India*. Asking the judge either to resign his post or, if he believed in the system, to give him (Gandhi) the severest penalty possible, Gandhi declared it to be "an honor to be disaffected towards a government which in its totality has done more harm to India than any previous system." [40]

Similarly, Germans prosecuted by the occupation powers during the *Ruhrkampf* used their trials as a means of pointing out the injustice of the French and Belgian seizure of the Ruhr. [41] After the abortive *Putsch* in 1923, Adolph Hitler made the most of his trial, which for the first time gave him an audience outside the frontiers of Bavaria; according to his biographer, Allan Bullock, "in his final speech he established a complete mastery over the court." [42] In the famous *Reichstag* fire trial in Nazi Germany in 1933, one of the accused, the Bulgarian Communist Georgi Dimitroff, served as his own lawyer, cleverly cross-examined Göring himself, taunted him into a rage, and succeeded in obtaining acquittal for himself and three others. [43]

Further examples of reverse trial continue to occur when political and moral issues are involved in the case and when the prosecuted persons are able to regain the initiative against their prosecutors. This method illustrates the potential of simple psychological intervention even when no other types of leverage are at the disposal of the accused.

161. Nonviolent harassment

This method consists of psychological harassment by a combination of actions which concentrate private and public pressures on one or more individuals engaged in activities which are detested. The actions which may be used to produce nonviolent harassment include stronger and more persistent use of "haunting" (constantly remaining physically near the person) and "taunting" (name-calling and accusations)—both of which have been discussed in mild forms as methods of nonviolent protest and persuasion. Nonviolent harassment has also utilized means of public communication such as posters and newspaper advertisements; the use of other such means would fall within this method. The objective of the combination of pressures is to induce the person to halt the behavior or action which is found objectionable; these are not the types of pressures likely to alter the opinion or beliefs of the person against which they are directed. This method has been termed nonviolent harassment by Carleton Mabee in *Black Freedom,* his study of nonviolent opposition to slavery in the United States. [44] The proposal to use this method was worked out in detail by Charles K. Whipple, who had been treasurer of the Nonresistance Society and was a contributor to William Lloyd Garrison's paper, *Liberator.* This method was to be used against slave hunters in Northern states hired to capture and return escaped slaves to their Southern owners. Whipple's proposal drew upon general recommendations by Garrison, Wendell Phillips and the Rhode Island Antislavery Society. The Boston Vigilance Committee debated and partially adopted the proposal, which was published in the *Liberator* and other antislavery papers in 1850-51. The recommendation was this:

> As soon as the kidnappers arrived in any town, large handbills should be posted in all the public places, containing their names, with a description of their persons and the business on which they come.

An attempt should be made to induce the landlord of any hotel or boarding-house to which they may go, to refuse them entertainment, on the ground of their being persons infamous by profession, like pick-pockets, gamblers, or horse-stealers.

If this proves unsuccessful, some of the committee of attendance should take lodging in the same house with the kidnappers, and take, if possible, sleeping rooms and seats at table directly opposite to them.

The doors of the house should be watched carefully, day and night, and whenever they go out, two resolute, unarmed men should follow each of them wherever he goes, pointing him out from time to time with the word SLAVE-HUNTER. They should follow him into every shop, office, or place of public dwelling, wait outside, watching all the avenues, and ready to renew the attendance when he comes out. If he takes a coach, they should follow in another; if he drives out of town, they should follow; if he takes a seat in a railroad car, they should go with him, and make him known as a slave-hunter to the passengers in the car, and to the people of the town where he stops. He should not have one moment's relief from the feeling that his object is understood, that he cannot act in secret, that he is surrounded by men who loathe his person and detest his purpose, and who have means at hand to prevent the possibility of success.[45]

Mabee reports that on the basis of this and similar proposals nonviolent attempts were made throughout the 1850s to protect fugitive slaves in the North.[46] For example, this method was used in Philadelphia when a Miss Wilson from Maryland arrived to locate her runaway slave. J. Miller McKim, an exponent of nonviolent methods who was in charge of the office of the Pennsylvania Antislavery Society, on hearing of her efforts to hire a local slave catcher, arranged for an abolitionist to pose as one. He was hired and obtained the name of the slave. McKim notified the fugitive, who went into hiding, and then prepared posters about three feet square, headed "BEWARE OF SLAVE-CATCHERS," which were posted about the city. Miss Wilson was named, as well as the slave, whom people were urged to hide, in accordance with a scriptural injunction. When she learned of the posters, Miss Wilson abandoned the hunt and returned to her home in Maryland.[47]

Similarly in Boston, when Charles Hobson from Virginia came to hunt his escaped slave, Henry Langhorn, abolitionists took an advertisement in the newspaper, mimicking the advertisement which Hobson had published seeking his slave; the abolitionists' advertisement described Hobson and stated that he was staying at the Tremont Hotel. They also posted about one hundred placards warning that Hobson was in town to catch a slave.

Unnerved, Hobson hurriedly departed for Virginia without Henry Langhorn. [48]

These cases of nonviolent harassment of slave catchers were not, however, widely imitated, and this method was not applied on a sufficiently large scale to test its potential in that situation.

PHYSICAL INTERVENTION

A second subclass of methods of nonviolent intervention consists of those predominantly characterized by the interference created by people's physical bodies, especially as they enter, or refuse to leave, some place where they are not wanted or from which they have been prohibited.

162. Sit-in

In a sit-in the interventionists occupy certain facilities by sitting on available chairs, stools and occasionally on the floor for a limited or unlimited period, either in a single act or in a series of acts, with the objective of disrupting the normal pattern of activities. The purpose may be to establish a new pattern, such as opening particular facilities to previously excluded persons, or to make a protest which may not be directly connected with the facilities occupied. This method has often been used in the civil rights movement in the United States.

In conception the method is not at all new, however. Mabee reports that as early as 1838 the Antislavery Convention of American Women adopted a comprehensive policy supporting sit-ins and ride-ins, but that there had been no systematic follow-up campaign. [49] Then, during the August 1841 meeting of the Massachusetts Antislavery Society, a "Garrisonian nonviolent actionist," Stephen S. Foster, impatient with regular political methods, moved a resolution which described the basis of sit-ins, ride-ins and related methods: "We recommend to [white] abolitionists as the most consistent and effectual method of abolishing the 'Negro-pew,' to take their seats in it, wherever it may be found, whether in a gentile synogogue [church], a railroad car, a steamboat, or a stage coach." [50] The exponents of nonviolent means within that Society split on the resolution, William Lloyd Garrison himself opposing it, although he personally participated in ride-ins, and the resolution was defeated. Nevertheless, the principle was applied in a series of ride-ins, as will be described under that method. [51]

An early, modified application of the sit-in occurred in Chicago in late 1869 or early 1870. Negro protests had failed to abolish the segregationist

Black Code and segregated education, Negro children being forced to attend the so-called Black School. The Negro parents and children then applied a form of the sit-in; since segregation was then the law, this method also involved civil disobedience. The parents simply sent the children to the school nearest their homes. Although the teachers did not assign the children to classes or give them lessons to do, "The children . . . attended daily, taking their seats in an orderly fashion throughout the controversy that ensued." The school board attempted to compromise by admitting only children with one-eighth Negro ancestry to the regular schools, but the Chicago Negroes invaded the offices of the board and of the Mayor, and the Black School was abolished.[52]

In 1938 Chippewa Indians from a reservation in the Cass Lake region of Minnesota, through their chiefs, had protested against the decision made by Commissioner of Indian Affairs John Collier to move the Bureau of Indian Affairs headquarters from the reservation to Duluth; the chiefs argued that this was a violation of the new United States policy of granting Indian self-government. Agency Superintendent Lewis Balsam, however, proceeded with the moving plans. Then several hundred Chippewa braves, painted and wearing traditional costumes, marched to the headquarters and danced around the building to the beat of drums. A group of Chippewa women followed, entering the office, and Balsam fled. The young braves then moved in, sitting on desks and filing cabinets, while a picket line formed outside. Commissioner Collier still insisted on moving the office to the city, but his superior, Secretary of the Interior Harold L. Ickes, ordered a tribal referendum on the issue, agreeing to accept its results.[53]

In 1960 American Indians of Chrokee ancestry, called Croatans, resorted to a sit-in after six years of unsuccessful efforts to gain admission to Dunn High School, in Dunn, Hartnett County, North Carolina. At the beginning of the 1960–61 school year nine Indian students had attempted to register for school at Dunn but had been refused, being told to attend instead the all-Indian high school, which meant a seventy-mile round-trip each day from Dunn. On August 31 seven Indian youths, accompanied by two adults, began a three day sit-in at Dunn High School. On the third day seven youths and five adults were arrested for trespassing. Promised an Indian school in Dunn by the autumn of 1961, they called off their action. However, in response to protests from across the United States, the local Mayor, G.F. Blalock, insisted that the problem was not the town's fault, and that the local citizens overwhelmingly favored admission of Indian students. In June 1961 the Hartnett County School Board announced that twenty Indians would be allowed to enroll in the Dunn High School during the next school year.[54]

The sit-in has been widely used in the United States to break down racial discrimination in restaurants and lunch counters. In this method the actionists progressively occupy a large number or all of the available seats and refuse to leave until the Afro-American members of the group are served, the restaurant closes, the group arrested, or a certain predetermined period of time elapses.

The Congress of Racial Equality used this method in Northern and border states during the 1940s and 1950s.[55] It first became widely practiced on a large scale in the South in early 1960, with sit-ins in Woolworth's in Greensboro, North Carolina, conducted by students of North Carolina Agricultural and Technical College. Shortly thereafter, high school and college students all over the South began to stage similar sit-ins at lunch counters, and a movement of major proportions developed.[56] The Southern Regional Council reported that within seven months at least 70,000 Negroes and whites had actively participated and 3,600 had been arrested.[57] A U.S. Supreme Court decision on December 11, 1961, outlawed the use of disorderly conduct statutes as grounds for arresting Negroes sitting in to obtain equal service.[58]

The basic principle may also be applied in other situations—for example, to protest segregated housing or to express various political grievances. For example, 801 demonstrators supporting the Free Speech Movement at the University of California at Berkeley were arrested on December 3, 1964, following a sit-in to support their demand for freedom of political action.[59] A student sit-in, called by the Student Council, was held in the administration building of City College in New York City in November 1966 to demand specific measures for increased student participation in administrative decisions for the college.[60] In June 1963 an all-night sit-in was held at the headquarters of the Boston School Committee in protest against the refusal of most of its members to admit the existence of *de facto* segregation in the school system.[61]

In 1964 delegates from the Freedom Democratic Party of Mississippi, which was predominantly Negro, claimed the seats of the regular Democratic Party delegation at the Democratic Party's National Convention, stating that only the Freedom Democratic Party was pledged to support the Democratic Party's national ticket. When their full claim was not granted, the Freedom delegates, aided by sympathetic delegates from other states, entered the convention hall during the evening sessions of August 25 and 26, and the F.D.P. representatives simply sat in the seats for the Mississippi delegation. After a brief attempt to remove them by force, the convention authorities left them alone, and the "regular" white Mississippi delegation had to sit elsewhere.[62]

In addition to student sit-ins in universities in recent years, there have also been sit-ins in mayors' and governors' offices, but these, and suggestions for sit-ins on Capitol Hill and in congressional offices, have been widely condemned and regarded as "the disruption of the governing process itself." [63]

A very different case occurred in Moscow in 1964. Forty-five Moroccan students began a sit-in and twenty-four hour fast at the Moroccan Embassy there on March 19 to protest the death sentences and severe imprisonments of alleged antigovernment plotters in Morocco. At Moroccan request, Soviet authorities expelled them from the Embassy. [64]

163. Stand-in

The stand-in occurs when direct actionists remain standing in an orderly quiet manner at a ticket office, admission entrance, appointment desk, doorway, or the like, as they seek to purchase a ticket, admission, an interview, or whatever when these have been refused to them. This method has been used particularly by civil rights actionists in the United States seeking to obtain equality of service for all potential customers. It has been applied especially in seeking admission to motion picture theaters and swimming pools. When admittance, purchase of a ticket, or the like is refused to the Negro, for example, all the direct actionists, including the person refused admission, wait patiently in line for admittance, refusing to leave until all are granted equal service, a specified period of time has elapsed, the group is arrested, or the facilities are closed. This method may be repeated until the policy is changed to allow all to use the facilities.

The stand-in was used, for example, in 1947 to end discrimination at the swimming pool in the Palisades Amusement Park, New Jersey. On Sundays the interracial Congress of Racial Equality (C.O.R.E.) groups "would remain peacefully lined up in front of the pool's ticket booth after being refused admission." Despite repeated beatings by park guards and police, and arrests, the C.O.R.E. stand-in was continued on Sundays throughout the summer. [65] It has been claimed that the enactment of the New Jersey civil rights bill in 1949 was partly due to the news reports and editorials published in newspapers in northern New Jersey as a result of the beatings and arrests during the summer of 1947. [66]

A different form of the stand-in was urged in 1837 for use in churches where Negroes were admitted but were assigned to segregated seating. In 1837 the periodical *Colored American* told its readers that if they were not allowed to sit where the whites did, they should "stand in the aisles and rather worship God upon your feet than become a party to your own degradation. You must shame your oppressors, and wear out prejudice by this holy policy." [67]

164. Ride-in

The ride-in, popularly known in the United States as the freedom ride, is a type of sit-in adapted to public transportation. It was widely used during the 1960s in the United States against racial segregation on buses, although its earlier use was more diverse. In this method Negroes and whites persist in sitting in sections of buses or other vehicles opposite to those assigned to them. Sometimes such actions have violated company regulations or local and state laws. More recently, since federal rulings have outlawed such segregation, ride-ins were taken to bring local practice into conformity with the law.

In 1841 when the ride-in campaign against frequent, but not universal racial segregation in transportation began in New England, the small minority of Negroes in those states (one percent in Massachusetts and about three percent in Rhode Island, for example) were highly discriminated against. On stagecoaches, Negroes, even in bad weather, might be refused rides completely, or be required to ride on top in the open. On steamboats they might be refused cabins or only be permitted to travel on deck with cattle. The new railroads enforced segregation of free blacks, while allowing slaves to ride with their Southern masters when visiting from the South. [68] The campaign against this discrimination and segregation was led by Garrisonian nonviolent abolitionists, Mabee reports, incuding Garrison himself, John Λ. Collins, active in the Nonresistance Society, and Frederick Douglass, former slave who became the famous advocate of abolition of slavery. [69]

In June and July 1841, while visiting Massachusetts, the young David Ruggles, a half-blind New York Negro who was very active in the struggle for rights of his people, set a personal example for the ride-ins. He insisted on buying a ticket for first-class accommodation on the steamer for Nantucket, and refused to move from a white car on the New Bedford Railroad. In both cases, he was physically attacked; his nonviolence did not prohibit his taking court action, however. Ruggles based his insistence on equal service on this belief: "While I advocate the principles of equal liberty, it is my duty to practice what I preach, and claim my rights at all times." [70] Following a protest meeting by New Bedford Negroes, chaired by the young Frederick Douglass, Garrison, Douglass and about forty black and white abolitionists boarded a steamer, also for Nantucket. The whole ship was segregated. When the captain refused to sail until the Negroes occupied the upper deck, some of the party left the ship; those remaining, obtained the captain's agreement that the whole group should ride on the upper deck. "As the steamer moved toward Nantucket the abolitionists cheerfully held a meeting . . . to protest the steamship company's already crumbling segregation policy," Mabee reports.[71]

A series of ride-ins on New England railroads took place in 1841. Sometimes whites rode in the Negro car, sometimes unaccompanied Negroes rode in white cars, and sometimes integrated groups or two or three rode in the white cars. Physical assault was commonplace. One of the participants, James N. Buffum, a Quaker, reported his view that the ride-in actions and the reactions of the railroad officials brought new converts to the cause; in Lynn, for example, and "even in Salem, where it has seemed as if nothing short of Almighty judgments could wake them from their guilty slumbers," people were aroused and talking of the "shameful" treatment of the "ride-inners." [72] A boycott of the segregated Massachusetts railroads was organized, people being urged to use unsegregated rail or stage service instead. Mabee writes that "it is doubtful that without the drama of the ride-ins, often heightened by the violence of the conductors, a boycott of significant proportions would have developed." [73] This boycott was strongly supported every week for a year, beginning in April 1842, by Garrison's *Liberator* and by the *American Antislavery Almanac*.[74] The combination of these nonviolent pressures, plus the strong possibility of legislation against such segregation, induced both the New Bedford Railroad and the Eastern Railroad quietly to end segregation.[75] Referring to the ride-ins by Negroes who had entered "the cars intended only for white passengers and allowed ourselves to be beaten and dragged out," Frederick Douglass said in 1849 that this had produced desegregation of the railroads "because the railroad companies became ashamed of their proscription." [76]

A few years later ride-ins were also used on horse-drawn cars in New York City and in Philadelphia. In 1854 and 1855 there were several instances of Negroes insisting on riding on the basis of equality in the horsecars, including members of the congregation of the highly respected Dr. Pennington, the Heidelberg-educated Negro moderator of the Presbyterian Church. Similar action occurred in Philadelphia in 1858 when the well-known Negro poet and Garrisonian Frances Watkins insisted on riding like any other passenger. Similar action occurred during the Civil War when a Negro businessman and his wife insisted on riding inside the car, not on the platform. In that case, in final exasperation the conductor opened all the windows, unhitched the horses, and abandoned the car.[77]

After the Civil War another ride-in was held in Louisville, Kentucky, in 1871, by newly freed Negro slaves who sought the end of segregation on the streetcars of the city. It began in January when Robert Fox paid his fare and insisted on sitting in the white section, refusing to move when ordered and finally being thrown off the car. He won a Federal District Court ruling in his favor, which was, however, ignored by the local streetcar company, which continued segregated seating; instead of throwing Negroes bodily out of the cars for refusing to sit where ordered, they simply halted the cars until the Negroes moved. After consultation with local Federal officials and white attorneys, local Negro leaders launched a full-scale ride-in. In May a young Negro boy sitting in the white section was evicted and beaten by a hostile white crowd, then arrested and fined in the city court, with the judge warning against further ride-ins. But the ride-in campaign continued as Negroes in streetcar after streetcar took "white" seats. The drivers then left the cars completely, and occasionally Negroes drove the cars themselves. White violence erupted, and a race riot threatened. Moderate Kentucky newspapers and many community leaders deplored the fighting, and the Republican gubernatorial candidate, John Marshall Harlan—a former slave owner—denounced the segregation policy. National attention grew. There were rumors that President Grant might send in Federal troops. Federal marshals and an attorney for the Federal government backed the Negroes. The streetcar company capitulated, and all city transit companies in Louisville abandoned segregation permanently.[78]

After the 1946 Supreme Court ruling against segregation in interstate travel, George Houser and Bayard Rustin in 1947 organized the first extended freedom ride, the group riding interstate buses throughout the upper South, insisting without violence on their newly awarded constitutional right to be seated without segregation.[79]

The big wave of freedom rides was launched, however, in 1961 under the sponsorship of the Congress of Racial Equality, then a nonviolent group led by James Farmer. On May 4 the interracial group left Washington D.C., originally intending to reach New Orleans. The group was subjected to a long series of arrests, harassments, and white mob violence, though it also gained increased support and wider sponsorship. The freedom ride, however, halted on May 28 in Jackson, Mississippi, where a jail-in campaign developed. At least a dozen of these ride-ins were held during the period, involving over a thousand persons representing four major organizations. Beginning on November 1 all interstate buses were required by federal regulation to display a sign: "Seating aboard this vehicle without regard to race, color, creed, or national origin, by order of the Interstate Commerce Commission." The following year this was also printed on all interstate bus tickets, and terminals for such buses had to post similar signs.[80]

165. Wade-in

The wade-in is a method designed to counter racial discrimination in the use of beaches which are physically accessible to the public (i.e., not surrounded by fences, etc.) and for which tickets are not required. The opponents of racial discrimination simply enter the area and make normal use of the beach and water without regard to restrictive customs or legal prohibition. An interracial group of seventy-five from the Youth Work Committee of the Chicago National Association for the Advancement of Colored People, for example, conducted a wade-in at Rainbow Beach on Lake Michigan, in the South Shore of Chicago, from July 16 to the end of the summer 1961.[81] The principle of such entry and use of facilities may be applicable to other restricted areas which are not fenced in, and is related to, but not identical with, nonviolent invasion, which is described below.

166. Mill-in[82]

In the mill-in the actionists gather in some place of symbolic significance or one which is related to the grievance, such as the offices of the opponent. They then remain there for a certain period, usually determined in advance. But instead of conducting a sit-in or a sit-down, they remain mobile. People may thus move within the building (or other place), and individuals may come and go during the mill-in. This method has been described as capable of achieving the goals of direct confrontation and intervention while being less likely to provoke serious repression than, say, a nonviolent occupation. The presence of a large number of "mill-inners" is likely to impede the normal operations of people who may be working in the building, but deliberate obstruction of their activities is not a part of this method.

The mill-in was used, for example, by the Afro-American Society of Tufts University and its supporters, who sought more minority employment in the construction of a dormitory on the campus at Medford, Massachusetts, in November 1969. After a large police contingent occupied the building site itself, the Afro-American Society held a mill-in at the university administration building, Ballou Hall, on Friday November 7 and again on Monday, November 10. *Criterion,* a Tufts alumni journal, describing the Friday action, reported:

> Approximately 400 students—50 blacks, 350 whites—and a few faculty members—gathered in front of Ballou Hall at 9:00 A.M. for a "mill-in." They divided into four equal groups, each assigned to approach one of four university administrators . . . . The peaceful "mill-in" was al-

lowed by University officials; there were no policemen inside or outside Ballou Hall . . . . Students peacefully occupied administrative offices, querying officials on issues surrounding the situation. A meeting
convened around 9:30 A.M. in the Coolidge room of Ballou and was
packed with about 300 students. They listened to President Hallowell
air the University's position for about one half hour.[83]

Students evacuated the room and building thirty minutes before normal
closing time. It is reported that normal administrative work in the building was "either slowed or halted completely" during the mill-in.[84]

167. Pray-in

In the pray-in persons enter, or attempt to enter, a church from which
they have been by custom or policy barred, in order to participate equally in the religious services. In cases where admission has been allowed but
seating has been segregated, participants in the pray-in sit in the pews reserved for others.

In early 1848 Frederick Douglass urged all Negroes to abandon the
separate black churches and instead to attend white ones, in "a massive
pray-in," as Mabee calls it. Douglass declared that Negroes "should go in
and take seats without regard to their complexion, and allow themselves
to be dragged out by the ministers, elders, and deacons. Such a course
would very soon settle the question, and in the right way."[85]

This massive action did not occur, but there were a number of individual cases of pray-ins reported from Philadelphia, New York state and
parts of New England. The reactions were not always friendly. For example, in Randolph, Massachusetts, sometime before 1835, a Negro family
purchased a pew in a white Baptist church; when they discovered one Sunday morning that the pew had been removed, they sat in its place on the
floor. The next Sunday, they discovered that even the floorboards had
been removed. When visiting the Marlborough Presbyterian church in
New York State in 1837, the white abolitionist Lewis Tappan joined with
the Negroes, who were served communion last; the minister was startled
and later resolved to serve all at the same time.

In 1838 a white minister in Newark, New Jersey, was driven out of
his pulpit after he had walked a black woman servant to church and
seated her with his wife. The only abolitionist congressman from New York
in 1840, Seth Gates, invited a visiting Negro abolitionist to sit with him
in his church pew in Genessee County, New York; the local newspaper
denounced Gates as an "amalgamator," but he was nonetheless reelected
to Congress. A young white Quaker was in 1840 reprimanded for sitting

with the blacks in the separate pews assigned to them; the youth was told he was "sitting in judgment" of the Friends who had assigned the pews. The Grimké sisters, Angelina and Sarah, new converts to Quakerism, insisted on sitting with the black women in the Philadelphia Meeting house they attended. Also scolded by the Quakers, the sisters replied: "While you put this badge of degradation on our sisters, we feel it is our duty to share it with them." A predominantly white Baptist church in Newport, Rhode Island, in 1858 refused to renew the lease on the pew of a white lady who had invited a black girl who was a member of the church to sit with her; the white woman brought a camp stool to church and sat in the aisle beside her former pew. [86]

During the civil rights actions of the 1960s, when Negroes sought admission to all-white churches in the South, they frequently knelt at the church entrance; this became known as a kneel-in. For example, one Sunday in February 1961, in Rock Hill, South Carolina, the city's first kneel-ins took place, at the same time that many students were being jailed for participation in sit-ins at lunch counters. The Negroes were admitted to three of the white churches but barred at two others. [87] In Birmingham, Alabama, in 1963 it was announced that part of the current campaign on Easter Sunday, April 14, would include mass attempts to worship at white churches. As had already been done on various occasions, the pattern was that when refused entrance to the churches, the Negroes would kneel on the church steps and pray. [88]

168. Nonviolent raids

In nonviolent raids, volunteers march to certain designated key points of symbolic or strategic importance and demand possession. This method usually involves civil disobedience and the risk of severe repression by police and troops. During the 1930–31 campaign in India, for example, quite a few of the seized Congress offices were reoccupied, and unorganized attempts to occupy government buildings occurred. [89] An even clearer example from that campaign was the effort to "seize" the Dharasana salt depot. Almost every day for a period of weeks volunteers marched in an orderly procession toward the depot and asked possession. Intending to take the salt stored there as an advanced method of defiance of the Salt Act (which was a major point of attack during that campaign), the volunteers met with severe repression. [90]

As the volunteers do not use violent methods of seizing or holding such places, their raids are not conducted with the main intent of actually gaining possession. Rather, nonviolent raids are intended more as a challenge to authority, a symbolic defiance of the established regime, and as a means of bringing into use some of the psychological mechanisms associated with self-suffering. In an extremely advanced stage of a nonviolent revolt, however, large masses of people might conceivably surround such "seized" points and effectively obstruct efforts by officials to recapture them, if helped by restrictions on the means of repression or assistance from the troops or police.

A variation on this method—seeking possession of merchandise rather than of a place—was practiced in Boston, Massachusetts Bay Colony, on January 18, 1770, in an attempt to deal with eight merchants who were violating the nonimportation agreement. The offending merchants had refused to reverse their behavior and to surrender the imported products to the committee of inspection. Arthur Schlesinger reports that:

> The whole body of more than a thousand persons then proceeded, in impressive and orderly array, to the houses or stores of each of these men; and, through William Molineux as spokesman, demanded that the goods, which had once been placed in the store, should be immediately deposited with the committee of inspection. Only Cary made the concession demanded.[91]

169. Nonviolent air raids[92]

Airplanes, balloons, or other air transport may be used to enter the air space of an opponent, without use or threat of any violence or destruction, to bring leaflets, or perhaps food and other gifts, to the population. (Air missions bringing supplies to break blockades are classed separately.) At times such a raid and dropping of leaflets may have an important psychological impact. An example of this occurred in the closing phase of the Kapp *Putsch*. On Tuesday, March 16, an airplane of the German government, which had fled to Stuttgart, appeared over Berlin, held by the putschists, to drop a leaflet, "THE COLLAPSE OF THE MILITARY DICTATORSHIP." Lieutenant-Colonel Goodspeed reports that "even in the fashionable sections of the city, the Berliners eagerly seized the printed sheets and, when they read them, cheered so loudly that officers of the Allied Commission of Control came hurrying to their hotel windows to see what was going on."[93]

Nonviolent air raids have often been small actions in overwhelmingly violent struggles—highly unfavorable conditions in which to produce results. For example, in late July 1965 United States planes dropped toys and clothes over villages near Hanoi in order to impress the civilian population of the good will of the United States.[94] And in South Vietnam U.S. planes some weeks later hovered above National Liberation Front positions, playing tape recordings of typical family noises and sounds. This was followed by a pitiful entreaty intoned by a Vietnamese woman: "Come home." U.S. officials believed this produced many deserters and called it a "humane form of terrorism." [95]

170. Nonviolent invasion

In nonviolent invasion a group of nonviolent volunteers deliberately and openly enter a forbidden area in order to demonstrate their refusal to recognize the right of the controlling regime or agency to exercise sovereignty or control over that area or to use it for a particular purpose. This method entails civil disobedience and the risk of severe repression. The mass nonviolent invasion of Goa in 1955 to defy the right of Portugal to exercise sovereignty over that part of India is perhaps a classic example of nonviolent invasion. [96] Other examples include attempts by pacifists to enter rocket sites near Omaha, Nebraska, in 1959, [97] and attempts to "reclaim" military land in Harrington, England, for peaceful purposes. [98] The attempt, in January 1960, to halt the French atomic test at Reggan, North Africa, by entering the forbidden area was intended to create nonviolent interjection, but as the volunteers did not come close to the actual test site this case was limited to a nonviolent invasion of French-controlled territory. [99] American opponents of nuclear weapons sought to halt Pacific nuclear tests by sailing into the prohibited area in 1958 and 1962. [100]

171. Nonviolent interjection

The method of nonviolent interjection involves placing one's body between a person and the objective of his work or activity, or sometimes between a soldier or a policeman and his opponent, or on other occasions in the path of a vehicle. This action is distinguished from the next method, nonviolent obstruction, in that the interjection does not constitute a sufficiently large or extensive physical obstruction that it cannot be overcome, removed, or surmounted. For example, with nonviolent interjection, persons or vehicles could simply proceed over the bodies, while with nonviolent obstruction they cannot do so. [101] The aim of nonviolent interjection is to persuade or otherwise induce the persons being impeded (soldiers, drivers, etc.) that they should desist from the activity which the actionists regard as immoral or illegitimate, or at least that the activity should not be continued at the price of imposing human suffering on the people who have intervened to bring it to a halt.

Since the possible results of this method are not achieved by imposing an insurmountable physical obstruction, the numbers of actionists are not decisive. A single person or a small group of people may, for example, lie or sit in front of a tank or train carrying war supplies in an effort to induce the driver to refuse to move the vehicle instead of inflicting injury or death on those lying or sitting in front of it. In fact, it has been argued that fewness of numbers increases the psychological or moral impact of the interjection. Bradford Lyttle distinguishes between individual nonviolent interjection (which he sees as running the greatest risk of injury or death because the individual may not be seen or may be thought to be bluffing) and group interjection (in which the risk of suffering or death for each individual taking part is less). Lyttle therefore suggests that individual nonviolent interjection may be more powerful. The examples of nonviolent interjection which are offered here are grouped into three types: intervention in social and employment activities, in actions of police and soldiers, and in halting vehicles.

In a rather atypical case, antiapartheid demonstrators sat down on the tennis court at Madserud Arena, Oslo, on May 13, 1964, to oppose the Davis Cup tennis match between Norway and the all-white South African team. [102] It is more common for this method to be used, however, as interjection between the actionists and the work or other activities of some group. For example, during the 1922 campaign in India, some students sat in the gateways of Calcutta University to block the passage of their fellow students. Urging them to refuse to attend classes, the demonstrators took the risk of being stepped on by those who persisted in entering the university. Similar means were used during the Indian nationalist struggles by women to halt the sale of liquor and by noncooperators to "persuade" government workers still loyal to the British *Raj* to resign their jobs. It is reported that Indian women used this method to induce their husbands working for the British to refuse to cooperate with the regime. [103] In 1957 striking hosiery workers in Reading, Pennsylvania, lay down on the sidewalks at factory gates, forcing the nonstrikers to choose whether they would walk over them in order to enter the factory or stay away from their jobs. [104]

Civil rights demonstrators in the United States have used nonviolent interjection as a strong means of influencing employers to hire more Negroes. In May 1963 Philadelphia chapters of the Congress of Racial Equality and the National Association for the Advancement of Colored People blocked the entry of white workmen at sites of allegedly discriminatory employment—calling this a "job blockade." (In this case there was some violence between the demonstrators and white construction workers.) Similar means were later successfully used in San Francisco to reach agreement from local hotels and car dealers to hire hundreds of Negroes; some demonstrators drew long jail sentences, illustrating that interventionist methods are often met with strong counteraction. The entrance to a New York City plumbers' union headquarters was also blocked, winning an agreement to admit Negro apprentices. [105]

Nonviolent interjection has also been used by white segregationists to block integration in the South; for example, in Greenwood, Mississippi, in the summer of 1964, a Negro couple and their son had been attempting to be served at a local cafe. Undaunted by a lawyer blocking the door one day, they returned the following day carrying a copy of the Civil Rights Act. This time, however, the proprietor herself stood in the door, effectively blocking it, and screaming at them to get out. Later, the couple told civil rights workers that next time they would go somewhere else. [106]

Nonviolent interjectionists have also attempted to interfere with the activities of police or soldiers, especially where they have attempted to arrest persons, or sometimes to prevent fighting. It has also been used to assist the escape of an apprehended Negro who was thought to be an escaped slave. One such example occurred in Boston in 1851, during the period of the Federal Fugitive Slave Law. Shadrach, a waiter in a Boston coffeehouse, had been arrested, Mabee reports, charged as an escaped Virginia slave, and brought to court. A group of from twenty to forty Negroes entered the courtroom and, laughing and jostling, moved about the room, hiding Shadrach among them long enough to rush him out of the room, thus enabling him to start the journey to Canada. Daniel Webster, then Secretary of State, called the rescue treason, and Senator Henry Clay thought the law should be made more severe. The American and Foreign Antislavery Society pointed out, however, that no weapons had been used and no one was injured, while Garrison pronounced this action by "unarmed friends of equal liberty" to be "an uninjurious deliverance of the oppressed out of the hands of the oppressor." [107]

When, in late winter or early spring of 1943, it became known in Bulgaria that the first deportations of Jews were being planned, "revolutionary elements in Sofia" issued an appeal for people to intervene to protect the Jews:

> Take your stand before your neighboring Jewish homes and do not let them be led away by force! Hide the children and do not give them to the executioners! Crowd the Jewish quarters and manifest your solidarity with the oppressed Jews! [108]

In the course of rivalries threatening newly independent Algeria with civil war, there were at the end of August and the beginning of September 1962 many instances in which unarmed local inhabitants barred the road between Oran and Constantine with their bodies and challenged the troops to use arms against them if they insisted on advancing toward rival troops. [109] In the Boghari area, south of Algiers, local inhabitants placed themselves between the pro-Ben Bella forces and opposition troops and demonstrated against any resumption in fighting. "Many of them lay down on the road." [110]

In June 1965 opposition Buddhists in Vietnam interjected themselves to prevent troops which were repressing Buddhist resistance from entering a pagoda by sitting in front of the gate of the National Buddhist Institute, Vien Hoa Doa. [111]

Nonviolent interjection has also been used in efforts to stop vehicles, such as automobiles, trucks and trains carrying goods the actionists did not wish to be delivered, construction machinery, and even tanks. On February 11, 1963, students sat on the road outside the Royal College at Nairobi, Kenya, to draw attention to the dangerous road-crossing conditions for undergraduates. [112] Women with baby carriages (prams), some with babies and older children, have often blocked highways and streets in the United States and England in efforts to have traffic lights or other safety devices installed to protect children and others from the traffic. At times this method may be used in a different issue, however, and in association with another method. In connection with the Glasgow school boycott of 1963 described in Chapter Four, against a dangerous unfenced canal, fifty mothers with prams and children blocked the canal bridge to traffic. [113]

In Palermo, Sicily, in 1963, an unemployed bricklayer linked hands with four of his seven children to form a human barrier across a busy street, protesting his being unemployed and "striking" to get a job. [114]

In Bombay, during the 1930-31 campaign a young man, Babu Ganu, attempted to stop a truck carrying boycotted cloth by lying in front of it and was killed when it ran over him. [115] There are several examples of this method in efforts to stop one type of construction or another. For example, in August 1958 at a missile base near Cheyenne, Wyoming, four persons attempted to stop trucks carrying supplies from entering the base; one was seriously injured. [116] Another example took place in England in December 1958 at a rocket site near a town called Swaffham. Direct actionists on two different occasions lay across the road and surrounded equipment in such a way as to force the workmen to choose between halting their work or injuring the demonstrators.[117] There were no serious injuries, the work was temporarily disrupted, and newspaper publicity was often sympathetic.

In 1958, in an effort to block work on a plan of the New York State Power Authority to flood 1,300 acres of Tuscaroras Indian nation land for a storage resevoir while legal action was being taken to stop the seizure of the land, members of this tribe on three separate occasions interjected their persons. Signs such as "WARNING. NO TRESPASSING. INDIAN RESERVE" and "MUST YOU TAKE EVERYTHING WE OWN?" were carried by bands of Tuscaroras in April 1958 as they blocked the entrance of surveyors and trucks by standing or lying down in front of them. State and county police arrested three of the demonstration leaders for unlawful assembly and disorderly conduct. Two of the men were tackled by police and dragged to the police wagon. Some scuffling between the police and Indian women and children occurred, although the interjection itself was nonviolent. In May surveyors again entered the reservation; Tuscaroras stood in front of their instruments to disrupt the survey work. Later, when bulldozers were sent in to clear land, the clearance crew consisting of Tuscaroras men stayed away from the job, and the work was stalled again. In the meantime their attorney, Mr. Grossman, was pursuing the legal battle. Edmund Wilson, in his *Apologies to the Iroquois,* reports that "the practical obstruction by one group of the Indians and the defense of them in their difficulties by Grossman gave pause to the Power Authority and influenced public opinion." In 1959 the Indians won their case when the Federal Power Commission refused to permit the New York Power Authority to build on Indian reservation land.[118]

While demonstrators in Cleveland, Ohio, on April 7, 1964, sought to disrupt construction of a new school in a Negro area—which was seen as an attempt to stop Negroes from attending predominantly white schools and to tighten segregation—the Rev. Bruce William Klunder, twenty-seven, a Presbyterian minister, threw himself on the ground behind a bulldozer which was moving in reverse to avoid three other demonstrators lying in front of it. The driver, not seeing Rev. Klunder, drove over him, and he was crushed to death. Rioting followed.[119]

In one small town in Slovakia during the Nazi occupation all the young men lay down on the railroad tracks to prevent a train from taking away the Jews.[120]

In 1953, when the Russians used tanks in Jena, East Germany, to disperse a crowd of 25,000 persons which were seeking the release of eight demonstrators who had been arrested during the uprising in June, "the crowd refused to budge. Women sat down in rows and forced the drivers to stop," Stefan Brant reports. By this means, and by maneuvering street-cars to block the tanks, the crowd held up the Russians for half an hour, at which time they temporarily withdrew. Eventually, the Russians dispersed the demonstrators by shooting over the heads of the crowd. [121]

172. Nonviolent obstruction

Nonviolent obstruction is similar to nonviolent interjection, except that the human bodies are used not only for psychological intervention but as a physical obstruction. [122] Such physical blocking occurs when the obstruction is undertaken by very large numbers or when the obstructors are so placed that the work, vehicle, police, troops, or the like cannot proceed even though they injure or kill the demonstrators. As in the previous method, the risk of arrest, injury, or death is involved. Such obstruction is unlikely to last very long unless: 1) the numbers are exceedingly large, are maintained over a long period, and are beyond the control of the personnel, equipment, and weaponry which the opponent is able and willing to apply; 2) the opponent is unwilling simply to kill all the obstructors by whatever means may be available; 3) the workers or the enforcement officials, police, or troops are, or become, sympathetic to the demonstrators; or 4) the demonstration of public opposition to the grievance, or to repression of the actionists, is strong enough to induce the opponent to abandon the objectionable activity or halt it for a time.

Various proposals for nonviolent obstruction to protect fugitive slaves in the United States were made between 1850 and 1852. The Rhode Island Antislavery Society, for example, decided that when it was impossible to hide slaves for whom warrants had been issued or to help them escape, "they shall be surrounded by a sufficiently numerous and influential Peace Committee to protect them from assault and capture." Wendell Phillips proposed that in a case where a fugitive was held in a courthouse, "hundreds of thousands" of people should nonviolently surround the building to prevent his return to the South by requiring officials "to walk over our heads." The periodical *National Antislavery Standard* argued that a phalanx of peaceful men, willing to give their lives, could protect an escaped slave even from military forces; it called for men who were ". . . unarmed but determined that no slave shall be taken . . . except over their bodies." This would, it continued, be a "revolution," ". . . the noblest the world ever saw, and it would, we cannot doubt, be effectual. We can hardly believe that armed citizen-soldiers would ride over and cut down their fellow-citizens standing and braving death with calm but desperate resolution lest a man should be taken among them and made a slave." [123]

It is not always easy to find the border-line between nonviolent interjection and nonviolent obstruction, as some of these cases may suggest. In Hungary, in early December 1956, seven hundred unarmed men and women blocked factory gates when police and two truckloads of Hungarian Army officers came to arrest three members of the workers' council at the *Danubia* textile factory. The arresting officers eventually left without the three men. [124] Another case of obstruction took place in Sunakawa, Japan, in 1956, when ten thousand people occupied a site intended for a United States air base; after several days of obstruction, plans for building the air base was abandoned. [125] In Brooklyn, New York, on July 22, 1963, about 1,250 persons took part in an effort to block public construction until more Negroes and Puerto Ricans were hired. More than two hundred obstructors were arrested, including at least ten ministers and church officials. Peter Kihss, of *The New York Times,* reports "In wave after wave for nearly eight hours Negro and white sympathizers darted in front of incoming construction vehicles to sit down or lie down in the roadway. They were picked up and taken away in patrol wagons—a dozen at a time." [126]

In the autumn of 1963, when white segregationist Mississippians feared that governor Ross Barnett might be arrested by federal marshals for contempt of a court order desegregating the University of Mississippi, Waskow reports, thousands of them sat down around the governor's mansion "to interpose their bodies—perhaps intending a 'not-quite-violent' resistance—between him and the forces of law and order." [127]

173. Nonviolent occupation

Nonviolent occupation may be used after a nonviolent invasion or a nonviolent land seizure, or by people who have been ordered to leave their land or building. Thus nonviolent occupation may involve technical trespass and the violation of other laws. Nonviolent occupation was successfully practiced by Bishop Ambrose during Easter week, 385 A.D., when he defied orders of the imperial government of the Roman Empire to surrender one of the larger churches in Milan to the Arian Christians. Although the church was surrounded by troops, Ambrose risked imprisonment and death, and continued to hold masses for five days. Finally the government ordered the troops withdrawn and the fines remitted, and, wrote Ambrose, "as soon as they heard, the troops rushed into the Church to receive the kiss of peace." [128]

During the 1928 Bardoli campaign in India, those peasants whose land was attached because of their refusal to pay taxes either refused to leave the land at all or returned to it. They cultivated it and planted crops, and insisted that whatever the current legal status might be, morally the land remained theirs and that they had a right to use it for constructive purposes. [129]

In August 1957 about two hundred Mohawk Indians, part of the Iroquois Confederacy, settled on the banks of the Schohari Creek, near Fort Hunter, New York; they said that they had been blasted from their homes by the construction of the St. Lawrence Seaway, and that the land they now occupied had belonged to the Mohawks under a treaty made in the 1700s. The Indians built a longhouse—the place of worship of the Handsome Lake religion—and half a dozen cabins. The Mohawks asserted they would recognize no local eviction proceedings, nor would they deal with local or state officials; as they were a nation they would deal only with the Federal government. [130]

The most dramatic nonviolent occupation by American Indians has been that of Alcatraz Island. On November 9, 1969, a few American Indians swam through the waters of San Francisco Bay and landed on the old island prison of Alcatraz, abandoned seven years before by the government. Eleven days later a hundred more joined them, and claimed the site by right of some old treaties that awarded all deserted areas within a tribe's original territory to the original inhabitants. The Indians wanted to make the area into an educational culture center for the American Indian and proved their determination by continued occupation of the island. Power and water were cut off by the authorities, but the inhabitants managed with two malfunctioning generators and the little drinking water that could be carried over in jugs. They were supported from the mainland by both Indians and non-Indians alike, who donated food, clothing and medical supplies. A small school was established, and many families took up permanent residence on "the Rock." It became a central focus of the new Indian movement and a source of pride as a successful intervention to protest the U.S. government's inadequacies in Indian affairs. Alcatraz was held by the Indians until the last fifteen were removed by Federal marshals on June 14, 1971. [131]

With Russian military units outside Czechoslovak government buildings in August 1968, government officials and legislators remained in their buildings and continued to act in their legitimate capacities. For example, in the afternoon of August 24, *Politika* reported:

The Government Presidium building is blockaded, tank guns are aiming at the building from all sides, guns stand in firing positions in the little park at Klarov. The Government Presidium is blockaded, but the Government is functioning. Twenty-two ministers meet, hold discussions, make decisions, report to the parliament on their activity, maintain contact with the new Party leadership. [132]

Politika also reported that the extraordinary twenty-sixth session of the National Assembly had already lasted four days:

The National Assembly building is surrounded by foreign troops, but the deputies are not leaving; they have imposed on themselves a house arrest. Acting on the summons by the Presidium, almost two hundred deputies from all over the Republic have reported in . . . an almost two-thirds majority. . . . On the first night, the deputies slept on the floor of their offices; for the following nights, they were able to get blankets and, more important, field cots for the women. Machine gun salvoes rattle under the windows of the National Assembly building at night. Supplies in the dining room are satisfactory. . . .

Neither the gun barrels aimed at the National Assembly windows nor the threat of arrest will force the deputies to capitulate. The permanent session is to continue until some solution to the aggression is found. [133]

SOCIAL INTERVENTION

Methods which take the form of direct intrusion in social behavior patterns, social occasions and social institutions are grouped as the third subclass of nonviolent intervention. In addition to these seven methods, certain others—such as a sit-in—produce social intervention, even though their dominant form is some other one, such as physical intervention, and hence they are grouped here in another subclass.

174. Establishing new social patterns

While social disobedience, a method of social noncooperation, consists of the refusal to obey various social customs, rules, regulations, practices, and behavior patterns, another method of social intervention consists of new ways of behavior which may positively contribute to the establishment of new social patterns. These may be unplanned actions by individuals or a series of individuals or groups. Or they may be actions planned as organized opposition. A wide variety of social patterns may be involved. It is, however, easily illustrated with behavior which replaces social patterns of inequality, hatred, or avoidance with new relationships of equality and respect. In the 1830s American abolitionists, sometimes naturally and without deliberation, sometimes as a conscious act, associated with Negroes, who even in Northern cities were normally socially boycotted. Mabee reports that on the proposal of Sarah Grimké, a Quaker, the Antislavery Convention of American Women in 1838 adopted a resolution which stated: "It is . . . the duty of abolitionists to identify themselves with these oppressed Americans, by sitting with them in places of worship, by appearing with them in our streets, by giving them our countenance in steamboats and stages, by visiting with them at their homes and encouraging them to visit us, receiving them as we do our white fellow citizens." [134] Some abolitionists did not approve of such practices, however, either because of a fear that they would provoke violence against abolitionists or against Negroes, or because of an opinion that the issues of slavery and racial prejudice should be kept separate. Among abolitionists the issue of public association with persons of another color was so sharp that there was fear in 1836 that the American Antislavery Society would split on it. [135]

Various abolitionists in Boston, Philadelphia, New York City and elsewhere engaged in "walk-alongs" (as Mabee calls them), in which they simply walked in the streets with persons of the other color, and often the other sex, sometimes arm in arm. This often upset people; the mayor of Philadelphia in 1839 urged Lucretia Mott not to do this because it offended the white rabble at a time when an anti-Negro riot was expected. However, she persisted in walking publicly with people regardless of color. After a meeting the Boston physician Dr. Henry Bowditch invited Frederick Douglass to walk home down Washington Street with him to dinner; Dr. Bowditch was afraid he would encounter his friends but Douglass later said that it was the first time a white had treated him as a man. In 1849 Douglass wrote in his periodical, *North Star,* that the way for abolitionists to remove prejudice was "to act as though it didn't exist, and to associate with their fellow creatures irrespective of all complexional differences. We have marked out this path for ourselves, and we mean to pursue it at all hazards." [136]

Mixed dining during the 1840 annual meeting in New York of the American Antislavery Society met with trouble from a mob, but by 1847 and 1858 similar events were not disturbed. [137] Private individuals "interdined," i.e., ate together in violation of taboos against social equality between their groups. To cope with prejudiced Quakers during a Friends Yearly Meeting, the Quaker Isaac Hooper invited his Negro Quaker guests, Mr. and Mrs. David Mapes, to join him for dinner and told the other guests that if they objected to joining them, they could eat later when the first group had finished. None did. [138] Various abolitionists entertained traveling abolitionists of a different color in their homes. However, in Pendleton, Indiana, a Quaker doctor who had been host to Frederick Douglass during his 1843 lecture tour was driven out of town by a mob. [139] Social equality within abolition societies was not fully accepted; about 1835 the Unitarian preacher William Ellery Channing, for example, advised against permitting Negroes to become members of such groups. That advice did not prevail, and Negroes held major offices in the national antislavery societies; but as late as the 1840s and 1850s Negroes sensed that they were not fully accepted. [140]

Interracial marriages occurred among abolitionists. Those marriages clearly set a different social pattern and violated the strong taboo against them. Such marriages were sometimes illegal, as they were in Massachusetts until repeal of the law in 1843. Both men and women married across the racial barrier, sometimes then having to face diverse pressures and sanctions. These included having to move elsewhere, social ostracism, physical assault, and loss of job. Nevertheless, since more male than female fugitive slaves reached Canada, the young men "frequently" married whites; in one year during the Civil War the city of Boston reported that sixteen percent of the Negroes who married that year were marrying whites. [141]

Another variation on this method has been the individual insistence on receiving equal treatment in public facilities, such as restaurants. For example, in 1837 Charles R. Ray and Philip Bell, the general agent and the proprietor of the *Colored American,* traveling up the Hudson on a steamer from New York City refused to have their tea in the kitchen, insisting on service in the dining cabin, even if they had to wait until the whites had had been served. Ray and Bell insisted: ". . . we do not like to be the agents of our own degradation." Similarly, until threatened with physical removal, Frederick Douglass, also on a Hudson River steamer, insisted on taking dinner like the other passengers. In Cleveland in 1857, Susan B. Anthony, the woman suffrage leader, and other delegates to an abolitionist convention refused to enter the dining room until a black abolitionist, William Wells Brown, was permitted to join them; the hotel backed down and provided equal service for the remainder of their stay. [142]

A number of these actions are almost identical with activities which have been undertaken in modern India for the eradication of untouchability and achieving communal unity. "Interdining" by people of various castes, untouchables and members of other religions has frequently occurred. Beginning in the 1930s Gora (born a Brahman), the prominent atheist Gandhian social revolutionary, organized intercaste and interreligious dining on a mass scale in India. Everyone brought his own provisions, and the cooking and dining were done without regard to caste or religious taboos, although intercaste dining was prohibited by orthodox Hindus. Special efforts were sometimes needed to overcome the hesitancy of lower-caste Hindus to eat with groups lower than themselves. Intermarriage has also been practiced and even encouraged as a means of ending untouchability. For example, Gora's children have been encouraged on that basis to marry outside the caste barriers, including with untouchables, and have done so. [143]

175. Overloading of facilities

Overloading facilities involves the deliberate increase of demands for services far beyond their capacity, so that the operation of the institution (government department, business, social service, and so on) is slowed down or paralyzed. Such overloading may be initiated by customers, the public, or employees of the institution. The objectives may vary and may include improved services, wage increases and political ends.

In 1965 at the Los Angeles County Hospital in California, for example, interns protesting pay policies initiated an overloading of facilities by admitting far more patients to the hospital than existing facilities could accommodate—even persons not needing hospitalization were admitted. This was called a heal-in. The interns' aim was to obtain a better bargaining position with the hospital administration. The hospital was filled with patients within four days, and the action cost the city around $250,000 in increased costs. [144]

A similar case occurred in Massachusetts at the Boston City Hospital in 1967, where it was called an "around-the-clock heal-in." This action was begun by 450 residents and interns at Boston City Hospital on Tuesday, May 16, 1967. The purpose of the heal-in was to dramatize salary demands by doctors at Boston teaching hospitals; at that time the take-home salary of an intern was only sixty dollars per week. The doctors felt that it would be in violation of their oaths to go on strike, so they chose instead to practice "ultra-conservative medicine" in order to overcrowd the hospital. Dr. Philip Caper, President of the House Officers' Association, said: "Everyone gets the best of care," which was ensured by having all the interns and residents work twenty-four hours a day. "Every patient who might benefit from hospitalization will be admitted, and no one will be discharged until he is completely well."

The heal-in was patterned after the similar action at the Los Angeles County Hospital eighteen months previously. The Boston City Hospital doctors began their heal-in as an unannounced experiment on Saturday, with 874 patients in the hospital. On Sunday there were 890, on Monday 924, and on Tuesday at 7 A.M. (after the main action was begun) there were 982. An unidentified doctor stated: "With 1,200 or more patients in the hospital the laundry will not be able to keep up, the kitchens will have trouble getting the food out, the X-ray and laboratory departments will be swamped, and people will begin to listen to our demands . . ." By Wednesday morning there were over 1,000 patients, and 1,075 on Thursday. The heal-in was supported by private doctors and house officers at the other major Boston hospitals. Action was taken only at Boston City Hospital because house officers there had full responsibility for medical procedure, unlike the private hospitals.

Countermeasures by the administration began Tuesday afternoon with an announcement that there were no more beds for male patients, which was disproved that evening by the admission of two more patients. They next tried to influence the chiefs of services to override the admittances, which these doctors refused to do on the grounds that these patients were indeed getting the best of care. The administration's final effort was to deny their competence to make salary changes. On the evening of Thursday, May 18, they relented and promised to make salary adjustments. The doctors ended the heal-in voluntarily that night. Observers felt that it was a "safe, effective way of backing up demands for higher wages." [145]

A student version of the method was applied in Japan in 1954. It was the practice in some private universities to admit more students than there were facilities, on the assumption that not all students would attend classes at the same time. The students organized a campaign of "united attendance" as a means of pressure against the university. [146]

176. Stall-in

The stall-in is a method that consists simply of conducting legitimate business as slowly as possible. This differs from stalling and obstruction, described in the previous chapter on political noncooperation, which is action by government employees to delay or prevent the implementation of some policy. The stall-in is undertaken by customers and clients for purposes which are likely to be social, but which may also include economic and political objectives. This method was applied in June 1964 by the Congress of Racial Equality against the Bank of America in San Diego, California, with C.O.R.E. customers taking thirty minutes to transact business normally done in about three. C.O.R.E. was seeking an end to discrimination in the bank's employment practices. [147] In conjunction with the 1938 Harlem Negroes' "black-out boycott" movement (see consumers' boycott above), bill payers by the hundreds went to the electric utilities offices, each paying in nickels and pennies. [148]

177. Speak-in [149]

A special form of nonviolent intervention occurs when actionists interrupt a meeting, church service, or other gathering for the purpose of expressing viewpoints on issues which may or may not be related directly to the occasion. Since the intervention is primarily interference with the social form of the meeting, this method can best be classed as one of social intervention, although it includes psychological and physical aspects also.

This form of action was often used by George Fox and other early Quakers. For example, in his *Journal* George Fox records how one Sunday (First-day) in 1649 he attended the Church of St. Mary in Nottingham, England, (a "steeplehouse," he called it, rather than a church) and was "moved" to speak during the regular service:

> Now as I . . . looked upon the town the greatest steeplehouse struck at my life . . . , a great . . . idolatrous temple. And the Lord said unto me, "Thou must go cry against yonder great idol, and against the worshippers therein." . . . . And when I came there, all the people looked like fallow land, and the priest, like a great lump of earth, stood in his pulpit above. He took for his text these words of Peter, "We have also a more sure word of prophecy, whereunto ye do well that ye take heed. . ." And he told the people that the Scriptures were the touchstone and judge by which they were to try all doctrines, religions, and opinions. . . Now the Lord's power was so mighty upon me . . . that I . . . was made to cry out and say, "Oh, no, it is not the Scriptures," . . . But I told them it was . . . the Holy Spirit, by which the holy men of God gave forth the Scriptures, whereby opinions, religions, and judgements were to be tried. . . . Now as I spoke thus amongst them, the officers came and took me away and put me into prison, a pitiful stinking place . . . [150]

In 1651 at Cranswick, in Yorkshire, one Sunday afternoon, a friend took Fox to meet the local priest, with whom he would talk after the service, which they attended. Fox records what happened:

And he took a text, which was, "Ho, everyone that thirsteth, let him come freely, without money and without price." And so I was moved of the Lord God to say unto him, "Come down, thou deceiver and hireling, for dost thou bid people come freely . . . and yet thou takest three hundred pounds off them for preaching the Scriptures to them. Mayest thou not blush for shame? . . . . And so the priest, like a man amazed, packed away; . . . And so after the priest had left his flock, I had as much time as I could desire to speak to the people, and I directed them to the grace of God that would teach them and bring them salvation. . .[151]

Fox did not always interrupt the regular services but sometimes waited until they had been completed, and then spoke to the priest and the people, as, for example, he did in Doncaster in 1652:

> . . . and after the priest had done I spoke to him and the people what the Lord God commanded me, and they were in a great rage and hurried me out and threw me down the stairs, and haled me before the mayor and magistrates . . . and they threatened my life if I ever came there again . . .[152]

During the antislavery campaign in the United States, actionists at times interrupted church services in order to denounce the lack of effective opposition to slaveholding, and also the refusal of many churches to accomodate antislavery meetings. Thus Mabee reports:

> One Sunday morning in 1841, a determined young Garrisonian, Stephen S. Foster, entered a Congregational Church in Concord, New Hampshire. In a lull in the service he rose and denounced the church for upholding slavery. The pastor asked Foster to stop speaking, but he continued until some of the congregation took him by the arms and led him out. In the afternoon Foster returned to another service and again spoke without permission. This time some of the congregation threw him down the stairs, and he was arrested for disturbing public worship.[153]

In using this method abolitionists were cautious to attempt a hearing through more agreeable means if possible:

> . . . Foster and his team never interrupted a worship service unless they had already tried and failed to win a hearing by permission, including attempts to secure the use of the church building to hold their own meetings.[154]

178. Guerrilla theater[155]

Guerrilla theater, another method of social intervention, means a disruptive skit, dramatic presentation, or similar act. It came to be used in the United States in the late 1960s. The disruption may be of speeches, lectures, or normal proceedings of some group or institution. (The term guerrilla theater is also used for a spontaneous style of stage theater, usually with a political theme.)

Two examples are provided by Jerry Rubin, one of the more dramatic self-styled revolutionaries who emerged in the late 1960s. In late 1967 a conference of college newspaper editors in Washington, D.C., was debating whether or not to take a stand on the Vietnamese conflict:

> Someone made a motion to table all resolutions and take no stand. The motion passed. Suddenly the lights went out and across the wall flashed scenes of World War II fighting, burning Vietnamese villages, crying Vietnamese women and napalmed children, image after image. The room echoed with hysterical screams, *"Stop it! Stop it!"*
>
> A voice boomed over a bullhorn: "Attention. This is Sergeant Haggerty of the Washington Police. These films were smuggled illegally into the country from North Vietnam. We have confiscated them and arrested the people who are responsible. Now clear this room! Anyone still here in two minutes will be arrested!"
>
> The editors fell over themselves rushing for the door. . . They believed they were going to be arrested for seeing a . . . film. They believe they live in a Nazi country. They accept it. [156]

Earlier, in August of that year, Rubin and some others had used a similar device to denounce the American preoccupation with money. Rubin and his friends did this at the New York Stock Exchange:

> The stock market comes to a complete standstill at our entrance to the top of the balcony. The thousands of brokers stop playing Monopoly and applaud us. What a crazy sight for them—longhaired hippies staring down at them.
>
> We throw dollar bills over the ledge. Floating currency fills the air. Like wild animals, the stockbrokers climb over each other to grab the money.
>
> *"This is what it's all about, real live money. Real dollar bills! People are starving in Biafra!"* we shout. . .
>
> While throwing the money we spot the cops coming. The cops grab us and throw us off the ledge and into the elevators. The stockbrokers below loudly boo the pigs. [157]

179. Alternative social institutions

One of the forms which nonviolent intervention may take is the building of new institutions. When their creation and growth produces a challenge the previous institutions, the new ones constitute nonviolent intervention. These new institutions intervene in various ways, such as by becoming competitive rivals of the opponent's institutions, by replacing them partly or completely, by providing institutional implementation of the actionists' principles or program, or by increasing the effectiveness of other methods of nonviolent action being used in the struggle. In any of these cases the opponent's institutions will no longer have the field to themselves, and the actionists will have intervened by offering substitute institutions. Alternative economic and political institutions are discussed later in this chapter. The focus here is on social institutions, which of course include educational ones.

It may be useful, however, to note briefly some of the reasons why new institutions may be launched. For example, in a long-term nonviolent struggle a necessary counterpart to noncooperation with certain established institutions may be the building up of alternative institutions, social, economic and political. This is often necessary in order to make noncooperation with institutions controlled by the opponent effective and in order to develop or maintain an alternative social order. Sometimes also this is done in order to prevent "contamination" by the institutions which are opposed, or to fulfill needs neglected by established bodies.

In the nineteenth century, during their resistance to Austrian rule, the Hungarians developed both social and economic institutions to combat the "Austrianization" of Hungary. These included the National Academy of Sciences, the National Museum, and the National Theater, while economic bodies included the Agricultural Union, the National Protective Union, and the Company of Commerce.[158] In 1905 in Ireland, Arthur Griffith developed a comparable Sinn Fein policy of building alternative educational, economic, political and diplomatic institutions for Ireland, built on the Hungarian pattern and designed to restore self-reliance and independence to the country.[159] Gandhi, too, developed the theory of alternative institutions as a crucial part of his constructive program.[160]

Sometimes, however, a resistance movement may select only a few institutions for parallel development. In the nineteenth century the American abolitionists and Negro churchmen, for example, protesting against segregation within the churches, withdrew from them and sometimes established new churches. This is how the African Methodist Episcopal Zion Church was established in 1821.[161]

In addition to privately teaching slaves and free Negroes to read and write, abolitionists and others before the Civil War sometimes established new schools, usually for Negroes but occasionally for an integrated enrollment. In many states both such private instruction and schools were forbidden by law. In breaking up a school for slaves, a grand jury in Lexington, Kentucky, argued that the school would enlighten ". . . the minds of those whose happiness obviously depends on their ignorance."[162] A Negro woman in Savannah, Georgia, taught a black school illegally for over thirty years; in other cases the teacher went to private homes, as in Petersburg, Virginia, where a mulatto secretly went from house to house at night to teach Negroes. In the late 1850s the abolitionist Rev. John G. Fee tried to create integrated schools in Kentucky; after his school building was burned by armed proslavery whites, Fee defiantly returned despite threats. He refused to carry weapons even for self-protection, and although frequently mobbed, he continued to create integrated schools. Catholics, Quakers and Negro church bodies supported several schools for free Negroes in Baltimore and Washington. Mobs broke up furniture and burned these schoolhouses, driving some teachers out of the capital city. After Quakers helped Myrtilla Miner to establish a normal school for Negroes in Washington in the early 1850s, boys on the street tormented the students, and a mob invaded the schoolroom. Miss Miner, however, "laughed them to shame; and when they threatened to burn her [school]house, she told them they could not stop her in that way, as another house, better than the old, would immediately rise from its ashes." A fire was set in 1860, but the building was nevertheless saved.[163]

Schools seem to be one of the most common social institutions for parallel development, for the remaining two examples refer also to them, in very different circumstances. During the German occupation of their country Polish citizens set up an educational system independent of Nazi control. In 1942 in the Warsaw district alone more than 85,000 children were receiving education in small secret sessions in private homes. Over 1,700 had by that date been graduated from high school, receiving innocently worded cards which were after the war to be exchanged for official diplomas.[164]

Alternative private school systems have been created in the U.S. South by prosegregationist whites in efforts to counter Federal court decisions ordering integration in public schools. In Virginia, in the autumn of 1958, for example, state aid to pay tuition for children in private schools was attempted. A Federal court ruling banning publicly paid teachers from operating private segregated schools (along with citizen support for the public schools and other factors) prevented these private schools from replacing integrated public ones. [165]

180. Alternative communication system [166]

Under political systems which have extensive control or monopoly over systems and media of communication, the creation by opposition groups of substitute systems of communication may constitute nonviolent intervention when they disrupt the regime's control or monopoly over the communication of information and ideas. This may involve newspapers, radio and even television. Systems for communication between individuals (as substitutes for the controlled postal or telephone system) may also be involved. Newspapers themselves, or radio broadcasts, as described in Chapter Three, are classed as methods of protest and persuasion; but when these are developed as alternative systems of communication on a sufficient scale to challenge the controlled ones, the intervention of these new systems disrupts the opponents control of these media. These new communication systems then become powerful tools of the nonviolent actionists; and, the opponent's control of communication of ideas and information having been broken, these systems in turn may enable the actionists in the future to resist and intervene in still other ways.

The underground newspaper systems cited in Chapter Three in certain Nazi-occupied countries were on a sufficient scale to constitute an alternative news communication system. This was clearly the case in the Netherlands. The very day after the German invasion the first hand-written underground bulletin appeared, and soon there were more handwritten or typewritten sheets or bulletins, called "snow-ball letters" (which readers were expected to copy and to pass on to friends). Major periodicals developed and grew to have very large circulations, especially considering the repressive conditions under which they were edited, published and distributed. *Vrij Nederland* with its local editions reached a circulation in September 1944 of one hundred thousand printed copies. *Het Parool* began as the first printed underground paper with six thousand copies, reaching a circulation of sixty thousand in 1944, and its daily news bulletins nearly reached a circulation of one hundred thousand. *Je Maintiendrai* grew from a small mimeographed sheet to a weekly which had a circulation of forty thousand in 1945. *Trouw* had a basic circulation of sixty thousand, but there were also about sixty local and regional editions; by

January 1945 the total circulation of all its editions and news bulletins was about two million. In 1944 *De Waarheid,* a weekly printed in Amsterdam and Rotterdam, may have reached one hundred thousand copies. *Ons Volk* reached a circulation of 120,000. In addition to these, various other clandestine periodicals and papers were published and circulated, and after confiscation of radios in May 1943 they grew rapidly; 150 separate such titles appeared in 1943, and between September 1944 and January 1945, 350 news bulletins appeared, "reaching a cumulative circulation of millions of copies." [167] With so extensive an alternative system of communication of political ideas, discussion of resistance tactics, and news, the illegal papers clearly rivaled the official ones and prevented the occupation forces from establishing a monopoly for the Nazi-controlled press and censored news reports.

Another type of alternative communication system is more specialized, involving the delivery of information and special messages to particular persons or groups, when the regular media for such communication, like the postal service, telephones and so on, are subject to interception or tapping.

The system of alternative radio broadcasting and television which operated in Czechoslovakia for a full two weeks, described briefly in Chapter Three, is the most advanced development thus far of such an alternative broadcast system operating within an occupied country. It operated longer under those conditions than had been believed possible, but as yet there has been relatively little attention to the technical, organizational and other requirements which might enable such a rival broadcasting system to continue to operate periodically over months or years to assist a resistance movement.

ECONOMIC INTERVENTION

Nonviolent intervention may also take economic forms. [168] The effect of some of the twelve methods in this subclass is, however, primarily psychological, while in other methods it is largely economic, often with political ramifications. Four of these methods are characterized by combined physical and economic characteristics: the reverse strike, the stay-in strike, nonviolent land seizures, and defiance of blockades. Four of these methods are simply disruptive of an opponent's economy, especially that of another country, and these usually involve government action, although they could in special circumstances be carried out by private groups; they are politically motivated counterfeiting, preclusive purchasing, seizure of assets in another country, and dumping of products on the international market to injure or destroy the economy of another country. These methods are far from forms derived from love of one's opponent and indeed have sometimes been used just prior to or during military conflicts by the belligerents themselves. These methods however do fulfill the technical characteristics of this class of methods within the technique of nonviolent action. The last grouping within economic intervention is primarily nongovernmental, and involves the creation, shifting, or increase of alternative purchasing, marketing, transportation and production capacity.

181. Reverse strike

While economic in form, the reverse strike is largely psychological in impact. As far is now known, the reverse strike is a relatively new form of nonviolent action, originating among agricultural workers in Italy around 1950, prior to the well-known use of the reverse strike in Sicily by the Italian exponent of nonviolent social change, Danilo Dolci. In using this method, the agricultural workers worked harder and longer than they were either required or paid to do. They did this to support their demand for pay increases and to place the employer in a difficult position to deny their requests.

The reverse strike has also been used to dramatize the need for jobs for unemployed men. In 1956 unemployed Sicilians led by Danilo Dolci used this method when they voluntarily repaired a public road in order to call attention to the severe unemployment in the area, the government's failure to deal adequately with it, and the constitutional guarantee of the right to work. On this occasion, Dolci and others were arrested. [169]

James Farmer reports that more recently (no date given) in Chicago a Congress of Racial Equality (C.O.R.E.) group organized unemployed Negro youths to work on a slum clean-up campaign and then left a bill at City Hall (which was never paid) enumerating the costs of the effort. They were, as Farmer puts it, "as it were doing public works before they were authorized." [170]

The first Sunday of the Russian occupation of Czechoslovakia, August 25, a majority of workers of the C.K.D., one of the country's largest machinery factories, including office workers, reported for an extra shift of work they called "Dubček's Sunday," to support the Dubček government by building the economy, instead of striking, which would have hurt the country itself, not the Russians. At the compressor plant, however, the instructions for the "Dubček shift" came too late and only about forty percent reported for work. [171]

Although the reverse strike *appears* innocuous and of little threat to the established order, it has at times in Italy been regarded by officials as sufficiently dangerous to merit the arrest, imprisonment and even shooting of reverse strikers by police.[172] Why this is so is difficult to answer unless defiant initiatives and intervention by workers is seen as more perilous than the halting of work by ordinary strikes.

182. Stay-in strike

In the stay-in strike—the term is used by both Peterson and Knowles[173] —the workers halt work but remain at the place of work, such as the factory, and refuse to leave until their demands are granted. This has been more frequently called a sit-down strike, but the term stay-in strike is recommended here as a more accurate (for the workers do not literally remain sitting down), and in order to avoid confusion with the sit-down described in Chapter Seven. When used by miners, this has been called a stay-down strike, since they remain down in the mines for its duration.

The stay-in strike has a number of advantages for the strikers: it leaves them in control of the means of production; it reduces the chances of strikebreakers being used to keep production going; and unless the stay-in strikers are attacked by police or troops, the chances of violence and sabotage in the strike are lessened.[174]

Joseph G. Rayback, in his *A History of American Labor*, reports that "women in the needle trades had engaged in at least one sit-down strike in the nineteenth century" and says that the method had been used in Poland and France, but that these cases were not remembered by the American trade unionists in the mid-1930s.[175] Although it is by no means clear, there is some evidence that the development of this method in the United States was influenced by the Gandhian struggles in India.[176]

Stay-in strikes were widely used in Europe and the United States during the 1930s. Rubber workers in Akron, Ohio, in 1936 conducted the first major American sit-down strike,[177] and the same year Cleveland auto workers conducted another.[178] In October 1936 the stay-in strike was used against the speedup at the General Motors plant in Anderson, Indiana,[179] and on November 13, the same year, it was used against the firing of union men at General Motors' Chevrolet plant in Flint, Michigan.[180]

It was, however, the strike by the United Automobile Workers against General Motors at Flint which made the stay-in, or sit-down, strike famous, Rayback reports. "The strike was something new because workers instead of walking out of the plant just sat at their workbenches . . . . The sit-down proved highly effective." The action was denounced by General Motors as an unlawful invasion of property rights and ejection of the workers was demanded. The company cut off heat in the plants, but the workers remained. Two waves of attack by Flint city police were repulsed violently by the strikers, first with coffee mugs, soft drink bottles, iron bolts and hinges, and then, against tear gas bombs, by fire hoses. Governor Frank Murphy refused to use the state militia to expel the strikers. The workers defied a court order for evacuation, saying that they were seeking to make General Motors "obey the law and engage in collective bargaining"; in defiance of the Wagner Act, the company had refused to discuss either union recognition or collective bargaining. On February 4, President Franklin D. Roosevelt requested that negotiations be resumed, and a week later an agreement was reached whereby the company recognized the union, dropped the injunction, and agreed not to discriminate against union members.

In April 1937 a short stay-in strike forced the Chrysler Corporation to come to terms, Rayback also reports. The strike innovation spread widely, so that between September 1936 and June 1937 almost five hundred thousand workers took part in stay-in strikes in rubber, textile, glass and many other industries. This type of action produced a strong reaction, however, from employers, newspapers, sections of the public, the United States Senate, and finally the American Federation of Labor (A.F.L.). The Congress of Industrial Organizations (C.I.O.) had primarily used it against companies which ignored or defied orders of the National Labor Relations Board; in the summer of 1937 the C.I.O. decided that the stay-in strike "was both unnecessary and impolitic," writes Rayback, and it was quietly abandoned. In 1939 the United States Supreme Court virtually outlawed this type of strike as trespass on private property. [181]

Whereas the stay-in strike in America was used only to press for particular demands concerning wages, working conditions and union recognition, the use of the method in Italy before Mussolini's rise to power was revolutionary—the workers hoped to take over the factories and run them themselves. [182] These cases were sometimes combined with violence.

There are a number of examples of the stay-down strike by miners. In 1934 the miners of Pecs, Hungary, conducted a combined stay-down and hunger strike in the mines. [183] The stay-down strike has also been used by coal miners in Poland and Wales, [184] including two cases of eight miners in September 1959 at the Great Mountain Colliery, Tumble, near Llanelly, South Wales, [185] and thirty-seven men at Groesfaen Colliery, Glamorgan, Wales in March 1960. [186]

In Bitterfeld during the East German Rising in June 1953, the stay-in strike was used as a method of nonviolent struggle which would be effective while keeping people off the streets and avoiding mass confrontations with Russian and East German police and troops. The head of the local strike committee later declared: "We appealed to the workers over the city radio to return to their firms but not to resume work." [187] Evaluating the general use of this method in that revolt, Rainer Hildebrandt writes: ". . . [in] some factories . . . the sit-down strike lasted several days, sustained no casualties and even got some workmates released who had been arrested for striking." [188]

183. Nonviolent land seizure

Another method of economic intervention occurs when people nonviolently expropriate and utilize land which by statute has belonged to someone else, with the intent of producing a *de facto* change of ownership and control. They hope that it will be recognized as a *de jure* change of ownership as well. Usually such land seizures are carried out by landless peasants against large landowners, frequently the same ones on whose land the peasants have previously worked. On other occasions, the seized land may be owned by the government, or may recently have been confiscated as punishment for popular antigovernment resistance, such as tax refusal.

The conditions under which nonviolent land seizures occur differ widely, sometimes even being undertaken with the approval of the government in power or with the encouragement of powerful groups in the society. It seems that the social and political situation is always complicated. They have occurred in diverse parts of the world, only a few examples of which are cited here.

The accounts of land seizures which are readily available are, as is the cases with many other methods, written with a focus which makes it difficult to determine whether the particular seizure was completely nonviolent, largely so, or mixed with significant violence; further research on such illustrative cases as are listed here might therefore require some modification in their descriptions.

As a few examples, we may cite peasant land seizures which occurred in Central and Southern Italy and in Sicily in 1919 and 1920. Christopher Seton-Watson reports that peasant land seizures began in August 1919 in the Roman Campagna.

Columns would set out at dawn from the villages, with banners and martial music, march to the selected estate, mark out the uncultivated land in strips or plots, and at once begin to dig or plough, to establish ownership. Often the land selected for seizure had been the object of bitter disputes for decades and was regarded by the peasants as rightfully theirs. [189] In September the government authorized the prefects to requisition uncultivated land; it was to be distributed to needy claimants if they organized themselves into cooperatives. In the spring of 1920 Catholic peasant leagues, frequently encouraged by parish priests, organized larger land seizures in Sicily. The government then said that only peasants capable of efficient farming would have their claims recognized. The total amount of land which permanently changed hands by land seizures was small. [190]

A large number of cases of land seizure have occurred in South America, especially in Colombia, Bolivia, Peru, Venezuela and Brazil. In Colombia peasant leagues in 1929 used land seizures and apparently defensive violence in Cundinamarca, Tolima and Valle and maintained on the former Viotá estates, in a mountainous area of over five hundred square kilometers, an independent communist republic for over twenty years. In 1933 the peasants took advantage of a Colombian law which made the landlord financially obligated to his tenants for improvements they made on his land. With and without permission, tenants planted coffee trees, making repossession by the landlord impossible without payment to the tenants. In the area of Cundinamarca these peasant actions were successful, and they kept the land. Somewhat later the Colombian Congress passed the Law 200, known as the López land reform. [191] The *Caja Agraria,* agricultural credit bank, legalized the seizure of various *haciendas* by buying them from the original owners and selling them on long-term credit back to the peasants who had occupied them; this would not have happened except for the peasants' action. [192]

About 1961 between five and six hundred peasant families invaded and seized the large abandoned *haciendas* of the area of Cunday. In this and two other areas the government's Land Reform Institute then divided the estates among a large number of peasant families. [193]

Miguel Urrutia reports that around 1967 land seizures were still being organized by peasant unions and that the Roman Catholic-oriented *Federación Agraria Nacional* (affiliated with the *Unión de Trabadores de Colombia)* had organized land seizures which had given *de facto* property rights to thousands of peasants. Such seizures have often been approved by Church advisors and led by priests. Nonviolent seizures were in some cases made legal by sales on credit by the landowner to the peasants, while in other instances the government's Land Reform Institute declares the invaded land a "land reform" area. In other cases, says Urrutia, "the peasants keep their land through force." [194]

Major land seizures have also occurred in Bolivia, often with government encouragement. In 1945 at a national congress of *campesinos* the Indians were urged by officials of the revolutionary nationalist government to strengthen their organizations as a step toward future actions to expropriate the *latifundios*—the large estates. However, later under a conservative government when Indians invaded the *haciendas* of the plateau they were cruelly repressed, Eduardo Arze-Loureiro reports. [195]

In 1952, after the elected Nationalistic Revolutionary Movement gained government power, the N.R.M. and government together set about urging the Indians to occupy the land. With help, agricultural unions were established, and land was distributed into family plots and collective fields.

> With surprising rapidity the land was taken and distributed, without violence, even before the promulgation of the Agrarian Reform Decree. The process took place almost simultaneously throughout the vast zone which is inhabited by 80 percent of the national population, and this with all its amplitude and with a stability that precluded the necessity for subsequent revisions. [196]

The feudal divisions of land use, between family plots and the landowners, were kept, but ownership was transferred to the family groups and the community respectively. "It has been a peaceful process," writes Arze-Loureiro, "although one of transcendent importance, because it has eliminated one rural social class, that of the *latifundistas,* and has converted the serf into the owner of his parcel and a member of an institution with common possessions and interests." [197] The large landowners retreated to the cities, where they turned to gaining control of the State apparatus by means of the *coup d'etat.*

Huntington reports that peasant land seizures in the Cuzco area of Peru and the growing strength of peasant organizations contributed to the passage of the 1960 land reform law in that country; [198] it is also reported that President Belaunde Terry had "encouraged landless Indians to seize untilled latifundios so as to force through Congress his land reform bill." [199] In 1962-63 in Peru a syndicate movement grew in the departments of Junin and Pasco in the Central Sierra. Doreen Warriner reports that these groups organized "numerous seizures or invasions of *haciendas* which had taken land from the Indians. ('Invasion' means that the Indians drive their cattle onto the disputed land, build huts and live there.)" [200]

After President Rómulo Betancourt of Venezuela returned to power in 1959, his government immediately began to distribute public lands and to approve of land seizures which had been organized by the syndicates. The 1960 Agrarian Reform Law, writes Warriner, "did not really initiate the reform: it regularized the preceding take-overs of land by the syndicates, and provided a mechanism by which syndicates could, in future, petition the National Agrarian Institute for the expropriation of estates." [201] She also reports that "Venezuela is the only country where a trade union movement has carried out a land reform . . ." [202]

In 1963-64 land invasions occurred in Brazil, especially of abandoned and uninhabited estates where opposition was unlikely. The Paraiba Valley was the scene of many of the land seizures. Police threw the invaders out most of the time but not always, as Warriner reports: "In one case where the invaders were backed by the railway workers' syndicate which threatened a railway strike if the invaders were expelled, the state government purchased the estate and handed it over to the invaders." [203] The Brazilian government agency *Superintendencia da Politica de Reforma Agraria* did expropriate some properties where land seizures had been attempted or had been successful. [204] The government of President Goulart was ousted by a *coup d'etat* in April 1964. Landowners' fear of a general upheaval is reported as one factor in its overthrow. Leaders of the syndicate movement were then imprisoned. [205]

184. Defiance of blockades [206]

In the course of international conflict, nations may attempt to exert political pressure by blockading opponents, to exclude certain "strategic goods" of a military nature or to cut off food and other necessary supplies, or both. Defying the blockade without the threat or use of military action, in order to bring food and related necessities to the cut-off population, then constitutes a method of economic intervention which third parties may use to support the besieged country. Such defiance may be made by both private and governmental bodies. Where governmental action is involved, there is always the possibility that even when there is no intent to threaten or use military support, the opponent may perceive this to be a possibility if he interferes with the defiance of the blockade. Also, as in the case of embargoes, there may be an implicit possibility of violent action by the government to support a method which is by itself nonviolent. These background conditions may have been present in the best-known example of blockade defiance, the Berlin Airlift of 1948-49. In it British and United States planes airlifted into Berlin food, fuel and other necessary supplies after the Soviet Union had imposed a blockade, which began on June 24, 1948, and continued until May 12, 1949. There does not, however, appear to have been an explicit threat of Western military action by the British or Americans, nor apparently were the supply planes armed. This case thus meets the criteria for classification as nonviolent action as well as do embargoes. Further study of this type of phenomenon is needed.

In addition to the Allied airlift, Germans themselves brought supplies to Berlin for several months. W. Phillips Davidson writes in his book *The Berlin Blockade* that owing to the currency reform it was profitable for West German farmers to increase production and to try to keep Berlin as a market.

> Enterprising truckers managed to evade Soviet controls and spirit produce from West Germany [across East Germany] to West Berlin, where it would command slightly higher prices. During the summer there were some days when fresh vegetables smuggled in from the west zones were available at such reasonable prices that the Magistrat [the executive branch of the Berlin city government] was hard pressed to dispose of those marketed through the usual channels.
>
> In addition, throughout the summer West Berliners were able to obtain a limited quantity of food and other supplies from the Soviet zone. Trucks drove out daily into the surrounding country-side and came back with vegetables. Individuals returned by boat, train, subway, or bicycle with wood, coal briquettes, potatoes, and sundries. [207]

In the autumn of 1948 Soviet officials moved to seal these holes in the blockade.

The vast bulk of supplies, however, were brought in by air; these included not only vast quantities of food, but even coal, machinery and electrical generating equipment. The record was set on April 16, 1949, when 12,490 tons were airlifted in twenty-four hours. Tonnage airlifted for the month of April alone was 235,000. [208]

185. Politically motivated counterfeiting

Politically motivated counterfeiting involves the deliberate distribution in one country of counterfeit money and other documents of economic importance by a hostile country. "It might be done either to disrupt the economy by monetary means," writes Professor Thomas C. Schelling, "or to create such a prevalence of counterfeit as to cause loss of confidence in the currency." [209] Murray Teich Bloom reports that "counterfeiting an enemy's coinage or currency has been a tactic of most wars since 1470 when the wily Duke Galeazzo Sforza of Milan used it against Venice." [210]

President Franklin D. Roosevelt is reported to have asked the British to consider counterfeiting German currency, but they refused, though they did make good facsimiles of Nazi ration stamps, which were airdropped in 1940. Counterfeit postage stamps for Germany and occupied France were also made, and used by secret agents and for mailing propaganda within these countries. It is also reported by Bloom (and denied by the former director of the Office for Stategic Services) that the United States made and distributed counterfeit Japanese currency. [211]

After 1943 the Germans circulated counterfeit British notes of various denominations. The very best quality notes were used in neutral countries and by German spies in enemy countries, the second best for paying off collaborators and Quislings in occupied countries, and notes of the third quality were to be dropped over England by plane to disrupt the British banking system. Others were unusable. The counterfeit money was distributed widely in North Africa after the Allied invasion, and in Portugal and Spain, among other places. The Bank of England suspected the scheme in April 1943. In 1944 alone the Nazis produced usable British currency worth about $277,500,000. Only a very few U.S. one hundred dollar bills were produced early in 1945. [212]

186. Preclusive purchasing

Preclusive purchasing is a intervention which involves "buying strategic commodities in world markets for the purpose of making them unavailable to the enemy." [213] During World War II, for example, the United States bought various minerals in Spain, Portugal and Turkey in order to ensure that they did not become available to the Axis powers. [214]

187. Seizure of assets

Another method of economic intervention involves the impounding or confiscating of assets, including "blocking the use of bank accounts, or of securities in brokerage accounts; preventing the payment of interest or dividends to enemy countries; abrogating patent or royalty rights and so forth." [215]

All Japanese assets in the United States were ordered frozen on July 25, 1941, and Britain and the Netherlands took similar action. Japan had signed a treaty with Axis powers in September 1940, and a treaty of neutrality with the Soviet Union in April 1941; after the German attack in June on Russia, Japan had made demands on the Vichy French government for still more bases in Indochina. Embargoes on shipment of various war materials to Japan had already been declared; petroleum supplies were particularly short. "In these circumstances," writes Thomas A. Bailey, "the Big Freeze was a blow hardly less jarring to the Japanese than their later assault on Pearl Harbor was to the Americans." [216] During World War II the freezing of assets of enemy countries was a standard practice. [217]

Following the nationalization of the Anglo-Iranian Oil Co. by the government of Iran under Mossadegh in 1951, one of Britain's actions was to freeze all Iranian deposits in British banks, thus bringing all of Iran's foreign trade to a standstill. [218]

188. Dumping

This is, writes Professor Schelling, the "deliberate sale [at below standard prices] of a commodity on world markets to depress price and reduce the earnings of another country." [219] It is, he writes, "most uncommon," partly because it is very expensive. The threat to dump agricultural products may be a very serious threat against countries whose economies are highly dependent on export of such products. When the Russians in the early 1950s sought to sell oil abroad, they were wrongly thought to be aiming at disrupting the oil market, and some also thought that the 1953-54 Russian gold sales were intended to cause confusion in foreign financial circles. [220]

Such examples involve government action which is likely to make possible faster and more complete results. However, there has been at least one abortive and somewhat ambitious attempt by private groups to undermine an economic system by dumping on the international market. This complex plan to end slavery in the United States by dumping cotton on the international market was developed, St. Clair Drake reports, by physician Martin R. Delaney and minister Henry Highland Garnet, founders of the African Civilization Society. Under a mandate by the Emigration Convention of 1854, Delaney went to Africa and signed an agreement with the rulers of Yoruba (now part of Nigeria) to allocate land for settlement by Negro freedmen from the United States. The plan was that these ex-slaves would teach Africans how to grow cotton. It would then be dumped on the world market at such a low price as to destroy the economic basis of the Southern plantation system. The result would be freedom for the slaves, cheaper cloth, and skills and prosperity for the Africans. The plans, and British financial support, ended with the outbreak of the Civil War. [221]

189. Selective patronage

As mentioned in the discussion of consumers' boycotts in Chapter Five, nonviolent campaigners in the United States have sometimes urged patronage of named firms, instead of boycott of others, in order to bypass antiboycott laws in some states. Selective patronage campaigns have, however, been used more widely, and with other motives, than those cases suggest. This method has been used in order to reward financially businesses which have pursued an approved policy, especially at times when such a policy was regarded by some as an economic risk.

Garrison and a group of abolitionists in 1834 deliberately chose to patronize a steamboat on the Delaware River which was not segregated, as some were; the route was slower and less direct, but they preferred to encourage the integration policy, and told the captain that because of it he had gained twenty-seven dollars worth of business. *The Liberator* reported their view that if the refusal to use segregated transportation, and the choice of integrated transportation, were "extensively imitated by antislavery men . . . every barrier of caste will soon be overthrown." [222]

When the people of one country are engaged in a struggle to attain independence from another country which has been ruling them, the economic means of action used often include campaigns to purchase the products grown or made in the dependent country. This is often the counterpart of an economic boycott, but in important ways differs from it. The object with a program of selective patronage of a county's own products is not simply to hurt the opponent country economically (which would be compatible with buying the boycotted products from other countries instead), but to build up the dependent country economically. This is sometimes seen as a necessary step toward full independence.

This was an important component of American colonial struggles before 1775. As resistance was organized in 1765 against the Stamp Act, for example, a campaign was launched to promote and develop alternative American products. [223] Although the policy did not originate with him, this movement was given impetus by a pamphlet by Daniel Dulany, who wrote: "By a vigorous Application to Manufactures, the Consequence of Oppression in the Colonies to the Inhabitants of Great Britain would strike Home and immediately . . ." [224] Various societies were organized to promote the manufacture and use of American products in preference to English ones, and descriptions of the domestic products were publicized in the newspapers. These American-made items included scythes, spades, shovels, wallpaper, liquors, cordials, cloth and clothing. The colonial production campaign included the promotion of American linen, made of native-grown-and-spun flax. Factory production of linen grew in Philadelphia and New York, while in Rhode Island women turned to spinning flax in their homes. A variety of American substitutes for tea—sage, sassafras and balm—were promoted as more healthful, and the eating of lamb was abandoned in order not to interfere with the production of American wool. [225]

During the Gandhian struggles against the British rule of India, an important component of the Indian means of action was the movement to increase Indian production and use of her own products. This was called *swadeshi,* and it had a philosophical as well as economic and political ramifications. Gandhi often preferred *swadeshi* to an economic boycott movement which he sometimes, especially earlier in his career, regarded as vindictive. *Swadeshi,* however, positively built up India's economy and independence, and reduced economic dependence on all foreign countries. [226]

Trade unions in the United States have often urged the purchase of products bearing the union label, as a means of supporting higher wages and improved working conditions. Myers and Laidler defined the union label as "a device which organized labor has developed to encourage the purchase of goods made under union conditions." [227] Looking something like trademarks, insignia, coats of arms, and the like, the union label is attached directly to the product where possible, or displayed where the item is sold, or shown on the packaging. Its presence shows that the article has been "produced by union labor under conditions required of union shops." [228] Trade unionists have been especially urged to purchase products bearing the union label, and conventions in the 1930s in the United States used to have a "union-label roll call" in which delegates using particular union-made items were asked to stand as the list of products was called. The union label began in 1875 among cigar factory workers in California and was originally used to identify cigars made by white workers. [229] One of the departments created in the merged A.F.L.-C.I.O. was a Union Label Department, in Washington, D.C., which provides lists of union-label products. [230] After the grape growers of California began signing union contracts with the United Farm Workers in 1970, the union label on boxes of grapes sold throughout the country became very important in determining which grapes should be purchased by supporters of the grape workers and which should still be boycotted.

190. Alternative markets[231]

Illegal or "black" markets, especially in wartime or during occupations, are usually associated with exploitative prices and selfish objectives.

In some cases, however, alternative illegal channels of buying and selling food and various other supplies may be created as a form of economic intervention. Apart from helping to meet needs of the populace and keeping goods out of the enemy's hands, there may be a wider political significance in such action. Against a totalitarian regime's attempts to control all economic life, thwarting that control by the maintainance of independent channels of distribution may become an important resistance objective.

This method has been used at least once in a struggle during an occupation, the German occupation of Norway. A.K. Jameson reports:

> The high moral tone of the whole movement is clearly shown in the way the black market was run. Producers of foodstuffs were supposed to hand over all their produce to government distributing agencies, but in fact they succeeded in keeping back quite a lot. In contrast to what happened elsewhere, however, this store was sold secretly at prices very little higher than those officially fixed and much of it was bought up by employers for the benefit of employees and by individuals for the maintainance of those hiding from the authorities. Practically no private profit was made from these transactions and hence the market had not the same demoralizing effects as it had in other occupied countries, and it ceased the moment the occupation was over. [232]

It is difficult without detailed research to judge whether this report may be too sweeping, although in any case it illustrates the potential of this method. In a wider discussion of production during this period, not limited to foodstuffs, Professor Erling Petersen points out that while many products were saved for the Norwegian economy by withholding them from the regular market, "in many cases" the main consideration was to get the high prices of the black market, with the "moral excuse" of keeping the products out of German hands. [233]

191. Alternative transportation system

Side by side with the boycott of a public transportation system, a parallel substitute system has occasionally been improvised. This occurred in the Montgomery, Alabama, bus boycott, already described in detail, almost immediately after its beginning. "In the early stages of the protest the problem of transportation demanded most of our attention," Dr. Martin Luther King, Jr., later wrote. For the first few days Negro taxi companies followed an agreement to carry passengers for the ten cent bus fare, but a law which set a minimum taxi fare of forty-five cents required that other arrangements be made. Drawing on experience during an earlier bus boycott in Baton Rouge, Louisiana, the Montgomery group quickly decided to set up a volunteer private car pool. The new transportation system established forty-eight dispatch and forty-two pick-up stations by December 13. Dr. King reports: "In a few days this system was working astonishingly well" and even impressed the white segregationists. During the next year fifteen new station wagons were purchased for the transport system.

The parallel transportation system was clearly seen by the Montgomery city officials and the bus company as a serious problem in itself. Four times the insurance on the vehicles was canceled and under the administration of Mayor Gayle the city's legal department took court action to ban the motor pool. But the United States Supreme Court decision that Alabama's state and local bus segregation laws were unconstitutional came before the local court's temporary injunction against the motor pool.[234]

192. Alternative economic institutions[235]

Although not all economic institutions created or used by nonviolent actionists constitute economic intervention, they do so when the economic institution is itself used in a conflict situation as a method of wielding power or influence. These new institutions may be concerned with production, ownership, or distribution of economic goods. The objectives may not only be economic but also be social and political.

For example, when consumers' or producers' cooperatives are engaged in conflict with capitalist or State industries, or when the cooperatives are being deliberately developed and expanded to replace the existing economic system, or part of it, they constitute economic intervention. For example, after the turn of the century the Swedish cooperative society *Kooperativa Förbundet,* having failed to lower the price of margarine by boycotting the products of the margarine cartel factories, purchased a small margarine factory, and later built a larger one, in order to enter the market itself at lower prices. The result was a sixty percent cut in the price of margerine, which saved Swedish consumers about two million dollars annually.[236] During the 1920s and 1930s K.F. bought or built plants for making other products, including light bulbs, tires, fertilizers, pottery and building materials. Usually when they captured fifteen to twenty-five percent of the market monopoly prices were broken.[237]

In Italy after 1890 the "Charity and Christian Economy" branch of the Roman Catholic activist organization *Opera dei Congressi* attempted to build up "a network of cooperatives, peasant unions, friendly societies, insurance and rural credit institutions." With continued expansion, these had the potential of becoming "the framework, prefabricated and tested by experience, of a new Catholic state, rising from the ruins of liberalism." [238] By 1912 this branch had 360,000 members.

The Southwest Alabama Farmers Cooperative Association, organized in 1967 by veterans of the Selma civil rights march, arranged for marketing of produce through cooperative channels. This, writes Michael Miles in the *New Republic,* "disrupted the system of exploitation of the black farmer, which depends on the identification of each farmer's cotton at the warehouse so that it can immediately be appropriated by his creditors . . ." [239] Other Southern black organizations attempting economic intervention include the Poor People's Corp., (Jackson, Mississippi), the Federation of Southern Cooperatives, and Crawfordville (Florida) Enterprises. [240] Such organizations have often encountered strong opposition but nevertheless increased the economic well-being and self-determination of their members.

POLITICAL INTERVENTION

This last subclass of methods of nonviolent intervention includes seven which are clearly political in form. The first five of these are acts by citizens, individually or in small or large groups, who attempt to intervene by disrupting the administrative or enforcement agencies of the government. The sixth method, work-on without collaboration, is undertaken by the government employees and officials, while the last one, dual sovereignty and parallel government, involves the shift of loyalties by citizens to a new rival government. All of these, in differing degrees and ways, intervene to disturb the working of the opponent's government and even to challenge its existence.

193. Overloading of administrative systems [241]

Administrative systems of governments may be overloaded by excessive compliance in providing them with diverse types of information which may be directly or indirectly related to their responsibilities, or in making an excessive number of enquiries of them, or by providing them with excessive numbers of suggestions, protests or statements. The resulting overloading of the administrative system may make the continuance of operations difficult or may slow its capacity to deal with its normal activities. This type of action is particularly likely to happen where the law or regulations which the administrative unit is implementing require frequent revision of data concerning personnel or other matters, or when complex systems of rules and regulations to be followed are subject to frequent change.

This method—called the comply-in—was applied in the United States in the spring of 1970 by the antiwar movement, as people were urged to comply with all the usually neglected provisions of the law concerning personal information. The *New York Times* quoted Mrs. Trudi Young, spokesman for the New Mobilization Committee to End the War in Vietnam, to this effect: "The [Selective Service] law also requires registrants to inform the draft boards within ten days of any change in address or status. This means changes in religion, mental attitude and everything else." Although almost entirely ignored by the Selective Service System itself, the law applies its regulations to all males born after August 30, 1922, not just to those up to twenty-five years of age. Mrs. Young continued:

> We want everyone to take this law so seriously that they inform their board of every single change, even if they're over age or have already completed their service. This means wives, mothers, and friends as well. They should submit documents attesting to any change in the status of a registrant. The Selective Service just cannot stand up, administratively, to absolute obedience to the draft law.

The paper quoted a Selective Service spokesman as saying that if thousands of overage men followed the law to the letter, "Lord help us." [242] This type of action is closely related to the "working-to-rule" strike described in Chapter Six.

In Massachusetts in June 1970, following the invasion of Cambodia by United States forces and the resultant protests, Colonel Paul Feeney of the Selective Service System in the state in an interview described the flood of mail which had poured into their offices:

> Some of the mail says "I've changed my status, I've moved from the first floor to the third floor." Or we'll get a letter saying, "I'm going to Europe." A few days later we'll get another letter saying, "I've changed my mind. I am not going to Europe."

One official estimated that perhaps a thousand man-hours had been lost by handling the excess mail. Officials ordered seven hundred thousand postcards which could quickly, yet legally, be used to respond to the increased quantity of mail. [243]

194. Disclosing identities of secret agents[244]

Where secret police and undercover political agents are employed, one means of dealing with them when they are discovered has been to publish their names, perhaps with other details, photographs and the like; this has the effect of making it extraordinarily difficult for those particular persons to continue their activities as secret agents. This may be applied to political agents which have infiltrated, or have attempted to infiltrate, resistance organizations, and may constitute an alternative to murdering them, a frequent practice by resistance movements in Nazi-occupied countries during World War II.

The publication of names and descriptions of slaveowners seeking their runaway slaves, described earlier in this chapter under nonviolent harassment, is very close to this method. In other cases the various other described forms of personal harassment were not used but placards were posted describing paid slave hunters; these instances are clearly within this method. Such a case occurred in Boston in 1850 when two slave hunters arrived to seize William and Ellen Craft; with the identities and objective of the hunters openly revealed, their effectiveness was reduced, and this helped to induce the slave hunters to leave town.[245]

In 1969 the *Los Angeles Free Press,* which opposed imprisonment for the use of nonaddictive drugs, published the names of over fifty state narcotics agents with their addresses and telephone numbers. The newspaper saw this as a political act, although officials took a different view. The California Attorney General then obtained an injunction against publication of more "confidential" documents of the state Justice Department, and the exposed agents as a group filed a suit for $25,000,000 against the newspaper, while the Attorney General filed another damage suit for the state.[246]

195. Seeking imprisonment

Imprisonment in civil disobedience is normally a secondary consequence of the peaceful breaking of a law or regulation, which act is seen to be of much greater importance than the imprisonment. However, on occasion imprisonment may be sought by the nonviolent actionists as a *primary* objective, especially when this is done in very large numbers. Actionists may deliberately disobey a particular regulation in order to be imprisoned, and may ask to be arrested even though police select others for arrest or even though the persons were not present on the original occasion. At times the objective is to fill the jails; that is called a jail-in.

Requests to be arrested usually occur as an expression of solidarity with associates already under arrest, but the intent may also be to demonstrate a lack of fear of arrest, to obtain the release of those already arrested, to clog the courts or fill the prisons, or to obtain wider publicity and increased resistance. During the Norwegian teachers' noncooperation struggle in 1942, the day after Quisling had personally stormed and raged at the teachers in the Stabekk school and ordered their arrest, teachers who had that day been absent went to the prison and demanded to be arrested also. [247]

In January 1959 women supporters of Dr. Banda and the Nyasaland African Congress rejected police orders to disperse as they marched toward the Zomba Government House to hear the results of talks between Dr. Banda and the Governor. An initial advance was followed by a clash and beatings of the women, and finally another advance;

> . . . in the end, the police arrested a few of them. The remainder protested. They began to protest physically and insisted that if some are arrested, then all must be arrested. . . So the police arrested them —36 in all. [248]

In France in 1959 a group under the auspices of *Action Civique Nonviolent* went to the Thol detainee camp, where North Africans were held without trial or hearing, and requested that they, too, be placed in the camp as witnesses against the flagrant miscarriage of justice. [249]

In 1961, in connection with a wave of freedom rides against racial segregation on buses, C.O.R.E. members, together with many volunteers, began to fill Mississippi jails—the jail-in being "aimed at making segregationist practices so expensive and inconvenient as to become unfeasible." The flood of prisoners cost the city of Jackson, Mississippi, alone over a million dollars in increased enforcement and imprisonment bills. [250] James Peck, a veteran of many nonviolent civil rights struggles, reports that the term jail-in was coined by newspapermen in February 1961 to refer to the increasing number of antisegregation Southern nonviolent student actionists who "to emphasize the injustice of being arrested for protesting racial descrimination, chose to remain in jail rather than pay fines or go out on bail." [251]

On March 25, 1960, four days after the shootings at Sharpeville, Philip Kgosana, a young Pan-Africanist leader led a march of 1,500 Africans from Langa location to the police station in nearby Capetown and demanded their arrest for refusing to carry the required passes. The police chief, however, turned them away, and they went home in an orderly manner. [252]

At the time of the arrest and trial of six members of the Committee of 100 in Britain in 1962, several other members of the Committee offered themselves for arrest as being equally guilty. [253]

In February 1964 Southern Rhodesian African women protested the lack of government action in providing roads, bridges and schools in the Tanda reserve by refusing to dip their cattle as required. Of the 172 women arrested, 150 refused to pay the imposed fine, choosing instead to serve the prison sentence. Another group of 158 was remanded for later sentencing. Three hundred more women also marched to the Meyo Court demanding to be placed under arrest. They were reinforced by still another angry group of 300 women, who arrived later with the same demand. [254]

196. Civil disobedience of "neutral" laws

Although civil disobedience is usually the disobedience of laws which are regarded as inherently immoral or otherwise illegitimate, at times nonviolent actionists may disobey or ignore laws and regulations which are regarded as morally "neutral." This is most likely to occur in the advanced stages of a nonviolent revolutionary movement (as in India under the British), or in cases where the nature of modern government, or of the issue itself, makes it difficult to noncooperate with or to disobey a law directly related to the grievance. An example of this was the issue of nuclear weapons in Britain in 1962.

In all modern States there are laws which exist simply to help the government exercise its authority, regulate the citizenry, and carry out its functions, but which neither prohibit people from committing some "inhuman" or "immoral" act, nor are themselves regarded as unjust or oppressive. These "neutral" laws are often of a regulatory character. While disobedience of laws which prohibit infliction of harm on other people does not fall within civil disobedience of any type, these "neutral" laws are violated in this extreme type of civil disobedience. The point then is not that the disobeyed law is itself wrong, but that the actionists have either rebelled against the government, or have found no other strong way to express their grievance.

Gandhi regarded this type of civil disobedience as justified at times, but as "a most dangerous weapon." It should be postponed, he maintained, when the opponent is in difficulties; at such times the *satyagrahi* ought not to harass him but rather seek to convert him. However, when the government is regarded as having become so unjust as to have forfeited all obligation to obedience, and the intention has become to destroy the government by noncooperation and disobedience, this type of civil disobedience may be justified. Gandhi believed that then the breach of such laws would not harm the people, but would merely make it more difficult for the government to carry out its administration, and that, when undertaken on a mass scale, such a breach would contribute to the government's dissolution.[255] This stage has thus far rarely been reached in actual campaigns, but during the 1930-31 Indian campaign it was closely approximated on several occasions.[256]

197. Work-on without collaboration

This method involves determined persistence by civil servants, government officials, and ordinary citizens in carrying out the legally established policies, programs and duties in indifference to, or defiance of, contrary measures from a usurping regime, which has seized the State apparatus in either a *coup d'etat* or a foreign invasion. This method thus differs from a selective refusal of assistance by government aides, a method of political noncooperation, which is a refusal to carry out particular instructions or orders, though the two methods may be related. The emphasis here is on the deliberate continuation of legitimate duties and tasks.

The clearest theoretical presentations of this method have been made by Dr. Theodor Ebert in discussion of the strategic problems of civilian defense—i.e., the prepared use of nonviolent action for purposes of national defense. Ebert writes: "Everyone should remain at his job and do his duty under the law and in the tradition of his country until physically removed by the occupation power." This would involve, Ebert writes:

> . . . a strict refusal at all levels to recognize the usurper's legality and to obey his orders. The constitution and the laws of the land should be defended as legitimate, and the occupiers regarded as unauthorized private persons whose orders must be ignored. Every member of parliament, minister, civil servant and ordinary citizen would become, in the event of occupation, a soldier on guard at his place of work. *In general, the emphasis should be more on a determined continuation of the existing social and political system, than on resignations and strikes* [italics added].

This method would thus involve "the deliberate continuation of ordinary social roles according to one's legal status . . ."[257]

> Dismissals by the new authorities are to be ignored and people are to attend to their work until physically restrained from so doing. When a leader is removed, his legitimate representative should take his place; and where no such person is available, the subordinates and

assistants are to act on their own responsibility, the usurper's appointees being ignored.[258]

Ebert argues that this method would cause the usurper "more technical and psychological difficulties than a strike or voluntary resignations," reduce opportunities for collaboration, force the opponent to leave legitimate holders of positions alone or face the difficult task of replacing an entire administration (especially difficult on the local level), reduce the risk of social and industrial chaos which is run in a prolonged general strike, and, finally, by the continuing struggle illustrate the objective of the conflict: "to ensure a society's right to order its affairs free from outside coercion."[259]

One interpretation of official policy which is very close to the work-on but not identical with it was issued in May 1943 in the occupied Netherlands. This was written by Bosch Ridder van Rosenthal, former Comissioner of the Queen for the province of Utrecht and a leading resistance leader. Rosenthal wrote a "Commentary," which was published in the underground press on the "Directives of 1937," issued by the Colijn government; Warmbrunn describes these as "a set of somewhat vague secret instructions for the conduct of civil servants in the event of a military occupation." He summarized them as instructing civil servants to continue their work if their service to the Netherlands population was greater than to the enemy; otherwise they should resign. The "Directive of 1937" assumed, however, that the occupier would respect the rules of the Hague Convention, and were so vague that decisions were left to each individual.[260] Also these directives were kept so secret that Prime Minister Gerbrandy (with the exile government in London) apparently did not learn of them until 1943![261]

However, in addition to urging officials to refuse to carry out actions which conflicted with the interests of the population, Rosenthal's "Commentary" urged them not to resign but "to wait for possible dismissal for their failure to implement 'illegal' German orders." "The assumption was that the German authorities might not dismiss all officials practicing such passive resistance." The "Commentary" also emphasized that the legal government of the Netherlands was the one in exile in London, and it was to it that loyalty was due. Specific impermissible types of assistance by civil servants to the Germans were also enumerated.[262]

On a minor scale many of the Norwegian teachers in the case described in Chapter Two conducted a work-on wthout collaboration; those who were not arrested when they returned to their schools repudiated membership in the fascist teachers' organization, explained to their classes their higher responsibilities, and continued to teach without regard to new fascist "obligations." [263]

198. Dual sovereignty and parallel government

This method involves the creation of a new government, or continued loyalty to an existing rival government to that of the opponent. If the parallel government receives overwhelming support from the populace, it may replace the opponent's established government. This extreme development of alternative political institutions has only rarely been deliberately initiated and developed; more commonly it has been an unanticipated product of a massive resistance or revolutionary struggle. Although the examples here refer to this type of situation, comparable cases of parallel government may also occur when the population of an occupied country continues to obey the legal government deposed by the invader and to deny the legitimacy of the invader's regime and hence disobey it.

When a nonviolent revolutionary movement seeking the abolition, not reform, of a regime, and possessing extensive popular support, reaches an advanced stage, it threatens the stability of the old regime by depriving it of the obedience and cooperation of the populace. At this point, the shifting of loyalty to a new authority and the creation, or acceptance, of some type of a parallel government is a necessary next step if the movement is to prove successful. This is both a logical consequence of the cooperation which has developed among the resisters themselves, and a step taken to maximize the impact of noncooperation and defiance against the old regime. A new sovereignty thus begins to replace the established one and a new political structure evolves to claim the support and allegiance of the populace. Although this tendency may be present without conscious intent, the resisters often deliberately attempt to establish a parallel structure to advance their policies. [264] A parallel government with widespread popular support can take over the governmental functions and eventually squeeze the tottering regime out of existence. [265]

This general phenomenon has occurred in a variety of situations and is by no means a product of twentieth century revolutions. Important elements of a parallel government emerged in 1575-77, for example, during the Netherlands' struggle against the Spanish king. [266] The characteristics of parallel government often occur during struggles of national liberation (especially at the time of a declaration of independence), and in domestic revolutions against a dictatorship or social system. As Crane Brinton has pointed out: "This is at once an institution and a process; or better, a process that works through a very similar set of institutions."

When another and conflicting chain of institutions provides another and conflicting set of decisions, then you have a dual sovereignty. Within the same society, two sets of institutions, leaders, and laws demand obedience, not in one single respect, but in the whole interwoven series of actions which make up life for the average man.

. . . the legal government finds opposed to it, once the first steps in actual revolution have been taken, not merely hostile individuals and parties—this any government finds—but a rival government, better organized, better staffed, better obeyed. . . . At a given revolutionary crisis they step naturally and easily into the place of the defeated government. [267]

The outcome of a contest between rival governments in ultimate terms is usually determined by their relative ability to procure the necessary support and obedience from the populace. This contest for obedience occurred, for example, when both the Japanese and the "Border Government" were trying to rule in North China in the late 1930s:

In this extraordinary situation there is a sense in which the rival govments were concerned . . . more with the problem of creating new bases for political authority, new concepts of political obligation, new relations between government and people, than with the mere exercise of authority. [268]

Parallel government may develop in revolutions in which violence plays an important role, as well as in conflicts in which violence is noticeably absent. Although the new government may continue to use violence after its victory, the emergence of dual sovereignty and parallel government is *not* intrinsically associated with violence and in fact depends almost entirely on the voluntary withdrawal of authority, support and obedience from the old regime and their award to a new body. Dual sovereignty and parallel government may thus be classified as a method of nonviolent action and occur in revolutionary struggles in which violence is largely or entirely absent.

Professor Brinton notes that the general phenomenon occurred in England in the conflict between Charles and the Long Parliament (albeit in the context of a civil war) during the 1640s. He mentions also the struggle of the American colonists, both before and after 1776, and the rival groupings of the French Revolution. [269]

Various organs of parallel government were of extreme importance in the American colonists' struggle. The Continental Association—the program of organized nonviolent resistance adopted by the First Continental Congress in the autumn of 1774, which its authors described as "a nonimportation, non-consumption, and non-exportation agreement"[270] illustrated this development well, while parallel government found also organizational expression in a variety of alternative quasi-governmental bodies. Gipson writes:

> Although the First Continental Congress was dissolved on October 26, 1774, the measures it had adopted were held by the patriots to be nothing less than the supreme law of the land, taking precedence over any measure or pronouncement of the individual colonial assemblies, not to mention the laws of Parliament relating to America. Therefore, it was not surprising that the Association adopted by the Congress was entered into and enforced with a high degree of unanimity.[271]

The extremity of the collapse of British colonial power at least in certain colonies *before* the War of Independence is testified to by two British governors. Governor Dunmore of Virginia wrote to Lord Dartmouth on December 24, 1774, that the Continental Association was being enforced "with the greatest rigour" and that "the Laws of Congress" (i.e., the First Continental Congress) were given by Virginians "marks of reverence which they never bestowed on their legal Government, or the Laws proceeding from it." Dunmore added:

> I have discovered no instance where the interposition of Government, in the feeble state to which it is reduced, could serve any other purpose than to suffer the disgrace of a disappointment, and thereby afford matter of great exultation to its enemies and increase their influence over the minds of the people.[272]

On September 23, 1775, Governor Wright of Georgia wrote in similar but more extreme terms, complaining also of intimidation and threats of destruction of property: "Government totally Annihilated, and Assumed by Congresses, Councils and Committees, and the greatest Acts of Tyranny, Oppression, Gross Insults &c &c &c committed, and not the least means of Protection, Support, or even Personal Safety . . ." Wright added on October 14: "The poison has Infected the whole Province, and neither Law, Government, or Regular Authority have any Weight or are at all attended to."[273] In some cases existing legal organs of local or provincial government *under* the British system were turned into parts of a system of parallel government *against* the British system, and in other cases new bodies helped serve this role, representative ones (such as certain provincial assemblies and the Continental Congresses) or self-selected ones (for example, the Sons of Liberty).[274]

Usually parallel government has been but one of many methods and types of action which emerge in the course of a very large struggle. There is at least one instance, however, in which during a significant period of a struggle this method became the predominant method of action relied upon by those opposed to the established order. This was in Rhode Island in 1841-42, during what became known as "Dorr's Rebellion," or, far less accurately, as "Dorr's War." [275]

In 1841 Rhode Island's government was still operating under the Charter granted by King Charles II in 1663. Under that Charter, representation in the legislature took no account of the shifts of population and the growth of certain cities; even more seriously, built-in property qualifications for voting disenfranchised three of every five adult white males (to say nothing of anyone else). From 1796 on, repeated attempts had been made to obtain a new constitution, or reapportionment in the legislature, or an extension of the suffrage, if not to all adult white citizens, at least to a few more. All these efforts had been defeated, obstructed or ignored by the legislature or the property-owning voters (called "freemen"). In January 1841 the General Assembly passed over the call to expand the suffrage and responded favorably to an appeal for a constitutional convention—but the delegates to it were apportioned exactly like the existing General Assembly, and existing restrictions on who could vote applied also to election of the delegates. Thus two of the main grievances were built into the convention, and power was clearly intended to be kept in the same hands.

In April, May and July mass meetings of suffragists were held in Providence and Newport. At the Providence meeting on July 5 a resolution was passed demanding a constitutional convention and expressing determination to put into effect a new constitution. On July 20 it was announced that on August 28 delegates to such a convention would be elected by all adult male citizens resident in the state; the constitutional convention would meet at Providence on October 4. Over 7,500 of over 25,000 potential voters—which included resident adult male citizens whether or not franchised under the constitution—participated in the election of delegates. The new constitution—called the "People's Constitution"—was completed by the Convention in mid-November; it extended voting to all adult resident white male citizens, reapportioned representation in the General Assembly, increased the separation between the legislative and judicial branches, and made certain other changes. In December 1841, in a referendum in which all resident adult white male citizens could take part, the new constitution was ratified by a vote of nearly 14,000 to 52 (with more than 10,000 potential voters not participating).

PART TWO: METHODS

But this was not the whole story, for another convention which had been called by the legislature in January—the "Freemen's Convention"—had also met in November; finally in mid-February 1842 it completed its new draft constitution. This also extended the suffrage to adult white male resident citizens but only reapportioned seats in the House of Representatives. A few weeks before, however, on January 12, the People's Convention had reassembled and declared its "People's Constitution" to be in force. Under attack by extremists on both sides, the "Freemen's Constitution," with the same enlarged electorate as had voted in the other referendum, was narrowly defeated by less than 700 votes of a total of about 16,700. The state Supreme Court unofficially denounced the "People's Constitution" as illegal, and in March a repressive "Algerine Law" was passed. This law imposed severe penalties, including the charge of treason, for people who participated in any elections not in accordance with previous statutes; even persons voting in elections held under the "People's Constitution" were to be punished.

Claiming popular sovereignty in a republic, the suffragists argued that their constitution was legal. Governor Samuel King of Rhode Island appealed to President Tyler, who replied on April 11 that he could not anticipate a revolutionary movement but that should an actual insurrection take place, Federal aid would be forthcoming; he also denied his right to judge on the merits of the conflict in the state, but added that he would continue to recognize the established government until advised that another had legally and peaceably been adopted by both the authorities and the people of the state. [276]

On April 18 elections were held for state offices under the "People's Constitution," including for members of both houses of the new legislature; all candidates were elected unanimously, but the leader of the movement, Harvard graduate Thomas Wilson Dorr, received only a little over 6,300 votes for governor, which did not help establish his authority. President Tyler's letter, the repressive Algerine Law, and perhaps other factors had caused many persons who were undecided to shift over to the "law and order" party. Many suffragists also weakened in their determination to go through with the new substitute constitution and government, and several of the earlier nominees of the suffragists for that election had even withdrawn.

On April 20, two days after the "People's Election," the regular election according to the regular Charter took place, and Governor King defeated his challenger, General Carpenter, who was originally to have been the candidate on the "People's ticket" by a margin of a little more than two to one. About seven thousand property-owning "freemen" had voted.

Despite the severity of the challenge by the new constitution and the elected substitute government, the established government was cautious in repressing the rival group for, as A.M. Mowry points out, they would have been acting against 180 of the state's most prominent citizens, backed by at least a large minority of the citizens of Rhode Island, over six thousand of whom had also laid themselves open to prosecution by voting in the "People's Election." [277] The Charter government was not certain that the state militia would come to its aid. [278] The situation was clearly regarded by both sides as grave, and there were signs both sides were preparing for military action.

On May 3, 1842, after Thomas Dorr and elected members of the new General Assembly paraded through the streets of Providence with a militia escort, they were inaugurated, and the Assembly received an inaugural address from Governor Dorr. The new officials, however, did not even attempt to gain access to and control of the State House, or to install a new judiciary. In his history Mowry says that it would have been "a peaceful, as well as an easy, task" to take possession of the State House, but instead of doing so the new legislature met in an empty foundry building, and after two days of action adjourned for two months. They had requested Governor Dorr to make known to the President, Houses of Congress, and governors of the states those changes which had taken place: they proclaimed the new government as duly organized, called for obedience, and repealed the Algerine Law and various other acts. Dorr later wrote that the failure to replace the old government by occupying the State House was "fatal." Mowry writes that "the old charter government had lost its force, and could accomplish little; the new charter government had yet to organize; and the charter officials were at Newport." [279]

However, on May 4, at Newport, the government elected under the old Charter met and organized, and passed a resolution against the new constitution and government under Governor Dorr; they particularly called attention to "the strong military force" supporting Dorr (the fairly small militia escort at the inauguration, which body had pledged obedience to Dorr as the state commander-in-chief). On this basis, the Charter legislature declared that an "insurrection" existed in Rhode Island and called for Federal intervention. [280]

Governor King sent a delegation to see President Tyler. Governor Dorr also sent various documents to President Tyler. Tyler, however, did not wish to intervene at the moment. On May 7, Dorr, wanted for arrest by the rival government, secretly left for Washington, D.C., to plead the case of the People's government in person, leaving his government in Rhode Island without effective leadership. During the brief stay of

Dorr and his colleagues in Washington, they scored no tangible successes with either executive or congressional officials.

In Rhode Island, within a week of the adjournment of the General Assembly under the People's Constitution, the new rival government was in a state of collapse. Arrests and resignations depleted its ranks.

There seems to have been no consideration given, either at an earlier or at this critical stage, to a campaign of noncooperation with the Charter government and persistent obedience to the People's government. Nor apparently was there any consideration of the possible negative effects that even the appearance of military action might have on many Rhode Islanders, or on Federal intervention (as President Tyler had already indicated). Instead, on his return from Washington, Governor Dorr sought support from the Democrats of Tammany Hall, and while in New York he explored the possibilities of military assistance from other states. He received offers from two commanders of regiments of New York state militia, and wrote the governors of Connecticut and Maine for military aid in case of Federal intervention.[281]

Arriving in Providence on May 16, Governor Dorr was welcomed by a crowd of about 1,200 persons, a quarter of whom were armed. The outcome of the contest was still unsettled, and even the loyalty of the militia was undetermined. There were no attempts to arrest Dorr on the sixteenth or seventeenth. Dorr then clearly shifted to military action, even if it was slightly comic. In a swift move, two field pieces were seized without a fight, but his men forgot to take the balls and shot for the cannons. The Charter government called the militia of Providence to readiness and summoned other outside companies to report to the city. Dorr determined to seize first the arsenal, then several other buildings and armories; otherwise, he thought, the whole campaign was lost.

About midnight on the seventeenth, with about 230 men and two cannons, Dorr's forces set out for the city arsenal in the midst of great confusion and a heavy fog, with many people flooding the streets, bells ringing, and uncertainty as to who was friend and who foe. When the arsenal commander refused to surrender, Dorr ordered the cannons fired, but either someone had tampered with them or the damp from the fog was as effective, and they only flashed twice but did not fire. Had they worked, and had troops in the well-armed stone arsenal returned fire, the attackers would quite probably have been annihilated. As the night went on, Dorr's volunteers melted away until by daylight not more than fifty remained. At about eight o'clock Dorr was given a letter stating that all the officers of his government who lived in Providence had resigned. Dorr was advised to flee and this he did, though later he reportedly regretted having done so. Members of the People's legislature repudiated the military actions. After a brief rally of his forces in Glocester late in June, Dorr escaped to New Hampshire.

While the tide of reaction was still strong, a new constitutional convention for Rhode Island was assembled that November. The Charter General Assembly authorized increased representation for Providence and Smithfield, and permitted all native-born adult male citizens to vote for delegates. The new constitution, with limited reapportionment, and a somewhat expanded but complicated system of suffrage rights, was adopted in November and went into effect in May 1843. Dorr's supporters boycotted the referendum, while many diehard supporters of the Charter opposed the constitution as too liberal. About 7,000 men, of a voters' list of over 25,000, voted in the referendum. Dorr returned to Providence to surrender in October 1843 and was sentenced to life imprisonment. After one year the new governor signed a bill releasing him, and in 1851 the General Assembly restored his civil and political rights. Despite the state Supreme Court's protest, the General Assembly in 1854 reversed his conviction for treason.

From the perspective of nonviolent action, this case illustrates the deliberate development of a parallel government by popular assembly and referendum and also its initial operation, although the events do not show how the later struggle might have been conducted nonviolently. The introduction of military action to defend the new constitution and government, and Dorr's appeals for Federal support, seem to have been remarkably ineffective. The events even suggest that the threat and use of military action were counterproductive. They may have caused those people who were wavering in loyalty to support the Charter government, and may also have caused even existing supporters of the People's government to withdraw, leaving it still weaker.

Some other very clear examples of parallel government occur in the Russian 1905 Revolution and in the 1917 Russian Revolution prior to the Bolshevik seizure of power from both the Provisional Government and the independent *soviets*. [282] The most famous such organ of the 1905 Revolution was the Council of Workingmen's Deputies of St. Petersburg, "at once general strike Committee, communal administration, organizer of nationwide revolt, temporary parliament of labor in particular and the Russian people in general, rival governmental power." [283]

For the St. Petersburg Soviet had astonishingly maintained itself as in some sort a rival authority to the government. It was to the soviet that the working population turned for advice or aid in the chaotic conditions in the capital; it was the soviet which gave instructions in the workers' quarters. Its executive committee negotiated directly with Prime Minister Witte on problems of transport and food supplies. The government's orders to the postal and telegraph workers could be issued only through the soviet. Even the city duma was obliged to carry out the instructions of the soviet, most conspicuously in allocating funds for the relief of the strikers' families.

For the time being at least the government could not but acquiesce. But so paralysing a form of dual power in the capital could not continue indefinitely. [284]

On trial for his role in the revolution, Trotsky told the court that the Council of Workingmen's Deputies "was neither more nor less than the self-governing organ of the revolutionary masses, *an organ of state power* . . . " [285]

This was by no means the only expression of parallel government during that revolution, however, as the Bureau of *Zemstvo* Congresses also exercised considerable authority at one time. [286] Entire districts established their own administrations independent of the central government, [287] especially certain nationalities as happened in Georgia, where the parallel government was maintained into 1906, [288] and the Mongol government which was elected and obeyed for some months toward the end of 1905. [289] Prior to these events, Marxist thought had given relatively little attention to this method as a means of carrying out a revolution, despite an early comment by Marx [290] and some significant discussion by the Menshevik Axélrod just prior to the 1905 revolution. [291]

Strong tendencies to develop alternative sovereignty and parallel government have emerged, unanticipated and unplanned, during large-scale nonviolent struggles, such as Western general strikes and Indian independence movements. Hiller, for example, noted the development of control organizations among strikers and wrote:

Control organizations, whether representing attempts to assert authority and enforce it by physical coercion or to "maintain order" while practicing economic non-participation, constitute usurpation of governmental functions. For example, the enrolling of an independent police force responsible to an upstart authority is a revolutionary act, and, if community-wide and permanent, constitutes an actual revolution. It signifies a new integration of society around the competing center of dominance in the social body. [292]

Crook points out that during the 1919 general strike in Winnipeg, Canada, a citizens' committee of one thousand ran the fire, water and police services, which is evidence that it had some of the qualities of a parallel government.[293] Hiller cites further examples of this kind of development during the general strikes in Seattle and the Italian general strike of 1904.[294]

Although the British General Strike of 1926 was not intended or pursued as a revolutionary strike for overthrowing the government, W.H. Crook concludes that:

> There can be just as little question that the *orders* of the General Council, as interpreted by the various strike committees throughout the nation and as put into practice by them, did logically constitute an attempt to set up a rival authority to that of the local and national governing bodies. This is particularly evident in the matter of *permits*. The General Council had apparently intended that the workers themselves should carry on, if not actually organize, the distribution of food and absolute essentials of life . . . . The Government, through Mr. Churchill, had tendered an emphatic refusal to enter "into partnership with a rival Government."[295]

The nascent forms of a parallel government were nearly or actually reached on several occasions in local situations during the Indian struggles, especially the 1930-31 campaign. In late April 1930, after the refusal of two platoons of the Garhwali Regiment to support the police against the nonviolent volunteers, troops were removed from Peshawar city completely. The Congress Committee then assumed virtual control of the city, including issuing instructions and patrolling the streets at night, for nine days. A contemporary British report also described the success of the local Muslim nonviolence organization, the Khudai Khidmatgar, in collecting land revenue owed to the government.[296] The authority of the old *panchayats* was restored in many places to replace the British judicial system. A program of "national education" was intended to replace the British schools.[297] In some cities volunteer corps were organized to direct traffic and to act as policemen. The Bombay Congress Committee worked out its own system of taxation for those citizens who would cooperate, and in a few instances even fined financial interests when they diverged from Congress policies.

Speaking of Bombay during the early period of the 1930 struggle, an eyewitness, H.N. Brailsford, wrote:

Bombay, one soon perceived, had two governments. To the British Government, with all its apparatus of legality and power, there still were loyal the European population, the Indian sepoys who wore its uniform, and the elder generation of the Moslem minority. The rest of Bombay had transferred its allegiance to one of His Majesty's too numerous prisoners. In Mahatma Gandhi's name Congress ruled this city. Its lightest nod was obeyed. It could fill the streets, when it pleased, and as often as it pleased, with tens of thousands of men and women, who shouted its watchwords. It could with a word close the shutters of every shop in the bazaar. When it proclaimed a *hartal* (a day of mourning), which it did all but every week, by way of protest against some act of the other government, silence descended upon the streets, and even the factories closed their doors. Only with its printed permit on a scrap of coloured paper, dare a driver urge his bullocks and his bales past its uniformed sentries, who kept watch, day and night, in every lane and alley of the business quarter. They had their guardrooms. Their inspectors entered every warehouse and shop, and watched every cotton-press. They would even confiscate forbidden goods, which a merchant had tried to smuggle past their patrols.[298]

At such points the program of building alternative institutions may culminate in a major challenge to the existence of the old institutions. In Gandhi's view this did not necessarily mean violence, for he repeatedly emphasized that any parallel government ought not rely on the usual governmental coercive powers but upon strictly nonviolent methods and popular support of the populace.[299]

In the relative absence of theoretical foundations and studies of the strategic role of parallel government in nonviolent struggle, these various developments may be highly significant. Parallel government in the context of nonviolent struggle may point to a type of institutional change which differs sharply from the *coup d'etat* on the one hand and the abortive collapse of the resistance movement on the other.

CONCLUSION

Any future revision of the listing in these past six chapters is certain to lead to considerable expansion. This listing itself has increased by one quarter since the 1968 version, and that had more than doubled in length since the author's first version, prepared in 1960;[300] the latter was itself vastly longer than any previous integrated list.[301] Future research should also produce further examples of the listed methods, which would make the illustrations more representative historically, geographically and politically.

These methods have all occurred spontaneously, or have been consciously invented, to meet the needs of an immediate conflict situation. They have then spread by imitation, perhaps being modified in the process to suit new circumstances. To my knowledge, however, no one has tried to compile as many *new,* previously unused, methods as possible which conceivably could be applied in future conflicts. This task is a logical next step in the conscious development of the technique of nonviolent action which has now begun. It may be particularly important in the possible extension of its applicability to new political situations and conditions.

These six chapters, which have examined minutely many specific methods at the disposal of the practitioner of nonviolent action, present a one-sided and somewhat static view of the conflict situation in which (at least) one side is using this technique. These many methods can be viewed as limited implementations of the theory of power presented in Chapter One —that all governments and hierarchical systems depend on the obedience, assistance and cooperation of the people which they rule and that these people have the capacity of limiting or withholding their contributions and obedience to the system. According to that theory, if the withholding is undertaken by enough people for a long enough period of time, then the regime will have to come to terms or it will be collapsed.

But of course only very rarely, if ever, do governments and other hierarchical systems face the extreme alternatives of complete support or none. Most frequently they receive partial support. Even when, in the end, the regime is destroyed by disobedience, noncooperation and defiance, this may follow only after a severe struggle in which the regime was supported sufficiently and long enough to inflict brutal repression against the nonviolent actionists. The simple enumeration of specific methods of this technique and exploration of their characteristics and application give less than one side of this picture. This is so because even that does not explore the psychological forces which may operate in these conflict situations nor does it take into consideration the extreme and often quick shifts in power relations which occur between the contesting groups.

Except for an introductory discussion in Chapter Two, what has been missing thus far in our examination of the basic nature and characteristics of the technique of nonviolent action has been an exploration of how it operates in struggle against a violent opponent and the several ways in which changes are finally produced. That is, we have not yet examined the technique's dynamics in struggle, its mechanisms of change, the specific factors which determine whether a given campaign will be a success or a failure or something in between. It is to these vital aspects of our subject which we now turn: how does nonviolent action work in struggle?

NOTES

1. Ch'ien Yung, *Li-yüan ts'ung hua*, chapt. 1, p. 11a-11b. I am grateful to Professor Wolfram Eberhard for both the example and the translation from the original Chinese text.

2. Personal letter, 19 November 1966.

3. Leon Trotsky, **My Life** (New York: Grosset & Dunlap, Universal Library, 1960), p. 25.

4. *Peace News*, 4 and 25 May, 24 August, 26 October and 14 December 1962, and 4 January, 29 March and 20 December 1963. For a Canadian example, see *ibid.*, 15 June 1962.

5. Whitley Stokes, ed., **Tripartite Life of St. Patrick** (London: H.M. Stationary Office, by Eyre and Spottiswoode, 1887), CLXXVII, pp. 219, 417 and 419.

6. Gipson, **The British Empire Before the American Revolution**, vol. XII, **The Triumphant Empire, Britain Sails into the Storm, 1770-1776**, pp. 240-241.

7. Paul Leicester Ford, ed., **The Works of Thomas Jefferson**, vol. II, pp. 9-10.

8. *Ibid.*, p. 10, n. 1.

9. B. O. Flower, "Jefferson's Service to Civilization During Founding of the Republic," in Andrew A. Lipscome, editor-in-chief, **The Writings of Thomas Jefferson** (Washington, D.C.: The Thomas Jefferson Memorial Association of the United States, 1903), vol. VII, p. vii.

10. Ford, ed., **The Works of Thomas Jefferson**, vol. II, pp. 10-11.

11. *Ibid.*, p. 11. n. 1.

12. Flower, "Jefferson's Service to Civilization During the Founding of the Republic," p. viii.

13. Ford, ed., **The Works of Thomas Jefferson**, vol. II, p. 12.

14. Gipson, **The British Empire . . .** , vol. XII, p. 233.

15. *Ibid.*, pp. 316-317 and Trevelyan, **The American Revolution** (New York: Longmans, Green & Co., 1908), p. 277.

16. *Peace News*, 20 April 1962.

17. *Ibid.*, 8 and 15 June 1962.

18. Giovanni Pioli, *Peace News*, 16 March 1956 and Mary Taylor, ed., **Community Development in Western Sicily** (duplicated; *Partinico: Centro studi e iniziative*

per la piena occupazione, 1963), pp. 5-6.

19. Helen Mayer, *Peace News*, 4 February 1966.

20. Hanh, "Love in Action," p. 12.

21. Patrick Joyce, **A Social History of Ancient Ireland** (London: Longmans, Green, 1903) vol. I, pp. 204-205.

22. Shridharani, **War Without Violence** (U.S. ed.: pp. 19-20; Br. ed.: p. 85.)

23. Seton-Watson, **The Decline of Imperial Russia**, pp. 68-69.

24. Prawdin, **The Unmentionable Nechaev**, p. 102.

25. P. Kropotkine (sic), **In Russian and French Prisons** (London: Ward and Downey, 1887), p. 76.

26. *Ibid.*, p. 101.

27. Issac Deutscher, **The Prophet Armed: Trotsky: 1879-1921** (New York and London: Oxford University Press, 1963), pp. 40-41.

28. Schapiro, **The Origin of the Communist Autocracy**, p. 205. See also I.N. Steinberg, **In the Workshop of the Revolution** (New York: Rhinehart & Co., 1953), pp. 167-172. (Cited by Miller, **Nonviolence**, pp. 174-175.)

29. Paul Barton, "The Strike Mechanism in Soviet Concentration Camps," in *Monthly Information Bulletin*, International Commission Against Concentration Camp Practices, no. 4, (Aug.-Nov., 1955) pp. 25-26.

30. Holt, **Protest in Arms**, p. 145. I am grateful to William Hamilton for this and certain other examples.

31. Bernard, **Social Control in its Sociological Aspects**, pp. 396-397; and S.K. Ratcliffe, "Hunger Strike," **Encyclopedia of the Social Sciences** (New York: Macmillan, 1935), vol. VII, pp. 532-533.

32. *Ibid.*, pp. 206-07.

33. Ratcliffe, "Hunger Strike," p. 533.

34. Mulford Sibley and Asa Wardlaw, "Conscientious Objectors in Prison," p. 304, in Lynd, ed., **Nonviolence in America.**

35. *The Times*, 2 May 1958.

36. *Observer*, 9 August 1959.

37. Louis Fischer, **The Life of Mahatma Gandhi**, (New York: Harpers, 1950), pp. 154-157 and Erik Erikson, **Gandhi's Truth: On the Origins of Militant Nonviolence** (New York: W.W. Norton & Co., 1969), pp. 255-392.

38. Sharp, **Gandhi Wields the Weapon of Moral Power**, pp. 227-289.

39. Venturi, **Roots of Revolution**, pp. 585-590.

40. Louis Fischer, **The Life of Mahatma Gandhi** (New York: Harpers, 1950), p. 203.

41. Sternstein, "The *Ruhrkampf* of 1923," p. 114.

42. Bullock, **Hitler**, p. 117.

43. Delarue, **The Gestapo**, pp. 38-39.

44. Mabee, **Black Freedom**, p. 301.

45. *Ibid.*, p. 302.

46. *Ibid.*

47. *Ibid.*, pp. 303-304.

48. *Ibid.*, p. 204. See also p. 311.

49. *Ibid.*, p. 115.

50. *Ibid.*

51. *Ibid.*, pp. 115-116.

52. From the account of a "Colored Old Settler," quoted by St. Clair Drake and Horace R. Cayton, **Black Metropolis: A Study of Negro Life in a Northern City** (New York: Harcourt, Brace, 1945), p. 44.

53. DeMarco, "The Use of Non-violent Direct Action Tactics and Strategy by American Indians,". MS. p. 6; her source is John R. Covert, "Indians Win Sit-Down Strike," *Philadelphia Evening Bulletin,* 19 April 1938.

54. DeMarco, *ibid.,* pp. 14-15. Her sources are the *Philadelphia Bulletin,* 7 September 1960 and the *New York Times,* 1 September 1961, p. 18.

55. See George Houser, **Erasing the Color Line** (Rev. ed., pamphlet; New York: Congress of Racial Equality, 1948); Farmer, **Freedom—When?**, pp. 61-62; and Peck, **Freedom Ride**, pp. 45-50, for descriptions of the 1942 Chicago restaurant sit-in—probably the first of its kind.

56. Patrick O'Donovan, *Observer,* 20 March 1960; and Jim Peck, *Peace News,* 4 March 1960. Merrill Proudfoot's **Diary of a Sit-in** (Chapel Hill, N.C.: University of North Carolina Press, 1962) contains a detailed account—from a religious perspective—of the campaign for the integration of lunch counters in Knoxville, Tennessee in July 1960. See also C. Eric Lincoln, "The Sit-in Comes to Atlanta," in Westin, ed., **Freedom Now**, pp. 259-265. On other cases see Peck, **Freedom Ride**, pp. 73-79 and 82-88.

57. Claude Sitton, "A Chronology of the New Civil-Rights Protest, 1960-1963," in Westin, ed., **Freedom Now**, p. 81.

58. Peck, **Freedom Ride**, p. 89.

59. *Peace News,* 11 December 1964.

60. *New York Times,* 10 and 12 November 1966.

61. Hentoff, **The New Equality**, p. 204.

62. Waskow, **From Race Riot to Sit-in**, pp. 267-275.

63. *Ibid.*, pp. 243-244.

64. *Peace News,* 3 April 1964.

65. James Peck, **Freedom Ride**, pp. 23-29. For another case see p. 44.

66. *Ibid.*, pp. 34-35.

67. Mabee, **Black Freedom**, pp. 127-38.

68. *Ibid.*, pp. 112-13.

69. *Ibid.*, p. 112.

70. *Ibid.*, p. 114.

71. *Ibid.*, p. 115.

72. *Ibid.*, p. 121.

73. *Ibid.*, p. 122.

74. *Ibid.*, pp. 123-24.

75. *Ibid.*, p. 125.

76. *Ibid.*, p. 126.

77. *Ibid.*, pp. 202-203.

78. Westin, "Ride-in's and Sit-in's of the 1870's," in Westin, ed., **Freedom Now**, pp. 69-70.

79. For an account, see Peck, **Freedom Ride**, pp. 14-27.

80. Lomax, **The Negro Revolt**, pp. 145-156, Miller, **Nonviolence**, pp. 313-316, and Peck, **Freedom Ride**.

81. *New York Times*, 9, 16, 23 and 24 July 1961
82. This section is based on a draft by Michael Schulter.
83. **Criterion**, November 1969, p. 4.
84. *Ibid.*, p. 1.
85. Mabee, **Black Freedom**, p. 128.
86. *Ibid.*, pp. 128-130.
87. Peck, **Freedom˙ Ride**, p. 98.
88. Anthony Lewis and *The New York Times,* **Portrait of a Decade: The Second American Revolution** (New York: Random House, 1964) p. 177.
89. Sharp, **Gandhi Wields . . .** , p. 177 and Shridharani, **War Without Violence,** U.S. ed., pp. 41-42; Br. ed., p. 57.
90. Sharp, **Gandhi Wields . . .** , pp. 132-151.
91. Schlesinger, **The Colonial Merchants and the American Revolution**, p. 176.
92. This section, and the Vietnamese examples, have been suggested by Michael Schulter.
93. Goodspeed, **The Conspirators**, p. 134.
94. *Newsweek*, 2 Aug. 1965, p. 10.
95. *Ibid.*, 4 October 1965, p. 40.
96. *The Times*, 19 and 20 May and 16 June 1955.
97. *Peace News*, 22 May, 10, 17, 24 and 31 July 1959.
98. *Ibid.*, 27 November and 4 December 1959, and 2 and 15 January, and 18 March 1960.
99. *Ibid.*, 2, 9 and 23 October, 13 and 27 November, 18 and 25 December 1959, 1 and 22 January and 10 June 1960.
100. *Peace News*, 20 June 1958, and 13 and 20 July 1962.
101. This definition is based upon a terminological refinement by Bradford Lyttle, **Essays on Nonviolent Action** (mimeo; Chicago, The Author, 1959), pp. 31-32.
102. *Peace News*, 22 May 1964.
103. Shridharani, **War Without Violence,** U.S. ed. p. 21; Br. ed., p. 41.
104. Myers and Laidler, **What Do You Know About Labor?**, p. 76.
105. Waskow, **From Race Riot to Sit-in**, p. 242.
106. Belfrage, **Freedom Summer**, p. 184.
107. Mabee, **Black Freedom**, p. 307.
108. Matei Yulzari, "The Bulgarian Jews in the Resistance Movement," in Suhl, ed., **They Fought Back**, p. 277.
109. *Guardian*, 1 September 1962.
110. *Ibid.*, 3 September 1962.
111. *Peace News*, 2 July 1965.
112. *Peace News*, 1 March 1963.
113. Isobel Lindsay, *Peace News*, 29 November 1963.
114. *Peace News*, 12 April 1963.
115. Sharp, **Gandhi Wields . . .** , pp. 166-167.
116. Lyttle, **Essays on Non-violent Action**, p. 34, and *Peace News*, 22 and 29 August 1958.
117. *The Times*, 8 December 1958, *Manchester Guardian*, 8 December 1958,

Observer, 21 December 1958, *The Times*, 22 December 1958 and *Manchester Guardian*, 22 December 1958.

118. This account is based on student paper by Margaret DeMarco, "The Use of Non-violent Direct Action Tactics and Strategy by American Indians," MS. pp. 15-17. Her sources are Edmund Wilson, **Apologies to the Iroquois** (New York: Farrar, Straus and Cudahy, 1960), the quotation being from p. 143, and the *Philadelphia Evening Bulletin*, 7 May 1958.

119. Benjamin Muse, **The American Negro Revolution: From Nonviolence to Black Power 1963-1967** (Bloomington and London: Indiana University Press, 1968), pp. 111-12.

120. Friedman, "Jewish Resistance to Nazism," in **European Resistance Movements**, p. 204.

121. Brant, **The East German Rising**, pp. 111-112.

122. Lyttle, **Essays on Non-violent Action**, p. 32.

123. Mabee, **Black Freedom**, pp. 300-301.

124. *Daily Mirror* (London), 7 December 1956.

125. *Peace News*, 26 October 1956 and 1 March 1957.

126. Peter Kihss, "Blockades in New York," in Westin, ed., **Freedom Now**, pp. 275-276.

127. Waskow, **From Race Riot to Sit-in**, p. 279.

128. John Morris, "Early Christian Civil Disobedience," in *Peace News*, 5 January 1962. This article contains a translation of Ambrose's letter to his sister describing the events.

129. Bondurant, **Conquest of Violence**, p. 57 and Desai, **The Story of Bardoli**, pp. 172 and 186.

130. *New York Times*, 17 August 1957, p. 17. This account is based on Margaret DeMarco's unpublished paper, "The Use of Non-violent Direct Action Tactics and Strategy by American Indians," MS. pp. 7-8.

131. This account has been prepared by Katherine Preston. For some coverage of the occupation at Alcatraz consult **Akwesasne Notes**, a resume of Indian affairs available from Mohawk Nation, via Roosevelttown, New York, 13683, and also **The Warpath**, published by the United Native Americans, Inc., P. O. Box 26149, San Francisco, California, 94126. Details of final removal are from *New York Times*, 14 June 1971.

132. Littell, ed., **The Czech Black Book**, p. 142.

133. *Ibid.*, pp. 147-48. See also pp. 164, 198, 204, 208, 223, 224 and 249.

134. Mabee, **Black Freedom**, pp. 91-92.

135. *Ibid.*, p. 93.

136. *Ibid.*, pp. 93-94.

137. *Ibid.*, p. 104.

138. *Ibid.*, p. 105.

139. *Ibid.*, p. 104.

140. *Ibid.*, p. 106.

141. *Ibid.*, pp. 107-09.

142. *Ibid.*, pp. 95-97.

143. G. S. Rao, **Gora—An Atheist** (Vijayawada, India: Atheistic Centre, 1970), pp. 4, 13-14, and 16; and personal conversations with Lavanam, one of the sons, in

1968, and Gora himself in 1970.

144. James Q. Wilson, "The Negro in Politics," in *Daedalus*, vol. 94, no. 4 (Fall, 1965), p. 973, n. 29. No other details are given.

145. This account has been drafted by Ronald McCarthy on the basis of reports in the *Boston Globe*, 16-19 May 1967. The quotations are respectively from the following issues: 16 May (morn. edition), 16 May (eve. ed.), 16 May (morn. ed.), *ibid.*, 18 May (eve. ed.), and 16 May (eve. ed.).

146. Shimbori, "Zengakuren", in *Sociology of Education*, vol. 37, no. 3 (Spring 1964), p. 247.

147. Michael Parkhouse, *Peace News*, 10 July 1964.

148. Botemps, **100 Years of Negro Freedom**, p. 254.

149. This section is based on a draft prepared by Michael Schulter.

150. John L. Nickalls, ed., **The Journal of George Fox** (Cambridge: [Cambridge] University Press, 1952), pp. 39-40.

151. *Ibid.*, p. 76.

152. *Ibid.*, p. 98.

153. Mabee, **Black Freedom**, p. 205.

154. *Ibid.*, p. 208.

155. This section is based on a draft by Michael Schulter.

156. Jerry Rubin, **Do It!** (New York: Simon and Schuster, 1970), pp. 133-135.

157. *Ibid.*, pp. 117-118.

158. Griffith, **The Resurrection of Hungary**, pp. xx, xxvi-xxvii, 7 and 170.

159. *Ibid.*, pp. 139-163.

160. Gandhi, **The Constructive Programme**.

161. Mabee, **Black Freedom**, pp. 127 and 133-135.

162. *Ibid.*, p. 140.

163. *Ibid.*, pp. 139-142. See also p. 149.

164. Karski, **The Story of a Secret State**, pp. 304-305 and 308.

165. Muse, **Virginia's Massive Resistance**, pp. 8, 15, 76-79, 111-118, and 148-159.

166. This section has been suggested by Michael Schulter.

167. Warmbrunn, **The Dutch Under the German Occupation 1940-1945**, pp. 221-258. The quotation is from p. 244.

168. My earlier drafts of discussions of nonviolent intervention did not include economic intervention as a distinct class within it. A student and friend at Harvard, Robert Reitherman, argued that this was unfortunate, and produced an independent study paper, "Nonviolent Economic 'Intervention' ", 15 pp., in March 1970, which was convincing.

169. Pioli, *Peace News*, 16 March 1956.

170. Farmer, **Freedom—When?** p. 105. No date is given for this example.

171. Littell, ed., **The Czech Black Book**, pp. 162 and 191. CKD, as it is now known under State ownership, was originally founded as a private firm *českomolavska-Kolben-Daněk*.

172. *Peace News*, 20 April 1956.

173. Peterson, **American Labor Unions**, p. 30, and Knowles, **Strikes**, pp. 10-11.

174. For further discussion of the sit-down strike, see Ligt, **The Conquest of Violence**, pp. 144 and 167; Edward Levinson, "Sit-down Strike," in E. Wight

Bakke and Charles Kerr, **Unions, Management and the Public** (New York: Harcourt and Brace, 1948), pp. 410-412; Coleman, **Men and Coal**, p. 164; Howe and Widick, **The U.A.W. and Walter Reuther**, pp. 47-65; Herbert Harris, **American Labor** (New Haven: Yale University Press, 1938); Peterson, **American Labor Unions**, pp. 222-225 and 268.

175. Joseph G. Rayback, **A History of American Labor**, p. 353.

176. Peterson, **American Labor Unions**, p. 223.

177. Peterson, **American Labor Unions**, p. 217 and *Newsweek,* vol. VII, no. 13 (28 March 1936), pp. 13-14.

178. Rayback, **A History of American Labor**, p. 353.

179. Levinson, "Sit-Down Strike," p. 410.

180. *Ibid.*

181. Rayback, **A History of American Labor**, p. 355 and Solomon Barkin, "Labor Unions and Workers' Rights in Jobs," p. 127, in Arthur Kornhauser, Robert Dubin and Arthur M. Ross, eds., **Industrial Conflict** (New York: McGraw-Hill, 1954) and references cited in n. 92.

182. Harris, **American Labor**, p. 294.

183. Ligt, **The Conquest of Violence**, p. 144.

184. Peterson, **American Labor Unions**, p. 223.

185. *Observer*, 6 September 1959.

186. *Ibid.*, 13 March 1960.

187. Quoted by Theodor Ebert, "Nonviolent Resistance Against Communist Regimes?" in Roberts, ed., **Civilian Resistance as a National Defence**, p. 193; Br. ed.: **The Strategy of Civilian Defence**, p. 193.

188. Rainer Hildebrandt, *Was lehrte der 17 Juni*, p. 7 (Berlin: the author, 1954), quoted by Ebert, *op. cit.*, p. 193.

189. Christopher Seton-Watson, **Italy From Liberalism to Fascism 1870-1925** (New York: Barnes and Noble, 1967, and London: Methuen, 1967), p. 521.

190. *Ibid.*, p. 522.

191. Miguel Urrutia, **The Development of the Colombian Labor Movement** (New Haven and London: Yale University Press, 1969), pp. 130-131. On the Viotá case, Urrutia cites José Gutiérrez, *LaReveldia Colombiana* (Bogotá: Tercer Mundo, 1962), pp. 83-96. From Urrutia's account it is difficult to determine the extent of violence in this case as his conception of violence (p. 128) includes the general strike and the "sit-in strike."

192. Samuel Huntington writes that Colombia's agrarian reform law of the 1930s was "primarily designed to legitimize peasant land seizures which had already occurred." Samuel P. Huntington, **Political Order in Changing Societies** (New Haven and London: Yale University Press, 1968), p. 393. See also p. 358.

193. Urrutia, **The Development of the Colombian Labor Movement**, p. 135.

194. *Ibid.*, p. 133.

195. Eduardo Arze-Loureiro, "The Process of Agrarian Reform in Bolivia, in T. Lynn Smith, ed., **Agrarian Reform in Latin America** (New York: Alfred A. Knopf, 1965), p. 133.

196. *Ibid.*, p. 136.

197. *Ibid.*

198. Huntington, **Political Order in Changing Societies**, p. 393.

199. John Gerassi, **Great Fear in Latin America** (New York: Collier, 1965), p. 139. I am grateful to Bob Reitherman for this reference.

200. Doreen Warriner, **Land Reform in Principle and Practice** (Oxford: Clarendon Press, 1969), p. 259. I am grateful to Jeffrey B. Peters for these references, and for encouraging the expansion of the discussion of nonviolent land seizures.

201. *Ibid.*, p. 353.

202. *Ibid.*, p. 351.

203. *Ibid.*, p. 289.

204. *Ibid.*, p. 290.

205. *Ibid.*, pp. 290-291.

206. This method has been suggested by Michael Schulter.

207. W. Phillips Davidson, **The Berlin Blockade** (Princeton, N.J.; Princeton University Press, 1958), p. 196.

208. *Ibid.*, p. 261.

209. Thomas C. Schelling, **International Economics**, p. 488.

210. Murray Teigh Bloom, "The World's Greatest Counterfeiters," *Harpers Magazine*, vol. 240, no. 1436 (July 1957), p. 47.

211. *Ibid.*

212. *Ibid.*, pp. 50-52.

213. Schelling, **International Economics**, p. 488.

214. *Ibid.*, p. 489.

215. *Ibid.*, p. 488.

216. Bailey, **A Diplomatic History of the American People**, p. 734.

217. Schelling, **International Economics**, pp. 488-489.

218. Nirumand, **Iran**, p. 55.

219. Schelling, **International Economics**, p. 488.

220. *Ibid.*, p. 489.

221. St. Clair Drake, "Negro Americans and the Africa Interest," in John P. Davis, **The American Negro Reference Book** (Englewood Cliffs, N.J.: Prentice-Hall, Inc., 1966), p. 675, n. 23. I am grateful to Robert Reitherman for this reference.

222. Mabee, **Black Freedom**, p. 99.

223. Morgan and Morgan, **The Stamp Act Crisis**, pp. 49-50; and Gipson, **The British Empire Before the American Revolution**, vol. X, **The Triumphant Empire: Thunder-Clouds Gather in the West, 1763-1766**, p. 361.

224. Gipson, *op. cit.*, p. 363.

225. Schlesinger, **The Colonial Merchants . . .**, p. 77.

226. See M. K. Gandhi, **Economics of Khadi** (Ahmedabad, India: Navajivan, 1941), esp. pp. 3-20, 26-29, 108-109, and 369-372; and Bondurant, **Conquest of Violence**, pp. 106-107, 126-127, and 180.

227. Myers and Laidler, **What Do You Know About Labor?**, p. 186.

228. Dale Yoder, **Labor Economics and Labor Problems** (New York and London: McGraw-Hill Co., 1939), p. 509.

229. *Ibid.*, pp. 309-310.

230. Myers and Laidler, **What Do You Know About Labor?**, pp. 32 and 187n.

231. This section is based on a draft by Michael Schulter.

232. A.K. Jameson, **A New Way In Norway** (pamphlet; London: *Peace News*, 1946 or 1947 [?]; also quoted in Mulford Q. Sibley ed., **The Quiet Battle** (Boston: Beacon Press, 1968), pp. 168-169.

233. Professor Erling Petersen, *"Økonomiske Forhold,"* in Steen, gen. ed., **Norges Krig**, vol. III, pp. 524-26.

234. King, **Stride Towards Freedom**, pp. 69-74 and 151-154.

235. This section draws heavily on Bob Reitherman's unpublished student independent study paper "Nonviolent Economic 'Intervention'," Harvard University, March 1970.

236. Wilfred Fleischer, **Sweden: The Welfare State** (New York: John Day, 1956), p. 76.

237. *Ibid.*

238. Seton-Watson, **Italy: From Liberalism to Fascism**, pp. 228-29 and 302.

239. Michael Miles, "Black Cooperatives," *New Republic*, vol. 159, no. 2 (21 September 1968), p. 22.

240. Art Goldberg, "Negro Self-Help," *New Republic*, vol. 156, no. 239 (10 June 1967), pp. 21-23.

241. This section is based on suggestions by Robin Remington and Michael Schulter.

242. *New York Times*, 3 March 1970, I am grateful to Robin Remington for this reference.

243. Interview with Colonel Paul Feeney, *Record American* (Boston), 27 June 1970.

244. This section is based on a proposal by Michael Schulter.

245. Mabee, **Black Freedom**, pp. 302-303.

246. *New York Times*, 13 August 1969, p. 39.

247. Sharp, **Tyranny Could Not Quell Them.**

248. Letter from H.B. Chipembere to M.W.K. Chiume, Appendix I, p. 145, **Report of the Nyasaland Commission of Inquiry.** See also p. 53.

249. *Peace News*, 6 May 1960.

250. Farmer, **Freedom—When?**, pp. 70-72.

251. Peck, **Freedom Ride**, p. 94.

252. Miller, **Nonviolence**, p. 280.

253. *Peace News*, 16 February 1962.

254. *Ibid.*, 6 March 1964.

255. Gandhi, **Non-violent Resistance**, p. 265; Ind. ed., *Satyagraha*, p. 265.

256. Sharp, **Gandhi Wields . . .**, pp. 152, 182, and 187-189.

257. Theodor Ebert, "Organization in Civilian Defence," in Roberts, ed., **Civilian Resistance as a National Defence**, p. 258; **The Strategy of Civilian Defence**, p. 258.

258. *Ibid.*, p. 262

259. *Ibid.*, pp. 260-261.

260. Warmbrunn, **The Dutch . . .**, p. 121.

261. *Ibid.*, p. 298. n. 4.

262. *Ibid.*, pp. 121-122.

263. Sharp, **Tyranny Could Not Quell Them.**

264. Bernard, **Social Control . . .**, pp. 126 and 186.

265. Shridharani, **War Without Violence**, U.S. ed., p. 42; Br. ed., p. 58.

266. Geyl, The Revolt of the Netherlands 1555-1609, pp. 138-139, 147-148, and 154.

267. Crane Brinton, The Anatomy of Revolution, pp. 139-141.

268. Taylor, The Struggle for North China, p. 199.

269. Brinton, The Anatomy of Revolution, pp. 142-143.

270. The full text is published in Schlesinger, The Colonial Merchants..., pp. 607-613.

271. Gipson, The British Empire..., vol. XII, p. 313.

272. Schlesinger, The Colonial Merchants..., p. 519.

273. *Ibid.*, pp. 551-552.

274. See *ibid.*, p. 136, 148-149, 428, 435-436, 452, 483-484, 494, 505, 509, 519, 522-523, 528-529, 549, 551, 563, and 580-581; Trevelyan, The American Revolution, pp. 270-271; Gipson, The Coming of the American Revolution, pp. 103, 180-181, 203, 222-223, and 228-230; Gipson, The British Empire Before the American Revolution, vol. XI, The Triumphant Empire, The Rumbling of the Coming Storm 1766-1770, p. 513; and *ibid.*, vol. XII, pp. 157, 160, 216-217, 222, 313, 315-316, 324 and 349.

275. I am grateful to Dennis Brady for calling my attention to this case. This account is based primarily on Irving Berdine Richman, Rhode Island: A Study in Separatism (Boston and New York: Houghton Mifflin Co., 1905), pp. 285-307, and Arthur May Mowry, The Dorr War or The Constitutional Struggle in Rhode Island (Providence, R.I.: Preston & Rounds, 1901), pp. 98-198 and 286-306, and also on Peter J. Coleman, The Transformation of Rhode Island 1790-1860 (Providence, R.I.: American History Research Center, Brown University Press, 1963), pp. 255-294. See also, e.g., Dan King, The Life and Times of Thomas Wilson Dorr with Outlines of the Political History of Rhode Island (Boston: the Author, 1859) and "A Rhode Islander," Might and Right (Providence: A.H. Stillwell, 1844). A larger literature is available.

276. Mowry, The Dorr War, p. 143.

277. *Ibid.*, p. 139.

278. *Ibid.*, p. 140.

279. *Ibid.*, p. 155.

280. *Ibid.*, p. 157.

281. *Ibid.*, p. 172.

282. See Charques, The Twilight of Imperial Russia, p. 243, Deutcher, Stalin, pp. 130, 134, 160-161, and 193, and Schapiro, The Communist Party of the Soviet Union, pp. 154, 159, 162 and 166.

283. Wolfe, Three Who Made A Revolution, p. 319.

284. Charques, The Twilight..., p. 134. See also Seton-Watson, The Decline of Imperial Russia, p. 227, and Harcave, First Blood, pp. 187-189, 195, 212-214 and 236.

285. Wolfe, Three Who Made a Revolution, p. 333.

286. Keep, The Rise of Social Democracy in Russia, p. 162.

287. Schapiro, The Communist Party..., p. 66.

288. Seton-Watson, The Decline..., p. 240, and Keep, The Rise..., p. 160.

289. Seton-Watson, The Decline..., p. 241.

290. Wolfe, Three Who Made a Revolution, p. 493.

291. Schapiro, The Communist Party..., p. 67, and Keep, The Rise..., p. 214.

292. Hiller, **The Strike**, p. 246.

293. Crook, "General Strike," p. 610.

294. Hiller, **The Strike**, pp. 244-249.

295. Crook, **The General Strike**, p. 402. See also Symons, **The General Strike**, pp. 89, 93, 118, 124-125, 138, 144, and 158-159.

296. Bondurant, **Conquest of Violence**, p. 137.

297. Sharp, **Gandhi Wields . . .** , p. 152.

298. H.N. Brailsford, **Rebel India** (New York: New Republic, Inc., 1931; and London: Leonard Stein [with Victor Gollancz], 1931) U.S. ed., pp. 4-5; Br. ed., p. 13.

299. See Pyarelal (Nayar), "Gandhiji Discusses Another 1942 Issue: Non-violent Technique and Parallel Government," reprinted from *Harijan*, in *The Independent* (Bombay), 25 March 1946.

300. Sharp, "The Methods of Nonviolent Resistance and Direct Action;" duplicated, 68 pp.; Oslo: Institute for Social Research, 1960). That paper contained sixty-three methods.

301. Indeed, some additional methods have already been suggested which have not been included here for one reason or another. These are: circulation of hostile rumours and jokes, the "rally" (which might possibly be classified separately from "assemblies of protest or support" and "protest meetings"), hoarding (under certain political and economic conditions), a noisy claque pro or con some cause involved in a meeting, packing a meeting with sympathizers, clogging the channels of justice (which here might be a part of "seeking imprisonment"), over-use of certain technical or mechanical (as distinct from social) facilities (as clogging a telephone switchboard with masses of calls), inviting martyrdom (if one separates the extreme forms— as daring soldiers or police to shoot one—from the general phenomenon which may occur with various methods), aesthetic display (art, music, poetry, drama) not itself containing protest but performed *in the name* of protest, subtle protest through artistic performance (as a few lines in a play). These have been suggested by John L. Sorenson while at the Defense Research Corporation; he also called my attention to several others which are included in the present classification.

PART THREE:
The Dynamics of Nonviolent Action

INTRODUCTION
TO PART THREE

An understanding of how nonviolent action "works," of its dynamics in struggle, and of its mechanics of change is of extreme importance. Without that insight our extensive catalogue of its methods will lack the vitality which is characteristic of social change and political conflict, and the view of power upon which this technique rests will remain an exercise for specialists in political philosophy. But with awareness of the dynamics of nonviolent action, we can understand the operation of this technique in society and politics, and evaluate intelligently its potential utility in various types of conflict situations.

The dynamics of nonviolent action is a relatively uninvestigated phenomenon. There have been important pioneers in the field—especially Richard Gregg,[1] E.T. Hiller,[2] and Leo Kuper,[3] and a few others who will be cited later. Certain activists in the application of the technique have also made significant observations on the subject, especially M.K. Gandi.[4]

In these final six chapters we shall draw on the insights of these theorists and activists. But primarily we shall draw on the events in several significant cases of nonviolent action to construct, largely by an inductive approach, an analysis of how this technique works. This analysis contains many hypotheses awaiting further critical examination and testing, including the use of a wider selection of case material.

Throughout the exploration of this topic, it is essential to remember that the operation of nonviolent action in struggle is always a dynamic process. It involves continuous change in the various influences and forces which operate in that process and are constantly influencing each other. No discussion in static terms of how nonviolent action works can be valid. Also, the process is very complicated; for reasons which will become clear, it is more complicated than conventional military warfare or even guerrilla warfare.

NOTES

1. Gregg, **The Power of Nonviolence.**
2. Hiller, **The Strike.**
3. Kuper, **Passive Resistance in South Africa.**
4. See, for example, M. K. Gandhi, **Non-Violence in Peace and War** (two vols.; Ahmedabad, India: Navajivan Publishing House, 1948 and 1949), and **Non-Violent Resistance;** Ind. ed.: **Satyagraha.**

9

Laying the Groundwork for Nonviolent Action

INTRODUCTION

Nonviolent action is a means of wielding social and political power, even though it does not involve its practitioners in the use of violence. If nonviolent action is capable of wielding power, it must be able with its power to act upon the power wielded by the opponent. This it does by means which differ radically from those involved in political violence, i.e., violence for political purposes. Nonviolent action can be viewed as acting against the opponent's power in two ways, either *indirectly* against it, or more *directly* than violence against it. We shall now see how this is the case.

CONFRONTING THE OPPONENT'S POWER

The opponent is frequently a government; where it is not, the opponent often has the support of the State machinery. In either case, the nonviolent group may find arrayed against it the government's troops, police, prisons and the like. In nonviolent action there is no attempt to combat these by using the same types of instruments, as would be the case if both sides were using violence. Instead, in strategic terms, the nonviolent group counters this expression of the opponent's power *indirectly,* in various ways. These weaken the opponent's relative power position rather than strengthen it by, for example, alienating existing support and undermining the opponent's ability (and at times weakening his will) to continue the policy and the repression. The opponent is usually well equipped to apply military and other violent means of combat and repression, as well as to fight violent and military means of struggle. Instead of meeting him directly on that level, where he is strong, nonviolent actionists rely on a totally different technique of struggle, or "weapons systems," which is designed to operate to *their* advantage. The whole conflict then takes on a very special assymetrical character; the combatants are fighting but they are using very different types of weapons. Given an extensive, determined, and skillful application of nonviolent action, the opponent is likely to find that nonviolent actionists' insistence on fighting with their choice of "weapons system" will cause him very special problems which will tend to frustrate the effective utilization of his own forces.

A close consideration of the strategic problems of military conflict shows that frontal resistance or attack may not necessarily be the wisest course of action—precisely because this is where the enemy has concentrated his strength. Napoleon wrote, for example:

> It is an approved maxim in war, never to do what the enemy wishes you to do, for this reason alone, that he desires it. A field of battle, therefore, which he has previously studied and reconnoitered, should be avoided, and double care should be taken where he has had time to fortify and entrench. One consequence deductible from this principle is, never to attack a position in front which you can gain by turning. [1]

This approach to strategy has been developed by the late Sir Basil Liddell Hart, who argued:

> . . . throughout the ages, effective results in war have rarely been attained unless the approach has had such indirectness as to ensure the opponent's unreadiness to meet it. The indirectness has usually been physical, and always psychological. In strategy the longest way round is often the shortest way home. . . .
>
> To move along the line of natural expectation consolidates the opponent's balance and thus increases his resisting power. . . . In most

campaigns the dislocation of the enemy's psychological and physical balance has been the vital prelude to a successful attempt at his overthrow.[2]

This indirect approach to conventional military strategy has been carried to a more extreme development in modern guerrilla warfare.

Nonviolent struggle carries indirect strategy still further, to the point where the military opponent is confronted not only with differing strategies but with a contrasting technique of struggle and a nonmilitary "weapons system." Nonviolent action involves opposing the opponent's power, including his police and military capacity, not with the weapons chosen by him, but by quite different means. (The possibility of both sides instead using nonviolent action is discussed briefly in Chapter Eleven.) The result of using nonviolent weapons against violent action may be a significant increase in the actionists' total combat effectiveness. In this special type of assymetrical conflict, the opponent's violent action is always confronted indirectly, i.e., not by the same type of action in direct confrontation but by nonviolent resistance and intervention. This can be viewed as an extreme development of indirect strategy as discussed above. Repression by the opponent is used against his own power position in a kind of political *jiu-jitsu,* and the very sources of his power (analyzed in Chapter One) thus reduced or removed, with the result that his political and military position is seriously weakened or destroyed. The opponent's balance is thereby dislocated, his resistance power· undermined, and in extreme cases his ability to continue the struggle eliminated.

There is also a sense in which nonviolent action impinges upon an opponent's power *more directly* than would violence. In varying degrees, depending upon a number of factors, nonviolent action is capable of striking at the availability of the sources of political power of the ruler: authority, human resources, skills and knowledge, intangible factors, material resources, and even sanctions themselves. The ruler's power, as discussed earlier, is dependent upon these sources. Through various processes which take place in a large-scale nonviolent struggle, the supply of those sources may be threatened, curtailed, or cut off. The degree to which the sources of power are restricted in individual cases varies considerably, of course. This potential of the nonviolent technique is illustrated most clearly perhaps in strikes and mutinies. For example, nonviolent actionists may try to destroy the opponent's army as an effective force of repression by inducing deliberate inefficiency and open mutiny among the soldiers, without whom there can be no army. In contrast, military actionists would usually fight that army intact and attempt to defeat it by destroying its weapons and killing its soldiers. Such attacks on them would usually reinforce, not disrupt or destroy, their obedience patterns.

Therefore, in the sense that nonviolent action cuts off the *sources* of the opponent's power, rather than simply combatting the final power product of those sources, nonviolent action is a more direct attack on an opponent's power than is violence.

RISKS AND VARIATIONS IN NONVIOLENT ACTION

As a substitute for violence in political conflicts, nonviolent action also involves risks. The first risk is possible defeat. This technique is not foolproof. The simple choice of nonviolent action does not guarantee success, especially on a short-term basis. This should not be surprising, since this technique too involves the matching of forces and must be ably and skillfully used if it is to produce success. No technique of struggle can guarantee success every time; after all, in cases in which both sides use violence, one of them usually loses.

Nonviolent action is not a safe means of struggle; there is no such thing. People are liable to be hurt and to suffer in various ways, including economic loss, physical injury, imprisonment, and even death; this is the second risk. There are, of course, risks in passivity—especially in letting an oppressive regime go unchallenged—and in any type of alternative violent action which might be taken. It is claimed, however, that the injuries, deaths, suffering and destruction are significantly less—even on the resisters' side alone—when one side relies on nonviolent action than when both sides use violence.[3]

A third risk is that political violence may break out during the use of nonviolent action. Gandhi recognized this risk and took measures to prevent the outbreak of violence, and to isolate and eliminate such violence if it occurred. This risk did not in his opinion mean that the nonviolent campaign should not be launched. His view was that the outbreak of political violence (with its consequent detrimental effects on all concerned) was far more likely if he did nothing in a tense conflict situation than it was if people were offered a nonviolent substitute course of action. Gandhi wrote in 1920:

. . . the risk of supineness in the face of a grave issue is infinitely greater than the danger of violence ensuing from organizing non-cooperation. To do nothing is to invite violence for a certainty.

. . . the only way to avoid violence is to enable them to give such expression to their feelings as to compel redress. I have found nothing save non-cooperation.[4]

He felt that with greater experience and with the accumulation of visible successes in nonviolent struggle, the chances that people would turn to violence in such a situation would be considerably reduced.

No two cases of nonviolent action are alike, and they may indeed differ radically from each other, as the illustrations in Chapter Two and the examples of various methods in Part Two illustrate. There are other important variations which need to kept in mind. The campaign may have been deliberately planned and prepared for, or it may have broken out spontaneously or "semi-spontaneously." There may be a clear leadership group, or not. The movement may start spontaneously and without leadership and end up organized and with leaders; or the process may be exactly the opposite. There may be general preparations which arouse the will to resist and give general ideas of how to do so, but the specific movement may start accidentally. Or the preparations may be for a very limited action, with people not knowing what to do in other situations. The range of methods applied may differ widely, as may the numbers of actionists involved and the intensity of the penalties they are willing to undergo. A given movement may avow "love" for the opponent or hatred as intense (at certain stages at least) as in many military conflicts. Nonviolent actionists may aim to convert or to coerce their opponent. The types of issues at stake and their relative importance to the contending groups may differ widely. Similarly, the composition and characteristics of the respective groups will differ from case to case, as will their resources, allies, strengths and weaknesses. The degree of severity of repression, too, will differ. Whether the police are partisan or neutral between the contending groups will be important. The extent and depth of understanding of the technique of nonviolent action among its practitioners will differ considerably, as will the degree and adequacy of the strategy and tactics used. Other important variables will add considerably to the difficulty of describing the various processes and mechanisms involved in the working of nonviolent action in conflicts.

Certain assumptions will therefore be made here in order to reduce somewhat the difficulties in the way of analysis. It is assumed, for example, that the methods used include those of noncooperation (not simply nonviolent protest and persuasion), and some methods of nonviolent intervention. The participation of fairly large numbers of people is assumed, which means that most of them are not believers in a creed enjoining nonviolence but are acting under a nonviolent discipline for the conflict's duration. It is also assumed that the struggle takes place where there are at least some civil liberties, although these may be reduced as the campaign continues. The use of nonviolent action against totalitarian systems requires separate discussion.

CASTING OFF FEAR

One of the prerequisites of nonviolent struggle is that the participants must cast off fear of acting independently and fear of the sufferings which may follow. A high degree of courage is required of nonviolent actionists. The accusation of cowardice, which has often been unjustly made against people who for conscientious reasons refuse to take part in war, cannot even be levelled against nonviolent actionists—except perhaps by those totally ignorant on the subject.

Indeed, Gandhi was most emphatic in his condemnation of cowardice, arguing that "cowardice and *ahimsa* [nonviolence] do not go together any more than water and fire." [5] The coward seeks to avoid the conflict and flees from danger, the nonviolent actionist faces the conflict and risks the dangers involved in pursuing it honorably. "Cowardice is impotence worse than violence," concluded Gandhi. [6] "Nonviolence cannot be taught to a person who fears to die and has no power of resistance . . ." [7] "There is hope for a violent man to be some day nonviolent, but there is none for a coward," [8] "Fear," argues Gregg, "develops out of an assumption of relative weakness." [9] The coward, being fearful, cannot use nonviolent action effectively. The nonviolent actionist must have confidence in the right and strength of his cause, in his principles, and in his technique of action.

The emphasis which Gandhi and other nonviolent actionists have placed on casting off fear has political roots and consequences. Despotism, they have insisted, could not exist if it did not have fear as its foundation. "The Government takes advantage of our fear of jails," argued Gandhi. [10] In the earlier theoretical analysis of the roots of political power, in Chapter One, it was emphasized that sanctions *themselves* do not produce obedience; but the *fear* of sanctions does. If there is great fear among the subjects, even minor sanctions may produce great conformity, while severe sanctions in face of a high degree of fearlessness may not secure the regime. This difference is crucial for the operation of nonviolent means of struggle in face of violent repression.

Nonviolent actionists have not been alone in pointing to the paralyzing political effect of fear and in arguing that liberation can only come after fear has been cast off. The nineteenth century Russian revolutionary Alexander Herzen, for example, devoted the first page of the first issue of his *Free Russian Press* (published in London in 1853) to this objective. [11]

If fear, then, plays an important role in maintaining oppressive regimes, the liberation of the subjects by their own efforts requires a change in them toward fearlessness and self-confidence. This view is also shared by advocates of violent revolution. Bakunin, for example, linked "mental liberation" with "socio-economic liberation." [12] The Russian Jacobin Petr Tkachev, from whom Lenin learned so much, argued for the need of fearlessness if revolution were to be possible: "When the people see that terrible power that they dreaded and before which they were accustomed to tremble and to denigrate themselves, is disorganized, split and befouled, when they see that they need not fear anybody or anything, then the accumulated bitterness will break out with irrestible force." [13] There were others. [14] Michael Prawdin writes that in Russia in early 1917 "the people had lost their fear of punishment and the bogey of the state had lost its power to terrify." [15]

Gandhi repeatedly emphasized the importance of this inner psychological change from fear and submission to fearlessness and self-respect as a necessary prerequisite of real political freedom. In this context, his emphasis on the primacy of "inner conditions" over "external conditions" gains new significance. Speaking of India's millions, Gandhi wrote: "We have to dispel fear from their hearts. On the day they shed all fear, India's fetters shall fall and she will be free." [16] This is not to say that fear must initially be *fully* cast off, and that only then can nonviolent action follow. Fear may be cast off by degrees, and certain groups in the population may become less afraid than other groups. Also, participation in nonviolent action often seems to lead to a loss of fear.

Casting off fear is closely tied to gaining confidence that one possesses power and can act in effective ways to change a situation. [17] This was apparently the case in Montgomery, Alabama, during the bus boycott. Martin Luther King, Jr. reported that when repression began, "a once fear-ridden people had been transformed. Those who had previously trembled before the law were now proud to be arrested for the cause of freedom." [18] It is clear that a great deal of the strength of the Norwegian teachers in their resistance to the Quisling regime lay in their open defiance and refusal to bow to fear. [19]

The qualities of bravery and courage are not, of course, limited to nonviolent action. They are present in other situations and certainly where people struggle heroically by violent means, as Gandhi often acknowledged [20] He argued, however, that "the use of nonviolence requires greater bravery than that of violence" [21] and that nonviolent struggle constitutes a weapon "of the stoutest hearts." [22] According to the theories of nonviolent action, violence is removed, not by yielding to it, but by remaining firm in its face. Courage in this technique is not simply a moral virtue; it is a practical requirement of the technique.

Assuming that the actionists maintain courage, the specific type of action possible will be determined by the *degree* to which the participants have become fearless. As E.D. Nixon said at the beginning of the Montgomery bus boycott: ". . . if we are afraid we might just as well fold up right now." [23] If the groups which have been dominated by the opponent are afraid, there can be no nonviolent action, no challenge to the opponent, and no willingness to risk his sanctions. If the nonviolent actionists become fearful in the midst of the struggle, then the movement collapses.

Fear interferes with or destroys the operation of most of the processes of change upon which nonviolent action depends, whether these be conversion of the opponent by convincing him of a new, more favorable, image of the grievance group, or be paralysis of the system by the massiveness of noncooperation despite repression. Fear may also contribute to the continuation of brutalities rather than their diminuation and cessation; *the shortest way to end brutalities is to demonstrate that they do not help to achieve the opponent's objectives.* Courage is required if the nonviolent struggle is to continue and to lead to the increasing strength of the nonviolent group and an undermining of the opponent's power.

Gandhi argued that bravery expressed nonviolently is more powerful than bravery expressed in violence. [24] The emphasis on fearlessness in Gandhian thought, and in various cases of nonviolent struggle, is well advised, for it is a casting off of one's fear—or at least the deliberate reduction and control of one's fear—which makes possible the challenge, the persistance in face of repression, and the capacity to bring into operation the sources of strength and change which can finally lead to victory. This courage makes possible nonviolent discipline in face of severe repression and provocation; and this nonviolent discipline is in turn necessary for the operation of the technique. The nonviolence in nonviolent action rests upon courage.

SOCIAL SOURCES OF POWER CHANGES

The total combat strength and military power of belligerents in conventional military wars are not determined solely by the leaders of the contending governents or even by the soldiers in the front lines. Actions of other sections of the populations, and at times the assistance of other countries in providing various types of necessary support, are also important. Because of this aid, combat strength in military war is variable and depends on the extent and type of support for and participation in the war effort. Similar variations occur in the combat strength of two contending groups when one of them relies on nonviolent action, but with important differences.

The variations in the respective power of the contending groups in this type of conflict situation are likely to be more extreme, to take place more quickly, and to have more diverse consequences. In addition, the nonviolent group may, by its actions and behavior, control the increase or decrease in the relative strength of the opponent group, and this to a much greater degree than occurs in purely military conflicts.

On both sides the leadership groups are dependent on a variety of types of support from large numbers of people and groups, many of which provide specialized types of assistance and serve other essential social roles. The conflict is therefore not one between two clear-cut groups of fixed composition and strength. *Instead, the power of both groups varies.* The process by which their relative and absolute power is altered is complicated, but it can be simply illustrated. The strength of the nonviolent group will be strongly influenced by the people who are actually carrying out the action: the men and women who refuse to work in a strike, the volunteers who disobey laws in a civil disobedience campaign, the people who refuse taxes, who parade in the streets, and who leave boycotted goods on the shelves. If they participate fully, and persist despite the punishments meted out to them, the nonviolent movement is likely to be strong. If significant numbers of the nonviolent actionists decide, however, not to continue to take part, then the nonviolent movement will be weakened.

The opponent group's leadership—say, the government—is similarly dependent on the participation of many people on its side, such as administrators, civil servants, soldiers, policemen, members of the prison system, and the like. All of these may of course not be directly involved in the struggle at any given point. They are, however, the agents (the term is used in a morally neutral sense) on whom the opponent relies in carrying out his policies and countermeasures. If they support the opponent and carry out his policies and instructions fully and efficiently, they will help to maintain or increase his relative power position. But this is not necessarily the case. There are examples of persons in such positions who become lax in carrying out their duties—for example, by not passing important information up the hierarchy, by not relaying orders clearly to their subordinates, by not carrying out their own responsibilities efficiently, or by refusing outright to obey. Should this happen on a widespread basis, the opponent's relative power position is likely to be significantly weakened. There are indications that such laxness in carrying out measures for the regime and against the opposition is likely to occur more frequently, extensively and seriously when the opposition is using nonviolent means of struggle than when it is applying some type of political violence.

The degree to which the participants on *each* side give their wholehearted assistance in behalf of their group's objective varies, therefore. This instability and variability of general participation on *both* sides is an important characteristic of conflicts in which one side uses nonviolent action. The course of the struggle is significantly determined by the supporters of each side. It is they who wage the actual struggle. Without their participation and active assistance neither the leadership of the nonviolent group nor that of the opponent group could increase or even maintain its power. This is a first source of the constant variation in the strengths of each side. There are two others.

Rarely, if ever, does either the nonviolent or the opponent group include the whole "population," or group of people, whom they purport to represent or serve. In a given nonviolent campaign the active participants are usually a relatively small percentage of the whole population in whose interests the nonviolent group claims to be acting. On occasion, of course, participation may be extraordinarily high. The small percentage of actual combatants is not peculiar to nonviolent action. Generally it is even more so in violent struggles, whether international wars or violent revolutions. The attitudes and activities of that wider population associated with the nonviolent struggle are, however, highly important: its approval or disapproval of the nonviolent campaign may influence the morale and hence the behavior of the active participants. If sympathetic, the wider group may provide funds, facilities and supplies, take less dangerous symbolic actions of support, or provide new volunteers for the more militant action; on occasion the whole group may move toward noncooperation with and defiance of the opponent. Conversely, their disapproval of the struggle and withholding of assistance may seriously weaken or undermine the nonviolent actionists. The degree of sympathy and support from the larger group is likely to be influenced by many factors, especially by the issues at stake, the behavior of the opponent group, and the behavior of the nonviolent actionists.

A similar dependence exists for the opponent, for the attitudes and actions of his usual or potential backers are also likely to influence his relative strength. It is on this general population that he is likely ultimately to depend for his financial and material resources, and (in many cases) the operation of the economic system. So, too, he will have to rely on that population for new recruits for the army, police, civil service and the like, and for the general approval of his policies. That approval—or disapproval—may significantly influence the morale and behavior of the officials, police and soldiers who implement the policies and carry out the repression. In some situations a change in attitude in the general population could lead to changes in government policy, and even to a change in government. Here, too, the degree of sympathy and support for the regime, its policies and its measures against the nonviolent actionists is likely to be influenced by the issues at stake and by the behavior of the opponent group and of the nonviolent group. As will become clear, there are important indications that the nonviolent group may be able directly and indirectly both to increase internal opposition to the opponent regime and also to encourage among that regime's general population sympathy and support for the nonviolent group; all this to a far greater degree than would be possible if the nonviolent group had used violence.

In summary, the degree to which the respective "populations" give or withhold their encouragement and assistance to the active protagonists is a very important factor in determining the relative strengths of the two protagonists and the outcome of the conflict. This is a second source of the constant variation in the relative strengths of the respective groups. There remains one more.

Usually this type of conflict occurs within a wider "universe." It may be national or international or both. The importance of national and world opinion to the outcome of the struggle varies considerably and can be highly exaggerated. Such opinion may at times, however, influence the morale of the respective groups, and hence the outcome of the conflict. Or, such opinion may at times take on more concrete expression: public statements by national leaders or pronouncements by international organizations, political intervention by national leaders, economic and other types of support for the nonviolent actionists, economic boycotts and embargoes against the opponent, diplomatic representations, severance of diplomatic relations, and various other forms, depending on the particular situation. These are often ineffective, but on occasion they may tip the scales to bring victory. As will be discussed briefly in Chapter Eleven, this factor was important in the 1963 Buddhist struggle in Vietnam and influential even in unsuccessful struggles.

Because of the variability of the strengths of the protagonists and the dependence of the leadership groups on various other groups, the objectives of the two groups, and their means of action, their wider strategies, tactics, specific methods, and behavior are all likely to have effects far beyond the particular time and place in which they occur. These effects will rebound to strengthen or weaken one group or the other. The ever-present potential for extreme variability in the power of the contending groups, and the widespread and complex character of the reverberations and influences of actions and their effects, are highly important in understanding how this technique of struggle works and why certain types of behavior may have consequences which would not otherwise be expected.

LEADERSHIP IN NONVIOLENT STRUGGLE

Socially significant nonviolent action does not just happen. In every case—whether such action occurs spontaneously, "semi-spontaneously," or is deliberately planned—considerable groundwork has prepared the way for the use of this particular technique of struggle. This groundwork may have been laid quite unconsciously as the result of a variety of influences. Frustration at the blocking of conventional channels of change, or at their uselessness in certain situations, may have finally led people to think of unorthodox ways of acting. The situation itself may have become unbearable or threatening, thus requiring radical action. Other types of action—such as violence—may have been defeated or may appear hopeless. An example of nonviolent action in some other place or time may suddenly be seen as relevant to the immediate situation. People may have grasped hope that something can be done to improve their lot and that they can do it. They may have lost their fear. New insights into accepted beliefs may have gained. The pleas or example of an apparently ignored minority may finally have produced results. New leadership may have arisen. There may have been other factors, but before socially significant nonviolent action can take place, *something* must have prepared the situation for it.

Unfortunately, we know very little of the conditions under which spontaneous cases occur and to what degree the groundwork for these can be consciously cultivated even though the actual resort to nonviolent action remains unplanned. Detailed comparative studies of cases of spontaneous nonviolent action might shed light on this and prove to be extremely important, especially for political situations which make it difficult to organize nonviolent action on a large scale. Such studies might also shed light on whether, and if so how, particular problems—such as strategy, discipline and tenacity—involved in spontaneous nonviolent action could be satisfactorily solved. For the sake of simplification, in these chapters we are assuming deliberate planning. We can therefore assume that some recognizable leadership for the movement exists.

The leadership group will usually initiate as well as plan and give continuing direction, at least in the early stages, to the nonviolent action, although in some cases it may be called to or assume its position after the action has begun. Leadership in such situations serves a very important role, especially where knowledge and understanding of the principles and practice of nonviolent action are not widespread and deep among the general population. Machiavelli pointed to the tendency of threats of disobedience to collapse if there is no effective leadership to assist in implementing them. [25] Recent struggles give evidence to support Machiavelli's view. For example, Eugen Stamm has argued that the decisive shortcomings of the 1953 East German Rising were "lack of organizational preparations; lack of central leadership; the incapacity of local strike leaders to keep in touch with one another." [26]

It would be rash, however, to say that without central leadership nonviolent struggle can never be successful. Much depends on the extent and depth of understanding of the nature and requirements of this technique of struggle. There is evidence that, in the late stages of a campaign, a nonviolent resistance movement can continue even after all the central leadership has been imprisoned or otherwise removed. If so, there is no intrinsic reason why a movement which started without central leadership could not be effective, given wide popular understanding of this type of action. It is not necessarily true that the stronger the leadership the better. For example, it has been argued that during the British General Strike of 1926 the General Council of the Trades Union Congress (influenced especially by Ernest Bevin) attempted too much centralized control. [27]

In most cases, however, some type of central leadership will be present and will be important for a variety of tasks. These would include working out strategy and tactics for action, negotiating with the opponent, encouraging willingness to resist, promoting discipline, choosing the best moment for action, and recommending continuing tactics and counterresponses as the struggle continues. Gandhi was, for example, convinced of the importance of strong leadership for a major movement using nonviolent action. He did not mean only the top leadership but also a larger band of well-trained volunteers "who thoroughly understood the strict conditions of Satyagraha. They could explain these to the people, and by sleepless vigilance keep them on the right path." [28] Referring to the participation of many thousands in the 1930–31 campaign, Gandhi said: "Their belief in nonviolence was unintelligent. . . . But their belief in their leaders was genuine." [29]

The main tasks of leadership in conflicts have been listed by Miller: to serve as spokesmen for those who are less articulate, to offer solutions to the problems they face, and to organize the implementation of those solutions. [30] Also, in the course of a struggle there will arise a host of problems and situations in which decisions based on knowledge and experience are to be preferred to decisions based on little understanding, or to no decisions at all because there is no one to take them.

The origins and structure of leadership in nonviolent struggles have differed widely. Where an existing organization resolves upon a course of nonviolent action, that body can itself provide a considerable degree of the leadership and organizational framework for the ensuing conflict. The Trades Union Congress and other trades union bodies served such roles in the British General Strike of 1926, for example (especially the General Council's Strike Organization Committee)[31] and the Indian National Congress, with Gandhi in a strong role, composed most of the leadership in the Indian struggles. The leadership has also taken the form of a self-selected group which operates an underground giving instructions for open nonviolent resistance by the general population, as in Finland in 1901.[32] A leadership committee may be elected by popular vote; a sixty-member committee to carry out the economic boycott against Great Britain was so elected at the City Hall in New York City on November 22, 1774.[33] In nonviolent action in support of the government, against invaders or *coups d'etat,* the top leadership may be the legal government and its ministers, as happened in the *Ruhrkampf* of 1923.[34]

In other cases, a self-selected leadership group may be formed shortly before or immediately after conflict has broken out into the open. At other times the people directly involved in the action may elect a leadership committee: frequently several such committees may federate to form a wider leadership committee. For example, in Halle, East Germany, where strikers were able to fall back on a long trade union tradition, local strike committees joined together on June 17, 1953, to form an Initiative Committee, which called a mass meeting and conducted negotiations for the successful occupation of a radio station and newspaper office.[35] During the student sit-in movement in 1960, in Raleigh, North Carolina, students from two colleges joined to set up leadership committees, composed of persons who had emerged "by natural selection." Elsewhere student presidents stepped into leadership in the new situation. In Raleigh, students formed a central Intelligence Committee (executive committee) with four specialized subcommittees to deal with particular tasks.[36] In Atlanta, Georgia, the 1960 sit-ins were led by a policy-making board of about fifteen members from six colleges, the Committee on Appeal for Human Rights; there was a general staff, a top officer called *"le Commandante,"* a "Deputy Chief of Operations," a field commander, deputy commander, and area commanders.[37] New leaders were also "thrown up out of the situation" in the bus boycott by the Africans of Alexandra Township near Johannesburg in 1957.[38] On May 20, 1917, mutinous French troops at the XXXIInd Corps replacement depot elected three delegates to present the officers with an ultimatum, and others a few days later elected "deputies" on the style of the Russian Soldiers' Councils.[39]

Top leadership in nonviolent action movements has so far taken one of three forms: group or committee leadership, an individual (especially Gandhi) acting much like a general in an army with all others carrying out orders, or a combination of the two. There are advantages and objections to all.

The individual leadership system makes it possible for the most experienced person with deepest insight into the technique, the social and political situation, the condition of the expected volunteers and general population, and other factors to work out the plans and strategy as a comprehensive whole. This is important, for the particular actions and stages of the movement can only be most significant if they are seen in relation to the wider movement to which they contribute. Gandhi argued that if the movement in crisis situations were to avoid temptations to resort to violence, or to take actions which might lead to violence, the leadership of the movement must be in the hands of those who believed in nonviolence as a moral principle. Also, in the preparation for a struggle there is often time for only limited detailed discussions and arguments in committee. Depending of course on the composition of the specific committee, such bodies can help; but they can also involve "interminable" discussions and arguments on trivial or irrelevant points. Sometimes such meetings can fairly be described as sessions in which mutual ignorance is pooled. There would be times in which to have the direction of a large-scale struggle in such hands could prove disastrous.

On the other hand, if no individual obviously stands well above the group in the qualities needed for this leadership position, it could be dangerous to give power of overall direction to one not prepared for it. Consequently, the alternative procedure—usually followed in the West—is for the leadership and planning to be in the hands of a special committee. The members may bring to it various backgrounds, skills, knowledge and insights, which ideally will combine to give the committee as a whole the qualities, skills and information to fulfill its tasks. The presence on the committee of members who lack the ability to listen to others, who talk incessantly, argue over irrelevancies, are unstable, arrogant, or simply difficult persons must be avoided. If so, and suitable persons who are capable of working smoothly together and of recognizing useful insights and suggestions from other members are included, then the group leadership will possess advantages over individual leadership and may usefully contribute to the further training of top leadership personnel. It is arguable which could operate best in crisis situations.

Even in the case of individual leadership, however, the situation is not as authoritarian as it appears at first sight, for the leader would be selected by the group concerned with the grievance and given authority to prepare plans for the action. For example, Gandhi was authorized by the

Indian National Congress—the nationalist party—to plan the civil disobedience campaign in 1930. But the leader's continued authority would always be subject to the continuance of the group's voluntary recognition of it. There is likely to be—often there must be—a pyramid of leadership with two or three or more ranks. But despite this hierarchical leadership structure, the leader cannot force his will upon those unwilling to accept it. The group could decline to accept the leader's plans. Any individual could decline to volunteer for the struggle, and at any time he could withdraw from the group if he could no longer conscientiously support the movement and its actions. As long as the volunteer remains a volunteer, however, he should carry out instructions. As Gandhi put it, he "may not remain a unit in his regiment and have the option of doing or not doing things he is asked to do."[40] In Western practice, people usually do not volunteer for a long-term nonviolent campaign, but for a specific demonstration or action, usually because long-term campaigns are rarely planned. Hence there is very little or no chance of their being ordered into a specific action of which they may disapprove, thus having to withdraw from the movement. But if a campaign or a more limited action has been carefully planned it is extremely important that all participants be willing to abide by the plans if the action is to be coherent and disciplined.

The nonviolent leadership has only nonviolent sanctions at its disposal for the enforcement of its decisions and instructions. These sanctions will be discussed in more detail later, but their relationship to the character of nonviolent leadership requires attention here. One sanction is the disapproval by other members of the nonviolent group. Sometimes social boycotts have been used. The leader himself has sanctions which only he can impose. For example, Gandhi first fasted and then called off the 1919 campaign against the Rowlatt Act because some demonstrators had resorted to violence.[41] When striking mill workers being led by Gandhi in Ahmedabad in 1918 began to go back on their pledges of behavior for the course of the strike, Gandhi's fast restored morale and adherence to their earlier promises.[42] However effective such extreme sanctions may sometimes be, they are clearly of a different character than the extreme sanctions at the disposal of leaders in a violent struggle—imprisonment or execution. This difference in enforcement sanctions is only one of the factors which separate the operation of military leadership and even the most authoritarian forms of leadership in a nonviolent movement. In addition, nonviolent leaders have frequently emphasized that they did not wish people to follow them blindly, but to follow only if convinced of the policy and proposed actions.[43]

One of the most important justifications for strong leadership in nonviolent struggles has been that only a few people had sufficient understanding of this technique to make wise decisions as to how to take action. It is very possible that widespread self-education and spread of knowledge about nonviolent action may facilitate the development of a more diffused system of leadership and increased self-reliance.

Whatever form it takes, the quality of the leadership for nonviolent action is very important in developing the movement along sound lines, gathering support, maintaining confidence, keeping up morale, and guiding it directly or with prepared plans through difficulties to a successful conclusion. The personal qualities of the leader or the leadership group and the perceived wisdom of their plans for action determine whether their guidance is accepted voluntarily by the participants in the struggle. If not, those "leaders" will be rejected and become unsuccessful claimants to leadership positions. Gregg lists as necessary qualities of nonviolent leaders a high degree of love, faith, courage, honesty and humility.[44] There are other qualities, however, which are highly important. Leaders for this type of struggle are likely to be most capable if they possess an active mind, have thorough expertise in the technique they are applying, are able to develop wise strategy, plans and actions, and understand the opponent's case, his psychology, resources, and the changing views and attitudes of his supporters. The nonviolent leader will need to understand the potentialities, limitations and nature of the volunteers, sympathizers and the population. His past record will also be important, especially his experience, service and integrity. He must be willing to accept sacrifice and to set an example for the movement.

In some cases the leadership will be more diffused and harder to locate—especially where the movement has been spontaneous rather than planned, and also in advanced stages of planned movements when the original leadership has been entirely removed. Leadership may then be provided by larger numbers of individuals and small groups who offer leads for action which are accepted and followed by others. The quality of this type of leadership is important too, for it must not lead in the wrong direction if the campaign is to be a success.

PREPARING FOR NONVIOLENT STRUGGLE

Whether a campaign is to be massive, including many millions of participants, or small, with only a handful of volunteers or even a single person, careful planning and preparations are essential. Gandhi's careful attention to detail in laying plans for *satyagraha* and in solving organizational problems has been acknowledged as one of the reasons for his effectiveness. This has not always been the case in nonviolent struggles, of course. Lindberg pointed out in 1937 that military campaigns have almost always been carried out by disciplined men acting under trained leaders, while nonviolent campaigns have never taken place under such favorable conditions. "They have always been characterized by inadequate preparations." However, since the time of Gandhi's major experiments with this technique in India, there has been increasing emphasis on the need for preparations if the technique is to be effective. As Lindberg wrote: "Every form of nonviolent campaign of a merely spontaneous character is threatened either by death in indifference in the course of a short time, or is threatened by a much too rapid growth and blooming in a transition to violence." [45] Investigation may show ways to combine general preparations for nonviolent struggle with spontaneity as to the exact moment and form of action; this might be especially useful in political situations where open advance preparations and organization are impossible. However, Gandhi and others who have given considerable thought to the problem would come very close to full agreement with Lindberg.

The exact order in which various types of preparation or actions are carried out, or ought to be carried out, for greatest effectiveness will vary with the particular situation. The order of the topics discussed here ought not therefore to be identified with an unchangeable pattern.

A. Investigation

Where the use of nonviolent action is contemplated, the movement will be strengthened by an advance investigation of alleged grievances. Few things can weaken such a movement as much as the revelation that the actionists did not really know the facts nor have accurate information on the situation they were complaining about. Where full and accurate information is not readily available, some type of investigation will have to be undertaken. That investigation should be as accurate and as fair as possible; this will help in the wide acceptance of its results. The investigation should not be limited only to the facts as seen by the group with the grievances, but should include the facts as seen by the opponent group and by third parties. Following the investigation, a statement of desired changes should be formulated. The greater the accuracy and fairness in the statement of grievances and of facts, and the greater the restraint shown in concentrating on only the clearest and most important demands, it has been said, the stronger the appearance of the nonviolent group's case and the weaker that of the opponent. Furthermore, basic issues should not be confused with secondary ones.

Sometimes in rigid political systems the facts may come to light not by an investigation—which might be impossible—but by simply "leaking out." For example, in Nazi Germany news of the gassing of mentally ill persons which began in September 1939 leaked out even though it was top secret; this led to significant protest from Roman Catholic church leaders until the euthanasia program was stopped in August 1941.[46]

After the information has been gathered by investigation or other means, the widest possible publicity is to be given to the facts of the case, the grievances, and the aims of the nonviolent group. This publicity is not part of the investigation, which is normally done quietly, but belongs in the phase of "generating cause-consciousness" which is discussed below. This publicity may itself bring pressure for a change. Even if it does not, the dissemination of the results of investigation will contribute to a stronger position for the nonviolent group during the ensuing struggle.

B. Negotiations

At this stage of the conflict negotiations with the opponent are usually undertaken or intensified, through personal meetings and letters, often unpublicized. Initiation of nonviolent action, especially in its more radical forms, is a serious undertaking. Efforts to solve the problem before taking direct action are desirable. In addition an effort at negotiations—whether or not immediately successful—may also *contribute* to a satisfactory resolution of the conflict. Negotiations in this context are therefore not seen as a full substitute for nonviolent action, but as a step which might make it unnecessary in some cases and more effective in others.

Where the issues at stake are serious, especially where they affect the relative power positions of the groups, it should not be surprising if a solution satisfactory to the nonviolent group is not reached by negotiation. The effort may, however, serve other purposes. Negotiation is one channel for maintaining contact between the two groups, helping the opponent understand the grievances, and communicating to him why nonviolent action is going to be taken. In negotiations the nonviolent group can also explain the type of struggle which will be used. Very important in some cases, negotiations may also help the opponent and the negotiators to achieve a relationship between human beings as such. This may counterbalance or prevent the mutual distortions of each other's images which often occur in conflict and which may reduce the chances of a settlement.[47] It is also important that the nonviolent group should make, and be seen to make, every effort at a settlement before launching direct action. This greatly increases its moral position, in its own eyes and in those of the opponent group and of third parties. It will also aid the perception that the more extreme action has been forced upon the nonviolent group and is therefore more justified.[48] When the nonviolent group begins direct action, that perception may influence various reactions and thus the relative support the two contending groups receive.

In negotiations, the representatives of the nonviolent group will make clear their minimum demands, as distinguished from secondary issues on which compromise may be possible, or which may even not be pressed. Where basic moral or political principles are involved they will not be subject to compromise, however. Once the demands are set, it is generally recommended that they be kept unchanged during the struggle, and not raised or lowered with variations in the nonviolent group's chances of victory. Usually, such changes in demands are likely to reduce sympathy and support for the nonviolent group, and lower its credibility.[49]

Preparation for nonviolent action is likely to increase the chances of successful negotiations, for the mere possibility of such struggle may on occasion encourage the opponent to make concessions.[50] This relationship is important at this stage of the conflict. The practitioner of this technique is much more realistic about the role of power than is his more naïve friend who favors negotiations as a *substitute* for open struggle. Negotiations do not take place in a vacuum, and they are rarely resolved solely on the objective merits of the respective arguments and evidence. Behind every case of negotiations is the stated or silent—but mutually understood—role of the relative power positions of the negotiators; that is, what each can do if no agreement is reached. Gandhi said, for example: "I do not believe in making appeals when there is no force behind them, whether moral or material."[51] The nonviolent actionists' capacity and willingness for further action distinguishes his approach from that of those who vaguely prefer peace and think that talking is a substitute for war. The nonviolent army, Gandhi said, "should be so well prepared as to make war unnecessary."[52] Theodor Ebert has called "a credible determination to fight a prerequisite for negotiations."[53] Ebert has pointed out that on some occasions Indian leaders demanded not only concrete promises in negotiations, but some "advance deeds as proof that the promises would later be kept," such as the release of political prisoners.[54]

All cases may not follow this pattern, of course. In actual events, negotiations may occur simultaneously with other actions, such as a strike or a civil disobedience campaign. Or the opponent may refuse to negotiate, demanding, for example, that the nonviolent group give up all plans for direct action, or, if such action has begun, declaring that he will not negotiate until it is called off. The nonviolent actionist will refuse to be intimidated or sidetracked by such tactics. However, Gandhi and others have emphasized that as long as the opponent does not impose unreasonable preconditions for negotiations, the nonviolent group should be willing and even eager to negotiate at any stage of the conflict, in the hope of finding an acceptable settlement which will make continued direct action unnecessary.

C. Sharpening the focus for attack

Nonviolent action is a technique of struggle in which the participants are able to advance their cause in proportion to the degree that the opponent's desire and ability to maintain the objectionable policy are weakened, and that the nonviolent group is able to generate the will and power to give it the internal strength to effect the change. The skillful choice of the point of attack is important in this connection. In intellectual arguments one often concentrates on the weakest links in the opponent's case. In war, instead of attacking with equal force on the whole front simultaneously, one usually concentrates forces on what are believed to be the enemy's weakest points in the belief that a breakthrough there will lead to a weakening or collapse of other sections of the front. So in a nonviolent struggle the nonviolent leadership will show wisdom in concentrating action on the weakest points in the opponent's case, policy, or system. This will contribute to the maximum weakening of his relative position and the maximum strengthening of that of the nonviolent group.

In nonviolent action it is necessary to have a pivot point on which to place the lever which is to remove the evil. The selection of this pivot or issue is very important for the whole consequent campaign. One does not, in Gandhi's view, launch a nonviolent campaign for such general objectives as "peace," "independence," "freedom," or "brotherhood." "The issue must be definite and capable of being clearly understood and within the power of the opponent to yield." [55] In applying this technique of struggle under less than perfect conditions, success may depend, Miller writes, on "phasing strategy in such a way as to score a series of minor gains or to secure a single major victory in the most accessible sector, rather than trying for a cluster of major objectives at the same time." [56] Whether the specific objective(s) chosen is (are) highly limited or very ambitious will hinge in part on the nonviolent group's assessment of its relative strength and capacity for action.

In a study of the defeated campaign in Albany, Georgia, in 1962, Professor Howard Zinn wrote:

There has been a failure to create and handle skillfully a set of differentiated tactics for different situations. The problem of desegregating Albany facilities involves various parties: some situations call for action by the city commission; some for decision by the Federal Courts; some for agreement with private businessmen. Moreover, there are advantages to singling out a particular goal and concentrating on it. This is an approach not only tactically sound for Negro protest but also creates a climate favorable to a negotiated solution. The community is presented with a specific concrete demand rather than a quilt of grievances and demands which smothers the always limited ability of societies to think rationally about their faults.[57]

Martin Luther King, Jr., reached a similar conclusion in the same case:

. . . we decided that one of the principal mistakes we had made there was to scatter our efforts too widely. We had been so involved in attacking segregation in general that we had failed to direct our protest effectively to any one major facet. We concluded that in hard-core communities a more effective battle could be waged if it was concentrated against one aspect of the evil and intricate system of segregation.[58]

Without question there were other serious causes of the Albany defeat, but those do not invalidate these observations.

Instead, then, of a campaign for some very general objective, Ebert writes: "In working out the staged plan, it is essential for the success of the campaign to find the correct point of attack or one flash-point among many in social relationships which symbolizes all the other conflicts."[59] In the Vykom campaign, sketched in Chapter Two, the issue was the right of people to use a road that led to their homes. In the 1930-31 independence movement the specific issue which initiated the campaign was that of the Salt Laws, which touched the lives of most of the people in India; other wider political aims were condensed into eleven demands.[60]

This is not a matter of being moderate in one's aims, but of concentrating one's strength in ways which will make victory more likely. The planners choose the point of attack, the specific aspect of the general problem which symbolizes the "evil" which is least defensible by the opponent and which is capable of arousing the greatest strength against it. Success in such limited campaigns will in turn increase the self-confidence of the actionists[61] and their ability to move effectively toward the fuller achievement of their larger objectives as they gain experience in the use of effective means of action to realize their aims.

The choice of the point of attack requires considerable understanding and a keen perception of the total situation. Amiya Chakravarty has described very well Gandhi's ability to combine short-run and long-run plans in the selection of a focal point for action. It sometimes happens, Chakravarty writes, that "in following one obvious remedial line we have hit upon a symptom which symbolizes, demonstrates and challenges a root situation." A series of attacks on these points makes it possible to move "from one total situation to another." The issue should be kept clear and clean, he continues, pointing out that, for example, segregation in opium parlors would be an erroneous choice as a point for attack on racial segregation, while the right to pray in unsegregated churches "would be an issue of overwhelming convergence." Repression against nonviolent actionists concentrating on such a point of attack could but strengthen their cause. "Again and again, Gandhiji showed an instinct, a spiritual instinct, for the right issue, for the converging issues which supported each other at a point." [62]

This approach to political action has strong support from a quite different source, namely, Lenin, who wrote: "The whole art of politics lies in finding and gripping as strong as we can the link that is least likely to be torn out of our hands, the one that is most important at the given moment, the one that guarantees the possessor of a link the possession of the whole chain." [63]

D. Generating "cause-consciousness" [64]

During the stage of investigation, publicity will usually, but not always, have been avoided. After the information has been gathered, however, and the minimum demands determined, it is necessary to publicize the facts, the issues and the arguments advanced by the nonviolent group. "The investigation into the causes of the conflict, the documentation of actual grievances and the resulting demands of the oppressed must be widely disseminated in a form which is comprehensible to the public and to the oppressor," writes Ebert. [65] The need for such a period of motivational preparation has been long recognized as important to a well-supported and sustained nonviolent movement. For example, in 1769, in correspondence with George Washington about the details and implementation of a nonimportation plan, his neighbor James Mason argued that it would be necessary to publish "something preparatory to it in our gazettes, to warn the people of the impending danger and to induce them the more readily and cheerfully to concur in the proper measures to avert it." [66]

This phase may begin prior to negotiations with the opponent, or it may occur simultaneously with negotiations, or follow them when they have failed. It may proceed by stages, moving from the effort to inform the public in general of the grievances, to encouraging people to feel that nonviolent action is needed to correct them, and finally to enlisting paricipants for the coming struggle. A very important part of this activity is aimed at arousing the feeling that something can and ought to be done, and at increasing confidence that this can and should be done along nonviolent lines.

A variety of means may be used for these purposes. Pamphlets, leaflets, books, articles and papers dealing with the issues and the implications of the dispute may be issued. Public meetings, speeches, debates, discussions on radio, television and before existing organizations may be held. Sometimes the cinema, theater, catchy songs, slogans and symbols may be used, as well as house-to-house canvassing, petitions and personal contacts. The degree to which specific means are used openly depends somewhat on the regime and political situation in the country. A properly conducted journal can be of immense help in such a campaign, as most leaders of political dissent, including Gandhi, have recognized.

The emphasis in this effort to arouse "cause-consciousness" must be placed on quality rather than on speed or quantity, and strict efforts must be made to avoid exaggerations, distortions and falsehoods. Neither should feelings of hatred or intolerance be aroused. Oppenheimer and Lakey write that, without compromising, it is important "to try to limit the amount of antagonism from potential allies." This involves both "cutting down on actions which can be misinterpreted to be hostile and negative" and also improving the interpretation of all activities. "Remember," they add, "that many people are only looking for an excuse *not* to support the movement." [67]

The duration of this stage of the movement will vary with the situation and previous work. [68] Sometimes, some of the publicity efforts started when the grievance group had not yet considered taking nonviolent action will be continued. Sometimes, also, widespread individual discontent will coalesce into general awareness of collective dissent. For example, before the East German Rising of June 16–17, 1953, workers had become increasingly vocal about their dissatisfaction with working conditions and with an increase in the work norms, which reduced wages but not the amount of work. They had managed to discuss their grievances, and the Rising itself was preceded by some sixty local strikes during the first half of June. [69]

Arousing "cause-consciousness" may be divided into several phases. Special efforts will be necessary to develop understanding of the issues. When the decision is finally made to launch nonviolent action and specific plans are announced, further efforts will be needed to inform the population and possible participants of the nature of the contemplated action, the requirements for its success, the importance of engaging or not engaging in particular acts, and similar points.

A variety of efforts may then be made to justify and legitimatize resort to direct action. Persons about to launch nonviolent action may regard themselves as acting in defense of the constitution and the law, while the opponent's actions are regarded as having no legal basis.[70] Alternatively, the action may be taken in an attempt to restore a system or constitution which was illegally and violently overthrown by the opponent. Justification may also be made in terms of democratic popular will against minority or foreign oppression, or in terms of the basic rights of man or of religious principles. Frequently, too, reliance on the technique of nonviolent action will be regarded as adding legitimacy and justification to the cause, especially when various means of violent action are regarded as inappropriate or wrong for social and political as well as moral reasons.

The nonviolent leaders may also at this stage warn of the hardship and suffering which will be incurred during the struggle. They may seek to arouse confidence that those penalties will be worth incurring, because this type of action is more likely than any other to procure victory. Sometimes such leaders and participants believe that the combination of a just cause and the use of this technique of action will in the long run ensure victory. Frederic Solomon and Jacob R. Fishman argued that the confidence of civil rights workers in inevitable desegregation—coming from a just cause and use of nonviolent action—was psychologically useful because "it heightens [their] own strength and resolve" and also "undermines that of the opposition."[71] Various types of symbolic action (among them methods described in Chapter Three) may be used at this stage to dramatize the issues, strike the imagination of the general populace, and arouse the will to take direct action.

E. Quantity and quality in nonviolent action

In planning and conducting nonviolent action very careful consideration must constantly be given to the relationship between the numbers participating in the conflict and the quality of their participation. This appears to be a more complex relationship than is recognized by those who argue that *only quantity* or *only quality* is important. The way in which this relationship is resolved and expressed has a very significant effect upon the whole course of the movement and its consequences. Clearly both are important, but they are not always equally important. Within certain limits the relationship between numbers and quality may vary considerably, changing with the situation, the stage of the movement, and the methods which are to be used. Certainly in a technique of action which in large degree depends for its effectiveness on the withdrawal of consent, cooperation and obedience, the numbers of participants are significant to its relative impact. But to concentrate on numbers alone may prove unwise because the effectiveness and consequences of nonviolent action are not in simple proportion to the numbers involved. If large numbers are involved, the strength thus demonstrated must be genuine if the movement is not to collapse in crises and if it is to persist and grow. The genuineness of this strength is in turn related to such factors as the degree of fearlessness, discipline, willingness to persist despite sanctions, and wisdom shown in the choice of strategy, tactics and methods of action. These are all closely associated with the quality of the movement.

In a sense nonviolent action is by its very nature qualitatively different from other means of struggle. It requires, for example, fearlessness and determination, an ability to maintain nonretaliation, sometimes forgiveness, and always nonviolence in face of the opponent's sometimes brutal repression. At the same time it requires courageous persistence in the intended course of action, and selfless commitment to the cause of the grievance group.

The degree of quality required in a given movement may vary with conditions, especially those conditions which may make it difficult to use this technique, and also with the type of opponent being confronted. In a labor strike, for example, under normal conditions in Western countries today, as long as the men stay away from work, their chances of success are high. They usually have some form of financial assistance to help them through the strike. The chances of severe repression by police or the military are now slight. Strikebreakers are rarer than before. Provocation to violence is usually no longer extensive. Objectives are usually quite limited and do not threaten the opponent seriously. The duration of the strike is not likely to be long. Under such conditions, the actionists can "get away" with a lower overall quality in the movement than would be desirable or necessary if contrasting conditions existed. This certainly does not mean that increased quality in behavior of participants under such conditions would not be desirable and even highly beneficial, but that it is no longer so necessary.

However, when the chances of success are not large, when repression may be severe, when the opponent provokes violence, when the objectives seriously threaten the opponent's ego or position, and the struggle may be a long one, then high quality in the movement becomes essential. The problem is how to achieve it. Sometimes people may out of desperation, newly gained confidence, courage, or intuition rise to the demands of the situation. On other occasions they may be willing to follow wise guidance from leaders who understand what is needed. Sometimes the development of quality behavior in large numbers of participants may follow a series of smaller demonstrations of brave and disciplined nonviolent action.

There is a tradition within nonviolent action, especially in the labor movement and among advocates of the general strike in achieving social revolution, which emphasizes the importance of numbers. So, too, there is another tradition (clearly expressed by Gandhi) which emphasizes the role of quality and the disproportionate effect which a small number of actionists may have. Gregg has argued that a minute force can lead to a large change and that frequently a weak stimulus may even be superior to a stronger one.[72] He speaks of the "primary influential power of disciplined individual persons."[73] Bondurant relates Gandhi's concepts of the power of the individual to his concern for individual freedom within society and to Western concepts of the dignity of the individual.[74] Fewer numbers of volunteers with fuller understanding of the nonviolent approach are likely, she explains, to prove more reliable in crises. Lakey suggests that quality may be more important, even at the cost of numbers, when the nonviolent group aims at persuading or converting the opponent. He writes:

This may be explained by recourse to our view that communication of images is an important part of any conflict. The image which is presented by the nonviolent actor is more important than the number of persons comprising the image. In Goffman's terms, the person for whom nonviolence is a matter of faith is more likely to give a "consistent performance"—thereby presenting a clear-cut image of suffering and courageous humanity. The fewer "slips" there are into angry retorts or frantic retreats, the more likely it is that the opponent and public will perceive in the campaigner an important common quality and respond to it with a lessening of violence.[75]

It may be useful briefly to survey Gandhi's views on the dependence of both success and numbers in nonviolent action on quality, since his conclusions differ considerably from the popular expectation. Numbers, Gandhi insisted, were not necessary in a just cause.[76] In a nonviolent struggle fewer *satyagrahis* would be needed than would regular soldiers in a violent conflict.[77] Nonviolent action of high quality and small numbers could have a powerful impact, he insisted.[78] "I attach the highest importance to quality irrespective almost of quantity . . ."[79] "Even a handful of true satyagrahis well organized and disciplined through selfless service of the masses, can win independence for India."[80] "I am convinced that there is safety in fewness so long as we have not evolved cohesion, exactness and intelligent cooperation and responsiveness."[81] Even a single perfect *satyagrahi,* Gandhi believed, could "defy the whole might of an unjust empire . . . and lay the foundation for that empire's fall or regeneration."[82] Unfortunately, Gandhi admitted, such perfection was not possible, but this did not alter the general principle of the overwhelming importance of quality in a nonviolent movement.

It is clear that Gandhi saw this quality as influencing the opponent and making him more likely to accept the demands of the nonviolent group, as paving the way for larger numbers when, inspired by the example, more people learned to cast off fear and to rely on disciplined nonviolent action to remedy the grievance.[83] Quality would be contagious and multiply; the number of nonviolent actionists enrolled under Gandhi's leadership in South Africa, for example, rose from sixteen to sixty thousand.[84] In contrast, undisciplined numbers would fade away. Furthermore, the growth in numbers was important for another reason. Even if it were possible for a single individual or a very few nonviolent actionists by their own actions to achieve the desired change, it would be wiser, Gandhi felt, for them to use their abilities to educate the masses of the people in the means by which they themselves could right their wrongs. The maintenance of quality was important in this. "Mass instruction on any other terms is an impossibility."[85]

In other words, the maintenance of high quality in nonviolent action is necessary at all stages; if this is done when the numbers are small, it will make possible a very considerable increase in the numbers of nonviolent actionists capable of the strength necessary for effectivenenss. Large numbers not able to maintain the nonviolent discipline, the fearlessness, and other necessary standards of behavior could only weaken the movement,[86] but large numbers capable of maintaining the necessary standards and discipline become "irresistable."[87]

In summary, because of the nature of the technique of nonviolent action itself, attention to the maintenance of the quality of the movement, including such factors as fearlessness and maintaining the nonviolent discipline, is always required. Large numbers may frequently be necessary to effect particular changes. However, such numbers can be obtained as reliable participants only by maintaining and not lowering the standards of the movement.

F. Organizing the movement

Some type of organization is usually helpful or necessary if the action campaign is to implement decisions and carry out specific tasks. Important jobs cannot be simply left to chance; they require efficient organization to ensure that they are done. Among the tasks of such an organization are those which relate to the public, the volunteers, the leadership and the movement as a whole. These tasks will include publicizing the facts and grievances, promoting sympathy for the nonviolent group and its aims, informing the public of the intentions of the nonviolent group and its plans for action, and mobilizing financial and other resources for the movement. Another group of tasks relating to volunteers includes recruiting participants for the campaign, preparing volunteers and potential participants for action, and training these volunteers for specific and immediate tasks. Also, when new sympathizers and supporters appear, it will be necessary to show them how to help the movement in specific ways and to incorporate them into groups of other active participants. Leadership and organization are related; the organization may provide in advance for several successive stages of leadership to replace immediately arrested leaders, and may determine the procedure for further selection of leadership as long as conditions permit its operation as a clear group. The organization may also provide the leadership with accurate information about the condition of the movement and various factors influencing it. Other tasks which the organization may tackle include steps to keep up the movement's morale, to maintain discipline, and to prepare participants to act without leaders in times of severe repression.

The degree to which such organization has been formal has in past campaigns varied considerably. The numbers involved, their understanding of the technique of action, whether they are used to working together, and the situation in which they are operating—all have an influence in this regard. Sometimes an organization may be set up on the spot, as by striking workers who have no trade union. Sometimes an existing organization may be turned to the new task of nonviolent action; there are sometimes advantages to that, especially as the body may already be a legitimate group with a definite place in the society. Sometimes local or regional or even central government may become the resistance organization, especially if such government is responsive to popular will. Local and regional government may be involved when the opponent is the central government; together with the central government, local and regional governments may be involved in facing an internal usurper carrying out a *coup,* or a foreign invader. On other occasions a new action organization for the specific purpose may be set up before nonviolent action is launched. Both tried and respected persons and leaders of other groups and new and hitherto inexperienced and unknown persons may help to build and operate the organization.

An organization for nonviolent struggle should not be unwieldy, it must not be corrupted, it should be able to put its full weight into the struggle without pursuing any basically inconsistent further objective, and it should be able to operate under a voluntary formal or informal discipline. [88] An effective system of communication between the various branches and levels of the direct action organization will usually be required. If the opponent's police measures and control of communications and transportation make such communication difficult or impossible, then the planners will need to determine in advance the points and issues on which opposition will be launched and how this will be done. Then, despite lack of contact between resistance groups, they may still be able to act, even as part of a joint action for the same objectives. [89]

Regardless of the precise form which organization takes in a particular conflict situation—and that subject itself merits detailed study[90]—the importance of organization for effective nonviolent action remains of high priority. As Gandhi wrote in 1920:

But the greatest thing in this campaign of non-cooperation is to evolve order, discipline, cooperation among the people, coordination among the workers. Effective non-cooperation depends upon complete organization. [91]

Ebert has supported this view:

The fact that the state of organization and advance preparation has been so decisive in past nonviolent campaigns suggests that nonviolent resistance can develop into an alternative to violent resistance only in so far as it assumes visible organizational shape and is adequately prepared. [92]

Sometimes part of the preparatory organizational work will include obtaining pledges to participate in the campaign. Such pledges will often include clauses committing the signer to abide by the movement's nonviolent discipline as a contribution to success. Pledges are not a recent innovation. Pledges, oaths and agreements to carry out resistance plans, especially for nonviolent economic resistance, were widely used during the struggle of the American colonists.[93] In 1775, for example, radicals in Virginia sought the signature of every inhabitant in the colony to the Continental Association resistance plan adopted by the First Continental Congress.[94] The Congress had in that document pledged continued adherence to the plan until repeal of the offending laws of Parliament had been achieved.[95]

Mass meetings have often been used to contact possible volunteers and to stimulate their willingness to join the coming struggle. If formal pledges are used in the campaign, signatures may then be sought. In other cases there have been no formal pledges, with reliance being placed instead on adherence to the general principles of the movement, high morale and group pressures to ensure continued participation and discipline. Where volunteers have continuing confidence in the efficacy of nonviolent action, considerable understanding of and experience in the use of this technique, and also a good grasp of the planned course of action, then the need for formal pledges may not be so severe. However, in light of existing experience, strong commitment of the volunteers to participation and adherence to the campaign's plans and standards remain crucial. Effective means for promoting these are therefore important at this and other stages of the struggle. In preparing the volunteers and the general population for the struggle, extreme attention must be given to three closely related qualities of this technique: fearlessness, nonviolence, and their corollary, openness or nonsecrecy.

OPENNESS AND SECRECY IN NONVIOLENT STRUGGLE

Secrecy, deception and underground conspiracy pose very difficult problems for a movement using nonviolent action. No matter from what ideological or philosophical position one starts there is often no easy solution to them.

Believers in nonviolence as a moral principle have often asserted that an associated principle—that of truthfulness—should also be accepted by persons using nonviolent means; they have therefore concluded that nonviolent action movements must never use secrecy. When based simply on assertions of moral principles, these arguments have generally had little influence on persons not sharing them. The relative success of these believers in influencing nonviolent action movements to operate openly and to reject secrecy is probably rooted less in the impact of their arguments than in the evidence provided by various campaigns and action projects that openness worked.

Nevertheless, some persons taking part in nonviolent struggle have at times tried to get the action organization to use secrecy and conspiratorial behavior. This has happened not only where the movement was under political dictatorship, where such an approach might seem reasonable, but even under relatively liberal political conditions, as in Britain. Within the anti-nuclear weapons Committee of 100 in its heyday, there were, for example, members who were acting, or pressing the Committee to act, by secret and conspiratorial means. They argued that it was naïve and "emotional" to attempt to apply such moral principles as openness and truthfulness to the hard reality of political struggle. The choice of tactics and the decision whether to be open or secretive must not, they maintained, be unreasonably restricted by emotion, religion or prejudices; practical answers to practical problems had to be worked out solely in light of the demands of the situation. However, if one asks what the consequences of secrecy and deception for the movement and the society are, or their effects on the dynamics of nonviolent action, or what the practical alternative means to openness in building and conducting an effective movement are, the weaknesses of the intellectual case for underground conspiratorial means become apparent.

In this section we shall look at the relationship between openness or secrecy and the dynamics of nonviolent action. We are not here concerned with moral imperatives to openness and truthfulness, but with the psychological, social and political effects of such behavior. The basic conclusion of this discussion will be contrary to what might commonly be assumed: the dynamics of this technique require that, in most situations at least, nonviolent action movements operate openly if they are to achieve their maximum strength and advantage in the struggle.

Openness in nonviolent action means that the organization backing the action act openly: that the names and activities of their leaders be revealed to the public and the opponent, that written protests be signed by the person or groups making them, that actions of protest, resistance and intervention be taken openly without attempt at deceit or hiding the behavior. Usually it has also even meant that the opponent and often the police be directly notified in advance, usually in writing, of the date, place, time, often the names of participants, and of the type of action to be taken. Gandhi was well known for this type of behavior, typified by his letter of March 2, 1930, to Lord Irwin, the Viceroy. In that letter Gandhi said that if his appeal for major political changes were not granted by March 11, he would, with his co-workers, begin his plan to disobey the provisions of the Salt Laws. On March 12, the names, ages, and identification of those who were to march with him to the sea to make salt were published in his paper, *Young India;* the plans included provision for immediate mass civil disobedience, should he be arrested at any point before he broke the law.[96] Similar plans for action in case openness led to early arrests were followed on other occasions. Similar openness has been used by American nonviolent civil rights groups. For a long period it was followed in South Africa by the African National Congress—for example, during the 1952 Defiance Campaign.[97] This openness in nonviolent action is not, however, something new introduced by Gandhi. Openness in defiance was a prominent feature of the Russian Revolution of 1905. Father Gapon himself told the Russian government of the plans for the march to the Winter Palace with a petition on January 9, 1905 (which became "Bloody Sunday");[98] liberals during the spring of 1905 were, in contrast to previous times, "operating virtually in the open";[99] instead of repeating the former practice of indoor and secret May Day celebrations in 1905, the socialists let it be widely known that they would conduct open demonstrations accompanied by political strikes (despite police arrests "the plans were carried out, with somewhat irregular success, in scores of places throughout the country").[100]

The problems of openness and secrecy under extreme dictatorships, especially totalitarian regimes, require special consideration. In this analysis we assume that the movement is not operating under such extreme difficulties. Improved understanding of the conditions and consequences of secrecy and openness in these milder situations may assist later examination of the problem under totalitarian conditions. However, it is not these extreme situations with which opposition groups are usually faced, even under milder dictatorships and colonialism and where civil liberties are in decline. Further, the answer to the problem of secrecy and openness in nonviolent action against totalitarian regimes does not necessarily determine the answer in the far greater number of situations more frequently faced.

However, the fact that open protest and resistance have taken place even under extreme totalitarian situations, when the actionists were improvising without special knowledge and understanding of this technique, shows that the case against the open operation of nonviolent action against totalitarian systems is not as firm and closed as many might believe. Indeed, the courage involved in such open action may strike especially hard at totalitarian systems, which are characterized by the instillation of fear and submissiveness in the subjects. Open defiance was a major characteristic of the East German Rising, for example, [101] and in the successful resistance in Berlin in 1943 to the deportation of Jews—especially those in mixed marriages—to the extermination camps, as described briefly in Chapter Two. In his study *The Final Solution,* Reitlinger cites Goebbels's entries in his diaries in March 1943 referring to these events, including the crowd demonstration against the evacuation of a home for aged Jews which resulted in the suspension of the whole action: "We can save it up for a week or two." Even Hitler's personal complaints to Goebbels at the continued presence in Berlin of Jewish intellectuals produced no results. Goebbels wrote: "After a terrific commotion in artistic circles, particularly among actors, a number of Jews married to Aryans had to be released." [102] Reitlinger concludes that this attempt to deport the partners of mixed marriages and their children, "like the euthanasia programme for the insane and incurable, was one of Hitler's defeats." [103] In the history of Nazism these were minor defeats, but these instances illustrate the simple point that openness in successful resistance was possible under even the conditions in the Third Reich.

Discussions in favor of secrecy in nonviolent action often seem to assume that it is not difficult to keep the opponent or the government from finding out what is to be kept secret. In many situations this is a very naïve assumption, both for small and large movements. While it may be possible to keep certain matters secret for some time, it is likely that sooner or later the police will learn not only the most important general intentions, but often the detailed plans as well. Modern electronic devices of various types may be used in addition to the older methods of opening the mail, telephone tapping, volunteer informers, planting of agents, spying and the like. If there are no secrets and planned action is not dependent on secrecy, such measures are not likely to impede the movement seriously. But when the implementation of plans for action depends on maintenance of secrecy, then such police methods may pose serious threats. Even under the Russian tsarist regime—which was scarcely as efficient as modern governments—police agents and spies penetrated the revolutionists' organizations continually, frequently rising to top positions of trust.[104] The British government apparently tried to have informers and agents in strike organizations during the General Strike of 1926.[105] In Nazi Germany opposition groups had immense difficulty in keeping resistance plans secret; informers and agents frequently penetrated underground groups and even operated inside concentration camps and prisoner-of-war camps.[106]

However, the most powerful single objection to secrecy in a nonviolent action movement is that secrecy is not only rooted in fear but that it contributes to fear. Fear is often a block to action even when people are stirred to indignation. As has been discussed earlier in this chapter, willingness to use nonviolent action depends in large degree upon the casting off of fear.

To produce change, nonviolent action operates on much more fundamental psychological, social and political levels than other techniques of action, especially more so than the several types of political violence with which conspiratorial behavior is usually associated. These more fundamental levels of operation in nonviolent action, which may produce shifts of loyalties and invisibly undermine the power of a hostile regime, often operate more quickly than dramatic acts which might only be possible by secrecy. But the more basic changes will be far more important. Therefore, it is highly dangerous to threaten the operation of those sometimes less obvious but much stronger forces by a secret effort to produce a quick temporary victory on some subordinate point. If the nonviolent actionists are to maximize their strength, they must act in harmony with the dynamics of this technique and its requirements. Especially important in these requirements are the maintenance of fearlessness and nonviolent discipline.

If—because of an inadequate understanding of their own technique and its dynamics, or because of the temptations of shortsighted expediency, or because of undisciplined behavior—the nonviolent actionists introduce into their struggle qualities and means appropriate to a violent struggle, they reverse important processes necessary for their success. At the same time they strengthen the opponent. The introduction of secrecy into a nonviolent action movement operates strongly against the maintenance of fearlessness and nonviolent discipline. Thus openness—that is, being truthful in statements and frank with the opponent and the public concerning intentions and plans—appears to be a corollary of the requirements of fearlessness and nonviolent discipline.

The openness of the movement and even its effrontery in daring to state its intentions publicly will have a significant impact on the nonviolent group itself, on the opponent, and on third parties. Conversely, resorting to secrecy, deception and underground conspiracy is likely to have a detrimental impact on all three groups.

Secrecy in a nonviolent action movement is likely to involve the leaders' going into hiding and seeking to avoid arrest. Whatever the leaders' motivation may be when this happens, the impression may spread that they are in fact seeking to avoid prison or other suffering. The lack of daring leadership by example is likely to have a disastrous effect on the willingness of others in lesser positions in the movement to do anything which might lead to danger or risks that the leaders are not taking. When such leaders are caught, sometimes the opponent may feel able to impose larger penalties on them under conditions which bring the leaders and movement less sympathy and support than if the punishments were imposed after open defiance. Leaders in hiding may even under some conditions become a liability to the movement. In contrast, imprisoned nonviolent leaders who have challenged the regime openly are more likely to be seen as heroes and martyrs, disturbing the complacent and inspiring the resisters.

When there are serious attempts to maintain secrecy in a nonviolent resistance movement, an atmosphere of fear spreads—fear that plans will be discovered, fear that hidden leaders will be captured, fear that the secret organization will be broken, fear that key members and masses of supporters will be imprisoned. As this happens among actual and potential supporters, the spirit of resistance is dampened. Instead of open nonviolent action demonstrating that repression is powerless, fear that secrets and plans will be revealed and that personnel will be captured permeates the movement; this leads to a kind of degeneration, demoralization and weakening which inevitably tends to undermine the movement.

Gandhi charged that resort to secrecy during the Indian 1932-33 struggle had been a prime cause for that movement's collapse. He said: ". . . the secrecy that has attended the movement is fatal to its success . . ." "There can be no doubt that fear has seized the common mass. The ordinances have cowed them down and I am inclined to think that the secret methods are largely responsible for this demoralisation."[107]

Certain theorists and practitioners of nonviolent struggle thus blame fear and other factors associated with secrecy for producing a series of undesirable influences which weaken the movement. It is significant that

Nehru—who, it is emphasized, did not share Gandhi's philosophical or religious beliefs nor his ethical commitment to nonviolence—had a similar view of the effects of secrecy during the campaigns of 1930-31 and 1932-33:

> Our experience of 1930 and 1932 showed that it was easily possible for us to organise a secret network of information all over India. Without much effort, and in spite of some opposition, good results were produced. But many of us had the feeling that secrecy did not fit in with the spirit of civil disobedience, and produced a damping effect on the mass consciousness. As a small part of a big open mass-movement it was useful, but there was always the danger, especially when the movement was declining, of a few more or less ineffective secret activities taking the place of the mass movement.[108]

Secrecy is most likely to be used by a movement to maintain itself when it feels too weak to operate openly. However, the secrecy may in fact lead to fewer participants rather than more,[109] not only because of the above factors, but also because, in many situations at least, the movement which is "security conscious" will have to reduce the number of people who plan and carry out policy. Under some conditions, numbers may also be reduced by the alienation of persons who were becoming sympathetic to the movement when it operated openly, but who distrust a secret political organization; this is especially likely to be the case where the nonviolent action is being applied in a society with a liberal democratic form of government.

The use of police spies, agents and informers is likely to seem more justified against a movement organized and operating on the basis of secrecy than against one which is not. Openness will not necessarily eliminate such agents. However, whether people see the use of police spies as justified or not justified, and whether or not sympathy is given to the police or to the nonviolent actionists, may influence the outcome of the conflict. It has also been suggested that secrecy concerning plans for nonviolent action may increase the chances of more brutal reaction from the opponent's forces than might have been the case had they known what to expect and had time to consider their counteraction carefully.

Secrecy may also threaten the very capacity of the movement to remain nonviolent—and this is crucial to the success of such a movement. This threat is most clearly illustrated by the problem of how to deal with an informer or police agent in possession of information which—it is believed—the opponent must not learn if the movement is to succeed. Various nonviolent types of persuasion and pressure might be used, plans could be changed, and the agent ostracized in the future once his identity is known (see Chapter Eight), but there is no nonviolent means of guaranteeing that the agent will not pass the information to the police or others. Past revolutionary and resistance movements using both secrecy and violence have not hesitated to murder the agent (or suspected agent, for it has sometimes proved later that the suspicions were unfounded). But resort to violence in a nonviolent action movement would reverse the operation of the mechanisms of change upon which that movement depends. The attempt to apply violence only on a very selective and restricted basis is likely to alter the conflict situation radically. It is likely to contribute to a major switch from the nonviolent technique to a violent one. In turn, that switch would enhance the opponent's relative power position, since he is better equipped to wage violent struggle.

In summary, a nonviolent movement which attempts to maintain a policy of secrecy concerning its planning, actions and organization faces problems and obstacles which are likely to prove insurmountable and which will, at best, severely threaten its requirements for casting off fear and the maintenance of nonviolent discipline. It is for such reasons that in their handbook for American civil rights demonstrators Oppenheimer and Lakey wrote:

> It is possible to confuse and delay the obtaining of "secret" information by your opponents in various ways. However, if your opponents are determined, this is pointless. It results in *inefficiency* because you have to cover up much that you do from your own members, *authoritarianism* because you cannot tell your members what is going on, and *mistrust*. In any case, your opponents, if they are determined, will plant "informers" and/or modern electronic devices in such a way that your activities will be an open book. You may as well open the book and be fully honest about your plans to begin with. You should try to plan tactics . . . which do not depend on secrecy for their value.[110]

Openness concerning intentions, plans, organizations and the like will also, it is argued, produce certain positive results which will help to strengthen the nonviolent group. This certainly does not imply that the movement will not face difficult problems, but openness contributes to the growth of *genuine* strength in the movement, as distinct from showy passing feats. In nonviolent action it is the buildup of genuine strength which is required; unreal appearances of strength are never lasting, and the movement may in fact be weakened if they are sought at the expense of undermining prerequisites of nonviolent power.

There are several specific ways, it has been argued, in which openness assists the nonviolent movement. Gregg, for example, feels that a policy of openness may promote wider knowledge of the existence, aims and activities of the resistance movement, and make the opponent's attempts at censorship and suppression of news more difficult.[111] It is true that open opposition is likely to become more difficult as the society becomes less democratic. But on the other hand, it also appears that the more monolithic a society, the greater the likely impact of any dissent. News of such opposition is likely to spread widely even when it is treated with silence in the official news media.

The contrast between the contending groups when one side relies upon nonviolent action is sharpened when that group also maintains a policy of truthful statements and openness concerning its intentions and plans. The contrast between the behavior of the conflicting groups is important in influencing the sympathies of third parties. Such sympathies are of course not decisive, but at times they may be important, especially when they take the form of concrete action against the opponent or in support of the nonviolent actionists. Sympathy and support may come as well from members of the broader grievance group who have not yet joined the struggle, and even from within the opponent's group itself. Therefore behavior which contributes to changes of perception and attitudes is very important. Here the visible contrast between the two groups plays a key role.

One side resorts to violence, brutality and repression; the other persists with courage in its action, accepts the suffering as the price of change, pledges itself anew to only nonviolent means, and refuses to retaliate. One group resorts to spies, deception, tricks and secrecy, while the other announces its intentions, plans, personnel and objectives publicly. One group demonstrates fear and uncertainty as to the present and future, while the other remains calm, determined, confident and fearless. In the process, the nonviolent group actively affects the power relationships between the groups. As the movement continues and the nonviolent actionists maintain their qualities and behavior, the perception that this movement differs qualitatively from the opponent group and from conventional political groups will gradually spread. This will, in turn, tend strongly to increase support for the nonviolent group from all sources and to weaken that for the opponent. The distinguishing qualities between the nonviolent group and the opponent will not appear so sharp if deception is used by both sides. Suspicions concerning the movement's real intentions, objectives and plans will spread, and sympathy for the actionists from third parties will be less likely.

Because nonviolent action is based upon that view of power which claims that all governments, hierarchical systems, oppression and injustice are ultimately dependent upon the submission, cooperation and assistance of the multitude of the citizens, subordinates and victims, it follows that the key to change by this technique lies in psychological and attitudinal changes among the subordinates. Feelings of apathy, impotence, fear and submissiveness will need to be shattered and replaced by their opposites. Gandhi implied that openness in defiance was necessary to break the habit of submissiveness and that a great deal of the effect of nonviolent action lay in the indifference of its users to measures for self-protection and in their willingness to take severe risks.[112] In the struggle to attain freedom, it was necessary to behave like free men: "A free man would not engage in a secret movement."[113] Openness, Gandhi argued, contributed to the morale of the rank and file of the movement, and enhanced their dignity and respect in their own eyes and in those of the opponent and third parties. A demonstration of confidence and daring is also often needed to inspire in others confidence and willingness to take risks. Gandhi insisted on this on several occasions:

No secret organization, however big, could do any good. . . . We have to organize for action a vast people that have been crushed under the heel of unspeakable tyranny for centuries. They cannot be organized by any other than open truthful means.[114]

No underhand or underground movement can ever become a mass movement or stir millions to mass action.[115]

Only open challenge and open activity is for all to follow. Real *Swaraj* [self-rule] *must* be felt by all—man, woman and child. To labour for that consummation is true revolution. . . . The millions of India would not have been awakened but for the open, unarmed struggle. Every deviation from the straight path has meant a temporary arrest of the evolutionary revolution.[116]

Once again Nehru's experience in open action showed him the psycologically liberating effects of struggle without secrecy, and also how this affected the British agents:

Above all, we had a sense of freedom and a pride in that freedom. The old feeling of oppression and frustration was completely gone. There was no more whispering, no round-about legal phraseology to avoid getting into trouble with the authorities. We said what we felt and shouted it out from the house-tops. What did we care for the consequences? Prison? We looked forward to it; that would help our cause still further. The innumerable spies and secret-service men who used to surround us and follow us about became rather pitiable individuals as there was nothing secret for them to discover. All our cards were always on the table. [117]

Honesty, openness and lack of secrecy may also have certain effects on the opponent group, at least under certain conditions. These will be especially important where the nonviolent group aims at changes in attitudes in the opponent, most clearly where conversion is attempted. This has been emphasized by Ebert:

So long as the oppressor fears the resistance fighters, i.e., so long as he is not convinced of their nonviolent attitude, he will be inclined to strengthen his own position. Only an open resistance organization can convince the oppressor that its professed belief and the demands which arise from it correspond to the true aims of the campaign. [118]

This does not mean that the opponent will immediately interpret the nonviolent group's motives, aims, intentions and plans correctly; only that this is more likely under conditions of openness than under conditions of attempted secrecy. Direct contact with the opponent group may be repeatedly sought as a means of avoiding or correcting distortions in perception which could seriously affect the course of the conflict. Advance notice to authorities of demonstrations, for example, may not only help to reduce brutalities by surprised police uncertain of what may happen, but may be interpreted as "clean fighting" and chivalry. These perceptions may contribute to increased respect for the nonviolent actionists among members of the opponent group. [119]

Usually there will be a time lag in changes in the opponent's perception of the nonviolent group, but constant repetition of behavior inconsistent with the opponent's view of members of that group may eventually lead to a correction of his perception. As Irving Janis and Daniel

Katz point out, openness may affect the opponent's view of the actionists, e.g., his view of their moral status:

> Revealing material that is ordinarily kept secret may influence the ri-
> vals' attitude concerning the *moral status* of the acting group (e.g.,
> they may become suspicious that something more important is being
> kept secret, or they may become much more respectful of the sincerity
> of the group). [120]

Openness may cause a distortion in perception of their strength in either
direction:

> Revealing tactical plans that will handicap the acting group may influ-
> ence the rivals' attitudes concerning the *strength* of the acting group
> (e.g., admission of one's plans may be perceived as signs of weakness
> and ineptness in conducting the struggle or as signs of an exception-
> ally powerful movement that is capable of being successful without re-
> sorting to secrecy). [121]

Similarly, Janis and Katz write, telling the opponent in advance of the
intended plans for nonviolent action "may have the effect of increasing or
decreasing the magnitude of frustration and the intensity of the aggressive
impulses aroused when the deprivations subsequently materialized." [122]
This refers to the opponent's *initial* response to the action. Specialists in
this technique have not claimed that openness always reduces hostility in
the initial stages of a conflict, but that it tends to do so over a period of
time.

There may also be even more important long-term consequences for
the society as a whole of an atmosphere of secrecy, distrust and fear, or
conversely of open expression of views and intentions, but these have as
yet received little attention.

BASIC ELEMENTS IN NONVIOLENT STRATEGY

The strategy and tactics of war have been carefully developed and
studied, and major attempts have been made to develop underlying theory.
Maxims, rules and systems for conducting war have been formulated in
response to "urgent want." [123] In the field of nonviolent action there
has been to date no comparable development. Gandhi made the most important conscious efforts to develop strategy and tactics in this technique
of struggle. He was, however, neither an analyst nor a theorist; hence,

despite his contribution in practice and his passing observations, the analysis and formulation of strategy and tactics have been left to others. Only comparatively recently has attention been turned to the examination of the problems and possibilities of strategy and tactics in nonviolent struggle against would-be internal dictators or invaders. [124] Attention is needed both to the broad field of strategy and tactics and to the specific problems which are likely to arise in facing particular opponents and in achieving particular objectives.

Strategy and tactics are of course present in various forms and degrees in many aspects of social life. They are, however, especially important in military action and nonviolent action, which are both techniques by which social and political conflicts are conducted when they have developed to the point of open struggle and a pitting of strength. There appear to be some points at which insights from military strategy may be carried over into nonviolent strategy; and there are also points at which military insights must *not* be carried over, because the nature and dynamics of the two techniques of struggle differ radically. This section is therefore not purely descriptive or analytical of existing observations on strategy in nonviolent action; it also involves the incorporation of principles of military strategy where these seem valid for the nonviolent technique, and where the military sources are clearer and more explicit than observations from nonviolent actionists.

Here are some brief definitions of basic strategic terms: grand strategy is the broadest conception which serves to coordinate and direct all the resources of the struggle group toward the attainment of the objectives of the conflict. Strategy, a more narrow term, is the broad plan of action for the overall struggle, including the development of an advantageous situation, the decision of when to fight, and the broad plan for utilizing various specific actions in the general conflict. Tactics refers to plans for more limited conflicts within the selected strategic plan. Fuller definitions of these terms are provided in the author's *An Abecedary of Nonviolent Action and Civilian Defense.*

A. The importance of strategy and tactics

Strategy is just as important in nonviolent action as it is in military action. While military strategic concepts and principles cannot automatically be carried over into the field of nonviolent action, the basic importance of strategy and tactics is in no way diminished. Attention is therefore needed to the general principles of strategy and tactics appropriate to this technique (both those peculiar to it and those which may be carried over from military strategy and other types of conflict). These aspects need to be considered, of course, within the context of the unique dynamics and mechanisms of nonviolent struggle.

People from a military background may find it strange to discover certain exponents of nonviolent means stressing the importance of strategy and tactics. And people from a background in religious or philosophical nonviolence may also be surprised to find strategy and tactics stressed instead of moral principles and conscience. Therefore, some brief discussion is needed of the function of strategy and tactics in nonviolent action.

In order to influence the outcome of a struggle, it is important to choose the course of action wisely and carry it out carefully and intelligently. It is quite inadequate simply to say that one will be moral and do what is right, for there may be several courses of action which are all morally "right"; what is "right" may involve maintaining or creating maximum opposition to "evil," and if so the problem is how to do this; in order to meet one's moral responsibility and maximize the effects of one's action, those actions must be carefully chosen and carried out at the right time. Specialists in the study and conduct of war have long since learned that the best results were not achieved simply by an uncontrolled outburst of violence and sacrifice. As Liddell Hart has said: ". . . the conduct of war must be controlled by reason if its object is to be fulfilled. . . . The better your strategy, the easier you will gain the upper hand, and the less it will cost you." [125] As in war, strategy and tactics are used in nonviolent action so that the courage, sacrifice, numbers, and so on of the nonviolent actionists may make the greatest possible impact.

The course of the struggle may take any of a wide variety of forms. depending on the strategies, tactics and methods chosen to meet the particular needs of the situation. The specific acts of protest, noncooperation and intervention in the course of a nonviolent campaign will be most effective if they fit together as parts of a comprehensive whole, so that each specific action contributes in a maximum way to the development and successful conclusion of the struggle. The optimal combination of specific actions is therefore best achieved where leaders with an adequate grasp of the situation and the technique are able to chart the course of the campaigns. "Only the general who conducts a campaign can know the objective of each particular move," wrote Gandhi. [126] Gandhi chose the issues, places, times and methods of action with extreme care, so that his movement was placed in the strongest position possible *vis-à-vis* the British, and so that the actions themselves conveyed the greatest understanding to his fellow Indians and aroused the maximum sympathy and support from everyone. Just as strategy is important in labor strikes,[127] so it is important in more highly developed types of nonviolent struggle—even more so when it is directed against extreme dictatorships.

There is ample historical evidence of the importance of strategy and tactics.[128] Sometimes this evidence is of a negative type, showing effects of the absence of strategy or of failure to make important decisions on strategic and tactical questions. Sometimes difficult problems which arose in the course of given conflicts could have been avoided or more satisfactorily resolved had there been greater understanding of the role and principles of nonviolent strategy. On other occasions, nonviolent campaigns have been continued after the point when achievement of almost all the objectives and demands was possible—far more than is usually the case in military conflicts; subsequent events then led to the defeat of the movement. Or in other cases the nonviolent movement *regarded* itself as defeated even though by normal standards it was victorious; as a result, that nonviolent action was eventually replaced by military action which was *believed* to be more effective. The American colonists' struggles against the British government can without difficulty be interpreted in this way. Considerable light would be shed on the problems and general principles of nonviolent strategy if careful strategic and tactical analyses were undertaken of a series of nonviolent struggles. It is also important to have acceptance by the grievance group of the strategy for the struggle; in the case of Finland in 1901, disagreement on *how* to deal with the opponent seems to have severely accentuated existing internal conflicts.[129]

B. Some key elements in nonviolent strategy and tactics

Despite the relative absence of strategic analyses of past nonviolent struggles and the lack of systematic studies of basic principles of nonviolent strategy, it is possible to list certain fairly clear general principles which have taken concrete form in particular struggles. Clausewitz wrote that in the case of war it was easier to make a theory of tactics than of strategy.[130] Both theories are very difficult in nonviolent action, and the list of principles offered here is necessarily incomplete and provisional.

1. The indirect approach to the opponent's power   The technique of nonviolent action can be regarded as an extreme development of "the indirect approach" to military strategy as formulated by Liddell Hart, and discussed earlier in this chapter.

Liddell Hart argued that direct strategy consolidates the opponent's strength, while an indirect approach is militarily more sound; generally effective results have followed when the plan of action has had "such indirectness as to ensure the opponent's unreadiness to meet it." Therefore, instead of a direct attack on the opponent's positions of strength, Liddell Hart emphasized the importance of psychological factors; the purpose of strategy then becomes "to diminish the possibility of resistance . . ." "Dislocation" of the enemy is crucial, he insisted, in achieving the conditions for victory, and the dislocation must be followed by "exploitation" of the opportunity created by the position of insecurity. It thus becomes important "to nullify opposition by paralysing the power to oppose" and to make "the enemy do something wrong." [131] These general principles are all applicable to the use of nonviolent action against an opponent using military means, so that the opponent's means of action are always confronted indirectly and his power of repression made to rebound against him in a kind of political *jiu-jitsu*. Finally, the very sources of his power are reduced or removed without having been confronted directly by the same means of action.

2. Psychological elements   Some of the psychological elements in military war have equivalents in "war without violence." But the carry-over is not automatic. For example, surprise has been regarded as an essential element in certain types of military strategy. In nonviolent action, however, such objectives as throwing the enemy off guard, benefiting from his incapacity to meet the attack, and so on, which surprise has been intended to produce, are likely to a significant degree to be achieved simply by insistence on using a technique different from that of the opponent in the struggle. At times, however, the element of surprise in nonviolent action may operate to the detriment of the nonviolent actionists, by increasing the possibility of jumpiness among troops which may in turn mean more severe repression and less chance of disaffection among them.

Morale among the actionists will be important in nonviolent conflict just as it is in military conflict. It will be crucial for the population as a whole to understand well that the opponent's military might does not give him either control or victory. Confidence in nonviolent action would be fundamental, along with the qualities of "a warlike people" as described by Clausewitz: "bravery, aptitude, powers of endurance and enthusiasm." [132]

3. Geographical and physical elements   Neither possession of nor gaining of control over particular places is regarded even in military war as important for its own sake but as "intermediate links," as "means of gaining greater superiority" so as finally to achieve victory.[133] While not to be *totally* ignored in nonviolent action, these elements assume a considerably lesser role, because the technique of struggle is dependent primarily upon the will and actions of human beings rather than on possession of geographical positions. It is possible, for example, for a territory to be physically occupied by troops without the regime which commands them having effective control over the population of the territory. Particular places, buildings and so on may on occasion become important in nonviolent action, especially where they have high symbolic value; in such cases, the methods of nonviolent obstruction, nonviolent raids and nonviolent invasion are likely to be applied. Even then, however, the physical possession of particular points is of secondary importance to the fulfillment of the conditions which make possible the operation of the mechanisms of change in nonviolent action. There are other geographical and physical elements; on occasion the terrain, time of day and weather may be important, and there may be "camps" for volunteers and hospitals to care for the wounded.

A careful nonviolent strategist is likely to be attentive to the choice of the place at which given acts of opposition are to be undertaken. Gandhi usually paid considerable attention to this point, as was illustrated by his plans for civil disobedience of the Salt Laws in 1930. As the place where he would make salt and spark the national struggle, Gandhi chose the little-known Dandi beach on the Gulf of Cambay, not significant in itself, but a point which allowed Gandhi and his followers to walk for twenty-six days—the now-famous Salt March—during which time he could arouse public interest and focus attention on his plans for civil disobedience.[138] Also during his investigation of the plight of the peasants in Champaran, Bihar, in 1917, when Gandhi expected arrest he went to Bettiah, preferring to be arrested among the most poverty-stricken peasants of the district.[135]

4. Timing   The timing of the implementation of tactics can be extremely important in nonviolent action. This timing may be of several types. For example, it is necessary to be able to judge when people are ready to take direct action, and also when a call for action would meet only a weak response or be ignored.[136] Timing needs to be considered in light of the whole situation; Nehru paid tribute to Gandhi's ability to do this when he wrote: ". . . he knows his India well and reacts to her lightest tremors, and gauges a situation accurately and almost instinctively, and has a knack of acting at the psychological moment."[137]

It has been argued that the Irish "No-Rent Manifesto" would have been more successful if issued in February 1881—as the extreme wing of the Land League wanted—instead of six months later, after the leaders had been jailed and reforms were dampening the will to resist. [138]

Sometimes the launching of nonviolent action may be timed to coincide with some significant day or occasion. The choice of April 6, 1930, as the start of the Indian civil disobedience campaign, for example, coincided with the beginning of National Week, which was observed in homage to the victims of the Amritsar Massacre of 1919. [139] Timing may also be important in another sense. The hour and minute at which given nonviolent actionists are to be at certain places and the synchronization of actions of various groups may be crucial; this has been the case in certain student actions in the U.S. South. [140]

In still a different sense, timing may refer to the choice of the stage at which to resist an opponent who is attempting to impose or extend his control over a society. On occasion, the opponent's demands and action may require prompt reaction and resistance if his efforts to establish or extend control are to be thwarted. In the case of an invasion, for example, this may be particularly true at three points. The first occurs after the formal seizure of power and the occupation of the country. The second is at the stage when the invader seeks the collaboration and assistance of important groups, such as police, civil service and trade unions. The last is at the point where he attempts to destroy the independent social institutions, bring all organizations and institutions under his control, and atomize the population. When each of these attacks occurs, it will be important that resistance be undertaken without delay and that people do not "wait and see" or just drift. Only prompt action can be effective. In other conflict situations, the timing of action at various stages of the struggle may also be important.

5. Numbers and strength   While numbers may be extremely important both in nonviolent action and in military action, [141] they are certainly not the only important factor and do not guarantee victory. It is fallacious to attempt "to analyze and theorize about strategy in terms of mathematics" and to assume that victory is determined simply by "a superior concentration of force at a selected place." [142] In nonviolent action—especially when nonviolent coercion is being attempted, as in a general strike or a mutiny—numbers may at times be decisive. But numbers must not be considered alone; large numbers may even be a disadvantage, either for tactical reasons or because discipline and reliability have been sacrificed to obtain them, as discussed earlier in this chapter. Particular tactics and methods may in the given circumstances have their own requirements concerning the numbers of actionists. Large numbers unable to maintain nonviolent discipline and to continue action in face of repression may weaken the movement, but with the necessary standards and discipline they may become "irresistible." [143]

6. The issue and concentration of strength   If there are to be wise strategy and tactics for conducting nonviolent action most effectively, then a careful selection of the points on which to fight is crucial, as discussed above. In conventional military campaigns, such points may in large degree be determined by consideration of topography, supplies and the like. But in nonviolent campaigns they are almost exclusively determined by political, psychological, social and economic factors.

There is no substitute for genuine strength in nonviolent action. If this is lacking, then the attempt to fight for an objective which is too vast to be achieved may be unwise. To be effective, nonviolent action needs to be concentrated at crucial points which are selected after consideration of one's own strength, the objectives and position of the opponent (including his weaknesses), and the importance of the issue itself. Napoleon's maxim that it is impossible to be too strong at the decisive point applies here as well. [144] In selecting that point consideration must also be given to the probable consequences if that particular battle is either lost or won. This is very closely related to the first of the axioms of military strategy and tactics outlined by Liddell Hart:

> *Adjust your end to your means.* In determining your object, clear sight and cool calculation should prevail. It is folly "to bite off more than you can chew," and the beginning of military wisdom is a sense of what is possible. So learn to face facts while still preserving faith: there will be ample need for faith—the faith that can achieve the apparently impossible—when action begins. Confidence is like the current in a battery: avoid exhausting it in vain effort—and remember that your own continued confidence will be of no avail if the cells of your battery, the men upon whom you depend, have been run down. [145]

There may be particular circumstances, such as the attempt to atomize the population, which may require that action be taken despite weaknesses; but even then consideration of one's real strength is required, and in formulating strategy and tactics an attempt should be made to see if the existing strength can be used to best advantage and the weaknesses either bypassed or urgently corrected.

"The principles of war, not merely one principle, can be condensed into a single word—'concentration.' But for truth this needs to be amplified as the 'concentration of strength against weakness.' " [146] This principle of military action applies also in nonviolent action and was stressed by Gandhi. Concentration in nonviolent struggles will primarily be on certain political, social or economic points which symbolize wider general conditions. This is related to another of Liddell Hart's axioms: "*Keep your object always in mind,* while adapting your plan to circumstances. Realize that there are more ways than one of gaining an object, but take heed that every objective should bear on the object." [147] Nonviolent actionists will seek to attack the specific aspect which symbolizes the "evil" they are fighting, which is least defensible by the opponent and which is capable of arousing the greatest strength among the nonviolent actionists and the wider population. Success on such a limited point will increase their self-confidence and ability to move forward effectively toward the fuller realization of their objectives. Having chosen the point for concentrated attack, they must not allow themselves to become sidetracked to a lesser course of action or a dead-end issue. [148]

7. The initiative   In nonviolent action it is highly important—even in defensive phases of the struggle—for the actionists to obtain and retain the initiative. "An able general always gives battle in his own time on the ground of his choice. He always retains the initiative in these respects and never allows it to pass into the hands of the enemy," wrote Gandhi. [149] One of the important distinctions indicated by Nehru between the 1930 campaign—which could be described at least as a "draw"—and the 1932 campaign, which was a clear defeat for the Indians, was that in 1930 the "initiative definitely remained with the Congress and the people" whereas "the initiative early in 1932 was definitively with the Government, and Congress was always on the defensive." [150] The nonviolent leadership group needs to be able to control the situation and to demonstrate that it has that control. [151] Nirmal Kumar Bose writes that a leader of a nonviolent campaign ". . . should not allow the adversary to dictate or force any step upon him . . . [nor] allow himself to be buffeted about by every temporary event." [152] Wherever possible, then, the nonviolent group, not the opponent, will choose the time, issue and course of action and seek to maintain the initiative despite the opponent's repression. In cases where the conflict has been precipitated by the opponent, as in a *coup d'etat* or invasion or when new repressive measures are imposed, the nonviolent actionists will endeavor to restore the initiative to themselves as quickly as possible.

C. The choice of weapons

In order to achieve optimal results, the choice of nonviolent weapons to initiate and conduct the campaign will need to be made carefully and wisely. It will be necessary to determine which of the specific methods of nonviolent action described in Part Two (and possibly other methods) are most appropriate to this particular conflict. This decision will need to be taken in the light of a variety of factors. These include the issues at stake, the nature of the contending groups, the type of culture and society of each, and the social and political context of the conflict. Other factors are the mechanisms of change intended by the nonviolent group (as to convert or to coerce), the experience of the nonviolent group, and their ability in applying nonviolent action. Finally, there are also the type of repression and other countermeasures expected, the ability of the nonviolent group to withstand them, and the intensities of commitment to the struggle within the nonviolent group. There are of course others.

The number of methods used in any single conflict will vary from only one to dozens. The choice of the specific methods to be used in a given campaign will be based on several factors. One of these is a judgment as to whether or not the basic characteristics of the method contain qualities desired for that particular conflict. For example, generally speaking, the methods of the class of nonviolent protest and persuasion (Chapter Three) are largely symbolic in their effect and produce an awareness of the existence of dissent. Their impact is proportionately greater under authoritarian regimes where opposition and nonconformity are discouraged and rare. Depending on the numbers involved, the methods of noncooperation (Chapters Four, Five, Six and Seven) are likely to cause difficulties in maintaining the normal operation and efficiency of the system. In extreme situations, these methods may threaten its existence. The methods of nonviolent intervention (Chapter Eight) possess qualities of both groups, but in addition usually constitute a more direct challenge to the regime. This class of methods makes possible a greater impact with smaller numbers, providing that fearlessness and discipline are maintained.

Moving from the class of nonviolent protest and persuasion to that of noncooperation and thence to nonviolent intervention generally involves a progressive increase in the degree of sacrifice required of the nonviolent actionists, in the risk of disturbing the public peace and order, and in effectiveness. The methods of noncooperation can be interpreted as withdrawal of cooperation from an evil system, and hence as having connotations of a defensive moral action. The use of this class of methods, as compared to nonviolent intervention, may also contribute to producing a *relatively* less explosive and dangerous social situation, in that they simply withdraw existing cooperation or withhold new forms of cooperation with the opponent.[153] The penalties and sufferings imposed directly or indirectly upon noncooperators, although severe at times, may be relatively less than those involved in nonviolent intervention. Also, the risk of such repression in any particular case may be less. It may also be easier to get people to refrain from doing something which has been ordered, i.e., to noncooperate, than to get them to do something daring which is prohibited.

For effective noncooperation, larger numbers of participants are usually required than for either symbolic protest or intervention, and the action usually continues over longer periods of time. Often a long duration is necessary for the noncooperation to achieve its impact. In 1930 Gandhi said that whereas the cooperation of three hundred million people would be necessary for a foreign-cloth boycott campaign to be successful, for the civil disobedience campaign an army of ten thousand defiant men and women would suffice.[154] Many of the methods of nonviolent intervention can only be practiced for limited periods of time. A continuous effect therefore is achieved only by constant repetition of the action. These methods therefore require more skilled, reliable and determined practitioners than methods of noncooperation. Because of this, the quicker methods of nonviolent intervention usually require considerable preparations in order to be successfully applied. Also, those methods are often best combined with other forms of nonviolent action. The movement using intervention methods, too, must be more highly disciplined and better led. "The quickest remedies are always fraught with the greatest danger and require the utmost skill in handling them."[155]

Another important factor in the selection of the specific methods to be used in the campaign is whether the actionists intend to produce change by the mechanism of conversion, accommodation, or nonviolent coercion. Within that context, the specific inducements for change by the opponent which the nonviolent group is attempting to produce may be important; these may include, for example, economic losses, weakening of political position, guilt feelings, new perceptions, and the like. Where conversion of the opponent is sought, such methods as the general strike, mutiny and parallel government are obviously not appropriate. But where nonviolent coercion is intended these may be precisely the methods needed, whereas forms which rely for their impact on psychological and emotional effects on the leaders of the opponent group may be a waste of time and effort. The problem is complicated, however, and frequently methods which apply differing pressures and use different mechanisms may be combined effectively within the same campaign. Fast rules are not possible.

In most cases more than one method will be used; then the order in which the methods are applied, the ways in which they are combined, and how they influence the application of other methods and contribute to the struggle as a whole become highly important. The methods to be used in a given situation must be considered not only for their specific and immediate impact on the conflict situation and the opponent. Also important is their contribution to the progressive development of the movement, to changes in attitudes and power relationships, to alterations in the support for each side, and to the later application and effects of more radical nonviolent methods.

Sometimes the combination of methods is relatively simple, especially in a local or limited type of action. Economic boycotts have been used, for example, in support of sit-ins against racial discrimination, and picketing is commonly used in support of strikes. When a general strike is used to support the mutiny of government troops, however, the situation begins to become more complicated, with larger numbers of methods likely to become involved quickly.

For large-scale planned campaigns against determined opponents the question of how to combine the use of several methods is not easy to answer; it must be considered in the context both of the overall strategy of the struggle and its more localized and restricted phases. In a long struggle phasing is highly important, and the choice and sequence of methods may be the most important single factor in that phasing. Waskow speaks, for example, of the " 'escalation' of disorder without violence." [156] The importance of this phased development of a nonviolent campaign has been stressed by specialists in Gandhi's type of nonviolent action, such as Bose[157] and Bondurant. As one of nine "fundamental rules" of *satyagraha* Bondurant lists:

> *Progressive advancement of the movement* through steps and stages determined to be appropriate within the given situation. Decision as to when to proceed to a further phase of the satyagraha must be carefully weighed in the light of the ever-changing circumstance, but a static condition must be avoided. [158]

It may, therefore, be determined that certain methods must precede others, in order that it may be possible later to use more radical forms.

Gandhi frequently used the response of the volunteers and public to some specific action as a means of testing whether or not some further, more radical, form of action were possible, in such terms as degree of commitment, willingness to act, ability to withstand the opponent's sanctions, degree of discipline, and ability to remain both fearless and nonviolent. In his testimony before the Hunter Committee in 1920, for example, Gandhi said:

> *Hartal* was designed to strike the imagination of the people and the government. . . I had no means of understanding the mind of India except by some such striking movement. *Hartal* was a proper indication to me how far I would be able to carry civil disobedience. [159]

He also used the consumer's boycott to test readiness for civil disobedience. Gandhi wrote in 1921: "It is my firm conviction that if we bring about a successful boycott of foreign cloth, we shall have produced an atmosphere that would enable us to inaugurate civil disobedience on a scale that no Government can resist." [160]

In May 1920 Gandhi had reported in *Young India* that the organizers of the coming noncooperation movement had decided that it should take place in four stages: 1) relinquishment of honorary posts and titles, 2) progressive voluntary withdrawal from government employment, 3) withdrawal of members of the police and the military from government service ("a distant goal"), and 4) suspension of payment of taxes ("still more remote"). [161] The first stage involved the minimum danger and sacrifice, [162] while the last two involved the greatest risks. [163]

The 1930-31 movement was planned with a different strategy. It began with methods of nonviolent protest, such as the Salt March itself and mass meetings, and mild forms of political noncooperation, such as limited withdrawals from the provincial legislatures—all involving small numbers of people. The mass movement itself began directly with civil disobedience of a law regarded as immoral, and then developed to include both milder forms of noncooperation and more radical forms of noncooperation and nonviolent intervention. [164]

D. Selecting the strategy and tactics

The general strategy, types of tactics, and choice of methods planned by the leaders in advance will usually determine the general direction and conduct of the campaign throughout its course. Their selection is therefore highly important. As in war, a large number of factors must be considered in the selection of strategy and tactics. However, the quite different dynamics and mechanisms of nonviolent struggle appear to make the interrelationships of these factors more intimate and complex than in military struggle.

Fundamental to this task is careful consideration of the opponent's primary and secondary objectives, and the various objectives of the nonviolent group. It will be highly important to evaluate accurately the opponent's and one's own strengths and weaknesses, and to take these into account in the formulation of strategy and tactics. Failure to do so may lead either to overly ambitious plans which fail because they are not based on a realistic assessment of possibilities, or to excessively timid plans which may fail precisely because they attempt too little. Evaluation of the strengths and nature of the opponent group may assist the nonviolent leadership in formulating a course of action most likely to produce or aggravate weaknesses and internal conflicts within it. Correct assessment of the weaknesses of the nonviolent group itself may be used in the selection of strategy and tactics which are intended to bypass them, and which may possibly also contribute to strengthening them. Estimates as to the length of the forthcoming struggle will be needed and will be important for outlining the course of action. But provision must also be made for an error of judgment in such estimates and for contingency tactics if the struggle turns out to be long instead of brief.

Careful consideration of other factors in the general situation will be necessary to determine whether conditions are suitable for the launching of nonviolent action, and, if so, what the general and specific conditions of the situation mean for the planning of the campaign. Sibley has emphasized that

> . . . the effective use of nonviolent resistance depends not only on adequate training and commitment, but also on the "objective" situation: external conditions must be ripe for effective campaigns, and if they are not, it is the part both of wisdom and of morality not to resort to nonviolent resistance. [165]

Gandhi insisted that in formulating and carrying out the strategy and tactics of the struggle the leaders need to be responsive to the demonstrated qualities of their movement and to the developing situation:

> In a satyagraha campaign the mode of fight and the choice of tactics, e.g. whether to advance or retreat, offer civil resistance or organize nonviolent strength through constructive work and purely selfless humanitarian service, are determined according to the exigencies of the situation. [166]

Strategy and tactics are of course interdependent. Precise tactics can only be formulated in the context of the overall strategy, and an intimate understanding of the whole situation and the specific methods of action which are open. Skillful selection and implementation of tactics will not make up for a bad overall strategy, and a good strategy remains impotent unless carried to fulfillment with sound tactics: ". . . only great tactical results can lead to great strategical ones . . ." [167]

Liddell Hart has suggested that the particular course of action should have more than one objective.

> *Take a line of operation which offers alternate objectives.* For you will thus put your opponent on the horns of a dilemma, which goes far to assure the chance of gaining one objective at least—whichever he guards least—and may enable you to gain one after the other.
>
> Alternative objectives allow you to keep the opportunity of gaining *an* objective; whereas a single objective, unless the enemy is helplessly inferior, means the certainty that you will not gain it—once the enemy is no longer uncertain as to your aim. There is no more common mistake than to confuse a single line of operation, which is usually wise, with a single objective, which is usually futile. [168]

To a large degree this frequently happens in nonviolent action anyhow without particular planning, since the nonviolent group aims at achieving both particular objectives and more general changes in attitudes and power relationships within each group and between the contending groups. These more general changes are likely to be taking place during the whole course of the conflict, and may be achieved to a considerable degree even in instances where the particular political goal is not won. However, attention is also needed to the possibility of applying Liddell Hart's strategic principle to concrete limited goals, so long as this does not violate the principle of concentration discussed previously.

The progressive development of the movement, partially characterized by the staged introduction of new methods of action (as discussed in the previous section), will also benefit from careful strategic planning. Such development will help to ensure that the alteration of methods and new courses of action will contribute to the maximum utilization of the actionists' forces, facilitate an improvement in their morale, and increase the chances of vistory. Without clear strategic insight, changes from one type of action to another may take place without good purpose or effect, and the discouraging results which may follow can lead first to increased uncertainty as to what to do, then to demoralization, and finally to disintegration of the nonviolent movement.

Strategic phasing of nonviolent campaigns is not new of course. However, greater understanding of the nature of the technique and of principles of strategy now make possible a fuller development and more effective utilization of such phasing than has been possible before. Three earlier examples of phasing are offered here. The provincial convention of Virginia, meeting in early August 1774, outlined a phased campaign of economic noncooperation to achieve its objectives. The convention set dates at which new phases of their campaign were to go into effect, subject to alterations agreed to by Virginia delegates in the Continental Congress. Starting at once, no tea was to be imported or used. If Boston were compelled to reimburse the East India Company for losses (as of tea in the Boston Tea Party), the boycott would be extended to all articles sold by the company until the money was returned. On November 1, an absolute boycott was to be imposed on all goods (except medicines) imported directly or indirectly from Britain, including all slaves from wherever they were brought. If colonial grievances were not corrected by August 10, 1775 (a year later), then an absolute program of nonexportation of all articles to Britain was to be imposed. The year interval before nonexportation took effect allowed for payment of debts to British merchants, and for Virginia tobacco growers to shift to crops which could be used at home. [169] This phased campaign drafted by Virginians foreshadowed the program adopted by the First Continental Congress.

A phased campaign of peasant action was issued in Russia by the Second Congress of the Peasants Union, meeting in Moscow in November 1905, during the revolution of that year. The Congress called for the use of methods of peaceful pressure (such as the peasants' collective refusal to buy or rent land from the landlords) to achieve the free transfer of land to the peasants. If these methods did not produce results, then the Union would call for a general agrarian strike to coincide with a general strike in the cities. If the tsarist government harassed the Union, it would call on the peasants to refuse to pay taxes or to serve in the armed forces. [170]

The Pan-Africanists in South Africa had planned their campaign of defiance of the Pass Laws in the spring of 1960 as simply the first stage of a three-front long-range struggle: 1) *political,* with the international aim of isolating South Africa (including United Nations condemnation and expulsion from the British Commonwealth) and the domestic aim of ending collaboration and submission by the African people upon which the government depended; 2) *labor,* the withdrawal of cheap African labor would bring an economic collapse, and therefore stay-at-home strikes were designed to induce industrialists to demand changes in government policies; and 3) *psychological,* the Africans "would discover the power they have even without weapons and they would never be the same again." Despite clear thought and certain planning for a phased campaign, however, the organization had not anticipated that the government would seize the initiative by declaring a state of emergency. [171]

While specific tactics for the later stages of the struggle cannot be formulated in advance, it is possible to explore a variety of general approaches for later consideration. Tactics for use in the early (and possibly intermediate) stages may, however, be successfully selected in advance if one has accurately anticipated the situation and form of attack.

A variety of approaches may be used in tactics, involving different fronts, groups, time periods, methods and other factors. For example, the brunt of the responsibility for carrying out the action may, after certain periods of time or certain political events, be shifted from one group to another, or different roles may be assigned to particular groups. The most dangerous tasks (involving, for example, the use of the most daring methods, such as those of nonviolent intervention) could be assigned to groups with especially high discipline, experience, skill, or training, while other important but less dangerous tasks could be undertaken by groups more typical of the general population. At times particular responsibilities would fall upon certain occupational or geographical groups because of the policies and actions of the opponent. Where the initiative lay with the nonviolent actionists, they could deliberately choose to undertake simultaneous actions on more than one front if their strength and the general situation were such as to make this wise. At times tactics could involve geographical fronts as well as political fronts, as in the use of nonviolent raids or obstruction; far more often, however, there would be no semblance of a geographical front and the resistance would be more diffuse and general, as in the case of a stay-at-home. The selection of tactics will be influenced significantly by the immediate and long-term political aims of the nonviolent actionists, and by the mechanisms through which change is sought. Various types of tactics will produce different problems for the usurper and have different effects on the nonviolent population.

Variation in tactics may be important in order to add variety and interest (and often newsworthiness) to the campaign. Such changes may serve other purposes, such as to involve new sections of the population, to augment psychological, political and economic pressures on the opponent, expand or contract the front and to test the discipline, morale and capacity of the nonviolent actionists. Tactical changes may be designed to achieve a variety of effects on the opponent, leadership, bystanders, or police and troops charged with repression. For example, Ebert points to the deliberate use in some cases of small groups of demonstrators (instead of large ones) and time gaps between demonstrations (instead of continuous ones), as means of reducing brutality in the repression by making it easier for the opponent's police and troops to see the actionists as individual human beings, and by allowing them time for reflection and reconsideration between particular demonstrations.[172]

The unrolling of the strategy and implementation of tactics in specific acts takes place in a context of a sensitivity and responsiveness to the developing conflict situation. Very careful and precise plans may have been prepared for commencing the attack. Following the beginning of the struggle, however, room must be allowed for flexibility in the further development, modification and application of the strategy and tactics.[173] Liddell Hart has emphasized the importance of flexibility in the formulation and implementation of the anticipated course of action:

> *Ensure that both plan and disposition are flexible—adaptable to circumstances.* Your plan should foresee and provide for a next step in case of success or failure, or partial success—which is the most common case in war. Your dispositions (or formation) should be such as to allow this exploitation or adaption in the shortest possible time.[174]

The capacity to respond to unforeseen (or unforeseeable) events must be acutely developed. Especially important is the response, morale and behavior of the nonviolent actionists and potential supporters. If they have proved too unprepared and weak to carry out the plans, the plans must be altered, either by taking "some dramatic step which will strike the imagination of the people, and restore confidence in the possibility of full resistance through nonviolence," or by calling a temporary retreat in order to prepare for a future stronger effort.[175] There is no substitute for, or shortcut to, strength in a movement of nonviolent action. If the necessary strength and ability to persist in face of penalties and suffering do not exist, that fact must be recognized and given an intelligent response. "A wise general does not wait till he is actually routed; he withdraws in time in an orderly manner from a position which he knows he would not be able to hold."[176] The leadership will, just as in a military conflict, need to recognize frankly the weaknesses in their volunteers and potential supporters and find ways of correcting these.[177]

The means for doing this will vary with the conditions of the given situation.

On the other hand, the struggle may reveal significant weaknesses in the opponent which may call for prompt alteration of the tactics and speeding up the tempo of the struggle. At times, too, the struggle may reveal the nonviolent actionists and the general population to be stronger than had been expected, and then it may be possible to make a more rapid advance on a sound basis than originally conceived.

THE ULTIMATUM

If negotiations with the opponent are not showing signs of producing satisfactory results, the strategy and early tactics must be settled, and various types of organizational preparations completed. In some types of nonviolent struggle—primarily Gandhian or neo-Gandhian—the next stage will be the issuance of an ultimatum to the opponent. In other traditions of nonviolent struggle there may be no ultimatum, because the idea is unknown, because the planners hope to take the opponent by surprise, because the conflict has already broken out spontaneously, or for some other reason. Where the ultimatum is used, however, it is very similar to ultimatums which in the old days used to be issued by governments before they declared war on their opponent: the demands are stated, and an offer is made to cancel plans for attack if the opponent grants those demands (or a major part of them) by a given day and hour.[178]

Like negotiations, the ultimatum is intended to influence both the opponent and the general public. Negotiations are aimed not only at influencing the opponent to grant the demands of the nonviolent group through greater appreciation of their justice and for other reasons, including that granting them may be the better part of political wisdom. Negotiations—especially long, sincere negotiations which have really sought a solution short of open struggle—may also help to put the adversary in the wrong in the eyes of all concerned and to bring sympathy to the nonviolent group for attempting diligently and patiently to find a peaceful settlement. Similarly, the ultimatum may be intended to encourage the opponent to agree to the demands, by telling him in clear terms the consequences of a failure to achieve a mutually agreed change in the matters at stake. At the same time, however, the ultimatum is also a means of showing everyone who may be interested that, while maintaining firmness and dignity, the nonviolent group is giving the opponent one last chance to settle the conflict peacefully. This may endow the nonviolent group with an aura of defensiveness—which may be psychologically advantageous in several ways—even while they are preparing for militant nonviolent action. An ultimatum may also be important in building up morale and willingness to act in the grievance group.

In its ultimatum the leaders of the nonviolent group list their grievances and demands without exaggeration. A time limit is set for the granting of these minimum demands. This ultimatum may be likened to a conditional declaration of war. The nonviolent group may in the ultimatum include assurances to the opponent intended to correct misunderstandings and remove fears he may have about the group and their objectives, and it may remind him that only nonviolent means are intended. Without compromising basic issues and principles, the ultimatum may be worded in such a way as to leave the opponent a way of saving face. The nonviolent group hopes that the opponent will grant the demands and that the threatened action will thus be avoided. If not, the time will have arrived for nonviolent action.

On occasion an ultimatum may take the form of a general public declaration—intended for the opponent and others—of what will happen if the demands are not met by a given date. This may be a part of a plan of escalation of resistance. This type of ultimatum was included in the plan for American colonial resistance, the Continental Association, adopted by the First Continental Congress. The nonimportation phase had already begun in late 1774, but the nonexportation phase was to be launched a year after the meeting of the Continental Congress—if victory had not by then been achieved:

> The earnest desire we have, not to injure our fellow-subjects in Great-Britain, Ireland, or the West-Indies, induces us to suspend a non-exportation until the tenth day of September, 1775; at which time, if the said acts and parts of acts of the British parliament herein after mentioned are not repealed, we will not, directly or indirectly, export any merchandise or commodity whatsoever to Great-Britain, Ireland, or the West-Indies, except rice to Europe. [179]

Ultimatums have also been issued in the course of unplanned nonviolent resistance, as during the French army mutiny in 1917 when defiant soldiers intended for the 162nd Regiment demonstrated on May 20 at the XXXIInd Corps replacement depot demanding more pay, more leave, and better food, and in the evening elected three delegates to present their ultimatum. [180]

The 1952 Defiance Campaign in South Africa was preceded by an ultimatum to the government from the African National Congress, which stated:

At the recent annual conference of the African National Congress held in Bloemfontein from 15th to 17th December, 1951, the whole policy of the Government was reviewed, and, after serious and careful consideration of the matter, conference unanimously resolved to call upon your Government, as we hereby do, to repeal the aforementioned Acts, by NOT LATER THAN THE 29TH DAY OF FEBRUARY 1952, failing which the African National Congress will hold protest demonstrations and meetings on the 6th day of April 1952, as a prelude to the implementation of the plan for the defiance of unjust laws. [181]

The classic ultimatum in the tradition of Gandhian nonviolent struggle remains Gandhi's letter to the British Viceroy, Lord Irwin, written on March 2, 1930. He began the long letter by addressing the representative of the King-Emperor simply as "Dear Friend." Gandhi then went straight to the point: "Before embarking on civil disobedience and taking the risk I have dreaded to take all these years, I would fain approach you and find a way out." No harm was intended to any Englishman, Gandhi continued, although he held British rule to be a curse. As no significant steps toward independence had been taken, there was now no option, he wrote, but to carry out the 1928 Indian National Congress decision to declare independence if the British had not acted in that direction by the end of 1929. Gandhi then stated why, as he saw it, the British had not acted: "It seems as clear as daylight that responsible British statesmen do not contemplate any alteration in British policy that might adversely affect Britain's commerce with India or require an impartial and close scrutiny of Britain's transactions with India." Unless something were done, Gandhi predicted, the already severe exploitation would continue and India would "be bled at an ever increasing speed."

This Gandhi could not tolerate: ". . . if India is to live as a nation, if the slow death by starvation of her people is to stop, some remedy must be found for immediate relief." He then rejected the proposed Round Table Conference as a remedy. "It is not a matter of carrying conviction by argument. The matter resolves itself into one of matching forces. Conviction or no conviction, Great Britain would defend her Indian commerce and interests by all the forces at her command. India

PART THREE: DYNAMICS

must consequently evolve force enough to free herself from that embrace of death." Indians advocating political violence were gaining support, Gandhi pointed out, while British-organized violence was inflicted on India. The answer to both, he asserted, was nonviolent struggle.

Gandhi then turned to his plan of action: "It is my purpose to set in motion that force as well against the organized violent force of the British rule as the unorganized violent force of the growing party of violence. To sit still would be to give rein to both the forces . . ." The civil disobedience and noncooperation which were contemplated were intended to convert the British, he continued. The civil disobedience plan would include attacking a number of specific injustices which he had outlined in the letter. When these were removed, he continued, "the way to friendly negotiation will be open. If the British commerce with India is purified of greed, you will have no difficulty in recognizing our independence." Gandhi then invited the Viceroy "to pave the way for an immediate removal of those evils, and thus open the way for a real conference between equals."

Gandhi, however, did not expect the British Empire to give way so easily, and he turned to the plan of resistance: "But if you cannot see your way to deal with these evils and my letter makes no appeal to your heart, on the 11th day of this month, I shall proceed with such co-workers of the Ashram as I can take, to disregard the provisions of the Salt Laws." If the Viceroy were to arrest him first, Gandhi expressed the hope there would "be tens of thousands ready, in a disciplined manner, to take up the work after me, and, in the act of disobeying the Salt Act to lay themselves open to the penalties of a law that should never have disfigured the Statute Book." Gandhi offered to discuss the issues if the Viceroy found substance in the letter. "This letter is not in any way intended as a threat but as a simple and sacred duty peremptory on a civil resister." [182] He signed the letter, "I remain, your sincere friend, M.K. Gandhi," and sent a young British Quaker to deliver it to Lord Irwin.

The nonviolent actionists are not naïve enough to expect that such an ultimatum will often lead to capitulation by the opponent. There may be various reasons for this. He may not, for example, see nonviolent action as a credible threat of which he need take notice. Even more often, however, the opponent is likely to see such a communication as an unjustified challenge to his authority, an affront to his dignity, and a usurpation of status, highly improper behavior for people of a subordinate position. The opponent may therefore become angry, he may break off any negotiations in progress, he may totally ignore the communication, or he may say it should have been directed to some subordinate official. Or he may, as did Lord Irwin, have his secretary send a terse four-line acknowledgment of the letter.

In such a case, the time has come for action. The nonviolent actionists will then speak of courage, daring and sacrifice, and call on the people opposed to the opponent's policies to combat them in open struggle, as did Mr. Ahmed Kathrada at the beginning of the 1952 civil disobedience campaign in South Africa:

> The time has come for action. For too long have we been talking to the white man. For three hundred years they have oppressed us . . . And, friends, after three hundred years I say that the time has come when we will talk to the white man in the only language he understands: the language of struggle. [183]

NOTES

1. Napoleon, **The Officer's Manual** or **Napoleon's Maxims of War** (New York: James G. Gregory, 1861) Maxim XVI, pp. 58-59.
2. B. H. Liddell Hart, **Strategy: The Indirect Approach** (New York: Frederick A. Praeger, 1954. Br. ed.: London: Faber and Faber, 1954), p. 25.
3. See Lindberg, *"Konklusionen: Teorien om Ikke-vold,"* p. 209 in Lindberg, Jacobsen and Ehrlich, **Kamp Uden Vaaben**; Oppenheimer and Lakey, **A Manual for Direct Action,** pp. 116-117; and Frederic Solomon and Jacob R. Fishman, "The Psychosocial Meaning of Nonviolence in Student Civil Rights Activities," *Psychiatry*, May 1964, pp. 91-99.
4. Gandhi, **Non-violent Resistance,** pp. 116-117; Ind. ed.: **Satyagraha,** pp. 116-117. See also pp. 362-363; Sharp, **Gandhi Wields the Weapon of Moral Power,** pp. 83 and 87; and Nirmal Kumar Bose, **Studies in Gandhism** (Second Edition); Calcutta: Indian Associated Publishing Co., 1947, p. 171.
5. Gopinath Dhawan, **The Political Philosophy of Mahatma Gandhi,** Ahmedabad, India: Navajivan, 1962, (Third Revised Edition), p. 72.
6. *Ibid.*
7. *Ibid.,* p. 73.
8. *Ibid.,* pp. 72-73. See also Gandhi, **Non-violence in Peace and War,** vol. II, pp. 5-6.

9. Gregg, The Power of Nonviolence, p. 50.
10. Gandhi, Non-violent Resistance, p. 172; Ind. ed.: Satyagraha, p. 172.
11. Venturi, Roots of Revolution, p. 92.
12. *Ibid.,* p. 432.
13. Prawdin, The Unmentionable Nechaev, p. 174.
14. There were several 19th century cases of such psychological and attitude changes among the peasants, some of them deliberately cultivated. See for example, Venturi, Roots of Revolution, pp. 64, 214, 576.
15. Prawdin, The Unmentionable Nechaev, pp. 171-172.
16. Gandhi, Non-violence in Peace and War, vol. II, p. 38.
17. See *Ibid.,* vol. I, p. 12.
18. King, Stride Toward Freedom; U.S. ed., p. 119; Br. ed., p. 140.
19. See Sharp, Tyranny Could Not Quell Them.
20. See Sharp, "Gandhi's Defence Policy," in Mahadevan, Roberts and Sharp, eds., Civilian Defence: An Introduction, pp. 15-52.
21. Gandhi, Non-violence in Peace and War, vol. I, pp. 131-132.
    See also pp. 76 and 151, and vol. II, pp. 38, 133, 233, and 247; Gandhi, Non-violent Resistance, p. 51; Ind. ed.: Satyagraha, p. 51; and Krishna Kripalani, ed., All Men Are Brothers: Life and Thoughts of Mahatma Gandhi as told in his Own Words (Paris: Unesco, 1958), p. 101; Ind. ed.: (Ahmedabad: Navajivan, 1960), p. 135.
22. Gandhi, Non-violence in Peace and War, vol. I, p. 109.
23. Quoted in King, Stride Toward Freedom, U.S. ed., pp. 46-47; Br. ed., p. 55.
24. See, e.g., Gandhi, Non-violence in Peace and War, vol. II, pp. 220-221.
25. See Machiavelli, The Discourses of Niccolo Machiavelli, vol. I, pp. 339-340.
26. Eugen Stamm and Helmut Kastner, Juni 53: Der Volksaufstand vom 17 Juni 1953 in Ost-Berlin und der Sowjetischen Besatzungszone (Bonn: *Bundesministerium für gesamtdeutsche Fragen,* 1961) p. 43. Quoted in Ebert, "Nonviolent Resistance Against Communist Regimes?" pp. 193-194. On the lack of leadership in that Rising, see Ebert's account, *ibid.,* pp. 177-179 and Brant, The East German Rising, pp. 73 and 113.
27. Symons, The General Strike, p. 137.
28. M. K. Gandhi, An Autobiography or the Story of My Experiments With Truth, (Ahmedabad, India: Navajivan, 1956) pp. 470-471.
29. Quoted in Miller, Nonviolence, p. 139.
30. *Ibid.,* p. 136.
31. Symons, The General Strike, p. 63.
32. Jutikkala, A History of Finland, p. 233.
33. Gipson, The British Empire Before the American Revolution, vol. XII, The Triumphant Empire, Britain Sails into the Storm, 1770-1776, p. 179.
34. Halperin, Germany Tried Democracy, pp. 251-259.
35. Ebert, "Nonviolent Resistance Against Communist Regimes?" p. 182.
36. Miller, Nonviolence, p. 307.
37. C. Eric Lincoln, "The Strategy of a Sit-in" p. 296, in Sibley, ed., The Quiet Battle.
38. Luthuli, Let My People Go, p. 179.
39. Watt, Dare Call it Treason, p. 185.

40. M. K. Gandhi, **Young India**, vol. II; quoted by Dhawan, **The Political Philosophy of Mahatma Gandhi**, p. 122.

41. See D. G. Tendulker, **Mahatma: Life of Mohandas Karamchand Gandhi** (Delhi: Government of India, Publications Division, 1960), vol. I, p. 255 and 261.

42. *Ibid.*, pp. 219-221.

43. See for example, Gandhi, **Non-violent Resistance**, pp. 30 and 301; Ind. ed.: Satyagraha, pp. 30 and 301; and Dhawan, **The Political Philosophy** ..., p. 120.

44. Gregg, **The Power of Nonviolence**, p. 49.

45. Lindberg, *"Konklusionen: Theorien om Ikke-vold,"* in Lindberg, Jacobsen and Ehrlich, **Kamp Uden Vaaben**, p. 208.

46. Guenter Lewy, **The Catholic Church and Nazi Germany** (New York and Toronto: McGraw-Hill, 1964, and London: Weidenfeld and Nicholson, 1964), pp. 263-267.

47. See Gregg, **The Power of Nonviolence**, pp. 56, 76 and 123, and Miller, **Nonviolence**, pp. 145-147.

48. See Bose, **Studies in Gandhism**, pp. 142-143.

49. *Ibid.*, pp. 138-139.

50. See M. K. Gandhi, **Satyagraha in South Africa** (Ahmedabad, India: Navajivan, 1950), p. xii.

51. Gandhi, **Non-violence in Peace and War**, vol. I, p. 52.

52. Quoted in Dhawan, **The Political Philosophy** ..., p. 216.

53. Theodor Ebert, "Theory and Practice of Nonviolent Resistance: A Model of a Campaign," manuscript, p. 138. Unpublished English translation (by Hilda Morris) of a doctoral thesis in political science presented at the University of Erlangen, Germany, 1965. Published as **Gewaltfrier Aufstand: Alternative zum Bürgerkrieg** (Freiburg: Verlag Rombach, 1968), and paperback abridgement (Frankfurt am Main and Hamburg: Fischerbücheri, GmbH, 1970).

54. *Ibid.*, p. 142.

55. Gandhi, quoted in Bose, **Studies in Gandhism**, p. 134. See also Gandhi, **Non-violent Resistance**, pp. 30 and 174; Ind. ed.; Satyagraha, pp. 30 and 174.

56. Miller, **Nonviolence**, pp. 168-169.

57. Howard Zinn, **Albany** (Atlanta: Southern Regional Council, 1962), p. 19, quoted in *ibid.*, p. 328. Miller also cites on this Wyatt Tee Walker, "Achievement in Albany," in **New South** (Atlanta), June, 1963.

58. Martin Luther King, Jr., **Why We Can't Wait** (New York: The New American Library, Signet Books, 1964), p. 54.

59. Ebert, "Theory and Practice of Nonviolent Resistance," MS. p. 171.

60. See Sharp, **Gandhi Wields** ..., pp. 56-57 and 59-60.

61. Gandhi, **Satyagraha in South Africa** (rev. sec. ed.; trans. from the Gujarati by Valji Govindji Desai; Ahmedabad, India: Navajivan, 1950), p. 46.

62. Amiya Chakravarty, **A Saint at Work: A View of Gandhi's Work and Message** (William Penn Lecture 1950; Philadelphia: Young Friends Movement of the Philadelphia Yearly Meetings, 1950), pp. 29-31.

63. V.I. Lenin, "What is to be Done? Burning Questions of Our Movement," in V.I. Lenin, **Selected Works in Three Volumes** (New York: International Publishers, and Moscow: Progress Publishers, 1967), vol. I, pp. 232-233. Also in Lenin, **Selected Works in Two Volumes** (Moscow: Foreign Languages Publishing House, 1950) vol. I, p. 379.

64. The term is used by Shridharani, War Without Violence, U.S. ed., p. 7; Br. ed., p. 30.

65. Ebert, "Theory and Practice of Nonviolent Resistance," MS.p. 128.

66. Schlesinger, The Colonial Merchants and the American Revolution, p. 136. "Preliminary agitation" took place that autumn in Providence, Rhode Island. See ibid., p. 153.

67. Oppenheimer and Lakey, A Manual for Direct Action, p. 50.

68. For other descriptions of this stage, see Shridharani, War Without Violence, U.S. ed., pp. 7-9; Br. ed., pp. 30-32 and Bose, Studies in Gandhism, pp. 139-142.

69. Ebert, "Nonviolent Resistance Against Communist Regimes?," pp. 176-177.

70. See, for example, Jutikkala, A History of Finland, p. 233, and Gipson, The Coming of the American Revolution, pp. 98, 182, 199 and 211.

71. Soloman and Fishman, "The Psychosocial Meaning of Nonviolence in Student Civil Rights Activities," Psychiatry, vol. XXVII, no. 2 (May 1964), p. 98.

72. Gregg, The Power of Nonviolence, pp. 114-120.

73. Ibid., p. 147.

74. Bondurant, Conquest of Violence, pp. 29-30.

75. George Lakey, "The Sociological Mechanisms of Nonviolent Action," (M.A. thesis in sociology, University of Pennsylvania, 1962), p. 53; also published in Peace Research Reviews (Oakville, Ontario: Canadian Peace Research Institute), vol. II, no. 6 (Dec. 1968), p. 34.

76. Gandhi, Non-violent Resistance, p. 33; Ind. ed.: Satyagraha, p. 33.

77. Ibid., p. 362.

78. See ibid., pp. 91 and 294.

79. Gandhi, quoted in Dhawan, The Political Philosophy . . . , p. 225.

80. Ibid., p. 225.

81. Ibid., p. 225.

82. Gandhi, Young India, vol. I, p. 262.

83. Gandhi, Non-violent Resistance, p. 295; Ind. ed.: Satyagraha, p. 295.

84. Dhawan, The Political Philosophy . . . , p. 225.

85. Bose, Studies in Gandhism, p. 129.

86. Gandhi, Non-violent Resistance, p. 288; Ind. ed.: Satyagraha, p. 288, and Dhawan, The Political Philosophy . . . , pp. 224-225.

87. Dhawan, The Political Philosophy . . . , p. 225.

88. See Gandhi, Non-violent Resistance, p. 296; Ind. ed.: Satyagraha, p. 296.

89. For a discussion of difficult problems of organization in "civilian defence" – i.e., prepared nonviolent action for purposes of national defence – see Ebert, "Organization in Civilian Defence," in Roberts, ed., Civilian Resistance As a National Defense, Br. title: The Strategy of Civilian Defence, pp. 255-273.

90. For suggestions on methods of organization for U.S. civil rights groups, see Oppenheimer and Lakey, A Manual for Direct Action, esp. pp. 42-55.

91. Quoted by Ebert in "Organization in Civilian Defence," in Roberts, ed., op. cit., p. 256.

92. Ibid., p. 257.

93. See Schlesinger, The Colonial Merchants . . . , p. 360, 370, 501 and 521, and Gipson, The British Empire Before the American Revolution, vol. XI, The Triumphant Empire: The Rumbling of the Coming Storm 1766-1770, pp. 143,

145, 181-182 and 187-188; and vol. XII, pp. 152-153 and 208.

94. Schlesinger, **The Colonial Merchants** . . . , p. 513.

95. *Ibid.,* p. 612.

96. See Sharp, **Gandhi Wields** . . ., pp. 61-72.

97. Luthuli, **Let My People Go,** pp. 117 and 160.

98. Harcave, **First Blood,** p. 84.

99. *Ibid.,* p. 142.

100. *Ibid.,* p. 150.

101. See Brant, **The East German Rising,** pp. 62, 66, 87-88, 91-95, 98-99, 104, 108, 111-112, 124, 136, and 140-141, and Ebert, "Nonviolent Resistance Against Communist Regimes?," MS. pp. 176-183.

102. Reitlinger, **The Final Solution,** p. 161.

103. *Ibid.,* p. 179.

104. See, for example, Prawdin, **The Unmentionable Nechaev,** pp. 153-155, 157, 159 and 160-61, and Charques, **The Twilight of Imperial Russia,** pp. 70, 83, 176, 186 and 201-202. For an instance of how a worker informant gave the police information which enabled them to crush a whole organization, see Venturi, **Roots of Revolution,** p. 533. These are simply examples which could be multiplied from other cases also.

105. Symons, **The General Strike,** p. 145.

106. See Wheeler-Bennett, **The Nemesis of Power,** pp. 550, 565, 593 and 628, and Delarue, **The Gestapo,** pp. 127, 193-194, 210, 227, 239, 272, 297, 304-305 and 316.

107. Bose, **Studies in Gandhism,** pp. 144-145.

108. Jawaharlal Nehru, **An Autobiography** (New edition; London: The Bodley Head, 1953), p. 337.

109. Bose, **Studies in Gandhism** and Gandhi, **Non-violence in Peace and War,** vol. II, p. 3.

110. Oppenheim and Lakey, **A Manual for Direct Action,** p. 48.

111. Gregg, **The Power of Nonviolence,** p. 80.

112. See Gandhi, **Non-violence in Peace and War,** vol. II, pp. 2-3.

113. Gandhi, quoted in Bose, **Studies in Gandhism,** p. 146.

114. Gandhi, **Non-violent Resistance,** pp. 379-380; Ind. ed.: **Satyagraha,** pp. 379-380.

115. Quoted in Dhawan, **The Political Philosophy** . . . , p. 223.

116. Gandhi, **Non-violence in Peace and War,** vol. II, pp. 50-51.

117. Nehru, **An Autobiography,** p. 69.

118. Ebert, "Theory and Practice of Nonviolent Resistance," MS. p. 116.

119. Gregg, **The Power of Nonviolence,** p. 80.

120. Irving L. Janis and Daniel Katz, "The Reduction of Intergroup Hostility: Research Problems and Hypotheses," **Journal of Conflict Resolution,** vol. III, no. 1 (March 1959), p. 87.

121. *Ibid.*

122. *Ibid.*

123. Clausewitz, **On War,** vol. I, p. 96.

124. This has been especially stimulated by examinations of how prepared nonviolent struggle might be used in national defence—i.e., "civilian defence". See, for example Sir Stephen King-Hall, **Defence in the Nuclear Age** pp.

196-205; (Nyack, N.Y.: Fellowship, 1959; Br. ed.: London: Gollancz, 1958), and Adam Roberts, "Civilian Defence Strategy," in Roberts, editor, **Civilian Resistance as a National Defense,** Br. ed.: **The Strategy of Civilian Defence,** pp. 215-254.

This chapter, however, is restricted to examination of basic principles of strategy and tactics in nonviolent action generally, and will not therefore examine how these principles might be applied in specific conflicts or for particular purposes.

125. Liddell Hart, **Strategy,** p. 369.

126. Gandhi, **Satyagraha in South Africa,** p. xi.

127. Hiller, **The Strike,** p. 126.

128. On strategic and tactical problems in the struggles of the American colonists, see Morgan and Morgan, **The Stamp Act Crisis,** pp. 174 and 240; Gipson, **The British Empire . . . ,** vol. XI, pp. 265-271; and Schlesinger, **The Colonial Merchants . . . ,** pp. 213-215, 218-220, 226-234, and 400-401.

On the lack of strategy in the East German Rising, see Brant, **The East German Rising,** pp. 73, 103 and 188-189.

On the lack of strategic planning for the *Ruhrkamf,* see Ehrlich (Raloff), *"Ruhrkampen,"* p. 184, in Lindberg, Jacobsen and Ehrlich, **Kamp Uden Vaaben.** Lack of advance strategic planning for certain aspects of the 1926 British General Strike is mentioned by Symons, in **The General Strike,** p. 51. On strategic and tactical questions in the spontaneous 1905 Revolution, see Schwarz, **The Russian Revolution of 1905,** pp. 99-112, and (on conflicting views on whether strikes should lead to a violent rising) pp. 132-143, and Harcave, **First Blood,** pp. 165-167, 175, 199-206, 209-210, and 215; p. 199 raises the question of when the optimum results might have been achieved by ending that particular struggle. On the tactical problem of what the *Duma* should have done when dissolved in February 1917, see Katkov, **Russia 1917,** pp. 293-294. On strategic and tactical planning of a sit-in campaign in Atlanta, see C. Eric Lincoln, "The Strategy of a Sit-in," in Sibley **The Quiet Battle,** pp. 296-297. On when to call off an African bus boycott in South Africa, see Luthuli, **Let My People Go,** p. 178.

129. See Jutikkala, **A History of Finland,** pp. 233-235.

130. Clausewitz, **On War,** vol. I, p. 107.

131. See Liddell Hart, **Strategy,** pp. 340-41, 25, 337, 349, 359 and 350.

132. Clausewitz, **On War,** vol. I, p. 183.

133. *Ibid.,* p. 173.

134. Sharp, **Gandhi Wields . . .** pp. 70-90.

135. *Ibid.,* pp. 14-15.

136. Miller, **Nonviolence,** p. 150.

137. Nehru, **An Autobiography,** p. 253.

138. Sheehy-Skeffington, **Michael Davitt,** pp. 120-121. On debate in 1775 on the timing of the American Colonists' nonimportation and nonexportation movement, see Schlesinger, **The Colonial Merchants . . .** pp. 414-421.

139. Sharp, **Gandhi Wields . . .** p. 84.

140. See Miller, **Nonviolence,** p. 308; and Lincoln, "The Strategy of a Sit-in," p. 297.

141. Clausewitz, **On War,** vol. I, p. 192.

142. Liddell Hart, **Strategy,** p. 342. See also Clausewitz, **On War,** vol. I, p. 97.

143. M. K. Gandhi, **Non-violent Resistance,** p. 288; Ind. ed.: **Satyagraha,** p. 288; and Dhawan, **The Political Philosophy . . . ,** pp. 224-5.

144. Clausewitz, **On War,** vol. I, p. 214.
145. Liddell Hart, **Strategy,** p. 348.
146. *Ibid.,* p. 347.
147. *Ibid.,* p. 348.
148. *Ibid.*
149. Bose, **Selections from Gandhi,** p. 202.
150. Nehru, **An Autobiography,** pp. 215 and 327-328.
151. Miller, **Nonviolence,** pp. 146 and 150.
152. Bose, **Studies in Gandhism,** p. 152.
153. Gandhi, **Non-violent Resistance,** p. 156; Ind. ed.: **Satyagraha,** p. 156.
154. Sharp, **Gandhi Wields** . . . , p. 72.
155. Gandhi, **Nonviolent Resistance,** p. 173; Ind. ed.: **Satyagraha,** p. 173.
156. Waskow, **From Race Riot to Sit-in,** p. 246.
157. Bose, **Studies in Gandhism,** p. 176.
158. Bondurant, **Conquest of Violence,** p. 38.
159. Gandhi, **Non-violent Resistance,** p. 25; Ind. ed.: **Satyagraha,** p. 25.
160, *Ibid.,* p. 173.
161. *Ibid.,* pp. 115-116.
162. *Ibid.,* p. 127.
163. *Ibid.,* p. 151.
164. Sharp, **Gandhi Wields** . . . , pp. 51-206.
165. Sibley, ed., **The Quiet Battle,** p. 371.
166. Bose, **Selections from Gandhi,** p. 202.
167. Clausewitz, **On War,** vol. I, p. 241.
168. Liddell Hart, **Strategy,** p. 348.
169. Schlesinger, **The Colonial Merchants** . . . , pp. 369-370.
170. Harcave, **First Blood,** pp. 219-220.
171. Interview with Pan-Africanist representative Peter Molotsi in Accra, 26 April 1960; reported in Gene Sharp, "No Co-existence with Oppression," *Peace News,* 13 May 1960.
172. Ebert, "Theory and Practice of Nonviolent Resistance," MS pp. 313-314.
173. See Liddell Hart, **Strategy,** pp. 343-344 and Clausewitz, **On War,** vol. I, p. 166.
174. Liddell Hart, **Strategy,** p. 349.
175. Bose, **Studies in Gandhism,** p. 153.
176. Gandhi, quoted in Bose, **Selections from Gandhi,** p. 202.
177. See Bondurant, **Conquest of Violence,** pp. 38-39 and Bose, **Studies in Gandhism,** p. 176.
178. On the nature and role of the ultimatum in satyagraha, see Shridharani, **War Without Violence,** U.S. ed., pp. 11 and 133-134, and Br. ed., pp. 33-34, 98 and 128, and Bondurant, **Conquest of Violence,** pp. 40 and 85.
179. Schlesinger, **The Colonial Merchants** . . . , p. 609.
180. Watt, **Dare Call It Treason,** p. 185.
181. Kuper, **Passive Resistance in South Africa,** p. 234; Appendix B, pp. 233-247, contains the full text of this exchange of letters with the government.
182. The full text is quoted in Sharp, **Gandhi Wields** . . . , pp. 61-66.
183. Kuper, **Passive Resistance in South Africa,** p. 114.

10

Challenge
Brings Repression

INTRODUCTION

The time comes when passivity, acquiescence and patience give way to open nonviolent struggle. This time for action may have been determined by various factors discussed in the previous chapter: tactical and strategic considerations, the opponent's actions, the absence of solutions through milder measures, and the state of mind of the grievance group.

This time for action is also the time for self-reliance and internal strengthening of the struggle group. During an Irish rent strike campaign in 1879 and 1880 Charles Stewart Parnell repeatedly called on the peasants to "rely on yourselves," not on any one else, to right their grievances:

> It is no use relying on the Government . . . You must only rely upon your own determination . . . . help yourselves by standing together . . . strengthen those amongst yourselves who are weak . . . ,

band yourselves together, organize yourselves . . . and you must win . . .

When you have made this question ripe for settlement, then and not till then will it be settled.[1]

Self-reliance and organization (or, occasionally, spontaneous united action) contribute to change by increasing the strength of the groups near the bottom of hierarchically organized social, economic and political systems. The dominant groups in such systems are usually well organized and capable of united action for their objectives. Subordinates in such systems are frequently not so. They may be large in numbers, and the dominant groups may be in fact dependent upon them. Yet the subordinates may often be incapable of effective joint action because they lack confidence in themselves, because they remain a mass of separated individuals and disunited groups,[2] and because they do not know how to act. Nonviolent action may change this situation. The grievance group may take joint action by a technique which mobilizes power among the subordinates and enables them to exert control over their present and future lives. Of course, to win, the actionists must do more; they must persist despite repression and must bring into operation the forces which can bring success.

A HALT TO SUBMISSION

Nonviolent action means that submission and passivity are cast off. Nonviolence, said Gandhi, "means the pitting of one's whole soul against the will of the tyrant."[3] Nehru's view was similar.[4] This determination to struggle will be expressed in the use of the psychological, social, economic and political forces at the disposal of the actionists. These forces operate in concrete ways utilizing the methods of action which have been described in detail in Chapters Three to Eight. This period is the time of the matching of forces. If advance planning has preceded action, now will be the time to disseminate precise instructions on what action should take place, when, and which persons and groups are to act. If advance pledges to act have been made, this is the time to put them into practice.

The initial forms of action in a nonviolent struggle may differ widely. Methods of nonviolent protest—marches, parades, display of flags and the like—often begin a campaign, or in other cases some type of psychological nonviolent intervention—such as fasts—may be used. Other struggles begin directly with noncooperation—civil disobedience or a large-scale strike, for example. Initial dramatic actions symbolic of the issues at stake, conducted in a disciplined manner, may strike the imaginations of all concerned, shatter inertia, awaken awareness, increase the morale of the grievance group, and set the tone for the struggle which has begun.[5]

Particular conflicts will differ widely in the pace with which the strategy is unrolled and the full strength of the movement is mobilized and applied. Sometimes a slow and deliberate development is most effective, while at other times it may be stunningly rapid. Since nonviolent campaigns differ widely, there are no universal steps or stages for them all. Therefore, in this and the next chapters the focus will be on the general processes, forces and mechanisms of change operating in this type of conflict. Their specific implementation will differ from case to case.

With the launching of nonviolent action, basic, often latent, conflicts between the respective groups are brought to the surface and activated. Through ensuing "creative conflict and tension"[6] it becomes possible to produce change to resolve the underlying conflict.

Unlike many religious pacifists, most exponents of nonviolent action would agree with Frederick Douglass:

> Those who profess to favor freedom and yet deprecate agitation, are men who want crops without plowing up the ground. They want rain without thunder and lightning. They want the ocean without the awful roar of its many waters. The struggle may be a moral one; or it may be a physical one; or it may be both moral and physical. But it must be a struggle. Power concedes nothing without demand. It never did and it never will.[7]

Indeed, nonviolent actionists insist that in sharp conflicts, only effective nonviolent struggle can lead to a satisfactory solution which avoids both passive submission and political violence.

In some cases members of the grievance group may become enthusiastic at the prospect of nonviolent hostilities. As tension increases, morale rises and large numbers of formerly passive people become determined to take part in the coming struggle. "Such enthusiasm in the face of future suffering may be due to the fact that a community which has been oppressed and humbled, looks forward to the opportunity of proving their full and equal worth in combat," writes Ebert.[8]

The changes which nonviolent struggle brings to the struggle group will be explored more fully in Chapter Fourteen, but a brief mention of them is required here. Some will be psychological—a shattering of attitudes of conformity, hopelessness, inertia, impotence and passivity. Others will be more directly political—learning how to act together to achieve objectives, the long-term results of which will obviously be most significant where success is achieved. Participation in nonviolent action may give people increased self-respect, confidence and an awareness of their own power. Thus, writes Hiller, "Recognition of laborers as formidable opponents undoubtedly helps to improve the status of every workingman. The strike, although it brings no material gain, is felt to bring a triumph if it brings this sense of importance." [9] The experience in India was similar. Jawaharlal Nehru wrote that Gandhi's example and leadership changed the millions in India from a demoralized mass of people without hope or capacity for resistance, into people with self-respect and capacity for self-reliant struggle against oppression. [10]

The withdrawal of consent, cooperation and submission will challenge the system. How seriously, will vary with the quality and forms of action, the numbers of the actionists, and their persistence in face of repression. The social and political milieu is also important. This includes: how much nonconformity the system can tolerate, how much support for, or hostility to, the regime there is, what the chances are of the resistance spreading, and how much the opponent's sources of power are threatened by the action. The final outcome of the challenge will be determined by some kind of balance between the seriousness of the challenge and the degree to which the social and political milieu favors each side. The opponent's own efforts are clearly important, but, *in themselves,* they are not decisive. Take repression, for example. To be effective, repression must produce submission. But at times it does not. Repression may even be counterproductive, and forces started by the nonviolent actionists and outside of the opponent's control may even reduce or destroy his *ability* to act. An end to the submission of the grievance group initiates changes which may bring fundamental alterations in the relations of the contending groups.

INITIAL POLARIZATION FOLLOWED BY SHIFTING POWER

The launching of nonviolent action will almost always sharpen the conflict, cause the conflicting groups to become more sharply deliniated, and stimulate previously uncommitted people to take sides. This polarization seems to be a quality of all forms of open conflict. [11] At the beginning of nonviolent struggle, Lakey observes, "those initially inclined toward the opponent tend to move closer to his position and support it, while those initially inclined toward the campaigner may move in the campaigner's direction." [12] The point at which this occurs varies. Oppenheimer and Lakey point out that the previous period of indifference is likely to be replaced by one of "active antagonism, the time when tide often runs highest against the movement." [13]

This polarization of support for the opponent is well illustrated by reactions in the 1952 Defiance Campaign in South Africa. Before the campaign, the Europeans were usually indifferent to the many prosecutions of Africans and other nonwhites for breaking the Pass Laws and certain other regulatory laws. However, when the *Apartheid* laws and regulations were deliberately and publicly disobeyed by the nonwhites who used jail-going as a protest, the Europeans' indifference was shattered, and they reacted "with active emotions of hate or sympathy." A related political shift occurred also; the opposition United Party, committed to white domination in a milder form than the ruling Nationalist Party, "moved toward the assimilation of its non-European policy with that of the Government, and United Party supporters moved into the ranks of the Nationalist Party." [14] In this case the struggle ended without a major reversal of this trend although, as discussed in Chapter Twelve, under certain circumstances which include continuation of the struggle, this polarization in favor of the opponent is likely to be a passing phenomenon. In the South African case it was not, since the campaign collapsed just as disunity of the opponent group had started to appear.

During this initial polarization, which may be short or long, it is especially important for the nonviolent actionists to be most careful in their behavior. "Actions which confirm the prejudices of the opponent will be seized upon and magnified; those which counter the prejudices will have more impact than ordinarily." At this stage, the grievance group will be worse off than before the campaign started since repression has been added to the initial grievances. If the struggle halts at this stage the grievance group will remain worse off than before. But a continuation of the struggle in a disciplined manner is likely to lead to a new stage, characterized by the disunity of the opponent. [15] In this new stage the opponent is likely to lose even support he had before the struggle while support for the nonviolent actionists may grow.

Seifert supports this view of the instability of the initial polarization, drawing largely upon the cases of minority nonviolent action for social reform. Because the first public reaction to the nonviolent challenge may well be negative, the actionists should attempt to keep to a minimum defection of this pre-campaign support for the desired changes. But, Seifert argues, there seems to be nothing the actionists can do to prevent a temporary strengthening of the opponent group. In addition, the supporters of change may become divided between nonviolent militants and more conventional moderates. After this initial stage, Seifert continues, the first shifts in favor of correcting the grievances "are likely to come at an agonizingly slow rate." A "tipping point" will come, however, after which the shifts in opinion, support and power will proceed at a rapid rate, and, for many, even become "the thing to do."

In the long run, therefore, successful nonviolent campaigns produce a strengthened solidarity among the nonviolent militants, a growth of wider support for correction of the grievance and a fragmentation and disintegration of support for the opponent. Seifert acknowledges, of course, that the factors making for this shift may not always be present; at times other factors, such as economic interests, may dictate a very rapid adjustment by the opponent to the new situation produced by the nonviolent challenge. [16]

This instability of the initial polarization, the tendency of a section of intermediary opinion to shift toward the nonviolent group, of the opponent's camp to split, and of support for the actionists' objectives to grow, are not inevitable. They appear to develop only so long as the group remains nonviolent. For reasons discussed in Chapter Eleven, if violence is used by or on behalf of the actionists the tendency toward both a relative and an absolute increase of their strength and support seems to reverse.

As intermediary opinion shifts toward the nonviolent actionists the new support may be expressed not by nonviolent action but by more conventional attacks on the grievances. This has occurred in several cases. Nonviolent sit-ins in the U.S. South, for example, are reported to have stimulated other less militant antisegregation action, such as voter registration, integration of schools and integration of all-white professional organizations. [17] There is other scattered evidence of this tendency. For example, the 1930-31 civil disobedience campaign in India prodded the Liberals (who had opposed it) to take stronger action by constitutional means, and to act as intermediaries in negotiations between the Indian National Congress and the British *Raj.* [18] The Defiance Campaign of 1952 in South Africa contributed significantly to the formation of the Liberal Party and the Congress of Democrats—both antiapartheid political groups. In that same campaign, the African National Congress experienced a jump from seven thousand to one hundred thousand in paid-up members. The objectives of the campaign also received support from various church groups not previously involved. [19]

Support for the nonviolent actionists and increased participation in the campaign itself are also likely to grow as the initial polarization is reversed. When these various changes take place, the extreme polarization which first occurred between the nonviolent group and the opponent is revealed as unstable. There tends to develop what Harvey Seifert has called the "progressive detachment of groups arranged in a spectrum of potential support." [20] The course of the struggle may be viewed as the attempt of the nonviolent actionists continually to increase their strength (numerical and otherwise), not only among their usual supporters and third parties but even in the camp of the opponent, and by various processes to reduce the strength of the opponent group.

During the campaign the respective strengths of the two contending groups are therefore subject to constant change, both absolutely and relatively. Such change takes place to a much greater degree and more quickly than it does in struggles in which both sides use violence.

The nonviolent actionists' behavior may therefore influence the strength or weakness of both their own group and also of the opponent. In addition the conduct of the nonviolent group will influence whether third parties turn to the support of either of the groups. The extreme and constant variability of the strength of both contending groups is highly important to the nonviolent actionists in choosing and applying strategy, tactics and methods. This highly dynamic and changeable situation means that particular acts within a nonviolent strategy may have extremely wide and significant repercussions on the power of each side, even more so than comparable acts in war. Each particular action, even a limited one, therefore needs to be selected and evaluated in terms of its wider influences on the overall struggle.

If possible, the specific acts should not only demonstrate the present strength of the actionists, but also help to increase their absolute power and to diminish that of the opponent. This may happen even when the immediate political objective has *not* been achieved. Naturally, short-term successes which also contribute to a favorable alteration of relative strengths are to be preferred if possible, but short-term successes at the *cost* of an unfavorable alteration of relative strengths are most questionable. It is possible to *appear* to lose all the battles except the last and yet clearly to win that last one because of the changes in relative strengths that have occurred during the previous battles.

Improvements in the relative strength of the nonviolent actionists after the initial polarization will be highly important in determining the course of events in the intermediate and later stages of the campaign. An increase in genuine strength of the nonviolent group at each stage will make it easier for the group to meet unforeseen circumstances, will maximize its relative strength in the next stage of the struggle, and will increase the possibility of full success.

THE OPPONENT'S INITIAL PROBLEM

The opponent's initial problem arises from the fact that the nonviolent action disrupts the status quo and requires of him some type of response. The type and extent of the disruption will differ. The opponent's tolerance will vary. And his reactions, both psychologically and in countermeasures, may range widely and may change as the struggle continues.

In mild cases, initiation of nonviolent action may disturb the existing situation only slightly. In extreme cases, however, it may shatter the status quo. The opponent will no longer be able to count on the submission of the members of the grievance group. He will no longer be able to assume they will do nothing fundamental to alter their plight; they are actively protesting, noncooperating and perhaps intervening to block implementation of his policies or to produce changes of their own. The opponent will have to respond to the new challenge. Generally he will try to end the opposition. To do so, the opponent will need to take a series of decisions about his own countermeasures. He will need to make similar decisions when the challenge is instead made by violent means, but, as later discussion will show, nonviolent means may be especially conducive to creating difficulties in making those decisions. Nonviolent action also tends to produce and aggravate conflicts within the opponent's camp about appropriate countermeasures.[21]

It is to the advantage of the nonviolent actionists to prevent and correct misperceptions of their intentions and activities. At the initial stage such misperceptions may cause the opponent group to make first responses which may be harmful to all concerned. If the misperceptions continue into later stages, they are likely to disturb—though not destroy—the normal operation of the mechanisms of change of nonviolent action, especially the processes associated with the conversion mechanism. Problems of accurate perception of nonviolent intentions existed even before Gandhi's campaigns. Nehru, who knew the English well, has written: "The average Englishman did not believe the *bona fides* of nonviolence; he thought that all this was camouflage, a cloak to cover some vast secret design which would burst out in a violent upheaval one day." [22] Past cases of violence during and following a nonviolent struggle therefore produce detrimental influences which the nonviolent group will need to counter, both at the initiation of the campaign and throughout its course. Frequently it will also be necessary to counter a general disbelief in the possibility of effective but strictly nonviolent struggle.

Sometimes—but not always—when confronted with nonviolent action the opponent and his officials become confused, especially when they have been taken by surprise by the events or when they are unfamiliar with this type of behavior. This confusion is not, of course, necessarily beneficial to the actionists and their cause. French army officers were, for example, confused and uncertain about what to do when faced with mass mutiny in 1917.[23] East German officials, police and Party leaders, especially on the local level, were confused and uncertain when confronted with strikes and demonstrations in June 1953.[24] Heinz Brandt—then secretary for agitation and propaganda in the Berlin organization of the Socialist Unity Party—has described the Party propagandists as "completely bewildered" as they witnessed the first "genuine working class movement" of their lives which, contrary to all they had been taught, was acting against the "workers' party."[25] Furthermore, a similar response came from higher officials: "Party and state officials were taken by surprise and increasingly paralyzed. A monstrous event was occurring before their very eyes: workers were rising against the 'worker-peasant' state. The world collapsed round their ears."[26] Workers rebelling against the Communist State often sang "The Internationale."[27] These events suggest that confusion may be especially likely when the nonviolent action takes the forms which shatter the perception of the world contained in official doctrines and ideology.

Confusion in the ranks of the opponent may have other sources as well. It may arise from excessive optimism and false confidence that others see his actions and policises as entirely good. When attempting to overthrow the Weimar Republic, Dr. Kapp "staked all on a great popular welcome, and when confronted with blank hostility, he showed himself bewildered, weak and helpless."[28] Nehru records British confusion and uncertainty as they faced the 1921 noncooperation movement:

> As our morale grew, that of the Government went down. They did not understand what was happening: it seemed that the old world they knew in India was toppling down. There was a new aggressive spirit abroad and self-reliance and fearlessness, and the great prop of British rule in India—prestige—was visibly wilting. Repression in a small way only strengthened the movement, and the Government hesitated for long before it would take action against the big leaders. It did not know what the consequences might be. Was the Indian Army reliable? Would the police carry out orders? As Lord Reading, the Viceroy, said in December 1921, they were "puzzled and perplexed."[29]

Sometimes in the past, one source of the opponent's confusion has been surprise at the explicitly nonviolent character of the action movement. Such surprise may or may not have helped the nonviolent group. However, with increasing use of the nonviolent technique, the surprise element has declined; it will finally disappear. Governments are also rapidly accumulating experience in dealing with this type of challenge.[30] Although these developments may reduce the brutality of repression, they will not necessarily reduce the effectiveness of the technique. The struggle potential of nonviolent action is not dependent upon surprise or novelty.

At times, instead, the opponent may be ignorant of its nature and workings. Ignorance of the power of nonviolent struggle may cause the opponent to be overconfident and hence to react extremely mildly to the nonviolent challenge. This reaction may also derive from misperceptions of the intentions of the grievance group, or in overconfidence rooted in belief in the regime's omnipotence, or in long absence of effective challenge. Tsarist officials clearly miscalculated the gravity of the spreading illegal strike movement in St. Petersburg in the first few days of January 1905, a short while before the march on the Winter Palace on Bloody Sunday.[31] Even in later months, despite events and warnings from advisers, tsarist officials again underestimated the seriousness of the trouble spots throughout the Empire. In both instances they did so because of overconfidence in the regime's ability to deal with trouble should it erupt.[32]

In other situations, the opponent may clearly recognize the danger to his system or policies which the nonviolent action poses. Any given nonviolent action will not, however, be equally threatening to all regimes. There are variations in tolerance, i.e., in the degree to which the opponent can safely ignore the challenge or take only mild action against it. Several factors will be involved: the issues at stake, the numbers involved, the methods of nonviolent action used, and the expected future course of the movement. The degree to which the opponent can tolerate dissent may also be influenced by the degree to which the society is democratic or nondemocratic. Gandhi argued for example: "A civil resister never uses arms and hence he is harmless to a State that is at all willing to listen to the voice of public opinion. He is dangerous for an autocratic State, for he brings about its fall by engaging public opinion upon the matter for which he resists the State."[33] Many systems will not, and some cannot, tolerate defiance without taking repressive counteractions.

This is not to say that all hostile responses to nonviolent challenges arise solely from an intellectual recognition of the objective dangers which they pose to the opponent's policies or system. Frequently, an opponent may react to nonviolent challenge emotionally, seeing it largely as an affront, an indignity, as offensive behavior, and as a repudiation of his authority and position. He may regard these aspects of the challenge as more important than the actual issues at stake. The opponent may then try to obtain either verbal acknowledgement of his authority and position, or a cancellation of the nonviolent campaign, or both, before he will consent to negotiations or reconsider the disputed policies. Even written protests and petitions, and correspondence concerning grievances between responsible bodies—which are far short of actual disobedience—may provoke this indignant reaction. Such mild acts by American colonists and their legislatures, for example, aroused highly emotional reactions in Britain, from the King and from members of both Houses of Parliament; until the colonials had acknowledged the supremacy of British laws and their responsibility to help support the government of the Empire, there was no disposition to consider objectively their grievances or petitions. [34]

Sometimes this reaction of indignation may accompany recognition that the nonviolent challenge is genuinely serious. The British government's reaction to the 1926 general strike, for example, was partially emotional, the strike being seen as an affront, as offensive, and as a repudiation of authority; but it was also rational, the strike being seen as a serious threat which had to be defeated in order to halt such challenges once and for all. In the days before the strike, the government broke off negotiations and demanded "an immediate and unconditional withdrawal of the instructions for a General Strike." [35] As the time for action came, even government supporters who had earlier favored conciliation hardened their position, and concluded that, once begun, the struggle had to be fought to an end. [36] At almost the last minute, Labour M.P. Arthur Henderson (who opposed the strike) attempted a final appeal for a settlement to Sir Winston Churchill (leader of Cabinet "hard-liners"). When Henderson arrived, however, Churchill asked: "Have you come to say that the strike notices are withdrawn? . . . No? Then there is no reason to continue this discussion." [37]

In many instances, the opponent may be less concerned with challenges to his dignity or authority and more with the immediate issues at stake. He may recognize that his interest will be better served by concentrating primarily or exclusively on the issues in dispute. This does not necessarily mean that he will take the nonviolent challenge without concern, especially if withdrawal of the subordinates' usual cooperation and support brings realization to a somewhat startled opponent that his power is in fact based upon the support which is now denied. For example, Watt reports that during the 1917 mutiny, French Army "officers suddenly found that they were not in control of their men . . ." [38] The Russian 1905 Revolution, concludes Katkov, brought to the tsarist government a "newly-discovered need for popular support . . ." [39] In his report to the Tsar on January 17, 1905, just over a week after Bloody Sunday, the Minister of Agriculture, Alexis Ermolov, reminded him that the strength of the throne was dependent on the support of the people. [40] Despite these insights the Russian government persisted in underestimating the power of various strike waves until they produced undeniable economic paralysis.

As already noted, the strong reactions to the British general strike of 1926 were in part rooted in a perception of the power of nonviolent economic struggle, which Conservatives saw as a challenge to the existence of the British constitutional system. An editorial written for the *Daily Mail* reflected this view. The general strike was not "an industrial dispute," it declared, but "a revolutionary movement" which, by inflicting suffering upon the general community, was intended "to put forcible constraint upon the Government." The general strike, the draft editorial continued, could "only succeed by destroying the Government and subverting the rights and liberties of the people." Therefore no civilized government could tolerate it, and "it must be dealt with by every resource at the disposal of the community." [41] With such a perception, the British government prepared to meet the crisis by withdrawing warships from the Atlantic fleet for use at home, dispersing soldiers and naval contingents to various parts of the country, and canceling all army and navy leaves. [42]

The Nazis also saw mass noncooperation in the form of the general strike as a dangerous weapon if used against them. For example on March 1, 1933, after the burning of the *Reichstag* (the German parliament building) on February 27, the Nazis issued a decree which provided punishments both for "provocation to armed conflict against the State" and for "provocation to a general strike." Delarue in his study, *The Gestapo*, writes, "What the Nazis feared the most was a general strike, which could be the sole effective weapon of the divided Left." [43]

Recognition of the power of nonviolent action will sometimes lead the opponent to make concessions in the hope of ending the challenge. The opponent may grant major demands claimed by the nonviolent actionists if they appear just to others and if he expects that otherwise the movement will grow and become increasingly difficult to control. He may see serious concessions to be in the long run the easiest way out. Or, he may hesitate to take such action because of fear that other groups with less justified claims might resort to similar means. While conceding demands, the opponent may seek to save face, as by suddenly discovering that a long-standing commission or board had just submitted its recommendations which included changes demanded by the nonviolent group: "If only they had been patient and trusted us . . . ."

At other times, the opponent will make major concessions only after a considerable period of struggle, that is, after he has recognized the real power of the movement. For example, the tsarist regime in 1905, especially during the Great October Strike, had "to become acquainted with the new force and form of the opposition and to meet unexpected problems." In the first days of the October strike, "the government seemed paralyzed; and in many ways it was." Very reluctantly, not knowing what else to do, the Tsar issued the imperial October Manifesto, in which he renounced his role as unrivaled autocrat, granted civil liberties and extension of the vote in principle to all, established that *Duma* (parliamentary) consent was required for all laws, and guaranteed effective popular supervision of appointed officials.[44] These concessions were, however, too mild to halt the revolution, for many people now aimed at bigger objectives.

Instead of major concessions, the opponent may offer comparatively minor ones. For example, after it was announced that the 1930-31 campaign in India would begin with civil disobedience of the Salt Act, the government referred the salt tax question to the Tariff Board; the aim was to lower the price of taxed salt to that of untaxed salt if the salt tax were abolished. Gandhi, however, affirmed that he would not be satisfied with this concession, and besides there were yet other forts to be stormed.[45] In a very different conflict, in early August 1953 during the peak of the strike in the Vorkuta prison camps, the State Prosecutor arrived with a retinue of generals from Moscow offering minor concessions: two letters could be mailed a month instead of a year, one family visit a year, removal of identification numbers from clothes, and removal of iron bars from windows. These were rejected in an open letter from the prisoners. Their reply was ignored and General Deravyanko traveled from camp to camp within the Vorkuta group promising better food, higher pay, shorter shifts, with "some effect on weaker and less politically active elements."[46] Often in ordinary labor strikes the employer offers certain limited improvements as a counter to trade union demands. The East German regime responded to the developing strikes and the Rising on June 16, 1953— which had been to a significant degree sparked by an increase in the amount of work required in the factories—by minor concessions. Very quickly government loud-speaker vans announced that the Politburo would "reconsider" the increased work norms, and later the same day the Politburo did in fact rescind them.[47]

Relatively minor concession, however, frequently will not satisfy a determined movement. The Diem regime in South Vietnam on several occasions responded unsuccessfully to the Buddhist campaign of 1963 with minor concessions and gestures of conciliation. These included removal of certain local government officials, apologies for the actions of some subordinate officials, renewal of talks with the Buddhists, release of some Buddhist prisoners, removal of barbed wire around pagodas.[48] Minor concessions are related to what has become called "tokenism" in the Afro-American freedom movement, i.e., minor changes intended simply to end protest and pressure, as Martin Luther King, Jr., described it.[49]

But concessions, large or small, may not weaken the resistance, but strengthen it. The concessions may give confidence to the actionists, as occurred in the East German Rising. Striking and demonstrating workers were elated by their first gains, and cancellation of the increased work norms brought confusion to Party members who had been defending them.[50]

Many opponents have difficulties in granting major concessions, or in acceding to all the actionists' objectives as long as they still have a choice. These difficulties may be rooted in beliefs, prestige, or in power considerations. Occasionally an opponent—however autocratic—may genuinely believe that concessions, compromise, or surrender are out of the question if he is to be "true" to his mission or duty. Such a belief was very important in the qualms of conscience which Tsar Nicholas II experienced before deciding to abdicate in March 1917.[51] The opponent's sincere belief that he is right and that his policies and repression are correct and necessary may be highly important factors in particular conflicts. Under certain conditions, international prestige may also discourage certain opponents from making major concessions.[52] In other cases concessions may be difficult because of the opponent's desire to appease some of his supporters who strongly oppose the nonviolent group.

Even more serious can be the opponent's fear that once he surrenders on some specific issues, he may have to surrender everything. This was a frequent reaction to the predominantly nonviolent economic and political resistance campaign of the American colonists prior to April 1775. For example, in England there was a strong feeling against the impending repeal of the disrupted Townshend duties on the grounds that, says Gipson, "the government could not give way without bringing about a disruption of the Empire."[53] In 1774 when repeal of the remaining tax on tea was being debated, Solicitor General Widderburn told Edmund Burke: ". . . if you give up this tax, it is not here you must stop, you will be required to give up much more, nay, to give up all." [54]

Rather than repression, the opponent may use psychological influences to induce the nonviolent actionists to be submissive again and to withdraw from the struggle. Usually the opponent may try to convince them that not only can the movement not succeed, but that it has already begun to lose strength. These tactics are commonly used in strikes, in the form of inspired reports that more and more of the strikers are returning to their jobs. In one major American steel strike, for example: "Full page advertisements begged the men to go back to work, while flaming headlines told us 'men go back to mills,' 'steel strike waning!' and 'mills operating stronger'; 'more men back at work'; and so forth." [55] At one point a false report of a settlement was issued in an attempt to bring the Montgomery bus boycott to an end. [56] In the Bardoli revenue refusal campaign in 1928 there were repeated attempts to induce key people to pay the land revenue which was being withheld in the hope that this would weaken the will of others. [57]

False rumors may also be spread about the movement, its intentions, and its leadership. [58] Attempts may be made to split off groups supporting the movement or to turn leaders against each other. [59] Or a more direct counterattack may be mounted, with the opponent making a major effort to justify existing policies and to show that there is no justification for the demands of the nonviolent group. This effort is intended to reduce the support that the nonviolent group can mobilize and retain.

It is common for nonviolent resistance to be met with repression when the opponent is unwilling or unable to grant the actionists' demands. Repression is an acknowledgement of the seriousness of the challenge. Sometimes the severity of repression will be in proportion to the seriousness of the nonviolent challenge, but this is by no means a standard pattern. In cases of civil disobedience, for example, in certain political situations, the fact that a law chosen for open disobedience is unimportant will not necessarily reduce the intensity of the opponent's reaction. [60] Gandhi acknowledged that when people practiced civil disobedience ". . . it was impossible for the Government to leave them free." [61] True, the opponent's need to bring an end to defiance may in certain situations be largely symbolic. But in other situations of widespread nonviolent action which is likely to become increasingly effective, the pressures on the opponent to halt it by some means or other will be overwhelming. Such strong pressures will especially occur where the system cannot stand major dissent.

For example, Luthuli pointed out that one reason for the South African Government's attempt to break the 1957 bus boycott by Africans living in Alexandra township, near Johannesburg, was that it needed "to break all demonstrations of African unity . . ." [62] (The boycott nevertheless succeeded.) "The first problem of an autocratic ruler is . . . how to maintain firm control of his subjects . . . ," Hsiao writes. [63] In any conflict situation, involving an autocratic regime or not, if the nonviolent opposition is widespread or especially daring, the opponent really cannot ignore it without appearing to be helpless in the face of defiance and thereby running the risk of its spread. He must then take some kind of counteraction. Sometimes he will respond with police action even to public declarations of opposition and of intent to carry out resistance at some future time. [64] Sometimes the opponent's need to act against the nonviolent challenge will to a significant degree be rooted in his reactions of fear and uncertainty in face of challenges to his dominance, authority, status and wealth. [65] Economic noncooperation (especially by tax refusal and rejection of the government's paper money) may so threaten the financial stability of the regime that it constitutes "a challenge that could not be ignored"—which was the case in Russia in December 1905. [66] Repeated American colonial campaigns of economic and political noncooperation finally confronted the British Parliament with ". . . the alternative of adopting coercive measures, or of forever relinquishing our claim of sovereignty or dominion over the colonies,"—as Lord Mansfield declared in February 1775, two months before the violence at Lexington and Concord. [67] The morning after the general protest strike against Nazi maltreatment of Jews began in Amsterdam on February 25, 1941, the German occupation officials realized that it constituted a major challenge. Originally planned for only one day, the strike had been extended, had spread to towns outside Amsterdam, and large crowds were continuing to demostrate within the city. "These constituted a serious threat to the occupying power, which could not tolerate a display of popular strength in defiance of its orders." Consequently Nazi officials ". . . felt that ruthless and quick action was needed, including the establishment of a state of seige during which harsher punishments would be meted out by summary courts." [68]

As these examples illustrate, an opponent who is unwilling to grant the demands of the nonviolent actionists, and who knows no other type of response to such a challenge, is likely to resort to sanctions. These sanctions will vary. In a strike, they may simply involve cutting off wages, or a lock-out. In other situations, however, when the opponent is the State, or has its support, the sanctions are likely to involve the use of the police, the prison system and the armed forces. This response is repression.

Whether the opponent uses repression or some other means, as long as the actionists persist in struggle while maintaining nonviolent discipline, the opponent will experience difficulties in dealing with that struggle. These difficulties are associated with the dynamics and mechanisms of the technique and their tendency to maximize the influence and power of the nonviolent group while undermining those of the opponent.

REPRESSION

Nonviolent actionists who know what they are doing will not be surprised at the repression inflicted by the opponent. "If we choose to adopt revolutionary direct action methods, however nonviolent they might be, we must expect every resistance," wrote Nehru.[69] The Buddhists struggling against the Diem regime in South Vietnam also expected repression.[70] Repression is especially likely when the nonviolent action takes forms and expressions which present a serious challenge to the opponent. As most political systems use some type of violent sanctions against dissidents, through police, prisons and the military forces, these are likely also to be used against the nonviolent challengers. In acute social and political conflicts the actionists must often pay a price in the struggle to achieve their objectives. Freedom is not free.

Once the opponent has decided to use repression, the questions are: what means of repression will he use, will they help him to achieve his objectives, and what will be the response of the nonviolent group and others to the repression. We turn first to the means of repression. Some of the sanctions which the opponent may use will be official while some may be unofficially encouraged. Sometimes there will be threats; other times the sanctions will be simply carried out. Some sanctions involve open police or military action (i.e., repression), others more indirect means of control and manipulation, and some even nonviolent sanctions. Many of the means of repression are also used in quite different conflict situations.

The sanctions the nonviolent actionist can expect will take many forms and involve different degrees of pressure. They may be discussed under eight general headings:

A. Control of communication and information

These methods will include: censorship of all means of public information and communication; suppression of particular newspapers, books, leaflets, radio and television broadcasts, etc.; dissemination of false news reports; severance of private communication between members and sections of the nonviolent group, as by intercepting mail and telegrams; and tapping telephone conversations and the like.

B. Psychological pressures

Although many other methods also have psychological influence, certain methods are intended to be primarily psychological. These include verbal abuse as name-calling, swearing, slander and rumors; ostracism; efforts to obtain defections and changes in plans by bribing key people, directly or indirectly, as with job offers; vague threats of various types of severe action if certain things are, or are not, done; threats of specific brutal actions; making "examples" of a few by severe punishment; retaliation against families and friends of resisters or other innocent people; and finally, severe mental pressures.

C. Confiscation

These methods include confiscation of property, funds, literature, records, correspondence, offices and equipment.

D. Economic sanctions

These range widely, from those imposed by courts and officials to popular economic boycotts. They include direct or indirect efforts to deprive nonviolent actionists of their livelihood, especially by dismissal from jobs and blacklisting; restrictions on trade, commerce, materials, supplies and the like; cutting off utilities, as water, gas and fuel; cutting off food supplies; consumer and other economic boycotts; individual fines and collective fines.

E. Bans and prohibitions

These are government orders which prohibit certain types of acts and activities. They include orders declaring organizations illegal; the banning of public meetings or assemblies; interfering with travel of nonviolent actionists; curfews; and court injunctions against certain behavior associated with the struggle.

F. Arrests and imprisonment

These are the sanctions which are commonly used to punish disobedience of the State's laws and regulations. They include: arrests for serious and minor charges related to the nonviolent action; arrests and legal harrassing on unrelated or imagined charges, as traffic violations; arrests of negotiators, delegations and leaders; and prison sentences of varying lengths.

G. Exceptional restrictions

These methods involve unusual or more severe forms of detention and restrictions on normal public liberties. They include: new laws or regulations to deal with the defiance; suspension of *habeas corpus* and other rights; declaration of martial law and states of emergency; mobilization of special forces, as "special constables" or "deputy sheriffs," and use of army reserves, territorial army, national or state guards, or other military units normally assigned to other duties; forced labor, as in prison camps and road gangs; prosecutions on charges more serious than for the simple act of resistance, as for conspiracy, and incitement; conscription of nonviolent actionists into armed forces, where they will be subject to court martial for indiscipline; mass expulsion of the resisting population; exile or other removal of leaders; detention without trial; and concentration camps.

H. Direct physical violence

These methods include official beatings and whippings; rough physical treatment, including manhandling, pushing, unofficial beatings including encouragement or permission for third parties (as hoodlums) to attack the nonviolent group physically; use of dogs, horses and vehicles against demonstrators; use of water from fire hoses, such instruments as electric cattle prodders and the like; bombings and other destruction of homes, offices and other buildings; individual assassinations; torture; shooting, discriminate or indiscriminate, of demonstrators or general population; executions, open or secret, individual, group, or mass; and bombings by airplanes.

Almost all of these have already been used in some cases of nonviolent action, and any of them—and others—could be used in extreme cases in the future. The amount and type of repression used by the opponent will vary with his perception of the conflict situation, the issues involved, his understanding of the nature of nonviolent action, and the anticipated results of the repression both in restoring "order" and in alienating needed cooperation, support, etc., of others. In small local cases of nonviolent action, the number of means of repression may be few, while in large movements a considerable number may be involved. In some situations the opponent may operate on the basis of an overall strategy against the nonviolent movement, while in other cases specific means of repression may be selected or improvised to deal with particular nonviolent acts only.

Seifert has pointed out that the severity of repression frequently tends to increase significantly as the campaign continues and as earlier forms of repression prove ineffective. For example, when the first Quakers came to Massachusetts Bay Colony in defiance of Puritan legal prohibitions, they were immediately imprisoned and deported. Later they were whipped in addition. Then ear-cropping was instituted, and finally the Quakers were banished under threat of execution. Between 1659 and 1661 four Quakers were hanged, including a woman. Over two and a half centuries later, when woman suffragists first picketed the White House while Woodrow Wilson was President, they were not interfered with officially for nearly six months, but after several stages of escalation of repression, prison sentences of six and seven months were given out. [71]

The introduction of special laws, edicts and ordinances to deal with various forms of nonviolent action is nothing new. Confronted with the noncooperation of the bakers of the city of Ephesus in the second century A.D., the Roman Proconsul of Asia issued an edict: "I therefore order the Bakers' Union not to hold meetings as a faction nor to be leaders in recklessness, but strictly to obey the regulations made for the general welfare and to supply the city unfailingly with the labor essential for bread-making." He threatened violators with arrest and a "fitting penalty." [72] Very strong Roman laws against strikes were issued about the middle of the fifth century, A.D. [73]

In modern times, strikes for the purpose of achieving wage increases and improved conditions were illegal for decades in many countries, and in many cases antistrike laws were only repealed after considerable struggle. Laws against economic boycotts are still on the books of many American states.

There is also a record of laws against various types of nonviolent action used to achieve political objectives. In a direct attempt to deal with economic resistance by the American colonists, Lord North sponsored bills which became law in March and April 1775, which provided that until the nonimportation campaign ended and peaceful conditions of business were restored, certain of the provinces would not be permitted to trade with any part of the world except the British Isles and the British West Indies, and after a short time with minor exceptions, those provinces would be prohibited from sending out fishing fleets also. One type of disruption of trade was to be matched by another type, to be backed by the means at the disposal of the British government. [74] One measure which Austria used to counter Hungarian economic nonviolent resistance around 1860 was to issue an ordinance declaring "exclusive trading" illegal. [75]

When the French and Belgian occupiers of the Ruhr were confronted with German government-sponsored nonviolent resistance, they issued innumerable regulations. "Soon there was nothing which was not forbidden or punishable under some regulation issued by General Degoutte or one of his subordinates," writes Grimm, who enumerates a multitude of aspects of life to which they applied. He concludes: ". . . finally [there was] a law for the suppression of passive resistance, which put an end to free speech and threatened with five years' imprisonment anyone evincing doubts about the justice and validity of the orders and directions issued by the occupation authorities. General Degoutte's decrees reached the remarkable number of 174." [76]

Two special laws were enacted in response to the South African 1952 civil disobedience movement. One of these, the Public Safety Act, No. 3 of 1953, provided the machinery for the introduction of wide emergency powers, the reorganization of the police and a change in their functions. This Act specified the conditions under which police violence might be used, and enabled the police to act before, rather than after, the event. [77] The other, the Criminal Law Amendment Act, No. 8, of 1953, is probably one of the first legislative acts created especially to deal with civil disobedience (as distinct from other forms of nonviolent action). This Act provides:

> Whenever any person is convicted of an offence which is proved to have been committed by way of protest or in support of any campaign for the repeal or modification of any law or the variation or limitation of the application or administration of any law, the court convicting him may, notwithstanding anything to the contrary in any other law contained, sentence him to (a) a fine not exceeding three hundred pounds; or (b) inprisonment for a period not exceeding three years; or (c) a whipping not exceeding ten strokes; or (d) both such fine and such imprisonment; or (e) both such fine and such whipping; or (f) both such imprisonment and such a whipping. [78]

Kuper reports that even more drastic penalties are imposed by the Act on persons convicted of promoting or assisting offenses by way of protest against any law.[79] In actual practice it was not necessary to use the new powers bestowed on the government by the new laws. The mere assumption of these powers had an effect.

Another Act already on the books, the Supression of Communism Act, could also be used against nonviolent action since charges of promoting "Communism" amazingly included "unlawful acts or omissions, actual or threatened, aimed at bringing about any *[sic!]* political, industrial, social or economic change." There were, of course, other South African laws against nonviolent action, such as the Native Labour (Settlement of Disputes) Act, which made strikes by Africans illegal.[80] One of the new laws decreed shortly after the end of World War II and the beginning of the occupation of the Eastern Zone of Germany by Soviet troops was one against "incitement to War, Murder and Non-cooperation."[81] The point is simply that special laws against various forms of nonviolent action are nothing new, but have occurred under diverse historical and political conditions.

Various other countermeasures may be used by the opponent along with repression. These differ widely, depending on the situation and forms of nonviolent action being fought. Countermeasures taken by the British government during the 1926 General Strike included a government newspaper, advance stockpiling of food, coal and fuel and the organization of alternative supplies and transportation. An unofficial Organization for the Maintenance of Supplies, said to include about one hundred thousand ready volunteers, was set up well in advance and its control was handed over to the government just before the outbreak of the strike.[82] The French during the Ruhr struggle also used various counter means to control the resistance as well as strictly violent repression. For example, they disbanded the police force of Essen and banished its members.[83] In other cases the opponent regime has responded by changes in its own structures and command system. This was illustrated during the February Revolution of 1917 by the Tsar's appointment of General Ivanov as Commander-in-Chief of the Petrograd garrison with full powers even over government ministers.[84] Very different countermeasures were used in South Vietnam in 1963 when the Diem regime in combatting Buddhist resistance attempted to show "popular support" for the government; rival pro-government Buddhist organizations were set up and "elections" were held which produced 99.8 percent of the votes for prominent government personalities.[85]

Some people (including certain pacifists) have seen the opponent's violent repression as created by the nonviolent group through its radical action; hence these people have often preferred milder means short of direct action. This reaction is, however, based upon both an inadequate understanding of the operation of the nonviolent technique and upon a very superficial view of political violence and the social system in which it is prominent. The absence of open violence by the ruler does not mean that violence is absent. Nor, if violence is the opponent's reaction to nonviolent action, does it mean that the nonviolent group created the violence. Rather, there is an intimate relationship between the kind of social system and the degree of violence the power holders in that system are prepared to use if it is challenged.

Political violence is not expressed only in beating, shooting or imprisoning people, but also in the readiness, threat and preparations to inflict such violence if the situation "requires" it. Political violence is also present in hierarchical political systems where status, wealth, effective decision-making and control are concentrated in an elite willing and able to use political violence to implement its will and to maintain dominance. In such a system, as long as the subordinates submit passively, there will be no need to implement the reserve capacity for violent repression and thus to show clearly the system's character and ultimate sanction. Nevertheless, the continuing domination by the elite through threats of violent sanctions for insubordination is from this perspective a case of constant political violence. Opponents of such systems describe them as "oppression," "exploitation," or "tyranny." In less extreme systems such as Western democracies, violence also remains the accepted sanction for dealing with law-breakers, insurrections, subversion, or external aggression.[86] The degree to which any particular political and social system depends for its existence upon covert or overt violence varies considerably. Where the degree of this dependence is small, where the citizens effectively influence and determine the government's policies, where there is confidence in ultimate sanctions other than violence for dealing with crises, there one can expect proportionately less violence in response to internal nonviolent action. Probably the chances of nonviolent action within the system will also be less. The converse would also follow.

When a system largely characterized by political violence is actively, albeit nonviolently, challenged, one can expect that the basic nature of that system will be more clearly revealed in the crisis than during less difficult times. The violence upon which the system depends is thus brought to the surface and revealed in unmistakable terms for all to see: it then becomes more possible to remove it.

In support of this view, Kuper argues that the 1952 response of hostility and violence from the South African whites to the civil disobedience had its roots in the nature of the oppressive system, which was revealed by nonviolent action: "The explanation of this violence lies in the nature of the domination itself." The original "naked force of conquest" had been translated into the sanctity of law. When the subordinate group challenged *any* law, even a trivial one, this was seen as "rebellion," and increased "force" was applied to suppress the rebellion. Kuper points out that civil disobedience brought the violence behind the law and the domination into actual operation. "Satyagraha strips this sanctity from the laws, and compels the application of sanctions, thus converting domination again to naked force." The nonviolent challenge had not created, but only revealed the violence. "Force is implicit in white domination: the resistance campaign made it explicit."[87] Kuper's observations on this point are consistent with Gandhi's conclusions. In Gandhi's view this process of making the violence inherent in the system explicit could be an important step in the destruction or radical alteration of the system. It could alienate support for the regime among its usual supporters and agents, promote greater solidarity and resistance within the subordinate group, arouse the opinion of third parties against the oppressor, and demonstrate that not even violent repression can compel the resisters to submit.

April Carter, an English direct actionist and political scientist, also supports this interpretation of violent repression against nonviolent actionists. She writes that civil disobedience is sometimes intended ". . . to force the opponent into overt use of the means of violence at his command," which reveals to the people and to the world at large the degree "to which the regime is oppressive and prepared to use violence to maintain itself." In that light, ". . . the true character of the South African Government was revealed at Sharpeville, the true character of segregation in the Deep South when the Freedom Riders were mobbed." The social violence inherent in *Apartheid* and segregation was made clear by those events, an important step toward changing the status quo.[88]

If one is not familiar with the workings of nonviolent action, the enumeration of the many possible means of repression and realization of the severe character of many of these, may prove rather staggering. It may then be difficult to see how one could hope for effectiveness from this technique. For example, during the Algerian War, Algerian nationalist leaders were asked why they had chosen to rely on political terrorism and guerrilla tactics instead of on massive nonviolent noncooperation. They replied that they had indeed tried strikes and boycotts which had been carried our relatively effectively. The French had not, however, responded nonviolently but with the use of military might and Algerian people had been injured. Therefore, they said, the Algerians, too, had turned to political violence. But, we may ask, if the nonviolent action had been so ineffective and harmless to the established system, why was the repression so harsh? Why should the French authorities (or anyone else) bother to repress actions which are supposedly so impotent?

The fact is, of course, that while it is true that the severity of the repression may be out of proportion to the seriousness of a threat, the repeated application of repression which has occurred against nonviolent action in Algeria, South Africa, Nazi Germany, India, the Soviet Union, East Germany, the Deep South, England, occupied Norway and many other places, is very strong evidence that nonviolent action does frequently pose a serious threat to the established order. This repression is a confirmation of and a tribute to the power of nonviolent action. Refusal to submit to this repression while maintaining nonviolent discipline is crucial if the desired shift in policies and power relationships is to be achieved.

The opponent's repression may succeed in defeating the nonviolent actionists and in restoring passive submission, as has happened in various cases. Whether this happens will in large degree be determined by the nonviolent actionists' response; if they become frightened and weaken in their resolve, then, just as in military combat, the front lines will fall back and the whole front will be threatened.

However, repression will not necessarily cause a collapse of nonviolent action. As was pointed out in Chapter One, if sanctions are to be effective, they must operate on the minds of the subjects, and produce fear and willingness to obey. However, these necessary intervening processes may not occur because of the nonviolent actionists' lack of fear, or because of their deliberate control of fear, or because of their commitment to some overriding loyalty or objective; when fear does not control the mind the repression may not succeed. Exponents of nonviolent action have stressed the limits of repression in obtaining submission and obedience. In 1917, Gandhi for example said that tyrannical rulers could not effectively use violent force against a nonviolent actionist who continued to refuse his consent and submission: ". . . without his concurrence they cannot make him do their will." [89] Since the ruler's sanctions are not effective in restoring submission and obedience unless the will of the nonviolent actionist is changed, the repression is not necessarily effective. It remains possible for the nonviolent actionists to achieve their objectives. "Nothing is more irritating and, in the final analysis, harmful to a government," wrote Nehru, "than to have to deal with people who will not bend to its will whatever the consequences." [90]

The opponent faces an additional problem in making repression effective: the means of repression are more appropriate to deal with violent opposition than with nonviolent action. Since, however, nonviolent action operates quite differently from violent action, repression used against the nonviolent group may fail to produce the desired results, and may even weaken the opponent, as we shall see. In contrast, when a movement of violent terrorism, or a military revolt is met with violent repression the two conflicting groups are applying essentially the same means of struggle. Violent repression then has a certain logic and a greater chance of effectiveness and is more likely to be justified in the eyes of the general population and third parties. This is not true when one side instead struggles nonviolently. This is not to say that violent resistance poses no threat to a regime, or that violent rebellion is always easily squashed, but it is to say that nonviolent struggle can be more difficult to deal with and that violent repression against it is less likely to be effective than against violent resistance.

One of the ways in which nonviolent action functions is to exhaust the opponents' means of repression and demonstrate their impotence. In this, the actionists' attitude of fearlessness is crucial. Without fear of sanctions, the sanctions lose their power to produce submission. The actionists may therefore—instead of fearing the repression—openly defy laws, seek imprisonment and may even ask the opponent to do his worst. The result may be to make repression impotent.

The peculiar problems of repression against a nonviolent movement were felt by the British in India during the 1930-31 struggle:

> . . . during the year there were violent disturbances and acts of terrorism in many parts of the country, but these the forces of law and order in India as elsewhere, were trained to counter. What perplexed them was the mobilization of inertia, the large crowds silently awaiting punishment, the well organized processions refusing to yield in face of attack. [91]

When people deliberately court arrest by practicing civil disobedience, imprisonment ceases to be a deterrent to their defiance. Indeed, imprisoned nonviolent resisters are sometimes more of a difficulty for the opponent than if they had been left safely in their homes. Other specific means of repression and other specific methods of action by the nonviolent group present their own difficulties for the opponent. Continued defiance by nonviolent noncooperation and intervention by hundreds, thousands, hundreds of thousands, and even millions of people despite the opponent's repression can create a political nightmare for an autocratic ruler. Not only is his repression then ineffective; it may even multiply the problems created by the nonviolent challenge.

PERSISTENCE

Faced with repression, nonviolent actionists have only one acceptable response: to overcome they must persist in their action and refuse to submit or retreat. As Gandhi put it, "In the code of the satyagrahi, there is no such thing as surrender to brute force." [92] Without willingness to face repression as the price of struggle, the nonviolent action movement cannot hope to succeed. Kuper argues, for example, that unwillingness to accept the vastly increased sanctions for violation of the laws in question was an important reason for the collapse of the 1952 Defiance Campaign. [93]

The opponent applying the repression is likely to be a believer in the effectiveness of political violence and to assume that repression, if severe enough, will produce submission. Therefore, as we have noted, once repression has begun, the opponent is likely to increase it when it is not immediately effective. [94] An unconsidered reaction by persons seeking to minimize suffering might then be to halt the nonviolent challenge and submit, or to seek a "compromise," or in effect a sell-out. This is a very shortsighted reaction, however. Such behavior confirms the opponent in his belief in the efficacy of repression, and encourages him to become increasingly brutal by showing him that sufficient cruelty will bring the nonviolent action to an end. Hence, stopping the movement in order to reduce repression while the actionists are still capable of continuing the struggle is likely in the long run to contribute to an increase in the extent and severity of repression against nonviolent action. Furthermore, a collapse of the movement at this stage will make it impossible to bring into operation the mechanisms of change upon which nonviolent action depends for success. It is necessary and possible at this point to break the usual repression-fear-submission pattern, that is, of repression producing fear, fear bringing submission, and submission causing a continuation of the objectionable policies or the intolerable regime.

Fearlessness, or deliberate control of fear, discussed in Chapter Nine is especially important at this stage of the struggle. Standing firm at this point will make it possible to refute stereotypes of the subordinate group. One of these may be that they are cowards: for example, " . . . that 'Negroes, like animals, will be scared away by a show of force.'" [95] Firmness will make it possible for mass noncooperation to produce its coercive effects. Under certain circumstances persistence may also contribute to sympathy and respect for the defiant nonviolent actionists.[96]

Submission to violence is contrary to the nature of the nonviolent technique. Nonviolently resisting volunteers must be able to stand against apparently overwhelming physical force. Throughout history there have been many instances of an individual or a small number of men standing firmly for their convictions, struggling to achieve a wider social end, or fighting to defend their people or principles against "impossible" odds. Defiance without retaliation may enable the nonviolent actionists to remove the policy or regime to which they object and to make the repression impotent. "Strength does not come from physical capacity. It comes from an indomitable will,"[97] wrote Gandhi. "No power on earth can make a person do a thing against his will. Satyagraha is a direct result of the recognition of this great law . . ."[98]

There are various examples of nonviolent actionists standing firm in face of repression. At Vorkuta, for example, when the Russian authorities on July 20, 1953, arrested the Pit No. 1 Strike Committee (recognized as the central leadership) even before the prisoners could initiate their strike, the prisoners' response was to elect a new committee. The strike was thus merely postponed for twelve hours. Later, when the Strike Committee went to meet officials for negotiations but never returned, the strikers nevertheless continued.[99] When, during the Montgomery boycott, white officials resorted to mass arrests and private persons resorted to bombings, the result was a demonstration of increased determination and fearlessness by the Afro-Americans.[100] "The members of the opposition . . . ," wrote Martin Luther King, "thought they were dealing with a group who could be cajoled or forced to do whatever the white man wanted them to do. They were not aware that they were dealing with Negroes who had been freed from fear. And so every move they made proved to be a mistake."[101] When the Ku Klux Klan rode through the Negro section, hoping to repeat its usual tactic of striking terror into the Negroes who would then lock their doors and darken their houses, they met with a surprise. The Negroes kept the lights on, the doors open, remained casual, as though watching a circus parade, some even waved to the cars. Nonplussed, the Klan disappeared into the night.[102]

The Quakers who kept coming with their religious message to Puritan Massachusetts Bay Colony were undeterred by deportations, whippings, imprisonments and even death penalties, as Seifert reports:

In spite of increasing severity, the same persons came back again and again "to look the bloody laws in the face." Although about sixty years of age, Elizabeth Hooton came to Boston at least six times, being expelled each time, and was four times whipped through several towns out of the jurisdiction. Even the death penalty proved to be no deterrent. While William Leddra was being tried for his life, Wenlock Christison, who had already been banished upon pain of death, walked calmly into the courtroom. Then while Christison was on trial, Edward Wharton, who had also been ordered to leave the colony or forfeit his life, wrote from his home in Salem that he was still there. Such a succession of applications for execution identified a people who were not to be turned aside by any terrors their persecutors might devise. [103]

There are many other examples of defiance in face of repression. In November 1905 the Central Bureau of the Union of Railroad Workers in tsarist Russia defiantly called for anti-government strikes in retaliation for the court-martial sentencing to death of a railroad engineer named Sokolov and others for their participation in a recent strike at Kushka Station on the Central Asian Railroad. [104] Reitlinger gives a large measure of credit for the saving of over 75 per cent of the Jews in France from the Nazi extermination plan to the refusal of Frenchmen to submit and comply in face of Gestapo terror and other intimidation: "the final solution . . . failed in France because of the sense of decency in the common man, who, having suffered the utmost depths of self-humiliation, learnt to conquer fear." [105] Although Russian tanks had been roaming the streets of Halle, East Germany, and the People's Police had been firing warning shots into the air, an estimated sixty thousand to eighty thousand people attended a mass antigovernment meeting in the market place on June 17, 1953. [106]

Examples of this refusal to submit to repression, and this assertion of fearlessness, could be multiplied. It is especially important that the leaders of the nonviolent struggle be, and be seen to be, courageous and unbowed in face of repression and threats of future punishments. Albert Luthuli's compliance with various restrictions imposed by the South African government, which removed him from active political work without placing him in prison, is therefore an example which ought *not* to be followed, and is a response to repression which may encourage submission by others and help to discredit nonviolent struggle as a militant and effective technique. [107]

Courageous persistence must, of course, continue to be expressed through disciplined nonviolent behavior if the movement is not to be seriously weakened. This leaves room for, and indeed often requires, flexible and imaginative responses suitable to the particular situation. In various cases the nonviolent actionists may make certain tactical moves to avoid unnecessary provocation of more severe repression. Miller writes, for example:

> We must be careful not to corner our opponent . . . Firmness should never become dogmatic rigidity. Although nonviolence places a premium upon the capacity of the nonviolent cadre to endure suffering, each team of cadres should have sufficient tactical flexibility to be able to choose whether to extricate the individual members from a catastrophic situation or, if this alternative is foreclosed, to endure martyrdom with a composure that may cause their attackers to repent afterward. [108]

Sometimes nonviolent actionists may alter their behavior at the moment when repression is likely to begin or has just begun. For example, in 1959, when ordered to disperse by police who prepared to make a baton charge, African women demonstrators at Ixopo, South Africa, went down on their knees and began to pray. In that instance at least the baton charge was not made and the "police hung around helplessly." [109]

Sometimes certain methods of action will by their nature be more difficult to deal with by repression and less likely to put resisters to the test of withstanding severe brutalities. Some strike leaders from the East German Rising concluded that strikers who had stayed at home or had conducted a stay-in strike at their jobs were more difficult for the regime to cope with than demonstrators in the streets who could usually be easily dispersed by tanks. Ebert calls this "the avoidance of mass confrontations, which is not the same thing as renouncing resistance." [110] Nonviolent actionists or others may appeal to the opponent's troops and police urging them to restrict their repression in some way. Such appeals were planned in Berlin in June 1953, but both a prepared broadcast in Russian to members of the Soviet occupation forces by the acting mayor of West Berlin, Ernst Reuter, and appeals by Russian émigrés at the border with East Berlin to Russian soldiers not to use violence against demonstrating workers, were blocked by Western officials in Berlin. [111] Flexibility and alternative responses to repression while continuing the struggle may at times depend upon the recognition that in a given conflict situation victory will not come quickly and the campaign may be protracted. [112]

Any possible variations in tactics in response to repression must not, however, alter the basic nonviolent counteraction to repression: persistence, determination, nonviolent discipline and an end to fearful cringing before the opponent's threats and punishments. With this response, change is possible, for "the grip of fear" is broken, [113] and "an immediate and relentless and peaceful struggle" is under way. Those words are from the call for resistance issued by Maxim Gorky and nine others shortly before their arrest the day after Bloody Sunday, 1905. [114]

THE NECESSITY OF SUFFERING

Facing repression with persistence and courage means that the nonviolent actionists must be prepared to endure the opponent's sanctions without flinching. The nonviolent actionists must be prepared to suffer in order to advance their cause. Some people may interpret this suffering in a metaphysical or spiritual sense, but this view is not necessary for the technique; it is sufficient if the volunteers see something of the contribution which withstanding repression makes to achieving their objectives. Nonviolent action has long been regarded as a "two-edged Sword"—a phrase used in 1770 by Governor Wright of Georgia to describe the colonists' nonimportation program. [115] While the analogy is accurate, it is not complete, for it may imply that direct actionists are likely to suffer only when they use the nonviolent technique, instead of violence, or when they do nothing. This is of course not true.

Political violence, too, especially in the forms of civil wars, terrorist movements. guerrilla war, violent revolution and international wars, involves the risk of suffering and usually high casualties. Accounts of certain nonviolent campaigns are sometimes gory with detailed descriptions of beatings and other brutal treatment of nonretaliating actionists, while histories of wars often cite casualties only in impersonal statistics. Such bloody events in nonviolent struggles are, of course, usually comparatively mild in both seriousness and extent compared with comparable scenes in major cases of political violence, accounts of which rarely describe in detail the human suffering which accompany them. Descriptions of brutalities incurred in nonviolent struggles are simply honest accounts of unpleasant events which for fairness should be balanced with equally detailed reports of suffering in violent conflicts. It is inappropriate for supporters of those violent means to object (as they sometimes do) to nonviolent action on the ground that somebody might get hurt. When only some form of direct action is judged to be an acceptable response to the situation, then suffering is an inherent consequence of that decision. The intelligent response is not to ask simply what means will most effectively release frustration and hatred. The likely consequences of violent action or of nonviolent action are also important. [116]

The fact that suffering is likely or inevitable with both violent and nonviolent action does not mean that there are no important differences.

Other questions remain, such as will there be more or less suffering with one technique or the other, and will the sacrifices incurred by use of each type of action really advance the long term objectives of the grievance group. There have been no careful comparative studies of casualties in violent and nonviolent struggles, but there are reasons for suggesting that both total casualties and suffering on both sides, and also those of only the nonviolent actionists and grievance group, are significantly less than when both sides use violence.

When both belligerents use violent methods, a pattern frequently occurs in which the violence of each side is met with counterviolence in a continuing cycle. Even without significant escalation in the severity and extent of its application, this process produces a continuing accumulation of violence, and of casualties and suffering until one side accedes. When, however, one side is fighting with a different, nonviolent, weapons system, the constant circle of violence is broken. Suffering will still occur, and at times it will be severe, but the substitution of nonviolent persistence for violent retaliation tends to reduce the severity of repression and to contribute in the long run to a reduction in political violence.

This break in the political violence cycle, produced by the willingness of the nonviolent group to accept nonretaliatory suffering as the price of achieving its goals, seems in that immediate struggle to reduce the casualties on both sides. Gregg, for example, argued in these terms:

> In the Indian struggle for independence, though I know of no accurate statistics, hundreds of thousands of Indians went to jail, probably not more than five hundred received permanent physical injuries, and probably not over eight thousand were killed immediately or died later from wounds. No British, I believe, were killed or wounded. Considering the importance and size of the conflict and the many years it lasted, these numbers are much smaller than they would have been if the Indians had used violence toward the British.[117]

There were, however, a few Indian policemen in British service killed in the conflict. But the total casualties were still very small, as compared with the 1857 Indian violent struggle against the British—the idea that Indians are somehow by nature nonviolent is just not true—or compared with the number of Algerian dead in the Algerian revolution against the French, estimated variously, but by some as high as nearly a million out of a population only ten times that size.

It also appears that the introduction of violence into a nonviolent struggle will increase the casualties. Bondurant writes: "A comparison of campaigns of civil disobedience which remained nonviolent with others in which satyagraha deteriorated into violence, indicates significantly greater incidence of injury and death in the latter cases."[118] In the series of strikes in Soviet prison camps, especially in 1953 and 1954, there appears to be a significant correlation between the degree of brutality used in repression and the casualties inflicted on the prisoners on the one hand, and the degree to which the prisoners remained nonviolent or resorted to serious violence against the prison camp officials, police and troops.[119] Nazi repression and retaliation for the two day strike in Amsterdam and nearby towns in protest against persecution of Jews were severe: several people were wounded in the streets; seven were killed on the second day; Himmler authorized brutalities and the arrest and deportation of one thousand strikers; over one hundred Communists and others suspected of instigating the strike were arrested; fines were imposed on Amsterdam and other municipalities; the mayors of Amsterdam and nearby Haarlem and Zaandam were dismissed and other Dutch officials were also accused of not making sufficient efforts to suppress the strike.[120] There seems no question however that a comparable two day violent Dutch uprising in the same area and by the same number of people would in light of Nazi actions elsewhere against violent resistance (Warsaw, for instance) have produced many times that number of dead, wounded and imprisoned.

In addition to human suffering, a variety of economic losses have also occurred during nonviolent resistance campaigns, as, for example, in the American colonists' struggles, and in the *Ruhrkampf*. Writing about the effects of the nonimportation movement in Boston in 1770, Samuel Adams said: "The Merchants in general have punctually abode by their Agreement, to their very great private loss."[121] Later, when the British closed the port of Boston in retaliation for the city's various and continued acts of defiance and noncooperation, it was not only the merchants who suffered economically. Hundreds of workmen were thrown out of jobs, and it proved necessary to find ways to feed the poor without giving in to the British.[122] However, the most severe example of economic suffering and dislocation accompanying nonviolent resistance is probably the *Ruhrkampf*. Much of the economic disruption of the German economy as a whole can be blamed, however, on the German government's decision to finance the resistance by unsupported paper money.[123] Within the Ruhr, shortages of milk in the cities endangered the health of children and of ill adults so severely that the death rate for children increased, and only evacuation of about a half million children to unoccupied Germany reduced their danger. Furthermore, in the occupied Ruhr district and the Rhineland, the number of unemployed reached two million out of a total population of about nine million.[124] An immense inflation took place throughout Germany with disastrous economic results.[125] But even in such a case, one does not have to be very imaginative to see that a military war for repossession of the territory (had Germany been then capable of it) could well have been still more disastrous economically, not only for the Ruhr which would have become a battleground but for all Germany because of the required financial expenditure, the likely destruction of the Ruhr's productive capacity, and the extreme loss of lives.

Not all suffering is the same, nor does it have the same effects. The suffering involved in nonviolent action has more in common with the suffering of certain violent resisters than with the suffering of helpless terrorized and submissive people. Accordingly, the results of suffering of courageous resisters are likely to differ radically from that of the submissive. Gandhi himself pointed to some instances of violence as being almost comparable to those of courageous nonviolence. These cases of violence involved great courage in defying overwhelming forces with very little or no hope of victory, and with the certainty of major suffering. A woman defending herself from rape, a single man (even with a sword) defending himself against a horde of fully armed bandits and killers, or the Poles who ". . . knew that they would be crushed to atoms, and yet they resisted the German hordes." All three cases, he said, had in common ". . . the refusal to bend before overwhelming might in the full knowledge that it means certain death."[126] Suffering endured in such courageous violence had more in common with suffering in nonviolent action than the latter had with that of the terrified, passive victim of brutalities. However, this is not, of course, to say that the social and political results would be the same with equally courageous violent and nonviolent resistance.

In common with participants in violent revolution and war, the nonviolent actionists must be willing in extreme crises to risk their lives.[127] Gandhi repeatedly emphasized that rather than submitting to the violence of the opponent, the nonviolent actionist must be willing to make severe sacrifices including, if need be, his own life.[128] Those planning nonviolent action will need to consider the degree of suffering the volunteers are willing to endure, as this may determine which methods of action can be used and how firmly the volunteers will be able to defy the opponent's repression. If the degree of expected tolerable suffering is low, then the volunteers may require further preparation, or they will have to limit themselves to milder forms unlikely to require serious sacrifice.[129]

People may remain nonviolent, not for moral or ideological reasons, but because they realize this behavior is necessary for the practical operation of the technique. "Without suffering," wrote Gandhi, "it is not possible to attain freedom."[130] It was from this perspective that Motilal

Nehru, father of the late Prime Minister, declared on the eve of his own imprisonment in 1930:

> We have not yet paid one hundredth part of the price of freedom and must go forward with unflinching step defying the enemy and all the cruel refinements of torture that he is capable of inventing. Do not worry for those who have been taken. See to it that every man, woman and child left behind gives a good account of himself or herself to the nation. [131]

This persistence through repression and willingness to suffer will have a number of effects. Two are: 1) the numerical or quantitative (sometimes almost mechanical) effect of many defiant subjects refusing to obey despite repression on the opponent's ability to control the situation and to maintain his policies, and 2) the psychological or qualitative (or moral) effect of the sacrifices on the opponent, his supporters, third parties and others. Both of these are complicated processes; frequently their operation depends on intervening processes, and in overcoming problems in accurate perception. We shall return to these effects and processes in the final chapters.

In many conflicts the repression and other counter action will be relatively mild or moderate. The intensity and extent of suffering among the actionists and the grievance group will therefore be within the range which can be withstood without extreme difficulty. However, in some cases there will be brutalities.

FACING BRUTALITIES

Brutalities may arise from three main general sources.

First, the regime may be one in which brutality is commonplace. Terror may be used against all opponents, real or imaginary, in an effort to make the regime omnipotent. Such regimes are usually described as tyrannical or, in extreme forms, totalitarian.

Second, a nontyrannical regime may, when effectively and fundamentally challenged, react with brutal repression. This may follow from a decision that only drastic action can crush the resisters (especially if milder measures have failed) or from exasperation at the actionists' defiant behavior or refusal to submit in face of less severe repression.

Finally, without orders from the regime, local officers, or individuals, in the army, police, or even the general public, may on their own initiative perpetrate brutalities on the nonviolent actionists. These brutalities may result from sadistic personalities, from frustration produced by the defiance, or from inner conflicts aroused by the situation and the qualities of the nonviolent actionists.

The first two sources may be described as official brutality and the third as unofficial brutality.

A. Official and unofficial brutalities

There must be no illusions. In some cases nonviolent people have not only been beaten and cruelly treated but killed, not only accidentally or as isolated punishment, but in deliberate massacres. Refraining from violence is not a guarantee of safety, although contrary to popular opinion it is arguable that nonviolent behavior has better "survival value" than violence. There are disturbing cases of major killings. The 1919 British massacre of at least 379 Indians (and wounding of 1,137) meeting peaceably in Jalianwala Bagh, Amritsar, is one such case. [132]

There have been some massacres of pacifists, although not always when engaged in nonviolent action. In the context of Ohio frontier wars and raids in 1782, two hundred white frontiersmen with full deliberation slaughtered a group of pacifist native American Indians, converts to the Moravian Church which held to nonresistant pacifism. These were wrongly believed to have killed a woman and her five children in a raid on a settler's farm. Twenty-nine men, twenty-seven women and thirty-four children (including at least twelve babies) were slaughtered two by two; almost all were then scalped by the whites. [133] Luthuli reports that in South Africa in 1924 "a hundred Hottentots were butchered for refusing to pay an incomprehensible tax on dogs." [134] It should be pointed out that the massacre of the Moravian Indians took place in the context of warfare, and involved mistaken identity. The victims were not engaged in nonviolent action as defined in this study although they were nonviolent. The case is included here simply to acknowledge that such events have occurred against peaceful people.

But the Indians in Amritsar were holding a peaceful protest meeting and the Hottentots were refusing to pay a tax—both methods of nonviolent action. The shootings on Bloody Sunday are another example. Massacres of nonviolent actionists can take place. Such killings also occur, probably much more frequently, when people resist violently, and even people who passively submit to their oppressors may die as victims of their policies and brutalities. There is no guarantee of safety as long as the underlying conditions contributing to brutality continue. If there is no immediate way to guarantee protection from brutalities, it is at least wise to be aware that they may occur against nonviolent actionists and to determine how to respond to them in accordance with the technique's requirements for effectiveness.

The more tyrannical the regime and system generally, the more probable will be extreme brutalities against the nonviolent actionists. Among all regimes and systems which to any considerable degree depend on violence, the common response when they are challenged, even though by nonviolent means, will be violence against the dissenters. As Bose put it, "the violence of the rulers, which was formerly implicit or camouflaged, now becomes explicit." [135] The degree of severity of repression and of brutalities will vary considerably. Frequently, the response may be quite out of proportion to the seriousness of the challenge. As Hiller pointed out: ". . . the stronger party (especially when it is irresponsible) tends to respond violently to a mild act of resistance or of assertion by the weaker, and especially by a despised party." [136]

Early in the conflict the opponent may have interpreted the actionists' nonviolence as cowardice or stupidity, only to discover it was neither. Continued nonviolent defiance may have proven to be difficult to crush and it may have come to threaten the opponent's continued dominance and control. When the opponent's will is thwarted, violent retaliation is a very likely response. [137] Brutalities may then be deliberate, as we have seen. Seifert has pointed to this type of motivation for brutalities: "This buildup in brutality may be the result of normal and rather rational goal-directed behavior." To the opponent, the established social order, institutions and policies may be good, and he may see the defeat of the resisters as the only way to protect them. "Since, so far as he knows, the only way to accomplish this defeat is to increase severity, he . . . becomes more repressive. This seems to him to be the best possible expedient among the choices available . . ." He is, "given his presuppositions . . . acting in a rational, defensible manner." [138] "Insofar as nonviolence is interpreted as a sign of weakness, it 'makes sense' to increase hostile pressure in the expectation that this will cause collapse of the resisters' cause." [139]

The degree of brutality inflicted as official policy will vary. It may be influenced by the degree to which the opponent understands what is happening, including his comprehension of the dynamics of nonviolent action, and the process of political *jiu-jitsu,* which will be discussed in Chapter Twelve. Confusion, uncertainty and fear will increase the likelihood of official brutalities.

Unauthorized and unofficial brutalities may also be committed on nonviolent actionists. Sometimes highly disproportionate repression may be quite accidental, especially when police or troops are threatened or attacked by undisciplined persons or groups, as was apparently the origin of the famous Boston Massacre of 1770. [140] Brutalities may be committed deliberately, although unofficially, for a variety of motives. A paternalistic ruler who has been rejected by his subjects may commit brutalities.

Within a paternalistic, imperialist framework he may have expressed considerable kindness to a subject race so long as its members stayed "in their place." He may even have thought he was requiring participation in God's own true religion, an essential to the eternal salvation of the resister. [141]

Such an opponent, shocked at having his supposed "good" acts denounced as "evil" by the subordinates, and his egoism revealed and rejected, may resort to extreme acts. "When anyone strips away our cherished self-images and exposes what we really are, he invites punishment." [142] This is closely associated with the wider phenomenon of status-usurpation by the nonviolent actionists.

The agents of repression, and the dominant group in general, may see the nonviolent actionists of the subordinate group as behaving in ways they have no "right" to behave. That is, they are no longer acting like subordinates, but have behaved like equals, no longer cowed and submissive, but erect and insistent. One Deep South store manager faced with a sit-in declared, "Who do these niggers think they are?" [143] Speaking of self-suffering produced by nonwhite civil disobedience in South Africa, Kuper argues that one reason it may alienate sympathy of the whites is that "there is a quality of impudence about it, of status-usurpation, when looked at from the point of view of the dominant group." [144] This, too, may be conducive to brutalities.

The individual policemen or soldiers and the lower rank officers may be in a very difficult position, which may press them toward extreme actions. Not only are they used to having people obey them in such situations, but they are themselves required to obey and carry out orders from their superiors. If they fail to do so, they may be subjected to reprimands, sanctions and withholding of promotions. They may have been given orders to prevent certain actions by the nonviolent group, or to disperse and halt the action if it has already begun. With the nonviolent group remaining fearless, refusing to obey their orders and standing firm, the police, or troops, may find their ability to cope with the situation by the usual permitted means of action blocked. Fearing the consequences of a failure to carry out their orders, the men and lower officers may in desperation or frustration resort to extraordinary means in an effort to complete the tasks commanded by their superiors.

When, despite normal sanctions and repression, the actionists remain fearless, continue their defiance while remaining nonviolent and refusing to be provoked into retaliation, the opponent's police, troops and the like are likely to become frustrated and irritated. Such behavior, in which people neither fear nor obey them, drastically reduces the ability of such agents to control the situation and to carry out their duties. In addition, as we have noted, they are likely to feel insecure when due deference is not given to their position. Irritation and inadequacy may lead to brutality. Seifert also describes this factor:

> When measures taken against resisters have proved ineffectual, and when an opponent faces a personal loss of status or threat to his personality, he may lay on all the harder. Feeling powerless and being unable to tolerate such a feeling of impotence, he resorts to force to give himself the illusion of strength. [145]

This seems to have happened in India in 1930-31. [146]

In his autobiography, Nehru describes an earlier occasion in 1928 when he and other nonviolent demonstrators were beaten seriously by both foot police and a large number of cavalry or mounted police. Some Indians were permanently injured but, though badly beaten and wounded, Nehru recovered fully. He wrote:

> But the memory that endures with me far more than that of the beating itself, is that of many of the faces of those policemen, and especially of the officers, who were attacking us. Most of the real beating and battering was done by European sergeants, the Indian rank and file were milder in their methods. And those faces, full of hate and blood-lust, almost mad, with no trace of sympathy or touch of humanity! [147]

On occasion it will be private individuals who commit brutalities. Such attacks sometimes occurred during lunch counter sit-ins in the United States South in 1960. One such instance was against high school anti-segregation sit-inners in Portsmouth, Virginia. The student sit-inners had not expected such violence and lacked both specific instructions and training to meet it. Hence, they finally reacted with violent retaliation. It started on February 15, 1960, when a group of young white hoodlums arrived on the scene to provoke violence and attack the sit-inners and other Negro youths. A participant, Edward Rodman, writes:

> Outside [of the store] the [white] boy stood in the middle of the street, daring any Negro to cross a certain line. He then pulled a car

chain and claw hammer from his pocket and started swinging the chain in the air.

He stepped up his taunting with the encouragement of others. When we did not respond, he became so infuriated that he struck a Negro boy in the face with the chain. The boy kept walking. Then in utter frustration the white boy picked up a street sign and threw it on a Negro girl. [148]

In other cases, brutalities may at times take place as a consequence of an inner moral or psychological conflict within the individual committing them, a conflict produced at least in part by the behavior of the nonviolent actionists. [149] Disturbed, consciously or unconsciously, by the challenge of the nonviolent group, their claims and behavior, and by the acts against them he is expected to perform, the individual agent may seek to dismiss this inner conflict or to assert his loyalty to the opponent by extra vigor in repression. Sometimes it is the situation which Seifert describes: ". . . he knows that the resisters are right, but he cannot bear the knowledge. Therefore he represses it and strikes those who irritate his conscience." [150] On other occasions, he may still think the opponent right, but may find himself inflicting punishment which he knows is reprehensible, especially against nonviolent persons:

But he has too much emotional capital invested in his policy to admit he has been wrong . . . When the opponent doubts the defensibility of terror, he may intensify it as a way of convincing himself that he was right all along. He may beat the more to try to avoid a feeling of guilt for those already beaten. [151]

In addition, some of the extreme aggression against the nonviolent group may be the result of their providing, apparently, a safe group on which to vent aggressions against other, known or unknown, persons or conditions. [152] Unless and until the nonviolent behavior of the actionists is perceived as bravery and strength, some persons may see it as weakness and therefore express irrational hostility because of their own inadequacies, as Seifert points out:

Some persons are basically cowardly, but put on an outer show of bravado. When they see action which they interpret as weakness or cowardice, they strike out at it as though despising it wholeheartedly. Not being able to strike at the weakness in themselves, they hit the harder at the resister. For such persons the sight of suffering endured may become provocative. Nonviolent resistance brings out the bully in those inclined to be bullies. [153]

A contrasting situation exists when the demonstrators do not firmly adhere to their nonviolent discipline, or when the police, troops, etc., on the spot do not understand that the group is going to remain nonviolent and is not attacking them violently. The police and others may then be inspired by fear in what they believe to be a highly insecure and threatening situation, especially if the group is large. This fear may lead them to inflict brutalities on the nonviolent group and to be generally hostile. [154] Such acts of violence may occur even in defiance of general orders from superior officers. Lord Hardinge, the British Ambassador to St. Petersburg, claimed, for example, that (contrary to a widely held belief) on Bloody Sunday 1905 it was Prince Vassiltchikoff, commander of the Guards Division, who was on the spot (not the Grand Duke Vladimir), who gave the order to fire on the peaceful demonstrators. Hardinge added that Prince Vassiltchikoff also disobeyed an order from the Grand Duke to stop firing, "saying he could not be responsible for the safety of his troops or of the town unless they used their arms." [155] Lord Hardinge's testimonial may or may not be true, but this is the type of situation in which police and troops immediately in charge of maintaining order or of inflicting repression may fear the worst and act accordingly.

There will be a strong tendency to brutalities when the agencies of repression include a considerable number of persons with strong sadistic tendencies. Katz and Janis have pointed "toward a fit between unusual institutional roles and basic personality patterns." "When an institution permits violence as part of its function, people will be attracted to this role who derive satisfactions from the nature of the work. Thus there is a self-selection process for brutal roles." Even when the person is not especially brutal on entering such institutions, there will be a strong tendency for him to change or leave; in either case those people with strong sadistic or hostile drives will tend to continue and dominate the organization. [156] While this tendency is not universal it may be sufficiently common to help to explain brutalities committed by police, and other official bodies when they do occur. Seifert has also discussed the tendency for individuals to be harsher in their behavior when they are acting as members of a group, with its backing and on the basis of institutional decisions, than they would be as single individuals. Private inhibitions are thus reduced, and "the barrier of institutional decision can insulate a person from emotional involvement." [157]

In some situations, there will also be a considerable possibility that brutalities may be perpetrated on nonviolent actionists by members of the general population and by special civilian groups and organizations, as well as mobs. This has happened frequently in the Deep South.[158] Such private brutalities may be entirely independent of the police, or with their conveniently remaining elsewhere during the attacks, or watching the attacks as passive bystanders. At other times, nonofficial brutalities may be perpetrated despite active attempts by the police to prevent them.

B. Remaining firm

Therefore, the informed actionist is not, in crisis situations, surprised by the occurrence of brutalities against the nonviolent group. As already noted, they may even be expected. Their occurrence in situations where many people would least expect them—as in India under British rule[159] or in the United States—should leave little doubt that they may certainly be expected in a system comparable to Nazi Germany or Stalinist Russia. The response of the nonviolent actionists—if the movement is to continue and not be crushed—must be essentially the same as to normal repression. Either to halt the action or to resort to violence would have serious consequences and would certainly rebound to the opponent's favor. To be effective, the actionists must persist through the brutalities and suffering and maintain their fearlessness, nonviolence and firmness.

This will doubtless mean considerable suffering until it becomes clear that the brutalities are not effective in cowing the actionists, that instead they may be weakening the opponent's position, or until there is a change of policy or attitude toward the nonviolent group and their demands. This process, it must be clear, will often take some time and it may be necessary to have repeated demonstrations to the opponent and his agents that brutalities will not crush the movement.[160] The price the nonviolent actionists may thus have to pay may be at times severe, but it is, in terms of the dynamics of nonviolent action, a price which sometimes must be paid if fundamental changes are to be made. This has military parallels, although there are significant differences.

The leadership in a nonviolent struggle will not, on the basis of any criteria, be wise to demand that the actionists undergo suffering, or court brutalities, beyond their abilities to bear them. Certainly a new course of action which is liable to intensify repression and brutalities must be considered most carefully, and if an unwise course of action has been started it should not be continued out of dogmaticism or stubbornness.

Wise leadership will take great care to avoid unnecessary brutalization of the opponent. It is also desirable to seek to remove motives or influences which might produce brutalities when this can be done without weakening the movement, or giving in to cruelties intended to induce submission. However, there should be no retreat when maintenance of a firm stand, or even still more daring action, is required.

There are occasions when, in Gandhi's view, the nonviolent actionists ought to intensify resistance in face of severe repression and be willing to court additional suffering. This would demonstrate, he maintained, first that the repressive might of the opponent was incapable of crushing the resistance. This would also set in motion a number of forces which would lead to a relative weakening of the opponent, to a strengthening of the nonviolent group and to increased support for the latter from third parties. This is involved in the political *jiu-jitsu* process which is examined in Chapter Twelve. Such provocative nonviolent action may also sometimes be deemed necessary for the internal strengthening of the nonviolent group. A demonstration by a smaller group of some daring form of fearless dramatic action which, if known in advance, may bring upon them "the most intense form of repression possible," [161] may contribute to improving morale and combating a growth of fear of repression.

The reasons for daring to take provocative nonviolent action and for risking cruel retaliation from the opponent are primarily concerned with the effects of such action on the nonviolent group, on the opponent, or sometimes on third parties, or a combination of these. In any case, the nonviolent group may deliberately seek to reveal to all the extreme brutality of which the opponent and his agents are capable. This type of provocative nonviolent action, it should be made clear, is especially Gandhian. Explicit advocacy of such a course, and theoretical justification for it, do not occur widely in other traditions of nonviolent action, although there are examples in actual practice.

Early in the Indian 1930-31 campaign scattered acts of brutality occurred against the nonviolent volunteers. Gandhi then decided that if this was going to happen anyhow, it would be best to challenge the regime in such a way that such brutality could be revealed publicly in unmistakable terms in order to alienate further support from the government. Gandhi wrote to the Viceroy:

> . . . I feel that it would be cowardly on my part not to invite you to disclose to the full the leonine paws of authority, so that the people who are suffering tortures and destruction of their property may not

feel that I, who had perhaps been the chief party inspiring them to action that has brought to right light the Government in its true colours, had left any stone unturned to work out the Satyagraha programme as fully as it was possible under given circumstances. [162]

He therefore planned a nonviolent raid to seize the government salt depot at Dharasana, an act which because of its daring and challenge would inevitably bring either Government acquiescence or—far more likely—severe repression and brutalities.

This example should make it clear, if there be still any doubt, that it is an error to equate being nonviolent with keeping the opponent "good-natured." The nonviolent strategist regards both the provocation of extreme repression in rare cases and the more usual willingness to withstand repression against more conventional nonviolent action, as interim stages, temporary phases, of a larger and more complicated process of change, a process which is necessary to alter an intolerable situation.

No opponent is likely to appreciate a serious challenge to his power or policies, even if the challenge is peaceful. The nonviolent actionist recognizes that the desired change may only come as the consequence of a difficult and temporarily disruptive struggle. Gandhi wrote:

Our aim is not merely to arouse the best in [our opponent] but to do so whilst we are prosecuting our cause. If we cease to pursue our course, we do not evoke the best in him but we pander to the evil in him. The best must not be confounded with good temper. When we are dealing with any evil, we may have to ruffle the evil-doer. We have to run the risk, if we are to bring the best out of him. I have likened nonviolence to a septic and violence to antiseptic treatment. Both are intended to ward off the evil, and therefore cause a kind of disturbance which is often inevitable. The first never harms the evil-doer. [163]

April Carter has drawn an analogy between the tensions and conflict involved in a civil disobedience struggle, and those the patient goes through under psychoanalysis, it being necessary in both cases to bring the conflict into the open and to experience it in order to remove it and allow a more healthy condition to be achieved. [164]

As the Gandhian nonviolent actionist understands the process, as long as the opponent is not simply becoming brutalized, and as long as the actionists are able to withstand the repression, there need be no alarm when the opponent temporarily becomes angry and inflicts repression, even brutalities. The situation must, however, be handled wisely and if the

PART THREE: DYNAMICS

above qualifying conditions no longer exist a change in tactics and methods may be urgently required. Barring that, the nonviolent actionists persist while remaining brave and nonviolent. If this can be achieved, there are good grounds for believing that the brutalities will be a temporary phase, though not necessarily a brief one. Seifert points out that while it is not always the case, ". . . it is entirely possible for the worst persecution to come shortly before capitulation by their opponents." [165]

The precise factors which may lead to a reduction or cessation of brutalities will vary widely with the particular situation. These factors will be closely associated with 1) the operation of one or more of the mechanisms of change discussed in later chapters, and especially 2) the ways in which repression may rebound against the opponent's position as will be discussed in Chapter Twelve. For example, members of the opponent group may learn that the nonviolent actionists are in fact both brave and strong. With nonviolent discipline, the opponent group may realize it need not fear a violent attack on itself, and hence its hostility may be reduced. [166] Gandhi argued that when the opponent's violence was met with nonviolence, the result would be finally be a weakening of the opponent's desire or ability to continue his violence; in this way nonviolence would "blunt the edge of the tyrant's sword." [167] An important factor in this process would be the opponent's realization that, rather than strengthening his position, his own repression and brutalities were reacting against him and weakening him, while increasing the relative strength of the nonviolent group.

The change will, however, come only if the nonviolent actionists and the wider grievance group are able to maintain and increase their solidarity. It is to this task and the means for doing so that the discussion now turns.

NOTES

1. From Parnell's speeches at Tipperary, on 21 September 1879, and at Ennis, on 19 September 1880, quoted in O'Hegarty, **A History of Ireland Under the Union, 1880-1922,** pp. 490-491.
2. For examples of this, see Franco Venturi, **Roots of Revolution,** pp. 490, 573 and 651, and Gipson, **The British Empire Before the American Revolution,** vol. XII, **The Triumphant Empire, Britain Sails into the Storm, 1770-1776,** p. 239.
3. Gandhi, **Non-violent Resistance,** p. 134; Ind. ed.: **Satyagraha,** p. 134.
4. Nehru, **An Autobiography,** p. 551.
5. Seifert, **Conquest by Suffering,** p. 64.
6. Farmer, **Freedom — When?,** p. 73. See also Kuper, **Passive Resistance in South Africa,** p. 74.
7. Quoted by Farmer, *loc cit.*
8. Ebert, "Theory and Practice of Nonviolent Resistance," MS p. 168.
9. Hiller, **The Strike,** pp. 22 and 88.
10. Jawaharlal Nehru, **India and the World: Essays by Jawaharlal Nehru** (London: Geo. Allen & Unwin, Ltd., 1936), p. 173. See also Diwakar, **Satyagraha,** p. 28.
11. Hiller, **The Strike,** p. 30.
12. Lakey, "The Sociological Mechanisms of Nonviolent Action" (thesis), p. 110; also in **Peace Research Reviews,** vol. II, no. 6 (Dec. 1968), p. 73.
13. Oppenheimer and Lakey, **A Manual for Direct Action,** p. 23.
14. Kuper, **Passive Resistance in South Africa,** pp. 22 and 180. See also pp. 154-159 and 178-180.
15. Oppenheimer and Lakey, **A Manual for Direct Action,** p. 23. See also Miller, **Nonviolence,** p. 311, and Luthuli, **Let My People Go,** p. 181.
16. Seifert, **Conquest by Suffering,** pp. 61-62. See also p. 46.
17. Lakey, "The Sociological Mechanisms of Nonviolent Action" (thesis), p. 110, and **Peace Research Reviews,** vol. II, no. 6 (Dec. 1968), pp. 73-74, cites: Paul Ernest Wehr, "The Sit-Down Protests: A Study of a Passive Resistance Movement in North Carolina" (unpublished M.A. thesis, University of North Carolina, 1960), and Martin Oppenheimer, "The Sit-In Movement: A Study in Contemporary Negro Protest" (unpublished Ph.D. dissertation, University of Pennsylvania, 1962), pp. 111 and 134.
18. See Sharp, **Gandhi Wields the Weapon of Moral Power,** p. 124. On their role in negotiations, see pp. 170, 178, 202-203, and 205-207.
19. See Kuper, **Passive Resistance in South Africa,** pp. 209, 146, and 146-149.
20. Harvey J. D. Seifert, "The Use by American Quakers of Nonviolent Resistance as a Method of Social Change" (unpublished Ph.D. dissertation, Boston University, 1940), p. 145.
21. On conflicts within the East German regime and in Moscow about the handling of the Rising, or as a consequence of it, see Ebert "Nonviolent Resistance

Against Communist Regimes?" pp. 186-187 and Brant, **The East German Rising,** pp. 167-175.

22. Nehru, **An Autobiography,** p. 70.
23. Watt, **Dare Call it Treason,** p. 182.
24. See Brant, **The East German Rising,** pp. 155-157 and Ebert, "Nonviolent Resistance Against Communist Regimes?" pp. 184-188.
25. Ebert, "Nonviolent Resistance Against Communist Regimes?" p. 184.
26. *Ibid.,* p. 187.
27. *Ibid.*
28. Wheeler-Bennett, **The Nemesis of Power,** p. 78.
29. Nehru, **An Autobiography,** p. 70.
30. Kuper, **Passive Resistance in South Africa,** p. 87. On Gandhi's views of the ways in which the government is unprepared for nonviolent action, essentially because it does not expect it, see Gandhi, **Satyagraha in South Africa,** p. 214.
31. Harcave, **First Blood,** pp. 76-77.
32. *Ibid.,* p. 169.
33. Gandhi, **Non-violent Resistance,** p. 174; Ind. ed.: **Satyagraha,** p. 174.
34. Gipson, **The British Empire Before the American Revolution,** vol. XI, **The Triumphant Empire: The Rumbling of the Coming Storm, 1766-1770,** pp. 151-152, and vol. XII, pp. 309-311.
35. Symons, **The General Strike,** pp. 47-48.
36. *Ibid.,* p. 52.
37. *Ibid.,* p. 53.
38. Watt, **Dare Call It Treason,** p. 186.
39. Katkov, **Russia 1917,** p. xxv.
40. Harcave, **First Blood,** p. 125.
41. Symons, **The General Strike,** p. 49.
42. *Ibid.,* pp. 52-53.
43. Delarue, **The Gestapo,** p. 8.
44. Harcave, **First Blood,** p. 189. On other instances of recognition by officials of the need to prevent spread of strikes, see also pp. 97, 174, and 196.
45. Sharp, **Gandhi Wields . . . ,** p. 81.
46. Gerland, "The Great Labor Camp Strike at Vorkuta," *Militant,* 7 March 1955.
47. Ebert, "Nonviolent Resistance Against Communist Regimes?" pp. 179 and 185. After the rising more significant concessions were made. See Brant, **The East German Rising,** pp. 163-164, and 166.
48. *Newsweek,* 17 June 1963, and *New York Times,* 19 July and 9 October 1963, cited in Roberts, "The Buddhist Revolt", MS pp. 13, 17 and 37.
49. King, **Why We Can't Wait,** pp. 30-32.
50. Ebert, "Nonviolent Resistance Against Communist Regimes?" p. 185. On elation and determination to continue the struggle in Russia after the "October Manifesto" see Harcave, **First Blood,** pp. 199-203.
51. Katkov, **Russia 1917,** pp. 322-323 and 332.
52. Jutikkala, **A History of Finland,** p. 229.
53. Gipson, **The Coming of the Revolution, 1763-1775,** p. 193.
54. Gipson, **The British Empire . . . ,** vol. XII, p. 130. For similar statements, see

also pp. 295 and 310-311, and Schlesinger, **The Colonial Merchants and the American Revolution,** pp. 537-538.

55. William Z. Foster, **The Great Steel Strike and Its Lessons** (New York: B. W. Huebsch, 1920), p. 116. I am grateful to George Lakey for this reference. See also Symons, **The General Strike,** pp. 158, 182-186 and 196.

56. King, **Stride Toward Freedom,** U.S. ed., pp. 100-102; Br. ed., pp. 118-120.

57. See Mahadev Desai, **The Story of Bardoli,** pp. 71-72, 88-89, 90, 94-95.

58. See King, **Stride Toward Freedom,** U.S. ed., 98-99; Br. ed., p. 116.

59. *Ibid.*

60. Kuper, **Passive Resistance in South Africa,** p. 86.

61. Gandhi, **Non-violent Resistance,** p. 208; Ind. ed.: **Satyagraha,** p. 208.

62. Luthuli, **Let My People Go,** p. 175.

63. Hsiao, **Rural China,** p. 3.

64. Luthuli, **Let My People Go,** p. 159. This refers to reaction to the issuing of the Freedom Charter in 1955.

65. Seifert, **Conquest by Suffering,** p. 49.

66. Harcave, **First Blood,** p. 232.

67. Gipson, **The British Empire** . . . , vol. XII, p. 287. On a similar warning by General Gage in 1767, see *ibid.,* vol. XI, p. 57.

68. Warmbrunn, **The Dutch Under German Occupation 1940-1945,** p. 110.

69. Nehru, **An Autobiography,** pp. 328-329.

70. Malcolm W. Browne (of Associated Press), *Japan Times,* 31 August 1963, quoted by Roberts, "The Buddhist Revolt," MS p. 45.

71. Seifert, **Conquest by Suffering,** pp. 39-40.

72. Buckler, "Labour Disputes in the Province of Asia Minor," p. 31. On other repression against strikes and tax refusal, see Rostovtzeff, **The Social and Economic History of the Roman Empire,** vol. I, p. 449.

73. Ramsay MacMullan, "A Note on Roman Strikes," *Classical Journal,* vol. LVIII (1962-1963), pp. 269-271.

74. Schlesinger, **The Colonial Merchants** . . . , pp. 538-539.

75. Griffith, **The Resurrection of Hungary,** p. 34.

76. Friedrich Grimm, **Vom Ruhrkrieg zur Rheinlandräumung** (Hamburg: *Hanseatische Verlagsanstalt,* 1930), p. 105. Quoted in translation by Sternstein, "The *Ruhrkampf* of 1923," pp. 121-122.

77. Kuper, **Passive Resistance in South Africa,** p. 63.

78. *Ibid.,* p. 62.

79. *Ibid.*

80. Luthuli, **Let My People Go,** p. 149.

81. Brant, **The East German Rising,** p. 20.

82. See Symons, **The General Strike,** pp. 20-22, 26-27, 94 and 154-155.

83. Halperin, **Germany Tried Democracy,** p. 250.

84. Katkov, **Russia 1917,** pp. 307-308.

85. *New York Times,* 30 September 1963, quoted in Roberts, "The Buddhist Revolt," *MS pp. 15 and 34.*

86. Bondurant, **Conquest of Violence,** p. 218.

87. Kuper, **Passive Resistance in South Africa,** pp. 86, 79 and 206.

88. April Carter, **Direct Action** (pamphlet; London:*Peace News,* 1962), p. 22.

89. Dhawan, **The Political Philosophy of Mahatma Gandhi**, p. 142.

90. Nehru, **Toward Freedom**, p. 249.

91. Gopal, **The Viceroyalty of Lord Irwin**, p. 64.

92. Gandhi, **Non-violent Resistance**, p. 81; Ind., ed.: **Satyagraha**, p. 81.

93. Kuper, **Passive Resistance in South Africa**, p. 86.

94. See Seifert, **Conquest by Suffering**, p. 39.

95. Oppenheimer and Lakey, **A Manual for Direct Action**, p. 23.

96. Fredric Solomon and Jacob R. Fishman, "The Psychosocial Meaning of Nonviolence in Student Civil Rights Activities," **Psychiatry**, vol. XVII, no. 2 (May 1964), p. 96.

97. Gandhi, **All Men Are Brothers** (Ahmedabad, India: Navajivan, 1960), p. 138.

98. Gandhi, **Non-violent Resistance**, p. 347; Ind. ed.: **Satyagraha**, p. 347.

99. Brigitte Gerland, "The Great Labor Camp Strike at Vorkuta," **Militant** (New York), 7 March 1955, p. 3

100. King, **Stride Toward Freedom**, pp. 106-122; Br. ed.: pp. 126-144.

101. **Ibid.**, U.S. ed.: p. 122; Br. ed.: p. 144.

102. **Ibid.**, U.S. ed.: p. 132-133; Br. ed.: p. 156. On other examples from the Afro-American movement, see Farmer, **Freedom—When?**, p. 10, and Solomon and Fishman, "The Psychosocial Meaning of Nonviolence in Student Civil Rights Activities," pp. 95-97.

103. Seifert, **Conquest by Suffering**, p. 41.

104. Harcave, **First Blood**, p. 231.

105. Reitlinger, **The Final Solution**, p. 328.

106. Ebert, "Nonviolent Resistance Against Communist Regimes?" p. 182.

107. Luthuli, **Let My People Go**, pp. 11, 78, 145-147, 150-153, 155-157, 161, 170, 209, 214-217, 226, and 229, and Appendix C, and also Sharp, "Problems of Violent and Nonviolent Struggle," **Peace News**, 28 June 1963.

108. Miller, **Nonviolence**, p. 162.

109. Luthuli, **Let My People Go**, p. 196.

110. Ebert, "Nonviolent Resistance Against Communist Regimes?" p. 193.

111. **Ibid.**, p. 192.

112. Ebert, "Theory and Practice of Nonviolent Resistance," MS pp. 438-439.

113. Brant, **The East German Rising**, p. 164.

114. Harcave, **First Blood**, p. 116.

115. Gipson, **The British Empire** . . . , p. 186 On economic hardships on the colonists of that campaign in 1770, see p. 273.

116. Niels Lindberg as early as 1937 attempted, and appealed for, a comparative evaluation on practical grounds of the advantages, disadvantages and consequences of nonviolent action, military resistance, terrorist resistance and guerilla war. See Lindberg, **"Konklusionen: Theorien om Ikke-vold,"** in Lindberg, Jacobsen and Ehrlich, **Kamp Uden Vaaben**, pp. 203-213.

117. Gregg, **The Power of Nonviolence**, p. 100.

118. Bondurant, **Conquest of Violence**, p. 229.

119. See **Monthly Information Bulletin** of the International Commission Against Concentration Camp Practices (August-November 1955), pp. 19-35, and 66-68.

120. Warmbrunn, **The Dutch** . . . , p. 110.

121. Schlesinger, **The Colonial Merchants** . . . , p. 183.

122. *Ibid.*, p. 315.

123. Ehrlich, *"Ruhrkampen,"* p. 189.

124. *Ibid.*, pp. 188-189.

125. Halperin, **Germany Tried Democracy**, pp. 252-254.

126. Gandhi, **Non-violence in Peace and War**, vol. I, p. 338. See also, pp. 43, 226, 278, 323, and 337-339. For other discussions of suffering in nonviolent action, see *ibid.*, vol. II, pp. 63, 145, 166 and 288; Gandhi, **Non-violent Resistance**; Ind. ed.: **Satyagraha**, p. 134, and 172; Gregg, **The Power of Nonviolence**, pp. 53, 78, 84, and 129-130; Bose, **Selections from Gandhi**, p. 183; Case, **Non-violent Coercion**, pp. 397-401; Dhawan, **The Political Philosophy** . . . , pp. 139-141; Kuper, **Passive Resistance in South Africa**, pp. 78-93, and Wolff, editor, **The Sociology of Georg Simmel**, pp. 224-249, esp. p. 226.

127. See Bondurant, **Conquest of Violence**, pp. 29 and 198 and Gandhi, **Non-violence in Peace and War**, vol. II, p. 21.

128. See Gandhi, **Non-violence in Peace and War**, vol. II, pp. 36, 59 and 63, and Bose, **Selections from Gandhi**, p. 189.

129. Gandhi, **Non-violent Resistance** p. 67; Ind. ed.: **Satyagraha**, p. 67.

130. *Ibid.*, p. 115.

131. *Young India* (weekly), 10 July 1930 nr. 28.

132. Sharp, **Gandhi Wields** . . . , p. 76.

133. Miller, **Nonviolence**, pp. 224-229.

134. Luthuli, **Let My People Go**, p. 92.

135. Bose, **Studies in Gandhism**, p. 161.

136. Hiller, **The Strike**, p. 151.

137. See Lakey, "The Sociological Mechanisms . . . " (thesis), p. 84; *Peace Research Reviews*, vol. II, no. 6 (Dec. 1968), pp. 54-55.

138. Seifert, **Conquest by Suffering**, p. 47.

139. *Ibid.*, p. 50. See also p. 49.

140. Schlesinger, **The Colonial Merchants** . . . , p. 180 and Gipson, **The British Empire** . . . , vol. XI, pp. 276-280.

141. Seifert, **Conquest by Suffering**, p. 47.

142. *Ibid.*, p. 48.

143. Quoted by Lakey, "The Sociological Mechanisms . . . " (thesis), p. 83; *Peace Research Reviews*, vol. II, no. 6 (Dec. 1968), pp. 54-55.

144. Kuper, **Passive Resistance in South Africa**, p. 89.

145. Seifert, **Conquest by Suffering**, p. 48.

146. See Gopal, **Viceroyalty of Lord Irwin**, p. 65.

147. Nehru, **An Autobiography**, p. 180.

148. Edward Rodman, "Portsmouth: A Lesson in Nonviolence," pp. 80-81, in Peck, **Freedom Ride.**

149. See Kuper, **Passive Resistance in South Africa**, p. 85.

150. Seifert, **Conquest by Suffering**, p. 48.

151. *Ibid.*, p. 50.

152. *Ibid.*, pp. 48-49.

152. *Ibid.*, pp. 48-49.

153. *Ibid.*, p. 50.

154. Lakey, "The Sociological Mechanisms . . . ," (Thesis) p. 85; *Peace Research Reviews*, vol. II, no. 6 (Dec. 1968), pp. 55-56.

155. Lord Hardinge of Penschurst, **Old Diplomacy: The Reminiscences of Lord Hardinge of Penschurst** (London: James Murray, 1947), p. 114.

156. Janis and Katz, "The Reduction of Intergroup Hostility," p. 99.

157. Seifert, **Conquest by Suffering**, p. 51.

158. Miller, **Nonviolence**, p. 164.

159. See Sharp, **Gandhi Wields** . . . , pp. 101-102; 104-105; 108-111; 115; 139-141; 142-144; 148-149; 162-166.

160. Gregg, **The Power of Nonviolence**, pp. 59, 83, 118, 120 and 126.

161. Bose, **Studies in Gandhism**, p. 153.

162. Sharp, **Gandhi Wields** . . . , p. 117.

163. Quoted in Bose, **Studies in Gandhism**, p. 168.

164. April Carter, **Direct Action** (pamphlet), p. 23.

165. Seifert, **Conquest by Suffering**, p. 63.

166. Gregg, **The Power of Nonviolence**, p. 48, and Janis and Katz, "The Reduction of Intergroup Hostility," **Journal of Conflict Resolution**, vol III, no. 1 (March 1959), p. 95.

167. Dhawan, **The Political Philosophy** . . . , p. 141.

11

Solidarity and Discipline to Fight Repression

INTRODUCTION

Faced with repression and suffering, the nonviolent actionists will need to stand together, to maintain their internal solidarity and morale, and to continue the struggle. As the opponent attributes violence to them and tries to provoke them to commit violence—with which he could deal more effectively—the nonviolent actionists will need to persist in reliance on their chosen technique of struggle and to maintain nonviolent discipline. As the conflict deepens, the nonviolent actionists will need to continue to pursue the struggle in order to bring into operation the changes that will alter relationships and achieve their objectives.

THE NEED FOR SOLIDARITY

The need for solidarity has been recognized in many campaigns, both in the initial stages and in the later more difficult phases. During the initial stages, when the effort is to rally as much support as possible, the nonviolent group is likely to identify with the grievance group as a whole and its needs. This will continue, Lakey points out, as long as the group of participants is growing; "little if any emphasis is placed on a boundary between the nonviolent actor and the public."[1] In some cases the whole population group is more or less involved, although not always equally so. In other cases, the nonviolent actionists may be a minority and a highly visible group, in comparison to the general population or even the group whose grievances are being championed.

Sometimes people will hesitate to commit themselves to nonviolent action unless they are convinced that there will be sufficiently solid support to make it effective. In the spring of 1768 New England merchants were, for example, cautious about a nonimportation campaign; they wanted assurances that merchants in the colonies down the coast would also take part. New York merchants made their adoption of the plan later that year dependent on continued support from Boston and the adoption of similar measures in Philadelphia.[2]

Nonviolent actionists will aim for the full participation which was shown at the beginning of the British General Strike of 1926:

> The workers' reaction to the strike call was immediate and overwhelming. There can be no doubt that its completeness surprised the Government, as well as the TUC. From district after district reports came into the TUC headquarters at Eccleston Square, sending the same message in various words: the men were all out, the strike was solid. This is a very rare thing . . . this one, almost unprepared and imperfectly coordinated, might have been expected to show signs of collapse from the start. Instead, the response was in effect complete.[3]

On June 16, 1953, similar solidarity was shown by East Berlin workers. Workers from *Volkseigener Betrieb Industriebau*'s Block 40 section were indignant at the approximately ten percent increase in their work norms, which had been announced by the ministerial council. At first it was decided to send delegates to Ulbricht and Grotewohl to protest the change, but, Ebert reports:

> At an improvised meeting a foreman said that it was time to act. All the workers should go, not just the delegates. One of the workers has described this decisive movement in the history of the uprising: "A colleague came forward. 'Take your choice. If you are with us, step over to the right: if not step over to the left.' The whole gang moved to the right." The uprising began in that instant. The workers re-

solved to protest openly. After that there was no turning back. The fact that they had all taken the same step gave them strength and confidence.[4]

It should not be assumed, however, that such initial unanimity will always be possible, nor that it is always required (however desirable it may be). If near unanimity of participation is not likely, or does not materialize, this fact will have to be considered in the selection, or modification, of the strategy, tactics and specific methods for the campaign. Where the active participants in the nonviolent struggle are only a section of the general population, deliberate efforts may be needed to strengthen their morale. This strengthening may involve developing the nonviolent actionists as a *self-conscious* group distinguished from the rest of the population. Lakey writes that this drawing of boundaries may happen "as soon as campaigners cease to be recruited at a high rate."[5] When maximum possible support has at that stage been rallied, the nonviolent group is likely without conscious influence to develop its internal solidarity as it faces the coming struggle. Deliberate efforts may also be made to develop and maintain group solidarity.

The maintenance of morale in nonviolent struggles is extremely important. There appear to be roughly four ways of doing this (and here we follow Hiller's analysis of morale-building in strikes[6] with some modifications and additions). These are: 1) maintaining rapport, feelings of group participation and group solidarity; 2) generating incentives to carry on the struggle; 3) lessening incentives to give it up; and 4) possessing or using restraints on participants wishing to abandon the struggle.

A. Maintaining rapport

The ability of the participants to face repression will be very significantly increased if they constantly feel that they are part of a much larger movement which gives them, personally, support and strength to carry on. Even when the individual is physically separated from the group, the awareness that others are continuing in solidarity with him will help him to resist temptations to submit. Regular contacts and demonstrations of "togetherness" are therefore important ways of maintaining group morale.[7] This explains the role of regular mass meetings during strikes.[8] During the Montgomery bus boycott, regular mass prayer meetings were held, first twice a week and later once a week.[9]

Other specific actions seemingly intended as resistance against the opponent or as an effort to reach the public may in reality help to maintain internal group solidarity and morale. For example, parades and marches may be used. As Hiller points out in the case of strikes: "March-ing before spectators is a declaration 'to the world' that one's lot has been cast with the group in its rivalry with others. Self-display before a public causes one to feel identified with those similarly placed and associ-ated." Picketing has an effect, not only on the public, strikebreakers, etc., but on the strikers themselves. Hiller describes this effect as being "more influential upon the strikers than upon the scab and the employer. The very antagonism which these efforts provide helps to maintain the conflict, boost morale, and lessen desertions." [10]

During the Indian 1930-31 campaign, for example, there were a sig-nificant number of parades, picketing, the hoisting or carrying of the In-dian national flag, the burning of foreign cloth and mass meetings. The *hartal* was not only a form of protest but also a means of keeping up morale. Singing was frequently used by large crowds in crisis situations. [11] At the beginning of the campaign, Gandhi, writing in *Young India,* stated that during the movement *satyagrahis* should find themselves:

1. In prison or in an analogous state, or
2. Engaged in civil disobedience, or
3. Under orders at the spinning wheel, or at some constructive work advancing *Swaraj* [self-rule]. [12]

Thus in the crises, work on the constructive program (intended to remove social evils, educate the people, and build new, self-reliant, institutions) also helped to keep people involved and active in the overall movement, whether or not engaged in civil disobedience. In 1952 mass meetings were used in South Africa both to build up a spirit of resistance and solidarity and to spread the objectives and plans of the civil disobedience movement. The campaign was preceded by a day of prayer in many African loca-tions throughout the country. [13]

In some situations temporary camps for volunteers may be set up, as in India in 1930. These are particularly necessary in combat situations, as during the nonviolent raid at Dharasana, [14] and serve not only to meet elementary physical needs but also to maintain group spirit.

Sometimes the wearing of certain symbols of unity will help people to identify with the movement and show their support for it. For example, Elizabeth Gurley Flynn tells how this worked in an American labor strike:

> The strike was in danger of waning for lack of action. We got every striker to put on a little red ribbon . . . and when they got out of their homes and saw the great body that they were they had renewed energy which carried them along for many weeks in the strike. [15]

Norwegians during the Nazi occupation wore paper clips in their lapels, a sign of "keep together," and students and pupils took to wearing necklaces and bracelets of paper clips. Red caps were worn as a sign of resistance. Pupils wore tiny potatoes on match sticks in their lapels. Every day they became larger, indicating that the anti-Nazi forces were growing. The smallest Norwegian coin, showing "H VII" for King Haakon VII, was brightly polished and worn. Flowers were widely worn on the King's seventieth birthday. Such symbolic actions not only irritated the Nazis—several hundred Norwegians were arrested for them—but also served to boost feelings of solidarity among the Norwegians. [16]

Explaining why a strikers' picnic was held on Sunday (when the strikers could have had a rest and break), Flynn pointed out that the reasons went "deep into the psychology of a strike." She then elaborated on the importance of conscious efforts to maintain solidarity if the strikers were to win. "You have got to keep the people busy all the time, to keep them active, working," she explained. This was the reason why the Industrial Workers of the World had "these great mass meetings, women's meetings, children's meetings . . . [,] mass picketing and mass funerals. And out of all this . . . we are able to create that feeling . . . 'One for all and all for one' . . . we are able to bring them to the point where they will go to jail and refuse fines, and go, hundreds of them, together . . ." [17]

B. Generating incentives

A second way of maintaining morale is to promote determination to carry on the struggle. The participants must believe that they have very good reasons for continuing, that their action is justified, that the objectives when won will be worthwhile, and that the means of action to achieve them have been wisely chosen. "The biggest job in getting any movement off the ground," wrote Martin Luther King, Jr., "is to keep together the people who form it. This task requires more than a common aim: it demands a philosophy that wins and holds the people's allegiance; and it depends upon open channels of communication between the people and their leaders." [18]

The leaders in Montgomery put much effort into explaining nonviolent action and "Christian love" in the mass meetings. Morale is likely to increase if the nature of the technique, the plan of action and tactics, the significance of the repression and the response to it are understood. Sometimes the opponent's repression will by its brutality make waverers more firm on their resolve. If the goals and means of struggle are, or can be, related to deep religious or philosophical convictions *already held* by the participants and the wider population, their resolve and morale are likely to be stronger.

C. Reducing grounds for capitulation

At certain stages in nonviolent campaigns, the participants may become discouraged or fatigued, and specific attention must then be given to counteract these conditions. Wise nonviolent leaders will have anticipated this development and may have tried to reduce its severity by advance measures. It is highly important that at least the original participants continue support and that none desert. The failure to maintain lasting internal solidarity among the inhabitants of the Ruhr led to serious weakening of the movement. "The united front against occupiers, which had been firm and strong at the outset, now began to disintegrate," writes Sternstein about the months of August and September, 1923. [19]

Where fatigue or monotony occur, special entertainment may be marginally useful. There was a considerable effort in this direction during the 1926 British General Strike. The General Council of the Trades Union Congress suggested the organization of sports and entertainment, and local Strike Committees organized concerts, football matches and other sports. In many cases strikers played football matches against teams of local policemen. All over Britain, local Strike Committees organized "Sport and Entertainment" sections. The Cardiff, Wales, Strike Committee advised the local men: "Keep smiling. Refuse to be provoked. Get into your garden. Look after the wife and kiddies. If you have not got a garden, get into the country, the parks and the playgrounds." [20]

Where, because of participation in the struggle, the nonviolent actionists and their families suffer from lack of food, housing, money and the like, or if they may do so in the future, there may be a major effort to supply these needs. This assistance would relieve the nonviolent combatants and their families of immediate worries, and enable them to carry on longer than otherwise possible. Such efforts to equalize the burdens and provide mutual help have been made in various recent campaigns, but the practice is an old one, having been used by American colonists. South Carolinians, for example, devised a scheme for equalizing the burdens which would come with the plan for economic resistance contained in the Continental Association; the possible adverse effects on rice planters were regarded as especially important. [21] When the British closure of the port of Boston brought economic hardship to the city's merchants and unemployment for workingmen, other cities and towns, and indeed other colonies at some distance, provided various forms of mutual help, ranging from free use of storerooms and wharves for Boston merchants in nearby Marblehead to financial assistance for Boston's needy. [22] Modern forms of such assistance have included legal representation, bail funds, financial assistance to families, and (where the campaign was in support of the government) advance guarantees of compensation for financial losses arising from the struggle. For example, the German Minister of Traffic, Gröner, in 1920 promised all staff members, officials and workers in the State railroads that in accordance with the policy of refusing all cooperation with French efforts to run the railroads in the Ruhr, the government would reimburse them for all injury and loss. This compensation policy was also extended to industrialists of the territory for their losses during the struggle, and 715,000,000 marks were later paid in compensation. [23] In other cases, where the resistance organization was a private one with little or no financial reserve, volunteers have sometimes been asked to sign a statement acknowledging that there will be no claim for, or pledge of, financial remuneration for any losses or difficulties arising from the struggle.

The sufferings incurred in the course of nonviolent struggle are sometimes interpreted by nonviolent leaders in ways which make them seem more bearable. Where this effort is successful, further grounds for capitulation will be reduced. Various speakers emphasized such interpretations during the 1952 South African Defiance Campaign:

> I know you will be called upon to make many sacrifices and you may have to undergo many sufferings. But what are these sufferings compared with the sufferings of other people in this country to-day . . . . Our people suffer every day, and it is all wasted. What we say is, suffer, but for a cause, and let us rather die for a good cause.

> If they put you in gaol, I ask you: is your condition better outside?

> They can bring their machine-guns, as they did on the first of May, and shoot us down—innocent men—without provocation. And what will happen to you if you die? I ask you. My friend, let me tell you that when you die they must take that chain off you and you will be free in your death.

> . . . their power is great. But are we going to be frightened of that power? . . . The power of man is greater than the power of machineguns . . . And if justice and truth is on our side, no machine, no police, no power can stop us from marching onwards. [24]

D. Restraints or sanctions

The last, most extreme, and least used, means of maintaining solidarity is the threat or use of nonviolent restraints or sanctions. Such restraints or sanctions may be applied to those who have refused to join the movement, or to members of the nonviolent group who have weakened and withdrawn from the campaign. These nonviolent sanctions differ radically from the sanctions for indiscipline applied in violent conflicts, which are imprisonment or execution.

The nonviolent alternative sanctions may under suitable circumstances be powerful and effective. Sometimes verbal persuasion is sufficient to restore adherence to the movement. When this is not adequate, other methods are available, including vigils, public prayers, picketing, fines, publication of names, suspension of membership, social boycott, economic boycott, fasting and nonviolent interjection. [25]

If such pressures are to be used, considerable care will be needed in their application. Intimidation and threats of physical harm must not be used, or the movement is likely to slide into a struggle with violence applied against one's own people. Rejection of threats is certainly a minimum limitation on sanctions for maintaining solidarity. Frequently nonviolent leaders insist that the attitude toward the persons whose behavior requires these pressures must be a benevolent one. Gandhi insisted, for example, that such means must be applied without vindictiveness or hostility. This is contrary to attitudes frequently accompanying Western labor conflicts when nonstrikers are ostracized or "sent to Coventry." Social boycotts, it should be remembered, do not require bitterness and hatred. In any case, supplies of food and all other necessities must be maintained; if necessary these must be provided to those who are being socially boycotted.

The activists among American colonists during their noncooperation campaigns against British laws, regulations and government probably still furnish the outstanding example of these types of restraints and sanctions. (This is not to deny that threats of physical violence were also on occasion used against recalcitrants.) For example, in 1769 residents of Massachusetts Bay Colony used various nonviolent methods against those not complying with the nonimportation campaign, including distribution of thousands of handbills urging people to shun the shops of merchants not abiding by the agreement, refusal to do business with any vessel which loaded forbidden goods at any British port, and publication in newspapers of the names of violators. [26]

This is, however, simply one illustration of many which might be offered. Various committees were set up throughout the colonies to enforce the provisions of the ongoing campaign, and these achieved considerable effectiveness.[27] In Connecticut the Continental Association was enforced by open, fair trials of persons accused of violations of its provisions.[28] In order to prevent a skyrocketing of prices as a consequence of short supplies during nonimportation, colonials controlled prices by instituting investigations (at times demanding examinations of accounts), publishing names of violators, and imposing economic boycotts on those who sought to profit from the crisis.[29] The most important nonviolent sanctions were the "naming" of people—i.e., publishing their names in newpspapers—imposition of social boycott, and in the case of merchants and traders, the application of secondary economic boycotts against them. In practice it was often difficult to separate the operation of the methods of "naming," social boycott and economic boycott.[30] One ultraradical wrote in late 1774:

> The [Continental] Congress, like other Legislative bodies, have annexed penalties to their laws. They do not consist of the gallows, the rack, and the stake . . . but INFAMY, a species of infamy . . . more dreadful to a freeman than the gallows, the rack, or the stake. It is this, he shall be declared in the publick papers to be *an enemy to his country* . . .[31]

In certain situations certain austerities adopted for resistance, including the ban against gambling, were also enforced by such means. The enforcement measures took a variety of additional forms depending on the situation, including dismissal from their jobs of ship captains or masters who had taken on prohibited goods and the refusal of lawyers to provide services for violators of the noncooperation plan.[32]

Enforcement of the nonimportation and other measures by such means was frequently effective. Banned goods were sometimes returned to England without being unloaded, while at other times such imports were unloaded but placed in storage for the duration of the campaign, or sold at auction for the benefit of the resistance movement.[33] Occasionally shopkeepers were "sentenced" to burn boycotted tea in their possession.[34]

The Lieutenant Governor of Massachusetts Bay, Thomas Hutchinson, writing of the period when he acted as Governor before General Gage replaced Governor Bernard, confirmed the effectiveness of the various means of enforcement:

> The design, at this time, was to enforce the compliance with the former subscription, and to compel all other persons to abstain from

importation. The first step for this purpose was the publication in the newspapers, of the names of such persons as were most notorious for persisting in importing goods contrary to the agreement of the merchants, "that there might be the concurrence of every person upon the continent in rendering their base and dangerous designs abortive." Many persons, at first, appeared determined not to submit to so arbitrary a proceeding, but the subscription was general, with few exceptions only.[35]

Hutchinson also offered several examples of pressures which involved a shift toward physical intimidation to enforce the noncooperation provisions.[36] Without doubt there was at times both a strong tendency for suppression of contrary opinions and violation of freedom of speech, and a development of quasi-military groups,[37] but such developments do not necessarily follow from the nonviolent enforcement of resistance policy: indeed, they need to be prevented.

In an unusual extension of this type of enforcement, colonies which were firmly supporting nonimportation applied secondary economic boycotts not only against towns where the expression of opposition was weak,[38] but even against whole colonies which had been lax in launching or maintaining noncooperation, especially Rhode Island, South Carolina and Georgia.[39]

During the Irish rent refusal campaign, Charles S. Parnell, Member of Parliament and President of the Land League, called for social boycott against Irishmen who did not maintain solidarity with their resisting compatriots. Parnell declared at Ennis on September 19, 1880:

Now what are you to do to a tenant who bids for a farm from which another tenant has been evicted? I think I heard somebody say shoot him. I wish to point out to you a very much better way—a more Christian and charitable way, which will give the lost man an opportunity of repenting. When a man takes a farm from which another has been evicted, you must shun him on the roadside when you meet him—you must shun him in the streets of the town—you must shun him in the shop—you must shun him on the fair-green and in the market place, and even in the place of worship, by leaving him alone, by putting him into a moral Coventry, by isolating him from the rest of his country, as if he were the leper of old—you must show him your detestation of the crime he has committed . . .[40]

Examples of the use of nonviolent interjection, for example, to press nonstrikers to stay away from work have also been offered in Chapter

Eight in the description of that method.[41] On occasion fasts have been used to maintain solidarity. For example, during the Ahmedabad textile workers' strike led by Gandhi in 1918, after four weeks the strikers became dispirited and some began to return to work. Gandhi regarded their weakening as a breaking of their pledge not to do so. Accordingly, he reminded the workers of their pledge and undertook a fast, saying, "unless the strikers rally and continue the strike till a settlement is reached, or till they leave the mills altogether, I will not touch any food." This restored morale and solidarity.[42]

In late 1930, when tax refusal was added to the methods of resistance used by the Indians and the government consequently seized properties of tax resisters, fasts were applied against fellow Indians who sought to profit from the struggle. In Siddapur *taluka* (subdistrict), in Kanara, Karnatak province, thirty-seven women fasted at the doors of persons who had bought the seized properties of tax resisters, and at Mavinagundi such a fast lasted thirty-one days.[43]

It is possible, of course, that in face of repression, despite such means of promoting solidarity, both determination and fearlessness may weaken and the movement may collapse. If, however, the nonviolent actionists remain determined and fearless, are willing to undergo the suffering and maintain their solidarity and high morale, it is highly likely that the movement will continue. This will present severe problems for the opponent. It will mean, among other things, that his effort to crush the movement by his strongest means of action—repression—will have failed. To achieve this, however, the actionists must maintain nonviolent discipline, for there are strong chances that the opponent will falsely attribute violence to them and seek to provoke them into committing it. That is to his advantage.

INHIBITING REPRESSION

The difficulties which the opponent faces in attempting to defeat a nonviolent action movement arise from 1) the fact that the opponent strongly tends to be more limited in the means of repression which he may use against nonviolent action than against violent action, and 2) the nature of his means of repression, which are generally most effective in dealing with *violent* action.

Extremely severe and brutal repression against a group pledged to nonviolence and to harm no one is much more difficult to justify to everyone concerned than is such repression against a group engaged in injuring and killing people. Awareness of this in advance, or as a result of experience, will in many cases cause the opponent to make his counteraction less severe than against violent actionists. He learns that disproportionate repression may react against him, not only in terms of opinion but also in weakening his own relative power position. This reaction includes increased support for the nonviolent group, less support for, and greater open opposition to, the opponent's policies, repression and regime generally.

Lakey puts it this way:

> . . . the strategy of the nonviolent actor is to limit the means of repression which can be included in the definition of the situation of the opponent. The nonviolent actor does this by persuading his opponent that some means are inappropriate for use against him. Even if the opponent has traditionally exploited or been violent against the campaigner, the latter seeks to protect an image of himself which will remove the justification for the opponent's violence. [44]

It is true that the British were far more brutal in putting down the Indian nonviolent movement than most people today realize. [45] However, it is also true that they were by no means as ruthless as they *could* have been, and as they in fact *were* in putting down the 1857 uprising in India and the Mau Mau movement in Kenya, or in the bombings of German cities in World War II. At least a major part of the reason for the comparative British restraint in dealing with the Indian nonviolent movement was that the Indians' continuing nonviolence limited the British in the means of repression which are effectively open to them. Focusing on labor strikes, Hiller points to the influence of the presence or absence of a public on the kinds of repression which may be used against strikers. [46]

Explaining the British Government's refusal to arrest Gandhi during his Salt March to the sea to commit civil disobedience in 1930, Gandhi said:

> . . . the only interpretation I can put upon this noninterference is that the British Government, powerful though it is, is sensitive to world opinion which will not tolerate repression of extreme political agitation which civil disobedience undoubtedly is, so long as disobedience remains civil, and, therefore, necessarily nonviolent. [47]

The degree to which a regime will feel able to defy world—or internal—opinion will of course vary, depending on several factors. These include the kind of regime it is, whether it thinks the events can be kept unknown, the degree to which it is threatened by the events, and whether opinion against the regime will be translated into assistance for the non-violent group and into actions against the opponent.

Censorship kept the news of the 1919 massacre of Jalianwala Bagh in Amritsar, India, from reaching the United States for eight months—but it did eventually leak out.[48] In dealing with the defiant nonviolently resisting Norwegian teachers Quisling could obviously have been more ruthless than he was and could have shot some or all of them. However, he was not really free to do so because he knew that if he took harsher measures against the teachers than sending them to concentration camps he might irrevocably increase public hostility to his regime and make forever impossible his hope of gaining the consent and cooperation he needed for establishing the Corporative State in Norway.[49]

The British in India clearly faced some very difficult decisions concerning what means of repression should be used and when they should be applied. Nehru described this situation in late 1921: "The nerves of many a British official began to give way. The strain was great. There was this ever-growing opposition and spirit of defiance which overshadowed official India like a vast monsoon cloud, and yet because of its peaceful methods it offered no handle, no grip, no opportunity for forcible repression."[50] Gopal, who had access to government correspondence and reports, describes some of the problems during the 1930-31 struggle and the differences of opinion within the government about measures of repression.[51] These are simply indicative of the general problem which an opponent faces when confronting nonviolent action. The decisions are difficult for him if he is to consider the effects of his action on his own position, strength and future; the responses offered to this problem may vary considerably.

In other cases, too, there is suggestive evidence that the maintenance of nonviolent discipline in face of repression tends significantly to restrict the repression and to cause especially difficult problems for the opponent. For example, in South Africa, in an effort to crush a strike by Africans which began on March 22, 1960 (the day after the shooting at Sharpeville), police invaded the Nyanga location near Capetown on April 4; for four days they unleashed a reign of terror including extensive whippings of men, use of batons and some shootings and killings. (This was after extensive unprovoked police brutality against Africans elsewhere, which had produced important white protests against the police.) Norman Phillips of the *Toronto Star* reports the inhibiting effects of nonretaliation even in this situation: "For sheer sadism, the closest comparison to what happened at Nyanga was when the Gestapo sealed off the Warsaw ghetto and began to annihilate it. Had Nyanga fought back, it, too, would have been wiped out; but the Africans employed nonaggressive tactics that puzzled the police." [52] The French commander confronted with nonviolent resistance in the Ruhr acknowledged that it was not very easy to crush the movement; he told the German author Friedrich Grimm: "You have no idea of the difficulties I had, nor of the opportunities you had of exploiting them." [53]

Sir Basil Liddell Hart offered further evidence of the special problems of repression against nonviolent actionists from German occupation experience in World War II:

> When interrogating the German generals after the Second World War, I took the opportunity of getting their evidence about the effect of the different kinds of resistance which they had met in the occupied countries.
>
> Their evidence tended to show that the violent forms of resistance had not been very effective and troublesome to them, except in wide spaces or mountainous areas such as Russia and the Balkans, where topography favoured guerrilla action. In the flat and thickly populated countries of western Europe, it rarely became a serious handicap unless and until the Allied armies were able, and close enough, to exert a simultaneous pressure.
>
> Their evidence also showed the effectiveness of nonviolent resistance as practised in Denmark, Holland and Norway—and, to some extent, in France and Belgium. Even clearer, was their inability to cope with it. They were experts in violence, and had been trained to deal with opponents who used that method. But other forms of resistance baffled them—and all the more in proportion as the methods were subtle and concealed. It was a relief to them when resistance became violent and when nonviolent forms were mixed with guerrilla action, thus making it easier to combine drastic repressive action against both at the same time. [54]

THE OPPONENT PREFERS VIOLENCE

Because of the special difficulties of repressing a nonviolent resistance movement, the opponent may seek to ease them by attributing violence to the nonviolent actionists. The British policy in 1930-31 was to publicize widely all the violence that occurred and, it often seemed, to issue deliberately false reports. The official report for the year, *India in 1930 -31,* stated that between April 6 and July 7, 1930, there was a considerable number of "riots and serious disturbances" and "disorders" throughout the country. Fifty-three such happenings were listed—with no attempt to distinguish between violent riots and nonviolent "disorders." [55] During the 1952 Defiance Campaign in South Africa, as we have seen, there was considerable attempt to identify the civil disobedience movement with the Mau Mau movement in Kenya. [56] The opponent may also plant incriminating evidence "proving" violent intentions and unsavory political associations within the nonviolent group. For example, according to Denis Warner in the *Daily Telegraph* (London) the South Vietnamese Diem regime planted weapons, explosives and "Communist propaganda" in the Xa Loi pagoda in Hué, in 1963. [57] This was to help "justify" severe repression, harsh raids, and large-scale arrests.

Frequently fearing nonviolent resistance more than violent resistance, officials have on occasion preferred that the actionists resort to violence. On the other hand, an opponent who genuinely holds humanitarian and moral views may be partially grateful that the actionists use nonviolent means. [58] However, if the opponent is more interested in maintaining policies which are difficult to justify, in preserving his dominance, and in crushing opposition than he is in upholding an ethical outlook, he may try to provoke violence. In the history of the labor movement, for example, there are frequent instances in which employers have found that resort to violence by the strikers was counterproductive for them but an advantage for the employers. [59] In the United States, Oppenheimer and Lakey report as follows: "Again and again in the civil rights struggle police have been itching to shoot into demonstrations but have not fired because they could not find the excuse of 'self-defense' or 'rioting.'" [60]

Toward the end of Gandhi's struggle in South Africa, one of the secretaries to General Smuts said to Gandhi: "I often wish you took to violence like the English strikers, and then we would know at once how to dispose of you." [61] Gopal reports that whereas the British found Gandhi's nonviolent action "bewildering," "nothing would have suited the British better than to have been confronted with a series of weak, armed rebellions . . ." [62] Benjamin Tucker argued: "There is not a tyrant in the civilized world today who would not rather do anything in his power to precipitate a bloody revolution rather than see himself confronted by any large fraction of his subjects determined not to obey." [63]

Even minor breaks in discipline and very limited violence may be the occasion for quite disproportionate response by the agents of repression; this happened both at Sharpeville in 1960 when stones were thrown at the police and in Birmingham, Alabama, in 1963, when initial taunting of the police produced high pressure water hosing against Negro demonstrators, a step which led to the Negroes' hurling stone paving-blocks at police in a struggle which lasted an hour-and-a-half.[64] Even a little violence will give the opponent the excuse for which he may well have waited to use his overwhelming violence and repression. Severe repression may, of course, occur even when nonviolent discipline is maintained; but in that case, the repression is more likely to rebound against the opponent's power, as is discussed in Chapter Twelve.

Where both sides rely on violence, despite their disagreements, "in reality they conduct their fight on the basis of a strong fundamental agreement that violence is a sound mode of procedure."[65] The use of nonviolent means against a violent opponent, however, creates a condition of disequilibrium within the dynamics of the conflict which operates to the benefit of the nonviolent group.

It is clear that Hitler and the Nazi regime generally regarded some type of "provocation" as necessary, or at least highly desirable, when they were about to launch some major international or domestic power grab which might otherwise have met with considerable opposition. If the provocation desired by the Nazis did not happen on its own, then it was "necessary" to fake a provocation. Detailed study of archives and documents might show whether or not the Nazis consciously applied this as a general practice to resistance movements of various types; this extensive research has not been possible. However, the available evidence shows that even in the Nazis' opinion provocation greatly facilitated international aggression, internal usurpation and brutalities against and murder of hated people. This Nazi desire for provocations adds plausibility to the view that violence used by or on behalf of nonviolent actionists is likely to be counterproductive and help the opponent to inflict overwhelming repression and brutalities. Since the Nazi regime would be expected to be most indifferent to a need for such "justification," these cases are especially significant. Several such instances will therefore be surveyed here. In all these the Nazis wanted violence from their opponents. If it did not happen anyhow, the Nazis either falsely attributed violence to the opposition or provoked them to commit it. Then the Nazis utilized such violence for their own political advantage.

In 1933 Hitler clearly saw provocation to be necessary if he were to use his precarious position as Chancellor representing a minority party in a coalition cabinet operating under a democratic constitution, to abolish the Weimar Republic and to establish a one-party Nazi system. Communist violence was seen as necessary for the "legal" destruction of the Communist Party, and the Nazis would accordingly wait.[66] The burning of the *Reichstag*, the parliament building, provided the occasion. Although one might expect such a dramatic act of presumed opposition to the Nazis to weaken them, it in fact strengthened them. Arriving at the burning building, Hitler declared: "This is a sign from God. No one can now prevent us from crushing the Communists with a mailed fist." [67] As far as the role which the fire played in the Nazi rise to power is concerned, it makes little or no difference whether one believes the fire was (as the Nazis said) started by the Communists as part of a plot, or was (as anti-Nazis said) started by the Nazis themselves for the purpose of blaming the Communists, [68] or was (as Fritz Tobias says) started only by Marius van der Lubbe. [69] The fact remains that the fire provided the necessary provocation which enabled the Nazis by several actions to rout the Communists, abolish constitutionally guaranteed liberties, arrest members of the *Reichstag,* and achieve passage of the disastrous Enabling Act—which suspended the constitution and made it possible for Hitler's National Socialist German Workers Party to become undisputed ruler of Germany.

In international adventures, Hitler always sought to shift the blame to someone else and to show that his peace-loving regime had only acted in the interest of order and self-defence after the most extreme provocation and, if possible, attack by his victims. On July 1, 1940, Hitler told the Italian ambassador, Dino Alfieri, "it was always a good tactic to make the enemy responsible in the eyes of public opinion in Germany and abroad for the future course of events. This strengthened one's own morale and weakened that of the enemy." [70] Accordingly, considerable preparations preceded the German occupation of Austria so that the act might appear, not as military aggression, but as an altruistic act intended to save Austria from violence and civil war; these preparations may even have included plans for the murder of the German Ambassador Franz von Papen. [71] The advance planning for the 1939 invasion and take-over of Czechoslovakia included extensive manipulation of the victim's internal situation designed to make it possible for Hitler to pose as the savior of the cruelly persecuted and terrorized German minority. By threats Hitler even gained the submission of the Czechoslovak government in order to maintain the appearance of "legality" for the actual occupation. [72] In the later case of Poland, the Nazis were not content with justification of the invasion on the basis of persecution of the German minority, but on August 31, 1939, even staged a fake border incident in an attempt to show that the Poles had attacked first and seized a German radio station near the border; as "proof" that Polish troops had made the attack, a dozen or so condemned German criminals in Polish uniforms were left dead, with appropriate wounds, at the scene.[73] The next day at dawn the German armies invaded Poland.

Acts of violence against Germans provided favorable opportunities for the Nazis to carry out the brutalities they wanted to commit. The murder of the young Ernst vom Rath, anti-Nazi third secretary at the German Embassy in Paris, in November 1938 by seventeen-year-old Herschel Gryszpan, son of one of the Jews who had been deported across the Silesian border, was met with "the week of broken glass." Well-organized "spontaneous" reprisals took place against Jews throughout Germany in what became the "first ruthless and undisguised suppression of Jews in Germany on a wholesale scale," and various anti-Jewish laws and economic measures were also then introduced.[74] The assassination of Reinhardt Heydrich on May 29, 1942, near the village of Lidice, Czechoslovakia, by agents from England was followed by the execution of 1,690 persons. These included 199 from Lidice (the village itself was razed to the ground), 152 Jewish hostages in Berlin, and 1,339 other persons in Prague and Bruenn.[75] Attacks on German soldiers and acts of sabotage in several occupied countries were met with brutal retaliation.[76] Hitler even regarded some provocation necessary for the planned extermination of Polish intellectuals, nobility, clergy and Jews. The original excuse, a faked rising in the Galician Ukraine, was set aside as the Nazis waited for a more favorable moment. The extermination was then "justified" by the claim that it was necessary to end agitation dangerous to the security of the troops.[77] It was clear that Hitler was quite conscious in his utilization of violent opposition as the occasion for disproportionately brutal retaliation; he said, for example, that partisan warfare launched in occupied areas of the Soviet Union "enables us to eradicate everyone who opposes us."[78]

These various cases show two simple points: 1) that even Hitler and his cohorts were strongly convinced that their own ruthlessness and agression would be much more easily committed and have greater success if it could be portrayed as retaliation for the violence of others, and 2) that the common assumption that violence by the grievance group can only strengthen their position and not weaken it is, in many situations, not true. This does not prove, of course, but it does make more plausible, the view that violence committed by or in support of nonviolent actionists operates to the advantage of the opponent, and is indeed precisely what he may want in order to consolidate his position and to apply ruthless repression.[79]

The opponent may therefore attempt to provoke the nonviolent actionists and grievance group to violence. This may be attempted in several ways. One of the common means is to make the repression so severe that the actionists break the nonviolent discipline spontaneously, or a group of them begins to advocate violent retaliation openly and to gain a following. This is how Gandhi interpreted the government's declaration of martial law and other harsh repressions in Bardoli in 1928 when the whole area was refusing to pay the land revenue: "It is evident that by the latest form of 'frightfulness' the Government is seeking to goad people into some act of violence, be it ever so slight, to justify their enactment of the last act in the tragedy."[80] This had already happened in 1919 during the *satyagraha* campaign against the Rowlatt Act when people in Ahmedabad, Viramgam, and other parts of the Gujarat heard of Gandhi's arrest. Gandhi later testified: "They became furious, shops were closed, crowds gathered and murder, arson, pillage, wirecutting and attempts at derailment followed."[81] Describing a scene in Bihar in 1930, Rajendra Prasad, later President of India, reported: "The police are, it seems, now determined upon provoking violence so that they get an excuse for using their guns."[82] Writing to the Viceroy after the beginning of the 1930-31 campaign, Gandhi once again commented on this tendency: "If you say, as you have said, that the civil disobedience must end in violence, history will pronounce the verdict that the British Government, not bearing because not understanding nonviolence, goaded human nature to violence which it could understand and deal with."[83]

Similar claims were made by African speakers early in the 1952 Defiance Campaign in South Africa:

> And the police who are supposed to uphold order but who only start riots, shot down a hundred at Bellhoek, May 1st, 1951! I don't need to remind you that in many African townships the police started the riots. If the Africans will not fight, the police make them fight.[84]

> They [the volunteers] must behave well as the police will provoke them. Tomorrow the police will say, *"Ek het 'n kaffer geskiet, hy het met'n klip gegooi."* ("I've shot a kaffir. He threw a stone at me.") But that policeman has never been injured. But what will they say now? *"Hoe gaan ons werk, kerels, die mense baklei nie."* ("What shall we do, chaps? These people don't fight.") You must give them that headache.[85]

Police in Birmingham, Alabama, on May 3, 1963, appeared to be deliberately provoking Negroes to violence, using first torrents of water from fire hoses, then dogs, then "a state police investigator deliberately swerved his car into the crowd." At that point the Negroes threw bricks and bottles at the police. After a settlement had been reached, white extremists unsuccessfully tried to get white leaders to provoke the Negroes to new violence as a pretext for repudiation of the agreement.[86]

The opponent may also employ spies and agents in an effort to defeat the nonviolent movement, including *agents provocateurs*. If the nonviolent action campaign is being operated without secrecy—as is common in nontotalitarian countries—spies and agents will not be much good for gathering secret information, for there will be none. They may, however, be useful in stirring up "jealousies and resentments among the campaigners and spreading morale-disturbing rumors."[87] The opponent may by such means make serious attempts to demoralize the movement internally, to divide it on policies or personal matters, or to bog down its policy-making meetings with endless bickerings or to prevent effective operation of the group's normal decision-making process.

Agents provocateurs may also be used in a deliberate attempt to provoke the group to violence. At an earlier stage of the labor movement, employers used *agents provocateurs* widely to combat the development of trade unions and to defeat particular strikes. One method is to place agents inside the nonviolent group. These agents then agitate for a switch to violence, or, defying group decision and discipline, commit violence themselves. The hope is to incriminate the whole group or to provoke wider violence. Sometimes they may operate outside the nonviolent group as such, and seek in difficult situations to provoke large nonviolent demonstrations into violence, or to commit acts of violence which, though actually separate from the plans of the nonviolent group, can be identified in the public's mind with their resistance.

This danger was emphasized by Gregg:

Who in this actual world of hard realities does or ever would for an instant fear this so-called weapon of nonviolent resistance?

The answer is known to every student of history, every detective, secret service man or C.I.D. officer, every really "hard-boiled" ruthless executive of an American industrial corporation which has had a strike of employees, every American trade union leader, every leader of a subject people striving for political freedom. The answer is that every "blood and iron" type of governor fears nonviolent resistance so much that he secretly hires *agents provocateurs* who go among the nonviolent resisters pretending to be of them, and invite them to deeds of violence or actually throw bombs or do deeds of violence themselves. This was the method of the tsarist government of old Russia. Rulers in power immediately make great outcry, stir up public indignation against the "miscreants," call out the police or soldiery, and "repress the uprising" with considerable brutality, meanwhile assuring the world that these are stern but necessary steps taken only in the interests of public safety, law and order. Those striving for freedom or more privileges are indeed often violent in the first instance. But if they are not violent, their opponents or the underlings of their opponents frequently stir up violence in order to take advantage of the public reaction against it. That they feel they need to adopt such tactics shows how much they fear nonviolent resistance.[88]

Kuper also points to the dangers of agents:

In certain circumstances, the rulers may incite the resisters to violence, by use of *agents provocateurs* and of extreme provocation, for two reasons. First, force is more readily mobilized against violence . . . Second, the severe repressive measures, which the ruler may wish to use and is organized to use, require some justification. The violence of the resisters is the best justification for violent counteraction; this explains the tendency of the ruling groups in South Africa to identify the passive resistance campaign with Mau Mau.[89]

Nehru claimed after the violence at Chauri-Chaura in 1922 that "numerous *agents provocateurs,* stool pigeons, and the like . . . [have] crept into our movement and indulged in violence themselves or induced others to do so."[90] In 1936, in his presidential address at the forty-ninth session of the Indian National Congress at Lucknow, Nehru again reported the existence of ". . . a wide network of spies, and [a] . . . tribe of informers and *agents provocateurs* and the like."[91] An examination of the relevant archives would be useful in checking these charges and possibly shedding more light on the subject. In England itself, during the 1926 General Strike, the British Army had agents all over the country who mixed with strikers; whether they would have been used to provoke violence is not clear, but certainly they were instructed to gather information and report current attitudes of strikers—a much milder role.[92]

In combatting the Finnish nonviolent noncooperation movement for independence from tsarist Russia, the Russian Governor-General of Finland, General Nikolai I. Bobrikov, arranged for *agents provocateurs* (hired by the Ochrana, the Russian secret police) to commit violence themselves against Russians, or to provoke the Finns to adopt violence. The aim was to help justify savage repression.[93] Despite the pleas of innocence of the last head of the police under the Tsar, A.T. Vassilyev,[94] there is impressive evidence that the Ochrana did use *agents provocateurs* against the Russian revolutionary groups,[95] in addition to very effectively infiltrating its agents into these groups in order to gain information.[96]

These means of counteracting a movement of nonviolent action will not necessarily be successful, however. Provocation is, indeed, highly dangerous for the opponent. If it should be publicly revealed (as is always possible) that he had deliberately attempted to provoke violence, this could disastrously affect his normal support and relative power position. Even if his agents do not publicly reveal their activities, there are other ways in which they may be unmasked (see Chapter Eight, on "disclosing identities of secret agents"), and in which their provocations may be blocked or nullified. The nonviolent group will need to give careful attention to this problem, and additional research and analysis on it are needed. The opponent's provocation to violence emphasizes still further the importance of strict adherence to nonviolent discipline. To resort to violence, declared Gandhi, is to "cooperate with the Government in the most active manner."[97] "Restraint under the gravest provocation," he insisted, "is the truest mark of soldiership." Just as even a novice in "the art of war knows that he must avoid the ambushes of his adversary," so nonviolent actionists must see every provocation as "a dangerous ambush into which we must resolutely refuse to walk."[98]

If the actionists can maintain such discipline under very difficult circumstances, they will not only help expose *agents provocateurs* and reveal the opponent, not only as an upholder of order, but as one who prefers resisters who injure and kill to disciplined nonviolent resisters; they may also help to prevent the most ruthless repression and to bring the actionists success. This is because nonviolent struggle, like other techniques for conducting conflicts, has requirements which must be fulfilled if it is to "work." One such requirement is that the nonviolent actionists and their supporters maintain nonviolent behavior.

THE NEED FOR NONVIOLENT BEHAVIOR

The requirement that volunteers maintain their nonviolent behavior is rooted in the dynamics of the technique of nonviolent action and is not an alien emphasis introduced by moralists or pacifists.[99] Without nonviolence, the opponent's repression will not rebound to undermine his power through political *jiu-jitsu* (discussed in Chapter Twelve), and the mechanisms of this technique (discussed in Chapter Thirteen) will not operate. This is not a new perception. In 1861 Francis Deák warned fellow Hungarians not to be betrayed into acts of violence nor to abandon legality (i.e., the old Hungarian constitution) as the basis of their struggle against Austrian rule: "This is the safe ground on which, unarmed ourselves, we can hold our own against armed force." [100] As Gandhi put it, "victory is impossible until we are able to keep our temper under the gravest provocation. Calmness under fire is a soldier's indispensable quality." [101] "Nonviolence is the most vital and integral part of noncooperation. We may fail in everything else and still continue our battle if we remain nonviolent." [102] Nonviolent conduct is "a strategic imperative." [103]

Nonviolent means are often perceived to be more legitimate (or sometimes less illegitimate) than violent means in the same situation, especially if the nonviolent ones seem effective. This reaction may be partly intuitive, partly emotional and partly rational. It is especially likely among third parties, usual passive supporters of the opponent, and members of the grievance group not yet participating in the struggle. These are precisely the groups whose shifts of position and loyalty may, as we shall see in later chapters, help to determine the outcome of the conflict.

Nonviolent behavior is likely to contribute to achieving a variety of positive accomplishments. Four of these are: 1) winning sympathy and support, 2) reducing casualties, 3) inducing mutiny of the opponent's troops and similar disaffection, and 4) attracting maximum participation in the nonviolent struggle. We shall consider each of these briefly here; and some of them will be discussed in more detail in the following chapter.

The sympathy and support which a nonviolent political stance tends to bring to the actionists has often been anticipated by groups using nonviolent means, even at times ones which did not exclude possible later use of violence. This was the case, for example, in the Suffolk Resolves passed by delegates in Suffolk County, Massachusetts Bay, in 1774. These Resolves were later approved by the First Continental Congress. While the Suffolk delegates clearly provided for military preparations in case hostilities broke out, they preferred peaceful forms of struggle which would bring respect and sympathy to the colonials.

> . . . we would heartily recommend to all persons of this community not to engage in any routs, riots, or licentious attacks upon the properties of any person whatsoever, as being subversive of all order and government: but, by a steady, manly, uniform, and persevering opposition, to convince our enemies that in a contest so important—in a cause so solemn, our conduct shall be such as to merit the approbation of the wise, and the admiration of the brave and free of every age and of every country. [104]

The tendency already discussed for the opponent's repression to be relatively limited against nonviolent actionists obviously only operates so long as they remain nonviolent. Even then, the limitations on repression are not complete, and brutalities may occur. The murder of three young civil rights workers in Mississippi in 1964 is evidence of the fact that brutalities must be expected, but does not refute this tendency on nonviolent behavior to limit the repression; in fact, Robert Moses, head of the Mississippi 1964 Summer Project, has stated: "One reason we've survived is that we haven't had guns and everyone knew it." [105]

A nonviolent stance in face of repression may help undermine the morale and loyalty of the opponent's police, troops and other important aides so much that they may mutiny or express their disaffection in other strong ways. One important example of such mutiny and disaffection occurred in Petrograd in the February 1917 Revolution and was largely responsible for the final disintegration of the Tsar's regime. This instance will be described in more detail in the following chapter on political *jiu-jitsu*. There seems little doubt that serious disaffection and mutiny are much more likely in face of heroic nonviolent resistance than in face of violence when the safety and lives of the police, troops and the like are threatened. When mutiny occurs on a large scale, it demonstrates that nonviolent behavior may deal with the opponent's violent repression in a fundamental and effective way.

There is one final reason why adherance to nonviolence strengthens the movement: the use of nonviolent action will allow the maximum degree of active participation in the struggle by the highest proportion of the population. [106] Nonviolent action can be actively applied by men and women, old and young, city dwellers and rural people, factory workers, intellectuals and farmers, educated and uneducated, able-bodied and the physically weak. Virtually no one in the population need be excluded. This makes possible a much higher number of active combatants than in any other technique. The realization of this potential hinges, of course, on people's will to act and on their skill and persistence in doing so, but the technique makes possible the participation of the highest numbers of all possible forms of struggle. This will not only increase the strength of the grievance group, but this large and diverse popular participation is also likely to cause especially severe problems for the opponent. There will be many more people against whom he must act. It will often be more difficult to separate "combatants" from "noncombatants." Application of his usual control measures and repression against the old, women, the young, handicapped people, etc.—the very groups usually excluded from active combat—is especially likely to provoke reactions which weaken his power position and strengthen that of the nonviolent group. (How this happens is discussed in the next chapter.) Maintenance of nonviolent behavior is therefore extremely important in this technique for practical reasons.

HOW VIOLENCE WEAKENS THE MOVEMENT

Political violence "works" in quite different ways from nonviolent action. The introduction of violence into a nonviolent campaign by the nonviolent actionists or the grievance group, or on their behalf, is highly dangerous because the process which in nonviolent action produce strength, and could lead to success, will thereby be reversed. This reversal is likely to lead to reduced strength for the nonviolent actionists, to increased effectiveness of the opponent's measures to retain or regain control, and to the defeat of the nonviolent group. "Two opposite forces can never work concurrently so as to help each other," stated Gandhi. [107] In his study of the strike, Hiller pointed out that violence "reverses the character of the response" to the resistance. [108] It is no accident that, as we have noted, opponents confronted with nonviolent action often attribute violence to the nonviolent group when it is not present, and that, when it occurs, they concentrate on it, and exaggerate its seriousness. One example, out of the many possible, is the reaction to the predominantly nonviolent East German Rising. On June 23, 1953, the official Communist paper *Neues Deutschland* sought to justify violent suppression by recounting alleged violent actions by demonstrators and strikers during the Rising: "On 17 June . . . Fascist hordes roamed the streets, murdering, pillaging, destroying and screaming." [109] Similarly, a few days after the event, the government described speakers who had actually advised disciplined behavior at a city strike meeting of twenty thousand in the Goerlitz town square as "fascist provocateurs, criminals and bandits," and charged that they had incited the crowd to sabotage and violence. [110]

The use of violence by the nonviolent actionists, or on their behalf, has a strong tendency to shift attention to that violence and away from the issues at stake in the conflict and from the nature of the opponent's system, and also away from the (usually much greater), violence of his repressive measures. The tendency for the basic issues to be lost sight of in such cases has been pointed out by Mulford Sibley in the case of labor strikes: "If strikers resort to violence, whether initially or in response to provocation, they simply provide an excuse for the government to use force against them; and once force has been employed, the original issues leading to the strike become confused or are often forgotten." [111]

The events which followed the bombing of policemen at a strike meeting in Haymarket Square, Chicago, on May 4, 1886, illustrate both that resistance violence may shift attention from the issues in the struggle and also become the "justification" for overwhelming repression. The bombing occurred during a large and reasonably effective strike movement in various cities for the eight-hour day. In Chicago the labor organizations which believed in violence headed the strike movement, and proviolence anarchists were very influential. The peaceful open-air strike meeting at Haymarket Square had been called after police had fired into a group of two hundred striking workers who had taunted and attacked nonstrikers at a Chicago plant. At least four workers were killed and many wounded. The bomb which was thrown by an unknown person into a group of policemen killed seven and wounded sixty-six; the police had been about to disperse the small remnants of the large meeting. Although the real identity and motives of the bomber could not be established, the blame was placed on anarchists and labor radicals.

The Haymarket bomb had many results, but the eight-hour day and stronger workers' organizations were not among them. Nor was an advance for anarchism. The dead and wounded workers felled by police firings immediately after the bomb exploded were only the beginning of the workers' casualties. "Stimulation of public hysteria became the main activity of the police," writes Yellen. [112] All strike leaders and twenty-five printers of a labor newspaper were arrested. Newspapers throughout the country demanded "instantaneous execution of all subversive persons . . ." There were many police raids; homes, offices and meeting halls were broken into and searched; evidence was often fabricated. Eight strike leaders were found guilty of the bombing and four were sentenced to hang, even though they had been tried primarily on their anarchist convictions rather than on evidence. The State's Attorney admitted they were "no more guilty than the thousands who followed them," and John Altgeld, later Illinois governor, denounced the trial as grossly unfair. There were more savage police attacks on strikers' gatherings; the workingmen's ranks were split; the "Black International" dwindled to a few intellectuals and anarchism never regained a hold on the American labor movement. For many years all radical theory and practice fell into disfavor with American labor organizations. The issue of the eight-hour day was lost, the strike movement for it collapsed, and even in most cases where the eight-hour day had been already granted, employers took it away. [113]

Some people advocate the use of violence for restricted and special use in a campaign in which overwhelming reliance is to remain on nonviolent methods. There is evidence, however, that when significant violence is introduced into a nonviolent action campaign, the result will be its collapse, or the abandonment of nonviolent methods, or at least considerably reduced nonviolent action and its subordination to violence as the dominant technique.

Violence by or on behalf of the nonviolent actionists may lead to the collapse of the nonviolent movement. After the peasants of Bardoli district in India had in 1928 successfully refused to pay land revenue increases, Gandhi said that if they had "committed one single act of violence, they would have lost their cause";[114] ". . . we capitulate miserably if we fail in adhering to nonviolence."[115] This is likely to lead to "disaster."[116]

The outbreak of violence in South Africa in 1952 played a very important role in the collapse of the Defiance Campaign. At the peak of the civil disobedience movement, after it had been in motion for about six months, a series of African riots broke out between October 18 and November 9. Six whites were killed and thirty-three Africans. The white dead included a nun who had been a missionary doctor to the Africans; her body was spoliated.[117] This contributed to the sensationalism and to feelings that repression was "justified." The precise causes of the riots are not clear. The resistance leaders demanded an enquiry, which the government refused. There was no evidence that the resistance movement was responsible, and there were suggestions that *agents provocateurs* may have been involved.[118] In any case, the effects of the riots "were to damp down the spirit of resistance."[119] It is possible, Kuper acknowledges, that the campaign was ready to decline anyhow, but even then the riots played an important role:

> In October the movement was still in full vigor. The number of resisters was the highest sent into action—2,354 . . . Probably as many as 1,000 defied the laws in the latter half of October. In November and December, however, the number of resisters fell to 280. Nor did the introduction of white resisters check the decline.[120]

For "all practical purposes," says Kuper, "the resistance campaign was at an end."[121] Other factors in this may include the impending general elections and the arrest of leaders, but,

> Clearly the riots played a decisive role. Quite apart from their effect on the resisters, the riots provided the opportunity for the Government to take over the initiative and to assume far-reaching powers with some measure of justification.[122]

This violence also assisted the Europeans' attempt to identify the civil disobedience movement, not with Gandhi, but with Mau Mau in Kenya.[123]

The transition between nonviolent struggle and violent struggle in the case of the American colonists illustrates that, on occasion at least, a gradual increase in readiness to use violence and the introduction of unplanned violence (Lexington and Concord) may alter the situation so drastically that even a carefully-planned, comprehensive and phased nonviolent campaign with wide popular backing may be abandoned for violence. This is especially likely when there is little deep appreciation of the practical advantages of nonviolent struggle, and when, despite using nonviolent means, people still regard violence as the most effective means of combat. Arthur Schlesinger, Sr., pointed out the vastly disproportionate effect of unplanned minor skirmishes in Massachusetts Bay on the carefully worked-out and phased program of hitherto effective economic noncooperation, the "Continental Association" adopted by the First Continental Congress. After February 1, 1775, ". . . British mercantile houses and manufactories became idle so far as American business was concerned. They were threatened with dull times and industrial depression at a time when their capital was more largely then usual tied up in American ventures." At this point limited firings took place between American irregulars and British troops. After four-and-a-half months of the noncooperation movement these events "changed the whole face of public affairs and rapidly converted the Association from a mode of peaceful pressure into a war measure." The military action at Lexington and Concord, and that which followed, convinced the radicals that ". . . the Association as a method of redress had suddenly become antiquated and that it must be altered, if not altogether abandoned, to meet the greatly changed conditions. This realization was at once acted upon by local committees and by Congress; and by the middle of 1775 the Continental Association was rapidly losing its original character." The political machinery of the Association turned increasingly to military preparations, so that by September 10, 1775, when the nonexportation phase of the noncooperation was to begin, the character of that measure was changed. "Thus, the bold experiment, inaugurated by the First Congress . . . was brought to a premature close by the call to arms."[124]

The introduction of violence is also likely to counter sharply, and to reverse, both the process of political *jiu-jitsu* and the operation of the very special mechanisms of change and dynamics of the technique of nonviolent action, discussed in later chapters. This tendency develops even when the violence is on the relatively small scale of rioting, injury, accidental loss of life in violent sabotage, or individual assassinations. For example, the whole conversion mechanism, which aims at a change of opinions, feelings and outlook, will be blocked. Violence will enable the opponent who had been unsettled by courageous nonviolence to resume his previous certainty and views, saying "I told you so . . ." [125] Also, the opponent's violence will no longer rebound against him by alienating his usual supporters, or by bringing sympathy and support from third parties. As resistance violence leads to a contraction of support for the nonviolent group in the grievance group, the opponent group and among third parties, the chances of change by nonviolent coercion are also almost entirely eliminated. With factors leading to both nonviolent coercion and conversion virtually eliminated, change by accommodation, which falls between them, also becomes most unlikely. Later we shall see in detail how these mechanisms are disrupted by resistance violence.

Success in nonviolent struggle depends to an extremely high degree upon the persistence of the nonviolent actionists in fighting with *their own methods,* and upon their refusing all temptation, whether caused by emotional hostility to the opponent's brutalities, by temptations of temporary gains, or by *agents provocateurs,* to fight with the opponent's "weapons system." If the nonviolent group switches to violence, it has, in effect, consented to fight on the opponent's own terms and with weapons where most of the advantages lie with him. This hands the initiative to the enemy, when the initiative should be retained by the nonviolent group, as we have already discussed. Luthuli points to this shift of initiative as a consequence of the riots, already described, which happened at the peak of the 1952 Defiance Campaign. Before they occurred, he wrote:

> The Defiance Campaign was far too orderly and successful for the Government's liking, and it was growing . . . . The challenge of nonviolence was more than they could meet. It robbed them of the initiative. On the other hand, violence by Africans would restore this initiative to them—they would then be able to bring out the guns and the other techniques of intimidation and present themselves as restorerers of order.
>
> It cannot be denied that this is exactly what happened, and at the moment most convenient for the Government. The infiltration of *agents provocateurs* in both Port Elizabeth and Kimberly is well attested. They kept well clear of the volunteers and the Congress. They did their work among irresponsible youngsters . . .
>
> It was all the Government needed. The riots and the Defiance Campaign were immediately identified with each other in the white South African imagination. The initiative was with the Government.

It is well known that the Government used its recovered initiative harshly and to the full . . . The activities of rioters provided the pretext for crushing nonviolent demonstrators. [126]

Violence by the actionists will also tend strongly to alienate existing support for the struggle by other members of the grievance group. Thus violence may weaken the unity and reduce the combat strength of the general grievance group. There are many examples of this from the history of the Russian revolutionary movement. [127] Katkov points out these effects on one revolutionary party:

The Socialist Revolutionary Party did not give up its terrorist activities until the double agent, Azef, who directed them, was unmasked in 1908. Terrorism, however, had sapped the organizational capacity of the party and alienated it from the masses, who never understood the purpose of political terror. [128]

Alienation of support by acts of violence also happened during the various struggles of the American colonists; initially it was mob disorders and intimidations which alienated people—especially merchants—who otherwise supported the objectives of the struggle. [129] The destruction of property belonging to someone else—as the dumping of tea into Boston harbor—also alienated other Americans who were not merchants:

. . . the Boston Tea Party was best calculated to enkindle the public mind; but, to the surprise of the radicals, there was no bursting forth of the flame that had swept over the country at the time of [the nonviolent campaigns against] the Stamp Act and again during the Townshend Acts, save in Massachusetts where the fuse had been carefully laid . . . The merchant class was generally shocked into remorseful silence . . . and many other people, more liberally inclined, were of their cast of mind. [130]

Even Benjamin Franklin called the tea destruction "an act of violent injustice on our part." [131] When military resistance broke out, even some radicals deserted the colonists' cause. [132] There had been a great degree of unity in implementing the earlier noncooperation campaigns. When violent resistance became dominant, Gipson points out, many Americans chose to be Loyalists and to fight for the King and the association with England—giving the contest "all the characteristics of a civil war in many parts of the country." Furthermore, he continues,

. . . there were vastly greater numbers of colonials hostile to the revolutionary movement. They stood aghast at the acts of terrorism performed by bands of rioters and vandals . . . To people of such conservative tendencies the patriotic cry of liberty was a mockery, when hand in hand with it went acts of violence designed to deprive them of all liberty because they disagreed on the great issue of the day. [133]

The earlier opposition of moderates to the Continental Association plan of resistance by economic noncooperation[134] had thus been multiplied and intensified by the switch to violence.

There is supporting evidence also from the contemporary Afro-American struggle in the United States that violence alienates support. [135] James Farmer, then National Director of the Congress of Racial Equality, predicted this process in 1965, before the large-scale urban riots; his warning has been largely fulfilled.

Widespread violence by the freedom fighters would sever from the struggle all but a few of our allies. It would also provoke and, to many, justify such repressive measures as would injure the movement. None would profit from such developments except the defenders of segregation and perhaps the more bellicose of the black nationalist groups. [136]

There is wide evidence in support of Farmer's view that violence by the grievance group tends to unleash disproportionately severe repression. Such repression would otherwise probably not have happened even though the opponent might well have liked to use it, and if it had happened in face of nonviolent resistance it would probably not have been effective. There are repeated examples of this. The firings at Lexington and Concord led to British occupation of Boston by troops, who turned it into an armed camp. [137]

Irish reforms, an end to English coercion, and the possibility of Home Rule were all destroyed by the assassinations in Phoenix Park, Dublin, on May 6, 1882, of two government officials. These occurred just when the coercion policy had been ended, the Irish leaders Parnell, Dillon and Davitt had been released from prison, and the strongest men in the government, including Gladstone, were coming around to Irish Home Rule. The assassinations were carried out by "The Invincible Society," a group of about twenty youthful Irish patriots. "The result was almost fatal to the national movement," writes O'Hegarty. [138] A new far more severe Coercion Act, which suspended the ordinary processes of law and civil liberties, was enacted. Conservative opinion hardened, and any step toward Home Rule became out of the question. "This year and next, Ireland was under the iron heel." [139] Morley, biographer of Gladstone, writes: "The reaction produced by the murders in the Park made perseverance in a milder policy impossible in face of English opinion, and parliament eagerly passed the Coercion Act of 1882." [140] "The Invincible Society" succeeded in aiding English imperialism with great effectiveness. "No worse blow could have been struck at Mr. Parnell's policy." [141]

Even the youthful Stalin warned workers against individual assaults on employers or managers—"economic terror"—which were becoming widespread, because they would recoil on organized labor. [142]

Casualties also tended to be much higher among violent resisters than among nonviolent resisters. During the 1905 revolution, for example, much greater numbers of dead occurred in instances of large-scale violence than in overwhelmingly nonviolent demonstrations and general strikes. Thus relatively brief violent rebellions in Lodz left three hundred dead; in Odessa, about two thousand dead; and in Moscow, one thousand dead. Nonviolent strikers and demonstrators were also killed, but not in such proportions, even though their challenge to the government's power was often far greater. [143]

The government-sponsored nonviolent noncooperation struggle against Franco-Belgian occupation of the Ruhr was detrimentally affected by the introduction into the struggle of acts of political violence, including destructive sabotage, attacks on French sentries and blowing up of bridges. The distinguished German historian, Erich Eyck, points to their counterproductive effects:

> Although such acts satisfied the bitter mood of many Germans, politically they were absurd, indeed suicidal. Only the politically immature could persuade themselves that these incidents would force France and Belgium to retreat. Their only consequence could be still worse sufferings for the unfortunate people of the occupied zones: arrests, expulsions, and executions . . . [Carl] Severing, [the Prussian Minister of the Interior], and the whole Prussian government were only doing their clear duty when they tried to stop as best they could this playing with fire. [144]

Similar evidence of the tendency for violent action to provoke strong repression may be found in reactions to the United States 1919 race riots, [145] and from the urban ghetto riots of the late 1960s.

Solomon and Fishman have also pointed to the tendency for violence to remove the limitations on the opponent's repression, while maintenance of nonviolence tends to restrict repression. In fact they describe this nonviolent technique as ". . . a means of directly asserting aggression while still trying to minimize provocation. When a group or individual wants to struggle against strong opposition which is capable of inflicting disastrous retaliation, the nonviolent mode of 'defiance' seems to provide a way of resolving the dilemma." [146] Violence by the subordinates, however, removes the limitations on repression imposed by the dynamics of nonviolent action.

Violence by, or in support of, the nonviolent actionists is also likely to bring an abrupt reversal of sympathy for them among the members of the opponent group, and especially end any internal opposition to the objectionable policies or repression. It was, for example, much easier for Englishmen to oppose colonialism and repression in India during the Gandhian struggles than in Kenya during the Mau Mau campaign. Members of the opponent group who have supported the policies and regime out of idealistic motives are especially likely to be alienated by violence; however, had nonviolent discipline been maintained, those people might have proved to be the least reliable of the opponent's supporters. Since nonviolent action operates to aggravate existing dissent in the opponent group, and to create within it support for the nonviolent group, such violence would be especially unfortunate. Increased solidarity in the opponent group behind the policies and repression will sharply reduce the chances of victory for the nonviolent actionists.

American colonial economic noncooperation had by early 1775 aroused British merchants, traders and investors with American connections into a considerable campaign against the Government and for repeal of the coercive acts of 1774. (Total export trade from England to the participating North American colonies dropped by nearly ninety-seven percent from 1774 to 1775.) The merchants carried on systematic activities to convince the King's ministers and Parliament to yield; these included many petitions and were similar to actions which had on earlier occasions brought changes in government policies for America. The ministry did not yield in response, but before the merchants' indignation against government coercive measures against the colonists could find new expressions, the merchants became reconciled to the situation and their opposition faded. One important factor in this was the improvement in mid-1775 in British business conditions as a result of increased European orders and improved payments of debts by American merchants. However, there was another equally important reason for the collapse of the support for the Americans by British merchants. Schlesinger writes: "undoubtedly the affair at Lexington and Concord in April sharpened the understanding of many of them as to the nature of the issues at stake." [147]

Resistance violence is especially likely to restore loyalty and obedience among any of the opponent's troops or police becoming disaffected by the nonviolent action. Soldiers under fire are likely to remain obedient, not mutiny. It is well known that ordinary soldiers will fight more persistently and effectively if they and their friends are being shot, wounded or killed. Resistance violence will tend to remove the influences producing sympathy for nonviolent actionists and shatter possible inner doubts about the issues of the conflict and the soldier's own duty. In nonviolent struggles in which success and failure hinge on whether the opponent's troops can be induced to mutiny, violence against them may spell defeat.

There is suggestive evidence of this counterproductive role of violence from the Moscow general strike and armed rising of December 1905. In the weeks prior to the Moscow strike there was considerable and widely scattered unrest in the armed forces, involving ". . . an unmistakable change in attitude toward authority. The results were mutinous and disorderly conduct that ranged from minor infractions to quite ominous outbreaks." [148] There had been several mutinies of both sailors and soldiers. These, added to lesser instances of insubordination, "made the navy practically worthless as a trustworthy fighting force . . ." [149] Disaffection in the army was widespread, even in the interior of the Empire. Although outright disobedience by soldiers was not so marked in those areas, ". . . there were good reasons for concern about the instrument upon which the regime would have to place its ultimate dependence, its armed forces." [150] Although the Menshevik and Bolshevik wings of the Social Democratic Party in Moscow were both agreed that "the Tsarist government was deliberately provoking the working class . . . ," both supported the plan for an armed rising; although the Bolsheviks favored an immediate armed rising, they agreed to the Menshevik proposal for "a general political strike which should transform itself into an armed uprising." [151] This was in response to the November 27 call from the St. Petersburg Soviet for a general armed rising, issued immediately before it was crushed. [152]

There was no reason to assume at the time that there was a serious chance of victory for an armed rising in Moscow. The militia of the Social Democratic Party in the city numbered only about one thousand, inadequately organized and armed and with less than twenty handmade bombs and grenades. The head of the militia himself opposed an armed rising, and others expressed doubts that the soldiers would support insurrection. [153] Very important, it has been reported that the tsarist government was deliberately provoking violence in order to be able to crush the revolution. [154] Once the decision had been made, workers, party revolutionaries and even Bolsheviks were all uneasy about the plan. They lacked enthusiasm and even believed in "the inevitability of defeat." [155] "Although damaging to the Government's prestige," Keep writes, a violent rising had "no chance of bringing about its overthrow . . ." [156]

Nevertheless, the Bolsheviks had taken the lead in pushing for an armed rising in Moscow. On the basis of available evidence, the Leninist Social Democrats did not seem to have compared the likely effect of an armed rising to alternative courses of action, on the chances of inducing a major mutiny of the Tsar's troops. The "Right Bolsheviks," however, apparently did. The Bolsheviks under Lenin were instead primarily concerned with gaining control of the situation for their own purposes and directing it as they chose to gain Bolshevik political objectives, regardless of the wishes of others or of effects on the revolution. [157] It is also clear the call of the Moscow Bolsheviks for an armed rising was not an "irresponsible" independent act of the local group, for on November 27 there had been a meeting of the Central Committee of the Social Democratic Party in St. Petersburg, attended by Lenin, at which preparations for an armed rising were discussed. [158]

It is difficult to document the Bolsheviks' motives for an armed rising launched when the loyalty of the troops still hung in the balance, and when the chances of mutiny were high while those of military victory were very small. Prawdin writes that "the real purpose of the Bolsheviks was to bring it home to the workers that they could not do without military organization and arms." [159] This interpretation is consistent with Lenin's comments on the need for violence, which he had written before the Moscow rising, [160] and with his comments on the rising written afterwards. [161]

The general strike phase of the Moscow insurrection began on December 7—four days after the mutiny of a regiment stationed in the city. The Social Democratic Party seems to have been either indifferent to the mutiny or incompetent in responding to it. The party offered no practical advice to the disobedient troops in their barracks—not even to become lost in civilian clothes among the general population. All they did was to advise restraint. The mutiny was then suppressed and several units were withdrawn from Moscow. [162] Then the general strike began, and during this phase, Harcave reports, "Two-thirds of the government troops . . . were judged unreliable; one whole regiment had actually undertaken to join the strikers before the fighting began, and had been prevented only by the interposing of loyal troops." [163] There were a number of instances of troops refusing to fire on demonstrators. [164]

The violent insurrection then developed. This included partisan warfare tactics, street barricades and sniper fire against the soldiers patrolling the city. In contrast to the earlier disaffection, disobedience and mutiny, the troops now obeyed orders. [165] The violent insurrection was defeated. "The Moscow rising was a failure," writes Seton-Watson," and it was clear that the revolution was over. The army's loyalty was by now ensured." [166] Other historians also point to the end of the Moscow rising as the beginning of the end for the revolution; Lenin's conclusion on that single point was identical. [167] Further research is needed, but provisionally the evidence suggests that: 1) the failure of the Moscow rising had a significant influence on the revolution as a whole, contributing to its defeat, 2) the Moscow rising was a failure because the troops, despite widespread unrest, did not mutiny, 3) the chance of large-scale mutinies of soldiers in Moscow would have been greater if revolutionary activities had been restricted to nonviolent ones not threatening the lives of the troops, and 4) had nonviolent discipline been more widespread and a nonviolent Moscow rising replaced the violent one, the tsarist system might have been destroyed in December 1905-January 1906. The popular view that violence in a resistance or revolutionary movement by definition adds to the power and chances of success of that movement can no longer be accepted.

SABOTAGE AND NONVIOLENT ACTION

Hostile conservative critics of nonviolent action sometimes argue that nonviolent struggle should be rejected because it is closely associated with sabotage or leads to sabotage. In contrast, others interested primarily in maximum effectiveness in struggle and who think themselves to be more realistic argue that sabotage should be used along with nonviolent action. Both views reveal an inadequate understanding of the nonviolent technique.

Sabotage, as used here, refers to acts of demolition and related destruction directed against machinery, transport, buildings, bridges, installations and the like. Because these are acts against *property,* they are not included in the definition of "violence" in this book. Such acts would, however, become "violence" if they bring injury or death to *persons,* or threaten to do so. Certain other types of action fall somewhere between sabotage and nonviolent action, such as removal of key parts from machinery and vehicles, removal or release in nondangerous ways of fuel for machinery and vehicles, removal of records and files for various government departments and offices (as police) and even their destruction by means which could not possibly cause physical injury to any persons. Such methods require separate consideration, and this discussion does not apply to them. Those methods are more likely to be compatible with nonviolent action, but are not always so in all situations. They, too, can be detrimental to effective nonviolent action under certain conditions.

Sabotage has on occasion followed nonviolent action, especially when the latter was not immediately effective, as in South Africa. Sabotage has also occurred during nonviolent resistance when there has been no decision to use only certain means of resistance, as in Norway during the Nazi occupation. Even there, however, much if not most of the sabotage was organized from England for Allied military purposes, not by resistance groups in Norway. Also, sabotage has on occasion been used during a consciously nonviolent struggle by persons and groups ignoring or defying the instructions of the leadership to eschew acts of demolition, as was the case in the *Ruhrkampf*. But sabotage has never, to my knowledge, been deliberately applied by a disciplined movement which has consciously chosen to fight by nonviolent action. Gandhi constantly emphasized that sabotage was contrary to this technique. [168] In terms of the principles, strategy and mechanisms of operation, sabotage is more closely related to violent than to nonviolent action. This is true even though the aim of the sabotage may be only the destruction of material objects without taking lives—such as an empty bridge as distinct from a bridge being crossed by enemy troops.

There are strong reasons why the introduction of sabotage will seriously weaken a nonviolent action movement. These are rooted in the differing dynamics and mechanisms of these two techniques. There are at least nine such reasons:

First, sabotage always runs the risk of unintentional physical injury or death to opponents or to innocent bystanders, as in attempts to destroy bridges, factories, etc. Nonviolent action, on the other hand, requires that its supporters refuse to use physical violence and instead protect the lives of opponents and others. Even limited injuries or deaths will rebound against the nonviolent movement.

Second, effective sabotage in difficult situations requires a willingness to use physical violence against persons who discover the plans and are willing and able either to reveal or to prevent them. These may be informers, guards, soldiers, or ordinary people. Nonviolent action, conversely, requires for success the strict maintenance of nonviolence.

Third, sabotage requires secrecy in the planning and carrying out of missions. As already discussed, secrecy introduces a whole series of disruptive influences. These include ultimate dependence on violence (instead of nonviolence), fear of discovery (in place of fearless open action), and wild suspicions among the opponents about the resisters' intent and plans which may increase brutalities and intransigence (in place of the usually openly announced intentions).

Fourth, sabotage requires only a few persons to carry it out and hence reduces the number of effective resisters, while nonviolent action makes possible a large degree of participation among the whole population.

Fifth, confidence in the adequacy of nonviolent action is a great aid to its successful application. The use of sabotage, however, demonstrates a lack of such confidence which is detrimental to effective use of nonviolent action.

Sixth, nonviolent action is based upon a challenge *in human terms* by human beings to other human beings. Sabotage relies on physical destruction of property, a very different approach likely to detract from the operation of the other, potentially more powerful, influences. [169]

Seventh, sabotage and nonviolent action are rooted in quite different premises about how to undermine the opponent. Nonviolent action produces withdrawal of consent by the subjects, while sabotage acts against the opponent by destroying property.

Eighth, where physical injury or death occurs to persons because of sabotage, whether accidental or deliberate, there is likely to be a relative loss of sympathy and support for the nonviolent group and/or an increase of sympathy and support for the opponent—the opposite of what is likely and necessary in nonviolent action.

Finally, therefore, sabotage is likely to result in highly disproportionate repression against the saboteurs or the general population, or both. [170] Contrary to the effects of repression against persistent nonviolent actionists, repression provoked by sabotage is not likely to weaken the opponent's relative power position.

That sabotage does not combine well with nonviolent action is amply illustrated by the 1923 Ruhr struggle. There is further evidence to support the view of Eyck quoted above that sabotage had detrimental effects. Not only were electricity and telegraph wires cut but also various objectives, such as railway lines, canal locks and barges, railway trestles and military trains carrying occupation troops were bombed. Ten Belgian soldiers were killed and forty wounded by the attack on the Rhine bridge near Duisburg. Other acts of violence included terrorist attacks against occupation soldiers, and suspected spies and traitors within the sabotage groups were sometimes murdered. [171] One reason for these developments was the Germans' lack of a plan for nonviolent resistance and their relative lack of effective leadership and organization. [172] Although sabotage and similar acts did harass the occupation officials, there is little indication that the acts were effective in limiting or reducing the occupiers' control or ability to achieve their objectives. However, sabotage had other effects, including extremely severe repression from the occupying forces who sometimes beat and killed people, including innocent bystanders. Also, the unity of the population of the occupied area—which had been achieved under the nonviolent resistance campaign—was destroyed. Repression included a widespread ban on road traffic which, according to Wentzcke, "heralded the end of passive resistance." Internationally, the moral isolation of France and the high degree of world sympathy which had been produced by the nonviolent resistance were not only erased, but to a significant degree reversed. [173]

For these reasons, the idea that sabotage is compatible with nonviolent action must be rejected, as either a false accusation of uninformed critics, or as a highly dangerous action proposal likely to disrupt the processes which could bring strength and victory.

OTHER WAYS TO SLIP INTO VIOLENCE

One reason why the most perceptive exponents and practitioners of nonviolent action have emphasized so strongly the firm and meticulous maintenance of nonviolent behavior is that without strict and conscious attention, the movement could easily slip into progressively greater reliance on violence without a prior conscious decision to do so. This may happen at a variety of points, a number of which are illustrated by instances in the American colonists' struggles. Their struggles probably provide the richest example of this type of development—from systematic and repeated noncooperation to a long war of independence.

Even while the colonists' struggle prior to April 1775 was overwhelmingly nonviolent, there were quite a few points at which actions were taken which were either themselves violent or which potentially set the stage for violence. Until Lexington and Concord, however, these did not expand sufficiently to alter the predominantly nonviolent character of the resistance. They are nevertheless instructive. During the opposition to the Stamp Act there was considerable use of personal and mob threats, physical intimidation, and destruction of personal and public property designed, for example, to induce newly appointed Stamp Distributors to resign their posts. [174] During the same period, there was a general tendency among undisciplined elements of the population to act in disregard of the recommended plans of those who had launched the campaign and had selected the means of action which were to be used. [175] Economic boycotts and nonuse of taxed imports lead to smuggling, and "smuggling proved to be the first channel through which violence was injected into the struggle." [176] Sometimes relatively insignificant behavior burst into violence, because "the high tension which public affairs had reached ripened the public mind for violence." [177] Some radicals, such as Thomas Mason, urged that a policy of disobedience to Parliament's laws be defended if necessary by "resort to armed resistance and secession . . ." [178] Sometimes delaying a decision or postponing action provided the necessary opportunity for advocates of violence to win the day. [179] The destruction of property rapidly escalated in seriousness, as from the dumping of tea in Boston harbor to the later burning of a tea-bearing vessel at Annapolis, Maryland. [180]

The exchanges of fire between British troops and colonial irregulars at Lexington and Concord were, as it happened, the actions which resulted in abandonment of a comprehensive plan of economic noncooperation before it had been fully applied and in its replacement by military means. The campaign of economic noncooperation embodied in the Continental Association had been signed by the members of the First Continental Congress on October 20, 1774. It was broadly divided into two phases, the nonimportation of British goods to begin from December 1, 1774, and the nonexportation of American goods to Britain to begin from September 10, 1775. [181] This remained the colonists' resistance strategy, even though tensions were sometimes high and though various groups were on their own initiative preparing for military conflict. In Massachusetts Bay the Provincial Congress took steps in February 1775 to prepare the militia and the "Minute Men" and to raise taxes to pay for weapons. [182] This was independent action taken outside the context of the Continental Association campaign of resistance adopted for all the colonies. Further preparations for military conflict were shortly taken by the Committee of Safety. When seven hundred British troops under orders to destroy the colonists' military supplies hidden at Concord met seventy-five Minute Men on the Lexington village green on April 19, there was an exchange of fire. This was probably initiated by an American who was not among the Minute Men; the latter fled, leaving dead and wounded on the green. Most of the Concord supplies were removed before the British arrived there, and the Minute Men with large reinforcements forced British troops to retreat under fire toward Boston. The Redcoats were continually fired upon by Americans hidden behind stones and trees, and only the arrival of British reinforcements made possible a fighting withdrawal to Charlestown, across the river from Boston. [183]

For the purposes of this study, the significance of these events is the effect that they had on the entire course of the American struggle. The large-scale preparations for military conflict in Massachusetts Bay were undertaken on the initiative of Massachusetts radicals only, and outside of the resistance measures outlined in the Continental Association. These had not even mentioned military resistance, neither to commend it, threaten it, nor to discourage it, except by implication in the statement that nonimportation, nonconsumption and nonexportation measures "faithfully adhered to, will prove the most speedy, effectual and peaceable measures . . ." [184]

Once military preparations against the British had begun in Massachusetts Bay it was to be expected that, short of immediate evacuation, the British would have to take counteraction. The British action was intended to be a. very limited one, to destroy supplies of American arms hidden at Concord, the exact location of which they knew from an informer. However, once each side had taken these steps the chances of avoiding an exchange of fire were few. (If the Concord supplies had all been moved, as most of them were, and hidden elsewhere and the Americans had themselves remained out of sight the British troops would have had to return to Boston without having accomplished their mission but also without military hostilities.) The consequence of general military preparations in *one* colony and the unplanned shift to military struggle on April 19 extended to all the colonies and altered the whole approach to the conduct of the conflict.

It is arguable that the American colonists could have won full independence more quickly, with more support within the colonies and from Englishmen, had they continued to rely upon the nonviolent methods of struggle they had so successfully used to that date. *De facto* British control in the colonies was already extraordinarily weak, owing to the Americans' political noncooperation, economic sanctions and development of alternative political institutions to which they gave loyalty. Governor Dunmore of Virginia wrote to Lord Dartmouth on December 24, 1774, that the Continental Association was being enforced there "with greatest rigour," that the "Laws of Congress" (the Continental Congress) received from Virginians "marks of reverence they never bestowed on their legal Government, or the Laws preceding from it." He added:

I have discovered no instance where the interposition of Government, in the feeble state to which it is reduced, could serve any other purpose than to suffer the disgrace of a disappointment, and thereby afford matter of great exultation to its enemies and increase their influence over the minds of the people.[185]

In South Carolina the British Government was so weak compared to the Continental Association that "ministerial opposition is here obliged to be silent," as the General Committee wrote at the time.[186] The Governor of Massachusetts Bay in early 1774 was already of the opinion that "All legislative, as well as executive power was gone . . . ."[187] Governor Gage made a similar report from there in September 1774, and by the end of October he had virtually no power except that of his troops.[188] By October 1774, the legal government in Maryland had virtually abdicated.[189] There are also other indications.[190]

By mid-April the nonimportation and nonconsumption phase of the Continental Association resistance plan had only been in operation about four-and-a-half months, and the more extreme nonexportation phase was not due to come into operation for almost another five months. The introduction of the unplanned but obviously significant violence of the Massachusetts Bay Minute Men in the colonists' struggle created a situation in which imitation of their action seemed natural, and a large-scale extension of military preparations and action seemed to be required—"seemed" is used since there was apparently no careful evaluation of the relative advantages of a major shift to military struggle as compared with an attempt to isolate the Lexington-Concord events and to continue to rely upon the established strategy of political and economic noncooperation along with a further development of parallel governmental institutions. One immediate result was confusion, as Robert R. Livingston put it during the Second Continental Congress, which opened on May 10, 1775: "We are between hawk and buzzard; we puzzle ourselves between the commercial and warlike opposition."[191] The uncertainty did not last long, however. Schlesinger summarized the change which took place:

> The tocsin of war, sounded on the historic April day at Lexington and Concord, wrought a radical change in the nature of the opposition directed by the Americans against the British measures. This did not mean that a struggle for independence had begun, but it did mean that armed rebellion had superseded commercial coercion as the dependence of the radicals in their struggle for larger liberties. Thereafter the Continental Association lost its distinctive character as a method of peaceful coercion; it became subordinated to the military necessities of the times.

The transformation which the Association was undergoing revealed itself in five ways: in the widespread adoption of defense associations; in the determination of the Georgian moderates to adopt the Continental Association as a deterrent to the more violent methods advocated by the radicals there; in the spontaneous action of the extra-legal bodies in the several provinces in taking on disciplinary and military functions; in the adoption, by provinces exposed to the perils of war, of non-exportation regulations prior to the time fixed in the Association; and in the important alterations made in the text of the original Association by the Second Continental Congress. [192]

This Second Congress regarded the Lexington events as a declaration of war, began to act like a government, and took direction of the rebellion. In June, 1775, already, George Washington was appointed Commander-in-Chief of the army of the United Colonies, and regulations were announced for the army and navy. On July 6 a declaration was issued which in effect said that the British use of military force required the colonists to change their means of struggle and to reply with military means also. [193]

THE NECESSITY OF DISCIPLINE

If the nonviolent struggle movement is to persist in face of repression, to remain nonviolent, and to carry through the campaign, discipline among the nonviolent actionists is required. Basically, this discipline consists of adherence to certain minimum standards of behavior. The degree and type of discipline required will vary depending on the situation and the nature of the nonviolent group and of the opponent. The absence of discipline will mean that effective use of this technique will become very difficult or impossible. This emphasis on discipline is not, as some might think, associated only with Gandhian nonviolence. The need for it was emphasized by the Danish exponent of nonviolent action, Nils Lindberg, before World War II on the basis of other considerations, [194] and very un-Gandhian East Germans called for discipline in the course of resistance during the rising of June 1953. [195] Although Gandhi antedates these instances, their emphasis on discipline is derived from other sources.

Discipline may be encouraged by leaders through instructions, appeals, pledges, as well as by discipline leaflets, marshals and other means, as discussed below, and, as we have already seen, various nonviolent sanctions may be applied in support of group decisions and discipline. However, in nonviolent action discipline cannot be imposed or forced upon the participants by the leaders; various means of encouraging discipline will be effective only to the degree that they influence or strengthen the will or conscience of the actionists. Despite important measures to promote and maintain discipline, including nonviolent sanctions, by the nature of the technique discipline in nonviolent action must be essentially the self-discipline of the participants.

Discipline in nonviolent action is, therefore, self-discipline and inner discipline. This is true whether the discipline has been promoted by the active leaders of the movement, or has been continued after all distinguishable leaders have been imprisoned, or has been developed intuitively in a spontaneous movement. But there are a variety of ways used to promote nonviolent discipline and there is room for comparative evaluation and choice among these alternative ways. But there must be some type of discipline. Those who out of ignorance or emotional reaction to discipline would ignore or abolish it in nonviolent action place the entire struggle in a perilous position. If their views predominate, effective nonviolent action becomes impossible. It is not necessary to agree with everything Gandhi said on the subject to appreciate his general assessment:

> Freedom of four hundred million people through purely non-violent effort is not to be gained without learning the virtue of iron discipline —not imposed from without, but sprung naturally from within. Without the requisite discipline, non-violence can only be a veneer. [196]

Continued participation in the struggle and refusal to submit to fear are the most crucial aims of discipline. After this, adherence to nonviolent behavior is the most important single aspect of discipline in this technique. Discipline serves other functions also, including increasing the actionists' ability to withstand severe repression. "A group of people who are acting under discipline are less likely to crack under pressure," argues Bradford Lyttle. Just as discipline helps military troops to continue to confront the enemy despite danger, discipline helps nonviolent actionists: "disciplined demonstrators can better resist charge by the police or attack by counter-demonstrators." Discipline, Lyttle writes, will help nonviolent demonstrators to remain calm and firm, and to react effectively in unexpected situations. [197]

Where discipline is weak or absent, there is danger that a nonviolent demonstration may, in a tense situation, lead to a major riot which would most likely both shift attention from the original grievance and also alienate support. Four days of riots in Negro areas of New York City in July

1964 were triggered in this way. On the evening of July 18, a rally was held by several city chapters of the Congress of Racial Equality (C.O.R.E.) to demand a civilian review board to examine cases of alleged police brutality and the removal of the police commissioner. The rally was held two days after an off-duty policeman had shot to death a youth who had attacked him in Harlem. About a hundred people were led by C.O.R.E. organizers to a Harlem police precinct station where they presented their demands. They then sat down in the street, announcing they would stay until at least some of the demands were met. When police tried to push some of the crowd back, several scuffles took place, but the organizers generally maintained control. They were, however, arrested, dragged into the police station, and, some reported, beaten. Its nonviolent leadership removed, the crowd began throwing bricks and bottles at the police, who charged into the crowd. Later a flaming bottle of gasoline was thrown at a police car, police fired at rioters, looting took place, and such activities continued during the night. In Harlem and the Negro ghetto of Bedford-Stuyvesant in Brooklyn similar violence took place, largely between Negro youths and white police, for the next four nights. [198] Had the experienced C.O.R.E. organizers not been arrested, or had the remaining sit-downers maintained discipline, the rioting would probably not have happened, and attention would have remained focused not on Negro rioting, but on charges of police brutality and demands for a civilian control board.

In addition to maintaining nonviolent behavior in organized planned demonstrations, discipline includes adherence to the plans and instructions for the action. If prospective nonviolent actionists do not have confidence in the judgment of those responsible for planning the nonviolent action, then they ought not to take part. If they do have confidence, then the plans and instructions ought to be carried out precisely.

Where advance planning is possible, it should be in the hands of those persons most qualified for the job on the basis of their knowledge of the technique, understanding of the situation and experience. Other important qualities include ability to express themselves and to get along well with others. Persons who accept the planners' recommendations, and therefore wish to participate in the action or campaign, should then have the humility to follow the recommended strategy and course of action. Almost always action should be limited to the forms prescribed for the particular conflict. Not everyone is equally capable of intelligent planning for group or mass nonviolent action, any more than everyone is equally capable of doing anything else. While knowledge of the dynamics, methods and strategy of this technique remains restricted, there are likely to be fewer capable planners. But when such knowledge increases and spreads, more and more persons will become capable of participating in formulation of wise plans for nonviolent struggle. It is either arrogance or deliberate disruption intended to help the opponent which causes a person to join a nonviolent group and then ignore the prepared plans for the struggle, insisting on doing whatever he or she pleases. To the degree possible, leaders should take participants into their confidence and explain to them the reasons for the choice of the given strategy and plans for action, along with discussion of anticipated difficulties and recommended ways of dealing with them. [199]

Well formulated plans take into consideration the best means for achieving maximum impact, given the numbers, strengths and qualities of the nonviolent actionists, the nature of the opponent, the issues, the conflict situation, and the requirements of this technique. If then some participants take other unplanned types of action, while claiming to be part of the planned action, the effectiveness of the whole operation may in serious instances be jeopardized unless the rest of the nonviolent group is able to isolate or to counterbalance the innovations. Undisciplined activities are likely to give the effect of disunity and dissension. As a result other participants may be placed in a situation for which they are not prepared, represented as supporting actions with which they do not agree, or confronted with unanticipated repression by police or troops responding to the unexpected.

Of course, in a given instance, the unplanned innovations may seem to do little harm, or even be beneficial. However, they intrinsically involve dangers. For example, unplanned types of action, or demonstrating at other places than those selected can greatly facilitate the outbreak of counterproductive violence among the grievance group and the application of effective repression by the opponent. Sometimes indiscipline and internal chaos may be promoted by well intentioned but confused people. At other times, they may be emotionally disturbed. On still other occasions, they may be undercover agents for the police or a hostile political organization. Small or large groups of bystanders—whether friendly or hostile—may also present special discipline problems requiring different types of control measures. [200]

Political groups with strong viewpoints, clear policy, internal discipline and ambitions far beyond the immediate demands of the struggle may also seek to "use" the conflict situation to their own advantage, even though promotion of their political advantage may require weakening of the nonviolent struggle and harming its cause, verbal pronouncements notwithstanding. Sometimes such political groups will promote indiscipline themselves and at other times they may try to capitalize on disruption and confusion introduced by others. Groups which have a strong doctrinal belief in the necessity of political violence, such as the Communists, are especially risky potential collaborators. Even when they do not seek to enter the nonviolent opposition movement their behavior may be disruptive. At the beginning of the general strike against the Kapp *Putsch* in Germany in 1920, the Communists refused to support it and thereby refused to act against the attempted military-monarchist seizure of power because they did not wish to help a capitalist republic. Later they supported the strike, but after the collapse of the *coup* the Communists tried to capitalize on the internal crisis by organizing violent rebellion in the Ruhr and by attempting their own *coup* in Sachsen. [201] Communists and their supporters in South Africa who used and supported nonviolent action at certain stages were prominent among those who later denounced nonviolent methods as having "failed" without offering comparative strategic analyses of the problems, advantages and disadvantages of various types of both nonviolent and violent struggle in the situation. The South African Communists' abandonment of nonviolent means could have been, and indeed was, predicted. [202]

Discipline is especially important when there is special danger that violence may break out and when participants lack experience and deep understanding of nonviolent technique. In addition to the multitude of statements by Gandhi on the importance of the volunteers' carrying out instructions, and obeying the rules and resolutions of their own group, [203] various Western groups have also stressed discipline. Peace action groups have often been especially articulate on this point. The 1962 discipline of New York City peace groups, for example, included this pledge:

We will adhere to the planned program of action for each demonstration, unless a change of plan is communicated to us by the demonstration's sponsors or by their representatives. We will not initiate any unannounced action, unless it has been explicitly approved by the sponsors.

We recognize that conducting an orderly demonstration depends upon mutual cooperation and respect between participants and those who have organized and are responsible for the demonstration. (If requests are made for action which you feel are unwise, you will have an opportunity to discuss your complaint fully with the responsible persons after the demonstration, if it is not possible at the time.) If a request is made which you cannot accept, please quietly disassociate yourself from the demonstration. [204]

The nonviolent group's standards for behavior of participants may cover not only the direct action stage, but also the period of imprisonment following arrests.[205]

Exponents of discipline in nonviolent action have argued that a disciplined movement (as compared to an undisciplined one) is more likely to win the respect of third parties and of the opponent,[206] achieve a greater recognition of the seriousness of purpose involved, be more inspiring and produce a greater impact.[207] Such discipline, Gregg argued, also contributes to inner growth and inner strengthening of individual participants.[208] It will also help to maintain social order even in the midst of major struggle and sharp political conflict. Though not easy, nonviolent discipline is quite within the capacities of the vast majority of people; Gregg argued that discipline in nonviolent action, once understood, is not necessarily more difficult than the quite different type of discipline which is often achieved among soldiers in war situations.[209]

PROMOTING NONVIOLENT DISCIPLINE

In some cases participants may intuitively, or by common accord, adhere to nonviolent discipline without formal efforts to promote it. Strong support for the objectives and general acceptance of nonviolent action as the means to achieve them may be sufficient to ensure the necessary degree of nonviolent discipline in the particular situation. This may be especially true if the participants are experienced in the use of nonviolent technique, if opposition is not strong, if the factors likely to produce violence are minimal, and if the actionists have a strong religious or moral preference for nonviolent means.

However, since the dangers to the movement of indisciplined action and of an outbreak of violence are so serious, one should not passively stand by and hope for the best even when such favorable conditions are present. A movement *may* come through safely, but every effort needs to be made to avoid those threats to success. Furthermore in the larger number of cases without those favorable conditions, stronger efforts still are needed to maintain nonviolent discipline. Some persons with anti-authoritarian personalities or *some* philosophical anarchists react very negatively to any type of discipline. To allow emotional reactions or inadequately considered philosophical generalizations to block efforts to promote nonviolent discipline is most unwise and irrational. There is nothing "wrong" with nonviolent discipline; it is necessary because it "helps prevent actions or reactions which bring disunity or disorder or which work against the objectives of the action [and] provides a way by which a group of people can do corporately what they wish to do," as Charles C. Walker has pointed out.[210]

Nonviolent discipline also frequently includes willingness to carry out humble and undramatic tasks, as well as the more visible and daring ones from which a greater personal sense of importance, recognition, or honor may result. Nonviolent actionists also need to be willing to try to improve their abilities and skills so as to be able to act with greater effectiveness. Dignified, calm behavior may frequently be a part of nonviolent discipline.[211] All this does not in any way imply submissiveness or cringing before the opponent and his police or troops; behavior will be polite but firm. Nonviolent actionists will treat the opponent and his agents as human beings, but the actionists will not be bullied.[212]

It follows from the need for nonviolent discipline that those persons or groups unwilling or unable to abide by it must be asked not to take part. They will help most by remaining outside the movement or withdrawing from it until they feel able to act in accordance with the required standards of behavior.[213] The maintenance of high standards for participants may initially reduce the numbers of nonviolent actionists. However, in the long run both larger numbers of participants and success in the struggle depend on maintaining the quality of the movement, as has already been pointed out. Reducing nonviolent discipline in order to bring in larger numbers will have serious detrimental effects on the movement. Gandhi argued, for example, that the lowering of the standards for volunteers late in the 1930–31 struggle seriously weakened the movement and led to *goondaism* (rioting or violent disorder) in some places.[214]

Persons not familiar with the past practice of nonviolent action are often highly skeptical that nonviolent discipline can be achieved on a group or mass basis. The assumption that only individuals are capable of disciplined nonviolent action is a denial of the facts. It is widely acknowledged that with group encouragement and support many individuals commit acts of violence which they never would commit, acting alone. Group encouragement and support help achieve a similar, but reverse, change in behavior in the case of nonviolent action. Individuals who are not pacifists, and who if attacked individually would reply with counter-violence, have with group encouragement, support and pressures successfully maintained nonviolent discipline even when physically attacked. This happens when the nonpacifist participant is able to see that nonviolent discipline and nonretaliatory persistence are necessary to advance the group's goals which which he shares.[215] There are cases of such group discipline even when advance instructions and training in nonviolent conflict behavior were minimal or absent.[216]

Nonviolent action almost always occurs in a situation of conflict and tension: it generally heightens such conditions rather than reduces them. Given that fact, it requires some skill to prevent violence and to maintain discipline. But it is possible to do this because not all conflict is violent and because tension and aggression can be released in disciplined nonviolent ways. Sometimes—but not always—in situations where the atmosphere strongly favors violence, or where violence has already broken out, nonviolent leaders have judged it best not to start a nonviolent campaign at that point, or to call off a current campaign, until a more propitious moment. For example, Gandhi suspended the campaign against the Rowlatt Bills in 1919 because of the outbreak of violence.[217] In the summer of 1939 Gandhi rejected suggestions that he organize mass nonviolent struggle, arguing:

. . . the atmosphere is surcharged with violence . . . nonviolent mass movement is an impossibility unless the atmosphere is radically changed . . . If any mass movement is undertaken at the present moment in the name of nonviolence, it will resolve itself into violence largely unorganized and organized in some cases. It will bring discredit on the Congress, spell disaster for the Congress struggle for independence and bring ruin to many a home.[218]

Ruling out mass nonviolent struggle did not, however, necessarily rule out all nonviolent action, as Gandhi had pointed out two weeks earlier: ". . . some active form of Satyagraha, not necessarily civil disobedience, must be available in order to end an impossible situation . . . There must be either effective nonviolent action or violence and anarchy within a measurable distance of time."[219]

Other methods may be used in advance to prevent the creation of an explosive situation. In 1769 during the nonimportation campaign to achieve repeal of the Townshend duties, the decision of Philadelphia merchants to refuse to allow any English goods not ordered before February 6, 1769 to be landed from the ships had this effect. As the goods were returned to England directly, there was no occasion for acts of violence against anyone for possession, use or attempt to sell the prohibited goods, nor for attempts to destroy the goods. It is uncertain whether this calming result was the intended consequence of banning the landing of boycotted goods, but it happened. Schlesinger concluded that in Philadelphia in 1769-70 ". . . the enforcement of nonimportation was free from all exhibitions of mob violence, largely because goods violative of the agreement were immediately re-shipped to Great Britain.'' [220] This prevention of provocative situations may contribute to nonviolent discipline.

Whenever two hostile crowds have gathered and may meet, the situation is ripe for violence. For example, in New York City on July 7, 1770, during that same campaign, crowds for and against the nonimportation policy encountered each other in Wall Street, "where stiff blows were exchanged with cane and club and the nonimporters finally dispersed." [221] Where opposing groups are likely to gather, or have already done so, nonviolent strategists seeking to maintain peaceful discipline will need to take counter measures. If the hostile group attacks, the nonviolent actionist will need strong self-discipline in order to prevent both a rout and violence. If the leaders wish to avoid a physical encounter, possible lines of action include movement of the nonviolent group away from the violent demonstrators, dispersal, or a switch to some other type of individual or small group nonviolent action. If the possible physical attack by the mob is to be confronted directly, the nonviolent leadership will need to be sure that the actionists will be capable of maintaining both discipline and nonviolence if the conflict is not to degenerate into flight or riot. Sometimes various novel acts may be applied at such a point, including singing religious or patriotic hymns, kneeling in prayer, and sitting down.

In many situations where conflict and tension are widespread the launching of militant nonviolent action may be regarded as a necessary step to prevent the outbreak of violence. Such action is aimed at providing alternative effective means for conducting the conflict and simultaneously releasing feelings of aggression and hostility which have accumulated within the grievance group. Militant nonviolent action may often be risky, but it may be the only alternative to passive submission on the one hand and allowing the forces of violence to gain the upper hand on the other. A decision to launch militant nonviolent action to prevent violence may be made when there is high tension but as yet no open conflict (either violent or nonviolent), or in a tense situation once the nonviolent struggle has begun.

It has been recognized for a long time that certain nonviolent activities may defuse potential violence. For example, in 1765, after Newport, Rhode Island, had already experienced one riot, another threatened as the tense local situation combined with the approach of November 1, when the hated Stamp Act was to go into effect. The result might have been a politically counterproductive explosion. Then, on that date, ". . . in order to forestall any possible riot, the Sons of Liberty attempted to divert popular feeling into an orderly demonstration, by staging a 'grand Funeral of Freedom'," as described in detail in Chapter Three. Many decades later, on a vastly larger scale, Gandhi sought to provide nonviolent means of struggle which would simultaneously be effective for achieving political ends and also would prevent political violence. While there were growing terrorist groups, Gandhi showed the effectiveness of nonviolent struggle and got the Indian National Congress—the nationalist party—to adopt it for achieving independence. Jawaharlal Nehru, who had been an advocate of violent revolution and who never became a believer in nonviolent doctrine, was among those who accepted the nonviolent technique for practical reasons.[222] Later, while the struggle continued, he wrote:

Terrorists have flourished in India, off and on, for nearly thirty years . . . terrorism, in spite of occasional recrudescence, has no longer any real appeal for the youth of India. Fifteen years' stress on nonviolence has changed the whole background in India and made the masses much more indifferent to, and even hostile to, the idea of terrorism as a method of political action. Even the classes from which the terrorists are usually drawn, the lower middle classes and intelligentsia, have been powerfully affected by the Congress propaganda against methods of violence. Their active and impatient elements, who think in terms of revolutionary action, also realize fully now that revolution does not come through terrorism, and that terrorism is an outworn and profitless method that comes in the way of real revolutionary action.[223]

James Farmer has strongly supported this analysis: ". . . rather than leading to riots, demonstrations tend to prevent them by providing an alternative outlet for frustration." Farmer then supported his view with evidence from New York City and Chicago. In the summer of 1963, in New York, for example, he maintained, "anger and frustration were just as high as they were to be in the riotous summer of 1964." However, in 1963 there were "hundreds of mass demonstrations" against discrimination in the building trades. Many unemployed youths who would otherwise have prowled the streets aimlessly, joined in the demonstrations. They picketed, climbed cranes, and blocked the bulldozers. Furthermore, these youths remained nonviolent. "They did not have to resort to throwing bottles and bricks, and they didn't." In the summer of 1964, however, there were few demonstrations, and there were riots.

Farmer denied a simple cause-and-effect relationship between organized nonviolent protest and avoidance of riots, ". . . but certainly there is some relationship. We have seen it countless times, in the South as well as the North." During the riots of 1964 Farmer walked the streets of Harlem and reported: "I saw more clearly than I have ever before how young men who feel that nothing is being done about grievances so deep they can barely articulate them, will finally spring to violence." He added: "I firmly believe that if Harlemites had been better trained in legitimate mass demonstrations (demonstrating *is* doing something)—and if the police had not acted so unwisely—the Harlem riots [of July 1964] could have been averted." As a general conclusion, Farmer continued: "One way to avert riots is to satisfy people that they can do something—not promise that things will be done, but satisfy them that *they can do something* without turning to self-defeating violence. One thing they can do is demonstrate." (Italics added). This was exactly what happened in the summer of 1965, and the riots which had been predicted did not occur.

Just as labor movement violence has been replaced by legitimizing strikes and other mass labor demonstrations, so racial violence can be replaced by ". . . legitimizing the techniques of mass action developed by the civil rights groups. It seems to me obvious that without demonstrations we will learn what violence and chaos really are. To inhibit mass demonstrations is madness." Of course, Farmer continued, where the only possible result of a demonstration is immediate mob violence it should not be held, but that certainly does not mean abandonment of "all but the most polite demonstrations of protest." Instead, he concluded, ". . . if demonstrations are in danger of courting violence, the remedy is not to stop demonstrating but to perfect our ability to control the more undisciplined participants and to spread our teaching." Farmer also points to the desirability of countering ill-advised demonstrations by the development and use of tactically sounder ones, rather than leaving people with the choice of doing nothing or participating in an unwise action. [224]

This discussion is not to imply that *any* form of nonviolent action can channel aggression and group hostilities away from violence. That obviously is not true, and careful consideration needs to be given to the selection of the precise ways most suitable for the particular situation. The remainder of this section is a survey of the types of efforts to maintain nonviolent discipline that have been used in the past. High morale is important in achieving and preserving nonviolent discipline. Walker emphasizes that high morale requires that participants believe they are members of a group which cares about them as individuals, which gives them the opportunity for creativity, active participation, overcoming obstacles and working together loyally with others who share their outlook and purposes.[225] Mass meetings may be held periodically—daily, weekly, or at some other interval—for the purpose of building morale, as well as increasing understanding of the nonviolent technique and disseminating information; mass meetings have been used in support of nonviolent action in the South, as during student sit-ins, and during the Montgomery bus boycott.[226]

The hope of achieving victory will often help maintain nonviolent discipline, especially among the less reliable elements, and may also help hold together the existing coalition of diverse groups behind the struggle. This was the case during the early stages of the 1905 revolution in Russia: ". . . as long as the possibility of peaceful political change remained in sight . . . the weakly united front of liberals and socialists continued." [227] When this united front dissolved and workers turned toward the more pro-violent socialists it was ". . . not so much because of the socialists' ideology as because of their vigorous tactics—which now seemed to many the only means of influencing events and achieving new victories." [228]

Morale will often be increased, also, by feelings among the actionists that some significant source of strength not available to their opponent is supporting them. In some cases these feelings may arise in part from a sense of the power of the technique of action they are using, or the justice of their cause, or the inevitability of their victory. In some cases, such feeling may be rooted in a belief that they have powerful friends whose influence and capacity may finally help to defeat their opponent. Norwegian participants in nonviolent struggle against Quisling's regime and the Nazi occupation frequently point to the importance to their morale of their belief that the Allies were waging a powerful military struggle against the Nazis; civil rights workers using nonviolent action in the Deep South gained inner strength not only from the rightness of their cause and the moral superiority of their methods, but also from ". . . an intimate sense of identification with public opinion and with the movement of the Federal Government—however slow. He [the civil rights worker] is isolated only from the immediate antagonistic community." [229] During the 1920 Kapp *Putsch,* Dr. Kapp and part of the army had to confront a determined population inspired by awareness that they were defending the Republic at the request of the constitutional government. As a result, "an inspired purposefulness reigned in the camp of Dr. Kapp's enemies." [230]

Where the nonviolent actionists are a distinct minority and also do not have access to these sources of feelings of strength, they will need to take compensating measures to support high morale. Such measures should not be simply gimmicks and should be able to survive crises. In any case, it would be dangerous and overly optimistic simply to count on high morale to achieve and maintain nonviolent discipline. There are other ways to promote this.

One of these is that active participants in the struggle, sympathizers and the general population understand well *why* the campaign needs to be kept strictly nonviolent. Such understanding has not always been achieved to a significant degree; instead, a few inadequate generalizations about nonviolence being "better" or "more moral" have often been regarded as sufficient. Fuller and politically more adequate explanation of the need for nonviolent discipline might be more effective both in avoiding scattered violence during the campaign and a later major switch to violence. The groups most likely to advocate or initiate violence are precisely those likely to be least influenced by vague generalizations and moral exhortations to be nonviolent.

As understanding of the reasons for the importance of nonviolent behavior for the operation of the technique spreads, it will be more and more difficult to provoke violence. Also, the chances are increased that if the opponent attempts to do precisely that, his efforts will be publicly exposed. Under this new discipline, violence against the opponent becomes "as traitorous to the cause as desertion is in the army."

> Once that understanding, attitude and discipline are attained among the group of nonviolent resisters, any *agent provocateur* who comes whispering among them or preaching violence, retaliation or revenge will be immediately known for what he is and repudiated. And the group will soon prove its tactics so clearly to the public that the latter will not be deceived by the act of an *agent provocateur* bomb thrower or inflammatory speaker.[231]

The need for outward discipline is thus likely to be reduced as the volunteers gain confidence in the adequacy of nonviolent action to further their cause.[232]

Good organization, wise leadership, carefully laid and intelligently formulated plans and effective means of communication within the movement will contribute significantly to the achievement and maintenance of nonviolent discipline. Conversely, the absence of these will greatly facilitate both indiscipline and violence. "Karl Ehrlich" (pseud. for Karl Raloff) attributed the development of terrorism during the *Ruhrkampf* to the absence of German plans for nonviolent resistance, and the relative absence of leadership and organization for the struggle.[233]

Organization, leadership, plans and communication involve attention to a considerable variety of particular problems and tasks. Strategy, tactics and methods always need to be carefully chosen, but when the atmosphere is especially conducive to violence special care in their choice and formulation will be needed. In some cases methods which rely on the high-quality action of a few people may be more appropriate than those that rely on large numbers of less disciplined participants.[234] For particularly difficult tasks the person or group to carry them out needs to be carefully selected on the basis of reliability and other qualifications, especially when the task is dangerous, or extremely important, as in starting the struggle,[235] or in shifting its direction at a critical point.

The degree to which regular participants in the action should be selected from among the volunteers, or that selection is possible, will differ from one conflict to another. So, too, will the degree and type of advance training of general participants differ. Detailed discussion of methods for training of both general participants and specialist personnel lies outside the scope of this study. Study groups, workshops, seminars and socio-drama have been used widely in the United States by civil rights groups.[236] Such methods, however, obviously only scratch the surface of the possibilities. Consideration of the purposes, levels and means of training large numbers of people or the whole population is essential.

Organizers, leaders and sometimes ordinary participants have used speeches, messages and on-the-spot pleas in efforts to prevent violence and maintain discipline. Initial calls for action and statements by leaders and spokesmen for the grievance group before or at the beginning of the struggle, often emphasize the nonviolent and disciplined nature of the coming action, with the intent of influencing the course of the movement and the behavior of possible participants. Such statements were made, for example, in South Vietnam at the start of the 1963 Buddhist anti-Diem struggle. The conflict began after shootings into crowds of Buddhists in Hué as they objected to restrictions on their religious freedom. The next day (May 9) a Buddhist leader, Thich Tan Chau, wrote a letter addressed to all monks, nuns, and other Buddhists in Vietnam asking support to ". . . protect our just religion in an orderly, peaceful, nonviolent manner." The following day the manifesto of demands to be the basis of the coming struggle, presented in Hué, declared that Buddhists "will use nonviolent methods of struggle."[237] Verbal pleas for nonviolent disciplined behavior, as many persons may expect, were often made by Gandhi,[238] by King,[239] and by leaders of the 1952 Defiance Campaign in South Africa.[240] Such calls have also been made in situations where they might be less expected. It is not so widely known that the manifesto issued by the Pan Africanist

Congress of South Africa before its 1960 campaign against the Pass Laws called for "absolute nonviolence." After several hours of intimidation of the orderly and disciplined seven thousand demonstrators at Sharpeville on March 21, some Africans broke discipline and began throwing stones at the police. (It was only at that point the police without warning began firing into the crowd with the deadly results that are so well known.) The Pan Africanists continued to seek nonviolent discipline, however, Philip Kgosana was notably successful in achieving this with very large demonstrations; on March 30 he led a disciplined peaceful thirty thousand Africans marching thirty abreast through Capetown. (He was later arrested as he led a deputation, when police broke their promise that the deputation would be received by officials. [241]

There were numerous verbal attempts to maintain nonviolent discipline during the 1953 East German Rising. It was repeatedly emphasized that this was a struggle against the East German Communist regime and that all possible steps should be taken not to provoke the Russians. For example, a speaker at a mass meeting of sixty thousand in Halle ". . . asked the crowd to observe strict discipline warning against panic buying, looting and violence—the Red Army, he told them earnestly, must be given no excuse to intervene." [242] It was a similar story in Goerlitz: "At no time had the demonstrators become involved with the occupation troops. Speaker after speaker had warned against provoking the Red Army into taking action and no one had contradicted them." [243] The leader of the insurgents at East Germany's largest chemical plant (the *Leunawerke* near Leipzig), Friedrich Schorn declared: "Everything is at stake. But violence isn't the answer . . . Let's keep order." When factory guards turned over their weapons, Schorn ordered them locked in a storeroom, instead of being used in the rising. When the plant's workers marched to Merseburg for a mass meeting, Schorn again urged the crowd to remain calm, even as Soviet troops advanced on the square where the meeting was being held. When some demonstrators began shouting and spitting at the Russians, signs of possible serious violence in that situation, Schorn after consultations with others urged the strikers to return to their respective factories but not to begin work. "They formed columns and marched off in perfect discipline." [244]

Sometimes more active intervention has been used to halt acts of violence or acts which might lead to serious violence even though they might in themselves not be very serious. For example, on one occasion after an initial clash between police and strikers outside the House of Ministries, in East Berlin, June 17, 1953, a few of the demonstrators tried to prevent others from throwing stones at the police.[245] Night patrols have also been used. In Newport, Rhode Island, on November 1, 1765, for example, as the Stamp Act went into force "the Sons of Liberty endeavored to maintain popular feeling against the Stamp Act without touching off another riot"; after the substitute nonviolent demonstration (in the form of a mock funeral described above) they also took other measures. "In the evening a number of persons patrolled the streets to prevent the gathering of a mob, and the night passed quietly."[246]

Effective organization and communication in the nonviolent group will contribute significantly to achieving and maintaining nonviolent discipline. Certain measures for organization and communication which appear to be directed solely to relations with the opponent or the press, for example, the selection of a spokesman to issue statements, answer questions and speak for the demonstrators during the confrontation[247] also are likely to promote group discipline.

Highly important in promoting nonviolent discipline will be ". . . clear lines of command and communication, and . . . a clear understanding by the participants of what they are to do in a variety of circumstances."[248] One of the most effective means of promoting nonviolent discipline in large scale nonviolent action demonstrations has been detailed instruction and discipline leaflets. Sometimes the detailed instructions for the particular action are combined with the general instructions about how to behave in crises, and sometimes they have been separate leaflets. Clear, simple explanations of the plans, of the nonviolent discipline, and of the reasons for them, combined with recommendations on how the actionist is expected to behave in various specific situations, may help remove much of the uncertainty and potential to violence. Where violence nevertheless breaks out, these detailed instructions may help prevent the nonviolent actionists from being blamed for the violence. Such instruction and discipline leaflets sometimes include brief explanations of why a particular course of action is recommended or rejected.

"Marshals" for demonstrations have also been used to help keep a given action nonviolent and disciplined. These marshals are usually especially experienced, able to remain calm and confident, and well versed in an understanding of the technique. The marshals receive special briefings on the plans and problems expected. They may be assigned to particular small groups of actionists, so that reliable persons who are able to set an example, offer advice and instructions, and relay detailed plans and lines for action to those near them are spread throughout a large demonstration. In the South African struggles in the early 1900s violence would sometimes have broken out but for the "most vigilant supervision," reports Gandhi. [249] In Britain the Direct Action Committee Against Nuclear War, the Campaign for Nuclear Disarmament, and the Committee of 100 all made extensive use of marshals to keep the demonstrations orderly and peaceful. On the Aldermaston marches, such marshals even assisted in directing traffic, relieving the police of some of their normal duties. These marshals played an extremely important role in promoting nonviolent discipline among large numbers of people who may have been new to both demonstrations and nonviolent action. As an extremely effective means to maintain nonviolent discipline, the use of marshals is likely to be adopted and refined increasingly by practitioners of nonviolent action. Marshals have also been used widely in the United States, especially for massive anti-Vietnam-War demonstrations in Washington, D.C. Agitation against marshals—they have been called "peace pigs"—may have various motives, some for destroying the movement, as may other pressures against nonviolent discipline discussed above. In the absence of extraordinary self-discipline and experience, however, efforts to undermine the moral authority and effectiveness of marshals can only benefit the opponent by increasing the chances of violence.

Organizers of nonviolent action have sometimes sought to promote nonviolent discipline by asking volunteers to promise, or to sign a pledge in advance, to adhere to a certain code of behavior. "Success depends entirely upon disciplined and concerted non-cooperation and the latter is dependent upon strict obedience to instructions, calmness and absolute freedom from violence," declared a statement issued in India by the Noncooperation Committee for public information and guidance in 1920. [250] There have been two types of these written standards—campaign pledges and demonstration pledges. In India far more than elsewhere, volunteers have been asked to pledge themselves to participate in a long-term struggle and to abide by certain standards of behavior while taking part. "Long-term" implies the duration of the campaign, from a few to many months. Formal pledges asked of persons volunteering to take part in a whole campaign have included a clause on nonviolent behavior and on obedience to orders. [251] The Indians have not, however, been the only ones to seek pledges for a whole campaign.

An attempt was made in New York during the boycott of tea in 1773 to obtain signatures to a pledge of nonviolent behavior during the struggle, as Schlesinger reports that "the more conservative merchants" saw a clear drift toward mob control. Four days after a mass meeting of two thousand endorsed a secondary boycott of persons helping introduce boycotted dutied teas, a few persons, including Isaac Low and Jacob Walton, sought signatures to a pledge not to resort to violence in opposing the introduction of the tea. Schlesinger reports that the project quickly made some headway, ". . . but was abandoned on the next day because of the excitement aroused by the receipt of news of the Boston Tea Party. From that moment, as Governor Tryon informed Dartmouth, all hope of a temperate opposition was gone." [252]

Codes of discipline for participants in particular demonstrations have been used both in Britain by the Direct Action Committee against Nuclear War and the Committee of 100,[253] and in the United States by peace groups.[254] Some of the basic points in various American peace and civil rights discipline codes have been listed by both Walker[255] and Miller.[256] For several years the Congress of Racial Equality used a general code of nonviolent discipline, and local groups have sometimes prepared their own codes, as that adopted by college students in Nashville, Tennessee, for use in lunch counter sit-ins.[257]

Often the intent to keep a resistance movement nonviolent has been partially frustrated by the arrest of the very resistance leaders capable of preventing violence. O'Hegarty reports this happened in Ireland following the arrests of Parnell, Dillon and other local and national leaders of the Land League in October 1881:

> Deprived of their leaders, deprived of their Organization, the people resisted as individuals, and resisted as families, and as communities. With no central direction or policy, violence and outrage and intimidation, the unarmed or poorly armed people's only defence against tyranny, soon held full sway.[258]

This is one reason why it is insufficient for nonviolent actionists to rely only on the established leaders. In any case, most such movements require a constant influx of new blood into the leadership group. Sometimes the recognized leadership may be arrested before it has been able to formulate plans. In other cases, at an advanced stage of a campaign all the leaders are likely to be imprisoned or otherwise removed. Whether leaders are arrested early or late, it is vital that the other persons be capable of stepping into leadership positions, and finally that the nonviolent actionists become capable of acting courageously and effectively in the absence of a recognizable leadership group.[259] This was emphasized by Gandhi. He spoke of the stage in a campaign ". . . where no one has to look expectantly at another, where there are no leaders and no followers, or where all are leaders and all are followers . . ." [260] He also said: "Discipline has a place in nonviolent strategy, but much more is required. In a satyagraha army everybody is a soldier and a servant. But at a pinch every satyagrahi soldier has also to be his own general and leader." [261]

While capable of free action the leaders will need to take steps to help people maintain the necessary nonviolent discipline when they must act without leaders. These steps will include both general instructions and specific training in the nature of nonviolent action, in the need for nonviolent discipline and in ways of maintaining it. Also important is the careful formulation of the initial stages of the campaign so that the early pattern can set the mood and serve as an example for the later stages.

In other situations, the opposite trend may develop: instead of all leadership being removed, the nonviolent forces may become so strong that characteristics of a parallel government emerge, [262] which help maintain nonviolent discipline. For example, during the Continental Association plan for economic nonviolent resistance, Connecticut colonial patriots in 1775 enforced compliance with the resistance provisions by open trials of persons accused of violating the resistance plans. The problem of enforcement was more difficult in that colony because it possessed no commercial metropolis but only several small river and coast towns. The movement started, Schlesinger reports, at a meeting of the committees of inspection of Hartford County on January 25, 1775. It was agreed that proceedings against a person accused of violating the noncooperation program should be conducted in an "open, candid and deliberate manner." Furthermore, formal summonses would be served upon him, containing the nature of the charge, and an invitation to defend himself before the committee six days or more later. Witnesses and other evidence were to be "openly, fairly and fully heard"; and conviction should be made only "upon the fullest, clearest and most convincing proof." New Haven, Fairfield and Litchfield counties adopted the same mode of procedure. Nor were these mere pious platitudes. Schlesinger reports that "trials of offenders by the committees of inspection bore every evidence of being fair and impartial hearings, although mistakes were occasionally made." [263]

REFUSAL TO HATE

It should be clear at this point that nonviolent action does not require its practitioners to "love" their opponent, nor to try to convert him. Clearly this technique has been applied by people who hated their opponent and desired to coerce him. Such emotions and attitudes can coexist with the use of nonviolent means.

However, it is also true that effectiveness with the nonviolent technique may be increased when the actionists are able to refrain from hatred and hostility. This is true for all three mechanisms of change, which are discussed in detail in Chapter Thirteen. Appeals to "love" the enemy may at times be emotionally or religiously motivated appeals of persons who are politically naïve. But it is often similarly naïve to dismiss pleas to regard members of the opponent group as fellow human beings and to treat them with respect, personal friendliness and even "love." If actionists are incapable of making this distinction between persons and the issues, and are able only to abstain from physical violence, they should be credited with that achievement rather than have their behavior and attitudes discredited because they were less than perfect. However, if in addition they can refrain from hostility, ill will and hatred, and perhaps even demonstrate personal goodwill for members of the opponent group, they may have much greater chances of success.

An absence of hostility and the presence of goodwill will facilitate the operation of the conversion mechanism. Repression against people who are not only nonviolent but also personally friendly while persisting in their firm action will often appear less justifiable than repression of hostile persons. Repression may still be applied, but the impact of the resulting suffering on the opponent group and on third parties is also likely to be greater. Where the conversion mechanism is not fully achieved, the nonhostile attitudes of the actionists may facilitate change by accommodation. An absence of personal ill will while fighting for the issue may increase the degree to which the opponent's repression rebounds to weaken his own political position. [264]

Even when nonviolent coercion is sought there are good reasons for deliberate efforts to minimize ill will, hostility and hatred by the nonviolent actionists toward the opponent group and to promote positive personal relationships. Such efforts may, for example, help undermine the loyalty of the opponent's police and troops, possibly leading to reduced efficiency in the carrying out of orders for repression, or even to open refusal to obey.

Gandhi is prominent among those who have argued that there is no room for hatred, malice or ill will in nonviolent action, and that they should be replaced by the gentleness, civility, compassion and love for the opponent. [265] This attitude has also been expressed in Western cases of nonviolent action as illustrated in discipline leaflets for demonstrations by American and British peace groups. A 1962 discipline leaflet adopted by New York City peace organizations include these sentences:

Our attitude toward persons who may oppose us will be one of understanding and of respect for the right of others to hold and express whatever views they wish.

We will not be violent in our attitude, make hostile remarks, shout or call names. If singing or chanting is indicated, it will be in a manner consistent with the nonviolent spirit of the demonstration.[266]

The discipline leaflet issued in Britain by the Committee for Direct Action Against Nuclear War (the predecessor of the Direct Action Committee Against Nuclear war) contained this request:

Do not use any language or take any action which is likely to provoke violence by others. A dignified bearing and courteous determination will greatly contribute to victory for this cause.

If you are jeered or called names, do not shout back or jeer those who differ from our views. Silence and a friendly smile are the best reply to hostility, as you continue [to act] as before the interruption.[267]

The nonviolent action movement against racial segregation in the Deep South placed very great importance on "love" for the white segregationists. "The nonviolent resister not only refuses to shoot his opponent but he also refuses to hate him," wrote Martin Luther King, Jr. "At the center of nonviolence stands the principle of love."[268] This extreme emphasis turned some people away from nonviolent means. When understood as a *requirement* for nonviolent action (rather than a helpful refinement), the demand for "love" for people who have done cruel things may turn people who are justifiably bitter and unable to love their opponents toward violence as the technique most consistent with bitterness and hatred. This confusion of secondary refinements with primary requirements and alienation of many potential users of the nonviolent technique has sometimes been aggravated by attempts of pacifists and believers in the principles of nonviolence to proselytize within nonviolent action movements, and to blur the distinctions between their beliefs and the nonviolent technique. Such efforts may in the long run impede rather than promote the substitution of nonviolent for violent means. Nevertheless, for the sake of effectiveness and beneficial long-term consequences, it is desirable for nonviolent actionists to minimize hostility and hatred and to maximize their goodwill for members of the opponent group while firmly continuing the struggle.

THE INEFFICACY OF REPRESSION

As we have already indicated, repression against a movement of non-violent action does not always produce the desired results. If the nonviolent actionists remain fearless, keep their nonviolent discipline, are willing to accept the sufferings inflicted for their defiance, and are determined to persist, then the opponent's attempt to force them to submit to his will is likely to be thwarted. He may be able to imprison them, to injure them, or even to execute them, but as long as they hold out, his will remains unfulfilled. Even if only a single person remains defiant, to that degree the opponent is defeated. The political potentialities of this thwarting of the opponent's will begin to assume much clearer forms when large numbers maintain this persistence, along with the other necessary qualities of nonviolent action. Where significant sections of the population continue defiance, the results will extend far beyond individual example and martyrdom, perhaps even to the point where the opponent's will is effectively blocked. That is, he is politically unable to carry out his plans even with the aid of repression.

He may arrest the leaders, but the movement may simply carry on without a recognizable leadership. He may make new acts illegal, only to find that he has opened new opportunities for defiance. He may attempt to repress defiance at certain points, only to find that the nonviolent actionists have gained enough strength to broaden their attack on other fronts so as to challenge his very ability to rule. He may find that mass repression fails to force a resumption of cooperation and obedience, but instead is constantly met by refusal to submit or flee, producing repeated demonstrations of impotence. Yet, not only may his repression prove inadequate to control his defiant subjects; his very agencies of repression may in extreme cases be immobilized by the massive defiance.

A. Arresting leaders is inadequate

It is natural for the opponent to believe that arresting the leadership will cause the movement to collapse. This was the view of Thomas Hutchinson, Lieutenant Governor of Massachusetts Bay Colony, when he attempted to counteract the campaign of nonimportation of British goods and other noncooperation; in 1769 and 1770 he urged passage by Parliament of an act to punish organizers and participants in such a movement. He denounced "the confederacy of merchants"—who were providing leadership—as unlawful and wrote that Parliament's laws would always be nullified in America ". . . if combinations to prevent the operation of them and to sacrifice all who conform to them are tolerated, or if towns are allowed to meet and vote that measures for defeating such acts are legal." [269] Operating on such a view, opponents confronted with nonviolent action have often seen their best immediate course of counteraction to be the arrest of the leaders and making the organization of this form of struggle illegal. In certain circumstances, this type of repression may be effective. This is most likely to happen when the movement does not genuinely have the strength it appeared to have, when the people are not fearless and when they do not understand how to conduct nonviolent action.

But when the movement does have strength, when the people are fearless, when they understand how to carry on, then the arrest of the leaders may prove a very inadequate means of crushing the movement. Repression is most likely to be made impotent when there has been a widespread and intensive program of public education in the use of nonviolent action or when the actionists have had considerable experience with the technique. Sometimes the example of a few and the intuition of others may suffice to continue resistance, but this is rare and dangerous; sound preparation is safer. Advance training and a widely distributed manual on how to use nonviolent action may help in compensating for the loss of the leadership. These aids may help the actionists to continue to struggle even though reserve layers of leadership have also been removed.

Provision of successive layers of leadership to replace those arrested, or otherwise removed by the opponent, seems to have been given the greatest attention during the Gandhian struggles in India. Not only was a secondary leadership prepared to take the place of the first-line leadership when it was arrested but a whole chain of successive layers of leadership was selected in advance, sometimes up to the thirtieth successive group, to take over direction of the movement as the previous groups were arrested. Sometimes there was, instead, a clear procedure for selecting later leaders, especially by having an existing leader appoint his successor. But, in a mass defiance campaign against an opponent intent upon repressing it ruthlessly, such measures are only stop gap measures. It is likely that sooner or later the continued operation of centralized leadership will become impossible.

In a struggle using political violence—violent revolution, civil war, or international war, for example—the leadership is in most situations kept back, out of danger. Indeed, the movement may depend upon the safety of the top leadership. In nonviolent action, by contrast, the leaders are usually the first victims of the opponent's repression. Having laid down the basic strategy, tactics and methods by which the struggle is to proceed, having helped to forge the organization to carry out those plans, and having emphasized the importance of fearlessness, persistance and maintenance of the nonviolent discipline, the leaders must *act* accordingly. They must by their own fearlessness, suffering and bearing set an example for the many who shall follow them. It is partly because the leadership will be so quickly removed from the scene that so much emphasis must be laid on the quality of the movement at the very beginning. Said Gandhi, ". . . clean examples have a curious method of multiplying themselves." [270] He emphasized the consequences of the importance of the quality of the participants in a nonviolent movement: ". . . mass instruction on any other terms is an impossibility." [271] The leaders, wrote Bose, ". . . are out of the picture at the first shot, only to leave their example to work as leaven in raising the masses." [272]

"There should be no demoralization when the leaders are gone, and there should be no surrender in the face of fire." [273] Rather than causing a slackening, the imprisonment or death of these and other participants in the struggle ought to cause an intensification of the fight: [274] ". . . surely the memory of imprisonment should act as a spur to greater and more disciplined action. We must be able to stand on our own legs without support even as we breathe naturally and without artificial aid." [275] This leads to a situation in which "self-reliance is the order of the day." [276]

These prescriptions by Gandhi for a successful major nonviolent action movement against severe repression were to a considerable degree filled during the 1930-31 independence campaign. Almost immediately after the launching of this struggle, the government began arresting and imprisoning prominent members of the nationalist party, the Indian National Congress. When Jawaharlal Nehru was sentenced to six months' simple imprisonment, there was a universal, spontaneous and complete *hartal.* He left a message for the people: "Keep smiling, fight on and get through the job." [277] When Gandhi was arrested and imprisoned without trial, there were *hartals* and demonstrations throughout the country and the remaining Congress leadership resolved to intensify the struggle by extending the areas of noncooperation and civil disobedience. [278] Gradually the various Congress organizations were declared illegal. They continued, nevertheless, to function for a considerable time with varying membership. After the Congress Working Committee had been effectively halted in its activities, ". . . civil disobedience lacked steering; but it had by now secured sufficient momentum to continue on its own." [279]

This broad self-reliance and continued resistance were deliberately promoted. In an article in *Young India* Jairamdas Daulatram wrote:

> The Government wishes to disorganize us. Each town, each village may have, therefore, to become its own battlefield. The strategy of the battle must then come to be determined by local circumstances and change with them day to day. The sooner the workers prepare for this state of things, the earlier shall we reach our goal. They should need little guidance from outside. [280]

This decentralization of the battle-planning must, he added, be accompanied by continued firm adherence to discipline and to nonviolence, and continued obedience to leaders as long as they remain at liberty. After nearly all the Congress organizations had been declared illegal, Vallabhbhai Patel declared that thereafter every home must be a Congress office and every individual a Congress organization. [281]

At Mathura when the leaders were all arrested before the plans for civil disobedience could be put into effect, the response was a spontaneous city-wide *hartal,* and a huge procession paraded through the city; eight thousand carried out civil disobedience in the form of making illegal salt. [282] In Bihar, with nearly all the leaders in prison, many more salt centers were opened illegally. [283] Referring to conditions throughout the country as a whole, Gopal commented: "The policy of arresting only the leaders was obviously ineffective in countering a movement which drew its strength from local organizations." [284]

This growth of decentralization and self-reliance developed to such a point that without fear of contradiction Gandhi was able to point to the difficulties of carrying on negotiations with the British when only members of the Working Committee had been released from prison. He maintained that evidently the authorities did not understand that the people as a whole had become so much affected by the movement that, no matter how prominent the leaders, they could not dictate a course of action if the masses were not in accord. [285] Such a development, if it should take place to a significant degree over a large area, would be most difficult to combat.

It would be an error to conclude that continued popular resistance despite arrests of leaders is only possible in India, or only with Gandhi as the inspiring leader even when in jail. There is scattered evidence from other conflicts that this continued resistance may occur in a considerable variety of situations. Officials have sometimes anticipated that increased resistance would result from the arrest of leaders and have accordingly acted with caution. For example, although the tsarist Minister of the Interior, Peter Svyatopolk-Mirsky, in January 1905 issued orders for the arrest of Father Gapon and nineteen of his lieutenants before the planned march to the Winter Palace in St. Petersburg, the Prefect of the capital, General Ivan Fullon, did not carry out the arrests, fearing that his police force could not handle the greater, potentially violent, tumult which he expected as the result of such arrests.[286] At Vorkuta in 1953, as noted earlier, the original strike committee was arrested even before the strike began, but the plans went ahead. In Montgomery, Alabama, during the 1957 bus boycott, there were mass arrests of the leadership. Rather than striking fear into the Negroes, the result was increased determination and fearlessness.[287]

Diffused leadership may also be required as a result of the very effectiveness of the nonviolent struggle. This is illustrated by the Russian 1905 Revolution. Only one newspaper was still being printed (a reactionary one in Kiev); telegraph communications were either cut or under government control; there was generally no public transportation operating; the postal system was almost paralyzed. All this meant that no strike leadership could be effective beyond the local area; consequently, resistance leadership was diffused, with leaders in each city acting in virtual isolation.[288]

B. Repression measures may become new points of resistance

Where the nonviolent actionists are strong, and other favorable conditions are present, various measures of repression may be utilized as new points at which to practice civil disobedience and political noncooperation. This is quite distinct from increasing the group's *demands,* which is regarded as generally unwise once the movement has begun. The extension of resistance to repression measures themselves also differs from expansion of other points of resistance and defiance.

It may have been planned, for example, that if the movement showed sufficient strength new methods of action would be used, or the same ones would be applied at new points. In other cases unexpected vigor and resiliance of the actionists and grievance group may make such an expansion of points of resistance possible and desirable. It must be emphasized that any extension of the points of resistance should only be launched if the movement has demonstrated unmistakably sufficient support, tenacity and discipline to warrant the extension; it would be a grave strategic error to overextend the fronts beyond the ability of the nonviolent group to hold them and to keep the initiative.

If the movement shows such nonviolent power and is even able effectively to extend the struggle against certain measures of repression themselves, the opponent will find the situation particularly frustrating. The more his countermeasures infringe on widely accepted standards of conduct and political practice, the more suitable they may be for selection as new points for nonviolent challenge. For example, in trying to combat the nonviolent movement, the opponent may restrict freedom of the press, or freedom of speech or assembly. Such counteractions and repression provide the nonviolent group with additional points at which to resist and defy the regime on issues which will have the sympathy and support of many people still outside the movement.

The 1930–31 struggle in India probably provides the best examples of the extension of resistance, both to more ambitious forms as part of a planned strategy, and also to the opponent's repressive measures themselves. For instance, Gandhi decided to escalate the massive individual violations of the Salt Laws (in which individuals or groups committed civil disobedience by boiling down sea water or digging salt) to large-scale nonviolent raids on government salt depots.[289] Following Gandhi's arrest, the Working Committee of the Congress expanded the scope of the campaign considerably, intensifying the salt raids and the boycott of foreign cloth, encouraging no-tax campaigns, expanding breaches of the Salt Act by manufacture, civil disobedience of the Forest Laws, initiating a boycott of British goods, banking and insurance, and urging the newspapers to noncooperate with new government restrictions on them.[290]

Among the government measures to deal with the civil disobedience movement was the Press Ordinance. This required all journals and newspapers to deposit a security with the government. If the publication then printed information or views ruled by the government to be subversive, the deposit was forfeited and publication was to cease. The Congress Working Committee urged the newspapers to regard this as a new point of refusal of cooperation with the government and to cease publication as a printed journal. Gandhi's own press closed, but *Young India* continued to be issued in duplicated form. Walls, sidewalks and paved roads served as blackboards for Congress notices. Handwritten and typed newspapers were copied and recopied and widely circulated. Various papers and news sheets appeared, all to be declared illegal. (However, most newspapers, but not all, complied with the government ordinance, thus not completing the extension of the defiance which was made possible by the measures.)[291] When public distribution of certain literature was made illegal, *satyagrahis* sometimes held public readings of the banned material, in a further act of civil disobedience. [292] Other extensions of resistance took place also. For example, at one point political prisoners in several jails in the Central Province were on hunger strike, [293] and elsewhere peasants unable to bear further repression went on a protest-migration *(hijrat)* to areas outside British control. [294] It is significant that during that campaign the United Provinces Government opposed the proposal that the central government should declare all Congress organizations illegal. The former felt that "such action was not justified by local conditions and might well revive an agitation which was more or less at a standstill [in the province]." [295] Gopal reports also that while the imposition of collective fines on villages and districts, and the introduction of whipping, had in limited localities helped to control the nonviolent movement, "elsewhere ordinances only seemed to serve the purpose of providing fresh opportunities for defiance; and when the ordinances lapsed the tendency to lawlessness was keener than before." [296]

If the nonviolent actionists' response to repression is an effective expansion of the points at which noncooperation and defiance are committed, and a significant increase in the numbers of active participants in the struggle, the opponent is faced with a strong movement whose opposition may become total. He is then in serious trouble. Very likely, he will in desperation intensify repression. Not only may this not work, but it may backfire to undermine his power position still further. Having failed to deal with the power of noncooperation and defiance, he may unwittingly have brought yet another force into operation against him: that of political *jiu-jitsu.*

NOTES

1. Lakey, "The Sociological Mechanisms of Nonviolent Action" (Thesis) p. 68; *Peace Research Reviews,* vol. II, no. 6 (Dec. 1968), p. 47.
2. Schlesinger, **The Colonial Merchants and the American Revolution,** pp. 113-115.
3. Symons, **The General Strike,** p. 62.
4. Ebert, "Nonviolent Resistance Against Communist Regimes?" p. 177.
5. Lakey, *loc. cit.*
6. Hiller, **The Strike,** pp. 83-84.
7. *Ibid.,* p. 82.
8. *Ibid.,* pp. 85-86.
9. King, **Stride Toward Freedom,** U.S. ed., p. 67; Br. ed., p. 79.
10. Hiller, **The Strike,** pp. 87 and 123.
11. See Sharp, **Gandhi Wields the Weapon of Moral Power,** pp. 41-210 *passim.*
12. Quoted in *ibid.,* p. 59.
13. See Kuper, **Passive Resistance in South Africa,** pp. 10-19 and 112-122.
14. See Sharp, **Gandhi Wields . . . ,** pp. 133 and 144-148.
15. Quoted in Hiller, **The Strike,** p. 94.
16. See Sharp, **Tyranny Could Not Quell Them.**
17. Quoted in Hiller, **The Strike,** p. 94.
18. King, **Stride Toward Freedom,** U.S. ed., p. 66; Br. ed., p. 78.
19. Sternstein, "The *Ruhrkampf* of 1923", p. 127. See also Ehrlich, "*Ruhrkampen,*" p. 191.
20. Symons, **The General Strike,** pp. 141-142.
21. Schlesinger, **The Colonial Merchants . . . ,** pp. 465-469.
22. *Ibid.,* pp. 314, 480, 485, 489, 514-515, 520 and 611.
23. Ehrlich, "Ruhrkampen" in Lindberg, Jacobsen and Ehrlich, **Kamp Uden Vaaben,** pp. 186 and 192.
24. Kuper, **Passive Resistance in South Africa,** pp. 112-113, 116, 119 and 121.
25. Lakey, "The Sociological Mechanisms . . ." p. 73.
26. Schlesinger, **The Colonial Merchants . . . ,** pp. 156-164.
27. See Schlesinger, **The Colonial Merchants . . . ,** pp. 186-187, 189, 192-193, 205-206, 208, 387, 427-428, 437-438, 441-443, 447 n.2, 498, 504-505, 611-612, and Gipson, **The British Empire Before the American Revolution,** vol. XII, **The Triumphant Empire: Britain Sails into the Storm, 1770-1776,** pp. 217-254.
28. Schlesinger, **The Colonial Merchants . . . ,** pp. 487-488.
29. See *ibid.,* pp. 516-517, 586-587, and 610-611.
30. See *ibid.,* pp. 82, 111-112, 122, 124, 139, 141-143, 146, 148-151, 153-154, 158, 162-164, 173-175, 177, 181-182, 184, 188-189, 195, 198, 203, 205-206,

208-209, 211, 215-219, 227-228, 367-370, 388, 454 n.1, 477-478, 481, 483, 486, 491, 493, 495, 507-508, 515, and 610-611; Gipson, **The British Empire Before the American Revolution,** vol. XI, **The Triumphant Empire: The Rumbling of the Coming Storm, 1766-1770,** pp. 183, 188, and 265n., and vol. XII, pp. 69, 196, 208, 252, and 254.

31. Schlesinger, **The Colonial Merchants . . . ,** pp. 432-433.

32. *Ibid.,* pp. 519, 524-525, 610 and 504-505.

33. In addition to above references, see *ibid.,* pp. 479ff, 489, 498-499, 520-521, 526, 551, and 611.

34. *Ibid.,* pp. 484 and 507.

35. Thomas Hutchinson, **The History of the Colony and Province of Massachusetts-Bay,** vol. III, p. 185. See also, pp. 191 and 193. Cambridge, Mass.: Harvard University Press, 1936. Some additional material on resistance is contained in Catherine Barton Mayo, ed., **Additions to Thomas Hutchinson's "History of Massachusetts Bay"** (Worcester, Mass.: American Antiquarian Society, 1949). I am grateful to Ron McCarthy for locating this.

36. See *ibid.,* vol. III, pp. 185-187 and 191-194.

37. See Schlesinger, **The Colonial Merchants . . . ,** pp. 81-82, 478, 542, 552-559, and 564.

38. *Ibid.,* pp. 363, 367 and 372.

39. *Ibid.,* pp. 189, 225, 267, 269, 360-362, 472, 483ff, 529, 531f, and 612.

40. O'Hegarty, **A History of Ireland Under the Union, 1880-1922,** p. 491. During this struggle violence became applied to a significant degree against Irishmen who did not support the campaign, or who weakened in their resolve. For some cases of this, see Forster, **The Truth About the Land League, Its Leaders and Its Teachings,** esp. pp. 70-71, and 84-85.

41. See above Chapter Eight, method 171, nonviolent interjection.

42. See Shridharani, **War Without Violence,** U.S. ed., pp. 86-87; Br. ed., pp. 90-93; Diwakar, **Satyagraha,** pp. 112-114; Gandhi, **An Autobiography,** pp. 427-428 and 430-432; and Erikson, **Gandhi's Truth,** pp. 351-362.

43. Sharp, **Gandhi Wields . . . ,** p. 183.

44. Lakey, "The Sociological Mechanisms . . . " (Thesis), p. 34; *Peace Research Reviews,* vol. II, no. 6 (Dec. 1968), p. 22.

45. See Sharp, **Gandhi Wields . . . ,** pp. 89-211.

46. Hiller, **The Strike,** p. 149.

47. Sharp, **Gandhi Wields . . . ,** p. 85.

48. See Gregg, **The Power of Nonviolence,** p. 79.

49. Sharp, **Tyranny Could Not Quell Them,** p. 16.

50. Nehru, **An Autobiography,** p. 70.

51. Gopal, **The Viceroyalty of Lord Irwin,** pp. 55, 58-59, 64-66, 69-70.

52. Norman Phillips, **The Tragedy of Apartheid** (New York: David McKay, 1960), p. 172.

53. Sternstein, "The *Ruhrkampf* of 1923", p. 132.

54. Liddell Hart, "Lessons from Resistance Movements—Guerilla and Nonviolent", p. 205. See also Sir Basil Liddell Hart, **Defence of the West: Some Riddles of War and Peace** (London: Cassell, 1950), pp. 53-57 (Chapter VII "Were we Wise to Foster 'Resistance Movements'?").

55. Government of India, **India in 1930-31, a Statement prepared for Presentation to Parliament etc.** (Calcutta: Government of India, 1932), pp. 69-72.

56. Kuper, **Passive Resistance in South Africa,** pp. 87 and 156.
57. *Daily Telegraph,* 4 September 1963; cited in Roberts, "The Buddhist Revolt," MS p. 25.
58. See, e.g., Sharp, **Gandhi Wields . . . ,** p. 98.
59. See, e.g., Hiller, **The Strike,** p. 164.
60. Oppenheimer and Lakey, **A Manual for Direct Action,** p. 116.
61. Dhawan, **The Political Philosophy of Mahatma Gandhi,** p. 141.
62. Gopal, **The Viceroyalty of Lord Irwin,** p. 5.
63. Quoted by de Ligt, **The Conquest of Violence,** p. 118.
64. Miller, **Nonviolence,** p. 336.
65. Gregg, **The Power of Nonviolence,** p. 44.
66. See Delarue, **The Gestapo,** pp. 6 and 40 (including a quotation to that effect from Goebbels).
67. *Ibid.,* p. 40.
68. See, e.g., Shirer, **The Rise and Fall of the Third Reich,** pp. 191-196, Delarue, **The Gestapo,** pp. 7-10 and 34-46, and Bullock, **Hitler,** pp. 262-274.
69. Fritz Tobias, **The Reichstag Fire.** New York: G.P. Putnam's Sons, 1964.
70. Quoted in Shirer, **The Rise and Fall . . . ,** p. 756.
71. See *ibid.,* pp. 336, 339, 342, and 345n., and Bullock, **Hitler,** pp. 427-428 and 433.
72. See Shirer, **The Rise and Fall . . . ,** pp. 304, 357, 361-363, 377, 383, 387-388, 406, 427, and 443-444, and Bullock, **Hitler,** 443-466 and 482-485.
73. Delarue, **The Gestapo,** pp. 173-176, Crankshaw, **Gestapo,** pp. 101-102 and 109-111, Shirer, **The Rise and Fall . . . ,** pp. 464, 472, 518-520, 546-547, 554 inc. n., 563, 577, 579 n., 582, 593-595, 602, 604 and 615, and Bullock, **Hitler,** pp. 376 and 546-547.
74. See Reitlinger, **The Final Solution,** pp. 10-15, Shirer, **The Rise and Fall . . . ,** pp. 430-435, Crankshaw, **Gestapo,** p. 160, Delarue, **The Gestapo,** p. 268 inc. n., Neumann, **Behemoth,** pp. 118-120.
75. Reitlinger, **The Final Solution,** p. 100.
76. See, e.g., *ibid.,* pp. 309, 330-331, 348, and 361.
77. See Delarue, **The Gestapo,** pp. 177 and 191-192, and Wheeler-Bennett, **The Nemesis of Power,** p. 461.
78. Shirer, **The Rise and Fall . . . ,** p. 941.
79. Another important example of the effect of revolutionary violence in making the regime stronger, more dictatorial and in uprooting opposition is the attempted assassination of Tsar Alexander II of Imperial Russia in 1866. That year Karakozov, an emotionally unstable member of a revolutionary group decided against the opinion of his fellow revolutionaries to assassinate Alexander II. This followed a period of liberalization and certain reforms approved by the Tsar. Karakozov's attempt to shoot the Tsar failed and he was seized.
     "The shooting made an enormous impression [writes Venturi]. It put an end to the few remaining traces of collaboration between the Emperor and the liberal intelligentsia in the direction of reforms—a collaboration that had made possible the freeing of the serfs and the subsequent changes in local administration and justice. A wave of indignation and fear destroyed any liberal dreams that still survived after the repression of 1862. And the period of what is traditionally called the 'White Terror' now began. Even men like Nekrasov, who had inherited the spirit of the Tsar's earliest years on the throne, bowed down and tried to save what could still be saved. They added their voice to the chorus

of protests against 'nihilism' and joined with the intelligentsia in a mass condemnation of the desperate and violent younger generation. Muravev, who in 1863 had crushed the Polish rebellion in blood, was put in effective charge of internal affairs. He organized a system of repression which aimed to root out the forces of revolution by striking the intellectual tendencies which had given them birth.

"The reaction went deep, and even spread to the people. Exact information is difficult to come by, but all sources are agreed that the peasants stood by the Emperor, often violently."

The workmen in the factories similarly rallied to the Tsar, he reports.

". . . the attempt on the Tsar's life did show how strong was the alliance between the monarchy and the mass of working classes and peasants. It was a bond which could not be cunningly exploited to incite violence against the nobles, as the revolutionaries had hoped. They must have realized now what an abyss still divided them from the people."

After Karakozov's arrest it was not long before the police were able to trace other members of the revolutionary group.

"The entire Moscow group was at once caught. The arrested were taken to St. Petersburg.

"The atmosphere of reaction and terror in which the enquiries were made inevitably had profound effects on the results. The extent of the arrests, which involved several hundred people, eventually provided the police with a large number of facts."

"The repression which followed Karakozov's attempt to kill the Tsar had one immediate and tangible effect. Between 1866 and 1868 there was not a single group in Russia able to carry out clandestine activities or make known its ideas by giving a more general significance to its internal debates."

Venturi, **Roots of Revolution**, pp. 345-350.

80. Gandhi, **Non-Violent Resistance**, p. 212; Ind. ed.: **Satyagraha**, p. 212.

81. *Ibid.*, p. 9.

82. Sharp, **Gandhi Wields . . .** , p. 103.

83. *Ibid.*, p. 118.

84. Kuper, **Passive Resistance in South Africa**, p. 239.

85. *Ibid.*, p. 131.

86. Miller, **Nonviolence**, p. 333 and 338.

87. Lakey, "The Sociological Mechanisms . . . ",(Thesis), p. 95; *Peace Research Reviews,* vol. II, no. 6 (Dec. 1968), p. 63.

88. Gregg, **The Power of Nonviolence**, pp. 87-88. The use of *agents provocateurs* against nonviolent campaigns is also briefly mentioned in Oppenheimer and Lakey, **A Manual for Direct Action**, p. 116 and Walker, **Organizing for Nonviolent Direct Action**, p. 26.

89. Kuper, **Passive Resistance in South Africa**, p. 87.

90. **Nehru, An Autobiography**, p. 81.

91. Nehru, **Toward Freedom**, p. 394.

92. Symons, **The General Strike**, pp. 112-113.

93. Miller, **Nonviolence**, p. 247.

94. Vassilyev, **The Ochrana**, pp. 63-78.

95. See, e.g., Katkov, **Russia 1917**, pp. xxvi, 288 and 419.

96. See, e.g., *ibid.*, pp. 28, 30-31, 33, 170, 288, 420.

97. Gandhi, quoted in Bose, **Selections from Gandhi**, p. 204.

98. *Ibid.*
99. It is sometimes assumed that this emphasis on keeping the struggle nonviolent is a recent innovation stemming from pacifist or Gandhian influences; this is not true. The degree to which the mass use of nonviolent means has been self-conscious has, of course, varied considerably. The nonviolent character of certain mass struggles has often been intuitive or spontaneous in nature and therefore with limited or no explicit efforts to keep it nonviolent. However, in several cases where the ethical view of nonviolence was minimal or absent there have been efforts to maintain nonviolent behavior. In the American colonists' struggles, for example, the noncooperation measures were often seen as a peaceful substitute for war, even though explicit attempts to prevent violence were comparatively limited. (See Gipson, **The British Empire . . .** , vol. XII, pp. 153 and 252-253.) But such efforts to keep the struggle peaceful were made in Virginia, New York and Massachusetts Bay. In this last colony, Lieutenant-Governor Hutchinson wrote in late 1773 of "the greater part" of the merchants, that "though in general they declare against mobs and violence, yet they as generally wish the teas may not be imported." (Schlesinger, **The Colonial Merchants . . .** , p. 283 n.2. See also pp. 93, 96, 129, 189-190, 283, 293, and 605, and Gipson, **The British Empire . . .** , vol. XII, pp. 201-202, and 246.)

The Finnish constitutionalists' struggle launched in 1901 against new Russian measures was based on the view, writes Jutikkala, that "the unarmed nation must carry on the struggle with all the means available, without, however, resorting to violence." (Jutikkala, **A History of Finland,** p. 233.) In the predominantly nonviolent Russian 1905 Revolution there were frequent explicit attempts to keep strikes and demonstrations nonviolent. Although significant spontaneous violence did occur, much of the violence can be traced to deliberate initiatives of students and Marxists—especially Bolsheviks; the political wisdom of those initiatives can be challenged most seriously. (See Harcave, **First Blood,** pp. 73, 90, 92-93, 100, 105-106, 116-117, 144, 171, 187 and 219; Schwarz, **The Russian Revolution of 1905,** pp. xi, 65, 68, 132-134, and 138-143; Keep, **The Rise of Social Democracy in Russia,** pp. 157, 159, 172-174, 187, 220, 222, 225-226, 228, 236, 258, 260, 263, 266, 270, and 289-290, and Lord Hardinge of Penschurst, **Old Diplomacy,** p. 114.

When the French and Belgians invaded the Ruhr, the proclamation to the entire German people from the President and government urged avoidance of counterproductive action: ". . . take no action which would harm our just cause. Anyone who . . . commits any rash and unconsidered action which in the end would only serve the enemy's ends would be deeply guilty. The public good depends on each and every person exercising the utmost self-control." (Sternstein, "The *Ruhrkampf* of 1923" p. 112.) In the predominantly nonviolent East German rising of 1953 there were spontaneous attempts to keep it nonviolent. (See Brant, **The East German Rising,** pp. 71, 73, 76, 84, 94, 99, 102-103, 115, 124, 126, and 190-191.) Ebert writes: ". . . in general the more reasonable elements among the workers managed to prevent acts of violence. The demonstrators locked up or destroyed any weapons they found." (Ebert, "Nonviolent Resistance Against Communist Regimes?" pp. 190-191.) These few examples illustrate that nonviolent discipline is not an alien emphasis introduced by moralists, but that other practitioners have perceived it to be a necessary aspect of the technique itself.

100. Griffith, **The Resurrection of Hungary,** p. 32. See also pp. 17 and 57.
101. Gandhi, **Non-violent Resistance,** p. 56; Ind. ed.: **Satyagraha,** p. 56. See also p. 187.

102. Gandhi, in Bose, **Selections from Gandhi,** p. 203.

103. The phrase is Miller's. Miller, **Nonviolence,** p. 155.

104. "Suffolk Resolves" Nr.18, **American Archives,** Fourth Series (Washington, D.C.: M. St. Clarke and Peter Force, 1937), vol. I, p. 778.

105. Oppenheimer and Lakey, **A Manual for Direct Action,** p. 121.

106. Lindberg, *"Konklusionen: Teorien om Ikke-vold"*, p. 209, in Lindberg, Jacobsen and Ehrlich, **Kamp Uden Vaaben.** Lenin also acknowledged this tendency in 1905 although he favored violence. See Lenin, "Lessons of the Moscow Uprising" in Lenin, **Selected Works in Three Volumes,** vol. I, p. 577.

107. *Young India* (weekly), 27 March 1930.

108. Hiller, **The Strike,** pp. 171-172.

109. Ebert, "Nonviolent Resistance Against Communist Regimes?" p. 191.

110. Brant, **The East German Rising,** p. 124.

111. Sibley, **The Quiet Battle,** p. 117.

112. Samuel Yellen, **American Labor Struggles** (New York: Harcourt, Brace & Co., 1936), p. 58.

113. This account is summarized from Yellen, *op. cit.,* pp. 39-71.

114. Gandhi, **Non-violent Resistance,** p. 218; Ind. ed.: **Satyagraha,** p. 218.

115. Gandhi, quoted in Bose, **Selections from Gandhi,** p. 203.

116. Gandhi, **Non-violent Resistance,** p. 288; Ind. ed.: **Satyagraha,** p. 288.

117. See Kuper, **Passive Resistance in South Africa,** p. 133-140.

118. See *ibid.,* pp. 140-143.

119. *Ibid.,* p. 140.

120. *Ibid.,* p. 143. On these riots and their effects, see also Luthuli, **Let My People Go,** pp. 127-128 and 130.

121. *Ibid.,* p. 144.

122. *Ibid.,* p. 145.

123. *Ibid.,* p. 156.

124. Schlesinger, **The Colonial Merchants . . . ,** pp. 475-476. For some specific examples of the abandonment or repeal of provisions of the Continental Association, see also pp. 566-568, 572, 583-585 and 589.

125. See Gregg, **The Power of Nonviolence,** p. 133,

126. Luthuli, **Let My People Go,** pp. 127-128.

127. See Yarmolinsky, **Road to Revolution,** pp. 9, 141-142, 161, 177-178, 227, 291; Seton-Watson, **The Decline of Imperial Russia,** p. 72; Schapiro, **The Communist Party of the Soviet Union,** p. 80 and Venturi, **Roots of Revolution,** pp. xxvi, 469 and 527. On the effects of arson, see Yarmolinsky, *op. cit.,* pp. 113-114, and on the effects of robberies, see Schapiro, *op.cit.,* pp. 97 and 104.

128. Katkov, **Russia 1917,** p. xxvi.

129. See Schlesinger, **The Colonial Merchants . . . ,** pp. 92-93.

130. *Ibid.,* pp. 298-299. See also pp. 300 and 308-309.

131. *Ibid.,* p. 299.

132. *Ibid.,* p. 542.

133. Gipson, **The British Empire . . . ,** vol. XII, p. 369.

134. See Schlesinger, **The Colonial Merchants . . . ,** pp. 435-439.

135. See, e.g., Waskow, **From Race Riot to Sit-In,** p. 261 for an early observation of this.

136. Farmer, **Freedom – When?**, p. 79.

137. Schlesinger, **The Colonial Merchants . . .** , p. 531.

138. O'Hegarty, **A History of Ireland Under the Union, 1880-1922,** p. 515.

139. *Ibid.,* p. 522.

140. John Morley, **The Life of William Ewart Gladstone** (New York & London: Macmillan & Co., 1903), vol. III, p. 70.

141. *Ibid.,* vol. III, p. 68.

142. Deutscher, **Stalin,** p. 102.

143. See Harcave, **First Blood,** esp. pp. 155-157, 177 and 238.

144. Eyck, **A History of the Weimar Republic,** vol. I, p. 237. See also Sternstein, "The *Ruhrkampf* of 1923" pp. 120 and 125. He reports especially the taking of hostages, and the deaths of 141 Germans from beatings, arbitrary executions, and firings from guards and patrols.

145. Waskow, **From Race Riot to Sit-in,** pp. 199-202.

146. Solomon and Fishman, "The Psychosocial Meaning of Nonviolence in Student Civil Rights Activities," *Psychiatry,* vol. XXVII (May, 1964), p. 95.

147. Schlesinger, **The Colonial Merchants . . .** , p. 539. See also pp. 536-540. There remained, however, other important British support for the Americans even after Lexington and Concord. See Gipson, **The British Empire . . .** , vol. XII, pp. 340-351.

148. Harcave, **First Blood,** p. 220.

140. *Ibid.,* p. 222.

150. *Ibid.,* p. 223.

151. Keep, **The Rise of Social Democracy in Russia,** p. 249.

152. *Ibid.,* pp. 239-242.

153. *Ibid.,* p. 248.

154. Henry W. Nevinson, who was at the time in Moscow as a special correspondent for the *Daily Chronicle* (London) reported the disaffection and untrustworthiness—prior to the rising—of the soldiers stationed in Moscow. Nevinson also wrote that on December 6 (19) – the day before the general strike began— ". . . the Government was only longing for disturbances as an excuse for military assassination." He reported that on Dec. 8 (21): "They [the revolutionists] were ill-armed, had only eighty rifles as yet; a good many revolvers certainly, but not enough arms. Besides, if the Government wanted a rising, they obviously ought not to rise. It is a bad strategist who lets the enemy dictate the time for battle."

"But the Government had determined that neither delay nor opportunity should be given. Their one thought was the urgent need of money, the power that commands force is the Government, and the power that commands money can command force; that was their just and simple argument. Their one hope was to stir up an ill-prepared rebellion, to crush it down, and stand triumphant before the nations of Europe, confidently inviting new loans in the name of law and order, so as to pay the interest on the old and 'maintain the value of the rouble.' For this object it was essential that people should be killed in large numbers . . . unless the slaughter came quickly the officials could not count upon their pay. The only alternative was national bankruptcy. . . . At all costs the people must be goaded into violence, or the Government's strategy would have failed." Nevinson, Henry W., **The Dawn in Russia or Scenes in the Russian Revolution** (London and New York: Harper & Bros., 1906), pp. 123 and 136-138.

155. Keep, **The Rise of Social Democracy in Russia,** pp. 250-251.
156. *Ibid.,* p. 243.
157. *Ibid.,* pp. 245-246.
158. Louis Fischer, **The Life of Lenin** (New York: Harper & Row, 1965 and London: Weidenfeld and Nicolson, 1965), p. 57.
159. Prawdin, **The Unmentionable Nechaev,** p. 148. Also on the Bolsheviks' view of the Moscow defeat as "beneficial," see Adam B. Ulam, **The Bolsheviks: The Intellectual and Political History of the Triumph of Communism in Russia** (New York: Macmillan, and London: Collier-Macmillian, 1965), p. 236. And Nevinson, **The Dawn in Russia,** pp. 198-199.
160. In July 1905 Lenin wrote: "The revolutionary army is required for the military struggle and the military leadership of the masses of the people against the remnants of the military forces of the autocracy. The revolutionary army is needed because great historical questions can be solved only by *violence,* and the *organisation of violence* in the modern struggle is a military organisation." Lenin, "The Revolutionary Army and the Revolutionary Government," in V. I. Lenin, **Selected Works,** vol. III, **The Revolution of 1905-07** (Moscow and Leningrad: Co-operative Publishing Society of Foreign Workers in the U.S.S.R., 1934 [?]), p. 313. See also p. 315.

In August he wrote: ". . . we must clearly and resolutely point out the necessity for an uprising in the present state of affairs; we must directly call for insurrection (without, of course, fixing the date beforehand), and call for the immediate organisation of a revolutionary army. Only a very bold and wide organisation of such an army can serve as a prologue to the insurrection. Only insurrection can guarantee the victory of the revolution . . ." Lenin, "The Boycott of the Bulygin Duma and the Insurrection" p. 327 in *op. cit.,* vol. III.
161. "The broad masses, however, were still too naive, their mood was too passive, too good-natured, too Christian. . . . they lacked . . . a clear understanding that only the most vigorous continuation of the armed struggle, only a victory over all the military and civil authorities, only the overthrow of the government and the seizure of power throughout the country could guarantee the success of the revolution." Lenin, "Lecture on the 1905 Revolution" (January 1917), in Lenin, **Selected Works in Three Volumes,** vol. I, p. 795. (Note: the Moscow 1934(?) edition refers to the seizure of power "over the whole state" instead of "throughout the country." See Lenin, **Selected Works,** vol. III, p. 10.)

". . . we should have explained to the masses that it was impossible to confine things to a peaceful strike and that a fearless and relentless armed fight was necessary. And now we must at last openly and publicly admit that political strikes are inadequate; we must carry on the widest agitation among the masses in favour of an armed uprising and make no attempt to obscure this question . . . We would be deceiving both ourselves and the people if we concealed from the masses the necessity of a desperate, bloody war of extermination, as the immediate task of the coming revolutionary action.

". . . Another lesson [of the December 1905 events] concerns the character of the uprising, the methods by which it is conducted, and the conditions which lead to the troops coming over to the side of the people. An extremely biased view on this latter point prevails in the Right wing of our Party. It is alleged that there is no possibility of fighting modern troops; the troops must become revolutionary. Of course, unless the revolution assumes a mass character and affects the troops, there can be no question of serious struggle. That we must work among the troops goes without saying. But we must not imagine that they will come over to our side at one stroke, as a result of persuasion of their own convictions. . . . But we shall prove to be miserable pedants if we forget that at a time of uprising there must also be a physical struggle for the troops."

"And the guerrilla warfare and mass terror that has been taking place throughout Russia practically without a break since December [1905], will undoubtedly help the masses to learn the correct tactics of an uprising." Lenin, "Lessons of the Moscow Uprising," in Lenin, **Selected Works in Three Volumes,** vol. I, pp. 579-582.

162. Keep, The Rise of Social Democracy in Russia, pp. 246-247.

163. Harcave, **First Blood,** p. 235. On the four phases of the rising, see Keep, **The Rise** ..., pp. 251-257.

164. Harcave, **First Blood,** p. 235.

165. Keep, The Rise ..., pp. 253-254.

166. Seton-Watson, **The Decline of Imperial Russia,** pp. 224-225.

167. Harcave, **First Blood,** pp. 238 and 243. Nevinson wrote: "The failure at Moscow fell like a blight upon all Russia, and all hope withered." (Nevinson, **The Dawn in Russia,** p. 198.) Lenin later wrote: "In October 1905, Russia was at the peak of the revolutionary upsurge ... the period of decline set in after the defeat of December 1905 ..." "The turning point in the struggle began with the defeat of the December uprising. Step by step the counter-revolution passed to the offensive as the mass struggle weakened." Lenin, "Revolution and Counter-Revolution," from *Proletary*, Nr. 17, 20 October 1907, in **Collected Works,** vol. 13, **June 1907–April 1908** (Moscow: Foreign Languages Publishing House, 1962), pp. 114 and 116.

168. "Sabotage, and all it means, including the destruction of property, is in itself violence," wrote Gandhi. Bose, **Studies in Gandhism,** p. 145.

169. See Gandhi, **Non-violent Resistance,** p. 378; Ind. ed.: **Satyagraha,** p. 378.

170. See *Ibid.,* p. 379.

171. See Halperin, **Germany Tried Democracy,** p. 250, Karl Ehrlich, *"Ruhrkampen,"* in Lindberg, Jacobsen and Ehrlich, **Kamp Uden Vaaben,** p. 187, and Sternstein, "The *Ruhrkampf* of 1923" pp. 123-126.

172. Ehrlich, "Ruhrkampen" p. 187.

173. On these negative influences of sabotage, see Sternstein, "The *Ruhrkampf* of 1923" pp. 124-126. The quotation from Wentzcke is on p. 125 from Paul Wentzcke **Ruhrkampf** (Berlin: Reimar Hobbing, 1930), vol. I, pp. 424-425.

174. See, e.g., Schlesinger, **The Colonial Merchants** ..., p. 71.

175. *Ibid.,* pp. 91-92 and 105.

176. *Ibid.,* p. 97. See also p. 103.

177. *Ibid.,* pp. 179-180.

178. *Ibid.,* p. 368.

179. *Ibid.,* p. 390.

180. *Ibid.,* pp. 391-392.

181. For the text of the Association, see *ibid.,* pp. 607-613.

182. Gipson, **The British Empire** ..., vol. XII, p. 316.

183. *Ibid.,* pp. 321-323.

184. Schlesinger, **The Colonial Merchants** ..., p. 608.

185. *Ibid.,* p. 519.

186. *Ibid.,* p. 529.

187. Gipson, **The British Empire** ..., vol. XII, p. 145.

188. *Ibid.*, pp. 163-164.
189. *Ibid.*, p. 197.
190. See, e.g., *ibid.*, pp. 320-349.
191. Schlesinger, **The Colonial Merchants . . .** , p. 563.
192. *Ibid.*, p. 541. See also p. 542. On various alterations in the earlier economic sanctions, see pp. 562, 566-568, 572-573, and 576.
193. *Ibid.*, p. 563.
194. See Lindberg,*"Konklusionen: Teorien on Ikke-vold,"* pp. 207-208 in Lindberg, Jacobsen and Ehrlich, **Kamp Uden Vaaben.**
195. See Ebert, "Nonviolent Resistance Against Communist Regimes?" p. 182.
196. Bose, **Selections from Gandhi,** p. 200.
197. Bradford Lyttle, "The Importance of Discipline in Demonstrations for Peace" (duplicated, 2pp. New York: Committee for Non-Violent Action, 1962).
198. Waskow, **From Race Riot to Sit-in,** pp. 255-257.
199. Lyttle, "The Importance of Discipline in Demonstrations for Peace."
200. Luthuli, **Let My People Go,** p. 120.
201. Ehrlich, *"Rene Sociale Klassekampe. Den Ikke-voldelige Modstand, Der. Kvalte Kapp-Kuppet,"* pp. 200 n. and 202, in Lindberg, Jacobsen and Ehrlich, **Kamp Uden Vaaben.**
202. See Kuper, **Passive Resistance in South Africa,** p. 93 and Sharp, "A South African Contribution to the Study of Nonviolent Action: A Review" p. 400, *Journal of Conflict Resolution,* vol. V, no. 4 (December, 1961).
203. For examples of Gandhi's views, see Bose, **Selections From Gandhi,** p. 189; Bose, **Studies in Gandhism,** p. 151; and Gandhi, **Non-violent Resistance,** pp. 57, 98, 100, 194-195, 302, 355 and 362-363; Ind. ed.: **Satyagraha,** same pp.
204. "Discipline for Public Witness Demonstrations" (leaflet).
205. For Gandhi's views on self-discipline in prison, see Gandhi, **Non-violent Resistance,** pp. 60-65; Ind. ed.: **Satyagraha,** pp. 60-65.
206. Gregg, **The Power of Nonviolence,** pp. 80-81.
207. Lyttle, "The Importance of Discipline in Demonstrations for Peace".
208. See Gregg, **The Power of Nonviolence,** p. 71.
209. *Ibid.*, p. 67.
210. Charles C. Walker, **Organizing for Nonviolent Direct Action** (pamphlet) (Cheney, Pennsylvania: The Author, 1961), p. 16.
211. See *ibid.*, pp. 20 and 22.
212. Oppenheimer and Lakey, **A Manual for Direct Action,** p. 108.
213. Gandhi, **Non-violent Resistance,** p. 333; Ind. ed.: **Satyagraha,** p. 333. The Committee of 100 during the period of its greatest strength repeatedly made the same request for its civil disobedience demonstrations.
214. Gandhi, **Non-violent Resistance,** p. 287; Ind. ed.: **Satyagraha,** p. 287.
215. See Gregg, **The Power of Nonviolence,** p. 118.
216. Luthuli paid strong tribute to the discipline of the inexperienced and largely untrained volunteers for the 1952 Defiance Campaign in South Africa, although this did not apply to the whole nonwhite population. See Luthuli, **Let My People Go,** pp. 118 and 125.
217. Gandhi, **Non-violent Resistance,** p. 25; Ind. ed.: **Satyagraha,** p. 25.
218. *Ibid.*, p. 299.
219. *Ibid.*, p. 297.

220. Schlesinger, The Colonial Merchants . . . , pp. 193-194. On other cases of reshipment of goods without information on its effect on mob violence, see also pp. 200-201, 217 and 426.

221. *Ibid.,* p. 226.

222. See his statement in Sharp, Gandhi Wields . . . , p. 49.

223. Nehru, An Autobiography, p. 175.

224. Farmer, Freedom – When? pp. 27, 28, and 32-34. On the effect of nonviolent action reducing the chances of violence, see also Waskow, From Race Riot to Sit-in, pp. 262 and 285.

225. Walker, Organizing for Nonviolent Direct Action, p. 28.

226. Miller, Nonviolence, p. 307 and King, Stride Towards Freedom, pp. 58-62 and 78-81.

227. Harcave, First Blood, p. 149.

228. *Ibid.,* p. 226.

229. Solomon and Fishman, "The Psychosocial Meaning of Nonviolence in Student Civil Rights Activities," p. 98.

230. Halperin, Germany Tried Democracy, p. 179.

231. Gregg, The Power of Nonviolence, p. 88.

232. See Gandhi, Non-violent Resistance, p. 151; Ind. ed.: Satyagraha, p. 151.

233. Ehrlich, *"Ruhrkampen,"* p. 187.

234. See Bose, Studies in Gandhism, pp. 143-144 and Gandhi, Non-violent Resistance, pp. 139-141 and 151; Ind. ed.: Satyagraha, pp. 139-141 and 151.

235. See Walker, Organizing for Nonviolent Direct Action, p. 20.

236. Oppenheimer and Lakey, A Manual for Direct Action, p. 84 and Miller, Nonviolence, pp. 306-308, and Walker, Organizing for Nonviolent Direct Action, pp. 9-11.

237. Quoted in Roberts, "Buddhism and Politics in South Vietnam" pp. 243-244.

238. Sharp, Gandhi Wields . . . , p. 81.

239. King, Stride Toward Freedom, U.S. ed., p. 51; Br. ed., p. 60. For an example of on-the-spot pleas for nonviolence from hostile crowds in Birmingham, Alabama, in 1963, see Miller, Nonviolence, pp. 334-336.

240. Kuper, Passive Resistance in South Africa, p. 119.

241. Miller, Nonviolence, pp. 278-280.

242. Brant, The East German Rising, pp. 102-103. See also p. 99.

243. *Ibid.,* p. 126.

244. Joseph Wechsberg, "A Reporter in Germany," pp. 38, 49 and 50 in *The New Yorker,* 29 August 1953, quoted in Miller, Nonviolence, pp. 352-353.

245. Brant, The East German Rising, p. 71.

246. Morgan and Morgan, The Stamp Act Crisis, p. 248.

247. Peck, Freedom Ride, p. 76 and Walker, Organizing for Nonviolent Direct Action, p. 20.

248. Oppenheimer and Lakey, A Manual for Direct Action, p. 87.

249. Gandhi, Non-violent Resistance, p. 35; Ind. ed.: Satyagraha, p. 35.

250. *Ibid.,* pp. 118-119. This view was repeatedly emphasized by Gandhi in very strong terms; see also, pp. 98 and 302.

251. See, for example, Gandhi, Nonviolence in Peace and War, vol. I, p. 154; Dhawan, The Political Philosophy . . . , pp. 211-213; Sharp, Gandhi Wields . . . , pp. 67-69 and 80-81; Gandhi, Non-violent Resistance, pp. 205-206; Ind. ed.:

Satyagraha, pp. 205-206; and Bondurant, **Conquest of Violence,** pp. 77 and 133-134.

252. Schlesinger, **The Colonial Merchants . . . ,** p. 293. In late June 1774 the town meeting of Portsmouth deliberately took various other measures—not involving pledges or codes of discipline—to prevent the outbreak of violence when dutied teas was landed, and at the town's insistence and expense re-exported so that it was not sold or used in Portsmouth. See *ibid.,* p. 303.

253. The Direct Action Committee Against Nuclear War issued a general but detailed discipline leaflet − "Demonstrators −" (1958?) intended both for organized demonstrations and for distribution during spontaneous demonstrations. That Committee also issued detailed briefings for participants on the particular plans and behavioral requirements for a given demonstration, as well as legal aspects and a guide for statements in court for those arrested. For example, for one action the following were issued: "Briefing for Non-Violent Obstruction at North Pickenham Rocket Base on Saturday December 6th" (25 November 1958), "Briefing on legal aspects of demonstration on December 6th" (4 December 1958), and "Explanatory statement to be made in Court" (n.d.). Discipline leaflets were also issued both for the National Committee of 100 and affiliated groups, as the Oxford Committee of 100. The Oxford leaflet differed from ·the D.A.C.A.N.W. leaflet not only in its brevity, but its recommendation that if violence broke out people should not physically place themselves between the fighters, but "immediately withdraw, leave an empty space, and sit down. Isolate the violence."

254. Twelve New York City peace organizations in 1962 issued a "Discipline for Public Witness Demonstrations" and a very detailed binding discipline code was issued by the Committee for Nonviolent Action for its long peace walk focusing on U.S. relations with Cuba: "Group Discipline − Principles of Conduct − or what have you for the Quebec-Washington-Guantanamo walk for peace − sponsored by CNVA."

255. Walker, **Organizing for Nonviolent Direct Action,** p. 16.

256. Miller, **Nonviolence,** pp. 155-156.

257. Sibley, **The Quite Battle,** pp. 299-300.

258. O'Hegarty, **A History of Ireland Under the Union 1880-1922,** p. 514.

259. This is discussed more fully in the last section of this chapter.

260. Bose, **Selections from Gandhi,** p. 203.

261. *Ibid.,*

262. See above pp. 479-491.

263. Schlesinger, **The Colonial Merchants . . . ,** pp. 488-489.

264. Thus Gandhi argued that the purer the suffering, the quicker would be the result. Gandhi, **Non-violent Resistance,** p. 188; Ind. ed.: **Satyagraha,** p. 188.

265. See, e.g., *Ibid.,* pp. 74, 93, 107, 162, 169, 179, 182, 193, 201-202, 207, 284-285, and 357.

266. "Discipline for Public Witness Demonstrations" (leaflet). New York: various peace organizations, 1962.

267. "Demonstrators − " (leaflet). London: Committee for Direct Action Against Nuclear War, 1958 (?).

268. King, **Stride Toward Freedom,** U.S. ed., p. 83; Br. ed.: pp. 97-98.

269. Schlesinger, **The Colonial Merchants . . . ,** p. 172.

270. Gandhi, **Non-violent Resistance,** p. 139; Ind. ed.: **Satyagraha,** p. 139.

271. Bose, **Studies in Gandhism,** p. 129.

272. *Ibid.,* p. 147.

273. Quoted in Bose, **Selections from Gandhi,** p. 202.

274. *Ibid.,* pp. 202-203.

275. *Ibid.,* p. 202.

276. *Ibid.,* p. 203.

277. Sharp, **Gandhi Wields . . . ,** p. 91.

278. See *ibid.,* pp. 118-127 and Gopal, **The Viceroyalty of Lord Irwin,** p. 71.

279. Gopal, **The Viceroyalty** . . . , p. 79.

280. Sharp, **Gandhi Wields . . . ,** p. 172. See also p. 177.

281. *Ibid.,* pp. 171-172.

282. *Ibid.,* p. 104.

283. *Ibid.,* p. 100.

284. Gopal, **The Viceroyalty** . . , pp. 77-78.

285. Sharp, **Gandhi Wields . . . ,** pp. 202-203. On this possibility, see also Symons, **The General Strike,** pp. 210-211.

286. Harcave, **First Blood,** p. 84.

287. King, **Stride Toward Freedom,** U.S. ed., pp. 115-122; Br. ed.; pp. 136-144.

288. Harcave, **First Blood,** pp. 186-187.

289. See Gopal, **The Viceroyalty** . . . , p. 70, and Sharp, **Gandhi Wields . . . ,** pp. 114ff.

290. See Gopal, **The Viceroyalty** . . . , p. 71, and Sharp, **Gandhi Wields . . . ,** pp. 125-127 and 174-176.

291. See Gopal, **The Viceroyalty** . . . , p. 77, and Sharp, **Gandhi Wields . . . ,** pp. 113-114, 132 and 183. For Gandhi's views on hand-copied newspapers in 1921, see Bose, **Selections from Gandhi,** pp. 200-201.

292. Sharp, **Gandhi Wields . . . ,** pp. 132 and 161.

293. *Ibid.,* p. 200.

294. *Ibid.,* pp. 198-200.

295. Gopal, **The Viceroyalty** . . . , p. 78.

296. *Ibid.,* p. 87.

12

Political Jiu-Jitsu

INTRODUCTION

Political *jiu-jitsu* [1] is one of the special processes by which nonviolent action deals with violent repression. By combining nonviolent discipline with solidarity and persistence in struggle, the nonviolent actionists cause the violence of the opponent's repression to be exposed in the worst possible light. This, in turn, may lead to shifts in opinion and then to shifts in power relationships favorable to the nonviolent group. These shifts result from withdrawal of support for the opponent and the grant of support to the nonviolent actionists.

Cruelties and brutalities committed against the clearly nonviolent are likely to disturb many people and to fill some with outrage. Even milder violent repression appears less justified against nonviolent people than when employed against violent resisters. This reaction to repression is especially likely when the opponent's policies themselves are hard to justify. Thus, wider public opinion may turn against the opponent, members of his own group may dissent, and more or less passive members of the general grievance group may shift to firm opposition. The effects of this process do not stop there, however. In addition to shifts of opinion *against* the opponent, positive sympathy in *favor* of the nonviolent actionists and their cause is also likely to develop. Most important, all these shifts in opinion may lead to action. The opponent may find more and more groups, even among his normal supporters, resisting his policies and activities; at the same time, increased active support for the nonviolent actionists and their cause may develop.

Thus, precisely because the actionists have rejected violence while persisting in resistance and defiance, the opponent's violence has certain effects on several social groups which tend to shift loyalties, social forces and power relationships against him and in favor of the nonviolent actionists. *Their nonviolence helps the opponent's repression to throw him off balance politically.*[2] *The nonviolent group is also able to gain far more support and power than if it had met violence with violence.*

Political *jiu-jitsu* does not operate in all nonviolent struggles. Most of the many specific methods of action listed in earlier chapters are independent of this particular process. If opponents become more sophisticated in dealing with nonviolent action, so that they drastically reduce, or even eliminate, violent repression and thereby political *jiu-jitsu,* the nonviolent actionists will still be able to win. They will still be able to utilize the many psychological, social, economic and political forces and pressures which the multitude of specific methods brings into play.

Political *jiu-jutsu* operates among three broad groups: 1) uncommitted third parties, whether on the local scene or the world level, 2) the opponent's usual supporters, and 3) the general grievance group. Now we shall explore the ways in which the views and actions of each of these three groups tend to shift away from the opponent and in favor of the nonviolent actionists. We shall begin with third parties whose potential influence is normally the smallest, then consider the opponent's usual supporters who are obviously very important, and conclude with the grievance group, whose role may be crucial.

WINNING OVER UNCOMMITTED THIRD PARTIES

Repression against nonviolent people may attract wide attention to the struggle and strong sympathy for the suffering nonviolent group among persons not involved in the struggle in any way. As the American sociologist Edward Alsworth Ross put it,

The spectacle of men suffering for a principle and *not hitting back* is a moving one. It obliges the power holders to condescend to explain, to justify themselves. The weak get a change of venue from the will of the stronger to the court of public opinion, perhaps world opinion.[3]

A. International indignation

Indeed, some of the main cases used in this study support this conclusion. For example, Bloody Sunday (1905) in St. Petersburg produced, reports Harcave, "immediate and bitter international revulsion" expressed in anti-tsarist demonstrations in England, Germany, Austria-Hungary, Sweden, France, Spain, Italy, Belgium, United States, Argentina and Uruguay.[4] Two days after the massacre, Kokovtsev, the Minister of Finance, reported to the Tsar that not only had the killings impaired morale at home, but that Russian financial credit abroad had been affected.[5] In other words, repression of nonviolent actionists had drawn even foreign "third parties" into the struggle against the regime (even if the creditors' motives were selfish).

Similar results have taken place in such contrasting cases as Germany and India. In 1923 government-sponsored nonviolent resistance in the Ruhr against the Franco-Belgian occupation produced wide sympathy for Germany, brought new discredit to the Treaty of Versailles, and alienated British opinion from the invaders at a time when France needed British support for the international security it wanted.[6] And in the thirties, British repression against nonviolent Indian volunteers helped move world opinion significantly toward the Indians.[7]

International indignation was also aroused by repression against nonviolent actionists in both South Africa and South Vietnam. Sometimes the actionists, aware of this process, have deliberately sought to arouse this international support, as they did in South Africa.[8] For example, the 1952 Defiance Campaign attracted world attention to *Apartheid* in South Africa and the plight of nonwhites there. Press reports hostile to the regime became common. Several Asian governments and African political groups expressed sympathy for the resisters. After India raised the matter in the United Nations General Assembly, a U.N. commission investigated the effects of *Apartheid* legislation.[9] This widespread disapproval of its policies, Kuper writes, posed two problems for the South African government: how to win over world opinion, and how to explain world condemnation to its own European population.[10] The government was more successful in the latter than in the former, but continued major efforts to win international acceptance indicate its importance to that regime.

Eight years later, in 1960, during another nonviolent campaign in that country, the killing of demonstrators at Sharpeville (where Africans had only thrown stones, and that without inflicting serious injuries) produced widespread condemnation and economic sanctions against the South African government. The extreme disproportion between the repression and the demonstrators' behavior shocked world opinion. The shootings had made clear, said Luthuli, "the implacable, wanton brutality of their regime." [11] Throughout far away Norway, for example, flags were flown at half-mast in mourning. The Legums report that the European population in South Africa was in 1960 "staggered by the unanimity of the world's reaction to Sharpeville." By December 1963, hostility at the United Nations had increased to the point that "South Africa stood alone in the face of the world's unanimous condemnation of its policies." The South African Europeans again "reacted with dazed incomprehension or truculent self-justification." [12]

Another quite different case, the 1963 Buddhist struggle against the South Vietnamese regime of President Ngo Dinh Diem, also illustrates that, by being nonviolent, the repressed group is likely to gain significant sympathy from third parties. By 1963 President Diem had for nine years had the support of the United States. Hedrick Smith reported in his article on Diem's overthrow in *The New York Times* series on *The Pentagon Papers* revelations that "until the eruption of Buddhist demonstrations against the Diem regime in May 1963, much of the American public was oblivious to the 'political decay' in Vietnam described in the Pentagon account . . ." [13]

But on May 8 government troops fired into a crowd of Buddhists in Hué who were displaying religious flags in defiance of a government decree. Armored vehicles crushed some of the demonstrators. Nine were killed and fourteen injured. [14] The Buddhist campaign followed, using nonviolent struggle and also suicide by fire, in which monks burned themselves with gasoline. During those weeks the United States government pressed the Diem regime to meet Buddhist demands. On June 12 the deputy U.S. Ambassador, William Truehart, warned Diem that unless the Buddhist crisis was solved the United States would be forced to dissociate itself from him. Finally, on August 15 Diem declared his policy always to have been conciliation with the Buddhists.

Only six days later, however, the South Vietnamese Special Forces, financed by the United States Central Intelligence Agency and commanded by Diem's very powerful brother, Ngo Dinh Nhu, conducted cruel and destructive midnight raids on Buddhist pagodas: 1,400 people, mostly monks, were arrested, many were beaten, and thirty Buddhists were killed. [15] On

August 29, United States Ambassador Henry Cabot Lodge cabled Secretary of State Rusk, in part: ". . . there is no possibility . . . that Diem or any member of the family can govern the country in a way to gain the support of the people who count, i.e., the educated class in and out of government service, civil and military—not to mention the American people. In the last few months (and especially days) they have in fact positively alienated these people to an incalculable degree." [16]

In addition to internal reactions, the pagoda raids brought deep world resentment against the Diem regime, including criticism from the Vatican, [17] plus open United States government criticism and hints that a change of government might not be unacceptable to Washington. [18] The United States government applied pressure to get the arrested Buddhists freed and their grievances corrected. The author of the Pentagon's account of this period wrote of the consequences of the pagoda raids as follows: "In their brutality and their blunt repudiation of Diem's solemn word to [retiring Ambassador] Nolting, they were a direct, impudent slap in the face for the U.S. For better or worse, the August 21 pagoda raids decided the issue for us." [19] Four days after the raids, on August 24, the initial State Department approval of a possible change in government was sent to Ambassador Lodge, signed by Acting Secretary George W. Ball. [20] Between late August and early October decisions were taken to cut various types of economic aid to the regime. [21] From August 24 on, with slight shifts from time to time, United States officials encouraged and, from behind the scenes, assisted an already initiated generals' *coup*. This took place on November 1, after the Buddhist campaign had undermined the moral authority of and support for the regime; Diem and his family were deposed and Diem himself was killed. [22]

South Vietnamese police were obviously aware during the Buddhist campaign that unfavorable news stories and especially photographs were dangerous to the regime. Although a complete news blackout to the outside world was not politically possible, the police took sporadic action against foreign reporters. On July 7 nine Western reporters and cameramen covering a Buddhist demonstration in Saigon were attacked by police. [23] Just before the crucial raids on Buddhist pagodas, many normal channels of communication with the outside world were cut off. [24] Also, on October 5 three American reporters were beaten by plainclothes police after resisting attempts to seize their cameras which had been used to photograph a political suicide by fire. [25]

Nonviolent action by the Buddhists has been credited with extreme importance, both in bringing this sympathy to the Buddhists and in arousing support within South Vietnam for a change in government. Denis Warner has written: "The physical weakness of the Buddhists was their moral strength. If they had had guns, the Ngo Dinhs could have crushed them and neither Vietnam nor the rest of the world would have cared; defenceless they proved beyond defeat." [26]

B. Factors determining the impact of third party opinion

The third parties whose opinions may shift may be local people, or from the wider region or nation, or as the above indicated, from the world as a whole. In any case, although these shifts of opinion are desirable and usually advantageous to the nonviolent group, they alone serve a limited role at best. There should be no naïve assumption that "public opinion" alone will triumph. Disapproval by third parties and condemnation by world opinion may be very important to some opponents. Both may, in certain cases at least, contribute to uncertainty about the type of counter-action and repression being used, and even about overall policies and objectives. [27] Hostile opinion may cause the opponent to try to justify his policies and measures, or to deprecate those of the nonviolent group. But world opinion on the side of the nonviolent group will *by itself* rarely produce a change in the opponent's policies. Frequently a determined opponent can ignore hostile opinion until and unless it is accompanied by, or leads to, shifts in power relationships, or threatens to do so.

Three groups of factors will determine whether or not the opponent is affected by changes in the opinion of third parties: 1) factors related to the nature of the opponent and of the conflict situation; 2) factors related to action based on the changed opinions; and 3) factors related to the effects of opinion changes on the nonviolent actionists themselves. We shall now consider these.

First, opponents are not alike. Some of them are far more sensitive to public opinion than others. A loss of prestige and the imposition of world censure may be an intolerable price for some opponents to pay, while others will be quite willing to do so if they see no other way to their objectives. There is probably a general correlation between the degree of democracy or autocracy in the opponent's regime or system on the one hand and the degree of responsiveness or unresponsiveness to wider opinion on the other. But this is clearly not an inviolate rule, and reverse combinations sometimes occur. At times even the Nazi regime seemed highly sensitive to public opinion. The nature of the regime, its ideology, its attitude to opposition in general, the role of repression, the social system and related factors may all be important in this context. In addition, some issues may be regarded by the opponent as sufficiently important to be worth the cost of alienated opinion.

Furthermore, not all third parties will be of equal importance to the opponent. Esteem and condemnation are clearly of greater significance in some cases than in others. If the opponent is in fact dependent on certain third parties, he is much more likely to be sensitive to shifts in their opinion than he would be otherwise.

Second, changes in third-party opinions are much more likely to be effective if the opinions are transformed into actions affecting the opponent's relative power position, either opposing the opponent's regime and its policies or supporting the nonviolent group and its policies. Both *who* takes the actions and *what* actions are taken are important. All action is not equal.

The proportion of successes among past cases of international nonviolent action, especially by third parties, is extremely small.[28] There are reasons for this. In the past most third-party and international nonviolent supporting actions have been either largely symbolic in character, or, when more substantial (economic sanctions), have not been applied on the systematic and sustained basis required for effectiveness.

International action by third parties has also sometimes been regarded as a *substitute* for effective struggle by the grievance group itself—as in the case of South Africa—when in fact there is a limit to what third-party nonviolent actions alone can do. The capacity of such actions is—and perhaps should be—limited. Reliance on others is not a source of salvation for people who feel themselves oppressed but who are at the moment unable or unwilling to take effective action themselves. It is in the nature of the nonviolent technique that the main brunt of the struggle must be borne not by third parties but by the grievance group immediately affected by the opponent's policies. For third-party opinion and actions to be most effective within the context of political *jiu-jitsu,* they must, regardless of their strength, play the auxiliary role of backing up the main struggle being conducted by the nonviolent actionists from the grievance group itself. Any other view may be dangerous, for overconfidence in the potential of aid from others may distract resistance efforts from their own most important tasks. In fact, third-party support is more likely to be forthcoming when nonviolent struggle by the grievance group is being waged effectively.

Foreign financial support for nonviolent actionists is one form which third-party assistance has taken. Gandhi argued, however, that nonviolent actionists should be financially (and in other ways) self-reliant, and that in some situations foreign funds could be misperceived or misrepresented and hence be counterproductive. Instead, complete financial self-reliance, even when more limited, could be a better policy, he felt. That view does not, of course, exclude other types of third-party supporting action, such as protests, public declarations and demonstrations, diplomatic representations and sanctions, and economic sanctions.

The final way in which shifts in third-party opinion clearly aid the nonviolent actionists is by boosting their morale and encouraging them to persist until they win. Conversely, strong third-party opinion supporting the nonviolent actionists and opposing the opponent's policies and repression may help to undermine the morale of the opponent group as a whole or perhaps primarily that of certain sections of that group.

C. The future of third party support

One reason for the limited use and effectiveness of third party and international supporting actions lies in their primitive state. Conscious attempts to maximize effectiveness of this aspect of the nonviolent technique have been extremely limited, especially when it comes to supporting action for a domestic nonviolent resistance movement.

Perhaps in the future other forms of third party action may be de-designed to help the grievance group and the nonviolent actionists to increase their nonviolent combat strength. These forms might, for example, include supply of literature and handbooks about nonviolent struggle, of printing facilities or services, radio broadcasting facilities and equipment, and bases and centers for study and training in this type of struggle. Additional possible forms may provide for communication among resisters, especially when under severe repression, and with the outside world. Third parties could also relay messages between the actionists and the opponent when regular communications were severed, and could at times bring them into direct touch.

Over the past fifteen years or so pacifists have discussed the possibility of third party action in the form of international nonviolent intervention on a politically significant scale. This proposal has usually taken the form of illegal nonviolent crossings of national borders in solidarity with an internal resistance group, especially in relation to (the former) Northern Rhodesia, South West Africa and South Africa, but such an invasion has not occurred. Such forms of international nonviolent action may be applied in the future, but they are likely to have very limited effectiveness.

The conscious development of third party and international support for a domestic nonviolent resistance movement raises, of course, a series of difficult problems which lie outside the scope of this study. Some of these are questions of political wisdom, others are practical questions of application and effectiveness. Such support may in the future have far-reaching implications and potentialities, but it can, and should be, primarily in assistance of an internal resistance movement.

AROUSING DISSENT AND OPPOSITION IN THE OPPONENT'S OWN CAMP

Violent repression of nonviolent actionists is far more likely to result in uneasiness and criticism within the opponent's camp than is violent repression of violent actionists. This is so for two general reasons. First, severe repression against nonviolent people is more likely to be seen as unreasonable, distasteful, inhuman or dangerous for the society. Such repression may also be seen by members of the opponent group as too high a price to pay for continued denial of the demands of the nonviolent group. Second, when the actionists are nonviolent instead of violent it is much easier for members of the opponent group to express their possible misgivings, to advise caution, or to recommend changes in the counteractions or in the policy which is at issue. Even without a change of opinion about the issues at stake, a perception within the opponent group that severe repression or brutalities are inappropriate against nonviolent people may detach support from the opponent and arouse active dissent. Seifert suggests that the most likely group to be alienated by violent countermeasures is the vast body of persons who are normally indifferent or apathetic about major issues. When repression becomes "nasty or annoying, they withdraw their support." [29] The violence of repression does not, of course, operate completely in isolation. The issues at stake—what are they, and how important?—and the wider public and international reactions to the conflict may also be significant in this process.

A. Questioning both repression and the cause

Opposition in Britain to British policies in India and to repressive measures against the Gandhian nonviolent struggles is often cited as a reason why nonviolent action could work in that special situation. However, criticisms in Britain, and even within its Parliament, of British policy in India were only in part a result of the nature of British society and institutions, though these were obviously important. These criticisms were also a consequence of the Indians' choice of nonviolent means, which made it easier for people at home to view British rule in India in an unfavorable light.

The Indians were well aware of this aspect of political *jiu-jitsu* and consequently sought to maintain their nonviolent discipline in order to create maximum dissent from British policy in Britain itself. V.J. Patel once made this perception explicit to the American journalist Negley Farson, who had questioned him concerning the program of action for the 1930 campaign. Patel, who had just resigned as Speaker of the Indian Legislative Assembly to show support of the noncooperation movement, said:

> I am going to make you beat me so outrageously that after a while you will begin to feel ashamed of yourself, and while you are doing it, I am going to put up such an outcry that the whole street will know about it. Even your own family will be horrified at you. And after you have stood this scandal long enough, you will come to me and say, "Look here, this sort of business cannot go on any longer. Now, why cannot we two get together and settle something?" [30]

In contrast, the violence of the Mau Mau movement during the Emergency in British-ruled Kenya was far less conducive to criticism and dissent within Britain, either concerning the anti-Mau Mau repression or British colonial policies in Kenya.

In this asymmetrical conflict situation—violent repression versus nonviolent struggle—some members of the opponent group may begin to question not only the *means* of repression, but their cause itself. This is a new stage, for they may then become willing to consider the claims of the nonviolent group. Conversion, or partial steps in that direction, then become possible. In certain conflicts such positive support within the opponent group may contribute to still stronger internal dissent and opposition. Not only is the repression seen as inappropriate or cruel, but even the cause for which it is used is rejected as unjust. Thus both the negative rejection of extreme repression and brutalities, and the positive espousal of some or all of the nonviolent actionists' cause, may lead to withdrawal of support for the opponent's policies and measures. The positive espousal of the actionists' cause may also lead to concrete assistance for it even within the opponent's own camp where he normally counts on solidarity in times of crisis. Seifert points out that nonviolent action is especially conducive to playing upon existing diversities within the opponent group, including age, sex, class, political allegiance, economic interest, ideology, personality type and many others. In fact, he writes:

> In the swing toward more sympathetic regard for the resisters and their rights, it is possible to speak of a spectrum of potential support . . . This continuum ranges from those individuals and groups most

predisposed to alter their position, through various intermediary group-ings, to those most rigid and tenacious in their condemnation of the resisters.[31]

This aspect of political *jiu-jitsu* may, in summary, contribute to sev-eral types of dissent and supporting reactions among members of the op-ponent group. These include: 1) feelings that the repression and possible brutalities are excessive and that concessions are preferable to their con-tinuation; 2) an altered view of the nature of the opponent's regime and leadership, possibly resulting in a new or greatly intensified conviction that important changes in its policies, personnel, or even the system itself are required; 3) active sympathy for the nonviolent group and their cause; 4) various resulting types of unease, dissidence and even defection and dis-obedience among members of the opponent group, including officials and agents of repression; and 5) various types of positive assistance for the cause of the grievance group and aid to the nonviolent actionists. One, two, or more of these may occur in the same situation, and at times mem-bers of the opponent group may begin with the first of these reactions and then move on to more extreme ones. Illustrations of these aspects of po-litical *jiu-jitsu* are diverse. First we shall focus on certain cases of attitude change, and then cite some cases where attitude change was followed by action.

B. Repression produces defections: three cases

Occasionally an opponent has recognized in advance that, if used, severe repression would cost him support in his own group and even arouse active opposition. Because of this recognition, he had limited his repression. The British government, in late 1765 for example, faced a very difficult problem in dealing with the American colonists' defiance of the Stamp Act and their use of the weapons of economic boycott, civil disobedience, and refusal to pay debts, for these methods stimulated important opposi-tion to the Stamp Act and support for the colonists in England itself. Giv-ing in to the colonists could set a dangerous precedent, but on the other hand, ". . . were it to attempt to enforce the Stamp Act by the sword . . . it risked uprisings in support of the colonials in many of the leading trading towns of England."[32]

More often, however, the realization that repression of nonviolent re-sisters could arouse significant opposition among the opponent's usual sup-porters has come only after the event. This was true in Russia in January 1905. Superficially, Bloody Sunday was a full victory for the tsarist regime:

it had been demonstrated that protest processions would not be allowed, petitions to the Tsar would not be received, and that tsarist troops could control the streets, ruthlessly routing dissident crowds. But the real result was very different and Bloody Sunday in fact inflicted a defeat on the regime from which it was never to recover.

Not only were the poor who had long believed in the Tsar and his concern for their welfare alienated from him—a point discussed later in this chapter—but the brutality of the repression aroused strong protest among several groups whose support the system required. Liberals who still did not favor revolution obtained 459 signatures for a letter to "Officers of the Russian Army," which declared Russia's need for bread, enlightenment, liberty and a constitution, and asked the officers: should their place be with the Tsar or ". . . with all of honourable and selfless Russia? As men of honour, you will not use arms against the unarmed, you will not take money from the people for its blood, which you have already spilled." The letter asked them to turn their arms against "the enemies of the people." [33] Not only did factory workers go on strike; there developed "what may be called a strike among the educated class, . . . generally peaceful but openly defiant." Lawyers refused to appear in the courts and formally protested against the "pitiless hand of the government." Medical, legal, pedagogical and agricultural societies denounced the regime, calling for a constituent assembly. Because of their participation in the repression of Bloody Sunday, guards officers were refused admittance to the Merchants Club. The Manufacturers Association voted to give financial help to the victims' families, to demand political reforms, and to take no action against workers on strike. A declaration that the events had created the need for a change in government was issued by sixteen members of the august Academy of Sciences, and signed first by 326 distinguished professors and lecturers and then by 1,200 of the country's most noted scholars. [34]

It is not widely recognized that French military action and brutal measures of repression against the nonviolent resistance in the Ruhr alienated Frenchmen at home and played a role in the 1924 electoral defeat of the government which had launched the invasion and been responsible for the repression. In the 1924 elections a coalition of the Left was victorious, and consequently in May Poincaré resigned. Halperin writes that this political upset was partly due to "a nation-wide revulsion against the methods he [Poincaré] had employed in dealing with the whole complex of Franco-German relations . . ." Many Frenchmen, Halperin reports, had begun to realize that both the occupation and "the policy of coercion" against the resistance had been mistakes. Not only had "France . . . failed to attain her objective" but "the invasion cost her more than she was able to get out of it."[35] Not only did Frenchmen at home change their attitudes toward the occupation and repression; so did many French occupation soldiers and civilian occupation aides. The German historian of this struggle, Friedrich Grimm, reports:

> The occupation had repercussions which no one had expected. Thousands of Frenchmen who went to the Ruhr as soldiers and civilians became *"advocats des boches,"* intercessors on behalf of the Germans. For the first time they saw the Germans as they really are . . .There were even many high-ranking officers who had soon to be replaced as unsuitable because of their friendly attitude towards the Germans . . .[36]

C. Four more cases of defections

Even the Nazis had on occasion to consider whether or not they might lose more support by acting against a defiant opponent than by giving in. After the failure of a number of written protests by Catholic and Protestant church leaders against the "top secret" program of systematic extermination of the incurably ill, Bishop Galen, speaking in the St. Lamberti Church in Münster on August 3, 1941, described in detail how the ill were being killed and their families deceived; Galen stamped the actions as criminal, and demanded that the killers be charged with murder. Copies of the Bishop's sermon were circulated throughout the country and among troops at the front. He became so popular that the government—at the height of its military victories—decided in its own interest not to punish him. Martin Bormann (Head of the Nazi Party Chancery) thought Bishop Galen should be executed, but propaganda chief Goebbels feared that if that happened, the population of Münster and perhaps of all Westphalia would be lost to the war effort. Even though Hitler was furious, he feared to make Bishop Galen a martyr; indeed a short while later a *Führerbefehl* was issued stopping the systematic extermination of the incurably ill. By then about seventy thousand had been gassed; only scattered killings occurred later.[37]

Brutalities against nonviolent Africans have aroused sympathies among the dominant Europeans—even in South Africa. Such sympathies developed, for example, during the successful 1957 bus boycott conducted by Africans living in Alexandra location near Johannesburg. Despite official threats, many European automobile drivers gave rides to the walking African boycotters. On the route the Africans had been systematically intimidated and persecuted by the police.[38] Also, after Sharpeville, unprovoked attacks —including whippings—by police against Africans in the Capetown area during an African strike, led to so many European bystanders phoning to report the attacks to Capetown newspapers that the switchboards were jammed; the President of the Cape Chamber of Industries, C.F. Regnier, personally pleaded with the Chief of Police, Col. I.P.S. Terblanche, to stop the assaults.[39]

In the United States also, nonviolent persistence against repression and brutalities in civil rights struggles led to considerable white support and participation in the actions and in other ways; later, when nonviolent means were less prominent and violence increased, this white support was drastically reduced.[40] When official repression and unofficial brutalities against disciplined and courageous nonviolent actionists became especially severe, Southern white communities and even the prosegregationist leadership sometimes split, and significant sections among them counseled moderation, concessions to the Negroes, and a halt to brutalities. Sometimes these defections began to operate behind the scenes before they became public.[41] There are several examples, including some from Montgomery, Atlanta and Birmingham.

After a federal court ordered an end to racial segregation on the buses of Montgomery, Alabama, at the end of the 1956-57 bus boycott, white extremists bombed two homes and four churches. Martin Luther King, Jr., reported that the next morning there were three major defections from the hard-line segregationists' camp. The editor of the *Montgomery Advertiser,* Gus Hall, in a strong editorial entitled "Is it safe to live in Montgomery?" argued that although he supported segregation, the bombings had shifted the issue, and he could not stomach these excesses. Several white clergymen issued a statement, repeated throughout the day by the distinguished Presbyterian minister Reverend Merle Patterson, denouncing the bombings as un-Christian and uncivilized. The businessmen's organization, the Men of Montgomery, also publically opposed the bombings. King wrote: "For the first time since the protest began, these influential whites were on public record on the side of law and order." [42] A few more bombings were attempted, but they were quickly halted. The bombings had lost important support for the extreme segregationists and, reports King, "it was clear that the vast majority of Montgomery's whites preferred peace and law to the excesses performed in the name of segregation." [43]

Later, in 1961, when anti-segregationist "freedom riders" were brutally beaten by white extremists in Atlanta, Georgia, with the police refusing to intervene, many Southern whites were again repelled. The Atlanta *Constitution* editorially criticized the police for not preventing the brutalities against the "freedom riders":

> If the police, representing the people, refuse to intervene when a man—any man—is being beaten to the pavement of an American city, then it is not a noble land at all. It is a jungle. But this is a noble land. And it is time for the decent people in it to muzzle the jackals.[44]

In May 1963 when police brutalities were committed against demonstrating Negro women and children during the civil rights struggle in Birmingham, Alabama, one of the effects was a withdrawal of the white business community from its firm support for segregation. Also, in contrast to earlier situations, most Birmingham whites no longer actively supported or participated in the repressive actions; instead "the majority were maintaining a strictly hands-off policy."[45] After returning from a tour of the Far East, the President of the Birmingham Chamber of Commerce, Sidney Smyer, said that his city had lost much prestige as a result of the violence there against freedom riders.[46]

A similar defection from the opponent's camp occurred in South Vietnam in 1963 in the campaign in which Buddhists charged they were discriminated against by the government, which favored the Roman Catholic minority. Although South Vietnamese Catholics might have been expected to support the Diem regime against the 1963 Buddhist campaign, many Catholics felt they could not support the repressive measures being used. The Roman Catholic Archbishop of Saigon, Nguyen Van Binh, circulated a pastoral letter in August appealing for religious tolerance, stating that some "confuse the political authority that governs Vietnam with the spiritual power that rules the Church in Vietnam."[47] Brutal repression during that struggle led to major defections from the Diem regime, both at the lower levels, and high in the regime; for example, the Foreign Minister and the Ambassador to the United States both resigned.[48] Actual defections of officials as a result of the operation of this aspect of political *jiu-jitsu* have also occurred in other cases.

D. The troops mutiny

Defections sometimes extend to police and troops who are charged with inflicting repression, as happened in the Vietnamese struggle. After the repression of Buddhist demonstrators in early June 1963, the *New York Herald Tribune* reported "growing unrest among army units in central Vietnam, whose ranks are mostly filled with Buddhists."[49] In August unrest was widely reported even among the wives of secret policemen, with the result that there was often plenty of warning of coming repression.[50] Army unrest extended even to the generals, producing, as we noted, a military *coup* when the government's moral authority had been undermined by the Buddhist campaign, a *coup* backed, but not instigated, by the United States.

Unease and disaffection among the opponent's agents of repression may be expressed by deliberate inefficiency in carrying out their duties. This inefficiency is especially likely if they are unwilling or unable to risk the penalties for open disobedience. In other cases, the police or troops may actually mutiny and defy orders to inflict repression. Both these types of behavior are discussed in Chapter Seven. Out of revulsion against severe repression against nonviolent actionists, regular troops, police and officers may deliberately but covertly restrict their assistance in it, or they may openly defy orders to carry out repression. Both types of behavior may, if sufficiently widespread or if they occur in crisis situations, severely reduce the repressive power of the regime.

The main example which will be offered here of the impact of troop mutiny in face of nonviolent action on the outcome of the struggle is from the February 1917 Russian revolution. This case is sufficiently important to merit detailed attention, especially since many people assume in ignorance that violence was necessary to destroy the tsarist regime.

Even Trotsky, who was no exponent of nonviolence, acknowledged after 1905 that victory or defeat in that revolution had hinged on whether the troops could be made sympathetic to the revolutionaries. He added that the greatest power did not lie in weapons, though they were useful:

Not the capacity of the masses to kill others but their great readiness to die themselves . . . assures in the last instance the success of a popular uprising . . . the soul of the soldier . . . must experience . . . a profound commotion . . . Even barricades . . . are of significance in reality above all as a moral force . . .[51]

The failure of the 1905 Revolution can be largely traced to the failure to win the soldiers over to massive disobedience on a large scale.

In contrast, large scale mutinies occurred in February 1917 and these were highly significant in the disintegration of the Tsar's power. One of the reasons for these mutinies was the "profound commotion" produced within and among the soldiers by the predominantly nonviolent behavior of the revolutionary people. It is true that for a time there was considerable restraint in the use of violence on *both* sides, and also that violence was used in Petrograd by *both* sides on a scattered basis. However, up to February 25 the government forces had orders not to use firearms on the demonstrating crowds except in self-defense. This made it possible for the demonstrators to talk with the troops. "The soldiers soon caught the mood of the crowd. To them they seemed to be peaceful demonstrators, against whom it would be an outrage to use arms." [52]

Even the Bolsheviks at this point tried to prevent violence by the revolutionaries—though Leninist doctrine stressed the importance of violence. The Bolsheviks in Petrograd now behaved very differently than they had in 1905. In February 1917 they saw prevention of violence against the troops as necessary to induce them to mutiny, after which, the Bolsheviks believed, the former soldiers would make effective military means available for the revolution; the Bolsheviks sought nonviolence only for tactical purposes. This does not, however, destroy the significance of these events. Katkov writes:

> . . . even the Bolshevik leaders seem to have done everything in their power to prevent shooting in the streets. [Alexandr] Shlyapnikov [one of three members of the Russian Bureau of the Central Committee of the Party] is most definite on this point. When workers urged him to arm the demonstrators with revolvers, he refused. Not, he says, that it would have been difficult to get hold of arms. But that was not the point:
>
> "I feared [says Shlyapnikov] that a rash use of arms thus supplied could only harm the cause. An excited comrade who used a revolver against a soldier would only provoke some military unit and provide an excuse for the authorities to incite the troops against the workers. I therefore firmly refused to give arms to anybody who asked for them, and insisted again and again that the soldiers must be brought into the uprising, for in this way arms would be provided for all workers. This was a more difficult decision to carry out than getting a couple of dozen revolvers, but it was a consistent programme of action." [53]

The Tsar had telegraphed an order on February 25 to Khabalov, commander of the Petrograd Military District, to "put an end as from tomorrow to all disturbances in the streets of the capital." Accordingly, the troops fired into demonstrating crowds in Znamensky and Kazansky Squares on the next day. There were many dead and wounded. Katkov reports the impact of the events on the soldiers who had obeyed orders:

> What cannot be too strongly emphasized is the effect of the shooting on the troops themselves . . . When at last they were ordered to open

fire on the same predominantly unarmed crowds they had previously fraternized with, they were appalled, and there is no reason to doubt General Martynov's estimate of the situation: "The overwhelming majority of the soldiers were disgusted with the role assigned to them in quelling the riots and fired only under compulsion." This applied in particular to the training unit of the Volynsky Regiment, consisting of two companies with two machine-guns, which had to disperse the demonstrations of Znamensky Square . . . leaving forty dead and as many wounded lying on the pavement. [54]

The result of this and other shootings was that "order had been restored." That was not, however, the end of the story.

The next day there was a brief mutiny of some members of the Pavlovsky Guards Regiment, two of whose companies had taken part in the shootings. Some went into the streets and called for an end to the bloodshed. [55] Much more significant, however, was the effect of the shootings on the soldiers of the Volynsky Regiment, who had fired on demonstrators in Znamensky Square.

After the officers had left the barracks, the men gathered to discuss the day's events. They could not understand why they had had to shoot . . . Nothing indicates that it was revolutionary conviction that led to the troops' momentous decision to refuse to fire on the demonstrating crowds. They were, far more probably, prompted by a natural revulsion against what they had been doing under the command of a most unpopular officer. Yet they must have known the risks they incurred in adopting a mutinous attitude. [56]

On Monday, the 27th, the day after the shootings, these same troops informed their officer of their refusal to go out into the streets. After he left them he was shot by an unknown assassin. The disobedient troops left their barracks, went into the streets, proclaimed their support for the people's rising, and tried to persuade other regiments to follow their example. Other units did indeed also mutiny, and troop reinforcements had a way of "dissolving" on the way to their destinations, merging with the anonymous crowd. It was not long before the Tsar's regime no longer had an effective military force at its command in the capital. [57] This evidence suggests that had the demonstrators at Znamensky Square fired on the soldiers of the Volynsky Regiment, and had other demonstrators also done so elsewhere, the Tsar's troops would have been more likely to remain loyal, and without their mutiny the Tsar's regime would probably not have disintegrated. The Tsar's capacity for violent repression was detroyed when the troops mutinied after shooting peaceful demonstrators. Exponents of nonviolent action see this process as important in revolutionary situations.

In a very different case, it is significant that the Garhwali mutiny in India in late 1930 occurred immediately after severe repression in Peshawar, where at least 30 and perhaps as many as 125 demonstrators had been killed.[58] "The 2/18th Royal Garhwal Rifles were ordered to Peshawar, but two platoons refused to proceed, on the ground that their duty was to fight enemies from abroad and not to shoot 'unarmed brethen'," writes Gopal.[59] The severe repression against peaceful demonstrators thus produced a situation of great potential gravity for the regime, although insufficient to destroy it.

Some cases of disaffection or open mutiny also occurred during the 1953 East German Rising. For example, as stronger action was taken against the rising, the Russians sent Polish tanks across the border at Goerlitz to disperse demonstrators. Thousands of the demonstrators greeted the tanks. An eyewitness to the encounter, Don Doane, an Associated Press correspondent, wrote:

> The senior Polish officer stepped out of his tank, faced the Germans —and saluted. "I don't fire on German workers," he said. The Germans returned his salute.
>
> When the Russians saw the Poles were not going to resist the Germans, they ordered the Polish troops back across the border and sent in Russian tanks.[60]

East German police and troops and even Russian troops sometimes proved unreliable when ordered to put down the predominantly nonviolent rising. Cases of disobedience of orders occurred both among East German police and Russian officers. The Russians frequently brought in fresh troops who had not previously been in East Germany and would presumably have less inhibitions against carrying out repressive measures against the population.[61]

E. Splits in the opponent regime

Not only may troops defect; splits over the conflict may develop between officials of the regime itself. This should be expected, for internal conflicts sometimes occur in a regime engaged in conflict, even when it is against a *violent* enemy. For example, significant conflicts over policy for the occupied sections of the Soviet Union occurred within the Nazi system—a regime in which most people would not expect to find internal disputes.[62] However, internal conflicts in the opponent group are much more likely when the other party to the conflict is *nonviolent*. This is because the actionists pose no *violent* threat (which usually unifies the opponent's camp), and also because counteracting a nonviolent campaign is especially difficult, conducive to different opinions on what to do, and later to recriminations over the failure of those counteractions. Some of the conflicts within the opponent group may thus be created by the problems of dealing with a nonviolent struggle group, while others may be rooted in earlier problems or rivalries within the regime which have been aggravated by the conflict.

Studies focusing on the relationships between splits within the opponent regime and the use of nonviolent struggle in actual historical cases remain to be undertaken. A comparative study might be undertaken of the opponent's internal conflicts on policy and repression in several cases, for example, the British in dealing with the Indian campaigns, the French in dealing with the Ruhr resistance, and the Norwegian fascists and German Nazis in dealing with the Norwegian resistance. Internal conflicts may be most expected when the campaign lasts some weeks or months, which gives time for conflicts arising over how to deal with the challenge to develop, or for control measures to fail and invite recriminations, or for old rivalries to take on new forms in the context of the struggle. However, the fact that splits among officials occurred almost immediately in the unexpected and very brief civilian insurrection of the East German Rising of June 16–17, 1953, suggests that splits within the opponent's regime may be extremely important in some cases of nonviolent struggle.

In the East German case some of the confusion and splits among officials and Party leaders focused on the problem of the appropriate counteraction, and both East German leaders and the Russians themselves thought that severe repression might cost them more than it would help in crushing the rebellion. The Socialist Unity Party's Central Committee later admitted that some Party organizations, organs, officials and members had given in "to panic and confusion," and that in "many cases" Party members had lost nerve and capitulated or even themselves taken part in meetings and demonstrations against the regime. Also, at the time, the Minister for State Security, Wilhelm Zaisser, and the Editor-in-Chief of the official paper *Neues Deutschland,* Rudolf Herrnstadt, formed a faction in the Politburo and the Central Committee with the intent of overthrowing Ulbricht.[63] Their reasons may not have been directly related to the rising itself, but the timing may be significant. From the beginning some Party officials favored violent repression, but others counseled against it. On June 16 the Russians first prohibited repressive police action against workers marching down the Stalinallee, believing it would be "provocative." Despite pressure from the chief of the East Berlin police, the Berlin district secretary of the Party refused to urge the Russians to permit strong repression, as he did not want to be regarded as a "worker slaughterer." [64] The nature of the East German and Russian regimes, and the rapidity with which internal confllcts appeared, suggest that investigation of the possible relationships between nonviolent struggle and splits in the opponent's camp may be highly important.

F. Provocation and appeals

Nonviolent actionists aware that brutal repression may produce unease, dissent and opposition within the opponent group have on occasion provoked the opponent to violence deliberately. For example, after British woman suffragists were maltreated by bystanders and police and then arrested, some suffragists concluded that their cause had gained more than it had lost by the events, and therefore they in the future deliberately provoked violent police reprisals in order to split the opponents of woman suffrage over the repression, embarrass the leaders of the political parties and get them to act on the demand for suffrage. [65] This type of provocation, however, has limited utility and contains its own dangers. Conversely, fearing the political *jiu-jitsu* effect of severe repression and not wanting opposition "at home," the opponent may try to prevent the facts from being discovered at all and to block thc dissemination of existing information. This interpretation was placed on British attempts in 1930-31 to block investigations into severe repression against Indian nonviolent actionists, as by arresting two unofficial committees before their enquiries into police excesses in Rampur, Gujarat, could begin. [66] Censorship may also be applied on a wide scale.

Nonviolent actionists may also encourage splits in the opponent group by quite different means, by direct appeals and efforts to persuade members of that group of the justice of the cause of the grievance group and to solicit their support for it. These efforts may take a variety of forms, including personal conversations, small and large meetings, distribution of literature, and many other means. Luthuli in South Africa, for example, took advantage of a number of opportunities to address all-white meetings and racially mixed gatherings in order to explain the conditions under which Africans were living and to plead their cause. [67] In 1920 the legal German government used leaflets called "The Collapse of the Military

Dictatorship" to spread President Ebert's stirring appeal to defeat the Kapp *Putsch*. Strikers handed the leaflets to troops, and a government plane dropped them over the capital, including over the soldiers barracks.[68]

As the examples in this section show, nonviolent action may accentuate and arouse internal dissent and opposition within the opponent's own group both without deliberate efforts by the nonviolent group to do so, and when the actionists consciously seek to produce such splits—and deliberate efforts are likely to help. The capacity of the nonviolent technique to create and aggravate internal problems for the opponent group puts nonviolent action in a special class among techniques of struggle. Violent techniques, in contrast, usually seem to presume that the opponent group is a fixed entity to be fought and defeated, not a group which could be split and within which major active support could be won. In this respect guerrilla warfare is closer to nonviolent action than other violent techniques, though still at a considerable distance. In conventional warfare, although splits in the opponent group are welcomed when they occur, the usual assumption is that they will not and that the group as a whole must be defeated; in addition, conventional warfare generally contributes to increased unity within the opponent group which rallies together against the dangers of enemy attack.

INCREASING SUPPORT AND PARTICIPATION FROM THE GRIEVANCE GROUP

There is a third way in which political *jiu-jitsu* causes the opponent's severe repression and brutalities to recoil against his power position. The repression may increase the resistance from the grievance group itself, instead of intimidating them into acquiescence. This process will be first illustrated with an example from the Russian revolutionary movement, and then the general process will be discussed with further examples.

A. The victory in Palace Square

Nineteenth century Russian revolutionaries had long been vexed with a severe problem: how to destroy the naïve faith in the Tsar held by the mass of the peasants and workers, how to make them see that the Tsar was not a benevolent well-intentioned father but the head of an oppressive social and political system, how to make them see the system in all its naked violence. Bakunin, for example, had written: "Above all we must destroy within the hearts of the people the remains of that unfortunate faith in the Tsar which for centuries has condemned them to terrible serfdom." [69] Violence by revolutionaries had failed to do this. In 1866, when Karakozov attempted to assassinate Tsar Alexander II, the result was a rallying of sympathy and support from the poor for the Tsar, while the revolutionaries lost both drastically. Venturi reports that ". . . all sources are agreed that the peasants stood by the Emperor, often violently." ". . . the attempt on the Tsar's life did show how strong was the alliance between the monarchy and the mass of working classes and peasants." [70] As long as the workers and peasants believed in the benevolence of the Tsar and consequently supported him, popular mass revolution in Russia would remain a utopian dream of isolated sectarians.

The killing and wounding of hundreds of peaceful marchers who were under instructions to remain nonviolent, which made January 9, 1905 famous as Bloody Sunday, destroyed that alliance of the poor with the Tsar. The sharp contrast between the brutal political violence of the regime and the nonviolence of the marching petitioners shattered the naïve belief of the peasants and workers in the benevolence of the Tsar. Only when that belief was shattered did a popular revolution by the masses of people become possible. The British Ambassador at St. Petersburg, Lord Hardinge of Penhurst, wrote that because of Bloody Sunday ". . . a gulf was created between the Emperor and his people and the story was spread that when his subjects came to present their grievances to the 'Little Father' they were mowed down by his troops." [71] Several historians have also pointed to this change and its significance. Schapiro: ". . . from this day on, . . . faith in the Emperor's love and care for his people was shattered." [72] Charques: ". . . it did perhaps more than anything else during the whole reign to undermine the allegiance of the common people to the throne . . ." [73] Harcave: "After January 9, the liberation movement could count on far greater support and more favorable conditions for expansion and action than ever before." "The socialists . . . had been given just what they had sought for years: an aroused working class." [74] Keep: "It dissipated what remained of peasant ways of thinking and opened their minds to revolutionary propaganda." [75] "Another event like Bloody Sunday might be sufficient to topple the government . . ." [76]

On January 17, six days after the shootings, Minister of Agriculture Alexis Ermolov in his regular report to the Tsar called the shootings a disaster for the government, warned that the army might disobey orders to shoot and that even if it remained loyal it might be inadequate to defeat a rising in the countryside. Ermolov reminded the Tsar that he depended on the people's support, which needed to be regained and maintained.[77]

In addition to turning the middle class, intellectuals, businessmen and nobility against the regime—as discussed earlier—Bloody Sunday began one of the great popular mass revolutions in history. The workers resorted to strike action—in the remainder of January alone more workers were on strike than the whole decade from 1894 to 1904.[78] For the first time in Russia's history the peasants began to act as an organized political force in opposition to the government.[79] The easy "victory" of the Tsar's troops in Palace Square reverberated throughout the Empire, shattered illusions, and recoiled in anger, determination and revolution. The "victory" in clearing the square had created the most important precondition for a mass revolutionary movement.

B. Strength needed to withstand repression

Of course severe repression does not always produce mass revolution or even increased resistance. As has been emphasized throughout this Part of the book, this technique has requirements which must be fulfilled if it is to be successful. The most important of these are the requirements associated with the nonviolent group itself. One of these is that people must not be intimidated by repression. Whether severe repression results in decreased or increased resistance depends to a considerable degree on how much suffering the actionists and the general grievance group are willing and able to endure as the price of change. If their conviction in the rightness of their cause is not strong, if their courage falters, or if the suffering is greater than their capacity to bear it, then whether or not more persons become alienated from the opponent, the numbers of actionists will not increase by additions from the general grievance group, and may even diminish. Under such conditions, growing severity of repression may lower morale in the grievance group and among the nonviolent actionists and reduce resistance. The weak may be weeded out.[80] This is one of the important reasons why numbers alone are not decisive in nonviolent action, and why there is no substitute in this technique for genuine strength. Submission to violence spells defeat.

But violent repression need not spell submission. Contrary to popular opinion, as we have already seen in Chapter Ten, how much suffering people can withstand is *not* determined only by the relative severity of the repression. The strength, resilience and will of the nonviolent group are also very important. In fact, severities and brutalities under certain conditions *increase* resistance and weaken the opponent. Machiavelli argued that when a ruler is opposed by the public as a whole and attempts to make himself secure by brutality, "the greater his cruelty, the weaker does his regime become." [81]

C. Repression may legitimize resistance

When violence is committed against people who are, and are seen to be, nonviolent, it is difficult for the opponent to claim "self-defense" for his use of extreme repression, or to argue that the severe repression was for the good of the society as a whole. Instead, the opponent is likely to appear to many people as a villain, and many will believe that the worst accusations against the opponent are being confirmed, and that they are witnessing "deepening injustice." [82]

When such extreme repression occurs, the chances of the nonviolent group agreeing to a compromise settlement far short of their avowed aims may be sharply reduced. Severe Puritan repression against Quakers in Massachusetts Bay Colony, for example, "made the Quakers all the more certain that the Puritans were anti-Christ." [83] British measures against Indians practicing civil disobedience made many Indians believe the worst possible interpretations of British motives and of the nature of the *Raj*.

When severe repression is directed against nonviolent actionists who persist in the struggle with obvious courage and at great cost, the actionists' persistence makes it difficult for the opponent to claim he has acted to "defend" or "liberate" the people concerned. Instead, it will be seen that the opponent could not win obedience and support on the basis of the merits of the regime and its policies and has therefore in desperation sought to induce submission by severe measures. He is seen as *unable* to rule without extreme repression. Concerning repression in India, J.C. Kumarappa made this point when he wrote in 1930 that "the Government . . . . is . . . demonstrating beyond a doubt its total incapacity to govern by civilized methods." [84] People whose lives have been affected by the grievances, who have nevertheless seen the opponent as benevolent and well-intentioned, may now shift. For them the opponent's positive image may be destroyed and they may become convinced that he deserves not obedience and cooperation but defiance and resistance.

One result of this increased alienation is that the *existing* group of nonviolent actionists may become more—not less—determined to continue their intended course and even to expand their efforts to bring about change. To be imprisoned for disobedience, for example, is interpreted not as a shame but as an honor. This shift took place both in India among nationalist resisters,[85] and in the United States among woman suffragists and civil rights workers.[86] "The result is both legitimization and intensification of revolt."[87] The effects of alienation from the opponent extend still further, however.

D. The numbers of resisters may grow

If determination and willingness to pay the price of resistance become great enough among members of the general grievance group, this increase in alienation from the opponent may mean that more members of that group become active participants in the struggle. The numbers of nonviolent actionists defying the opponent may then increase. This is in line with Gregg's view that in nonviolent action the suffering and even death of the volunteers in face of the opponent's repression are likely to produce new volunteers to take the place of the fallen.[88]

The opponent's problems in dealing with this development will be multiplied because this nonviolent technique can, far more than violence, involve as active participants *all* sections of the population—not only able-bodied young men, but women, the young, and the old.[89] In India in 1930 for example, at Mahuva in Kathiawad, Gujarat, four thousand women and children went on a fast in sympathy with the picketers of shops selling foreign cloth. The dealers in foreign cloth then stopped sales.[90] Also in that campaign, thousands of women took an active part in picketing, parades and in civil disobedience against the Salt Act and other types of noncooperation. This participation of women, usual in Indian society, was difficult for the police to deal with.[91] During the Korean struggle in 1919-22 against Japanese rule, not only women but school children took part in the nonviolent protest campaign. It was reported that police attacked them with drawn swords, beat them, and as a punishment publicly stripped girls taking part in the protest. As a result Koreans were still further alienated from the regime.[92]

Increased resistance has sometimes resulted also when brutal repression has been applied against violent resistance or against mixed violent and nonviolent resistance. There are cases in which the violence of the repression was highly disproportionate to the lesser violence of the resistance. The Nazis encountered this general phenomenon on a number of occasions. In occupied areas of the Soviet Union, they were ruthless in repression, seized people for slave labor in Germany, exterminated many prisoners of war, and did many other such things. The result was not, however, passive submission to Nazi rule, but flaming resentment and resistance. Dr. Otto Bräutigam, deputy leader of the Political Department of Rosenberg's Ministry for the Occupied Eastern Territories, in a confidential report to his superiors, wrote that German policy and practice in the occupied Soviet Union had "brought about the enormous resistance of the Eastern peoples." [93] Shooting of innocent hostages was widely used in Nazi-occupied Europe to terrorize the population into submission and to halt various acts of opposition, usually sabotage or acts of violence. The results were often the opposite of those intended, however. The policy of shooting hostages led to protests to Keitel from both the Commander of the *Wehrmacht* (German Army) in the Netherlands and from the military Governor of Belgium, General Falkenhausen. The latter wrote to Field Marshall Keitel in September 1942, as follows:

> The result is undoubtedly very unsatisfactory. The effect is not so much deterrent as destructive of the feeling of the population for right and security; the gulf between the people influenced by Communism and the remainder of the population is being bridged; all circles are becoming filled with a feeling of hatred towards the occupying forces, and effective inciting material is given to enemy propaganda. Thereby military danger and general political reaction of an entirely unwanted nature . . .[94]

In Denmark, the Nazis were unable to destroy a single Danish resistance organization of any importance throughout the occupation, although they were able to arrest, deport and execute members of those organizations. The Danish occupation historian de J. Hæstrup writes: "It seems that suppression only gave birth to more vigorous resistance. The view might be different in other countries where conditions were more cruel, but the Danish conclusion must be that suppression is a two-edged sword." [95]

Although, as the above cases indicate, a *jiu-jitsu* effect increasing, not reducing, resistance *may* operate in cases of mixed violent and nonviolent resistance, or of repression highly disproportionate to the resistance violence, the *jiu-jitsu* effect is both more frequent and more intensive in cases of exclusively nonviolent action. This is so contrary to the popular assumption that power accrues to the violent, that several cases will now be described or cited in which repression against nonviolent action produced not passive submission but increased alienation and resistance.

In addition to the events of 1905, described earlier in this section, there are many other Russian examples of repression leading to increased alienation of the population and to intensified resistance. Thus, for example, the tsarist regime used the army to intervene in 269 industrial disputes between 1895 and 1899. Keep writes:

... some officers seem to have taken it for granted that bloodshed was an unfortunate but necessary means of intimidating "rebellious elements" into submission. Naturally, where shooting took place, this served to embitter the atmosphere still further. Often it provoked action by workers in other enterprises, which it was the main aim of the military to prevent.[96]

When police used whips to quell student disturbances at St. Petersburg University in 1899, the result was a student strike all over Russia.[97]

The old statement that the blood of the martyrs is the seed of the Church is thus not at all a sectarian religious saying for the comfort of the believers. It is a profound statement about a likely consequence of brutal repression against nonviolent people who stand firm in their convictions—a statement with wide political implications far beyond the treatment of unwanted religious groups. In his tirade against the German philosopher Eugen Dühring, Frederick Engels, no less, argued that Dühring's anti-religious extremism would in fact help religion to survive: ". . . he incites his gendarmes of the future against religion, and thereby helps it to martyrdom and a prolonged lease on life." [98] In the 1920s the Communist Party of the Soviet Union, having ignored Engels' warning, found it difficult to ignore the demonstrated validity of his opinion. "The party," writes Schapiro, "could persecute priests and preach atheism, but the communists were soon to discover that religion thrives on persecution." [99]

The sixteenth century Inquisition begun by Charles V in the Netherlands, if not increasing public defiance, at least added to the numbers of heretics. Pieter Geyl writes:

... after the first deaths by fire—the victims were two Antwerp Augustinian monks, burnt at Brussels in 1523—the number of the martyrs kept steadily growing . . . . And yet this horror . . . achieved no more than that the opinions which it was intended to kill were driven underground. Men who could have given a lead kept quiet or left the country, but the spectacle of the martyrs' sufferings and courage made many thousands of simple souls take the new heresy into their hearts. In the parlour and the market place, in the workshop and in the meetings of the Rhetoricians, passionate discussions went on about the problems of faith. Souls that were inaccessible to the learning of the humanists now thirsted after the new doctrine.[100]

In the American colonies, too, the English soon found that their attempts to force the colonials to obey and to halt political and economic noncooperation by military means or by threats of new punishment usually only heightened the spirit of defiance. The unplanned Boston Massacre heightened the spirit of opposition and increased the practice of resistance not only in Massachusetts Bay but throughout the American colonies—even though the British troops had been provoked. In Boston the deaths of those shot by the troops were deliberately used to arouse more general opposition to the British rule. [101] The commanding officers finally acceded to the demand of the Boston town authorities, supported unanimously by the Council of Massachusetts Bay, that British troops be withdrawn from the city; they were transferred to Castle William in the harbor, [102] a result which the colonials could not easily have achieved by military means. Other colonies also reacted very strongly to the news [103] and the Massacre gave considerable impetus to the economic boycott movement. [104]

Although relatively mild by contemporary standards of State repression, the coercive acts enacted by Parliament in the spring of 1774 evoked widespread opposition and a significant increase in resistance, which they had been intended to quell. The new acts were designed to alter the Massachusetts constitution and destroy the independence of the town meetings in order to halt unrest and to punish the refusal of compensation to the East India Company for the losses inflicted at the Boston Tea Party. While these acts led to a tendency for merchants to side with the government more than they had earlier, the general effect of the coercive acts was to win converts to the radical position, to make the issues at stake in the conflict clearly political, and to increase hostility to the English government. Dr. Benjamin Franklin was one of many who, though antagonized by the earlier destruction of tea in Boston harbor, found the new acts even more offensive. [105] The closing of the port of Boston and transfer of the provincial capital from the city also aroused widespread indignation, opposition and resistance (not all nonviolent), instead of achieving the intended reimbursement for property losses and passive submission. [106] These acts against Boston were cited as a reason for the Continental Association program of noncooperation. [107] "The Coercive Acts made open rebellion inevitable." [108] Gipson also writes concerning the situation in September 1774: "Only the removal of the pressures brought to bear upon Massachusetts Bay to compel its obedience to the will of the government of Great Britain could now stem the revolutionary tide." [109]

During the nonviolent resistance to the Kapp *Putsch* there were several similar instances. When pro-Kapp *Freikorps* troops on March 14, 1920, occupied the offices of two newspapers supporting the legal Government, *Freiheit* and *Vorwärts,* the result was not the submission of all associated with newspaper publishing, but a strike of all the printers in Berlin.[110] One morning the Kapp group arrested all the ministers of the Prussian Government—which controlled a major section of Germany. Immediately, the railroad workers threatened to strike unless Minister Oesser —in charge of railroads—were released; he refused to leave unless the other ministers were also released, and they were all let go.[111] It is true that the *Putsch* was ill planned and inefficiently carried out. It would be a mistake, however, to attribute its collapse to faint-heartedness of Dr. Kapp in face of resistance, for he finally ordered that all strikers be shot (only to find that his own troops would not carry out the order).[112]

While French repression was sometimes effective during the *Ruhrkampf,* at other times it was not. In one case, for example, after an occupation ultimatum of twenty-four hours had expired, French troops evicted thousands of families of striking railworkers from their homes and left them in the streets. The German workers, however, did not return to their jobs. In fact German Transportation Minister Gröner instructed not only the workers, but also all higher functionaries and civil servants of the railroads in the occupied territory to refuse all cooperation with the French. Furthermore, Gröner promised them financial compensation for possible losses.[113]

Indians struggling nonviolently against British rule often found that severe repression, and especially brutalities (even when provoked), helped the independence movement by increasing the number of Indians opposed to the *Raj* and willing to resist it. The shootings at Jallianwala Bagh, Amritsar, in 1919 were unprovoked. They permanently alienated many Indians from British colonial rule. On an official goodwill visit for Britain sometime after the Amritsar shooting, the Duke of Connaught observed: "Since I landed I have felt around me bitterness and estrangement between those who have been my friends. The shadow of Amritsar has lengthened over the face of India."[114] Those shootings, which came to be called a massacre, helped to complete Gandhi's own disaffection from the British Empire for which he had once had warm and sympathetic feelings. Disillusioned with the manner in which Prime Minister David Lloyd George handled the killings and the question of reparations, Gandhi wrote in December 1920 that his "faith in the good intentions of the Government and the nation which is supporting it" had been "completely shattered.''[115] In the coming years India and Britain were to experience the full effects of his alienation.

Severe unprovoked repression occurred during the 1930-31 campaign, but sometimes the Indians used nonviolent means that were deliberately provocative. A young Indian in Bombay attempted to stop a truck delivering foreign cloth by lying in front of it and was killed when the truck ran over him. Then the population throughout Bombay Presidency became indignant and the boycott of foreign cloth became highly successful.[116] After reporting a number of police brutalities against the nonviolent actionists, H. N. Brailsford commented:

> The importance of such affairs . . . was psychological. They helped to discredit the Government during the critical time when the masses were hesitating whether they should unreservedly support Congress. The privations . . . suffered by the main body . . . of the political prisoners in jail had the same effect.[117]

Specific provocative tactics were sometimes chosen to arouse extreme repression and discredit the regime. In Gandhi's view, nonviolent provocation was intended: 1) to reveal clearly the inherent violence upon which the British Empire rested; 2) to exert moral pressure on the British to change their attitudes; 3) to make clear to the world the nature of the empire in India and the determination of Indians to be free; and 4) very important, to expose the nature of the British system to the Indians themselves, thereby alienating them from it and increasing their resolution to destroy it.

The nonviolent raids on the salt works at Dharasana that year, described briefly in Chapter Eight, were deliberately planned by Gandhi with the knowledge that they would provoke extreme repression. He expected such repression to put the British *Raj* in a very bad light, strengthening the Indian position while weakening the British. Concerning this instance, J. C. Kumarappa has written:

> Dharasana raid was decided upon not to get salt, which was only the means. Our expectation was that the Government would open fire on unarmed crowds . . . . Our primary object was to show to the world at large the fangs and claws of the Government in all its ugliness and ferocity. In this we have succeeded beyond measure.[118]

Madeline Slade wrote: "India has now realized the true nature of the British *Raj,* and with that . . . the *Raj* is doomed.''[119]

At the end of the 1930-31 struggle Britain still remained established in India, but from an Indian perspective Britain had not won. A psychological change had taken place which was comparable to that in Russia on Bloody Sunday 1905. Rabindranath Tagore described the change in these words:

> Those who live in England, far away from the East, have now got to realize that Europe has completely lost her former moral prestige in Asia, she is no longer regarded as the champion throughout the world of fair dealing and the exponent of high principle, but as the upholder of Western race supremacy and the exploiter of those outside her own borders.
>
> For Europe, this is, in actual fact, a great moral defeat that has happened. Even though Asia is still physically weak and unable to protect herself from aggression where her vital interests are menaced, nevertheless, she can now afford to look down on Europe where before she looked up. [120]

The effort by Soviet officials in East Germany to avoid provoking further resistance by overreaction to the initial demonstrations and strikes of the 1953 rising has already been noted. [121] While later intervention of the Soviet military forces defeated the demonstrators and strikers, on at least two occasions during those June days severe repression led to increased resistance. In the case of demonstrations in smaller towns near the zonal border on June 18, "it was largely the news of the brutal suppression of the strikes in the big industrial centers which drove the people into open resistance." [122] Similarly, when the news of the execution in Jena of a young motor mechanic reached Erfurt, "the employees of three large factories joined the strike." [123]

The Diem regime's repression of Buddhist resisters in 1963 greatly alienated other South Vietnamese from the regime and increased resistance instead of quelling it; conversely a reduction in repression seemed to reduce resistance. *The New York Times* on August 5 reported: "Some observers feel that the Buddhist movement has slowed down in the last two weeks because the Government had been shrewder and less repressive in handling the Buddhists." [124] One result of the severe pagoda raids the night of August 20–21 was a wave of revulsion against the government throughout the country. [125] Surveying the campaign and the effects of severe repression against nonviolently defiant Buddhists, David Halberstam concluded:

> Often the Government broke up their demonstrations with violence and bloodshed, and as Bull Connor and his police dogs in Birmingham were to etch indelibly the civil rights movement in the minds

of millions of Americans, so the Buddhists used the Government's repeated clumsiness to commit their people further to their cause and to strengthen the movement. "There is blood on the orange robes," a spokesman would say at a demonstration, and the emotional response was always astonishing.[126]

As Halberstam suggests, this general phenomenon has also occurred repeatedly in the United States in nonviolent struggles against racial discrimination and segregation. Both arrests and unofficial extremist violence failed to intimidate Negroes in Montgomery, Alabama, or to cause them to halt their famous bus boycott. Instead, the opposite results were achieved, as Dr. King reported: "Every attempt to end the protest by intimidation, by encouraging Negroes to inform, by force and violence, further cemented the Negro community . . ."[127] When mass arrests came, the results were anything but those desired by the white officials: "Instead of stopping the movement, the opposition's tactics had only served to give it greater momentum, and to draw us closer together."[128]

Various types of official and unofficial counteractions against the student sit-ins in 1960 were followed not by acquiescence but increased demonstrations. On successive days in late March, in Baton Rouge, Louisiana, seven and nine student sit-inners, respectively, were arrested. The results: 3,500 students marched through the center of town to the State Capital.[129] On April 19 in Nashville, Tennessee, the home of a well-known Negro attorney defending the sit-inners was bombed. The result: a few hours later 2,500 unintimidated demonstrators marched on City Hall.[130] The 1961 Freedom Rides began with thirteen people, with the organizers hoping there would still be that many at the end. Then one bus was burned in Anniston, Alabama, and the actionists on the other bus were cruelly beaten. The result: ". . . we were deluged with letters and telegrams from people all over the country, volunteering their bodies for the Freedom Rides," James Farmer reported. Hundreds of people inexperienced in nonviolent action arrived, and it became possible to begin filling the jails of Mississippi with opponents of segregation.[131]

Birmingham, Alabama, in the spring of 1963, also experienced this phenomenon of severe repression increasing resistance, especially when school children were arrested and police dogs were used against them. One of the effects was, writes Waskow, that, "it swiftly involved many more Negroes in active, vigorous support of the movement for integration—since that movement now meant not only an abstract demand for social change, but the concrete and immediate protection of their children."[132] In addition, the Birmingham struggle provoked new Negro demonstrations and demands throughout the South and also in Northern ghettos.[133]

After James Meredith was shot and wounded by a fanatical white supremacist in June 1966, the march through Mississippi—which he had only just begun with a tiny handful of supporters—became the biggest since the march from Selma to Montgomery, Alabama. *Newsweek* wrote that the three shotgun blasts "reverberated across the nation," echoing other cases of brutalities against Negroes and several civil rights martyrs, and once again leading to government action. "It was the same dark counterpoint of nonviolent protest and violent response that produced the Civil Rights Acts of 1964 and 1965." President Johnson called the shooting an "awful act of violence," and Congress began to move more quickly on civil rights legislation. Emanuel Celler, aged chairman of the House of Representatives Judiciary Committee, commented: "There are times when the civil-rights movement has no greater friend than its enemy. It is the enemy of civil rights who again and again produces the evidence . . . that we cannot afford to stand still." [134]

To avoid misunderstanding, let it be emphasized again that whether repression crushes or increases resistance to the opponent depends on a variety of conditions other than the repression itself. To a large degree these may be within the control of the nonviolent actionists and the general grievance group for which they are acting. Severe repression and brutalities against nonviolent people have lead to increased resistance by more people in too many cases in diverse circumstances for this result to be dismissed as an isolated and atypical occurrence. Instead, it is an important part of the general process by which nonviolent action combats repression and brutalities, using them to weaken the power position of the opponent and to strengthen that of the nonviolent actionists through the workings of political *jiu-jitsu.*

LESS SEVERE REPRESSION AND COUNTER-NONVIOLENCE?

Some opponents, or some members of the opponent group, sometimes realize that severe violence against nonviolent actionists is counterproductive. When the repression or brutalities have already been committed, this realization may lead to private recriminations and disagreements among officials within the opponent group. Where the realization preceeds the repression, there may be experiments in less severe counteractions or even counter-nonviolence.

Where the realization by some members of the opponent group that severe action is counterproductive follows the event, a reversal of steps already taken may not follow. In fact, there may be a great show of determination and haughty rejection of protests about the repression at the same time that the leadership of the opponent group realizes that the severity of the repression was a mistake. An example of this is official Nazi reaction to the mass arrests of Norwegian students at the University of Oslo November 30, 1943 under the orders of *Reichskommissar* Josef Terboven. The arrests followed a long conflict with the students, faculty and administration of the University on one side, and the Germans and their supporters in the Norwegian fascist party *Nasjonal Samling* on the other.[135] The immediate cause was a fire set November 28, in the *Aulaen*, a large hall in the main University building, located near the Palace. The Nazis charged that students had set the fire as part of their protest, and the Norwegians charged it was a Nazi provocation.[136] Action against students was decided upon. Warnings to students to escape were possible because of information leaked from German officers to the underground Homefront Leadership, and other warnings from high *Nasjonal Samling* sources. Nevertheless, between 1,100 and 1,200 male students were arrested, of whom about 700 were deported to Germany.[137] The University was closed.

Propaganda chief Goebbels, Interior Minister Himmler and Hitler himself all concluded that Terboven's action was excessive and more detrimental to Germany's position than milder action would have been. Goebbels wrote in his diary on December 5 and 6, 1943:

The Fuehrer was somewhat put out—and rightly so—that this question was handled with a sledge hammer. The Fuehrer is also skeptical about the success to be expected. Undoubtedly it would have been possible to achieve an essentially greater effect with less effort, for there are only a couple of dozen rebels among Oslo students who could have been arrested without the public noticing it. Most decidedly it was a big mistake to arrest all students of Oslo. Terboven is especially to be blamed for not having informed the Fuehrer before acting. The whole affair would have run an entirely different course had he done so.

. . . the whole Oslo affair stinks. The Fuehrer, too, is quite unhappy about the way it was handled. He received two representatives of Terboven and gave them an energetic scolding. Terboven has once more behaved like a bull in a china shop. Himmler is furious about the effects of Terboven's action. He was going to enlist about 40,000 to 60,000 volunteers in Norway during the coming months. Prospects for this seemed to be excellent. By Terboven's stupid action a good part of the plan has fallen in the water. [138]

There was no public apology or reversal of Terboven's action, however. Despite considerable turmoil in both Sweden and Finland about the arrests, Hitler ordered Foreign Minister Ribbentrop to reject the Swedish Government's official protest "in the sharpest language." Accordingly Ribbentrop gave the Swedish Chargé d'Affaires in Berlin "a very juicy and cutting reply." "Naturally we can't beat a retreat on this Oslo student question now," wrote Goebbels. "But it would have been better to think matters over before rather than after." [139]

In other cases there have been advance attempts to reduce the extent or intensity of the repression. In the United States in 1937 when confronted with unusual strike action in which workers occupied factories and unemployed coal miners simply appropriated coal, both industrialists and government officials sometimes found it best not to take severe repressive action.

> . . . General Motors evidently feels it would lose public support by evicting the strikers from the plants by force. Even though the sit-downers . . . are manifestly trespassers on others' property, the public is averse to violence and apt to blame the side which begins it, whatever the legal rights may be. For that reason, coal operators and public officials in Pennsylvania are shrugging their shoulders while unemployed miners dig and sell anthracite which does not belong to them. [140]

In South Africa also there were several instances in 1952 in which, despite advance notice from the volunteers, the police refused to arrest actionists committing civil disobedience, sometimes even when they paraded past the police in defiance of curfew regulations. In other isolated cases, the police cordoned off areas where civil disobedience might be committed in order to thwart the defiance of the laws without making arrests. In another case, at Mafeking, volunteers were convicted but not imprisoned. [141] Police in Britain sometimes refused to arrest large numbers of supporters of the Committee of 100 who were committing civil disobedience during their anti-nuclear campaigns.

Sometimes, in the midst of a struggle, the opponent has made a generous and challenging gesture or appeal intended to put the leadership of the nonviolent group in a situation in which they almost had to respond in a conciliatory way. In January 1931—in the midst of the nonviolent

Indian rebellion—the British Viceroy of India, Lord Irwin, in a speech to the Central Legislature, paid high tribute to Gandhi's spiritual force and invited his cooperation in constitutional revision and in the restoration of friendship between the British and Indian peoples. Later, he unconditionally released Gandhi and his chief colleagues and again made the Congress Working Committee a legal body. This clearly put the pressure for the next move on the Congress. [142]

In some instances another type of gesture has been offered. One cold winter day President Wilson invited the woman suffragists who were picketing him into the East Room of the White House to warm up. (They refused the invitation.) [143] In August 1966 United States Air Force police abandoned their guns in dealing with an attempted nonviolent invasion of a base by two hundred demonstrators, mostly children. The group was protesting a decision of the Armed Services Committee of the House of Representatives to block for five years use of the base for low and middle-income housing. The demonstrators were stopped at the entrance but, after a conference with the head of the group, Air Force officers invited them in for a free tour of the base in Air Force buses. The Associated Press dispatch called the counteraction "one of the coolest bits of public relations in military history." [144]

There is another type of response to nonviolent action which, though relatively undeveloped, may in future decades become as significant as violent repression, or more so. The British (both in India and in the American colonies) and the American segregationists have been pioneers in this response. It involves confronting nonviolent action with counter-nonviolent action. For example, on one day during the nonviolent raids on the Dharasana salt depot in 1930, the police stopped the nonviolent volunteers on the road before they could reach the salt mounds and, when the Gandhian raiders sat down in protest, the police did the same. For some hours the two groups sat facing each other, until the patience of the police expired and they again resorted to violent methods to remove the sit-downers. [145] Later in Bombay, police also sat down in front of thirty thousand people sitting in the street after their procession had been halted. After hours and much rain, during which the volunteers passed their food, water and blankets to the police, the police gave in and the procession ended in a triumphant march. [146]

After several bitter experiences of the effectiveness of the American colonists' nonviolent economic noncooperation, the British attempted to apply similar economic measures against the Americans, albeit *after* the colonists had largely shifted to reliance on violence following the skirmishes at Lexington and Concord on April 19, 1775. The measure was Lord North's Prohibitory Bill, introduced on November 20, 1775, and given the royal assent on December 22. It provided for the prohibition of all trade and intercourse with the colonies: it also provided for the appointment of commissioners with authority to exempt from that prohibition any person, group or colony which they determined to be at peace with His Majesty. Other important concessions to the colonists were also promised by Lord North. The trade ban, however, was not to be enforced nonviolently but by seizures by the navy of vessels and cargoes, and allowance for impressment of crews of seized ships. This Act was regarded by many as "a declaration of perpetual war" against the colonies. [147]

In the United States civil rights struggles, there has been a very large number of examples of forms of nonviolent action used by segregationists. Sometimes these have taken rather simple forms, such as closing down businesses or making gestures of conciliation. For example, the bus terminal facilities in Montgomery, Alabama, were closed in May 1961, just before the arrival of Freedom Riders intent on violating segregation practices there. [148] In Orangeburg, South Carolina, the management of a lunch-counter where students were holding a sit-in responded, first by a temporary closure, then by removing seats, and finally by closing completely for two weeks. [149] The Maryland State Guard in Cambridge, Maryland, in May 1964, asked demonstrators to sing a few songs, led the group in prayer, and then politely asked them to disperse. [150] Imitation by segregationists of the same forms of nonviolent action being used by the integrationists has also occurred. For example, the Ku Klux Klan members in Atlanta, in late 1960, imitated student picketers by appearing dressed in full K.K.K. regalia to hold a counter-demonstration wherever they learned the students were demonstrating. They also threatened to call a white boycott against any store that desegregated its eating facilities in response to the student pressures. [151] During the Freedom Rides to integrate busses, a group of American Nazis sent a "hate bus" from Washington, D.C. to New Orleans, where they were jailed for "unreasonably" alarming the public; in protest the Nazis went on a fast. [152] Economic pressures have been widely used against opponents of segregation in the South.

Such cases of counter-nonviolence may be the first feeble attempts to move toward a new type of conflict situation in which *both* sides to a conflict will rely on nonviolent action as their ultimate sanction. If that were to occur widely, it would have the deepest social and political implications and ramifications. Many people, of course, will object to their opponents' doing anything to defend or advance viewpoints or practices which they reject as undemocratic or unjust. However, agreement on issues within a reasonable period of time is often impossible. In this situation the conflicting groups still hold contradictory views which each believes must not be compromised. Is it then preferable that the group whose views one detests continues to use murder and terror or instead adopts economic boycotts and other nonviolent methods? Although powerful, those nonviolent methods do not involve killing but allow a continuation of the conflict by nonviolent means—which may bring into play various human influences leading to its ultimate resolution. This special type of conflict situation requires thoughtful analysis. [153] One important question is: what factors would be most important in the dynamics of this technique and in determining success in that special conflict situation? [154] This speculative exploration lies outside the scope of the present study, however. For the more limited purposes of this book, these developments show on the one hand a variation in the usual pattern of nonviolent action being met with violent repression. They also indicate that the opponent sometimes perceives that even from his perspective a nonviolent response is preferable. This perception may be based on a recognition that repression, especially when brutal, does not always strengthen the side which uses it; it sometimes strengthens the apparently defenseless nonviolent actionists.

By choosing to fight with a technique which makes possible political *jiu-jitsu,* the nonviolent actionists unleash forces which though often less immediately visible and tangible may nevertheless be more difficult for the opponent to combat than violence.

ALTERING POWER RELATIONSHIPS

The power of each contender in a conflict in which nonviolent action is used by one side, or by both, is continually variable, as was pointed out at the beginning of Chapter Nine. Far more than in violent conflict, the nonviolent actionists are able to exert considerable control not only over their own group's power, but directly and indirectly over the power of the opponent group. This the nonviolent actionists do by the effects which their behavior has on the social sources of each group's power. As discussed in this chapter, the availability of these sources of power is regulated, among other ways, by the operation of political *jiu-jitsu,* which affects the roles of third parties, the opponent group itself and the grievance group. Each of these groups of people exercises influence and control over the distribution of power by making available their cooperation with one side or the other, or by restricting or withholding cooperation from one or the other.

Shifts in power relationships as a consequence of political *jiu-jitsu* will not always be immediately apparent; sometimes they may be obvious and dramatic only after they are completed, as when the army has mutinied. Nor are these shifts all-or-nothing changes. The steps may be partial ones, and may be expressed in a variety of ways. For example, persons and groups who once supported the opponent fully may simply become uncertain, take up neutral positions, and refrain from offering major help to either side. On the other hand, persons who were formerly indifferent or neutral may through this process move toward the nonviolent group, either offering it minor or major assistance or simply withdrawing cooperation with the opponent. There is a considerable variety of other ways in which changes in feelings, attitudes and opinions stimulated by the opponent's repression may shift the social sources of power; some of these shifts may be decisive.

Political *jiu-jitsu* is one of the important factors which break up and reverse the initial polarization, discussed in Chapter Ten, when at the very beginning of the campaign the opponent is likely to gain support. As the changes which have been described in this chapter occur, that initial polarization is revealed as highly unstable. As attitudes shift, and as actions are brought into line with the new attitudes, the relative power positions of the protagonists also shift. What Seifert called (as we already noted) the "progressive detachment of groups arranged in a spectrum of potential support" may develop. [155]

The power shifts produced by political *jiu-jitsu* do not operate in isolation. They are concurrent with the other ideational, psychological, social, economic and political influences and pressures induced by the operation of the methods of nonviolent protest and persuasion, noncooperation and nonviolent intervention—the methods described in detail in Chapters Three to Eight. A period in which the balance of forces may seem to be in the opponent's favor, or one in which the contending forces seem approximately equal, may therefore be followed by the build-up and extension of the forces supporting the nonviolent struggle, while those supporting the opponent's violent regime disintegrate.

The Kapp *Putsch* provides an example. After initial success (seizure of the capital and flight of the legal government), followed by uncertainty (as noncooperation was launched), support for the *Putsch* bit by bit collapsed as key groups (previously either pro-Kapp or discreetly undecided) shifted loyalty to the legal government. Three *Reichswehr* commanders, previously uncertain, announced support for the legal government. Britain announced it would never recognize the usurping regime. The Nationalist Party, which had given the rebels limited support, urged Kapp to withdraw. The powerful National Association of German Industries, after initial reservation about the general strike, formally denounced the Kapp regime. The hitherto neutral Security Police demanded Kapp's resignation. Kapp resigned and flew to Sweden, leaving General von Lüttwitz as his heir. But even Lüttwitz's troops and regimental officers did not help: the Potsdam garrison mutinied against the usurpers, and most of his officers favored calling off the *Putsch*. "The General was somewhat bewildered at the way in which the whole structure of the conspiracy had suddenly crumbled around him." [156]

Mass nonviolent struggle may become so overwhelming that it is impossible to crush. It may also undermine the very power of the opponent, so that even if he wants to continue fighting the movement, he is no longer effectively able to do so. Massive defiance of the people can make a government powerless. Whether this potential will be fully realized will depend on the circumstances. Influential will be the degree to which, by its nonviolent discipline, persistence, and choice of strategy and tactics, the nonviolent group promotes the operation of political *jiu-jitsu*.

This is one of the ways in which change may be achieved by nonviolent action, although, as we noted, nonviolent struggle can be successful even if the political *jiu-jitsu* is reduced or eliminated by an opponent's restraint in counter measures. We shall next consider in more detail the effects of the application of nonviolent action, and the nature and requirements of the three mechanisms by which change may be achieved with its effective use—conversion, accomodation and nonviolent coercion.

NOTES

1. In his 1935 study, **The Power of Nonviolence** (pp. 44-45), Richard Gregg described nonviolent action as "moral *jiu-jitsu*." He referred to the moral or psychological effects of nonviolent persistence on the people carrying out the repression themselves. For the purposes of this study of the social and political dynamics of the technique, "social *jiu-jitsu*" or "political *jiu-jitsu*" is a much more important process. It incorporates "moral *jiu-jitsu*" when it occurs as part of a much broader process. A violent opponent facing a determined and disciplined nonviolent struggle movement can never really come to grips with its kind of power, and the more he tries to do so by means of his violence and brutalities, the more he loses his political balance.

2. The use of repressive violence against persistent nonviolent actionists rebounds against the opponent's very sources of strength. "The might of the tyrant recoils upon himself when it meets with no response, even as an arm violently waved in the air suffers dislocation," Gandhi said. (Gandhi, **Nonviolent Resistance**, p. 57; Ind. ed.:**Satyagraha**, p. 57.) But the process is more complex than that. Nehru came closer in his description:

   > Naked coercion . . . . is an expensive affair for the rulers. Even for them it is a painful and nerve-shaking ordeal, and they know well that ultimately it weakens their foundations. It exposes continually the real character of their rule, both to the people coerced and the world at large. They infinitely prefer to put on the velvet glove to hide the iron fist. Nothing is more irritating and, in the final analysis, harmful to a Government than to have to deal with people who will not bend to its will, whatever the consequences. (Jawaharlal Nehru, **An Autobiography**, p. 393.)

3. Ross, "Introduction," in Case, **Non-violent Coercion**, p. iv. See also Sharp, **Gandhi Wields the Weapon of Moral Power**, p. 186. Gregg, (**The Power of Nonviolence**, p. 86) and Hiller, (**The Strike**, p. 169) have also pointed to the tendency for the opponent's repression against nonviolent actionists to arouse public opinion and enlist it in sympathy for the nonviolent group.

4. Harcave, **First Blood**, p. 116.

5. *Ibid.*, p. 121.

6. Halperin, **Germany Tried Democracy**, p. 288.

7. Sharp, **Gandhi Wields . . . .** , pp. 123 and 151.

8. Kuper, **Passive Resistance in South Africa**, p. 132. The nonwhite campaigners had even organized special "U.N.O. batches" of volunteers to commit civil disobedience just before the U.N. General Assembly discussed apartheid.

9. **Ibid**, pp. 164-165.

10. **Ibid.**, p. 166.

11. Luthuli, **Let My People Go**, p. 222. For his comment on world attention on the Treason Trial, see p. 181.

12. Colin and Margaret Legum, **South Africa: Crisis for the West** (New York and London: Frederick A. Praeger, 1964), p. 75.

13. *The Pentagon Papers* as published by *The New York Times* (New York, Toronto, London: Bantam Books, 1971), p. 163.

14. *Ibid.*, p. 165.

15. *Ibid.*, p. 166: also *The New York Times* 24 August 1963, and *Daily Telegraph* (London), 24 August 1963, cited in Adam Roberts, "The Buddhist Revolt," MS p. 25.

16. *The Pentagon Papers*, p. 197.

17. *Observer* (London), 8 September 1963, cited in Roberts, "The Buddhist Revolt," MS p. 27.

18. *New York Times*, 26 and 27 August, cited in *ibid.*, MS p. 26.

19. *The Pentagon Papers*, p. 166.

20. *Ibid.*, pp. 194 and 168.

21. *Ibid.*, pp. 172-178.

22. *Ibid.*, pp. 168-232.

23. *The Times* (London), 8 July, 1963 and *The New York Times*, 6 October, 1963, cited by Roberts, "The Buddhist Revolt," MS p. 16.

24. *New York Times*, 23 August 1963, cited in *Ibid.*, MS p. 24.

25. *New York Times*, 5 and 6 October, 1963, cited in *Ibid.*, MS p. 36.

26. Roberts, "The Buddhists, the War, and the Vietcong," p. 215. Denis Warner's quotation is from his book **The Last Confucian** (London and Baltimore, Md.: Penguin Books, 1964), p. 221.

27. Gregg, **The Power of Nonviolence**, pp. 45-46.

28. See Peter Wallensteen, "Characteristics of Economic Sanctions," *Journal of Peace Research*, 1968, no. 3, p. 251.

29. Seifert, **Conquest by Suffering**, p. 58.

30. Sharp, **Gandhi Wields . . .**, p. 124. When charged with causing feelings of contempt toward the government, J.C. Kumarappa claimed in court that it was not he but "the accredited agents of this Government that bring it into disrepute." *Ibid.*, p. 209.

31. Seifert, **Conquest by Suffering**, p. 56.

32. Gipson, **The Coming of the Revolution**, p. 108. Gipson cites Walpole's **Memoirs** as authority for that statement. During the period of the Continental Association program of colonial resistance, adopted by the First Continental Congress, in 1774-1775, wide public support for the colonists' grievances continued in England. See Gipson, **The British Empire Before the American Revolution**, vol. XII, **The Triumphant Empire, Britain Sails into the Storm, 1770-1776**, pp. 259-290.

33. Harcave, **First Blood**, pp. 94-95.

34. **Ibid.**, pp. 100-110.

35. Halperin, **Germany Tried Democracy**, p. 288.

36. Quoted in Sternstein, "The *Ruhrkampf* of 1923," p. 129.

37. Lewy, **The Catholic Church and Nazi Germany**, pp. 265-267.

38. Luthuli, **Let My People Go**, p. 176.

39. Miller, **Nonviolence**, pp. 280-281.

40. This white help was so widespread that the following are only scattered examples: there was significant white participation in the 1961 freedom rides (*ibid.*, pp. 313-317); the United Auto Workers and National Maritime Union provided bail money for jailed Birmingham Negroes in 1963 (*ibid.*, p. 337);

especially in 1963 there was significant endorsement of nonviolent action against segregation and discrimination from major religious denominational bodies and active participation in various demonstrations of major church leaders and a multitude of clergymen – who were sometimes arrested and imprisoned (*ibid.*, pp. 208-211 and 309).

41. Oppenheimer and Lakey, A Manual for Direct Action, pp. 23-24.
42. King, Stride Toward Freedom, pp. 166-167.
43. *Ibid.*, p. 10.
44. Seifert, Conquest by Suffering, p. 58; quoted from The Freedom Ride, p. 6, a "special report" issued by the Southern Regional Council, May, 1961.
45. King, Why We Can't Wait, pp. 100-101.
46. Miller, Nonviolence, p. 315.
47. *New York Herald Tribune,* 21 August 1963, quoted in Roberts, "The Buddhist Revolt," MS p. 23.
48. Roberts, "Buddhism and Politics in South Vietnam," pp. 246-247.
49. *New York Herald Tribune,* 5 June 1963, quoted by Roberts, "The Buddhist Revolt," MS p. 10.
50. *New York Times*, 26 August 1963, cited in *ibid*.
51. Wolfe, Three Who Made a Revolution, pp. 333-334.
52. Katkov, Russia 1917, p. 263.
53. *Ibid.*, pp. 263-264.
54. *Ibid.*, pp. 269.
55. *Ibid.*, pp. 270.
56. *Ibid.*, p. 272.
57. *Ibid.*, pp. 272-284.
58. Gopal, The Viceroyalty of Lord Irwin, pp. 68-69.
59. *Ibid.*, p. 69.
60. Associated Press dispatch, datelined Berlin, 22 June 1953, quoted in Miller, Nonviolence, p. 352.
61. Ebert, "Nonviolent Resistance Against Communist Regimes?" pp. 189 and 192, and Brant, The East German Rising, pp. 149-152.
62. See Dallin, German Rule in Russia, 1941-1945.
63. See Ebert, "Nonviolent Resistance Against Communist Regimes?" p. 183. He cites Martin Jänicke, Der dritte Weg: Die Antistalinistische Opposition gegen Ulbricht seit 1953 (Cologne: Neuer Deutsche Verlag, 1964), p. 38.
64. Ebert, "Nonviolent Resistance Against Communist Regimes?" p. 186.
65. Eleanor Flexner, Century of Struggle (Cambridge, Mass.: Harvard University Press, 1959), pp. 250-251.
66. Sharp, Gandhi Wields . . . , p. 180.
67. Luthuli, Let My People Go, pp. 211-214.
68. Wheeler-Bennett, The Nemesis of Power, p. 79, and Goodspeed, The Conspirators, p. 134.
69. Venturi, Roots of Revolution, p. 433.
70. *Ibid.*, p. 348.
71. Lord Hardinge of Penschurst, Old Diplomacy, p. 114.
72. Schapiro, The Communist Party of the Soviet Union, p. 65.
73. Charques, The Twilight of Imperial Russia p. 113.

74. Harcave, First Blood, pp. 98 and 114. See also p. 110.
75. Keep, The Rise of Social Democracy in Russia, p. 154. See also p. 158.
76. Harcave, First Blood, p. 114.
77. *Ibid.*, pp. 124-125.
78. *Ibid.*, p. 104.
79. *Ibid.*., p. 171-172.
80. Seifert, Conquest by Suffering, p. 42.
81. Machiavelli, The Discourses of Niccolo Machiavelli, vol. I, p. 254.
82. Seifert, Conquest by Suffering, p. 43.
83. *Ibid.*, p. 42.
84. Sharp, Gandhi Wields . . . , p. 186.
85. *Ibid.*, p. 176.
86. Seifert, Conquest by Suffering, p. 45.
87. *Ibid.*
88. Gregg, The Power of Nonviolence, p. 133.
89. Gandhi, Non-violence in Peace and War, vol. I, p. 130.
90. Sharp, Gandhi Wields . . . , p. 196.
91. *Ibid.*, p. 106.
92. Brockway, Non-co-operation in Other Lands, pp. 62-65. Brockway's account is mostly based on F. A. Mackenzie's Korea's Fight for Freedom.
93. Shirer, The Rise and Fall of the Third Reich, p. 941. See also Dallin, German Rule in Russia, 1941-1945, *passim,* and Crankshaw, The Gestapo, pp. 230-231.
94. Crankshaw, The Gestapo, p. 214.
95. de J. Haestrup, "Exposé," in European Resistance Movements 1939-1945, p. 160.
96. Keep, The Rise of Social Democracy in Russia, p. 40. See also Schapiro, The Communist Party . . . , p. 28.
97. *Ibid.*, p. 70. For other examples of the general phenomenon, see also pp. 72, 98 and 216, and Katkov, Russia 1917, p. 420.
98. Frederick Engles, Anti-Dühring (Moscow: Foreign Languages Publishing House, 1954), p. 440.
99. Schapiro, The Communist Party . . . , p. 347.
100. Geyl, The Revolt of the Netherlands 1555-1609, p. 56. Later under Philip in 1565 there was another lesson that repression may produce the opposite to the intended results. See *ibid.*, pp. 78-79.
101. Gipson, The British Empire Before the American Revolution, vol. XI, The Triumphant Empire: The Rumbling of the Coming Storm 1766-1770, pp. 282-283.
102. *Ibid.*, p. 278; and Gipson, The Coming of the Revolution 1763-1775, pp. 201-202.
103. Gipson, The British Empire. . . , vol. XI, p. 305.
104. *Ibid.*, p. 190, and Schlesinger, The Colonial Merchants and the American Revolution, pp. 155, 181-186 and 194.
105. Schlesinger, The Colonial Merchants . . . , pp. 305-311.
106. *Ibid.*, pp. 353, 360, 363, 366, 367, 373, 397, 425 and 430-431. It also produced, it is claimed, the first explicit call for an American union, from the town meeting of Providence, Rhode Island, a week after the news of the Boston

Port Act reached America. Gipson, **The British Empire** . . . , vol. XII, p. 157.

107. *Ibid.,* p. 608.

108. Gipson, **The Coming of the Revolution,** p. 227.

109. Gipson, **The Bristish Empire** . . . vol. XII, p. 160. There were, of course, other instances when punishments, or threats, produced increased defiance. For example, in 1774 Brigadier Ruggles, a magistrate at Hardwicke, Massachusetts Bay threatened to jail any man who signed a Covenant not to purchase or use British goods, a hundred men defiantly signed it. (Schlesinger, **The Colonial Merchants** . . . , p. 323.) In the summer of 1774, Salem held a town meeting in defiance of the Governor's orders. (Gipson, **The British Empire** . . . , vol XII, p. 157.)

110. Goodspeed, **The Conspirators,** p. 132.

111. Eyck, **A History of the Weimar Republic,,** vol. I, p. 151.

112. Wheeler-Bennett, **The Nemesis of Power,** p. 79.

113. Ehrlich, "Ruhrkampen," in Lindberg, Jacobsen and Ehrlich, **Kamp Uden Vaaben,** p. 186.

114. Quoted in Case, **Non-Violent Coercion,** p. 381.

115. *Ibid.,* pp. 381-382.

116. Sharp, **Gandhi Wields** . . . , p. 167.

117. *Ibid.,* p. 193. See also pp. 165-166.

118. *Ibid.,* p. 151.

119. *Ibid.,* p. 151.

120. *Ibid.,* p. 157.

121. Ebert, "Nonviolent Resistance Against Communist Regimes?" pp. 186 and 190.

122. Brant, **The East German Rising,** p. 92.

123. *Ibid.,* p. 113.

124. Quoted in Roberts, "The Buddhist Revolt," MS p. 20.

125. Roberts, "Buddhism and Politics in South Vietnam," p. 246.

126. David Halberstam, **The Making of a Quagmire** (New York: Random House and London: The Bodley Head, 1965), p. 215.

127. Quoted in Peck, **Freedom Ride,** p. 57.

128. King, **Stride Toward Freedom,** p. 143.

129. Major Johns, "Baton Rouge: Higher Education – Southern Style," p. 89, in Peck, **Freedom Ride.**

130. Paul Laprad, "Nashville: A Community Struggle," in Peck, **Freedom Ride,** p. 87.

131. Farmer, **Freedom -- When?,** pp. 69-70.

132. Waskow, **From Race Riot to Sit-in,** p. 234.

133. *Newsweek,* 27 May 1963, cited in Ebert, "Theory and Practice of Nonviolent Resistance," MS p. 397.

134. *Newsweek,* 20 June 1966, pp. 27-31.

135. On the over-all struggle, see Sverre Steen, *"Universitetet i Ildlinjen,"* in Steen, gen. ed., **Norges Krig,** vol. III, pp. 127-194.

136. See *ibid.,* pp. 182-184.

137. *Ibid.,* pp. 186 and 190.

138. Lochner, ed., **The Goebbels Diaries,** pp. 542-544.

139. *Ibid.*

140. "Editoral Research Reports," *St. Louis Post-Dispatch* 20 January 1937; quoted in Bernard, Social Control in its Sociological Aspects, p. 389.

141. See Kuper, Passive Resistance in South Africa, pp. 82, and 125-126, and Luthuli, Let My People Go, p. 118.

142. Gopal, The Viceroyalty of Lord Irwin, pp. 98-100.

143. Seifert, Conquest by Suffering, p. 38.

144. *Baltimore Sun*, 2 August 1966.

145. Sharp, Gandhi Wields . . . , pp. 136-137.

146. *Ibid.*, pp. 166-167.

147. Gipson, The British Empire . . . , vol. XII, pp. 346-349.

148. Lomax, The Negro Revolt, p. 155.

149. Miller, Nonviolence, pp. 308-309.

150. Oppenheimer and Lakey, A Manual for Direct Action, p. 87.

151. C. Eric Lincoln, "The Strategy of a Sit-in,", in Sibley, ed., The Quiet Battle, pp. 295 and 298.

152. Lomax, The Negro Revolt, pp. 151-155.

153. For an interesting discussion on this, see Waskow, From Race Riot to Sit-in, pp. 276-303.

154. Gregg suggests that in such conflicts with both sides using nonviolent action, success would go to the side with the greatest understanding of nonviolent action, the best discipline, and preparations, the most self-purification and love, the best understanding of society, the greater inner unity and strength, and the more respect from the other side and from the public. Gregg, however, emphasizes the mechanism of conversion and gives very little consideration to the wider social, economic and political pressures, often coercive, which may be involved in nonviolent action. Hence, further analysis is required. See Gregg, The Power of Nonviolence, pp. 99-100.

155. Harvey J.D. Siefert, " The Use by American Quakers of Nonviolent Resistance as a Method of Social Change," MS p. 145.

156. Wheeler-Bennett, The Nemesis of Power, p. 80. For the specific cited changes in loyalty, see pp. 79-81.

13

Three Ways Success
May Be Achieved

INTRODUCTION

Nonviolent struggle can only be successful when the necessary conditions exist or have been created. Despite the improvised character of most nonviolent action in the past, successes from which we can learn have occurred. Even failures can provide important insights. As understanding of the requirements for effectiveness grows, the proportion of successes is likely to increase. The question then increasingly becomes *how* success can be achieved.

The influences, causes and processes involved in producing success in nonviolent conflict are diverse, complicated and intermeshed. The determining combination of influences, pressures and forces will never be precisely the same, the possible combinations being infinite. It would be a distortion to impose on them an unnatural uniformity or an artificial simplicity.

It is, however, possible to distinguish three broad processes, or mechanisms, by which the complicated forces utilized and produced by nonviolent action influence the opponent and his capacity for action and thereby perhaps bring success to the cause of the grievance group. These are *conversion, accommodation* and *nonviolent coercion,* [1] which we introduced briefly in Chapter Two. Other consequences of nonviolent struggle, affecting the actionists themselves and the long-term distribution of power in the society, will be discussed in the next chapter.

In *conversion* the opponent has been inwardly changed so that he wants to make the changes desired by the nonviolent actionists. In *accommodation,* the opponent does not agree with the changes (he has not been converted), and he could continue the struggle (he has not been nonviolently coerced), but nevertheless he has concluded that it is best to grant some or all of the demands. He may see the issues as not so important after all, the actionists as not as bad as he had thought, or he may expect to lose more by continuing the struggle than by conceding gracefully. In *nonviolent coercion* the opponent has not changed his mind on the issues and wants to *continue* the struggle, but is *unable* to do so; the sources of his power and means of control have been taken away from him without the use of violence. This may have been done by the nonviolent group or by opposition and noncooperation among his own group (as, mutiny of his troops), or some combination of these.

Advocates and practitioners of nonviolent action have differed in their attitudes to these mechanisms. All too often their attitudes have been oversimplified, focusing primarily on the extremes of complete conversion or full nonviolent coercion. Thus, exponents of a nonviolence derived from religious conviction who emphasize conversion frequently see nonviolent coercion as closer to violence than to their own beliefs. Exponents of nonviolent coercion (say, use of the general strike to achieve social revolution) often deny even the possibility of conversion, and see that approach as alien to their own efforts. There are also middle positions. The choice of a preferred mechanism will influence the conduct of the struggle, including the strategy, tactics and methods used, the public statements made, the "tone" of the movement, and the responses to the opponent's repression. A choice or preference by actionists of one of these mechanisms is possible and even necessary, whether on ethical or strategic grounds. In practice, however, matters are rarely clear and simple between pure conversion and strict coercion, as exponents of these extreme mechanisms would have us believe. Not only may the mechanisms be variously combined and play different roles in the various stages of the struggle; different persons and subgroups within the opponent group may be diversely affected or even unaffected by the nonviolent action. We shall return to the ethical significance of these complexities later. First we must examine the three broad mechanisms of change themselves.

CONVERSION

"By conversion we mean that the opponent, as the result of the actions of the nonviolent person or group, comes around to a new point of view which embraces the ends of the nonviolent actor." [2] This change may be influenced by reason, argumentation and other intellectual efforts. [3] It is doubtful, however, that conversion will be produced solely by intellectual effort. Conversion is more likely to involve the opponent's emotions, beliefs, attitudes and moral system.

A. Seeking conversion

While Gandhi did not in certain circumstances rule out actions which produced change by accomodation or even nonviolent coercion, [4] he sought to achieve the change as far as possible by means which did not "humiliate" the opponent "but . . . uplift him." [5] Gandhi's statements provide good illustrations of this objective of conversion. He wrote to the Viceroy in 1930: "For my ambition is no less than to convert the British people through nonviolence, and thus make them see the wrong they have done to India." [6] On another occasion he wrote that a *satyagrahi* never seeks to influence the "wrong-doer" by inducing fear; instead the appeal must always be "to his heart. The Satyagrahi's object is to convert, not coerce, the wrong-doer." [7] The aim of nonviolent action with this motivation is thus not simply to free the subordinate group, but also to free the opponent, who is thought to be imprisoned by his own system and policies. [8]

In line with this attitude, while maintaining their internal solidarity and pursuing the struggle, the nonviolent actionists will emphasize that they intend no personal hostility toward the members of the opponent group. Instead, the actionists may regard the conflict as a temporary, but necessary, disruption which will make possible deeper unity and cooperation between the two groups in the future. [9] Gandhi said: "My non-cooperation is non-cooperation with evil, not with the evil-doer." He added that he wished by noncooperation to induce the opponent to cease inflicting the evil or harm so that cooperation would be possible on a different basis. [10] "My non-cooperation is with methods and systems, never with men." [11] This aim of conversion has in certain situations had significant effects on the opponent group. Replacement of hostile personal attitudes by positive attitudes will reduce the pressure on the opponent group to be defensively aggressive. "Thus the opponents may be influenced to engage in fewer acts of provocative hostility, and, in the long-run, some of their leaders and part of the membership may even become motivated to live up to the other group's view of them as potential allies." [12]

The extreme Gandhian emphasis on conversion is translated into action only rarely. However, efforts to convert sometimes occur in the absence of such a doctrine, and conversion sometimes occurs without conscious efforts. Also, conversion of *some* members of the opponent group (say, soldiers) may contribute to change by accommodation or nonviolent coercion.

Conversion efforts may sometimes take place side by side with the application of other nonviolent pressures, such as economic or political noncooperation. For example, even as Philadelphia merchants were in late 1765 cancelling orders already placed with British merchants and launching a campaign of economic noncooperation in an effort to obtain repeal of the Stamp Act, they sent a memorial to British merchants in which they urged those same merchants to help the Americans achieve repeal of the Act and the removal of certain commercial restrictions. [13] Almost exactly three years later under comparable conditions a similar memorial was sent from Philadelphia, seeking support for repeal of the Townshend duties. [14]

The opponent group of course consists of many members and a variety of subgroups, and the nonviolent group will be unable to apply equal influences for conversion to all of these. Furthermore, the nonviolent group may deliberately choose to concentrate its efforts to achieve conversion on certain persons or subgroups in the opponent camp. When the most direct personal contact in the course of the struggle occurs between the nonviolent actionists and the opponent's agents of repression—his police and troops—the actionists may attempt to convert these agents, instead of the general public or the policy makers. For example, during the resistance to the Kapp *Putsch,* striking workers carried on an open discussion with troops serving the usurpers who, it soon turned out, could no longer completely rely on their own soldiers. [15] Even in the East German Rising in 1953 demonstrators and strikers made significant, spontaneous and repeated appeals to police and troops, although there was no systematic effort to win them over. [16]

Variations will also occur in the type of influences utilized to induce conversion. One approach may be to change the social situation drastically, eliminating the opponent's power or profits, in order that he may see the ethical issues in his past policies in a new light. For example, when an oppressor's economic gains are eliminated he may find it easier to see that exploitation is morally wrong. Gandhi sometimes spoke of this path to attitude change.

More often, however, nonviolent groups which have sought to convert have emphasized direct appeals to their opponent's better nature, as Gandhi put it. [17] These appeals have not only been made with words, as in the Philadelphia examples, but have primarily utilized emotional pressures induced through the nonviolent actionists' own self-suffering, either at the opponent's hands (as in withstanding repression) or at their own hands (as in fasts). It is important to understand the rationale underlying this view.

B. The rationale of self-suffering

All nonviolent actionists who understand their technique accept the necessity of willingness to suffer and to persist in the face of repression. As has been discussed earlier, such willingness is the necessary price for maintaining resistance and possibly also a way to neutralize or immobilize the opponent's repression. Suffering in the context of the conversion mechanism is more than that, however. *Some* nonviolent actionists see an *additional* reason for acceptance of such nonretaliatory suffering: to them it is the main means by which the opponent may be converted to their views and aims. (Other nonviolent actionists, of course, reject that objective as undesirable, unnecessary or impossible, and instead stress change by accommodation or nonviolent coercion.)

Advocates of suffering to achieve conversion maintain that on some issues a strictly rational appeal to the opponent's mind will be inadequate, and insist that it is then necessary to appeal also to his emotions. Gandhi repeatedly argued along these lines:

> I have found that mere appeal to reason does not answer where prejudices are age-long and based on supposed religious authority. Reason has to be strengthened by suffering and suffering opens the eyes of understanding. [18]

> . . . if you want something really important to be done you must not merely satisfy reason, you must move the heart also. The appeal of reason is more to the head but the penetration of the heart comes from suffering. It opens up the inner understanding of man. [19]

He identified the appeal to the hearts of the opponent group as "evoking the best that is in them." [20] Bondurant explains it in these words: "Suffering operates in the satyagraha strategy as a tactic for cutting through the rational defenses which the opponent may have built in opposing the initial efforts of rational persuasion . . ." In other words, suffering "acts as a shock treatment . . ." [21]

It must be clear that just any kind of suffering is not likely to set in motion the processes which may lead to changes in the opponent's feelings, beliefs and attitudes. The suffering of nonviolent actionists has little or nothing to do with the suffering of those who passively accept their fate. For suffering to lead to conversion, Lakey points out, the opponent must experience feelings of identification with the nonviolent group. This identification in turn, he argues citing Freud, requires a new perception of a common quality between the two groups. Such perception depends not only on the actual suffering but on the way in which the nonviolent actionists behave prior to and during such suffering. Therefore, he continues, suffering by people who have demonstrated their bravery, openness and honesty, goodwill and nonviolent determination is far more likely to produce a significant sympathetic response in the opponent than is suffering by people who behave like cowards, and cringe, flee, lie and hate. [22]

The opponent's initial reactions to the suffering of nonviolent actionists may vary widely from situation to situation. Initial reactions are, however, often unstable and may be reversed. Self-suffering is likely to shatter normal indifference to the particular issue, producing instead (as it did in South Africa) extremes in reactions, "active emotions of hate or sympathy." [23] In face of challenge, as noted earlier, the opponent group may first unite, [24] but in face of the nonviolent actionists' suffering and other influences, that initial unity may be shattered as the actionists' demonstrated bravery and sincerity arouse sympathetic interest. [25]

The initial reaction of the general public may also be split, with the suffering evoking resentment among some, and pity among others. [26] This pity may lead members of the public to see the suffering actionists as men of integrity, determination and goodwill, [27] even while not agreeing with them. Suffering for a cause may also help move public opinion on the issues at stake, [28] as was discussed in the previous chapter. That shift may in turn influence the attitudes of members of the opponent group to the issues at stake. It is in the nature of conversion of this type that a considerable number of influences will operate simultaneously and often unconsciously, over a period of time.

It is unlikely to be easy to endure the suffering which can induce conversion. The actionists may be helped to continue their struggle and to maintain the necessary discipline by awareness that their courageous suffering without counter-violence may help both to frustrate and immobilize the opponent's repression and also to contribute to changes of attitudes and feelings. Hiller has pointed out correctly, however, that the sacrifice required of actionists must be "bearable," or depression will set in and their will will be broken.[29] It is not solely the opponent who determines what is bearable, however. The sufferings which one group may find trivial may be intolerable to another. It is also true and very important that the sufferings which one group will find intolerable may be quite acceptable to another as the price of change. The will power, determination, beliefs and emotional response of the nonviolent actionists will help to determine, sometimes decisively, how much suffering is tolerable as the price of change.

Gregg also has pointed out that when nonviolent actionists understand the role of suffering in the dynamics of their type of struggle, and regard suffering as not simply a necessary risk, as in war, but also as an effective weapon for strengthening their cause, casualties will not lower their morale.[30] Voluntarily accepted suffering for the sake of winning goals may instead enhance morale and unify the actionists and others in support of their objectives.[31] Summarizing the Gandhian view of suffering in this context, Kuper writes: "Hence, suffering being positively desired by the resisters becomes an armour against the tyrant rather than a weapon in his hands."[32]

In most types of nonviolent action suffering is not deliberately courted but neither is it avoided when it is a consequence of other appropriate stages of the campaign.[33] There are, however, certain forms of Gandhian *satyagraha* which at times do seek suffering by provocative acts of physical nonviolent intervention or by fasts, for example. Even in these, however, Gandhi insisted that the suffering not to be sought for its own sake and argued that previous personal and social preparation were important in order to achieve maximum beneficial effects. Even in such cases of nonviolent provocation there is little sign that actions are undertaken for masochistic purposes. In their study of student civil rights workers in 1963 (especially of some who took dangerous actions and were severely attacked), Drs. Solomon and Fishman, both psychiatrists, reported: "Only very rarely have we heard of a personally masochistic demonstrator—emphasis in the movement is always on group values and goals."[34]

C. The barrier of social distance

The "social distance" between the contending groups—the degree to which there is or is not "fellow feeling," mutual understanding and sympathy—is important in the operation of self-suffering as a tool for converting members of the opponent group. At one extreme, if members of the nonviolent group are not even regarded as fellow human beings, the chances of achieving conversion by nonviolent suffering are likely to be nil. This barrier needs to be examined.

The closeness or distance between the contending groups will help to determine the effect of the suffering of the nonviolent group on members of the opponent group. If the opponent group sees the grievance group as members of "a common moral order," this perception is likely to encourage better treatment and a more sympathetic response to their challenge. Conversely, if the subordinates are regarded as outside such a common moral order, or as traitors to it, or as inferiors or nonhumans, the opponent group is more likely to be both cruel and indifferent to their sufferings.

Citing Simmel's analysis, Kuper points out that the possibility of conversion through suffering in nonviolent action will be influenced by the structure of the social system.[35] Kuper argues that whether the members of *both* the dominant and subordinate groups in the system are recognized as full human beings, or are regarded simply as members of some category, will be important. Not only will the perception by the dominant group of the subordinates as a class of inferior creatures block sympathy and empathy for their suffering, but also, if the members of the opponent group see *themselves* not as individuals but as members of some overriding collectivity, they will be less responsive to the sufferings of nonviolent actionists. Seeing themselves simply as parts of a very important whole (party, race, etc.) members of the opponent group will be likely to surrender their own sense of responsibility, standards of behavior, and right of moral judgment to the group, and to hide behind the policy or decision of their government, party or other collectivity. Suffering then becomes institutionalized, and may take relatively impersonal forms. Brutalized elements of the population become the agents for inflicting severe repression or brutalities on the nonviolent group, and the average citizen may be protected from emotional involvement by an insulating barrier of institutional procedures. Arguments that the members of the grievance group are inherently inferior may be consciously used to keep the average citizen indifferent to their suffering.

The greater the social distance, the fewer the "reality checks" on each group's picture of the other,[36] and the more likely that the conflict can proceed with relative indifference to the human suffering involved. Censorship and other controls over the media of communication may increase the difficulties of using suffering to overcome the social distance between the two groups.[37] Conversely, the more sympathetic feelings the two groups have for each other, the more difficult it will be for the opponent to use violence against the nonviolent group.

Illustrations of how subordinate groups can be treated inhumanly because they are regarded as nonhuman or outside the common moral order can be found in the behavior toward the Negro by the Ku Klux Klan member, toward the Jew by the Nazi, and toward the "enemy" in many wars. Even within the institution of slavery, the degree of cruelty varied, with the same social distance, being generally less when the master knew the slave personally, and greatest when slave traders or overseers regarded the slave simply as a commodity or as a subhuman species.[38] When people were "debtor slaves," i.e., were bound into slavery in their own country because of debts, they were usually treated more considerately than were foreign slaves.[39]

Within the context of nonviolent action, a similar difference has occurred in repression and attitudes toward actionists who were members of the opponent's own people and toward actionists who were foreigners. For example, Harvey Seifert reports that during the New England Puritans' persecution of Quakers from 1656 to 1675 officials distinguished foreign Quakers from colonists who had become Quakers, penalties for colonist-Quakers being consistently more lenient than for Quakers who came from outside.[40]

The role of social distance as an insulator against influence by suffering helps to explain why governments sometimes use police and troops who have as little as possible in common with the people they are to repress. For example, the Soviet government used non-Russian speaking troops from Far Eastern sections of the U.S.S.R., who could therefore not talk with Russian-speaking Hungarians, to repress the Hungarian 1956 revolution, after there had been considerable unrest and defections among the Russian and Ukranian troops previously utilized.

Where a large social distance exists, the opponent may be insulated against empathy for the suffering nonviolent actionists by various interpretations of the suffering. Such misperceptions may be especially frequent in societies in which people already suffer a great deal *involuntarily* in the course of normal living.[41] When the actionists deliberately court suffering for a cause, the opponent may, initially at least, regard their act of defiance which leads to suffering and the actionists' taking the initiative themselves in inviting suffering, as a kind of impudence and status-usurpation.[42] By defying the opponent's expectations the challenge by self-suffering may therefore initially produce, not sympathy or pity, but hostility.[43] Alternatively, the nonviolent suffering may initially be interpreted as cowardice, the result of a "mental condition," or ridiculous. When the opponent group believes its dominance to be for the benefit of the subordinates, it may interpret the nonviolent suffering as an attempt to exploit its good nature by trying to arouse sympathy for a "bad" cause, or as the result of the subordinates being misled by subversive or foreign influences.[44] For example, the South African 1952 civil disobedience campaign was described by government supporters to be the result of Mau Mau influence, Russian Communism and Indian imperialism.[45]

After a time, certain misperceptions of the self-suffering of nonviolent actionists may be recognized by members of the opponent group as inaccurate. Other misperceptions may, however, not be so quickly corrected. Which each of these will be, and why, will vary with the particular case. When the social distance between the groups is considerable, all of the misperceptions of the grievance group and the actionists are likely to aggravate the difficulty of converting members of the opponent group by sacrificial suffering. That effort may still have some effect on some members of the opponent group, especially over a long period of time.[46] But for short-term or less costly changes it may at times be necessary to bring the other mechanisms of change into operation also.

Recognizing the importance of social distance, nonviolent actionists have taken a number of steps to overcome and remove it. When members of the grievance group have seen certain of their traits to be undesirable in themselves and also objectionable to others—such as lack of cleanliness, rudeness, etc.—they may make deliberate efforts at self-improvement, as Gandhi often urged. Participation in the struggle by persons with high prestige and status may also help to penetrate the barrier of social distance.[47] When the barrier involves language and lack of acquaintance with the people and issues at stake, the nonviolent action involving self-suffering may be used as a means of communication. Gregg pointed to this possibility: "Nonviolent resistance . . . uses facial expressions, bodily gestures and the tone of voice, just as in all personal communication . . . . conduct . . . itself may be a rapid, accurate, and efficient means of communication."[48] Even Gregg, who strongly favored conversion, recognized that this process may take place slowly or incompletely.

The opponent's fear of the challenge to the status quo, or his perception of the nonviolent group as a dangerous one with secret intentions and plans, work against the conversion. The nonviolent group which seeks a change in attitudes will need to relieve or counteract such fears. Nonviolent behavior is important here, but other means may also be helpful. For example, when the opponent is afraid of large numbers, a specific demonstration may be restricted to high quality action by a few actionists in order to minimize, or remove, that impediment to the influence of self-suffering.[49] Miller has succinctly pleaded for this approach:

> It is our task in any encounter with the opponent to strip away his fears and apprehensions and to deprive him of any rationalizations he may be using to distort the facts. It is distinctly to our advantage if we can summon sufficient empathy to see matters from his point of view so that we can help him to see the situation as it actually is.[50]

In some cases, the self-suffering of the nonviolent actionists may itself finally break down the social distance between the groups, as a result of repeated actions which finally explode the old stereotypes of the group and gradually arouse respect from the opponent group. Some of the initial negative reactions to the suffering may gradually be modified and reversed. The fact that the suffering is *voluntarily* accepted,[51] and that the actionists repeatedly demonstrate great bravery and heroism, may finally become decisive.

Just as an absence of respect for nonviolent actionists is a serious impediment to conversion by the self-suffering of the actionists, so a growth of respect can be an important step toward changed perceptions of the grievance group and the issues at stake. Respect does not automatically come with nonviolent behavior. Very courageous nonviolent actionists often gain respect from others, but in achieving that change it seems that while their nonviolence is important, their courage is primary. Indeed, their nonviolence may be perceived as a higher type of bravery. Their courage is more akin to the courage of brave violent fighters than to the behavior of people who use no violence but behave cowardly. Opponents are most unlikely to respect people who submit helplessly, or cringe or plead in fear of punishment. Respect for men with courage, and contempt for people who cringe, are especially likely responses from certain personality types which are most likely to be brutal in dealing with dissenters and resisters.

Bravery is so important in the context of nonviolent action that it has much in common with extreme courage demonstrated by violent resisters. The capacity of great bravery expressed in violence to arouse admiration from the most unlikely people is illustrated by the responses of two high Nazis to the Jews of the Warsaw ghetto rebellion of 1943. Even Adolph Eichmann, working hard at the extermination program, declared in total violation of Nazi racial theories that some of those Jews were "important biological material." That is, they had by their bravery demonstrated sufficient biological superiority to be important for "breeding" future generations, rather than being so biologically inferior and contaminating as to require extermination, as the Nazi ideology maintained. The Nazi police chief, S.S. Major-General Krueger, of the *General Government* (in the remnant of Poland), praised the endurance of the defiant Jews also.[52]

In a different situation, Hitler too seemed moved by the courage of a rebel, in this case a defiant Nazi, Hans Frank, *Reichskommisar* for Justice for Germany and Governor-General of occupied Poland. Frank had split with the S.S. and after a personal friend, who was a Nazi official in Poland, had been executed without trial, Frank went on a stormy speaking tour of German universities in July 1942, advocating a return to constitutional rule. This was an act of defiance for which Frank might well have been executed, but although he was removed as *Reichskommisar* for Justice, Frank was kept as Governor-General and even won his fight with the S.S. Reitlinger writes that "Hitler had an uncanny respect" for a man who could remain defiant in the face of death.[53]

These instances are very different from ideal nonviolent action; the Warsaw Jews were clearly violent and Frank was scarcely a model nonviolent actionist. But these instances do show that bravery and defiance can sometimes win respect even from the most unlikely persons. Some people have argued that by expressing heroism and courage nonviolently, nonviolent actionists may be braver than even courageous practitioners of violence, and thereby gain respect from the opponent through demonstrated courage, sincerity, nonretaliation and self-sacrifice.

Such bravery is likely to violate the opponent's stereotype of the nonviolent group. Some members of the opponent group may, Seifert suggests, feel more threatened by such an unexpected response, and hence react with more intense aggression, but others who are more open may begin to change to bring their perceptions closer to reality. The impact of such a dramatic demonstration and suffering, "combined with a comparative absence of personal threat, make this outcome more likely," Seifert writes. "Although perceptions always remain somewhat distorted, under these circumstances it is harder to maintain the bias of old steotypes in full force . . . Under the conditions created by nonviolent resistance, man's capacity for unreality is more likely to be limited."[54]

Farmer reports that newspaper and television accounts of the 1960 sit-ins in the United States presented images which reversed the common stereotypes of Negroes—stereotypes which extended beyond cowardice and passivity. The students taking part in the sit-ins were well-dressed, well-mannered, studious and quiet, while the crowds of white boys outside were disorderly and trying to start trouble.[55] Solomon and Fishman made similar observations; the movement was destroying both the *Southern* stereotype of the "contented Negro," and the *national* stereotype of the "violent Negro."[56]

When nonviolent actionists seek conversion through self-suffering, Miller argues, it is necessary to make "a maximum effort to establish rapport and to present the opponent with an image that commands respect and can lay a basis for empathy."[57] If a change of image and a growth of respect take place it may become possible for the opponent to "identify" with the suffering nonviolent actionist despite the former extreme social distance between the two groups. Such a breakdown of social distance has occurred both outside and within the context of nonviolent action.[58] The social distance between the orthodox Brahman Hindus and the untouchables in South India in the 1920s was about as great as can be imagined. Yet the 1924–25 Vykom temple-road *satyagraha* campaign ended sixteen months after it began with the Brahmans changing their attitude. This campaign, which was described in Chapter Two, persisted despite beatings, prison sentences, tropical sun and floods. The actionists sought not simply the right of the untouchables to use a road which passed the temple, but that the Brahmans should willingly agree to that change. In the end, the Brahmans said: "We cannot any longer resist the prayers that have been made to us, and we are willing to receive the untouchables."[59] This illustrates that under certain circumstances conversion is possible despite extreme social distance. For these cases, and the many more in which the barriers to conversion are not so high, it is important to examine *how* this conversion takes place.

D. Conversion through self-suffering

Because there has been so little research on conversion in nonviolent action it is impossible here to offer a full and accurate analysis of how conversion is achieved, when it is, or to give full consideration to all the important variations within this mechanism. It is, however, possible to summarize present insights into the process which raise hypotheses for further research and add to our understanding of the dynamics of the technique.

Conversion is, of course, not a single precise phenomenon. It includes various types of changes varying in their rational and emotional components, operating on different people, and differing with the length of time the change has been in operation.

Conversion includes various changes in the opponent's attitudes, beliefs, feelings and world views. There may be changes in opinions and reactions toward the grievance group, for example, or toward themselves, or toward the issues at stake in the conflict, toward the repression, their own social system, or, finally, toward their own belief system or that of the actionists. The conversion may be primarily focused on one of these or involve all of them to a significant degree, or a combination of several of them.

Conversion results from differing influences and also varies in the degree of rationality and nonrationality involved; it seems to range on a continuum from a relatively rational change of attitude on the specific issue at stake to a change almost exclusively in the person's emotions and deepest convictions. The latter type may involve a revulsion against past policies and behavior, contrition and repentence, and a change in an entire outlook on life, including the adoption of new beliefs. This type is apparently much the rarest type of conversion, although it is the type most often discussed in the writings of actionists who believe in principled nonviolence and who seek conversion. Most cases of conversion fall at various points between these extremes.

Nor will all members of the opponent group be equally converted simultaneously. Some may not change at all. Although members of the general public of the opponent group may change their views and feelings toward the conflict or the grievance group and even ordinary soldiers may do so, the persons occupying the top political positions may not be moved in the slightest. Nonviolent actionists, far more than their violent counterparts, view their opponent as a heterogeneous group. Although headed sometimes by strong leaders who may be hard to influence, the actionists see the opponent group as consisting of diverse subgroups and people who may be far less committed to the objectionable policies than are the leaders. These sub-parts of the opponent group may be much more susceptible to influence in favor of the nonviolent group, and their conversions may prove to be highly important.

Furthermore, conversion of any type takes place over a time span and the process goes through various stages. This means that if the process is interrupted or halted at a certain point, although the opinions and feelings of the person will differ from what they were previously, they will also differ from those which would have developed had the conversion process been completed.

Although believers in principled nonviolence derived from religious sources most often are the exponents of conversion, this mechanism occurs in the absence of such beliefs and even when conversion is not deliberately sought. For example, most of the attitudes thought to be needed to achieve conversion were apparently absent in the Irish peasants' boycott of the now famous Captain Boycott, mentioned briefly earlier. Although economically ruined by the peasants' action in 1879, he returned in 1883 from New York to Ireland, but this time as a *supporter* of the Irish cause.[60] This does not show that the peasants' boycott alone had changed his opinions, but that his personal experience was bound to have played a role in his thinking about conditions in Ireland.

Theory and opinions from Gandhi and others on how conversion operates may best be understood if an example of change by conversion is described first: the Quakers' struggle in Puritan Massachusetts Bay Colony, 1656-75.[61] When the Quakers attempted to proselitize in Puritan Massachusetts they became involved in a nonviolent action campaign for religious liberty. The Puritans regarded Quakerism as a "sink of blasphemies" and Quakers themselves as "ravening wolves." They were accused of defiance of the ministry and the courts, naked dancing, and a plot to burn Boston and kill the inhabitants. Perhaps most important, a grant of religious toleration would have ended the Puritan theocracy and political ideal. The Puritans believed they had a religious duty to persecute those who spread religious "error."

Two women Quakers were the first to arrive; they were sent back to England on the next boat. Two days later eight more Quakers arrived; despite harsh penalties the numbers constantly increased as they waged "a direct frontal attack." They met in private homes, tried to speak after sermons in churches, spoke during their own trials and from their jail cell windows, issued pamphlets and tracts, returned to the colony in defiance of the law, held illegal meetings, refused to pay fines, and when imprisoned refused to work at the cost of food being denied them. Despite expulsions, whippings through towns and executions, the Quakers repeatedly returned. One already banished on pain of death walked calmly into the court where another was on trial for his life.

Initially the general public and the theocratic leaders were united in favor of the persecution. Gradually, however, a split developed as the public began to see the Quakers in a new light. Sympathizers began to pay the jailers' fees and at night passed food to the Quakers through jail windows. The bearing of the Quakers as they were whipped and executed convinced people that they had "the support of the Lord" and were "the

Lord's people." The Governor expressed his determination to continue executions so long as the Quakers persisted.

Public unease increased. After a time that same governor even threatened to punish a jailer who had nearly killed an imprisoned Quaker by beating. The law on banishment under pain of death was modified to allow trial by jury. Later, opposition to enforcement of the law grew and after a woman Quaker was executed discontent increased. Finally, even the General Court (the legislature) began to weaken. The death penalty was virtually abolished. Although the laws became milder, it was difficult to obtain constables to enforce them. By 1675 in Boston the Quakers were holding regular Meetings undisturbed. The Quakers were now included in the category of human beings and a "common moral order," and religious liberty was then not far behind.

In a very different case, despite his rejection of nonviolence as a moral principle and his emphasis on economic and political forces, Nehru's experience forced him to conclude that something like conversion did at times take place in nonviolent struggle:

That it has considerable effect on the opponent is undoubted. It exposes his moral defences, it unnerves him, it appeals to the best in him, it leaves the door open for conciliation. There can be no doubt that the approach of love and self-suffering has powerful psychic reactions on the adversary as well as on the onlookers.[62]

All writers on conversion by nonviolent action seem to see self-suffering by the actionists as the dominant factor which initiates conversion, but there are differences on whether the suffering directly initiates conversion or whether it does so indirectly. Sometimes such suffering is seen to operate *directly* on the consciences of members of the opponent group, and at other times the suffering is seen first to influence wider public opinion which then causes members of the opponent group to experience inner emotional conflict and to question their previous opinions and beliefs.

Gandhi sometimes spoke of this *indirect* type of conversion. In the case of the Vykom *satyagraha,* already described, he said: "The method of reaching the heart is to awaken public opinion."[63] The opponent's violence, then, first puts him in a bad light in the eyes of observers, and their disapproval contributes to the beginnings of inner uncertainty in the opponent himself. As Gregg put it:

With the audience as a sort of mirror . . . the attacker with his violence perhaps begins to feel a little excessive and undignified—even a little ineffective—and by contrast with the victim, less generous and in fact brutal. He realizes that the onlookers see that he has misjudged the nature of his adversary, and realizes that he has lost prestige. He somewhat loses his self-respect . . .[64]

The sufferings of the nonviolent actionists may also be a *direct* stimulus to inner change in the opponent, especially when the social distance between the groups is not great or can be overcome with time. Voluntary suffering for a belief or ideal, argues Gregg, is likely to induce in others feelings of "kinship with the sufferer"[65] and sympathy for him. If the severity of their suffering disturbs the opponent, awareness that granting the demands of the nonviolent actionists can quickly end the suffering may stimulate change. When the opponent starts to wonder if the demands of the nonviolent group are justified, he is on the way toward conversion.

The existence of a complex of strong emotions, which may swing between opposites, was regarded by Case as another factor facilitating conversion; this is said to make possible sudden rushes of sympathetic emotions such as admiration, remorse, compassion and shame. The changed views may focus on the violence of the repression or on the issues at stake.[66]

Among the possible effects of the self-suffering of nonviolent actionists on the members of the opponent group are three: the sincerity of the actionists may become clear; their courage and determination may bring reluctant respect; and the old image of the group may be replaced by a new, more favorable, one.

Willingness to endure sacrifices—such as poverty, injury, imprisonment and even death—in furtherance of their beliefs or cause is likely to demonstrate the sincerity of the nonviolent actionists. Sacrifices incurred in *violent* conflict also demonstrate sincerity, as already discussed, but, it is argued, sympathy for the actionists is more likely when they are not also inflicting suffering on the opponent.[67] "To be willing to suffer and die for a cause is an incontestable proof of sincere belief, and perhaps in most cases the only incontestable proof."[68] Willingness of leaders of social movements to make visible personal sacrifices for their cause has also been called a test of their sincerity.[69]

If the opponent recognizes the sincerity of the nonviolent group, this may be a very important step toward respect for them and toward a reconsideration of the issues. Gandhi saw respect of the opponent for the nonviolent actionists as an achievement which heralded approaching success. He argued that at the approach of this stage, the nonviolent actionists must conduct themselves with special care.

Every good movement passes through five stages, indifference, ridicule, abuse, repression, and respect. . . . Every movement that survives repression, mild or severe, invariably commands respect which is another name for success. This repression, if we are true, may be treated as a sure sign of the approaching victory. But, if we are true, we shall neither be cowed down nor angrily retaliate and be violent. *Violence is suicide* . . . power dies hard, and . . . it is but natural for the Government to make a final effort for life even . . . through repression. Complete self-restraint at the present critical moment is the speediest way to success.[70]

The self-suffering of the nonviolent actionists may also contribute to changes in the opponent group's perception of themselves. At times, instead of seeing themselves as the brave heroes courageously defending their loved ones, principles and society against vicious attacks, the events may break through their psychological defences and force them to recognize that it is *they* who have harshly attacked courageous men standing firmly for their cause without either threats or retaliation. On one occasion King expressed his confidence in the power of such self-suffering to bring inner disturbance to the perpetrators of such cruelties.[71]

In certain circumstances repression of the nonviolent group may lower the self-esteem of members of the opponent group. This change may affect their will to continue the repression and the struggle generally, especially if the opponent's objectives are difficult to justify.

Intermediary stages of the conversion mechanism may lead to reduced violent repression. While continued and increasingly severe violence is more likely against a violent action group—violence thrives on violence—violent repression tends to be reduced when confronted with nonviolent resistance. Another source of reduced repression is the growth of respect for the nonviolent actionists which may, according to Gregg, lead the opponent unconsciously to imitate them by reducing his own violence.[72] The absence of violence from the actionists may also lead individual members of the opponent group to reject a violent response; for example, during a lunch counter sit-in in Tallahassee, Florida, in February 1960, when tough-looking characters entered the store and looked as if they might attack the sit-inners, the waitress asked them to leave, and when some made derogatory remarks, she told them, "You can see they aren't here to start anything."[73]

In some instances the opponent's anger at the nonviolent group may prove to be physically and emotionally exhausting. Such exhaustion, combined with new inner uncertainties, may lead him to make mistakes in calculation and judgment, or may reduce his ability to make crucial decisions.[74]

When the influences which may bring about conversion are first set into operation the opponent is unlikely to be conscious of them. Gandhi described this conversion process as three-fourths invisible, its effect being in inverse ratio to its visibility. This led, he argued, to more effective and lasting change in the long run.[75] These inner influences may grow until the opponent realizes that he has doubts and has begun to question the rightness of his attitudes and behavior. When he becomes aware of these inner conflicts, the conversion process has already reached an advanced state. "If you want to conquer another man," wrote Gregg, "do it . . . by creating inside his own personality a strong new impulse that is incompatible with his previous tendency."[76] This inner conflict may be increased because the opponent finds that his usual outlook on life, his ways of behaving and responding to subordinates, opponents and crises—in which he has always had confidence—have failed to produce the expected results. In a very real sense this places him in a new world which requires that he reconsider many things.[77]

The willingness of nonviolent actionists to suffer rather than to submit may therefore lead the opponent to look once again at his dogma and policies, as Case suggests.[78] Initially, he may have intended to revel in their correctness, but now he may see them differently. Attitudes and feelings may then change, including some which seemed rigid. Some changes will appear as apparently sudden reversals of outlook.[79]

Such results will, of course, not take place easily, or even at all. There will be strong counterpressures, psychological, economic, political or other, to continue the old policy and activities, and the opponent may decide to do so no matter what the cost. He may also become brutalized and callous to the sufferings of others, and his mind may become closed to rational arguments.[80]

In order to avoid such brutalization, advocates of conversion in non-violent action have often counseled restraint, and recommended that the opponent not be pushed too far at a single point. They have urged that he not be required to choose too often between being repeatedly brutal and acquiescing to demands. Whole campaigns, and even individual demonstrations, may therefore be planned to be implemented in phases which are intended to reduce hatred, to avoid extreme fury, and to provide time for one phase to work before the next begins. Such a phased campaign gives the opponent opportunity for reflection and thought, and is an effort to show him that not he personally but his policy is under attack. The choice of methods, the numbers participating at a given time and point, the tactics employed, attitudes conveyed, and even small personal gestures, may all be important in this attempt. These refinements may facilitate the operation of the conversion mechanism despite unfavorable circumstances by showing the opponent the sincerity of the actionists and by removing his misconceptions about them and their objectives.

As the opponent's first point of reference is himself,[81] he must keep a favorable self-image. His justification for the policy at issue and his dismissal of the grievance group as nonhuman or as outside the common moral order may have helped him to do this. If as a result of the nonviolent group's self-suffering, he begins to doubt his policy and also begins to see the members of the grievance group as fellow human beings, it will be difficult to keep that favorable self-image. In order to do so he must then change the policy and cease certain behavior.

The conflict may thus be resolved by a change of the opponent's will, aims and feelings. "He ceases to want in the same way the things he wanted before; he ceases to maintain his former attitude toward the resisters; he undergoes a sort of inner conversion."[82] The inner conflicts and uncertainty—which are certainly not easy to bear—may lead the opponent to become receptive to suggestions from the nonviolent group as to an honorable way out of the particular conflict,[83] as well as to new ideas which may lead to more fundamental conversion.[84] In such circumstances the opponent may be considerably more subject to influence and suggestion than the nonviolent group.[85] Gregg also argues that the emotional and moral perturbation taking place in the opponent during the struggle may bring to the surface "moral memories" which he had long since forgotten and which had ceased to influence his behavior; these, he suggests may also influence the opponent to make a more humane response to the conflict.[86] The conversion process may finally lead the opponent to come to see the situation "in a broader, more fundamental and far-sighted way . . ."[87] Gregg describes this change confidently in these words:

> Nonviolent resistance demoralizes the opponent only to re-establish in him a new morale that is finer because it is based on sounder values. Nonviolent resistance does not break the opponent's will but alters it; does not destroy his confidence, enthusiasm and hope but transfers them to a finer purpose.[88]

Gandhi's views on this mechanism may be illuminating. Although he fully recognized the importance of power in social and political conflicts and in certain circumstances justified action which would produce nonviolent coercion, Gandhi had full confidence in the power of voluntary suffering to convert the opponent. "Given a just cause, capacity for endless suffering and avoidance of violence, victory is certain." Another path was concentration over a long period on the reform of the nonviolent group itself; this would produce various influences and finally result in the opponent being "completely transformed." [89]

The results of voluntary suffering might not appear at once, [90] and especially difficult cases might require extreme suffering. This did not, however, alter his view: even "the hardest heart" must melt before "the heat of nonviolence," and there was no limit on the capacity of nonviolence to generate heat. [91] Gandhi credited the brave suffering of the Boer women of South Africa in concentration camps set up by Lord Kitchener with changing the English attitude toward the Boers and making changes possible in British government policy for that country. [92] Gandhi applied this same principle in India, incorporated in nonviolent action. He wrote in 1930: "If the people join me as I expect they will, the sufferings they will undergo, unless the British nation sooner retraces its steps will be enough to melt the stoniest heart." [93]

When results from voluntary suffering were not immediately forthcoming, Gandhi, perhaps using circular logic, explained that there had been not enough suffering, or not enough time, or the suffering had not been pure enough. Granted the quality of the suffering, however, Gandhi saw an almost mathematical relationship between the suffering and the results. "Success is the certain result of suffering of the extremest character, voluntarily undergone." [94] "Progress is to be measured by the amount of suffering undergone by the sufferer, the purer the suffering, the greater is the progress." [95] At times he even defined the technique of *satyagraha* as "a method of securing rights by personal suffering . . ." [96]

It is not necessary to share Gandhi's extreme view of the power of voluntary suffering to achieve conversion to recognize that under some circumstances this mechanism may be effective. However, an oversimplified view of conversion, whether held by exponents of that mechanism, or by sceptics, is bound to lead to misunderstanding and the unwarranted dismissal of conversion as a genuine mechanism of change in certain circumstances. It is important to recognize, as Ebert points out, that "if it occurs at all, it does so by way of intermediate stages." [97] Furthermore, there are distinguishable factors which may influence the operation of the conversion mechanism, and it is to these that our attention now turns.

E. Some factors influencing conversion

The factors influencing the operation of the conversion mechanism in nonviolent action may be roughly divided into external factors and internal factors—external factors being those inherent in the conflict situation and outside the direct control of the nonviolent group, and internal factors being those under the direct control of the nonviolent group and involving either its internal condition or the activities and gestures it may make in efforts to convert the opponent.

1. External factors   These factors will include the following:

(a) The degree of conflict of interest. If the issue at stake in the conflict is highly important to the opponent, the nonviolent actionists can reasonably expect that it will be more difficult to convert him to their point of view than if the issue at stake is of relatively little importance to the opponent. Janis and Katz describe this as "the degree of conflict of interest relative to the community of interest between the competing groups." [98] The gravity of the issues at stake, and the likely consequences if the demands of the nonviolent group are granted, may significantly influence the resistance of members of the opponent group to efforts to convert them.

(b) Social distance. In accordance with the earlier discussion, whether or not the subordinates are regarded by the opponent as members of a common moral order will be an important factor influencing the possibility of conversion.

(c) The personality structure of the opponents. Certain types of personalities may be particularly susceptible to conversion by nonviolent self-suffering, while others may be extremely resistant to such influences. (This does not imply that sadists, for example, would simply revel in the opportunity to inflict cruelties against nonviolent actionists, for other factors in the situation, especially the absence of masochistic fear, cringing, etc., among them, may make the relationship unsatisfactory for sadists.) Research, which takes into consideration both existing knowledge of personality structure and change, and also the nature of this technique of struggle, could contribute significantly to understanding the personality factor.

(d) Beliefs and norms—shared or diverse. If the opponent and the nonviolent actionists share common beliefs and norms of behavior, they will provide "a higher tribunal, standing above the parties" to which the nonviolent group can appeal with the expectation of understanding and perhaps sympathy. [99] Where such common ideals and standards are absent, however, and especially where the opponent group is committed to belief in the right or duty of domination, there will be "formidable barriers" to the conversion of the opponent.[100]

(e) The role of third parties. Whether or not the opponent group cares about praise or condemnation from third parties, and whether and how those groups respond to repression of the nonviolent actionists, will frequently be an important factor influencing conversion.

These five factors may at times be supplemented by others. Even when these five factors are unfavorable to conversion, a nonviolent group might be able to achieve conversion anyhow. However, the combination of a high degree of conflict of interest, great social distance, unfavorable personality types in the opponent group, absence of shared beliefs and moral standards, and unsympathetic third parties would make conversion exceedingly difficult.

2. Internal factors   According to Gandhian thinking, there are at least eight factors influencing conversion which are under the control of the nonviolent group.[101]

(a) Refraining from violence and hostility. If the nonviolent group wants to convert the opponent, it generally emphasizes the importance of abstention from physical violence and also from expressions of hostility and antagonism toward the opponent. Deliberate rejection of violence in favor of nonviolent means is regarded as having an important psychological impact on the opponent which may influence his conversion,[102] removing or reducing his fear of the grievance group, and hence increasing his ability to consider its arguments and to respond sympathetically to its plight. Gandhi believed that when the Englishmen came to feel that their lives were protected, not by their weapons but by the Indians' refusal to harm them, "that moment will see a transformation in the English nature in its relation to India . . . ."[103] When an opponent feels a campaign to be a personal attack on himself—psychological if not physical—he is more likely to resist changes in his outlook and policies, and to be more impervious to appeals from the actionists and third parties, than when the actionists are able to convince him they bear no personal hostility and are concerned only with policies.[104]

(b) Attempting to gain the opponent's trust. Trust of the nonviolent actionists may significantly increase the chances of conversion. This trust may be consciously cultivated, in at least four ways. 1) Truthfulness, in the sense of accuracy of one's word. Statements to the opponent and to the public should be as correct as possible. In describing the grievance, for example, the facts should not be exaggerated or falsified. All statements to the opponent should be accurate with no attempt at deception. 2)

Openness concerning intentions. Truthfulness is carried to the point of telling the opponent one's plans for action and broader intentions.[105] In addition to the factors discussed in Chapter Nine openness also has beneficial psychological influences on the opponent. 3) Chivalry. If the opponent experiences some unrelated difficulty, such as a natural disaster, the nonviolent action may be postponed, or he may even be offered assistance. This "don't hit a man when he's down" behavior may help gain his trust and promote conversion.[106] 4) Personal appearance and habits. Offensive appearance and behavior may, as Sir Herbert Read, the anarchist, observed, "create a barrier of suspicion and reserve which makes the communication of any truth impossible."[107] To gain trust, the actionists may try to make their appearance and behavior inoffensive without compromise on the issues at stake. If the opponent does gain more trust in the actionists, his own insecurity may be reduced, and hence his desire for dominance.[108]

(c) Refraining from humiliating the opponent. Humiliation is an unlikely step toward sympathy, voluntary change and conversion. Therefore, if the nonviolent group aims at conversion, it must refrain "from any action that will have the effect of humiliating the rival group."[109]

This implies various "do's" and "don'ts" for the nonviolent actionist. For example, *don't* rely on numbers to convert the opponent. Numbers as such may inspire fear, and hence work against conversion. Even an outward "victory," produced by massive numbers may produce only obstinacy or bitterness. *Do* rely on the power of a few determined, nonviolent, self-sacrificing volunteers, or even a single one. Gandhi believed one actionist might "induce a heart change even in the opponent who, freed from fear, will the more readily appreciate his simple faith and respect it."[110] Seeking conversion, actionists also sometimes may refrain from pressing home a "victory" within their reach while persisting in action, as at Vykom, until the opponent is ready to agree to the objective.

(d) Making visible sacrifices for one's own cause.[111] If the suffering is to have the greatest impact on the opponent, it should, argued Gandhi, be offered by people directly involved in the grievances. This is more likely to be perceived as sincerity, and therefore influence conversion, than if they are unwilling to do so, or if some other people are taking the risks. Even major sacrifices by other people who are, or are regarded as, "outsiders," may have comparatively little effect. Their participation may even arouse hostility as "outside intervention" and "trouble-making." The opponent may even see the whole campaign as originating with outsiders, not with the people directly affected by the grievance.[112]

Generally, in Gandhi's view, outside aid should be limited entirely to expressions of sympathy. When the aim is conversion of the opponent, sympathetic nonviolent action should be offered only in special circumstances. During the Vykom *satyagraha,* a Christian became leader of the nonviolent actionists at one point. Gandhi then urged that participants should be limited to Hindus (including untouchables).

The silent loving suffering of one single pure Hindu as such will be enough to melt the hearts of millions of Hindus; but the sufferings of thousands of non-Hindus on behalf of the "untouchables" will leave the Hindus unmoved. Their blind eyes will not be opened by outside interference, however well-intentioned and generous it may be; for it will not bring home to them the sense of guilt. On the contrary, they would probably hug the sin all the more for such interference. All reform to be sincere and lasting must come from within. [113]

Self-sufficient nonviolent action by members of the grievance group was also necessary, Gandhi argued, to show the opponent his dependence on that group and that "without the cooperation, direct or indirect, of the wronged the wrong-doer cannot do the wrong intended by him." [114]

There are also some indications from the experience of nonviolent action movements in the Deep South that outsiders may arouse more antagonism than local people in initiating projects.

(e) Carrying on constructive work. Constructive program work and other efforts at self-improvement within the subordinate group may help to achieve conversion. Janis and Katz describe such work as "maintaining a consistent and persistent set of positive activities which are explicit (though partial) realizations of the group's objectives." [115] Such work may demonstrate sincerity and social concern. "Participation *(as individuals)* in wider community activities which are widely regarded as necessary in the common welfare" is listed by Robin Williams as one means by which a vulnerable minority group can reduce the majority's hostility towards it. [116]

It is relatively difficult to dismiss humanitarian and constructive work and to distort the motives behind it; when people who engage in such work are also practicing nonviolent action, the opponent may take their statements and behavior more seriously.

(f) Maintaining personal contact with the opponent. Nonviolent actionists seeking to convert the opponent repeatedly emphasize the importance of maintaining personal contact with him. Such contact may at times also be maintained by personal letters, or by discussions and conferences. Such contact may help keep personal relations friendly despite the conflict and achieve maximum accurate understanding of the other's views, motivations, aims and intentions. [117] Personal contact may at times contribute to conversion by both emotional and rational processes.

(g) Demonstrating trust of the opponent. The nonviolent group seeking to convert the opponent will, in Gandhian thinking, adopt "a consistent attitude of trust toward the rival group and [take] overt actions which demonstrate that one is, in fact, willing to act upon this attitude." [118] When the nonviolent group has high expectations of the opponent's intentions and future behavior, those expectations, it is believed, may encourage him to live up to them. Such high expectations of the opponent may also place the nonviolent group in a favorable light with third parties. The actionists do not, however, play down their indictment of the opponent's policies, or temporize about the justification for nonviolent action. [119] However, negotiations and other means of settling the conflict short of direct action will be fully explored, and the nonviolent group will deliberately appeal to the best in the opponent to facilitate a response in similar terms. All suggestions by him for negotiations will be seriously explored, even when they may be intended as diversions from the direct action campaign. [120] It is, of course, not necessary to suspend direct action for negotiations to take place, and if, after an agreement has been reached, the opponent does not fulfill his pledges, nonviolent action can always be resumed.

(h) Developing empathy, good will and patience toward the opponent. Conversion will be helped if the actionists can achieve an inner understanding of the opponent, ". . . a high degree of empathy with respect to the motives, affects, expectations, and attitudes of the members of the rival group." [121] With such empathy, the nonviolent actionists may be more able to anticipate the opponent's moves and reactions, and will also have a more sympathetic understanding of his outlook, feelings and problems—while disagreeing with him on policy.

The actionists can then refrain from action which would needlessly antagonize the opponent and, positively, in small ways—a glance, tone of voice, letter—or in large ways communicate the nonviolent actionists' lack of personal hostility and even their personal friendship in the midst of battle. This may aid the opponent's conversion. Demonstrated respect for the individual members of the opponent group, and understanding of their outlook and problems may in turn make them more sympathetic and less hostile to the nonviolent challengers.

The expression of personal goodwill for the opponents may express itself in such ways as continuation of personal friendships in the midst of the struggle or efforts not to inconvenience the opponent. Bondurant reports instances in India "of proper satyagrahis refusing to take action in the mid-day sun because of the hardship this would work on European opponents who were less accustomed to extreme heat, and again, of satyagrahis postponing an action to spare the Englishman for his Easter Sunday services and celebration." [122] When the police raided the *satyagrahis* camp at Dharasana in 1930, following two days of bloody repression which had turned the camp into a hospital, one of the *satyagrahis* wrote: "Some twenty policemen surrounded us. We were going on with our own work. As it was hot we gave our police brethren a drink of cold fresh water. On the mornings of the 21st and 22nd, we had given them our blood as patiently and quietly." [123] Nonviolent actionists intent upon converting the opponent must be willing to demonstrate considerable patience with him. This patience with him as an individual is combined with impatience with his policies.

F. Conversion may not be achieved

There are a variety of reasons why the self-suffering of nonviolent actionists may not convert the opponent. Sometimes only partial success may be achieved, while in other cases the struggle may end without outward indications that any degree of conversion has been achieved. Such factors as the conflict of interest, the social distance, absence of shared beliefs and norms, and the personality structure of members of the opponent group may have established a broad and deep chasm between the groups, so unfavorable to conversion that the suffering of the nonviolent group is insufficient to achieve conversion. Even Gregg—who stresses conversion —admits that "in the case of a very proud and obstinate opponent, there may have to be a complete outward defeat before the change of heart really takes place . . ." [124] Others acknowledge that certain groups may be especially difficult, or impossible, to convert. Miller singles out unofficial and anonymous attackers drawn from "the worst elements among the opponent's masses" who may bomb, shoot, beat and kill nonviolent actionists (he recommends appeals to "the more responsible elements in their community to quarantine them.") [125] Members of a terroristic secret police, such as the Gestapo, must also be expected to be nearly immune to conversion attempts, while ordinary conscript soldiers may be vulnerable. While it is easy on the one hand to dismiss the possibilities of conversion with excessive enthusiasm, it would also be naïve not to recognize that in some cases conversion will never take place.

Frequently all three mechanisms of change operate in the same situation. In many campaigns success cannot be attributed solely to conversion or nonviolent coercion, or even to the middle mechanism, accommodation. Instead, change may be produced by some combination of these mechanisms.

Sometimes, for example, although conversion is attempted, the conflict may produce other forces of change which contribute to accommodation or nonviolent coercion so rapidly that the aims of the actionists will be achieved before the conversion process has had time to work. In those cases in which the passive acquiescence of the grievance group has in the past been largely responsible for the grievance, their noncooperation and defiance may in itself be sufficient to abolish the objectionable policy or practice. The halt to their submissiveness may result from a "change of heart" within the members of the *grievance group*, rather than the different type of "change of heart" in the *opponent group*, which is more often discussed in the literature. The withdrawal of support by the grievance group may have a rapid impact on the operation of the system. "The unifying power of nonviolent resistance may often take effect more rapidly than does the breaking down of the morale of the opponents." [126]

Some advocates of conversion as the only ethical or moral mechanism in nonviolent struggle have a very simplistic view of the nature of change in nonviolent action, of possible courses of action, and of the ethical problems posed by the differing mechanisms. Some of these are revealed by the power of noncooperation even when conversion is sought. Extreme exponents of conversion reject all change which is not willingly agreed to by the opponent leadership. But where the victims of an objectionable policy have ended it by noncooperation and such moralists still insist on conversion, they must also advocate a resumption of cooperation and continuance of the "evil" to which they object until the leaders of the opposition group are converted. Should the grievance group, with its new sense of self-respect, courage and determination, then be counseled to continue to submit while the opponent's domination or objectionable social practices continue?

Related ethical problems concerning conversion are raised when some members of the opponent group are converted while others, such as the top officials or leaders, have not been changed. The effort to achieve conversion is not likely to win over *all* members of the opponent group simultaneously. The opponent's troops, administrators and general population may be converted before the top leaders. Soldiers, for example, carrying out repression against the nonviolent actionists may, despite their discipline and habits of obedience, come to question the use of such repression against nonviolent people. Such questions, combined perhaps with fraternization with the nonviolent group, may lead them to think for themselves, and then to lower their morale and finally to question orders, disobey and perhaps even mutiny.[127] A similar process may take place among the opponents' administrators, home civilian populations, and even officers. When such members of the opponent group begin to protest at the opponent's policies and finally refuse to obey orders, should they resume their roles as tools for maintaining the objectionable policies until their top officials have been converted?

Nonviolent actionists may, of course, not even attempt to convert the opponent. Or they may be willing to try to do so, while being ready after a certain point to use full nonviolent coercion. Nonviolent action can achieve social and political objectives by means other than conversion.

Difficulties in producing conversion have led many exponents and practitioners of nonviolent action, among them James Farmer, to reject the attempt to achieve it, and to concentrate on change by accommodation or nonviolent coercion: "In the arena of political and social events, what men feel and believe matters much less than what, under various kinds of external pressures, they can be made to *do.*"[128] Attention now turns to the mechanisms of change by *accommodation* and *nonviolent coercion.*

ACCOMMODATION

Accommodation as a mechanism of nonviolent action falls in an intermediary position between conversion and nonviolent coercion. In accommodation the opponent is neither converted nor nonviolently coerced; yet there are elements of both involved in his decision to grant concessions to the nonviolent actionists. This may be, as has been suggested, the most common mechanism of the three in successful nonviolent campaigns.[129] In the mechanism of accommodation the opponent resolves to grant the demands of the nonviolent actionists without having changed his mind fundamentally about the issues involved.[130] Some other factor has come to be considered more important than the issue at stake in the conflict, and the opponent is therefore willing to yield on the issue rather than to risk or to experience some other condition or result regarded as still more unsatisfactory. The main reason for this new willingness to yield is the changed social situation produced by the nonviolent action. Accommodation has this in common with nonviolent coercion. In both mechanisms, action is "directed toward . . . a change in those aspects of the situation which are regarded as productive of existing attitudes and behavior." [131] This means that the actionists

. . . operate on the situation within which people must act, or upon their perception of the situation, without attempting directly to alter their attitudes, sentiments or values. The pressure for a given type of behavior then comes either from (a) revealing information which affects the way in which individuals visualize the situation, or from (b) actual or potential alteration of the situation itself. [132]

In nonviolent coercion the changes are made when the opponent no longer has an effective choice between conceding or refusing to accept the demands. In accommodation, however, although the change is made in response to the altered situation, it is made while the opponent still has an effective choice before him, and before significant nonviolent coercion takes place. The degree to which the opponent accepts this change as a result of influences which would potentially have led to his conversion, or as the result of influences which might have produced nonviolent coercion, will vary. Both may be present in the same case. Sometimes other factors not capable of leading to either extreme may contribute to achieving accommodation.

A. Violent repression seen as inappropriate

The opponent may become convinced that despite his view of the rights and wrongs of the issues at stake in the conflict, continued repression of the nonviolent group by various types of violence is inappropriate. The suffering of the nonviolent actionists may have moved him to the point where, although not converted, he sees them as fellow human beings against whom the continued infliction of violence is no longer tolerable. Or he may feel that his violence is losing him "face" among third parties whose opinions may be important to him, and that if he continues the repression, he will lose still more. As Seifert explained it,

Humanitarians in government or in the general population may oppose the cause of the resisters, but also want to protect an image of themselves as decent, tolerant persons. In order to protect the second . . . they may yield on the first. For them the costs of terrorization and brutality have become greater than the costs of . . . whatever the resisters were contending for. Or opponents may . . . no longer consider the central issue to be as important as they once did . . . They would still like to have their own way on [it] . . . but . . . continuing the struggle is not worth the trouble. [133]

The change of opinion among Montgomery, Alabama, whites is an example of this type of accommodation. While still favoring segregation at the end of the bus boycott, many of them could no longer countenance extreme violence, such as bombings and shootings, to support it.[134] A similar reaction was noted by correspondent Negley Farson in India in 1930. His dispatch published on June 23 said:

"Where is this going to end? What can we do with people like this?" These are some of the questions which at clubs, home, offices and on the streets Europeans in Bombay are now asking each other, many of them appalled by the brutal methods police employ against Mahatma Gandhi's nonviolent campaign.[135]

Four days later it was reported that the very Englishmen who had six weeks earlier been the "damn-well-got-to-rule" type had now come to say, "Well, if the Indians are so determined to have dominion status as all this, let them have it and get on with it."[136] A similar development occurred in the American woman suffrage movement. Seifert reports that many people

. . . who objected to militant tactics or to woman suffrage, . . . objected even more to cruel handling of them . . . . The suffragists quoted an unnamed congressman as saying, "While I have always been opposed to suffrage I have been so aroused over the treatment of the women at Occoquan [a prison] that I have decided to vote for the Federal Amendment" . . . . When a choice had to be made between supporting the cause of the militants and cruelly suppressing them, many people preferred the former.[137]

The opponent may thus find that, although he is perfectly capable of continuing the repression and although he still has not agreed with the demands of the nonviolent actionists, "the campaigner is not really so bad after all and that, all things considered it 'costs too much' to suppress the campaigner."[138] He may thereby end the still unresolved inner conflict produced by the behavior of the nonviolent actionists.[139]

B. Getting rid of a nuisance

Sometimes opponents may grant the actionists' demands, or make major concessions, simply because they regard the group, or certain consequences of the conflict, as a nuisance which they wish to end. Lakey has argued that "when the campaigner succeeds in projecting an image of himself as a 'nuisance' and not as a 'threat,' he is close to a resolution of the conflict." [140] Seifert writes that some Americans may favor accommodation in face of nonviolent action because, for example, they are more devoted to orderly community life than to the issues, because they want quiet and an end to continued demonstrations; even segregationist parents may prefer open integrated schools to closed segregated ones. With these priorities, such persons "therefore detach their support from repressive policies." [141]

Sometimes when repression against nonviolent actionists is proving unsuccessful and frustrating, the government may itself conclude that the group is more of a nuisance than a threat, and that therefore partial or full concessions are in order.

The toleration of Christians in the Roman Empire seems to have resulted from this type of accommodation. The edict of toleration, issued by the Roman Emperor Galerius in April 311 A.D. frankly admitted that the attempt to get the Christians to return to the State religion, which had been reinforced by bloody repression, had not been successful. In granting toleration, the Emperor appears not to have been motivated by a sudden conversion to the principle of religious liberty, much less being coerced into making concessions. Rather, it appears, he wished to end the constant source of irritation posed by the Christians who would not bend to the Emperor. The reconsideration of the status of the Christians was made, the edict stated, in the context of various other arrangements "which we are making for the permanent advantage of the state." The edict spoke of the "willfulness" and "folly" of the Christians who "were making themselves laws for their own observance . . . and in diverse places were assembling various multitudes." Although in face of the repression many had given in and others had been "exposed to jeopardy," "very great numbers" had refused to yield. The edict stated that therefore, following the pattern of clemancy and pardon granted to others in the past, "Christians may exist again, and may establish their meeting houses, yet so that they do nothing contrary to good order." [142] There is other evidence that this edict was not, as the Christians then claimed, an act of repentance, but an act of State policy influenced by the lack of success of the policy of repression. [143]

C. Adjusting to opposition in his own group

As discussed repeatedly above, one likely consequence of nonviolent action is to create or deepen internal dissension and opposition over policies and repression within the opponent's group. These internal disagreements may become so serious that the leaders of the opponent group find it to their domestic political advantage to grant some or all of the demands of the nonviolent actionists. This is especially likely if such opposition is expected to grow, and it therefore seems best to cut the ground from under it. In some extreme cases failure to do so could result in the power-holders' being removed from their official positions. In such cases, Seifert points out, the officials "would prefer to continue the suppression, but they cannot do so and remain in office." Given that choice "they unwillingly give up the repression." [144] This does not imply that such internal opposition within the opponent's own group will always be successful, nor that a change in government will never be involved.

Although such opposition was a very important factor in achieving repeal of laws against which the American colonists were using economic and political noncooperation, Lord Chatham's plan of conciliation (which would have made the colonies autonomous, but subordinate, states within the Empire) failed to win approval of Parliament in early 1775, a crucial period before a major shift in the colonies to violent struggle. [145] As has already been shown, however, opposition in the opponent's own camp was highly important in achieving the withdrawal of French forces from the Ruhr, following electoral defeat for the French government produced in part by dissension over the occupation and repression. (German willingness to call off the noncooperation was obviously also important.) There are wide variations in the extent of internal opposition which is required to produce change and the forms in which it may be expressed.

D. Minimizing economic losses

The opponent may find it to his interest to accommodate to the demands of the nonviolent actionists, without either conversion or nonviolent coercion, if his economic position is important to him and the struggle is affecting his wallet more than would concessions. This is an extremely common motive in settlements of strikes and economic boycotts, when the objectives are improved wages and working conditions.(Various illustrations of this factor in accommodation may be found in Chapters Five and Six.)

Economic motives for settlement may also be important, however, in other cases where they are less obvious, and even when economic demands are not present or are secondary. Thus in American civil rights campaigns both economic boycotts of white-owned stores and peaceful demonstrations which discourage shoppers from buying in the area where they were held have sometimes helped Southern white businessmen to favor concessions to the Negro demands. [146] For example, during a sit-in campaign in Atlanta between November 25 and mid-December 1960,

Christmas buying was down sixteen percent, almost ten million dollars below normal.

Repeal of the Stamp Act, achieved partly because of support from British merchants, was certainly influenced by the effects of the American colonists' cutting off trade and refusing to pay commercial debts to those merchants. A Bristol merchant reported in August 1765, for example: "The present Situation of the Colonies alarms every Person who has any Connection with them . . . . The Avenues of Trade are all shut up . . . . We have no Remittances, and we are at our Witts End for Want of Money to fulfill our Engagement with our Tradesmen."[147] The merchants' petitions for modification or repeal of the relevant acts emphasized this economic motivation,[148] and the repeal statute itself stated that continuation of the Stamp Act would be accompanied by ". . . many Inconveniences, and may be productive of Consequences greatly detrimental to the Commercial Interests of these Kingdoms . . ."[149]

Economic motives for a settlement proved effective in achieving a victory for African bus boycotters in South Africa in 1957. Africans reported for work as usual during the boycott, but walking ten miles or more each way between their homes in Alexandra township and their jobs in the city of Johannesburg inevitably reduced their productivity. Despite the obstinacy of the Nationalist government, businessmen and industrialists became worried, and their intervention finally led to a settlement which gave victory to the Africans, as Luthuli reports:

> A stage was reached when an honorable conclusion became a possibility, as a result of a set of proposals made by the Chamber of Commerce—the fatigue of workers was not doing production any good. To put it briefly, the Chamber of Commerce appeared willing to do what the adamant Government refused to do, which was to subsidise the [bus] company indirectly rather than place a new burden on poor folk.[150]

E. Bowing gracefully to the inevitable

In other instances of accommodation, the opponent may concede because he sees inevitable defeat. He may, therefore, wish to bow to change gracefully, avoiding the humiliation of defeat and perhaps salvaging more from the situation than might be possible at a later stage. The degree of choice the opponent has in such a situation may vary. In some cases, the social and political situation may have so changed that while the opponent cannot be said to be nonviolently coerced it would nevertheless be most difficult for him to pursue an earlier intended course of action. This happened, for example, to the recommendations of the British government's Simon Commission concerning the future political development of India. The Commission had begun its work early in 1928, and, in face of widespread boycott and refusal of assistance by the Indians, concluded its work over a year later. By the time its report was published in June 1930, however, the three-month-old national civil disobedience movement had so changed the Indian political situation that it was impossible for the British even to attempt to follow the Commission's recommendations. "The report . . . was dead before it was born." [151]

In other cases, the opponent may decide to accommodate himself to the nonviolent actionists while he still has some freedom of action. If he expects the nonviolent movement to grow significantly in strength, he may be inclined to accede to the demands voluntarily. Strength may include numbers but, as discussed earlier, encompasses much more.

In some situations, the opponent may accede relatively easily to the demands of the nonviolent actionists if he anticipates that otherwise he will face a really powerful movement capable of causing considerable difficulties and perhaps of winning despite repression. The motivation for accommodation in this case may not be simply to bow to the inevitable, but to prevent the activists and the rest of the population from realizing by experience the power of which they are capable when united in nonviolent noncooperation and intervention.

This motivation is illustrated in Faulkner's novel, *A Fable,* which describes troops of both sides in World War I defying their generals, mutinying and bringing the war to a sudden halt. The threat implied in the troops' action was deeper than the mere stopping of the war, however. The more severe threat was the possibility that troops and people generally would learn that they were *able* to stop wars if they wanted to do so. The group commander in the novel saw this clearly:

> We can permit even our own rank and file to let us down on occasion; that's one of the prerequisites of their doom and fate as rank and file forever. They may even stop the wars, as they have done before and will again; ours merely to guard them from the knowledge that it was actually they who accomplished that act. Let the whole vast moil and seethe of man confederate in stopping wars if they wish, so long as we can prevent them learning that they have done so. [152]

After a struggle has reached an advanced stage, the opponent's fear of the awareness of people's knowledge of their own power may make him determined *not* to make concessions. For example, in January 1775

Lord Chatham's plan of conciliation with the American colonies was opposed in the House of Lords by the Earl of Suffolk for essentially this reason: victories for the colonists would give them confidence to demand independence. Suffolk condemned the First Continental Congress, which had adopted a noncooperation program:

> . . . the whole of their deliberations and proceedings breathed the spirit of unconstitutional independency and open rebellion . . . . Now, therefore, was the time to assert the authority of Great Britain, for . . . every concession on our side would produce a new demand on theirs; and in the end, bring about that state of traitorous independency, at which it was too plain they were now aiming. [153]

Fear that the people would learn their power also appears to have been one of the major obstacles to reaching a settlement of the Bardoli peasants' revenue-refusal campaign in 1928, waged against the government of Bombay Presidency. In this instance nearly the entire population of 87,000 had stood together and effectively blocked the government's will. More extreme repression might have caused the local campaign to spread to all India. There seemed little the government could do except to concede defeat. But that was difficult. Therefore, though the settlement finally agreed upon meant in practice that the government would grant the peasants' demands, it did not openly state that the demands were granted. The government was much concerned with "saving face" and with finding a formula which would grant the demands of the *satyagrahis* without directly admitting the government's defeat. This was done by establishing an Enquiry Committee whose eventual recommendations meant that there was virtually no increase in the revenue in Bardoli. [154] It is difficult to avoid the conclusion that it was not simply an empty gesture to support the prestige of the government, but a desire not to admit defeat in face of determined nonviolent action—an example which in the India of unrest and turmoil of 1928 might have had the most dangerous consequences for the British *Raj*.

The factors influencing accommodation may be summarized as the degree of conflict of interest, all factors influencing the conversion mechanism, actual and potential support for the nonviolent actionists and their cause in the opponent's group and among third parties, the degree of effectiveness of the opponent's repression and other countermeasures, economic losses produced by the conflict, the estimated present and future strength of the nonviolent actionists, and the estimated chances of victory and defeat and their consequences.

But not even accommodation may be achieved, for there are clearly some types of opponents who may be unwilling to grant any demands of the nonviolent group. Even if they know that they may be finally defeated, such opponents may prefer to remain firm to the end. For these cases, too, the question arises as to whether nonviolent action can win except by a change of will in the opponent? Is there such a thing as *nonviolent coercion?*

NONVIOLENT COERCION

In some cases of nonviolent action, the opponent is neither converted nor does he decide to accommodate to the actionists' demands. Instead he may be determined to win full victory against them. Under some circumstances he may do so, or he may at least achieve temporary success in crushing the actionists. Failure of both conversion and accommodation does not, however, always mean victory for the opponent. The demands of the nonviolent group may also be achieved *against* the will of the opponent, that is, he may be *nonviolently coerced.* This type of nonviolent change has often been neglected in favor of the other two mechanisms.

As James Farmer has pointed out, when change by conversion and accommodation is believed to be unrealistic, neglect of the mechanism of nonviolent coercion has left the field clear for advocates of violence:

> Perhaps we at CORE have failed to show how effective and virile nonviolence can be . . . . We must show that nonviolence is something more than turning the other cheek, that it can be aggressive within the limits a civilized order will permit. Where we cannot influence the heart of the evil-doer, we can force an end to the evil practice. [155]

Roughly speaking, nonviolent coercion may take place in any of three ways: 1) the defiance may become too widespread and massive to be controlled by the opponent's repression; 2) the noncooperation and defiance may make it impossible for the social, economic and political system to operate unless the actionists' demands are achieved; 3) even the opponent's ability to apply repression may be undermined and may at times dissolve. In any of these cases, or any combination of them, despite his resolution not to give in, the opponent may discover that it is impossible for him to defend or impose his objectionable policies or system. In such an instance, the change will have been achieved by nonviolent coercion.

A. The concept of nonviolent coercion

The concept of coercion is not limited to the effects of threat or use of physical violence. Neither the *Oxford Dictionary* nor the *Webster Dictionary* suggests that its definition is restricted to the impact of that pressure or force which comes from physical violence. On the contrary, it is often made clear that coercion can be effected by nonphysical pressures including moral force.[156] Instead of violence, the key factors in coercion are: 1) whether the opponent's will is blocked despite his continued efforts to impose it, and 2) whether the opponent is *able* to act in an effort to implement his will. These two aspects are emphasized by Paullin and Lakey. "Coercion is the use of either physical or intangible force to compel action contrary to the will or reasoned judgement of the individual or group subjected to such force."[157] "Coercion . . . is taking away from the opponent either his ability to maintain the status quo or his ability to effect social change."[158] The concept of "coercion" is thus a very broad one, which clearly includes the imposition of certain conditions by means of nonviolent action without the opponent's agreement.

There is, however, a vast difference between nonviolent coercion and what might be called violent coercion. As Bondurant points out: "The difference between violent coercion in which deliberate injury is inflicted upon the opponent and nonviolent coercion in which injury indirectly results is a difference of such great degree that it is almost a difference of kind."[159] Involved in the former is the deliberate intention of *inflicting* physical injury or death; in the latter, the coercion largely arises from noncooperation, a refusal of the nonviolent group to submit despite repression, and at times removal of the opponent's ability to inflict violence: "nonviolent coercion forces the opponent to accept the [nonviolent actionists'] demands even though he disagrees with them, has an unfavorable image of [the nonviolent group], and would continue resisting if he could."[160] In such cases the nonviolent actionists have so grown in numbers and strength, or the opponent's sources of repressive sanctions have been so weakened, or both, that the opponent is unable to continue to impose his will on the subordinates.[161] The opponent can no longer wield power contrary to the wishes of the nonviolent group.

Nonviolent coercion is not simply a creation of theoretical speculation. Nor is it even a forecast of future potentialities of the technique based on extensions of previous experience. Despite the improvised nature of most past cases of nonviolent action, nonviolent coercion has sometimes occurred. In other cases it has nearly taken place. Noncooperation has sometimes been so effective that temporary paralysis of the opponent's power has been achieved, but total collapse of his regime did nevertheless not result. The regime may have regained ground because of the actionists' failure to capitalize strategically on the situation, the introduction of resistance violence or other disruptive influences, or some other factor. For example, as descibed earlier, effective British power in several of the American colonies was for a time paralyzed and it even collapsed in the face of noncooperation.

A similar situation existed at certain points in the Russian 1905 Revolution. *The Times* in London reported at the end of October: "The nation is still in passive revolt, and the Government is incapable of enforcing even the semblance of authority." [162] The Great October Strike, described above, was so effective and inclusive that the government was for a while unable to govern.

For five days Nicholas II and his advisors found themselves virtually isolated at Peterhof, facing a country that appeared to be gripped by some strange paralysis. It was this situation that in the final instance induced the Tsar to issue the constitutional manifesto of 17 October—a turning-point in the 1905 revolution and a landmark in Russian history. [163]

The 1920 Kapp *Putsch* against the new Weimar Republic is a much clearer case of this mechanism. The general strike and political noncooperation made it impossible for the usurpers to govern, despite their successful occupation of Berlin. They were unable to win the assistance of those persons and groups whose help was essential. Without that assistance and the submission of the people, the Kappists remained an impotent group, pretending to govern a country whose loyalty and support were reserved for the legal government. The *Putsch* therefore simply collapsed.

Despite a limited amount of violence, the February 1917 Russian Revolution, to which reference has repeatedly been made above, provides another example of success through nonviolent coercion. There were massive strikes—on February 28 nearly a quarter of a million were on strike in Petrograd alone. There were massive peaceful street demonstrations in which the people talked with the soldiers trying to win them over, and even the Bolshevik leaders tried to prevent violence, which they saw would only provide an excuse for extreme repression. Revulsion at obeying orders to fire on such crowds contributed to unrest and to the mutiny of the Tsar's troops. When reinforcements were sent to replace ineffective or disobedient troops, they dissolved into the crowds. Soon organized government forces ceased to exist. The Commander of the Petrograd Military District, General S.S. Khabalov, was unable even to rely on the troops which had not disappeared. When he realized his powerlessness, he "probably did not even know to whom he could have surrendered." Meeting on the 27th, the Council of Ministers experienced "a sense of impotence and lassitude." Rodzyanko, Chairman of the Duma Committee, declared "the old regime has turned out to be impotent," while others asserted that it had fallen. On the night of March 2, Nicholas II quietly signed an act of abdication for himself and his son. The Tsarist government had been "dissolved and swept away." [164]

Economic shutdowns and other noncooperation produced two other cases of nonviolent coercion, the nonviolent paralysis in 1944 of the dictatorships of Martinez in El Salvador and of Ubico in Guatamala, described in Chapter Two. These cases involved far less violence than the February 1917 revolution, and their coercive character is unmistakable.

B. Withdrawing the sources of political power

The theoretical analysis of the sources of political power and their withdrawal by noncooperation, which was developed on Chapter One, now merges with our analysis of the dynamics of nonviolent struggle. In this section we shall recall the sources of political power which have already been discussed and examine how each of these may be restricted or severed by nonviolent action. Some of the examples which illustrate the restriction or severance of the particular source of power are from cases of nonviolent coercion, while others simply show the potential of nonviolent struggle to affect the particular power source. The discussion in this section will show the practical relevance of the earlier power analysis and will also help to explain how nonviolent coercion is possible. It is precisely the remarkable convergence of the necessary sources of political power with the ways in which nonviolent action strikes at the opponent's strength and position which gives this technique the potential for high effectiveness and greater political power than violence.

As the analysis in Chapter One showed, political power emerges from the interaction of all, or several, of the following sources of power, each of which derives from the cooperation, support and obedience of the subjects: *authority, human resources, skills and knowledge, intangible factors, material resources* and *sanctions*. As was noted, changes in the degree to which these sources are available to the ruler will determine the degree of the ruler's political power. Our earlier catalogue of the methods of nonviolent action and our analysis of the dynamics of this technique show that these sources are potentially highly vulnerable to a widespread, yet qualitative, application of nonviolent action.

It is the capacity of the nonviolent technique to cut off these sources of power which gives it the power of coercion. The precise ways in which these sources of power are restricted or severed, and the extent to which they are cut, will vary. This technique can both restrict and sever the availability of those sources of power to the opponent, and also reveal the the loss of those sources by other means. This technique becomes coercive when the people applying it withhold or withdraw to a decisive degree the necessary sources of the opponent's power. Nonviolent action makes possible "coercion through nonparticipation." [165] This potential is of the greatest political significance and requires detailed attention, even at the risk of repeating points made earlier, to show how each of these sources of power may be cut off.

1. Authority   Nonviolent action affects the opponent's authority in three ways: 1) it may show how much authority the opponent has *already* lost, and a demonstrated major loss of authority will by itself weaken his power; 2) nonviolent action may help to undermine his authority *still further;* and 3) people who have repudiated his authority may transfer their loyalty to a rival claimant in the form of a parallel government, which may in turn weaken his authority yet more as well as create or aggravate other serious problems. Any of these consequences for the opponent's power may be serious.

Bloody Sunday—which produced a loss of authority—was followed by a warning to the Tsar from Minister of Finance Vladimir Kokovstev that something had to be done at once to regain public confidence, and also by the expressed fear of Count Witte, chairman of the Committee of Ministers, that the "aureole of the ruler would be destroyed" if Nicholas II did not publicly dissociate himself from the day's events. [166] Their warnings proved correct. Katkov points also to the Russian liberals' campaign over some years of denouncing and discrediting the autocracy, that is destroying its authority, as paving the way for the success of the February 1917 "popular rising and the mutiny of the Petrograd garrison [which] resulted in the bloodless collapse of the monarchy . . ." [167]

In his account of the East German Rising, Brant observes:

To the people of the Soviet Zone it [the declaration of the state of emergency by the Red Army, not the East German regime] was confirmation of what they already knew: after seven years in command the Red republicans were still dependent on power lent them by their protectors. But lasting domination depends less upon power than upon authority; power demands constant submission, and submission can quickly turn to mutiny. Authority requires and is granted respect, which in time of trouble and unrest is confirmed in willing obedience. [168]

In an extreme case, loss of authority in a system or regime may lead to recognition of the authority of a rival, nascent regime, and therefore the transfer of loyalty and obedience from the old to the new government. (At times loyalty may also be transfered, not to a rival regime, but to a more abstract authority, as a religious or moral system, or to a principle or ideology.)

A parallel government will emerge only in unusual instances of nonviolent action in clearly revolutionary situations. To be successful, the new government must possess widespread and deep support, and the old regime must have lost its authority among the vast majority of the populace. However, when a parallel government develops in a serious way, the opponent's *remaining* authority and power will also be severely threatened.

Such a parallel government obviously faces a number of difficult problems, and whether it succeeds or not will depend on how they are answered. Little analytical work has been done to date on the factors leading to success or failure of this particular method, or on the ways in which, when successful, the replacement may take place.

2. Human resources   Nonviolent action may also cut off the human resources necessary to the opponent's political power. Usually, in "normal times," rulers assume that they will receive general obedience and cooperation among the subjects who will obey and do all the things that need to be done to maintain them as rulers and to enable the system to operate. The widespread practice of nonviolent action, however, may shatter that assumption. The sheer numerical multiplication of noncooperating, disobedient and defiant members of the subordinate group and general population is likely not only to create severe enforcement problems but also to influence the ruler's power position. Nonviolent action is likely to lead not only to an increase in the refusal of consent among the subordinates directly affected by the grievance, but also to a related withdrawal of consent among the opponent's usual supporters (assuming there is a distinction between the two.)

This withdrawal of human resources will be most effective in 1) conflicts within the opponent's country in which the noncooperation of his own home population denies him the only available source of the human assistance he requires, and 2) in conflicts, as in a foreign occupation, in which the opponent is denied the assistance of *both* population groups, that is his usual supporters (the home population) and the grievance group (the people of the occupied country). However, even when two population groups are involved, and only *one* of these (as in an occupied country) withholds its human assistance, the noncooperation may nevertheless prove effective given the presence of certain other favorable conditions.

The increased withholding of human resources both in absolute and proportionate terms may lead to a disastrous situation for the opponent. These human resources, along with other sources of power, are likely to be reduced simultaneously with an increase in the demands upon that power which have been produced by the growth of noncooperation and defiance. The opponent then may lose control of the situation and the regime may become powerless. When this happens in politics nonviolent action has produced in the political arena results comparable to an effective strike in the industrial arena. Nonparticipation may paralyze the opponent's political system. This potentiality was clearly foreseen by Gandhi:

I believe, and everybody must grant, that no Government can exist for a single moment without the cooperation of the people, willing or forced, and if people suddenly withdraw their cooperation in every detail, the Government will come to a stand-still. [169]

For major periods during the Russian 1905 Revolution the situation was completely out of the control of the government and the police were powerless to intervene, so massive was the popular defiance. [170]

In face of massive nonviolent defiance in Peshawar in April 1930 and the Garwali mutiny, already cited, the British temporarily gave up the attempt to control the city and withdrew their troops, abandoning the city for nearly ten days until reinforcements were available. [171]

The Devlin Commission's report to the British Government in 1959 revealed that the real reason for the 1958 Emergency in Nyasaland (now called Malawi) was fear that widespread African noncooperation and disobedience would lead to collapse of the government—not the "murder plot" which was so widely publicized at the time. By early March the situation reached the point where "the Government had either to act or to abdicate." [172] The Commission declared: "The decision to suppress Congress, we think, owed more to the belief that its continued activities were making government impossible than to the feeling that it was, or might be, a terrorist organization." [173]

3. Skills and knowledge   People do different jobs, have different skills and knowledge, and a particular regime or system needs some of these more than others. A withdrawal, therefore, by key personnel, technicians, officers, administrators, etc., of their assistance to the opponent (or their *reduced* assistance) may have an impact on the opponent's power quite disproportionate to the numbers actually noncooperating.

Refusal of assistance by key subjects may make it difficult for the opponent to develop and carry out policies appropriate to the situation he faces. This may lead to the acceptance of policies which prove to be political mistakes or to an inability to implement chosen policies, or difficulties in doing so.

For example, during the Inquisition imposed by Spain's Charles V on the Netherlands which Spain then ruled, the opposition of officials and magistrates, as well as of regular citizens, seems to have been decisive in blocking its implementation. In 1550 there was an attempt to impose the most severe measure yet, the "edict of blood," which imposed the death sentence for all trespasses. It proved, however, impossible to carry out the edict on a large scale. Pieter Geyl reports that both officials and magistrates opposed it and declined to give their cooperation. "In the opinion of those who designed the system, religious persecution in the Netherlands never worked anything but defectively." [174]

Gandhi maintained that if the Indians who held official posts under the British *Raj* were to resign them, the result would probably be the end of foreign rule without the need for the noncooperation of the masses. The alternative for Britain, he said, would be a pure despotic military dictatorship which, he argued, Britain did not dare contemplate. [175] Pleas were often made during the Indian struggle for officials to resign. [176] The key contribution made to the defeat of the Kapp *Putsch* by the noncooperation of civil servants and the refusal of experts to join the new cabinet has already been described above. The German government in 1923 recognized the special role of civil servants in the official passive resistance struggle against the French and Belgian occupation of the Ruhr, as it forbade all State, provincial and local authorities and civil servants from obeying the occupation officials' orders. [177]

Doubtless in some political and social situations the chances of the administrators and officials—the bureaucracy—shifting their loyalty are greater than in other situations, but if it happens, it may prove decisive. The opponent's political power may be weakened also by internal conflicts within his own regime, both at upper and lower levels. These conflicts may be independent of the nonviolent action, or may be accentuated by it, or perhaps even created by it—as on such questions as whether to make concessions and what repression should be applied. While the regime may give the impression to the outside world that it is firmly united, the actual situation may be quite different, with or without a major nonviolent action movement.

The theoretically omnipotent Russian Tsar, for example, in 1904 could neither impose his will on his advisors nor stop their intrigues and disputes.[178] The split inside the Soviet Communist Party and the regime in 1924-27 is another example.[179] Various splits also occurred within the Nazi regime over policy and administration of the occupied areas of the Soviet Union.[180] Khrushchev's admission of disputes within the Russian leadership on how to react to the Hungarian Revolution is confirmation that such conflicts may exist in response to a major challenge outside the regime. The mere existence of such internal conflicts under various conditions may accentuate the impact of nonviolent action.

The analysis of the dynamics of nonviolent action suggests that for a variety of reasons such internal conflicts may be *more* probable in face of major nonviolent action, although documentary proof is at present not available. Where they occur, such internal conflicts in the opponent's regime will affect detrimentally the degree to which the regime's full potential of skills, knowledge, insight, energy, etc., is available for dealing with the challenge.

4. Intangible factors   Such factors as habits of obedience, political beliefs and the like may be significantly threatened by widespread nonviolent action. Such a movement involves the destruction of the habit of *unquestioning* obedience and the development of conscious choice to obey or disobey. This development would tend to make the opponent's political power more dependent upon the active and deliberate support of the subjects.

Nonviolent action may also be associated with changes in outlook and political beliefs. Nonviolent action in some situations (not necessarily the majority) *reflects* the spread among the subjects of views which challenge officially blessed doctrines. In most situations, however, the actionists are likely to be concerned instead with either particular grievances or a single broad political principle or objective, or with both. Even such cases may contribute to *further* erosion of unquestioning belief in an official doctrine. In such a struggle, events may refute official dogmas. For example, effective nonviolent challenge to the dictatorship may refute the view that violence is omnipotent. Or, the doctrine that the dictatorship reflects the will of the "people," or is a "workers' State," may be questioned when the general population, or the workers, demonstrate in the streets against it, go on strike, or noncooperate politically. Or, a belief that the dictatorship is benevolent and humanitarian may be shattered by repression against nonviolent people whose demand seems reasonable. The degree to which members of the population as a whole, and particularly members of the dominant group (the government, the Party, etc.) will be able and willing to re-examine the official political ideology will vary. At times firm adherence to the official ideology may ensure that repression is swift and harsh, although this may be a temporary phase. In other conflicts the actionists may be seen as trying to implement the "real" principles underlying official doctrines, while the existing regime is viewed as violating and distorting them to support despicable policies.

This discussion is only illustrative of ways nonviolent action may alter the intangible factors which help to secure the subjects' obedience and to preserve the ruler's power.

5. Material resources   Nonviolent action also may regulate the degree to which material resources are available to the opponent. These resources include control of the economic system, transportation, means of communication, financial resources, raw materials, and the like. The capacity of nonviolent action to impose economic penalties on the opponent should already be clear, for of the 198 methods of this technique described in earlier chapters 61 are directly economic, boycotts, strikes or intervention. In addition certain other methods may also have indirect economic effects, as from political disruption or by increasing costs of enforcement, or by losing goodwill for the opponent, or public confidence, so that third parties withhold loans, investments, trade and the like. A view popular among economic determinists—that nonviolent action is inevitably ineffective and irrelevant because financial and material factors determine the course of politics—is therefore based upon a fundamental gap in their understanding of this technique.

The Townshend duties, against which the American colonists complained so harshly, had been imposed to reduce the burdens on the British taxpayer by raising revenue in North America. The colonists' campaign of noncooperation not only blocked achievement of that objective, but also imposed additional economic losses on the Mother Country. A correspondent (probably Benjamin Franklin) pointed out in the London *Public Advertiser* on January 17, 1769, that only a maximum revenue of £3,500 had been produced in the colonies, while the British business loss due to the American nonimportation and nonconsumption campaign was estimated at £7,250,000. He also pointed to the possibility of war if the policy were continued, which would take the British at least ten years to win, cost at least £100,000,000, and leave a loss of life and a legacy of hatred. In Britain by that time, says Gipson, ". . . most men in public life were persuaded that to attempt to collect such duties in face of colonial opposition was economically unsound and politically unwise." [181]

It would be possible to offer innumerable examples from the two centuries since 1769 in which nonviolent action has inflicted such material losses on opponents that their economic, and consequently their power position, were both placed in jeopardy. Many examples described in Chapters Five and Six are of this type, especially of generalized strikes, general strikes and economic shutdowns.

However, only one more example of how nonviolent action affects the economic resources of the opponent will be offered: the nonviolent Indian struggles against British rule. These economic losses are in the main attributed to three sources: direct revenue refusal, increased expenditure for administration and enforcement, and deliberate economic boycotts.

During the Indian 1930-31 struggle, as a result of tax refusal and boycott of goods providing government revenue, and with increased expenditure to deal with the civil disobedience movement, the British regime faced deficits in the provincial governments. At various times the government of the Punjab faced a deficit of Rs. 10,000,000, the Bombay government faced a deficit of Rs. 10,250,000, the Central provinces Rs. 5,000,000, Madras Rs. 8,700,000, Bengal Rs. 9,482,000 and Bihar Rs. 4,200,000. [182] Gandhi's *Young India* commented: "When we check the nourishment from passing from the victim to the parasite the latter naturally weakens and dies while the former revives." [183] It is clear that revenue refusal was an important aspect of that movement. [184]

Year	Total Exports of the United Kingdom to British India in Millions of Pounds
1924	90.6
1925	86.0
1926	81.8
1927	85.0
1928	83.9
1929	78.2
1930 (boycott year)	52.9 [185]

People who argue that Gandhi's nonviolence had nothing to do with the British leaving India, that the real reasons were instead economic, erroneously assume that there was no contact between the two. There was, however, a close relationship, which included an immediate reduction of trade and profits.

A survey of exports to India over several years is instructive.

For certain specific items the decrease in imports from Great Britain between 1929 and 1930 ranged from eighteen percent to forty-five percent.[186] The Secretary of State for India told the House of Commons at the end of 1930 that the general depression in world trade accounted for a drop of twenty-five percent in exports to India, while he credited a drop of a further eighteen percent to the Congress' boycott.[187] Even eighteen percent is a significant figure, but the boycott may have been even more effective. Imports of British cotton cloth to India dropped far more that year than imports of cotton cloth from all foreign countries combined.[188] Between October 1930 and April 1931, when the boycott was at its height, there was a decline of eighty-four percent in imports of British cloth. Lancashire millowners and workers petitioned the Secretary of State for India to "do something about India." [189]

These cases are simply illustrative, and quite mild at that. Large-scale strikes and economic shutdowns affect much more severely the economic resources available to the opponent and the degree of political power he can wield, as the Great October Strike of 1905 or the 1944 economic shutdowns in El Salvador and Guatemala illustrate. International consumers' boycotts and embargoes may also influence the outcome of the struggle.

6. Sanctions　　Even the opponent's ability to apply sanctions may on occasion be influenced by nonviolent action. We saw in Chapter One that fear of the ruler's sanctions is one of the reasons for obedience. We also noted that the threat or use of sanctions does not necessarily produce obedience, and that they can be neutralized by massive defiance.

In addition, sanctions as a source of the ruler's power may be reduced or removed by nonviolent action by those who help to provide the sanctions. Usually, this means that police and troops carry out orders for repression inefficiently, or disobey them completely. Sometimes the actions of others may also cut off the supply of weapons and ammunition, as when foreign suppliers halt shipments, or when strikes occur in domestic arms factories and transport. These means of control may be very important in certain situations.

The opponent's ability to apply sanctions may also be influenced by the degree to which his agents of repression—police and troops—are willing to carry out orders. In some situations there may be too few such agents because they have not volunteered or because conscripts have refused duty. In other situations, the existing police or troops decline to carry out orders efficiently, or refuse them completely—i.e. mutiny. Mutinies have occurred in wartime, in face of violent revolution, and in cases of mixed violent and nonviolent struggle.

As we have already discussed, there is good reason to believe that mutiny is much more likely in face of nonviolent resistance. The troops or police then do not face injury or death from the "rebels" and they must decide whether to obey orders to inflict severe repression against *nonviolent* people. Laxity in obedience and finally open mutiny will only occur in special circumstances, however. Police and troops will vary in their sensitivity or callousness to the sufferings they inflict on the nonviolent group. The potential for reduced reliability of the agents of repression nevertheless exists; this may be descibed as a tendency in nonviolent conflicts. Gandhi was quite convinced that soldiers who wound and kill nonviolent actionists undergo a traumatic experience which in time will bring them to contrition: ". . . an army that dares to pass over the corpses of innocent men and women would not be able to repeat that experiment." [190]

Efforts to convert the opponent group may produce both laxity in obeying orders for repression and open mutiny among police and troops, which may lead to nonviolent coercion of the opponent leadership. In other cases, mutiny may occur without conscious efforts at conversion. In any case, disobedience by the agents of repression will reduce the opponent's power, in some cases decisively. Widespread mutinies of Russian troops during the revolutions of 1905 and February 1917 have already been described above. [191] In the latter case they played a major role in achieving the disintegration of the tsarist regime.

The Nazis recognized well that if they lost control of the Army their power would be drastically weakened; Goebbels reveals that in early February 1938 the Nazis feared most of all not a *coup d'etat* but the collective resignation of all high-ranking officers [192]—a form of noncooperation.

During the predominantly nonviolent East German Rising of June 1953 police sometimes withdrew completely or willingly gave up their arms. Among the East German armed forces there were some cases of mutiny and laying down of arms. There were even evidences of sympathy from Russian soldiers and of reluctance to fire on the civilians. The overwhelming number of Russians who obeyed orders apparently suffered reduced morale. [193] It is reported that some one thousand Soviet officers and other ranks refused to fire at demonstrators, and that fifty-two Party members and soldiers were shot for disobeying orders. [194]

Large-scale deliberate inefficiency among troops and police is likely to reduce the regime's power. When officials realize that obedience is uncertain, especially if small mutinies have already occurred, they may hesitate before ordering severe repressive actions which might provoke mutiny. That hesitation also limits sanctions as a source of power. A major mutiny is bound to alter power relationships radically, and the opponent is unlikely then to be able to withstand the demands of the nonviolent actionists. In fact, his regime may then disintegrate.

C. Some factors influencing nonviolent coercion

There is no single pattern for producing nonviolent coercion. The factors which produce it occur in different combinations and proportions; there appear to be at least eight such factors. The role and combination of these will not be the same when the nonviolent coercion has been largely produced by mutiny, for example, as when the coercion has been achieved by economic and political paralysis. The contribution of each factor will depend upon the degree to which it regulates one or more of the opponent's necessary sources of power.

Generally speaking, nonviolent coercion is more likely where the *numbers* of nonviolent actionists are very large, both in absolute numerical terms and in proportion to the general population. It is then possible for the defiance to be too massive for the opponent to control; paralysis by noncooperation is more likely. There, too, may be a greater chance of interfering with the sources of power which depend upon manpower, skilled or unskilled.

The *degree of the opponent's dependence* on the nonviolent actionists for the sources of his power is also important. The greater the dependence, the greater the chances of nonviolent coercion. It therefore becomes important to consider exactly *who* is refusing assistance to the opponent. "The extent of nonparticipation required to produce measurable political effects varies with the strategic position of the strikers," argued Hiller.[195] Under certain circumstances the opponent may be relatively indifferent to large numbers of noncooperating subjects and in other circumstances he may be nonviolently coerced by the action of a relatively few.

The *ability* of the nonviolent group *to apply the technique* of nonviolent action will be very important. The role of fighting skill here is comparable to its importance in any other type of combat. Skill here includes the capacity to choose strategy, tactics and methods, the times and places for action, etc., and ability to act in accordance with the dynamics and requirements of this nonviolent technique. Ability to apply nonviolent action skillfully will help to overcome the weaknesses of the nonviolent group, to capitalize on the opponent's weaknesses, and to struggle against the opponent's countermeasures.

Whether or not nonviolent coercion is achieved will also depend on *how long* the defiance and noncooperation can be maintained. A massive act of noncooperation which collapses after a few hours cannot nonviolently coerce anyone. Willingness and ability to maintain nonviolent action for a sufficient duration despite repression are necessary to reduce or sever sources of the opponent's power.

The sympathy and support of *third parties* for the nonviolent group may be important in producing nonviolent coercion if the opponent depends on them for such things as economic resources, transportation facilities, military supplies and the like. Such supplies may then be cut off and his power position thereby undermined.

The *means of control and repression* which the opponent can use, and for how long, in an attempt to force a resumption of cooperation and obedience are also important. Even more important is the actionists' response to them.

The final factor contributing to nonviolent coercion is *opposition within the opponent group* either to the policies at issue or to the repression, or to both. The number of dissidents, the intensity of their disagreement, the types of action they use, and their positions in the social, economic and political structure will all be important here. On occasion splits in the ruling group itself may occur. Should this happen, or should a general strike or major mutiny of troops or police take place in opposition to repression of the nonviolent actionists, it would be a major factor in producing nonviolent coercion.

A SUCCESSFUL CONCLUSION?

Contrary to a popular view, skillfully applied nonviolent action may offer greater chances of success than would political violence in the same situation. However, the simple choice of nonviolent action as the technique of struggle does not and cannot guarantee victory, especially on a short-term basis. Changes will take place when significant nonviolent struggle occurs, but there is no certainty that these changes will always be for the better, from the perspective of the actionists. Nor are the results of such conflicts always full defeat or full success, but *as in all conflicts* they are frequently mixtures of the two in differing proportions. The results of many cases of nonviolent struggle might be spread along a continuum with complete defeat and complete success at opposite poles, and a draw falling at the midpoint. This allows for various intermediary types of results, such as partial failures and partial successes, which is where most of the cases would fall. The terms "success" and "failure" will both require examination since, as we shall note, they are usually far less precise and lucid than they first appear. The risk of defeat and its possible consequences will be considered first.

A. The risk and nature of defeat

Defeat in immediate political terms is always possible in nonviolent action, just as it is in war or in other types of political violence. "Defeat" here indicates failure to achieve the objectives of the struggle. During the analysis in this Part, stress has repeatedly been laid on the need to develop various qualities and to fulfill a number of conditions if the actionists are to wield maximum power. If these requirements have not been met in sufficient degree, there is no reason to expect success. If the grievance group does not as yet possess sufficient internal strength, determination and ability to act to make this technique effective against their opponent, then the simple verbal acceptance of nonviolent action will not save them. There is no substitute for genuine strength in nonviolent action and if the subordinates do not possess sufficient to cope with the opponent, they cannot be expected to win until they develop that strength.

Comparative studies are urgently needed of cases of "failure" and "success" to see whether common features are present within each group and if so what they are. It might then be possible to seek ways to counter weaknesses and to overcome especially difficult external circumstances.

The possibility of defeat is not a characteristic limited to this technique, however. Comparative evaluations of nonviolent and violent means must take into consideration that political violence is often defeated also. By conventional standards, does not one side lose in each international war, civil war and violent revolution? Such defeats have usually been explained as resulting from certain weaknesses or inadequacies, such as lack of fighting spirit, insufficient or poor weapons, mistakes in strategy and tactics, or numerical inferiority. Comparable weaknesses may also lead to defeat in nonviolent action. The common practice of explaining defeats of political violence in terms of such *specific* shortcomings while blaming defeats of nonviolent action on the presumption of its *universal* impotence is both irrational and uninformed.

The precise consequences of defeat will vary from case to case depending on the particular conditions in each situation. In some cases there may be physical suffering and mental anguish. At times defeat will bring economic losses and worsened conditions, as for the defeated British miners in 1927. Defeat may also be followed by new legal restrictions and prohibitions designed to place the government in a more advantageous position to prevent or control future nonviolent action. The defeat of the British General Strike of 1926 was followed by the harsh Trade Disputes and Trade Union Act of 1927,[196] and the Defiance Campaign of 1952 in South Africa was followed by the Criminal Law Amendment Act, No. 8 of 1953 and the Public Safety Act, No. 3 of 1953.[197]

Where defeat leads to demoralization and loss of confidence in the effectiveness of nonviolent action, the chances of a later resort to this technique may be drastically reduced. This was the case, writes Symons, after the British 1926 General Strike: "One thing Governments, Conservative, Labour or National, could feel happily sure: the trade unionists would never again attempt to engage in a General Strike." [198] Previous successes or failures in the use of nonviolent action are likely to influence whether or not the technique is used again, and, if so, may also help to determine the outcome of those later campaigns.

It does not follow, however, that defeats are necessarily always total and permanent. There are two relevant perspectives here: first, it is sometimes better to have fought and lost than not to have fought at all, and second, even in the midst of defeat there may occur less obvious changes which contribute to a later success for the nonviolent group.

Nehru expressed the former view well, when it was becoming obvious that the current civil disobedience campaign (of 1932-34) was not going to win. He wrote in prison in 1933:

Outside, the struggle went on, and brave men and women continued to defy peacefully a powerful and entrenched government, though they knew that it was not for them to achieve in the present or the near future. And repression . . . demonstrated the basis of British rule in India. There was no camouflage about it now . . . It was better that we should be governed thus, we thought, than . . . sell our souls and submit to spiritual prostitution. . . . [T]he cause went on despite setbacks; there could be no failure if ideals remained undimmed and spirits undaunted. Real failure was a desertion of principle . . . and an ignoble submission to wrong. Self-made wounds always took longer to heal than those caused by an adversary.

There was often a weariness at our weakness . . . and yet . . . . it was good to feel oneself to be a member of a gallant band.[199]

Obviously defeat alone does not determine whether the actionists become demoralized and nonviolent action is abandoned permanently. Defeat can also be seen as a lost battle, leaving for the future the winning of the war. Other factors make the difference in perspective. One of these may be an awareness that the side effects of even defeated nonviolent action can be important. Sometimes in conventional war the cost of success is so great that the victor has won only a Pyrrhic victory, which contributes to the relative strengthening and final victory of the defeated side. A comparable situation sometimes also occurs in nonviolent action. The actionists appear to be defeated, but the opponent's power is in the process weakened, or the subordinates' determination and ability to resist are significantly strengthened.

L. de Jong has observed that the mass strikes in the occupied Netherlands against Nazi rule in February 1941, 1943 and again in September 1944 were met with "great ferocity." Although there were no changes for the better in German policy, the strikes were "a tremendous stimulant to solidarity" of the Dutch people and offered ". . . convincing proof of the will to resist animating the majority of the people . . ."[200]

Although not immediately successful, if the nonviolent actionists increase their spirit of resistance, expand their organizational strength, improve their skill in applying this technique, and gain sympathy and friends which may be useful in the future, then even defeat may become a prelude to success.

B. A draw or an interim settlement?

During difficult stages of the struggle various steps can be taken to maintain a high level of participation and high morale among actionists. These steps may include phasing the strategy and tactics, varying the specific methods used, shifting the degrees of involvement and of risk for various groups, and attempting to win certain smaller interim goals or partial successes. If spirits are sagging, or fear of repression is increasing, some form of fearless, dramatic and dangerous action may be undertaken by a few reliable people in an effort to restore morale and confidence and to rally continued participation.

If such steps are not taken, or are not successful, however, the actionists may have to face the reality that, despite their achievements, they do not as yet have sufficient strength to win. In any contest of strength there are likely to be periods of increased and reduced direct involvement, high and low morale, growing strength and loss of vitality. In reference to military war Clausewitz pointed to the need always to allow for a line of retreat in case of necessity.[201] He also spoke of the need to provide rest for certain population and reserve groups while others take up the most exhausting action and thus keep up constant pressure on the opponent.[202] In nonviolent struggle, the "troops" may also become afflicted with "war-weariness" and reach a limit to their capacity for tension and suffering. This was the situation by late January 1931 in India after ten months of the civil disobedience campaign, reports Gopal. "Repression," Gandhi had earlier argued, "does good only to those who are prepared for it."[203] Not all nonviolent actionists have an equal capacity for suffering, and the capacity of the same person may vary at different stages within a particular movement. "Suffering has its well-defined limits. Suffering can be both wise and unwise, and, when the limit is reached, to prolong it would be not unwise but the height of folly."[204] This must be considered by leaders who plan and launch a campaign and who can influence the time and circumstances of its termination.

If the participants are not capable of further voluntary suffering without demoralization then tactical or even strategic changes may be necessary. "A wise general does not wait till he is actually routed; he withdraws in time in an orderly manner from a position which he knows he would not be able to hold," wrote Gandhi.[205] It may be wise to halt the current phase of the movement while one is still strong enough to achieve a negotiated settlement, or an unwritten one, with certain gains.

In other situations, when the actionists would have to give up or compromise on *essentials,* there may be no formal or informal truce. Instead, the nonviolent group may simply make a major change in strategy and take steps to provide rest for the combatants while attempting to make the situation more propitious for major action at a future date. There is no standard rule for determining when to call a formal halt to the campaign under honorable conditions with partial gains, and when to continue the defiance by the many in spirit and by only a few in action. Careful assessment of the particular circumstances is required.[206] If a temporary halt is to be called, it should be done at the most favorable moment. One factor in the choice of that moment will be the opponent's readiness to negotiate and to offer significant concessions.

The opponent, too, may have good reasons for wishing to end the struggle. The course of the struggle may have placed him in an insecure position from which he may wish to extricate himself. While the nonviolent actionists had been unable to win, the opponent may have been unable to crush the movement and may have found the losses due to the conflict unacceptable. The opponent may therefore seek, by means other than repression, a resumption of cooperation and obedience. He may be willing to make certain concessions, either explicit ones or in substance.

This may well involve formal negotiations with the nonviolent actionists. For example, Lord Irwin, the British Viceroy, at the end of the 1930–31 struggle made determined efforts to settle the conflict and to obtain the resumption of cooperation by the Congress with the British regime. It is clear that these efforts were in large degree politically motivated by the need for an end to the noncooperation.[207] Where such efforts take place they may be encouraged by the actions of less extreme groups which did not participate in the nonviolent action movement, but urged the opponent to grant concessions and offer a settlement as did the Indian Liberals in 1930–31.[208]

Following the negotiated settlement at the end of the 1930–31 struggle, Gandhi said in his Press statement:

> It would be folly to go on suffering when the opponent makes it easy for you to enter into a discussion with him upon your longings. If a real opening is made, it is one's duty to take advantage of it, and in my humble opinion, the settlement has made a real opening. Such a settlement has necessarily to be provisional, as this is. The peace arrived at is conditional upon many other things happening. The largest part of the written word is taken up with what may be called, "terms of truce." [209]

It should be stressed again that the nonviolent actionists may compromise on secondary, nonessential, matters, but will not on essentials or give up fundamental principles or demands. They may, however, state in a document that disagreements on such points continue, although direct action on them is being suspended for the time being. The policies of compromise and of this type of interim settlement are quite different.[210] Compromise requires willingness on each side to give up part of their aims and objectives, on essential as well as unessential issues. Nonviolent actionists see such compromise at times as morally and politically unacceptable. For example, how does one "split the difference" on such issues as freedom of religion or speech, equal treatment of minorities, international aggression, the existence of a dictatorship, and the like? Compromise on basic issues is thus rejected both as a substitute for nonviolent struggle and as a means of settling a nonviolent campaign. Nonviolent actionists are willing to negotiate, but not on essentials—even when they cannot be won.

Even the occurrence of negotiations may mark a recognition of changes which the nonviolent action has produced in the relationships between the opponent and the nonviolent group. If a government, or other powerful opponent, agrees to negotiate it is usually because the opponent recognizes that the other side is able to wield effective power. This capacity to wield power will also influence the course and outcome of the negotiations. For example, Gandhi argued that the struggle must continue unabated during the 1931 negotiations, since any slackening at that stage would lead to a prolongation of the struggle.[211]

In certain political circumstances, such negotiations may themselves be a major concession by the opponent and a recognition of the new status of the subordinates. In 1931, for example, "the Congress was negotiating with the Government on what was virtually an equal footing."[212] Gandhi came to the Viceroy as the representative of India to negotiate with the representative of the British Empire. Sir Winston Churchill condemned the "nauseating and humiliating spectacle of this one-time Inner Temple lawyer, now seditious fakir, striding half-naked up the steps of the Viceroy's palace, there to negotiate and to parley on equal terms with the representative of the King-Emperor."[213] While the British in that year had not been converted, nor yet forced to give full independence, they found it necessary to negotiate and thus give a kind of *de facto* recognition to India as a separate political unit. The terms of the truce and the specific concessions—either direct concessions or ones granted in substance without officially conceding the demands of the nonviolent actionists[214]—important though they were, were secondary to this more fundamental recognition in the change of the relationship between Britain and India. The settlement itself "was framed in the form of a treaty to end a state of war." Gandhi saw its most important feature to be the recognition of the Indian National Congress as the intermediary between the people and the government. Members of the government in London privately expressed disapproval of the acceptance of "the unique and semi-sovereign position of the Congress."[215]

Formal negotiations and agreements are not the only ways to produce a truce or interim settlement. Such negotiations or agreements do not create the changes in the relationships but reflect and result from them.

Such formal bargaining at the conference table may, of course, not occur at all. The opponent may refuse to negotiate or make significant concessions, or other political circumstances may be difficult. In such cases a tacit truce may develop and informal understandings may become the equivalent of a settlement. For example, the opponent may call a halt to arrests for certain types of nonviolent action, especially if he has not been able effectively to halt them anyhow and if the wider public has clearly expressed its belief that on these issues justice lies with the actionists. The nonviolent group, in turn, might refrain from launching new types of action, or might halt its most ambitious methods, such as nonviolent raids or civil disobedience of regulatory laws. Gains already achieved toward the long run wider objectives might then be tacitly accepted—such as advances in free speech, freedom of the press, desegregation and the like—without the opponent abandoning his intent to block full realization of wider objectives and without the nonviolent group disavowing its intent to implement the full goals.

For the nonviolent group, the period following such a truce or interim settlement will be difficult. They will need as a minimum to maintain their existing position and marginal gains; at best they need to utilize this as a period for regrouping and gaining new strength. If they can do that, then later under more favorable conditions the nonviolent actionists will be stronger and can press more effectively to their full goal.

Pressures to renew the attack along exactly the same line will have to be resisted.[216] So also must be pressures to jump to the offensive too soon and without good reason to believe that one's relative strength has in the interim been significantly increased. Clausewitz' insights on war are applicable here:

> The first movements [after a lost battle] should be as small as possible, and it is a maxim in general not to suffer ourselves to be dictated to by the enemy. This maxim cannot be followed without bloody fighting with the enemy at our heels, but the gain is worth the sacrifice; without it we get into an accelerated pace which soon turns into a headlong rush, and costs merely in stragglers more men than rear-guard combats, and besides that extinguishes the last remnants of the spirit of resistance.[217]

In nonviolent action where morale and psychological influences are so important, very careful consideration must be given to trying to understand and solve these problems. Periods of retreat, and even times of defeat, must be turned into opportunities for the recovery of strength, confidence and determination, and for preparations for more favorable action. As Nehru pointed out, one should not count on a chance "irrepressible upheaval of the masses," although it might occur, but instead anticipate "a long struggle with ups and downs and many a stalemate in between, and a progressive strengthening of the masses in discipline and united action and ideology." [218]

To some degree, increased understanding of the nature of the technique combined with advanced training, wise strategy and careful preparations will make major successes by campaigns of shorter duration more likely. These campaigns may involve larger numbers of participants, applying more extensive, disciplined and persistent noncooperation and defiance.[219] Even if increased knowledge of this technique brings shorter and more successful conflicts, there will still be cases in which the nonviolent actionists must regroup and strengthen themselves and the wider grievance group. If a given campaign is not successful, the actionists' attitude in such a case generally is that the people are externally defeated for the time being, but internally still determined and defiant. They may be, for example, a "subjected but unconquered people," [220] who in time will translate their inner spirit of independence and opposition into an overthrow of the external subjugation.

Strategy and tactics during the period of regrouping and regaining strength will be of particular importance. One should never remain completely passive, for the population must not sink again into submissiveness. In such periods nonviolent action may be continued by individuals or reliable small groups especially committed and prepared to act. Sometimes large numbers or even masses of people may be involved in limited actions of a symbolic nature which, although clearly showing the feelings and views of the participants and hence perhaps improving morale, involve a minimum of risk to the participants. Demonstrations, protest or resistance may be used briefly or occasionally. Various methods of nonviolent protest, or even protest strikes, may be used on such occasions. National days, religious holidays, anniversaries of events related to the struggle and the like, may provide occasions for these limited acts of mass participation. For example, although the South African Defiance Campaign was really over, on June 26, 1953, the first anniversary of its launching, Albert Luthuli in a message to Africans and their allies appealed to them to light bonfires or candles or lanterns outside their homes, "as a symbol of the spark of freedom which we are determined to keep alive in our hearts, and as a sign to freedom-lovers that we are keeping the vigil on that night." [221] Such limited acts of protest or resistance must be continued until the time for more severe struggle comes. Organizational work and training in nonviolent action will also be highly important during such a period. Where appropriate local issues require remedies, and the necessary support, determination and resistance capacity are present, local campaigns may be highly important for correcting the particular grievance. They may also help to maintain the spirit of resistance, improve morale by producing victories, and train people by participation and example for wider future campaigns. Ebert calls these "continuity or revival struggles" or "local continuity actions." [222] The nonviolent group may also use the period for trying to undermine both the opponent's belief in the rightness of his policies and his confidence that he can win; they may also try to improve his attitudes toward the grievance group and the nonviolent actionists in particular. If such efforts are successful to a significant degree, then when struggle is resumed, the opponent group may lack both the will power to refuse the demands and also the determination to impose severe repression.

In a different type of situation, when the nonviolent group wins its full objectives as the result of a series of struggles each of which achieves part of the full aim, the points actually won by each particular conflict are likely to correspond to more basic changes in attitudes, power positions and other relationships between the contending groups. If so, those limited successes are likely to be genuine and lasting, ones which cannot be easily taken from them by anyone, as they could if they had been given as an edict or a gift without struggle.

C. Success

Most of this chapter has been devoted to evaluations of the ways in which nonviolent action may make the changes which produce success by the three mechanisms of change. It is possible that the most successful cases of nonviolent action involve optimal combinations of the three mechanisms. A considerable number of the illustrative cases of nonviolent action which have been offered in the book as a whole were successful. It has also been shown that a few cases of nonviolent struggle—as in the Ruhr—which are commonly regarded as complete failures instead achieved a considerable degree of success. The time has come to offer some final observations on the nature of success with this technique, and the ways in which it may occur.

PART THREE: DYNAMICS

In internal political conflicts and in international wars the terms "success" and "failure" or "victory" and "defeat" are widely used in very diverse senses, some quite clear, others imprecise or misleading. In violent struggles attention is frequently paid only to that side which succeeds in crushing the combat forces of the other and to that side which surrenders. Is that a sufficient criterion for success? What is the situation when, despite military victory, the political objectives or war aims of the winning side are not achieved? Or are won only in part? What if the military struggle ends in a stalemate, but one side gets most or all of its political objectives? Many other similar questions could be asked. Examinations of violent struggles in which it is presumably clear who won and lost, to determine whether goals of each side were achieved or not, are revealing.

It is important to see the problem of defining "success" in nonviolent action in this wider context. Precise thought and careful criteria are needed in order to determine intelligently whether given cases of nonviolent action have, or have not, succeeded, and to what degree.

As is often the case with violent struggles, it is not always possible to conclude categorically that a particular nonviolent action movement has been a clear "success" or "failure." Elements of both success and failure may be present in the same situation. The particular struggle must often be seen in the wider context of a series of campaigns and of its contribution to the later struggles and relationships. Even though all the goals may not have been won at a particular stage, it is possible that the struggle may have paved the way for their later achievement. Much more work on the nature and conditions of success in nonviolent struggle is needed. Understanding of this technique could be considerably advanced by a comparative study of cases of nonviolent action in terms of the results which were produced. Such a study might take into consideration such factors as these: 1) were the goals of the nonviolent group achieved? fully? in part? as the result of nonviolent action? as the result of other means or factors? immediately, or some time after the struggle? 2) which mechanisms of change operated? 3) were the nonviolent group and the grievance group strengthened or weakened internally as a result of the campaign? 4) was the basis laid for later or wider achievement of their objectives, or both? 5) were there changes in attitudes and perceptions toward the issues and toward the various groups? 6) were there additional subtle and indirect effects, and if so of what types? 7) were there lasting effects on the social structure or social system generally, and if so of what kind? 8) what was the cost of the achievements, and how do they compare with the cost of other efforts to achieve similar results? Doubtless other relevant questions might also be added.

That type of study cannot, however, be attempted here. For our purposes "success" in nonviolent action will be measured by whether the avowed goals of the nonviolent group were achieved as a consequence of the struggle, either at its end or shortly thereafter. Where all (or almost all) of their goals or demands are achieved, then the movement is described as *a full success*. Where only some of those goals are achieved, the movement is described as *a partial success*. Both of these may be achieved by any one, or any combination, of the three mechanisms of change discussed above, conversion, accommodation and nonviolent coercion.

If the nonviolent actionists have persisted on their chosen course despite repression, and have achieved a significant number of the factors upon which change hinges, then they are in sight of a victorious conclusion of the struggle. This is a crucial period, and a dangerous one. The opponent, sensing his imminent defeat, may make special exertions and take unexpected measures to defeat the actionists. Members of the nonviolent group, sensing victory, may become victims of overconfidence, carelessness and reduced determination. Gandhi clearly warned that ". . . the danger is the greatest when victory seems the nearest. No victory worth the name has ever been won without a final effort, more serious than all the preceding ones." [223]

Where full success is achieved, or a partial success in which most of the goals are won, there is no single formula with which the campaign is ended. Indeed, some cases are successful even before direct action is launched, at the stage of negotiations. James Farmer reports significant cases of desegregation and of opening employment to Negroes during negotiations because the opponent was familiar with other cases of successful nonviolent action for similar objectives by the Congress of Racial Equality (C.O.R.E.) These "victory before struggle" cases included, for example, the desegregation of all sixty-nine Howard Johnson restaurants in Florida, the ending of employment discrimination at various Sears Roebuck stores, and at the First National Bank in Boston. [224]

Attention here, however, is on the more common cases in which success follows only after struggle. As might be expected, with a technique as broad and diverse as nonviolent action and with the multitude of possible variables, there is no uniform pattern for the successful conclusion. At times conflict situations, especially international ones, may be so complex that it is difficult to disentangle the relative roles of nonviolent action and other factors in producing the change, as for example the conclusion of the Hungarian struggle against Austrian rule. In other cases the proportionate role of the nonviolent action will be clearer. The mechanism with which change has been effected—conversion, accommodation or nonviolent coercion—will influence the manner of conclusion. Negotiation with a formal settlement is possible in all three mechanisms.[225] Some negotiations will be real bargaining sessions, but others will simply formalize the changes already agreed or recognized as inevitable. Those nonviolent groups which seek conversion of the opponent, or at least accommodation, may be only satisfied by a settlement which involves real agreement with the opponent.[226]

In certain instances of conversion or accommodation, there may be no formal negotiations or settlement. The opponent may simply grant the full, or essential, demand. Where a full success is achieved by nonviolent coercion, negotiations may produce a formal surrender to the actionists' demands. In other cases, the nonviolent group may even refuse to negotiate with the opponent, on the ground that he deserves no recognition at all; this was the case in 1920 when the legitimate Ebert government in Germany refused negotiations with Lüttwitz, who headed the putschists after Kapp fled to Sweden.[227]

In some cases of nonviolent coercion there may be no agreement or negotiation at the end of the struggle because of the impact of a major mutiny of the opponent's troops and police, an economic shutdown, massive popular noncooperation and an effective parallel government. The opponent's power may have disintegrated and collapsed, and the people's loyalty shifted to the new regime or system.

D. Toward a genuine solution

Advocates of the use of nonviolent action in place of techniques of violence have sometimes argued that the results achieved by nonviolent action are likely to be more permanent and satisfactory than those achieved by violence. Gregg, for example, wrote that victory achieved by violence is likely to result in hatred and desire for revenge, which may in turn lead to a new war to achieve revenge or restitution. The results of a successful nonviolent struggle, Gregg maintains, are quite different; it is likely there will be "no aftermath of resentment, bitterness, or revenge, no necessity for further threats of force."[228] The solution has been reached on a deeper level, with better feelings on both sides and fewer ill effects. The readjustment of relationships, he says, is more likely to be permanent.[229] Gandhi was of the opinion that even the sufferings of nonviolent actionists inflicted by repression did not lead to bitterness which would cause lasting tension and hostility.[230] King also pointed to increased respect in the opponent group for the nonviolent actionists after their demands had been won, and a lack of bitterness toward them; he attributed the lack of bitterness to "our insistence on nonviolence" and the resulting absence of casualties among the opponent group.[231] Others, too, have maintained that changes won by nonviolent action are much more lasting both than those won by violence and also than those which have been bestowed without struggle.

Such claims merit investigation. Comparative studies of the results of cases of successful violent action and successful nonviolent action have yet to be undertaken. They could, however, help significantly an intelligent evaluation of the relative merits of the contrasting techniques. The analysis in the preceeding chapters, however, suggests that successful nonviolent action may well produce a number of long-term beneficial results.

For example, the likelihood of bitterness, hatred and desire for revenge may be indeed reduced, especially where the conversion and accommodation mechanisms have operated to any considerable degree. The incidence of political violence may be reduced in the future also. The defeated opponent may be less likely to use violence in new attempts to impose policies on people who do not want them, because he has learned that violence is not omnipotent. The grievance group, having won nonviolently, may be less inclined to use violent means in future conflicts if feasible nonviolent strategies can be developed. Under some conditions the nonviolent struggle may have had lasting repercussions on the opponent group, such as stimulating new ways to achieve their objectives, bringing new outlooks and goals, or modifying the system itself. To the degree that the nonviolent action has been able to remove the grievances which provoked the nonviolent action, these will not provide issues for future conflicts.

Where changes have been achieved in accommodation or nonviolent coercion because of power changes, a lasting alteration in the power relationships of the contending groups is likely. This, too, may contribute to more equitable and less contentious relationships in the future. Many of the most important changes are within the grievance group itself. It is to those changes, and the changes in power relationships, to which we now turn in the concluding chapter.

NOTES

1. This roughly follows Lakey's similar discussion of three mechanisms, except that I have offered a substitute title for the second and modified its description slightly. See Lakey, "The Sociological Mechanisms of Nonviolent Action" p. 23; *Peace Research Reviews*, vol. II, no. 6 (Dec. 1968), p. 14. Earlier writers have usually not included this intermediary mechanism, jumping directly from conversion by suffering to nonviolent coercion. See, for example, Kuper, **Passive Resistance in South Africa**, pp. 77-78, and Bondurant, **Conquest of Violence**, p. 11.

2. Lakey, "The Sociological Mechanisms . . ." p. 20; *Peace Research Reviews,* vol. II, no. 6 (Dec. 1968), p. 12.

3. See Case, **Non-violent Coercion**, pp. 397-398.

4. Gandhi did not like the term "nonviolent coercion" but sometimes spoke of "compelling change" and of "compulsion."

5. Gandhi, **Non-violence in Peace and War**, vol. I, p. 44.

6. Sharp, **Gandhi Wields the Weapon of Moral Power**, p. 65.

7. Gandhi, **Non-violent Resistance** p. 87; Ind. ed.: **Satyagraha**, p. 87. See also Gopal, **The Viceroyalty of Lord Irwin**, 1926-31, pp. 4-5.

8. See Kumarappa's statement in Sharp, **Gandhi Wields** . . . , pp. 190-191.

9. Gregg, **The Power of Nonviolence**, p. 85.

10. Quoted in Bose, **Studies in Gandhism**, p. 162.

11. *Ibid.*

12. Janis and Katz, "The Reducation of Intergroup Hostility," *Journal of Conflict Resolution*, vol. III, no. 1 (March 1959), p. 95.

13. Schlesinger, **The Colonial Merchants and the American Revolution**, p. 79.

14. *Ibid.*, p. 127.

15. Ehrlich, *"Den Ikke-voldelige Modstand, der Kvalte Kapp-Kupet,"* p. 201.

16. See Ebert, "Nonviolent Resistance Against Communist Regimes?" pp. 180, 188, and 191-193.

17. Gandhi, **Non-violence in Peace and War**, vol. I, p. 412.

18. Gandhi, **Non-violent Resistance**, p. 194; Ind. ed.: **Satyagraha**, p. 194.

19. Gandhi quoted in Bose, **Studies in Gandhism**, p. 162. See also Bose, **Selections from Gandhi**, p. 146.

20. Gandhi, **Non-violent Resistance**, p. 202; Ind. ed.: **Satyagraha**, p. 202.

21. Bondurant, **Conquest of Violence**, pp. 227-229. See also Seifert, **Conquest by Suffering**, pp. 69-70.

22. Lakey, "The Sociological Mechanisms . . . ," pp. 30-33; *Peace Research Reviews,* vol. II, no. 6 (Dec. 1968), pp. 19-20.

23. Kuper, **Passive Resistance in South Africa**, p. 22.

24. *Ibid.*, p. 178.

25. Hiller, The Strike, p. 159.

26. *Ibid.*, pp. 169-171.

27. Case, Non-violent Coercion, p. 400.

28. *Ibid.*, pp. 399-400.

29. Hiller, The Strike, p. 91.

30. Gregg, The Power of Nonviolence, p. 78.

31. *Ibid.*, p. 84.

32. Kuper, Passive Resistance in South Africa, p. 79.

33. Seifert, Conquest by Suffering, p. 18.

34. Frederick Solomon and Jacob R. Fishman, "The Psychosocial Meaning of Non-violence in Student Civil Rights Activities," *Psychiatry,* vol. XXVII (May 1964), p. 99.

35. Kuper, Passive Resistance in South Africa, pp. 87-91.

36. See Wolff, ed., The Sociology of Georg Simmel, pp. 224-249.

36. See Janis and Katz, "The Reduction of Intergroup Hostility," p. 88.

37. See Kuper, Passive Resistance in South Africa, p. 131.

38. E. Franklin Frazier, Race and Culture Contacts in the Modern World (Boston: Beacon Press, 1957), pp. 49-50.

39. Bernard J. Stern, "Slavery, Primitive," in Encyclopedia of the Social Sciences, (New York: The Macmillan Co., 1934), vol. 14, p. 73.

40. Harvey Seifert, "The Use by American Quakers of Nonviolent Resistance as a Method of Social Change," MS p. 41.

41. Kuper, Passive Resistance in South Africa, pp. 84-85.

42. *Ibid.*, p. 89.

43. Lakey, "The Sociological Mechanisms . . . ," pp. 83-84; *Peace Research Reviews,* vol. II, no. 6 (Dec. 1968), pp. 54-55.

44. Kuper, Passive Resistance in South Africa, pp. 85 and 89.

45. *Ibid.*, p. 91.

46. Hiller, The Strike, p. 170.

47. Kuper, Passive Resistance in South Africa, p. 85, and Gandhi, Non-violent Resistance, pp. 62-63; Ind. ed.: Satyagratha, pp. 62-63.

48. Gregg, The Power of Nonviolence, pp. 54-55.

49. Gandhi, Non-violent Resistance, p. 294; Ind. ed.: Satyagraha, p. 294.

50. Miller, Nonviolence, p. 146.

51. Kuper, Passive Resistance in South Africa, p. 85.

52. Reitlinger, The Final Solution, p. 277.

53. *Ibid.*, pp. 38-39 and 157-158.

54. Seifert, Conquest by Suffering, p. 68.

55. Farmer, Freedom – When?, pp. 67-68.

56. Solomon and Fishman, "The Psychosocial Meaning of Nonviolence in Student Civil Rights Activities," *Psychiatry,* vol. XXVII (May 1964), p. 97. See also Miller, Nonviolence pp. 312-313.

57. Miller, Nonviolence, p. 173.

58. McCleery has cited such a case in a Southern prison, where a Negro had defied officials: "In North Carolina, a Negro who had remained defiant through a reported 26 days in 'the hole' (solitary confinement) and repeated beatings was held in high respect by the predominantly Southern, white, members of his

group." Richard H. McCleery, "Authoritarianism and the Belief System of Incorrigibles," in Donald R. Cressey, ed., **The Prison: Studies in Institutional Organization and Change** (New York: Holt, Rinehart and Winston, 1961), p. 283. I am grateful to George Lakey for this reference.

59. Bondurant, **Conquest of Violence**, pp. 46-52.

60. Lindberg, *"Eksempler fra Irland,"* in Lindberg, Jacobsen and Ehrlich, **Kamp Uden Vaaben**, pp. 161-162.

61. Seifert, "The Use by American Quakers of Nonviolent Resistance as a Method of Social Change," pp. 22-54.

62. Jawaharlal Nehru: **An Autobiography**, p. 545.

63. Gandhi, **Non-violent Resistance**, p. 191; Ind. ed.: **Satyagraha**, p. 191.

64. Gregg, **The Power of Nonviolence**, p. 45.

65. *Ibid.*, p. 53. See also p. 78.

66. See Case, **Nonviolent Coercion**, p. 398. Gandhi describes how his wife's resistance and suffering in response to his efforts to dominate her "ultimately made me ashamed of myself, and cured me of my stupidity in thinking that I was born to rule over her, and in the end she became my teacher in non-violence. And what I did in South Africa was but an extension of the rule of satyagraha which she unwillingly practised in her own person." Gandhi, **Non-violence in Peace and War**, vol. I, p. 174.

67. Gregg, **The Power of Nonviolence**, p. 78.

68. *Ibid.*, p. 47. See also p. 133.

69. Bondurant, **Conquest of Violence**, p. 227, Janis and Katz, "The Reduction of Intergroup Hostility," p. 91, and Bose, **Studies in Gandhism**, p. 147, and Bertrand Russell, **Roads to Freedom: Socialism, Anarchism and Syndicalism** (London: Geo. Allen & Unwin, 1918), p. 14.

70. Quoted in Bose, **Selections from Gandhi**, p. 204.

71. King, **Stride Toward Freedom**, p. 177; Br. ed.: p. 207.

72. Gregg, **The Power of Nonviolence**, p. 54.

73. Peck, **Freedom Ride**, p. 75.

74. Gregg, **The Power of Nonviolence**, pp. 45-46.

75. Gandhi, **Non-violence in Peace and War**, vol. I, pp. 128-130.

76. Gregg, **The Power of Nonviolence**, p. 53.

77. *Ibid.*, pp. 44-45.

78. Case, **Non-violent Coercion**, p. 400.

79. Gregg, **The Power of Nonviolence**, pp. 55-56.

80. Lakey, "The Sociological Mechanisms . . ." (thesis), p. 33; *Peace Research Reviews,* vol. II, no. 6 (Dec. 1968), p. 21.

81. Lakey, "The Sociological Mechanisms . . . ," p. 87; *Peace Research Reviews,* vol. II, no. 6, p. 57.

82. Gregg, **The Power of Nonviolence**, p. 83.

83. *Ibid.*, pp. 46-47.

84. *Ibid.*, pp. 52-53.

85. *Ibid.*, p. 46.

86. *Ibid.*, pp. 56-57.

87. *Ibid.*, p. 97.

88. *Ibid.*, p. 73.

89. Gandhi, **Non-violence in Peace and War**, vol. II, p. 64.

90. *Ibid.,* vol. I, p. 178.
91. *Ibid.,* vol. I, p. 180.
92. Gandhi, Satyagraha in South Africa, pp. 16-17.
93. Quoted in Sharp, Gandhi Wields . . . , p. 65.
94. Quoted in *ibid.,* p. 117.
95. Gandhi, Non-violent Resistance, p. 113; Ind. ed.: Satyagraha, p. 113. See also pp. 188-189.
96. *Ibid.,* p. 17.
97. Ebert, "Theory and Practice of Nonviolent Resistance," MS p. 297.
98. Janis and Katz, "The Reduction of Intergroup Conflict," p. 88.
99. Kuper, Passive Resistance in South Africa, p. 90. Kuper cites Wolff, ed., The Sociology of Georg Simmel, pp. 195-197.
100. Kuper, Passive Resistance in South Africa, p. 91.
101. The outline of these eight factors is based upon Janis and Katz, "The Reduction of Intergroup Conflict," p. 86, who based their listing upon Arne Naess' analysis of Gandhi's norms of action. See Naess, "A Systematization of Gandhian Ethics of Conflict Resolution," *Journal of Conflict Resolution,* vol. I (1957), pp. 140-155.
102. Gandhi, Non-violence in Peace and War, vol. II, p. 91.
103. Gandhi, Non-violent Resistance, p. 154; Ind. ed.: Satyagraha, p. 154.
104. Lakey, "The Sociological Mechanisms . . ." (thesis), p. 37; *Peace Research Reviews,* vol. II, no. 6 (Dec. 1968), p. 24.
105. Janis and Katz, "The Reduction of Intergroup Conflict" p. 86.
106. Bondurant, Conquest of Violence, pp. 119-120.
107. Miller, Nonviolence, p. 168.
108. Gregg, The Power of Nonviolence, p. 133.
109. Janis and Katz, "The Reduction of Intergroup Conflict," p. 86.
110. Gandhi, Non-violent Resistance, p. 295; Ind. ed.: Satyagraha, p. 295.
111. Janis and Katz, "The Reduction of Intergroup Conflict," p. 86.
112. Oppenheimer and Lakey, A Manual for Direct Action, pp. 21-22.
113. Gandhi, Non-violent Resistance, p. 181; Ind. ed.: Satyagraha, p. 181.
114. Quoted in Bose, Studies in Gandhism, p. 127.
115. Janis and Katz, "The Reduction of Intergroup Conflict" p. 86.
116. Williams, The Reduction of Intergroup Tensions, p. 77.
117. Janis and Katz, "The Reduction of Intergroup Conflict," p. 86.
118. *Ibid.*
119. See Gandhi's letter to Lord Irwin, in Sharp, Gandhi Wields . . . , pp. 61-66.
120. Gregg, The Power of Nonviolence, pp. 78 and 55.
121. Janis and Katz, "The Reduction of Intergroup Conflict," p. 86.
122. Bondurant, Conquest of Violence, p. 120 n.
123. See Sharp, Gandhi Wields . . . , p. 145.
124. Gregg, The Power of Nonviolence, p. 83.
125. Miller, Nonviolence, p. 164.
126. Gregg, The Power of Non-violence, p. 85.
127. *Ibid.,* pp. 73-76.
128. *Ibid.,* p. 17.

129. Lakey, "The Sociological Mechanisms . . ." (thesis), p. 21; *Peace Research Reviews*, vol. II, no. 6 (Dec. 1968), p. 12.

130. Lakey, "The Sociological Mechanisms . . . ," p. 22; *Peace Research Reviews*, vol. II, no. 6, p. 13. Lakey described this mechanism as "persuasion," interpreted as persuasion to discontinue resistance to the efforts of the nonviolent actionists, rather than persuasion over the demands and issues at stake. In my slightly different interpretation of this mechanism, emphasizing the importance of adjustment to a changed social situation, the term "accommodation" may be more descriptive. See Farmer, Freedom – When? p. 41.

131. Williams, The Reduction of Intergroup Tensions, p. 14.

132. *Ibid.,* p. 17.

133. Seifert, Conquest by Suffering, pp. 73-74.

134. King, Stride Toward Freedom, pp. 8 and 140-144; Br. ed.: pp. 10 and 164-168.

135. Sharp, Gandhi Wields . . . , p. 165.

136. *Ibid.,* p. 166.

137. Seifert, "The Use by American Quakers of Nonviolent Resistance as a Method of Social Change," MS p. 94.

138. Lakey, "The Sociological Mechanisms . . ." (thesis), p. 23; *Peace Research Reviews*, vol. II, no. 6 (Dec. 1968), p. 14. For Gandhi's similar view, see Gandhi, Non-violent Resistance, p. 121; Ind. ed.: Satyagraha, p. 121.

139. Lakey, "The Sociological Mechanisms . . . ," p. 36; *Peace Research Reviews*, vol. II, no. 6, p. 23.

140. Lakey,"The Sociological Mechanisms . . . ," pp. 22-23; *Peace Research Reviews*, vol. II, no. 6, p. 13.

141. Seifert, Conquest by Suffering, p. 74.

142. "The Toleration Edict of Galerius, 30 April 311," in J. Stevenson, ed., A New Eusebius: Documents Illustrative of the History of the Church to A.D. 337 (London: S.P.C.K., 1957), p. 296.

143. See Hans Lietzmann, From Constantine to Julian (London: Lutterworth Press, 1960), p. 72. I am grateful to J. D. Kemp for this and the above reference.

144. Seifert, Conquest by Suffering, p. 73.

145. Gipson, The British Empire Before the American Revolution, vol. XII, The Triumphant Empire, Britain Sails into the Storm, 1770-1776, pp. 277-307.

146. Seifert, Conquest by Suffering, p. 74.

147. Gipson, The Coming of the Revolution, 1763-1775, p. 106.

148. *Ibid.,* p. 107.

149. *Ibid.,* p. 115.

150. Luthuli, Let My People Go, p. 177.

151. Gopal, The Viceroyalty of Lord Irwin, 1926-1931, p. 91.

152. William Faulkner, A Fable (New York: Random House, 1954), p. 54.

153. Gipson, The British Empire . . . , vol. XII, p. 279.

154. See Bondurant, Conquest of Violence, pp. 53-64, esp. pp. 60-61 and 64, and Mahadev Desai, The Story of Bardoli, esp. pp. 256-263.

155. Farmer, Freedom – When? p. 101.

156. In addition to those dictionaries, see Case, Non-violent Coercion, p. 403, and Horace M. Kallen, "Coercion," Encyclopedia of the Social Sciences, vol. III, pp. 617-619.

157. Theodor Paullin, Introduction to Non-violence, p. 6. Philadelphia: Pacifist

Research Bureau, 1944. Paullin defines "force" as "physical or intangible power or influence to effect change in the material or immaterial world." Elliott's definition of "force" is similar: ". . . force need not be limited to physical coercion. Any form of willed compulsion, whether it uses economic means or even moral pressure may become political force if it is used to accomplish political ends." W. Y. Elliott, "Political Force," Encyclopedia of the Social Sciences (New York: Macmillan, 1935), Vol. VI, p. 338.

158. Lakey, "The Sociological Mechanisms . . . (thesis), p. 18; *Peace Research Reviews*, vol. II, no. 6 (Dec. 1968), p. 10.

159. Bondurant, Conquest of Violence, p. 9.

160. Lakey, "The Sociological Mechanisms . . . ," p. 23; *Peace Research Reviews*, vol. II, no. 6, p. 13.

161. Some believers of nonviolence as a moral principle reject such "nonviolent coercion." Gandhi and some of his interpreters have often argued in these terms, although they have admitted that satyagraha contained a justifiable "compelling element." On Gandhi and "nonviolent coercion," see Bose, Studies in Gandhism, pp. 223-224; Dhawan, The Political Philosophy of Mahatma Gandhi, pp. 133-134, 254, and 261-266; Shridharani, War Without Violence, pp. 291-292, Br. ed.: pp. 249-250; Diwakar, Satyagraha, pp. 44 and 61; Bondurant, Conquest of Violence, pp. 9-11 and 173; and Johan Galtung and Arne Næss, Gandhis Politiske Etikk (Oslo: Tanum, 1955), pp. 223 and 258-259.

On the other hand, it has been argued, by Bondurant, Case and others, that it is precisely the combination of coercion and nonviolence which is so important, and which makes the ideals politically relevant, their achievement possible, and also makes the application of nonviolent means acceptable to people who would otherwise use violence. Case writes: "Perhaps it is only through a working partnership of seemingly incongruous forms of behavior as nonviolence and coercion that the problems of social collision can be permanently solved." (Case, Non-violent Coercion, p. 413. See also pp. 3, and 403-404.)

162. Crook, The General Strike, p. 165.

163. Keep, The Rise of Social Democracy in Russia, p. 222. See also Harcave, First Blood, pp. 191-197.

164. Katkov, Russia 1917, pp. 249, 263-264, 269-276, 278-281, 284, 288, 296, 340-344 and 364.

165. This is Hiller's phrase. See Hiller, The Strike, p. 125.

166. Harcave, First Blood, p. 121.

167. Katkov, Russia 1917, p. 423.

168. Brant, The East German Rising, p. 155.

169. Gandhi, Non-violent Resistance, p. 157; Ind. ed.: Satyagraha, p. 157. Sometimes specific tactics and methods of nonviolent action are used to make the optimal use of numbers in order to bring about the collapse of the government, as by massive nonviolent raids on government salt depots in India in 1930. "Such a widening of the salt campaign, by substituting collective action for individual breaches of the law, directly challenged the Government's ability to maintain the public peace." Gopal, The Viceroyalty of Lord Irwin, p. 70.

170. Schapiro, The Communist Party of the Soviet Union, p. 66, and Charques, The Twilight of Imperial Russia, pp. 119, 125 and 132. See also, Katkov, Russia 1917, p. 262.

171. Gopal, The Viceroyalty of Lord Irwin, p. 69.

172. Report of the Nyasaland Commission of Inquiry, p. 74.
173. *Ibid.*, p. 88.
174. Geyl, The Revolt of the Netherlands (1555-1609), pp. 55-56.
175. Gandhi, Non-violent Resistance, p. 121; Ind. ed.: Satyagraha, p. 121. See also Bose, Selections from Gandhi, p. 199.
176. Gopal, The Viceroyalty . . . , p. 80.
177. Sternstein, "The *Ruhrkampf* of 1923," p. 114. See also pp. 111, 115, 117, 123, and 132-133.
178. Seton-Watson, The Decline of Imperial Russia, p. 214.
179. Schapiro, The Community Party of the Soviet Union, pp. 286-308.
180. Dallin, German Rule in Russia, 1941-1945, *passim.*
181. Gipson, The Coming of the Revolution, 1763-1775, p. 193.
182. Sharp, Gandhi Wields . . . , pp. 190, 179, 200, 210, 189, and 204, respectively.
183. *Ibid.*, p. 179.
184. *Ibid.*, pp. 106, 126-128, 134, 160, 175, 182-183, 190, 192-193, 196, 205, and 211, and Gopal The Viceroyalty . . . , pp. 79-80 and 86-87.
185. Shridharani, War Without Violence, p. 24; Br. ed.: p. 43.
186. Gopal, The Viceroyalty . . . , p. 97, based on telegrams of the Viceroy to the Secretary of State.
187. Cited by Kumarappa in *"Young India"*, and quoted in Sharp, Gandhi Wields . . . , p. 186.
188. Shridharani, War Without Violence, p. 25; Br. ed.: p. 44; Shridharani reports that these figures are based upon the Statistical Abstract for the United Kingdom 74th number, and Trade and Navigation, The United Kingdom.
189. Shridharani, War Without Violence, p. 25, Br. ed.: p. 44.
190. Gandhi, Non-violent Resistance, p. 361; Ind. ed.: Satyagraha, p. 361.
191. See also Katkov, Russia 1917, pp. 262, 274, 276-282, and 340-341.
192. Görlitz, The German General Staff, p. 319. See also p. 341.
193. Stefan Brant, The East German Rising, pp. 86, 106, 149-153. On the behavior of the East German police and troops, and the Russian troops during the rising, see also Ebert, "Nonviolent Resistance Against Communist Regimes?" pp. 187-190.
194. *Das Parlament* (Bonn), 15 June 1955. Cited in Ebert, "Theory and Practice of Nonviolent Resistance," MS p. 254.
195. Hiller, The Strike, p. 233.
196. Symons, The General Strike, pp. 224-227.
197. Kuper, Passive Resistance in South Africa, pp. 62-63.
198. Symons, The General Strike, p. 228.
199. Nehru, An Autobiography, p. 360.
200. L. de Jong, "Anti-Nazi Resistance in the Netherlands," in European Resistance Movements, 1939-1945, p. 142.
201. Clausewitz, On War, vol. I, pp. 249-250.
202. *Ibid.*, pp. 231-234.
203. Gopal, The Viceroyalty . . . , p. 100.
204. Sharp, Gandhi Wields . . . , p. 220.
205. Bose, Selections From Gandhi, p. 154. See also p. 153.
206. Opposite views were, for example, offered by Nehru in differing conditions.

Nehru, An Autobiography, pp. 405-406, and Ebert, "Theory and Practice of Nonviolent Resistance," MS pp. 427-430 and 437-439.

207. Gopal, The Viceroyalty ..., pp. 97-100 and Sharp, Gandhi Wields..., p. 203.

208. Sharp, Gandhi Wields..., pp. 124, 202 and 207, and Gopal, The Viceroyalty ..., pp. 92-94.

209. Sharp, Gandhi Wields..., pp. 220-221.

210. Bondurant, Conquest of Violence, pp. 196-197.

211. Sharp, Gandhi Wields..., p. 207.

212. Gopal, The Viceroyalty..., p. 101.

213. Sharp, Gandhi Wields..., p. 206.

214. See ibid., pp. 213-219, or Gopal, The Viceroyalty ..., pp. 140-144.

215. Gopal, The Viceroyalty ..., pp. 112-113.

216. Liddell Hart, Strategy: The Indirect Approach, p. 348.

217. Clausewitz, On War, vol. I, pp. 306-307.

218. Nehru, An Autobiography, p. 339.

219. See Ebert's discussion of a nonviolent Blitzkrieg strategy for use in national defense through prepared nonviolent resistance (civilian defense), in his chapters "Preparations for Civilian Defense" p. 155 and "Initiating Popular Resistance to Totalitarian Invasion," in Mahadevan, Roberts and Sharp, eds., Civilian Defence: An Introduction, pp. 159-161.

220. O'Hegarty, A History of Ireland Under the Union, p. 487. This discussion draws upon Ebert, "Theory and Practice of Nonviolent Resistance," MS pp. 431-438.

221. Kuper, Passive Resistance in South Africa, p. 145.

222. Ebert, "Theory and Practice of Nonviolent Resistence" MS p. 435.

223. Bose, Selections from Gandhi, p. 203.

224. Farmer, Freedom — When?, pp. 38-39.

225. For some general observations on the role of negotiations in civil rights struggles, see Oppenheimer and Lakey, A Manual for Direct Action, pp. 24-25.

226. See Gandhi's view, Bose, Selections from Gandhi, p. 187.

227. Halperin, Germany Tried Democracy, pp. 181-182.

228. Gregg, The Power of Nonviolence, p. 98.

229. Ibid., pp. 61-62, 98, 100-101 and 120. Aldous Huxley argued that the results of nonviolent action were preferable to those of violence because "... the means employed inevitably determine the nature of the result achieved ..." Aldous Huxley, Ends and Means: An Enquiry into the Nature of Ideals and into the Methods Employed for Their Realization (New York: Harper Bros., 1937 and London: Chatto and Windhus, 1948), p. 55.

230. Gandhi, Non-violent Resistance, p. 31; Ind. ed.: Satyagraha, p. 31.

231. King, Stride Toward Freedom, p. 148; Br. ed.: p. 174.

14

The Redistribution
of Power

INTRODUCTION

The nonviolent technique of action inevitably has important effects on the nonviolent group itself and on the distribution of power among the contenders in the conflict and within the wider system. These consequences of the technique require consideration. As is the case with all other areas which this study has been exploring, very little research has been carried out on these subjects. This discussion must, therefore, be limited to those effects which are now fairly clear. Further investigation may correct possible errors in our present understanding, reveal other important effects, and explore the complexities of these consequences of nonviolent action.

EFFECTS ON THE NONVIOLENT GROUP

Reference has already repeatedly been made to the fact that the strength of the nonviolent actionists may grow as the struggle proceeds, both in comparison to their earlier strength and to the capacity of their opponent. Although some of this strengthening of the nonviolent group may be temporary, other aspects of this increased internal strength are likely to last. There are also other important effects of the use of this technique. For example, to start with, the people end their submissiveness and learn a technique of action which shows them they are no longer powerless. They are also likely to experience a growth of internal group solidarity. Certain psychological changes will occur which spring from their new sense of power and their increased self-respect. Finally, members of the group which uses nonviolent action seem during and after the struggle to cooperate more on common tasks. We shall now explore these, and related, consequences in more detail.

A. Ending submissiveness

Participation in nonviolent action both requires and produces certain changes in the previous pattern of submissiveness within the grievance group. A change of the opponent's outlook and beliefs may or may not be an objective of the campaign, but some kind of "change of heart" must take place in the nonviolent group and in the wider grievance group. Without it there can be no nonviolent action. Without a change from passive acceptance of the opponent's will, from lack of confidence and helplessness and a sense of inferiority and fear, there can be no significant nonviolent action and no basic transformation of relationships.

Erik Erikson has pointed out the close association between hierarchical systems and the subordinate's view of himself:

Therapeutic efforts as well as attempts at social reform verify the sad truth that in any system based on suppression, exclusion, and exploitation, the suppressed, excluded, and exploited unconsciously believe in the evil image which they are made to represent by those who are dominant.[1]

As long as members of the subordinate group regard themselves as inferiors, are submissive, and behave in a deferential and humiliating manner to members of the dominant group, repeating the customary habits of acknowledging inferiority (the lowered eyes, and "Yes, sir," for example), they confirm the dominant group's view of them as inferiors and as creatures or persons outside the "common moral order."[2] Submissive behavior by the subordinates helps to support the views which serve to "justify" the established system. Also, such a pattern of submission makes possible the system's continuation, for that behavior helps the system to operate smoothly.

Gregg related this self-image to an inability of subordinates to act to change their condition. He argued that an inferiority complex created in childhood and regularly reinforced in later years is "the most potent of all methods of restraining independent creative action among individuals and masses of people. It makes them feel utterly helpless and in times of crisis it creates a fatal hesitation and lack of confidence."[3] Use of nonviolent action requires at least a partial end to the former pattern of self-deprecation and submission. Gregg has argued that people using nonviolent action also cease to experience such social weaknesses as lack of self-respect, dislike of responsibility, the desire to be dominated, and political and economic ignorance.[4]

B. Learning a technique which reveals one's power

One of the most important problems faced by people who feel that they are oppressed, or that they must oppose dominant "evil" policies and systems, is: *how can they act?* Nonviolent action provides a multitude of ways in which people, whether majorities or minorities, can utilize whatever potential leverage they may possess to become active agents in controlling their own lives. People learn a "new" way of acting which immediately frees them from feelings of helplessness. As the movement develops and they become a formidable force, they become freed from the sense of impotence and they gain confidence in their own power. The specific ways this operates differ with the situation and the leverages utilized—labor, buying power, public sympathy, self-sacrifice, political behavior and the like. But to gain a sense of power, it is often necessary to learn how to use the leverage effectively. As they learned how to strike, industrial workers realized they could act together effectively, instead of being individually helpless. They learned to wield power by withdrawing their labor in order to gain certain objectives from their employers. During the rise of industrialism, workers did not always have this knowledge and ability. They were often unfamiliar with earlier cases of strikes. We frequently forget that this type of nonviolent action also had to be learned, experimented with, and tested in struggle.

As strikes became more widespread the participating workers gained confidence in their ability to improve their lot by their own efforts, and this example stimulated other workers to form unions and similarly to withdraw their labor in case their demands were not met. The workers had to achieve group solidarity, learn how to act, and be willing to undergo temporary suffering during the struggle as the price of winning improvements in their condition and status. These are qualities common to most instances of nonviolent action.

This process among industrial workers took place in a variety of situations and countries. In Russia, for example, industrial workers began to learn the weapon of the strike about 1870.[5] In the following three decades the process which we have described in general terms above occurred. "The modest ameliorations [produced by the strikes] were often in practice nullified by evasion and corruption, but," writes Schapiro, "they taught the workers the important lesson that they could improve their lot by striking."[6] The strikes in the late 1890s not only gave the workers confidence that they could achieve immediate concessions but also made them aware that they possessed the power, given time, to make much more fundamental changes in the system. "By making concessions only when faced with organized force [in the form of strikes], it [the autocracy] nurtured the hope that the fortress could one day be stormed."[7] Strikes became commonplace at the beginning of the 1905 revolution. Although usually spontaneous and unorganized, each strike "helped to impress the 'strike habit' more firmly on Russian workers" and strikes spread.[8] The workers were soon convinced that this was an appropriate form of action for more fundamental changes. The process continued to develop, and in a few months the Great October Strike dramatically demonstrated the increased use of the weapons of noncooperation against the government. Both supporters of strikes and of the autocracy had to take notice of the change which had been introduced.[9]

The success of the noncooperation against the 1920 Kapp *Putsch* gave even the calmest and most responsible labor leaders an unexpected sense of great power (sometimes they forgot the roles in that struggle played by others: civil servants, the Berlin population, etc.). The labor leaders then sought to use this power in bargaining to achieve their own political demands. Despite only partial success in that effort "many workers and their leaders . . . nourished long memories of how effective their weapon had been."[10]

The Indian experiments under Gandhi produced a similar sense of power among nonviolent actionists as they learned a "new" way to act. Gandhi often described a nonviolent action campaign as a means by which the people would generate the strength to enable them to advance toward achieving their political goals.[11] It was through noncooperation, Gandhi said, that people come to realize "their true power."[12] Referring to the experience of the Bardoli revenue-refusal campaign of 1928, he pointed to the importance of the participants learning the lessons "that so long as they remain united in nonviolence they have nothing to fear" and that they could wield "the unseen power of nonviolence." [13] At the beginning of the 1930–31 struggle, Gandhi wrote: "The mission of the Satyagrahis ends when they have shown the way to the nation to become conscious of the power lying latent in it." [14] Gandhi insisted that nonviolent action enables people to feel their own power, and added that "possession of such power *is* independence." [15]

The phenomenon is not new. It occurred also as a result of the American colonists' successful noncooperation campaign against the Townshend Acts (September 1767 to April 1770). Schlesinger writes: "The workingmen had emerged from the struggle against the Townshend duties conscious for the first time of their power in the community." [16] The South African civil disobedience campaign by the Indian minority in 1908 (against registration certificates, similar to the present passes) gave the Indians "some consciousness of their strength." [17] The mutiny of the 2nd Division of the Colonial Infantry (Tenth French Army) in May 1917 gave the defiant soldiers a similar awareness. So many mutinied that they were not generally punished, but were instead talked into returning to the trenches—with the important difference that they were not required to make the almost suicidal attack on German trenches.

And the soldiers sensed with an ominous thrill that they could defy their officers, could shrug off the faceless inevitability of discipline with near-impunity, could refuse to attack. In short, it was up to the troops themselves whether they would live or die. And, marveling at this simple but heretofore unsuspected truth, they marched forward to share it with the Army. [18]

Reluctant support for this view of the effect of nonviolent struggle came from Lenin who was firmly committed to violence for revolutionary aims. Writing of the impact of the mass strike on the exploited class during the 1905 revolution, Lenin observed that ". . . only the struggle discloses to it the magnitude of its own power . . ." [19]

The capacity of nonviolent action to give the people who use it increased power has been described by Seifert as a general characteristic of the technique. Nonviolent resistance movements, he writes, "have demonstrated that the powerless can wield power and that social means can be democratized." People who have been politically subjugated and economically dispossessed "have accomplished on country roads and city streets" the power changes usually associated "only with paneled board rooms and marble legislative halls." A chief result of resistance campaigns, Seifert continues, has been to "give to disprivileged groups the conviction that there is something they can do about their plight. Nonviolent strategies have given a powerful voice to those otherwise inarticulate." [20]

Individual nonviolent campaigns may be primarily intended to strengthen the subordinate group through the learning and use of nonviolent struggle, even though their avowed objectives are to win concessions from the opponent. The strengthening of the subordinates will be the most fundamental of these changes and have lasting consequences.

C. Increasing fearlessness

That the grievance group needs to cast off fear in order to use nonviolent action effectively has already been discussed. The other side of the story is that experience in the use of nonviolent action tends to increase the degree of fearlessness among the actionists. It may be that initially both fear and anger among nonviolent actionists must be consciously controlled.[21] Discipline and training may assist in this, as they do in military conflict. The nonviolent actionists learn, through explanation, training, example and experience, that they can remain firm in face of the opponent's repression, that he is not omnipotent, even that his violence betrays his weakness.[22] The actionists learn that if they act together and refuse to be terrorized, they are powerful. Imprisonment and other suffering can be withstood. In common with heroes of violent combat, they also risk death as a chance not too high to take on behalf of fundamental principles and goals. Casualties are interpreted as assertions of the dignity and importance of individuals[23] who refuse to bend in face of wrong and who struggle with others to achieve their objectives. Hence, casualties may simply prod the others to make still stronger efforts.

Beyond this conscious discipline there appears, however, to be a stage in which the nonviolent actionists do not have to control their fear because they cease to be fearful. Gandhi has pointed out that in actual cases people who had previously been "fear-stricken" of the government had "ceased to fear" its officials.[24] Interpreting the 1930-31 Indian campaign, Gregg wrote that its activities had been intended to end the fear of the government among the masses and "to stimulate courage, self-reliance, self-respect and political unity." He concluded that these aims had been largely achieved.[25] It might be possible to dismiss the testimony of both Gandhi and Gregg on the ground that, as believers in an ethic of nonviolence, they were not objective observers. However, Nehru, who was never such a believer and only reluctantly came to accept the practicality of nonviolent struggle, pointed to the same effect. He wrote that "the dominant impulse" in British-ruled India was "fear, pervasive, oppressing, strangling fear." Sources of this fear were the army, the police, the widespread secret service, the official class, laws, prisons, the landlord's agents, moneylenders, unemployment and starvation. "It was against this all-pervading fear that Gandhi's quiet and determined voice was raised: Be not afraid." It was not quite so simple, Nehru admitted, but in substance this was accurate. Although "fear builds its phantoms . . . more fearsome than reality itself," the real dangers, when calmly faced and accepted, lose much of their terror. Nonviolent struggle resulted in the lifting to a large degree of that fear from the people's shoulders.[26]

Noncooperation gave the masses "a tremendous feeling of release . . . , a throwing-off of a great burden, a new sense of freedom. The fear that had crushed them retired into the background, and they straightened their backs and raised their heads."[27]

There is evidence that not only masses of people but even individual actionists lose fear in the midst of nonviolent struggle. After being personally beaten by a mounted policeman using a *lathi,* Nehru wrote that he forgot the physical pain in the "exhilaration that I was physically strong enough to face and bear *lathi* blows."[28] Other participants in nonviolent defiance, too, he reported, experienced a growth of inner "freedom and a pride in that freedom. The old feeling of oppression and frustration was completely gone."[29]

Experience in the American nonviolent civil rights movement was similar. As a result of participation in the Montgomery, Alabama, bus boycott, wrote King, "a once fear-ridden people had been transformed."[30] The 1960 sit-ins created, wrote Lomax, a new type of Negro: "They were no longer afraid; their boldness, at times, was nothing short of alarming."[31] Student sit-inners and freedom riders frequently experienced a "strange calm" immediately before especially dangerous actions. Physical injury was feared more than death, and when lives were indeed in danger, the actionists tended to think: "One of us is going to die, I bet, but it's not going to be me; it's going to be him, the next guy." When these student nonviolent actionists did face the prospect of their own deaths, they felt it might arouse sympathy for their cause and they were sometimes inspired by heroes who had died in *violent* campaigns against oppression.[32]

The development of fearlessness is seen both as having important consequences for the personal growth of the individual actionists, as they develop such qualities as self-sacrifice, heroism and sympathy,[33] and also as having far-reaching social and political implications. Absence of fear may not only threaten the particular hierarchical system being opposed. It will greatly enhance the ability of those people to remain free and to determine their own future.

D. Increased self-esteem

If hierarchical systems exist in part because the subordinates submit as a result of seeing themselves as inferiors, the problem of how to change and end the hierarchical system becomes twofold: first, to get the members of the subordinate group to see themselves as full human beings, not inferiors to anyone, and, second, to get them to behave in ways consistent with that enhanced view of themselves, i.e., to resist and defy the patterns of inferiority and subordination.

People who are not, and do not regard themselves as, inferior must not behave as though they were: they must act to refute those conceptions and to challenge the social practices based on those views.[34] Some change of self-perception among at least certain members of the subordinate group must precede action, and further changes or extensions of those changes among more members of the subordinate group are likely to occur as a result of participation in nonviolent struggle.

An improved self-image often must precede action against the stratified system, and indeed an enhanced view often requires such action. When people who have accepted domination come to see their previous submission as unworthy of their new estimate of themselves, they must bring their behavior in line with their enhanced self-image. They must cease cooperation with that system, noncooperate with and disobey its behavior patterns, and the established "rules" which symbolize and perpetuate the inferior status. Self-image and resistance are thus seen to be closely linked. Lakey points out that "there is a tendency for the initiators of campaigns of exploited groups to be persons closest to the exploiting group in status in terms of self-image." [35] This changed behavior by the subordinates may then be important in changing the views of them held by members of the dominant group, who are confronted by behavior which refutes their stereotyped and distorted picture of the subordinate group.

The focus here, however, is primarily on the changes in self-perception which participation in nonviolent struggle has on the nonviolent actionists and other members of the subordinate group. Behavior which itself defies and refutes the former self-image of the subordinates becomes a major factor in spreading and deepening their new enhanced view of themselves. Even the very initiation of action and tackling the underlying conflict may improve the self-image of members of the subordinate group. To many of them it may come as a revelation that they are capable of standing up to the opponent, and that by acting together they become formidable challengers of whom notice must be taken. They then gain a new sense of importance.[36] By their action they throw off and refute the opponent's image of themselves as inferior and stand up to him as equals. They demonstrate courage and determination. Even injuries and deaths incurred in struggle are not viewed as cruelties inflicted on helpless victims but as the price of change paid by determined resisters struggling to alter their present condition and to create their own future. These people who have been subordinates are no longer a passive mass of malleable humanity, but men and women acting powerfully against conditions they oppose. They have learned to rely on themselves, and to shape their own lives.

Willingness to undergo punishment without retaliation does not destroy this new image. There is a crucial difference in the self-esteem of the person who suffers because he is punished for defying a law which he regards as violating his dignity, and he who suffers out of passive acquiescence to the same law which he regards in the same way, as Luthuli said: "Nationalist laws seek to degrade us. We do not consent. They degrade the men who frame them. They injure us—that is something different."[37] Because of the importance of this element, although Indian civil disobedience prisoners in 1930 had been instructed by Gandhi to obey most prison rules, they were not to submit to orders which were "contrary to self-respect," nor would they submit "out of fear." During that campaign the Indians outside of prison refused to cooperate with the British census because, they reasoned, as long as they remained a subject people such a census was in their eyes like a "stocktaking" of "slaves."[38]

Standing up against the opponent and fighting back by *some* means, even if violent ones, may contribute to greater self-respect. For example, Negroes of Washington, D. C. who fought back violently when attacked during the 1919 riots gained increased self-respect.[39] However, there are indications that when the struggle is conducted by nonviolent means the group will gain additional self-respect not only because they are struggling instead of submitting but also because they are acting with means which are seen to be ethically superior.[40] Nehru records, for example, that in the Indian nonviolent struggles the Indians saw their goal and their nonviolent type of struggle as better than the goal and methods of their British rulers, and this gave the Indians "an agreeable sense of moral superiority over our opponents."[41]

An enhanced view of themselves and a new sense of their own importance has been noted among strikers and other nonviolent actionists.[42] Hiller points out that increased self-esteem may result from success.[43] But success is not the only factor, for Hiller also indicates, as does Lakey,[44] that even when the nonviolent group is not successful, increased self-confidence and less inner tension tend to develop.[45]

The capacity of nonviolent action to change the participants themselves was, writes James Farmer, one of the reasons why the early Congress of Racial Equality (C.O.R.E.) concentrated on nonviolent direct action projects instead of working for new laws and court decisions:

> CORE . . . wanted to involve the people . . . personally in the struggle for their own freedom . . . [I]n the very act of working for the impersonal cause of racial freedom, a man experiences . . . a large measure of private freedom . . . which, if not the same thing as freedom, is its radical source.

Having described a courageous initial attempt at nonviolent defiance by Negroes of Plaquemine, Louisiana, Farmer pointed to a change within them:

> Gradually, during . . . those two violent days, they made the decision to act instead of being acted upon . . . [They] refused to be victimized any longer by the troopers, [and] had been transformed into a community of men, capable, despite the severest limitations, of free and even heroic acts. Their subsequent activity at the polls and in initiating a school boycott suggests that this kind of freedom, though essentially personal, will inevitably lead to social action, and that freedom once won is not readily surrendered.[46]

Nehru described the change wrought by Gandhi on the Indian millions as one "from a demoralized, timid and hopeless mass, bullied and crushed by every dominant interest, and incapable of resistance, into a people with self-respect and self-reliance, resisting tyranny, and capable of united action and sacrifice for a larger cause.[47] Describing a similar change among the fifty thousand Negroes of Montgomery, Alabama, during the year-long bus boycott, King wrote that they "acquired a new estimate of their own human worth."[48] Seen in this context certain instances of Gandhi's moralizing have strong political implications. He insisted on dignity, discipline and restraint which would bring the Indians self-respect. Their self-respect would bring them the respect of others, and this would bring them freedom. "To command respect is the first step to *Swaraj* [self-rule]."[49]

The growth of self-esteem, with its impact on the opponent, the subordinate group, and the ability and determination of that group to defy the behavior patterns of inferiority, may have highly significant long term consequences.

E. Bringing satisfaction, enthusiasm and hope

Despite the dangers and hardships encountered in the struggle, non-violent actionists may find the overall experience a satisfying one. The precise source of the satisfaction has varied, but it has occurred in diverse cases, including the pro-Jewish strikers of Amsterdam in February 1941:

> To those who had participated, the strike provided a sense of relief, since it represented an active repudiation of the German regime. . . . In the strike the working population of Amsterdam had discovered its own identity in defiance of the occupying power.[50]

Tens of thousands of British citizens found the 1926 General Strike to be "the most enjoyable time of their lives."[51] A high society lady from Washington, D.C., who supported woman suffrage by doing picket duty, maintained that "no public service she had ever done gave her such an exalted feeling."[52] In England, woman suffragist public demonstrations had a similar effect on the actionists; Mary Winsor wrote that "to make women feel at ease in the streets of the city helped to break the sex dominance that man had set up."[53] Nehru wrote: "In the midst of strife, and while we ourselves encouraged that strife, we had a sense of inner peace."[54]

Of similar experiences in the United States, Farmer has observed that tens of thousands of young Negroes who participated in marches, sit-ins, or went to jail experienced "the joys of action and the liberating effect" of working to determine their own future. Consequently, "they began to regard themselves differently." ". . . men must achieve freedom for themselves. Do it for them and you extinguish the spark which makes freedom possible and glorious . . ." The many Negroes who participated in the nonviolent civil rights movement, Farmer continued, achieved "a measure of spiritual emancipation" which no legal document could give them: "The segregation barriers . . . . have ceased to be an extension of their minds . . . They do not feel inferior . . . We feel dignified . . ." People who had formerly felt little and insignificant changed as a result of taking part in nonviolent struggle, he reports, so that afterwards they "in their own eyes, stand ten feet tall." Farmer quotes a student in Atlanta: "I, myself, desegregated that lunch counter on Peachtree Street. Nobody else. I did it by sitting-in, by walking the picket line, by marching. I didn't have to wait for any big shots to do it for me. I did it myself." Farmer adds: "Never again will that youth and the many like him see themselves as unimportant." [55]

Participants in nonviolent action may also experience increased enthusiasm, dedication and hope.[56] Luthuli concluded that the 1952 Defiance Campaign in South Africa "had succeeded in *creating* among a very large number of Africans the spirit of militant defiance. The Campaign itself came to an untimely end, but it left a new climate, and it embraced people far beyond our range of vision. Since then there have been a number of unexpected demonstrations, especially among women." Luthuli goes on to cite several instances in which Africans after that campaign was over applied nonviolent action and "the refusal to comply" because they had caught the "mood" of the campaign "and sometimes its technique." [57]

The 1962 civil rights campaign among Mississippi Negroes (which consisted largely of the "freedom registration" and "freedom ballot") "energized Negroes who had never before dreamed of participating in their state's political process . . ." [58] The 1961 Freedom Riders "went back to their homes with a deep and abiding commitment to the movement of the sort that only direct participation can inspire." The gains that were won through nonviolent action also produced a "sense of possibility . . . in the ghetto." [59] Hope was restored, or perhaps born.

Lenin was no friend of nonviolent action, but in his "Lecture on the 1905 Revolution" he acknowledged the role which some methods of this technique played in radically altering the attitudes of the masses. Before January 9, 1905 the revolutionary party in Russia, he writes, "consisted of a small handful of people . . ." Within a few months "slumbering Russia became transformed into a Russia of a revolutionary proletariat and a revolutionary people." How had this transformation come about? What were its methods and ways? Lenin had no doubt, although the answer was contrary to his elitist conception of revolution. "The principal means by which this transformation was brought about was the *mass strike.*" The social content of that 1905 revolution, he wrote, was a *"bourgeois-democratic* revolution" but "in its methods of struggle it was a *proletarian* revolution." It was this type of action which had made the change: ". . . the specifically proletarian means of struggle—namely, the strike—was the principal instrument employed for rousing the masses . . ." This struggle had imbued the masses with "a new spirit." "Only the struggle educates the exploited class." Only struggle reveals to that class the extent of its own power, while it also "widens its horizon, enhances its abilities, clarifies its mind, forges its will . . ." Even reactionaries had to admit, concluded Lenin, that the year 1905 had "definitely buried patriarchal Russia." [60]

F. Effects on aggression, masculinity, crime and violence

Participation in nonviolent action has at times reversed or demonstrated a reversal of the usual assumed relationships between nonviolent behavior and human aggressiveness, masculinity, crime and future violence.

The use of nonviolent struggle by multitudes of ordinary people should make it clear beyond dispute both that human beings are not by nature too aggressive to use such means, and that human aggressiveness can be expressed nonviolently. It is fairly obvious that aggressiveness and feelings of hostility may be expressed in economic boycotts which inflict financial losses on the opponent, and that demonstrators who sit down in the street may realize that by this nonviolent act they are being more difficult to deal with than if they had used violence. There are also indications that the show of friendliness toward opponents may be associated with contempt for them, and that even extreme gestures of humanity in nonviolent action may at times derive from feelings of aggressiveness. Solomon and Fishman point to this association in their studies of American student civil rights actionists: "The friendliness of demonstrators toward their foes . . . sometimes is displayed at moments when the students *feel* the most hostile and contemptuous." They cite an instance in which a member of the American Nazi Party, carrying and shouting extremely offensive racial expressions, taunted a civil rights picket line near Washington, D.C. One student demonstrator wanted for the first half hour to hit the Nazi, but for the sake of the movement he didn't. Then, the student started smiling at the Nazi every time he saw him. In a quarter of an hour, the Nazi started smiling back, but then felt ridiculous for not hating the student enough, got mad, and left. That student had found in other cases also that friendly behavior to hecklers made them "quite exasperated at themselves." He adopted a Mississippi journalist's motto: "I always love my enemies because it makes them mad as hell." [61]

Nonviolent action has also been used by groups which have been famous for their very aggressive behavior and violence. Bondurant points to the case of the Pathans, in the North-West Frontier Province of British India. She quotes William Crooke's observation of their nature, published in 1896: "The true Pathan . . . is cruel, bloodthirsty and vindictive in the highest degree . . . . He leads a wild, free, active life in the rugged fastnesses of his mountains; and there is an air of masculine independence about him . . ." Bondurant quotes others who have said that war has traditionally been the "normal business of the land" among the Pathans, who had "no hesitation to kill when the provocation causes sufficient wrath." It should also be noted that the Pathans were Muslims, adherents of a religion widely regarded as approving of war for a good cause. Yet among these Pathans, Khan Abdul Ghaffar Khan, "the Frontier Gandhi," organized a powerful movement of the Khudai Khidmatgar, or Servants of God, which was pledged to complete nonviolence and whose members became some of the bravest and most daring and reliable nonviolent resisters of India's struggle for independence. Bondurant writes: "The achievement of the Khudai Khidmatgar was nothing less than the reversal in attitude and habit of a people steeped in the tradition of factious violence . . . . The instrument for this achievement was a Pathan version of satyagraha." [62] It seems clear from this extremely important case that there was no basic change in the "human nature" of the Pathans, but that the aggressiveness, bravery and daring of those people found new nonviolent expressions through the nonviolent technique.

Jerome D. Frank, Professor of Psychiatry at Johns Hopkins University, writes that nonviolent action struggles have also broken "the psychological link between masculinity and violence, thus circumventing one of the major psychological supports for war." He points to Kenneth Boulding's "First Law": "What exists, is possible." Frank continues: "Nonviolent action exists and has succeeded under some circumstances, and this alone destroys the contention that nonviolent methods of conflict are hopelessly at variance with human nature." The Indian campaigns under Gandhi and the American nonviolent civil rights struggles, in very different societies with quite unlike traditions,

. . . have reversed the relationship between masculinity and violence, and shown that this may be based more on cultural expectations than on the usually assumed biology of maleness. They succeeded in establishing group standards in which willingness to die rather than resort to violence was the highest expression of manly courage.

Frank cites as supporting evidence the findings of two studies of participants in the American sit-in movements and Freedom Rides, which ". . . have revealed that by refusing to resort to violence, the participants gain a heightened feeling of manliness and a sense of moral superiority over their opponents, who in effect, act out their own aggressive impulses for them."[63]

Nonviolent action may also help reduce crime and other anti-social behavior among the general grievance group. At the end of the Montgomery, Alabama, Negro bus boycott, King observed a decline in heavy drinking, crime and divorce among the Negroes, and in the number of fights on Saturday nights.[64] Others reported the same trend from other cities. Hentoff wrote:

> Significantly, again and again in recent years, when a large section of a Negro community has been caught up in a movement against discrimination, the crime rate in that community has gone down and remained down so long as mass action continues.[65]

Mrs. Gloria Richardson, Chairman of the Cambridge, Maryland, Non-Violent Action Committee, said in 1963:

> It's funny, but during the whole time we were demonstrating actively, there were almost no fights in this ward and almost no crime. . . . Now they've gone back to fighting each other again. They've been thrown back to carrying a chip on their shoulder.[66]

Farmer cited both the above cases also, pointing in addition to Jackson, Mississippi, which before the 1961 Freedom Rides had "a shocking incidence of petty and violent crime of Negro against Negro. When the Freedom Buses came, the city united in support and the crime rate dropped precipitately." He added: "Whenever people are given hope and the technique to get the heel off their necks, crime will decline."[67] Solomon and Fishman also cited reports of sharp decline in crime and delinquency during public protest campaigns, noting generally: "The movement provides a release of pent-up resentment and anger in a socially and politically advantageous and morally superior manner. . ."[68] There has also been a psychiatric study on this result of nonviolent action.[69]

Participation in nonviolent action, under some circumstances at least, may contribute to an extension of the areas of life in which the person may feel able to act nonviolently, instead of violently, and to an increased sympathy for nonviolence as an overall moral principle. Lakey reports changes among participants in the sit-in movement in the Deep South: some began taking part while being rather hostile and aggressive persons, but later came gradually to "accept the Gandhian values of nonviolent action as a part of their everyday behavior."[70] This is in line with Gregg's view that "in actual life action often precedes and clarifies thought and even creates it."[71] Similar developments in some individual participants of the British Committee of 100 civil disobedience demonstrations were reported.

Of course, such changes may not take place at all, or if they do, they may occur only among a small percentage of the actionists; this will depend on various factors. Given sufficient time and favorable experiences (not necessarily pleasant ones), such changes are likely, however, among *some* of the participants. A process of "emotional relearning" may take place in which, by testing out a new way of behaving, the actionist learns that his earlier fears about the consequences of nonviolent behavior may not in fact materialize.[72] Janis and Katz have suggested that the prospect of taking part in a future act of violence in a conflict situation may produce at least a small degree of anticipatory guilt feelings, and hence emotional tension; they add that this inner tension may be reduced by a group decision to abstain from violence and to use "an effective form of nonviolent action instead." They argued that even when the group's approval of nonviolent behavior is only lip service, that approval may increase the individual's self-esteem concerning his own adherence to nonviolence. The combination of this reduced inner tension and this increase in self-esteem for his own nonviolence, may make the individual increasingly sympathetic to nonviolent behavior more generally.

If each act of abstention [from violence] is rewarded in this way, a new attitude will gradually tend to develop such that the person becomes increasingly more predisposed to decide or vote in favor of nonviolent means. Perhaps under these conditions, good moral "practice makes perfect."

Even where success is ambiguous, they argued, this type of process is likely to take place among those members of the group "who have a relatively low need for aggression," and people who, without thinking, formerly accepted violent methods may instead accept nonviolent methods for dealing with opponents.

Other factors and processes are of course involved in such a change. Just as the person may have inner hesitations about using violence, he may also be apprehensive about using nonviolent means only, Janis and Katz continued. Such a pressure against nonviolence may arise, for example, from the widely accepted view that violence is the only suitable response in severe conflicts, or from such a question as "Am I a sissy?" The person using nonviolent action may therefore have to justify to himself his participation in a campaign which rejects violence or withdraw from the struggle. Janis and Katz have argued that the process set in motion by this is likely to "contribute to two types of attitude change: 1) reduced hostility toward the rival group, and 2) more favorable evaluations of the desirability of using positive [i.e., nonviolent] means in general." [73] Gregg argued that nonviolent action is also less exhausting and requires less emotional energy than violence: [74] if so, this factor too may make the nonviolent actionist sympathetic to use of nonviolent methods in other areas of his life.

There may also be certain social-psychological effects of adherence to nonviolent methods on the group as a whole. Janis and Katz have suggested that reliance on nonviolent action may strengthen the group's commitment to its avowed goal, whereas reliance on violence may lead to the original goals being abandoned and to other "corrupting" effects. [75]

On a more conscious and rational level, participation in nonviolent action may convince people that such behavior may be practical and effective in conflicts in which they have presumed only violence to "work." Moral imperatives to refrain from violence—contained in various philosophical and religious systems to which lip-service is widely paid—are often violated because people believe that nonviolent behavior is not practical in serious social, political and international conflicts. [76] If people become convinced by participation, observation and new knowledge that nonviolent action is practical, it may be used in more serious conflict situations, and the tension between a desire to adhere to a nonviolent ethic and a wish to be effective in real conflicts may be reduced or removed. This process will not, of course, operate unless concrete and practical nonviolent courses of action are worked out to deal with each conflict situation.

G. Increased group unity

The effectiveness of nonviolent action is increased when the actionists and the general grievance group possess a high degree of internal unity. In addition, the use of nonviolent action in itself contributes significantly to the growth of such internal solidarity. This growth has often been seen in the labor movement. Conflict, said Hiller, "solidifies the group." "Under attack, strikers perceive the identity of their interests." Comradeship is generated in the group during the conflict and a feeling of elation is produced by acting with the whole group. "Mutual stimulation increases the readiness to act." [77]

There is evidence that the nonviolent actionists are likely to find it easier to achieve and maintain group unity than is the opponent group; and also easier than if they use violent means. Violence is likely to exclude certain persons from full participation, both because of age, sex, physical condition and the like, and because of beliefs, or simple distaste and revulsion against the use of violence in the conflict.

For example, there was much greater unity among the American colonists during the predominantly nonviolent campaigns against English laws and policies than there was later, after the struggle had shifted to a military confrontation. The Morgans point out that the colonies had never been able to unite for any purpose, even against the French and Indians in war, prior to the Stamp Act struggle. Not only did the Stamp Act Congress show this unity: the solidarity of merchants in several cities in supporting nonimportation agreements, despite temptations to profit by violating them, was also new. A proposal for an intercolonial union was making rapid progress when the Stamp Act was repealed. Joseph Warren in March 1766 wrote that Grenville's legislation had produced ". . . what the most zealous Colonist never could have expected. The Colonies until now were ever at variance and foolishly jealous of each other, they are now . . . united . . . nor will they soon forget the weight which this close union gives them." [78] Further noncooperation followed, and greater unity among the colonies. This unity grew, so that during the deliberations of the First Continental Congress in 1774 (which drafted the most ambitious noncooperation campaign yet), Patrick Henry of Virginia was able to declare: "The Distinctions between Virginians, Pennsylvanians, New Yorkers, and New Englanders, are no more. I am not a Virginian, but an American." [79]

The initial period of the 1905 Revolution in Russia, which was significantly more nonviolent than the concluding period, produced a "strong feeling of camaraderie and unity," wrote Harcave. It was possible to achieve a common front uniting everyone from revolutionaries to conservatives against the regime, under the limited but common conviction that it was impossible to continue without change.[80] It was under the program urged by Gandhi and the application of nonviolent action to achieve independence that the Indian National Congress was transformed from a very small group of intellectuals who met for discussions and consideration of resolutions once a year into a mass membership political party engaged in active struggle with the British Empire. During this same period, despite diverse linguistic, cultural and religious groups, very considerable if inadequate steps were taken in developing Indian unity. The 1952 South African Defiance Campaign also saw increased solidarity and a sense of power among the nonwhites. The various nonwhite Congresses were strengthened, and in particular the number of paid members of the African National Congress jumped from seven thousand at the beginning of the campaign to one hundred thousand at the end.[81] The South African 1957 bus boycott by Alexandra township Africans also produced similar effects. African National Congress leader Walter Sisulu said later that "the bus boycott has raised the political consciousness of the people and has brought about a great solidarity and unity among them." [82] Repeatedly, the use of nonviolent action against racial discrimination and segregation in the United States led to a significant increase in Negro unity. The June 1963 Boston Negro boycott of the public schools, in protest against *de facto* racial segregation, produced this result, as Noel Day, one of its leaders, pointed out: "The boycott was a success in terms of getting the Negro community organized for action. It was never as united before the boycott as it has been since." [83] Feelings of group unity are closely associated with increased cooperation, self-help and organization within the grievance group.

H. Increased internal cooperation

The withdrawal of cooperation from the opponent and his system by nonviolent actionists does not lead simply to chaos and disorganization. On the contrary, such noncooperation and defiance are balanced by increased cooperation within the grievance group in general and among the nonviolent actionists in particular. The effective conduct of a nonviolent action movement requires considerable organization, cooperation and self-help.

At the same time, increased cooperation within the grievance group is required in order to provide alternative ways of meeting those social needs formerly met by the institutions with which cooperation has been now refused. The reverse side of noncooperation is cooperation, and that of defiance is mutual aid. These make it possible both to preserve social order and to meet social needs during and following a nonviolent action movement. Without such positive efforts, even though the nonviolent action were effective and successful—which is doubtful—the result would be social chaos and collapse which would lead the way toward quite different results than those intended by the nonviolent group, unless there were a prompt resumption of cooperation under the old system. The alternative arrangements for preserving social order and meeting human needs depend upon the willingness of the grievance group to give them their cooperation and to make them a success.

The close relationship between noncooperation and cooperation was repeatedly emphasized by Gandhi:

> The movement of non-cooperation is one of automatic adjustment. If the Government schools are emptied, I would certainly expect national schools to come into being. If the lawyers as a whole suspended practice, they would devise arbitration courts . . . [84]

Bondurant makes the same point: ". . . the non-cooperation of satyagraha has the necessary concomitant of cooperation among the resisters themselves . . . for establishing a parallel social structure, [and] also in . . . conversion of the system against which the group is resisting." [85]

This building up of cooperation to fulfill the social needs formerly met by the opponent's institutions is illustrated by the Montgomery bus boycott. With the decision of the Negroes to refuse to ride on the segregated buses, fifty thousand people were left without a public transportation system. This was one of the first problems to be tackled by the planning committee. Through a series of efforts, they established a highly efficient alternative transportation system. The importance of this rival institution was clearly recognized by the city officials who made repeated efforts to crush it. [86]

There is considerable variation in the degree to which this balancing of noncooperation with cooperation is consciously developed or just "happens" without advance consideration. There are even some cases in which a broad program of social change and development based on this developing cooperation has been thought out and deliberately promoted to take place both between and during nonviolent action struggles. A whole series of alternative national Hungarian cultural, educational, economic and political institutions were built up during Hungarian opposition to Austrian rule in the mid-nineteenth century, especially during the passive resistance phase from about 1850 to 1867. It is clear that these alternative institutions were important in the continuation of Hungary as a nation and in its ability to resist domination from Vienna.[87]

In India, Gandhi also developed his "constructive program"[88] on the need for parallel substitute institutions to replace those of the opponent. With this theory and program, new institutions and social patterns need not wait for the capture of State machinery: far better, they could be initiated immediately, Gandhi maintained. Social "evils" were to be attacked directly by nonviolent action when necessary. Along with such struggle, however, had to go the broader educational and institutional work, a balancing cooperation to meet social needs. To the extent that there is support for this constructive program and that it succeeds, the new efforts will gradually weaken and replace the former system. Also in Gandhi's view, as it showed results that constructive program would increase support for the resistance movement by showing that change was both desirable and possible. Gandhi constantly pressed for constructive work, both between and during direct action struggles. He believed it helped to train volunteers, to educate the masses, and was a necessary accompaniment to all nonviolent action struggles except in cases of a local specific common grievance.[89]

Both Gandhi and the Hungarians in the mid-nineteenth century apparently had an explicit theory about the need for alternative social institutions. However, even in the absence of such theories, nonviolent action struggles tend to be accompanied by increased cooperation within the grievance group expressed in organizational, institutional and often economic forms. Some type of compensating process seems to be involved: noncooperation with certain institutions tends to produce increased alternative cooperation with other institutions, even if these have to be created especially for the purpose.

Economic noncooperation campaigns by American colonists against England, for example, led to strong efforts to build up American self-sufficiency in both agriculture and manufactures.[90] Strikes and political noncooperation in the Russian Empire in 1905 were balanced by a growth of organizational strength among the revolutionaries, especially among trade unions and the creation of *soviets* (councils) as institutions of direct popular government.[91] A logical consequence of this development of internal cooperation and of alternative institutions for meeting social needs and maintaining social order in a revolutionary situation is dual sovereignty and parallel government.

I. Contagion

When nonviolent action is used with at least moderate effectiveness, the technique will tend to spread. The same people may use it again under other circumstances, and the example set may be followed by other people in quite different circumstances. This effect of contagion is not unique to nonviolent action—political violence too seems to be contagious—but the spread of nonviolent action is important, especially because that technique enhances the power of the nonviolent actionists. Those consequences, as we shall see, are different from those of political violence.

The royal governors of American colonies claimed that it was the contagious example of Boston's initial defiance of the Stamp Act (not strictly nonviolently) which had set off resistance in their colonies, too, and produced the situation in which no one was willing and able to put the Act into operation on November 1, 1765, when it was to come into force. Reports which exaggerated the radical nature of resistance in Virginia led to resistance in other colonies more extreme than had actually occurred in Virginia.[92]

Success in achieving repeal of the Stamp Act paved the way for the colonists to use comparable methods when facing new grievances, such as the Townshend taxes. The very influential "Letters from a Farmer in Pennsylvania" (authored anonymously by John Dickinson) reminded the American colonists of the previous effectiveness of their legislative petitions and nonimportation agreements, and urged that those means of protest be revived against the new Townshend Acts. Arthur Schlesinger wrote: "These articles were read everywhere and helped to prepare the public mind for the mercantile opposition of the next few years."[93]

This additional colonial experience with noncooperation made possible in turn the development of a more comprehensive program of such resistance embodied in the Continental Association, adopted by the First Continental Congress. It was, wrote Schlesinger, in part "the standardization and nationalization of the systems of commercial opposition which had hitherto been employed on a local scale." There was, however, a significant difference, for initiative and control had been seized by the radicals, who were now using the weapons which the merchant class had earlier developed and used for their own purposes; the radicals "had now reversed the weapons on them in an effort to secure ends desired solely by the radicals."[94]

There were repeated instances during the 1905 Revolution in which strikes and other forms of struggle spread by imitation. Small successes from strikes earlier in the year led to expansion of trade union organizations and more use of strikes. Similarly, limited political successes have sometimes prodded resisters and revolutionaries to press on to larger objectives. The Tsar's October Manifesto which granted civil liberties and a limited *Duma*, wrested from the Tsar by the Great October Strike which had paralyzed the country and the government, convinced the revolutionaries that they had the power to press on. The majority considered, Harcave reported, that they had won "a preliminary victory" which should be followed "by a final assault on autocracy."[95]

To my knowledge, studies have not been made specifically on the contagion effect of the nonviolent technique. However this contagion seems to operate even across national borders and around the world as descriptions of nonviolent struggles are relayed by radio, television and newspapers. Printed accounts in books or pamphlets may also serve a similar purpose at times. When nonviolent struggles are failures, contagion is not likely to occur; but when successes follow each other nonviolent action may spread and the use of the technique may multiply almost geometrically.

J. Conclusion

The bulk of the earlier analysis in this Part was focused on the dynamics of nonviolent struggle in terms of its effects on the opponent. That is obviously an extremely important aspect of the technique. However, as the discussion in this section has shown, the effects of this technique on its practitioners are far-reaching and in light of the analysis of power on which this technique rests, may in the long run be the most important. For if people are strong and know how to resist effectively, it becomes difficult or impossible for anyone to oppress them in the first place. Future analysis of the dynamics of nonviolent action may, therefore, give more attention to the changes the technique produces among the nonviolent actionists than to the immediate effects on the opponent. The strengthening of the grievance group is bound to alter power relationships in lasting ways.

DIFFUSED POWER AND THE NONVIOLENT TECHNIQUE

Tocqueville pointed out that a society needs strong social groups and institutions capable of independent action and able to wield power in their own right; when necessary, these may act to control the power of the established government or any possible domestic or foreign usurper. If such groups (*loci*-or places-of power) are not present to a significant degree, it may prove extraordinarily difficult or impossible for that society to exercise control over its present ruler, to preserve its constitutional system, and to defend its independence.[96] People are better able to act together against the ruler or usurper when they can act through groups, organizations and other institutions than when each person is isolated from all others, and no group of them has collective control over any of the sources of the power of the State.

According to this view, lasting capacity for popular control of political power, especially in crises, requires the strengthening of such nongovernmental groups and institutions in the normal functioning of the society in order that in crises they will be able to control the sources of political power, and therefore control rulers who do not wish to be controlled. In this establishment of effective control over the political power of rulers, questions of social organization and of political technique converge.

There may be a causal connection between the relative concentration or diffusion of power in the society and the technique of struggle, or final sanction, relied upon by that society to maintain the social system or to change it. Political violence and nonviolent action may produce quite different effects on the future concentration of power in the society. Therefore, the choice between the various political techniques will become that society's ultimate sanction and technique of struggle and may help to determine the future capacity of that society to exercise popular control over any ruler or would-be ruler.

This brief discussion necessarily deals in broad generalizations and tendencies, which may not give full appreciation to the complexities of a given case. It may be remembered not only that many other factors may be operating in a given situation, but that under particular conditions the tendencies discussed here might not be realized.

A. Violence and centralization of power

It has been widely recognized that violent revolutions and wars have been accompanied and followed by an increase both in the absolute power of the State and in the relative centralization of power in its hands. This recognition has by no means been limited to opponents of political violence and centralization. Following successful violent revolutions, the new ruler may in some cases behave in a more humanitarian and self-restrained way than the former regime, but this is not always so, and there is nothing in the new structure which requires it. Furthermore, the increased power of the new government frequently puts the general populace in a more unfavorable position to exert control over it in the future than the populace was under the old regime. The weakening of other social groups and institutions and the concentration of increased power in the hands of the State—whoever might hold the position of ruler—thus generally has not brought to the subjects increased ability to control political power. This process, Jouvenel has argued, laid the foundation for the monolithic State.[97]

The centralizing effect of conventional war has similarly been widely recognized. This has been especially obvious in the twentieth century, but the tendency was apparent earlier.[98] Technological changes and the breakdown of the distinction between civilians and the armed forces have accentuated this tendency. Effective mobilization of manpower and other resources into an efficient war machine, the necessity of centralized planning and direction, the disruptive effect of dissension, the need for effective control over the war effort, and the increase in the military might which is available to the government, all contribute to the strong tendency of modern war to concentrate more and more effective power in the hands of the ruler—whoever occupies that position. There seems to be a causal connection between the use of political violence and the increased centralization of power in the government. Political violence, therefore, even when used against a particular tyrant, may contribute to increased difficulties in controlling the power of future rulers of that society and in preventing or combatting future tyranny.

There are various factors in the dynamics of political violence which appear to influence this connection; all of these seem to be aggravated by modern developments in technology and political organization. For example, centralized control of the preparations for and the waging of violence is generally necessary if the violence is to be applied efficiently. In order to provide control over the preparations and waging of violence, centralized control of the weapons (and other material resources), the active combatants, and the groups and institutions on which these depend, is also required.

The combination of all these types of control means increased power before and during the struggle for those exercising that control. The controllers will also be able to use violence against the population to maintain that control. After a successful violent struggle, the group which controlled the conduct of the struggle, and which now controls the State, is likely to retain at least most of the power which they accumulated during the conflict. Or, if a *coup d'etat* takes place, others will obtain control of that increased power. In addition, when violent revolutionaries take over the old State, now strengthened by the additional centralized power accumulated by them during the violent conflict, the overall effective power of the new ruler will be increased, compared to that of the old one.

Furthermore, the power of the State is likely also to be increased relatively as a result of the destruction or weakening during the struggle of the effective *loci* of power—the independent institutions and social groups. The combination of an increase in the power of the State and a weakening of the *loci* of power among the people will leave the subjects under the new regime relatively weakened *vis à vis* the ruler, compared with their condition before the change. In addition, the new regime which was born out of violence will require continued reliance on violence, and therefore centralization, to defend itself from internal and external enemies. In a society where subjects and ruler alike regard violence as the only kind of power and the only effective means of struggle, the subjects may feel helpless in face of a ruler which possesses such vast capacity to wield political violence. Technological developments in modern weaponry, communications, police methods, transportation, computers and the like all contribute to the further concentration of control of effective political violence and to a diminution of what can be called freedom or democracy. All these various factors and related ones may thus help to reduce the capacity of subjects to control political power in a society which has relied upon violence as its supreme sanction and technique of struggle.

B. Nonviolent action and decentralization of power

Nonviolent action appears to have quite different long term effects on the distribution of power in the society. Not only does this technique lack the centralizing effects of political violence, but nonviolent action appears by its very nature to contribute to the diffusion of effective power throughout the society. This diffusion, in turn, is likely to make it easier in the long run for the subjects to control their ruler's exercise of power in the future. This increased potential for popular control means more freedom and more democracy.

There are several reasons why widespread use of nonviolent action in place of political violence tends to diffuse power among the subjects.

These reasons have to do with the greater self-reliance of the people using the technique, as related to leadership, weapons, the more limited power of the post-struggle government, and the reservoir capacity for nonviolent struggle which has been built up against future dangers.

Leadership in nonviolent struggle, although important, is an unstable and often temporary phenomenon, while the dynamics of the technique promote and even require greater self-reliance among the participants. The chances of continuing domination by a leadership group are thereby drastically reduced. Although strong leadership may play an important role in initiating the movement and setting its strategy, as the struggle develops the populace takes up its dominant role in carrying out the noncooperation or defiance, and the original leadership is often imprisoned or otherwise removed by the opponent. A continuing central leadership group then ceases to be so necessary or even possible in many situations. The movement thus tends to become self-reliant, and in extreme situations effectively leaderless. Under severe repression, efficiency in nonviolent action requires that the participants be able to act without reliance on a central leadership group.

A nonviolent struggle movement cannot be centrally controlled by regulation of the supply and distribution of weapons to the combatants and populace, because in nonviolent action there are no material weapons. There are, it is true, a multitude of nonviolent "weapons"—the many specific methods examined in Chapters Three to Eight—but their availability cannot be centrally controlled. The nonviolent actionists depend not on weapons which can be restricted or confiscated or ammunition which may not be freely available, but on such qualities as their bravery, ability to maintain nonviolent discipline, skill in applying the technique and the like. These qualities and skills are likely to develop with use, so that during and at the end of a nonviolent struggle the populace is likely to be more self-reliant and powerful than in a violent struggle when the fighting forces are dependent on the supply of equipment and ammunition. This is important for the distribution of power in the post-struggle society, for people who have, or believe they have, no independent capacity for struggle are likely to be treated by elites as a passive populace to be controlled and acted upon, not as people capable of wielding effective power for their own objectives.

Irving L. Janis and Daniel Katz have suggested that the choice of violent action or nonviolent action may also have significant effects on the *type* of leadership likely to arise in the movement, to be perpetuated in it, and to carry over into the post-struggle society. Violence, they suggest, tends to result in a more brutal, less democratic leadership than does nonviolent action, and also in the long run reduces adherence to the movement's original humanitarian goals as motivating principles for both leaders and participants. "That individuals and groups can be involved in anti-social practices in the interests of desirable social goals and still maintain these goals in relatively pure fashion is a doctrine for which there is little psychological support." They add that ". . . repeated behavior of an anti-social character, though originally in the interests of altruistic social goals, will probably lead to the abandonment of those goals as directing forces for the . . . leaders as well as the followers within any group or organization." Social approval for violence, they continue, is likely to increase the amount of violence in the society by weakening super-ego controls and by releasing latent violence. Where the violence becomes institutionalized, Janis and Katz conclude, even assuming the political "success" of the movement, it tends to lead to rigidity and to the filling of political and social positions involving violence with individuals whose basic personality patterns (deriving satisfaction from such work) are reinforced by rewards of status, salary and social approval.[99]

Nonviolent leaders do not use violent sanctions to maintain their positions and hence are more subject to popular control than leaders of violent movements which may apply violent sanctions against internal opposition. During nonviolent campaigns, their leaders depend for their positions upon voluntarily accepted moral authority, acceptance of their political and strategic judgment, and popular support—not upon any capacity to threaten or use violence against the participants themselves. After the struggle, the leaders who do not accept official positions in the State will have no means of violence for use against the populace to maintain their leadership positions or to impose a nondemocratic regime. In such cases as national independence struggles or social revolutions in which some of the leaders after the conclusion of the conflict accept official positions in the State, that capacity of the State for violence against the populace, as we have seen, will be more limited than it would have been had the struggle been violent. After the nonviolent struggle, then, the State power remains unenlarged while the popular capacity for resistance has increased; greater chances for future popular control and a greater degree of diffused power therefore exist.

Whereas violent struggles tend to erode or destroy the independence of the society's *loci* of power, with nonviolent struggle those groups and institutions are likely to have been strengthened. That increased capacity will in turn contribute to greater institutional vitality, capacity for opposing autocratic tendencies, and to the general diffusion of power in the post-struggle society.

It cannot be expected that a nonviolent campaign for specific objectives will be followed immediately by that society's full rejection of violence in all situations. However, effective use of nonviolent struggle may be a step in the direction of increased substitution of nonviolent for violent sanctions in that society. Increased confidence and understanding of the potential and requirements of the nonviolent technique will need to be accompanied by efforts to work out specific strategies to deal with specific issues, since lasting substitution hinges on the nonviolent alternative being, and being seen to be, effective for each specific conflict. That is, replacement of violence with nonviolent action is likely to be a continuing series of particular substitutions instead of a single sweeping adoption of nonviolent means, regardless of the reason it might be chosen. In addition, changes won by nonviolent means are unlikely to be seen to "require" violence to maintain them, in contrast to changes won by violence. When, to cite a third possibility, the changes have been "given" by the opponent without struggle by the grievance group, those changes may be taken away, either by the donor or some other group, as easily as they were received. However, changes won in struggle by nonviolent action are accompanied by the capacity developed in struggle to defend those changes nonviolently against future threats. Such changes achieved by nonviolent action are therefore likely to be relatively lasting, and not to require political violence to maintain them. [100]

Members of grievance groups which have, respectively, used violent struggle and nonviolent struggle successfully, are likely—following the conflicts—to have different perceptions of their own power in the new situation. With confidence in violence as the real type of power, after a nominally successful violent struggle which has, for example, changed the elite which controls the State, the populace viewing the concentrated capacity for violence held by the new government is likely to see it in comparison as relatively helpless in any possible serious struggle against it. A quite different situation is, however, likely to follow a successful nonviolent struggle. Training in nonviolent "battle" contributes to increased future capacity to apply the technique in crises and to the ability of that populace to control whatever ruler may seek to impose his will on the people. Nirmal Kumar Bose has written that experience using nonviolent action puts people "on their own legs." In contrast to violence which, when all accept it as the "real" power, gives the upper hand to the group which uses it most effectively, nonviolent struggle distributes power among all. Given determination and bravery, every person can apply the nonviolent technique which brings power to each actionist. Consequently, Bose continued, in a nonviolent revolution power "spreads evenly among the masses . . ." [101] This is, of course, a tendency and not a nothing-or-all process. The degree to which power is diffused among the populace, and whether in the course of time this continues and grows or is diminished and largely lost, is dependent on the course of that nonviolent struggle and later events. However, experience in the effective use of nonviolent action "arms" the populace with knowledge of how to wield nonviolent weapons; this technique thereby tends toward the diffusion of power throughout the society and contributes decidedly toward the capacity of the populace to control the ruler should he on future occasions alienate the support of the majority of the subjects. All these indications are suggestive that nonviolent action and political violence may contribute to quite different types of societies.

Gregg argued in the 1930s that the adoption of nonviolent action in place of violence might break the constant circle of the violence of one group leading to violence by the other, and also break the frequent escalation in the extent and severity of violence. [102] If valid, the social consequences of breaking the spiral of violence are obviously important for reducing the amount and intensity of violence, especially political violence. Since violence may be particularly compatible with hierarchical and especially dictatorial systems, the ramifications of such breaks in the spiral of violence may be wide and profound.

CONCLUSION

This book has been an exploration of the nature of nonviolent struggle. We began with an examination of political power, which has been often assumed to derive from violence and to be ultimately controlable only by still greater violence. We discovered that political power derives instead from sources in the society which may be regulated or severed by the withholding or withdrawal of cooperation by the populace. The political power of governments may in fact be very fragile and even the power of dictators may be destroyed by withdrawal of the human assistance which has made their regime possible. At least that was the theory.

The technique of nonviolent action is rooted in that theory of power.

We surveyed its basic characteristics and sketched part of the history of its development. Then we turned to an examination in detail of the multitude of specific methods which fall within that technique, under the general classes of nonviolent protest and persuasion, noncooperation and nonviolent intervention. These methods make possible the application of diverse leverages against the opponent in the effort to achieve the objectives of the actionists: psychological, ideational, economic, social, political, physical and other leverages. Attention then shifted to the complex ways in which this technique may operate in conflict with a violent opponent. The groundwork which may precede the launching of nonviolent action was examined, and some of the basic requirements for the effective use of the technique. Then we focused on the initial impact which the launching of nonviolent action may have on the social situation and the opponent, to the probability of repression and the need for a determined, yet nonviolent, continuation of resistance. The opponent's repression, we saw, may rebound to weaken his power position through the process of political *jiu-jitsu*.

Instead of nonviolent action achieving change in one simple way, we discovered that there were three main processes, or mechanisms, by which change was produced, ranging from conversion of the opponent, so that he now agrees with the nonviolent group—probably the rarest type of change—to nonviolent coercion on the other extreme in which changes are forced, albeit nonviolently, on the opponent, with accommodation falling at midpoint and being the most usual mechanism. Nonviolent struggle also brings changes of various types to the nonviolent group itself, as we examined in this concluding chapter. These changes are especially associated with a new sense of self-respect, self-confidence, and a realization of the power people can wield in controling their own lives through learning to use the nonviolent technique. These changes within the nonviolent group gain greater significance in light of the analysis of power in the first chapter which showed it to derive ultimately from the people who are ruled or otherwise subordinated. The changes in the nonviolent group, the relative strengthening of the non-State institutions of the society in which nonviolent action is used, and the development of a nonviolent struggle capacity by which the opponent's violence may be made impotent, combine to redistribute power in that society.

This book has thus been limited to an attempt to understand the nature of the technique of nonviolent action. Despite its widespread application on many issues against diverse opponents, nonviolent struggle has remained an underdeveloped political technique, largely neglected not only by the officials of governments and leaders of the society's dominant institutions but also by social reformers, avowed revolutionaries, even pacifists, and very importantly also by academics. We are only becoming aware of the past history of this type of conflict and of the vast armory of nonviolent weapons it utilizes. The ways it operates in major struggle to produce change are still new to us and its long term possibilities and significance are still primarily matters of speculation rather than careful analysis based on adequate understanding. One thing is, however, abundantly clear: this is a significant technique of great past importance and of considerable future potential.

As the brief historical survey of the development of this technique showed, nonviolent struggle has in the past century undergone major innovations, development and expansion as compared at least to what we know of its previous history. Certain other characteristics of this same century stand in sharp contrast: the extension and growth of control by centralized States, the development and expansion of depersonalized industrial production, the emergence of total war with World War I and then with World War II the invention of nuclear and other weapons of mass destruction, the development in the 1920s and 1930s of modern totalitarian systems, the deliberate extermination of whole population groups, and the mass killings of still more millions in pursuit of domestic political objectives or in the course of war. Even many of the rebels against the old order have adopted its belief in the omnipotence of political violence, now in the forms of guerrilla warfare, domestic repression, or even nuclear weapons. There have been other similar developments in political violence. Yet it was in this same century that nonviolent action became more significant and powerful than in any previous era.

Nonviolent struggle may now be entering a new phase of its development. One of the most important factors in this phase is the conscious effort to increase our knowledge and understanding of the nature of the technique, to improve its effectiveness, and to extend the areas in which it may be substituted for violence, even as a replacement for military defense. This new phase has begun, but only just, and it remains to be seen how and to what extent it will develop. Once again, it is remarkable that this development in nonviolent alternatives should begin at the same time that important trends in politics, technology, social control, social organization and violence are moving in the opposite direction: toward capacity for super destruction, toward vast State controls over institutions and people, toward computer and other technological aids to regimentation, toward psychological and chemical control of people's behavior, toward an increased police capacity for political surveilance, toward centralized control of the economy by small elites, and even toward genetic control of future mankind. For those of us who still believe that human dignity, creativity, justice and freedom are important, the nonviolent technique of struggle may provide one of our last hopes for effective reversal of the current directions toward dehumanization, regimentation, manipulation, and the dominance of political structures of violence and tyranny.

Such a hope may or may not be achieved, for between our present condition and the current underdeveloped status of the nonviolent technique on the one hand, and a reversal of present trends, on the other, lies a great gap. All the requirements for filling that gap are not yet clear, but it is possible to indicate at least a few of them which are directly associated with nonviolent action.

One step is clearly research and analysis on the nature of this technique. The insights, theories and hypotheses of this study require continual testing, evaluation and modification in light of other cases of nonviolent action, future experience and further research. This book has been intended to stimulate further explorations of the politics of nonviolent action. These explorations include opening this field to a greater degree than hitherto to academic investigation. This is only the beginning.

A related step involves efforts to explore and develop various extensions in the practical application of this technique in place of violence in a variety of specific tasks for meeting pressing problems. These vary widely and may include its potential for securing rights for suppressed minorities, for obtaining, maintaining or extending civil liberties, for expanding social justice, for restructuring social, economic or political institutions, for disintegrating and replacing political dictatorships, for achieving social revolution with freedom, for preventing internal usurpations by *coup d'état* and other political violence, and even as a substitute for military defense in deterring and defeating foreign invasions and foreign-aided *coups*. These and various other areas for basic research and investigation of policy alternatives are outlined elsewhere as parts of a comprehensive program which needs to be launched.[103] Needless to say, this research, analysis and policy exploration must include attention to weaknesses, limitations and possible undesirable ramifications of the nonviolent technique, as well as its more positive potentialities.

Another step is public education using various media to share widely the information we now have or soon gain about the nature of nonviolent action, its requirements and know-how, as well as new proposals for its application to problems for which people now rely upon violence. One of these areas of possible future application would be "civilian defense"—the use of prepared nonviolent resistance to defeat domestic usurpations and foreign invasions. Others might focus on current or anticipated problems of a country or area, such as conflicts of color, poverty, freedoms, institutional restructuring, prevention and disintegration of tyranny and many others. Courses in nonviolent alternatives in schools and universities at all levels would be an important part of such public education and would help develop qualified future researchers on these phenomena.

Then too, there is the field of action. Many people would place this first. While in some ways it is primary, it is given a slightly lower priority here since nonviolent action which is ill-conceived, based on ignorance of the requirements of the technique or of the conditions and issues of the conflict, on poor strategy and tactics and similar inadequacies is likely to be counterproductive in advancing the adoption of nonviolent alternatives. On the other hand, until and unless people have themselves gained experience in the use of this technique for limited objectives, and have observed others applying it also effectively, they will be unlikely or may even be unable to use it in the more difficult and crucial conflicts.

Attention is also needed to the ways in which nonviolent action may be related to milder peaceful ways of action and to regular institutional procedures, either private or governmental ones, for nonviolent action is not a substitute for, but an aid to, other peaceful ways of dealing with problems and carrying out common tasks where they are responsive to popular control.

There are other important things to be done. Each person who is familiar with the needs of his neighborhood, people, country and world will be able to propose and tackle additional problems.

For all its many pages and hundreds of thousands of words, this book is not the last word on nonviolent action. It is hoped that instead it may turn out to be one of the first in this new stage of the development of nonviolent alternatives. If we are to gain new knowledge and increased understanding, and if deliberate efforts are to be made to apply nonviolent action in place of violence in the crucial conflicts of today and tomorrow, then the responsibility must fall on all of us who see these as tasks which need to be accomplished. This means the responsibility is ours. It falls on each of us, on me and on you.

NOTES

1. Erik Erikson, **Identity and the Life Cycle**, in *Psychological Issues* (New York: International Universities Press, 1959), vol. I, monograph 1, p. 31.
2. Lakey, "The Sociological Mechanisms of Nonviolent Action" (thesis), p. 43; *Peace Research Reviews*, vol. II, no. 6 (Dec. 1968), p. 26.
3. Gregg, **The Power of Nonviolence**, pp. 85-86.
4. *Ibid.*, p. 133.
5. Venturi, **Roots of Revolution**, p. 445.
6. Schapiro, **The Communist Party of the Soviet Union**, p. 20.
7. *Ibid.*, p. 28.
8. Harcave, **First Blood**, p. 133.
9. *Ibid.*, p. 189.
10. Eyck, **A History of the Weimar Republic**, vol. I, p. 154.
11. See Gandhi, **Non-violent Resistance**, p. 356; Ind. ed.: **Satyagraha**, p. 356, and Sharp, **Gandhi Wields the Weapon of Moral Power**, pp. 72 and 100.
12. Gandhi, **Non-violent Resistance**, p. 154; Ind. ed.: Satyagraha, p. 154.
13. *Ibid.*, p. 218.
14. Sharp, **Gandhi Wields . . .** , p. 71.
15. Bose, **Selections from Gandhi**, p. 205.
16. Schlesinger, **The Colonial Merchants and the American Revolution**, p. 280.
17. M. K. Gandhi, **Satyagraha in South Africa**, p. 203.
18. Watt, **Dare Call it Treason**, p. 183.
19. Lenin, "Lecture on the 1905 Revolution," in Lenin, **Selected Works in Three Volumes**, vol. I, p. 792.
20. Seifert, **Conquest by Suffering**, p. 174.
21. Gregg, **The Power of Nonviolence**, p. 55. Gregg also argues that fear, anger, and hatred are closely related emotionally, and that therefore the capacity to control or replace one of them is associated with the capacity similarly to deal with the others. See pp. 66-67.
22. Lakey, "The Sociological Mechanisms . . ." (thesis), p. 63; *Peace Research Reviews*, vol. II, no. 6 (Dec. 1968), p. 43.
23. See Bondurant, **Conquest of Violence**, p. 29.
24. Gandhi, **Non-violent Resistance**, p. 8; Ind. ed.: **Satyagraha**, p. 8.
25. Gregg, **The Power of Nonviolence**, p. 64.
26. Jawaharlal Nehru, **The Discovery of India** (New York: John Day, 1946), p. 361.
27. **Nehru, An Autobiography**, p. 69.
28. *Ibid.*, p. 178.
29. Nehru, **Toward Freedom**, p. 129.

30. King, **Stride Toward Freedom,** p. 119; Br. ed.: p. 140. See also Peck, **Freedom Ride,** pp. 51-54.

31. Lomax, **The Negro Revolt,** p. 137.

32. Frederic Solomon and Jacob R. Fishman, "The Psychosocial Meaning of Nonviolence in Student Civil Rights Activities," *Psychiatry,* vol. XXVII (1964), p. 96.

33. See Hiller, **The Strike,** p. 19.

34. See Gandhi, **Satyagraha in South Africa,** p. 199.

35. Lakey, "The Sociological Mechanisms of Nonviolent Action," p. 45; *Peace Research Reviews,* vol. II, no. 6, p. 28.

36. Hiller, **The Strike,** pp. 22 and 168-169.

37. Luthuli, **Let My People Go.** p. 10.

38. Sharp, **Gandhi Wields . . . ,** pp. 67-68 and 188.

39. Waskow, **From Race Riot to Sit-in,** p. 37.

40. Gregg, **The Power of Nonviolence,** p. 85.

41. Nehru, **An Autobiography,** p. 70.

42. Lakey, "The Sociological Mechanisms . . ." (thesis), pp. 44-45; *Peace Research Reviews,* vol. II, no. 6 (Dec. 1968), pp. 27-28.

43. Hiller, **The Strike,** p. 19.

44. Lakey, "The Sociological Mechanisms . . . ," p. 74; *Peace Research Reviews,* vol. II, no. 6, pp. 51-52.

45. Hiller, **The Strike,** p. 88.

46. Farmer, **Freedom – When?** pp. 17-18.

47. Nehru, **India and the World,** p. 173.

48. King, **Stride Toward Freedom,** p. 7; Br. ed.: p. 9.

49. Sharp, **Gandhi Wields . . . ,** pp. 44-45.

50. Warmbrunn, **The Dutch Under German Occupation, 1940-1945,** p. 111.

51. Symons, **The General Strike,** p. 53.

52. Inez Haynes Irwin, **The Story of the Woman's Party** (New York: Harcourt, Brace and Co., 1921), p. 219. I am grateful to George Lakey for this and the next reference.

53. Mary Windsor, "The Title is Probably This Long," *The Annals of the American Academy of Political and Social Science,"* (Season, 1914).

54. Nehru, **An Autobiography,** p. 70.

55. Farmer, **Freedom – When?** pp. 67 and 80-81.

56. Ebert, "Theory and Practice of Nonviolent Resistance," MS p. 249.

57. Luthuli, **Let My People Go,** p. 136.

58. Waskow, **From Race Riot to Sit-in,** p. 264.

59. Farmer, **Freedom – When?** pp. 72 and 76.

60. Lenin, "Lecture on the 1905 Revolution," in Lenin, **Selected Works in Three Volumes,** vol. I, pp. 789-792.

61. Solomon and Fishman, "The Psychosocial Meaning of Nonviolence in Student Civil Rights Activities," *Psychiatry,* vol. XXVII (1964), p. 97.

62. Bondurant, **Conquest of Violence,** pp. 131-145. Quotations are respectively from pp. 132 and 144.

63. Frank, **Sanity and Survival,** pp. 270-271. He cites C. M. Pierce and L. J. West,

"Six Years of Sit-ins: Psychodynamic Causes and Effects," in *International Journal of Social Psychiatry*, vol. XII (1966), pp. 29-34, and Solomon and Fishman, "The Psychosocial Meaning of Nonviolence in Student Civil Rights Activities."

64. King, **Stride Toward Freedom**, pp. 177-178.

65. Hentoff, **The New Equality**, p. 55.

66. *Ibid.*

67. Farmer, **Freedom – When?** pp. 35-36.

68. Solomon and Fishman, "The Psychosocial Meaning of Nonviolence in Student Civil Rights Activities," p. 99.

69. F. Solomon, W. L. Walker, G. O'Connor, and J. R. Fishman, "Civil Rights Activity and Reduction in Crime Among Negroes," *Archives of General Psychiatry*, vol. XII (March 1965), pp. 227-236.

70. Lakey, "The Sociological Mechanisms . . . (thesis), pp. 74-75; *Peace Research Reviews*, vol. II, no. 6, p. 52.

71. Gregg, **The Power of Nonviolence**, p. 63.

72. See Janis and Katz, "The Reduction of Intergroup Hostility" p. 93.

73. *Ibid.*, pp. 93-95.

74. Gregg, **The Power of Nonviolence**, pp. 45, 47, and 60-61.

75. Janis and Katz, "The Reduction of Intergroup Hostility" pp. 88 and 90-93.

76. See Sharp, "The Need of a Functional Substitute for War" *International Relations* (London), vol. III, no. 3 (April 1967), pp. 187-207.

77. Hiller, **The Strike**, pp. 30, 90, 19 and 17.

78. Morgan and Morgan, **The Stamp Act Crisis**, pp. 368-369.

79. Gipson, **The British Empire Before the American Revolution**, vol. XII, **The Triumphant Empire: Britain Sails into the Storm, 1770-1776**, p. 244. On other general indications of this tendency, see Schlesinger, **The Colonial Merchants . . .** , pp. 371ff. and *passim.*

80. Harcave, **First Blood**, pp. 116-117.

81. Kuper, **Passive Resistance in South Africa**, p. 215 and 146. See also Luthuli, **Let My People Go**, pp. 125 and 192.

82. Miller, **Nonviolence**, p. 275. See also Luthuli, **Let My People Go**, p. 180.

83. Hentoff, **The New Equality**, p. 205. For mention of a similar effect in Chicago, see p. 206.

84. Gandhi, **Non-violent Resistance**, p. 152; Ind. ed.: **Satyagraha**, p. 152.

85. Bondurant, **Conquest of Violence**, p. 186. See also Hiller, **The Strike**, p. 31.

86. King, **Stride Toward Freedom**, pp. 46, 65, and 69-74, 120-122 and 152-154.

87. Griffith, **The Resurrection of Hungary**, p. 170.

88. On the theory and content of the constructive program, see M. K. Gandhi, **Constructive Programme: Its Meaning and Place** (pamphlet; Ahmedabad: Navajivan Publishing House, 1941 and later), and Sharp, "The Constructive Programme," *Mankind* (Hyderabad), vol. I, no. 12 (July 1957), pp. 1102-1112, and Dhawan, **The Political Philosophy of Mahatma Gandhi**, pp. 190-208.

89. Gandhi, **Constructive Programme**, pp. 5 and 30 (1957 edition), and Dhawan, **The Political Philosophy of Mahatma Gandhi**, pp. 191-193.

90. See Gipson, **The Coming of the Revolution, 1763-1775**, pp. 181 and 187, and Schlesinger, **The Colonial Merchants . . .** , pp. 97, 106-107, 109-110, 112, 117, 121-123, 128, 130-131, 140, 143, 147, 151-152, 243, 369-370, 482, 492,

500-502, 517-518, 524, 528 and 610.

91. See Harcave, **First Blood**, pp. 110-111, 134, 143-144, 154, 171, 176-177 and 215.

92. Morgan and Morgan, **The Stamp Act Crisis**, pp. 203 and 243.

93. Schlesinger, **The Colonial Merchants . . .** , p. 114.

94. Schlesinger, **The Colonial Merchants . . .** , pp. 423-424 and 432.

95. Harcave, **First Blood**, pp. 77, 79-81, 179, 181, 183-184, 225 and 174. The quotation is from p. 200.

96. Tocqueville, **Democracy in America**, vol. I, pp. 9, 92-93, 333-334, and vol. II, pp. 93, 258, 271-272, and 296. See also Jouvenel, **Power**, pp. 244-246 and Gaetano Mosca, **The Ruling Class** (New York and London: McGraw-Hill, 1939), p. 134.

97. Jouvenel, **Power**, pp. 18-22 and 244-246.

98. Quincy Wright, **A Study of War** (Chicago: University of Chicago Press, 1942), vol. I, pp. 232-242, 302 and esp. 311; Bronislaw Malinowski, "An Anthropological Analysis of War," *American Journal of Sociology*, vol. XLVI, no. 4, esp. p. 545; and Malinowski, **Freedom and Civilization** (New York: Roy Publishers, 1944), esp. pp. 265 and 305.

99. Irving L. Janis and Daniel Katz, "The Reduction of Intergroup Hostility," in *Journal of Conflict Resolution,* vol. III, no. 1 (March 1959), pp. 90-91.

100. See Sharp, **Gandhi Wields . . .** , p. 125, and Gandhi, **Non-violence in Peace and War**, vol. I, pp. 87 and 235, and vol. II, p. 340. Gregg writes: "Reforms will come to stay only if the masses acquire and retain the ability to make a firm veto by mass nonviolent resistance. . . . Hence reformers would be wise to lay less stress upon advocacy of their special changes and concentrate on the teaching of nonviolent resistance. Once that tool is mastered, we can make all sorts of permanent reforms." Gregg, **The Power of Nonviolence**, p. 146.

101. Bose, **Studies in Gandhism,** p. 148.

102. See Gregg, **The Power of Nonviolence**, p. 134.

103. See Sharp, **Exploring Nonviolent Alternatives** (Boston: Porter Sargent, 1970), pp. 73-113.

Appendix:
Summary of Factors Determining the Outcome of Nonviolent Struggles

The factors which determine the outcome of nonviolent struggles may be grouped in four classes: the factors associated with the social system, the opponent group, third parties and the nonviolent group. Those associated with the social situation are the most stable ones, within the limitations of which nonviolent action must usually operate. Long-run changes in these are possible, but within the time span of a nonviolent action struggle they cannot be relied upon, except in certain circumstances (item A.4, below). The remaining factors in the other three groups are mostly highly variable during the course of the struggle. The very nature of the dynamics of nonviolent action not only depends upon such changes but produces them, probably to a much greater degree than in comparable violent struggles. Almost all of these will constantly vary during the struggle; the only question is whether the changes will strengthen relatively the nonviolent actionists or their opponent.

A. *Factors in the social situation.*
    1. The degree of conflict of interest between the two groups.
    2. The social distance between the groups.

3. The degree to which beliefs and norms are shared by the two groups.
4. The degree to which the grievance group (and in some cases the opponent group) consists of atomized individuals with most social and political power concentrated in a center, or of social groups and institutions (*loci* of power) capable of wielding and withholding power.

B. *Factors associated with the opponent group.*
1. The degree to which the opponent is dependent for his sources of power upon those withdrawing their cooperation and obedience.
2. The degree of noncompliance which the opponent can tolerate without his position being seriously endangered; the less nonconformity and dissent normally allowed, the greater challenge it will be when it does occur.
3. The degree to which the opponent and the opponent's usual supporters are convinced of the rightness of their views and policies and/or their necessity in the situation.
4. The degree of conviction among the opponent and his usual supporters in the rightness of and justification for the means of repression used against the nonviolent actionists.
5. The means of control, including repression, which the opponent may use in an effort to defeat the nonviolent challenge.
6. How long the opponent can continue to maintain his position and power in face of the nonviolent action.
7. The degree to which the opponent's agents of repression, administrators and other aides serve him efficiently or refrain from doing so, whether by deliberate inefficiency or by mutiny.
8. The degree and type of support or opposition within the opponent group for the opponent's policy and repression of the nonviolent group; this refers to the general population as distinguished from special agents, aides, etc.
9. The opponent's estimate of the future course of the movement, the chances of victory or defeat, and the consequences of either.

C. *Factors associated with third parties.*
1. The degree to which third parties become sympathetic to either the opponent or the nonviolent group.
2. The degree to which the opinions and good will of third parties are important to the opponent and to the nonviolent group respectively.
3. The degree to which third parties move from a noninvolved position to active support for, or to noncooperation with, or obstruction of, either of the contending groups.
4. The degree to which either of the contending groups will be assisted by such support or hindered by such noncooperation or obstruction.

D. *Factors associated with the nonviolent group.*
1. The opportunity and ability to organize nonviolent action *or* to act spontaneously on a group level in accordance with the requirements of nonviolent action.
2. The degree to which the nonviolent actionists and the general grievance group are convinced of the rightness of their cause.
3. The degree of confidence in nonviolent action among the nonviolent

actionists and the general grievance group.

4. The choice of the methods of nonviolent action, especially whether these are symbolic or involve noncooperation and intervention, and whether they are within the capacity of the nonviolent actionists.

5. The degree of soundness of the strategy and tactics chosen or accepted for the struggle.

6. Whether the demands of the nonviolent group are within their capacity to achieve them.

7. The relative ability of the nonviolent actionists to practise the technique as influenced, for example, by their past experience or their understanding of it.

8. The degree of voluntarily accepted discipline within the nonviolent group, so that the plans are carried out effectively, with a maximum of clarity and unity of action.

9. The numbers of nonviolent actionists, seen within the context of the quality of the movement and the mechanism by which change is sought.

10. The degree to which the nonviolent actionists are aided or hindered by the general grievance group, on whose behalf they may be acting.

11. The balance between the degree of terror the opponent is able and willing to use and the degree of determination to act (regardless of sanctions), due to fearlessness, courage or willingness to accept suffering as the price of change.

12. The length of time that the nonviolent actionists are able and willing to continue their course of action.

13. The ability of the nonviolent actionists to keep the struggle nonviolent.

14. The capacity of the nonviolent actionists to maintain openness and nonsecretiveness in their actions in normal circumstances.

15. The presence and quality of some type of effective leadership, formal or informal, or the ability of the actionists to act with unity, and discipline, and wisely chosen strategy, tactics and methods without a significant distinguishable leadership group.

16. The degree to which the nonviolent actionists can demonstrate the attitudes and actions which may help convert the opponent.

17. The degree to which the nonviolent actionists and the general grievance group control their own sources of power or to which these are subject to control by the opponent.

Most of these factors, especially in the last three groups, it is emphasized once again, are potentially subject to considerable and constant variation during the course of the nonviolent action struggle. The outcome is then determined by the direction and extent of these changes. The degree to which these factors, directly or indirectly, are subject to the control of the members of the grievance group is disproportionately high in nonviolent action as compared with the factors influencing the outcome of struggles using violent techniques.

Bibliography

Abramowitz, Isidore, **The Great Prisoners: The First Anthology of Literature** **Written in Prison.** New York: E.P. Dutton and Co., 1946.

Aczell, Tamas and Tibor Meray, **The Revolt of the Mind: A Case History of Intellectual Resistance Behind the Iron Curtain.** New York: Frederick A. Praeger, 1959. London: Thames & Hudson, 1960.

Adams, Henry, **History of the United States During the Second Administration of Thomas Jefferson,** vol. II. New York: Charles Scribner's Sons, 1890.

Agar, Herbert, ed., **The Formative Years,** vols. I and II. Edited from the writings of Henry Adams. Boston: Houghton Mifflin, 1947. London Collins, 1948.

Alinsky, Saul, a conversation with Marion K. Sanders, "The Professional Radical, 1970," *Harpers Magazine,* vol. 240, no. 1436 (January 1970), pp. 35-42.

American Archives, Fourth Series, vol. I, no. 18. Washington, D.C.: M. St. Clarke and Peter Force, 1937.

American Foreign Policy, 1950-1955: Basic Documents, vol. II. Washington, D.C.: Department of State, 1957.

American Foreign Policy: Current Documents, 1956. Washington, D.C.: Department of State, 1959.

American Foreign Policy: Current Documents, 1960. Washington, D.C.: Department of State, 1964.

Amundsen, Sverre S., general editor, **Kirkenes Ferda, 1942.** Oslo: J.W. Cappelens Forlag, 1946.

Aptheker, Herbert, **American Negro Slave Revolts.** New York: International Publishers, 1964.

"A Rhode Islander." See "Rhode Islander."

Austin, John, **Lectures on Jurisprudence of the Philosophy of Positive Law.** Two vols. Fifth edition. London: John Murray, 1911 (orig. 1861).

Baer, G. W., **The Coming of the Italian-Ethiopian War.** Cambridge, Mass.: Harvard University Press, 1957.

Bagby, Jeanne, "Witness Against Germ Warfare," *Christian Century*, vol. 76, 23 September 1959.

Bailey, Thomas A., **A Diplomatic History of the American People.** Sixth edition. New York: Appleton-Century-Crofts, 1958.

Bakke, E. Wight and Charles Kerr, **Unions, Management and the Public.** New York: Harcourt, Brace & Co., 1948.

Barbash, Jack, **Labor Unions in Action: A Study of the Mainsprings of Unionism.** New York: Harper and Bros., 1948.

Barker, J. Ellis, **Modern Germany: Its Rise, Growth, Downfall and Future.** New York: E. P. Dutton & Co., 1919.

Barnard, Chester I., **The Functions of the Executive.** Cambridge, Mass.: Harvard University Press, 1948.

Barraclough, Solon L., "Agricultural Policy and Land Reform." Duplicated MS. 106 pp. Conference on Key Problems of Economic Policy in Latin America, University of Chicago, 6-9 November 1966.

———, "Farmers' Organizations in Planning and Implementing Rural Programs." Duplicated MS. 22 and iv pp. Prepared for a study being edited by Professor Raanan Weitz.

Barton, Paul, "The Strike Mechanism in Soviet Concentration Camps," in *Monthly Information Bulletin of the International Commission Against Concentration Camp Practices* (now titled *Saturn*), (Brussels), no. 4 (August-November 1955).

Bauer, Raymond A. and Alice H., "Day to Day Resistance to Slavery," *Journal of Negro History,* vol. XXVII, no. 4 (Oct. 1942), pp. 388-419.

Belfrage, Sally, **Freedom Summer.** New York: Viking Press, 1965.

Bennett, Jeremy, "The Resistance Against the German Occupation of Denmark 1940-5," in Adam Roberts, ed., **Civilian Resistance as a National Defence,** pp. 154-172.

Bentham, Jeremy, **A Fragment on Government.** London: Oxford University Press, Humphrey Milford, 1931 (orig. 1891).

Berger, Carl, **The Korea Knot: A Military-Political History.** Philadelphia: University of Pennsylvania Press, 1950.

Berger, Suzanne, **Peasants Against Politics: Rural Organization in Brittany 1911-1967.** Cambridge, Mass.: Harvard University Press, 1972.

"The Berkeley Free Speech Controversy," prepared by "A Fact-Finding Committee of Graduate Political Scientists." Duplicated. Berkeley, Calif: The Authors, 1964.

Bernard, L.L., **Social Control in Its Sociological Aspects.** New York: Macmillan, 1939.

Blaustein, Albert P. and Clarence Clyde Ferguson, Jr., **Desegregation and the Law: The Meaning and Effect of the School Segregation Cases**. New Brunswick, New Jersey: Rutgers University Press, 1957.

Bloom, Murray Teigh, "The World's Greatest Counterfeiters," *Harpers Magazine*, vol. 215, no. 1286 (July 1957), pp. 47-53.

Blum, Robert, **The United States and China in World Affairs**. Ed. by A. Doak Barnett. New York: McGraw-Hill (for the Council on Foreign Relations), 1966.

de La Boétie, Etienne, *"Discours de la Servitude Volontaire,"* in **Oeuvres Completes d'Etienne de la Boétie**, pp. 1-57. Paris: J. Rouam & Coe., 1892.

———, **Anti-Dictator: The "Discours sur la servitude volontaire" of Etienne de la Boétie**, New York: Columbia University Press, 1942.

Bondurant, Joan V., **Conquest of Violence: The Gandhian Philosophy of Conflict**. Princeton, New Jersey: Princeton University Press. London: Oxford University Press, 1958.

Bontemps, Arna, **100 Years of Negro Freedom**. New York: Dodd, Mead & Co., 1962.

Borton, Hugh, **Peasant Uprisings in Japan of the Tokugawa Period**. Second Edition. New York: Paragon Book Reprint Corp., 1968. First published in *The Transactions of the Asiatic Society of Japan* (Second Series), vol. XVI, 1938.

Bose, Nirmal Kumar, **Selections from Gandhi**. Ahmedabad: Navajivan, 1948.

———, Studies in Gandhism. Calcutta: Indian Associated Publishing Co., 1947.

Brailsford, H.N., **Rebel India**. New York: New Republic, Inc., 1931. London: Leonard Stein (with Victor Gollancz), 1931.

Brant, Stefan, **The East German Rising**. New York: Frederick A. Praeger, 1957. London: Thames and Hudson, 1955.

Brinton, Crane, **The Anatomy of Revolution**. New York: Vintage Books, 1962.

Brockway, A. Fenner, **Non-co-operation in other Lands**. Madras: Tagore & Co., 1921.

Browne, Edward G., **The Persian Revolution of 1905-1909**. Cambridge: University Press, 1910.

Buckler, W. H., "Labour Disputes in the Province of Asia Minor," in W.H. Buckler and W.M. Culder, eds., **Anatolian Studies Presented to Sir William Mitchell Ramsay**. Manchester: University Press, 1923.

Bullock, Alan, **Hitler: A Study in Tyranny**. Revised edition. New York: Harper and Row, 1962. London: Odhams, 1964.

Busk, Sir Douglas, **The Craft of Diplomacy: How to Run a Diplomatic Service**. New York: Frederick A. Praeger, 1967.

Carter, April, **Direct Action** (pamphlet). London: Peace News, 1962.

Case, Clarence Marsh, **Nonviolent Coercion: A Study in Methods of Social Pressure**. New York: The Century Co., 1923.

Catt, Carrie Chapman and Nettie Rogers Shuller, **Woman Suffrage and Politics: The Inner Study of the Suffrage Movement**. New York: Charles Scribner's Sons, 1923.

Chakravarty, Amiya, **A Saint at Work. A View of Gandhi's Work and Message** (pamphlet). William Penn Lecture 1950. Philadelphia: Young Friends Movement of the Philadelphia Yearly Meetings, 1950.

Chang, Chung-li, **The Chinese Gentry: Studies in their Role in Nineteenth-**

Century Chinese Society. Seattle: University of Washington Press, 1955.

Charques, Richard, The Twilight of Imperial Russia. Fair Lawn, N.J.: Essential Books, 1959. London: Phoenix House, 1958.

Chaudury, P.C. Ray, Gandhiji's First Struggle in India. Ahmedabad: Navajivan, 1955.

Clark, Evans, ed., Boycotts and Peace. New York and London: Harper & Bros., 1932.

von Clausewitz, General Carl, On War. Three volumes. Trans. by Col. J.J. Graham. Edited by Col. F.N. Maude. New York: Barnes and Noble, 1956. London: Routledge and Kegan Paul, 1956.

Coleman, McAlister, Men and Coal. New York: Farrar and Reinhart, 1943.

Coleman, Peter J., The Transformation of Rhode Island 1790-1860. Providence, R.I.: American History Research Center, Brown University Press, 1963.

Commager, Henry Steele, ed., Documents of American History. New York and London: Appleton-Century-Crofts, 1948.

Comte, Auguste, The Positive Philosophy of Auguste Comte. Two volumes. London: George Bell & Sons, 1896.

Contempt (no author). Chicago: Swallow Press, 1970.

Coser, Lewis, The Functions of Social Conflict. Glencoe, Ill.: The Free Press, 1956.

Cottam, Richard W., Nationalism in Iran. Pittsburg: University of Pittsburg Press, 1964.

Cowell, F.R., The Revolutions of Ancient Rome. New York: Frederick A. Praeger, 1962. London: Thames and Hudson, 1962.

Craig, Gordon A., "Totalitarian Diplomacy," in Lawrence W. Martin, ed., Diplomacy in Modern European History, pp. 74-92. New York: Macmillan, 1966. London: Collier-Macmillan, 1966.

Crankshaw, Edward, Gestapo: Instrument of Tyranny. New York: Viking Press, 1956. London: Putnam, 1956.

Cremeans, Charles D., The Arabs and the World: Nasser's Arab Nationalist Policy. New York and London: Frederick A. Praeger (for the Council on Foreign Relations), 1963.

de Crespigny, Anthony, "The Nature and Methods of Non-violent Coercion," Political Studies, (London), vol. XII, no. 2 (June 1964), pp. 256-265.

Cressey, Donald R., ed., The Prison: Studies in Institutional Organization and Change. New York: Holt, Rinehart and Winston, 1961.

Crook, Wilfred H., Communism and the General Strike. Hamden, Connecticut: The Shoestring Press, 1960.

———, "General Strike," Encyclopedia of the Social Sciences, vol. VI, pp. 607-612.

———. The General Strike: A Study of Labor's Tragic Weapon in Theory and Practice. Chapel Hill: University of North Carolina Press, 1931.

Dallin, Alexander, German Rule in Russia, 1941-1945: A Study of Occupation Policies. New York: St. Martin's Press, 1957. London: Macmillan, 1957.

Daniels, Dan, "Non-violent Actions in Canada," in Our Generation Against Nuclear War (Montreal), vol. III. no. 1 (June 1964).

Davidson, Philip, Propaganda and the American Revolution. Chapel Hill: University of North Carolina Press, 1941.

Davis, John P., **The American Negro Reference Book**. Englewood Cliffs, N.J.: Prentice-Hall, 1966.

Davison, W. Phillips, **The Berlin Blockade**. Princeton, N.J.: Princeton University Press, 1958.

Deanesly, Margaret, **A History of the Medieval Church, 590-1500**. London: Methuen & Co., 1965.

Delarue, Jacques, **The Gestapo: A History of Horror**. New York: William Morrow, 1964.

DeMarco, Margaret, "The Use of Non-violent Direct Action, Tactics and Strategy by American Indians." Unpublished student research paper. Upland School of Social Change, Chester, Pa., July 1968.

"Demonstrators—" (leaflet). London: Committee for Direct Action Against Nuclear War, 1958.

Department of State, United States Government. See also **American Foreign Policy**. Department of State *Bulletin*, vol. XLVI.

Desai, Mahadev, **The Epic of Travancore**. Ahmedabad: Navajivan, 1937.

——, **The Story of Bardoli**. Ahmedabad: Navajivan Publishing House, 1929.

Deutsch, Karl W., "Cracks in the Monolith: Possibilities and Patterns of Disintegration in Totalitarian Systems," in Carl J. Friedrich, ed., **Totalitarianism**, pp. 308-333. Cambridge, Mass.: Harvard University Press, 1954.

Deutscher, Isaac, **The Prophet Armed: Trotsky: 1879-1921**. New York and London: Oxford University Press, 1963.

——, **Stalin: A Political Biography**. New York and London: Oxford University Press, 1961.

Dhawan, Gopinath, **The Political Philosophy of Mahatma Gandhi**. Third revised edition. Ahmedabad: Navajivan, 1962.

"Discipline for Public Witness Demonstrators" (leaflet). New York: various peace organizations, 1962.

Diwakar, Ranganath R., **Satyagraha: Its Technique and History**. Bombay: Hind Kitabs, 1946.

Drake, St. Clair, and Horace R. Cayton, **Black Metropolis: A Study of Negro Life in a Northern City**. New York: Harcourt Brace, 1945.

Dulles, Forster Rhea, **Labor in America: A History**. New York: Thomas Y. Crowell, Co., 1949.

Dunne, John Gregory, **Delano: The Story of the California Grape Strike**. New York: Ferrar, Straus & Giroux, 1967.

Ebert, Theodor, "Effects of Repression by the Invader," *Peace News* (London), 19 March, 1965.

——, "Nonviolent Resistance Against Communist Regimes?," pp. 175-194, in Roberts, ed.: *Civilian Resistance as a National Defence*, pp. 175-194.

——, "Organization in Civilian Defence," in Roberts, ed., *ibid.*, pp. 266-273.

——, "Theory and Practice of Nonviolent Resistance: A Model of a Campaign". MS. Unpublished English translation (by Hilda Morris) of a doctoral thesis in political science presented at the University of Erlangen, Germany, 1965. A revision of this thesis has now been published entitled: **Gewaltfrier Aufstand: Alternative zum Bürgerkrieg**. Freiburg: Verlag Rombach, 1968. Paperback abridgement: **Gewaltfrier Aufstand: Alternative zum Bürgerkrieg**. Frankfurt am Main and Hamburg: Fischerbücherei GmbH, 1970.

Ehrlich, Karl, (pseud. for Karl Raloff), "*Den Ikke-Voldelige Modstand, Der*

Kvalte Kapp-Kupet," in Ehrlich, Lindberg and Jacobsen, **Kamp Uden Vaaben,** pp. 194-202.

———, *"Ruhrkampen,"* in Ehrlich, Lindberg and Jacobsen, **Kamp Uden Vaaben,** pp. 181-193.

Ehrlich, Karl, Niels Lindberg and Gammelgaard Jacobsen, **Kamp Uden Vaaben: Ikke-Vold som Kampmiddel mod Krig og Undertrykkelse.** Copenhagen: Levin & Munksgaard, Ejnar Munksgaard, 1937.

Elliott, W. Y., "Force, Political," **Encyclopedia of the Social Sciences,** vol. VI, p. 338. New York: Macmillan, 1935.

Engels, Frederick, **Anti-Dühring.** Moscow: Foreign Languages Publishing House, 1954.

Erikson, Erik, **Gandhi's Truth: On the Origins of Militant Nonviolence.** New York: W. W. Norton & Co., 1969.

———, **Identity and the Life Cycle,** in *Psychological Issues,* vol. I, monograph 1. New York: International Universities Press, 1959.

European Resistance Movements, 1939-1945. First International Conference on the History of the Resistance Movements held at Liège-Bruxelles-Breendonk, 14-17 September 1958. (No editor listed.) Oxford: Pergamon Press, 1960.

Eyck, Erich, **A History of the Weimar Republic,** vol. I, **From the Collapse of the Empire to Hindenburg's Election.** Cambridge, Mass.: Harvard University Press, 1962.

Fairbank, John King, **The United States and China.** Cambridge, Mass.: Harvard University Press, 1958.

Farmer, James. **Freedom—When?** New York: Random House, 1965.

Faulkner, William. **A Fable.** New York: Random House, 1954.

Fehrenback, T. R. **This Kind of War.** New York: Macmillan, 1963.

The Fifty States Report. Submitted to the Commission on Civil Rights by the State Advisory Committees, 1961. Washington, D. C.: U.S. Government Printing Office, 1961.

Fischer, Louis. **The Life of Lenin.** New York: Harper and Row, 1965. London: Weidenfeld and Nicolson, 1965.

———, **The Life of Mahatma Gandhi.** New York: Harpers, 1950.

Fitch, John A., "Strikes and Lockouts," **Encyclopedia of the Social Sciences,** vol. XIV, p. 422. New York: Macmillan, 1935.

Fleischer, Wilfred, **Sweden: The Welfare State.** New York: John Day, 1956.

Flexner, Eleanor, **Century of Struggle.** Cambridge, Mass.: Harvard University Press, 1959.

Fogg, Richard W., "Jazz Under the Nazis," in **Music 66,** *"Down Beat's* Annual,"* 1966, pp. 97-99.

Foley, Hamilton, **Woodrow Wilson's Case for the League of Nations.** Princeton, N.J.: Princeton University Press, 1933. London: Humphrey Milford, Oxford University Press, 1933.

Follett, Mary, **Creative Experience.** New York and London: Longmans, Green & Co., 1924.

Fontaine, André, **History of the Cold War: From the October Revolution to the Korean War 1917-1950.** New York: Pantheon Books, 1968.

Ford, Paul Leicester, ed., **The Works of Thomas Jefferson.** New York and London: G. P. Putnam's Sons, 1904.

Forster, H. O. Arnold, *The Truth About the Land League, Leaders and its Teaching* (pamphlet). London: National Press Agency, Ltd. (published for the Property Defence Association), 1883.

Foster, William Z., **The Great Steel Strike and Its Lessons**. New York: B. W. Huebsch, 1920.

Fox, George. See Nickalls, J.L., ed.

Frank, Jerome D., **Sanity and Survival: Psychological Aspects of War and Peace**. New York: Random House, and Vintage Books, 1968.

Frazier, E. Franklin, **Race and Culture Contacts in the Modern World**. Boston: Beacon Press, 1957.

Friedman, Philip, "Jewish Resistance to Nazism: Its Various Forms and Aspects," in **European Resistance Movements, 1939-1945**, pp. 195-214.

Friedrich, Carl J., ed., **Totalitarianism**. Cambridge, Mass.: Harvard University Press, 1954.

Fromm, Erich, **Escape from Freedom**. New York: Holt Rinehart and Winston, 1961. British ed.: **The Fear of Freedom**. London: Routledge and Kegan Paul, 1961.

Galenson, Walter, **Labor in Norway**, Cambridge, Mass.: Harvard University Press, 1949.

Galtung, Johan, "On the Effects of International Economic Sanctions, with Examples from the Case of Rhodesia," **World Politics**, vol. XIX, no. 3 (April 1967), pp. 378-416.

Galtung, Johan and Arne Naess, **Gandhis Politiske Etikk**. Oslo: Tanum, 1955.

Gandhi, M.K., **An Autobiography or the Story of My Experiments with Truth**. Ahmedabad: Navajivan Publishing House, 1956.

——, **The Constructive Programme** (pamphlet). Ahmedabad: Navajivan, 1941.

——, **Economics of Khadi**. Ahmedabad: Navajivan, 1941.

——, **Hind Swaraj or Indian Home Rule**. Ahmedabad: Navajivan, 1958.

——, **Non-violence in Peace and War**. Two volumes. Ahmedabad: Navajivan, 1948 and 1949.

——, **Non-violent Resistance**. New York: Schocken Books, 1967. Indian ed.: **Satyagraha**. Ahmedabad: Navajivan, 1951.

——, **Satyagraha in South Africa**, Trans. from the Gujarati by Valji Govindji Desai. Revised second edition. Ahmedabad: Navajivan, 1950.

——, **Young India**, vol. I. Triplicane, Madras: S. Ganesan, 1922.

Gerassi, John, **Great Fear in Latin America**. New York: Collier, 1965.

Gerland, Brigitte, "How the Great Vorkuta Strike was Prepared," and "The Great Labor Camp Strike at Vorkuta," in **The Militant** (New York), 28 February and 7 March 1955.

Gerth, Hans and C. Wright Mills, **Character and Social Structure**. New York: Harcourt, Brace & Co., 1953. London: Routledge and Kegan Paul, 1954.

Gerth, Hans, and C. Wright Mills, editors, From **Max Weber: Essays in Sociology**. New York: Oxford University Press, Galaxy Books, 1958 (orig. 1946). London: Kegan Paul, Trench, Trabner and Co., 1948.

Geyl, Pieter, **The Revolt of the Netherlands 1555-1609**. New York: Barnes and Noble, 1958. London: Ernest Benn, 1962.

Gipson, Lawrence Henry, **The British Empire Before the American Revolution**, vol. X, **The Triumphant Empire: Thunder-clouds Gather in the West, 1763-1766**, vol. XI, **The Triumphant Empire: The Rumbling of the Coming Storm, 1766-1770**, and vol. XII, **The Triumphant Empire: Britain Sails into the Storm, 1770-1776**. New York: Alfred A. Knopf, 1961-1965.

——, The Coming of the Revolution, 1763-1775. New York and Evanston: Harper Torchbooks, 1962.

Gleditsch, Nils Petter, ed., Kamp Uten Våpen: En Antologi. Oslo: Pax Forlag, 1965.

Godwin, William, Enquiry Concerning Political Justice and its Influence on Morals and Happiness. Two volumes. London: G. G. and J. Robinson, 1796.

Goldberg, Art., "Negro Self-Help," New Republic, vol. 156, no. 23 (10 June 1967), p. 6.

Goldhamer, Herbert and Edward A. Shils, "Power and Status," American Journal of Sociology, vol. XLV, no. 2 (September, 1939), pp. 171-180.

Goldman, Emma, The Individual Society and the State (pamphlet). Chicago: Free Society Forum, n.d.

Goodspeed, D.J., The Conspirators: A Study of the Coup d'Etat. New York: Viking Press, 1962. Toronto: Macmillan Co. of Canada, 1962.

Goodrich, Leland M., Edvard Hambro and Anne Patricia Simons, Charter of the United Nations: Commentary and Documents. Third and revised edition. New York and London: Columbia University Press, 1969.

Gopal, S., The Viceroyalty of Lord Irwin, 1926-1931. London: Oxford University Press, 1957.

Gordon, King, U. N. in the Congo: A Quest for Peace. New York: Carnegie Endowment for International Peace: 1962.

Görlitz, Walter, History of the German General Staff, 1657-1945. Trans. by Brian Battershaw. New York: Praeger, 1962.

——, ed., The Memoirs of Field-Marshal Keitel. Trans. by David Irving. New York: Stein and Day, 1966.

Government of India, India in 1930-31, A Statement prepared for Presentation to Parliament in accordance with the requirements of the 26th section of the Government of India Act (5 & 6 Geo. V, Chapter 61). Calcutta: Government of India, Central Publication Branch, 1932.

Grant, Joan, ed., Black Protest: History, Documents, and Analyses 1619 to the Present. Greenwich, Conn.: Fawcett, 1968.

de Grazia, Sebastian, The Political Community: A Study of Anomie. Chicago: University of Chicago Press, 1948.

Green, Thomas Hill, Lectures on the Principles of Political Obligation. London: Longmans, Green & Co., 1948 (orig. 1882).

Gregg, Richard, The Power of Nonviolence. Second revised edition. New York: Schoken, 1966. London: James Clarke & Co., 1960.

Griffith, Arthur, The Resurrection of Hungary: A Parallel for Ireland. Third edition. Dublin: Wheland & Son, 1918.

de Haèstrup, J., "Expose," in European Resistance Movements 1939-1945, pp. 150-162.

Halberstam, David, The Making of a Quagmire. New York: Random House, 1965. London: The Bodley Head, 1965.

Hall, Fred S., Sympathetic Strikes and Sympathetic Lockouts, New York, published Ph.D. dissertation in Political Science. New York: Columbia University, 1898.

Halperin, S. William, Germany Tried Democracy: A Political History of the Reich from 1918 to 1933. Hamden, Conn. and London: Archon Books, 1963 (orig. 1946).

Hanh, Thich Nhát, "Love in Action: The Nonviolent Struggle for Peace in Vietnam" (duplicated pamphlet) Paris (?): Overseas Vietnamese Buddhists Association, 1967.

Harcave, Sidney, **First Blood: The Russian Revolution of 1905**. New York: Macmillan, 1964. London: Collier-Macmillan, 1964. Paperback edition entitled: **The Russian Revolution of 1905**. New York: Collier-Macmillan, 1970.

Hardinge of Penschurst, Lord, **Old Diplomacy: The Reminiscences of Lord Hardinge of Penschurst**. London: John Murray, 1947.

Hare, A. Paul, and Herbert H. Blumberg, eds., **Nonviolent Direct Action: American Cases: Social-Psychological Analyses**. Washington, D.C. and Cleveland: Corpus Books, 1968.

Harris, Errol E., "Political Power," *Ethics*, vol. XLVIII, no. 1 (October 1957), pp. 1-10.

Harris, Herbert, **American Labor**. New Haven: Yale University Press, 1938.

Heath, Dwight B., Charles J. Erasmus and Hans C. Buechler, **Land Reform and Social Revolution in Bolivia**. New York: Frederick A. Praeger, 1969.

Helset, Major General Olaf, *"Idrettsfronten,"* in Steen, gen. ed., **Norges Krig**, vol. III, pp. 7-34.

Hentoff, Nat, **The New Equality**. New edition. New York: Viking Press, 1965.

Higgins, Trumbull, **Korea and the Fall of MacArthur: A Precis in Limited War**. New York: Oxford University Press, 1960.

Hilberg, Raul, **The Destruction of the European Jews**. London: W. H. Allen, 1961.

Hildebrandt, Rainer, **2 x 2 = 8: The Story of a Group of Young Men in the Soviet Zone of Germany** (pamphlet). Bonn and Berlin: Federal Ministry for All-German Affairs, 1961.

Hillenbrand, Martin J., **Power and Morals**. New York: Columbia University Press, 1949.

Hiller, E. T., **The Strike: A Study in Collective Action**. Chicago: University of Chicago Press, 1928.

Hirst, Margaret E., **The Quakers in Peace and War**. New York: George H. Doran Co., 1923. London: Swarthmore Press, 1923.

Hitler, Adolph, **Mein Kampf**. New York: Reynal and Hitchcock, 1941.

Hobbes, Thomas, **Leviathan**. New York: Everymans E. P. Dutton, 1950. Oxford: Clarendon Press, 1958.

Hoffman, Frederik, "The Functions of Economic Sanctions: A Comparative Analysis," *Journal of Peace Research*, 1967, no. 2, pp. 140-160.

Holmsen, Andreas, **Norges Historie Fra de Eldste Tider til 1960**, (Third Edition). Oslo and Bergen: Universitetsforlaget, 1964.

Holt, Edgar, **Protest in Arms**. London: Putnam & Co., Ltd., 1960.

Holter, Harriet, "Disputes and Tensions in Industry," reprint from *Scandinavian Democracy* (Copenhagen), 1958.

Hoskyns, Catherine, **The Congo Since Independence: January 1960-December 1961**. London: Oxford University Press, 1965.

Houser, George, **Erasing the Color Line** (pamphlet). Revised edition. New York: Congress of Racial Equality, 1948.

Howe, Irving and B. J. Widick, **The U.A.W. and Walter Reuther**. New York: Random House, 1949.

Høye, Bjarne and Trygve M. Ager, **The Fight of the Norwegian Church Against Nazism.** New York: Macmillan, 1943.

Hsiao, Kung-ch,üan, **Rural China: Imperial Control in the Nineteenth Century.** Seattle: University of Washington Press, 1960.

Huntington, Samuel P., **Political Order in Changing Societies.** New Haven and London: Yale University Press, 1968.

Hurum, Hans Jørgen, **Musikken Under Okkupasjonen, 1940-1945.** Oslo: H. Aschehoug, 1946.

Hutchinson, Royal D., **The Radio and the Resistance: A Case Study from Czechoslovakia.** Hellerup, Denmark: Institute for Peace and Conflict Research, 1970.

Hutchinson, Thomas, editor, **The Complete Poetical Works of Percy Bysshe Shelley.** Oxford: Clarendon Press, 1904.

Hutchinson, Thomas, **The History of the Colony and Province of Massachusetts-Bay.** Edited by Laurence Shaw Mayo. Cambridge, Mass.: Harvard University Press, 1936. See also C.B. Mayo, ed.

Huxley, Aldous, **Ends and Means: An Enquiry into the Nature of Ideals and into the Methods Employed for their Realization.** New York: Harper Bros., 1937, and London: Chatto and Windus, 1948.

India in 1930-31. See Government of India.

Irwin, Inez Haynes, **The Story of the Woman's Party.** New York: Harcourt, Brace and Co., 1921.

Jacob, Philip E., See Sibley and Jacob.

Jameson, A.K., **A New Way in Norway** (pamphlet). London: Peace News, 1946 or 1947.

Janis, Irving L. and Daniel Katz, "The Reduction of Intergroup Hostility: Research Problems and Hypotheses," in *Journal of Conflict Resolution*, vol. III, no. 1 (March 1959), pp. 85-100.

Jensen, Magnus, "*Kampen om Skolen*," in Sverre Steen, gen. ed., **Norges Krig**, vol. III, pp. 73-110.

⸺, **Norges Historie: Norge Under Eneveldet, 1660-1814.** Oslo and Bergen: Universitetsforlaget, 1963.

de Jong, L., "Anti-Nazi Resistance in the Netherlands," in **European Resistance Movements 1939-1945**, pp. 137-149.

de Jouvenal, Bertrand, **On Power: Its Nature and The History of its Growth.** Trans. by J.F. Huntington. Boston: Beacon Paperback, 1962. British edition: **Power: The Natural History of its Growth.** London: The Batchworth Press, 1952 (1945).

⸺, **Sovereignty: An Enquiry Into the Political Good.** Chicago: University of Chicago Press, 1959. London: The Batchworth Press, 1952.

Joyce, Patrick, **A Social History of Ancient Ireland**, vol. I. London: Longmans, Green, 1903.

Jungk, Robert, **Brighter than a Thousand Suns: The Story of the Men Who Made the Bomb.** New York: Grove Press Black Cat Edition, n.d.

Jutikkala, Eino, **A History of Finland**, with Kauko Pirinen. Trans. by Paul Sjöblom. New York: Frederick A. Praeger, 1962. London: Thames and Hudson, 1962.

Kallen, Horace M. "Coercion." **Encyclopedia of the Social Sciences**, vol. III, pp. 617-619. New York: Macmillan, 1935.

Karski, Jan, **Story of a Secret State.** Boston: Houghton Mifflin, 1944.

Katkov, George, **Russia 1917: The February Revolution.** New York: Harper

& Row, 1967.

Keep, J.H.L., **The Rise of Social Democracy in Russia**. Oxford: Clarendon Press, 1963.

Kendall, Carlton W., **The Truth About Korea**. San Francisco: Korea National Association, 1919.

King, Dan, **The Life and Times of Thomas Wilson Dorr with Outlines of the Political History of Rhode Island**. Boston: The Author, 1859.

King, Martin Luther, Jr., **Stride Toward Freedom: The Montgomery Story**. New York: Ballantine Books, 1958. London: Victor Gollancz, 1959.

——, **Why We Can't Wait**. New York: Signet Books of The New American Library, 1964.

King-Hall, Sir Stephen, **Defence in the Nuclear Age**. Nyack, N.Y.: Fellowship, 1959. London: Victor Gollancz, 1958.

Kirchhoff, Hans, Henrik S. Nissen, and Henning Pulsen, **Besaettelsestidens Historie**. Copenhagen: Forlaget Fremad, Danmarks Radios Grundbøger, 1964.

Knapp, Wilfrid F., **A History of War and Peace 1939-1965**. London, New York and Toronto: Oxford University Press, 1967.

Knowles, K.G.J.C., **Strikes—A Study in Industrial Conflict with Special Reference to British Experience Between 1911 and 1945**. New York: Philosophical Library, 1952. Oxford: Basil Blackwell, 1954.

Koestler, Arthur, **Reflections on Hanging**. New York: Macmillan, 1967.

Korbel, Josef, **The Communist Subversion of Czechoslovakia 1938-1948: The Failure of Coexistence**. Princeton, New Jersey: Princeton University Press, 1959.

Kornhauser, Arthur, Robert Dubins, and Arthur M. Ross, eds., **Industrial Conflict**. New York: McGraw-Hill.

Krehbiel, Edward B., **The Interdict: Its History and its Operation**. Washington, D.C.: American Historical Association, 1909.

Kripalani, Krishna, ed., **All Men Are Brothers: Life and Thoughts of Mahatma Gandhi as told in his Own Words**. Ahmedabad: Navajivan, 1960. (Also, Paris: Unesco, 1958.)

Kropotkine, P. (sic), **In Russian and French Prisons**. London: Ward and Downey, 1887.

Kuper, Leo, **Passive Resistance in South Africa**. New Haven, Conn.: Yale University Press, 1957. London: Jonathan Cape, 1956.

Laidler, Harry, "Boycott," **Encyclopedia of the Social Sciences**, vol. II, pp. 662-666. New York: Macmillan, 1935.

——, **Boycotts and the Labor Struggle, Economic and Legal Aspects**. New York: John Lane Co., 1913.

——, See also James Myers and Harry Laidler.

Lakey, George, "Cultural Aspects of the American Movement for Woman Suffrage, Militant Phase." Duplicated MS. Philadelphia, 1968.

——, "The Sociological Mechanisms of Nonviolent Action." Duplicated M.A. thesis in Sociology, University of Pennsylvania, 1962. Published in *Peace Research Reviews* (Oakville, Ontario: Canadian Peace Research Institute), vol. II, no. 6, whole number, (Dec., 1968)..

Lasswell, Harold D., **Power and Personality**. New York: Norton, 1948.

Lees, Hannah, "The Not-Buying Power of Philadelphia Negroes," *The Reporter*, vol. 24, no. 10 (11 May 1961), pp. 33-35.

Lefebre, George, **The French Revolution from its Origins to 1793**. New York: Columbia University Press, 1962. London: Routledge & Kegan Paul, 1962.

Legum, Colin & Margaret, **South Africa: Crisis for the West**. New York and London: Frederick A. Praeger, 1964.

Leiss, Amelia, C., ed., **Apartheid and United Nations Collective Measures**. New York: Carnegie Endowment for International Peace, 1965.

Lenin, Nikolai (sic), **The Essentials of Lenin in Two Volumes**. London: Lawrence and Wishart, 1947. (N.B.: Lenin is now usually called V.I. Lenin.)

Lenin, V.I., **Collected Works**. Moscow: Foreign Languages Publishing House, 1962.

———, **Selected Works**. Moscow and Leningrad: Co-operative Publishing Society of Foreign Workers in the U.S.S.R., 1934(?).

———, **Selected Works in Three Volumes**. New York: International Publishers, and Moscow: Progress Publishers, 1967.

———, **Selected Works in Two Volumes**. Moscow: Foreign Languages Publishing House, 1950.

Lewis, Anthony and *The New York Times*, **Portrait of a Decade: The Second American Revolution**. New York: Random House, 1964.

Lewis, Flora, **A Case History of Hope: The Story of Poland's Peaceful Revolutions**. New York: Doubleday & Co., 1958. British edition: **The Polish Volcano: A Case History of Hope**. London: Secker & Warburg, 1959.

Lewy, Guenter, **The Catholic Church and Nazi Germany**. New York and Toronto: McGraw-Hill Co., 1964. London: Weidenfeld and Nicolson, 1964.

Liddell Hart, Sir Basil, **Defence of The West: Some Riddles of War and Peace**. New York: William Morrow Co., 1950. London: Cassell, 1950.

———, "Lessons from Resistance Movements—Guerilla and Nonviolent," in Roberts, ed., **Civilian Resistance as a National Defence**, pp. 195-211.

———, **Strategy: The Indirect Approach**. New York: Frederick A. Praeger, 1954. London: Faber and Faber, 1954.

Lipscome, Andrew A., editor-in-chief, **The Writings of Thomas Jefferson**. Washington, D.C.: Thomas Jefferson Memorial Association of the United States, 1903.

Littell, Robert, ed., **The Czech Black Book: Prepared by the Institute of History of the Czechoslovak Academy of Sciences**. New York, Washington and London: Frederick A. Praeger, 1969.

Lloyd, Clifford, **Ireland Under the Land League: A Narrative of Personal Experiences**. Edinburgh and London: William Blackwood & Sons, 1892.

Lochner, Louis P., ed., **The Goebbels Diaries, 1942-1943**. Garden City, N.Y.: Doubleday & Co., 1948.

Locker-Lampson, G., **A Consideration of the State of Ireland in the Nineteenth Century**. New York: E.P. Dutton & Co., 1907. London: Archibald Constable, 1907.

Loh, Robert (as told to Humphrey Evans), **Escape From Red China**. New York: Coward-McCann, 1962.

Lomax, Louis E., **The Negro Revolt**. New York: Signet Book, New American Library, 1963.

Luihn, Hans, **De Illegale Avisene: Den Frie, Hemmlige Pressen i Norge Under Okkupasjonen**. Oslo and Bergen: Universitetsforlaget, 1960.

Luthuli, Albert, **Let My People Go: An Autobiography**. New York McGraw-

Hill Book Co., Inc., 1962. London: Collins, 1962.

Lynd, Staughton, ed., **Nonviolence in America: A Documentary History.** Indianapolis: Bobbs-Merrill Co., 1966.

Lyttle, Bradford, **Essays on Non-violent Action** (duplicated booklet). Chicago: The Author, 1959.

——, "Haymarket; Violence Destroys a Movement" (duplicated). New York: Committee for Nonviolent Action, 1965.

——, "The Importance of Discipline in Demonstrations for Peace" (duplicated). New York: Committee for Nonviolent Action, 1962.

Mabee, Carleton, **Black Freedom: The Nonviolent Abolitionists from 1830 Through the Civil War.** New York: Macmillan, 1970. Toronto: Macmillan, 1970. London: Collier-Macmillan, 1970.

Machiavelli, Niccolo, **The Discourses of Niccolo Machiavelli.** London: Routledge and Kegan Paul, 1950.

——, **The Prince.** New York: E.P. Dutton Everyman's Library, 1948. London: J.M. Dent & Sons, Everyman's Library, 1948.

MacIver, R.M., **The Modern State.** Oxford: Clarendon Press, 1926. New York and London: Oxford University Press, 1964.

——, **The Web of Government.** New York: Macmillan, 1947.

Macmullen, Ramsay, "A Note on Roman Strikes," *Classical Journal*, vol. LVIII (1962-1963), pp. 269-271.

Mahadevan, T.K., Adam Roberts and Gene Sharp, eds., **Civilian Defence: An Introduction.** New Delhi: Gandhi Peace Foundation and Bombay: Bharatiya Vidya Bhavan, 1967.

Malinowski, Bronislaw, "An Anthropological Analysis of War," *American Journal of Sociology*, vol. XLVI, no. 4, pp. 521-549.

——, **Freedom and Civilization.** New York: Roy Publishers, 1944.

Maritain, Jacques, **Man and the State.** Chicago, Illinois: University of Chicago Press, 1954. London: Hollis & Carter, 1954.

Matthiessen, Peter, **Sal Si Puedes: Cesar Chavez and the New American Revolution.** New York: Random House, 1969.

Mayer, J.P., ed. and trans., **The Recollections of Alexis de Tocqueville.** New York: Meridian Books, 1959.

Mayo, Catherine Barton, ed., **Additions to Thomas Hutchinson's "History of Massachusetts Bay."** Worcester, Mass.: American Antiquarian Society, 1949.

McWilliams, Carey, **Factories in the Field: The Story of Migratory Farm Labor in California.** Boston: Little, Brown, & Co., 1939.

Menashe, Louis and Radosh, Ronald, eds., **Teach-ins: U.S.A.: Reports, Opinions, Documents.** New York: Frederick A. Praeger, 1967.

Michels, Robert, "Authority," **Encyclopedia of the Social Sciences,** vol. I, p. 319. New York: Macmillan, 1935.

Mikes, George, **The Hungarian Revolution.** London: Andre Deutsch, 1957.

Miles, Michael, "Black Cooperatives," *New Republic*, vol. 159, no. 12 (21 September 1968), pp. 21-23.

Miller, William Robert, **Nonviolence: A Christian Interpretation.** New York: Association Press, 1964.

Mills, C. Wright. See Hans Gerth and C. Wright Mills.

de Montesquieu, Baron. **The Spirit of the Laws.** Trans. by Thomas Nugent. Intro. by Franz Neumann. New York: Hafner Publishing Co., 1959.

Monthly Information Bulletin of the International Commission Against Con-centration Camp Practices, no. 4, Aug.-Nov. 1955. Now titled *Saturn*.

Morgan, Edmund S. & Helen M., **The Stamp Act Crisis: Prologue to Revolution**. New revised edition. New York: Collier Books, 1963.

Morley, John, **The Life of William Ewart Gladstone**, vol. III. New York and London: MacMillan & Co., 1903.

Morris, John, "Early Christian Civil Disobedience," *Peace News* (London), 5 January 1962.

Mosca, Gaetano, **The Ruling Class**. New York and London: McGraw-Hill, 1939.

Mowat, Charles Loch, **Britain Between the Wars 1918-1940**. London: Methuen & Co., 1955.

Mowry, Arthur May, **The Dorr War or the Constitutional Struggle in Rhode Island**. Providence, R.I.: Preston & Rounds, 1901.

Muse, Benjamin, **The American Negro Revolution: From Nonviolence to Black Power, 1963-1967**. Bloomington and London: Indiana University Press, 1968.

——, **Virginia's Massive Resistance**. Bloomington: Indiana University Press, 1961.

Myers, James and Harry W. Laidler, **What Do You Know About Labor?** New York: John Day, 1956.

Naess, Arne, "A Systematization of Gandhian Ethics of Conflict Resolution," *Journal of Conflict Resolution*, vol. I (1957), pp. 140-155. See also Johan Galtung and Arne Naess.

Napoleon, **The Officer's Manual** or **Napoleon's Maxim of War**. New York: James G. Gregory, 1861.

Nayar, Pyarelal. See Pyarelal.

Nehru, Jawaharlal, **An Autobiography**. New edition. London: The Bodley Head, 1953.

——, **The Discovery of India**. New York: John Day, 1946.

——, **India and the World: Essays by Jawaharlal Nehru**. London: Geo. Allen & Unwin, Ltd., 1936.

——, **Toward Freedom: The Autobiography of Jawaharlal Nehru**. Revised edition. New York: John Day Co., 1942.

Neumann, Franz, **Behemoth: The Structure and Practice of National Socialism 1933-1944**. New York: Octagon Books, 1963.

——, **The Democratic and the Authoritarian State: Essays in Political and Legal Theory**. Glencoe, Ill.: The Free Press and Falcon's Wing Press, 1957.

Neustadt, Richard E., **Presidential Power: The Politics of Leadership**. New York and London: John Wiley and Sons, 1960.

Nevins, Allan and Henry Steele Commager, **America: The Story of a Free People**. Boston: Little, Brown and Co., 1943.

Nevinson, Henry W., **The Dawn in Russia or Scenes in the Russian Revolution**. New York and London: Harper & Bros., 1906.

Nicholson, Harold, **Diplomacy**. Second edition. London; New York and Toronto: Oxford University Press, 1960 (orig. 1950).

Nickalls, John L., ed., **The Journal of George Fox**. Cambridge: University Press, 1952.

Niebuhr, Reinhold, **Moral Man and Immoral Society**. New York: Charles Scribner's Sons, 1960 (orig. 1932). London: S.C.M. Press, 1963.

Nirumand, Bahman, **Iran: The New Imperialism in Action**. New York and London: Modern Reader Paperback, 1969.

O'Hegarty, Patrick Sarsfield, **A History of Ireland Under The Union, 1880-1922**. With an Epilogue carrying the story down to the acceptance in 1927 by De Valera of the Anglo-Irish Treaty of 1921. London: Methuen Press, 1952.

Olmsted, Frederick Law, **A Journey in the Seaboard Slave States, with Remarks on Their Economy**. New York: Dix and Edwards, 1956. London: Sampson Low, Son & Co., 1956.

Oppenheimer, Martin and George Lakey, **A Manual for Direct Action**. Chicago: Quadrangle Books, 1965.

Oxford English Dictionary. See **Shorter Oxford English Dictionary on Historical Principles**.

Pattabhi Sitaramayya, Bhagaraju, **The History of the Indian National Congress, 1885-1935**, vol I. Madras: Working Committee of the Congress, 1935.

Paullin, Theodor, **Introduction to Nonviolence** (pamphlet). Philadelphia: Pacifist Research Bureau, 1944.

Peck, Graham, **Two Kinds of Time**. Boston: Houghton-Mifflin, 1950.

Peck, James, **Freedom Ride**. New York: Simon and Schuster, 1962.

The Pentagon Papers as published by "The New York Times." New York, Toronto and London: Bantam Books, 1971.

Perkins, Dwight H., **Market Control and Planning in Communist China**. Cambridge, Mass.: Harvard University Press, 1966.

Perlman, Selig, **A History of Trade Unionism in the United States**. New York: Macmillan Co., 1923.

Peters, William, **The Southern Temper**. Garden City, New Jersey: Doubleday & Co., 1959.

Peterson, Florence, **American Labor Unions: What They Are and How They Work**. New York: Harper and Bros., 1945.

———, **Survey of the Labor Economics**. Revised edition. New York: Harper and Bros., 1951.

Phillips, Ulrich Bonnell, **American Negro Slavery: A Survey of the Supply, Employment and Control of Negro Labor as Determined by the Plantation Regime**. New York: Peter Smith, 1952 (orig. 1918).

Phillips, Norman, **The Tragedy of Apartheid**. New York: David McKay, 1960.

Pigors, Paul, **Leadership or Domination**. Boston: Houghton Mifflin Co., 1935. London: George G. Harrap, 1935.

Plamenatz, John, **The Revolutionary Movement in France 1815-1871**. London: Longmans, Green and Co., 1952.

Post, R. H., "Mourning Becomes Patriotic," in *Win* (New York), vol. 3, no. 13 (July 1967), p. 23.

Postgate, R. W., ed., **Revolution from 1789 to 1906**. New York: Harper Torchbooks, 1962.

Prasad, Rajendra, **Satyagraha in Champaran**. Ahmedabad: Navajivan, 1949.

Prawdin, Michael, **The Unmentionable Nechaev: A Key to Bolshevism**. London: Allen and Unwin, 1961.

Proudfoot, Merrill, **Diary of a Sit-in**. Chapel Hill, North Carolina: University of North Carolina Press, 1962.

Pyarelal, "Gandhiji Discusses Another 1942 Issue: Nonviolent Technique and

Parallel Government," reprinted from *Harijan* in *The Independent* (Bombay), 25 March 1946.
——, **Mahatma Gandhi: The Last Phase**, vol. I. Ahmedabad: Navajivan Publishing House, 1956.
Radosh, Ronald. See Lewis Menashe and Ronald Radosh.
Roloff, Karl. See Karl Ehrlich.
Ramachandran, G. and T. K. Mahadevan, eds., **Gandhi: His Relevance for Our Times**. Revised and enlarged second edition. Berkeley, Calif.: World Without War Council, 1971 and Bombay: Bharatiya Vidya Bhavan and New Delhi: Gandhi Peace Foundation, 1967.
Rao, G. S., **Gora—An Atheist**. Vijayawada, India: Atheistic Centre, 1970.
Ratcliffe, S. K., "Hunger Strike," **Encyclopedia of the Social Sciences**, vol. VII, pp. 532-533. New York: Macmillan, 1935.
Rayback, Joseph G., **A History of American Labor**. New York: Macmillan, 1964.
Reitlinger, Gerald, **The Final Solution: The Attempt to Exterminate the Jews of Europe 1939-1945**. New York: A. S. Barnes, 1961.
Remington, Robin Alison, ed., **Winter in Prague: Documents on Czechoslovak Communism in Crisis**. Cambridge, Mass. and London: M.I.T. Press, 1969.
Report of the Advisory Commission on the Review of the Constitution of Rhodesia and Nyasaland, Cmnd. 1148. London: H. M. Stationery Office, 1960.
Report of the Nyasaland Commission of Inquiry, Cmnd. 814. London: H. M. Stationery Office, 1959.
Report of the Special Committee on the Problem of Hungary, General Assembly, Official Records: Eleventh Session, Supplement No. 18 (A/3592). New York: United Nations, 1957.
Reynolds, Lloyd G., **Labor Economics and Labor Relations**. Englewood Cliffs, New Jersey: Prentice-Hall, 1959.
"A Rhode Islander," **Might and Right**. Providence: A. H. Stillwell, 1844.
Richman, Irving Berdine, **Rhode Island: A Study in Separatism**. Boston and New York: Houghton Mifflin Co., 1905.
Roberts, Adam, "Buddhism and Politics in South Vietnam," in *The World Today* (London), vol. 21, no. 6. (June 1965), pp. 240-250.
——, "The Buddhist Revolt: The Anti-Diem Campaign in South Vietnam in 1963." London: The Author, duplicated MS, 1964.
——, "The Buddhists, the War, and the Vietcong," in *The World Today*, vol. 22, no. 5 (May 1966), pp. 214-222.
——, co-ed., **Civilian Defence: An Introduction**. See Mahadevan, T. K.
——, "Four Strategies in Resisting Invasion," unpublished MS.
——, ed., **Civilian Resistance as a National Defence: Non-violent Action Against Aggression**. Harrisburg, Pa.: Stackpole Books, 1968. British ed.: **The Strategy of Civilian Defence: Non-violent Resistance to Aggression**. London: Faber & Faber, 1967. Paperback ed.: **Civilian Resistance as a National Defence**. Baltimore, Maryland, Harmondsworth, Middlesex, England and Ringwood, Victoria, Australia: Penguin Books, 1969.
——, See also Philip Windsor and Adam Roberts.
Robertson, J. R., "On-the-Job Activity," in E. Wight Bakke and Charles Kerr, **Unions, Management and the Public**.
Rosenthal, Mario, **Guatemala: The Story of an Emergent Latin-American**

Democracy. New York: Twayne Publishers, 1962.

Rostovtzeff, M., **The Social and Economic History of the Roman Empire**, vol. I. Second edition revised by P. M. Fraser. Oxford: Clarendon Press, 1956.

Rousseau, Jean Jacques, "The Social Contract" in **The Social Contract and Discourses**. New York: E. P. Dutton & Co., Everyman's Library, 1920. London: J. M. Dent & Sons, Ltd., Everyman's Library, 1920.

The Royal Institute of International Affairs, **International Sanctions**. London: Oxford University Press, 1938.

———, **Sanctions**. Second edition. London: Royal Institute of International Affairs, 1935.

Rubin, Jerry, **Do It!** New York: Simon and Schuster, 1970.

Rudé, George, **The Crowd in The French Revolution**. Oxford: Clarendon Press, 1959.

Rudlin, W. A., "Obedience, Political" in **Encyclopedia of the Social Science**, vol. XI, p. 415. New York: Macmillan, 1935.

Russell, Bertrand, **Authority and the Individual: The Reith Lectures for 1948-1949**. New York: Simon and Schuster, 1949. London: George Allen and Unwin, 1949.

———, **Power: A New Social Analysis**. New York: W. W. Norton & Co., 1938. London: George Allen and Unwin, 1938.

———, **Roads to Freedom: Socialism, Anarchism and Syndicalism**. London: George Allen and Unwin, 1918.

Salvemini, Gaetano, **The French Revolution, 1788-1792**, Trans. I. M. Rawson. New York: Henry Holt and Co., 1954. London: Jonathan Cape, 1963.

Schapiro, Leonard, **The Communist Party of the Soviet Union**. New York: Random House, 1960. London: Eyre & Spottiswoode, 1960.

———, **The Origin of the Communist Autocracy, Political Opposition in the Soviet State, First Phase 1917-1922**. Cambridge, Mass.: Harvard University Press, 1955. London: G. Bell & Sons, The London School of Economics and Political Science, 1956.

Schelling, Thomas C., **International Economics**. Boston: Allyn and Bacon, 1958.

Schlesinger, Arthur M., **The Colonial Merchants and the American Revolution 1763-1776**. New York: Frederick Ungar, 1966.

Schneider, Ronald M., **Communism in Guatemala 1944-1954**. New York: Frederick A. Praeger, 1958.

Scholl, Inge, **Six Against Tyranny**, Trans. by Cyrus Brooks. London: John Murray, 1955.

Scholmer, Joseph, **Vortuka**. New York: Holt, 1955.

Schwarz, Solomon M., **The Russian Revolution of 1905: The Workers' Movement and the Formation of Bolshevism and Menshevism**, Trans. by Gertrude Vakar. Preface by Leopold H. Haimson. Chicago and London: University of Chicago Press, 1967.

Schweitzer, Arthur, **Big Business in the Third Reich**. Bloomington, Indiana: Indiana University Press, 1964. London: Eyre and Spottiswoode, 1964.

Segal, Ronald, ed., **Sanctions Against South Africa**. London and Baltimore, Md.: Penguin Books, 1964.

Seifert, Harvey, **Conquest by Suffering: The Process and Prospects of Nonviolent Resistance**. Philadelphia: Westminster Press, 1965.

——, "The Use by American Quakers of Nonviolent Resistance as a Method of Social Change." Unpublished Ph.D. dissertation, Boston University, 1940.

Seton-Watson, Christopher, **Italy From Liberalism to Fascism, 1870-1925.** New York: Barnes and Noble, 1967. London: Methuen, 1967.

Seton-Watson, Hugh, **The Decline of Imperial Russia.** New York: Frederick A. Praeger, 1952. London: Methuen & Co., 1952.

Sharp, Gene, **An Abecedary of Nonviolent Action and Civilian Defense.** Cambridge, Mass.: Schenkman, 1972.

——, "Can Non-violence work in South Africa?" "Problems of Violent and Non-violent Struggle," "Strategic Problems of the South African Resistance," and "How Do You Get Rid of Oppression?" in *Peace News* (London) 21 and 28 June, 5 July, and 25 October, 1963.

——, co-ed., **Civilian Defence: An Introduction.** See T.K. Mahadevan, Adam Roberts and Gene Sharp.

——, "The Constructive Programme," *Mankind* (Hyderabad), vol. I, no. 12 (July 1957), pp. 1102-1112.

——, "Creative Conflict in Politics," *The New Era*, January, 1962. Pamphlet reprint edition: London: Housmans, 1962.

——, "Dilemmas of Morality in Politics," *Reconciliation Quarterly* (London), First Quarter 1965, no. 128, pp. 528-535.

——, "Ethics and Responsibility in Politics: A critique of the present adequacy of Max Weber's classification of ethical systems," *Inquiry* (Oslo), vol. VII, no. 3 (Autumn 1964), pp. 304-317.

——, **Exploring Nonviolent Alternatives.** Boston: Porter Sargent, 1970.

——, **Gandhi Wields the Weapon of Moral Power: Three Case Histories.** Introduction by Albert Einstein. Ahmedabad: Navajivan, 1960.

——, "Gandhi's Defence Policy," in T. K. Mahadevan, Adam Roberts and Gene Sharp, eds., **Civilian Defence: An Introduction,** pp. 15-52.

——, "Gandhi's Political Significance Today," in G. Ramachandran and T.K. Mahadevan, eds., **Gandhi,** pp. 44-66.

——, "The Meanings of Nonviolence: A Typology (revised)," *Journal of Conflict Resolution*, vol. III, no. 1 (March 1959), pp. 41-66. See latest revision "Types of Principled Nonviolence."

——, "The Methods of Nonviolent Resistance and Direct Action" Duplicated MS. Oslo: Institute for Social Research, 1960.

——, "The Need of a Functional Substitute for War," *International Relations* (London), vol. III, no. 3 (April 1967), pp. 187-207.

——, "Non-violence: Moral Principle or Political Technique?" *Indian Political Science Review* (Delhi), vol. IV, no. 1 (Oct. 1969-Mar. 1970), pp. 17-36.

——, "The Political Equivalent of War—Civilian Defence," *International Conciliation*, Whole Number, no. 555. New York: Carnegie Endowment for International Peace, November 1965.

——, "A South African Contribution to the Study of Nonviolent Action: A Review," in *Journal of Conflict Resolution*, vol. II, no. 4 (Dec. 1961), pp. 395-402.

——, "The Technique of Nonviolent Action," in Adam Roberts, ed., **Civilian Resistance as a National Defense,** pp. 87-105.

——, "Types of Principled Nonviolence," in A. Paul Hare and Herbert H.

Blumberg, eds., **Nonviolent Direct Action**, pp. 273-313.
——, **Tyranny Could Not Quell Them** (pamphlet). London: Peace News, 1958 and later editions.
Sheehy-Skeffington, F., **Michael Davitt: Revolutionary, Agitator and Labour Leader**. London and Leipsic: T. Fisher Unwin, 1908.
Shimbori, Michiya, "Zengakuren: A Japanese Case Study of a Student Political Movement," in *Sociology of Education*, vol. 37, no. 3 (Spring 1964), pp. 229-253.
Shirer, William L., **Berlin Diary, The Journal of a Foreign Correspondent, 1934-1941**. New York: Alfred A. Knopf, 1941.
——, **The Rise and Fall of the Third Reich**. New York: Simon and Schuster, 1960. London: Secker and Warburg, 1962.
——, **The Shorter Oxford English Dictionary on Historical Principles**, vol. II. Third edition revised. Oxford: Clarendon Press, 1959.
Shridharani, Krishnalal, **War Without Violence: A Study of Gandhi's Method and Its Accomplishments**. New York: Harcourt, Brace, and Co., 1939. London: Victor Gollancz, 1939. Reprinted with an Introduction by Gene Sharp, New York: Garland, 1972. Revised and enlarged paperback edition: Chowpatty and Bombay: Bharatiya Vidya Bhavan, 1962.
Shuller, Nettie Rogers. See Carrie Chapman Catt and Nettie Rogers Shuller.
Sibley, Mulford Q. and Asa Wardlaw, "Conscientious Objectors in Prison," in Lynd, ed., **Nonviolence in America**.
Sibley, Mulford Q. and Philip E. Jacob, **Conscription of Conscience: The American State and the Conscientious Objector, 1940-1947**. Ithaca, N.Y.: Cornell University Press, 1952.
Sibley, Mulford Q., ed., **The Quiet Battle: Writings on the Theory and Practice of Nonviolent Resistance**. Garden City, N.Y.: Anchor Books, Doubleday, 1963.
Sitaramayya. See B. Pattabhi Sitaramayya.
Skodvin, Magne, "Det Store Fremstøt," in Steen, gen. ed., **Norges Krig**, vol. II, pp. 573-734.
——, "Norwegian Nonviolent Resistance During the German Occupation," in Roberts, ed., **Civilian Resistance as a National Defense**, pp. 136-153.
Smith, T. Lynn, ed., **Agrarian Reform in Latin America**. New York: Alfred A. Knopf, 1965.
Solomon, Frederic and Jacob R. Fishman, "The Psychosocial Meaning of Nonviolence in Student Civil Rights Activities," *Psychiatry*, vol. XXVII, no. 2 (May 1964), pp. 91-99.
Solomon, F., W. L. Walker, G. O'Connor and J. R. Fishman, "Civil Rights Activity and Reduction in Crime Among Negroes," *Archives of General Psychiatry*, vol. XII (March 1965), pp. 227-236.
Spitz, David, **Democracy and the Challenge of Power**. New York: Columbia University Press, 1958.
Stalberg, Benjamin, **Tailor's Progress: The Story of A Famous Union and the Men Who Made It**. New York: Doubleday, Doran and Co., 1944.
Steen, Sverre, gen. ed., **Norges Krig 1940-1945**. Three volumes. Oslo: Gyldendal Norsk Forlag, 1947-50.
Steinberg, I.N., **In the Workshop of the Revolution**. New York: Rinehart & Co., 1953.
Steiner, Stan, **The New Indians**. New York: Harper & Row, 1968.

Stern, Bernard J., "Slavery, Primitive," **Encyclopedia of the Social Sciences,** vol. 14, pp. 73-74. New York: Macmillan, 1935.

Sternstein, Wolfgang, "The *Ruhrkampf* of 1923: Economic Problems of Civilian Defence," in Roberts, ed., **Civilian Resistance as a National Defense,** pp. 106-135.

Steuben, John, **Strike Strategy.** New York: Gaer Associates, 1950.

Stevens, Doris, **Jailed for Freedom.** New York: Boni and Liverwright, 1920.

Stevenson, J., ed., **A New Eusebius: Documents Illustrative of the History of the Church to A.D. 337.** London: S.P.C.K., 1957.

Stokes, Whitley, ed., **Tripartite Life of St. Patrick.** London: Her Majesty's Stationery Office, by Eyre and Spottiswoode, 1887.

Suhl, Yuri, ed., **They Fought Back: The Story of the Jewish Resistance in Nazi Europe.** New York: Crown Publishers, 1967.

Sykes, Brigadier-General Sir Percy, **A History of Persia.** Two volumes. London: Macmillan & Co., 1963.

Symons, Julian, **The General Strike: A Historical Portrait.** London: The Cresset Press, 1957.

Taber, Robert, **M-26: Biography of a Revolution.** New York: Lyle Stuart, 1961.

Taft, Philip, **The A. F. of L. in the Time of Gompers.** New York: Harper and Bros., 1957.

Taubenfeld, Rita Falk and Howard J. Taubenfeld, "The 'Economic Weapon': The League and the United Nations," *Proceedings of the American Society of International Law,* 1964, pp. 183-205.

Taylor, George R., **The Struggle for North China.** New York: Institute of Pacific Relations, 1940.

Taylor, Mary, ed., "Community Development in Western Sicily." Duplicated. Partinico: Centro studi e iniziative per la piena occupazione, 1963.

Tendulkar, D. G., **Mahatma: Life of Mohandas Karamchand Gandhi.** Eight volumes. Delhi: Publications Division, Ministry of Information and Broadcasting, Government of India, 1962.

Thayer, Charles W., **Diplomat.** New York: Harper & Bros., 1959.

Thompson, Daniel, **The Negro Leadership Class.** Englewood Cliffs, New Jersey: Prentice-Hall, 1963.

Thoreau, Henry David, "On the Duty of Civil Disobedience" (pamphlet). Intro. by Gene Sharp. London: Peace News, 1963. Or, in **Walden and Other Writings of Henry David Thoreau.** New York: Random House, 1937.

Tobias, Fritz, **The Reichstag Fire.** New York: G. P. Putnam's Sons, 1964.

de Tocqueville, Alexis, **Democracy in America.** Translated by George Lawrence. Edited by J. P. Mayer. Garden City, N. Y.: Anchor Books, Doubleday & Co., 1969.

Tolstoy, Leo, **The Kingdom of God is Within You.** New York: Thomas Y. Crowell, 1899. London: William Heinemann, 1894.

———, **The Law of Violence and the Law of Love.** Translated by Mary Koutouzow Tolstoy. New York: Rudolph Field, 1948. Also published in a different translation in *The Fortnightly Review.* London: Chapman & Hall, 1909.

———, "A Letter to a Hindu: The Subjection of India—Its Cause and Cure," with an Introduction by M. K. Gandhi, in Leo Tolstoy, **The Works of**

Tolstoy, vol. XXI, **Recollections and Essays**, pp. 413-432. Translated by Mr. and Mrs. Aylmer Maude. London: Oxford University Press, Humphrey Milford, 1937. Also in Kalidas Nag, **Tolstoy and Gandhi**. Patna, India: Pustak Bhandar, 1950.

Trevelyan, Sir George Otto, **The American Revolution**, vol. I. New edition. New York, London and Bombay: Longmans, Green & Co., 1908.

Trotsky, Leon, **My Life**. New York: Universal Library, Grossett & Dunlap, 1960.

Ulam, Adam B., **The Bolsheviks: The Intellectual and Political History of the Triumph of Communism in Russia**. New York: Macmillan, 1965. London: Collier-Macmillan, 1965.

Ullstein, Heinz, **Spielplatz Meines Lebens: Erinnerungen**. Munich: Kindler Verlag, 1961.

United Nations. See **Report of the Special Committee on the Problem of Hungary**.

Urutia, Miguel, **The Development of the Colombian Labor Movement**. New Haven and London: Yale University Press, 1969.

Vali, Ferenc A., **Rift and Revolt in Hungary: Nationalism versus Communism**. Cambridge, Mass.: Harvard University Press. London: Oxford University Press, 1961.

Vassilyev, A.T., **The Ochrana: The Russian Secret Police**. Edited and with an Introduction by Rene Fülöp-Miller. Philadelphia and London: J.B. Lippincott Co., 1930.

Venturi, Franco, **Roots of Revolution: A History of the Populist and Socialist Movements in Nineteenth Century Russia**. New York: Alfred A. Knopf, 1960. London: Weidenfeld and Nicolson, 1960.

Walker, Charles C., **Organizing for Nonviolent Direct Action** (pamphlet). Cheney, Pennsylvania: The Author, 1961.

Wallensteen, Peter, "Characteristics of Economic Sanctions," *Journal of Peace Research* (Oslo), 1968, no. 3, pp. 248-267.

Walter, E. V., "Power and Violence," *American Political Science Review*, vol. LVIII, no. 2 (June 1964), pp. 350-360.

Walters, F. P., **A History of the League of Nations**. London: Oxford University Press, 1960.

Warmbrunn, Werner, **The Dutch Under German Occupation 1940-1945**. Palo Alto, California: Stanford University Press. London: Oxford University Press, 1963.

Warner, Denis, **The Last Confucian**. London and Baltimore, Md.: Penquin Books, 1964.

Warriner, Doreen, **Land Reform in Principle and Practice**. Oxford: Clarendon Press, 1969.

Washington, H. A., ed., **The Writings of Thomas Jefferson**. Washington, D.C.: Taylor and Maury, 1853.

Waskow, Arthur I., **From Race Riot to Sit-in: 1919 and the 1960s**. Garden City, N.Y.: Doubleday, 1966.

Watkins, Frederick, ed., **Hume: Theory of Politics**. Edinburgh: Thomas Nelson & Sons, Ltd., 1951.

Watt, Richard M., **Dare Call It Treason**. New York: Simon and Schuster, 1963.

Webb, Sidney and Beatrice, **The History of Trade Unionism**. Revised edition to 1920. New York: Longmans, Green & Co., 1920.

Weber, Max, "Politics as a Vocation," in H. H. Gerth and C. Wright Mills, eds. and trans., **From Max Weber: Essays in Sociology**, pp. 77-128. London: Kegan Paul, Trench, Trabner & Co., 1948.

Wechsberg, Joseph, **The Voices**. Garden City, N. Y.: Doubleday, 1969.

Westin, Alan F., ed., **Freedom Now: The Civil-Rights Struggle in America**. New York: Basic Books, 1964.

Wheeler-Bennett, John W., **The Nemesis of Power: The German Army in Politics, 1918-1945**. New York: St. Martin's Press, 1953. London: Macmillan, 1953.

Williams, George Huntston, "The Ministry and the Draft in Historical Perspective" in Donald Cutler, ed., **The Religious Situation—1969**. Boston: Beacon Press, 1969.

Williams, Robin M., **The Reduction of Intergroup Tensions**. New York: Social Science Research Council, 1947.

Willigan, J. Dennis, S.J., "Sanctuary," *Union Seminary Quarterly*, vol. XXV, no. 4 (Summer 1970).

Wilson, James Q., "The Negro in Politics," *Daedalus*, vol. 94, no. 4 (Fall 1965).

Windsor, Philip and Adam Roberts: **Czechoslovakia 1968: Reform, Repression and Resistance**. New York: Columbia University Press, 1969. London: Chatto & Windus, 1969.

Wolfe, Bertram D., **Three Who Made a Revolution**. New York: Dial Press, 1948. London: Thames and Hudson, 1956.

Wolff, Kurt H., ed. and trans., **The Sociology of Georg Simmel**. Glencoe, Ill.: Free Press, 1950.

Wolman, Leo, **The Boycott in American Trade Unions**, Johns Hopkins University Studies in Historical and Political Science, series XXXIV, no. 1, 1916. Baltimore, Md.: Johns Hopkins Press, 1916.

Woodward, E. L., **French Revolutions**. London: Oxford University Press, Humphrey Milford, 1939.

Wright, Quincy, **A Study of War**. Two volumes. Chicago: University of Chicago Press, 1942.

Wyller, Thomas Chr., **Nyordning og Motstand: Organisasjones Politiske Rolle Under Okkupasjonen**. Oslo: Universitetsforlaget, 1958.

Yarmolinsky, Avrahm, **Road to Revolution: A Century of Russian Radicalism**. New York: Macmillan and Co., 1959. London: Cassell, 1957.

Yellen, Samuel, **American Labor Struggles**. New York: Harcourt, Brace & Co., 1936.

Yoder, Dale, **Labor Economics and Labor Problems**. New York and London: McGraw-Hill Co., 1939.

Yunus, Muhammed, **Frontier Speaks**. Bombay: Hind Kitabs, 1947.

Zinn, Howard, **Albany**. Atlanta: Southern Regional Council, 1962.

Ziskind, David, **One Thousand Strikes of Government Employees**. New York: Columbia University Press, 1940.

Index

African slaves, 124.
Afro-Americans, 5, 70, 73, 95-97, 98, 134, 138, 166, 198, 199, 203, 223-224, 235, 239-240, 243, 335-337, 371-372, 373-377, 378, 379-380, 383-384, 386, 388, 391-392, 395, 398-399, 402, 411, 414-415, 472, 534, 548, 559-560, 569 n. 102, 591, 616-617, 640, 670, 671, 689-690, 700 n. 40; 713, 716-717, 737, 766, 771 n. 58, 785, 786-788, 791, 795, 796. See also Negroes.
Afro-American Society of Tufts University, 378-379.
Aga Bey, Lydia (Asia Minor), 124.
Agents provocateurs, 112, 592-594, 601, 627.
Ager, Trygve M., 122.
Agrarian Reform Decree, Bolivia, 407.
Agrarian Reform Law, Colombia, 441 n. 192.
Agrarian Reform Law, Venezuela, 408.
Agricultural strikes, 261-264.
Agricultural union, 398.
Ahimsa (nonviolence), 212, 456.
Ahmedabad, India, 466, 583, 591.
Ahmedabad, India, Municipal Board of, 339.
Ahmedabad strike, 367, 583.
Akron, Ohio, 277, 403.
Akwesasne Notes, 439 n. 131.
Alabama, 95, 151, 159, 201, 233, 414-415.
Albany, Georgia, 138, 471-472.
Albany County, New York, 226.
Albrecht, Emil, 325.
Alcatraz Island, 389, 439 n. 131.
Aldermaston Atomic Weapons Research Establishment, 148.
Aldermaston march, 171, 631.
Alexander II, Tsar, 645 n. 79, 679.
Alexander, King of Serbia, 344.
Alexandra, South Africa, 223, 464, 536, 669, 738, 795.
Alfieri, Dino, 589.
Algeria, 363, 385, 544-545, 552.
Algerian nationalists, 73, 544.
Algerian War, 310, 544, 552. See also France.
Algerine Law, of Rhode Island, 427, 428.
Algiers, Algeria, 165, 385.
Alien and Sedition Acts, U.S., 338.
Alinsky, Saul, 139.
Allied Commission of Control, 381.
Allied "terror fliers," 324.
Allies, 87, 90, 267, 312, 324, 409, 586, 626.

All-Russian Peasant Union, 237.
All Souls College, Oxford, Preface.
Almon, John, 317.
Alternative communication system, 400-401.
"Alternative Days" strike. See Strike, limited.
Alternative economic institutions, 415-416.
Alternative institutions, 433, 797.
Alternative markets, 413-414.
Alternative political institutions, 423.
Alternative social institutions, 398-400, 797.
Alternative transportation system, 414-415, 796.
Alternatives to violence, Preface.
Altgeld, Governor John, 598.
Ambrose, Bishop, 388.
America, 70, 76, 90, 132, 171, 212, 229, 233, 245, 250 n. 49, 265, 382, 397, 404, 425, 671, 689, 736, 794. See also United States of America, South America, Latin America and individual countries.
American Antislavery Almanac, 376.
American Antislavery Society, 391.
American Cigar Makers Union, 269.
American colonists, 4, 70, 73, 74, 76, 124, 140-141, 157, 160, 165, 185-186, 224, 225, 229, 231, 234, 238-239, 241-242, 246-247, 266, 274, 287, 299, 308, 337, 361-362, 352 n. 169, 412, 424, 481, 495, 507, 511, 519 n. 132, 519 n. 142, 531, 534-535, 536, 540, 551, 553, 569 n. 115, 578-579, 580-582, 595, 600, 602-603, 605, 646 n. 99, 648 n. 147, 611-615, 622-623, 631-632, 633, 636, 667, 685, 693, 708, 713, 737, 738, 740, 743, 750, 781, 794, 797-798.
American Congress of Deputies for All the Colonies, 362.
American Federation of Labor, 404.
American Federation of Labor and Congress of Industrial Organizations, 297.
———, Union Label Department, 413.
American and Foreign Antislavery Society, 384.
American Nazis, 694, 789.
American Railway Union, 233.
American War of Independence, 221, 264, 337, 425, 611.
Americus, Georgia, 243.
Ami du Peuple, 35.
Amnesty International, 172.

Avignon, France, 151.
Axelrod, P.B., 431.
Axis Powers, 410.
Aynu'd-Dawia. See Hamíd, Grand Visier Abdu'l.
Azef, Yevno, 602.
Bailey, Thomas A., 343, 411.
Baku, Russian Empire, 168, 268.
Bakunin, M.A. 456, 678.
Ball, George W., U.S. Acting Secretary of State, 661.
Ballou Hall, Tufts University, 378-379.
Balogh, Peter, Deputy Bishop, 309.
Balsam, Lewis, 372.
Baltic Brigades, 80, 81.
Baltimore, Maryland, 159, 399.
Banda, Dr. Hastings Kamuzu, 419.
Bank of America, 395.
Bank of England, 410.
Banners, 126, 152, 154, 156.
Banning of meetings, 86, 538.
Bans and prohibitions, 538.
Bantu education, South Africa, 298.
Baptist Church, 379-380.
Barbar, E.C., 210-211.
Barbash, Jack, 280 n. 5, 261.
Barcelona, Spain, 222.
Bardoli, India, 212, 591, 599.
Bardoli Satyagraha Campaign, 1928, 146, 212, 299, 389, 535, 740, 781.
Bargon, Werner von, 314.
Barker, J. Ellis, 303.
Barnard, Chester I., 14, 16, 17, 23, 51 n. 17, 52 n. 24, 54 n. 46.
Barnett, Ross, Governor, 388.
Baroda, India, 212.
Barraclough, Solon L., 262, 281 n. 27.
Barton, Paul, 366.
Basques, 171.
Bast (Sanctuary), 206-210.
Batista regime, Cuba, 153.
Baton Rouge, Louisiana, 415, 689.
Batum, Russian Empire, 268.
Bauer, Raymond and Alice, 270, 272.
Baum group, 125, 128, 314.
Baum, Herbert, 161.
Bauman, Nicholas, 160.
Bavaria, Germany, 331, 369.
Baxter & Co., 233.
Beatings, 86, 548, 551, 556, 559.
Beck, Ludwig, Colonel-General, 295.
Bedford-Stuyvesant, Brooklyn, New York, 617.
Begar, 264.
Belfast, Northern Ireland, 260.
Belgium, 74, 82, 189, 190, 206, 237, 259,

305, 314, 368, 586, 604, 659.
Belgrade, Yugoslavia, 340, 344.
Belief in nonviolence, Preface.
Belize, British Honduras, 155.
Belleville Township High School, St. Louis, 197.
Bellhoek, South Africa, 591.
Bell, Philip, 392.
Belorussia, 43.
Ben Bella, 385.
Benedict XV, Pope, 204.
Bengal, India, 156.
Bentham, Jeremy, 53 n. 33.
Berea, Ohio, 200.
Bergen, Norway, 241.
Berger, Suzanne, 189.
Beria, L.P., 94.
Berlin, Germany: general, 120, 125, 128, 161, 314, 321, 381; and Kapp *Putsch*, 4, 79-81, 170, 686, 743, 780; and Jewish resistance, 89, 164, 484; Airlift, 408; East, 161, 170, 550, 574; West, 409, 550.
Berlin, Sir Isaiah, Preface.
Ber Mark, Professor, 125, 126, 161.
Bernadotte, Folke, Count, 331.
Bernard, L.L., 366.
Bernard, Sir Francis, Governor of Massachusetts Bay, 165, 581.
Betancourt, Rómulo, President of Venezuela, 248, 408.,
Bettiah, Champoron, India, 497.
Bevin, Ernest, 463.
Biafra, 397.
Bihar, India, 497, 591, 639.
Birmingham, Alabama, 138, 150, 380, 587, 591, 653 n. 239, 670-671, 688-689, 700 n. 40.
Bishop, Corbett, 200-201.
Bismark, Prince Otto von, 302-303.
Bitterfeld, East Germany, 405.
Blacklisting, 538.
Blacklisting of traders, 244-245.
Black Markets, 413.
Black-Out Boycott, 223, 395.
Blalock, Mayor G.F., 372.
Blanco, Hugo, 262.
Blaustein, A.P., 335-336.
Blockade, British of Germany, 344.
Blocking of Lines of Command and Information, 321-323.
Bloemfontein, South Africa, 512.
Bloody Sunday, January 9, 1905; 4, 78, 122, 168, 190, 266, 483, 530, 532, 551, 556, 561, 659, 667-668, 679-680, 688, 745.

Bloom, Murray Teich, 409-410.
"Blowing In the Wind" (song), 129.
Bobrikov, General Nikolai I., 593.
Bock, Field-Marshal Fedor von, 322.
Boddie, Jan, Preface.
de la Boétie, Etienne, 17, 24, 34, 35, 36, 54 n. 52, 60 n. 158.
Boghari, Algeria, 385.
Bohemia, 234; Catholic newspapers in, 234; National Socialists in, 234.
Bolivia, 246, 406-407; *coup d' état* in, 407; Ministry of Rural Affairs, 262.
Bolsheviks, 4, 79, 160, 328, 430, 606-607, 646 n. 99, 649 n. 159, 673, 743. See also Communist Party, Soviet Union.
Bombay, India, 155, 311, 385, 432-433, 687, 693, 735, 740, 751.
Bombay Congress Committee, 432.
Bombay Presidency, British India, 687.
Bombing (as sabotage), 3, 12, 77, 96-97, 139, 539, 548, 598, 610, 670, 689, 735.
Bombings, U.S. of Vietnam, 342.
Bondurant, Joan V., 146, 211, 299, 477, 519 n. 182, 503, 552-553, 709-710, 731, 742, 774 n. 161, 790, 796.
Books, publication and distribution of, 127.
Bordeaux, France, 326.
Border Government, North China, 232, 424.
Bormann, Martin, 324, 669.
Borisov, U.S.S.R., German Army Group Center at, 320.
Borton, Hugh, 212-213.
Bose, Nirmal Kumar, 500, 503, 509, 557, 563, 638, 805-806.
Bose, Subhas Chandra, 86.
Boston, Massachusetts, 137, 141, 157, 165, 274, 361, 381, 720; and occupation of Boston by British, 338, 553, 578; Boston School Committee, 373; Boston City Hospital, 393; Boston Massacre, 557, 685.
Boston Edison Company, 131.
Boston Globe, 297, 394.
Boston Port Act and Bill, 361-362, 702 n. 106.
Boston Tea Party, 507, 602, 612, 632, 685.
Boston University, 205.
Boston Vigilance Committee, 369-370.
Boulding, Kenneth, 790.
Bowditch, Dr. Henry, 391.
Boycott: general, 12, 71, 76, 77, 126, 719. See Social boycott, Economic

boycott and Political boycott. See also Noncooperation; Social noncooperation; Economic noncooperation; Political noncooperation; all specific methods under those classes; also Primary and Secondary boycotts.
Boycott, Captain, 220, 719.
Boycott of elections, 291-292.
Boycott of government departments, agencies and other bodies, 295-297.
Boycott of government employment and positions, 292-295.
Boycott of government-supported organizations, 199, 298, 302.
Boycott of legislative bodies, 289-291.
Boycott of social affairs, 196.
Boycott, political. See Political boycott and Political noncooperation.
Boycott, social. See Social boycott, Boycott of social relations, and Selective social boycott.i,
Brady, Dennis, Preface.
Braemer, General Friedrich, 326.
Brailsford, H.N., 432-433, 687.
Brahmins, 83, 393, 717.
Brandeis University, Preface, 198.
Brando, Marlon, 319.
Brandt, Heinz, 172, 529.
Brant, Stefan, 170, 172, 303, 386-387, 519 n. 132, 542, 550, 566 n. 21, 567 n. 47, 629, 688, 745-746.
Bratislava, Slovakia, 234, 313.
Brauchitsch, Commander-in-Chief Walter Von, 295, 322.
Bräutigam, Dr. Otto, 683.
Brazil, 262, 406, 408; coup d'etat in, 262.
Brest, Katherine, Preface.
Breton peasants, 189.
Brewers' Association, U.S., 231.
Brewers' Employers' Association, Germany, 222.
Brezhnev, Leonid I., General Secretary, Communist Party of the Soviet Union, 126.
Brinton, Crane, 337, 423-424.
Bristol, James, 243.
Bristol, Rhode Island, 185.
Britain (also British, England and English): American colonists' struggles against, 4, 76-77, 124, 137, 141, 158-159, 160, 165, 172, 185, 221, 224-226, 229, 231, 238-239, 246-247, 274, 287, 299, 361-363, 412-413, 424-425, 464, 507, 531, 534-535, 540-541, 553, 578, 699 n. 32, 702 n. 109, 708, 738, 740, 750-751, 794. See also American colo-

Champs Elysées, Paris, 310.
Chaney, James, 198.
Chang Chung-Li, 155, 242.
Changes in diplomatic and other representation, 340-341.
Channing, William Ellery, 392.
Chapman, Colin, 100.
Charles I, King of England, 424.
Charles II, King of England, 426.
Charles V, King of the Netherlands, 684, 748.
Charleston, South Carolina, 141, 221.
Charlestown, Massachusetts, 613.
Charles University, Czechoslovakia, 127, 162.
Charques, Richard, 261, 287, 430-431, 679.
Chase Manhattan Bank, 237.
Chase, William, 205.
Chatham, Lord (William Pitt, First Earl of Chatham), 737, 740.
Chauri-Chaura, India, 593.
Chavez, Cesar, 263.
Chelm Telegraph Station, Poland, 304.
Chemin des Dames, France, 166.
Chernigov, Russia, 261.
Chernyshevsky, N. G., 128, 163.
Cherokee Indians, 2372.
Cheyenne, Wyoming, 385.
Chicago, Illinois, 139, 198, 233, 236, 371-372, 402, 437 n. 55, 598, 624, 813 n. 83; City Hall of, 139.
Ch'ien Yung, 359.
Chikuni, Northern Rhodesia, 197.
Childs Security Corp., 233.
China, 73, 76, 131, 155, 196-197, 210, 212, 220, 229, 233, 234-235, 242, 246, 272, 277, 303-304, 307-308, 350 n. 88; Nationalist China, 343, 345-346; People's Republic of China, 145, 167, 272-273, 306, 323, 343, 346; Labor Insurance Regulations, 272; Health Committee of Trade Unions, 273.
China, North, 211, 307-308, 424. See also Occupations, Japanese of China.
Chipembere, H.B., 419.
Chippewa Indians, 288, 372.
Chipping Norton, England, 235.
Chita, Russian Empire, 333.
Chōcen, Czechoslovakia, 327.
Chōsan. See Desertions.
Christian Action, 138.
Christian II, King of Denmark, 241.
Christians, 368, 736.
Christiansand, Norway, 305.
Christison, Wenlock, 549.
Cherokee Indians, 372.

Chrysler Corporation, 404.
Chungking, China, 308.
Churches, 121, 191, 199, 204-205, 294, 469. See also names of individual churches, religions and denominations.
Church of Dolores, Cuba, 153.
Church of San Francisco, Guatemala City, Guatemala, 92.
Churchill Boulevard, Warsaw, 144.
Churchill, Winston, 87, 432, 531, 761.
Chu Van An High School, Saigon, 136.
Cierna, Czechoslovakia, 327.
Cinema Strike, 196.
Circulation of hostile rumors and jokes, 445 n. 301.
Citizens' alternatives to obedience, 303-319.
Citizen Army, Ireland, 161.
Citizens' catechism, 186.
City College of New York, 205, 373.
Civil disobedience, 4, 41, 67, 73, 84, 85-86, 118, 122, 129, 153, 162, 167, 304, 308, 310, 312, 315, 372, 382, 418, 420, 459, 466, 470, 483, 487, 497, 504, 512-513, 522, 533, 535, 541, 544, 546, 552, 558, 576, 584, 599-600, 622, 638-639, 640-641, 642, 652 n. 213, 667, 681, 682, 692, 698 n. 8, 762, 785, 792; defensive, 316; in India, 42, 497-498, 502, 739, 751, 757, 759; against "illegitimate" laws, 315-319; against "neutral" laws, 420-421; purificatory, 316; reformatory, 316; revolutionary, 316.
Civil liberties, 455, 483.
Civil Rights Act, 1964, U.S., 384, 690.
Civil rights campaigns, U.S., 74, 95-97, 134, 159, 198, 233, 371, 380, 383, 475, 483, 488, 498, 517 n. 94, 534, 587, 596, 603, 625, 626, 628, 632, 670, 671, 682, 688, 690, 694, 711, 722, 737-738, 766 n. 225, 783, 787-788, 789, 790.
Civil servants, 40, 81, 82, 297, 293, 323, 328, 459, 460, 498, 748.
Civil war: general, 3, 34, 551, 637, 756; Austria, 589; England, 970; Holy Roman Empire, 192; U.S., 203, 376, 392, 399, 411.
Civilian defense, 421, 496, 517 n. 93, 519 n. 128, 776 n. 219, 810.
Civilian insurrection, 90.
Civilian Public Service, 200.
Civilian resistance, 90, 100, 155, 505, 513, 530.
Civilian Resistance, Directorate of Poland, 188.

ČKD, Czechoslovak factory, originally Ceskomolavska-Kolben-Danék, 402, 440 n. 171.

Clarke, Moira, Preface.

Clausewitz, General Carl von, 495, 496, 506, 759, 762.

Clay, Senator Henry, 384.

Cleveland, Ohio, 386, 392, 403.

Clogging the channels of justice, 445 n. 301.

"Closely Watched Trains," (film), 301.

Clyde, Scotland, 235.

Codex juris cannonici, 204.

Coercion, 12, 26, 27-28, 30, 42, 58 n. 122, 67-68, 83, 245-246, 367, 431, 433, 536, 548, 703 n. 154, 742, 807.

Coercion by direct physical violation, 12, 27, 30. See also Nonviolent coercion.

Coercion Act, Ireland, 603.

Coercive acts, colonial America, 685.

Coffin, Rev. William Sloane, 204.

Cohoes, New York, 236.

Coimbra, Portugal, 195.

Colijan government, Netherlands, 422.

Collaborators, 188-189, 410.

Collective disappearance, 210-211.

Collective indiscipline. See Mutinies.

Collier, John, Commissioner of Indian Affairs, 372.

Collins, John A., 375.

Colombia, 406.

Colombo, Ceylon, 267.

Colonialism: in Africa, 43, 293, 297, 483; Nazi, 43, 483.

Colored American, 374, 392.

Cominform, 347.

Commando order, Nazi, 353 n. 182.

Commissar Decree, Nazi, 322.

Committee of Correspondence, 165.

Committee for Direct Action Against Nuclear War, 635.

Committee for Nonviolent Action, 653 n. 254.

Committee of 100, Britain, 145, 167, 419-420, 482, 631, 632, 652 n. 213, 653 n. 253, 692, 792.

Committee on Appeal for Human Rights, Atlanta, Georgia, 464.

Committee of Observation and Prevention, American colonies, 274.

Committee of Safety, Massachusetts Bay Colony, 612.

Commodus, Emperor of Rome, 123, 201.

Communication, means of, 11, 15, 78, 100, 125, 369, 400, 474, 627, 640, 712, 714, 750, 802.

Communism, 5, 39-40, 93, 125, 172, 260, 297, 343, 532, 619, 714; Belgian Communists, 683; Hungarian Communists, 125; South African Communists, 619. See also Communist Parties and individual countries.

Communist Party, Czechoslovakia, 98-100; Extraordinary Fourteenth Congress of, 99-100, 121, 129, 170, 173 n. 19, 234, 260, 288; All-Unit Committee of, 173 n. 19, 288, 301; University Committee of, 174 n. 19; Presidium, 131, 310, 327, 390; Presidium of the Central Committee, 131, 174 n. 19; Presidium of the Prague City Committee of the National Front, 173 n. 19; Party Presidium, 99; Presidium of the Prague City Committee of the Communist Party, 131.

Communist Party, East Germany. See Socialist Unity Party, East Germany.

Communist Party, Poland, 316.

Communist Party, Hungary, 125.

Communist Party, Soviet Union, 39, 40, 170, 171, 684, 749, 753. See also Bolsheviks.

Communist Party, United States, 263.

Communist Party, Yugoslavia, Central Committee of, 340.

Company of Commerce, Hungary, 398.

Compliants, Finland, 186.

Compliance (pattern of), 15, 25, 26, 57 n. 110.

Comply-in, 417.

Compromise, 3, 65, 81, 100, 534, 547, 695, 760.

Comte, Auguste, 11, 49 n. 5; 49 n. 8; 49 n. 9.

Concentration camps, 88, 485, 585, 725.

Concessions, 45, 86, 94, 202, 207, 213, 258, 268, 283 n. 89; 470, 532-534, 567 n. 47; 694, 737, 739, 748, 759-761, 780, 782.

Conciliation, 65, 534.

Concord, New Hampshire, 199, 396.

Concord, Massachusetts, 246, 287, 536, 600, 603, 605, 611-614, 694.

Confiscation, 86, 538.

Conflict: acute, 3, 537, 793; scale of, 793; responses to, 65; in democratic system and dictatorships, 71; facing conflicts, 74; armed, 53; military, 111, 782; violence in, 133, 695, 792, 794, 801-802; international, 793; noncooperation in, 183; nonviolent action and assumptions about, 109, noncooperation in, 183, differences in development of strategy, 523; sharpened by

nonviolent action, 524; within opponent camp, 675-676; Gandhi's use of nonviolent action in 82-83; conclusion of conflict and concentration of power, 799-806; underlying, 785, 810; violent, 133, 551, 695, 782, 802.
Confronting the opponent's power, 451-454.
Confucius, 359.
Congo, 237.
Congregational Church, Concord, New Hampshire, 396.
Congregational Church, Plymouth, New Hampshire, 199.
Congress of Democrats, South Africa, 526.
Congress of Industrial Organizations (CIO), 404.
Congress of the People at Kliptown, Johannesburg, South Africa, 123.
Congress of Racial Equality (CORE), 134, 139-140, 373-374, 377, 383, 395, 402, 419, 617, 632, 741, 766, 786.
Congress of the United States of America, 126, 245-247, 338, 379, 428, 690. See also House of Representatives, Senate, and United States of America.
Congressional Union, 126.
Connaught, Duke of, 686.
Connecticut, 429, 581, 633. See also individual towns and cities.
Connor, Bull, 138.
Conscientious objector(s), U.S., 200, 265, 366.
Conscription, 260, 312, 539; resistance to, 125, 149, 204-205, 261, 312, 314, 507, 752.
Consent, 25, 27, 28, 29, 30-31, 58 n. 123; 59 n. 128; 44.
Consent, withdrawal of, 3, 13, 30, 47, 476, 524. See also Obedience.
Conser, Walter, Preface.
Conservation Department, State of Washington, 318.
Conservatives, England, 532.
Consolidated Edison Co., 223.
Conspiracy, 80, 81, 322.
Constantine, 385.
Consumer boycott, 221-224, 231-232, 234, 358, 395, 412, 504, 538.
Constitution, Atlanta, Georgia, 671.
Constitutionalists, Finland, 186.
Constitutional Movement, Persia, 206.
Continental Association, 5, 186, 224, 225, 229, 234, 424-425, 481, 511, 578, 581, 600, 603, 612-615, 633, 648 n. 124; 685, 699 n. 32; 798. See also Continental Congress.

Continental Congress, First, 5, 224-225, 229, 239, 274, 317, 424, 481, 507, 511, 581, 595, 600, 612, 699 n. 32; 740, 794, 798. See also Continental Association and Continental Congress, Second.
Continental Congress, Second, 123, 614-615. See also Continental Congress, First.
Control of communication and information, 538.
Control of political power: general, 3, 7, 13, 33, 34, 35, 52 n. 23; 54 n. 47; traditional means, 32-33.
Conversion, 69, 83, 85, 358, 363, 367, 455, 458, 477, 501, 502, 528, 601, 634, 666, 697, 703 n. 154; 706-733, 734, 737, 741, 753, 766, 767, 768, 769 n. 1.
Cooperation: power dependent upon, 8, 12, 13, 16, 18, 22, 23, 24, 27, 28, 29, 30, 42, 44, 47, 59 n. 144; 59 n. 145; 64, 423, 490, 695, 744, 746, 747; sanctions dependent on, 14, 15, 112, 755, 760; refusal of, 31, 34, 40, 41, 69, 80-81, 82, 183, 681, 686, 785. See also need for in Gandhi's view, 43, 78; among nonviolent actionists, 423, 778, 795-797. See also Noncooperation.
Copenhagen, Denmark, 274, 275, 277, 305.
Corporative state, Norway, 5, 70, 88, 89, 298, 585.
Corvées, India, 264; Russia, 270.
Cossacks, Russia, 163, 207, 333.
Cottam, Richard, 210.
Council of Art and Culture, Poland, 316.
Council of Limoges, 193.
Council of Massachusetts Bay, 685.
Council of Union of Liberation, Russia, 168.
Council of Workingmen's Delegates or Deputies of St. Petersburg, Imperial Russia, 430-431.
Coup d'etat: general and resistance to, 9, 25, 34, 294, 328, 421, 433, 464, 480, 500, 753, 802, 809; in Guatemala, 93; in Czechoslovakia, 98-99, 234; in Brazil, 262, 408; in Russia, 328; in Bolivia, 407; in South Vietnam, 672; in Sachsen, Germany, 619; in Germany, see Kapp *Putsch*.
"Coventry, Send to," 508.
Craft strike, 265.
Craft, William and Ellen, 418.
Craig, Gordon A., 342.
Cranswick, Yorkshire, England, 395.

92, 93, 96, 133, 316, 487, 543, 662, 781, 802, 804.

Demonstrations: advance notice of, 491; time gaps between, 509, 723; of unity, 536; repression of, see Repression; nonviolent demonstrations defusing violence, 623-625, 629; promoting nonviolent discipline in, 630, see also Nonviolent discipline: by third parties, 664; in periods of regrouping, 763; for particular demonstrations, see group of demonstrators, or place of demonstration. For particular types of demonstrations and examples of them, see all specific methods of the class nonviolent protest and persuasion, and all other methods of nonviolent action which operate primarily by calling attention to the grievance, viewpoint, etc., especially methods of social noncooperation, and the sub-classes of symbolic strikes, rejection of authority and often many of the methods of nonviolent intervention.

Demonstration, strike. See Protest strike.

Demonstrative funerals, 159-162.

Demoralization, 100.

Denmark, 87, 129, 136, 150, 194, 196, 231, 251 n. 64; 274, 275, 586, 683. See also Occupation, German of Denmark.

Department Deutschland, Nazi Germany, 325.

Department of Defense, U.S., Preface.

Deportation, 305, 312-313, 314, 321, 325, 326, 332, 484.

Deputations, 130-131.

Deravyanko, General, 533.

Desegregation, 97, 335, 388, 475, 788.

Despotism, 128, 339, 456. See also Dictators, Tyrants, Tyranny, Totalitarianism.

Desertions, 212-213. See also protest emmigration.

Destruction. See Material destruction.

Destruction, of own property, 140-142, 359.

Detailed strike, 268-269.

Detention camps, 86, 312.

Detroit, Michigan, 205.

Deutsch, Karl W., 15, 23, 52-53 n. 31.

Devlin Commission, 747.

De Waarheid 401.

Dharasana Salt Depot, 380, 564, 687, 731.

Dharasana salt raids, 311, 330, 687, 693.

Dhawan, Gopinath, 565, 813 n. 88.

Dhurna (or "Sitting Dhurna"), 364, 367.

Dickenson, John, 798.

Dictators (also dictatorship), 5, 29, 38, 71, 75, 90, 91, 92, 97, 298, 423, 482, 483-484, 493, 495, 744, 748, 749, 760, 806, 809. See also Tyranny, Totalitarianism, Oppression.

Diefenbaker, Prime Minister John, 140.

Diels, Rudolf, 330.

Diem, Ngo Dinh, 151, 660-661.

Diem Regime, 136, 137, 138, 279, 534, 537, 542, 587, 660-661, 671, 688.

Diet, Finland, 131.

Dillon, John, 603, 632.

Dimitroff, Georgi, 369.

Direct action, 537, 543, 544, 551, 797.

Direct Action Committee Against Nuclear War, 128, 148, 289, 631, 632, 653 n. 253.

Directives of 1937, Netherlands, 422.

Directorate of Civilian Resistance, Poland, 188.

Direct physical violence, 539-540.

Disarmament conference, 1933, 345.

Discipline: general, 54 n. 51; 333, 763, 782, 787; necessity of in nonviolent action, 615-620. See also Nonviolent discipline and Self-discipline.

Disclosing identities of secret agents, 418.

Discountenancing, 185.

Discrimination, 95, 358, 373, 375, 378, 419, 791, 795.

Disguised disobedience, 306-308.

Disobedience, 46, 285, 576; withdrawal of obedience, 12, 20, 21; and sanctions and repression, 27, 28, 32, 35, 58 n. 122, 58 n. 123, 204, 681; relationship to obedience and enforcement, 15, 35; and self-confidence, 23; always exists, 25; and self-interest, 27; potential and limits of, 32, 35, 45, 82, 84; perceived threat of, 45, 61-62 n. 201; ethical justification of, 45; resistance by, 47, 84; disintegrates political power, 63, 434, 753; by ruler's agents, 77, 667, 675, 753. See also specific methods subclassed as "Action by Government Personnel," and fraternization, 146. See also Fraternization, to military system, 204-205; judicial, 329. See also Judicial noncooperation; and leadership, 426. See also all the following particular methods: Social disobedience, Nonobedience, in absence of direct supervision, Popular nonobedience, Disguised disobedience, Refusal of an assemblage or meeting to disperse, Sitdown, Noncooperation with conscription and deportation, Hiding escape and false identities, Selective refusal of assistance by government aides, Blocking lines of command and information, Stalling and obstruction, General administrative noncooperation, Judicial noncooperation, Deliberate inefficiency and selective noncooperation by enforcement agents, Mutiny, Quasilegal evasions and delays, Noncooperation by constituent governmental units, Disclosing identities of secret agents, Seeking imprisonment, Civil disobedience of "neutral" laws, Work-on without collaboration, Dual sovereignty and parallel government.

Display of flags and symbolic colors, 135-136, 522.

Displayed communications, 126.

Displays of portraits, 143.

Disputes and Trade Union Act of 1927 Britain, 133.

Diwakar, Ranganath R., 85.

Doane, Don, 675.

Dobrolubov, N.A., 163.

Dolci, Danilo, 363, 402.

Domestic embargo, 244.

Dominican Republic, 248.

Donbas, U.S.S.R., 150.

Don Cossack region, Russian empire, 261.

Dorr's rebellion, Rhode Island, 426-430.

Dorr, Governor Thomas Wilson, 427-430.

Douglass, Frederick, 375-376, 379, 391-392, 523.

Doukhobors, 140, 141.

Dracy, France, 327.

Draft card burning, 142.

Draga, Queen of Serbia, 344.

Drake, St. Clair, 411.

Dresden, Germany, 80.

Drill Hall, Johannesburg, 150.

Dual sovereignty and parallel government, 4, 69, 79, 93, 232, 416, 423-433, 502, 633, 745, 746, 767.

Dubček, Alexander, First Secretary, Communist Party of Czechoslovakia, 98-99, 100, 111, 121, 122, 143.

Dubček, regime, 98, 100, 122, 173 n. 19, 402.

Dubček shift, 402.

Dubček's Sunday, 402.

Dublin, Ireland, 161, 227, 300.

Duc, Venerable Thich Quang, 138.

Dühring, Eugen, 684.

Duisburg, Germany, 610.

Dulany, Daniel, 76, 412.

Dulles, John Foster, 248, 343.

Duluth, Michigan, 372.

Duma of Imperial Russia, 152, 160, 191, 238, 242, 290, 291, 519 n. 132, 533, 799.

Dumbarton Oaks conversations, 346.

Dumping, 411.

Dunmore, Governor John Murray, 137, 425, 613-614.

Dunn, North Carolina, 372.

Dunn High School, North Carolina, 372.

Duplex Printing Co., 221.

Durban, South Africa, 200, 167.

Dutch. See Netherlands.

Dutchess County, province of New York, 226.

Dutch Reformed Church, 122.

Duy Tan Clinic, 363.

Dylan, Bob, 129.

Earthwriting, 130.

Eastern Railroad, Massachusetts, 376.

Eastern Transvaal, South Africa, 223.

East Europeans, 42-43. See also individual countries.

East German Peace Council, 172.

East German rising, 1953, 5, 93, 125, 143, 172, 277, 298, 405, 463, 474, 484, 515 n. 30, 519 n. 132, 533-534, 550, 597, 566 n. 21, 615, 629, 647 n. 99, 675, 676, 688, 708, 745-746, 753.

East Germany, 97, 121, 125, 136, 148, 153, 170, 172, 213, 242, 303, 529, 545, 566 n. 21, 675-677, 688, 745.

East India Company, 224-225, 361, 507, 685.

East Indies, 221.

East Prussia, 213.

Eberhard, Prof. Wolfram, 350 n. 88, 359.

Ebert government, Germany, Weimar Republic, 4, 40, 80, 81, 339, 767.

Ebert, President Friedrich, 80, 170, 678.

Ebert, Theodor, Preface, 421-422, 470, 472, 473, 480, 491, 509, 515 n. 30, 517 n. 93, 523, 529, 550, 566 n. 21, 567 n. 47, 567 n. 50, 574-575, 647 n. 99, 764, 775 n. 193, 776 n. 219.

Eccleston Square, London, 574.

Economic boycotts: general characteristics, 219-221; methods of, defined with examples, 221-248; general, 4, 70, 77, 86, 95, 118, 185, 186, 196, 258, 338, 461, 503, 538, 580, 667, 695, 737, 750, 789; relation to selective patronage, 412-413; laws and other countermeasures against, 540-541, 685; and smuggling, 612; American colonial, 580-582, 667, 750; See also American colonies, Britain—American colonists' struggles against, and specific methods described in Chapter Six. Indian, 641, 751. See also Britain–Indian struggles against, and India. See other specific cases in which economic boycotts were prominent.

Economic noncooperation, methods of, 257-285; general, 69, 184, 186, 219-248, 279, 507, 536, 600, 603, 605, 612, 614, 666, 685, 693, 708, 737, 797. See also economic boycotts and strikes.

Economic shutdown, 236, 266, 278-279, 744, 751, 752, 767.

Egmont Count of, Netherlands, 294.

Egypt, 125, 155, 190, 197, 201, 202, 204, 241, 295. See also Occupation, British and French of Port Said, Egypt.

Ehrlich, Raloff (pseud. for Karl Raloff), 519 n. 132, 627.

Eichman, Lt. Col. Karl Adolph, 326, 715.

Eilifsen, Gunnar, 332.

Eisenhower, President Dwight D., 36-39, 133.

Eisenbach, East Germany, 143.

Ekaterinoslav, Russia, 268.

Elbe River, 328.

Elites, 49 n. 6.

Elliott, W.Y., 774 n. 157.

El Salvador, 70, 74, 90, 91, 97, 292, 744, 752.

Embargo Act U.S., 245-246.

Embargoes: general, 12, 64, 408, 461, 752; enforced by blacklisting of traders, 244-245; for individual embargoes, see names of countries involved. See also the types of embargoes: Domestic embargo, International sellers' embargo, International buyers' embargo, International trade embargo, and Total international embargo.

Emerson, Ralph Waldo, 60 n. 158.

Emigration Convention of 1854, 411.

Enabling Act, Germany, 589.

England. See Britain.

Engels, Frederick, 684.

Ennis, Ireland, 582.

Ephesus, in Asia Minor, 231, 540.

Erfurt, Germany, 688.

Erikson, Erik, 778.

Ermolov, Alexis, Minister of Agriculture, 532, 679.

Esbjerg, Denmark, 279.

Essen, Germany, 149, 542.

Establishing new social patterns, 390-393.

Establishment strike, 267.

Ethical problems, Preface.

Ethiopia, 246.

Europe, 4, 192, 205, 212, 245-246, 290, 403, 417, 433, 525, 559, 586, 659, 669, 688. See also Occupation. German of Europe, and individual countries.

Euthanasia program, Nazi Germany, 469, 484.

Evasion, 320.

Excommunication, 191-193, 199.

Executions, 12, 466, 580, 604, 636, 638.

Exploitation, 44.

Expulsion from international organizations, 346-347, 445 n. 301.

Extermination camps, 484.

Eyck, Erich, 40, 81, 604, 610, 780.

Faber-Castell, Graf, 330.

Fabian tactics. See Stalling and obstruction.

Failure. See Outcome of the conflict, and Defeat.

Fairbank, John K., 220.

Fairfield County, Connecticut, 633.

Falkenhausen, General Alexander von, Military Governor of Belgium, 683.

Fanueil Hall, Boston, Massachusetts, 141, 165, 308.

Farm Workers' Strike, 262-264.

Farmer, James, 134, 139-140, 240, 377, 402, 419, 437 n. 55, 523, 569 n. 102, 603, 624-625, 689, 716, 733, 741, 766, 786-788, 791.

Farson, Negley, 666, 735.

Fascism (and fascists), 70, 88, 89, 122, 237, 331-332, 422; Norwegian fascists, 676, 691.

Fasts, 134, 137, 145, 359, 360-367, 466, 522, 580, 583, 682, 694, 709, 711. See also Fast of moral pressure, Hunger strike, Satyagrahic fast and Troscad.

Fast of moral pressure, 360-361.

Faulkner, William, 739.

Faupl, Mr. (A.F.L.-C.I.O.), 297.

Fear, 18-19, 20, 25, 26, 32, 55 n. 61, 58 n. 123, 111, 313, 456-457, 462, 476, 484, 485, 486, 489-490, 610, 616, 707, 714-715, 727-728, 740, 745; casting off of, 456-458, 478, 485, 488.

Fearlessness, 478, 481, 485, 489, 501, 504, 583, 636-638, 640.

Fear of Sanctions. See Sanctions, fear of.

February Manifesto (Tsar Nicholas II), 186.

Federación Agraria Nacional, Colombia, 406.

Federal Correctional Institution, Danbury, Connecticut, 265.

Federal Power Commission, U.S., 386.
Federation of Rhodesia and Nyasaland, 127, 242, 292-293, 296.
Federation of Southern Cooperatives, 416.
Fee, Rev. John G., 399.
Feeney, Colonel Paul, 417.
Fejto, François, 289.
Fender, B.E.F., Preface.
Ferguson, C.C., Jr., 335, 336.
Ferrer, Francisco, 230.
Fifeshire, Scotland, 273.
Filipino migrant workers in U.S., 263.
"Final Solution" (extermination of Jews), 89, 327, 484. See also Extermination camps, and Jews.
"Financial Manifesto" of the St. Petersburg Soviet, 237, 244.
Financial resources, 11, 460, 750.
Fines, 86.
Finkelstein, Marina S., Preface.
Finland, 125, 131, 149, 185-186, 278, 291, 312, 339, 346, 352 n. 169, 464, 495, 647 n. 99, 692.
Finland, Parliament, 339.
Finnish Nonviolent Noncooperation Movement for Independence, 593.
Firmness in face of repression, 562-565.
First National Bank, Boston, Massachusetts, 766.
First National City Bank of New York, 237.
Fish-ins, 318-319.
Fishman, J.R., 475, 569 n. 102, 604, 626, 711, 717, 783, 789-791.
Flags, 135-136, 162, 660.
Flekkefjord, Norway, 305.
"Flight" of workers, 201-204.
Flint glass makers, England, 268-269.
Flint, Michigan, 269, 403.
Florida, United States, 766.
Florida Board of Education, 336.
Florida, Spanish, 204.
Florida's pupil assignment law, 336-337.
Flower, B.O., 362.
Flynn, Elizabeth Gurley, 576-577.
Fogg, Richard W., 306.
Fortera, Richard, Preface.
Fonzo, Jenny, Preface.
Ford Foundation, Preface.
Force. 15, 27, 28, 29, 33, 34, 41, 43-44, 49-50 n. 5, 50 n. 15, 51 n. 17, 58 n. 122, 58 n. 123, 774 n. 157. See also Power, Violence, Coercion, and Nonviolent coercion.
Forced labor, 313, 325.
Forest laws, civil disobedience campaign against (India), 641.

Formosa (Taiwan), 346.
Forster, H.O. Arnold, 643 n. 40.
Fort Detrick, Maryland, 148
Fort Hunter, New York, 389.
Fort Jameson Schools, Northern Rhodesia, 197.
Forward, 306.
Foster, Stephen S., 371, 396.
Foster, William Z., 535.
Fox, George, 395-396.
Fox, Robert, 377.
France, vessels and trade banned by U.S. embargo policy, 246; nonviolent action against possible counter-revolutionary blockade, 247; National Assembly, 305, 309; nonviolent action during French Revolution, 137, 305. See also French Revolution; nonviolent action during 1848 revolution, 168, 305. See also French Revolution of 1848; Advocates of general strike, 276; boycotts of elections, 291; sit-down strikes, 403; fourteenth century protest music, 151-152; "red cap of liberty," 136; 1917 army mutinies, 144, 166, 334-335, 464, 511, 529, 532, 781; occupation and administration in Ruhr, 1923; see Ruhrkampf; miscellaneous, 363, 659, 794; resistance during Nazi occupation, 163, 586; pro-Jewish resistance in occupied France, 305, 549; pro-Jewish demonstration in Vichy France, 121; stalling and obstruction to save Jews in Vichy France, 325, 326-327; Vichy French government. Conseil de Ministres, 327; Commissariat aux Questions Juives, 326; Japanese demand Indo-China bases of, 410-411; repression in Algeria, 545. Algerian War casualties 552; refusal to pay U.N. contributions, 237; atomic test at Reggan, North Africa, 382; anti-detention demonstrations, 310, 419, fasts, 363. See also Occupation, Italy of France and German of France and Breton peasants.
Franco, General Francisco, 97.
Frank, Jerome D., 790-791, 813 n. 63
Frank, Reichkommissar Hans, 716.
Frankken, Gau, Nazi Germany, 320.
Franklin, Benjamin, 602, 685, 750.
Franz, Obersharführer, 150.
Franz Josef, Emperor of Austria, 135, 164, 286.
Fraternization, 118, 146, 198, 332, 673, 733, 789.
Frazer, Edwin, 130.
Frederick, Maryland, 148.

Freedom, 29, 58 n. 122, 59 n. 143, 94, 100, 123, 124, 133, 457, 490-491.
Freedom ballot, 134, 788.
Freedom buses, 791.
Freedom charter, 1955, South Africa, 568 n. 64.
Freedom democratic party of Mississippi, 135, 373.
"Freedom registration," 134, 788.
Freedom rides, 95, 375, 419, 544, 670-671, 689, 694, 700 n. 40, 783, 791.
"Freedom schools," New York, 198.
Freemen's constitution, Rhode Island, 427.
Freemen's convention, Rhode Island, 427.
Free press, 92, 120, 305, 641.
Free Russian Press, 456.
Free speech movement of University of California at Berkeley, 373.
Freiheit, 686
Freikorps troops, Germany, 80, 686.
French Canadians, 314.
French Revolution of 1789, 241, 305, 424.
French Revolution of 1848, 168.
Friederick II, 193.
Freud, Sigmund, 710.
Friends committee on national legislation, 132.
Fromm, Fritz, 322.
Frubel, Stanislaw, 314.
Fugitive slave law, (United States), 313, 384.
Fullon, General Ivan, 640.
Functional alternative to violence, Preface.
Funerals. See Political mourning, Mock funerals, Demonstrative funerals, and Homage at burial places.
Fürth, Germany, 320.

Gage, General and Governor Thomas, 124, 274, 338, 581, 568, 614.
Galen, Bishop, 669.
Galerius, Roman Emperor, 736; Toleration Edict of, 736.
Galician, Ukraine, 590.
Gandhi, Prime Minister Indira, 290.
Gandhi, Mohandas, K.: general, 5, 34, 42, 60, 87, 111, 143, 187, 360, 363, 433, 449, 464, 524, 567 n. 30, 600, 619, 654 n. 250, 655 n. 291, 719, 735, 772, 790; and nonviolent struggle, 4; role of consent, 27, 31-32, 78, 545, 729; on acceptance of sanctions, 56; on role of education, 57 n. 100; power of non-cooperation, 41, 46-47, 707; power of

nonviolence versus violence, 113, 587; withdrawal of cooperation, 59 n. 144; 59 n. 145, 747; on slavery, 59 n. 143; on resignation of officials, 748; struggles in South Africa (1906), 79; contribution to nonviolent technique, 82-83; theory of power, 83-86; on conversion of opponent, 83, 753; and satyagraha, 85, 548; 1930-31 Independence Campaign, 86-87, 153; grand strategy of, 87; 'walking tour,' 156; knowledge of nonviolent conflicts, 73-74; influence of experiments, 98; social boycott, 187, 229; coping with repression, 211, 759; protest emigration (*hijrat*), 212; economic boycott, 229-230; use of *hartal* by, 278, 504; reverse trial, 368; satyagrahic fast, 367, alternative social institutions, 398, 798; on dangers of secrecy, 486; on need for openness and risk-taking, 483, 490; civil disobedience, 315, 316, 483, 497, 504; of 'neutral" laws, 420-421. See also Civil Disobedience. On nonviolent strategy and tactics, 492, 505; on leadership needed for optimal success, 494; choosing place of struggle, 497; necessity of discipline, 615, 616, 619; promoting nonviolent discipline, 621, 622, 624, 629, 631; on discipline and numbers of actionists, 499, 502; need for nonviolent behavior, 595, 599; quantity and quality of nonviolent action, 477, 478, 638; concentration of strength, 500; numbers and discipline varying with method, 502; initiative, 500; phased development of nonviolent action, 502, 503-504, 759; halting submission, 522, 524; risk and prevention of violence, 454, 465; cowardice, 456; casting off fear, 457, 782, 783, 785; nonviolence requires greater bravery, 457, 458; suffering, 554, 563, 655 n. 264, 724-725, 728. See also Suffering. Leadership, 463, 494, 465, 632-633, 638; inadequacy of arresting leaders, 638; dependent on group for leadership authority, 465-466; nonviolent sanctions of leadership, 466, 580; obedience of volunteers, 466; preparation for nonviolent struggle, 467-468; negotiations, 470, 471; focal point for action, 471, 473; need for organization, 480; recognizing weakness of own movement, 509, 759; letter of ultimatum, 512-513; force of public opinion, 530, 584; dissatisfaction with concessions, 533; opponents' reaction to civil disobedience, 535; maintaining rapport, 576, 583; limits to effectiveness of opponents' violence, 544, 545, 698 n. 2; inhibiting repression, 584, 753; persistence, 547, 548; opponent prefers violence, 591; avoiding hatred, 634; resisting provocations to violence, 594; violence weakens movement, 597, 599; provocative nonviolent action, 563, 564, 687; nonviolence weakens opponent, 565; sabotage, 609, 651 n. 168; need for financial self-reliance, 663; escalation of disobedience, 641; reaction to Amristar shooting, 686; counter-nonviolence, 693; seeking conversion, 707, 709, 720, 723, 724-725, 727, 728; rationale of self-suffering, 709, 711; overcoming social distance, 714; sense of nonviolent power, 780, 781; increasing self-respect of Indians, 786; reversal of perceptions of masculinity and violence by, 790; effect on Indian National Congress, 795; increasing internal cooperation, 796; constructive program, 797, 813 n. 88; effect of nonviolence on British trade, 751-752; negotiated settlement, 760, 761; struggle during negotiations, 761; dangers of overconfidence, 766; aftermath of repression, 767-768; nonviolent coercion, 769 n. 4, 774 n. 161; effect of wife on, 771 n. 66; respect of opponent for actionists, 721; need for self-sufficient nonviolent action, 728, 729; *Young India*, 751.

Gandhian(s), 73, 131, 393, 563, 564, 693, 792.

Gandhian struggles, India, 74, 79, 83, 403, 413, 510, 512, 528, 665, 677.

Ganu, Babu, 385.

Gapon, Father Georgii, 155-156, 483, 640.

Garhwali Mutiny in India, 675, 747.

Garhwali Regiment, 335, 432.

Garnet, Henry Highland, 411.

Garrison, William Lloyd, 369, 371, 376, 384, 412.

Garrisonian nonviolent actionists, 371, 375, 396.

Gaspée, 299.

Gates, Seth, 379.

Gauche Dynastique, 168.

Gauldal, Trøndelag, Norway, 253 n. 119.

Gaul, 124.

Gayle, Mayor, 415.

Gazette, official newspaper of Persia, 207.

Gazetteer, Britain, 317.

General administrative noncooperation, 328.

General Assembly, Rhode Island, 426, 428-430.

General Committee, South Carolina, 614.

General Council's Strike Organization Committee, Britain, 464.

General Court, Massachusetts Bay Colony, 720.

General Governement, in Nazi-occupied Poland, 127.

General Motors, 269, 403, 403-404, 692.

General Agrarian Strike, Russia, 507.

General strike: general, 45, 80, 133-134, 165, 259, 265, 271, 275-277, 278, 289, 422, 431, 441 n. 191, 477, 498, 507, 751, 815-817; "localized," 275; and nonviolent coercion, 502, 706, 755; and economic shutdown, 279; economic, 276; political, 276; revolutionary, 276; in support of hunger strike, 366; in support of mutiny, 503; feared as powerful weapon, 532; measures against, 542, 593; and parallel government, 432; against Kapp *Putsch*, Germany 1920, 40, 41, 80, 619, 743. See also Kapp *Putsch*. Turned into armed rising, 79; Czechoslovakia 1968, 260; Britain 1926, 271, 432, 463, 464, 485, 519 n. 128, 531, 532, 542, 574, 578, 593, 757, 787; Belgian general strikes, 276; Russian general strikes, 604, 606, 607-608, 649 n. 154; Great October Strike, Russia 1905, 139, 152, 166, 276, 533, 743, 752, 780, 799; Guatemala 1944, 93; during Hungarian Revolution 1956, 93; Haiti 1956, 266; Ghana (then called Gold Coast) 1949, 788; Italy 1904, 432; Netherlands, 536.

Genessee County, New York, 379.

Geneva, Switzerland, 131, 297.

Geneva Committee of Parents, London, 131.

George III, King of England, 317, 363.

Georgia, Russian Empire, 242, 296, 431.

Georgia, United States, 200, 202, 221, 582, 615.

Gerbrandy, Prime Minister P. S., 422.

Gerland, Brigitte, 533.

Germany: general, 342, 545, 554, 562, 584, 659, 676, 682, 781, 787; submarine campaign 1917, 344; military attaché von Papen, 341; official backing for nonviolent action, 5; Weimar Republic. See Kapp *Putsch* and *Ruhrkampf*; abolition of Weimar Republic and Reichstag fire, 588-589; plantations in Guatemala, 90; assets frozen in U.S. 1941, 341; Nazi system: deportations of Jews, 153, 313, 314. See also Jews. Euthanasia program, 469; jazz banned, 306-307; and Portuguese cinemas, 233; pro-Jewish resistance in, 89-90, 136, 304, 305, 325-326. See also Jews. And right of resistance, 45; provocation by violence desired by, 588-589; Minister of War, 296; Ministry of Justice, 320-323; Minister of Economics, 244; East Ministry, 323; Order Police, 321; War Office, 320-322; Army High Command (O.K.H.), 295, 321-322; High Command of the Armed Forces (O.K.W.), 321; Foreign Office, 325, 327; Army band, 307; German Democratic Republic, Politbureau of, 533-534, 676. See also East Germany and Socialist Unity Party. West German farmers and Berlin blockade, 409; methods: public speeches, 119-120; pastoral letters, 122; slogans and symbols, 125-126; posters, 126; leaflets etc., 128; wearing of symbols, 136; silence, 170; social boycott, 189; consumers boycott, 222, 223; slowdown strike, 270-271; selective strike, 275; general strike, 276-277; refusal of industrial assistance in, 236; revenue refusal, 242; domestic embargo, 244; boycott of government employment etc., 293, 295; boycott of government agencies, 296; disguised disobedience, 306-307; "escape," 314; selective refusal of assistance by government aides, 320, 321; blocking lines of command and information, 321-322; stalling and obstruction, 323-324; noncooperation by constituent government units, 337; withdrawal from international organizations, 345; reverse trial, 368; nonviolent air raid, 381; political counterfeiting, 410. See also Berlin Airlift, Kapp *Putsch*, *Ruhrkampf*, East German Rising, Invasions, Occupations, Nazis, Hitler, Colonization, names of specific organizations and persons, or of occupied countries and cities.

Gerth, Hans, 18, 54 n. 51.
Gestapo, 88, 89, 90, 164, 306, 327, 331, 585, 549, 731.
Geyl, Pieter, 287, 684, 701 n. 100, 748.
Ghana (Gold Coast), People's Party Convention, 788.
Ginty, J. P., 273.
Gipson, Lawrence Henry, 124, 186, 239, 299, 317, 362, 425, 519 n. 132, 534, 602, 568 n. 67, 569 n. 115, 667, 685, 699 n. 32, 750-751.
Gladstone, William, 603.
Glasgow, Scotland, 197, 233, 270, 385.
Glazunov, Ilya, 311.
Glocester, Rhode Island, 430.
Goa, 382.
"Go-Home-Early" strikes. See Strikes, limited.
"Go-Slow" strike. See Strike, slowdown.
Godwin, William, 22, 29, 31, 32, 35, 50 n. 15, 55 n. 65.
Goebbels, Joseph, 120, 122, 164, 233, 270, 320, 323-324, 484, 644 n. 66, 669, 691-692, 753.
Goering, Hermann, 236, 324, 369. See also Hermann-Goering Works (steel plant).
Goerlitz, East Germany, 597, 629, 675.
Goffman, Erving, 477.
Going-limp, 200, 205, 300.
Goldhamer, Herbert, 52 n. 23.
Goldman, Emma, 55 n. 65.
Goodman, Andrew, 198.
Goodspeed, Lt. Col. D. J., 41, 81, 381.
Goodyear rubber workers, 267.
Gopal, S., 546, 585, 587, 638-639, 642, 675, 739, 759, 761.
Gora, 393.
Gordon, King, 237.
Gorky, Maxim, 551.
Görlitz, Walter, 170, 321, 322, 324, 353 n. 182.
Gothenburg, Sweden, 275.
Goulart, President of Brazil, 408.
Gounaris, M., 344.
Government: general, 78; and nonviolent action, 67, 98; depends on cooperation and consent, 64, 84; prevention of collaborationist, 99-100; resistance to, 85, 86, 88, 91-92; refusal to pay debts of, 237-238; revenue refusal and, 240-241, 242; blacklisting of traders by, 244-245; international sellers' embargo by, 245; reverse trial against, 368.
Governments-in-exile, 5, 87. See also individual countries.

Hannecken, General Hermann von, 321.
Harassment. See Nonviolent harassment and Psychological harassment.
Harbin, U.S.S.R., 333.
Harcave, Sidney, 139, 156, 160, 168, 266, 276, 287, 333, 353 n. 226, 483, 519 n. 132, 536, 567 n. 44, 567 n. 50, 606, 607, 626, 659, 679, 780, 794, 799.
Hardinge, Lord of Penschurst, 561, 679.
Hardwicke, Massachusetts Bay, 702 n. 109.
Harlan, John Marshall, 377.
Harlem, New York City, 223, 228, 395, 617, 625.
Harold, Hardråde, 251 n. 64.
Harrington, England, 289, 382.
Harris, Errol E., 29-30, 47, 48 n. 4, 49 n. 5, 51 n. 17, 52 n. 27.
Harris, Herbert, 267.
Hartal, 199, 277-278, 504, 576, 639.
Hartford County, Connecticut, 633.
Harteneck, General, 43.
Hartnett County School Board, North Carolina, 372.
Harvard University, Preface, 297, 427.
Harvard Divinity School, 205.
"Haunting" officials, 145-146, 369.
Haverhill, Massachusetts, 273.
Havlin, James, Preface.
Haymarket Square, Chicago, Bombing in, 598.
Hawaii, 205.
Hawaii, University of, 205.
Hawaii, University Resistance Group of, 205.
Heal-in, 393-394.
Hearn, John, Preface.
Heath, William, 341.
Heidelberg, Germany, 376.
Helset, Olaf, 194-195.
Henderson, Arthur, M.P., 539.
Henry IV, Emperor of the Holy Roman Empire, 192.
Henry, Patrick, 361, 794.
Hentoff, Nat, 791, 813 n. 83.
Hermann- Göring Works, 236.
Hernandes Martinez. See Martinez.
Heroes' Square, Budapest, 163.
Herrnstadt, Rudolf, 676.
Herst, Pawel, 316.
Herzen, Alexander, 163, 456.
Het Parool, 400.
Heydrich, Reinhardt, 325, 590.
Hiding, escape and false indentities, 313-314.

Hijrat, 211-212, 642.
Hijrat-i-Kubrá ("The Great Exodus"), 208.
Hilberg, Raul, 173 n. 7, 306, 322, 323.
Hildebrandt, Rainer, 148-149, 405.
Hillenbrand, Martin J., 7, 33, 34, 48 n. 1.
Hiller, E. T., 267, 269, 431, 449, 525, 557, 575-576, 584, 597, 698 n. 3, 711, 745, 754, 786, 794.
Himalayas, 264.
Himmler, Heinrich, 553, 691.
Hind Swaraj or Indian Home Rule by M. K. Gandhi., 84.
Hindu-Muslim unity, Gandhi's campaign for, 367.
Hindus, Orthodox, 83, 148, 156, 368, 393, 729.
Hingst, *Stadtkommissar*, 325.
Hipp, Jutta, 307.
Hird, 88, 196, 332.
Hiroshima Day, 117.
Hitler, Adolf: general, 90, 119, 126, 170, 484; government depends on consent, 29, 43; limits on imposition from above, 46; and Quisling's Corporate State, 89; public hostility to, 170; opposition to, 293, 295, 320-322, 324, 327; and Commando Order, 353 n. 182; reverse trial, 368; withdrawal from international organizations, 345; use of provocation, 588-590; less severe repression by, 669, 691; admiration of courage by, 716.
Hoarding, 445 n. 301.
Hobbes, Thomas, 18, 19, 45, 46, 58 n. 123, 61-62 n. 201.
Hobson, Charles, 370.
Hoepner, Colonel General Erich, 322.
Holland. See Netherlands.
Holland, Ambassador Jerome, 341.
Holmsen, Andreas, 251 n. 64, 253 n. 119.
Holt, Edgar, 161, 260, 366.
Homage at burial places, 162-163.
Homefront leadership, Norway, 691.
Home rule, Hungary, 135.
Home rule, Ireland, 260, 603.
Honan, China, 146.
Hong Kong, 220.
Honington, England, 145.
Honoring the dead, 157.
Hooper, Isaac, 392.
Hoorn, Count of, 294.
Hooton, Elizabeth, 549.
Hoover- Stimson Doctrine, 343.
Hopei-Chahar Political Council, 307.
Hostages, 313, 328.
Hoth, 320.

Hottentots, 556.
House of Burgesses, Virginia. See Virginia.
House of Commons, Britain, 124, 132, 316-317, 366, 752.
House of Lords, Britain, 316, 740.
House of Ministries, East Berlin, 629.
House(s) of Parliament, London, 141, 531.
House of Parliament, Persia, 210.
House of Representatives, Massachusetts Bay, 362-363.
House of Representatives, United States, 135, 427, 693; Judiciary Committee of, 690; See also Congress.
Houser, George, 377, 437.
Howard Johnson Restaurant, 766.
Høye, Bjarne, 122.
Hradec, Czechoslovakia, 328.
Hsiao, Kung-Chuan, 217 n. 107, 242, 301-302, 307, 536.
Hudson River, New York, 392.
Hué, Vietnam, 138, 158, 279, 628, 660.
Hué, University of, 138, 293.
Huerta, Victoriano, 342.
Human resources as source of power, 11, 453, 744, 746-747.
Hume, David, 19, 20-21, 22, 44-45, 46, 50 n. 15, 54 n. 51, 55 n. 70, 56 n. 85.
Humorous skits and pranks, 148.
"Hundred Flowers Blossoming," China, 167.
Hundred Years' War, 151.
Hungary: general, 74, 135, 659, 713; alternative national institutions, 398, 796-797; army officers, 388; assemblies of protest or support in, 164; Calvinists, 309; economic boycott against, 230; boycott of legislative bodies in, 290; home rule in, 135; homage at burial places in, 163; fraternization in, 146; nonviolent resistance in, 76-77; boycott of government employment and positions in, 293; revenue refusal in, 242; noncooperation with conscription and deportation in, 312; nonviolent obstruction in, 388; countering economic nonviolent resistance of, 541; nonviolence urged for, 594; silence used in, 170; Parliament of, 164; Protestants' resistance to Austria in, 157, 309; Revolution of 1956-57, 93, 97, 99, 146, 170, 200, 212, 288, 343, 713, 749; struggle against Austrian rule, 594-595, 767, 796.
Hunger strike, 360, 363-364, 365-367, 404, 642. See also Fasts.

Hunter Committee, 504.
Huntington, Samuel, 407, 441 n. 192.
Hurum, Hans Jørgen, 149.
Hus, Jan, Statue of, 162-163.
Husak, Gustav, 99.
Hutcheson, Federal Judge Sterling, 240.
Hutchinson, Governor Thomas, 172, 308, 581-582, 636, 646 n. 99.
Huxley, Aldous, 776 n. 229.
Ickes, Harold, 372.
Imám-Jum'a, 206.
Imám Rizá, Shrine of, 206.
Imes, Rev. William Lloyd, 223.
Imperial Parliament, Vienna, 290.
Imprisonment, 12, 86, 466, 540, 541, 548, 555, 580, 620, 636, 638, 689, 721, 782, 785, 803.
Imprisonment of leadership. See Leadership, jailing of.
Inaction, 64, 65-66.
Independence, 3, 87, 781. See also Home rule and individual countries.
Independence Day, January 26, 1930, India, 84, 135.
India: general, 74, 468, 545; British, 642 (United Provinces Government), 529 (Indian Army), 290 (National Legislative Council), 290 (Provincial Legislative Councils), 85 (Penal Code), 41 (Legislative Assembly), see also Britain; castes, 393; South India, 82, 148, 210; national flag, 576; uprising of 1857, 552, 584; British problem of repression, 546, 559, 681, 682, 686-8; casualties, 552; camps for volunteers, 576; pledges of nonviolent discipline, 631; decentralization of later resistance organization, 639; Gandhi on noncooperation for independence, 84-85, 748; Gandhi on fearlessness for independence, 457; Tolstoy on voluntary subjection of, 30, 78; need for cooperation of subjects, 41-42; subjection and English education, 57 n. 100; historical context for Indian struggles, 79; force needed for freedom, 85, 512-513; terrorism, 85-86, 624; violent revolution, 86; nonviolent action adopted as weapon, 87; panchayats, 133; untouchability violated, 198; negotiations by leaders, 470; negotiations with Britain, 761; secret resistance network, 487; strategies of campaigns, 504; Britain's economic ties, 512-513; people transformed into resisters, 524, 529, 780-781, 783, 786; resisters' sense

of liberation, 490-491, 783, 787; Simon Commission, 739; Secretary of State for, 752; effects of boycott on exports to, 752; international support, 650; counter-nonviolence by British, 693; conversion of British desired, 707, 725, 727; "imperialism," 714; challenging British ability to rule, 774 n. 169; constructive program, 797; nonviolent campaigns, general, 172, 211, 297, 383, 431, 432, 464, 552, 605, 637, 665, 676, 686, 687, 782-783, 786, 790; nonviolent campaign 1919, 278; nonviolent campaign 1920, 229; nonviolent campaign 1922, 383; nonviolent campaign 1930-31, 4, 15, 86-87, 126, 143, 155, 187, 212, 229, 234, 278, 290, 294, 311, 318, 335, 340, 380, 385, 421, 432-433, 463, 466, 472, 487, 498, 500, 504, 526, 533, 546, 563, 576, 584, 585, 586, 591, 621, 638, 641-642, 666, 682, 687-688, 735, 751, 760, 781, 782; nonviolent campaign 1932-33, 230, 486-487, 500; see also Ahmedabad, Champaran, Vykom, Bardoli, Jallianwala Bagh, Northwest Frontier Province, Gandhi, *satyagraha* and Britain, Indian struggles against; refusal of assistance to enforcement agents, 299; deliberate inefficiency by enforcement agents, 330; posters, 126; picketing, 133; display of flags, 135; destruction of own property, 141; renouncing honors, 171-172; "haunting" officials, 145; social boycott, 185; social disobedience, 198; *hijrat*, 211-212; trades boycott, 234; *hartal*, 277-278; boycott of government body, 295; *dhurna*, 364; hunger strike, 367; fast, 682; satyagraphic fast, 367, 583; reverse trial, 368; nonviolent invasion, 382; nonviolent interjection, 383; establishing new social patterns, 392; selective patronage in, 413; civil disobedience of neutral laws, 420-421; dual sovereignty and parallel government, 432-433; revenue refusal, 583. For other specific methods and additional listings for these (especially civil disobedience), see above India, nonviolent campaigns, esp. 1930-31. See also entries for particular places, organizations, persons, officials, Indian National Congress, Lord Irwin, Gandhi, and *satyagraha*.
Indian National Congress, 84-85, 86, 87, 126, 340, 380, 463, 466, 500, 512, 526, 593, 622, 624, 638, 639, 641, 642, 752, 760, 761, 795; All-Indian Congress Committee, 42; Working Committee, 84, 187, 230, 638, 639, 641, 693; Peshawar Committee, 432.
Indians, American, 288, 318-319, 372, 389, 439 n. 131, 556.
Indians, Bolivia, 407.
Indians, Peru, 407.
Indo-China, 411.
Indoctrination, 20, 23.
Indonesia, 233, 345.
Industrial Workers of the World, 267, 318, 577.
Industry Strike, 265, 267-268.
Influence, 14, 20, 34, 38, 112, 118, 289, 293.
Informers for police, 484-485, 487, 488, 491, 518 n. 108. See also Agents provocateurs.
Inhibition of repression in nonviolent action, 583-594.
Initiative, as an element in nonviolent struggle, 500.
Inner discipline. See Self-discipline.
Innocent II, Pope, 193.
Innocent III, Pope, 193.
Inquisition, Netherlands, 684, 748.
Institute for Social Research, Oslo. Preface.
Institutions: power dependent on cooperation by, 8, 13, 15, 17, 29, 38; governmental, 7; nongovernmental, 22 (seek cooperation of individuals), 198, 199 (resistance to), 302 (key to resisting occupations), institutional arrangements to restrain governments, 33; efforts to change, 68; and petitions, 123; declarations by, 121.
Institutional Procedures of Governments, 65, 67.
Intangible factors in producing obedience, 11, 453, 744, 749-750.
Integration, racial, 96, 239-240, 383-384, 399-400, 412, 526.
Interdict, 192-193.
Interjection. See Nonviolent interjection.
International Association of Machinists, 221.
International Buyers' Embargo, 246.
International Commission on Concentration Camp Practices, 95.
International Consumers' Boycott, 230, 752.
International Economic Boycott, 230, 251

200, 223, 464, 536, 669, 738.
John, King of England, 193.
Johnson, President Lyndon B., 341, 690.
Joint Boycott Committee, South Africa, 223.
Jong, L. de, 270, 282 n. 62, 284 n. 125, 313, 758.
Journeymen Stone Cutters Association, 231.
Jouvenel, Bertrand de, 16, 18, 19, 20, 24, 27, 34, 35, 36, 51 n. 17, 51 n. 19, 54 n. 50, 55 n. 63, 56 n. 74, 57 n. 105, 60 n. 158, 801.
Joyce, Patrick, 364.
Judenrat (Jewish Council) of Athens, 313.
Judicial Noncooperation, 328-330.
Jungk, Robert, 324.
Junin, Peru, 407.
Jutikkala, Eino, 186, 312, 646 n. 99.
Kádár regime, Hungary, 343.
Kagal, 149-150, 186.
Kaluga, Russia, 168.
Kanara, India, 210.
Kao-Yu District, China, 155.
Kapp, Dr. Wolfgang, 40-41, 80, 81, 277, 339, 529, 626, 686, 696-697. See also Kapp *Putsch*.
Kapp *Putsch*, 4, 36, 40-41, 70, 79-81, 170, 276, 277, 328, 339, 344, 381, 529, 619, 626, 677-678, 686, 696-697, 708, 743, 748, 767, 780.
Karakozov, D. V., 645 n. 79, 679.
Karski, Jan, 126, 137, 144, 157-158, 196, 232.
Kashmir, 135.
Kathrada, Ahmed, 514.
Katkov, George, 191, 333, 519, 532, 602, 673-674, 744, 745.
Katyn graves, 344.
Katz, Daniel, 491-492, 561, 708, 726, 728, 729-730, 772 n. 101, 792-793, 803-804.
Kaunda, President Kenneth, 293.
Kazan, Russia, 261.
Kazansky Square, Petrograd, 673.
Keep, J.H.L., 273, 333, 607, 649 n. 163, 679, 684, 743.
Keitel, Field-Marshal Wilhelm, 170, 322, 324, 683.
Kellogg-Briand Pact, 343.
Kennedy, President John F., 139.
Kentucky, United States, 377, 399.
Kentucky Resolutions, 338-339.
Kenya, 294, 666.
Kerensky, Alexander, 328.
Kerry Volunteers, Ireland, 366.

K.G.B. – Committee for State Security, Soviet Union, 99.
Kgosana, Philip, 419, 629.
Khabalov, General S. S., 334, 673, 743.
Khan Abdul Ghaffar Khan, 790.
Kharkov, Russian Empire, 261.
Kharkov Prison, 365.
Kherson, Russian Empire, 360, 365.
Khrushchev, Premier Nikita, 342, 749.
Khudai Khidmatgar, 432, 790.
Kiangsu, China, 155, 236.
King, Rev. Martin Luther, Jr.: general, 111, 569 n. 102; bus boycott in Montgomery, Alabama (1955-56), 95-96, 249 n. 18, 414; on casting off fear, 457, 458; sharpening the focus for attack, 472; on 'tokenism,' 534; on generating incentives, 577; pleas for nonviolent behavior, 628; nonviolence and love urged by, 635; segregationist defections reported by, 670-671; effects of repression against, 689; and self-suffering, 722; and effects of nonviolence on opponent, 678; and effects of nonviolence on Negroes, 786-787, 791.
Kitchener, Lord H. H., 725.
Kiev, Ukraine, 168, 261, 268, 318, 640.
Kihss, Peter, 388.
Kilmallock, Ireland, 189.
Kimberly, South Africa, 601.
King, Governor Samuel, 427-428.
Kirchhoff, Hans, 279.
Kirkenes, Norway, 88.
Klarov, Czechoslovakia, 390.
Klunder, Rev. Bruce William, 386.
Knapp, Wilfrid, Preface, 342, 345.
Kneel-in, 380.
Knights of Labor, 222, 231, 236.
Knowless, K.G.J.C., 233, 261, 271.
Knoxville, Tennessee, 437 n. 566.
Koch, *Reichskommissar* Erich, 323.
Koestler, Arthur, 329.
Kokovtsev, Russian Minister of Finance, 659, 745.
Kolin, Czechoslovakia, 328.
Koller, General Karl, 324.
Kooperativa Förbundet, 415.
Korbel, Josef, 163, 222, 234, 271.
Korea, 152, 172, 682.
Korean War, 345.
Kossuth, Louis, 77.
Kostroma, Russian Empire, 168.
Kota-Kota District, Nyasaland, 310.
Kotgiri, India, 264.
Krasnoyarsk, Russia, 333.

Lidice, Czechoslovakia, 590.
Lidova Demokracie, 144, 301.
Lie, Jonas, 332.
Life, 176 n. 67.
Liggett & Meyers Tobacco Co., 222.
Lightning strike. See Quickie walkout.
Limburg, Netherlands, 274.
Limerick, Ireland, 185.
Limited strike, 273-274.
Limoges, Council of, 193.
Lincoln, C. Eric, 437 n. 56.
Lindberg, Niels, 102 n. 3, 468, 569 n. 116, 615.
Lippmann, Horst, 307.
Lisbon University, 311.
Litchfield County, Connecticut, 633.
Literature and speeches advocating resistance, 289.
Lithuania, 287.
Littell, Robert, 129, 144, 147, 151, 162, 178 n. 152, 190.
"Little Wolves, The," 126, 143.
Liuzzo, Mrs. Violet, 159.
Liverpool, England, 233, 238.
Livingston, Robert R., 614.
Livingstone, Arthur, 15, 50 n. 13, 53 n. 32.
Llanelly, Wales, 404.
Lloyd, Clifford, 299.
Lloyd-George, Prime Minister David, 686.
Lobbying. See Group lobbying.
Local government noncooperation. See Noncooperation by constituent governmental units.
Locker-Lampson, G., 353 n. 212.
Lockout, 235-236, 536.
Lodge, Ambassador Henry Cabot, 661.
Lodz, Poland, 311, 604.
Loh, Robert, 167, 272-273.
Lohse, *Reichskommissar* Heinrich, 325-326.
Lomax, Louis, 783.
Lombardy, Italy, 192-193.
London, England, 87, 96, 131, 138, 139, 152, 155, 167, 188, 193, 222, 238, 296, 338, 456, 761.
London Public Advertiser, 750.
Long Parliament, England, 424.
López Land Reform, Colombia, 406.
Los Angeles, California, 142, 393-394.
Los Angeles Free Press, 418.
Louis XVI, King of France, 309.
Louis, President Pierre, 277.
Louisville, Kentucky, 376-377.
Louis XV, King of France, 294.
Low, Isaac, 632.

Lowndesboro, Alabama, 159.
Loyalists in American colonies, 602.
Loyal Nine, 157. See also Sons of Liberty.
Lubbe, Marius van der, 589.
Lu Chia-shu, 359.
Lucknow, India, 593.
Ludendorff, General Eric von, 80.
Luga, Russian Empire, 334.
Lusaka, Zambia (formerly Northern Rhodesia), 243.
Luther, Martin, Head of *Department Deutschland,* 325.
Luthuli: general on South African resistance, 138, 150, 464, 536, 550, 556, 677, 763; on "Freedom Charter," 123, 568 n. 64; burns pass book, 142; on mourning, 158; calls off potato boycott, 223; compliance with restrictions, 549; government provocation of violence, 601; on discipline of volunteers, 653 n. 216; on Sharpeville, 660; bus boycott, 738; on self-esteem of the disobedient, 785; results of Defiance Campaign, 788.
Lüttwitz, General Freiherr Walter von, 30, 81, 339, 697, 767.
Lynching, 324.
Lynn, Massachusetts, 376.
Lyons, France, 121.
Lysa nad Labem, Czechoslovakia, 328.
Lysistratic nonaction, 191.
Lyttle, Bradford, 383, 616.
Mabee, Carleton, 199, 313, 369-371, 375-376, 379, 391, 396, 399.
Machiavelli, Niccolo, 34, 35, 36, 51 n. 17, 55 n. 61, 462, 680.
MacIver, R.M. 22, 23, 25, 49 n. 5, 50 n. 9, 51 ns. 17 and 19, 56 n. 74.
Madera, Francisco, 343.
Madison, President James, 140, 144, 246-247, 338.
Madrid, Spain, 289.
Madrid University, 311.
Maserud Arena, Oslo, 383.
Mafeking, South Africa, 692.
Mafia, 363.
Magliore, General Paul E., 266, 279.
Magna Charta, 193.
"*Magna Charta* of Persia," 209.
Mahuva, Gujarat, India, 682.
Maine, U.S., 429.
Majlis, 210.
Malawi, 747. See also Nyasaland.
Malaysia, 345.
Malcolm, Major-General Sir Neill, 344.
Malik, Ambassador Jacob, 345.

Manchester, England, 167, 238-239.
Manchukuo, 343.
Manchuria, China, 343.
Mandal, Norway, 305.
Manege Gallery, Moscow, 311.
Manifestos, Guatemalan, 91; Vietnamese Buddhist, 628; of Tsar Nicholas II, 131.
Mansfield, William Murray, First Earl of, 536.
Manufacturers Association, Russian Empire, 668.
Mao Tse-Tung, 145.
Mapes, Mr. & Mrs. David, 329.
Marat, Jean-Paul, 35.
Marblehead, Massachusetts, 141, 155, 579.
Marburg, University of, 120.
Marches, 69, 78, 80, 81, 95, 118, 142, 152, 164, 170, 310-311, 522, 576, 787-788.
Maritain, Jacques, 11, 34.
Marlborough Presbyterian Church, New York, 379.
Marshals, for demonstrations, 630-631.
Martial Law, 91-92, 277, 279, 591.
Martin, Governor Josiah, 317.
Martinez, Maximiliano Hernández, 91, 744.
Martynov, General, 674.
Martyrs, 92. See also Political *jiu jitsu*, and Suffering.
Marx, Karl, 431.
Maryland, 76, 148, 157, 186, 614, 694.
Masaryk, Thomas Garrigue, 163.
Mashad, Persia, 206.
Masjid-i-Shah. See Royal Mosque.
Masjid-o-Jami (Mosque of Assembly), Persia, 208.
Mason, James, 473.
Massachusetts, 131, 274, 361, 371, 375-376, 392-393, 417, 602, 685. See also Massachusetts Bay Colony.
Massachusetts Bay Colony, 124, 137, 140-141, 172, 186, 317, 381, 540, 548, 580, 600, 612-614, 647 n. 99, 681, 685, 719-20.
Massachusetts Institute of Technology, student center, 205.
Material Destruction, 65-66.
Material Resources, 11, 453, 460, 744, 750-752, 755.
Mathura, India, 639.
Matilda, Countess of Tuscany, 192.
Mattarella, Italian Minister for Foreign Trade, 363.
Mau Mau movement, Kenya, 584, 587,

593, 600, 605, 666, 714.
Mavinagundi, India, 583.
May Day Celebrations, Russia, 483.
Mayer, J.P., 305.
Mayfield Borough, Pennsylvania, 266.
Mayo County, Ireland, 220.
McCleery, Richard H., 771 n. 58.
McKim, J. Miller, 370.
McSweeney, Lord Mayor Terence, 366.
McWilliams, Carey, 262-263.
Mead, William, 329.
Mecca, Saudi Arabia, 211.
Mechanisms of change, 69-70, 435, 523, 528, 537, 547, 565, 697. All of Chapter Thirteen.
Medford, Massachusetts, 297, 378.
Medico-Surgical Academy, St. Petersburg, 168.
Medina, Saudi Arabia, 211.
Meetings, 86, 95, 96, 329, 341, 481, 504, 512, 575-577, 626; banned, 92, 318. See also Assemblies of protest or support, Protest meetings, Camouflaged meetings of protest and Teach-ins.
Memorial de los 311, Guatemala, 91, 92.
Mennonites, 213.
Men of Montgomery, The, 670.
Mensheviks, 79, 296, 365, 606.
Merchants Club, St. Petersburg, 190, 668.
Merchants General Strike, 236.
Merchant Guilds, China, 220.
Mercury, The, 159.
Meredith, James, 690.
Merseburg, East Germany, 629.
Mestek, Karel, 188.
Methods of nonviolent action, 40, 82, 93, 113-115, 445 ns. 300 and 301, 501-504, 506, 575, 580, 617, 628, 638, 706, 792, 793. See also Nonviolent protest and persuasion, Noncooperation and Nonviolent intervention.
Mexican migrant workers, U.S., 263.
Mexico, 342.
Michels, Robert, 28.
Michigan, 200.
Middlesex Journal, 317.
Migrant Workers, U.S., 263-264.
Milan, Italy, 192, 388.
Milan, Michigan, 200.
Miles, Michael, 416.
Military Action, replaced by nonviolent action, 76; international economic sanctions as substitute for, 247; blockade defiance without, 408; in Rhode Island struggle, 428-430; should be

compared with nonviolent action, 569 n. 116; not mentioned in "Continental Association," 613, French in Ruhr alienates support, 668; crushed in Hungary as general strike continues, 93; both sides use knowledge of to defeat other, 111; may be defeated, 71; conceptual tool for exists, 73; economic intervention used in, 402; nonviolent air raids used in, 381.

Military means and forces, 3, 63, 75, 76, 453; in *coups d'etat*, 80-82, 671-672, 743, see also *coups d'etat*; in occupations, 31, 42-44, 84, 98-101, 121, 141, 146-147, 149, 162-164, 178 n. 152, 189-190, 261, 274, 300, 337-338, 388, 550, 557, 590, 600, 606, 668-669, 686; as internal police, 31, 92, 94, 146, 156, 206, 208, 304, 385, 387, 429, 532, 56', 593, 629-630, 660, 668, 671-675, 684, 688, 713, 775 n. 193; in revolutionary role, 428, 600, 612-613, 649 n. 160, 650 n. 161; similarity to nonviolent action, 616. See also repression, mutiny, deliberate inefficiency and selective noncooperation by enforcement agents.

Miller, William Robert, 1-8, 151, 309, 352 n. 169, 463, 471, 550, 591, 595, 632, 653 n. 239, 715, 717, 731.

Miller, Webb, 330.

Mill-in, 378-379.

Mills, C. Wright, 18, 54 n. 51.

Milner, Lord, 295.

Milorg, 332.

Miner, Myrtilla, 399.

Ming Dynasty, 350 n. 88.

"Minute Men," 612, 614.

Miramar Naval Air Station, San Diego, California, 130.

Mirza, Crown Prince Mohamed Ali, 206.

Mirza, Nasru'lláh Khán, 209.

Mississippi, 134-135, 198, 373, 388, 419, 596, 689-690, 788-789.

Missouri Pacific Railroad, 268.

Mobilization committee to end the war in Vietnam, 417.

Mock awards, 131.

Mock election, 134-135.

Mock funeral, 157-159, 630.

Mogilev, Russia, 191.

Mohammed, 211.

Mohawk Indians, 389.

Molineux, William, 381.

Molotsi, Peter, 508, 519 n. 175.

Mommsen, Theodor, 76.

Monashki, 94.

Monckton Commission, 126, 188, 197, 296.

Montague, F.C., 57 n. 105.

Montesquieu, Charles Louis, de Secondat Baron de, 12, 53 ns. 33 and 63.

Montgomery Advertiser, 670.

Montgomery, Alabama, 73, 95, 96, 159, 233, 249 n. 18, 670, 690, 694; bus boycott, 5, 95, 222, 414-415, 457, 535, 548, 575, 577, 626, 640, 670, 689, 735, 783, 786, 791, 796.

Montgomery, Field Marshal Sir Bernard Law, 282 n. 62.

Moral *jiu-jitsu*, 657 n. 1.

Morale, 88, 99, 467, 479, 481, 490, 508, 511, 529, 573, 596, 625, 626, 664, 711, 724, 733, 758, 762-764; maintenance of, 575-583.

Moral obligation to obey, 20-22, 24, 27, 55 n. 65.

Moravany, Czechoslovakia, 327.

Moravian Church, 556.

Moravian Indians, 556.

Morgan, Edmund S. & Helen M., 159, 306, 315, 337, 352 n. 169, 519 n. 132, 630, 794.

Morioka, Japan, 213.

Morley, John, 603-604.

Morocco, 374.

Mosca, Gaetano, 47, 56 n. 82.

Moscow, Russia, 39, 78, 79, 94, 98, 100, 121, 131, 148, 153, 160, 166, 168, 171, 260, 261, 276, 289, 310, 320, 366, 368, 374, 507, 533, 604, 646 n. 79, 650 n. 159, 651 n. 167.

Moser, Nazi Gauleiter for Warsaw, 158.

Moses, Robert, 596.

Moslems. See Muslims.

Mossadegh's government, Iran, 234, 411.

Motorcade, 156.

Mott, Lucretia, 391.

Mountjoy Gaol, Ireland, 366.

Mowat, Charles Lock, 188.

Mowry, A.M., 428.

Mpopoma, Southern Rhodesia, 191.

Mujtahids, 208.

Mullaney, Father Anthony, 205.

Mullás, 206-210.

Multi-industry strikes, 275-277.

Munich, Germany, 126, 128.

Munro, Sir Thomas, 210.

Münster, Germany, 669.

Muravev, M.N., 645 n. 79.

Murcia, Spain, 289.

Murphy, Governor Frank, 404.

Mushiru 'd-Dawla, 209.
Music, American, 129. See also performances of plays and music, and singing.
Muslims, 155, 156, 368, 432, 433, 790.
Mussolini, Benito, 88, 326, 404.
Mutiny: general, 112, 113, 118, 146, 332-333, 453, 498, 502, 503, 595, 596, 671-672, 696, 706, 708, 733, 739, 753, 754, 755, 767; sanctions against, 24; Kapp *Putsch* 1920, 708; India 1930, 335, 432, 675, 747; Russia 1905, 79, 333-334, 354 n. 226, 606-608; Russia 1917, 596, 672-675, 743-744, 753; France 1917, 144, 166, 334, 464, 511, 529, 781; East Germany 1953, 675, 745.
Muzaffaru'd-Din, Shah of Persia, 206-210.
M.V.D., Ministry of Internal Affairs, U.S.S.R., 94.
Myers, J., 318, 413.
Myshkin, Ippolit Nikitch, 368.
Naess, Arne, Preface, 722 n. 101.
Nage, Premier Imre, 200.
Naidu, Sarojini, 311.
Nairobi, Kenya, 385.
"Naming," 581-582.
Nantucket, Massachusetts, 375.
Napoleon I, Emperor of France, 93, 452, 499.
Nashville, Tennesse, 223-224, 632, 689.
Nasjonal Samling, 193-195, 331-332, 691.
National Academy of Sciences, Hungary, 398.
National Agrarian Institute, Venezuela, 408.
National American Woman Suffrage Association, 154.
National Antislavery Standard, 387.
National Assembly, Czechoslovakia, 99, 173 n. 19, 188, 390.
National Assembly, France, 241.
National Association for the Advancement of Colored People, 378, 383.
National Association of German Industries, 697.
National Buddhist Institute, Vien Hoa Doa, 385.
National Consultative Assembly, Persia, 210.
National consumers' boycott, 228-230.
National Farm Workers Association, U.S., 263.
National Labor Relations Board, U.S., 404.
National Land League, Ireland, 227.

National Liberation Front, Vietnam, 296, 342, 381.
National Maritime Union, U.S., 700.
National Museum, Czechoslovakia, 143, 260.
National Museum, Hungary, 398.
National Palace, Guatemala City, 91.
National Protective Union, Hungary, 398.
National Theatre, Hungary, 398.
National University, Guatemala, 197, 268.
National Wages Agreement of 1924, Britain, 233.
"National Week," Indian, 498.
"National Work Effort," Norway, 332.
Nationalist Party, Germany, 697.
Nationalist Party, South Africa, 525.
Nationalistic Revolutionary Movement, Bolivia, 407.
Nationalists, Irish, 160, 366. See also Ireland.
Nationalists, African, 785. See also individual countries.
Nationalists, Indian, 135, 187, 295. See also India.
Nationalists, Puerto Rican, 291.
Native Labour (Settlement of Disputes) Act, South Africa, 542.
Natural Resources, 11.
Nazis: general, 172, 397, 545, 562; nonviolent resistance in countries occupied by, 5; and cooperation of populations, 42-43; Hitler's regime, 45; Norwegian occupation by, 5, 47, 74, 88, 126, 149, 626; Polish occupation by, 127, 188, 399; Danish occupation by, 150; Czechoslovakian occupation by, 163; occupation of Soviet Union by, 322; struggles against, 87-90; methods used against: public speeches, 119-120; protest against propaganda campaigns of, 127-128; illegal newspapers, 129; performances of plays and music, 149; singing, 150; political mourning, 158; homage at burial places, 163; social boycott, 188; producers boycott, 232; revenue refusal to pro-Nazi leaders, 242; limited strike, 274; resignation, 293, 295; boycott of government departments and agencies, 296; disguised disobedience, 306-307; noncooperation with conscription and deportation, 312; escape, 314; selective refusal of assistance by government aides, 320-321; blocking of lines of command and communication, 321-323; stalling and obstruction, 323-327; deliberate

inefficiency and selective noncooperation by enforcement agents, 330-332; reverse trial, 369; nonviolent interjection, 386; alternative social institutions, 399; alternative communication system, 400-401; politically motivated counterfeiting, 410; general strike, 532, 536; openness and secrecy in resistance against, 484, 485; provocation by, 588-590; persistence against, 549; repression by, 553; morale in struggle against, 626; susceptible to public opinion, 662; defections from, 669; internal disputes of, 675, 676, 749; resistance spurred by repression by, 682-683; less severe repression urged by, 691; influence of Gandhi on resistance against, 98; swastika of, 126; domestic embargo used by, 244; interest payments refused by, 239; anti-Jewish measures of, 325-326; attitude toward Jews, 713; Labor Front of, 296; investigation of, 469. See also Germany, Hitler, Colonization and Invasions.

Nechaev, Sergei, 365.

Necker, Jacques, Minister of Louis XVI of France, 54 n. 51.

Negotiations, 65, 67, 77, 86, 90, 95, 100, 273, 277, 331, 341, 510, 514, 531, 639, 730, 759, 761, 766, 767, 776 n. 225; as preparation for nonviolent struggle, 470, 474, 510.

Negroes. See Afro-Americans.

Nehru, Jawaharlal: general, 42, 555, 776 n. 206; on power of noncooperation, 41; on length of struggles, 763; advocate of violence, 86; on nonviolent method of Gandhi, 87; on openness and lack of secrecy, 487, 490-491; halting submission, 522, 524; on timing of tactics, 497; on initiative in nonviolent action, 500; on repression, 537; on British perception of nonviolence, 528, 529; ineffectiveness of repression, 545-546, 585, 698 n. 2; beaten by police, 559, 783; on agents provocateurs, 593; effect of nonviolence on terrorism, 624; hartal used to protest imprisonment of, 638; reducing fear through nonviolence, 783; on nonviolence and self-respect, 786; nonviolent struggle brings satisfaction, 787; on nonviolent conversion, 720; on effect of defeat on later success, 757-758; photograph displayed, by supporters, 143.

Nehru, Motilal, 554-555.

Nekrasov, Nikolai A., 645 n. 79.

Neo-Gandhian struggles, 510.

Nepszabadsag, 289.

Netherlands: general, 129, 586; and nonviolent resistance, 87; resistance to Spanish rule 1565-1576, 4, 76, 287, 294; resistance to Inquisition, 684, 748; Nazi repression of strike in, 553; methods used in: strikes, 87, 758; letters of opposition and support, 120, 122; wearing of symbols, 136; vigils, 147; student strike, 197; industry strikes, 267; general strike, 277; producers' boycott, 232; seizure of assets by, 410; work-on without collaboration, 422; hiding, escape and false identities, 313-314; alternative communication system, 422; parallel government, 423; Commander of the *Wehrmacht* in, 683; repression brings solidarity in, 758; government-in-exile, 267, 422. See also Occupation, German of Netherlands.

Neues Deutschland, 597, 676.

Neumann, Franz, 18, 270-271, 283 n. 89.

Neurath, Foreign Minister, 295.

Neustadt, Richard, 36-39.

Nevinson, Henry W., 648-649 n. 154, 649 n. 167.

Newark, New Jersey, 379.

New Bedford, Massachusetts, 375.

New Bedford Railroad, 375-376.

Newbern, North Carolina, 318.

Newbury Church, Massachusetts Bay Colony, 140.

New Delhi, India, 290, 294, 367.

New England, 376, 379, 574, 794. See also individual colonies and states.

New Forward, 306.

New Hampshire, 186, 199, 225, 275, 430.

New Haven County, Connecticut, 633.

New Jersey, 157, 225, 374.

New Jersey Civil Rights Bill of 1949, 374.

New Orleans, Louisiana, 166, 377, 694.

Newport, Rhode Island, 158, 221, 380, 426, 428, 623, 630.

New Republic, 416.

New signs and names, 143-144.

Newsletter, National Strike Information Center, 198.

Newspapers, 128-129, 188, 306, 369, 377, 400, 542, 799. See also names of individual newspapers.

Newsweek, 690.

Newton, Isaac, 73.

New York City, 142, 198, 205, 226, 228, 375, 376, 379, 384, 391, 392, 616-617, 619, 654 n. 254, 719; colonial, 124, 141, 165, 186, 239, 265, 274, 413, 464, 574, 623, 647 n. 99, 794.
New York Herald Tribune, 671.
New York, Province of, 225, 226; General Assembly of, 337.
New York State, 230, 236, 379, 386, 429.
New York Times, 142-143, 388, 417, 660, 688.
New Zealand, 312.
Ngo Dinh Diem, President. See Diem, Ngo Dinh. (Most Vietnamese names are, however, here listed in the standard way by the first name of the series.)
Ngo Dinh Nhu, 660.
Nguyen Thanh Le, 342.
Nguyen Van Binh, Archbishop of Saigon, 671.
Nicolson, Harold, 344.
Nicholas, Robert Carter, 362.
Nicolas II, Tsar of Russia, 4, 79, 131, 156, 186, 191, 238, 312, 334, 530, 532, 533, 534, 542, 659, 668, 672-674, 678-680, 743-745, 749, 799.
Niedzialkowski Avenue, Warsaw, 144.
Nikolaev, Russia, 268.
Nivelle, General Robert, 335.
Nixon administration, 341.
Nixon, E. D., 458.
Nizhny Province, Russian Empire, 261.
N.K.V.D. (People's Commissariat of Internal Affairs), U.S.S.R., 365.
Noakhali, Bengal, India, 156.
Nolting, Ambassador Frederick E., 661.
Nonconformity, 524, 816.
Nonconsumption of boycotted goods, 186, 224-225, 229, 425, 613-614, 750.
Noncooperation: general, 4, 71, 114, 117, 429, 434, 455, 460, 522, 544, 763, 807; defined, 69, 183; and nonviolent action, 64, 67, 595; compared with nonviolent protest and persuasion, 118, 119, 169; compared with nonviolent intervention, 357; covert, 5; social, 169, 184, 188, 192, 211, 390, Chapter 4; political, 143, 184, 188, 212, 347, 504, 797, Chapter 7; economic, 184, 797, Chapter 5, 6; personal, 200, 201; by citizens with government, 289-303; works despite sanctions, 17; and habitual obedience, 25; and withdrawal of consent, 32; withdrawal of cooperation, 45, 46, 69, 84, 114, 183, 257, 285, 476, 501, 531, 696, 747,

806; withdrawal of support, 34, 85, 657, 666; popular, 41, 45, 767; and control of political power, 32, 44, 47; clues on political impact of, 36; as weapon of choice, 502; as intangible factor, 749; methods of: excommunication and interdict, 191; student strike, 196, 197; stay-at-home, 199; *hijrat*, 211, 212; social boycott used to encourage, 185, 187; producers' boycott, 231; withdrawal of bank deposits, 236; domestic embargo, 244; blocking lines of command and communication, 322; by constituent governmental units, 337-340; and removal of signs, 143; and fraternization, 146; with social events, 184; and alternative social institutions, 398, 796-797; and seeking imprisonment, 419; and civil disobedience of neutral laws, 420; reasons for nonrecognition of, 72; singing used against, 149; assemblies in support of, 164; persuasion by, 383; avoiding violence through, 454; aimed at conversion of opponent, 513, 706, 707, 732; as problem for opponent, 528, 532, 546-547, 747, 753; laws against, 540, 542; as defensive moral action, 501; when most effective, 494; action against refusal to engage in, 580-582; as substitute for war, 647; government-sponsored, 337, 604; effectiveness depends on organization, 480, and nonviolent coercion, 742-743, 744, 754, 755; and withdrawal of human resources, 746; altering power relationships through, 696; and withdrawal of skills and knowledge, 748; sensing power of, 739, 780, 781; and firmness, 548; discipline needed for success of, 631; increasing the use of, 638, 642, 780; increasing fearlessness through, 783; and self-image, 784; relation to cooperation, 795-796, 797; in absence of leadership, 803; and third parties, 818; and settlement, 760; Gandhi on, 84-85, 454, 480, 707, 748, 796; Gandhi's use of, 82, 84; Shelley on, 35; Nehru on, 41; by American colonies, 352 n. 169, 553, 580, 582, 600, 602, 611, 633, 636, 647, 685, 740, 743, 750, 781, 794, 797, 798; during American Revolution, 77, 337; in Northern Rhodesia and Nyasaland, 188, 747; in Guatemala 1944, 97; in Germany, 604; and

German generals' plot 1939, 322; against Kapp regime, Germany 40-41, 80, 696, 748; during the *Ruhrkampf* 1923, 82; in Egypt 1919, 97; in 1930-31 Indian campaign of Gandhi, 504, 682, 760; Noncooperation Committee in India 1920, 631; in Ephesus, Second Century A.D., 540; in Russia 1905, 797. See Economic boycotts, Strikes, Social noncooperation, and specific methods within those categories.

Noncooperation Committee, India, 631.

Noncooperation, general administrative. See General administrative noncooperation.

Noncooperation, judicial, 328-330.

Noncooperation with conscription and deportation, 311-313.

Noncooperation with social events, customs and institutions, 193.

Nonexportation, 186, 229, 239, 425, 507, 511, 600, 612, 615.

Nonimportation, 140-141, 186, 225, 229, 239, 425, 511, 540-541, 553, 574, 580-582, 612-614, 622, 636, 750-751, 794, 798.

Non-Importation Act, U.S., 246.

Non-Intercourse Act, U.S., 246.

Nonobedience, 350 n. 88. See also Popular nonobedience.

Nonobedience without direct supervision, 304.

Nonparticipation, economic, 431.

Nonrecognition, 72-74.

Nonresistance Society, 199, 375.

Nonsecrecy, in nonviolent struggle, 481-492.

Nonviolence: general, 47, 70, 83, 94, 111, 141, 387, 615, 794, 790; and political behavior, 65; and nonviolent action, 68, 71; and nonviolent coercion, 774 n. 161; and violence, 72, 77, 187, 528, 543, 552, 553, 565, 622; sometimes premeditated, 5; association with effective action, 82; and power of actionists, 110, 526, 781; and splits in opponent's group, 676; opponent's response to, 531, 557; repression of brings outrage, 657; and third parties, 660; produces unity, 794; and conversion, 719, 720; and element of surprise, 530; and increased self-esteem, 792; and Gandhi, 751-752, 771 n. 66; Gandhi on, 187, 229, 522, 565, 622, 725, 781; Nehru and ethic of, 87, 720; and Indian Campaign, 1930-31, 85; and anti-*Apartheid* movement, 123; and anti-slavery protests, 370; and anti-segregation protests, 375-376.

Nonviolent action, technique of. See Table of Contents.

Nonviolent air raids, 381-382.

Nonviolent *Blitzkrieg*, 776 n. 219.

Nonviolent coercion: general, 193, 455, 501, 709, 725, 737, 738, 769 n. 1; defined, 69, 706, 742-744; mechanism of change, 69, 71, 502, 697, 706, 732, 733, 734, 766, 767, 769 n. 1, 807; factors influencing, 754-755; economic boycott as form of, 220; linked to nonviolent intervention, 358; linked to conversion, 708, 732, 733; and numbers, 498; violence undermines, 601; and refusal to hate, 634; and negotiations, 767; alters power relationships, 768; and Gandhi, 769 n. 4.

Nonviolent discipline: general, 93, 101, 130, 264, 466, 573-642, 703 n. 154; necessary part of nonviolent technique, 455, 648 n. 99; need to maintain, 485, 537, 545, 549, 583, 638, 639; related to planning action, 462, 466; role of organization, 479, 480; and secrecy, 488; codes and pledges of, 481, 619, 631-632, 654 n. 254; and numbers 476, 478, 498, 501; and leadership, 638, 639, 817; possible without training, 620, 653 n. 216; and repression, 113, 537, 583, 585, 587, 591, 594, 657, 711; and nonviolent intervention, 501, 502, 508; prerequisite for shifts in power, 70, 545, 657; as test for future action, 504, 640; tested by tactical changes, 508; undermines opponent's support, 605, 666; promoting, 620-633; impact of, 565, 620, 710-711; and political *jiu-jitsu*, 697; as self-reliant weapon, 803; voluntarily accepted, 817; in Czechoslovakia 1968, 130; urged by Cesar Chavez, 264. See also Discipline, Codes of.

Nonviolent harassment, 369-371, 418.

Nonviolent interjection, 310, 382-387, 580, 582.

Nonviolent intervention: general, 64, 67, 321, 347, 494, 504, 528, 817; defined, 69; as class of methods, 114, 357-445; 455, 807; compared with other classes of methods, 117, 118, 119, 310, 358, 501-502; physical, 358, 371-390; political, 416-433, 461; psychological,

358, 359-371, 522; social, 358, 390-401; economic, 401-416; method of indirect confrontation, 453; when most effective, 494; and openness, 482; creates difficulties for opponent, 557, 739; responsibility assigned to particular group for, 508; and third party action, 664; and power shifts, 696; and suffering, 711; against Kapp *Putsch*, 81.

Nonviolent invasion, 69, 140, 378, 382, 388, 664.

Nonviolent land seizure, 388, 401, 405-408, 441 n. 192.

Nonviolent militants, 526.

Nonviolent obstruction, 69, 310, 320, 382, 387-388, 497, 508, 816.

Nonviolent occupation, 378, 388-390.

Nonviolent protest and persuasion: defined, 68-69; and nonviolent action, 67; as class of methods, 114-115, 117-182, 502, 763-764, 807; protest and persuasion compared, 173 n. 1; functions of, 118; related to methods of noncooperation, 118, 119, 193, 258, 277, 501; related to methods of intervention, 119, 357, 360, 369, 501; as weapons of choice, 501; as initial form of action, 504, 522; impact of varies, 118-119; may provoke indignation, 531; relation to violence, 624-625; need for openness, 492.

Nonviolent raids, 380, 497, 508, 564, 576, 641, 687, 762, 775 n. 169.

Nonviolent resistance. See Table of Contents for diverse aspects of nonviolent action.

Nonviolent strategy. See Strategy, nonviolent.

Nonviolent struggle: general, 69, 73, 74, 75, 86, 777-778, 783, 799, 803, 806, all of Part Three; neglect by historians, 72; economic. See Table of Contents for economic methods of noncooperation and intervention; expansion of, 76-78, 808; effectiveness of, 82, 523; methods used during, 133, 225, 398, 405, 431, 433, 522; timing of, 521; effect on actionists, 523-524, 781, 782, 784-785, 788, 807; and polarization, 524-525; innovations in, 808; power of ignored, 74, 530; difficulties in dealing with, 537, 698 n. 1; price of, 537; increasing strength during, 526; and leadership, 549, 562, 803, 804; violence detrimental to, 528; must continue de-

spite repression, 547, 550; suffering during, 551-552, 562; effects on aggression and violence, 789-790, 804-805; effects on masculinity, 790; and need for constructive work, 797; and diffusion of power, 803-804, 805-806, 807; as substitute for violence, 98, 808-809; factors determining outcome. See Outcome of the conflict; effect of Gandhi on, 98; Frederick Douglass on, 523. See also Violent struggle, Struggle, and listings in Table of Contents, especially Part Three.

Nonviolent weapons. See Methods of nonviolent action.

"No-Rent Manifesto," Ireland, 498.

Norfolk, England, 128.

Norkus, Eckhardt, 125.

North Africa, 202, 410, 419. See also individual countries.

North Africans in France, 310.

North Carolina, 124, 317, 336-337, 771 n. 58. See also individual towns and cities.

North Carolina Agricultural and Technical College, 373.

North Carolina State Advisory Committee, 336.

North Carolina Supreme Court, 336-337.

Northern California Committee for the Abolition of Nuclear Weapons, 133.

North Korea, 345.

Northern Rhodesia, 126, 177 n. 121, 188, 197, 242, 293, 296, 664.

North, Lord Frederick, 317, 540, 694.

North Star, 391.

North Vietnam. See Vietnam, North.

North-West Committee of 100, Britain, 167.

North-West Frontier Province of British India, 790.

Norway: general, 97, 586; nonviolent protest in, 120-121, 122, 126, 127, 129, 136, 149, 164; nonviolent resistance against Nazis in, 5, 47, 74, 87, 88-89, 609, 676; social noncooperation in, 189, 193-195, 196; political noncooperation in, 298, 310, 330-331; economic noncooperation in, 267, 268, 275, 277; nonviolent intervention used in, 383; solidarity against Nazis, 577, 626; protest against Sharpeville massacre, 660; Church and Education Department, 121; Sports Association of, 194; Army of, 195; Supreme Court, 329; Department for Labor Services and Sports, 194; peasants of, 231, 241, 253 n. 119; teachers' protests, 1942, 70, 88, 237, 419, 422, 457, 585; Quisling regime, 70, 120, 122, 196, 298, 457, 626; Quisling's Education Department, 88. See also Occupation, German of Norway.

Norway-Denmark, 305, 414, 691-692.
Noske, Minister of Defense Gustav, 80.
Notre Dame Cathedral, Paris, 136.
Nottingham, England, 395.
Nova Scotia, 275.
Novgorod, Russia, 261.
Nuclear disarmament symbol, 130, 360.
Nuclear testing, 131, 310.
Nuclear weapons, 3, 9, 259, 311, 324, 808.
Numbers and strength, in nonviolent struggle, 498-499.
Nyanga, South Africa, 585-586.
Nyasaland, 126, 188, 296, 747. See also Malawi.
Nyasaland African Congress, 242, 419.
Nyasaland Commission of Inquiry, 310.
Obedience: general, 20; sources of power depend on, 12-16, 18, 28, 744, 746, 817; as habit, 19, 25, 51 n. 17, 749; essentially voluntary, 26-30; not equally given, 30; and sanctions, 12, 14, 15, 19-20, 26, 28, 752; not inevitable, 18, 25, 57 n. 110; not uniform, 26; withdrawal of, 31, 32, 34, 45, 63, 817; different from coercion, 27; ruler's use of, 24; role of self-interest, 22, 27; varies with strength of reasons given, 31; interdependent with enforcement, 15; springs from fear, 18; and psychological identification with ruler, 23; and intangible factors, 749, 750; and zone of indifference, 23; and absence of subjects' self-confidence, 23-24; and common good, 20-21, 56 n. 74; and ruler's legitimacy, 21; and suprahuman factors, 21; and authority, 746; and conformity of commands to accepted norms, 21; duty of, 45; of many to the few, 54 n. 51; and repression, 112; and moral obligation, 20-22, 55 n. 65. See also individual authors.

The Observer, 171.
Occupations: general, 39, 40, 42, 44, 64, 71, 74, 82, 101, 118, 122, 126, 127, 136, 137, 143, 144, 147, 190, 211, 296, 298, 300, 302, 323, 325, 328, 414, 421, 423, 498, 686, 746. See also Nonviolent occupations; military, 129,

189, 422; British of Boston, 337, 603; British of India, 82, 330, 339, 585. See also India. British and French of Port Said, 190; French and Belgian of Germany, 126, 149, 287, 296, 541, 578, 604, 610, 659, 668, 737, 748. See also *Ruhrkampf*; German of Austria, 589; German of Czechoslovakia, 163, 177, 222, 271, 301; German of Denmark, 136, 189, 196, 277, 683; German of Europe, 87, 232, 270, 418, 586, 683; German of France, 305, 314, 326, 410; German of Netherlands, 231, 270, 274, 282 n. 62, 305, 313, 422, 536, 758; German of Norway, 47, 74, 88, 126, 129, 149, 170, 193, 294, 330, 314, 545, 577, 609, 626; German of Poland, 126, 127, 137, 143, 188, 222, 399, 716; German of Russia, 42-43, 322, 682-683, 749; Italian of France, 326; Japanese of China, 211, 231, 232; Russian of Czechoslovakia, 100, 144, 147, 300, 327-328, 402; Russian of Germany, 542, 550. See also Military forces, Occupations.

Ochakov, 287.
Ochrana, 330, 333, 593.
"October Manifesto" of Tsar Nicholas II, 79, 152, 291, 533, 567 n. 50, 799.
Odense, Denmark, 275.
Odessa, Russia, 168, 268, 276, 604.
O'Donovan, Patrick, 437 n. 56.
Oesser, Rudolf, 686.
Office of Strategic Services, U.S., 410.
O'Hegarty, P. S., 603, 632, 763.
Ohio, 200, 556.
Ohio State University, Preface.
Oklahoma, 335.
Olbricht, Friedrich, 322.
Olmstead, F. L., 203.
Olomouc, Czechoslovakia, 327.
Omaha, Nebraska, 382.
Omission, Acts of, 68.
Ons Volk, 401.
Open letter, 120.
Openness and secrecy in nonviolent struggle, 481-492.
Opera Dei Congressi, 416.
Oppenheimer, Martin, 300, 474, 488, 517 n. 94, 525, 547, 587, 630, 776 n. 225.
Opponent: general, 65, 67, 78, 92, 496, 500, 503, 508, 521, 564, 778, 786, 792, 795, 800, 816,; effect of nonviolent action on, 68, 69, 508, 754, 795, 799; violence of, 71, 547, 554, 698 n. 1, 807; repression by, 500, 536, 542,

546, 547, 551, 555, 557, 558, 559, 563, 698 n. 3, 803, 817; initial problem, 528-537; action against, 495, 496, 498, 506, 524, 527, 537, 563, 569, 785, 789, 807; actionists' evaluation of, 505; and polarization, 528; appeals to, 550, 562; cooperation used against, 795, 796; weakening of, 510, 565, 807; effect of ultimatum on, 510, 511, 513-514; and political *jiu-jitsu*, 496, Chapter 12; enthusiasm against, 787, 791; conversion of, 817; opponent group, 83, 84, 125, 491, 505, 525, 526, 737, 794, 816.

Oppression, 44, 46-47, 92, 124, 232, 491.

Oran, Algeria, 385.

Orangeburg, South Carolina, 694.

Organization for the Maintenance of Supplies, Britain, 542.

Organization of American States, 248.

Organizing the nonviolent movement, 479-481.

Oriel College, Oxford, Preface.

Oriente Province, Cuba, 153.

Orlov, Province, Russian Empire, 261.

Oslo, Norway, 89, 159, 196, 331-332, 691.

Ostland, German occupation of U.S.S.R., 325.

Østlandet, Norway, 332.

Ostministerium, in German occupation of U.S.S.R., 323, 326.

Ostracism, 184, 188, 189, 538, 580. See also Social boycott.

Outcome of the conflict, summaries of factors influencing: in nonviolent conversion, 726-731; in accommodation, 740; in nonviolent coercion, 754-755; factors associated with the nonviolent group, 816-817; factors associated with the opponent group, 816; factors associated with third parties, 816; factors in the social situation, 815-816.

Overloading of administrative systems, 416-417.

Overloading of facilities, 393-394.

Over-use of certain technical or mechanical facilities, 445 n. 301.

Oxford University, Preface, 169.

Oxyrhynchus, Egypt, 266.

Pacifism, 68, 71, 74, 514, 542, 556, 621, 635.

Packing a meeting with sympathizers, 445 n. 301.

Paint as protest, 143-144.

Pakistan, 135.

Palach, Jan, 142, 162, 171.

Palermo, Sicily, 385.

Palffy, Governor, 135.

Palisades Amusement Park, New Jersey, 374.

Palme, Swedish Premier Olof, 341.

Pamphlets, 127.

Pan-Africanists, 419, 507, 628.

Pan Africanist Congress, South Africa, 142, 318, 628.

Panchayats, 133, 295, 432.

Papacy, 191-192. See individual popes.

Papal Nuncio, 279.

Papen, Franz von, 119-120, 341, 589.

Parades, 69, 86, 91, 117, 142, 154-155, 311, 318, 459, 552, 575-576, 682.

Paraguay, 246.

Paraiba Valley, Brazil, 408.

Parallel government. See Dual sovereignty and Parallel government.

Parallel social structure, 796.

Pardubice, Czechoslovakia, 328.

Paris, France, 136, 166, 261, 294, 305.

Parks, Rosa, 95.

Parlements of France, 294.

Parnell, Charles S., M.P., 227, 521-522, 582, 603, 632.

Parthian expedition, 124.

Pasco, Peru, 407.

Pass laws, South Africa, 507, 525.

Passive resistance, 82, 93, 175 n. 51, 193, 201, 220, 271, 272, 278, 279, 338, 422, 541, 611, 748, 797.

Passivity, 64-65, 70, 522.

Pastoral letters, 121, 122.

Patel, Valiabhbhai, 187, 639, 666.

Pathans, 790.

Patterson, Rev. Merle, 670.

Pavel, Minister of Interior Josef, 288.

Paul, King of Greece, 290.

Paullin, Theodor, 742, 774 n. 157.

Pavlovsky Guards Regiment, Russian Tsarist regime, 674.

Peace News, 385.

"Peace of God," 193.

Pearl Harbor, Hawaii, 411.

Peasant strike, 261-262.

Peasant's Union, Russia, 261, 507.

Pechersky, Alexander, 150.

Peck, Graham, 146, 307-308.

Peck, James, 419, 437 ns. 55 and 56.

Pecs, Hungary, 404.

Peking, China, 167, 343.

Pemberton, Dr., 172.

Pendleton, Edmund, 315.

Pendleton, Indiana, 392.

Penn, Governor John of Pennsylvania, 299.
Penn, William, 329.
Pennington, Dr., 376.
Pennsylvania, 157, 186, 213, 267, 794. See also individual cities.
Pennsylvania Antislavery Society, 370.
Pentagon Papers, 660, 661.
Penza, Province, Russian Empire, 261.
"People's Police," East Germany, 197, 549.
People's Ticket, Rhode Island, 427.
People's United Party, British Honduras, 155.
People's Will, *Narodya Volya*, terrorist section, 163.
Pepsi-Cola Company, 224.
Performances of plays and music, 149.
Perkins, Dwight H., 306.
Perón's dictatorship, Argentina, 158.
Persia, 205-210, 217 n. 90.
Persia, Islamic leaders of, 205.
Persia, Shah of, 205-210.
Persian Courts of Justice, 209.
Persian Revolution 1905-06, 205-210.
Persistence, 547-551.
Persuasion, 47, 67, 125, 133, 477, 488. See also Nonviolent protest and persuasion.
Persuasion, verbal, 65-67.
Peru, 262, 406, 407.
Peshawar, Northwest Frontier Province, British India, 335, 432, 675, 747.
Pesth County Council, Hungary, 286.
Pesth, Hungary, 135.
Pétain, General Henri, 327, 335.
Peter-Paul Fortress, St. Petersburg, 365.
Petersburg, Virginia, 399.
Petersen, Erling, 414.
Peters, William, 249 n. 18.
Petition(s), 78, 123-124, 125, 131, 202, 207, 531, 605, 738.
Petöfi, Sandor, 163.
Petrograd, Russia, 191, 596, 673, 743, 745. See also St. Petersburg.
Petrov, Anton, 261.
Philadelphia Meeting House, 380.
Philadelphia, Mississippi, 233.
Philadelphia, Pennsylvania, 127, 140, 142, 157, 165, 186, 200, 224, 225, 239, 306, 376, 379, 383, 391, 413, 574, 622, 708, 709.
Philip II, King of Spain and ruler of the Netherlands, 294, 701 n. 100.
Phillips, Norman, 585.
Phillips, U.B., 202-203.

Phillips, Wendell, 369, 387.
Phoenix Park, Dublin, 603-604.
Picketing, 86, 117, 132-134, 145, 147, 277, 358, 503, 576, 577, 580, 682, 693, 788, 789.
Pierce, C.M., 813 n. 63.
Pigors, Paul, 54 n. 49.
Pilgrim Baptist Church, Birmingham, Alabama, 138.
Pilgrimage(s), 118, 156, 206, 264.
Ping-fang, Hupeh, China, 301-302.
"Placard of Dismissal," 287.
Placards. See Posters.
Planchart, Alejandro, 151.
Plaquemine, Louisiana, 786.
Plastiras, Colonel, 344.
Playboy, 140.
Plymouth, New Hampshire, 199.
Podolak, Boris, 365.
Podolia, Province, Russian Empire, 261.
Poincaré, Premier Raymond, 668.
Poland: general, 129, 150, 153, 170, 173 n. 7, 297, 309, 327, 403, 404, 554, 675; action against Nazi occupation of, 127, 137, 143-144, 173 n. 7, 188, 196, 232, 304, 399; Nazi propaganda division in, 173 n. 7; government-in-exile, London, 344; Embassy in Hungary, 170; Directorate of Civilian Resistance, 188; Council of Art and Culture, 316; Polish Rebellion, 646 n. 79. See also Occupation, German of Poland.
Polarization, 524-527.
Poliakiewicz, Simcha, 314.
Police: general, 3, 51, 445 n. 301, 480, 498, 616; opponent's power depends on support of, 459; effectiveness depends on public support, 15, 460; and propaganda, 20; disobedience, 63, 504, 596, 671, 672, 752, 753, 754, 755, 767; noncooperation of, 330, 332; collaboration of, 498; relation to contending groups, 455, 606; and internal problems of actionists, 618; and repression, 166-167, 380, 476, 536, 537, 550, 555, 557, 558, 561, 618, 713; nonviolent opposition to, 398, 452, 453, 509, 550, 558, 579, 616, 621; and methods of nonviolent protest, 146, 300; and methods of noncooperation, 185, 187, 188-189, 235; and methods of nonviolent interjection, 382, 384, 403, 418; provocation toward, 677; relation to openness and secrecy of actionists, 483, 484, 487, 488, 491, 518 n. 104; conversion of,

708; Tolstoy on, 44; in various countries: Cuba, 153; India, 42, 83, 187,
311, 318, 330, 432, 529, 552, 559,
591, 682, 687, 693, 731, 735, 783;
Germany, 80, 90, 288, 302, 354 n.
216, 542; East Germany, 161, 197,
405, 529, 629, 675, 677, 708, 753,
775 n. 193; Guatemala, 90, 91, 92;
Russia, 94, 197, 333, 365, 483, 485,
553, 561, 593, 640, 646 n. 79, 684;
Ireland, 161, 188-189; South Africa,
138, 223, 419, 541, 550, 587, 591,
629, 670, 692; Nyasaland, 310, 419;
United States, 138, 166, 319, 374,
378, 386, 397, 404, 587, 677, 692;
Spain, 171; Finland, 278; France, 310,
326, 327; Belgium, 312; Italy, 326,
363, 403; Brazil, 408; Norway,
330-332; Netherlands, 330; Hungary,
388; Japan, 682; South Vietnam, 661.
See also specific methods, individual
countries and particular struggles.
Policy of austerity, 225-226.
"Polite procrastination," 323. See Stalling
and obstruction.
Political boycott, 285. See also Political
noncooperation.
Political *jiu-jitsu*, 110, 112, 113, 453, 496,
557, 563, 596, 600, 642, 657-697, 698
n. 1; 807.
Political mourning, 157-158.
Political noncooperation: general, 69, 184,
394, 504, 737: defined, 285-286;
methods of, 285-347; related to methods of social noncooperation, 193,
195, 199, 212, 213; related to methods
of economic noncooperation, 240,
279; compared with methods of nonviolent intervention, 394, 421; effect of,
536, 613, 614, 743; and sanctions, 12;
practiced under repression, 640; and
nonviolent protest, 118, 129, 133,
143; conversion by, 70; Continental
Association, program of, 186. See also
Noncooperation and specific struggles.
Political violence, Preface; defined, 543;
compared with nonviolent action, 459,
485, 523, 679, 755, 756, 802, 805,
806; effect of nonviolent action on,
809; effect on nonviolent action, 513;
linked to kind of social system, 543;
800, 806, 808; relation to centralization of power, 800-801, 802; and repression, 545, 547, 552; and suffering,
551, 552; contagion of, 798; exposure
of leadership, 637; in Latin America,

90. See also Violence, Repression and
individual countries.
Politically-motivated counterfeiting,
409-410.
Politika, 327, 389-390.
Poltava, Province, Russian Empire, 261.
Ponce, General, 92.
Poor People's Corporation, Jackson, Mis-
sissippi, 416.
Popular nonobedience, 304-306, 308, 312.
Populists, Russia, 128, 163.
Port-au-Prince, Haiti, 279.
Port Elizabeth, South Africa, 138, 167,
200, 601.
Portsmouth, New Hampshire, 159, 653 n.
252.
Portsmouth, Virginia, 559.
Portugal, 195, 233, 237, 243, 291, 297,
347, 382, 410; Minister of Education,
311; opposition, 291; recognition of
Republic, 344.
Postal service, 86.
Posters, 126, 127, 132, 152, 154, 156,
171, 188, 369, 370.
Posters and other displayed protest, 117.
Potsdam Garrison, 697.
Powell, Rev. Adam Clayton, 223.
Power: general, 4, 5, 6, 13, 40, 72, 79, 81,
85, 124, 431, 532, 659, 706; social
power defined, 7; political power defined, 7-8; nature of, 8, 48 n. 4, 49 n.
5, 523; social roots of, 10-16; sources
of, 11-12, 16, 28, 69, 453; monolith
theory of, 9-10, 44; pluralistic-dependency theory of, 9, 39; relation to authority, 13; depends on consent, 3, 13,
16, 25, 29, 49 n. 8, 51 n. 17, 53 n. 33,
54 n. 51, 55 n. 61, 61 n. 201, 63, 490,
524, 745; depends on interaction, 11,
16, 17-18, 25, 26, 49-50 n. 9, 52 n. 23,
54 n. 47, 744; and nonviolent action,
3, 7-8, 64, 65-67, 69, 70, 76, 97, 110,
112, 113, 321, 451, 453-454, 470,
471, 485, 489, 490, 579, 657, 658,
698 n. 1, 743, 756, 816; and nonviolent coercion, 744-745; control of,
10, 18, 29, 32, 36, 39, 41, 47, 50 n.
13, 817; theory of nonviolent control
of, 32-34; technique of control of,
43-48, 461, varies with control of social forces, 15-16; social sources of
power changes, 458-461; altering relationships of, 695-697; power problem,
36-38, 39; Gandhi's theory of, 83-86,
724-725; withdrawing sources of, 47,
64, 85, 112, 453-454, 706, 744-754;

816; and sanctions, 14, 19; and repression, 35, 496, 588, 594; shifts in, 434, 524, 527, 537, 657, 658, 662, 690, 758, 767; redistribution of, Chapter 14; indirect approach to, 495-496; and political *jiu-jitsu,* 496, 690, 768; and concessions by opponent, 532, 543, 588, 594, 739; and conversion of opponent, 725; role in negotiations, 470; compared with authority, 745; and violence, 683; as factor in social situation, 618; awareness of, 739, 740; and Jouvenal, 54 n. 50; Weberian 'types', 56 n. 86.

Prace, 301.

Prague, Czechoslovakia, 73, 127, 129, 131, 136, 142, 151, 162, 163, 188, 189, 234, 260, 300, 310, 327, 328, 590; Lord Mayor of, 288; City Committee of the Communist Party, 131; Praha-Vrsovice railroad depot, 127.

Prasad, Rajendra, 591.

Prawdin, Michael, 457, 607.

Prayer and worship, 137-139, 480.

Pray-in, 379-380.

Preclusive purchasing, 410.

Prelouc, Czechoslovakia, 328.

Preparations for nonviolent struggle, 467-481.

Presbyterians, 376, 386, 670.

Press Ordinance, India, 641.

Preston, Katherine, 439 n. 131.

Pretoria, South Africa, 164, 167, 223.

Primary boycott, 220-221.

Prince Edward County, Virginia, 239.

Princeton, New Jersey, 140.

Princeton University, 144.

Principled nonviolence, Preface.

Prison, 77, 125, 138, 200, 452, 486, 491, 537, 576, 771 n. 58.

Prison camps, 93.

Prisoner-of-war camps, 485.

Prisoners and political prisons, 90, 93, 94, 265, 328, 470, 642.

Prisoners' strike, 265.

Producers boycott, 231-232.

Professional strike, 265-266, 334.

Prohibitory Act, Britain, 247, 694.

Propaganda, 20, 89, 120, 127, 146, 148, 332, 529, 683.

Property, 11.

Protest. See Nonviolent protest and persuasion.

Protest disrobing(s), 140, 177 n. 121, 359.

Protest emigration, 202, 204, 211-213. See also *hijirat.*

Protest meetings, 117, 165-167, 445 n. 301. See also Assemblies of protest or support, Camouflaged meetings of protest and Teach-ins.

Protest strike, 259-261, 763.

Protestants, 669.

Protopopov, Minister of the Interior, 190.

Proudfoot, Merrill, 437 n. 56.

Providence, Rhode Island, 141, 185, 205, 299, 426, 428-430, 517 n. 66, 702 n. 106.

Prussia, 213, 604, 686.

Psychological changes in nonviolent actionists, 777-793.

Psychological harassment, 369.

Psychological identification with ruler, 23, 24, 27.

Public opinion, 92, 110, 113, 119, 316, 321, 337, 340, 530, 584-585, 589, 626, 657, 659, 662, 710, 698 n. 3, 720.

Public Safety Act, No. 3 of 1953, South Africa, 541, 757.

Public statements, 122, 461, 511.

Publication of names, 186.

Puerto Rico, 388.

Puget Sound, State of Washington, 319.

Pullman Palace Car Co., 233.

Punjab, India, 751.

Puritans, 362, 540, 548, 681, 713, 719, 720.

Putrament, Jerzy, 316.

Quakers. See Society of Friends.

Quang Nang Province, South Vietnam, 296.

Quantity and quality in nonviolent action, 475-479.

Quantri, South Vietnam, 138.

Quasi-legal evasions and delays, 335-337.

Quebec, Canada, 264.

Quickie walkout, 261.

Quillayute River, State of Washington, 319.

Quisling, Vidkun, 5, 88, 89, 331, 410, 419, 585. See also Norway, Quisling regime.

Qum, Persia, 207, 208, 209, 210.

Radhakrishnan, President S., 290.

Radio, 129, 190, 799.

Radio Prague, 162.

Rainbow Beach, Lake Michigan, 378.

Rajasthan, India, 290.

Raleigh, North Carolina, 464.

Rally, 445 n. 301.

Rampur, Gujarat, India, 677.

Randolph, A. Philip, 223.

against revolutionaries, 646 n. 79; violence of actionists provides excuse for, 597, 603, 604, 605, 743; *agents provocateurs* used to justify, 593, 599; sabotage increases, 610, 611; undisciplined action facilitates effective, 618; opponent's means of and cause questionable, 665-667; problems in opponent's exercise of, 596, 665, 676-677, 752, 753, 755, 816; actionists provoke, 677, 687; increases resistance, 678, 682, 690, 740; strength needed to withstand, 680, 758-759; may legitimize resistance, 681; reduction of, 477, 565, 722; less severe forms and counter-nonviolence, 502, 690-695; and psychological effects, 698 n. 1, 722; and institutionalized indifference, 712; and differential treatment, 713; and mechanisms of success, 706, 708, 740, 722; neutralization through self-suffering, 709, 710-711; need for self-reliance against, 803; and nonviolent coercion, 741, 753, 755; inefficacy of, 636-642; solidarity and discipline needed to fight, 573-642; limitations on against nonviolent actions, 583-586; may become new point of resistance, 640-642; political *jiu-jitsu* a means to counter, 657, see also Political *jiu-jitsu*. See also Violence, Violent action and struggle, Sanctions and Political *jiu-jitsu*.

Republican Party, U.S., 134, 245, 246.

Resistance: general, 23, 35, 36, 76, 80, 81-82, 89, 98, 99, 113, 146, 185, 187, 196, 302, 312, 313, 321, 332, 418, 423, 452, 453, 480, 484, 485, 488, 498, 508, 586, 639, 640-642, 658, 763-764, 786; conditions when impossible, 56 n. 82, 524; and repression, 35; continuing under repression, 680-688, 709, 785; people adverse to, 21; right of, 45-46; by noncooperation, 47; corporate, 48; violent, 87; contagious, 798-799; advocacy of, 289; symbolic, 136, 360; economic, 76, 481, 534, 540, 578; and constructive program, 795-797; capacity for expanded, 804. See also Passive resistance and listings in Table of Contents.

Restraints or sanctions for solidarity of actionists, 580-583.

Restricted strike, 268-275.

Reverse strike, 114, 401, 402-403.

Revolutionary strike, 432.

Revolutionary struggle. See Struggle, revolutionary.

Reuter, Ernst, 550.

Revenue refusal, 84, 86, 240-243.

Reverse trial, 368-369.

Révész, Imre, 309.

Revolution: general, 33, 34, 78, 80, 97, 296, 332, 423, 424, 457, 460, 488, 551, 554, 753, 756; nonviolent, 78, 79, 806; social, 97, 477, 706, 809; right of, 45; and parallel government, 424; and centralization of power, 800, 802; and general strike, 532; and terrorism, 624; and leadership, 637; nonviolent, 86; Lenin on, 650-651 n. 160, 651 n. 161; support for violent, 86; Russian, 128, 456, 602; socialist, 291.

Reynolds, Lloyd G., 132-133.

Rhineland, German, 81, 259, 553.

Rhode Island, 225, 299, 337, 362, 375, 413, 426, 427, 428-429, 430, 582; Supreme Court, 427, 430; parallel government (Dorr's Rebellion), 426-430. See also individual towns, cities and persons.

Rhode Island Antislavery Society, 369, 387.

Rhodesia. See Southern Rhodesia and Northern Rhodesia.

Ribbentrop, Foreign Minister Joachim, 325, 326, 692.

Richardson, Gloria, 791.

Ride-in, 371, 375.

Riga massacres, 325.

Rinde, Erik, Preface.

Rioting, 3, 34, 77, 587, 591, 599, 600, 601, 603, 604, 616, 623-625.

Risør, Norway, 305.

Roberts, Adam, Preface, 173 n. 1.

Robin Moor, 341.

Rock Hill, South Carolina, 380.

Röchling concern, 236.

Rodman, Edward, 559.

Rodzyanko, M. V., 190, 744.

Rogers, abolitionist editor, 199.

Roman Campagna, Italy, 405.

Roman Catholic Church, 122, 234, 366, 399, 406, 416, 669. See also individual churches, clergy, popes, etc.

Roman Catholic Law, 204.

Roman Catholic minority, South Vietnam, 671.

Roman consuls, 75.

Rome: general, 192; ancient, 4, 57 n. 105, 75-76, 124, 266; Roman Empire, 123-124, 312, 388; toleration of Christians in Roman Empire, 736; Roman Republic, 212; Roman Proconsul of Asia, 231, 540; Minister of Food, 266; plebians of, 73, 75, 212; measures against nonviolent action in, 540.

Romsdal, Norway, 241.

Roosevelt, President Franklin D., 262, 404, 410.

Rose, Debby, Preface.

Rosenberg, Alfred, 43, 323, 325, 683.

Rosenthal, Bosch Ridder van, 422; commentary by for Netherlands government, 422.

Rosenthal, Mario, 92-93.

Ross, Edward Alsworth, 658-659, 698 n. 3.

Rostov-on-Don, Russia, 168, 276.

Rostovtzeff, M., 124, 201, 202, 568 n. 72.

"Rotation" hunger strike, 366.

Rothwell, Margaret, Preface.

Rotterdam, Netherlands, 126, 401.

Round Table Conference on India, 187, 230, 512.

Rousseau, Jean-Jacques, 24, 36, 50 n. 14, 51 n. 17.

Rowlatt Bills, India 1919, 278, campaign against, 466, 622.

Royal College, Nairobi, Kenya, 385.

Royal Garhwal Rifles, British India, 675.

Royal Irish Constabulary, 188.

Royal Mosque, Persia, 206.

Rubin, Jerry, 397.

Rude gestures, 145.

Rude Pravo, 147, 174 n. 19, 260-261, 301.

Rudlin, W. A., 15, 25.

Ruggles, Brigadier, 702 n. 109.

Ruggles, David, 375.

Ruhr, Germany and *Ruhrkampf*, 74, 81-82, 126, 149, 161, 164, 189, 190, 223, 259, 267, 275, 287, 296, 306, 353 n. 216, 368, 464, 519 n. 132, 541, 542, 553-554, 578, 579, 586, 604, 609, 610-611, 619, 627, 647 n. 99, 659, 668-669, 676, 686, 737, 748, 764.

Ruler: general, 29, 30, 82; defined, 49 n. 6; and theory of power, 9, 10, 11; sources of power, 11-12, 50; authority depends on obedience, 12-13, 14, 16, 18, 25, 31, 32, 34, 35, 44, 49 n. 8, 50 n. 15, 51 n. 19; needs assistance of subjects, 13-14; depends on bureaucracy, 36; obedience to essentially voluntary, 27, 28, 30; use of sanctions, 14, 35; ruler-subject relationship, 15-18, 29,

44, 52 n. 23, 54 n. 49; authority depends on fear, 18; and subjects' sense of moral obligation, 20-21; and self-interest of subjects, 22; psychological identification with, 23; and subjects' lack of self-confidence, 23-24; obtaining agents and functionaries, 24; nonviolent action against, 78, 84, 321, 453; nonrecognition of nonviolent action, 72; use of deception by, 44-45; self-restraint of, 33; dissolution of power, 63, 78; violence against, 34.

"Running-sore" strike. See Limited strike.

Russell, Bertrand, 24, 172.

Russia: general, 36, 43, 73, 74, 77, 94, 125, 162, 170, 202, 206, 209, 213, 226, 233, 234, 248, 312, 320, 328, 339, 346, 374, 389, 409, 430, 457, 507, 536, 545, 550, 562, 567 n. 50, 586, 590, 629, 647, 650 n. 160, 651 n. 161-n.167, 675, 677, 678, 682, 688, 713, 745, 780; methods of nonviolent action used in and by, 122, 128, 129, 131, 139, 147, 148, 150, 152, 155-156, 189-190, 190-191, 201, 202, 236, 237, 238, 261, 270, 276, 287, 291, 296, 364-366, 368, 386-387, 402, 411, 430; Imperial Russia, 78-79, 131, 197, 202, 268, 276, 278, 305, 312, 318, 330, 530, 645, 646 n. 79, 797; Tsarist regime, 4, 74, 79, 149, 152, 155-156, 163, 166, 242, 279, 290, 330, 484, 507, 530, 532, 533, 592, 593, 596, 606-608, 649-650 n. 154, 659, 667-668, 672, 674, 679, 680, 684, 753; Russian troops, 162, 163, 178 n. 152, 189-190, 405, 550, 668, 680, 753; Russian army, 149, 629, 668; Jews in, 150, 330; invasion of Czechoslovakia 1968, 4, 5, 98-101, 123, 136, 188-190, 288; May Day celebrations 1905, 483; repression of actionists in, 548; "great trials of 1877," 368; trial of "the fifty," 368; "trial of the hundred and ninety-three," 368; police, 330, 593, 684; trade unions, 797: Pit No. 1 Strike Committee, 548; Council of Ministers, 744; Minister of War, 334; Ministry of Public Welfare, 328; Ministers of Education and Health, 131; U.S.S.R. Ministry of Culture, 331; Ministry of Education, 131, 293; Second Congress of the Peasants Union, 507; Provisional Government, 328, 430; Central Bureau of the Union of Railroad Workers, 549; Manufacturers Association, 668; Merchants Club, 668; Kushka Station, 549; Academy of Sciences, 668; Bureau of the Central Committee of the Party, 673. See also Union of Soviet Socialist Republics, Occupation, German of Soviet Union, Russian of... specific methods of nonviolent action and Russian Revolutions of 1905, 1917.

Russian peasants, 228.

Russian Revolution of 1905, 4, 5, 78, 79, 139, 152, 166, 168, 197, 209, 236, 237, 242, 260, 261, 276, 296, 305, 306, 312, 333, 430, 431, 483, 507, 519 n. 132, 532, 533, 604, 606-608, 626, 640, 647 n. 99, 650 n. 160, 651 ns. 161 and 167, 672, 743, 747, 573, 780, 781, 788-789, 794, 798.

Russian Revolution of February-March 1917, 4, 5, 79, 333, 430, 519 n. 132, 542, 569, 596, 672, 743, 744, 745, 753.

Russian Socialist Federated Soviet Republic (R.S.F.S.R.), 39, 40.

Russian Soldiers' Councils, 464.

Russification, 279.

Russo-Japanese War, 78, 312.

Rustin, Bayard, 377.

Sabotage, 82, 274, 323, 403, 590, 597, 600, 604, 651 n. 168, 651 n. 173, 683; and nonviolent action, 608-611.

Sachsen, Germany, 619.

Sacramento, California, 264.

Sacred Mount, Rome, 75-76.

Saigon, Vietnam, 136, 661.

St. Donats Holiday Estates, Nash, Wales, 227.

St. Hedwig's Cathedral, Berlin, Germany, 120.

St. Lamberti Church, Münster, Germany, 669.

St. Lawrence Seaway, 389.

St. Louis, Missouri, 197.

St. Patrick, 361.

St. Petersburg, Russian Empire. 73. 78, 122, 155, 160, 162, 166, 168, 190, 197, 260, 266, 273, 333, 339, 368, 530, 645 n. 79, 659; Soviet of, 237, 242, 430, 606. See also Petrograd and Leningrad.

Salem, Massachusetts, 141, 317, 376, 549, 702 n. 109.

Salt Acts, British India, 86, 380, 483, 497, 513, 533, 641, 682.

Salt March of 1930, India, 4, 86, 153, 497, 504, 584, 775 n. 169. See also India, Gandhi, Indian National Congress and Britain.

Salvador. See El Salvador.

Salvemini, Gaetano, 137, 309.

Samara Province, Russian Empire, 261.

Sanctuary, 204; Christian examples, 204-205; Islamic examples (Persia 1906), 205-210.

Sanctions: defined, 12; social, 183-213; religious, 191-193; international, 12, 346, 663; diplomatic, 340-347, 664; economic (general), 141, 219-284; 401-416, 613, 652 n. 192, 664; (against nonviolent actionists) 538, (international), 132, 244-248, 251 n. 55, 409-411; nonviolent, 12, 537, 805, (to support nonviolent discipline), 466, 615-616; nonviolent action as, 165, 694; fear of as source of a ruler's power, 12, 14, 19, 22, 25, 27, 30, 55 n. 61, 453, 456, 744; nonviolent fearlessness makes impotent, 546, 752. See also Fearlessness. Fear of produces obedience, 19-20, 24, 27-28, 30, 456; and pattern of submission, 14, 15, 16-17, 23, 25-26, 35; must operate on will of subject, 26-29, 111, 545; willingness to undergo in resistance, 30-31, 32, 458, 476, 504, 551, 817; unwillingness to undergo in resistance, 547; derive from obedience and cooperation, 14-15, 21; nonviolent action may restrict opponent's, 752-754; against nonviolent action, 536-546; police and troops subject to, 558; and negotiations, 67. See also Repression, Obedience, Disobedience, Suffering, Self suffering, and Violent sanctions.

San Diego, California, 130, 395.

San Francisco Bay, 389.

San Francisco to Moscow Peace March, 153.

Sans-Culotte, 136.

Santiago, Cuba, 153, 154.

Saratov Province, Russian Empire, 168, 261.

Sargent, Porter, Preface.

Satyagraha: theory of power, 83, 85, 548, 711, 774 n. 161, 781; dynamics of, 211, 367, 707, 709-710, 725, 771 n. 66; and Dharsana raid, 311; and preparations, 467, 503, 505; reveals implicit violence, 544; casualties in, 553; widespread leadership in, 633; by Pathans, 790; at Vykom, 82; parallel social structures, 796; need for few

numbers, 478; and constructive program, 576.
Satyagrahic fast, 360, 363, 367.
Savannah, Georgia, 399.
Saxony, Germany, 192.
Scandinavia, 276, 321. See individual countries.
Scandinavian Airlines System, 267.
Scavenius, Premier Erik, 294.
Schacht, Minister of Economics Hjalmer H. G., 295.
Schalburgkorps, 277.
Schapiro, Leonard, 170, 648 n. 127, 679, 684, 780.
Scheetz, John W., 297.
Schelling, Thomas C., Preface, Introduction, 245, 409-411.
Schlesinger, Arthur, Sr., 137, 141, 160, 185, 221, 274-275, 318, 381, 511, 519 n. 142, 600, 602, 605, 612, 613, 614-615, 622-623, 632, 633, 652 n. 220, 653 ,n. 252, 702 ns. 106 and 109, 781, 798.
Schlegelberger, Franz, 320.
Scholl, Hans and Sophie, 175 n. 51.
Scholl, Inge, 175 n. 51.
School boycott. See Student strike.
Schorn, Friedrich, 629.
Schuster, Alvin, 143.
Schwerner, Michael, 198.
Schweitzer, Arthur, 236.
Sears Roebuck, 766.
Seattle, Washington, 275, 432.
"Secessions," Greek, 201. See also Protest emigration.
Secondary boycott, 220, 221, 581.
Seeking imprisonment, 418-420, 445 n. 301, 546.
Segregation, 75, 95, 96, 133, 198, 239, 265, 335-336, 373, 375-377, 384, 398, 399, 412, 419, 544, 635, 670, 689, 693, 694, 788.
Seifert, Harvey, 525, 527, 540, 548-549, 557, 558, 559, 560, 561, 565, 665, 666, 681, 682, 696, 713, 716, 734-736, 737, 782.
Seizure of assets, 410-411.
Selective patronage, 412-413.
Selective refusal of assistance by government aides, 320-321.
Selective Service, U.S., 142, 417.
Selective social boycott, 190-191.
Selective strike, 274-275.
Self-confidence, 23-24, 27, 29, 472, 500, 524, 786, 807.
Self-discipline, 199, 616, 623. See also

Discipline and Nonviolent discipline.
Self-exposure to the elements, 359-360.
Self-immolation, 138, 142, 162, 171.
Self-interest, 22, 24, 27.
Self-reliance, 227, 467, 521, 524, 529, 782, 786, 803.
Self-respect, 3, 31, 721, 778, 779, 782, 785, 786, 787, 807; lack of, 212.
Self-restraint in rulers, 33.
Self-retribution, 359.
Self-sacrifice, 67, 126, 716. See also Suffering, Self-suffering, Brutalities and Persistence.
Self-suffering: and conversion, 707, 771 n. 66; rationale of, 709-711; and social distance, 711-717; conversion through, 717-733. See also Suffering and Conversion.
Selma, Alabama, 233, 416, 690.
Senate, Roman, 76.
Senate, United States, 139, 404.
Sendai, Japan, 213.
Seoul, Korea, 152.
Septimius, Roman Emperor, 124.
Serbia, 290.
Sered Camp, Bratislava, Czechoslovakia, 313.
Serfdom, 318.
Serrano, Guatemalan opposition spokesmen, 92.
Seton-Watson, Christopher, Preface, 312, 405-406, 416, 608.
Severance of diplomatic relations, 12, 344-345, 461.
Severance of funds and credit, 239-240.
Severing, Carl, Prussian Minister, 604.
Seyss-Inquart, Arthur, *Reichskommissar*, 120.
Sforza, Duke Galeazzo, 410.
Shadrach, 384.
Shah, 'Abdul'-Azím, a holy shrine, 206.
Sharpeville, South Africa, 158, 200, 419, 544, 585, 587, 629, 660, 670.
Shelepin, Aleksandr, 121.
Shelley, Percy B., 35.
Shia, sect of Islam, 208.
Shils, Edward A., 52 n. 23.
Shimbori Michiya, 155.
Shlyapnikov, Alexandr, 673.
Shootings, 86, 96, 674, 683, 684. See also Repression.
Shridharani, Krishnalal, 364, 752.
Sibley, Mulford, 505, 597.
Sicherheits-Dienst, S.D., 161.
Sicily, 363, 402, 405-406.
Siddapur *taluka*, Kanara, India, 583.

Sports strike, 195.
Spy flights, 342.
S.S. (*Schutzstaffel*), Nazi, 89, 90, 330, 716.
St. Catherine's College, Oxford, Preface.
Stabekk School, Stabekk, Norway, 419.
Stack, Austin, 366.
South Africa, 98, 132, 142, 148, 150, 155, 164, 200, 223, 237, 240, 251 n. 55, 275, 298, 347, 383, 507, 536, 542, 544, 545, 549-550, 556, 558, 585-586, 609, 660, 663, 669-670, 677, 710, 783, 781; Ghandi in, 79, 82, 478, 587, 630-631, 771 n. 66, 795; 1952 Defiance Campaign, 137-138, 142, 167, 483, 514, 525, 544, 576, 599, 659, 692; South African "Freedom Charter," 123; See also Suppression of Communism Act, Criminal Law Amendment Act, Universities Apartheid Bill.
South America, 276, 406. See also individual countries.
Staffordshire, England, 235.
Stalin, Josef, 49 n. 6, 94, 141, 148, 340, 342, 347, 562, 604.
Stall-in, 394-395.
Stalling and obstruction, 323-328, 335, 394.
Stamm, Eugen, 463.
Stamp Act Congress, 794.
Stamp Act, 70, 157, 158, 185, 221, 225, 229, 231, 238-239, 241, 266, 306, 337, 412, 602, 611, 623, 630, 667, 708, 738, 794, 798.
Stand-in, 374-375.
Stang, Axel, 194.
Stanley, Governor Thomas, 240.
The State: general, 9, 10, 17, 22, 25, 57 n. 105, 67, 81, 199, 328, 451, 532; and "force," 15, 26, 49 n. 5; violence and origin of, 20; violence and centralization in, 800-802; obedience to, 26; control of, 34; Hitler on restructuring of, 46; dependence on authority, 50 n. 14; 51 n. 19, 52 n. 24; 53 n. 33; sanctions to induce obedience, 123 n. 61, 536-537. See also Sanctions. Dissolution of, 62 n. 201; and civil resistance, 530.
State Department, U.S., 661.
States General, France, 137.
"Statement of the 342," by Russian academics, 122.
Stauffenberg, Count Claus von, 322.
Stavanger, Norway, 196.

Stay-at-home, 170, 199-200, 259.
Stay-at-home strikes, 507, 508.
Strategy, 48, 67, 101, 455, 462, 518 n. 24, 519 n. 22, 523, (definition) 493; importance of, 493-495, 628, 756, 763; elements of, 495-500, (geographical) 496-497, (psychological) 490, (timing) 497-498; choice of weapons, 501-510; Gandhi's attention to, 82, 84, 85-86, 87, 492-493; grand strategy, 87, (definition) 493; and concentration of strength, 499-500; and influence of actionist behaviour, 527.
Stay-down strike, 403.
Stay-in strike, 401, 403-405, 550.
Steblova, Czechoslovakia, 328.
Steel strike, U.S., 535.
Steiner, Stan, 191, 319.
Sternstein, Wolfgang, 149, 287-288, 578, 648 n. 144.
Steuben, John, 265.
Stevenage, Hertfordshire, England, 259.
Stevens, Edmund, 145.
Stock Exchange, New York City, 397.
Stralsund shipyard, East Germany, 143.
Strikes: general references and diverse cases, 4, 5, 67, 71, 73, 77, 87, 91, 97, 113, 118, 124, 125, 172, 219, 257-279, 282 n. 62, 421, 453, 459, 474, 479, 522, 529, 534, 544, 550, 553, 629, 686, 747, 749, 750, 752; defined, 257-258, 280 n. 5; as sanction, 12; learning how to use, 779-780; "flight" as precursor of, 201-204; violence in, 597-598; illegal, 45; injunction against ignored, 318; countermeasures and repression against, 535, 536, 540, 568 n. 72, 584, 585-586, 640, 686, 688, 692, 758, see also Repression; reduced violence against, 476; perceptions of power of, 532-533; morale and solidarity in, 575-583, 794; strategy in, 495, 519 ns. 127 and 128; settlements of, 737; control organizations in, 431-432, 797; as repudiation of authority, 531; and self-respect, 524, 786; increased self-confidence from, 798-799; Lenin on impact of, 781, 788-789; Lenin on limits of, 650-651 n. 161; and picketing, 132-133, 134, 503; and social boycott, 184; and stay-at-home, 199; and appeals to mutiny, 677-678; and lockout, 235; and nonviolent interjection, 383; and fast, 466; combined with economic boycott, 232-233, 258, 227-279; in

1905 Revolution, 78-79, 139, 431, 483, 530, 532, 549, 567 n. 44, 647 n. 99, 650 n. 161, 668, 780, 788-789; see Russian Revolution of 1905. In resistance to Kapp *Putsch*, 80-81, 743; see Kapp *Putsch*; at Vorkuta, 93-95, 533, 548; see also Vorkuta. See also specific methods of the strike, invidual countries, places etc. for other specific cases.

Strike breakers, 263, 476, 576.
Strike by resignation, 273.
Strike committees, 94, 95, 464, 578; at Vorkuta, 548.
Strik-Strikfeldt, Captain Wilfried, 43.
Student strike, 93, 196-198.
Struggle, general, 85, 101, 109, 110, 526, 531, 533, 547, 547 n. 50, 564; characteristic of nonviolent action, 65-67, 71-72, 87, 548; and anarchism, 67; forms of imitated, 798; violent, 802, 803, 805, 815; military, 71; and nonviolent action, 97-98; withdrawal from, 535, 793; testing nonviolent action in, 779; means of, 546.
Stuttgart, Germany, 80, 381.
Submission of subjects: sanctions to induce, 14; psychological means to induce, 16; indirect economic rewards induce, 22; moral obligation induces, 20; lack of self-confidence induces, 24; alien education induces, 57 n. 100; basic to nondemocratic rule, 78, 84, 490, 745; needed to preserve government *per se*, 45; pattern of, 14, 543; to oppression destructive of society, 46; suffering of submissive people, 554; psychological and attitudinal changes halt, 31-32; rejection basic to nonviolent action, 64-65, 67, 70, 87, 522, 523, 549, 785; pattern of submissiveness ended, 778-779; withdrawal of, 31, 34-36, 84, 521-524, 528, 778; repression to force resumption of, 32, 545, 681, 683, 684; to violence spells defeat, 680; repression may fail to induce, 111-112, 546-547, 683-687. See also Sanctions, Obedience, Passivity, Repression, Disobedience, Noncooperation.
Subordination, 58 n. 122, 779.
Subversion, 36.
Success-failure, factors influencing. See Outcome of the conflict, factors influencing.
Suffering: penalty for disobedience, 29;

impact of, 634; acceptance as price of defiance, 636; capacity to endure, 680, 759; in nonviolent action (general), 638, 550, 769 n. 1; necessity of, 551-555; Gandhi on purity in, 655 n. 264; inflicted by general strike, 532. See also Self-suffering and Conversion.
Suffolk County, Massachusetts Bay, 595.
Suffolk, Henry Howard, Twelfth Earl of, 740.
Suffolk Resolves, 595.
Suhl, Yuri, 314.
Sumter County Civil Rights Movement, 243.
Sunakawa, Japan, 388.
"Sundays Only" strikes. See Strike, limited.
Sunday Times (London), 145, 162.
Sung Cheh-yuan, General, 307.
Suppliers and handlers boycott, 232-234.
Suppression, 541, 683, 688, 778. See also Repression.
Suppression of Communism Bill, South Africa, 199-200, 542.
Surrender, 534.
Suspension of social and sports activities, 193-196.
Svoboda, 127.
Svoboda, President Ludvik, 99, 100, 143.
Svyatopolk-Mirsky, Peter, 640.
Swadeshi, 413.
Swaffham, England, 385.
Swaraj, 41, 490, 576, 787.
Sweden, 81, 231, 241, 276, 341, 415, 659, 692, 697, 767.
Switzerland, 303.
Sykes, General Percy, 208, 209.
Symbolic Acts, 114, 117, 135-145, 287, 475, 576-577.
Symbolic lights, 142-143.
Symbolic public acts, 135-136.
Symbolic reclamations, 145.
Symbolic sounds, 144.
Symbolic strikes, 259-261.
Symbolic withdrawal, 172.
Symbols, 125, 126, 130, 136.
Symons, Julian, 134, 518 n. 105, 519 n. 128, 531, 574, 757.
Sympathetic, strike, 233, 267-268.
Syndicalists, 276.
Taber, Robert, 153-154.
Tabriz, Persia, 206.
Tagore, Rabindranath, 176, 688.
Tallahassee, Florida, 722.
Tambov Province, Russian Empire, 261.
Tamils, 135.

bers of, 235-236; demands met with limited offers, 533; learning how to strike stimulates, 779; picketing by, 132; strikes without, 479; role against invade, 498; growth of strength, 45; perception of strikes and economic boycotts as powerful, 77; choice of protest strike, 259; choice of detailed strike, 269; agricultural, 262-264. See also Agricultural unions. See also names of individual unions and specific methods of the strike, Economic boycott and Economic intervention.

Trades Union Congress, Britain, 233, 432, 463, 574, 578.

Trafalgar Square, London, 138, 167.

Trail, British Columbia, 140.

Transportation, means of, 11, 414, 415, 750, 755.

Trans-Siberian Railway, 333.

Trans-Tisza Church District, Hungary, 309.

Trappeto, Sicily, 363.

Travancore, South India, 83.

Treblinka extermination camp, 314.

Treaty of Medicine Creek of 1845, 318.

"Treaty Treks," 319.

Treaty of Versailles, 659.

Trebova, Czechoslovakia, 327.

Tremont Hotel, Boston, 370.

Trevelyan, Sir George Otto, 178 n. 128, 338.

Trinian, King of Ireland, 361.

Troscad, 364.

Trotsky, Leon, 360, 365, 431, 672.

Trouw, 400-401.

Troy, New York, 236.

Trubetskoi bastion, 365.

Trubetskoi, Prince, 160.

Truehart, Ambassador William, 660.

Trujillo, President Rafael, 248.

Truman, President Harry, 36-38.

Tryon, Governor William, 632.

Tsarskoe Selo, Russia, 139, 191.

Tsektran, 170, 293.

Tsibulsky, Boris, 150.

Tucker, Benjamin, 587.

Tu Dam pagoda, 138.

Tufts University, Preface, 297, 378.

Tuileries, Paris, France, 305.

Turkey, 410.

Turning one's back, 172.

Tuscaroras Indians, 386.

Tyler, President John, 427, 428, 429.

Tyranny, 24, 29, 30, 44, 46-47, 76, 87,

207, 211, 490, 809, 810. See also Totaltarianism, Dictatorship, Oppression.

"U2" plane, United States, 342.

Ubico, General Jorge, 90-93, 197, 268, 744.

Uganda, 291.

Uitenhage, South Africa, 137.

Ukraine, 43, 320, 323. See also individual cities.

Ulbricht, Walter, 303, 574, 676.

Ullstein, Heinz, 89-90.

Ultimatum in nonviolent action, 510-514.

"Underground Railroad," 204.

Union label, 413.

Union of Soviet Socialist Republics (U S.S.R.): early problems in control of bureaucracy, 39-40; absence of cooperation with German occupation, 42-43; strikes at Vorkuta prison camps, 93-95; appeals to officials and citizen of to withdraw troops from Czechoslovakia, 121; justifications for invasion rejected in Czechoslovakia, 129; nuclear tests protested, 139; rude gesture in Sino-Soviet Conflict, 145; soldiers fraternized with during Hungarian Revolution, 146; Czechoslovak employees of Radio Moscow, 289; dissent in *Tsektran*, 293; conflict with Yugoslavia, 340; delays and cancellation of diplomatic events by, 342; K.G.B. (State police), 98-99; troops of, 121, 122, 127, 128; Embassies of (Czechoslovakia), 131; (East Germany), 170; (Britain), 139; (Norway), 159, 310; withholding of diplomatic recognition from, 343; reaction to withholding of recognition from Hungarian Kádár regime, 344; breaks diplomatic relations with Polish government in exile, 344-345; and Katyn graves, 344-345; withdrawal from international organizations by, 345.

Unions. See Trade unions, Agricultural unions, and names of individual unions.

Union of Bulgarian Writers, 121.

Union Pacific Railroad, 231.

Unitarian Church, 392.

United Auto Workers, 269, 403, 700 n. 40.

United Brotherhood of Carpenters & Joiners, 231.

United Colonies, North America, 615.

ing of), 139; (peace delegation of), 342; peace talks, 342; South Vietnam (peace delegation), 342; (Special Forces), 660; Viet Cong (National Liberation Front), 136; Buddhist struggles in South Vietnam, 136-137, 151, 288, 363, 385, 461, 534, 537, 542, 628, 659, 660-662, 671, 688-689; Buddhist noncooperation with N.L.F., 296; U.S. alienated from Diem by repression of Buddhists, 660-661.
Vigilantes, 263.
Vigils, 69, 117, 147-148, 580.
Vilna, Lithuania, 287, 326.
Violence: defined, 608; defined by some as that disliked, 64; unusual definition, 441 n. 191; physical struggle, 523; shown within spectrum of social and political action, 66 Chart Two; not part of nonviolent action, 64, 84, 634; sabotage tied to, 609; dichotomy of violent and nonviolent social behavior untenable, 64-65; relation to material destruction, 65, 66 Chart Two; refraining from aids conversion, 727; and hostility, 727; Lenin committed to, 781; view that power comes from, 109, 683, 749, 793, 805, 806; power potential of, claimed exceeded by nonviolent action, 744; public adverse to, 692, 794; against violence reinforcing, 112, 722; nonviolent action against breaks circle of, 806; and "human nature," 72; diverse attitudes toward revealed by anthropologists, 72; Western civilization biased toward, 72-73; nonrational belief in, 73; none in civil disobedience, 316; of opponent's domination, 513; of system revealed by nonviolent action, 543-544, 557, 678-680; abstention from no guarantee of safety, 556-557; abstention from rewarded, 792; opponent prefers by resisters, 586-594; users of vulnerable, 110; need to prevent in nonviolent action, 465, 526, 595-608, 620, 647-648 n. 99, 722, 725, 727. See also Nonviolent discipline. By resisters reduces support in opponent's camp, 461; by resisters reinforces troop's loyalty, 606; warned against in Czechoslovakia, 130; factors likely to produce in nonviolent action, 608-615, 620; (spontaneity), 486; (improvization), 627; in nonviolent action loses support, 670; choice of methods to reduce chances

of, 403; means to prevent in nonviolent action, 618-633, 653 ns. 220 and 224, 654 ns. 252, 253, and 254; preventing in February 1917 Russian Revolution, 673, 743; expected by British in India, 528; attributed to nonviolent actionists, 573, 583; provocation of opponent to with nonviolent action, 476, 573, 583, 590-594; by resisters causes even radicals to desert American colonial cause, 602; nonviolent struggles tinged with, 97, 319, 404, 644 n. 40, 743; nonviolent struggles mixed with, 87, 94, 101, 146, 223, 235, 354 n. 226, 405, 424, 466, 519 n. 128, 580, 610. See also Violent action and struggle, Violent sanctions, Military struggle, Power, Conflict, War, Political violence, Struggle.
Violent action and struggle: and monolith view of power, 8-9, 678; forms of in conducting conflicts, 3, 34; has received disproportionate attention, 74; qualities and means appropriate to differ from those in nonviolent struggle, 485; defiance by may bring self-respect, 785; heroes of may inspire nonviolent actionists, 783; replacement in a series of particular nonviolent substitutions, 805, 808, 809, 810; meaning of success and failure in, 765; risks in compared to nonviolent struggle, 110; motives for substituting nonviolent action for, 67-68; conditions under which nonviolent action substituted for, 480; incapacity for leads to nonviolent means, 209; rejected for nonviolent means, 77, 98, 101, 318, 475; courageous but hopeless cases (compared to nonviolence), 554; (bridge social distance), 715-716; threat of may induce concessions, 258; opposition terrorism strengthens regime, 645-646 n. 79; unsuccessful cases idealized, 77; nonviolent action commonly unfairly compared with, 74; practical limitations of recognized, 97; time to achieve results, 70; usual means of repression designed to defeat, 111; enforcement problems against differ from those against nonviolent action, 111; group unity in less than in nonviolent action, 794; and centralization of power, 800-802; population less self-reliant than in nonviolent action, 803; may reduce population's perception of

own power, 805; less control over opponent's power sources than with nonviolent action, 817; percentage of combatants lower than in nonviolent struggle, 460, 682; more soldiers required in than in nonviolent struggle (Gandhi), 478; change in relative strengths of protagonists slower than in nonviolent action, 527; used to control rulers, 34, 46, 47; not needed to collapse rulers, 34; weakens *loci* of power, 804; and centralization of power, 800-802; maintenance of contrast from in nonviolent action essential, 113, 489; results claimed less permanent and satisfactory than with nonviolent action, 767-768, 776 n. 229, 806; efficiency increased by conscious efforts, 3; nonviolent coercion occurs without, 706, 742; advocates of aided by neglect of nonviolent coercion, 741; worst aspects avoided by nonviolent coercion, 774 n. 161; seen closer to nonviolent coercion than latter to religious nonviolence, 706, 774 n. 161; suffering during, 551; limited social distance reduces, 713; movements may murder police agents, 488; may be defeated, 71; influences type of leadership, 803-804; comparison of casualties with nonviolent struggle, 552-553; shift to from nonviolent means (American colonials), 536, 614-615; (Algeria), 545; bravery in less powerful than in nonviolent action, 458; advocates of in India gain, 513; in extermination camp, 304; not unconditionally excluded by American colonists, 595; not way for India's freedom, 84; and parallel government, 424; to defend land seizures, 406; in Polish resistance, 223; to back embargoes, 408; to back blockade defiance, 408; ineffective for Czechoslovakia 1968, 100-101; less effective against Nazi occupation than nonviolent resistance, 586; comparison of possible costs of in Ruhr with nonviolent *Ruhrkampf*, 553-554; not needed to destroy tsarist system, 672; in 1905 Revolution, 5, 61, 78-79, 519 n. 128, 648 n. 106, 649-650 n. 154, 650 n. 160, 650-651 n. 161. See also Russian Revolution of 1905. See also Violence, Violent Sanctions, Military struggle, Power, Conflict, War, Political violence, Struggle.

Violent sanctions: general, 12, 19, 109, 466, 537, 543, 804, 805; not needed against passive submission, 543; threat of as sanction, 543; capacity to wield removed, 742, 752-754; for disobedience in violent conflicts, 580; to produce obedience, 55 n. 61; capacity for provided by cooperation, 44; may increasingly be replaced by nonviolent sanction, 805. See also Sanctions.

Viramgam, India, 591.

Virginia: general, 370, 384, 399, 481, 507, 613, 647 n. 99; House of Burgesses, 137, 239, 361; Virginia Resolutions, 338; colonists' parallel government, 424-425.

Vi Vill Oss et Land, 47.

Volhynia Province, Russia, 261.

Volkseigener Betrieb Industrie-bau, 547.

Voluntary exile, 211.

Volynsky Regiment, Russia, 333, 674.

Vorkuta prison camp, U.S.S.R., 93, 94, 265, 365, 533, 548, 553, 640.

Vorwärts, 686.

Voter Registration campaign, Mississippi, 198.

"Voters' Veto" campaign, Britain, 292.

Vrij Nederland, 400.

Vu Van Mau, 137.

Vykom Satyagraha Campaign, India, 82, 148, 472, 717, 720, 728, 729.

Wabash Railroad Company, 231.

Wade-in, 378.

Wagner Act, United States, 404.

Wagner, Mayor Robert, 228.

Wait-in, 139.

Wales, 242, 404. See also individual towns or cities.

Wall Street, New York City, 623.

Walk-alongs, 391.

Walk-outs, 169-170.

Wallace, Governor George, 233.

Wallensteen, Peter, 248.

Walker, Charles C., 621, 625, 632.

Walpole, Horace, 238, 699 n. 32.

Walter, E. V., 54 n. 47.

War: general, 35, 42, 97, 553, 750, 790, 794, 808; and monolith theory of power, 9-10; substitute for, 29, 245, 247, 470, 647 n. 99; as sanction, 12, 36; as control, 32, 34; similarity to nonviolent action, 67, 452, 471, 494, 496, 504-505, 509, 527, 551, 554, 620, 637-638, 678, 711, 756, 758, 762; study of, 73, 75, 492; support for by populace, 460; adoption of by

American colonists, 614-615. See also Violence, shift to. As seedbed for future wars, 767; centralizing effect of, 801; not simply uncontrolled outburst of violence, 494. See also Violence, Violent action and struggle, and Military struggle.
"Walter Ulbricht," The (ship), 143.
Watton, Jacob, 632.
Wardel, Lydia, 140.
Warmbrunn, Werner, 267, 282 n. 62, 283 n. 85, 314, 401, 422, 536, 787.
Warner, Denis, 587, 662.
Warpath, The, 493 n. 131.
Warren, Joseph, 794.
Warriner, Doreen, 407-408.
Warsaw, Poland, 126, 143, 157, 314, 399, 553, 585.
Warsaw Treaty Organization, troops of, 98, 121, 122, 127, 128.
Washington, D.C., U.S.A., 38, 132, 141, 154, 169, 341, 374, 377, 397, 399, 413, 428, 631, 661, 694, 785, 787, 789; police of, 397.
Washington, George, 238, 341, 473, 615.
Washington State, Supreme Court of, 319.
Waskow, Arthur, 133, 134, 224, 374, 503, 689, 788.
Watkins, Frances, 376.
Watt, Richard M., 144, 166, 334, 532, 781.
Weapons: relation to cooperation, 15, 59, n. 144; "weapons systems," 110, 112, 113, 452-453, 601; choice of, 501-504. See also Strategy.
Wearing of symbols, 136.
Weber, Max, 53 n. 33, 56 n. 86.
Webster, Secretary of State Daniel, 384.
Webster Dictionary, 742.
Wechsberg, Joseph, 629.
Wedderburn, Solicitor General, 535.
Weimar Republic. See Germany, Weimar Republic.
Weisse Rose, 126, 128.
Weizäcker, Baron Ernst von, 325.
Welhaven, Kristian, 331.
Wenceslas Square, Prague, 136, 142-143, 151, 260.
Wenceslas, Statue of, 136, 143.
Wentzcke, Paul, 611.
Westchester County, New York, 226.
West, L.J., 813 n. 63.
Westminster, London, 152.
Westmoreland County, Virginia, 239.
Westphalia, Germany, 669.
Wharton, Edward, 549.

Wheble, John, 317.
Wheeler-Bennett, John, 321-322, 344.
Whipple, Charles K., 369.
White House, 133, 540, 693.
White Terror, 646 n. 79.
"Wildcat" strike, 258, 261.
Wilhelm II, Emperor, 80, 302.
Wilhelm Tell, 149.
Wilkes, John, 317.
William, Frederick, 213.
Williams, Robin, 729, 734.
Wilmington, North Carolina, 159.
Wilson, Edmund, 386.
Wilson, President Woodrow, 126, 133, 141, 247, 342, 344, 540, 693.
Winnipeg, Canada, 275, 432.
Winsor, Mary, 787.
Winter Palace, St. Petersburg, 78, 155, 190, 483, 530, 640.
Withdrawal from government educational institutions, 297.
Withdrawal from international organizations, 345.
Withdrawal from social institutions, 199.
Withdrawal from social system, 184, 199-200.
Withdrawal of authority, 424.
Withdrawal of bank deposits, 236.
Withdrawal of cooperation. See Noncooperation.
Withdrawal of economic cooperation. See Economic noncooperation.
Withdrawal of labor. See Strikes.
Withdrawal of obedience. See Disobedience and Civil disobedience.
Withholding of allegiance, 286-288.
Withholding of cooperation, 36, 295. See also Noncooperation.
Withholding of diplomatic recognition, 342-344.
Witte, Prime Minister, Count S.Y., 431.
Wolfe, Bertram D., 430-431.
Wolff, Kurt H., Preface.
Wolman, Leo, 220, 222, 230.
Woman suffrage: in United States, 126, 133, 141, 154, 540, 682, 693, 735, 787; in Netherlands, 147; in England, 366, 677.
Wood, Amos, 199.
Woodlawn Organization, 139.
Woodward, E. L., 291.
Woolworth's, 373.
Workmen's boycott, 230-231.
Work-on without collaboration, 416, 421-422.
"Working-to-rule" strike, 271, 417.

Acknowledgments

Appreciation is gratefully acknowledged to the authors and publishers whose works are quoted in this volume. Complete publication details are provided in the footnotes and bibliography.

Aptheker, Herbert, *American Negro Slave Revolts.* Copyright © 1963 by International Publishers, Inc. New York: International Publishers, 1964. Permission courtesy of International Publishers, Inc.

Bailey, Thomas A., *A Diplomatic History of the American People.* Sixth edition. Copyrighted. New York: Appleton-Century-Crofts, 1958. Permission courtesy of Appleton-Century-Crofts.

Bauer, Raymond A. and Alice H. Bauer, "Day to Day Resistance to Slavery," *Journal of Negro History*, vol. XXVII, no. 4 (Oct. 1942), pp. 388-419. Copyright © 1942 by the Association for the Study of African-American Life and History, Inc. Permission courtesy The Association for the Study of African-American Life and History, Inc., and Raymond A. and Alice H. Bauer.

Blum, Robert, *The United States and China in World Affairs.* ed. by A. Doak Barnett. Copyright © 1966 by the Council on Foreign Relations. New York: McGraw-Hill (for the Council on Foreign Relations), 1966. Permission courtesy McGraw-Hill Book Co.

Bondurant, Joan V., *Conquest of Violence: The Gandhian Philosophy of*

Conflict. Copyright © 1958 by Princeton University Press. Princeton, New Jersey: Princeton University Press. London: Oxford University Press, 1958. Passages reprinted by permission of Princeton University Press.

Borton, Hugh, *Peasant Uprisings in Japan of the Tokugawa Period.* Second Edition. New York: Paragon Book Reprint Corp., 1968. First published in *The Transactions of the Asiatic Society of Japan* (Second Series), vol. XVI, 1939. Passage reprinted courtesy of Paragon Book Reprint Corp.

Brant, Stefan, *The East German Rising.* Translated and adapted by Charles Wheeler. Copyright © 1955 by Stefan Brant. New York: Frederick A. Praeger, 1957. London: Thames and Hudson, 1955. Permission courtesy of Praeger Publishers, Inc.

Brinton, Crane, *The Anatomy of Revolution.* Copyright © Prentice-Hall Inc. Englewood Cliffs, N.J. New York: Vintage Books, 1962. Passages reprinted with permission of Prentice-Hall, Inc.

Case, Clarence Marsh, *Nonviolent Coercion: A Study in Methods of Social Pressure.* Copyright 1923. New York: The Century Co., 1923. Permission courtesy of Appleton-Century-Crofts, Inc.

Charques, Richard, *Twilight of Imperial Russia.* Copyright © 1958 by Richard Charques. Fair Lawn, N. J.: Essential Books, 1959. London: Phoenix House, 1958. Permission courtesy of Dorothy Charques.

Clark, Evans, ed., *Boycotts and Peace.* New York and London: Harper & Bros., 1932. Permission courtesy Harper & Row Publishers, Inc.

Crankshaw, Edward, *Gestapo: Instrument of Tyranny.* Copyright 1956. New York: Viking Press, 1956. London: Putnam, 1956. Permission courtesy of Edward Crankshaw.

Crook, Wilfrid H., *The General Strike: A Study of Labor's Tragic Weapon in Theory and Practice.* Chapel Hill: University of North Carolina Press, 1931. Passages reprinted by permission of the Shoe String Press, Inc., present copyright owner.

Dallin, Alexander, *German Rule in Russia, 1941-1945: A Study of Occupation Policies.* Copyright 1957. New York: St. Martin's Press, 1957. London: Macmillan, 1957. Permission courtesy of St. Martin's Press and Macmillan, London and Basingstoke.

Daniels, Jonathan, *Frontiers on the Potomac.* New York: Macmillan, 1946. Permission courtesy of Brandt & Brandt.

Davison, W. Phillips, *The Berlin Blockade: A Study in Cold War Politics.* Copyright © 1958 by the Rand Corporation. Princeton, N. J.: Princeton University Press, 1958. Passage reprinted by permission of Princeton University Press.

Deanesly, Margaret, *A History of the Medieval Church, 590-1500.* London: Methuen & Co., 1965. Permission courtesy of Associated Book Publishers Ltd.

Delarue, Jacques, *The Gestapo: A History of Horror.* New York: William Morrow, 1964. Passages reprinted courtesy of Macdonald & Co. (Publishers) Ltd.

Ebert, Theodor, "Theory and Practice of Nonviolent Resistance," unpublished English translation of a doctoral thesis presented at the University of Erlangen, Germany, 1965. Permission courtesy of Theodor Ebert.

Eyck, Erich, *A History of the Weimar Republic,* Vol. I. *From the Collapse of the Empire to Hindenburg's Election.* Copyright © 1962 by the President and Fellows of Harvard College. Cambridge, Mass.: Harvard University Press, 1962. Permission courtesy of Harvard University Press.

Farmer, James, *Freedom—When?* Copyright © 1965 by the Congress of Racial Equality, Inc. New York: Random House, 1965. Permission courtesy of James Farmer and Random House.

Faulkner, William, *A Fable.* Copyright © 1950, 1954 by William Faulkner. New York: Random House, 1954. Permission courtesy of Random House, Inc.

Fogg, Richard W., "Jazz Under the Nazis," in *Music 66, "down beat'*s Annual," 1966, pp. 97-99. Copyright © 1966 by *down beat,* 1966. Permission courtesy of *down beat.*

Frank, Jerome D., *Sanity and Survival: Psychological Aspects of War and Peace.* Copyright © 1967 by Jerome D. Frank. New York: Random House and Vintage Books, 1968. Permission courtesy of Jerome D. Frank.

Friedrich, Carl J., ed., *Totalitarianism.* Copyright © 1954 by President and Fellows of Harvard College. Cambridge, Mass.: Harvard University Press, 1954. Permission courtesy of Harvard University Press.

Gandhi, M. K., *An Autobiography, The Constructive Programme, Economics of Khadi, Hind Swaraj, Non-violence in Peace and War,* Two vols., *Satyagraha, Satyagraha in South Africa, Young India,* Vol. I; publication details as cited in the bibliography; Gandhi's works are copyrighted by Navajivan Trust, Ahmedabad, India, and the passages reproduced in this volume are reprinted with the permission and courtesy of Navajivan Trust.

Gipson, Lawrence Henry, *The British Empire Before the American Revolution,* vols. X, XI and XII (see Bibliography). Copyright © by Alfred A. Knopf, 1961, 1965 and 1965 respectively. New York: Alfred A. Knopf, 1961-1965. Permission courtesy of Alfred A. Knopf, Inc.

———, *The Coming of the Revolution, 1763-1775.* Copyright © 1954 by Harper and Brothers. New York and Evanston: Harper Torchbooks, 1962. Permission courtesy of Harper & Row, Publishers, Inc.

Goodspeed, D. J., *The Conspirators: A Study of the Coup d'Etat.* Copyright © 1962 by D. J. Goodspeed, 1962. New York: Viking Press, 1962. Toronto: Macmillan Co. of Canada, 1962. Permission courtesy of Viking Press and of Macmillan (London and Basingstoke).

Gopal, S., *The Viceroyalty of Lord Irwin, 1926-1931.* Copyright 1957. London: Oxford University Press, 1957. Permission courtesy of Oxford University Press.

Görlitz, Walter, ed., *The Memoirs of Field-Marshal Keitel.* Trans. by David Irving. Copyright © 1965 by William Kimber and Co., Ltd. Passages reprinted with permission of William Kimber and Co., Ltd., and Stein and Day Publishers.

Gregg, Richard B., *The Power of Nonviolence.* Second revised edition. Copyright © 1935, 1959, 1966 by Richard B. Gregg. New York: Schocken, 1966. London: James Clarke & Co., 1960. Permission courtesy Schocken Books Inc. for Richard B. Gregg.

Halberstam, David, *The Making of a Quagmire.* Copyright © 1964, 1965 by David Halberstam. New York: Random House, 1965. London: The Bodley Head, 1965. Permission courtesy of Random House.

Halperin, S. William, *Germany Tried Democracy: A Political History of the*

Reich from 1918 to 1933. Copyright © 1946 by Thomas Y. Crowell Co. Hamden, Conn. and London: Archon Books, 1963 [1946]. Used with permission of Thomas Y. Crowell Co.

Harcave, Sidney, *First Blood: The Russian Revolution of 1905.* Copyright © 1964 by The Macmillan Co. New York: Macmillan, 1964. London: Collier-Macmillan, 1964. Permission courtesy of The Macmillan Co.

Harris, Errol E., "Political Power," *Ethics*, vol.XLVIII, no. 1 (Oct. 1957), pp. 1-10. Copyright © 1957 by the University of Chicago Press. Permission courtesy of University of Chicago Press.

Hentoff, Nat, *The New Equality.* New Edition. Copyright © 1964 by Nat Hentoff. New York: Viking Press, 1965. Permission courtesy of Nat Hentoff.

Hiller, E. T., *The Strike: A Study in Collective Action.* Copyright © 1928 by University of Chicago Press. Chicago: University of Chicago Press, 1928. Permission courtesy of University of Chicago Press.

Hsiao, Kung-ch,üan, *Rural China: Imperial Control in the Nineteenth Century.* Copyright © 1960 by University of Washington Press. Seattle: University of Washington Press, 1960. Permission courtesy of University of Washington Press.

Janis, Irving L. and Daniel Katz, "The Reduction of Intergroup Hostility: Research Problems and Hypotheses," in *Journal of Conflict Resolution,* vol. III, no. 1 (March 1959), pp. 85-100. Excerpts are reprinted by permission of the present publisher, Sage Publications Co., Inc. and the authors.

Karski, Jan, *Story of a Secret State.* Boston: Houghton Mifflin, 1944. Permission courtesy Houghton Mifflin Co.

Katkov, George, *Russia 1917: The February Revolution.* Copyright © 1967 by George Katkov. New York: Harper & Row, 1967. Permission courtesy of George Katkov.

Keep, J. H. L., *The Rise of Social Democracy in Russia.* Copyright © 1963 Oxford University Press. Oxford: Clarendon Press, 1963. Permission courtesy of the Clarendon Press.

King, Martin Luther, Jr., *Stride Toward Freedom: The Montgomery Story.* Copyright © 1958 by Martin Luther King, Jr. New York: Harper & Row and Ballentine Books, 1958. London: Victor Gollancz, 1959. Permission courtesy of Harper & Row, Publishers.

———, *Why We Can't Wait.* Copyright © 1963, 1964 by Martin Luther King, Jr. New York: Signet Books of The New American Library, 1964. Permission courtesy of Harper & Row, Publishers, publishers of the hardcover edition.

Knapp, Wilfrid F., *A History of War and Peace: 1939-1965.* Copyright © 1967 by Royal Institute of International Affairs. London, New York and Toronto: Oxford University Press (issued under the auspices of the Royal Institute of International Affairs), 1967. Permission courtesy of Wilfrid F. Knapp.

Koestler, Arthur, *Reflections on Hanging.* Copyright © 1957 by The Macmillan Co. New York: Macmillan, 1967. Permission courtesy of The Macmillan Co.

Korbel, Josef, *The Communist Subversion of Czechoslovakia, 1938-1948: The Failure of Coexistence.* Copyright © 1959 by Princeton University Press, 1959. Excerpts reprinted by permission of Princeton University

Press and Oxford University Press.

Kuper, Leo, *Passive Resistance in South Africa*. New Haven, Conn.: Yale University Press, 1957. London: Jonathan Cape, 1956. Permission courtesy of Yale University Press and Leo Kuper.

Lasswell, Harold D., *Power and Personality*. Copyright © 1948 by W. W. Norton & Co., Inc. New York: W. W. Norton & Co., 1948. Permission courtesy W. W. Norton & Co., Inc.

Lenin, V. I., *Selected Works in Three Volumes*. English language translations copyrighted. New York: International Publishers, and Moscow: Progress Publishers, 1967. Passages reprinted with permission of International Publishers, Inc.

Liddell Hart, Sir Basil, *Strategy: The Indirect Approach*. Coprighted. New York: Frederick A. Praeger, 1954. London: Faber & Faber, 1954. Permission courtesy of Lady Kathleen Liddell Hart.

Littell, Robert, ed., *The Czech Black Book: Prepared by the Institute of History of the Czechoslovak Academy of Sciences*. Copyright © 1969 by Praeger Publishers, Inc., New York. New York, Washington and London: Frederick A. Praeger, 1969.

Lochner, Louis P., ed., *The Goebbels Diaries, 1942-1943*. Copyright © 1948 by the Fireside Press, Inc. Garden City, New York: Doubleday & Co., 1948. Permission courtesy of Doubleday & Co., Inc.

Loh, Robert (as told to Humphrey Evans), *Escape from Red China*. Copyright © 1962 by Robert Loh and Humphrey Evans. New York: Coward-McCann, 1962. Passages reprinted by permission of Coward, McCann and Geoghegan, Inc.

Luthuli, Albert, *Let My People Go: An Autobiography*. Copyright © 1962 by Albert Luthuli. New York: McGraw-Hill Book Co., Inc., 1962. London: Collins, 1962. Used with permission of McGraw-Hill Book Co., Inc.

Mabee, Carleton, *Black Freedom: The Nonviolent Abolitionists from 1830 Through the Civil War*. Copyright © 1970 by Carleton Mabee. New York: Macmillan, 1970. Toronto: Macmillan, 1970. London: Collier-Macmillan, 1970. Permission courtesy of The Macmillan Co.

MacIver, R. M., *The Web of Government*. Copyright © 1947, 1965 by Robert MacIver. New York: Macmillan, 1947.

Miller, William Robert, *Nonviolence: A Christian Interpretation*. Copyright © 1964 by National Board of Young Men's Christian Association. New York: Association Press, 1964. Permission courtesy of Association Press.

Morgan, Edmund S. and Helen M., *The Stamp Act Crisis: Prologue to Revolution*. New, revised edition. Copyright © 1953 by the University of North Carolina Press; Copyright © 1962 by Edmund S. Morgan. New York: Collier Books, 1963. Permission courtesy of Edmund S. Morgan, the University of North Carolina Press and the Institute of Early American History and Culture, Williamsburg.

Mosca, Gaetano, *The Ruling Class*. Introduction by Arthur Livingstone. Copyright © 1939 by McGraw-Hill. New York and London: McGraw-Hill, 1939. Permission courtesy McGraw-Hill Book Co.

Jawaharlal Nehru, *An Autobiography* (sometimes cited as *Jawaharlal Nehru: An Autobiography*). New edition. London: The Bodley Head, 1953. Excerpts quoted with permission of The Bodley Head and the John Day Company. U.S. copyright: Copyright © 1941, The John Day Company.

Renewed 1968 by Indira Gandhi.

———, *Toward Freedom: The Autobiography of Jawaharlal Nehru.* Revised edition. Copyright 1941, The John Day Company, New York: John Day Co., 1942. Permission courtesy of The John Day Co., Ind., publishers.

Neumann, Franz, *Behemoth: The Structure and Practice of National Socialism, 1933-1944.* Copyright © 1942, 1944 by Oxford University Press, New York. New York: Octagon Books, 1963. Passages reprinted courtesy of Farrar, Straus & Giroux, Inc.

Neustadt, Richard E., *Presidential Power: The Politics of Leadership.* Copyright © 1960, 1964 by John Wiley & Sons, Inc. New York and London: John Wiley and Sons, 1960. Permission courtesy John Wiley & Sons, Inc.

Nicholson, Harold, *Diplomacy.* Second edition. Copyrighted 1950, 1960. London, New York and Toronto: Oxford University Press, 1960 [1950]. Permission courtesy of Oxford University Press.

Nickalls, John L., ed., *The Journals of George Fox.* Cambridge: University Press, 1952. Quotations reprinted by permission of Cambridge University Press.

Oppenheimer, Martin and George Lakey, *A Manual for Direct Action.* Copyright © 1964, 1965 by Martin Oppenheimer, George Lakey, and the Friends Peace Committee. Chicago: Quadrangle Books, 1965. Permission courtesy of Quadrangle Books.

Peace News (London), passage from issue of July 2, 1965. Permission courtesy of Peace News Ltd.

Peck, Graham, *Two Kinds of Time.* Copyright © 1950 by Graham Peck. Houghton Mifflin, 1950. Permission courtesy of Houghton Mifflin Co.

•Peck, James, *Freedom Ride.* Copyright © 1962 by James Peck. New York: Simon & Schuster, 1962. Permission courtesy Simon & Schuster.

The Pentagon Papers as published by "The New York Times", Copyright © 1971 by The New York Times Company. New York, Toronto and London: Bantam Books, 1971. Permission courtesy of *The New York Times.*

Prawdin, Michael, **The Unmentionable Nechaev: A Key to Bolshevism.** Copyright 1961. London: Allen and Unwin, 1961. Permission courtesy of Reneé C. Prawdin.

Rayback, Joseph G., *A History of American Labor.* Copyright © 1959, 1965 by Joseph G. Rayback. New York, Macmillan, 1964. Permission courtesy of The Macmillan Co.

Révész, Imre, *History of the Hungarian Reformed Church.* Washington, D.C.: Hungarian Reformed Federation of America, 1956. Passage reprinted from p. 128. Courtesy of the Hungarian Reformed Federation of America.

Reynolds, Lloyd G., *Labor Economics and Labor Relations.* Copyright © 1949 by Prentice-Hall, Inc. Englewood Cliffs, New Jersey: Prentice-Hall, 1959. Permission courtesy of Prentice-Hall, Inc.

Roberts, Adam, "Buddhism and Politics in South Vietnam," in *The World Today* (London), vol. 21, no. 6 (June 1965), pp. 240-250. Permission courtesy of Adam Roberts.

———, *Civilian Resistance as a National Defence.* Harrisburg, Pa., Stackpole Books, 1968. Original British edition: *The Strategy of Civilian Defence.* Copyright © 1967 by Adam Roberts, 1967. London: Faber & Faber, 1967. Permission courtesy of Adam Roberts.

Rosenthal, Mario, *Guatemala: The Story of an Emergent Latin American Democracy.* Copyrighted, New York: Twayne Publishers, 1962. Permission courtesy of Twayne Publishers, Inc.

Rostovtzeff, M., *The Social and Economic History of the Roman Empire,* Vol. I. Second edition revised by P. M. Frazer. Copyright © 1957 by Oxford Universtiy Press. Oxford: Clarendon Press, 1956. Permission courtesy of Clarendon Preess.

Rubin, Jerry, *Do It!* New York: Simon and Schuster, 1970. Permission courtesy of Jerry Rubin.

Schapiro, Leonard, *The Communist Party of the Soviet Union.* Copyright © 1960, 1971 by Leonard Schapiro. New York: Random House, 1960. London: Eyre & Spottiswoode, 1960. Permission courtesy of Leonard B. Schapiro.

Schelling, Thomas C., *International Economics.* Copyright © 1958 by Allyn and Bacon, Inc. Boston: Allyn and Bacon, 1958.

Seifert, Harvey, *Conquest by Suffering: The Process and Prospects of Nonviolent Resistance.* Copyright © 1965 by W. L. Jenkins. Philadelphia: Westminster Press, 1965. Permission courtesy of the Westminster Press.

Seton-Watson, Christopher, *Italy From Liberalism to Fascism, 1870-1925.* Copyright © 1967 by Christopher Seton-Watson. New York: Barnes and Noble, 1967. London: Methuen, 1967. Permission courtesy of Christopher Seton-Watson.

Shirer, William L., *The Rise and Fall of the Third Reich.* Copyright © 1959, 1960 by William L. Shirer. New York: Simon and Schuster, 1960. London: Secker and Warburg, 1962. Permission courtesy of Simon and Schuster.

Shridharani, Krishnalal, *War Without Violence: A Study of Gandhi's Method and Its Accomplishments.* New York: Harcourt Brace and Co., 1939. London: Victor Gollancz, 1939. Permission courtesy of S. K. Shridharani.

Soloman, Frederic and Jacob R. Fishman, "The Psychosocial Meaning of Nonviolence in Student Civil Rights Activities", *Psychiatry*, vol. XXVII, No. 2 (May 1964), pp. 91-99. Permission courtesy of *Psychiatry: A Publication.*

Steiner, Stan, *The New Indians.* Copyright © 1968 by Stan Steiner, 1968. New York: Harper & Row, 1968. Permission courtesy of Stan Steiner and Harper & Row.

Suhl, Yuri, *They Fought Back: The Story of Jewish Resistance in Nazi Europe.* New York: Crown Publishers, 1967. London: MacGibbon and Kee, 1968. Permission courtesy of Yuri Suhl.

Sunday Times (London), a passage from the issue of March 19, 1967. Permission courtesy of the *Sunday Times.*

Symons, Julian, *The General Strike: A Historical Portrait.* Copyright © 1957 by Julian Symons. London: The Cresset Press. 1957. Permission courtesy of the Cresset Press, and Julian Symons.

Tabor, Robert, *M-26: Biography of a Revolution.* Copyrighted 1961. New York: Lyle Stuart, 1961. Permission courtesy of Lyle Stuart, Inc.

Taylor, George R., *The Struggle for North China.* Copyright © 1940 by the Secretariat, Institute of Pacific Relations. New York: Institute of Pacific Relations, 1940. Permission courtesy of William L. Holland, Editor, *Pacific Affairs.*

Ullstein, Heinz, *Spielplatz meines Lebens: Erinnerungen.* Copyright © 1961 by Kindler Verlag München. Munich: Kindler Verlag, 1961. Permission courtesy of Kindler Verlag. English translation in text by Hilda von

Klenze Morris.

Vassilyev, A. T., *The Ochrana: The Russian Secret Police.* Edited and with an Introduction by Rene Fülöp-Miller. Copyright © 1930 by J. B. Lippincott Co. Philadelphia and London: J. B. Lippincott Co., 1930. Passage reprinted by permission of J. B. Lippincott Company.

Warmbrunn, Werner, *The Dutch under German Occupation 1940-1945.* Copyright © 1963 by Board of Trustees of the Leland Standford Junior University. Stanford, California: Stanford University Press, 1963. London: Oxford University Press, 1963. Passages reprinted with permission of Stanford University Press.

Warriner, Doreen, *Land Reform in Principle and Practice.* Copyright © 1969 by Oxford University Press. Oxford: Clarendon Press, 1969. Permission courtesy of Clarendon Press.

Waskow, Arthur I., *From Race Riot to Sit-in: 1919 and the 1960s.* Copyright © 1966 by Doubleday and Co., Inc. Garden City, N. Y.: Doubleday, 1966. Permission courtesy of Doubleday & Co.

Wheeler-Bennett, Sir John W., *The Nemesis of Power: The Germany Army in Politics, 1918-1945.* New York: St. Martin's Press, 1953. London: Macmillan, 1953. Permission courtesy of Sir John Wheeler-Bennett.

Williams, Robin M., *The Reduction of Intergroup Tensions.* New York: Social Science Research Council, 1947. Permission courtesy of Robin M. Williams.

Wolfe, Bertram D., *Three who Made a Revolution.* Copyrighted. New York: Dial Press, 1948. London: Thames and Hudson, 1956. Permission courtesy of Bertram D. Wolfe.

Zinn, Howard, *Albany.* Atlanta: Southern Regional Council, 1962. Permission courtesy of Howard Zinn.